American Schools of Oriental Research
Special Volume Series
No. 1

Series Editor: Eric M. Meyers

David Noel Freedman

The Word of the Lord Shall Go Forth

Essays in Honor of David Noel Freedman in Celebration of His Sixtieth Birthday

edited by

Carol L. Meyers and M. O'Connor

Published for the
American Schools of Oriental Research
by
EISENBRAUNS
Winona Lake, Indiana

Library of Congress Cataloging in Publication Data:
Main entry under title:

The Word of the Lord shall go forth.

(Special volume series / American Schools of Oriental Research; no. 1)
Bibliography: p. 719
1. Bible. O.T.—Criticism, interpretation, etc.—Addresses, essays, lectures. 2. Inscriptions, Semitic—Addresses, essays, lectures.
3. Freedman, David Noel, 1922- . I. Meyers, Carol L.
II. O'Connor, M. III. Freedman, David Noel, 1922- . IV. Series:
Special volume series (American Schools of Oriental Research); no. 1.
BS1188.W66 1983 221.6 83-20589
ISBN 0-931464-19-6

The American Schools wish to thank the following, who have given them permisson to reproduce copyright poems or portions thereof:

Gary Snyder: "What You Should Know to be a Poet," "Everybody Lying on Their Stomachs," and "Regarding Wave," from Gary Snyder, *Regarding Wave,* Copyright © 1968, 1970 by Gary Snyder; "Source" from Gary Snyder, *Turtle Island,* Copyright © 1974 by Gary Snyder; all printed by permission of New Directions Publishing Corporation; and "Water" from Gary Snyder, *Riprap* (San Francisco: The Four Seasons Foundation), Copyright © 1959 by Gary Snyder; reprinted by permission of the author.

Wallace Stevens: "Thirteen Ways of Looking at a Blackbird," "Notes Toward A Supreme Fiction," "Of Modern Poetry," from Wallace Stevens, *The Collected Poems of Wallace Stevens,* Copyright © by Elsie Stevens and Holly Stevens; and "Of Mere Being" from Wallace Stevens, *Opus Posthumous,* Copyright © 1957 by Elsie Stevens and Holly Stevens; all reprinted by permission of Alfred A. Knopf, Inc.

*This volume has been made possible
through the generous support of
The Zion Research Foundation
and
several ASOR trustees*

Preface

It is indeed an occasion for rejoicing when a new publication series is inaugurated with a book such as this. As David Noel Freedman relinquishes the reins of ASOR publications after six active years at the helm as First Vice President for Publications, it is altogether fitting to honor this man who has lifted ASOR books and journals to their highest level of distinction. That his sixtieth birthday coincides more or less with the conclusion of his term as chief publication officer of ASOR, and that his successor in that capacity is also editor of the Special Volumes Series, are coincidences that should not go unnoticed. Indeed, David Noel Freedman's utter commitment to seeing scholarship through to its ultimate form, the published word, has been the determining factor influencing my decision to take over the publication reins from him.

This Festschrift therefore celebrates an important transition in David Noel Freedman's life. ASOR is proud to provide this vehicle for conveying its appreciation to him for his decades of service to the organization. The contents of this magnificent volume speak for themselves; they constitute the most appropriate form of tribute we can provide.

I would like to thank the editors of this volume, Carol Meyers and M. O'Connor, for their extraordinary efforts in making this book possible. In many ways, they represent in their young scholarly lives what David Noel Freedman has sought to inspire these many years. Philip J. King, as President of the American Schools of Oriental Research, is to be commended for so graciously encouraging this work and facilitating its publication. Special thanks also go to Susan Leeb, production manager of ASOR, for her superb work on this volume. David Drake, of Durham, Wendy Laura Frisch, of Huntington Woods, K. A. Palka, of Stevens Point, and Philip Schmitz, of Ann Arbor, provided assistance with a difficult set of proofs. The editors regret that it has not been possible to provide indexes for the volume. Finally, we are all deeply grateful to those friends, especially the Zion Research Foundation, a nonsectarian foundation for the study of the Bible and the history of the Christian Church, whose generosity made possible publication of this volume.

Eric M. Meyers

Durham, North Carolina
28 January 1982

Foreword

Words at their best, well-crafted into cogent patterns, reflect both the thought processes that produce them as well as sensitivity to the mindset of those that will hear or read them. Words are the mediating devices of human culture, and the scholar who best understands them and their unique power stands to use them in ways that will mark him among the formative figures of his discipline. David Noel Freedman is such a scholar. We seek to honor him here with words gathered in recognition of the way his scholarly and personal contributions have involved us all.

David Noel Freedman's work on ancient Hebrew poetry must be placed at the forefront of work on Hebrew literature. He has brought clarity of analysis to a field floundering in the frustrations of dealing with an ancient system of literary expression, and he has opened wide the way for future research. That he has accomplished this is a measure of his own brilliance and perseverance.

He has not, despite attention to words and syllables, stopped with them, for reasons hinted at in the preface to the Authorized Version of the English Bible (1611).

> Thus to minse the matter [of absolute consistency in translational equivalents], wee thought to savour more of curiositie then wisedome, and that rather it would breed scorne in the Atheist, then bring profite to the godly Reader. For is the kingdome of God become words or syllables?

Freedman's specialized contributions are only the core of his work. He has meant much more to his students and colleagues, to the scholarly community, and also to the general public. In an ardent manifestation of energy and concern, he has sought to share with others his insights into poetry and countless other dimensions of biblical literature and religion. He has used multifarious avenues of communication. Throughout his professional career he has been extraordinarily active in editing and publication. He has been a tireless lecturer to classes, to scholarly gatherings, and to popular audiences. He has been a willing and able consultant to media productions dealing with the biblical world. He has himself crafted, and has helped to shape, a stunning assortment of works which have assured that the words of biblical scholarship have truly "gone forth."

The diversity of Freedman's talents is reflected here by the range of topics in this volume. We did not specially solicit essays related to his primary area of scholarship, yet we received such, along with many others dealing with topics for which he has a vital concern. David Noel Freedman's personal encouragement to students and junior scholars as well as his thoughtful cooperation and collaboration with colleagues is likewise reflected here, in the size of the volume and in its multinational character. Even so, only a small portion of the community of Professor Freedman's scholarly friends is represented here.

We wish to celebrate with this Festschrift the first sixty years of David Noel Freedman's life. His accomplishments in that span have been monumental, and we hope that he gains much satisfaction from this appreciation.

In our greeting to Professor Freedman we are joined by two who had intended to contribute to this volume but were prevented by death from doing so. Monsignor Patrick W. Skehan, who was among Freedman's teachers at Johns Hopkins, died on 9 September 1980. Professor John Bailey, who was for the last decade of his life Freedman's colleague at the University of Michigan, died on 11 December 1980. Their passing has not deprived them of their share in our celebration.

Carol Meyers
M. O'Connor

Durham, North Carolina
31 January 1982

While this volume was in proof we received news of the death of Mitchell Dahood on 2 March 1982 in Rome. Father Dahood did not live to see his contribution to this volume in print, but his delight in having been able to participate in this tribute to his friend cannot be marred by his untimely passing.

25 March 1982

CONTENTS

II. The Prose of the Hebrew Bible

III. History and Institutions of Israel

Abbreviations

The abbreviations are those used in the *Bulletin of the American Schools of Oriental Research* (printed in #222, 1976) and, for rabbinic materials, the *Journal of Biblical Literature* (printed in volume 95, 1976); classical abbreviations follow Liddell, Scott, Jones, and Lewis and Short.

Biblical Texts

BH^3 / K	R. Kittel, P. Kahle, et al., eds. 1937. *Biblia Hebraica.* Stuttgart: Württembergische Bibelanstalt.
BHS	K. Elliger, W. Rudolph, H. P. Rüger, G. E. Weil, et al., eds. 1977. *Biblia Hebraica Stuttgartensia.* Stuttgart: Deutsche Bibelstiftung.

Biblical Translations

AV/KJV	The Authorized *or* King James Version, 1611.
RV	The Revised Version, 1885.
RSV	The Revised Standard Version, 1952/1957.
BJ	La Sainte Bible . . . de Jerusalem, 1955.
JB	The Jerusalem Bible, 1968.
NEB	The New English Bible, 1970.
NAB	The New American Bible, 1970.
TEV/Good News	The Good News Bible [of the American Bible Society]: The Bible in Today's English Version, 1976.
JPS/NJPS	The (New) Jewish Publication Society of America (Torah, 1965; Prophets, 1978; Writings, 1982).
NIV	The New International Version, 1978.

Reference Works

AHw	W. von Soden. 1956-1981. *Akkadisches Handwörterbuch.* Wiesbaden: Harrassowitz.
ANEP	J. B. Pritchard. 1969. *The Ancient Near East in Pictures Relating to the Old Testament*[2]. Princeton: Princeton University Press.
ANET	J. B. Pritchard, ed. 1969. *Ancient Near Eastern Texts Relating to the Old Testament*[3]. Princeton: Princeton University Press.
BDB	F. Brown, S. R. Driver, and C. A. Briggs. 1907. *A Hebrew and English Lexicon of the Old Testament . . . Based on the Lexicon of William Gesenius.* Oxford: Clarendon.

CAD I. J. Gelb, A. L. Oppenheim, E. Reiner et al., eds. 1955-. *The Assyrian Dictionary of the Oriental Institute of the University of Chicago.* Chicago: The Oriental Institute.

CAH^3 I. E. Edwards, C. J. Gadd, N. G. L. Hammond, and E. Sollberger, eds. 1970-75. *The Cambridge Ancient History^3.* Vol. I, part 1, 1970; vol. I, part 2, 1971; vol. II, part 1, 1973; vol. II, part 2, 1975. Cambridge: Cambridge University Press.

CTA A. Herdner. 1963. *Corpus des tablettes en cunéiformes alphabétiques découvertes à Ras Shamra-Ugarit de 1929 à 1939.* Institut Français d'archéologie de Beyrouth/Bibliothéque archéologique et historique 89, Mission de Ras Shamra 10. Paris: Imprimerie Nationale and Paul Geuthner.

GKC E. Kautzsch. 1910. *Gesenius' Hebrew Grammar.* Trans. A. E. Cowley. Oxford: Clarendon.

KAI H. Donner and W. Röllig. 1962-71. *Kanaanäische und Aramäische Inschriften.* Bd. 1, 1962, 1971^3; Bd. 2, 1964, 1968^2; Bd. 3, 1964, 1969^2. Wiesbaden: Harrassowitz.

KTU M. Dietrich, O. Loretz, and J. Sanmartín, with H.-W. Kisker. 1976. *Die keilalphabetischen Texte aus Ugarit. Einschliesslich der Keilalphabetischen Texte ausserhalb Ugarit. 1. Transkription.* Alter Orient und Altes Testament 24. Kevelaer and Neukirchen-Vluyn: Verlag Butzon und Bercker and Neukirchener Verlag.

UT C. H. Gordon. 1965. *Ugaritic Textbook.* Analecta Orientalia 38. Rome: Pontificium Institutum Biblicum.

Sharing the Results of Scholarly Research

Philip J. King
Boston College, Chestnut Hill, Massachusetts

Scholarship of its nature is an enterprise which must be shared; it is too vast to be done effectively in isolation. Certainly individuals may conduct original research in the privacy of libraries or laboratories, but they must communicate their findings to colleagues for testing and refinement. Guilds have been established to provide the community of scholars with such fora, enabling them to do together what none can do alone. If, in addition, scholarship is to maintain vitality and relevance, its practitioners must share their conclusions not only with peers but also with a wider audience. For this reason a publication program is an intrinsic part of the structure of every learned society. In the course of their professional careers scholars may even be affiliated with several overlapping guilds, as they go about their research and share their conclusions through publication.

David Noel Freedman, whom we honor by this festschrift, is a distinguished scholar whose academic career conforms well to the pattern just described. Not content merely to be a member of his guilds, he has assumed a leading role in them, often functioning as officer or trustee. As a specialist in the related fields of Bible and the Ancient Near East, he has been actively engaged both in the Society of Biblical Literature and the American Schools of Oriental Research, two learned societies with shared interests from the time of their inception to the present. The most appropriate way to lend perspective to the scholarly attainments of Freedman is to sketch him against the background of the American Schools of Oriental Research, the guild with which he has been more intimately connected in the recent past, especially as vice president in charge of its publication program and editor of its journals.

The American Schools of Oriental Research, known simply by its acronym ASOR, is a consortium of over 140 universities, colleges, museums, and professional schools in the United States and Canada, with research interests in the Near East. Its primary purpose is to initiate, encourage, and support research into, and public understanding of, the peoples and cultures of the Near East, from earliest times to the modern period. ASOR has been actively engaged in the Near East and the eastern Mediterranean basin since its founding at the turn of the century. As of 1983, in addition to supporting research centers in Jerusalem, Baghdad, Amman, and Nicosia, ASOR is overseeing about 35 archeological projects in six countries of the Near East and the Mediterranean littoral: Syria, Jordan, Egypt, Israel, Cyprus, and Tunisia. In the past ASOR has also sponsored research in countries such as Turkey, Iraq, and Saudi Arabia, and aspires to do so in the future.

ASOR owes its existence in large measure to the Society of Biblical Literature, as history attests. At the 29th meeting of the Society, held in Hartford on June 13, 1895, Joseph Henry Thayer, New Testament professor at Harvard University, delivered the presidential address, entitled "The Historical Element in the New Testament." In the course of his presentation he commented:

> But I am impatient to reach a suggestion which I will frankly confess has with me for the moment vastly more interest and attraction than any other; is it not high time that an *American School for Oriental Study and Research* should be established in Palestine? This is no new idea. Others besides myself, no doubt, have been cherishing it as a secret hope for years. . . . Indeed, so alluring are enterprises of this sort at present, so great their promise of usefulness alike to Biblical learning and missionary work, that—as you are aware—a French Catholic School of Biblical Studies has established itself already in Jerusalem, whose quarterly "Revue Biblique," printed in Paris, is in its fifth year and deserves the respectful attention of scholars. . . . Shall the countrymen of Robinson and Thomson, Lynch and Merrill, Eli Smith and Van Dyck, look on unconcerned? Shall a society, organized for the express purpose of stimulating and diffusing a scholarly knowledge of the Sacred Word, remain seated with folded hands, taking no part or lot in the matter? (Thayer 1895: 16)

With this eloquent challenge Thayer planted the ASOR seed, but five years elapsed before it took root—in 1900 ASOR was born in Jerusalem.

While ASOR's conception can be traced indirectly to several national organizations of its kind already established in the Near East during the 19th century, its direct lineage resides in three learned societies—the American Oriental Society, organized in 1842; the Archaeological Institute of America, founded in 1879; and the Society of Biblical Literature and Exegesis, formed in 1880. ASOR has much in common with each of these parent organizations, but it also has a unique role to fulfill, as the constitution states:

> The main object of said School shall be to enable properly qualified persons to prosecute Biblical, linguistic, archaeological, historical, and other kindred studies and researches under more favorable conditions than can be secured at a distance from the Holy Land.

The American Oriental Society was established "for the cultivation of learning in the Asiatic, African, and Polynesian languages." The Archaeological Institute of America was formed "for the purpose of promoting and directing archaeological investigations and research." The Society of Biblical Literature and Exegesis was founded "for the purpose of promoting a thorough study of the Scriptures by the reading and discussion of original papers." These statements of purpose demonstrate the convergence of interests among these various organizations, while in addition, ASOR's special emphasis on the Near East stands out.

From its inception ASOR has worked cooperatively with the Archaeological Institute of America and the Society of Biblical Literature and Exegesis in the area of publications. The original regulations governing publication of articles produced under the auspices of ASOR stated that they

> may be published in either the Journal of the Society of Biblical Literature and Exegesis or in the Journal of the Archaeological Institute of America, the Journal of the Institute having a prior claim on such material produced by the School or as a result of its explorations as is of a distinctly archaeological and non-Biblical character.

Charles C. Torrey, a member of the Yale faculty and a leading biblical scholar, traveled to Jerusalem in the summer of 1900 to establish ASOR's first overseas research institute; he remained in residence for a year, serving as director of the fledgling center. It was clear from the beginning that long-term directors were preferable to annual appointees, but it was impossible at that time to find a qualified scholar with the luxury of an extended leave from a teaching position back home. Consequently, in the years before World War I, the Jerusalem School was administered by annual directors, several of whom were outstanding biblical and oriental scholars. Since in most cases it was their first experience in Palestine, they were unfamiliar with the land, its people, their languages and customs. So they made an intensive effort to correct their deficiency by organizing field trips to important historical sites, by arranging both formal and informal meetings with the local people, and by availing themselves of language tutors in modern Arabic and Hebrew.

In keeping with the venturesome nature reflected in his prolific writings, Torrey launched the School's pioneer archaeological program by excavating a series of Phoenician rock tombs at Sidon on the Mediterranean coast. A detailed, illustrated report of this initial undertaking appeared as the lead article in the first of ASOR's series *The Annual of the American School of Oriental Research in Jerusalem*, inaugurated in 1920 under the editorship of Torrey; it marked the first time ASOR published research papers in its own name, independently of the journals of its parent societies. The *Annual* was instituted to guarantee the regular publication of the scholarly research generated by ASOR appointees, especially the directors of the overseas centers.

In addition to Torrey's excavation report, the first volume of the *Annual* contained contributions from three other early directors of the Jerusalem School, based on research accomplished while they resided in Jerusalem. Hinckley G. Mitchell, professor of Old Testament and biblical languages at Boston University and director of the school in 1901–1902, was the author of the second article—a detailed study of the walls of Jerusalem, illustrated with 71 plates. Lewis B. Paton, prominent Old Testament scholar of the Hartford Theological Seminary, who directed the Jerusalem School in 1903–1904, contributed the third article, entitled "Survivals of Primitive Religion in Modern Palestine." Warren J. Moulton of the Bangor Theological Seminary, who had been a special student in Jerusalem in 1902–1903, and afterward director of the School in 1912–1913, authored the final paper of the first *Annual*, concerned with archaeology and epigraphy, specifically cupmarkings, pyxes, and figurines, as well as a Caesarean and a Nabatean inscription.

The second volume of the *Annual*, edited by Moulton, was issued as a double number (II and III) for the years 1921 and 1922; it contained, among others, articles by two ASOR members who became scholars of great renown, not only in ASOR circles but in the wider orbit of biblical and Near Eastern studies—James A. Montgomery and William F. Albright. Since that time the *Annual* has appeared on a regular basis, communicating the results of significant research by ASOR scholars; often but not always, the contents have been in the form of preliminary or final excavation reports. The series of *Annuals* is an excellent index of the development of Syro-Palestinian and Mesopotamian archeology in terms of both method and interpretation. Even today an archeologist cannot afford to neglect those volumes of the *Annual* where Albright described in detail the pottery of Tell Beit Mirsim.

Albright and Freedman are to be counted among the ASOR scholars who have edited *Annuals* in the service of their colleagues. Of the recent volumes edited by

Freedman for example, number 43 is a compilation of five preliminary excavation reports dealing with Early Bronze Age Bab edh-Dhrâʿ in Jordan, the Lydian site of Sardis in modern Turkey, the excavations at Meiron in Upper Galilee, Tell el-Hesi in Israel, and the ancient site of Carthage; number 44 is an archeological report on the Tabqa Dam Project in the Euphrates Valley, an international salvage operation initiated by the Syrian government when important archeological sites became endangered by the construction of the High Dam at Tabqa.

The last director of the Jerusalem School prior to the outbreak of World War I was James A. Montgomery, professor at the Philadelphia Divinity School and the University of Pennsylvania. A distinguished biblical scholar, he was invited to join the Society of Biblical Literature and Exegesis in 1892, and at the time of his death in 1949 he ranked as its senior member; in 1918 he was elected president of the Society. He also served as president of the American Oriental Society in 1926–1927, and was ASOR's president for 13 years, from 1921–1934. In addition, he was editor of the professional journals of these three learned societies: the *Journal of Biblical Literature* in 1909–1913; the *Journal of the American Oriental Society* in 1916–1921, and again in 1924; and the *Bulletin of the American Schools of Oriental Research* in 1919–1930. His study on the *Book of Daniel* in the prestigious *International Critical Commentary* series has been acclaimed its outstanding volume. Few scholars have contributed so much to biblical scholarship, and few have served ASOR so well and so long.

Besides his own research, writing, and editing, Montgomery found time to encourage younger scholars in these same endeavors, especially William F. Albright, who embarked upon his scholarly career as the Joseph Henry Thayer Fellow in Jerusalem with the blessing of Montgomery, at the time chairman of ASOR's managing committee. From then on, he groomed and promoted Albright, helping to shape the destiny of the scholar who became the foremost orientalist of our time. Albright readily acknowledged his indebtedness to Montgomery by dedicating his *Archaeology and the Religion of Israel*, which appeared in 1942, to him with this tribute:

> The dedication of this book to my former chief and my friend of many years, Professor James Alan Montgomery of the University of Pennsylvania, is only a slight token of my respect and affection for him. His careful scholarship, catholic spirit and broad culture have long adorned every institution or organization with which he was connected.

The year 1919 signaled, besides the reopening of the Jerusalem School after the armistice, the appearance of the first number of the *Bulletin of the American Schools of Oriental Research*, abbreviated *BASOR*, with Montgomery as editor. Originally intended as a newsletter from Jerusalem, it was unpretentious, consisting of a mere four pages. The first issue was a summary of the School's beginnings and an expression of its hopes for the future; it also described the School's plan for a cooperative venture with its British counterpart, as well as the inevitable appeal for funds to support the joint enterprise. The second and following numbers of *BASOR* were more ambitious, reporting on recent discoveries and other events of general interest; this augured well for the future of this publication. Six decades later it is not only ASOR's professional journal, but also the premier scholarly publication in its field.

William F. Albright directed the School in Jerusalem from 1921–1929, and again from 1933–1936, one of the most productive periods in ASOR's history. During his long tenure at the School, he offered formal courses in biblical and archeological studies, led exhaustive field trips throughout the Near East, conducted several field excavations and surveys, and also managed to find time to cultivate cordial relations with the other national institutes in Jerusalem. Much of the material in the early issues of *BASOR* is based on the whirlwind activities of Albright as director in Jerusalem.

When Montgomery relinquished the editorship of *BASOR* at the end of 1930, Albright succeeded him and continued vigorously in that post for 38 years, retiring reluctantly in 1968 when his eyesight began to fail. Remarkably, he edited 152 of the 200 issues published in the first half-century of the journal's existence. It was more than fitting that *BASOR* 200 (December 1970), the issue marking the golden jubilee of the quarterly, was dedicated to Albright. Since 1968 *BASOR* has had a succession of highly respected editors—Delbert R. Hillers of The Johns Hopkins University (1969–1974); David Noel Freedman (1974–1978); and currently William G. Dever of the University of Arizona.

BASOR 215 (October 1974), edited by Freedman, appeared in an enlarged format to accommodate diagrams, photographs, plans, and maps, which are an indispensable part of archeological reporting in our day—the first major change in the journal in 50 years. Dever, a leading Syro-Palestinian archeologist, is maintaining the high standard that has made *BASOR* a respected archeological periodical.

Under the editorship of Albright *BASOR* became an extension of his personality and a chronicle of his scholarly research with most of the contents emanating from his prolific pen; but he also dedicated a large amount of space to reporting and evaluating the projects of others. It is hard to find a better way to trace the history of Near Eastern archeology and related disciplines than by reading the back issues of *BASOR*, or at least by perusing *BASOR*'s indexes. The careful reader of the *BASOR*s of Albright's day will see how he established Syro-Palestinian archeology as a science by constructing, through the application of the twin principles of stratigraphy and typology, the framework for the chronology of that region. Tell Beit Mirsim, situated about 12 miles southwest of Hebron, was Albright's laboratory between 1926 and 1932; there he dated the occupation of the mound by the pottery fragments that lay within, and at the same time helped to fill in the gaps of Petrie's ceramic index. *BASOR*, and also the *Annual*, were the media Albright utilized to communicate the results of his excavations.

BASOR and the *Annual* also served the next generation of Jerusalem directors after Albright as the vehicle for sharing the results of their scholarly investigations. Director Nelson Glueck, for example, described in great detail his extraordinary explorations in Transjordan, the Jordan Valley, and the Negev for three decades beginning in 1932. These reports on his surface surveys have proved invaluable to present-day archeologists who are retracing Glueck's steps as they make their own regional survey of those same desolate areas.

With the passing years *BASOR* inevitably became a more technical journal than envisioned by its founders; rapid developments in the field of archeology forced *BASOR* into a more scientific mold, putting it out of the reach of the non-professional. No longer suitable to the popular audience originally envisioned, another organ had to be created for the general reader, as well as those engaged in teaching and preaching the Bible. Millar Burrows, President of ASOR, pointed to the problem; then to fill the void, G. Ernest Wright, a versatile scholar keenly interested in both archeology and biblical studies, founded *The Biblical Archaeologist* in 1938. Possessing the ability to share the results of scientific research in nontechnical language, a rare gift among scholars, Wright was ideal for the new undertaking.

The first number of the new magazine, composed of four pages, appeared in February 1938; it stated that publication would be quarterly, at a subscription rate of 50 cents a year. Despite its unprepossessing format, the journal was praised as readable and reliable. That first issue consisted of two articles—one by Albright entitled, "What Were the Cherubim?," and the other by Wright on "Herod's Nabataean Neighbor," this second inspired, no doubt, by Glueck's 1937 excavation of the Nabatean temple at Khirbet et-Tannur, situated southeast of the Dead Sea. This was the first of 36 articles which Wright contributed to *The Biblical Archaeologist* in as many years.

As editor of this journal, Wright was assisted by Albright, Burrows of Yale, and Ephraim A. Speiser of the University of Pennsylvania. Emily Wright, the editor's spouse, also rendered invaluable assistance in launching *The Biblical Archaeologist* and maintaining its momentum. Through the years many others have contributed significantly to the growth of the magazine, especially Edward F. Campbell of McCormick Theological Seminary, a former student of Wright who shared his mentor's interests in biblical archaeology. In 1959 Campbell became the editor, while Wright remained on the board until 1963; then he resigned after 25 years of editorial service. Others who played important roles in the life of *The Biblical Archaeologist* were Frank M. Cross, H. Darrell Lance, Floyd Filson, and Lee Ellenberger, and notably its most recent editor, David Noel Freedman.

With Freedman as editor, *The Biblical Archaeologist* for March 1976 appeared in new dress—an elegant and enlarged format, as well as other features that appeal to a popular audience. Confronted with a problem similar to the one Wright faced in 1938, he had to revamp the journal, stripping it of scientific trappings, to make it more attractive for the ordinary reader. Assisted by the late H. Thomas Frank of Oberlin College, an experienced popularizer of biblical archeology, Freedman began to publish articles of more general interest, written in a straightforward style free of jargon. The more technical offerings focusing on details of field archeology—the diet of specialists—were assigned to *BASOR*. Timely articles on the remarkable discovery of the Ebla library at Tell Mardikh in Syria, the icons and manuscripts found at St. Catherine's Monastery in the Sinai, and the Coptic library uncovered at Nag Hammadi in Upper Egypt have helped *The Biblical Archaeologist* to maintain its reputation as a leading journal in the field. For several years now, *The Biblical Archaeologist* has been published with the financial assistance of the Zion Research Foundation of Boston, which has been supporting ASOR projects on a regular basis since the twenties.

As time passed several articles printed in *The Biblical Archaeologist* were judged to be of permanent interest, requiring a more durable and at the same time more accessible form. Freedman responded; in collaboration with Wright and Campbell he assembled the more valuable essays and edited them in four volumes with the title *The Biblical Archaeologist Readers*. The first appeared in 1959, edited by Freedman and Wright; the latter three have been published intermittently with Freedman and Campbell as editors. The steady demand for these reprints attests to the abiding interest of a wide audience in the archeology and history of the Near East.

In the realm of popular publications there is also the ASOR *Newsletter*. As a supplement to *The Biblical Archaeologist* it informs the ASOR community quickly of exciting and unexpected developments in the field; it keeps them abreast of the activities at the overseas research centers; it is also a vehicle of communication between the administrative offices in the United States and ASOR's widely scattered constituency. The *Newsletter* came into being almost by accident in the forties when Nelson Glueck was long-term director of the school in Jerusalem. As a way of sharing the adventure of his pioneer explorations in Transjordan, he would circulate among friends occasional letters written in his lively style. His descriptions were so detailed that the letters home became a permanent record of his expeditions. ASOR's president, Millar Burrows, found these privately circulated reports so informative that he just presumed to distribute them more widely. Again the reception was so enthusiastic that Glueck consented to a general mailing among ASOR members; the *Newsletter* then became a regular feature from 1948 to the present. From time to time, the format of the Newsletter has undergone change, but the content has remained basically the same. James W. Flanagan of the University of Montana, current editor of the *Newsletter*, is responsible for the new graphic design, as well as the timely articles with illustrations and photographs. As a colleague of Freedman at the University of Michigan a decade ago, Flanagan learned about all aspects of publication; he also has the advantage of being a biblical scholar with extensive experience in dirt archeology.

In 1920, Albert T. Clay, professor of Assyriology at Yale, made an official visit to Iraq to determine through reconnaissance whether the time was ripe for establishing an American School of Oriental Research in Mesopotamia. Taking a long range point of view, he reported on the opportunities of excavating in that land:

> My own observations would lead me to believe that, with ten well-equipped expeditions, working continuously in the Near East, after a period of not twenty-five or thirty years, but after five hundred and twenty-five, there will be sufficient important tells left to keep the excavators busy for the centuries which follow (1920: 62).

The unsettled political situation in Iraq made it impossible to inaugurate ASOR's Baghdad School until 1923, when George A. Barton of the University of Pennsylvania became the first director, and Clay the resident professor. During the academic year 1924–1925, Edward Chiera of the University of Pennsylvania (later of the University of Chicago) went to Baghdad as annual professor. A leading Assyriologist, he excavated at Yorghan Tepe, the ancient Hurrian city of Nuzi in northeastern Iraq, a site rich in cuneiform tablets. In 1927, Chiera published a hundred of those tablets in a volume entitled *The Joint Expedition with the Iraq Museum at Nuzi*, the first in the Baghdad School series; others followed.

Although the Baghdad School was unable to sustain its ambitious publications program, it continues to make a substantial contribution to Mesopotamian scholarship through the pages of the *Journal of Cuneiform Studies*, the first American journal of its kind devoted exclusively to the dissemination of material from the cuneiform civilizations of the Ancient Near East. A highly specialized periodical intended for Assyriologists, it has a limited circulation, but at the same time is a valuable service to scholarship. The *Journal of Cuneiform Studies* was launched in 1947 by Albrecht Goetze, both an archeologist and Assyriologist from Yale, who served as director of the Baghdad School from 1947–1956. For 24 years he continued to edit the journal, with the assistance of two distinguished colleagues, Thorkild Jacobsen of Harvard and Abraham J. Sachs of Brown. Ephraim Speiser, professor at the University of Pennsylvania and author of the commentary on *Genesis* in *The Anchor Bible* series, paid tribute to the *Journal of Cuneiform Studies* in these words:

> It is . . . gratifying to make formal acknowledgement at this time of the founding of the *Journal of Cuneiform Studies* under the sponsorship of our Schools. The need for such a journal could scarcely be overstated. Before the war Europe had a monopoly on such periodicals as were devoted mainly to the study of the various ancient lands which utilized cuneiform writing as their common culture denominator. As a result of the specialization we now enjoy a greater insight than would have been possible otherwise, not only into the life and role of Sumer, Babylonia, and Assyria, but also into the legacy of the Elamites and the Hittites, the Hurrians and the Urartians, as well as the rich literature of Ugarit. Much of that fruitful activity was curtailed by the War, and some of it was cut off altogether. For various reasons it became our responsibility to maintain the volume and the quality of this important effort (1946: 6).

Today the *Journal of Cuneiform Studies* is ably edited by Erle Leichty of the University of Pennsylvania, with the assistance of Hans G. Güterbock, Jerrold S. Cooper and Maria deJ. Ellis.

Of all the publications ASOR has sponsored, none has been as exciting as the Dead Sea scrolls project. In 1948 Millar Burrows announced to the world through the pages of *The Biblical Archaeologist* the remarkable and unexpected discovery of these ancient manuscripts, which bridge a gap of a thousand years in the textual history of the Hebrew Bible. From the moment the scrolls came to public attention ASOR was involved in their identification, decipherment, and dissemination. Burrows, as well as John C. Trever and William H. Brownlee, both appointees in residence at the Jerusalem School when the scrolls came to light, were associated from the beginning with the publication of this invaluable material.

With the permission of the archbishop of the Syrian Orthodox Monastery of St. Mark in Jerusalem, who possessed the manuscripts, Burrows, assisted by Trever and Brownlee, edited the great Isaiah Manuscript (1QIsa^{a}) and the Habakkuk Commentary (1QpHab); then in 1950, ASOR published their results as volume I of *The Dead Sea Scrolls of St. Mark's Monastery*. The following year the plates and transcriptions of the Manual of Discipline (1QS) appeared as volume II.

In retrospect it is amazing that only 2000 copies of these two volumes were printed, given the unique value of the scrolls. Twenty years later, when they had gone out of print, ASOR issued a new edition entitled *Scrolls from Qumran Cave I*, edited by Frank M. Cross, David Noel Freedman, and James A. Sanders, and published jointly by the Albright Institute of Archaeological Research (formerly the American School in Jerusalem) and the Shrine of the Book in Jerusalem, with the aid of a grant from the Zion Research Foundation of Boston. It is a deluxe edition of the same three scrolls. Superior to its predecessor, this volume is enhanced by photographs of the scrolls in both black-and-white and color, reproductions made by Trever, a skilled photographer, when the scrolls were first brought to the Jerusalem School for scholarly evaluation in 1948. This edition has become an indispensable tool for the scholar since the original manuscripts can no longer be consulted directly; exposure to the atmosphere would cause irreparable damage.

By publishing the scrolls of Cave 1 so quickly, Millar Burrows set an example of promptness to his colleagues; for this, in the words of Freedman, Burrows "deserved a halo and a medal." He also produced a two-volume work on the Dead Sea Scrolls which has served as a handbook for students over a long period of time. In 1941 ASOR published Burrows' first-rate book, *What Mean These Stones?*, in which he surveyed excavations in the Near East, explaining their significance for biblical studies.

Several other ASOR scholars, notably Frank M. Cross, the late Patrick W. Skehan, James A. Sanders, and John Strugnell, working with colleagues from several other countries, have been engaged in editing the vast literature discovered since 1947 in the 11 caves located near the Wadi Qumran northwest of the Dead Sea. Freedman has been entrusted with publishing a manuscript containing a portion of Leviticus in paleo-Hebrew script. This scroll was among the contents of Cave 11 discovered by the Bedouin in 1956. ASOR's work on the Dead Sea scrolls has been facilitated by generous financial support from one of its trustees, Elizabeth Hay Bechtel, who has dedicated herself to the preservation of ancient manuscripts.

The history of ASOR attests that James A. Montgomery and William F. Albright were the two guiding spirits of the organization, especially in the first half of the 20th century. As long-term officers and in light of their scholarly attainments, both charted the course ASOR was to follow for several decades; in the process they encouraged younger ASOR members to participate by sharing the results of their own research. Judging from the thoughtful memorial tributes David Noel Freedman forged for Montgomery and Albright, not only did he consider them the leading lights of ASOR, but also his own career was profoundly influenced by them. Biography says more about the biographer than biographee! The parallels between their lives and his make it evident that he deliberately emulated them, and history will demonstrate that he did so well. Without question Albright has been the dominant influence on Freedman; Montgomery has served secondarily, reflected through Albright. There is so much common ground—they have all served as presidents or vice-presidents of ASOR, the Society of Biblical Literature, and other learned organizations; they have edited prestigious journals, in addition to their own contributions to the pages of these journals.

In 1956 Freedman, in partnership with his mentor Albright, undertook an enormous project—editing *The Anchor Bible*—a series of volumes, some 70 in number, each consisting of a fresh translation with an introduction, notes, and commentary on the books of the Bible. With the death of Albright in 1971 Freedman assumed total editorial responsibility; meanwhile 35 books have appeared, and the remaining 35 are in preparation.

The Anchor Bible marks a new day in ecumenical cooperation—the unbiased commentaries in this series are prepared by competent Protestant, Catholic, and Jewish scholars to serve the needs of an interfaith audience. At an earlier time biblical scholars customarily worked within their own traditions, oblivious of colleagues of other religious affiliations. With the advent of ecumenism the Bible became the bond effectively unifying scholars in their pursuit of truth through objective research. Albright did much to foster this cooperative spirit among scholars of the major biblical faiths, while Freedman has continued to promote the interfaith dialogue among peers.

Protestant in upbringing, Albright had a special appeal for Jews and Roman Catholics; his respect for the biblical tradition inspired confidence in the more conservative religious groups in the United States. As professor at The John Hopkins University, Albright trained several Roman Catholic priests in Near Eastern studies; they became prime movers in the renaissance of biblical studies among Roman Catholics in the fifties, and Freedman recruited several of them as contributors to *The Anchor Bible* series.

Albright's influence on Jewish scholars both at home and in Israel was also strongly felt. In 1969 the city of Jerusalem formally acknowledged its indebtedness to him by conferring a high honor—the title *yaqqir Yerušalayim*, Notable of Jerusalem. Freedman, himself both a Jew and a Presbyterian, continued to foster this relationship by inviting several Jewish and Israeli scholars to write for *The Anchor Bible*. Cyrus Gordon, a distinguished Jewish scholar, spoke for many of his community when he observed: "*The Anchor Bible* constitutes the outstanding biblical commentary of our generation."

Besides editing *The Anchor Bible*, Freedman has also coauthored the *Hosea* volume of the series with Francis I. Andersen of Australia. Dedicated to the memory of the first coeditor of the series, William F. Albright, it is a new translation with introduction and commentary on one of the more difficult books in the Hebrew canon. Preserving the literary integrity of Hosea, despite its textual obscurities, the authors have produced an insightful commentary that will help the reader to understand the prophet in the sociological context of the 8th century B.C.E.

In 1969 David Noel Freedman edited, with Jonas C. Greenfield of the Hebrew University in Jerusalem, *New Directions in Biblical Archeology*, a collection of essays by a broad spectrum of leading scholars on recent discoveries in biblical archaeology, with half the essays devoted to the Dead Sea scrolls. Based on his demonstrated competence as a biblical scholar and his field experience in archeology at the site of Ashdod, one of the five cities of the Philistines, Freedman was well qualified to edit these timely papers.

Freedman made a remarkable contribution to biblical and archeological research by preparing a comprehensive bibliography of the published works of William F. Albright, consisting of almost 1100 items. One of the most prolific scholars of his generation, Albright's articles touch on almost every aspect of Near Eastern studies and related fields. A glance at the titles alone is a review of the growth of Near Eastern studies during the last 50 years. The arduous effort invested in compiling such an exhaustive list of items means this project was a labor of love, as every scholar who utilizes it will recognize. In acknowledgement of the intrinsic value of this bibliography and the diligence of the editor who prepared it, ASOR published it as a special volume in 1975.

There appeared in 1980 a collection of Freedman's own articles, written during the sixties and seventies, which focus on Hebrew poetry. The alliterative title of the volume, *Pottery, Poetry, and Prophecy*, suggests the breadth of the author's scholarly concern. At first glance the three areas in the title may not seem to be related, but upon reflection there is a great deal of overlap. Although the poetry of the Bible has always been Freedman's prime concern, he did not pursue it isolated from other areas of Near Eastern research; nor can any scholar afford to be so narrow. To illustrate: when archeologists unearth literary documents like the collections found at Ugarit,

Nuzi, Mari, and Ebla, the specialist in Hebrew Bible stands to gain many insights from this cognate literature of ambient cultures.

In this assemblage of 20 essays, Freedman shares his insights gained over three decades, including the technique of syllable counting as a way of identifying metrical structures. He will not be surprised if some dissent at this point, for he is quite ready to rethink the issues he raises in this collection of creative studies.

Freedman's bibliography far exceeds the books and articles noticed here; there are several other significant pieces, some in prominent places, such as his exhaustive article on the "Pentateuch" in the *Interpreter's Dictionary of the Bible*; others of equal value appear in obscure journals. Those who have found them undoubtedly read them with profit.

Apart from *The Anchor Bible*, Freedman's most lasting contribution to Near Eastern scholarship continues to be made through the ASOR publications. In addition to overseeing the production of all ASOR's books and journals, and thereby guaranteeing a high level of scholarship, Freedman has put his own stamp on those journals which he had edited, especially *BASOR* and *The Biblical Archaeologist*, impressing them with renewed vitality. As ASOR's vice-president for publications, he also inaugurated several new series consisting of special volumes, dissertations, and monographs. Unfortunately, after an auspicious beginning, financial constraints have made it necessary to curtail the publications program for a time, a setback familiar to many learned societies at present.

If sharing scholarly research through publication is an ideal to be achieved, few have tried as hard as David Noel Freedman. Not content to devote himself exclusively to personal research, he has generously assisted others in publishing the results of their scholarly investigations. An editor is by definition an unselfish and committed person. Freedman's tireless effort in editing the *Journal of Biblical Literature*, the *Bulletin of the American Schools of Oriental Research, The Biblical Archaeologist*, and *The Anchor Bible* speaks eloquently for itself.

This essay would be incomplete if it did not consider another timely issue bearing directly on publications. Almost every extraordinary archeological discovery in modern times, notably when literary remains have been involved, has occasioned controversy among scholars. In view of the novelty of the finds there have been serious differences about authenticity, dating, and historical value, as well as other critical questions. For example, when several hundred texts were unearthed in the royal archives at Ugarit, the site of modern Ras Shamra in Syria, there was disagreement among the early epigraphers about how to decipher the writing on the tablets. Also the Dead Sea scrolls occasioned serious dispute about their antiquity though Albright publicly declared for an early date from the moment he examined the first fragmentary evidence, stating:

> There is no doubt in my mind that the script is more archaic than that of the Nash Papyrus. . . . I should prefer a date around 100 B.C. . . . What an absolutely incredible find! And there can happily not be the slightest doubt in the world about the genuineness of the manuscript (Albright apud Trever 1948: 55).

Recently the remarkable discovery of the Ebla tablets has been engulfed in controversy centering on the same issues; Freedman has been in the midst of the fray. As in the other cases, the controversy will eventually subside, and the truth will prevail, long after the question of who was right and who was wrong has been forgotten. Lest valuable time and energy be exhausted on useless disputing in the future, it would seem best, as Freedman has advocated, to publish the literary remains immediately, without transcription or translation, simply the plates, to give all qualified scholars equal opportunity to try their hand at decipherment and interpretation. And that may be the most effective way to put an end to proprietary attitudes vis-à-vis scrolls, manuscripts, inscriptions, and tablets.

References

Clay, A. T.
1920 Annual Report of The American Schools of Oriental Research. . . Committee on Mesopotamian Archaeology. *Bulletin of the American Institute of Archaeology* 11: 62–64.

Speiser, E. A.
1946 Report of the Director of The Baghdad School. *Bulletin of The American Schools of Oriental Research* 104: 5–6.

Thayer, J. H.
1895 The Historical Element in The New Testament. *Journal of Biblical Literature* 14: 1–18.

Trever, J. C.
1948 The Discovery of The Scrolls. *Biblical Archaeologist* 11: 46–57.

I. Hebrew Poetry and Prophecy

Isaiah 33: An Isaianic Elaboration of the Zion Tradition

J. J. M. Roberts
Princeton Theological Seminary, Princeton, New Jersey

Since Hermann Gunkel's famous article of 1924, Isaiah 33 has generally been treated as a unit, as a "prophetic liturgy"—a judgment that confirms Sigmund Mowinckel's earlier treatment of the chapter as a "coherent eschatological piece," the "portrayal of a single author," in the "form of a liturgical communal lament with a prophetic response" (1921: 235).* Hans Wildberger reverts to breaking the passage up into individual units, but even he admits that it is probable that the three parts of Isaiah 33 grow out of the same situation and stem from the same author (1979: 1286). Given that admission, it is difficult to justify his splintering the piece.

Though the chapter uses different genres, these are woven together in a way that provides a logical and coherent development of thought. Verse 1 opens with a *hôy* oracle formally addressed to the enemy. As in Isa 10: 5–22, however, the real audience is Judah; the *hôy* oracle actually functions to comfort the oppressed people. In verse 2 the author moves from this word of comfort to direct petition of Yahweh. His request is bolstered by a reference to God's acts of deliverance in the past (vv 3–6). That past security of Zion serves as a foil against which the present need brought on by the treacherous enemy stands out more clearly (vv 7–9). This lament, in turn, is answered by an oracle in which Yahweh promises to rise up again, as he did in the past, and destroy the enemy (vv 10–12). The oracle continues in vv 13–16 with a renewed call to attention. Yahweh wants everyone to grasp what he is doing, because his deliverance of Jerusalem will be such as to provoke a religious reform among the city's survivors—a reform he characterizes by quoting from the entrance liturgy genre. That leads, quite logically, into a description of life in the purified Jerusalem of this age of salvation (vv 17–24). The coherence provided by this logical development is further strengthened by recurring themes and vocabulary items that tie the different sections together.

If there has been considerable scholarly agreement to treat Isaiah 33 as a unit, however, there has been far less agreement concerning its date and authorship. Up until the late nineteenth century it was generally taken as Isaianic and connected to Sennacherib's assault on Jerusalem. The tide began to shift against that view with Bernhard Stade's arguments against Isaianic authorship in 1884, and though such recent scholars as Franz Feldmann (1925: 396–98), Joseph Ziegler (1948: 98–102), Angelo Penna (1958: 299–300), and H. L. Ginsberg (1971: 59) still argue for its authenticity, the modern tendency is to date it much later. Mowinckel placed it in the time of Josiah (1921: 235, n. 1), R. E. Clements thinks of the Babylonian exile (1980a: 265), Wildberger of the Persian period (1979: 1288), and others of the Hellenistic if not the Seleucid era (Kaiser 1973: 271).

Yet, as Paul Auvray points out (1972: 293), the arguments against the chapter's authenticity are hardly decisive. The repeated claim that the allusions to the enemy are too vague to be Isaianic is simply false. In some oracles Isaiah names the Assyrians, but in others the enemy is not named at all (1: 5–9, 18–20; 3: 1–15; 3: 24–4: 1; 5: 26–30; 28: 11; 29: 1–8). There is no clear pattern of specificity in Isaiah's references to the enemy; it varies from oracle to oracle. Moreover, if chapter 33 were composed during the seige of Jerusalem, the original audience would have found it quite specific enough. The composite, liturgical character of Isaiah 33 is an argument against Isaianic authorship only if one persists in fragmenting Isaiah's speeches into their smallest divisible units. If one recognizes larger liturgical settings (see Kaiser 1963: 10, on Isa 1: 2–20) or even speeches composed of several genres (see my forthcoming study of Isa 1: 2–20), Isaiah 33 no longer appears so isolated. Stade's argument from vocabulary (1884: 264–65) hinges on the antiquated notion that the Psalms are basically late post-exilic compositions. Once that notion is rejected, there is hardly anything left to discuss. Finally, as I will attempt to show in the following exegesis, the theology of Isaiah 33 is completely consistent with Isaiah's views. Once one has recognized the temporal priority of the Zion tradition (Roberts 1982b) and Isaiah's dependency on that tradition (von Rad 1965: 156–60), there remains no compelling reason to deny the Isaianic authorship of Isaiah 33.

The Text

1. Ho! You destroyer who yourself have not been destroyed,
You betrayer whom they have not betrayed—
When you have finished destroying, you will be destroyed.
When you have ceased[1] betraying, they will betray you.
2. O Yahweh, be gracious to us; we wait for you.
Be our support[2] in the morning,
Even our salvation in the time of stress.
3. At the sound of your thunder[3] the peoples fled;
At your rising up[3] the nations were scattered;
4. And spoil was gathered as grasshoppers gather,
As locusts leap, one leaped upon it.[4]
5. Yahweh was exalted. Yes, he dwelt on the height.[5]
He filled Zion with justice and righteousness.
6. [6]Yahweh, faithfulness to your covenant was her wealth,
Her salvation was wisdom and devotion,
The fear of Yahweh was her treasure.[6]
7. But now the Arielites[7] cry without,
The messengers of Shalem[8] weep bitterly.
8. The highways are desolate,
The wayfarer has ceased.
He has broken the covenant,
He has rejected the treaty,[9]
He has disregarded the tribute.[10]
9. The land is dried and withered,
Lebanon is disgraced and mouldering,
Sharon has become like a desert,
Bashan and Carmel are stripped bare.
10. "Now I will arise," says Yahweh,
"Now I will exalt myself,

Now I will raise myself up.
11. You conceive stubble,
You give birth to chaff,
My[11] breath like a fire will devour you,
12. And the peoples will be burnings of lime,
Cut-down thorns which are set on fire.
13. Hear, you distant ones, what I have done;
Acknowledge, you near ones, my might."
14. Sinners in Zion are afraid,
Trembling has seized the impious:
Who among us can live with this devouring fire?
Who among us can live with this never-dying blaze?
15. The one who walks in righteousness,
And who speaks uprightly,
Who refuses the profit from oppression,
Who shakes out his hands from taking a bribe,
Who closes his ears from participating in plots to shed blood,
Who shuts his eyes from contemplating evil.
16. Such a one will dwell in the heights.
His fortress will be the citadels of the cliffs,
His bread will be given him,
And his water assured.
17. Your eyes will gaze upon the king in his beauty;
You will see a land that stretches afar.
18. Your heart shall muse on the terror:
Where is the one who counted?
Where is the one who weighed?
Where is the one who counted the towers?
19. The barbarian people you will no longer see,
The people whose speech was too difficult to comprehend,
Who stammered in a tongue you could not understand.
20. Gaze upon Zion, the city of our assembly!
Your eyes shall see Jerusalem
As a secure habitation,
A tent which one does not move,
Whose tent pegs will never be pulled up,
And none of its ropes shall be broken.
21. No, there Yahweh is majestic,
A reservoir[12] of rivers for us,
Of streams broad and wide,
Where no rowing ship can go,
Nor stately craft can pass.
22. For Yahweh is our judge,
Yahweh is our commander,
Yahweh is our king,
He will save us.
23. Their[13] tackle ropes hang loose,
They cannot hold firm the socket of their mast,
They cannot spread the sail.
Then prey will be divided,
Booty in abundance,
The lame will divide the spoil.
24. And no inhabitant will say, "I am sick."
The people who live therein will be forgiven of sin.

Textual Notes

1. Reading *kkltk* with 1QIsa[a]. For the pairing *tmm*/*klh* see also Isa 16: 4; Lam 3: 22.

2. Either read *zĕrōʿ-m*, a substantive with enclitic *mem*, the suffix being understood from the suffix on the parallel term, *yšwʿtnw* (Irwin 1977: 138), or correct to *zrʿnw*. The Syriac, Targum, and some manuscripts of the Vulgate support the correction to *zrʿnw*.

The JPS translation suggests emending the imperative *hyh*, "Be," to the perfect *hyt*, "You have been." The change would be easy enough in the late script, and contextually it is beguiling, but there is no versional evidence for the correction, and it is not necessary to make sense of the passage.

3. The precise meaning of *hmwn*, "sound, murmur, roar, crowd, abundance," depends on one's understanding of the parallel term *mrwmmtk*. BDB's traditional treatment of it—the preposition *mn*, followed by an abstract noun used as an infinitive formed from the *Pôlēl* stem of *rwm*, plus the pronominal suffix—seems preferable to the numerous emendations suggested. Syriac, the later Greek translations, and the Vulgate all understood the word as a derivative from *rwm*. Moreover, there seems to be a play on this word in verse 10, where the author uses the *Pôlēl* imperfect of *rwm* to announce just such a rising up of the deity as indicated in v 3. Yahweh's rising up implies judgment and is traditionally clothed in the imagery of the thunderstorm (Isa 2: 19, 21; 29: 6; 30: 27–33; Pss 46: 7; 76: 7, 10). In that setting the translation of *hmwn* as "thunder" seems appropriate, and the suffix is understood from its occurrence with the parallel term.

4. The text of verse 4 is very difficult. I read *wĕʾussap šālāl kĕmô ʾosep heḥāsîl*/*kĕmô šaq gēbîm šôqēq bô*.

5. Gunkel corrected the participles *niśgāb* and *šōkēn* to perfects (1924: 178), but since the tense of a participle must be derived from the context (Kautzsch and Cowley 1910: 356, par. 116d 2), and since both the preceding (*nddw, npṣw, wʾsp, šwqq*) and the succeeding verbs (*mlʾ*) are perfects, one may translate *nśgb* and *škn* as referring to past time even if the vocalization as participles is preserved.

6. Verse 6 presents a textual crux that is impossible to resolve with any degree of certainty. The present text is hardly correct, but no correction is likely to receive common assent. One is tempted to simply leave the verse untranslated, but that would obscure the fact that the general drift of the passage is clear enough. The verse forms a tricola, and any analysis should begin with the last unit, since it is clearest: "The fear of Yahweh was her treasure." The pronominal suffix on "treasure" is masculine in Hebrew, but it is difficult to take Yahweh as the antecedent given the second masculine singular reference to him earlier in the verse. The antecedent should be Zion and therefore feminine. It is possible that the original suffix was the feminine *–â*, written *h*, which an early scribe misread as a *mater* for the masculine suffix *–ô*. The letter *h* was used as a *mater lectionis* for both *–â* and *–ô* from the time of Isaiah to the Exile (Cross and Freedman 1952: 49, 53), and there is other evidence in Isaiah for textual corruption due to uncertainty over whether to read *h* as *ô* or *â* (e.g., Isa 30: 33—*topotô* for *topteh*, *mĕdūrātô* for *mĕdūrātâ*, and *bô* for *bâ*).

If this emendation is correct, the second line should probably be divided and corrected to read as *yšwʿth ḥkmh wdʿt*. The suffix *h* probably dropped out by haplography after the adoption of the square script due to its similarity to the following *ḥ*. The anomalous form *ḥkmt* is perhaps due to the following *dʿt*, but one should not rule out the possibility that it is a rare but nonetheless correct form.

Unfortunately, the first line remains problematic. Neither the opening third masculine singular perfect, which clashes with the second masculine singular suffix on *ʿtyk*, nor the word *ʿtyk*, "your times," seems fitting. Radical emendation seems necessary. The 1QIsa[a] reading *ʿdym* in v 8 suggests the possible correction of *ʿtyk* to *ʿdyk*, "your covenant." One could solve the problem of the masculine verb by a transposition, *whyh ḥsnh ʾmwnt ʿdyk*, "Her wealth was faithfulness to your covenant," but the 1QIsa[a] reading *yhyh* suggests an easier correction which would have the merit of preparing for the second person suffix: *yhwh ʾmwnt ʿdyk ḥsnh*, "O Yahweh, faithfulness to your covenant was her wealth."

7. Reading *ʾrʾlym* with a few manuscripts and connecting it to *ʾryʾl* (29: 1), which is clearly a name for Jerusalem.

8. One should probably read *šālēm*, attested as a poetic name for Jerusalem (Ps 76: 3). Even if the reading *šālôm*, "peace," is correct, it probably represents a play on the proper name and should be regarded as an intentional double entendre, a device found elsewhere in Isaiah. Note, for example, his play on the meanings of *dlq* in 5: 11: "Ho, you who rise early in the morning that they might chase (*yrdpw*) beer,/Who tarry late in the evening that wine might chase/inflame them (*ydlyqm*)."

9. Reading *ʿdym* with 1QIsa^{a} and interpreting it in light of the Aramaic cognate and the parallel with *bryt*.

10. Reading *ʾnwš* as cognate with Ugaritic *unuššu*, following Hillers (1971: 257–59).

11. Reading *rwḥy kmw ʾš tʾklm*. The scribe was apparently influenced by the second masculine plural suffix on the verb to misread the first *km* as the same suffix.

12. Reading *miqwē-m* for MT *mĕqôm* with Irwin (1977: 158–59).

13. Correcting *ḥblyk* to *ḥblyhm* to agree with *trnm*, "their mast."

Commentary

The identity of the destroyer in verse 1 remains subject to debate. Duhm's equation of the enemy with Antiochus Eupator (1892: 216) places the text too late to be credible in view of the date of the Qumran scrolls. Wildberger thinks of the early Persian period (1979: 1288), but against such an identification is the fact that the Persians did not plunder Jerusalem; thus Wildberger is forced to turn this passage into a generalized judgment on a world oppressor in whose fall all, including Israel, will suffer (1979: 1291–92). With more reason Clements assigns the whole of chapter 33 to the age of the Babylonian Exile (1980a: 265). Hab 2: 5–8, which appears to speak of Babylon, contains a similar thought, and Isa 21: 2, which is usually dated to the Babylonian Exile, also mentions the "betrayer who betrays and the destroyer who destroys." It is possible that Isaiah 21 should be dated earlier in the Assyrian period, however (Macintosh 1980: 118, for parts of the chapter; Erlandsson 1972: 92), and Habakkuk could be reusing a motif taken from Isaiah. The general thought of the verse is the same as that found in Isa 10: 5–22, where Assyria is expressly identified as the enemy. There the emphasis is on God's use of unwitting Assyria as his tool to punish Israel, while in Isaiah 33 the prophet emphasizes the destroyer's actions without specifically referring to God's motive for permitting them; in both cases when the destroyer has finished his task, he in turn will be destroyed (Isa 10: 12).

The term *bwgd* includes the notion of treachery or betrayal (Irwin 1977: 137); it should not be reduced to a mere synonym of *šdd*. That raises the issue of its referent. If one thinks of the Assyrian period and interprets v 8 as referring to the same incident, one may find its background in the events recorded in 2 Kgs 18: 17–37. The literary character of this account and its relationship to the preceding account in 2 Kgs 18: 13–16 is debated. For the most recent discussion and literature, see Clements (1980b).

Read on the flat, 2 Kgs 18: 17ff. suggests that after Hezekiah submitted to Sennacherib's demands, Sennacherib raised them. The relationship between the events recorded in the two accounts may be far more complex, but if 2 Kgs 18: 17ff. is not taken as its sequel or dismissed as historicized legend, it can hardly refer to the same event as 2 Kgs 18: 13–16, since the outcome is totally different. Despite Clements's claims (1980b: 18–19), our historical knowledge of the events of 701 B.C.E. are not sufficient to rule out a serious check to Assyrian hopes, compatible with the highly theologized account in 2 Kgs 18: 17ff. Sennacherib did not capture Jerusalem as even his own bombastic account makes clear, and it should be noted that Hezekiah's tribute did not reach him until after he had returned to Nineveh (Luckenbill 1924: 33–34, lines 37–49). Nor can the hypothesis of a second campaign against Jerusalem be ruled out (Bright 1972: 296–308)—an hypothesis which would provide a striking context for the oracle in Isa 21: 1–10, if it is interpreted as referring to the fall of Babylon in 689 B.C.E. (Erlandsson 1972: 91). Either reconstruction seems historically preferable to dismissing 2 Kgs 18: 17ff. as sheer legend, and either would offer a setting in which a Judean prophet could characterize renewed or heightened Assyrian pressure on Judah as treachery.

In v 2 the prophet switches from his direct address of the enemy to invoke Yahweh on behalf of his community. As the text stands, the petition extends through v 2. The emendation of *hyh* to *hyt* discussed in the notes, if accepted, would indicate a switch from the imperative of request to past tense narration.

Even if one does not accept this emendation, however, the perfects in v 3 should be taken as indicating genuine past tense narration, not as precative perfects continuing the imperatives of the prayer (so Irwin 1977: 140), nor as a present or future description of the plight of the nations (so Wildberger 1979: 1289). The prophet is reciting the claims of the Zion tradition as they are found, for example, in the quite ancient Psalm 76. It is the same ancient tradition that the author of Psalm 48 refers to when he says, "As we have heard, thus we have seen" (Ps 48: 9). For that Psalmist an ancient tradition was confirmed in a contemporary experience, and in similar manner our prophet is quoting the ancient tradition as a background for his prediction of the outcome of the present conflict. His use of the *Pôlēl* of *rwm* in the oracle of salvation (v 10) resumes *rwmmt* in this verse and is a way of underscoring his point. As Yahweh saved Zion in the past, so he will save her now.

The image in verse 4 appears to mean that Israel swarmed over the booty left by the nations who fled and were scattered just as grasshoppers or locusts swarm over a field. Again the booty motif, if not the locust imagery, is rooted in the Zion tradition. Note the form *ʾštwllw* in Ps 76: 6 and the division of the spoil (*šll*) mentioned in Ps 68: 13.

V 5 celebrates Yahweh's former victory over his enemies with hymnic participles that describe him as exalted (*nśgb*) and dwelling on the height (*škn mrwm*). The designation *mrwm* can refer to either heaven (Ps 102: 20) or to an earthly height (Isa 22: 16; 26: 5; Hab 2: 9; Obad 3), and it often refers specifically to the temple mount (Isa 33: 16; Jer 17: 12; 31: 12; Ezek 20: 40; 34: 14). Classical temple theology did not clearly distinguish terrestrial from celestial (Amos 1: 2; Joel 4: 16 compared to Jer 25: 30; Ps 18: 10 compared to Pss 20: 3, 7; 50: 2; see Mettinger 1982), but *mrwm* here undoubtedly involves the concept of God's abode on the sacred mount (Isa 8: 18), since the last half of the verse speaks of his largess to Zion. When the verb *škn* is used of God's dwelling, it normally refers to his dwelling in Jerusalem (1 Kgs 6: 11–13; 8: 12–13 = 2 Chr 6: 1; Isa 8: 18; Ezek 43: 5–9; Joel 4: 17, 21; Zech 2: 14, 15; 8: 3; Pss 68: 17, 30; 74: 2; 135: 21; 1 Chr 23: 25) or at least to his earthly dwelling among men (Exod 24: 16; 25: 8; 29: 45; Num 5: 3; 35: 34; Ps 78: 60). Moreover, a nominal form (*mśgb*) of the root employed here to speak of Yahweh's elevation (*śgb*) is used in two of the Zion Songs to describe the exalted deity's protection of his city (Pss 46: 8,12; 48: 4). That nominal form also occurs later in this chapter, in v 16, where the prophet picks up on three of the terms used here (*nśgb—mśgbw, škn—yškn, mrwm—mrwmym*). One should note that the prophet continues to play on the root *rwm*.

Verse 5a prepares for 5b and 6. It was Yahweh's presence in and love for Zion which filled it with justice and righteousness (cf. Ps 132: 13–18). V 6 is textually uncertain, but it appears to be developing the preceding thought further. Jerusalem's wealth, salvation, and treasure were all rooted in her special relationship to Yahweh. In this context both *ḥkmh* and *dʿt* have a theological specificity; it is not just any wisdom or knowledge, but what Hosea refers to as *dʿt ʾlhym*, "the knowledge of God" (Hos 4: 1). That Isaiah was familiar with Hosea's concept seems clear from a comparison of Hos 4: 6 and Isa 5: 12–13.

After this petition grounded in Yahweh's past graciousness to Jerusalem, the prophet turns to the situation of need that provoked the petition and in so doing picks up part of the thought of v 1. The *hn* in v 7 appears to indicate a contrast between the former happy situation of Zion and the present situation of desperate need. The word is used elsewhere to introduce a statement set in contrast to a preceding clause (Isa 50: 1, 2, 9). Unlike the good old days, the present inhabitants of Jerusalem cry and weep bitterly because of the danger which has stopped travel. The term *ḥṣh*, "without," does not mean "outside the city," as though these mourners were exiles, but "outside, in the streets," where public mourning customarily took place (Amos 5: 16; Isa 15: 3; 24: 11).

It is not entirely clear why the messengers of Shalem weep. The line could refer to messengers from Jerusalem who had been turned back from their mission by besieging forces (cf. Luckenbill 1924: 33, lines 29–30), in which case the reference to the ceasing of travel is particularly appropriate. V 7b could also refer to such messengers returning with new and harsh demands from consultation with the Assyrian overlord. Sennacherib mentions the messengers Hezekiah sent to Nineveh to bear tribute and make submission as a vassal (Luckenbill 1924: 34, lines 48–49), and this background could explain the word play with *šālôm*, "messengers of peace." Finally, the line could refer to Judean messengers bringing word of the collapse of Hezekiah's ally, Babylon (Isa 21: 1–10).

In the present context the third masculine singular perfects of v 8b can only refer back to the treacherous destroyer of v 1. "He has broken the treaty, / He has rejected the treaty, / He has disregarded the tribute" would be appropriately said of Sennacherib if, as 2 Kgs 18: 17 suggests, Sennacherib went back on his word after the capitulation of Hezekiah. Given that scenario, Duhm's objection that it was Hezekiah, not Sennacherib, who had broken the covenant (1892: 218), falls by the way. The imagery of languishing woodlands or pasture is often associated with the covenant curses (Hos 4: 3; Isa 24: 1–6; Jer 23: 10; 12: 4), but that would not fit here if the Assyrian is the covenant breaker. The imagery also appears in theophanies (Nah 1: 4; Amos 1: 2), and in descriptions of a land ravaged by foreign enemies (Isa 19: 1–15) or by natural disaster under the figure of a foreign enemy (Joel 1: 10–12). Ravaging by a foreign enemy must be what is involved here.

It is possible, however, that the present text represents Isaiah's own reworking of an originally independent oracle, thus involving what Holladay calls a "self-extended oracle" (1978: 84). Verses 7–16, with slight changes, could be read as a judgment oracle against Judah, her plight described in traditional terms as due to her breach of covenant (reading three infinitive absolutes: *hāpēr, maʾōs, ḥāšōb*; see Hillers 1971). In this case, v 11 would originally have referred to Israel's plans as worthless (cf. 30: 1–5; 31: 1–4), and God's devouring fire would have originally burned his own people (reading *ʿammît* + enclitic *mem*) to lime (cf. 5: 23–24). If that were the original setting of vv 7–16, they have been altered to fit into the present larger context.

Yahweh's rising up in v 10 picks up the thought of v 3, binding the two units together. As in the past, so in the present, Yahweh, without assistance, will rise up to defeat his enemies. The vain plans of God's enemies (Isa 7: 7; 8: 9–10; 10: 7–11) and the burning up of the Assyrians (Isa 10: 16–18; 29: 5–6; 30: 27–28, 30, 33; 31: 9) are motifs running through Isaiah's thought.

V 13 calls upon all people, both those close at hand and those far away, to pay attention to what God has done. The reference is clearly to his projected judgment mentioned in the preceding verses, *pace* Vermeylen (1978: 433). Isaiah had constantly complained that his contemporaries did not pay attention to Yahweh's work (Isa 5: 12; 22: 11; 28: 21–22). On occasion they even mocked Isaiah by urging Yahweh to hurry it up (5: 19). But once Yahweh has acted, Isaiah says, those in Jerusalem who have seen his intervention first hand will no longer scoff at the prophet. They will react in terror at the majesty of this devouring fire and with trembling ask who can live in this God's presence (v 14). The reference to fire and furnace resumes the thought of vv 11–12 and demonstrates the interconnection of these verses despite the putative introductory formula in v 13.

The question and answer in vv 14–16 is modeled on the entrance liturgies, such as Psalms 15 and 24. Isaiah apparently adopted this form, which was at home in the pre-Isaianic Zion tradition and tied to its festival processions (Psalm 24; Cross 1973: 91–94; Roberts 1982, 1983), to give expression to what he understood as the result of God's purging of Jerusalem. The moral transformation of Zion's survivors is expressed here in traditional terms, though rooted in a new experiential awareness of God's character as mediated through his actions in history. Note how the language of v 16 reiterates the description of the past security of Zion (*škn mrwm—mrwmym yškn; nśgb—mśgbw; ʾmwnt—nʾmnym*), providing another link to tie the chapter together.

Vv 17–24 present a vision of Jerusalem after the terror has passed. In those days Israel will see the true king even as Isaiah saw him in the temple, and the presence of Yahweh, Immanuel, will mean the absence of the enemy. The people will look around in wonder at the disappearance of the enemy (cf. 29: 7–8). That people of strange speech whom Yahweh had used to instruct Israel (28: 11) will no longer be present. Though neither chapter 28 nor 33 names this people of barbaric tongue, the reference in 33: 19 clearly depends on 28: 11, and both refer to the Assyrians, whose language the average Judean could not understand. Even the Judean officials who were prepared to discuss terms with the Assyrian representative are represented as asking for the discussion to take place in Aramaic, not Assyrian (2 Kgs 18: 26).

Ps 48: 13–14, which seems close to Isa 33: 18, is probably dependent on Isaiah, not the other way around. Isaiah is presenting a future projection, but the Psalmist is apparently referring to something that has already happened. The Psalmist has just experienced what the ancient tradition affirmed (Ps 48: 9), and as a result of God's victory he calls upon his audience to walk around and inspect the recently delivered Zion (Ps 48: 13–14). Isaiah, in contrast, is speaking of a future deliverance, and he apparently refers to the enemy's hostile inspection of Zion, though the JPS translation suggests an alternate understanding. The close resemblance between Psalm 48 and Isaiah 33 suggests that they date from the same period, and it is possible that the Psalmist, having experienced the deliverance of Jerusalem and familiar with the slightly earlier oracle of Isaiah, formulated his hymn of thanksgiving in words appropriated from that oracle.

In v 20 Isaiah continues with an appeal to gaze upon the now secure Jerusalem. It is first pictured under the image of a permanently fixed tent. Then the prophet shifts to the imagery of the city as the paradisaical abode of Yahweh, the reservoir of broad rivers. This motif, rooted in the Zion tradition (Roberts 1982), is expanded by reference to another motif of the Zion tradition, the assault of the enemy kings on Zion. In the mythological antecedents of that motif these "men of the seashore" apparently came by ship to attack Baal's mountain (Roberts 1982). Ps 48: 8 speaks of Yahweh smashing the ships of Tarshish, and Isaiah elsewhere in a highly mythological context speaks of Yahweh's day against all the ships of Tarshish and dhows of Arabia (2: 16). The motif is clearly mythological in origin and secondarily applied to Jerusalem, since Jerusalem is neither on the coast nor subject to waterborne assault. Nonetheless, Isaiah uses this motif metaphorically to underscore Zion's future security. Though Yahweh's abode will be the source of wide streams, those rivers will never again be the avenue for arrogant human assaults on God's city. Because Yahweh is Zion's judge, ruler, king, and deliverer, enemy ships will never threaten her. Hostile fleets will be wrecked before endangering Jerusalem; they will serve only to fatten Zion's inhabitants with their plundered goods. Even the lame will find a share in the abundant wealth left abandoned by Zion's defeated foes. Note how the motif of plunder resumes the thought of 33: 4.

Finally, and as if to correct the notion suggested by the mention of the lame, Isaiah promises that the inhabitants of this purified Jerusalem will not suffer illness, for they will be a forgiven people, unlike the battered and sick Zion of the period before God's purging judgment (Isa 1: 5–6).

If these words were spoken by Isaiah in the context of the Assyrian crisis, as this paper has argued, many of Isaiah's expectations were not fulfilled. Whatever the nature of Yahweh's deliverance of Jerusalem, it did not have the permanently transforming effect upon Judah's inhabitants that Isaiah predicted. All Zion's sinners did not give up their sins, and Jerusalem did not ever after remain secure. Yahweh did not become transparently present for his people, and Jerusalem fell to her enemies again and again. The vision's failure to be realized in contemporary reality, however, is no reason to deny the vision to Isaiah. Most Old Testament prophetic visions of salvation were not realized in the time and to the extent expected by their biblical authors. Isaiah simply joins Ezekiel, Second Isaiah, and others among the prophets whose glorious visions for the future failed to materialize, or perhaps more adequately stated, are yet to be realized in a transformed and more glorious manner (Roberts 1979).

Note

* It is a real pleasure to present this study to David Noel Freedman, a long-time friend and one of the most stimulating and creative scholars I have ever had the pleasure to know.

References

Auvray, P.
1972 *Isaïe 1–39*. Sources Bibliques. Paris: Librairie Lecoffre.

Barth, H.
1977 *Die Jesaja-Worte in der Josiazeit*. Wissenschaftliche Monographien zum Alten und Neuen Testament 48. Neukirchen-Vluyn: Neukirchener Verlag.

Bright, J.
1972 *A History of Israel*². Philadelphia: Westminster.

Clements, R. E.
1980a *Isaiah 1–39*. New Century Bible Commentary. Grand Rapids: Eerdmans.
1980b *Isaiah and the Deliverance of Jerusalem*. Journal for the Study of the Old Testament Supplement Series 13. Sheffield: JSOT Press.

Cross, F. M.
1973 *Canaanite Myth and Hebrew Epic: Essays in the History of the Religion of Israel*. Cambridge: Harvard.

Cross, F. M., and Freedman, D. N.
1952 *Early Hebrew Orthography*. American Oriental Series 36. New Haven: American Oriental Society.

Duhm, B.
1892 *Das Buch Jesaia*. Handkommentar zum Alten Testament. Göttingen: Vandenhoeck und Ruprecht.

Erlandsson, S.
1970 *The Burden of Babylon*. Coniectanea Biblica. O. T. Series 4. Lund: Gleerup.

Feldmann, F.
1925 *Das Buch Isaias*. Exegetisches Handbuch zum Alten Testament 14. Münster: Verlag der Aschendorffschen Verlagsbuchhandlung.

Fohrer, G.
1960–64 *Das Buch Jesaja*. Zürcher Bibelkommentare I-III. Zürich-Stuttgart: Zwingli Verlag.

Ginsberg, H. L.
1971 First Isaiah. Vol. 9, pp. 49–60 in *Encyclopaedia Judaica*. Jerusalem: Keter Publishing House.

Gunkel, H.
1924 Jesia 33, eine prophetische Liturgie: Ein Vortrag. *Zeitschrift für die Alttestamentliche Wissenschaft* 42: 177–208.

Hillers, D. R.
1971 A Hebrew Cognate of *unuššu*/*'unṯ* in Is 33: 8. *Harvard Theological Review* 64: 257–59.

Holladay, W.
1978 *Isaiah: Scroll of a Prophetic Heritage*. Grand Rapids: Eerdmans.

Irwin, W. H.
1977 *Isaiah 28–33: Translation with Philological Notes*. Rome: Biblical Institute Press.

Ishida, T., ed.
1982 *Studies in the Period of David and Solomon and Other Essays*. Winona Lake, Indiana: Eisenbrauns.

Kaiser, O.
1963–1973 *Der Prophet Jesaja*. Das Alte Testament Deutsch 17–18. Göttingen: Vandenhoeck und Ruprecht.

Kautzsch, E., and Cowley, A. E.
1910 *Gesenius' Hebrew Grammar*. Oxford: Clarendon Press.

Kissane, E. J.
1941 *The Book of Isaiah, I.* Dublin: Browne and Nolan Limited.

Luckenbill, D. D.
1924 *The Annals of Sennacherib.* Oriental Institute Publications 2. Chicago: University of Chicago Press.

Macintosh, A. A.
1980 *Isaiah xxi: A Palimpsest.* Cambridge: Cambridge University Press.

Mettinger, T. N. D.
1982 YHWH SABAOTH—The Heavenly King on the Cherubim Throne. Pp. 109–38 in Ishida 1982.

Mowinckel, S.
1921 *Psalmenstudien II: Das Thronbesteigungsfest Jahwäs und der Ursprung des Eschatologie.* Kristiania: J. Dybwad. Rpt., 1966, Amsterdam: P. Schippers.

Penna, A.
1958 *Isaia.* La Sacra Bibbia. Rome: Marietti.

von Rad, G.
1965 *Old Testament Theology.* II. New York: Harper and Row.

Roberts, J. J. M.
1979 A Christian Perspective on Prophetic Prediction. *Interpretation* 33: 240–53.

1981 The Teaching Voice in Isaiah 30: 20–21. Pp. 130–137 in *Christian Teaching: Studies in Honor of LeMoine G. Lewis,* ed. E. Ferguson. Abilene, Texas: Abilene Christian University.

1982 Zion in the Theology of the Davidic-Solomonic Empire. Pp. 93–108 in Ishida 1982.

1983 The Divine King and the Human Community in Isaiah's Vision of the Future. In *The Quest for the Kingdom of God: Essays in Honor of George E. Mendenhall,* ed. H. B. Huffmon, F. A. Spina, and A. R. W. Green. Winona Lake, Indiana: Eisenbrauns.

Skinner, J.
1925 *Isaiah.* The Cambridge Bible for Schools and Colleges. Cambridge: Cambridge University Press.

Stade, B.
1884 Miscellen. *Zeitschrift für die Alttestamentliche Wissenchaft* 4: 256–71.

Vermeylen, J.
1978 *Du prophete Isaïe a l'apocalyptique: Isaïe, I-XXXV, miroir d'un demi-millenaire d'experience religieuse en Israël.* I-II. Etudes Bibliques. Paris: Libraire Lecoffre.

Wildberger, H.
1979 *Jesaja.* Biblischer Kommentar Altes Testament. Neukirchen-Vluyn: Neukirchener Verlag.

Ziegler, J.
1948 *Isaias.* Echter-Bibel. Würzburg: Echter-Verlag.

Isaiah 55: Invitation to a Feast

Richard J. Clifford
Weston School of Theology, Cambridge, Massachusetts

Even in a biblical book as dominated in recent decades by the form-critical method as Second Isaiah, one can still find passages where the form has not been sufficiently investigated and where valuable suggestions from the pioneer era of form criticism have gone undeveloped. Such a passage is Isaiah 55. Unexplored comparative evidence exists which can, in the writer's opinion, assist in resolving several longstanding problems of the chapter, viz., the relation of vv 1–3a to vv 3b-5, the significance of vv 6–11, and the relation of the whole chapter to Second Isaiah's message. It is a pleasure to dedicate this study to David Noel Freedman, who has made many contributions to the study of Hebrew rhetoric and poetry.

J. Begrich, the first scholar systematically to work through Second Isaiah with the then-new tools of form criticism, correctly noted that the call in vv 1–3a according to its form was an invitation by Wisdom to a banquet, comparable to Proverbs 9 and Sir 24: 19–22. Such invitations typically begin as an offer of food and drink to the hungry and thirsty and end as an offer of life. Begrich was puzzled by the connection of vv 1–3a, the invitation, to vv 3b-5, the extension of the Davidic covenant to those invited, since he thought the covenant had nothing to do with wisdom teaching (Begrich 1938: 59–60). Had the relevant Ugaritic texts been sufficiently deciphered for comparison in 1938, Begrich might have seen that the genre of invitation to a feast is not "a relatively late attested form of wisdom teaching" (Begrich 1938: 59) but is simply a formula of invitation to a sacral feast found in a variety of literatures from the Late Bronze Age to the second century B.C.E. In one Ugaritic text, for instance, the formula "Ho, eat of food," etc., occurs in the rubrical beginning of a ritual, and in another, in the narrative of a legend. Recent scholarship has acknowledged Begrich's acute observations but has not explored them further. His suggestion of an invitation to a banquet has been set alongside another one without a final decision being made in favor of either. The other suggestion, at least as old as Franz Delitzsch, has it that the verses mimic the cry of the water seller in the market place (1890: 325). J. Muilenburg is typical of moderns on the form: "The cry may therefore be reminiscent of the water seller, though the wisdom provenance seems clear in view of the parallels."[1]

Before comparing other texts in which the formula of invitation occurs, we must first eliminate from serious consideration the view that the cry of invitation is the cry of the water seller. First, to my knowledge, there is no ancient evidence for water sellers' cries. Second, the twice repeated cry, "Come and buy," in MT, allegedly imitating the repeated shouts of the eastern marketplace, is simply an instance of dittography and should be excised. Textual evidence from Qumran, the Greek versions, and parallelism within the verses, all strongly suggest the following translation.

Ho, all who thirst, come to the waters,
  and those who have no money, come!
Buy food[2] for no money,
  for no payment, wine and milk.
Why do you spend money for what is not food,
  your riches for what does not satisfy?
Listen attentively to me and eat choice food,
  let yourself enjoy the richest viands.
Incline your ear and come to me,
  hear and you shall live.

With the water seller gone from the scene, we may now turn to the ancient parallels of the feast. Two of the three apposite parallels come from Ugarit, which means that they antedate ca. 1200 B.C.E. and are part of the same cultural milieu as the Bible. The first is part of an opening rubric welcoming the royal party to what seems to be a rite, perhaps a *hieros gamos*. The main body of the text describes El having sexual relations with two females who shortly after give birth to the giants *Šḥr wŠlm*.

lḥm blḥm ʾay	Eat of bread, ho!
wšty bḫmr yn ʾay	and drink of the liquor of wine, ho!
šlm mlk šlm mlkt	Greetings, O King! Greetings, O Queen!
ʿrbm wṯnnm	and processionists and garrison![3]

Ugaritic *ʾay* is cognate to Hebrew *hôy*.[4] The king and queen of Ugarit are greeted upon their arrival at the place, presumably in the temple, where the ritual is to be reenacted. The connection of the formula with entry into a sanctuary is to be noted. It will be argued below that the formula in Isaiah 55 similarly invites listeners to a sacred place.

The second Ugaritic text is from the legend of Aqhat and is part of the narrative which describes the adventures of the young man Aqhat, his father Danil and his sister Paghat, and the activities of the gods, El and his court and Anat. The goddess Anat gives a banquet and invites her guests, among whom is Aqhat, inexperienced in dealing with the passionate goddess. She offers him eternal life with the gods in exchange for his wonderful bow.[5]

l}ḥm {blḥm ʾay}	"Eat of bread, ho!
{šty bḫmr yn} ʾay	Drink of the liquor of wine, ho!
š{ty bkrpnm yn(?)}	Drink goblets of wine (?),
bḥ}rb mlḥ{t qṣ mrʾi}	with beautiful knife slaughter (?) fatlings."
{tšty krpnm} yn	They drink goblets of wine,
bks ḫ{rṣ dm ʿṣm}	in cups of gold, the juice of vine stocks.

The following lines, too broken for continuous translation, show the goddess in the course of the banquet. The arrival of the young man with his bow and arrows has stirred her. Excitedly she offers him gold and silver if he will give it to her. The young man demurs, offering instead to furnish the raw materials of a bow so that she can have her own made. But she insists on his bow and soon raises her bid recklessly—life with the gods.

{tšu gh} wtṣḥ	She raises her voice and cries,
šmʿ mʿ {laqht ǵzr}	"Hear, O Aqhat the hero,
{i}rš ksp watnk	ask silver and I will give it to you,
{ḫrṣ waš}lḥk	gold, and I will bestow it on you.
wtn qštk {lʿnt}	Only give your bow to Anat,
{tq}ḥ {q}ṣʿtk ybmt limm	let Ybmt limm take your darts."
wyʿn aqht ǵzr	And Aqhat the hero said,
adr ṯqbm (b/d)lbnn	"I will vow trees from Lebanon,
adr gdm brumm	I will vow sinews from wild bulls,
adr qrnt byʿlm	I will vow horns from wild goats,
mtnm bʿqbt ṯr	tendons from the hocks of bulls.
adr bǵl il qnm	I will vow 'cradles' from sucking lambs.
tn lkṯr wḫss	Give these to Koshar-wa-Hasis.
ybʿl qšt lʿnt	He will make a bow for Anat,
qṣʿt lybmt limm	darts for Ybmt limm."
wtʿn btlt ʿnt	And Virgin Anat answered,
irš ḥym laqht ǵzr	"Ask for life, O Aqhat the hero,
irš ḥym watnk	ask for life and I will give it to you,
blmt wašlḥk	not-dying and I will grant it to you.
ašsprk ʿm bʿl šnt	I will cause you to count years with Baal,
ʿm bn il tspr yrḫm	with the sons of El you will count months.
kbʿl kyḥwy yʿšr	For Baal, when he gives life, gives a feast,
ḥwy yʿšr wyšqynh	for the one brought to life he gives a feast and makes him drink.
ybd wyšr ʿlh	He sings, he serenades him,
nʿm{n wt}ʿnynn	with sweetness does he sing.
ap ank aḥwy aqht ǵzr	And I will bring you to life, O Aqhat the hero."

The goddess invites her guests to her banquet to partake of food and drink. She ends by offering to one of her guests eternal life. It is crucial to this paper's argument to understand the kind of life the goddess offers. It is transference to the divine world, the only place where eternal life could be enjoyed. Aqhat's response reflects the ancient Near Eastern view that man as man in this world must someday die: "Mortal man, how can he attain everlasting life?/How can man attain an eternal destiny?" Aqhat recognizes that he would have to leave his status as mortal man and join the divine assembly in order to avoid death and live forever. Eternal life is life *with* the gods, life *in* the divine realm.

The important corollary to the assertion that "life" is life in the divine world is that one "lives" when one is admitted into the holy place, which is the extension of the divine world into the profane world of mortal human beings. W. Zimmerli has noted that behind the priestly declaratory formula "He shall surely live" lies a cultic understanding of "life." "'Life' is especially the gift given in the sphere of the sanctuary as the place of God's presence. . . . This becomes clear behind the polemical *torah* of Amos: Seek me, and you will live, but do not seek Bethel . . . (Amos 5: 4f). Behind it there echoes the priestly *torah* 'Seek Bethel, and you will live'" (Zimmerli 1979: 376).

The third text with affinities both to the Aqhat text and to Isaiah 55 is Prov 9: 1–6+11 and 13–18. In one panel of the diptych (vv 1–6+11), Dame Wisdom invites her guests to her new palace to eat and drink (*lĕkû laḥămû bĕlaḥămî uštû bĕyayin māsāktî*) and live (*wiḥĕyû*). In the opposite panel, Dame Folly issues a counter-invitation. The life that Wisdom offers at her banquet is an extended and blessed life *with* her, *in* her palace. Only by rejecting (*ʿizbû*) Dame Folly can one accept the life of wisdom. One enters Dame Wisdom's world and leaves behind the world of folly.

> Wisdom has built her palace,
> she has set up her seven columns.
> She has dressed her meat, mixed her wine.
> Yes, she has set her table.
> She has sent her maids,
> she calls at the highest places in the city:
> "Whoever is inexperienced, let him turn in here,
> to whomever lacks understanding I say,
> 'Come, eat of my food,
> and drink the wine I have mixed.
> Leave behind folly and live,
> walk in the path of insight.
> For with me your days will be multiplied,
> and the years of your life increased.' "[6]

The above parallels argue powerfully that Isaiah 55 too is an instance of the form of invitation to a feast where life, or proximity to the deity, is proffered. As in the invitations in Aqhat, Proverbs 9 (and Sir 24: 19–22), the language in Isaiah moves from the offer of food and drink to the offer of a "higher good," life. In the Aqhat text the invitation is to eternal life with the gods in the heavenly world. In Proverbs it is to long life, a full life, through association with Dame Wisdom in her palace and world.

In Isaiah 55, we will argue, the life that is offered is proximity to the deity in the deity's shrine. The demonstration of this proposition, which for all its seeming novelty was already suspected by Begrich,[7] will be in two propositions: 1) the call to the waters is really a summons to the shrine of the deity and hence to the realm of life, and 2) Yahweh's covenanting with those invited associates them *with* himself.

There can be little doubt that the people are invited to the shrine of Yahweh, Zion. The Hebrew and Ugaritic function of the formula is to invite to a holy place, i.e., a dwelling of the gods, and we should expect the same function here. Commentators generally agree that chapters 54 and 55 are closely related, largely through the persistence in both chapters of the covenant theme (Muilenburg 1956: 642 and Melugin 1976: 170–75). But chap. 54 tells Mother Zion to enlarge the place of her tent because her children are to return to her in great numbers. Chap. 55 invites those children to return. Perhaps the best indication that vv 1–5 invite the hearers to come to the shrine is the parallelism between these verses and vv 6–11. Second Isaiah elsewhere makes use of parallelism of structure, i.e., two sections of approximately equal or proportionate length (measured in cola) which make parallel statements. The device is certainly not confined to Second Isaiah (cf. Prov 9: 1–6 + 11 // 13–18) but there are several good instances in our poet, 41: 1–20 // 41: 21–42: 9 and 48: 1–11 // 12–22. The number of cola in Isaiah 55 are proportionately parallel: vv 1–5 (18 cola); vv 6–11 (21 cola), and vv 12–13 (9 cola).

In the face of considerable scholarly disagreement regarding the form(s) and unity of vv 6–11, these verses must be clarified before they can shed light on vv 1–5, the chief object of our inquiry. As has long been noted, Jer 29: 10–14 forms a parallel both in expression and substance and will aid considerably in understanding vv 6–11.

> For thus says the Lord: When seventy years are completed for Babylon, I will visit you, and I will fulfill to you my promise and bring you back to this place (*hammāqôm hazzeh*). For I know the plans (*maḥăšābōt*) I have for you, says the Lord, plans for welfare and not for evil, to give you a future and a hope. Then you will call upon me (*ûqrāʾtem ʾōtî,* cf. *qĕrāʾūhû* of v 6) and come and pray to me, and I will hear you. You will seek me and find me (*umṣāʾtem,* cf. *bĕhimmāṣĕʿô* of v 6); when you seek me (*tidrĕšūnî,* cf. *diršû* of v 6) with all your heart. I will be found by you (*wĕnimṣēʾtî lākem*), says the Lord, and I will restore your fortunes and gather you from all the nations and all the places where I have driven you, says the Lord, and I will bring you back to the place (*hammāqôm*) from which I sent you into exile.

Jeremiah teaches that Babylon was the place where Israel had to endure separation from Yahweh's presence as punishment for its sins. Only after the seventy years are completed and Yahweh brings them back to "this place," Hebrew idiom for shrine, will Israel be able to call upon, to seek Yahweh and actually to encounter him. Second Isaiah held the same theology of presence as Jeremiah. Yahweh would reveal his glory only in Zion—hence his constant call to return there. The Jeremiah text suggests that the traditional translation of Isa 55: 6a, "Seek the Lord while he may be found," is faulty. The verse should be read, "Seek Yahweh *where* he may be encountered, call upon him *where* he is present (*qārôb*)." Yahweh has returned to Zion, and Israel must go there if it is to encounter him. If v 6 is the summons to the sanctuary like the summons behind Amos 5: 4, then v 7 fits naturally as the completion of that summons, the "Thora-liturgie" or "Einzugsliturgie" exemplified in Psalms 15 and 24 and in Isa 33: 14–16. Those entering the sanctuary must lay aside all unworthy conduct before being admitted to the holy place. Vv 8–11 can hardly be dissociated from vv 6–7. The verses make no sense by themselves. As a *Heilsorakel* (so Begrich and others) they are without context. But as the elaboration of the holiness of the sanctuary which demands a putting aside of mere human devices in order to encounter the divine will and purpose, the verses make perfect sense. The parallel in thought to vv 1–5 is impressive. The first strophe summons the hearer to the divine dwelling and insists on receptivity to divine wisdom as the condition for life with Yahweh. The movement of the second strophe is the same: the summons to the sanctuary, the insistence upon turning from evil, the movement from food ("and gives seed to the sower and bread to the eater") to life as association with Yahweh through commission ("prosper in what I have sent it").[8]

It was necessary to establish that both vv 6–11 and vv 1–5 are invitations to seek the divine presence in the shrine in order to clarify the controverted vv 3b-5.

> I will make with you (pl.) an everlasting covenant,
> the enduring grace to David.[9]
> As I appointed him witness to peoples,
> prince and commander of peoples,
> so you (sg.) shall summon nations (*gôy,* coll.) you knew not,
> nations (*gôy,* coll.) that did not acknowledge you shall run to you—
> because of Yahweh your God,
> because of the Holy One of Israel,
> for he has imparted his glory (*pēʾărāk*) to you.

As has been learned from the parallel passages, the life which is offered is life *with* the deity. In this text Yahweh's covenanting with his people constitutes that divine association. The vocabulary is Davidic. Just as Yahweh once "found," "loved," "chose," and "swore to" David in such passages as Pss 78: 67–72; 89: 20–28; 132: 11–12, 17; 1 Sam 16: 1–13; and 2 Sam 7: 8, i.e., Yahweh consecrated or associated David with himself, so he does now with those who hear the summons.

It is not quite accurate to say with most recent commentators that the old covenant with David is here "democratized." The role of David that is transferred is quite limited and its limits are shown both by the two psalms cited in the text, Psalms 18 and 89, and by the Deutero-Isaian use of *ʿēd,* "witness." In Psalm 18 (paralleled in 2 Samuel 22), the king thanks God for rescuing him in battle. After describing how Yahweh had made him triumphant over his enemies, he declares

> You rescued me from the strife of peoples (*ʿam,* coll.),
> you set me at the head of nations (*gôyîm*).
> Peoples (*ʿam,* coll.) I did not know serve me;
> as soon as they hear of me they obey me (vv 44–45a).

The Davidic king, rescued by Yahweh's power, demonstrates to his enemies by his victory over them that his god rather than the gods of his enemies is superior in the heavenly world. As Yahweh's earthly regent, the Israelite king reflects, or witnesses to, Yahweh's superiority in the heavenly world. He becomes "the head of nations." The other kings come to recognize his true status.

Psalm 89, the other psalm cited (cf., e.g., Ps 89: 2–5 and 29 with Isa 55: 3b), is similar. As recent studies have made clear, Ps 89: 2–38 is a unity and proclaims that the kingship resulting from the cosmogonic victory of Yahweh in vv 6–19 is shared point by point with the Davidic ruler and his "sons" in vv 20–38. "The king, true lieutenant of Yahweh on earth, possesses power directly proportionate to the divine power. It is in this kind of perspective that one can understand the seeming excess of royal claims. We will see in fact that the different promises which concretize the royal 'election' are only a slightly weakened echo of the manifestations of the divine power about which the preceding cosmic hymn sings."[10] V 28, "Yes, I make him my first born, the highest (*ʿelyôn*) of the kings of the earth," expresses succinctly the belief that the Davidic king reflects among earthly kings the ascendancy of Yahweh among the deities in heaven: both Yahweh and his regent are "most high" in their respective spheres.

That the Davidic role in Isaiah 55 is to be interpreted in the limited fashion suggested by the psalms is supported by the use of the word *ʿēd,* "witness," within chapters 40–55. The word occurs outside of chap. 55 in two passages, 43: 9–10 and 44: 8–9 (Clifford 1980b), in which Israel is called upon to testify on Yahweh's behalf, and the nations (or their idols) are called to testify on behalf of their gods. Israel testifies that Yahweh is the only deity, i.e., the only deity who is able to fulfill his word of promise. In contrast, the nations (or their idols) are silent when called upon to testify because their gods have done nothing. In v 4, "witness" (in this sense) and "leader and commander" are parallel.[11] Israel's prosperity, visible to the nations especially in its new exodus-conquest, witnesses Yahweh's superiority and hence Israel's primary place among the nations. Israel elsewhere in Second Isaiah is a light to the nations.[12] The same glory that once surrounded the Davidic king, making him

ʿelyôn, "most high" among the kings of the earth, is now imparted to obedient Israel. Yahweh has imparted his glory (*pēʾēr,* v 5) to Israel. The passage is an instance of language once used of Israel's leaders in pre-exilic times, e.g., the language of servant, prophet, king, now being used of Israel. Yet it is not for all the people but only for those who are obedient and who heed the invitation to come to the feast in Zion.

In summary, Isaiah 55 is a unified poem in three strophes, vv 1–5, 6–11, 12–13, summoning the exiles to end their separation from Yahweh's presence by leaving Babylon and coming to Zion. The exiles are to come to the waters (cf. Isa 12: 3), to enjoy without payment a rich feast, to seek Yahweh where he may be encountered, in a word, to live—by being in holy Zion associated with Yahweh. Like David, whom Yahweh chose *at the term of the exodus-conquest* (2 Sam 7: 8–16; Pss 78: 43–72; 89: 1–38 esp. v 20), those of the exiles who heed the invitation to make the new exodus-conquest will find themselves "found," "chosen," "loved," "covenanted with." In short, they will find themselves brought near, consecrated, so that the glory or heavenly luster of Yahweh will shine forth to the nations.

Notes

1. Muilenburg 1956: 643. Other commentators also compare the cry of the water seller and the invitation to the banquet without adverting to the incompatibility of the two *Sitze* or exploring in much detail the call to the feast: C. R. North 1964: 255; C. Westermann 1969: 281–82; R. Melugin 1976: 25–26.

2. I emend MT *šibrû weʾĕkōlû / ûlkû šibrû bĕlôʾ kesep ûblôʾ mĕḥîr yayin wĕḥālāb,* "Buy food and eat / and come buy food for no money and for no payment, wine and milk," to *šibrû ʾōkel bĕlôʾ kesep / ûblôʾ mĕḥîr yayin wĕḥālāb,* "Buy food for no money / and for no payment, wine and milk." The Old Greek, represented particularly by the uncials A and Q, *badisantes agorasate kai piete aneu arguriou kai timēs oinou kai stear,* "Come buy and drink without money and payment wine and fat [*ḥēleb* for MT *ḥālāb*]," reflects the Vorlage *lkw šbrw ʾklw blwʾ ksp wblwʾ mḥyr yyn wḥlb.* The Greek translator has "improved" the awkward *ʾklw . . . yyn,* "eat . . . wine," to a smoother *piete . . . oinou,* "drink . . . wine," on the basis of his memory that Isaiah elsewhere uses "drink" with "wine." Examples of this tendency in the Isaiah translator have been collected by Ziegler (1934: 134–75). The hexaplaric recension reflects MT. At Qumran, 1QIs[b] is missing v 1 but 1QIs[a] has *šbwrw blwʾ ksp wblwʾ mḥyr yyn wḥlb.* OG and 1QIs[a] thus agree against MT on a short text–either *šbrw blwʾ ksp* etc. of 1QIs[a] or *šbrw ʾkl blwʾ ksp* [pointing *ʾkl* as the noun *ʾōkel,* "food," rather than the verb *ʾākal,* "to eat," and assuming that the translator missed the idiom *šibrû ʾōkel* and took both words as verbs]. Certainty is impossible since *šābar* is hapax in Isaiah and occurs elsewhere, e.g. in the Joseph story, both absolutely and with *ʾōkel* as object, with no difference in meaning. I prefer as original *šibrû ʾōkel bĕlôʾ kesep* because of the idiom, attested in Deut 2: 6 (cf. 2: 28) *ʾōkel tišbĕrû mēʾittām bakkesep,* "you shall buy food from them with money"; and more persuasive still, because of the clear parallelism between v 1b and v 2a, "Buy food without money . . ." and "Why do you spend money for what is not food?" Note too the play on words in *ʾōkel bĕlôʾ kesep,* "food without money," in v 1a and *kesep bĕlôʾ leḥem,* "money without bread," in v 2a.

3. CTA 23 (= UT 52 = KTU 1.23) 6–7. The text is much controverted. For bibliography, see Clifford 1975b.

4. The use of Ugaritic *ʾay* is like several uses of *hôy* in the Hebrew Bible, the use in Isaiah 55 and the three uses in Zech 2: 10–11 (MT), which are probably to be taken as cries of invitation to come to Zion where there will be a banquet (cf. Jer 31: 10–14). For the phenomenon of *he-ʾalep* interchange, see Greenstein 1973.

5. CTA 17 (= UT 2 Aqht = KTU 1.17) 6.2–5, 17–33. Most of the restorations can be made

with a good degree of certitude through comparison with other stereotyped passages. For the discussion of the text and of the restorations, see Clifford 1975a.

6. See further Clifford 1975a. I follow NAB in placing v 11 after v 6. Proverbs has attracted many single proverbs into itself, a process discernible in the additional proverbs in the LXX of this chapter.

7. "Second Isaiah departs significantly from the model he is imitating regarding that which one is invited to. For his message in content has nothing to do with the content of wisdom teaching. Thus one can readily understand when vv 3b-5 have been separated from 1–3a (e.g., by P. Volz). But objectively the verses are indispensable to each other. For the call to hear demands the delineation of what one is to hear. On the one hand, vv 1–3a, which avoid every contentual reference to wisdom, remain purely formal and thus unintelligible. Correspondingly vv 3b-5 taken by themselves do not yield satisfactory sense." Begrich 1938: 60.

8. Vv 12–13, describing the embarking on the journey homewards to Zion, are part of the same poem which invites its listeners to Zion. The miraculously transformed way, sign of the new exodus–conquest and of the new creation (victory over sterility), will become the memorial of divine victory, like the twelve stones of Josh 4: 5–7.

9. The attempts of Caquot (1965) and Beuken (1974) to interpret *ḥasdê dāwid hanneʾĕmānîm* as a subjective genitive, "the reliable manifestations of David's loyalty" (Beuken) have been effectively disposed of by Williamson (1978).

10. J.-B. Dumortier 1972: 187. See also J. M. Ward 1961 and R. J. Clifford 1980a.

11. The attempt of Beuken (1974: 55–57) to deny the parallel are extraordinarily forced.

12. The notorious crux *bĕrît ʿam,* lit. "covenant of people," may be illuminated by Isa 55: 3b-5 and Psalms 18 and 89, and by the Deutero-Isaian use of *ʿēd.* The alternation in the passages between plural and singular-as-collective in the nouns for "nations" (*ʿam, gôy, gôyîm, lĕʾummîm*) renders less anomalous the parallel use of *ʾôr gôyîm* and *bĕrît ʿam* in 42: 6 and 49: 6–8. These other passages suggest that *ʿam* in the phrase *bĕrît ʿam* is collective and means "peoples," and not simply Israel. Moreover, since the *bĕrît* in Isa 55: 3b is intended to show forth to the nations the glory of Yahweh, then *bĕrît ʿam* makes sense as "covenant of (*or* for) the peoples," parallel to *ʾôr gôyîm,* "light to the nations." The "light of (*or* for) the nations" is the heavenly glory proper to Yahweh that has been imparted to the holy city (Isa 60: 1) and to the returned exiles (Isa 55: 5).

References

Begrich, J.
1938 — *Studien zu Deuterojesaja.* Rpt., 1969, Theologische Bücherei 20. Munich: Kaiser.

Beuken, W. A. M.
1974 — Isa. 55, 3–5: The Reinterpretation of David. *Bijdragen* 35: 49–64.

Caquot, A.
1965 — Les "Graces de David." A propos d'Isaie 55/3b. *Semitica* 15: 45–69.

Clifford, R. J.
1975a — Proverbs IX: A Suggested Ugaritic Parallel. *Vetus Testamentum* 25: 298–306.

1975b — Recent Scholarly Discussion of *CTCA* 23 (*UT* 52). Vol. 1, pp. 99–106 in *Society of Biblical Literature 1975 Seminar Papers,* ed. G. W. MacRae. Missoula, MT: Scholars Press.

1980a — Psalm 89: A Lament over the Davidic Ruler's Continued Failure. *Harvard Theological Review* 73: 35–48.

1980b — The Function of Idol Passages in Second Isaiah. *Catholic Biblical Quarterly* 42: 450–64.

Delitzsch, F.
1890 — *Biblical Commentary on the Prophecies of Isaiah.* Edinburgh: T. & T. Clark.

Dumortier, J.-B.
1972 Un rituel d'intronisation: Le Ps LXXXIX: 2–38. *Vetus Testamentum* 22: 176–96.

Greenstein, E. L.
1973 Another Attestation of Initial *h*/ʾ in West Semitic. *Journal of the Ancient Near East Society of Columbia University* 5 (Gaster volume): 157–64.

Melugin, R.
1976 *The Formation of Isaiah 40–55.* Beihefte zur Zeitschrift für die Alttestamentliche Wissenschaft 141. Berlin: de Gruyter.

Muilenburg, J.
1956 The Book of Isaiah. Chapters 40–66. Vol. 5, pp. 381–773 in *The Interpreter's Bible,* ed. G. A. Buttrick et al. New York: Abingdon.

North, C. R.
1964 *The Second Isaiah.* Oxford: Clarendon.

Ward, J. M.
1961 The Literary Form and Liturgical Background of Psalm LXXXIX. *Vetus Testamentum* 11: 320–29.

Westermann, C.
1969 *Isaiah 40–55.* Old Testament Library. Philadelphia: Westminster.

Williamson, H. G. M.
1978 "The Sure Mercies of David": Subjective or Objective Genitive? *Journal of Semitic Studies* 23: 31–49.

Ziegler, J.
1934 *Untersuchungen zur Septuaginta des Buches Isaias.* Alttestamentliche Abhandlungen 12/3. Münster: Aschendorff.

Zimmerli, W.
1979 *Ezekiel 1.* Hermeneia. Philadelphia: Fortress.

MSRT HBRYT, "The obligation of the covenant," in Ezekiel 20: 37

Moshe Greenberg
The Hebrew University of Jerusalem

As editor of the Anchor Bible, David Noel Freedman has for years given unstintingly of his energy and wisdom to aid and encourage those charged with producing the volumes of that series. Since I have been a particularly avid recipient of his thoughtful supercomments on my irregularly delivered copy, I am grateful for the opportunity to express my deep appreciation in the following study of a hard phrase in the book of Ezekiel. I hope to show that (at least in this instance) for Ezekiel, as for Hosea, "it [is] more consistent with good scholarship to deal as faithfully as possible with a text that exists, than to create one which might serve our purposes better, but the interests of serious scholarship and the study of this book less well" (Andersen and Freedman 1980: 67).

In Ezek 20: 32–38 the prophet declares in God's name that a compulsory exodus will be imposed on the apostate exiles.

> 32 And what has entered your minds shall never be—your thinking, "We shall become like the nations, like the families of the earth, serving wood and stone." 33 By my life—declares the Lord YHWH—with a strong hand and with an outstretched arm and with outpoured fury I will be king over you! 34 I will take you from among the peoples and gather you from the lands through which you have been scattered with a strong hand and an outstretched arm and outpoured fury. 35 I will lead you into the wilderness of the peoples and enter into judgment with you there face to face. 36 As I entered into judgment with your fathers in the wilderness of Egypt so will I enter into judgment with you—declares the Lord YHWH. 37 *whʿbrty ʾtkm tḥt hšbṭ whbʾty ʾtkm bmsrt hbryt* 38 And I will purge you of those who rebel and transgress against me; I will take them out of the land of their sojourn but they shall not come onto the soil of Israel; and you shall know that I am YHWH.

Even a sampling of translations made during the past decade and a half alone reveals a remarkable variety of interpretations of the transliterated line.

NAB	I will count you with the staff and bring back but a small number.
NEB	I will pass you under the rod and bring you within the bond[a] ([a]*Or* muster) of the covenant.
NJPS	I will make you pass under the shepherd's staff[h] ([h]*I.e. to be counted;* see Lev. 27.32), and I will bring you into the bond[i] ([i]*Meaning of Heb. uncertain*) of the covenant.
Good News	I will take firm control of you and make you obey my covenant.

Only the first and last of these are outspokenly clear about the imagery and parallelism, yet they diverge widely as to meaning and even as to the underlying text. NAB's "count" goes with "small number" and omits "covenant"; Good News has "take control" corresponding to "make obey." The other two translations are less decisive. NEB's "pass under the rod" here seems deliberately vague when contrasted with its rendering of the same idiom in Lev 27: 32: "every creature that passes under the counting rod"; evidently this is meant to allow an ambiguity answering to its alternative renderings of *msrt* in the second part of the verse. The footnote "muster" (see below, on Ben-Ḥayyim's proposal) goes with a counting rod, while "bond (of the covenant)" goes with "under the rod" in the sense of subjection to authority. NJPS is very specific in the first part of the verse: not only "shepherd's staff" (so too at Lev 27: 32), but also a footnote, "to be counted"; however it admits to uncertainty regarding the non-parallel "bond (of the covenant)."

The history of interpretation of this verse shows a similar vacillation.

G(reek)	*kai diaxō hymas hypo tēn rabdon mou kai eisaxō hymas en arithmō* and I will pass you under my rod and lead you in by number (no equivalent of "covenant")
S(yriac)	*wʾʿbrkwn tḥyt šbṭʾ wʾʿlkwn bmrdwtʾ ddytyqy* and I will pass you under the rod and make you enter the chastisement of the covenant
T(argum)	*wʾnyḥ ʿlykwn gzyrt dyny wʾʿyl ytkwn bmsrt qymʾ* and I will impose (lit., make rest) on you my decreed judgment and make you enter into the tradition of the covenant
V(ulgate)	*et subiiciam vos sceptro meo, et inducam vos in vinculis foederis* and I will subject you to my scepter (= authority) and lead you into the bonds of the covenant

Medieval Hebrew commentators follow similarly divergent lines of interpretation, with the early French charging *msrt* with ambiguity.[1] Thus Rashi glosses "*under the rod:* You will be subject to me and my chastisement (*mwsry*, foreshadowing *msrt*). *bmsrt hbryt*: the covenant I transmitted (*msrty*) to you." Kara connects v 37a with v 38 and explicitly interprets *msrt* twice: "*under the rod:* in order to purge you of those who rebel and transgress against me. *bmsrt hbryt*: in the covenant I transmitted (*msrty*) and made for them (read: for you) which disciplines (*mysr*) you there (*sic!*) so that you will never more violate my covenant." Eliezer of Beaugency glosses *msrt* "reproof" (*twkḥt*), as though from *ysr*. Kimḥi follows Spanish-Jewish philologists (see below), paraphrasing "I will bind (*ʾʾsr*) you into the covenant so that you will never be freed from it."

Since the 19th century, the few scholars who have stayed with MT regard *msrt* as a derivative of *ʾsr*, "to bind" (like Kimḥi). For Valeton (1893: 256) v 37b meant, "the relation into which YHWH brings Israel. . . is a bond which forever after keeps Israel back from pagan ways" (cf. Kara), while Kraetzschmar rendered the word "fetter" (*Fessel*), explaining it as the covenant curse (*ʾālā*) "to and by which Israel is bound." But the typical modern scholar assumes that MT is in some disorder, since (1) the ancient versions (notably G) point to a text other than it, and (2) an acceptable meaning, meeting the standards of univocality and parallelism of the two halves of the verse, cannot readily be extracted from it. Accordingly, one is justified in altering the received text—a license that has produced a proliferation of conjectural emendations, some ephemeral, other still embraced, as witness the modern translations adduced above.

Regarding *šbṭ*, in the first part of the verse, scholars are divided between the conception of T, V, and Rashi, that it is the rod of authority or chastisement (e.g.,

Cornill, Jahn; cf. Good News), and the suggestion of Lev 27: 32 that it is a shepherd's counting rod (e.g., Smend, Davidson, Rothstein, Cooke, Fohrer, Auvray, Zimmerli, Carley).

The unique *msrt hbryt* has generated a variety of recourses. An early modern minimalist departure from tradition, changing the meaning but not the vocalization, was Luzatto's proposal that *msrt* (derived from *ʾsr*) means "pen, enclosure," while *bryt* here has the unique sense of "selection"—a derivative of *brr* like the immediately following word in the next verse (38), *wbrwty*, "I will purge." Accordingly, the figure of a shepherd counting sheep in the first part of the verse is continued in the second with the animals herded into an enclosure for the purpose of being sifted as they exited. Hitzig[2] and Graetz[3] conjectured that the original expression of sifting was *bĕmasrat habborit* "I will lead you) into the pan (= crucible; cf. *maśret* of 2 Sam. 13: 9) of purging (lit., detergent)" —a solution to which Herrmann still had recourse. The combination of consonantal conservatism and vocalic free-wheeling reappeared in Tur-Sinai's invention (1967: 315), *māsorĕt hibbārut*, "the muster (see Ben-Ḥayyim, below) of purgation."

The majority of critics, however, regarded the omission of *bryt*, "covenant," in G as pointing to a superior text, MT's sequence *bryt* [38] *wbrwty* having arisen from dittography. Detached, the hapax *msrt* was disposed of in two ways, in accord with the alternatives inherent in the first part of the verse. Smend supposed that G *en arithmō* reflected an original Heb. *bĕmispār* "by number" (cf. G at 2 Sam 2: 15), and he is followed by most moderns (Fohrer, Auvray, Zimmerli, Wevers; so too RSV). Cornill, looking for a word graphically closer to MT, lit on *mwsr* (*musār*), "chastisement," as a parallel to rod (see ahead); Ehrlich (1912: 77) argued for **mosĕrĕt*, "halter, rein."[4]

Progress from this juncture requires reconsideration of lexical and hermeneutical assumptions. The lexical treatment of *msrt* is hampered by its being a hapax and by the absence hitherto of external evidence for a contextually suitable meaning. (Later Heb "tradition," though reflected in T and in Theodotion's *paradosis*, like Rashi's reliance on the [later] verb *māsar*, "to transmit, deliver" [cf. AV margin: "a delivery"], does not offer a persuasive basis for interpretation.)

The morphology of the word as a derivative of *ʾsr*, "to bind," was explicated by the 10th c. Spanish-Jewish philologian Judah Ḥayyuj (1870: Heb 27); his treatment was restated by his disciple, Jonah ibn Janaḥ (1964: 259), who refers to

> the absorption of the *ʾalep* of *ʾkl*—the first radical—in the *kap* of *makkolĕt* ("provision," 1 Kgs 5: 25)—evolved out of **maʾkolĕt* after the pattern of *maḥgorĕt* ("girding," Isa 3: 24). The *ʾalep* was attenuated and absorbed, as was attenuated the *ʾalep* of *ʾsr* in the pronounciation of *māsorĕt*—evolved out of **maʾsorĕt*—except that there was no compensatory lengthening of [lit., no *dageš* appears in] it[s second radical].

Moshe ben Sheshet observed that elision of the *ʾalep* was compensated for by lengthening the preceding vowel to *qāmes*; he compared *hāsûrîm* (Qoh 4: 14) for **haʾăsûrîm*, "the imprisoned." For yet a third instance of elision of the *ʾalep* in this root, one may compare *wysr* in Exod 14: 25, for which the Samaritan has *wyʾsr* —reflected in G and S, "he bound"—i.e. he clogged (the wheels), preferable to MT's vocalization, "he removed."

Ḥayyuj linked the meaning of *msrt* with the usage in Num 30: 11 of *ʾissār*, namely, *wʾsrh ʾsr (ʾissār) ʿl npšh bšbwʿh*, "she imposes (lit., binds) an obligation on herself by oath." Ehrlich (1901: 323) implictly follows him in his translation of the second part of our verse, "I will force you to comply with the obligations of the covenant." "Obligation" (from Lat. *obligo*, "to tie, bind up" = *ʾsr*), whether abstract ("constraining power") or concrete ("bounden duty"), is a sense agreeable to the meanings of words occurring in this pattern; e.g., *maḥgorĕt*, "girding" (abs.; some say, "girdle" conc.); *malkodĕt* "trap" (conc.); *makkolĕt* "provision" (conc.); *maśkorĕt* "hire" (conc.); *maḥloqĕt* "division" (conc. in Bib. Heb., abs. in Post-Bib. Heb., "disagreement"). The rendering by "bond(s)" is a metaphoric equivalent.

Why has this solution, which admittedly "gives good sense" (Streane's interpolation in Davidson's commentary), failed to persuade moderns? For one thing, because *msrt* remains a hapax. For another, because of alleged contextual ineptness: "bond, obligation" is not a good parallel to *šbṭ* (taken, as it usually is, as "counting rod"), nor is the sequence of v 37–38 satisfactory—first entry into the covenant, then purge of sinners. On both counts, however, new considerations can be offered.

The lexical data bearing on biblical *msrt* may be added to by inclusion of a speical usage of a Mishnaic idiom, *msrt byd x*, usually meaning "X has a tradition (concerning some fact or law)." While this meaning is assured, and the sense of *msrt* in this idiom clearly linked with Mishnaic *māsar* "transmit," a variant in an early anecdote gives a glimpse of another possibility, strikingly apt for the biblical context. Testimonials concerning the trade secrets of temple guilds recur several times in talmudic literature. A descendant of a guild of incense-makers, upon being asked once to identify a certain aromatic herb replied: *msrt bydy mʾbwty šlʾ lhrʾwth lbyryyh* (*y. Šeqal.* 5.2; *y. Yoma* 3.9). This has usually been rendered, "I have a tradition from my fathers not to show it to a soul." However in two variants (*b. Yoma* 38a; *t. Kippurim* 2.7), in place of the *msrt* phrase appears, *šbwʿh hʾy bydynw*, "We are under oath (not to show etc.)." That *šbwʿh* "oath" should be synonymous with a derivative of *ʾsr* conforms with the combinations *ʾsrh . . . bšbwʿh* and *šbwʿt ʾsr* (*ʾissār*) in Num 30: 11, 14 (the latter phrase means "sworn obligation"). Applying the talmudic synonymy to our biblical phrase, *msrt hbryt* would mean effectively *šbwʿt hbryt*—a happy combination as shown by (1) the parallelism of *šbwʿh* and *bryt* in Ps 105: 8–10 (= 1 Chron 16: 15–17), and (2) the equivalence of *šbwʿh* and *ʾlh* in the sense of solemn sanctions of a covenant in Neh 10: 30 and Dan 9: 11. The full clause *hbyʾ bmsrt hbryt* would then combine the sense of *hbyʾ bʾlh,* "to impose an oath upon", (Ezek 17: 13) and *hbyʾ bbryt*, "to impose a covenant upon (= bind by covenant)" (1 Sam 20: 8); cf. *bʾ bʾlh wbšbwʿh,* "to take an oath with the sanction of a curse." Its translation would be "to impose upon one the obligation/oath of the covenant."[5]

Can a decision be made between "obligation" and "oath"? Just as biblical *šbwʿh* and *ʾsr* (*ʾissār*), though closely related, are not identical, so talmudic *šbwʿh* and *msrt,* though exchangeable in a specific context, may not be identical. It may be assumed that the appeal to God or to some dread sanction that is essential to *šbwʿh* is absent in derivatives of *ʾsr*; only the notion of binding obligation remains common to both. Our choice falls, then, on "obligation" as the precise meaning of biblical *msrt,*[6] and we submit that this biblical sense survived in the speech of the descendant of the temple guild recorded in the talmudic anecdote: "I am under an ancestral obligation (*msrt bydy mʾbwty*)," he said, "not to show [that herb] to a soul." The variant *msrt*/*šbwʿh* in this anecdote survived to provide a mate for the biblical hapax; otherwise, *msrt* in later

Hebrew was invariably associated with the later *māsar,* "to transmit" (but see Ben-Ḥayyim, below).

The attractiveness of this proposal is enhanced by doubts about the alternatives. The most appealing has proven to be based on G *en arithmō* with no equivalent of MT *hbryt.* This has been retroverted into Heb *bmspr*, and for the sense of *hby*ʾ *bmspr* 1 Chr 9: 28 and Isa 40: 26 have been compared. 1 Chr 9: 28 says of those in charge of the temple vessels that "they received them back (into the storerooms) by number and issued them by number" (*bmspr yby*ʾ*wm wbmspr ywṣy*ʾ*wm*), meaning that they checked to see that the full number issued came back. That in Isa 40: 26 the same is meant when God is said to bring out all the stars by number (*hmwṣy*ʾ *bmspr*) is shown by the conclusion, "Not one of them fails to appear." Our passage, taken in isolation can perhaps bear the meaning, especially if "pass under the rod" means "check out one by one." But in context that meaning is unsuitable: when in v 37 God declares that he will enter into judgment with the returning exiles as he did with the generation of the Exodus, he intends the contrary from seeing that the full complement of exiles returns—as is made explicit in v 38. Zimmerli does not ease this difficulty when he renders "exactly counted," thus making the second part of the verse "entirely parallel" with the first. Others (e.g., Auvray) follow Smend, who gave *bmspr* the sense of *mspr,* "few in number"—a sense it cannot bear alone (Smend compared 5: 3f, where however *m*ʿ*ṭ bmspr,* "a few in number," appears).

Even without indicating the semantic difficulty of the retroversion **bmspr*, Cornill doubted that out of it MT might have arisen; today we are in a position to argue that G *en arithmō* is simply a translation of Heb *bmsrt.* The rare MT verb *wymsrw* in Num 31: 5 is rendered in G *exērithmēsan,* "they counted"; scholars have deemed MT corrupt and emended it to *wysprw,* supposedly retroverting G (see BHS). But Z. Ben-Ḥayyim (1957) has pointed out that in the Aramaic of the Samaritan Targum *msr* regularly translates Heb *pqd,* "to count, muster"; one need go no further to explain the relation of G to MT. We submit that just as G *exērithmēsan* in Num 31: 5 is accounted for as an Aramaizing interpretation of Heb *wymsrw,* so G *en arithmō* here is accounted for as an Aramaizing interpretation of Heb *bmsrt,* which stood in G's *Vorlage* as it does in MT. By such an interpretation the second part of the verse would offer a kind of parallel to the counting image suggested in the first part. It would have been the only way to make sense of the text, if G's *Vorlage* did not contain the word *hbryt*—as apparently it did not—perhaps by error of haplography due to its similarity to the following *wbrwty.* Our evaluation of G's reading of the latter part of the verse depends finally on our understanding of the entire verse, to which we now turn.

Having secured a better foundation for the reading *msrt* and having argued that *msrt hbryt* means "the obligation of the covenant," we must address ourselves to the alternative meanings that have been assigned to the first part of the verse. At this juncture the larger context must be considered. God's judgment in the new exodus is compared to his judgment in the old (v 36); this invites us to compare the two exoduses in their entirety.

old (vv 5–29)	*new* (vv 32–41)
Israel was addicted to Egypt's idols (7–8).	Exiles intend to assimilate to the gentiles' worship of wood and stone (32).

In the wilderness, God gave them his laws.	In the wilderness of the peoples
They disobeyed him, so he purged the fathers and, since the sons continued disobeying, he punished them with bad laws and a defiled cult.	God will purge the rebels.
In the land they worshiped at *bāmôt*.	In the land they shall worship on God's holy mountain.

Now, the beginning and end of both processes are manifestly parallel: intention to assimilate to the gentiles' worship // addiction to Egypt's idols, and worship at the *bāmôt* // worship at God's holy mountain. Purging the fathers in the wilderness is also parallel to the future purge of rebels in the wilderness of the nations. By elimination, we conclude that God's past lawgiving in the wilderness has its future analogue in his imposing the "obligation of the covenant" on the "judged" nation. But how is it that the renewed covenant obligation (v 37b) precedes the purging (v 38)? We contend that it does not, but that v 37a describes, not merely a counting, but a process of selection that quite suitably precedes v 37b, and is preparatory for it.

In his Leviticus commentary, Elliger argued that the phrase "all that passes under the rod" in the tithe law of 27: 32 must have a special technical significance connected with the arbitrary selection of animals expressly ordained in v 33: "There shall be no inquiry as to whether it [the tenth animal] is good or bad." The Mishnaic passage to which he directs the reader confirms his supposition that we have here a mechanical tithing procedure and not a usual mode of mere counting.

> They lead the cattle into the pen and make a small outlet for them so that no two can go forth together. And they count with a rod: one two three four five six seven eight nine, and the one that comes out tenth is marked with a red mark, and it is said, "This is tithe" (*m. Ber.* 9.7; Danby translation).

Ezekiel's echo of the Leviticus phrase must, accordingly, signify not mere counting, but selection and thinning; cf. Kara's gloss, drawing on the expression of purgation in v 38. Kimḥi and Malbim took the same line.

> *Kimḥi* As when counting sheep, one holds a staff and counts one by one, setting the tenth apart as tithe, so shall I count you off so that the sinner shall be destroyed.
>
> *Malbim* He uses the figure of the shepherd who passes his flock under his rod to count them for tithing; thus (with Israel) only a tenth will be holy and they shall remain in the faith. Those he will cause to enter into the new covenant, alluded to in chap. 16 [:60ff.].

We conclude, then, that v 37a describes the sifting and selection of those who will be made to accept the obligations of the covenant in v 37b. The two parts of the verse are not synonymous but sequential, like the two parts of v 35. V 38, which speaks only of purging, is thus an elaboration (and a return to the topic) of v 37a, its conclusion serving to close the entire section with an echo of its beginning: "for I will take them out the land of their sojourn" // "I will take you from among the peoples . . . gather you . . . from the lands" (v 34). The future will recapitulate the past, with its redemption, its covenant, and its land-entry; but rebels—the present audience of the prophet—will be purged, and that cardinal point is not only made in v 37a but enlarged upon in v 38, which terminates the first, pre-land-entry stage of the redemption.

Having argued for this basic, single, contextually defined meaning, we cannot ignore the battery of phonetic and associative features that complexify the signification of this passage. The threefold occurrence of *nšpṭ*, "to enter into judgment," in the preceding verses strengthens the notion of punishment contained in *šbṭ*—a rod for beating. The assonance of *bryt* and *wbrwty* supports the express message that the covenant will be only for the survivors of the purge. Perhaps the most interesting overtone is the evocation by *šbṭ*—*msrt* of the pair *šbṭ mwsr*, "rod of discipline" (Prov 22: 15), in parallelism in Prov 23: 13 ("Do not withhold *mwsr* from a lad / If you beat him with a *šbṭ* he will not die") and 13: 24 ("He who withholds his *šbṭ* hates his son / But he who loves him starts each day with *mwsr*"). This association determined S's translation of *msrt* as *mrdwtʾ* "discipline" and Eliezer's gloss *twkḥt* "reproof" and Cornill's emendation to *mwsr*. But we must not confuse levels of signification; the first reading of "to pass under the rod" evokes the tithing process, as the first reading of "to make enter *msrt hbryt*" conveys the imposition of covenantal obligation. It is only when the association with *šbṭ mwsr* dawns on us—and that is promoted by the proximity of *nšpṭ*—that the overtone of discipline and chastisement so congenial to the context is realized.

Yet another resonance is supplied by God's assertion of royal authority in v 33 ("I will be king over you"); to royal idiom belongs also the political terms *mrdym wpšʿym by,* "those who rebel and transgress against me," in v 38. The combinations *šbṭ mlkwt*, "royal scepter" (Ps 45: 7), and *šbṭ mšlym,* "rulers' scepter" (Isa 14: 5), link our *šbṭ* with subjugation to kingly authority—a nuance which "pass under" reinforces (compare Ps 125: 3, "the rod/scepter of the wicket shall not rest (*ynwḥ*) upon [= wield authority over] the portion of the righteous," with T here, *ʾnyḥ gzyrt dyny*). This is what T and V heard in our *šbṭ* and what led some moderns to emend *msrt* to that other metaphor of control, *mwsrwt* "(yoke) cords." However, *šbṭ* is never paired with *mwsrwt,* as it is with *mwsr,* hence this resonance is weaker.

The unusual variety of intepretations given to our verse leads us to suspect that the choice of the rare word *msrt* may have been dictated by the richness of overtones created by its pairing with *šbṭ*. None of the commoner substitutes (*šbwʿh, ʾlh* or even *ʾsr*) would have had this effect. It is deserving of notice that we have come to realize the richness of the text through observing its reception by many readers—translators and commentators, not one of whom exhausted its manifold message. Our readiness to assume several simultaneous levels of signification enables us to exploit and affirm the value of the rich heritage of interpretation without being limited by its simpler view of meaning.

Our attentiveness to word-play and association in this passage seems justified by their frequency throughout this oracle. In v 29, the phonetic elements of *hbmh,* "the high-place shrine," are embedded in a disdainful question which the noun is thenceforth to evoke—as it were its poetic etymology: *MH hbmh ʾšr ʾtM HBʾyM šM,* which Moffat cleverly rendered "What is the high place you hie to?". The manifold repetition of *šm* in this and the preceding verse relates the polluted *bmh* worship of the past ("there!"—five times in anger) with the pure worship on God's holy hill in v 40 ("there"—three times in approbation). *gbʿh rmh* of v 28 contrasts with *hr mrwm-* of v 40, and the topic, with its lexical elements (*bʾ*) *šm*, calls up associations with the law of centralized worship in Deuteronomy 12 (note especially vv 2 [*hhrym hrmym, hgbʿwt*], 5 [*wbʾt šmh*], 6 [*whbʾtm šmh*], and repeated *šm*(*h*) in 7, 11, 14).

In v 40 a striking alliteration occurs, *bʾrṣ šm ʾrṣm*, "In the land, there will I take delight in them"—emphasizing the link between God's acceptance of Israel's worship and its location in the holy land. The people's saying in v 32, "We shall become like the nations," unmistakably evokes the old popular cry of the people asking Samuel for a king (1 Sam 8: 19): "No! But let a king be over us, so that we too may be like all the nations. . . ." The association with the ancient rebel cry is made vivid by God's angry retort here (v 33), "By my life . . . I will be king over you. . .!" Amidst such a display of verbal devices and associations, it is not straining to find them in our passage. The emphasis that is achieved in the first part of the oracle by a threefold repetition of the people's defiance is, in the account of the future purgative exodus, achieved by overloading the language; repetition is exchanged for supercharged compression.

The foregoing essay at interpreting a passage in Ezekiel 20 treats the oracle as a whole—as it appears in MT. This is not the way of modern analytical-critical commentators (e.g., Fohrer, Cooke, Eichrodt, Wevers, Zimmerli). But in the face of the evidence (and I have by no means exhausted it) that our oracle is a subtly integrated composition, it seems rash, if not naive, to resort to simplifying emendation and dissolution of the text in order to "relieve its tensions." It may be that the present text is the result of stratification, but it is an organic stratification, consisting of traditional components reused and reshaped in new connections, and of new elements, maybe of separate temporal provenience yet connected thematically to produce a new whole, in which the central message has been enriched by combination.

I am aware of an almost unbearable tension between the impulse to dissect the text on the basis of a standard of simplicity, univocality, strict consistency and coherence on the one hand, and the call of the text to interpret it as a designed, integrated complex on the other. Modern students have so long yielded to the first impulse that the approach to the text as it has confronted the historic community of Bible readers is virtually barred to them. This has created a cultural discontinuity whose scope and inevitability one is reluctant to admit. The above exercise is an attempt to adjust one's mind, through activating an appreciating-integrating critical faculty, to the signals that emanate from the received Hebrew taken as a whole. How much that adjustment hobbles the analytical-critical faculty nurtured by contemporary Bible criticism, and at what cost to historic truth—the presumed stages of evolution of the text—are matters that still have to be worked out. Until an appreciating-integrating holistic criticism has produced a considerable body of commentary and theory, on a level of philological competence equal to the best analytical criticism, an illuminating discussion and clarification of issues raised by each approach will not come about.

Notes

1. Unless otherwise indicated, references by name only are to commentators on Ezekiel and their comments on the passage in question. Publication data appear in the bibliography.

2. Cited by Smend 1880.
3. Cited by Tur-Sinai 1954: 382.
4. Variations on these last two conjectures occur; e.g., Jahn—(*šbṭ{y}* "my scepter" (= G) and) *msr{w}t{y}* "my bands"; Perles (1922: 103f)—*moserot* "bands," glossed by *hbryt,* which represents Akkadian *birītu* "fetter"; G. R. Driver, cited by Zimmerli— **mosĕrĕt* "chastisement."
5. Not, as Kraetzschmar (1896: 167 fn) paraphrased it, "to cause the *ʾālâ* (covenant-curse) to take effect upon," i.e., to punish in accord with the sanctions. That this is an error is clear from *hbyʾ bʾlh* in Ezek 17: 13. By such an interpretation Kraetzschmar sought to make v 37b parallel to v 37a, which he explained as "separating the goats from the sheep," comparing Jer 33: 13; but neither Jer 33: 13 nor any other passage associates "passing under the rod" with that activity.
6. The exchange of *msrt*/*šbwʿh* in Mishnaic Hebrew favors Kraetzschmar's equation of *msrt* with *ʾlh*. Nevertheless we prefer "obligation," because Israel's obedience to God in the future as Ezekiel depicts it in 11: 19–20 and 36: 26–36 will require no enforcement by oath-sanctions, since the restored Israelites will be constitutionally incapable of disobedience.

References

Andersen, F. I., and Freedman, D. N.
1980 *Hosea.* Anchor Bible 24. Garden City, NY: Doubleday.

Auvray, P.
1957 *Ézéchiel.* La sainte Bible. Paris: Cerf.

Ben-Ḥayyim, Z.
[AM] 5717/[CE] 1957 *mswrh wmswrt. Leshonenu* 21: 283–92 (briefly in English in 1958. *Scripta Hierosolymitana* 4: 212–13).

Carley, K.
1974 *The Book of the Prophet Ezekiel.* The Cambridge Bible Commentary. Cambridge: Cambridge University Press.

Cooke, G. A.
1937 *A Critical and Exegetical Commentary on the Book of Ezekiel.* International Critical Commentary. New York: Scribners.

Cornill, C. H.
1886 *Das Buch des Propheten Ezechiel.* Leipzig: Hinrichs.

Davidson, A. B.
1916 *The Book of the Prophet Ezekiel.* Revised A. W. Streane. Cambridge Bible for Schools and Colleges. Cambridge: Cambridge University Press.

Ehrlich, A.
1901 *Mikrâ ki-Pheschutô. Dritter Theil, Die Propheten.* Berlin: Poppelauer.
1912 *Randglossen zur Hebräischen Bibel. Fünfter Band, Ezechiel und die kleinen Propheten.* Leipzig: Hinrichs.

Eichrodt, W.
1970 *Ezekiel.* Trans. C. Quin. Old Testament Library. London: SCM Press. Originally 1966.

Elliger, K.
1966 *Leviticus.* Handbuch zum alten Testament. Tübingen: Mohr (Siebeck).

Eliezer of Beaugency
1909 *Kommentar zu Ezechiel und den xii kleinen Propheten von Eliezer aus Beaugency. Lieferung I: Ezechiel,* ed. S. Poznański. Warschau: "Hazefira."

Fohrer, G.
1955 *Ezechiel.* Handbuch zum alten Testament. Tübingen: Mohr (Siebeck).

Hayyuj, Judah
1870 *Two Treatises on Verbs Containing Feeble and Double Letters by R. Jehuda Ḥayug of Fez,* ed. J. W. Nutt. London: Asher.

Hermann, J.
1924 *Ezechiel.* Kommentar zum alten Testament. Leipzig: Deichert.

Ibn Janaḥ
1964 *spr hrqmh . . . lr{by} ywnh ʾbn jnʾḥ* ed. M. Wilensky. Vol. 1. Jerusalem: Academy of the Hebrew Language.

Jahn, G.
1905 *Das Buch Ezechiel.* Leipzig: Pfeiffer.

Kara, Joseph see *Mikraʾot Gedolot*

Kimḥi, Joseph see *Mikraʾot Gedolot*

Kraetzschmar, R.
1896 *Die Bundesvorstellung im alten Testament.* Marburg: Elwert.
1900 *Das Buch Ezechiel.* Handkommentar zum alten Testament. Göttingen: Vandenhoeck und Ruprecht.

Luzatto, S. D.
1876 *pyrwšy šd"l z"l ʿl yrmyh yḥzqʾl mšly wʾywb.* Lemberg: Menkes.

Malbim, M. L.
1964 *yḥzqʾl ʿm pyrwš mrʾh yḥzqʾl {nbyʾym wktwbym . . . wpyrwš . . . mqrʾy qwdš* 7}. New York: Grossman. Originally 1874.

Mikraʾot Gedolot
1911 *mqrʾwt gdwlwt:yḥzqʾl.* Lublin: Schneidmesser and Herschenhorn (includes commentaries of Rashi, Joseph Kara, David Kimḥi).

Moffat, J.
1954 *A New Translation of the Bible, Containing the Old and New Testaments.* New York: Harper and Row.

Moshe ben Sheshet
1871 *A Commentary upon the Books of Jeremiah and Ezeqiel by Mosheh ben Shesheth,* ed. S. R. Driver. London: Williams and Norgate.

Perles, F.
1922 *Analekten zur Textkritik des alten Testaments, Neue Folge.* Leipzig: Engel.

Rashi see *Mikraʾot Gedolot*

Rothstein, D.
1922 Das Buch Ezechiel (Hesekiel). Bd. I, pp. 838–1000 in *Die heilige Schrift des alten Testaments,* ed. A. Bertholet, E. Kautzsch. Tübingen: Mohr (Siebeck).

Smend, R.
1880 *Der Prophet Ezechiel.* Zweite Auflage. Kurzgefasstes exegetisches Handbuch. Leipzig: Hirzel.

Tur-Sinai, N. H.
1954 *hlšwn whspr: krk hlšwn.* Jerusalem: Mosad Bialik.
1967 *pšwṭw šl mqrʾ* iii/2. Tel-Aviv: Kiryat Sepher.

Valeton, J. J. P.
1893 Das Wort *bryt* bei den Propheten und in dem Ketubim—Resultat. *Zeitschrift für die Alttestamentliche Wissenschaft* 13: 245–79.

Wevers, J. W.
1969 *Ezekiel.* The Century Bible: New Series. London: Nelson.

Zimmerli, W.
1955–69 *Ezechiel.* Biblischer Kommentar xiii/1–2. Neukirchen-Vluyn: Neukirchener Verlag.

The Minor Prophets and Ebla

Mitchell Dahood
late of the
Pontifical Biblical Institute, Rome

In collaboration with Francis I. Andersen, David Noel Freedman has recently published a major commentary on Hosea (Andersen and Freedman 1980). The manuscript was obviously in press just when some important Ebla tablets were being published, with the result that the index lists only one reference to Ebla. Had more Ebla material been available at the time of composition, Freedman would surely have exploited it for its possible relevance to Hosea study; Freedman's empathy for the new epigraphic finds from Tell Mardikh is well known. The Ugaritic texts, however, have been put to extensive use. The preface reports that both are currently at work on the Anchor Bible volume containing the commentary on Amos and Micah, and that Andersen will write the commentaries on Joel, Obadiah, Jonah, Nahum, Habakkuk, and Zephaniah. To make some of the Ebla material available for their consideration, the writer presents, in appreciation for what he has learned from the Hosea volume, the following comments on the Minor Prophets prompted by the published Ebla documents. Unless indicated otherwise, the translations of the Hosea passages are those of Andersen and Freedman.

Hos 5: 14 *kî ʾānōkî kaššaḥal lĕʾeprayim*
wĕkakkĕpîr lĕbêt yĕhûdâ
I am like a lion for Ephraim,
and like a tawny lion for the house of Judah.
(my translation)

The authors follow tradition when rendering second-colon *kĕpîr* by 'young lion,' but no Hebrew lexicon furnishes an etymological basis for this translation. The Ebla bilingual vocabulary TM.75.G.1678 obv. III 6 translates Sumerian URUDU, "copper," by *kà-pá-lum*, which can be taken as *kaparum*, given the frequent writing of *–lum* for *–rum*. When discussing commercial relations with Cyprus, Pettinato (1979c: 206) observes, "It is interesting to point out that the Eblaite term to indicate copper was precisely *Kaparum*, whose root relates to that of Cyprus." Having a characteristic reddish-brown color, *kaparum*, "copper," supplies the lacking etymology of Heb *kōper*, "henna," a reddish-brown dye or cosmetic, as well as of *kōper*, "price for ransom of a life." The root meaning of *kpr* is apparently "to be reddish brown," and this sense would serve to define *kĕpîr*, here rendered "tawny lion"; it may also be translated "copper-colored lion." The city name *kĕpîrâ* in Josh 9: 17; 18: 26 may well describe the color of the city's terrain. The etymology of the theological verb *kipper*, "to compose a difference" (so Brichto 1976: 19–55, esp. 26–27, 35), must now be reconsidered. The term may well be Canaanite and commercial in character—like Ugar *pdy*, "to redeem"—rather than Akkadian or Arabic as current theories would have it.

At this point in their commentary the authors offer an excursus on "lion," observing that Hebrew has at least six words for "lion," five of them occurring in Job 4: 10–11. Of these six Hebrew words at least three occur in personal names from Ebla. Thus the apocopated PN *a-rí* in *MEE* 2,33 obv. III 8[1] may be equated with Heb *ʾărî*, "lion," and the PN *a-da-rí* in *MEE* 2,32 obv. VIII 5 lends itself to the interpretation *hadd-ʾarī*, "Hadd is a lion." Heb *šaḥal*, "lion," imparts meaning to the PN *ša-al/šaḥal/* in *MEE* 2,19 rev. II 15; note the denominative verb form occurring in the PN *iš-al-da-mu/yišḥal-damu/*, "Damu is a lion," in *MEE* 2,12 obv. V 5. Here predicated of the popular vegetation god Damu, *šaḥal* is employed in the simile in Hos 5: 14 wherein Yahweh compares himself to a *šaḥal*. Heretofore unwitnessed outside Hebrew, *šaḥal*'s appearance in the Tell Mardikh tablets points to a special lexical kinship between Elbaite and Hebrew. The root of the third word for "lion," namely *lābîʾ* (Hos 13: 8), can be recognized in the PN *íl-ba-šum/yilbaʾ-šum/*, "The Name is a lion" (*MEE* 2,20 obv. VIII 8) when the latter is compared with the Ugaritic PNN *šmlbʾu*, "The Name is a lion," in UT 2085: 13,14, and *bn šmlbʾi* in UT 303: 5.[2] Since this root is also predicated of Damu in *MEE* 2,39 rev. VI 7, *íl-ba-da-mu/yilbaʾ-damu/*, "Damu is a lion," the interpretation of *iš-al-da-mu* cited above takes on conviction.

Hos 9: 4 *kīleḥem* (MT *kĕleḥem*) *ʾônîm lāhem*
kol-ʾōkĕlāyw yiṭammāʾû
Indeed, the food of idols is theirs.
All who eat of it become unclean.

The commentary correctly notes that the interpretation of the first line depends on the meaning of *ʾônîm*, but less soundly states that *ʾôn*, "vigor, wealth," which has the masculine plural *ʾônîm*, does not make sense here. Hence the authors describe *ʾônîm* as a plural of *ʾāwen*, "wickedness" (Andersen and Freedman 1980: 526). But a strong case can now be made for taking plural *ônîm* as the plural of *ʾôn*, "vigor, wealth," to designate either "idols" or a specific deity. The incantation tablet TM.75.G.2038 rev. II 3 mentions the composite deity ^{d}*a-dar-wa-an*, which I have normalized *hadar-wa-ʾān*, "Splendor and Vigor" (*apud* Pettinato 1979d: 345). There I commented, "In Biblical Hebrew both *hādār* and *ʾôn* are predicated of Yahweh, and since many of his attributes were at one time Canaanite deities, it would seem that *hādār* and *ʾôn* also enjoyed divine status. . . . The double-barrelled divine name ^{d}*a-dar-wa-an* recalls such compound divine names as *kṯr w ḫss* and *mt w šr*, made famous by the Ugaritic texts. . . . This usage places Eblaite within the Canaanite ambience." The determinative preceding ^{d}*a-dar-wa-an* identifies the divine rank of *an*, and this in turn helps recognize him in Ugaritic PNN where the precise writing of consonants shows them to be identical with those of Heb *ʾôn*, "vigor"; thus *ḥlʾan*, "Powerful is Vigor"; *krʾan*, "The Lamb of Vigor"; *tran*, "The Dove of Vigor."

Hos 9: 11 *ʾeprayim kāʿôp yitʿôpēp kĕbôdām*
O Ephraim, like a bird their Glory will fly away.

The authors point out that in Hosea "Glory" can be a name for the pagan god that replaces Yahweh (4: 7; 10: 5). The background of this alternation can be seen in the cultic text TM.75.G.2238 obv. VIII 23 (Pettinato 1979a: 165), *[d]kà-pá-tù*, /*kabādu*/, "Glory." This root is predicated of Il in the PN *kab-da-ìl*(AN) /*kabda-ʾil*/, "Il is glorious" (*MEE* 2,11 obv. III 3). The biblical implications of this Eblaite datum have recently been studied by F. de Meyer (1980: 225–28), whose identification of *kābôd* in Ps 85: 10 with Yahweh Himself confirms the pre-Eblaite observation of Lipiński (1969: 97–98) on this verse.

Hos 10: 13 *kî bāṭaḥtā bĕdarkĕkā*
bĕrōb gibbôrêkā
For you trusted in your own power,
in the large numbers of your crack troops.

At the beginning of the second colon the translators have inserted an "and" which is not in the Hebrew text and which I have accordingly omitted. One must agree, though, with their rendition of *darkĕkā*, "your own power," on the basis of Ugar *drkt*, "dominion, power, authority." This respect for the consonantal text contrasts with the attitude of Wolff (1965: 232,234) who prefers to emend *drkk* to *rkbk*, "deine Streitwagen," "on the authority of the LXX and because the two words are graphically close." He concludes, "Darum dürfte auch die in Ugarit häufige Form *drkt* (= Herrschergewalt, Herrschaft) nicht ohne Weiteres hebr. *drk* gleichzusetzen sein."

This word now probably occurs in Eblaite as a synonym of *mlk*, "kingship," which is the first half of the Ugaritic pair *mlk*//*drkt*. Fronzaroli (1979a: 6) cites the bilingual tablet TM.75.G.20001+20003 rev. XI 11–12, where Sumerian n a m . e n, "kingship," is translated into Eblaite *ma-lí-gú-um* (see Dahood *apud* Watson 1981: 101, n. 5). In the same tablet (rev. IX 13–14) is registered the equivalence n a m. n a m. e n = *du-da-lí-gú-um*, which Fronzaroli normalizes *tumtallik-um*, "exercise of kingship," and parses as the *Piʿel* infixed *-t-* form of *mlk*, with the total assimilation of the *m* to the following dental *t*. Another explanation, however, is at hand; given that *lí* is often written for *ri* (Pettinato 1979c: 68; Fronzaroli 1979a: 10), *du-da-lí-gú-um* may be normalized *tudarrik-um*, a *Piʿel* infinitival form of *drk*, from which Ugar *drkt*, "dominion," derives. Since both nouns occur in the same bilingual tablet, they should be taken as synonyms from different roots, namely *mlk* and *drk*, rather than as offshoots of the same root *mlk*. This amounts to saying that Ebla had literary word pairs[3] that continued into the second and the first millennia. For the Ugaritic and Hebrew documentation of the poetic pair *mlk*//*drkt*, see Dahood and Penar (1972: 264).

Hos 11: 16 *wĕḥālâ ḥereb bĕʿārāyw*
And the sword will be active in his cities.
(my translation)

Andersen and Freedman render "The sword will damage his cities," and comment, "In *ḥlh* we meet once more a verb containing the consonants *ḥ–l* which offer so many possibilities. We read a form of *ḥly*, 'to be weak,' with the LXX and Vulgate." A more promising avenue is opened up by the middle weak root *ḫyl*, from which biblical *ḥayil*, "strength," derives, and which seems to underlie the following PNN from Ebla: *ḫa-la-il* /*ḫāla-ʾil*/, "Il is strong" (*MEE* 2,19 obv. IV 17); *ḫal-šum*, "The Name is strong" (*MEE* 2,19 obv. X 13); *ḫa-la-bí-du*[KI] /*ḫāla-pīd(u)*/, "Strong is

Misfortune"[4] (*MEE* 2,1 rev. I 11); *ḫal-za-um* /*ḫāl-zaʿūm*/, "Strong is the Angry One" (*MEE* 2,22 obv. X 11). The recognition of this root helps interpret the Ugaritic PNN *yḫl*, "Ya is strength" (UT 1078: 8), whose meaning may be compared with Eblaite *ḫālaʾil*, "Il is strong," and with biblical *ʾăbîḥayil*, "My father is strength"; *ḫlʾan*, "Strong is Vigor" (UT 1102: 19). Hebrew lexica recognize this verb in Ps 10: 5, *yāḥîlû*, and Job 20: 21, *yāḥîl*; both are probably *Qal* forms, though some authorities take them as *Hipʿil*. In our passage *ḥālâ* parses as the feminine *Qal* and is complemented by the prepositional phrase *bĕʿārāyw*, "is active in his cities." In the Andersen-Freedman version the preposition is unaccounted for: "The sword will damage his cities."

Hos 12: 2 *ûbĕrît ʿim-ʾaššûr yikrōtû*
wĕšemen lĕmiṣrayim yûbāl
They make a treaty with Assyria,
and oil is carried to Egypt.
(my translation)

The commentary notes first that D. J. McCarthy has argued from Assyrian texts that oil could be used in covenant-making and, second, that it would be a mistake to link the covenant exclusively with Assyria, and the oil with Egypt. "Both are tied to both, and we must suppose that the oil ceremony is a part or consequence of making a covenant" (p. 605). The correctness of these comments is borne out by two bilingual vocabularies cited by Pettinato (1980a: 50) where Sumerian g i š - d u g - g í d - d u is translated *kà-ra-tum*. Pettinato recognizes in *karatu* Heb *krt*, "to cut," as well as the technical term for making an alliance, and for Sumerian g i š - d u g - d u suggests the literal translation "to carry the jar." He does not discuss the meaning of g í d in the full formula g i š - d u g - g í d - d u = *kà-ra-tum*, but if g í d here bears its usual meanings, "to be long, distant," then the whole formula would signify "to carry the jar afar." This equation of "to carry the jar afar" with the verb "to cut" has a striking counterpart in the balancing cola of the Hosean verse, where the parallelism of making a treating and carrying oil has hitherto defied explanation for lack of biblical and extrabiblical parallels. Despite their third-millennium provenance the bilingual vocabularies from Ebla establish their biblical relevance by filling this lacuna. Here Ebla and the Bible are mutually defining; since oil was carried in jars, the biblical statement "Oil is carried to Egypt" helps to interpret Eblaite "to carry the jar afar."

Hos 12: 12 *gam mizbĕḥôtām kĕgallîm*
ʿal talmê śādāy
Their altars, too, are like stone heaps
upon the furrows of the field.
(my translation)

The phrase *ʿal talmê śādāy* has been rendered by Andersen-Freedman "beside furrows of the fields" because "the reference to 'furrows of the field' is part of the description of the stone heaps, not information about the location of the altars." This interpretation obliges them to render *ʿal* "beside," since the stone heaps were not upon the plowed land. But if *ʿal* is given its prima facie meaning "upon," the prophet is stating that the altars upon the furrows are as abundant as the stone heaps, whose location on the edges of the field required no description. With the knowledge that the Canaanites worshipped the god "Furrow," the exegete comes to understand why the backsliding Israelites excoriated by Hosea built so many altars upon the furrows: to promote the fertility of the soil. Among the Eblaite PNN attesting the veneration of "Furrow" are *ir_x-kab-du-lum /yirkab-tulum/*, "Furrow rides" (*MEE* 2,38 rev. IV 5); *dur-du-lum /tur-tulum/*, "Dove of Furrow" (*MEE* 2,37 obv. III 2); *eb-du-lum /ʾeb-tulum/*, "Bud of Furrow" (*MEE* 2,43 rev. VI 7); *i-bí-íb-du-lum /ʾibīb-tulum/*, "Furrow has made buds" (*MEE* 2,37 obv. IV 12)[5]; *sá-bí-íb-du-lum /sabīb-tulum/*, "All round is Furrow" (*MEE* 2,21 obv. IX 2).[6] Ugaritic supplies the normalization of *du-lum* as *tulum*, "furrow."[7] As Gordon (1965: 498) has observed, "The pers. n. *iytlm* (1076: 3–6) suggests that *tlm* is the name of a god; cf. *iybʿl, iyzbl*, etc." The PN *ibrtlm*, "Ox of Furrow" (UT 1141: 3), may serve to explain the statement immediately preceding our couplet: *baggilgal šĕwārîm zibbēḥû*, "In Gilgal they sacrificed bulls" (Hos 12: 12). These animals were apparently sacred to the vegetation deity Furrow, and in the Ebla PN *yirkab-tulum*, "Furrow rides," the animal that carries the god is doubtless the one which plows the field, namely, an ox.[8] The personification of weeping furrows in Job 31: 38 reflects the Canaanite conviction that they were alive.

Joel 1: 1 *dĕbar yhwh*, "The word of Yahweh"
2: 12 *nĕʾūm yhwh*, 'The oracle of Yahweh"

The prebiblical history of the important Hebraic terms *dābār* and *nĕʾūm* is coming into view with the publication of the Ebla records. One of the most surprising place names that has emerged is *é-da-bar*^{KI}, "The Temple of the Word" (*MEE* 1, 6523), where one can see the Canaanite forerunner of OT *dābār*, which in texts such as Isa 29: 21; Amos 6: 13; Ps 56: 5,11, may even designate God Himself, and of the Johannine *Logos*. The existence of this root is also known from the bilingual vocabulary TM.75.G.2284+ rev. VII 2–3 where Sumerian e m e - b a l, "translator," is rendered *tá-da-bí-lu /tadabbiru/*, a *Piʿel* infinitival form of *dbr*.[9] In *MEE* 2,2 obv. XII 5 the PN *da-bí-ru_x /dābiru/* may parse as the *Qal* active participle, Heb *dōbēr*; in the *Qal* conjugation the only forms preserved in Hebrew are the active and passive participles, and one possible instance (Ps 51: 6) of the construct infinitive.

The divinized Oracle can probably be identified in the toponyms *wa-lí*(NI)*-ni-um*^{KI} */walī-niʾum/*, "A Kinsman is the Oracle" (*MEE* 2,32 obv. VI 6), where *walī* is equated with Ugar *yly* "kinsman"//*aḫ; ba-ḫa-ni-um*^{KI}*/pāḫa–niʾum/*, "The Oracle has inspired" (*MEE* 1,732), where the two components are mutually defining. At first blush such names for cities or towns appear unlikely, but among the thousands of published personal and place names from Ebla there is usually no palpable difference between them either in form or signification, and were it not for the determinatives accompanying place names, one would be hard put to tell which is which. The same obtains in Hebrew where many PNN are also place names; e.g. *bilʿām; dān; dĕbîr; yiśrāʾēl; lābān; rimmôn; tirṣâ*.

In the bilingual TM.75.G.2001+ obv. XV 4 Sum p à d, "to recite, conjure," is translated into Eblaite as *na-ù-um /naʾum/*. Hence "to recite" may be the basic meaning of the root *nʾm*; in Late Hebrew *nûm*, with the elision of the *aleph*, means "to say."

Of course the divinization of *dabar*, "Word," and *niʾum*, "Oracle," must be evaluated within the wider context of Canaanite theology where the Name is an autonomous god (e.g. *ṭubī-šum*, "My good is the Name," in *MEE* 2,1 obv. IX 9; cf. UT 127: 56). The Voice too has been given divine status, as may be deduced from the PN *ib-tá-ra-gú* /*yibtaraʾ-gūl*/, "The Voice has created," in *MEE* 2,7 obv. XIV 14.[10] Cf. also the toponym *é-ba-rí-um*^{KI} /*É bāriʾum*/, "Temple of the Creator" (*MEE* 2,40 rev. IV 10), which recalls *é-da-bar*^{KI}, since the Word is creative (Ps 33: 6).

At Ugarit, as well, the Voice was considered divine, as is manifest in the following PNN: *abg*, "My father is the Voice" (UT 1064: 12); *lg* "Belonging to the Voice" (UT 2080: 10); *ṯbg*, "Return, O Voice" (UT 2068: 21), whose interpretation has been clarified by the syllabically written Ebla toponym *šu-bí-gú*^{KI} in *MEE* 1, 6522. This last example further illustrates the interchangeability of PNN and GNN; in Ugaritic *ṯbg* is a PN but it is a GN in Eblaite. Cf. also *gmn*, "The Voice is destiny" (UT 1143: 8), and *gdn*, "The Voice is judge" (UT 311: 8).

Joel 4: 3 (EVV 3: 3) *wayyittĕnû hayyeled bazzônâ*
They sold a boy for a harlot.

Till now unwitnessed outside Hebrew, *zônâ*, "harlot," turns up in *MEE* 2,43 obv. VII 7–VIII 3, g u r$_8$ g í n - d i l m u n k ù: b a b b a r *za-na a-zi-du* e - g i$_4$ - m a š k i m *en-na-da-gan* 10 g í n - d i l m u n k ù: b a b b a r *al-ma*, literally, "20 Dilmun shekels of silver for a harlot Azidu the commissioner Egi (has paid); Enna-Dagan 10 Dilmun shekels of silver for a maiden (has paid)." Here the contrast between *zana* and *alma* makes it evident that the former equals Heb *zônâ* (long *a* in Eblaite becomes long *o* in Hebrew), while the latter identifies with Heb *ʿalmâ*, "maiden."[11] This same tablet furnishes equally interesting data in rev. I 7–8, k u$_5$ k ù: b a b b a r *sá-ba* "30 (shekels) of silver for a slave girl," where *sá-ba* looks like an attempt to realize *šabḫa*, Heb *šipḥâ*, and in rev. II 9–III 4, 9 g í n - d i l m u n k ù: b a b b a r n ì - z i d u m u - m í *áš-ti-ḫa-zu-wa-an*^{KI}, "9 Dilmun shekels, payment for a girl from Hazuwan." Thus the successive mention of *zana*, *ʿalma*, *šabḫa* and Sum d u m i - m í, "girl," shows that these lines deal with the sale of young women.

Joel 4: 13 (EVV 3: 13) *šillĕḥû maggāl*
Swing the sickle.

Both these terms probably find their counterparts in the Ebla records. In the PN *iš-la-ma-lik* /*yišlaḫ—malik*/,"Malik sends" (*MEE* 2,2 rev. III 4) and *iš-la-yà* /*yišlaḫ—yāl*/, "Ya sends" (TM.75.G.336 obv. I 9), one recognizes the root *šlḫ*, so frequent in Hebrew, less well documented in other languages. In *MEE* 2,19 rev. VII 12–13 the term LÚ *ma-gal-lu* is preferably understood as "man of the sickle" rather than "il dependente del 'mercante' "(i.e., *magallu* equals *makkāru)*, as proposed by Pettinato (1980a: 139). Cf. also the PN *ma-gal-lu* in TM.75.G.336 obv. VI 8. In the bilingual vocabulary *MEE* 1,1263 rev. II 7, cited by Pettinato (1980a: 55), Sum d u b - n a g a r u r u d u is translated *ma-ga-lí*(NI); Pettinato hazards no translation but does note that it must be a small instrument used by the metalworker. Heb *maggāl*, "sickle," may prove relevant to future discussion of both the Sumerian term, whose meaning is unknown, and its Eblaite equivalent. A dislegomenon (also in Jer 50: 16), *maggāl* is found only in Hebrew and Aramaic and possibly in Ugar *bʿl gml*, which a couple of scholars have rendered "Lord of the Sickle" (see Gordon 1965: 380).

Amos 1: 8 *wĕhikrattî yôšēb mēʾašdôd. . .*
wahăšîbôtî yādî ʿal-ʿeqrôn
And I will cut off the king from Ashdod. . .
I will turn my hand against Eqron.

Among the toponyms listed by Pettinato in his *Catalogo* (1979b: 262) under no. 6535 one reads *šè-da-du*^{KI} and in the next line *é-ga-ru*$_x$*-nu*^{KI}. Since *šè* has also the value *éš*, the first GN may be read *éš-da-du*, "Ashdod,"[12] and inasmuch as *é* must often be read *ʾà*, the second term can be spelled *ʾà-ga-ru*$_x$*-nu* /*ʿaqarunu*/ "Ekron," Akkaron in the LXX and Amqarruna in Akkadian. This line of reasoning is sustained by *MEE* 2,50 obv. V 10–11, e n *ʾà-ga-ru*$_x$*-nu*^{KI}, "the king of Eqron." Having a king, Eqron must have been an important city-state in the middle of the third millennium B.C. This site is not mentioned in any Egyptian or Akkadian texts of the second millennium, while the earliest previous reference to Ashdod dates to the middle of the second millennium. These new epigraphic finds will eventually necessitate rewriting the history of ancient Canaan. For instance, it has been maintained that Eqron was first established in the 12th century B.C. (Wright 1966: 76).

Amos 5: 8 *ʿōśēh kîmâ ûkĕsîl*
Who made the Pleiades and Orion.

Found here and in Job 9: 9, *kîmâ*, "Pleiades," may shed light on the meaning of the GN *ki-ma*^{KI} in TM 75.G.2231 obv. IV 14; this tablet is the geographical gazetteer published by Pettinato (1978: 56). Corroborating this equation is the city name in *MEE* 2,39 obv. X 18; XI 13, *zu-ḫa-lum*^{KI}, whose phonemes coincide with those of *zuḫal*, the Arabic name for the planet Saturn. The naming of cities after celestial bodies reflects an interest in astronomy, and the toponym *zuḫal(um)* may point to the origin of some of the planet names in Arabic. Wellhausen (1887: 171) connected Arabic *zuḫal*, "Saturn," with 1 Kgs 1: 9, *ʾeben hazzōḥelet*. Heb-Arab *zaḥal(a)*, "to withdraw," would explain remote Saturn's name, "one who withdraws."

Amos 5: 16 *wĕqārĕʾû ʾikkār ʾel-ʾēbel*
ûmispad ʾēl (MT *mispēd ʾel*) *yôdĕʿê nehî*
And they will summon the farmer to mourning,
and to the solemn lament the professional wailers.

MT *mispēd ʾel* creates grammatical problems which are sometimes resolved by simply inverting the order of the words to read *ʾel mispēd*, "to the lament." May one consider repointing prepositional *ʾel* to the substantive *ʾēl* and explain *ûmispad ʾēl* as a construct chain with a superlative function, sharing the preposition *ʾel* of the first colon. Hence "and to the solemn lament." In consequence the chiastic sequence comes to light: *ʾikkār: ʾel ʾēbel*//*ûmispad ʾēl: yôdĕʿê nehî.*

Since the publication of the Ugaritic texts expressing the superlative by the construct + genitive *il*, as in *ṯlḥn il*, "a gorgeous table" (Gordon 1965: 113–14), this phenomenon has received more attention from Hebraists. This Northwest Semitic usage recurs frequently in Ebla economic texts where the construct chain t ú g *ì-lí*, literally "garment of god," really describes the top quality of the material, as observed by Pettinato (1976: 12, n. 7) and Dahood (1978: 96–97). This small but significant syntactic practice argues for the Canaanite classification of Eblaite.

Amos 5: 21 *wĕlōʾ ʾārîaḥ bĕʿaṣṣĕrōtêkem*
And I take no pleasure in your festal gatherings.

There is some dispute whether the form *ʾārîaḥ* derives from *rûaḥ*, "to breathe," or is a denominative from *rêaḥ* "scent, odor." But there is no doubt that here and in Isa 11: 3 the form is *Hipʿil* and the meaning "to take pleasure." To interpret an Eblaite PN the text of Isa 11: 3 bears special importance: *wahărîḥô bĕyirʾat yhwh*, "and his pleasure will be in the fear of Yahweh." Here *hărîḥô* parses as the *Hipʿil* infinitive construct followed by the masculine singular suffix of the third person. The same form, followed by the first-person singular suffix may occur in the Ebla PN *a-rí-ḫi-il* /*harīḫī-ʾil* /, "My pleasure is Il" (*MEE* 2,21 obv. I 2).

The number of *Hipʿil* forms in Eblaite continues to grow. To the instances already examined[13] one may add the irrefragable example furnished by a bilingual tablet, *MEE* 1, 1263 obv. I 9'-10', where š à - z u, "midwife," is translated *mu-li-tù* /*mūlittu* < *mūlidtu*/. In the bilingual *MEE* 1,1438 rev. II 19'-20', š a - z u is translated *mu-li-tum* (Pettinato 1980a: 292–93). This form can scarcely be confused with the *Piʿel* feminine participle of *wld* which appears as *mu-wa-li-tum* /*muwallittum* < *muwallidtum*/, "the woman giving birth," namely "the mother" (*MEE* 2,2 obv. VI 2). The GN *mú-rí-gú*^{KI}/*mūrī-gūl*, "My Teacher is the Voice," in TM.75.G.1591 rev. X 4'[14] clarifies the meaning of the toponym in Gen 22: 2, *ʾel ʾereṣ hammōrîyâ*, where unanalyzed *mōrîyâ* interprets as "My Teacher is Yah." Both Eblaite *mūrī* and Heb *mōrī* parse as *Hipʿil* participles of *wry*, "to teach." Similarly the toponym *mu-ší-lu*^{KI} in TM.76.G.523 obv. VIII 12[15] parses as the *Hipʿil* participle of *wšy*, "to be victorious, successful" (cf. Heb *tûšiyyâ*), so that the name signifies "Il grants victory," and prompts the explanation of biblical *mōšeh*, heretofore lacking an etymology, as a hypocoristicon whose divine component is lacking. The full form was probably **mōše-yāh*, "Yah grants victory"; see further below on Mic 6: 4.

Amos 6: 7 *wĕsār mirzaḥ sĕrûḥîm*
And the sprawlers' banquet will cease.

After the thorough study of the term *mrzḥ* by Pope (1977: 214–22), one needs but add its occurrence in *MEE* 2,46 rev. I 1–2, *in* u d *mar-za-u*$_9$, "on the day of his banquet," a formula that resembles *MEE* 2,2 obv. IV 15–17, *in* u d *maš-da-ù* d u m u - n i t a - *sù*, "on the day of his son's feast," where *mašda* equates with biblical *mišteh*, "feast, drink."

Found only in Hebrew otherwise, the verb *sār*, "to cease, pass away," crops up in the PN *sar-du-du* /*sār-dūdu*/, "The basket has passed on" (*MEE* 2,21 obv. III 10). This striking PN juxtaposes two roots that cooccur in Ps 81: 7, "I removed (*hăsîrôtî*) the burden from his shoulder./His hands were freed from the basket (*dûd*)." With the birth of a son the heavy work symbolized by the basket (Exod 1: 11–14) passes from the father to the son. Compare the name of Isaiah's son *šĕʾār yāšûb*, "A remnant shall return," in Isa 7: 3.

Amos 6: 13 *haśśĕmēḥîm lĕlōʾ dābār*
You who rejoice in the non-Word

As noted above at Joel 1: 1, biblical *dābār* sometimes designates Yahweh Himself; the present text apparently illustrates this usage. Just as in Deut 32: 21 *lōʾ-ʾēl* means "a non-god, something that is not a god," so here *lōʾ dābār* can be taken as a pagan deity, the rival of the true *dābār*, who is the God of Israel. For further discussion of this usage in Hosea, consult Andersen and Freedman (1980: 477–78, 650).

Obad 4 *wĕʾim-bên kôkābîm śîm qinnekā*
And if your nest has been set among the stars

The *Qal* passive form *śîm* here, in Job 20: 4 as well as in Phoenician (Dahood 1962: 64), sheds light on the Ebla toponym *zi-mi-da-nu*^{KI} /*śīm—ʾētānu*/, "Founded by the Perennial" (*MEE* 2, 2 rev. II 1). On *ʾêtān* as a divine epithet, see below on Mic 6: 2.

Obad 7 *lōḥĕmekā* (MT *laḥmĕkā*) *yāśîmû māzôr taḥtêkā*
Those who dine with you have set a trap under you.

The occurrence of dative suffixes in Ugaritic has triggered a series of articles and notes on dative suffixes in Biblical Hebrew, and now the appearance of this usage in Eblaite underscores the relationship between these members of the Canaanite family. In the juridical text TM.75.G.1766, published by Fronzaroli (1979a: 3–16), occurs the Sumerian verb ì . n a . s u m followed by the Semitic suffix *–kum* (obv. II 4); the syntagm means "he is giving to you," an unlikely construction in Sumerian but quite normal in Canaanite. The first to recognize this dative suffix was W. G. Lambert in a paper read at the congress on *La Lingua di Ebla* held in Naples, 21–23 April 1980.

Hence Davies (1977: 484–87) appears ill advised to suggest that the participle *lōḥămê* should be inserted before MT *laḥmĕkā* to restore the original text of Obad 7. The simple repointing of *laḥmĕkā* to participial *lōḥĕmekā* and the parsing of the suffix as datival can achieve the same result. The Masoretic uncertainty vis-à-vis this compact construction is bared at Job 3: 24 where MT *laḥmî* repointed to *lōḥămay* yields the superior version, "For in front of those dining with me my sighing comes; /my groans pour out like water."[16]

Obad 20 *ʿad - ṣārĕpat*
as far as Zarephath

Till now the earliest mention of Zarephath dated to a fourteenth century B.C. papyrus text, but like Ashdod and Eqron, discussed above at Amos 1: 8, the city's documentation actually goes back to circa 2500 B.C. In TM.75.G.2231 rev. I 10–11, the geographical gazetteer, one sees *za-ra-ba-ad*^{KI} /*ṣarapāt*/ listed twice, as noted by Maloney (1980: 59). In line 4 of the same column the city *gub-lum*^{KI}, "Byblos," is mentioned. There has been considerable dispute about the reading[17]; since the sign in question has the values DU and GUB, the city name has also been read *du-lu*^{KI}. Can this dispute be resolved? Since Zarephath is situated on the coast between Sidon and Tyre, it would appear that *gub-lum*^{KI}, also situated on the Phoenician coast, should be read instead of *du-lu*, about which nothing is known from ancient texts. Furthermore, in the tablets published thus far *gub-lum*^{KI} is mentioned some 40 times; from *MEE* 2,39 obv. III 16–17, e n *gub-lu*^{KI}, "the king of Byblos," and *MEE* 2,41 obv. IX 2–3, *ma-lik-tum gub-lu*^{KI}, "the queen of Byblos," one learns that Byblos had a king and a queen. Hence it must have been an important city-state in 2500 B.C.; this accords with the information emanating from third-millennium Egyptian texts. Purported *du-lu* remains to be heard from in ancient Near Eastern texts. Hence the conclusion that Ebla carried on international trade through the port city of Byblos appear justified. At this time Ugarit seems not to have been a significant center, being mentioned only once in the published tablets, in TM.75.G.2231 obv. I 5, *u*$_9$*-ga-ra-at*^{KI}, which looks like a plural form, signifying "Fields."

The brief book of Jonah contains several uncommon words and hapax legomena that turn up in the Tell Mardikh tablets. The space available permits discussion of only several verses which may suffice, however, to suggest the origins of the Jonah story.

Jonah 1: 3 *wayyāqom yônâ librōaḥ taršîšāh . . .*
wayyēred yāpô
And Jonah got up to flee to Tarshish . . .
and he went down to Joppa.

As noted elsewhere (Dahood 1978: 85) the PN *yônâ*, literally "Dove," had no counterpart in ancient records until the publication of the PN *wa-na* in TM.75.G.336 obv. III 3. The name recurs in *MEE* 1, 5043 obv. III 5 and *MEE* 2,22 obv. X 2, but whether it refers to one or several persons cannot be made out. Fronzaroli's effort (1977: 33) to explain *wa-na* as Anatolian appears misplaced.

With the identification of the geographical preformative *tar-*, "Emporium," in such toponyms as *tar-ba-ru-tim*^{KI} /*tār-barūt-im*/, "Food-emporium," in TM.75.G.2231 obv. VII 6,[18] it becomes possible to interpret much-canvassed *taršîš* as "Emporium of Linen/Alabaster." Since Heb *šēš* means something white, such as "linen" or "alabaster," the toponym *taršîš* may describe a place where some white substance was manufactured and traded. If *taršîš* is to be identified with Tartessus in southeastern Spain, the *–šîš* component may well refer to the white metal, namely, silver. According to Jer 10: 9 Tarshish exported finely wrought silver, and according to Ezek 27: 12, silver, iron, tin, and lead.

One of the frequently mentioned toponyms in *MEE* 2 is transliterated *i-NI-bu*^{KI} by Pettinato, but since the sign NI carries also the value *yà*, the name is preferably normalized *ʾī–yapu*, "Joppa by the Sea," wherein initial *ʾī-* is interpreted in the light of the Hebrew word for "coast, island." Cf. Ezra 3: 7, *ʾel-yām yāpōʾ*, "to the Sea of Joppa." In the large tablet TM.75.G.1591, discussed by Pettinato (1978: 52–54), which lists 78 cities receiving goods from Ebla, Joppa is written *i-yà-pu*^{KI} in obv. III 10. In its brisk trade with Egypt Ebla needed good ports along the coast; to judge from the published materials, Byblos, as noted at Obad 7, was the important port on the northern coast and Joppa was the chief station on the southern shore of the Mediterranean.

Jonah 1: 5 *wĕyônâ yārad ʾel yarkĕtê hassĕpînâ*
wayyiškab wayyērādam
But Jonah had gone down into the hold of the ship
where he lay down and fell into a deep sleep.

The hapax *sĕpîna*, "ship," may help interpret the toponym *su-bí-nu*KI /*supīnu*/ in *MEE* 2,37 obv. VIII 6 where it occurs as the next city after *gub-lu*KI in line 4. Since Byblos was a port, *supīnu* "Fleet,"[19] would have been an apt name for a city on the coast where ship-building may have been the chief industry.

Heretofore exclusively Hebrew, *rādam*, "to fall into a deep sleep," finds a counterpart in the bilingual vocabulary *MEE* 1, 1263 rev. VI 7–8, where Sum m a-m u, "night, sleep," answers to Eblaite *ra-da-mu* /*radām-u*/.[20] This lexical isogloss underscores the close relationship between Eblaite and Biblical Hebrew, especially between Ebla, Genesis and Job; the noun *tardēmâ*, "deep sleep," recurs twice in both these books.

Jonah 1: 6 *rab haḥōbēl*
the captain

Again without cognates in other languages, *ḥōbēl*, "sailor," probably occurs in *MEE* 2,30 rev. VIII 7–8 where a certain *ip-ṭù-lu* is described as 1 ú *a-bí-lu*. Since Sum 1 ú often precedes professional terms, participial *a-bí-lu* can tentatively be normalized *ḥābil-u* and identified with *ḥōbēl*, "sailor."[21]

Jonah 2: 1–2 *wayĕhî yônâ bimĕʿê haddāg . . .*
wayyitpallēl yônâ . . . mimmĕʿê haddāgâ
And Jonah was in the belly of the fish. . . .
Then Jonah prayed . . . from the belly of the fish.

Why the author first employs masculine *dāg* and, immediately after, feminine *dāgâ* when speaking of the same creature cannot clearly be made out. Here it suffices to observe that the Heb-Ugar noun *dāg* now appears as a deity in the GN *ba-ti-dag*KI, "Houses of the Fish-god" (TM.75.G.2231 rev. II 5), probably a fishing village on the Mediterranean coast. As a consequence two Ugaritic PNN become intelligible: *abdg*, "My father is the Fish-god" (UT 1046: 2), and *nbdg*, "Fruit of Fish-god" (UT 400 I 18). A fish-goddess was also venerated at Ebla, as may be deduced from the PN *en-da-ga* /*ḥēn-dagā*/, "Grace of Fish-goddess" (*MEE* 2, 37 obv. II 14).

Jonah 2: 3 *mibbeṭen šĕʾôl šiwwaʿtî*
From the bosom of Sheol I cried for help.

The GN *ši-a-la*KI in *MEE* 1, 1027 becomes particularly relevant in its potential correspondence to Heb *šĕʾôl*, which till now has lacked convincing cognates. If normalized *šiʾāla*, the Ebla name answers to Heb *šĕʾôl*, long *a* in Eblaite becoming long *o* in Hebrew. In the Masoretic tradition the initial vowel has been reduced to a vocal *shewa* in *šĕʾôl*; Eblaite *šiʾāla* serves to recover the quality of the initial vowel. Moreover, the feminine ending of *šiʾāla* classes it with Heb *šĕʾôl*, which is also feminine though lacking the feminine ending.

That the Hebrew netherworld should take its name from a city on earth accords with the derivation of Gehenna from the *gêʾ hinnōm*, "Valley of Hinnom."

Jonah 3: 3 *wĕnînĕwēh hāyĕtâ ʿîr gĕdôlâ lēʾlōhîm*
Now Nineveh was a large city belonging to the gods.

Versions and commentators do not agree in their analysis of *lēʾlōhîm*. RSV, for instance, takes it as a superlative, "Now Nineveh was an exceedingly great city," and the New International Version (1978) offers, "Now Nineveh was a very large city," but with the note, "Or *a city important to God*," attempting to come to terms with the preposition of *lēʾlōhîm*. A new insight is afforded by some Ebla proper names that contain as their first component the *lamed* of property or ownership. Thus *la-da-ad* /*la-daʿat*/, "Belonging to knowledge" (*MEE* 2,16 obv. III 6); *la-ti-a-at* /*la-diʿāt*/, "Belonging to knowledge" (*MEE* 1, 1009); *la-ma-il* /*lamā-ʾil*/, "Belonging to Il" (*MEE* 1, 929; cf. Prov 31: 4, *lĕmôʾēl*); *la-la-at*KI /*la-lahaṭ*/, "Belonging to Flame" (TM.75.G.2231 obv. VI 21; cf. Ps 104: 4); *la-da-i-in*KI/ *la-ṭāḥin*/, "Belonging to the Grinder" (*MEE* 1, 4967). Though one may argue about the interpretation of *da-i-in* in the last name, the prepositional nature of *la-* is clear because the god ᵈ*da-i-in* is documented in *MEE* 1, 4967. I suspect that ᵈ*da-i-in* is the epithet of a grain god such as Dagan.[22] Note also Ugar *lg*, discussed above at Joel 1: 1.

Jonah 4: 8 *wayĕman ʾĕlōhîm rûaḥ qādîm ḥărîšît*
God ordered a scorching east wind.

It seems rather odd that *qādîm*, which alone or with *rûaḥ* designates the most violent wind in Western Asia and surrounding countries, is known only from Biblical Hebrew. The origin of this term has at least become manifest in *MEE* 1, 138, a document dated DIŠ m u *kà-tim* /*qadīm*/ i t u *ì-la-mu*, "The year of the east wind, the month of October-November."[23] The phonemes of *kà-tim* /*qādīm*/ answer fully to Heb *qādîm*, while the phrase "year of the east wind" recalls Isa 27: 8, *bĕyôm qādîm*, "on the day of the east wind." Just as Amos 1: 1 dates the prophet's call to "two years before the earthquake," so the Ebla tablet is dated to a year remembered for a unusually pernicious and persistent scirocco. This must be judged a very telling lexical isogloss, linking Eblaite and Biblical Hebrew and distinguishing them from other ancient Semitic languages.

Mic 6: 2 *šimʿû hārîm ʾet-rîb yhwh*
wĕhāʾētānîm mōsĕdê ʾāreṣ
Hear, O mountains, the argument of Yahweh,
and of the Perennial, O foundations of earth!

When *ʾētānîm* is parsed as the majestic plural of the adjective *ʾētān*, "perennial," the composite divine title *yhwh ʾētānîm* and the chiastic structure of the verse come to light. The adjective *ʾētān* can be identified in the hypocoristicon *i-da-nu* /*ʾētānu*/, whose divine component is lacking (TM.75.G.336 rev. II 9). *i-da-nu* is taken to be identical with the biblical hypocoristicon *ʾêtān* in Ps 89: 1.[24] The juxtaposition of Perennial and foundations of the earth calls to mind the place name *za-mi-da-nu*KI, discussed above at Obad 4, and the phrase *ʾêtān môšābekā*, "perennial is your abode," in Num 24: 21. Prov 9: 10, *yhwh*//*qĕdōšîm*, illustrates the pattern of composite divine names that we purport to find in *yhwh*//*ʾētānîm*, while Gen 49: 24 and Prov 13: 15 witness other instances of the divine epithet *ʾêtān*.[25]

Mic 6: 4 *wāʾešlaḥ lĕpānêkā ʾet mōšeh*
And I sent Moses before you.

The important Northwest Semitic root *šlḥ* appears in several Ebla PNN such as *iš-la-ma-lik* /*yišlaḥ–malik*/, "Malik sends" (*MEE* 2,2 rev. III 4), and *iš-la-yà* /*yišlaḥ–yā*/, "Ya sends" (TM.75.G.336 obv. I 9), as noted above on Joel 4: 13.[26]

In a paper read at the *XXVII*ème *Rencontre Assyriologique Internationale* held in Paris, 30 June–5 July 1980, I proposed to explain the name *mōšeh* through the new evidence offered by the Ebla tablets. Briefly it is this. The comparison of the PN *i-ší-lum* (*MEE* 2,7 obv. XIII 4) with the toponym *mu-ší-lu*KI in TM.76.G.523 obv. VIII 12, suggests that the root underlying both names is *wšy*, "to be successful, victorious," preserved in Ugar *tšyt*, "victory," and Heb *tûšiyyâ*, "success." Thus the first name would be normalized *yiši-ʾilu(m)*, "Il is victorious," and *mūšīlu* signify "Il grants victory," with *muši* parsed as the *Hipʿil* participle of *wšy*.[27] The Canaanite etymology of Moses's name should not engender surprise. His wife's name, *ṣippōrâ*, is Canaanite, signifying "Bird," and that of his son *gēršōm* can now be explained, thanks to divinized Eblaite *šum*, "Name," as "Client of the Name."

Nah 1: 1 *naḥûm hāʾelqōšî*
Nahum the Elkoshite

Just as the divine epithet *raḥûm* means "Merciful" or "Compassionate," so *naḥûm* probably signifies "Consoler" as descriptive of God. Cathcart (1973: 37–38) has collected Northwest Semitic cognates of the late second and first millennia, and now third millennium parallels may be added. The PN in *MEE* 2,30 obv. I 7, *kà-na-um* /*ka-naḥūm*/, "Like the Consoler," seems to be a prayer that the child so named be like the consoling god.[28] Unable to cope with the Old Akkadian name *i-ti-na-um* /*ʾitti-naḥūm*/, "With me is the Consoler," which he termed "ununderstandable," Gelb (1957: 198) proposed to emend it to *i-ti-na-*< *bu* >*?–um* /*iddin-abum*/. Taken as Canaanite, the name is quite comprehensible and requires no emending.

Nah 3: 4 *baʿălat kĕšāpîm*
mistress of sorceries

Well attested in Akkadian and lately documented in Ugaritic as *kṯp*, "sorcerer," the root *kšp* now probably occurs as a professional term in *MEE* 2,8 rev. II 13, l ú *ga-šè-bù* /*qāšipu*/, "sorcerer," a participial formation comparable to l ú *ḥābilu*, "sailor," examined above at Jonah 1: 6.

Hab 1: 14–17 He has made (*wattaʿăśeh*) men like fish of the sea,
like sea creatures that have no ruler (*mōšēl*).
All of them he pulls up with his fishhook (*ḥakkâ*),
he drags them away with his net;
he gathers them into his dragnet,
and so he rejoices and exults.

> Therefore he sacrifices to his Net (*ḥermô*),
> and burns incense to his dragnet,
> for by these his portion is fat,
> and his food succulent (*maʾăkālô bĕrīʾâ*).
> O Most High Just One (*haʿal kēn*),
> is he to keep on emptying his net,
> destroying nations, sparing (*yaḥmôl*) no one?

Some of the mysterious elements in this description of the Chaldean invader are clarified when data from Ebla are taken into consideration. As noted by Dahood (1979a: 101), Ebla verb forms with preformative *t-* for the third masculine singular confirm the earlier analysis by van Dijk (1969: 446) of v 14 *taʿăśeh*, whose subject is the third-person invader and not second-person Yahweh. The Northwest Semitic root of *mōšēl*, "ruler," now appears in the PN *il-maš-il* /*ʾil-māšil*/, "Il is the Ruler" (*MEE* 2,35 rev. II 8). Found only here, and in Isa 19: 8 and Job 40: 25 with the specific meaning "fishhook," *ḥakkâ* appears in the professional term l ú *ag-ga* /*ḥakka*/, "fisherman" (literally "man of the fishhook"), in *MEE* 2,8 obv. X 11. The doubling of the second consonant in *ag-ga* lends conviction to its equation with Heb *ḥakkâ*, heretofore an exclusively Hebrew vocable. Commentators find obscure the statement "He sacrifices to his Net," but the knowledge that the Canaanites worshipped a god called "Net" reduces the obscurity. Thus *MEE* 1, 1570 mentions ^{d}*ir-mu* which may be normalized *ḥirmu*, "Divine Net," and the PN *i-ti-ir-mu* /*ʾitti-ḥirmu*/ "With me is the Divine Net" (*MEE* 1, 1008) was doubtless borne by a fisherman.

My student E. Zurro has observed that the phrase "his food is succulent" juxtaposes two roots that recall the two definitions of "food" given by two different scribes at Ebla. As the equivalent of Sumerian n ì - g é m e, "food," one scribe listed Eblaite *a-kà-lu* /*ʾakalu*/, "food," whereas the other gave *bù-ur-tum* /*būrtum*/, "sustenance."[29] The unexplained phrase *haʿal kēn* at the beginning of v 17 is parsed as vocative *ha-* followed by the composite divine title *ʿal kēn*, "Most High Just One."[30] Both components occur in Eblaite. Thus *a-lu-a-ḫu* /*ʿalu-ʾaḫu*/, "The Most High is a brother" (TM.75.G.336 rev. I 7); *a-ga-ma-al* /*ḥakama-ʿal*, "Most High is wise" (*MEE* 1,758); and *ki-ni-lum* /*kin-ʾilum*/, "Just is Il" (TM.75.G.336 rev. III 10). Finally, the root *ḥml* of *yaḥmôl*, which has no certain cognates in other languages, probably occurs in the PN *a-mu-lu* /*ḥamūlu*/ "Spared" (TM.75.G.1764 rev. X 5); it evokes the ancient Hebrew name *ḥāmûl*, "Spared," in Gen 46: 12.

Hab 2: 2 *ûbāʾēr ʿal-hallūḥôt*
lĕmaʿan yārûṣ qōrēʾ bô
And make it clear upon the tablets,
that one may read it on the run.

Plural *lūḥôt*, "tablets," sheds light upon the Eblaite toponym *lu-ḫa-tù*^{KI}/*luḫātu*/. The name may refer to a special industry of the city, such as that of producing tablets, planks, or plates, since these are the meanings borne later on by Heb *lūḥôt*. Or again, it may refer to the contours of the terrain on which the city was founded, as suggested by the Moabite place name *maʿălēh hallûḥît* in Isa 15: 5.

The verb *qārāʾ*, "to read," can probably be identified in *MEE* 1,6459 obv. I 1–6, *en-ma*/*i-bí-sí-piš*/*ší-in*/ e n /*wa*/ABxÁŠ.ABxÁŠ/ *qì-lu-ma*, "The grace of Ibbi-Sipiš to the king and the elders: read!" Pettinato (1980a: 232–33) renders somewhat differently: "Così Ibbi-Sipiš al sovrano e agli Anziani: state attenti!" In the position where the imperative *ší-ma*, "Hear!," normally occurs, one has *qì-lu-ma*, which Pettinato relates to Akk *qâlu*, "to listen, be silent." Given the frequent writing *lu* for *ru*, *qì-lu-ma* may also be read *qirū*ʾ*-ma*, plural imperative, with enclitic *–ma*, of *qārā*ʾ, "to read." As in the biblical passage, it is a matter of reading from clay tablets.

Hab 3: 5 *lĕpānāyw yēlek dāber*
wĕyēṣēʾ rešep lĕraglāyw
Before him marches Pestilence,
and Plague goes out from his feet.

Here the Prophet depicts Yahweh's victory over the gods of the pagans; two of Canaan's leading deities, Pestilence and Plague, have become Yahweh's attendants. In the Ebla records the former is called ^{d}*da-bí-ir* d i n g i r - *eb-la*^{KI}, "Dabir the god of Ebla," an indication that he was probably the tutelar deity of the capital (Pettinato 1979c: 268). His companion ^{d}*ra-sa-ap*, the god of the plague, was equally popular (Pettinato 1979a: 109) and one of the four city gates was dedicated to him; the other three gates were consecrated to Dagan, Baal, and Sipiš.

Hab 3: 15 *dāraktā bayyām sûsêkā*
ḥōmer mayim rabbîm
You drove your horses across the sea,
the basin of mighty waters.

There is no consensus regarding the meaning of the second colon, but I construe it all in apposition to *yām*, "sea." The definition of *ḥōmer* as "basin" proposed by Dahood (1964: 408; 1977: 330) has recently been examined by Tsumura (1981: 169 and n. 13) who adopts the Jerusalem Bible translation of *ḥōmer mayim rabbîm*, "the surge of great waters," but appends the note, "Or 'wine-bowl.' It may be that the word *ḥōmer*, being a *polyseme* with meanings of 'foaming' and 'clay' (for a bowl), is used in a twofold sense, the 'sea' being explained as both 'the *foaming* of great waters' and 'the *bowl* of great waters' in terms of a single Hebrew word *ḥōmer*." What the prophet had in mind was doubtless the Mediterranean, to this day called the "Mediterranean Basin."

Ebla now weighs in with the place name *ḫi-mu-ru*^{KI} in the geographical gazetteer, TM.75.G.2231 obv. IX 2; if related to our word, *ḫimurru*^{KI} would describe the concave shape of the land on which the town was situated. Names of vessels are occasionally used to express topographic features; thus Arabic *ṣa*ʿ, "a narrow depressed piece of ground," can be equated with Ugaritic *ṣ*ʿ, "bowl."

Zeph 1: 12 *ʾăḥappēś ʾet-yĕrûšālaim bannērôt*
I will search Jerusalem with lamps.

Heretofore an exclusively Ugaritic and Hebrew word, *nēr*, "lamp," appears both in the singular and the plural in Ebla toponyms. The attractive place name *gú-ne-er*^{KI} /*gū-nēr*/, "The Voice (cf. Ugar *g*) is a Lamp" (TM.75.G.2231 obv. IX 8), calls to mind the phrase of Ps 119: 105, *nēr-lĕraglî dĕbārekā*, "A lamp to my foot is your word." Corresponding to Hebrew plural *nērôt* is the toponym *ne-ra-at*[KI] /*nērāt*/, "Lamps" (*MEE* 1,817). A number of Ebla toponyms bear names associated with the names of the products manufactured there; e.g., *lu-ḫa-tu*[KI], "Tablets," discussed above at Hab 2: 2; *ni-zi-mu*[KI] /*nizimu*/, "Ring" (TM.76.G.189; see Pettinato 1979c: 211 for text), a segholate formation equatable with Heb *nezem*, "ring"; *zi-gi-nu*[KI] /*śikkīn*/, "Knife" (TM.75.G.2231 obv. IV 6) where the working of vocalic harmony aligns the form with Arabic *sikkīn*, "knife," in contrast to Heb *śakkîn*, "knife," a hapax legomenon in Prov 23: 2.

Hag 1: 1 *bĕyad-ḥaggay hannābîʾ*
through the prophet Haggai

The noun underlying the name *ḥaggay* can be identified in the personal names *ʾà-gi-a-lum* /*ḥaggī-ʿalum*/, "My Feast is the Most High" (TM.75.G.336 rev. III 8); *ʾà-ki-a* /*ḥaggī-yā*/, "My Feast is Ya" (*MEE* 1,6519), with the variant spelling *a-gi-yà* in *MEE* 2,26 rev. III 6.

Zech 2: 15 (EVV 11) *wĕnilwû gôyīm rabbîm ʾel-yhwh bĕyôm hāhûʾ*
wĕhāyû lî lĕʿām
ûšĕkīnātî (MT *wĕšākantî*) *bĕtôkēk*
wĕyādaʿat kî-yhwh ṣĕbāʾôt šĕlāḥānî ʾēlāyik
Many nations shall come over to Yahweh on that day,
and they will become his people.
But his glorious presence will be in your midst,
and you will know that Yahweh of Hosts
has sent me to you.

To achieve concord of persons, the versions resort to emendation, altering *lî* to *lô* and *šākantî* to *šākēn* or *šākĕnû*.[31] Northwest Semitic philology, however, can explain the suffix of both *lî* and *škntу* as third masculine singular, as in Phoenician, and in consonantal *škntу* recognize the postbiblical word *šĕkīnâ*, "glorious presence," attested in Talmudic and Rabbinical writings. In v 14 the text translates, "Shout aloud and rejoice, daughter of Zion; for, behold, I am coming and I will dwell (*wĕšākantî*) in your midst, says Yahweh"; in v 15 the Prophet announces to Zion that though many peoples will attach themselves to the Lord of Israel, Zion will remain his preferred abode.

The noun *šĕkīnâ* may also be present in the Ebla toponym read *ši-ki-na-at*[KI] by Pettinato (1979b: 93) but *ba-gi-na-at*[KI] by Archi (1980: 11). In the photograph published by Archi (Fig. 4a) the initial sign is doubtful; Pettinato's reading *ši-ki-na-at*[KI] issues in a comprehensible name but Archi's *ba-gi-na-at*[KI] does not immediately elicit a recognizable Semitic root. Our interpretation of Zech 2: 15 *škntу*, "his glorious presence," does not, however, depend upon the reading of disputed Ebla toponym *ši-ki-na-at*[KI].

Mal 3: 10 *wahărîqōtî lākem bĕrākâ*
ʿad-bĕlî-dāy
And I will pour out for you a blessing
until my abundance is no more.

For the second colon various versions have been proposed, such as NEB's "as long as there is need," and NIV's "that you will not have room for it." Comparison with Ps 72: 7, *ʿad-bĕlî yārēaḥ*, "till the moon is no more" (so NIV), argues that *ʿad-bĕlî-day* should be rendered accordingly. Among the more than 500 gods venerated by the Eblaites figures the deity *dī*, "Abundance," who may be identified in such personal names as *ṭù-bí-dì* /*ṭūbī-dī*/, "My good is Abundance" (TM.74.G.120)[32]; *íl-gú-uš-ti* /*yilquš-dī*/, "Abundance is the latter rain" (*MEE* 2,1 obv. VII 13). The second name, whose verb *yilquš* contains the root found in Heb *malqôš*, "latter rain," is particularly relevant since our verse specifically deals with rain, "And see if I will not open for you the windows of heaven, and pour out for you a blessing until my abundance is no more."[33]

Eblaite *dī* would be the contracted form of Heb *day*, whose construct is *dê*, "abundance." Since many of Yahweh's attributes were formerly names of independent Canaanite deities, *dāy* in Mal 3: 10 parses in the same manner as *yārēaḥ*, also a Canaanite deity, in Ps 72: 7, *ʿad-bĕlî yārēaḥ*, "till the moon is no more."

Albright (1968: 264) closed his analysis of Canaanite polytheism and its impact on Yahwistic religion with the following statements: "But significant pagan influences always came from the older and richer cultures, not from the nomads and semi-nomads of Sinai and North Arabia, as romantically imagined by many biblical scholars. It is high time that we turn from such imaginative fantasies to the real world of antiquity, which has so much to tell our world of today." How much more can we learn today from the real world of urbanized Canaan, thanks to the startling epigraphic discoveries at Ebla!

Notes

1. *MEE* 2 = Pettinato 1980a; *MEE* 1 = Pettinato 1979b.
2. UT = Gordon 1965.
3. Though no literary texts have yet been published, Ebla surely possessed mythological literature similar to that preserved at Ugarit. This claim takes rise from the striking PN *iš-tá-bá-má* recurring in *MEE* 2,37 obv. IV 1; 41 obv. IX 12; obv. X 3, which can be normalized *yištabama*, an infixed *-t-* form of *šbm*, "to muzzle"; the divine element is lacking in this hypocoristicon. The first person of this root and conjugation occurs in UT ʿnt:III: 37, *lʾištbm tnn*, "Indeed, I have muzzled Tannin," where the goddess ʿAnath speaks. One may parse Elbaite *ištabama* as first person singular, making it identical to the Ugaritic form, but the prevailing model in PNN is verb plus third-person name of god, such as above-cited *yilbaʾ-damu*, "Damu is a lion." Unable to cope with the uncommon sequence of signs *iš.tá.PA.má*, Pettinato (1980a: 256) decided that the signs should not be read in the order written but rather thus: PA.*iš-tá-má*. Since PA is a sumerogram signifying u g u l a, "superintendent," and the PN *iš-tá-má* is attested elsewhere in the tablets, Pettinato rendered the signs "the superintendent Ištama," with the comment that "no other explanation seems possible to me." The Canaanite approach to the tablets produces simpler and more elegant results.
4. Comparing *pīd(u)* with biblical *pîd*, "misfortune, disaster," a poetic word occurring thrice in Job (12: 5; 30: 24; 31: 29) and once in Proverbs (24: 22). Just as the Canaanites worshipped *gad*, "Fortune," so too they venerated its rival *pīd*, "Misfortune."
5. Parsing *ʾibīb* as *Piʿel* denominative from *ʾeb*, "bud" (root *ʾbb*); for other examples of *Piʿel* forms in Eblaite, see Dahood (1981: in press).
6. If adverbs and prepositions are a crucial criterion for classifying a language, then *sābīb*, "about, around," heretofore attested only in Hebrew, merits due consideration in future discussions.
7. The vocalization *tulum* vis-à-vis Heb *telem*, "furrow," compares with that of *ṣulum*, "Image," vis-à-vis Heb *ṣelem*. The god "Image" can be provisionally identified in the toponym *ša-nap-zu-lum*KI /*šanab-ṣulum*/, probably signifying "The Window of Image" (*MEE* 2,41 obv. VIII 9). The Hebrew

synonym of *ṣelem*, "image," namely *dĕmût*, "likeness," is revered as a god in the cultic texts TM.75.G.1764 obv. X 10; 2075 obv. VI 14; 2238 rev. II 16', published by Pettinato (1979a: 110–11), where the name is written ^{d}*ti-mu-tu /dimūt-u/*, "Likeness." Consult Dahood (1979b: 308) on Gen 1: 26.

8. The existence of the Canaanite god "Furrow" helps interpret the Ugaritic PN *grgš*, "Client of Clod," where *gš* is read in the light of Heb *gûš*, "clod, lump." Thus another Canaanite vegetation deity comes to light.

9. Fronzaroli's attempt (1980: 94–95) to derive *tá-da-bí-lu*, from **ʾpl*, "to reply," appears infelicitous.

10. For other instances see my note *apud* Pettinato (1980c: 216,n.35a).

11. The feminine ending *–a* in both *zana* and *alma* (Ugar *ǵlmt*, Phoen *ʿlmt*) suggests that Eblaite is an early form of Hebrew.

12. Prof. Pettinato accepts (oral communication) my proposal to read *éš-da-du*[KI] for *šè-da-du*[KI].

13. In Dahood (1981: in press).

14. The place names in this tablet were published by Pettinato (1978: 52–54).

15. The text can be found in Pettinato (1979c: 232).

16. On Job 30: 4 *lḥmm*, see Ceresko (1980: 50–52).

17. Thus in the Preface dated September 1979 to the English edition of his book Matthiae (1981:11) writes, "Byblos most probably does not appear in the texts, for the place name initially identified with it now appears to be an upper Mesopotamian centre that must be read as Dulu." Cf. Archi (1980: 3) who also favors the reading *du-lu*[KI].

18. Other instances of *tar* are cited in Dahood (1982) where the etymological basis of *tār* is examined. On *barūt*, "food," see *būrtum*, treated at Hab 1: 14–17 below.

19. Just as masculine collective *ʾŏnî* signifies "ships, fleet," whereas feminine *ʾŏnîyâ* denotes a single ship, so masculine *supīnu* may have designated "Fleet" in Eblaite, while feminine *sĕpînâ* in Hebrew referred to a single ship. It is worth noting that the toponyms *a-nì*[KI] in TM.75.G.2231 obv. IX 23 and *ṣí*[KI] in rev. I 6 may belong to the category of naval terms if these names identify with the parallel pair in Isa 33: 21, *ʾŏnî*, "ship"//*ṣî*, "vessel."

20. Contrast Pettinato's attempt (1980a: 31) to decipher *ra-da-mu* as an infixed *-ta-* conjugation of Akk *ramāmu*, "to love."

21. Fronzaroli (1979b: 79) reports that the professional term *mallāḫ–um*, "mariner," is found at Ebla. Ezek 27: 27, *mallāḥayik wĕḥōbĕlāyik*, "your mariners and sailors," is now seen to be employing two ancient Canaanite terms when describing the gang of the ship Tyre.

22. But one should not exclude a possible connection with Heb. *dōḥan*, "millet"; the cognate was *dôḥînāʾ* in Aramaic, close to the Eblaite vocalization.

23. Recognizing in *ì-la-mu* the adjective *ʿilāmu*, a synonym of *ʾêtān*, "perennial," which in 1 Kgs 8: 2, *yeraḥ hāʾêtānîm*, "the month of perennial streams," designates October-November.

24. Fronzaroli (1979a: 7) also understands *i-da-nu* as a hypocoristicon, though he does not associate it with the biblical PN *ʾêtān*.

25. In Gen 49: 24 I propose to read *wattĕšōbēb ʾêtān* (MT *wattēšeb bĕʾêtān*) *qaštô*, "And the Perennial renewed [cf. Ps 23: 3, *napšî yĕšôbēb*, where Yahweh is the subject] his bow"; cf. NEB, which recognizes that *ʾêtān* is a divine epithet, though it understands the colon differently. In Prov 13: 15 the reading of the second colon, which would restore the word balance to all four cola of vv 15–16, would be: *wĕderek bōgĕdîm ʾêtān killā* (MT *kol*, in v 16), "But the way of the faithless the Perennial demolishes." Cf. note 23.

26. This derivation supersedes my earlier explanation (1978: 106).

27. See the discussion of *Hipʿils* above, at Amos 5: 21.

28. Compare the Ugaritic PNN *kdn*, "Like the Judge"; *kkn*, "Like the Honest One"; *knʿm*, "Like the Gracious"; *ky*, "Like Ya," etc.

29. See Pettinato (1979c: 262). The existence of such synonyms shows that the Eblaites had word pairs that formed the basis of the Canaanite parallelistic poetry inherited by Ugaritic and biblical poets alike, as noted above.

30. For other instances see Viganò (1976: 177).

31. The NEB correctly maintains the third person in the disputed phrases "and become his people, and he will make his dwelling with you," but at the cost of three consonantal emendations, as explained in the critical apparatus published by Brockington (1973: 264).

32. For the text see Pettinato (1975: 370).

33. The sentiment expressed by the PN "Abundance is the latter-rain" recalls *sar-mi-lu /zarmī-ʾilu/*, "My downpour is Il" (*MEE* 2,7 obv. II 11), and of Ugaritic *gmm*, "The Voice is water" (UT 309: 10).

References

Albright, W. F.
1968 *Yahweh and the Gods of Canaan: A Historical Analysis of Two Contrasting Faiths*. Garden City: Doubleday.

Andersen, F. I., and Freedman, D. N.
1980 *Hosea*. Anchor Bible 24. Garden City: Doubleday.

Archi, A.
1980 Notes on Eblaite Geography. *Studi Eblaiti* II/1: 1–16.

Brichto, H. C.
1976 On Slaughter and Sacrifice, Blood and Atonement. *Hebrew Union College Annual* 47: 19–55.

Brockington, L. H.
1973 *The Hebrew Text of the Old Testament: the Readings adopted by the Translators of the New Engish Bible*. Oxford and Cambridge: the University Presses.

Cathcart, K. J.
1973 *Nahum in the Light of Northwest Semitic*. Biblica et Orientalia 26. Rome: Biblical Institute Press.

Ceresko, A. R.
1980 *Job 29–31 in the Light of Northwest Semitic*. Biblica et Orientalia 36. Rome: Biblical Institute Press.

Dahood, M.
1962 Northwest Semitic Philology and Job. Pp. 55–74 in *Gruenthaner Memorial Volume: The Bible in Current Catholic Thought*, ed. J. L. McKenzie. New York: Herder and Herder.
1964 Hebrew-Ugaritic Lexicography II. *Biblica* 45: 393–412.
1977 Rev. Lemaire. *Inscriptions hébraïques. I: Les ostraca. Orientalia* 46: 329–31.
1978 Ebla, Ugarit and the Old Testament. Pp. 81–112 in *Congress Volume: Göttingen 1977*. Supplements to Vetus Testamentum 29. Leiden: Brill.
1979a Third Masculine Singular with Preformative *t-* in Northwest Semitic. *Orientalia* 48: 97–106.
1979b The Ebla tablets and Old Testament theology. *Theology Digest* 27: 303–11.
1981 The Linguistic Classification of Eblaite. In *Atti del Convegno Internazionale su La Lingua di Ebla 21–23 aprile 1980*, ed. L. Cagni. Napoli: Istituto Universitario Orientale.
1982 Some Preformatives in Eblaite Place Names. *De la loi au Messie: Mélanges Henri Cazelles*, ed. A. Caquot and M. Delcor. Alter Orient und Altes Testament 14. Neukirchen-Vluyn and Kevelaer: Neukirchener Verlag and Butzon und Bercker.

Dahood, M., and Penar, T.
1972 Ugaritic-Hebrew Parallel Pairs. Pp. 71–382 in *Ras Shamra Parallels I*. Ed. L. R. Fisher. Analecta Orientalia 49. Rome: Pontifical Biblical Institute.

Davies, G. I.
1977 A new Solution to a Crux in Obadiah 7. *Vetus Testamentum* 27: 484–87.

van Dijk, H. J.
1969 Does Third Masculine Singular TAQTUL Exist in Hebrew? *Vetus Testamentum* 19: 440–47.

Fronzaroli, P.
1977 L'interferenza linguistica nella Siria settentrionale del III millennio. Pp. 27–43 of *Interferenza Linguistica: Atti del Convegno della Società Italiana di Glottologia*. Perugia, 24–25 aprile 1977. Ed. R. Ajello. Pisa: Giardini Editori.
1979a Un atto di donazione dagli archivi di Ebla (TM.75.G.1766). *Studi Eblaiti* I/1: 3–16.
1979b Problemi di fonetica eblaita I. *Studi Eblaiti* I/5–6: 65–95.
1980 Gli equivalenti di EME-BAL nelle liste lessicali eblaite. *Studi Eblaiti* II/6: 91–95.

Gelb, I. J.
1957 *Glossary of Old Akkadian*. Materials for the Assyrian Dictionary 3. Chicago: University of Chicago Press.

Gordon, C. H.
1965 *Ugaritic Textbook*. Analecta Orientalia 38. Rome: Pontifical Biblical Institute.

Lipiński, E.
1969 *La liturgie penitentielle dans la Bible*. Lectio Divina 52. Paris: Cerf.

Maloney, P. C.
1980 The Raw Material. *Biblical Archaeology Review* VI #3 (May/June): 57–59.

Matthiae, P.
1981 *Ebla: An Empire Rediscovered*. Garden City: Doubleday.

Meyer, F. de
1980 *kbd* comme nom divin en éblaite, ougaritique et hébreu. *Revue théologique de Louvain* 11: 225–28.

Pettinato, G.
1975 Testi cuneiformi del 3. millennio in paleo-cananeo rinvenuti nella campagna 1974 a Tell Mardīkh = Ebla. *Orientalia* 44: 361–74.
1976 Carchemiš-Kar-Kamiš. Le prime attestazioni del III millennio. *Oriens Antiquus* 16: 11–15.
1978 L'Atlante Geografico del Vicino Oriente Antico attestato ad Ebla e ad Abū Ṣalābīkh (I). *Orientalia* 47: 50–73.
1979a Culto ufficiale ad Ebla durante il regno di Ibbi-Sipiš. *Oriens Antiquus* 18: 85–215, 10 plates.
1979b *Catalogo dei testi cuneiformi di Tell Mardikh-Ebla*. Materiali epigrafici di Ebla 1. Napoli: Istituto Universitario Orientale di Napoli.
1979c *Ebla: Un impero inciso nell'argilla*. Milano: Mondadori.
1979d Le collezioni é n - é - n u - r u di Ebla. *Oriens Antiquus* 18: 329–51.
1980a *Testi amministrativi della biblioteca L. 2769*. Materiali epigrafici di Ebla 2. Napoli: Istituto Universitario Orientale di Napoli.
1980b Bollettino militare della campagna di Ebla contro la città di Mari. *Oriens Antiquus* 19: 231–45.
1980c Ebla and the Bible. *Biblical Archeologist* 43: 203–16.

Pope, M. H.
1977 *Song of Songs*. Anchor Bible 7C. Garden City: Doubleday.

Tsumura, D. T.
1981 Twofold Image of the Wine in Psalm 46: 4–5. *Jewish Quarterly Review* 71: 167–75.

Viganò, L.
1976 *Nomi e titoli di YHWH alla luce del semitico del Nordovest*. Biblica et

Orientalia 31. Rome: Biblical Institute Press.

Watson, W. G. E.
1981 Reversed Rootplay in Ps 145. *Biblica* 62: 101–2.

Wellhausen, J.
1887 *Skizzen und Vorarbeiten. Drittes Heft: Reste arabischen Heidentums*. Berlin: Reimer.

Wolff, H. W.
1965 *Dodekapropheton I. Hosea*². Biblischer Kommentar Altes Testament 14/I. Neukirchen Vluyn: Neukirchener Verlag.

Wright, G. E.
1966 Fresh Evidence for the Philistine Story. *Biblical Archaeologist* 29: 70–86.

The Use of *tôrâ* in Haggai 2: 11 and the Role of the Prophet in the Restoration Community

Eric M. Meyers
Duke University, Durham, North Carolina

Haggai prophesied in the days just prior to the rebuilding of the Second Temple. The period of his tenure was marked by an economy that could barely support the tiny Restoration community, which occupied little more than Jerusalem and environs (Hag 1: 6) (Broshi 1978; Eisman 1978). The Judean community was apparently at first preoccupied with personal welfare over against that of the public domain, for the former Temple was still in "shambles" when Haggai began to prophesy, each man rushing about his *own* house instead of rebuilding the Temple of Yahweh (1: 9). Haggai finally succeeded in arousing the conscience of the community, however, and the people "gave heed to the voice of Yhwh their God and to the words of the prophet Haggai when Yhwh their God sent him. . ." (1: 12). In this endeavor Haggai eventually enjoyed both political and clerical support.

> [14]Thus Yhwh roused the spirit of Zerubbabel ben Shealtiel, the governor of Judah, and the spirit of Joshua ben Jehozadak, the high priest, and the spirit of all the rest of the people, so that they began to do the work on the House of Yhwh of Hosts their God [15]on the twenty-fourth day of the sixth month in the second year of King Darius.[1]

Within a month's time (2: 1) work on the Temple had apparently progressed, but it is quite clear that Haggai had to work constantly at inspiring the reluctant workers (2: 3–5). The response was positive, for in just a short while (2: 6) heaven and earth were to announce the day of completion and rededication, when God's presence would fill the rebuilt Temple (2: 7).

> "The glory (*kābôd*) of this latter House will be greater than that of the former," spoke Yhwh of Hosts, "and I will grant well-being through this place"—saying of Yhwh of Hosts (2: 9).

It is quite understandable that the *kābôd* of the Second Temple was construed to be greater than that of the First Temple from the perspective of the Restoration community, but it does not seem possible to imagine that the 515 Temple was as physically glorious as the one the elders of the community would have remembered to have stood in 587 (Ezra 6: 13–18). According to Ezra the rededication of the Temple occurred on the third of Adar in the sixth year of the reign of Darius (Ezra 6: 15), i.e., in the very early spring of 515. According to the book of Haggai, that prophet's activities were limited to the second year of Darius; Zechariah continued until the fourth year of Darius (Zech 7: 1).

In short, the context of Haggai's exhortations is the second regnal year of Darius,

520 B.C.E., before the rededication in 515 B.C.E. It is a crucial period in the history of Israel and it provides us with a unique opportunity to observe the post-exilic prophet at work rebuilding a society as well as a physical House. These were troubled times not only from an economic standpoint but also because there were enemies from without who opposed the work; the Samaritans even succeeding in bringing the work to a temporary halt (Ezra 4: 1–24). The reestablishment of the community along the lines enumerated in Ezra 6: 16–18 demonstrates clearly how notions of legitimacy and priestly or Levitical rule came to dominate at this time (Myers 1965: 51–53). Indeed, the priests were returned to their divisions and the Levites to their positions for the divine service according to the Law of Moses (Ezra 6: 18; cf. Exodus 29; Leviticus 8; Numbers 3: 5–39; 8: 5–22).

The oracle of Hag 2: 10–14 thus offers an opportunity to examine, from a prophetic point of view, the process of restoring a community. That the concerns of Haggai intersect with those of the priests has led some critics to accuse Haggai, and Zechariah as well, of selling out to the establishment, thereby sowing the seeds of the demise of prophecy, which had heretofore been unattached to any arm of the religious establishment and which had been characterized by its visionary and antiestablishment nature (Hanson 1975). The present oracle, and in particular the unique usage of *tôrâ* in 2: 11, demonstrates very much the contrary, to wit, post-exilic prophecy went hand-in-hand with priestly concerns and provided the critical linkage between two disparate loci of society which come together in the Restoration period for a little while but remain together forever in the history of Judaism, where the sage or rabbi is the true inheritor of the biblical prophet. Such an assertion has been one of the hallmarks of Jewish scholarship for many years. Indeed, a contemporary scholar has referred to Pharisaism—that form of classical Judaism whose primary function was to interpret Hebrew jurisprudence—as "prophecy in action" (Finkelstein 1970). Although the present essay dissociates itself with such an absolutist approach, it does propose to see an epoch of continuity-with-change in the post-exilic period when prophecy declines. Despite the demise of classical prophecy, Judaism in the Second Temple period survives many critical challenges, and it was in no small measure because the sages saw themselves as heirs to the prophets (*m. Sanh.* 11a; *m. B. Bat.* 12b).

> [10]On the twenty-fourth day of the ninth month, in the second year of Darius, the word of Yhwh came to the prophet Haggai: [11]"Thus spoke Yhwh of Hosts, 'Ask the priests for a ruling (*tôrâ*) (on this), [12]"If someone carries sacral meat in the corner of his garment and with its corner touches bread, pottage, wine, oil, or any foodstuff, will it be sanctified?"'" The priests replied and said, "No." [13]Then Haggai said, "If a person defiled by contact with a corpse touches any of these, will it be defiled?" The priests replied and said, "It will be defiled." [14]Then Haggai replied and said, "So is this people and so is their nation before me,"—saying of Yhwh—"and so is all the work of their hands; whatever they offer there is defiled." (Hag 2: 10–14)

The first point to be considered is the use of the word *tôrâ* in 2: 11. There are 220 biblical occurrences of the word, of which approximately 52 may be translated "law," "statute," "judgment," or "ruling." In the remainder of instances its attestation must be associated with a book of statutes and commandments which Moses gave to Israel. There is no doubt that in the present case *tôrâ* without the definite article is being used in the narrowest legal sense and that its inspiration is the legal texts of the Pentateuch, e.g., Exod 12: 49; Lev 7: 7; Num 15: 16, 29. The list of passages could be greatly lengthened, especially if one were to count instances with the definite article or in the defined state where the meaning is similar or if one were to count plurals. It is our contention, however, that the use of *tôrâ* in Hag 2: 11 is part of a new idiom *š'l tôrâ*, which is also attested, in a slightly different form, in Mal 2: 7 (*bqš tôrâ*) and that this idiom is what might be called—for lack of any other better technical term—"proto-rabbinic," the predecessor of *pĕsaq dîn.*[2]

In Haggai the priests are "asked" to make a "ruling," to render a decision on a matter of ritual purity. The idiom thus refers in a most explicit way to an activity of the priests which was probably carried out in the Court of the Priests on the Temple grounds (cf. Zech 7: 3). That the priests had functioned as interpreters of the Law for some time is evident from Deut 17: 9,11 and Ezek 44: 23–24 (cf. 22: 26) and implicit in many pentateuchal passages. The Court of the Priests is said to have existed into rabbinic times (e.g., *m. Roš Haš.* 1.7, cf. also Zar-Kavod 1970: 8). What is absolutely clear from the present instance is that the prophet fully expects the people to turn to the priests and their court for a ruling regarding ritual purity. Haggai does not utilize the opportunity to expand on the meaning of ritual fitness; his statement rather reflects a kind of nuts-and-bolts attitude, with a rather reflective, summary conclusion (2: 14). When Haggai offers his somewhat redundant conclusion, ". . . whatever they offer there is defiled" (2: 14), he is both supporting and promulgating the priestly decision offered just before. Indeed, the force of the *wy'n* in 2: 14 is quite clearly to indicate, indeed to underscore the prophet's role in supporting and mediating the priestly decision to the people. Thus Haggai both assents to the *tôrâ* which is factually accurate and apt as well as concurring in the belief that all the people were impure as a result of their behavior.

The appearance of the word *tôrâ* in the singular, without the definite article, and with the verb of questioning *š'l*, enables us to posit a parallel usage in Mal 2: 7: "For the lips of a priest keep knowledge, so that people seek (*bqš*) a ruling (*tôrâ*) from his mouth." The meaning of the idiom here is also to be construed in a most literal vein: the Levitical covenant that is renewed in Mal 2: 4–5 elevates the priest to the role of a sage who functions expeditiously within society to maintain standards and to interpret the Law and to render specific rulings when need be. It is such a "teaching priest" who is anachronistically referred to by the Chronicler (2 Chr 15: 3) in the reign of King Asa.

The idiom "to ask (*or* seek) a ruling" from the priest(s) is, therefore, a creation of the post-exilic prophets and as such documents how closely prophecy and priesthood drew together in this period. That it draws upon earlier precedents has already been noted. The fact that the idiom already begins to take shape in earlier strata of biblical literature and ultimately assumes a technical place in rabbinic literature, however, enables us to locate the present usage in a period that is pivotal both for the history of Israel and the history of biblical language (Hill 1981). Possible earlier idioms that might have influenced this development include Num 27: 21 and 2 Sam 16: 23.[3]

The continuation of Mal 2: 7 in 2: 8 seems to suggest that improper teaching or interpretation of the Torah caused many to stumble. Thus, as the priests were invested with more and more authority, their capacity to violate the "covenant of Levi" was increased proportionately. In a sense the Malachi passage shows how the priest comes to displace the messenger of Yahweh. The messenger now is clearly the priest (2: 7), through whom correct ruling(s) and instruction are mediated. There can be no doubt that the teaching role of the priest is one of the most significant aspects of all post-exilic Judaism and one of the central leitmotifs of Temple Judaism (Begrich 1936).

It is usually assumed that the book of Malachi is to be dated later than Zechariah; indeed we subscribe to the opinion that it is to be dated to the first half of the fifth century B.C.E. (Hill 1981). Zechariah, at least chapters 1–8, dates to the period just prior to the rededication of the Temple in 515 B.C.E. (Ackroyd 1975; Mason 1977). The social situation of that period is such that the prophet (Zech 7: 2–4) himself feels constrained to answer an inquiry that is directed to both prophet and priest. Indeed, Zechariah not only answers the inquiry of the delegation from Bethel but does so by remembering the words of former prophets (7: 7), responding with a prophecy that is Deuteronomic in its style and intent, rather than with a strict ruling (7: 9–10). The prophet Zechariah both speaks like and behaves like a priestly sage; while still a prophet in this regard, he is more akin to Haggai than to Malachi, who concludes by announcing the primacy of Moses, the quintessential lawgiver, over the eschatological prophet, Elijah (Mal 3: 22–23). To be sure, Moses is also a prophet without equal, but it is statutes and judgments, not prophecies, that (3: 22) constitute the "Law of Moses."

With the isolation of a new idiom for seeking a priestly ruling attested in the post-exilic prophets Haggai and Malachi, and with the realization that Zechariah's roles as priest and prophet are beginning to merge, we may examine the full context of Haggai's oracle in order to assess its meaning early in the post-exilic period. The priests do indeed render a judgment regarding sacral flesh (2: 12) and defilement by contact with an unclean body or corpse (2: 13). But the prophet goes much further in his oracle. In addition to reporting the decision of the priestly court he also renders judgment on the people of his day (2: 14) for not adhering to standards of Levitical purity.[4] "This people and this nation" are none other than the Jews of the Restoration community, a position championed by Y. Kaufmann years ago (1977 trans.) and more recently by S. Talmon (1961: 343) and H. May (1968). Thus Haggai is still fulfilling an oracular or prophetic function ("saying of Yhwh," 2: 14) while at the same time assuming the role of the teaching priest. Judging from the examples we have already provided, these aspects of late biblical prophecy remained in dynamic tension till the very end of the prophetic movement itself. This development may tentatively be assigned to the first half of the fifth century B.C.E., taking Malachi as the last of the prophets. It is our opinion that so-called Deutero-Zechariah also belongs in this period, with a terminus of 475 B.C.E. These dates have been independently arrived at in a recent study by Hill (1981: 132–33).

P. Hanson has been an especially harsh critic of Haggai and Zechariah:

> Haggai and Zechariah, though using the forms and phrases of prophetic eschatology and exercising the prophetic functions of anointing the King and sanctifying the priesthood, placed prophecy in the uncritical service of a particular system. In giving Yahweh's unquestioned sanction to a particular human institution, and to particular priestly and royal officials, they were wedding their fate to the fate of that institution and those officials, and were giving up the independent stance always maintained by the classical prophets vis à vis the institutions of the temple and royal court. They were giving up the revolutionary element which was always an essential ingredient in genuine

> prophecy, an element stemming from a vision of Yahweh's order of mercy and justice which called into question every human institution and every human officebearer (1975: 247).

Such a view of late biblical prophecy is too severe; in our opinion it simply does not accord with the data. Haggai has not sold out to the establishment. Indeed, he is attempting to outline for the community the details of a cult that carries no unconditional guarantees: sacral flesh cannot convey holiness to the enumerated items, and, contrariwise, defilement by a corpse may be transmitted to such items, which thereby lose their sacred quality. The issue in Haggai is purely and simply a question of ritual fitness—defilement is not an issue of idolatry or sin. It is plainly an issue that requires a "ruling" or a decision, a *tôrâ*. Haggai refers the people to the priestly court and conveys the results of the priestly decision to the people in his dual role as prophet and as teacher, one who uses the priestly rulings as a vehicle for his prophetic message.

There is another point to this oracle: it was presented before the Temple was rebuilt, at a time when there was perhaps some unclarity as to the validity of certain ritual requirements and in particular as to the status of the purity issue posed in the oracle. Kaufmann plausibly suggests (1977: 260) that a temporary sacrificial cult did in fact exist prior to 515 B.C.E. The result of Haggai's clarification is dramatic and immediate: the people take the rebuke to heart and carry on with the building effort. The rebuilt Temple contains only the potential and promise of fitness for the coming of a new age. In that new time, ushered in by Zerubbabel in Hag 2: 23, presumably the community will have seen fit to prepare itself through purification of its social and religious life.

Such a vision does not in our opinion appear to be a sellout to the religious establishment. The religious establishment was at this time being refined, and the prophet is utilizing his high office to influence as best he can the character and quality of the religious life. That the content of Haggai's vision is priestly or pentateuchal does not gainsay his utter devotion to speaking out against ritual abuses which he believed must be corrected in order to prepare the way for the coming of a new day. That day was to be not any ordinary day but rather a day in which all people will share in God's glory (Hag 2: 7). The peace that will be provided by the restored Temple (2: 9) is a universal peace despite the fact that the entire book is cast in what seems to be the particularistic language of priestly concerns such as ritual fitness.

To our mind Hag 2: 6–9 and 2: 20–23 truly constitute visionary passages grafted in the context of late biblical prophecy onto the more mundane ritual concerns of post-exilic life. But it is the overall combination which gives Haggai its unique post-exilic flavor. Hanson's view that such a wedding of themes ultimately contributes to the disappearance of prophecy must be rejected as well.[5] The flurry of exilic and post-exilic canonical activity attests to a creative spurt in Israel's history that must be regarded as one of the most positive of all responses to the Exile. Here we must look to the work of our teacher, David Noel Freedman, whose view of the prophetic canon enables us to view in a constructive way the dynamic social context which brought these writings to definitive form in the time of the early Second Temple (1963, 1975, 1976). In many ways Freedman is followed by D. L. Petersen (1977). The great flurry of canonical activity before and after Haggai, lasting into the fifth century, could well have created the situation in which prophecy was eschatologized in Mal 3: 23 and perhaps in Joel 3: 1. In such a view prophecy cannot be said to have been swallowed up by the cult. Rather, just as the rabbis assert in *'Abot* 1: 1, the sages received their inspiration from the prophets. Prophecy passes on its function to the priest, and sage or wise man. It does not die; it is reborn. The rabbinic view thus is one of peaceful transition, a view we believe comports well with all the data.

Hag 2: 11, therefore, provides a critical datum in assessing the status of the role of the prophet in the Restoration community. Haggai is not, to be sure, a priest in the sense that Ezekiel was. Still, their common concerns are many, and their devotion to the role of the Temple in society is complete. *Tôrâ* has moved from designating the word of God, as in much of the prophetic literature, to designating the regulations for specific cultic or ritual practices, as in the pentateuchal literature (e.g., Lev 6: 2, 7, 18; Num 5: 29). But even more than this, the prophet by conveying a priestly ruling also appears as a mediator between the priests and the people.

In Haggai we have discovered a unique instance of an idiom that may be called "proto-rabbinic," an early *pĕsaq-dîn* form. This form, indeed the very idiom with the verb "to ask" (*š'l*), occurs frequently in the rabbinic literature, in both Aramaic and Hebrew (Jastrow 1950: 1506–8), attesting a linguistic continuity that parallels the continuity between the prophets and the sages or the men of the Great Assembly. We hope this study will contribute to yet another reassessment of late biblical prophecy, one which is sensitive both to the priestly concerns of nascent Judaism and to the prophetic ideals, however muted and recast they may be in the last of the prophets.

Notes

1. All quotations from Haggai are taken from the author's forthcoming Anchor Bible commentary on *Haggai, Zechariah, and Malachi* in preparation with Carol L. Meyers, co-editor of this volume. I am much indebted to her for her collaboration in that undertaking and to D. Noel Freedman for inviting us to write it.

2. This term is derived from the Aramaic usage of Hebrew *psq*, "to separate, divide, part *or* distribute." In rabbinic parlance it often has a halachic nuance, "to decide *or* adjudge." To render a specific opinion or judgment would be the intention of our proposed proto-rabbinic idiom, *pĕsaq dîn*. Although the specific idiom does not occur as such in the ancient literature, to anyone familiar with rabbinic law the expression clearly conjures up the image of "rendering a judgment." The proposal to use this term is tentative and is meant only to be suggestive of the process being referred to in Haggai. The reader is referred to the references in Jastrow (1950: 1199–1201) for full citations.

3. These two examples illustrate how the verb *š'l*, "to question," is used in a narrow, technical sense, first in the matter of a "ruling" (*mišpaṭ*) regarding the Urim, and second regarding the "word" (*dĕbar*) of the Lord.

4. Although the rabbis sometimes conceded a hiatus between biblical, canonical prophecy and the period of the sages, the dominant view was that expressed in *'Abot* 1: 1: "Moses received the *Torah* on Sinai and passed it on to Joshua; Joshua to the elders; the elders to the prophets; and the prophets passed it on to the men of the Great Assembly." The traditional view is that the men of the Great Assembly were the first rabbis. Indeed, so strong is the link between prophet and sage or rabbi in the rabbinic literature that the prophets are often infused with an inspired function as authoritative interpreters of law, as is the case in Hag 2: 11 and as is suggested by the priestly concerns of Ezekiel. On the legal functions of the prophets in the Babylonian Talmud, see e.g., *b. B. Qamma'* 82a; or *Mek. bĕšallaḥ* 1. See also Finkelstein (1970: *passim*).

5. It is quite conceivable that because of the ascendancy of wisdom literature and its concerns in the early post-exilic period that we are witnessing a kind of double merger in the later prophets between wisdom/cult and prophecy. That is to say, there is clearly an overlap in the function of prophet as teacher/sage and the prophet as interpreter of the Law. It is also clear to us that nowhere is cult so closely associated with prophet as in the later prophets. The growing influence of the sage or wisdom teacher in this period surely facilitated the process whereby wisdom themes were incorporated into the tradition. The rabbinic view of prophecy supports both the view offered in this paper as well as the view that postulates wisdom as a major contributor to the peaceful decline of prophecy. The sapiential character of late prophecy is best preserved in the book of Daniel, which is apocalyptic and yet part of *Kethubim*. It is important to note that the rabbinic view of prophecy also reflects the merger of wisdom with prophecy. Hence, there is a tendency in the Targumim to add prophetic headings to wisdom books (e.g., Ecclesiastes).

References

Ackroyd, P.
1975 *Exile and Restoration.* Old Testament Library. Philadelphia: Westminster.

Begrich, J.
1936 Die priesterliche Tora. Pp. 63–88 in *Weiden und Wesen des Alten Testament*, ed. P. Volz, F. Stummer, and J. Hempel. Beihefte zur Zeitschrift für die Alttestamentliche Wissenschaft 66. Berlin: Töpelmann.

Broshi, M.
1978 Estimating the Population of Ancient Jerusalem. *Biblical Archeology Review* 4: 10–15.

Eisman, M.
1978 A Tale of Three Cities. *Biblical Archeologist* 41: 47–60.

Finkelstein, L.
1970 *New Light From the Prophets.* New York: Basic Books.

Freedman, D. N.
1963 The Law and the Prophets. *Supplements to Vetus Testamentum* 9: 250–165.
1975 "Son of Man, Can These Bones Live?": The Exile. *Interpretation* 29 [#2: The History of Israel and Biblical Faith: In Honor of John Bright]: 171–86.
1976 Canon of the Old Testament. Pp. 130–36 in *The Interpreter's Dictionary of the Bible/Supplementary Volume*, ed. K. Crim et al. Nashville: Abingdon.

Hanson, P. D.
1975 *The Dawn of Apocalyptic.* Philadelphia: Fortress Press.

Hill, A. E.
1981 *The Book of Malachi: Its Place in Post-Exilic Chronology Linguistically Reconsidered.* Michigan Dissertation.

Jastrow, M.
1950 *A Dictionary of the Targumim, the Talmud Babli and Yerushalmi, and Midrashic Literature.* New York: Pardes Publishing House.

Kaufmann, Y.
1977 *History of the Religion of Israel, Vol. IV.* New York: Ktav Publishing.

Mason, R.
1977 *The Books of Haggai, Zechariah and Malachi.* Cambridge: Cambridge University Press.

May, H. G.
1968 "This People" and "This Nation" in Haggai. *Vetus Testamentum* 18: 190–97.

Myers, J. M.
1965 *Ezra-Nehemiah.* Anchor Bible 14. Garden City: Doubleday.

Petersen, D. L.
1977 *Late Israelite Prophecy: Studies in Deutero-Prophetic Literature and in Chronicles.* Society of Biblical Literature Monograph 23. Missoula: Scholars Press.

Talmon, S.
1961 Synonymous Readings in the Textual Traditions of the Old Testament. Pp. 335–83 in *Studies in the Bible*, ed. C. Rabin. Scripta Hierosolymitana 8. Jerusalem: Magnes.

Zar-Kavod, M.
1970 *Commentary on Haggai in the Twelve Minor Prophets.* Jerusalem: Mossad Harav Cook (Hebrew).

Dating the Book of Malachi: A Linguistic Reexamination

Andrew E. Hill
Trinity College, Deerfield, Illinois

I

The date of the book of Malachi and its relation to the other biblical writings has long been the subject of research and debate in the field of biblical scholarship.* In his classic work on Malachi, A. von Bulmerincq (1921: 87–97) outlines possibilities for the dating of Malachi which range from the 6th to the 2nd centuries B.C. All subsequent studies on the date of this last book of the Minor Prophets follow one or another of seven chronological positions worked out by von Bulmerincq (see Hill 1981: 14–25). The present article complements research on Malachi's oracle and its chronological relationship to the other post-Exilic prophetic books, Haggai and Zechariah, by presenting a purely linguistic analysis of the text. This approach contrasts sharply with previous investigations of Malachi, which have relied largely on thematic studies, ritual practices, and lexical parallels, as well as on descriptions of the religious, social, and political conditions within the post-Exilic Jewish community recorded in the post-Exilic prophets and Ezra and Nehemiah, to date the prophecy of Malachi. The linguistic analysis characteristic of this study is based upon the *typological* approach of R. Polzin (1976) and involves systematic application of nineteen grammatical and syntactic categories developed by Polzin for the express purpose of distinguishing the relative chronological relation of Early and Late Biblical prose. Polzin's target corpus was the so-called P strand of Biblical Hebrew. My study applies Polzin's methodology to the book of Malachi, working with Polzin's already established corpora as well as with the dated texts of Haggai and Zechariah 1–8 as control corpora (since the validity of the 520 B.C. dates in the superscriptions to the two books is now almost universally acknowledged by biblical scholars). Through the application of these nineteen categories Polzin produces a typological continuum of Biblical Hebrew narrative prose, demonstrating the relative chronological relationships of the corpora selected for analysis. My typological examination of the post-Exilic prophets endeavors to place Malachi onto this continuum, and extends the field of study to include prophetic prose.

The methodology of the typological linguistic analysis has a direct bearing on the notion of chronology used in the present article. Previous research on Malachi, utilizing such criteria as thematic similarities and lexical parallels, has sought to relate the book to certain post-Exilic *events* which have absolute historical dates and stipulate a definite chronology. On the other hand, the linguistic analysis characteristic of the typological method seeks to relate Malachi to other pieces of post-Exilic (as well as pre-Exilic and Exilic) *literature*. I have deliberately avoided the several acknowledged chronological complexities of the post-Exilic period. The emphasis here is rather on chronological relationships within the framework of the relative dating schematic yielded by typological analysis. Fortunately, in the case of the post-Exilic prophets, this gap between relative and absolute dating is minimized by the exact dates of Haggai and Zechariah 1–8.

Since Polzin structured his typological method for the analysis of Biblical Hebrew prose, it is necessary to establish that Haggai, Zechariah, and Malachi are indeed prose, so as to avoid the pitfalls of comparing dissimilar materials. This is particularly apropos in light of the recent study of F. I. Andersen and D. N. Freedman (1980: 57–66). They conclude from "prose-particle" counts of individual chapters that Hosea is a mixture of varying degrees of prose and poetry, a mixture of a type which appears to be characteristic of the 8th-century Hebrew prophets. The problem of prose-poetry discrimination is by no means a simple one and I would concur with J. Hoftijzer, who states,

> The boundaries of what is poetry are not easy to delimit, as we are very badly informed about the nature of Hebrew poetry. We know practically nothing with any certainty about the accentuation, the metre, the rhythm or any other system whereby poetry was differentiated from ordinary prose (1965: 50).

In his monograph on the particle *ʾet*, Hoftijzer traces its use through most of the Hebrew Bible. Based upon his analysis of *ʾet syntagmemes* (i.e., the particle *ʾet* and the word or group of words following it), Hoftijzer (1965: 76–77) concludes Haggai, Zechariah 1–8, and Malachi, at least in respect to their density of *ʾet syntagmemes*, are "comparable to [prose] narrative material." Concerning Zechariah 9–14 Hoftijzer (1965: 77) states, "We can conclude that in Deutero-Zechariah the *ʾet syntagmeme* density is like that of narrative [prose] material, with the exception of Zech. ix where it agrees with that in poetic material."

In the main, this treatment is corroborated by an analysis of the post-Exilic prophets based on the "prose-particle" counting method of Andersen & Freedman (1980: 57–66); here the total number of occurrences of the particles *ʾet*, *ʾăšer*, and the definite article is set in proportion to the total number of words per chapter of a given text. In general these particles are typical of Hebrew prose and atypical of Hebrew poetry. According to Andersen & Freedman the frequency of these particles is high in prose (on a percentage basis 15% or more of all words), while the frequency of these particles in poetry is much lower (5% or less of all words) (1980: 60). Haggai, Zechariah, and Malachi demonstrate "prose-particle" frequencies very near or above 15%, while Zechariah 9–14 exhibits similar ratios except in chapter nine, which has a "prose-particle" frequency of less than 4%. Given this further evidence, it would seem safe to conclude Haggai, Zechariah 1–8, and the target corpus of Malachi are representative of Hebrew prose, while Zechariah 9–14 appears to be a mixture of prose and poetry. This last datum is crucial to any consideration of the position of Zechariah 9–14 in post-Exilic literature.

The linguistic analysis of Biblical Hebrew is by no means a new development in biblical studies. A. Kropat (1909) was one of the pioneers in the linguistic analysis of Biblical Hebrew, and his work has become the *Grundlage* for the subsequent linguistic research of scholars such as A. Hurvitz and R. Polzin. Unfortunately, much of the work in the field of biblical studies which seeks to employ a linguistic approach has been devoid of contact with the larger discipline of linguistics in general, and historical linguistics in particular. In an attempt to broaden the horizons of those who undertake linguistic and typological analyses of the Hebrew Bible, I have oriented my research to several of the basic principles upon which the discipline of historical linguistics is founded, including general concepts of language contact and language change, and the comparative method of language analysis (see further Hill 1981: 5–9).

Modern typological approaches to language (including Polzin's) stem from similar historical linguistic research dating back to the early nineteenth century (cf. Lehmann 1962: 51–54). According to Lehmann,

> Given adequate descriptions we could type languages for their phonological, morphological, syntactic and semantic structures, with no attention to the frequency of selected features in texts. At present, however, analysis of frequency of selected features is the most promising approach. It must be tested on a variety of languages and refined. . . . Although the chief aim of typology is classification of languages, it promises new techniques for historical study [of how languages change]. . . . Typological classification applied at selected stages of languages would enable us to mark their development on the basis of verifiable criteria (1962: 61).

I concur whole-heartedly with Lehmann, and have chosen to adapt Polzin's typological approach to the problems inherent in the dating of post-Exilic Biblical Hebrew material for the reasons Lehmann cites. Granted that typological linguistic research is still in its infancy in biblical scholarship, nonetheless, it promises to offer a viable and much needed alternative to methodologies presently used in biblical studies. However, lest enthusiasm for "some new thing" displace necessary caution and reserve, R. J. Jeffers and I. Lehiste (1979: 119) point out that the incorporation of typological factors into linguistic studies "by no means presents a panacea" for students of historical linguistics. Notwithstanding this caution, I believe that the present study, through the utilization of typological methodology, can make a valuable contribution to the overall understanding of Malachi's relationship to Haggai and Zechariah 1–8 and 9–14 and to its place in the chronology of post-Exilic literature.

II

In his book *Late Biblical Hebrew: Toward an Historical Typology of Biblical Hebrew Prose,* Robert Polzin (1976) attempts to characterize and classify several major stages of Biblical Hebrew on the basis of nineteen different grammatical and syntactic categories. By systematically applying these nineteen categories to selected texts Polzin seeks to differentiate Early Biblical Hebrew from Late Biblical Hebrew on a relative chronological scale. The focal point of Polzin's research (the unknown as it were) is the portion of the Hebrew Bible traditionally called the Priestly Document (or P). Of the four recognized strands of P (the base text P^g, its supplement P^s, The Lawcode P^t, and the Holiness Code P^h) Polzin (1976: 85–90) concentrates on the bulk of the largest two, P^g and P^s. In addition, Polzin utilizes, in establishing the pre-Exilic end of his continuum, selections from the Pentateuchal parts of the Yahwist and Elohist traditions (JE), the Court History (CH, roughly 2 Samuel 13– 1 Kings 1), and the Deuteronomist (Dtr, i.e., the framework of Deuteronomy and parts of the Deuteronomic History); the post-Exilic part of his continuum is keyed to the non-synoptic portions of Chronicles (Chr), all of Ezra (Ezr), the memoir portions of Nehemiah (N^1), the non-memoir portions of Nehemiah (N^2), and all of Esther

(Est) (for the specific contents of each of the designated corpora see Hill 1981: 27–34). Polzin analyzes these corpora typologically for the purpose of determining whether the distinction of P versus non-P is a valid one and whether a typological characterization of the delineated corpora can yield criteria sufficient for the establishment of a dating scheme exhibiting the relative chronological relationship of each of the corpora, with an emphasis on the position of the "unknowns," P^g and P^s. In each case the typological research of Polzin offered an affirmative answer. Granted this fact, it is reasonable to assume typological methodology will yield criteria sufficient for the establishment of a relative dating scheme when applied to other texts as well. My analysis of the post-Exilic prophets from the typological perspective is built upon just this premise. The nineteen diagnostic features of Late Biblical Hebrew (LBH), grammatical and syntactic, developed by Polzin for the typological analysis of Biblical Hebrew prose are listed below. According to Polzin (1976: 1–2), the non-synoptic portions of the Books of Chronicles represent the best example of LBH, and Polzin's nineteen categories were largely developed on the basis of the language of the Chronicler (for a detailed and critical evaluation of Polzin's typological categories see Hill 1981: 38–45). The nineteen typological categories are recorded here in Polzin's system of enumeration:

A. Features of Late Biblical Hebrew (LBH) not attributable to Aramaic influence:
   1. Radically reduced use of *ʾet* with pronominal suffix.
   2. Increased use of *ʾet* before a noun in the nominative case: *ʾet* emphatic.
   3. Expression of possession by prospective pronominal suffix with a following noun, or *lĕ* plus noun or *šel* plus noun.
   4. Collectives are construed as plurals almost without exception.
   5. A preference for plural forms of words and phrases which the earlier language uses in the singular.
   6. The use of an infinitive absolute in immediate connection with a finite verb of the same stem is almost completely lacking in the Chronicler; the infinitive absolute used as a command is not found at all in Chronicles.
   7. The Chronicler's use of the infinitive construct with *bĕ,* and *kĕ*: as Segal (1927) points out, the later books of the OT show less frequent use of the infinitive construct with *bĕ,* and *kĕ*; even in the cases when LBH does use the introductory infinitive with *bĕ,* and *kĕ,* the usage is different than earlier constructions.
   8. Repetition of a singular word = Latin *quivis* [to express distributives].
   9. The Chronicler shows a merging [i.e., a tendency to replace] the third feminine plural suffix with the third masculine plural suffix.
   10. The first person singular imperfect with the *–āh* (the lengthened imperfect or cohortative) is found but once in the Chronicler's language.
   11. The use of *wayhî* greatly recedes in Chronicles and in the younger language.
   12. In appositional relationship, the Chronicler prefers to place the substantive before the numeral and almost always puts it in the plural; this is contrary to the older practice of putting the number first.
   13. The Chronicler shows an increased use of the infinitive construct with *lĕ.*

B. Features of Late Biblical Hebrew (LBH) attributable to Aramaic influence:
   1. In citing material and its weight or measure, the Chronicler often has the order, material weighed or measured + its weight or measure (+ number).
   2. *lĕ* is used often as a mark of the accusative.
   3. *min,* "from," the *nun* is often not assimilated before a noun with an article.
   4. The Chronicler uses the emphatic *lĕ* before the last element of a list.
   5. In an attributive usage, *rabbîm* is twice placed before the substantive.
   6. The use of *ʿad lĕ* [for "up to, until"].

The purpose in distinguishing the A and B classes is "not only to describe a certain feature as late, but to attempt also to further describe its nature" (Polzin 1976: 9–10). Polzin pursues this distinction in the nature of LBH features as a result of his interest in determining whether or not a given feature represents a proto-Mishnaic or Mishnaic characteristic. The differentiation of Aramaic and Mishnaic features important for his study will not be part of the analysis of the post-Exilic prophets. The presence of a given LBH feature means an overwhelming presence in the text under consideration, perhaps with occasional exceptions. Unique features, those typological categories rendering data deviating radically from the expected norm in the selected texts, are also denoted.

Polzin's research can be summarized with the typological continuum of Biblical Hebrew he offers as a result of his systematic application of the nineteen aforementioned grammatical and syntactic categories to the specified corpora. Corpora with slashes are more or less homogeneous. (In fairness to Polzin, as well as to the writer, I encourage the reader to examine both Polzin's work and my own full-scale adaptation of it.)

JE/CH/Dtr	P^g	P^s	Chr	Ezr/N^2	N^1	Est

JE/CH/Dtr: twelve stable features of Classical BH are present (contra A.1, A.2, A.3, A.4, A.5, A.6, A.7, A.8, A.9/B.1, A.11, A.12, A.13)

P^g: four features of LBH are present (A.3, A.4, A.6, A.9); seven features of Classical BH remain (contra A.2, A.5, A.7, A.8, A.11, A.12, B.1)

P^s: eight features of LBH are present (A.2, A.3, A.4, A.7, A.9, A.11, A.12, B.1); two features of Classical BH remain (contra A.5, A.8)

Chr: thirteen features of LBH are present (A.1, A.2, A.3, A.4, A.5, A.6, A.7, A.8, A.9, A.11, A.12, A.13, B.1); no features of Classical BH remain

Ezr/N^2: ten features of LBH are present (Ezr: A.3, A.4, A.5, A.6, A.7, A.8, A.9, A.11, A.12, B.1; N^2: A.1, A.2, A.3, A.4, A.5, A.6, A.7, A.11, A.12, B.1); no features of Classical BH remain

N^1: eight features of LBH are present (A.3, A.5, A.6, A.8, A.9, A.12, A.13, B.1); six features of Classical BH are present (whether they remain or, as Polzin would have it, reappear) (contra A.1, A.2, A.4, A.7, A.11, A.12)

Est: six features of LBH are present (A.1, A.5, A.7, A.8, A.13, B.2); six features of Classical BH are present (whether they remain or, as Polzin would have it, reappear) (contra A.4, A.6, A.9, A.11, A.12, B.1)

These data prompt Polzin (1976: 112) to conclude:

> Classical BH seems to have remained generally stable for a considerable period of time. It seems probable from the data presented that the grammatical/syntactic nature of P^g and P^s places them between classical BH and the LBH of Chronicles. Moreover, the data suggest that P^s is typologically later than P^g.

Polzin claims that the presence of Classical BH features in N^1 and Est is attributable to the "marked tendency toward archaizing" in the later stages of the post-Exilic period (1976: 74). This tendency culminated in the "neo-classical" writings of Qumran which "are archaistic attempts at classical Hebrew which are betrayed by late Aramaisms, 'proto-mishnaic' features, and LBH features" (Polzin 1976: 7). I shall return to this point of his treatment below.

III

Having established this necessary background to the typological method characteristic of this study, I can now outline my adaptation of Polzin's typological methodology in the analysis of the post-Exilic prophets.

The texts under investigation include the target corpus of Malachi (54 verses and 1255 words), and the control corpora of Haggai (38 verses and 822 words), Zechariah 1–8 (121 verses and 2465 words), and Zechariah 9–14 (90 verses and 1987 words), as well as the corpora analyzed by Polzin. The restricted size of the text samples constitutes the fundamental problem of the present study. Unfortunately there is just no more text with which to work; nonetheless all conclusions must be balanced against the very limited target and control corpora size.

Large portions of my analysis are based on the computations of Y. T. Radday in his *Analytical Linguistic Key-Word-In-Context Concordance to the Books of Haggai, Zechariah and Malachi* (1973). To ensure uniformity in each of the corpora, the individual texts of the post-Exilic prophets have been treated *in toto,* that is, without deletions (of so-called "obvious late additions," cf. Andersen & Freedman 1980: 57–77) or emendations of the basic text found in *BHK* (and supplemented when necessary by the readings of the more recent *BHS*). Unlike Polzin, I have based my typological analysis of the post-Exilic prophets on word-samplings-per-text rather than verse-samplings-per-text. This, coupled with the utilization of Radday's Computer Bible volume on the post-Exilic prophets, lends greater precision to the typological analysis and increased accuracy and reliability of the statistical data, features which are crucial given the limited sample sizes of the selected texts.

Finally, for comparative purposes, I have expanded Polzin's work where possible by statistically projecting his data, clarifying and supplementing his ratios and figures whenever possible, and incorporating statistical projections of the typological analysis of the post-Exilic prophetic texts. I have also included N^1 and Est on the Biblical Hebrew continuum. (See Hill 1981: 45–83 for specific statistical data resulting from the typological analysis of the post-Exilic prophets.)

Before I set forth the conclusions prompted by the systematic and detailed typological analysis of the post-Exilic prophets, I want to put the research into perspective by providing an overview of the categorical relationships of the post-Exilic prophets to each other and to the various corpora of Polzin. The additional prophetic books of Joel and Jonah were also typologically analyzed and they are used here solely for comparative purposes.

Observations and tentative conclusions based on the typological analysis of the post-Exilic prophets fall into two categories: (1) those involving the relationship of the post-Exilic prophets to the several established corpora of Polzin, and (2) those involving the relationship of the post-Exilic prophets to each other, especially the position of Malachi in the chronology of post-Exilic literature.

First, even cursory observation reveals that the post-Exilic prophets are similar to the material in the sector labeled LBH on Figure 1. It is also clear, in terms of the total number of LBH features exhibited, that the post-Exilic prophets align themselves closely with Polzin's P^g corpus. This corpus contains four LBH features and seven Classical BH features, while the post-Exilic prophets contain anywhere from three to five LBH features and eight to ten Classical BH features. Typologically, this

FIGURE 1

	A 1	2	3	4	5	6	7	8	9	10	11	12	13	B 1	2	3	4	5	6	
JE	p	p	p	p	p	p	p	p	p		p	p	p							Polzin's Classical BH
CH	p	p	p	p	p	p	p	p	p		p	p	p							
Dtr	p	p	p	p	p	p	p	p			p	p	p	p						
Pg	o	p	x	x	p	x	p	p	x		p	p	o	p						Polzin's LBH
Ps	o	x	x	x	p	o	x	p	x		x	x	o	x						
Chr	x	x	x	x	x	x	x	x	x		x	x	x	x						
Ezr			x	x	x	x	x	x	x		x	x		x						
N^2	x	x	x	x	x	x	x				x	x		x						
N^1	x̲	x̲	x	x̲	x	x	x̲	x	x		x̲	x	x	x						Polzin's "archaizing" LBH
Est	x			x̲	x	x̲	x	x	x̲		x̲	x̲	x	x̲	x					
Hag	p	x	p	x	p	x	x	p	p	*x*	p	p	x	p	*p*	*p*				Post-Exilic Prophets
Zech 1–8	p	x	p	p	p	p	x	p	p	*x*	p	p	x	p	*p*	*p*				
Zech 9–14	x	p	p	p	p	p	x	x	p	*p*	x	p	o	p	*p*	*p*				
Mal	p	p	p	p	p	x	x	p	p	*p*	x	p	o	p	*p*	*p*				
Joel	x	p	p	p	p	x	x	p	p		x		p		*p*	*p*				Additional Prophets
Jonah	x	p	x	p		x	x	p	p		p		x		*p*					

p = feature of Classical BH
p = feature of Classical BH in prophets, included for comparative purposes, not a part of Polzin's research or final typological tabulations
x = feature of LBH
x = feature of LBH in prophets, included for comparative purposes, not a part of Polzin's research or final typological tabulations
x̲ = Polzin's LBH "archaizing" feature
o = unique feature

places the post-Exilic prophets more or less contemporary with P^g and prior to P^s (which contains eight features of LBH and retains but two Classical BH features).

Polzin offers no attempts at correlating the typologically defined corpora with concrete historical time periods. The tentative suggestions to be made here are intended solely to furnish some kind of provisional chronological framework for understanding the relative associations established by the typological analysis. Although the official demise of the period of Classical BH no doubt came with the fall of the Judean monarchy in 586 B.C., the roots of LBH can probably be traced to times before the destruction of Jerusalem. A round figure for the beginning of the LBH period would be ca. 600 B.C. It is likely that the P^g corpus, to which the post-Exilic prophets are typologically similar, dates to the Exile. If this is the case the post-Exilic prophets demonstrate considerable continuity with Exilic LBH, a conclusion not totally unexpected. P^s, the late typological boundary of the post-Exilic prophetic writings, proves to be more difficult to date. I prefer to date P^s to the period of Ezra's and Nehemiah's influence on the restoration community, sometime ca. 460–430

B.C. (cf. S. R. Driver 1922: 135–59); however, a date for P^s of 400–350 B.C., supported by many biblical scholars, is also plausible. Thus, the post-Exilic prophets can be placed within the broad boundaries of a period extending from ca. 600 to 400–350 B.C. Even from this sweeping and somewhat detached chronological perspective, it is already possible to eliminate suggestions to date Malachi to the later Greek period or to the Maccabean period.

Secondly, Figure 1 illustrates the basic homogeneity of the post-Exilic prophets. All four corpora exhibit a low density of LBH features (from 3 to 5) and a relatively high density of Classical BH features (from 8 to 10). A more careful examination of the typological data from the analysis of the post-Exilic prophets reveals that Haggai, Zechariah 1–8, and Malachi exhibit like ratios in four features (A.1, A.8, A.11, and A.13), while Zechariah 9–14 and Malachi also yield similar results in four categories (A.7, A.10, A.11, and A.13). Zechariah 1–8 and 9–14 show some relationship in being similar for three categories (A.6, A.9, and A.11). Haggai and Malachi are similar in two features (A.6, A.11), while Haggai and Zechariah 1–8 exhibit similar ratios only in one feature (A.7). This last fact offers a useful caution regarding typological methodology, given that one would expect the greatest correlation between the two corpora dated to exactly the same year. No doubt the dissimilarities here are largely the product of the characteristics and peculiarities of individual style. This discrepancy serves to underscore further the need for reserve in attempting to draw conclusions from typological data.

In respect to actual absolute dating, the typological method permits only approximations. Haggai and Zechariah 1–8 can be dated assuredly to 520 B.C. Typologically, nothing precludes one from dating Malachi to the same general time frame. Clearly, Malachi must be dated between 520 B.C. and the date of the P^s corpus since typologically Malachi lies between Hag/Zech 1–8 and P^s on the BH continuum (below). Dating P^s, as stated earlier, is problematic given the limited nature of the typological evidence and the obscurity of the historical record. If P^s does indeed date to the time of Ezra's activity in post-Exilic Jerusalem, as suggested earlier, then P^s can be dated sometime shortly after 458 B.C., perhaps even as late as Nehemiah's first visit to Jerusalem in 445 B.C. (This last date is the subject of much dispute since there is no consensus on the date of Ezra's return to Jerusalem. I follow Cross [1975], who defends the traditional view that Ezra preceded Nehemiah and Ezra's return should therefore be dated to the reign of Artaxerxes I and not to the reign of Artaxerxes II Memnon.) Hence, I would date Malachi's discourse somewhere between the works of Haggai and Zechariah, 520 B.C., and the activity of Ezra, 458 B.C. The conclusions of von Bulmerincq (1921:42–49), who dated Malachi's oracle to ca. 480 B.C., and the conclusions of D. N. Freedman (1962 and 1976), who places the composition of the post-Exilic prophets and their incorporation into the canon at ca. 500 B.C., prove to be consonant with my analysis.

Given the typological similarities of Zechariah 9–14 to the other post-Exilic prophets, it is apparent that this corpus must also be dated to the same approximate time period (i.e., 520–458 B.C.). I am well aware that this contradicts the opinion of most scholars on the date of Zechariah 9–14. However, in view of the typological homogeneity of the post-Exilic prophets, there seems to be little room for recourse to other alternatives, although the prose-poetry mixture of Zechariah 9–14 may suggest some qualification of this conclusion (cf. Kirkpatrick 1915: 442–56; see also Hanson

FIGURE 2
Typological Continuum of Biblical Hebrew

JE/CH/Dtr	P^g	Hag/Zech 1–8	Mal/Zech 9–14	P^s	Est/N^1	Ezr/N^2	Chr
					[?]		

JE—12 stable Classical BH features (contra A.1, A.2, A.3, A.4, A.5, A.6, A.7, A.8, A.9, A.11, A.12, A.13)

CH—12 stable Classical BH features (contra A.1, A.2, A.3, A.4, A.5, A.6, A.7, A.8, A.9, A.11, A.12, A.13)

Dtr—12 stable Classical BH features (contra A.1, A.2, A.3, A.4, A.5, A.6, A.7, A.8, A.11, A.12, A.13, B.1)

P^g—4 features of LBH are present (A.3, A.4, A.6, A.9); 7 features of Classical BH remain (contra A.2, A.5, A.7, A.8, A.11, A.12, B.1); 2 unique features appear (cf. A.1, A.13)

Hag—5 features of LBH are present (A.2, A.4, A.6, A.7, A.13); 8 features of Classical BH remain (contra A.1, A.3, A.5, A.8, A.9, A.11, A.12, B.1)

Zech 1–8—3 features of LBH are present (A.2, A.7, A.13); 10 features of Classical BH remain (contra A.1, A.3, A.4, A.5, A.6, A.8, A.9, A.11, A.12, B.1)

Mal—3 features of LBH are present (A.6, A.7, A.11); 9 features of Classical BH remain (contra A.1, A.2, A.3, A.4, A.5, A.8, A.9, A.12, B.1); 1 unique feature appears (cf. A.13)

Zech 9–14—4 features of LBH are present (A.1, A.7, A.8, A.11); 8 features of Classical BH remain (contra A.2, A.3, A.4, A.5, A.6, A.9, A.12, B.1); 1 unique feature appears (cf. A.13)

P^s—8 features of LBH are present (A.2, A.3, A.4, A.7, A.9, A.11, A.12, B.1); 2 features of Classical BH remain (contra A.5, A.8); 3 unique features appear (cf. A.1, A.6, A.13)

Est—6 features of LBH are present (A.1, A.5, A.7, A.8, A.13, B.2); 6 features of Classical BH remain (contra A.4, A.6, A.9, A.11, A.12, B.1)

N^1—8 features of LBH are present (A.3, A.5, A.6, A.8, A.9, A.12, A.13, B.1); 5 features of Classical BH remain (contra A.1, A.2, A.4, A.7, A.11)

Ezr—10 features of LBH are present (A.3, A.4, A.5, A.6, A.7, A.8, A.9, A.11, A.12, B.1); no features of Classical BH remain

N^2—10 features of LBH are present (A.1, A.2, A.3, A.4, A.5, A.6, A.7, A.11, A.12, B.1); no features of Classical BH remain

Chr—13 features of LBH are present (A.1, A.2, A.3, A.4, A.5, A.6, A.7, A.8, A.9, A.11, A.12, A.13, B.1); no features of Classical BH remain

1975: 280–401, who dates parts of Zechariah 9–14 to this same time frame, ca. 520–475 B.C.).

The expanded typological continuum of Biblical Hebrew prose is included above. I have altered Polzin's continuum slightly, as I disagree with him on the placement of Ezr/N^2 and Est/N^1. I prefer to place Ezr/N^2 before Chr since it yields fewer LBH features than does Chr. I place Est/N^1 (tentatively) before Ezr/N^2 and Chr on the hypothesis of alternative language development in the Jewish community which remained in Babylon after the establishment of the restoration community in Palestine. In opposition to Polzin, I view Esther and the memoirs of Nehemiah not as late "archaizing" works, but as works of Babylonian origin or background. The Classical BH features contained in these works may not be deliberate archaizing tendencies of a later period, but features characteristic of the written language of the Jewish community remaining in Exile. I would say the Classical BH features *remain* in Est and N^1, whereas Polzin would say they *reappear*. I have qualified the position of Est and N^1 on the continuum with a question mark because it is impossible to be sure that the written language of the Jewish Babylonian community underwent a development parallel to and distinct from that of the written language of the restoration community in Palestine (see Hill 1981: 136–37 for a further discussion of these problems).

IV

Based upon evidence of a typological analysis of the post-Exilic prophets, Malachi most likely dates to the period of "pre-Ezra decline" (ca. 520–450 or better 515–458 B.C.). Even though the Temple had been rebuilt and the sacrificial system restored, the vision of Ezekiel's Temple-state quickly faded amidst the stark reality of Persian domination and the problems of mere survival in a city surrounded by foreigners (see further Hanson 1975: 280–86). Malachi and Zechariah 9–14 exhibit considerable typological continuity with Haggai and Zechariah 1–8; both were probably composed during the early years of the period of "pre-Ezra decline."

It is likely that Exilic Hebrew was largely maintained (at least as the written language) in the official and religious circles of the restoration community by the first generation returnees from Babylon. This would account for the striking typological similarities of the post-Exilic prophets to each other and to Polzin's P^g corpus. Those original returnees probably influenced the restoration community for a maximum of fifty or sixty years; a *terminus ad quem* of ca. 475 B.C. for Malachi and Zechariah 9–14 may be suggested. After ca. 475 B.C. written works would and do reflect the language changes absorbed by the second generation writers of the post-Exilic community (e.g., P^s). The multiple problems of unraveling complex language changes in the post-Exilic period notwithstanding, continued refinement of the typological method and further typological analysis of the Old Testament may well confirm these exploratory studies and at the same time generate new evidence that will address the questions arising from this investigation.

Note

*This offering in honor of David Noel Freedman summarizes, in part, the writer's University of Michigan dissertation, *The Book of Malachi: Its Place in Post-Exilic Chronology Linguistically Reconsidered*, to which Dr. Freedman made valuable contributions.

References

Andersen, F. I., and Freedman, D. N.
1980 *Hosea*. The Anchor Bible 24. New York: Doubleday.

Bee, R. E.
1979 A Study of Deuteronomy Based on Statistical Properties of the Text. *Vetus Testamentum* 29: 1–22.

Bulmerincq, A. von
1921 Einleitung in das Buch des Propheten Maleachi. *Acta et Commentationes* B/1–3: 3–140.
1922 Einleitung in das Buch des Propheten Maleachi. *Acta et Commentationes* B/1–3: 141–224.

Cross, F. M.
1975 A Reconstruction of the Judean Restoration. *Journal of Biblical Literature* 94: 4–18.

Driver, S. R.
1913 *Notes on the Hebrew Text and the Topography of the Books of Samuel.* Oxford: Clarendon.
1922 *An Introduction to the Literature of the Old Testament*[2]. New York: Scribners'.

Dumbrell, W. J.
1976 Malachi and the Ezra-Nehemiah Reforms. *Reformed Theological Review* 35: 45–52.

Elliger, K.
1956 *Das Buch der Zwölf.* Das Alte Testament Deutsch XXV. Gottingen: Vandenhoeck & Ruprecht.

Fischer, J. A.
1972 Notes on the Literary Form and Message of Malachi. *Catholic Biblical Quarterly* 34: 315–20.

Freedman, D. N.
1962 The Law and the Prophets. *Vetus Testamentum Supplement* 9: 250–65.
1976 Canon of the Old Testament. Pp. 130–36 in *The Interpreter's Dictionary of the Bible Supplementary Volume,* ed. K. Crim et al. Nashville: Abingdon.

Givón, T.
1977 The Drift from VSO to SVO in Biblical Hebrew: The Pragmatics of Tense-Aspect. Pp. 181–254 in *Mechanisms of Syntactic Change,* ed. C. Li. Austin: University of Texas.

Greenberg, J.
1963 Some Universals of Grammar with Particular Reference to the Order of Meaningful Elements. Pp. 58–90 in *Universals of Language,* ed. J. Greenberg. Cambridge: MIT.

Hanson, P. D.
1971 Jewish Apocalyptic against its Near Eastern Environment. *Revue biblique* 78: 31–58.
1975 *The Dawn of Apocalyptic.* Philadelphia: Fortress.

Hill, A. E.
1981 *The Book of Malachi: Its Place in Post-Exilic Chronology Linguistically Reconsidered.* Michigan Dissertation.

Hoftijzer, J.
1965 Remarks Concerning the Use of the Particle *'t* in Classical Hebrew. *Oudtestamentische Studien* 14: 1–99.

Hurvitz, A.
1968 The Chronological Significance of Aramaisms in Biblical Hebrew. *Israel Exploration Journal* 18: 234–40.
1974a The Date of the Prose-Tale of Job Linguistically Reconsidered. *Harvard Theological Review* 67: 17–34.
1974b The Evidence of Language in Dating the Priestly Code; A Linguistic Study in Technical Idioms and Terminology. *Revue biblique* 81: 24–56.

Jeffers, R. J., and Lehiste, I.
1979 *Principles and Methods for Historical Linguistics.* Cambridge: MIT.

Justus, C. F.
1979 The Textbook of Historical Linguistics: Summary of the Past or Guide to the Future? *Romance Philology* 33: 299–309.

Kirkpatrick, A. F.
1915 *The Doctrine of the Prophets.* London: Macmillan.

Kropat, A.
1909 Die Syntax des Autors der Chronik. *Beihefte zur Zeitschrift für die Alttestamentliche Wissenschaft* 16: 1–94.

Lehmann, W. P.
1962 *Historical Linguistics: An Introduction.* New York: Holt, Rinehart & Winston.

Lehmann, W. P., and Malkiel, Y., eds.
1968 *Directions for Historical Linguistics: A Symposium.* Austin: University of Texas.

Mendenhall, G. E.
1961 Biblical History in Transition. Pp. 32–53 in *The Bible and the Ancient Near East: Essays in Honor of William Foxwell Albright,* ed. G. E. Wright. New York: Doubleday.

Mitchell, H.G.; Smith, J. M. P.; and Bewer, J. A.
1912 *A Critical and Exegetical Commentary of Haggai, Zechariah, Malachi and Jonah.* The International Critical Commentary. Edinburgh: T. & T. Clark.

Neil, W.
1962 Malachi and Zechariah. Pp. 228–32 in Vol. III and pp. 943–47 in Vol. IV of *The Interpreter's Dictionary of the Bible,* ed. G. A. Buttrick et al. Nashville: Abingdon.

Parunak, H. V. D.
1979 *Linguistic Density Plots in Zechariah.* The Computer Bible XX. n. p.: Biblical Research Institute.

Polzin, R.
1976 *Late Biblical Hebrew: Toward an Historical Typology of Biblical Hebrew Prose.* Harvard Semitic Monographs 12. Missoula: Scholars Press.

Rabin, C.
1970 Hebrew. Pp. 304–46 in *Current Trends in Linguistics* IV, ed. T. Sebeok et al. The Hague: Mouton.

Radday, Y. T.
1973 *Analytical Linguistic Key-Word-In-Context Concordance to the Books of Haggai, Zechariah and Malachi.* The Computer Bible IV. n. p.: Biblical Research Institute.

Radday, Y. T., & Wickmann, D.
1975 Unity of Zechariah Examined in the Light of Statistical Linguistics. *Zeitschrift für die Alttestamentliche Wissenschaft* 87: 30–55.

Segal, M. H.
1908 Mishnaic Hebrew and its Relation to Biblical Hebrew and Aramaic. *Jewish Quarterly Review* 20: 647–737.
1927 *A Grammar of Mishnaic Hebrew.* Oxford: Clarendon.

Sellin, E.
1930 *Das Zwölfprophetenbuch.* Kommentar zum Alten Testament XII. Leipzig: Deichertsche.

Smith, G. A.
1896 *The Book of the Twelve Prophets.* New York: Armstrong.

Spoer, H.
1908 Some New Considerations Towards the Dating of the Book of Malachi. *Jewish Quarterly Review* 20: 167–86.

Torrey, C. C.
1898 The Prophecy of Malachi. *Journal of Biblical Literature* 17: 1–15.

Wachowicz, K.
1977 The Synchronic Description and Historical Change. Pp. 445–56 in *Current Issues in Linguistic Theory*, ed. P. J. Hopper. Amsterdam: Benjamins.

Weinreich, J.; Labov, W.; & Herzog, M.
1968 Empirical Foundations for a Theory of Language Change. Pp. 95–188 in Lehmann & Malkiel 1968.

Widengren, G.
1977 The Persian Period. Pp. 489–538 in *Israelite and Judaean History*, ed. J. H. Hayes & J. M. Miller. Philadelphia: Westminster.

Psalm 2 and Bēlit's Oracle for Ashurbanipal

Helmer Ringgren
Uppsala Universitat

In several articles (Ringgren 1971, 1977) I have insisted on the necessity of using correct methods in comparing biblical and extra-biblical materials. It is not sufficient to point to a "parallel" in the texts; we should also ask what is the *Sitz im Leben* of the extra-biblical text, and what are possible connections between the two. This might be a fairly easy task in most cases, but there are some in which it is extremely difficult. In this article I should like to discuss an example of the latter kind.

A distinctive and difficult oracle directed to Ashurbanipal by Bēlit (or Ninlil), probably early in his reign, shows considerable affinity with Psalm 2.* The text of the oracle is extremely difficult, since it contains several words which are otherwise unknown or the exact meaning of which it is difficult to ascertain. The following translation, therefore, must be regarded as purely tentative.

1. [^{d}] *Bēltu* (NIN.LÍL) *kab-ta-at* (or [^{mí}] *Bēltu-kab-ta-at*) ^{mí}*ra-gi-in-tú*
2. [*ma-*]*a a-bat šarri* (LUGAL) ^{d}*Bēltu* (NIN.LÍL) *ši-i ma-a la ta-pal-laḫ* ^{m}*Aššur-ban-aplu* (AN.ŠÁR.DÙ.A)
3. [*ma-a?*] *šá a-di ki-i šá aq-bu-u-ni ip-pa-šu-u-ni ad-da-nak-kan-ni*
4. [*ma-a*] *a-di ina muḫḫi* (UGU) *mārē* (DUMU.MEŠ) *šá* NÌ *šaptê* (NUNDUM.MEŠ) (or *šá* [LÚ] *šá* SU$_6$.MEŠ or *šá* LIMMU NUNDUM.MEŠ) *ina muḫḫi* (UGU) *ḫal-pe-te šá rēšāni* (LÚ.SAG.MEŠ)
5. [ ]-*kid? šarru-u-tú ina muḫ—ḫi-šú-nu tu-up-pa-šú-u-ni*
6. [ ] *šarru-ka ina bīt* (É) *ridu*(UŠ)-*u-ti*
7. [ ]-*a-ti* ^{túg}*pi-tu-tu i-rak-kas*
8. [ ].MEŠ *šá mātāti* (KUR.KUR) *a-na a-ḫi-iš i-qab-bu-u-ni*
9. [*ma-a? ni*]-*il-lik ina muḫḫi* (UGU) ^{m}*Aššur-ban-aplu* (AN.ŠÁR.DÙ.A) *šarri* (LUGAL)-*ši-i gaš-ra-ši*[-*i*]
10. [ ].MEŠ *ana abbī* (AD.MEŠ)-*ni* AD.AD.MEŠ-*ni i-ši-mu-u-ni*
11. [ ]·*ina bir-tu-*⌜*ú*⌝-*ni lip-ru-us*
12. ⌜^{d}*Bēltu* ([^{d}NIN].LÍL) *taq-ti*$_4$-*bi ma-a* [ ] *šá mātāti* (KUR.KUR)
13. [*a*]-*saḫ-ḫu-pá-a-ni* [*ad?-dan-iš* [ ] KASKAL.MEŠ *ina šēpā* (GÌR.II)-*šú-nu ašakkan* (GAR^{an})
14. [*ma-*]*a šá-ni-tu laq-bak-ka ma-a ki-i* ^{kur}*Elam*^{ki} ^{kur}*Gi-mir a-*[ ]
15. ⌜*e*⌝-*ta-al-la gi-ṣu a-šab-bir-ma a-mur-din-nu a-na ni-ip-ši a-nap-pa-áš*
16. [*ma?-*]*a dam-mu ma-a-te a-na šar-bi ú-ta-ra*
17. *ḫal-la-la-at-ti en-gur-a-ti*
18. *at-ta ta-qab-bi ma-a mi-i-nu ḫal-la-la-at-ti en-gur-a-ti*
19. *ḫal-la-la-at-ti ina* ^{kur}*Mu-ṣur e-rab en-gur-a-te u-ṣa-a*

20. *ma-a šá* ^{d}*Bēltu* (NIN.LÍL) *ummu* (AMA)*-šú-ni la ta-pal-laḫ šá bēlit* (GAŠAN) *Erba-ìl ta-ri-su-ni la ta-pal-laḫ*
21. *ma-a ki-i ta-ri-ti ina muḫḫi* (UGU) *gi-iš-ši ia-ga-tuš-ši-ka* (or *gi-iš-ši-ia anaššīka* (ÍL^{ši}*-ka*))
22. *ma-a* ^{giš}*šu-kur-ra ina bi-rit tulê* (UBUR.MEŠ)*-ia a-šak-kan-ka*
23. *šá mu-ši-ia e-rak* AN*-ṣar-ka šá kal u*$_4$*-me ḫi-il-pa-ka ad-dan*
24. *šá kal-la-ma-ri un-na-ni-ka ú-ṣur ú-ṣur up-pa-áš-ka*
25. [*ma-a*] *at-ta la ta-pal-laḫ mu-u-ri šá ana-ku ú-rab-bu-u-ni*

Translation

1. Bēlit is mighty—a sibyl.
2. Thus the word of Bēlit herself for the king: Fear not, O Ashurbanipal!
3. As I have spoken, it will come to pass: I will give (it) to you.
4. (You will rule) over peoples of (all) languages, over the armament (?) of princes.
5. You will exercise sovereignty over them.
6. [I gave you] your sovereignty in the *bīt ridûti.*
7. [   ] a fillet he binds on.
8. [The king]s of the lands spoke, each to his neighbor:
9. "Come, [let us rise] against Ashurbanipal, her (Assyria's?/ Bēlit's?) mighty king.
10. [The destinie]s of our fathers (and) our grandfathers they (the Assyrians) have fixed.
11. Let [his might?] among us be dissolved."
12. Bēlit spoke thus: [The kings] of the lands
13. [I] will overthrow (?), put fetters (?) on their feet.
14. Thus for the second time I proclaim to you: As with Elam and Gimir I [shall proceed].
15. I will arise; I will shatter the thorns; I will open (my way) through the brambles.
16. With blood I shall turn the land into mud.
17. "Like someone walking furtively, like someone walking proud (?)!"
18. You say, What's that— "Like someone walking furtively, like someone walking proud (?)!"?
19. (I explain:) Like someone walking furtively, he will enter Egypt. Like someone walking proud (?), he will come out (of Egypt).
20. Bēlit is his mother: fear not! The Mistress of Arbela bore him: fear not!
21. As she that's given birth (cares for) her child (?), so I care for you.
22. I have set you as an amulet (?) between my breasts.
23. All night I am awake, I keep watch over you. All day I give you milk.
24. In the early morning I (?) heed your supplication, I (?) heed your conduct.
25. Fear not, my foal, whom I myself have reared.

Jastrow, who, to my knowledge, is the only scholar who has dealt extensively with this text, points out that it may be regarded as having been composed of several independent oracles (Jastrow 1912: 170–74). On the other hand, the text has been preserved for us as a single composition, was probably edited with a definite purpose and, consequently, can reasonably be discussed as a self-contained unit. Jastrow also points out that the introductory phrase, *Bēlit kabtat,* is reminiscent of the acclamation of many collective laments (1912: 170 n. 4). The oracle may then be regarded as a kind of answer to such a lament, as a typical *šîr tākilti,* or oracle of help (Jastrow 1912: 145, 173). The text is tripartite.

Lines 1–7. It is uncertain whether the word *rāgintu* (from *ragāmu*, "to cry") is an epithet of the goddess or refers to a prophetess who delivered the oracle. In any case, the oracle appears as the word of the goddess (cf. Ps 110: 1) and is introduced by the typical "Fear not." It goes on to insist on the reliability of the divine word: "As I have spoken, it will come to pass." Then there is a promise of world dominion: Ashurbanipal shall rule over all peoples. Such promises formed part of the ritual of coronation. It is logical, therefore, that there follows a reference to the king's installation in the *bīt ridûti,* i.e., the temple in which kings were given their royal authority. There also seems to be an allusion to the putting on of a (royal) headgear.

Lines 8–19. The next section begins with a description of the situation at hand: some vassal princes are rebellious and want to throw off the Assyrian yoke. The context seems to indicate that the reference is to disturbances in Egypt mentioned in much the same words in the annals of Ashurbanipal. The events can be dated to the year 667 B.C.E. (Jastrow 1912: 172). The oracle proclaims that the goddess will defeat the rebels, even if many details remain obscure.

Lines 20–25. A general assurance of divine protection and assistance rounds out the text: the goddess is the king's mother and will care for him like a child; she will protect him and listen to his prayers. Finally, the phrase "fear not" is repeated.

The contents of the oracle may be summarized.

1. World dominion
2. Allusions to coronation
3. Rebellion of the princes
4. Promise of victory
5. Sonship
6. Protection

For comparison the contents of Psalm 2 can be summarized in the same manner.

1. Rebellion of the princes (vv 1–3)
2. Allusions to coronation (v 6)
3. Sonship (v 7)
4. World dominion (v 8)
5. Promise of victory (v 9)

All the major points occur in both documents, though in somewhat different order.

Some additional details should be noted. Jastrow points out that oracles of this kind were sometimes written down for the king on a *ṭuppu adê*, "tablet of law," i.e., a document vested with special authority. This is reminiscent of the fact that Yahweh's oracle to the king of Israel is referred to as *ḥoq* in Ps 2: 7. Further, line 3 of the oracle contains the word *addanakkanni,* "I shall give/grant (it) to you," corresponding to *ʾettenâ* in Ps 2: 8. Another interesting expression is *elatallâ* in line 15; this is similar to a usage in Ps 12: 6:

> "Because the poor are despoiled,
> because the needy groan,
> I will now arise," says Yahweh.

The situation is not quite comparable, but it is clear that Psalm 12 quotes an oracle in which Yahweh proclaimed his readiness to intervene, in much the same way as does the goddess in our oracle. Thus *ʿattâ ʾāqûm* reflects a divine reaction similar to the *elatallâ* of the oracle.

Further, the rebellion of the princes is described in the third person in both cases, and the promise of victory is given in a first person oracle. In Psalm 2 it is Yahweh who tells of the installation of the king; in our oracle, too, it seems that Bēlit refers back to the coronation. In Psalm 2 it is the king who refers to his being made the son of Yahweh; in the oracle, on the other hand, the mention of sonship seems to be part of the divine word. Although the goddess is referred to in the third person in line 20, the next line has her speaking in the first person.

Thus, the conditions reflected in the documents under discussion are similar. In both cases a threat from rebellious princes is met with reference to the king's legitimate installation and to his divine sonship. Furthermore, the king is promised victory over his enemies. A major difference is that the Assyrian oracle can be exactly located in history, while the Israelite psalm lacks an identifiable historical background.

Before discussing the possible relationship between the two texts, another fact must be noted. There is an obvious similarity in structure between Psalm 2 and the second Suffering Servant Song in Isaiah 49 (Kaiser 1959: 32ff.). Here we find the following main points.

1. Yahweh called me from the womb (Isa 49: 1)
2. He made me a sword and an arrow (49: 2)
3. He said to me: You are my servant (49: 3)
4. I thought: I have labored in vain (49: 4)
5. My right is with Yahweh (49: 4)
6. Yahweh gives him a task to perform (49: 6)

Thus, in a situation that seems hopeless, the Servant refers back to his royal destination (he was called in the womb) and his being proclaimed the servant of Yahweh, the phrase *ʾattâ ʿabdî* obviously reflecting the oracular *ʾattâ benî* of Psalm 2. On this ground he is convinced of divine assistance and ultimate success in performing his task. (On the "Do not fear" formulas in Akkadian oracles and Second Isaiah, see Ringgren 1977: 38–39).

This Deutero-Isaiah passage seems to suggest that the composition in Psalm 2 set a pattern in Israel. The Assyrian oracle, on the other hand, seems to be unique in its cultural sphere. It is true that that promise of victory forms part of Mesopotamian coronation rituals and that Assyrian kings were always eager to stress that they carried out their military campaigns at the order of (or at least with the consent of) their gods; but the combination of features that makes our oracle comparable to Psalm 2 has no counterpart in any other Akkadian oracle. Could it be, then, that the oracle to Ashurbanipal was taken over in Israel, for instance, under Manasseh or Josiah and set a pattern there? The difficulty with such a hypothesis is the impossibility of finding an historical context that would have prompted the borrowing. It may be that the Assyrian oracle is not so unique as it seems but is more or less typical of Mesopotamian royal ideology, though this cannot be shown. We might instead assume that the general views of the king's role in both Mesopotamia and Israel were so similar that two almost identical patterns independently appeared in similar situations. At the present state of our knowledge, no definite answer is possible, though it is certain that the similarity between the two texts can hardly be a coincidence.

Note

**The Text:* K.833. *First publication:* Strong 1894, copy, p. 645; transcription, p. 633; commentary, pp. 634–35. *Second publication:* Craig 1895, plates 26–27, with corrections in Craig 1897: x. *Major discussion:* Jastrow 1912: 170–74. *Current translation:* R. H. Pfeiffer, "An Oracular Dream Concerning Ashurbanipal," ANET 450–51. *Other references:* Jastrow 1912: 170, n. 1; Borger 1967: 67. The transliteration of the Akkadian text was prepared by M. O'Connor and L. E. Fyfe, both of whom suggested improvements in the translations.

References

R. Borger
1967 *Handbuch der Keilschriftliteratur I. Repertorium.* Berlin: De Gruyter.

J. A. Craig
1885 *Assyrian and Babylonian Religious Texts. I.* Assyriologische Bibliothek 13/I. Leipzig: Hinrichs.

M. Jastrow, Jr.
1912 *Die Religion Babyloniens und Assyriens. II.* Giessen: Ricker (Töpelmann).

O. Kaiser
1959 *Der Königliche Knecht.* Forschungen zur Religion und Literatur des Alten und Neuen Testaments NF 32. Göttingen: Vandenhoeck und Ruprecht.

H. Ringgren
1971 Remarks on the Method of Comparative Mythology. Pp. 407–11 in *Near Eastern Studies in Honor of William Foxwell Albright,* ed. H. Goedicke. Baltimore: The Johns Hopkins Press.

1973 *Religions of the Ancient Near East.* Trans. J. Sturdy. Philadelphia: Westminster.

1977 The Impact of the Ancient Near East on Israelite Tradition. Pp. 31–46 in *Tradition and Theology in the Old Testament,* ed. D. A. Knight. London: SPCK.

S. A. Strong
1894 On Some Oracles to Esarhaddon and Ashurbanipal. *Beiträge zur Assyriologie* 2: 624–45.

New Exodus, Covenant, and Restoration in Psalm 23

Michael L. Barré, S. S.
St. Patrick's Seminary, Menlo Park, California
and
John S. Kselman, S. S.
The Catholic University of America, Washington, D. C.

I. Introduction

Few of the psalms have been studied as frequently and as intensively as Psalm 23. In his commentary E. Beaucamp (1976: 115) lists more than thirty articles on this psalm published between 1934 and 1972. Since the first volume of Beaucamp's commentary was published in 1976, he could not take account of the most recent and most illuminating study of Psalm 23, the one by D. N. Freedman (1980). Freedman argues that the unifying theme of the poem is the new exodus, a theme whose closest parallels are from the literature of the seventh-sixth centuries B.C.E. Among the texts he considers that have significant thematic parallels to Psalm 23 are these.

Yahweh as shepherd (Ezek 34: 11–16, 25–31; Isa 40: 11; 49: 10; Jer 31: 10).

lacking nothing (Deut 2: 7; Neh 9: 21). The text from Deuteronomy is especially significant because, as Freedman notes (1980: 285), it relates directly to the Exodus experience: "For Yahweh your God has blessed you in all the work of your hands; he knows your going through this great wilderness; these forty years Yahweh your God has been with you; you have lacked nothing." In addition to the theme of lacking nothing (*lʾ ḥsrt dbr*) it mentions two other themes of Psalm 23, the divine presence (*yhwh ʾhlyk ʿmk*) and safe passage through dangerous terrain.

lying down in verdant pastures (Ezek 34: 14–15).

leading and guiding to water and rest (Jer 31: 9; Ps 95: 6–11).

passage through darkness (Jer 2: 6). Another parallel to Ps 23: 4, not noted by Freedman, is Ps 138: 7:

> *ʾm ʾlk bqrb ṣrh tḥyyny ʿl ʾp ʾyby tšlḥ ydk wtwšyʿny ymynk*
> Though I walk in the midst of trouble, you preserve my life; you stretch out your hand against the wrath of my enemies, and your right hand delivers me.[1]

Compare Ps 23: 4–5:

> *gm ky ʾlk bgyʾ ṣlmwt . . . šbṭk wmšʿntk*
> *hmh ynḥmny . . . ngd ṣrry*
> Even when I walk in the valley of deep shadow . . .
> your rod and your staff—they alone vindicate me
> . . . in the sight of my foes.[2]

the banquet (Jer 31: 9–14; Ps 78: 19).

Because Psalm 23 lacks clear historical references to the Exodus (as in, e.g., Psalm 78), the centrality of the new exodus theme is not immediately apparent. The problem is this: Although shepherd imagery dominates the first half of the poem, what relation to the exodus theme do we find with the abrupt change to the image of Yahweh as divine host in vv 5–6? As Freedman has shown (1980: 275–76), once the *topos* of the new exodus is recognized, the difficulty of the two conflicting images (Yahweh as shepherd and Yahweh as host) disappears, and the unity and coherence of Psalm 23 become clear.[3] The opening words of Ps 23: 5 (*tʿrk lpny šlḥn*, "You spread a table before me") allude directly to Ps 78: 19, where, in the context of the murmuring tradition of the wilderness period, the psalmist cites the people's complaint: "And they spoke against God, saying, 'Is El able to *spread a table* in the wilderness (*lʿrk šlḥn bmdbr*)?'" Psalm 78 describes Yahweh as the shepherd of his people, leading them out of Egypt (vv 52–53). Finally, Freedman has argued that the concluding statement in Psalm 23 about dwelling in the house of Yahweh is a reference to the goal of the Exodus, settlement in the land of promise.[4]

In this paper we hope to sustain and to extend Freedman's analysis by demonstrating that in addition to the relatively common seventh-sixth century themes of the new exodus, the new trek through the wilderness, and the restoration and resettlement in the land, the psalmist has employed in v 6a the rare theme of the new covenant, appropriately placed between God's provisioning of his people in the wilderness (v 5) and the peaceful dwelling of Israel in the land (v 6b). We shall attempt to demonstrate this by considering both biblical and extra-biblical evidence that will shed new light on v 6, and especially on the verb *yrdpwny*. Finally, on the basis of this evidence we shall show that the exilic author of Psalm 23 has reused traditional royal language and motifs in a new, democratized context, like another exilic author (Isa 55: 1–3), who reapplies the language of the Davidic covenant to Israel in exile.

We propose the following translation of Psalm 23.

1 Yahweh himself is my shepherd;
  I lack nothing.
2 In grassy meadows he makes me lie down.
  Beside tranquil waters
    he guides me;
3   he restores my life;
    he leads me
  in straight paths, for his name's sake—
4 even when I walk through the valley of deep darkness—
    I fear no evil, for you are with me.
  Your rod and your staff—
    they alone vindicate me.
5 You spread a table before me
    in the sight of my foes;
  You anoint my head with oil,
    my cup runs over.
6 (Henceforth) may only (your) covenant blessings pursue me
    all the days of my life;
  And may I dwell in Yahweh's house
    forevermore.

II. The Biblical Evidence

In discussing parallels to *ynḥny* of Ps 23: 3, Freedman makes the following observation: "Another parallel is to be found in Ps. 143: 10(-11): 'Let your good spirit lead me [*tanḥēnī*] into the level land'. . . . The first words of the next verse (Ps. 143: 11) are *lĕmaʿan šimkā,* which may belong with the preceding lines, as in Ps. 31: 4 and our passage [Ps 23: 3]" (1980: 290). The three passages in Psalms 23, 31, and 143 to which Freedman refers do show remarkable similarities.

Ps 23: 3	*ynḥny bmʿgly ṣdq lmʿn šmw* He leads me in straight paths, for his name's sake.
Ps 31: 4	*wlmʿn šmk tnḥny wtnhlny* For your name's sake, lead and guide me.
Ps 143: 10–11	*rwḥk ṭwbh*[5] *tnḥny bʾrṣ myšwr lmʿn šmk* May your good spirit lead me in a level land for your name's sake.

All of them use the verb *nḥh* and *lmʿn šmk/šmw,* while Psalms 23 and 143 share a third element: *bmʿgly ṣdq* = *bʾrṣ myšwr.*[6] And there may be yet another element common to all three passages, not pointed out by Freedman.

Ps 23: 3	*ky ʾth ʿmdy*	For you are with me.
Ps 31: 5	*ky ʾth mʿwzy*	For you are my refuge.
Ps 143: 10	*ky ʾth ʾlhy*	For you are my God.[7]

The pattern of conjunction *ky* + second person masculine singular pronoun (referring to God) + predicate with first person singular suffix is the same in all three: in Psalm 23 and 31, it follows the line about leading (*nḥh*) for the sake of the name, while in Psalm 143 it precedes that line.

In addition to the elements shared by Psalm 23 and 143 summarized above, there are also in Psalm 143 two instances where we find a *reversal* of the situation pictured in Psalm 23.

Ps 23: 2–3	*ʿl my mnḥwt ynhlny npšy yšwbb* Beside tranquil waters he guides me; he restores my life.
Ps 143: 6–7	*npšy bʾrṣ*[8] *ʿyph . . . klth rwḥy* My life in an arid land . . . my spirit fails.

Over against the waters that revive the poet's life in Psalm 23 is the arid land of Psalm 143, where the psalmist's spirit fails (note *wttʿṭp ʿly rwḥy* in v 4).

Ps 23: 6	*ʾk ṭwb wḥsd yrdpwny kl ymy ḥyy* *wšbty bbyt yhwh lʾrk ymym* (Henceforth) may only (your) covenant blessings pursue me, all the days of my life; And may I dwell[9] in Yahweh's house forevermore.
Ps 143: 3	*ky rdp ʾwyb npšy* *dkʾ lʾrṣ ḥyty* *hwšybny bmḥškym kmty ʿwlm*

For an enemy has pursued me
  (lit., "my soul");
he has crushed my life to the netherworld,
he has made me dwell in darkness
like those long dead.

In place of pursuit by the covenant blessings of goodness and kindness and dwelling in Yahweh's house forever is the negative image of Psalm 143, pursuit by the enemy of the psalmist, who makes the psalmist dwell in the netherworld with the dead (Dahood 1970: 323; Tromp 1969: 40). Such contrasts are not unexpected, in that Psalm 23 (a song of trust) and Psalm 143 (a lament) represent two contrasting literary types. What is striking, however, is that the reversal is expressed in language that is common to both poems: *npšy, yrdpwny/rdp, ḥyy/ḥyth, wšbty/hwšybny.*

The other passage that, like Psalm 143, forms the reverse of Ps 23: 6 is Ps 7: 5–6.

ʾm gmlty šwlmy rʿ wʾḥlṣh ṣrry ryqm
yrdp ʾwby npšy wyśg
wyrms lʾrṣ ḥyy wkbdy lʿpr yškn

If I have repaid my ally with treachery,
and rescued my foe . . .,
let an enemy pursue and overtake me;
let him trample my life to the netherworld;
let him cause me to dwell in the dust.[10]

In Psalm 7 as in Psalm 143, the enemy of the psalmist pursues him to the netherworld and overtakes him.[11]

In addition to the parallels in Psalms 7 and 143, there are several points of contact between Psalm 23 and Lamentations 3. Lam 3: 6 (*bmḥškym hwšybny kmty ʿwlm*) is identical (save word-order) to Ps 143: 3c, discussed above. In his commentary, D. R. Hillers writes: "Through vs. 9, the dominant theme of Lam 3 might be called *a reversal of the Twenty-third Psalm:* the Lord is a shepherd who misleads, a ruler who oppresses and imprisons" (1972: 65 [emphasis added]). Although Hillers does not point to specific parallels in support of his observation, presumably he is thinking of such texts as the following.

Lam 3: 1	the rod of his anger (*bšbṭ ʿbrtw*) = reversal of
Ps 23: 4	*šbṭk wmšʿntk hmh ynḥmny*
Lam 3: 2	walking in darkness, not light (*wylk ḥšk wlʾ ʾwr*) = reversal of
Ps 23: 4	*gm ky ʾlk bgyʾ ṣlmwt lʾ ʾyrʾ rʿ* *ky ʾth ʿmdy*
Lam 3: 6	dwelling in darkness of netherworld (*bmḥškym hwšybny kmty ʿwlm*) = reversal of
Ps 23: 6	*wšbty bbyt yhwh lʾrk ymym*
Lam 3: 9	he has twisted my path (*ntybty ʿwh*) = reversal of
Ps 23: 3	*ynḥny bmʿgly ṣdq*

To Hillers' observation we would only add that the "reversal of Psalm 23" motif may extend beyond v 9.

Lam 3: 15	he has sated me with bitter food, made me drink my fill of wormwood (*hśbyʿny bmrwrym hrwny lʿnh*) = reversal of
Ps 23: 5	*tʿrk lpny šlḥn . . . kwsy rwyh*
Lam 3: 17	I have rejected peace, forgotten good (*wtznḥ—m*[12] *šlwm npšy nšyty ṭwbh*) = reversal of
Ps 23: 6	*ʾk ṭwb wḥsd yrdpwny*

Finally, at the end of the chapter we find one more important reversal, of Ps 23: 6.

Lam 3: 65–66	*ttn lhm mgnt lb tʾltk lhm* *trdp bʾp wtšmydm* Give them hardness of heart as your curse upon them; May you/it pursue them in anger and destroy them.[13]

Here it is not the covenant blessings (*ṭwb wḥsd*) but God's curse that is to pursue and destroy,[14] a motif whose importance will become clear below.

To conclude this part of the discussion, one further passage may be cited.

Hos 8: 1b-3	*yʿn ʿbrw bryty wʿl twrty pšʿw* *ly yzʿqw ʾlhy ydʿnwk yśrʾl* *znḥ yśrʾl ṭwb ʾwyb yrdpw* Because they transgressed my covenant and rebelled against my law, while they cried out to me, "O God of Israel, we know you!"— because Israel has rejected the good [i.e., the covenant] an enemy will pursue him.[15]

It is worth noting that the phrase *znḥ yśrʾl ṭwb* shares with Lam 3: 17 *znḥ* and *ṭwb*, and that *ʾwyb yrdpw* echoes both Pss 7: 5 and 143: 3 (*yrdp*/*rdp ʾwyb npšy*). As in the passages from Psalms and Lamentations, the point here is that Hos 8: 1–3 constitutes a reversal of Ps 23: 6. Also striking is the explicitly covenantal context of the prophetic oracle (McCarthy 1972; 1978: 220, 289 [on Hosea 8]). In addition to *bryty, ydʿnwk* and *ṭwb* seem also to be from a covenantal *Sitz im Leben,* as a number of scholars have demonstrated.[16] Further, J. Tigay (1970) has argued (correctly, in our view) for the covenantal background of Ps 7: 5–6.

To summarize the discussion thus far, there appear in Psalms, Lamentations, and Hosea passages related to Psalm 23 in a way that might be termed "parallelism by reversal," where one finds the antithetic or opposite of the sentiment expressed in Psalm 23, and particularly in v 6 of that psalm. In Pss 143: 3; 7: 5–6; Lam 3: 65–66; and Hos 8: 1–3, a recurring element has been the verb *rdp,* several times in a clearly covenantal context. In Psalms 7 and 143, the psalmist, pursued by an enemy even to the netherworld, cries out for divine aid. In Hosea 8, the prophet pronounces judgment upon Israel for breach of covenant: "Because Israel has rejected the good [i.e., the covenant], an enemy will pursue him." And in Lam 3: 65–66, the poet prays: "Give them [his enemies] back, Yahweh, what they have coming, for what their hands have done. Give them hardness of heart, as your curse upon them! May you [Yahweh; or "May it" (the curse)] pursue them in anger and destroy them."[17] On *rdp* in Ps 23: 6 Freedman comments:

> The association of the divine virtues [i.e., *ṭwb wḥsd*] with the verb *rdp* here is distinctive and exceptional. . . . In the background is the mythological picture of the principal deity accompanied by lesser divine beings who . . . will leave their posts in the heavenly court, and accompany the Psalmist throughout his life (1980: 297–98).[18]

Certainly this understanding of *ṭwb wḥsd* is possible. And in its favor one might point to Ps 35: 5–6.

> *yhyw kmṣ lpny rwḥ wmlʾk yhwh dwḥh*
> *yhy drkm ḥšk wḥlqlqwt wmlʾk yhwh rdpm*
> Let them be like chaff before the wind,
> with the angel of Yahweh driving them;
> Let their way be dark and slippery,
> with the angel of Yahweh pursuing them.

In place of *ṭwb wḥsd* we have the hendiadys *ḥšk wḥlqlqwt,* and pursuit (*rdpm*) not by divine virtues serving as the psalmist's "guardian angels" but by a hostile member of God's divine court, as his agent in meting out punishment.[19]

Despite this possible parallel, we believe that a better interpretation can be provided for Ps 23: 6 on the basis of Freedman's understanding and analysis of Psalm 23 as a song of the new exodus and restoration to the Promised Land. Given these sixth-century themes as the unifying elements of Psalm 23—Yahweh's guidance of Israel through the wilderness (vv 1–5) into the land of promise (*byt yhwh* in v 6b)[20]—we think it more natural to see in *ṭwb wḥsd* a reference not to guardian angels, but to the covenant, appropriately placed between God's care for his people in the wilderness and their entrance into the land.

Certainly there is no difficulty in understanding *ṭwb wḥsd* as covenant terminology, implying the blessings of the covenant, and even as a virtual synonym for *bryt.*[21] The difficulty for this covenantal interpretation lies in the verb *rdp*: why does this verb occur in Ps 23: 6 and elsewhere (Psalm 7, Hosea 8) in covenantal contexts?[22] Freedman speaks of *rdp* as "distinctive and exceptional" because of its generally negative connotation.

> Normally the worshipper is encouraged or advised to pursue such qualities as a goal of life, and acquire them for himself: e.g., Ps. 38: 21 (*ṭōb*); Prov. 21: 21 (*ṣĕdāqāh wāḥesed*); Ps. 34: 15 (*šālōm*); Isa. 51: 1 (*ṣedeq*); Deut. 16: 20 (*ṣedeq*). In Ps. 23, the situation is reversed: the Psalmist will be accompanied by divine goodness and mercy (1980: 297–98).[23]

What Freedman does not point out is that, of 140 occurrences of the verb *rdp* in the Hebrew Bible, only in a few cases (Judg 3: 28; 2 Kgs 5: 21; Hos 2: 9; 6: 3; [12:2?]) is it used in a non-hostile sense when the object of *rdp* is a person or persons.[24] Indeed, what one might expect in place of *rdp*, a negative verb with overtones of hostility, would be a verb like *nṣr*, with its positive sense of "guard, preserve," as we shall demonstrate in Section III of this paper. The fact that we find in Psalm 23 such an unexpected verb as *rdp* signals its importance, given the fact that other alternatives (like *nṣr*) were available to the poet.

We can now proceed to suggest a context for the verb *rdp* that explains why the psalmist chose it over other available possibilities. Significantly, and coincidentally with the *Wortfeld* of Psalms 7, 23, and Hosea 8, the suggested context is covenantal. Note first the catalogue of curses attendant upon breach of covenant in Deuteronomy 28.[25] Specifically we are referring to Deut 28: 2 and 15, where the alternatives placed before Israel are obedience to the covenant and blessing, or disobedience and curse.

Deut 28: 2	*wbʾw ʿlyk kl hbrkwt hʾlh whśygk* *ky tšmʿ bqwl yhwh ʾlhyk* And all these blessings shall come upon you *and overtake you,* if you obey the voice of Yahweh your God.
Deut 28: 15	*whyh ʾm lʾ tšmʿ bqwl yhwh ʾlhyk . . .* *wbʾw ʿlyk kl hqllwt hʾlh whśygwk* But if you will not obey the voice of Yahweh your God . . . then all these curses shall come upon you *and overtake you.*

The verb *hśyg*, which occurs here, is important because of its frequent collocation or parallelism with *rdp*.[26] It is not so much a synonym as a complementary term, a verb expressing the consequence of *rdp* (i.e., pursue to overtake, a hendiadys for "capture" or the like).[27]

But the most important text for our purposes is Deut 28: 45, which comes at the end of the long series of curses that begins in 28: 15. Deut 28: 45 repeats the language of v 15 more emphatically.

> *wbʾw ʿlyk kl hqllwt hʾlh wrdpwk whśygwk ʿd hšmdk ky lʾ šmʿt bqwl yhwh ʾlhyk*
> All these curses shall come upon you *and pursue you and overtake you,* till you are destroyed, because you did not obey the voice of Yahweh your God.

In this passage, which probably serves as an inclusion with v 15, the curses for breach of covenant come upon those who have not obeyed the commandments of Yahweh. Not only is *hśyg* used, as in vv 2 and 15, but also *wrdpwk . . . ʿd hšmdk* (a collocation we have noted in Lam 3: 66). M. Weinfeld's remarks on this passage deserve to be quoted in full.

> The treaty curses are likewise described as possessing an independent power of their own to *pursue* those who violate the treaty. Thus, in the Hittite treaties, we repeatedly encounter the formula: 'And the *curses* shall *pursue* you relentlessly.' Similary we read in the epilogue of the Code of Hammurabi: 'May they (the curses) quickly *overtake* him', and in the Esarhaddon annals: 'the oaths of the great gods which they violated *overtook* them.' This conception also finds expression in various passages in the deuteronomic covenant . . . (1972: 108–09 [emphasis added]).

The deuteronomic passages he cites are Deut 29: 19 (*wrbṣh bw kl hʾlh hktwbh bspr hzh,* "And every oath written in this document will come upon him"), and the two passages with which we are concerned, Deut 28: 15 and 45.

The relevance of these passages to Psalm 23 should now be clear. In v 6 the psalmist uses *rdp*, a verb that has close associations with the language of treaty and covenant, particularly the language of curse for covenant violation. In a daring reversal, he prays that it not be the covenant curses, but only (*ʾk*) *ṭwb wḥsd* that "pursue" him (so to speak) throughout his life; here *ṭwb wḥsd* is a surrogate for the covenant and includes the blessings attendant upon obedience to the covenant stipulations.

III. Extra-Biblical Parallels

In the present section of this paper we shall consider vv 5–6 in greater detail and shall see further evidence for the understanding of *yrdpwny* adopted here. In particular, we shall attempt to shed light on this part of Psalm 23 by considering a number of extra-biblical parallels; in this connection note that several earlier studies have brought ancient Near Eastern material to bear on the interpretation of this psalm (Greenfield 1978; Waldman 1979). We shall present evidence to show that vv 5–6 can be correctly understood only when one realizes that the poet has reused traditional *royal* motifs here and fitted them to an exilic setting. Thus the banquet scene is properly a royal banquet, where the (divine) overlord reconfirms the rule of his vassal-king. "Goodness and kindness" are the blessings of the Davidic covenant which safeguard the king. The hope of dwelling "forevermore" in Yahweh's house is also a royal theme, whose precise meaning we shall elucidate presently. All of these motifs have been "democratized" by the poet so that they now speak to the situation of exiled Israel: the royal banquet becomes a metaphor to describe Yahweh's provision for his people in their return to and resettlement in the Promised Land; the covenant blessings now refer to the beneficial effects of the Sinai covenant, and the poet prays that from now on only these "pursue" the exiles; the longing to dwell in Yahweh's "house" (= "temple" in the royal context) becomes a hope for remaining forever in the Promised Land.

Despite the general persuasiveness of Freedman's thesis that Psalm 23 is to be understood in the context of the exodus tradition, some difficulties arise in the second half of the poem (vv 5–6). First, if the poet wants to call to mind in v 5 the feeding in the wilderness, why does he use language that rather suggests a royal banquet? True, *tʿrk lpny šlḥn* does allude to Ps 78: 19 (Freedman 1980: 295–96); but the rest of Ps 23: 5 does not seem to fit the wilderness experience.[28] Second, how is *ngd ṣrry* related to the motif of feeding in the desert? Freedman adduces little in the way of cogent parallels on this point. Third, the phrase *wšbty bbyt yhwh* in v 6 is also problematic. On Freedman's reading it would refer to Yahweh's domain rather than his temple (1980: 300). The instances where *byt yhwh* has this meaning were collected and commented upon above. But there is still a question to be answered: Why does the poet use this unusual expression if he "is affirming that he will dwell in Yahweh's holy land for the rest of his life?" (1980: 300).

One is on the way toward resolution of these difficulties once one realizes that vv 5–6 are not a free composition by the psalmist; rather he has adapted traditional imagery to suit his purpose. Specifically, we shall show that the poet has drawn upon the language of royal psalmody and reinterpreted that language and imagery to fit his overall theme of what we shall term the restoration (i.e., the return to and resettlement in the Promised Land).[29] This means that we are to understand and interpret vv 5–6 on two levels: the level of an earlier, royal setting, in which the speaker is the king, and the motifs are drawn from the ideology/theology of monarchy; and that of an exilic setting, the level intended by the author of Psalm 23 in its present form.

We turn first to v 5. While "spreading a table" may point to the Exodus setting of Ps 78: 19, the other images in this verse are hardly suggestive of such a setting. Rather they are reminiscent of royal banquets mentioned in Mesopotamian sources. In the following account Esarhaddon describes the banquet he gave at the dedication of his new palace in Calah.

lúGAL.MEŠ *ù* UN.MEŠ KUR-*ia* DÙ-*šú-nu*
ina gišBANŠUR *ta-ši-la-a-ti ta-kul-ti (u) qí-re-(e)-ti*
ina qer-bi-šá ú-še-šib-šú-nu-ti-ma
ú-šá-li-ṣa nu-pa-ar-šú-un
GEŠTIN.MEŠ *ku-ru-un-nu am-ki-ra ṣur-ra-šú-un*
Ì.SAG *ì-gu-la-a muḫ-ḫa-šú-nu ú-šá-áš-qi*
(Borger 1967: §27 A, VI 49–53)

All the nobles and people of my land
I seated at a festive *table,* at a guest-meal,
in its [the new palace's] midst;
I caused their hearts to rejoice,
I *drenched*[30] their bowels with wine,
I poured choice *oil* (and) perfumed *oil* on their *heads.*[31]

Here, as in Ps 23: 5, there is mention of a table of rich fare, superabundant drink, and anointing with (fine) oil. In both texts the exuberance bespeaks a "royal" host. But who is the "guest" in Ps 23: 5, who declares "You spread a table before me"?

On the basis of several ancient Near Eastern parallels we suggest that the speaker is the king, in his role as vassal of Yahweh. In the royal inscriptions of Sargon II, the king recounts his treatment of a loyal vassal in these words.

šá m*Ul-lu-su-nu* LUGAL *be-lí-šú-nu*
BANŠUR *tak-bit-ti ma-ḫar-šú ar-ku-su-ma* . . .
(Thureau-Dangin 1912: 12.62)

As for King Ullusunu, their lord,
I spread a rich *table before him* . . . .

The phrase *paššūr* . . . *maḫaršu arkussuma* is precisely equivalent (save for the change of person) to *tʿrk lpny šlḥn*. By being the honored guest at this "vassal-oath renewal,"[32] not only does the vassal reaffirm his loyalty to his overlord, but the latter implicitly reaffirms the vassal king's rule at the same time.

The expression *ngd ṣrry,* which seems awkward in the context of feeding in the wilderness,[33] may also allude to a setting where a vassal king is the subject (see Eaton 1976: 37). In an often cited passage from the Amarna correspondence a vassal city writes to Pharaoh:

LUGALru EN-*nu* . . . *ia-di-na*
NÍG-BA *a-na* ÌR-*šu ù ti-da-ga-lu*
LÚ.MEŠ *a-ia-bu-nu ù ti-ka-lu ep-ra*
(Knudtzon 1915: §100.31–36)

May the king our lord . . . give a
gift to his servant/vassal so that
our enemies may see (it) and be
humiliated (lit., eat dust) (see CAD D 21b).

The closest OT parallel to this passage is Ps 86: 16b-17, where the king (see Dahood 1968: 292) asks the divine overlord to send his "servant/vassal" (*ʿbdk*) a sign of his covenant favor (*ʾwt lṭwbh*) so that his enemies may see it and be ashamed. Another parallel is Mic 7: 16–17. Here the prophet asserts that when Yahweh brings his people out of exile "the nations will see (it) and be ashamed" and will "eat dust like the serpent."[34] In Psalm 23 *ngd ṣrry* may reflect both the royal setting (as in Psalm 86) and the exilic setting (as in Micah 7) at the same time.

Thus on the level of royal imagery we may see Ps 23: 5 as describing a banquet in which the overlord (Yahweh) wines and dines his vassal (the king) and reaffirms him as vassal king. The reference to anointing the head with oil in this verse is perhaps a double-entendre: on the more natural reading it would refer to part of the festive ritual of a banquet; but it may also allude to the anointing of the king. Freedman (1980: 297) accepts this latter interpretation with some reservation: ". . . the passage [Ps 23: 5b] evokes Ps 133: 2 . . . and to a lesser extent Ps 89: 21 (the anointing of the king)." The association of ideas in the two psalms indicates that Ps 89: 21–25 may be a more instructive clue to the meaning of Ps 23: 5 than Freedman allows. After mentioning the anointing (*bšmn . . . mšḥtyw;* cf. *dšnt bšmn* in Ps 23: 5b), Psalm 89 goes on to assert that Yahweh will destroy the king's enemies (*ṣryw,* v 24; cf. *ṣrry* in Ps 23: 5b) and that his covenantal *ʾmwnh wḥsd* will be with him (v 25; cf. *ṭwb wḥsd yrdpwny* in Ps 23: 6a).

Given the plausibility of a level of royal imagery in Ps 23: 5, can one justify the postulate of a reinterpretation of this imagery on the part of the poet in the direction of the new exodus/restoration theme? Besides Ps 78: 19, where *ʿrk šlḥn* refers to the Exodus experience, an even more enlightening parallel is Isa 55: 1–3, another exilic poem which joins the theme of God's provision for his people in the new exodus with that of covenant (as in Ps 23: 5–6) and which moreover announces explicitly that the covenant blessings extended to the house of David will now be applied to the whole (exilic) people.

> Ho, everyone who thirsts,
>   come to the waters;
> and he who has no money;
>   come, buy and eat!
> Come, buy wine and milk
>   without money and without price.
> Why do you spend your money
>   for that which is not bread,
> and your labor
>   for that which does not satisfy?
> Hearken diligently to me,
>   and eat what is *good* (*ṭwb*),
>   and delight yourselves in *fatness* (*dšn*).
> Incline your ear, and come to me;
>   hear, *that your soul may live;*
> And I will make with you
>   an everlasting covenant,
>   my sure covenant blessings for David.[35]

Several comments are in order. First, Isa 55: 1–3 refers more clearly than Ps 23: 5 to the new exodus experience. Yet even in this Deutero-Isaiah passage the language is indirect; and as Ps 23: 5 is patterned on royal banquet imagery, unrelated to exodus terminology, so for Isaiah 55 the principal model seems to be either a royal banquet (Sanders 1978) or the banquet given by Wisdom in Prov 9: 1–6 (Begrich 1938: 53). Second, both passages show affinities to Psalm 89[36] and all three passages (Psalms 23,

89, and Isaiah 55) use similar language to speak of new exodus and covenant blessings (*ʾmwnty wḥsdy* in Ps 89: 25; *ḥsdy dwyd* in Isa 55: 3; *ṭwb wḥsd* in Ps 23: 6). On the level of the new exodus/restoration imagery Ps 23: 5 points not only to a new provisioning of the people in the wilderness on their return journey, but also a reversal of the "hunger and thirst" synonymous with the exile (cf. Deut 28: 48). The fate of the people, who had broken the covenant and had been cursed with the loss of "grain, wine, and oil" (Deut 28: 51; cf. 38–40) so that they were "in want of everything" (Deut 28: 48, *bḥsr kl;* cf. *lʾ ʾḥsr* in Ps 23: 2), will be reversed: now food, wine, and oil will be superabundantly available to God's people when they re-enter the Promised Land.[37]

The connections between Ps 23: 5–6a and Ps 89: 21–25 suggest that v 6a, which mentions *ṭwb wḥsd* (= *ʾmwnty wḥsdy* of Ps 89: 25a), likewise belongs to a royal setting. On the level of royal imagery Ps 23: 5a expresses the hope that the blessings of the Davidic covenant will ever accompany the king.

We have seen that the use of *rdp* in v 6a is unexpected and points to a reversal of the language of curse in Deut 28: 45. But how can this verse then be explained on the level of royal imagery? In what context would the king pray for the covenant *blessings* to "pursue" him? Several explanations are possible. We have postulated that the author in vv 5–6 is using material from royal psalmody and reinterpreting it in light of the new exodus/restoration theme. Despite our earlier discussion of *rdp,* is it possible that this verb could have a positive connotation here? We have noted that the verb does occur occasionally in a positive sense. It is also true that in Akkadian, *redû,* a semantic equivalent of *rdp,* occurs in a positive sense in a passage quite similar to Ps 23: 6a.

> *u_4-me-šam-ma da-me-eq-ti u ba-laṭ*
> ZI-*ia li-ir-te$_9$-dan-ni*
> May good luck [lit., "goodness"]
> and health [lit., "the life of my
> soul"] *follow* me every day.[37a]

Thus on the level of royal imagery it is not impossible that *rdp* could have a neutral sense in Psalm 23. But on the whole this is unlikely. The fact is that nowhere else in the Hebrew Bible is *rdp* governed by a covenantal hendiadys; and where *rdp* is associated with covenant language the nuance is always negative.

We shall now attempt to demonstrate that the poet has deliberately introduced the verb *rdp* in order to create a more obvious connection with the new exodus/restoration motif. We have already noted that an alternative to this verb was available to him. As indicated above, one might have expected *nṣr,* "guard, preserve," in place of *rdp* with its hostile connotation. The verb *nṣr,* in fact, does occur in several Psalm passages and a verse from Proverbs, passages that are structurally quite similar to Ps 23: 6a.

Ps 23: 6a	*ʾk ṭwb wḥsd*	*yrdpwny*
Ps 25: 21a	*tm wyšr*	*yṣrwny*
Ps 40: 12b	*ḥsdk wʾmtk*	*tmyd yṣrwny*[38]
Ps 61: 8b	*ḥsd wʾmt*	*mn ynṣrhw*[39]
Prov 20: 28a	*ḥsd wʾmt*	*yṣrw mlk*

In all these texts the subject of an imperfect verb with personal object is a hendiadys;

in all but one (Psalm 25) the hendiadys is composed of two terms often associated in a covenantal context. In every case but one (Psalms 23) the verb is *nṣr*. All the verbs are jussive[40] except in Proverbs 20. In two instances (Psalm 61, Proverbs 20) the object is explicitly the king. The word-order is identical in every case: hendiadys + verb (imperfect) + object. In Ps 40: 12 *tmyd* is virtually synonymous with *kl ymy ḥyy* in Ps 23: 6a.

Of these texts Ps 61: 8 merits closer attention. The entire bicolon, with the preceding v 7, reads as follows.

ymym ʿl ymy mlk twsyp
šnwtyw kmw dr wdr
yšb ʿwlm lpny ʾlhym
ḥsd wʾmt mn ynṣrhw

Add (more) days to the lifetime of the king;
Let his years be like eternity!
Let him dwell in the presence of God forever;
Command (your) covenant blessings
(ever) preserve him!

Except for *mn*,[41] the passage is not problematic. It is commonly assumed that in the first colon of v 8 *yšb* refers to the king's reign: "Let him sit enthroned before God forever."[42] But if one retains the neutral translation "dwell,"[43] v 8a could be interpreted in a sense identical with that of Ps 23: 6b. Further, the expression *lpny ʾlhym,* "in the presence of God," should be understood in a specific sense here. In some OT passages the equivalent phrase *lpny yhwh*[44] means "in the holy place, temple, etc."[45] If the phrase has this meaning here (and we shall present further evidence that this is in fact the case), then Ps 61: 8 expresses in reverse order the same thought as in Ps 23: 6.

Ps 61:	8a	dwelling forever in Yahweh's presence (= temple)
	8b	preserved (*nṣr*) by covenant blessings (*ḥsd wʾmt*)
Ps 23:	6aα	"pursued" (*rdp*) by covenant blessings (*ṭwb wḥsd*)
	6bα	dwelling forever in Yahweh's temple (*byt yhwh*)

That Ps 61: 8a has reference to the temple is suggested by v 5a: *ʾgwrh bʾhlk ʿwlmym,* "Let me dwell in your tent forever."[46] As S. Mowinckel (1962: 1.226) and M. Dahood (1968: 84) have shown, this is a royal psalm, and so both vv 5a and 8a refer to the king.

The presence of *nṣr* in all these texts, and particularly in Ps 61: 8 with its virtual equivalence to Ps 23: 6b, suggests that the poet has chosen *yrdpwny* in place of expected *y(n)ṣrwny* in order to create another "reversal"; as v 5 "reverses" the Exodus motif of hunger and thirst because of the loss of grain, wine, and oil among the exiles, so in v 6a (on the level of new exodus/restoration imagery) it is covenant blessings, rather than curses, that "pursue" God's people.

The intermediate stage between the royal imagery (with *y(n)ṣrwny*) and the phraseology of Ps 23: 6a may be seen in Zech 1: 6.

ʾk dbry wḥqy . . . hlwʾ hśygw ʾbtykm

Indeed, have not my covenant stipulations[47] . . . *overtaken* your fathers?

Note that the word-order in this passage is almost identical to that of Pss 25: 21a;

40: 12b; 61: 8; Prov 20; 28a: hendiadys + verb + object. In Psalm 23 instead of these violated covenant demands (*dbry wḥqy*) which spelled expulsion from the land, the poet prays that only (*ʾk*)[48] Yahweh's covenant blessings (*ṭwb wḥsd*)[49] "pursue" him and allow him permanent residence in the Promised Land; here he speaks in the name of the exilic community. He uses *rdp* (rather than *nṣr*) because the covenant curses had been pursuing and indeed were still pursuing the exiles. Under these circumstances he could hardly express the hope that the covenant blessings would "preserve" them, since they had already felt the full wrath of the curses, as Zech 1: 6 shows. Thus, while *nṣr* would be appropriate in a royal setting, the author of Psalm 23 found *rdp* more suitable to his purpose. It was too late for this exilic poet to pray that the covenant blessings *preserve* him; but he could pray that, in place of the curses (Deut 28: 45), the blessings and these only now *pursue* him.

In this connection it is important to note that in the Hittite vassal treaties the equivalents of *nṣr* and *rdp* were the very terms used with blessings and curses respectively. "If you {do such-and-such in violation of the treaty}, may the(se) oath(-god)s pursue you."[50] "If you {obey the treaty stipulations}, may the(se) oath(-god)s preserve you."[51] In Akkadian copies of the Hittite treaties one finds *liṣṣurū,* from *naṣāru,* "to guard, preserve."[52] This explains the consistent use of *nṣr* in passages related to covenant blessings (Psalms 25, 40, 61; Proverbs 20).[53] In the Aramaic Sefîre treaties too *nṣr* is used in the treaty blessing[54] as is the Ugaritic cognate *nǵr* in a closely related passage.[55] Thus it is clear that *nṣr* had become a technical term both in East and West Semitic for the action of treaty-blessings. Returning to Ps 23: 6a, we may schematize what the psalmist has done here as follows.

Royal Context	Exilic Context	Restoration Context
May the covenant blessings preserve the king.	The covenant curses have pursued/overtaken the exiles.	(In place of the curses) may the covenant blessings "pursue" the exiles.

Hence this choice of *yrdpwny* over *y(n)ṣrwny* is a clear indication within Psalm 23 of its exilic *Sitz im Leben.*

Against this background, we can now raise the question: Precisely what does Ps 23: 6b mean? First, what does it mean on the level of royal imagery to "dwell in the house of Yahweh forevermore?" The specific intent of the verse on this level is not as straightforward as it might at first seem. As Freedman has pointed out, people did not dwell in the temple on a permanent basis (1980: 300). Nor has Dahood's thesis, that the poet expresses the hope of dwelling "in God's celestial abode" (1966: 149), proved convincing. One clue may be the parallelism of the concepts of dwelling in Yahweh's temple and being preserved by covenant blessings. This parallelism is obvious in Ps 61: 8, where the two ideas form one bicolon. In Ps 23: 6, however, each concept occurs in the first half of a bicolon. Yet since *kl ymy ḥyy* (6aβ) and *lʾrk ymym* (6bβ) are synonymous,[56] it is likely that dwelling in Yahweh's temple (6bα) and being preserved by covenant blessings (6aα) are parallel and thus synonymous as well. If this is correct, then the king's "dwelling" in the temple is somehow closely connected to the covenant blessings.

If such a connection does exist, how are we to interpret, on the level of royal imagery, the preservation by covenant blessings in v 6bα? One way to proceed would be to reverse the image: if covenant curses were to pursue the king, what would be the result? First, as we have seen, the reversal of this image is found in Pss 7: 6, 143: 3, and Lam 3: 6: to dwell (not in the house of Yahweh but) in the netherworld. This evokes the idea of sickness or death. Second, the reverse of dwelling in the temple is surely being excluded from it. Thus it could be that the king is praying that he never be excluded from Yahweh's "temple" (Ps 23: 6b) or from his "presence" (Ps 61: 8a) by reason of some illness or disease.

Evidence that this is the correct understanding of Ps 23: 6b is found in several texts that associate the king's sickness with his exclusion from the temple. In 2 Kgs 20: 5–6 Isaiah tells Hezekiah in Yahweh's name: ". . . behold, I will heal you; on the third day you shall go up to the house of Yahweh. And I will add fifteen years to your life."[57] The text implies that the king was not permitted to enter the temple until his affliction had been cured. From 2 Kgs 20: 7 (= Isa 38: 21) we learn that Hezekiah's illness was some kind of skin disease (*šḥyn*).[58] Even more significant is the account of Uzziah, who was "excluded from Yahweh's house" because of a similar affliction. We read in 2 Chr 26: 16–20 that Uzziah had been stricken with leprosy by Yahweh because the king had arrogantly appropriated certain priestly functions. The account continues (vv 20b-21a):

> . . . for Yahweh had afflicted him. And King Uzziah was a leper till the day of his death, and being a leper he had to dwell in a/the house of quarantine,[59] for he had been cut off from the temple of Yahweh.

One important aspect of this account has apparently gone unnoticed: vv 20b-21a clearly reflect not only the wording but even the sequence of details in the treaty-curse specific to the moon-god Sin—the curse of leprosy.

2 Chr 26: 20b-21a	Sin Treaty-Curse
. . . for *Yahweh* had afflicted him. And King Uzziah was a *leper*	May *Sin* . . . clothe him with *leprosy;* May he be unclean
till the day of his death,	*till the day of his death;*[60] *As long as he lives* may he be deprived of
and . . . in a/the *house* of quarantine	his own *house* . . .[61]
he had to *dwell*	May he have to *dwell*
(Josephus, *Ant* 9.10, says that Uzziah had to dwell *outside the city {exō tēs poleōs}*[63]),	*outside his own city;*[62]
for he had been *cut off* from the *temple* of Yahweh.	May he [Sin] *cut off*[64] his access to *temple* and palace.[65]

In the account of Uzziah we have the clear case of a king upon whom the dreaded curse of leprosy had fallen and who therefore was no longer allowed to "dwell" in Yahweh's temple. Given this negative parallel, the meaning of *yšb* in Pss 23: 6 and 61: 8 on the level of royal imagery becomes clear: it simply means that the king has access to the temple, to Yahweh's saving presence there. Akkadian texts containing this curse do not use the verb "dwell" but speak of one's being excluded from "access" (*erēbu*—lit., "entering"), "standing" (*mazzassu*), or "walking" (*italluku*) in the temple.[66]

A significant variant to being cut off from "temple and palace," the standard wording of this curse, is found in the vassal-treaties of Esarhaddon. There the curse reads, "[May he cut off] your entering *into the presence of the gods* or king."[67] It is precisely this phrase that appears in Ps 61: 8: "Let him [the king] dwell *in the presence of God* forever." This variant provides further evidence that *lpny ᵓlhym* in Ps 61: 8 = *bbyt yhwh* in Ps 23: 6.

It is not far-fetched to think that OT writers were familiar with such curses, especially at the time of the exile and later. Weinfeld asserts that in Deuteronomy 28

> not only are the curses of leprosy [v 27], blindness, exposure of the slain, sexual violation of the wife, pillage, and the enslavement of children common to both [Deuteronomy 28 and the vassal-treaties of Esarhaddon]. They occur in almost identical order. . . .
>
> Although the order of curses in Deuteronomy seems to have no plausible explanation, the sequence in *VTE* is based on the hierarchy within the Assyrian pantheon (1972: 118–19).

Thus in Ps 23: 6 ("May I dwell in the house of Yahweh forevermore") the king is praying that he not be excluded by such a curse from the presence of Yahweh. Such royal prayers are not confined to the OT. Two interesting parallels—especially to Ps 61: 7–8—are found in the inscriptions of Assurbanipal. The first is addressed to Nabu, the patron god of scribes, who writes the tablets of destiny.

> *ina ti-kip* ŠANTAK$_4$-*ki-ka ke-e-ni*
> TI UD.MEŠ-*iá* GÍD.MEŠ *li-ṣa-a šap-tuk-ka*
> *italluku* (DU.DU^{ku}) É.ZI.DA *ina* IGI DINGIR-*ti-ka*
> *li-lab-bi-ra* GÌR^{II}-*a-a* (Streck 1916: 2.274: 15–18)
>
> With a (mere) dot of your faithful stylus
> may (the decree for) a *life* of *long days*
> go forth from your lips for me;
> may my feet grow old *ever walking*[68] *in (your temple)* Ezida, *in your divine presence.*

The second prayer is addressed to Ištar.

> *ia-a-ti* ^{md}*Aš-šur*-DÙ.IBILA *pa-liḫ* DINGIR-*ti-ki* GAL^{ti}
> *ba-laṭ* UD.MEŠ GÍD.MEŠ DÙG.GA *lìb-bi qí-šim-ma*
> *italluku* (DU.DU^{ku}) É.MAŠ.MAŠ *lu-lab-bi-ra* GÌR^{II} *-a-a*
> (Streck 1916: 2.276: 16–18)
>
> To me, Assurbanipal, who worships your great divinity,
> grant a *life* of *long days* (and) happiness;
> may my feet grow old *ever walking in (your temple)* Emašmaš.

In both of these texts the Assyrian king is praying to be spared the curse of disease that would exclude him from the deity's presence. In other words, Assurbanipal is praying for long life and (with reference to walking in the temple) good health for a long time to come, as in Pss 23: 6; 61: 8. Note the expressions "a *life* of *long days* (cf. Ps 23: 6: *ḥyy* // *ᵓrk ymym*) and *"in your divine presence"* (cf. Ps 61: 8: *lpny ᵓlhym*). Other Akkadian royal prayers use similar language.[69]

It may be that in Ps 61: 8 and (on the level of royal imagery) Ps 23: 6 the king is praying to escape other diseases or afflictions besides leprosy. Ancient Near Eastern curses threatened other misfortunes that would likewise exclude a king from the temple. We learn from 2 Sam 5: 8 that "the blind and the lame shall/may not enter into the 'house.'" The LXX translates the last phrase as *eis oikon Kyriou,* "into the house of the Lord," which probably gives the intended sense of *hbyt* in this passage. In one important collection of Hittite curses the oath-breaker is threatened, "May these oath(-god)s seize him and blind his army."[70] In the vassal-treaties of Esarhaddon the curse of the sun-god Šamaš reads in part, "May he take away from you the power of sight—wander ever in darkness!"[71] Deut 28: 28–29, which is actually based on this curse (Weinfeld 1972: 117–21), says, "May Yahweh afflict you . . . with blindness . . . may you grope at noonday as the blind grope in darkness. . . ."

Thus far we have considered Akkadian texts where the king prays not to be excluded from the deity's presence or temple. But the Sin curse cited above also threatens exclusion from palace as well. One of the variations of the curse reads, "May he be deprived of *his own house*" (CAD Z 156b); this was certainly the fate of Uzziah, for example, who had to live in a "house of quarantine" outside the city. Hence we might expect to meet instances in which the king prays not to be driven out of his own house/palace. In the inscription of Esarhaddon cited earlier in connection with the royal banquet motif, such a prayer follows immediately on the banquet scene.

ina qí-bit ^{d}*Aš-šur šàr* DINGIR.MEŠ
ù DINGIR.MEŠ KUR *Aš-šur*^{ki} DÙ-*šú-nu*
ina ṭu-ub UZU.MEŠ *ḫu-ud lìb-bi*
nu-um-mur ka-bat-ti
še-bé-e lit-tu-ti qé-reb-šá da-riš
lu-ur-mì-(i-)ma lu-uš-ba-a la-la-a-šá
(Borger 1967: §27 A, VI 54–57)

By the command of Assur, king of the gods,
and all the gods of Assyria,
may I in health, happiness, exhiliration,
(and) fullness of old age *forever dwell* in it
[my new *palace*] (and) enjoy its splendor.

This text from the inscriptions of Esarhaddon presents the same sequence of details as in Ps 23: 5–6: royal banquet, blessings, prayer for long life in a house/temple.

Another feature common to Pss 23: 6, 61: 8, and the pertinent lines of Assurbanipal's prayers (that he might walk in the presence/temple of the deity throughout a "life of long days") is that these verses come at the end of the text. This is the standard position of blessings for the king in West Semitic royal inscriptions.[72] Hence we are to understand Ps 23: 6 as a blessing for the king like Ps 61: 8. The verbs are therefore to be taken as precatives, as in all the other texts mentioned above. Freedman has argued that in Ps 27: 4 (*šbty bbyt yhwh // kl ymy ḥyy*) "instead of the infinitive construct, *šibtī*, it is better to read *šabtī*, as in Ps. 23, and interpret the verb as the precative perfect" (1980: 299). We agree with his interpretation of Ps 27: 4 but would go further and argue for the same interpretation of the verb in Ps 23: 6. Because this verse is in fact a blessing and is synonymous with Ps 61: 8 (where *yšb*[73] and *ynṣrwhw* are jussive), *yrdpwny* and *šbty* ought also to be translated as precatives.

This interpretation of the syntax of the verbs in these passages from the Psalter, and indeed, our whole interpretation of Pss 23: 6, 61: 8, is further confirmed by a final and remarkable parallel, this time from a West Semitic royal document. The king of Ugarit concludes a letter to the king of Egypt with these words.

p. l. ḥy. np{šy.[74] *ar}š*
l.pn. bᶜ{l.} ṣpn. bᶜly
w.urk. ym. bᶜly
l.pn. amn. w.l.pn. il. mṣrm.
dt. tǵrn npš. špš. mlk. rb. bᶜly
(UT 1018.17–24)

And indeed {I pr]ay for the *life* of {my] sou[l}
in the presence of Baᶜ{al] Saphon, my lord;
and for *length of days* for my lord[75]
in the presence of Amun and
in the presence of the gods of Egypt—
may these (gods) *preserve* the life of the Sun,
the Great King, my lord.

This brief passage contains no less than four examples of verbatim correspondence to Psalms 23 and 61: (1–2) the formulaic word-pair "life" // "length of days" (as in Ps 23: 6b), (3) the use of "in the presence of" with divine names (as in Ps 61: 8a), and (4) the verb *nǵr* (= Hebrew *nṣr*) in the third person plural jussive (as *ynṣrhw* in Ps 61: 8b). This, we may recall, is the same verb found in the blessing in the Sefîre treaty (Old Aramaic *nṣr*), the Hittite treaties (Akkadian *naṣāru*), and several Psalms passages related to Ps 61: 8 (i.e., 25: 21; 40: 12). The Ugaritic passage comes at the end of the text and is a prayer for blessing, as is true in the case of Pss 25: 21, 61: 8, the prayers of Assurbanipal cited above, and—in our view—Ps 23: 6. The intention of the prayer may be seen from the expressions *ḥy. np{šy}, urk. ym,* and *tǵrn npš. špš:* good health (*ḥy npš* = Akkadian *balāṭ napišti*)[76] and long life (*urk ym<m>*). That *ḥy (npš) // urk ym<m>* means long-lasting health is also evident from KAI 26 A III 3–5, where the word-pair occurs with *ḥym* juxtaposed to *šlm,* "well-being."[77] The concluding petition that the gods of Egypt "preserve the life" of the Pharaoh is also a request for continued good health. This serves to corroborate our thesis that in Ps 23: 6 (on the level of royal imagery) what the king is really praying for is that Yahweh grant him a long, healthy life.

As the king prays in Ps 23: 6 that he never be excluded from Yahweh's house, so the psalmist prays in the name of the exiles that they never again be excluded from the Promised Land. This prayer is no expression of pious sentimentality but is uttered in light of the traumatic experience of exile and deportation. The same thought is expressed in the conclusion to the hortatory section of Deuteronomy (30: 19–20).

> I call heaven and earth to witness against you this day, that I have set before you life and death, *blessing and curse;* therefore choose life . . ., loving Yahweh your God, obeying his voice, and cleaving to him; for that means *life* to you and *length of days,* that you may *dwell in the land* which *Yahweh* swore to give your fathers, Abraham, Isaac, and Jacob.

To summarize our discussion of vv 5–6, we have argued that the psalmist here has artfully reworked the language, imagery, and motifs of royal psalmody and theology. The result is that, as in other exilic writings, language once applied to the Davidic king (royal imagery) is now applied to the exilic community (restoration imagery). The two levels of discourse in these verses may be illustrated as follows.

	Royal Imagery	Restoration Imagery
5	The god (Yahweh) fetes the king with a sumptuous banquet in the sight of his foes; the banquet reaffirms the overlord-vassal relationship between god (Yahweh) and king.	Yahweh fetes the returning exiles with sumptuous provisions to the envy of the nations; the feast reaffirms Yahweh's provident concern for his covenant people.
6	The king prays that the (Davidic) covenant blessings preserve (**ynṣrw*) him always; the king prays that he may always dwell in Yahweh's temple— i.e., that he may never be excluded from the divine presence.	The exiles pray that from now on only the covenant blessings pursue (*yrdpw*) them always (not the curses!); the exiles pray that they may always dwell in Yahweh's "house"— i.e., that they may never again be excluded from the Promised Land.

IV. Conclusion

In the conclusion to his study of Psalm 23, Freedman makes the following observation.

> The language of the Psalm . . . bears marked resemblances to the distinctive vocabulary and ideas of the exilic period, with special interest in a new Exodus, a new march through the wilderness, and a new settlement in the promised land. In addition, the wilderness experience has been idealized with respect to past history, and projected into the future, e.g., the "waters of contention" have become the "waters of repose" (1980: 301).

It is the contention of this paper that Ps 23: 6 adds to the above series of motifs the notion of covenant, so that the complete sequence in Psalm 23 is new exodus, new march through the wilderness, *new covenant* (i.e., renewal of the Sinai covenant combined with the blessings of the Davidic covenant), and new settlement in the Promised Land. Like the other motifs, the new covenant was also promised by a prophet of the seventh-sixth centuries; like the wilderness experience, the new covenant is an idealization of the old, projected into the future.

> The days are coming, says the Lord, when I shall make a new covenant with the house of Israel and the house of Judah. It will not be like the covenant I made with their fathers the day I took them by the hand to lead them forth from the land of Egypt; for they broke my covenant, and I had to show myself their master, says the Lord. But this is the covenant which I will make with the house of Israel after those days, says the Lord. I will place my law within them, and write it upon their hearts; I will be their God and they will be my people (Jer 31: 31–34).[78]

And how was this new covenant in Jeremiah an idealization of the old Sinai covenant? In the words of B. W. Anderson:

> Jeremiah's final understanding of the covenant relationship . . . exhibits a polarity: on the human side the covenant was broken and . . . could not be repaired by covenant ceremonies; on the divine side, however, the relationship was grounded in Yahweh's *ʾahăbat ʿôlām,* his everlasting love which is not conditioned by human behavior. Considering this polarity, it is not surprising

> that the prophet's theology begins to move away from the Mosaic covenant toward the Davidic covenant with its unconditional promises of grace . . . (1976: 353).

Commenting on the unprecedented notion of a new covenant written on the hearts of the people, W. L. Holladay writes:

> The old contract is a dead letter; it is in the wastebasket, so God is going to draw up a new one which is different from the old one in crucial respects. . . . God will draw up a new sort of contract for a new sort of relationship altogether, so that all the old difficulties will be gone and forgotten (1974: 119–20).

Because the notion is so unprecedented and so radically new, Holladay concludes, "But Jeremiah's vision of a new covenant is laid aside, never to be touched again in the Old Testament" (1974: 120). If the analysis of Ps 23: 6 in this paper has merit, perhaps the author of the psalm represents a single exception to Holladay's statement, an author who like Jeremiah looked to a new and eternal covenant, and celebrated it in his poem.

Notes

1. Note the similarity in structure common to

Ps 23: 4	*gm ky ʾlk bygʿ ṣlmwt // lʾ ʾyrʾ rʿ*
Ps 138: 7	*ʾm ʾlk bqrb ṣrh // tḥyny . . .*
Ps 27: 3	*ʾm tḥnh ʿly mḥnh // lʾ yyrʾ lby*

In this connection note several further links between Psalms 27 and 23.

	Psalm 27		Psalm 23
1	*yhwh ʾwry*	1	*yhwh rʿy*
4	*šbty bbyt yhwh*	6	*wšbty bbyt yhwh*
	kl ymy ḥyy		(= v 6aβ)
6	*wʿth yrwm rʾšy*	5	*tʿrk lpny šlḥn*
	ʿl ʾyby sbybwty		*ngd ṣrry*
11	*wnḥny bʾrḥ myšwr*	3	*ynḥny bmʿgly ṣdq*
	lmʿn šwrry		*lmʿn šmk*

2. In place of the hendiadys of protective rod and staff, it is Yahweh's (left) hand and right hand, another hendiadys, that protects the psalmist in Psalm 138 against the wrathful enemies. The connection between the divine shepherd's implements in Psalm 23 and the divine hands that wield them in Psalm 138 should be noted.

3. Other scholars (e.g., Merrill 1965) have been unsatisfied with an analysis of the poem as composed of two conflicting images but have not been able to demonstrate convincingly its unity. In the most recent extensive study of the psalm (Mittmann 1980), the author argues that, once the *Gattung* of Psalms 23 is correctly identified as *Danklied,* the second image of Yahweh as host is seen to be not an image at all, but an institutional reality: the sacrifice and meal of the *tōdâ* ritual, at the conclusion of which the *Danklied* is sung. For a similar understanding of the psalm, see Vogt 1953.

4. Freedman (1980: 298–99) proposes several solutions for the analysis of *wšbty* in Ps 23: 6, of which the most compelling would seem to be deriving the form from *šwb* II, a byform of *yšb* (cf. *ṭwb* and *yṭb*); so also Andersen 1970: 273. In the commentary on Hosea co-authored by Andersen and Freedman (1980), two other possible instances of *šwb* II have been identified: in Hos 11: 11 (p. 592) and 12: 10 (p. 618). For further evidence that *wšbty* here is derived from this root, see below, n. 73.

5. Note the appearance of *wrwḥk hṭwbh* in an Exodus context in Neh 9: 20.

6. Psalm 23 shares with Psalm 31 the pair *nḥh // nhl*. For *ṣdq // myšwr*, cf. Isa 11: 4; Prov 1: 3; 2: 9. Note also Ps 27: 11: *hwrny yhwh drkk // wnḥny bʾrḥ myšwr lmʿn šwrry*; Ps 5: 9: *yhwh nḥny bṣdqtk lmʿn šwrry // hwšr lpny drkk;* Ps 67: 5: *ky tšpṭ ʿmym myšwr // wlʾmym bʾrṣ tnḥm.*

7. Pss 31: 5 and 143: 10 are both part of a formulaic system that includes Pss 71: 5; 91: 9; 43: 2; 25: 5 as well. See Culley 1967: 52 #34.

8. Dahood 1970: 324: "With 11QPs[a] and many manuscripts we read *bʾrṣ* for *kĕʾereṣ*. . . ."

9. For this translation, see below, p. 112.

10. For this understanding of Psalm 7, see Tigay 1970: 178–86. We read *kĕbēdî* for MT *kĕbôdî*, with Dahood (1966: 43), and understand *lʾrṣ//lʿpr* as references to the underworld. Note also his comment (1970: 323): "Where our poet [in Ps 143: 3] uses the verb *hōšîbanī*, 'He made me dwell,' Ps vii uses *yaškēn*, 'Let him cause [my liver] to dwell' (vs. 6) in a very similar context." For the synonymity of *hwšybny* and *yškn*, cf. *yšb // škn* in Judg 5: 17; Isa 13: 20; 32: 16; Ps 69: 36–37, and the collocations in Isa 32: 18; Ps 68: 17.

11. Psalm 69 is another lament that, like Psalm 143, shares a number of motifs with Psalm 23. Like Psalm 143, Psalm 69 presents in the lament section a series of negative or contrasting images.

Ps 69: 20	*ngdk kl ṣwrry* (cf. 23: 5: *ngd ṣrry*)
Ps 69: 23	*yhy šlḥn lpnyhm* (cf. 23: 5: *tʿrk lpny šlḥn*)
Ps 69: 25	*wḥrwn ʾpk yśygm* (cf. 23: 6: *ʾk ṭwb wḥsd yrdpwny;* on the synonymity of *rdp // hśyg*, see below, p. 103, and nn. 14, 26, 38; and note *rdpw* in v 27)
Ps 69: 29	*wmḥw mspr ḥyym* (cf. 23: 6: *wšbty bbyt yhwh // kl ymy ḥyy*).

And in the thanksgiving section of the psalm (vv 31–37) there is a positive parallel to Ps 23: 6.

Ps 69: 36–37 *wyšbw šm* [i.e., in Zion and the cities of Judah, v 36] *wyršwh wzrʿ ʿbdyw ynḥlwh wʾhby šmw yšknw bh.*

12. For the analysis of MT *wtznḥ mšlwm* as verb + enclitic *mem* with *šlwm* as direct object, see Hummel 1957: 105; adopted by Hillers (1972: 55).

13. Note in this connection Lam 1: 3, where the verbs *rdp* and *hśyg* appear: *glth yhwdh mʿny wmrb ʿbdh // hyʾ yšbh bgwym lʾ mṣʾh mnwḥ // kl rdpyh hśygwh byn hmṣrym*, "Judah has gone into exile after suffering and after much toil. She dwelt among the nations but found no rest. All who pursued her cornered her in narrow straits" (translation from Hillers 1972: 1). This text exhibits the same kind of reversal of Psalm 23 as does Lamentations 3: Judah in exile is denied rest and is overtaken by hostile pursuers.

14. For *rdp // hšmyd* cf. 2 Sam 22: 38; and note the variant in Ps 18: 38: *rdp // hśyg*. Geller (1979: 66) writes: "The variant *ʾšmydm* has been chosen over *ʾśygm* of Ps. 18. Since *hśyg* is common after *rdp*, *ʾšmydm* may be lectio difficilior." All three forms occur in Deut 28: 45 (*wrdpwk // whśygwk ʿd hšmdk*). We will have occasion to return to *rdp* + *hśyg* later in this paper; see below, n. 26.

15. Andersen and Freedman (1980: 481) suggest a different translation for v 3: "The Good One [i.e., Yahweh] rejects Israel. As an enemy he will pursue him." However, they recognize the possibility of the translation proposed here, given the syntactic ambiguity of the line (p. 491). Another possibility would be to understand *yrdpw* as precative ("May an enemy pursue him"), as we shall suggest *yrdpwny* and *wšbty* are to be understood in Ps 23: 6. Finally, note that Emmerson (1975: 704) identifies *ʾwyb yrdpw* as a covenant curse.

16. On *ydʿ* as covenant terminology, see Huffmon 1966: 31–37; see Freedman 1972: 536 on the structure of Hos 8: 3. On *ṭwb* in Hos 8: 3 as a synonym for *bryt*, see Fox 1972: 42. Johag (1977) is a good review of the evidence from the OT and the ancient Near East. In this connection, the pair *šlwm // ṭwb* in Lam 3: 17 is interesting, given the appearance of these words as treaty terminology. See Moran 1963; Hillers 1964a (although this pair passes without comment in his work on Lamentations); Croatto 1968; Weinfeld 1973.

17. By analogy with Deut 28: 45, where the subject of *rdpwk* is *hqllwt* ("All these *curses* shall come upon you and *pursue* you"), and with a number of the extra-biblical parallels to be adduced below, we are tempted to understand the verb *trdp* as third person feminine singular, with *tʾltk* as subject ("May it [the curse] pursue them in anger") rather than second person masculine singular ("May you pursue. . . ."). However, in defense of the second person understanding of RSV, NEB, NAB, JB, AB, and TEV,

note Lam 3: 43, where *wtrdpnw* must mean "and *you* [Yahweh] have pursued us." It may also be worth recording a reversal of Psalm 23 in this same chapter of Deuteronomy: compare *ʿl my mnḥwt ynhlny npšy yšwbb* (Ps 23: 2–3) with *wlʾ yhwh mnwḥ . . . wntn yhwh lk šm . . . wdʾbwn npš* (Deut 28: 65).

18. So also Eaton 1976: 153: "A tendency to personify the covenant-graces appears fairly clearly in a number of passages; they take the form of angelic beings commissioned by God to accompany and guard his king." In addition to Ps 23: 6, Eaton cites Pss 21: 4; 40: 12; 42: 9; 43: 3; 54: 7; 59: 11; 61: 8; 91: 4. On Pss 40: 12 and 61: 8, see below.

19. Tromp's observation is apposite: "In Accadian incantations persecution is one of the favorite occupations of the demons. The Angel of Yahweh has a similar task in Ps 35: 5 . . ." (1969: 204).

20. For *byt yhwh* as "Yahweh's domain, i.e., the land of Yahweh," see Freedman 1980: 300, where he refers to *byt yhwh* in Hos 8: 1 and 9: 3–4, where *ʾrṣ yhwh* is parallel to *byt yhwh* (see also Andersen and Freedman 1980: 520). Andersen (1970: 273) translates Ps 23: 6 "And I shall reside on Yahweh's estate for the duration of my lifespan." Cf. *byt* = land of Yahweh in Hos 9: 15; Zech 9: 8. In Jer 12: 7 *byt* // *nḥlh* occurs in a context that may be covenantal (cf. *ṭwb* in 12: 6). See also Johnson 1970 and Clements 1965: 73–75. For parallels to *kl ymy ḥyy* and dwelling in the land *lʾrk ymym,* note Deut 4: 40 *(wlmʿn tʾryk ymym ʿl hʾdmh ʾšr yhwh ʾlhyk ntn lk kl hymym),* 5: 30 *(lmʿn tḥywn wṭwb lkm whʾrktm ymym bʾrṣ ʾšr tyršwn),* and 30: 20 *(ky hwʾ ḥyyk wʾrk ymyk lšbt ʿl hʾdmh ʾšr nšbʿ yhwh . . . ltt lhm);* cf. also Deut 5: 16; 6: 2; 11: 9; and Tawil 1974; Weinfeld 1972: 308–9.

21. See Weinfeld 1973: 192 n. 35: "Ps. 25: 7 speaks about remembering of *ṭwb* and *ḥsd* which are none other than the ancient gracious covenant, see v. 6. Compare Ps. 23: 6. . . ."

22. In addition to Psalm 7 and Hosea 8, two other passages where *rdp* appears in a covenantal context might be noted. First, in Amos 1: 11b: *ʿl rdpw bḥrb ʾḥyw wšḥt rḥmyw,* "Because he pursued his brothers with the sword and utterly destroyed his allies." Fishbane (1970 and 1972) argues that the pair *ʾḥyw* // *rḥmyw* is synonymous, meaning "covenant partner." As a parallel to *rdp* // *šḥt,* note *rdp* + *hšmyd* in Deut 28: 45; Lam 3: 66 and *rdp* // *hšmyd* in 2 Sam 22: 38 (= Ps 18: 38). The second passage is Ps 83: 16: *kn trdpm bsʿrk wbswptk tbhlm,* "[O my God—v 14] pursue them with your tempest and rout them with your storm." Roberts (1976: 130) has described Psalm 83 as "a prayer for help against rebellious vassals"; since covenant was the ordinary instrument for linking overlord to vassal, here too, as in Amos 1: 11, the punishment for violation of covenant is described by the verb *rdp.*

23. Freedman 1980: 297–98. To Freedman's list should be added Prov 15: 9 (*mrdp ṣdqh*). Note also *ṣdqh* as subject of *hśyg,* a synonym of *rdp,* in Isa 59: 9.

24. Mittmann (1980: 16) states the issue accurately: "Das Weg- und Wandermotif der ersten Strophe nimmt die zweite andeutend wieder auf im Ausdruck *rdp* 'verfolgen,' der hier zunächst befremdet, weil er sonst in der Regel im Sinne der feindlichen Nachstellung gebraucht ist und mit *ṭōb* und *ḥesed* nicht recht zu harmonieren." He goes on to claim that the tension between the verb *rdp* and its subject *ṭwb wḥsd* is intended: *rdp* "lässt den dunkeln Hintergrund der Bildvorstellung von V. 4a noch einmal an- und mitklingen: nicht Unheil verfolgt den Gerechten, selbst wenn der Weg durch das Tal der Finsternis führt, sondern Heil und Hilfe" (pp. 16–17). As we hope to show, Mittmann is correct about this intended tension.

25. For a general treatment of Deuteronomy 28, see Hillers 1964b: 30–42.

26. For *rdp* + *hśyg* in prose, see Gen 31: 23, 25; 44: 4; Exod 14: 9; Deut 19: 6; 28: 45; Josh 2: 5; 1 Sam 30: 8; 2 Kgs 25: 5 (= Jer 39: 5 = 52:8). For examples in poetry, see Exod 15: 9; Hos 2: 9; Ps 18: 38; Lam 1: 3.

27. The close association, if not exact synonymity, of *rdp* and *hśyg* allows one to recognize the striking parallel to Ps 23: 6 in Zech 1: 6: *ʾk dbry wḥqy . . . hlwʾ hśygw ʾbtykm.* On this text, see below, pp. 108–9.

28. As Freedman himself notes, "the key term *midbār* 'wilderness' is omitted, or not used" here (1980: 296).

29. Among those who have argued for the royal character of this psalm are Merrill 1965 and van Zyl 1963.

30. Note that Hebrew *rwh* (as in Ps 23: 5) likewise means "drench" in the *Piʿel* and *Hipʿil*. Cf. Jer 31: 12, which says that the "soul" of the exiles shall be "like a watered [*rwh*] garden"; and v 14, where Yahweh promises, "I will drench [*wrwyty*] the soul(s) of the priests with *dšn*" (cf. *dšnt* in Ps 23: 6).

31. For the continuation of this text, see below p. 112.

32. That the scene described here is in fact a "vassal oath renewal" has been argued most recently by Sheriffs (1979: 56). See also Cogan (1974: 49), who describes this scene as "suggestive of *adū* oath

ceremonies."

33. For an alternative proposal for *ngd ṣrry,* see the Appended Note.

34. For this translation, and a treatment of the relation of this cuneiform passage to the two texts mentioned, see Barré 1982.

35. *ḥsdy dwyd.* For evidence that "David" here should be understood as an objective genitive, see Williamson 1978.

36. On the relationship between Psalm 89 and Isa 55: 1–5, see Eissfeldt 1962.

37. This motif of superabundant provisioning is also present in Ps 78: 15–16, 25–29.

37a. For this text and translation, see CAD D 65b. Note, however, that the same form of this verb (Gtn form of *redû*) occurs regularly in a hostile sense, where the appropriate translation would be "pursue" (see AHw 966b). But in the Akkadian passage under discussion the meaning is clearly positive; it should be kept in mind that *redû* occurs far more frequently with a positive connotation than does Hebrew *rdp* (see AHw 965–66).

38. Ps 40: 12 is a significant parallel to Ps 23: 6 because in the following verse (13) we read *hśygwny ʿwnty; hśyg,* a frequent parallel to *rdp,* has here a first person singular suffix, as does *rdp* in Ps 23: 6. Because his iniquities have *overtaken* the author of Psalm 40, he prays that Yahweh's *ḥsd* and *ʾmt* protect him, a sentiment similar to that in Ps 23: 6 and expressed in similar language.

39. See Fitzgerald 1972: 90, 92.

40. That this is also the case with *yrdpwny* in Ps 23: 6 will be demonstrated below (see p. 112).

41. The latest attempt to solve this problem is that of Dahood (1979: 419). He translates Ps 61: 8b, "May the kindness and fidelity of Destiny [reading *mĕnī* for MT *man*] safeguard him." However, we accept the traditional parsing of *mn* in this verse as an apocopated *Piʿel* imperative from *mnh,* with the meaning here perhaps "bid, command" (see *HALAT* 567a). Some support for this interpretation may be found in an inscription of Sennacherib. Like the Esarhaddon text cited earlier, this inscription recounts a banquet given at the dedication of a royal palace.

> *i-na taš-ri-it* É.GAL *šá ba-ḫu-la-te* KUR-*ia ú-ša-aš-qa-a muḫ–ḫa-ši-in* GEŠTIN.MEŠ *du-uš-šú-pu*
> <*ṣur*>*-ra-ši-in am-kir i-na qí-bit* AN.ŠÁR *a-bu* DINGIR.MEŠ *ù* ^{d}*Iš-tar šar-ra-ti* ^{d}ALÀD *dum-qi*
> ^{d}LAMMA *dum-qi qé-reb* É.GAL *ša-a-tu da-riš liš-tab-ru-ú a-a ip-par-ku-ú i-da-a-ša* (Luckenbill 1924: 125.51–53)

> At the dedication of the palace I poured wine on the heads of the people of my land;
> I drenched their bowels with mead. *By the command* of Assur, father of the gods, and Ištar, the queen,
> may a good tutelary god and a good protecting god remain forever in that palace— may they never withdraw from its side.

Like Ps 23: 5–6, this prayer describes a royal banquet followed by a prayer to be protected by a beneficent *šēdu* and *lamassu* (who, like *ṭwb wḥsd,* often occur in literature as a *pair* of deities) *at the command* of the supreme deities, Assur and Ištar. Similarly—if our understanding of *mn* is correct—Yahweh is asked to *command* the twin covenant blessings *ṭwb wḥsd* to accompany the king (see also Eaton 1976: 153).

42. So NAB; similarly RSV, JB, TEV, Kraus 1972: 432, Dahood 1968: 83.

43. So NEB.

44. We would not expect *lpny yhwh* in Psalm 61 in any case, since this is part of the Elohistic psalter. See Kraus 1972: 432 and his note.

45. See van der Woude 1976: 2.458. Some of the examples he cites are Josh 18:6; Judg 20: 23, 26; 1 Sam 1: 12; 11: 15; 15: 33; 2 Sam 7: 18; 2 Kgs 19: 14.

46. Other, more distant connections with Psalm 23 are *tnḥny* (Ps 61: 3; cf. *ynḥny* in Ps 23: 3); *mpny ʾwyb* (Ps 61: 4; cf. *ngd ṣrry* in Ps 23: 5).

47. The term *dbry* here is best taken as referring to the commandments of Yahweh in the covenant rather than his prophetic "predictive" words. Note the close connection with *ḥqy* and the use of *dbr(ym)* elsewhere, especially in Deuteronomy, to denote the commandments (see Schmidt 1978: 116–18). An interesting parallel to the notion of Yahweh's words or commandments "overtaking" those who disregard them is found in an inscription of Esarhaddon, where a penitent vassal declares to the king:

māmīt ilāni rabûti ša ētiqu amat šarrūtika ša amēšu ikšudānni yâti, "The oath of the great gods, which I transgressed, and your royal *word/command,* which I disregarded, have *overtaken* me" (Borger 1967: §68.23).

48. The word *ʾk* in this verse is often indifferently translated either "surely" (RSV) or "only" (NAB). In the present context the latter interpretation is to be preferred.

49. We should probably understand *ṭwb wḥsd* as having the force of "*your* goodness and kindness," i.e., "your covenant blessings," given the second person cast of the poem from v 4 on: *ʾth, šbṭk, umšʿntk, tʿrk, dšnt* (so L. Alonso Schökel 1981: 109, 116, who translates "Tu bondad y lealdad me siguen"). Note that the LXX renders *wḥsd* as *kai to eleos sou.* One might even argue that the suffixes of *šbṭk wmšʿntk* are double-duty, serving to qualify *ṭwb wḥsd,* the only other hendiadys in the poem. For the association of *šbṭk wmšʿntk* with *ṭwb wḥsd* on structural grounds, see Milne 1974–75: 238–39, 243–44. The possibility of a connection between them is reinforced when one recognizes a wordplay based on sequence of consonants: in *šbṭk* the consonant sequence *b-ṭ-k* is echoed chiastically in the sequence *k-ṭ-b* of *ʾk ṭwb.* This is only one instance of assonance and wordplay in Psalm 23. Others include *rʿy* and *rʿ,* where the similarity in sound is in counterpoint to the opposition in meaning ("my shepherd" vs. "evil"); the consonant sequence *n-ḥ* in *mnḥwt, ynḥny,* and (reversed) *šlḥn; š-b* in *yšwbb, šbṭk, wšbty* (and the similar *p-š* in *npšy*); *r-k* in *tʿrk* and *lʾrk; m-ʿ-n-š* of *lmʿn šmw* and *m-š-ʿ-n* of *mšʿntk;* the consonants *b-m-g-l-ṣ* of *bmʿgly ṣdq* in v 3a repeated in *bgyʾ ṣlmwt* (where again similarity of sound contrasts with opposition in meaning); and the syllable *maʿg-* echoed in *gam* of the next line.

50. In Hittite the word is *parḫiškandu,* from the iterative stem of *parḫ–,* "to chase, pursue" (= Hebrew *rdp*): F3 §§10.25; 15.25; 17.21; 18.30; 19.8; 20.15; 22.33; 28.5; F5 §§9.57; 13.2; 16.30; 17.56, 60. In Akkadian copies of Hittite treaties one finds *likaššid-* from *kašādu* (D), "to chase, pursue": Wl rev 69; W2 rev 34. (In Mesopotamian documents *kašādu* [G], "overtake" [= Hebrew *hśyg,* as in Zech 1: 6], also appears in treaty contexts: cf. Borger 1967: §68.23; *ABL* 350 rev 4–5; 584 rev 4; CAD E 390a; K 278b.) In the curses one also encounters Hittite *(arḫa) ḫarninkandu* from *(arḫa) ḫarnink-,* "to destroy": F4 §§19.9; F5 §21.37; F6 §§10.10; 14.31; 19.69; 24.7; 26.2; 40.33; 45.57; KBo IV 10 rev 7, 20, 27; KBo VIII 35 rev 35 vs II 18. The Akkadian equivalent is *liḫalliqū-* from *ḫalāqu* (D), "to destroy": Fl §20.26; W2 rev 53; W3 rev IV 52; W4 rev 16. Note that the Hebrew equivalents, *ʾbd* and *(h)šm(y)d,* also occur in the context of covenant curses (Deut 28: 20, 22 [with *rdp*], 24, 45 [with *rdp*], 48, 51, 61, 63).

51. In Hittite the word is *paḫšandaru* from *paḫš-,* "to preserve, protect" (= Hebrew *nṣr*): F4 §20.45; F5 §21.44; F6 §11.12; KBo IV 10 rev 10; KBo VIII 35 vs II 15.

52. Fl §21.32; Wl rev 72; W2 rev 36, 55; W4 rev 20.

53. But in Psalm 25 *tm wyšr* do not constitute a covenantal hendiadys like *ṭwb wḥsd* or *ḥsd wʾmt.* Perhaps the use of *tm wyšr* with *nṣr* is patterned on the use of the covenantal expressions with this verb, a likelihood in view of the high degree of covenantal language in Psalm 25.

Ps 25: 4	*drkyk yhwh hwdyʿny*	(cf. Ps 23: 4: *ynḥny bmʿgly ṣdq*)
Ps 25: 5	*ky ʾth ʾlhy yšʿy*	(cf. Ps 23: 4: *ky ʾth ʿmdy*)
Ps 25: 6	*rḥmyk//ḥsdyk*	}
Ps 25: 7	*kḥsdk//lmʿn ṭwbk*	}
Ps 25: 10	*kl ʾrḥwt yhwh ḥsd wʾmt*	} (cf. Ps 23: 6: *ṭwb wḥsd*)
Ps 25: 21	*tm wyšr*	}

54. Sefîre I C 15–16 (= KAI 222 C 15–16): *yṣrw ʾlhn mn ywmh wmn byth* (see Fitzmyer 1967: 20). Fitzmyer translates, "May (the) gods keep [all evils] away from his day and his house" (p. 21). But in the blessings section of the Hittite treaties—and this treaty shows a number of affinities to the Hittite treaty form—the object of *paḫšandaru/liṣṣurū* is always the vassal and his wife, household, possessions, etc. (see the texts cited in nn. 51–52). The translation by Gibson (1975: 33) may be helpful: "May the gods keep (him) all his days and his house as long as it lasts!" On this rendering of *mn ywmh,* see Gibson 1975: 43; cf. *mymyk* in 1 Sam 25: 28.

55. See below, pp. 112–13.

56. "Life" // "length of days" is one of the most widely distributed paratactic word-pairs in Semitic literature. It occurs in Hebrew (Deut 30: 20; Ps 21: 5; Prov 3: 2), Ugaritic (UT 1018.18–21), Phoenician (KAI 26 A III 3–5), and Akkadian (*balāṭu // arāk ūmī;* see CAD A/2 223–24).

57. Note the correspondence of this passage to Ps 61: 7–8:

2 Kgs 20	Psalm 61
6 *whspty ʿl ymyk* *ḥmš ʿśrh šnh* And I will *add* fifteen *years to your days.*	7 *ymym ʿl ymy mlk twsyp* *šnwtyw kmw dr wdr* *Add* (more) days *to the days of the king;* Let his *years* be like eternity!
5 *bywm hšlyšy tʿlh* *byt yhwh* On the third day you will go up to *the temple of Yahweh.*	8 *yšb ʿwlm lpny ʾlhym* Let him dwell forever *in the presence of God.*

For the connection between the "third day" and recovery from sickness, cf. Hos 6: 2 (see Barré 1978: 139–40).

58. This is the same word found in Deut 28: 27 in the Hebrew version of the treaty-curse associated with the Moon god Sin; see Weinfeld 1972: 117–18 and n. 6. Moreover, in 4QPr Nab 2, the Aramaic cognate *šḥnʾ* describes the affliction of Nabonidus, which was also apparently connected with the curse of Sin; see Weinfeld 1972: 121 n. 2.

59. MT *byt hḥpšwt* (= Kethib; Qere = *byt hḥpšyt* as in 2 Kgs 15: 5). On this disputed term see Myers 1974: 151.

60. *Sîn . . . saḫaršuppâ . . . lilabbišma adi ūmi šīmatišu ay ībib* (*BBS* §7 II 16–17).

61. *adi ūm balṭu bīssu lizammima* (CAD Z 156b).

62. *ina kamât ālišu lîšib* (*BBS* §11 III 5).

63. Note that the Targum on this verse has *br myrwšlm,* "outside of Jerusalem," not found in the MT. See Le Déaut and Robert 1971: 2.140.

64. For this translation of *liḫalliq* in this curse, see Postgate 1969: 74.

65. Ištar, the daughter of Sin, is invoked as follows in a Neo-Assyrian curse: *Ištar . . . saḫaršuppâ limallišu ana ekurri ekalli erēbšu liḫalliq,* "May Ištar . . . fill him with leprosy; may she cut off his access to temple and palace" (Postgate 1969: §37.14′–16′). The curse of Sin reads similarly: *Sîn . . . {saḫar}šuppû . . . luḫal{lip}šu{nu} mazzassašunu issu ekurri ekalli luḫalliq,* "May Sin . . . clothe them . . . with leprosy; may he cut off their standing from temple and palace" (*BRM* 4.50: 16–18; see AHw 638a). Note also *VTE* 419–20: *Sîn . . . saḫaršuppê liḫallipkunu ina maḫar ilāni u šarri erābkunu {liḫalliq},* "May Sin . . . clothe you with leprosy; may he cut off your entering into the presence of the gods or the king." Instead of *liḫalliq,* Wiseman's text (1958: 59) reads *ay iqbi,* "May he forbid [lit., not command] . . . ." But all of the fragments containing this line (27, 28B, 29, 35, 56) break off before the verb; *ay iqbi* is evidently Wiseman's conjectural restoration. Given the texts cited in this note, perhaps the restoration *lu/liḫalliq* should be preferred.

66. For texts containing *erēbu/erābu* and *mazzassu,* see the previous note. For *italluku,* note the curse found in Neo-Assyrian royal grants with the king as subject, but clearly patterned on the Sin curse: *qereb ekurri ekalli italluka lizamme{šu},* "May he forbid him to walk in temple or palace" (Postgate 1969: §§9.62; 10.62; 12.62).

67. *VTE* 420. For the text, see n. 65.

68. The verb here (*italluku*) is in the Gtn-stem, which has an iterative or "habitative" nuance; see *GAG* §91e.

69. In one royal prayer the king prays, *maḫarka namriš atall{uk}a lušbi,* "May I find fulfillment ever walking radiantly in your presence" (Ebeling 1953: 64.22). On the royal character of this prayer, see Seux 1976: 291 n. 1.

70. The text reads: *nan kē lingaiš appan{d(u)} nu apēlla tuzzin dašuwa{ḫḫandu};* see Oettinger 1976: 6.24.

71. *VTE* 423–24. Reading with Borger (1961: 187): *niṭil ēnēkunu liššima ina eklēti itallakā.*

72. KAI 4.3–6 (note *yʾrk . . . ymt.yḥmlk* [lines 3–5], "May [the gods of Byblos] *lengthen the days* of Yehimilk . . ."); 5.2 (restored); 6.2–3 (note *tʾrk . . . {ymt.ʾ}lbʿl* [lines 2–3], "May [the Lady of Byblos] *lengthen* [*the days* of ʾE]libaʿal . . ."); 7.4–5; 10.8–11 (strictly speaking, this votive inscription ends with line 11; what follows is a curse directed against those who would tamper with the objects described in the inscription proper); 12.4; 18.8; 25.5–7 (note *ʾrk ḥy* [line 7], "*length of life*"); 26 A III 2–11 = C III 16–IV 12 (here, as in KAI 10, the blessing ends the royal inscription proper; it is followed by a curse

against whoever does harm to the inscription); 38.2; 39.3; 215.22–23; 217.7–9.

73. The fact that *yšb* in Ps 61: 8 (= Ps 23: 6b) is unquestionably from the root *yšb* < **wšb* settles the question of whether *šbty* in Pss 27: 4; 23: 6 is from *šwb* (I), "return," or from a by-form of *yšb*. Cf. the parallel Esarhaddon text: *qerebša dāriš lurmīma,* "May I *dwell* within it forever."

74. Gordon (1965: 219) reads *np[š? a?]rš;* the transliteration in *PRU II* 34 has *np[š . . . a(?)]rš*. But there is room on the copy (see *PRU II* 34) for *y* and the word-divider following *np[š]*. Since the king of Ugarit wishes Pharaoh long life in the presence of his [i.e., Pharaoh's] gods, the corresponding wish for *ḥy npš* in the presence of the Ugaritic god must refer to the king of Ugarit. Thus one should restore *ḥy. np[šy. a]rš.*

75. Literally, "and for the length of the days of my lord."

76. Even by itself *balāṭu* can mean "good health" (see CAD B 46); when followed by *napišti* it always has this specific nuance (see CAD A/2 223–24; 47–49).

77. Similarly Akkadian *balāṭu* is often paired with *šulmu*/*šalāmu;* see CAD B 46–50.

78. It is worth noting that in Jeremiah 31, along with the prophet's announcement of a new covenant, we find these parallels to Psalm 23: *ʾwlykm ʾl nḥly mym bdrk yšr* (v 9); *wšmrw krʿh ʿdrw* (v 10); *nhrw ʾl ṭwb yhwh* (v 12); *wrwyty npš khnym dšn* (v 14).

Appended Note

In the text of this paper we have presented evidence from the OT and extra-biblical sources that would seem to shed light on the meaning of *ngd ṣrry* in the context of Psalm 23. Notwithstanding its plausibility, "in the sight of my foes" strikes one as somehow out of place in a banquet scene. We therefore propose for consideration an alternative interpretation of this phrase.

One striking parallel to Ps 23: 5–6 adduced above is Esarhaddon's inscription describing the dedication of his new palace in Calah, in which he describes a royal banquet, prays for blessings for himself, and expresses the hope of dwelling forever in his palace. As regards the royal banquet itself, this text mentions the following details: seating the guests at a festive table, causing their hearts to rejoice, drenching their "bowels" with wine, and anointing their heads with oil. Only the first and last of these seem to be echoed in Psalm 23 (vv 5aα, 5bα), although "I drenched their bowels with wine" is similar to "My cup runs over."

But does the parallel extend further? One term that invites closer inspection is *ṣurrašun,* "their bowels." It is also found in other royal documents describing royal banquets.[1] Given the similarities already noted between Esarhaddon's inscription and Ps 23: 5–6, one is tempted to ask: Could there be a connection between *ṣurrašun* and *ṣrry*? Dahood has noted a number of passages in the Psalter where Hebrew *ṣrr* appears to be equivalent to Akkadian *ṣurru* (1966: 38 [Ps 6: 8], 63 [Ps 10: 5], 189 [Ps 31: 11]; 1968: 161 [Ps 69: 20]).

Understanding *ṣrry* as "my heart" (lit., "my bowels, innards") rather than "my foes" necessitates a reconsideration of *ngd*. The problem could be solved by reading **ngr* for *ngd,* presuming an early scribal confusion of *daleth* and *resh*. If **ngr* is the correct reading, it would be easy to explain why this relatively rare verb (10 × in the MT) would have been read by a copyist as *ngd*. This has actually happened in Ps 77: 3, where for MT *ngrh* (*niggěrâ*) the LXX has *enantion autou* (= *negdô*) and the Syriac *ngdtny*. We would parse **ngr* here as a *Nipʿal* infinitive absolute (*niggōr*); the verb is not attested in the *Qal*. On this reading Ps 23: 5 could be translated as follows.

You spread a table before me,
my heart overflows;
You anoint my head with oil,
my cup runs over.

**ngr* could be similar in meaning to *amkir(a)* in the Assyrian royal inscriptions ("I drenched"); *makāru* properly means "flood, irrigate" (CAD M/1 125a).[2] The Hebrew verb is found in only one other passage with a part of the body as subject: in Lam 3: 49 it occurs with *ʿyny* (*ʿyny ngrh wlʾ tdmh . . .*, "My eye will stream without stopping . . ."). Lamentations 3, it will be remembered, is the chapter containing a number of "reversals" of the imagery in Psalm 23. Could *ʿyny ngrh* be a reversal of Ps 23: 5aβ? It may be significant in this connection to note that *ʿyny* and *ṣrry* are parallel in Ps 6: 8 (Dahood 1966: 38).

The proposed **ngr ṣrry* would seem to fit the banquet context better than *ngd ṣrry*. It would also produce a number of interesting stylistic patterns. The first would involve the syntax of v 5.

5aα	verb + prepositional phrase + object
5aβ	verb + subject
5bα	verb + prepositional phrase + object
5bβ	subject + verb.[3]

The syntax of each bicolon is thus identical, except for the reversal of subject and verb in 5bβ. Note also

5aα	SUBJECT: Yahweh (second person)
5aβ	SUBJECT: my heart (third person + first person suffix)
5bα	SUBJECT: Yahweh (second person)
5bβ	SUBJECT: my cup (third person + first person suffix)

If we consider the nouns in v 5 which are not preceded by prepositions, the following pattern emerges.

5aα	NOUN: something associated with a banquet (*šlḥn*)
5aβ	NOUN: a part of the body (*ṣrry*)
5bα	NOUN: a part of the body (*rʾšy*)
5bβ	NOUN: something associated with a banquet (*kwsy*).

Here two sets of parallel terms, *šlḥn* // *kwsy*[4] and *ṣrry* // *rʾšy*,[5] are arranged chiastically.

The suggested emendation also produces a sonant pattern (*-ṓ, -áy*) in v 5a: *taʿărṓk lĕpānáy šulḥān* // *niggṓr ṣōrĕrāy*. There is also a triple *r* pattern in *niggōr ṣōrĕrāy*. Compare the *-ō, -ī* pattern and the triple *š* sound in v 5b: *diššantā baššemen rōʾšî* // *kōsî rāwāyâ*.

Notes

1. See Luckenbill 1924: 116.75–76: *ṣurrašin* (variant: *ṣurrašun*) *amkir*; 125.52: *ṣurrašin amkir*.

2. Actually *ngr* would seem to fit better with *kwsy* and *rwh* with *ṣrry*. The phrase *kwsy ngrh* would mean "My cup is spilling over, pouring over." Note Ps 75:9, where the two terms occur together: *ky kws byd yhwh . . . wygr mzh . . .*, "For (there is) a *cup* in Yahweh's hand . . . and he will *pour* from it. . . ." And *rwh ṣrry* would mean, "My heart [lit., bowels] is drenched." Compare *amkira ṣurrašun* in the Esarhaddon inscription, "I drenched their bowels (with wine)." Could the psalmist have switched the terms for poetic effect? This appears to be the case in, for example, Ps 1: 1: *ʾšry hʾyš ʾšr lʾ hlk bʿṣt ršʿym wbdrk ḥṭʾym lʾ ʿmd . . .*, "Happy the man who does not *walk* in the council of the wicked, nor *stand* in the way of sinners . . . ." One would expect *hlk* with *drk* (cf. 1 Kgs 18: 6; 2 Kgs 1: 18; 16: 3; 21: 22, etc.) and *ʿmd* with *ʿṣh* (cf. *ʿmd* with synonymous *swd* in Jer 23: 18, 22).

3. It is better to parse *rwyh* as a verb rather than as the *hapax legomenon rĕwāyâ* (noun) with the MT. We would read *rāwāyâ;* cf. *ḥāsāyâ napšî* in Ps 57: 2. In this way v 5b would begin and end with a perfect verb: *dšnt . . . rwyh*.

4. In *RSP I* 379 Dahood claims that *šlḥn* and *kwsy* are in parallelism in Ps 23: 5 and notes the parallelism of Ugaritic *ṯlḥny* and *ks* in *CTA* 4 III.15–16 (in the context of a divine banquet).

5. Note the parallelism of "their hearts/bowels" (*ṣurrašun*) and "their heads" (*muḫḫašunu*) in the Esarhaddon inscription cited above (p. 105) and in the Sennacherib inscription cited in n. 41 (see also Luckenbill 1924: 116.75–76).

References

ABL
Harper, R. F. 1892–1914. *Assyrian and Babylonian Letters Belonging to the Kouyunjik Collection of the British Museum.* 14 vols. Chicago: University of Chicago.

Alonso-Schökel, L.
1981 *Trienta Salmos: Poesia y Oracion.* Estudios de Antiguo Testamento 2. Madrid: Ediciones Christiandad.

Andersen, F. I.
1970 Biconsonantal Byforms of Weak Hebrew Roots. *Zeitschrift für die Alttestamentliche Wissenschaft* 82: 271–74.

———, and Freedman, D. N.
1980 *Hosea.* Anchor Bible 24. Garden City, NY: Doubleday.

Anderson, B. W.
1976 Exodus and Covenant in Second Isaiah and Prophetic Tradition. Pp. 339–60 in *Magnalia Dei: The Mighty Acts of God: Essays on the Bible and Archaeology in Memory of G. Ernest Wright,* ed. F. M. Cross et al. Garden City, NY: Doubleday.

Barré, M. L.
1978 New Light on the Interpretation of Hosea VI 2. *Vetus Testamentum* 28: 129–41.
1982 A Cuneiform Parallel to Ps 86: 16–17 and Mic 7: 16–17. *Journal of Biblical Literature* 101: 271–75.

BBS
King, L. W. 1912. *Babylonian Boundary-Stones and Memorial Tablets in the British Museum.* London: Oxford University.

Beaucamp, E.
1976 *Le Psautier: Ps 1–72.* Sources bibliques. Paris: Gabalda.

Begrich, J.
1938 *Studien zu Deuterojesaja.* Beiträge zur Wissenschaft vom Alten und Neuen Testament 25 [4th series]. Stuttgart: Kohlhammer.

Borger, R.
1961 Zu den Asarhaddon-Verträgen aus Nimrud. *Zeitschrift für Assyriologie* 54 [Neue Folge 20]: 173–96.
1967 *Die Inschriften Asarhaddons Königs von Assyrien.* Archiv für Orientforschung, Beiheft 9. Osnabrück: Biblio-Verlag [reprint of the 1956 edition].

BRM
Clay, A. T. 1923. *Babylonian Records in the Library of J. Pierpont Morgan.* Vol. 4. New Haven: Yale University.

Clements, R. E.
1965 *God and Temple.* Philadelphia: Fortress.

Cogan, M.
1974 *Imperialism and Religion: Assyria, Judah and Israel in the Eighth and Seventh Centuries* B.C.E. Society of Biblical Literature Monograph Series 19. Missoula, MT: Scholars Press.

Croatto, J. S.
1968 ṬŌBÂ como "amistad (de Alianza)" en el Antiguo Testamento. *Annali dell'istituto orientali di Napoli* 18 [new series]: 385–89.

Culley, R. C.
1967 *Formulaic Language in the Biblical Psalms.* Toronto: University of Toronto Press.

Dahood, M.
1966 *Psalms I: 1–50.* Anchor Bible 16. Garden City, NY: Doubleday.
1968 *Psalms II: 51–100.* Anchor Bible 17. Garden City, NY: Doubleday.
1970 *Psalms III: 101–150.* Anchor Bible 17A. Garden City, NY: Double-

day.

1979 Stichometry and Destiny in Psalm 23, 4. *Biblica* 60: 417–19.

Eaton, J. H.

1976 *Kingship and the Psalms.* Studies in Biblical Theology 2/32. London: SCM.

Ebeling, E.

1953 *Die akkadische Gebetsserie "Handerhebung" von neuem gesammelt und herausgegeben.* Berlin: Akademie-Verlag.

Eissfeldt, O.

1962 The Promises of Grace to David in Isaiah 55: 1–5. Pp. 196–207 in *Israel's Prophetic Heritage: Essays in Honor of James Muilenburg,* ed. B. W. Anderson and W. Harrelson. London: SCM.

Emmerson, G. I.

1975 The Structure and Meaning of Hosea VIII 1–3. *Vetus Testamentum* 25: 700–10.

F Friedrich, J. 1926–1930. *Staatsverträge des Hatti-Reiches in hethitischer Sprache.* Part 1: Mitteilungen der vorderasiatisch-ägyptischen Gesellschaft 31/1 (1926); Part 2: Mitteilungen der vorderasiatisch-ägyptischen Gesellschaft 34/1 (1930).

Fishbane, M.

1970 The Treaty Background of Amos 1: 11 and Related Matters. *Journal of Biblical Literature* 89: 313–18.

1972 Additional Remarks on *Rḥmyw* (Amos 1: 11). *Journal of Biblical Literature* 91: 391–93.

Fitzgerald, A.

1972 A Note on G-Stem *ynṣr* Forms in the Old Testament. *Zeitschrift für die Alttestamentliche Wissenschaft* 84: 90–92.

Fitzmyer, J. A.

1967 *The Aramaic Inscriptions of Sefîre.* Biblica et Orientalia 19. Rome: Pontifical Biblical Institute.

Fox, M.

1973 *Ṭôb* as Covenant Terminology. *Bulletin of the American Schools of Oriental Research* 209: 41–42.

Freedman, D. N.

1972 The Broken Construct Chain. *Biblica* 53: 534–36. Pp. 339–41 in *Pottery, Poetry, and Prophecy: Studies in Early Hebrew Poetry.* Winona Lake: Eisenbrauns.

1980 The Twenty-Third Psalm. Pp. 275–302 in *Pottery, Poetry, and Prophecy: Studies in Early Hebrew Poetry.* [Originally, 1976, pp. 139–66 in *Michigan Oriental Studies in Honor of George Cameron.* ed. L. L. Orlin et al. Ann Arbor, MI: Department of Near Eastern Studies, University of Michigan.]

GAG Soden, W. von. 1969. *Grundriss der akkadischen Grammatik.* Analecta Orientalia 33. Rome: Pontifical Biblical Institute.

Geller, S. A.

1979 *Parallelism in Early Biblical Poetry.* Harvard Semitic Monographs 20. Missoula, MT: Scholars Press.

Gibson, J. C. L.

1975 *Textbook of Syrian Semitic Inscriptions: 2: Aramaic Inscriptions.* Oxford: Clarendon.

Greenfield, J. C.

1978 Notes on the Asitawada (Karatepe) Inscription. *Eretz-Israel* 14: 74–77 [Hebrew; English summary on p. *125].

HALAT Baumgartner, W., *et al.* 1967– . *Hebräisches und aramäisches Lexikon zum Alten Testament*^{3}. Leiden: Brill.

Hillers, D. R.
1964a A Note on Some Treaty Terminology in the Old Testament. *Bulletin of the American Schools of Oriental Research* 176: 46–47.
1964b *Treaty-Curses and the Old Testament Prophets.* Biblica et Orientalia 16. Rome: Pontifical Biblical Institute.
1972 *Lamentations.* Anchor Bible 7A. Garden City, NY: Doubleday.

Holladay, W. L.
1974 *Jeremiah: Spokesman out of Time.* Philadelphia: United Church Press.

Huffmon, H.
1966 The Treaty Background of Hebrew *Yādaʿ*. *Bulletin of the American Schools of Oriental Research* 181: 31–37.

Hummel, H.
1957 Enclitic *Mem* in Early Northwest Semitic, Especially in Hebrew. *Journal of Biblical Literature* 76: 85–107.

Johag, I.
1977 *ṭwb*—Terminus Technicus in Vertrags–und Bündnis–formularen des alten Orients und des Alten Testaments. Pp. 3–23 in *Bausteine biblischer Theologie: Festgabe für G. Johannes Botterweck zum 60. Geburtstag dargebracht von seinen Schülern,* ed. H.-J. Fabry. Bonner Biblische Beiträge 50. Cologne/Bonn: Peter Hanstein Verlag.

Johnson, A. R.
1970 Psalm 23 and the Household of Faith. Pp. 255–71 in *Proclamation and Presence: Old Testament Essays in Honour of Gwynne Henton Davies,* ed. J. I. Durham and J. R. Porter. London: SCM.

KBo *Keilschrifttexte aus Boghazköi.* Leipzig/Berlin.

Knudtzon, J. A.
1915 *Die El-Amarna-Tafeln.* Vorderasiatische Bibliothek 2. Leipzig.

Kraus, H.-J.
1972 *Psalmen: 1–63.* 4th ed. Biblischer Kommentar: Altes Testament 15/1. Neukirchen-Vluyn: Neukirchener Verlag.

Le Déaut, R., and Robert, J.
1971 *Targum des Chroniques (Cod. Vat. Urb. Ebr. 1).* 2 vols. Analecta Biblica 51. Rome: Biblical Institute Press.

Luckenbill, D. D.
1924 *The Annals of Sennacherib.* Oriental Institute Publications 2. Chicago: University of Chicago.

McCarthy, D. J.
1972 *bĕrît* in Old Testament History and Theology. *Biblica* 53: 110–21.
1978 *Treaty and Covenant: A Study in Form in the Ancient Oriental Documents and in the Old Testament*[2]. Analecta Biblica 21A. Rome: Pontifical Biblical Institute.

Merrill, A. L.
1965 Psalm XXIII and the Jerusalem Tradition. *Vetus Testamentum* 15: 354–60.

Milne, P.
1974–75 √ Psalm 23: Echoes of the Exodus. *Sciences Religieuses/Studies in Religion* 4: 237–47.

Mittmann, S.
1980 Aufbau und Einheit des Danklieds Psalm 23. *Zeitschrift für Theologie und Kirche* 77: 1–23.

Moran, W. L.
1963 A Note on the Treaty Terminology of the Sefire Stelas. *Journal of Near Eastern Studies* 22: 173–76.

Mowinckel, S.
1962 *The Psalms in Israel's Worship.* 2 vols. New York: Abingdon.

Myers, J. M.
1974 — *II Chronicles.* Anchor Bible 13. Garden City, NY: Doubleday.

Oettinger, N.
1976 — *Die Militärischen Eide der Hethiter.* Studien zu den Boğazköy-Texten 22. Wiesbaden: Harrassowitz.

Postgate, J. N.
1969 — *Neo-Assyrian Royal Grants and Decrees.* Studia Pohl Series Major 1. Rome: Pontifical Biblical Institute.

PRU II — Virolleaud, C. 1957. *Le palais royal d'Ugarit II. Textes en cunéiformes alphabétiques des archives est, ouest et centrales.* Mission de Ras Shamra 7. Paris: Imprimerie nationale/Librairie C. Klincksieck.

Roberts, J. J. M.
1976 — The Religio-Political Setting of Psalm 47. *Bulletin of the American Schools of Oriental Research* 221: 129–32.

RSP I — Fisher, L. R., ed. 1972. *Ras Shamra Parallels: The Texts from Ugarit and the Hebrew Bible. Vol. 1.* Analecta Orientalia 49. Rome: Pontifical Biblical Institute.

Sanders, J.
1978 — Isaiah 55: 1–9. *Interpretation* 32: 290–95.

Schmidt, W. H.
1978 — *dābhar.* Vol. 3, pp. 94–125 in *Theological Dictionary of the Old Testament,* ed. G. J. Botterweck and H. Ringgren, trans. J. T. Willis et al. Grand Rapids, MI: Eerdmans.

Seux, M.-J.
1976 — *Hymnes et prières aux dieux de Babylonie et d'Assyrie.* Littératures anciennes du Proche-Orient 8. Paris: Editions du Cerf.

Sheriffs, D. C. T.
1979 — The Phrases *ina IGI DN* and *lipĕney Yhwh* in Treaty and Covenant Contexts. *Journal of Northwest Semitic Languages* 7: 55–68.

Streck, M.
1916 — *Assurbanipal und die letzten assyrischen Könige bis zum Untergange Niniveh's.* 2 vols. Vorderasiatische Bibliothek 4. Leipzig: Hinrichs.

Tawil, H.
1974 — Some Literary Elements in the Opening Sections of the Hadad, Zākir, and the Nērab II Inscriptions in the Light of East and West Semitic Royal Inscriptions. *Orientalia* 43: 40–65.

Thureau-Dangin, F.
1912 — *Une relation de la huitième campagne de Sargon.* Textes cunéiformes du Louvre 3. Paris: Librairie Paul Geuthner.

Tigay, J. H.
1970 — Psalm 7: 5 and Ancient Near Eastern Treaties. *Journal of Biblical Literature* 89: 178–86.

Tromp, N. J.
1969 — *Primitive Conceptions of Death and the Nether World in the Old Testament.* Biblica et Orientalia 21. Rome: Pontifical Biblical Institute.

Vogt, E.
1953 — The "Place of Life" of Ps 23. *Biblica* 34: 195–211.

VTE — Wiseman, D. J. 1958. *The Vassal-Treaties of Esarhaddon.* London: British School of Archaeology in Iraq. [= *Iraq* 20 (1958) Part I.]

W — Weidner, E. F. 1923. *Politische Dokumente aus Kleinasien: Die Staatsverträge in akkadischer Sprache aus dem Archiv von Boghazköi.* Boghazköi-Studien 8. Leipzig: Hinrichs.

Waldman, N. M.
1979 A Biblical Echo of Mesopotamian Royal Rhetoric. Pp. 449–55 in *Essays on the Occasion of the Seventieth Anniversary of the Dropsie University 1909–1979,* ed. A. Katsh and L. Nemoy. Philadelphia: Dropsie University.

Weinfeld, M.
1972 *Deuteronomy and the Deuteronomic School.* Oxford: Clarendon.
1973 Covenant Terminology in the Ancient Near East and Its Influence on the West. *Journal of the American Oriental Society* 93: 190–99.

Williamson, H.
1978 "The Sure Mercies of David": Subjective or Objective Genitive? *Journal of Semitic Studies* 23: 31–49.

van der Woude, A. S.
1976 *pānīm* Angesicht. Vol. 2, cols. 432–60 in *Theologisches Handwörterbuch zum Alten Testament,* ed. E. Jenni and C. Westermann. Munich: Kaiser Verlag/Zurich: Theologischer Verlag.

van Zyl, A. H.
1963 Psalm 23. Pp. 64–83 in *Studies on the Psalms: Papers Read at the 6th Meeting Held at the Potchefstroom University for the C. H. E. 29–31 January 1963,* ed. P. A. H. de Boer. Die Ou Testamentiese werkgemeenschap in Suid-Africa. Potchefstroom: Pro Rege-Pers Beperk.

Studies in the Structure of Hebrew Verse: The Prosody of Lamentations 1: 1–22

Frank Moore Cross
Harvard University, Cambridge, Massachusetts

Since the eighteenth century the study of Hebrew poetry has tended to focus on the semantic symmetries of Hebrew verse: binary structures conventionally termed *parallelismus membrorum*. Fault has been found with the term "parallelism," which indeed fails to comprehend the full binarism of Hebrew poetry, even at the lexical and semantic level. However, alternate terms are unlikely to replace the traditional term which has been taken up enthusiastically in the comparative study of a wide range of orally-composed literatures which exhibit similar features. Intense scholarly energy has also been directed toward the analysis of auditory features of Hebrew poetry in inconclusive searches for the structure of Hebrew meter. A variety of systems have been proposed. The dominant system, usually called after the names of Ley and Sievers, postulates an accentual rhythm, in which the basic units are cola of three stressed syllables or alternately cola of two stressed syllables, given the notation 3 + 3 or 2 + 2. More loosely Hebrew meter has been described as "word" meter, basic units of three words or two words which may be given the same notation. Much poetry of the early period (i.e., the era when oral composition was lively and flourishing) can be fitted to these systems presuming some minor use of poetic license. The real difficulty with these systems of metrical analysis is that they fail to reflect the full or precise symmetries of early Hebrew verse and wholly break down when applied to late Hebrew verse, in which new prosodic canons rooted in written composition evolved and became dominant.[1]

The papers of the late Roman Jakobson dealing with "grammatical parallelism" in traditional (oral) poetry have greatly deepened our insight into "the refinement in 'verbal polyphony' and its semantic tension." Jakobson showed how "Pervasive parallelism inevitably activates all the levels of language—the distinctive features, inherent and prosodic, the morphologic and syntactic categories and forms, the lexical units and their semantic classes in both their convergences and divergences acquire an autonomous poetic value" (Jakobson 1966: 423). His illustrations come from Finnish, Chinese, and especially Russian and Hebrew traditional poetry. His work has stimulated a number of recent studies of Canaanite (Ugaritic) and Hebrew poetry which have tightened our controls upon the prosodic canons of Hebrew poetry as well as extended our understanding of its complexity.[2]

I wish to present in this paper the first of two studies of a complex verse form first isolated in Budde's study of the meter of laments, and since commonly called Qinah meter.[3] Here I shall take up the acrostic lament found in the first chapter of Lamentations making use of new textual resources found in 4QLam[a]. David Noel

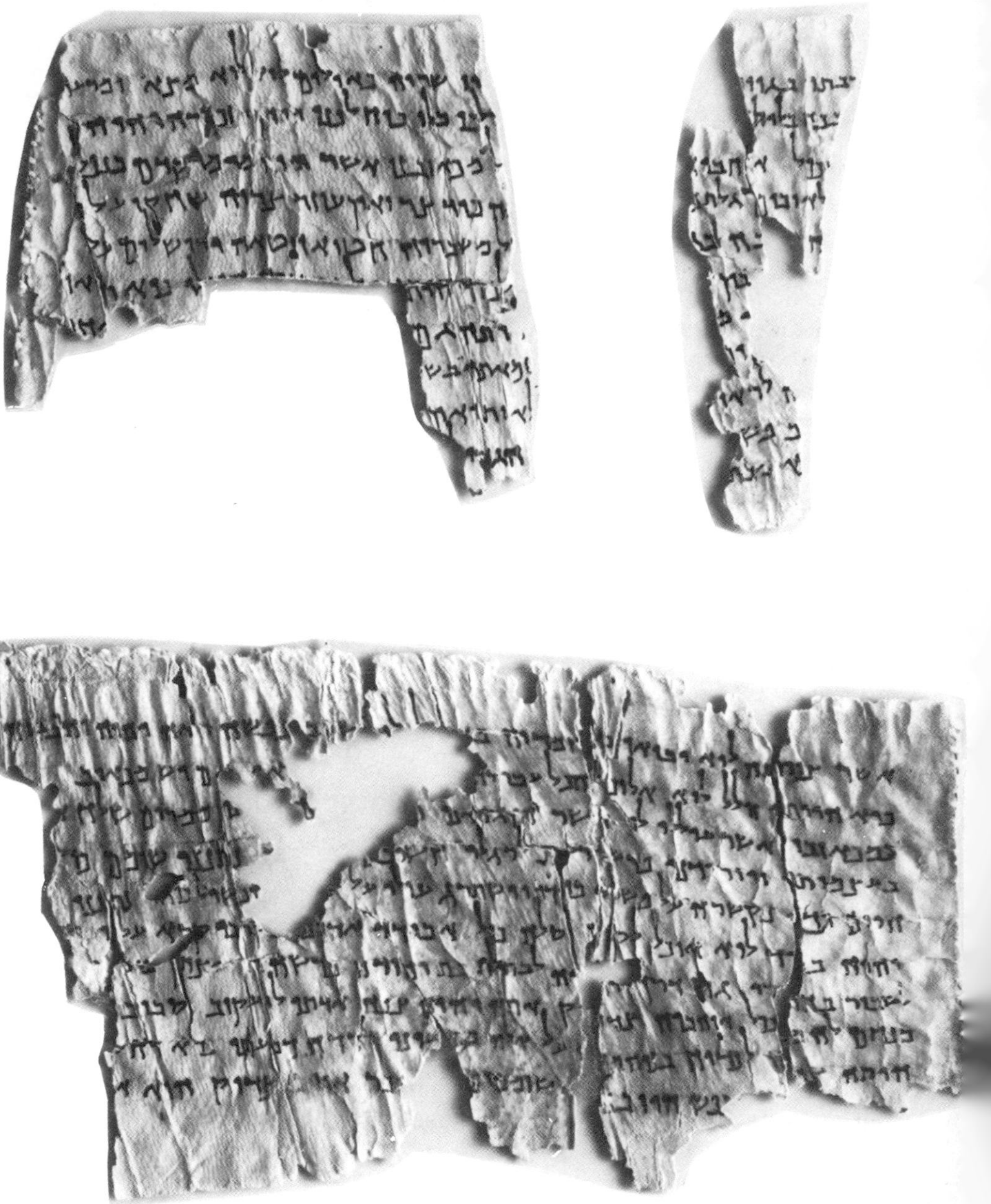

4QLamentations[a]. Photograph, Department of Antiquities, State of Israel.

Freedman's contributions to the study of the acrostic lament are well known (Freedman 1972a, b). I have been pleased, therefore, to prepare this study as an act of homage to Professor Freedman, a cherished friend, frequent coworker, and respected colleague of thirty-five years. In the second paper (to appear in the anniversary volume for George Mendenhall) we shall turn to a more traditional and superior exemplar of the verse form preserved in the Psalm of Jonah.

In our first study of ancient Yahwistic poetry, Noel Freedman and I recognized two basic building blocks of Hebrew and Ugaritic poetry, the so-called three-stress colon and the so-called two-stress colon, structured to form balanced or symmetrical bicola and tricola (Cross and Freedman 1975: 8–12). At the same time, we observed that apparent violations of the balance of stress often occurred without violating the canons of symmetry. "It may be very difficult or impossible to assign the same number of stresses to parallel cola; at the same time they may have an equal number of syllables and balance perfectly. Thus it appears that a deep sense of symmetry is the guiding principle of metrical structure, and that the stress pattern (3: 3; 2: 2) is only the most convenient . . . method of expressing this symmetry" (Cross and Freedman 1975: 9).

As an alternate to accentual balance, we have searched for syllabic symmetry of one kind or another. Here the difficulties are different, but no less formidable. Syllabic symmetry obtains, with extraordinary frequency, between the cola in a single bicolon or single tricolon, but rarely persists throughout a sequence of bicola or tricola. An example may be taken from CTA 23: 49–51 (cf. 55–56).

yáhburu šapatêhúmā yíšša[qu]	11
hín šapatāhúmā matuqatā́mi	11
matuqatāmi kalarammānīma	11
bámā nášaqi wa-hárī	8
ba-ḫúbuqi ḫimḫámatu	8

He bowed, he kissed their lips;
Behold their lips were sweet,
Sweet like pomegranates.

In kissing there was conceiving,
In embracing, heat of conception.

The symmetry of the first tricolon is clear, eleven syllables to the colon (though the stress pattern is asymmetrical); the bicolon is symmetrical, but with eight syllables to the bicolon. Another example is found in CTA 2.4.23–27 (cf. 13–18).

wa-yírtaqiṣ ṣamdu badế báʿli	10
{kámā} nášri ba-ʾuṣbaʿā́tihu	10
yálimu qúdquda zubū́li {yámmi}	11
bêna ʿênếmi ṯápiṭi náhari	11
yapársiḫu yámmu	6
yaqíllu la-ʾárṣi	6

tinnaǵiṣna pinnấtihu 8
wa-yádlupu taműnihu 8
yaqúṯṯu báʿlu wa-yáštī yámma 10
yakálliyu ṯấpiṭa náhara 10

The mace swooped in the hands of Baʿl,
Like a vulture in his fingers.

He smote the back of Prince Sea,
Between the eyes of Judge River.

Sea fell,
Sank to the earth.

His joints trembled,
His frame collapsed.

Baʿl crushed and drank Sea,
He annihilated Judge River.

The first and second bicola have long cola; each is symmetrical; and the fifth bicolon, with long cola, is symmetrical. The third bicolon with short cola is balanced, as is the fourth, again with short cola, but the balance is limited to the bicolon. In the same general context (CTA 2.4.10) is this marvelously assonant bicolon.

tíqqaḥa múlka ʿālámika 9
dárkata dấta dārdấrika 9

May you take thy eternal kingship,
Thy rule which will be forever.

Thus we have discovered sequences of individually symmetrical bicola, but having syllable counts 6: 6, 8: 8, 9: 9, 10: 10, and 11: 11.[4]

My conclusion has been that the ancient Canaanite and Hebrew poets were not counting syllables, at least in the pattern familiar in other oral, syllabic verse. It must be emphasized, moreover, that the oral formulae of Ugaritic and early Hebrew meter are binary, not chronemic as in Greek epic verse. These are constructed in pairs: word, phrase, and colon pairs, including paired epithets and proper names, complementing grammatical parallelism at every level.

It has been my practice for many years, therefore, to use a notation *l(ongum)* and *b(reve)* to label respectively the long colon and the short colon fundamental to Hebrew verse, a notation which leaves open the question of auditory (stress/quantitative) rhythm.[5] Often it is useful to note the syllable count in verse as an indication of its levels of balance in a bicolon or tricolon, or in a couplet or triplet of more complex structure, but such counts imply in my analysis no theory of chronemic meter.

In archaic poetry the standard verse forms are the *l:l* and *l:l:l*. In lyric poetry one often finds b:b::b:b, or better 2(b:b), and b:b::b:b::b:b, i.e., 3 (b:b). The simple verse b:b exists but is rare. In verse composed of b units, parallelism is ordinarily between two bicola forming a couplet (b:b // b:b), but parallelism also appears not infrequently between the cola (b // b), which, along with the regularity of the caesural pause, confirms the analysis that the unit is a short colon.

In such early poems as the Song of the Sea and the Lament of David, one finds the combination of these verse forms, often referred to as "mixed meter," usually in sequences of couplets and triplets, e.g., 2(b:b)–*l*:*l*–3(b:b)–*l*:*l*:*l*, etc. (Cross 1973: 126).

The complex verse form found *inter alia* in Lamentations 1 and the Psalm of Jonah—Budde's "Qinah meter"—was first analyzed in stress notation as 3:2; alternately it has been described as 5:5. Each description has merit, each defects. The dominant structure I shall argue is *l*:b::*l*:b (using our notation) in which grammatical and semantic binarism is chiefly between corresponding bicola. However, "internal" parallelism between the "mixed" (long and short) cola of the individual bicolon is not infrequent, especially in older, orally-composed verse of this type. While *l*:b::*l*:b is the most frequent verse pattern, there are also variant patterns: *l*:b::b:*l*, b:*l*::*l*:b, etc. In the older examples of this complex verse the variant patterns are used more widely than in later verse, and with greater effect.

The analysis of the prosody of Hebrew verse has always been complicated by two difficult, but necessary tasks: the establishment of a sound text, and the reconstruction of the early Hebrew language in which the poetry was composed. In fact, progress in the study of Hebrew prosody has been slow in direct relation to the data available for textual and historico-linguistic research. To be sure there are scholars—frequently those with a traditional approach to the received text—who choose to ignore these tasks in their analysis and then issue pronouncements, usually asserting the "irregularity" of Hebrew prosody. Such analyses, unless designed for an apologetic end, serve little purpose. No one seriously doubts that verse preserved in a corrupt text in "modernized" Hebrew is irregular. At the same time the interdependence of the tasks of analysis and reconstruction, prosodic, textual, and historico-linguistic, involves the student of Hebrew poetry in the circular reasoning inevitable in all complex inductive research. Accordingly, premature or forced theories proliferate, and progress toward sound results is halting. Fortunately, epigraphic research is producing rich new data for the reconstruction of the history of the Hebrew dialects, and new textual resources are greatly facilitating our understanding of the textual history of biblical works. More rapid progress in the study of Hebrew prosody may thus be anticipated.

2. The Lamentations manuscript published here, 4QLam^{a}, is inscribed in a Herodian script belonging to the tradition I have termed "vulgar semi-formal" (Cross 1961: 173–81). Its leather is tan or beige and rough in texture. Portions of three columns of Chapter 1 of Lamentations are preserved: Column I (of the material extant), containing eleven lines of script (1: 1aβ-6); Column II, containing also eleven lines of script (1: 6–10); and Column III, containing ten lines of writing (1: 10–16). A small fragment from later in the scroll (2:5) also is extant. We do not possess the first column(s) of the scroll. Column III is substantially preserved, albeit in shrunken and wrinkled condition, and with lacework produced by worms. It measures about 10 cm. high (the width of the scroll), the lined portion forming a column of writing about 15 cm. broad, 7 cm. high. Column II was about 8 cm. broad, as was Column I, to judge in the latter case from its reconstruction. In

antiquity these measurements undoubtedly would have been larger; they have been reduced by the shrinkage of the leather. Irregular shrinkage, it should be noted, has produced vertical splitting of the leather. The orthographic style of the manuscript is the late, full Palestinian type which developed in Maccabean times (Cross 1966: 89). There follows a reconstruction of its text.

Column I (Lam 1: 1aβ-6)

1 [היתה כאלמנה] רׄבתי בגוים֯ [שרתי במדינות]
2 [היתה למס בכה ת]בכה בלילה֯ [ודמעתה על]
3 [לחיה אין לה מנחם] מ֯כול או֯הביה֯ [כול רעיה]
4 [בגדו בה היו לה] לאיבים גלתהׄ [יהודה מעני]
5 [ומרוב עבודה היא]ה י֯[ש]בׄה בג[וים לוא מצאה]
6 [מנוח כול רדפיה השיגוה] בין [המצרים דרכי]
7 [ציון אבלות מבלי בא]י מ[ועד כול שעריה]
8 [שוממים כוהניה נאנ]ח֯ים [בתולותיה נוגות]
9 [והיאה מר לה היו צר]יה לראוש֯ [איביה שלו]
10 [כיא יהוה הוגה על רו]ב פשע֯[יה עולליה הלכו]
11 [שבי לפני צריה ויצ]א מבת [ציון כול הדרה]

Column II (Lam 1: 6-10)

1 [ה]יו שריה כאילים לואׄ לוא מצא ומרעה
2 [ו]יׄלכו בלי כוח לפני רודף זכו֯רה יהוה
3 [כו]ל מכאובנו אשר היו מימי קדם בנפל
4 [עמ]ה ביד צר ואין עוזר צריה שחקו על
5 [כו]ל משבריה חטוא חטאה ירושלים על
6 [כן] לנוד היתה֯ [כו]ל [מכב]ד֯י֯ה֯ ה֯ז֯י֯לו כיא ראו
7 [ע]ר֯ותה גם [היאה נאנחה ותשב] א֯חור֯
8 טׄמאתה בש[וליה לוא זכרה אחריתה ותרד]
9 [פ]לאות ואין [מנחם לה ראה יהוה את עניי]
10 [כי] הגד֯יל [אויב ידו פרש צר על כול]
11 [מחמ]ד֯יה כיא ראתה גוים באו מקדשה]

Column III (Lam 1: 10-16)

1 אשר צויתה לוא יבואו מחמדיה באו֯כ֯ל להׄשיב נפשה ראה יהוה והבטה
2 כיא הייתי זולל לוא אליכ[ן]הכול עבריׄ דׄ[רך הביטו ור]אוׄ אם יש מכאוב
3 כמכאבי אשר עוללו לי אשר הוגירני י[הוה ביו]ם [חרו]נו ממרום שלח אׄ[ש]
4 בעצמותי ויורידנו פרש רש֯ת לרגלי הׄשיבנׄיׄ [אחו]ר֯ נתנני שומם כול
5 הׄיום וד[ו]י נקשרה על פשעי בידו וישתרג עולו על צ֯[וארי] הׄכשיל כוחׄי נתנני
6 יהוה ביד לוא אוכל לקו֯םׄ סלה כול אבידי אדו֯נ֯יׄ ב֯קרבי קרא עלי מׄו֯[עד]

7 לשבור בחורי גת דרך יה̊ו̊ה לבתו̊לת בת יהודה פרשה / / /* ציון בי̊[דיה אין]
8 מנחם לה מכול אוהביה צדיק אתה יהוה צפה אדוני ליעקוב סביב[יו צריו]
9 היתה צי̇ון לנדוח בניהמ̇ה̊ על אלה בכו̊ עיני ירדה דמעתי כיא רחק̇ [ממני]
10 מ̊[נחם משיב] נפש היו בני̊ שוממים [כיא] ג̇בר אויב צדיק הוא א[דוני כיא]

*erasure

3. In the following notes we shall take up the verses of the acrostic *seriatim*, giving special attention to (1) textual problems and (2) problems of poetic artifice.

Verse 1 א

How alone does she sit,	איכה ישבה בדד	[7]	*l*	1.
The city (which was) mistress of people.	העיר רבתי עם	[6]	b	2.
She has become as a widow,	היתה כאלמנה	[7]	*l*	3.
(One who was) mistress among the nations.	רבתי בגוים	[6]	b	4.
(One who was) princess among the provinces,	שרתי במדינות	[7]	*l*	5.
She has become a serf.	היתה למס	[5]	b	6.

The structure of the triplet is *l*:b::*l*:b::*l*:b. The syllable count reveals the symmetry of the verse. If one attempts to scan either in stress or "word" meter he must resort to license in each of the three bicola. Parallelism is elaborately structured. Correspondence is between the first, third, and sixth cola, and between the second, fourth, and fifth cola.

1.	איכה ישבה בדד	2.	העיר רבתי עם
3.	היתה כאלמנה	4.	רבתי בגוים
6.	היתה למס	5.	שרתי במדינות

Cola 1, 3, and 6 possess the parallel verbal elements, and metaphors of the sad end of the personified city. Cola 2, 4, and 5 list epithets of the city reflecting her former estate. The correspondence of colon 1 and 6 is chiastic, colon 1 an *l* in first position in the bicolon, colon 6 a b in second position in its bicolon; at the same time, first and last, the cola yield cyclic structure, an *inclusio*. Colon 3 (*l*) and colon 6 (b) beginning with the repetition of *hyth* form a similar chiasm in position; colon 4 (b) and colon 5 (*l*) are positionally chiastic. Repetition of *rbty* is to be noted, tying together structurally cola 2 and 4 as does the repetition of *b* in *rbty bgwym* and *śrty bmdynwt*; the repetition of the archaizing forms *rbty—rbty—śrty* further links cola 2, 4, and 5. These repetitions, including that of *hyth* initially in colon 3 and colon 6, create auditory as well as semantic and grammatical correspondence. The first two words of colon 1 and colon 3 end in the syllable *-â* as does the first word of syllable 6. While this may not be conscious artifice, it should be noted since in Israel's early poetry studied sequences of phonemic and syllabic assonance (parallelism) abound. Finally we should not forget the commonly recognized formulaic pair *ʿm-gwym* extended here in the triplet with *mdynwt* (cola 2, 4, 5).

These observations make clear that the parallelistic structure is far more intricate than the simple semantic correspondence of the three bicola (1–2 // 3–4 // 5–6). The poet consciously manipulates both the short (b) cola and the long (*l*) cola for "dense" poetic structure.

The expression *rbty ʿm* has traditionally been taken to mean "full of people" and been compared to *rbt bnym ʾmllh* (1 Sam 2:5). Recently it has been argued that *rbty* must be taken as the familiar epithet *rbt* "lady, mistress" (McDaniel 1968: 29–31). The correspondence with *rbt bgwym* and especially *śrty bmdynwt* requires this understanding of *rbty* in my opinion, but I see no reason to exclude a play on alternate idiomatic meanings of *rbt* in the second colon.[6]

Verse 2 ב

She weeps bitterly in the night;	בכה תבכה בלילה	[7]	*l*	1.
Tears are on her cheek.	דמעה על לחיה	[5]	b	2.
There is none to comfort her	אין לה מנחם	[5]	b	3.
Among all her lovers.	מכל אהביה	[6]	*l*	4.
All her friends have deceived her;	כל רעיה בגדו בה	[8]	*l*	5.
They have become her enemies.	היו לה לאיבים	[7]	b	6.

In colon 1 we have restored the earlier orthographic form of *bkh* (MT *bkw*); in colon 2 we prefer *dmʿh* to *wdmʿth*.[7] The repetition of the pronoun is tautological and awkward. Moreover, the colon appears to have been influenced by a text like that of 4QLam in v 16 where *bkw* and *dmʿty* stand in parallelism (see below). There is no direct textual support of our preferred reading. 4QLam has been reconstructed to conform to MT, but this is arbitrary. We cannot distinguish between readings differing only by a letter or two in length. The Greek text of Lamentations is of relatively little use; it belongs to the *kaige* (Proto-Theodotionic) school which corrected to a Hebrew text of Proto-Rabbinic type (Barthélemy 1963: 33, 47). The secondary introduction of the conjunction *w* at the beginning of cola is, of course, extremely frequent, as has been shown in the study of texts in parallel transmission.[8]

The structure of the triplet is *l*:b::b:*l*::*l*:b. There is "internal" parallelism between colon 1 and colon 2 as well as between colon 5 and colon 6. In the first instance the formulaic pair *bky* // *dmʿ*, well known in both Ugaritic and Hebrew poetry, is noteworthy. The second and third bicola of the triplet are intricately linked by parallelism and chiasm. Colon 3 and colon 6, positionally chiastic, are bound by the opposition *ʾyn lh – hyw lh*. Colon 4 and colon 5, positionally chiastic, begin with *(m)kl ʾhbyh* and *kl rʿyh*. *ʾhb* and *rʿ* form a formulaic pair in Hebrew poetry, and in the present instance *ʾhbyh* is juxtaposed to *ʾybym* in colon 6, an extension of the formulaic pair with an antonym which at the same time produces assonance between the final members of each bicolon (*ʾhb* / *ʾyb*). The repetition of the syllable/word *-lâ* / *lāh* is hardly fortuitous in colon 1 (*blylh*), colon 3 (*lh*), and colon 6 (*lh*), with its cyclic distribution. The colon *ʾyn lh mnḥm* is repeated in variant forms at intervals throughout the lament: v 9 (*ʾyn mnḥm lh*), v 17 (*ʾyn mnḥm lh*) and v 21 (*ʾyn mnḥm ly*).

The distribution of this colon in its variations is interesting: twice in vv 1–11 (Part I, prevailingly 3rd person), and twice in vv 12–22 (Part II, prevailingly 1st person). Further it appears first in the second triplet from the beginning of the poem (v 2 *ʾyn lh mnḥm*), last in the second but final triplet (v 21 *ʾyn mnḥm ly*). Such long range repetition suggests that the lament was composed in writing, as does the use of certain prosaic elements necessary to the structure of the poem, elements absent or excessively rare in older, orally-composed verse. This is not surprising. In the sixth century we find evidence broadly of major transformations and new configurations of poetic genres and styles—imitative of old oral forms in part, and still using language originating in oral formulae, but anticipating many elements of later poetry certainly composed in writing— which mark a watershed in the evolution of biblical poetry.

Verse 3 ג

Judah is gone into exile out of (great) affliction,	גלתה יהודה מעני	[9]	*l*	1.
And out of abundance of servitude.	ומרב עבדה	[6]	b	2.
She herself sits among the nations;	היאה ישבה בגוים	[8]	*l*	3.
She has found no rest.	לא מצאה מנוח	[6]	b	4.
All who pursued her have overtaken her,	כל רדפיה השיגוה	[9]	*l*	5.
Within the straits.	בין המצרים	[5]	b	6.

We have chosen the archaic, long form of the pronoun *hyʾh* in colon 3 with 4QLam. To be sure, at Qumrân there is a secondary multiplication of such forms; on the other hand MT has tended to level through the short forms even in poetic contexts where the form properly survived. The bicola in this triplet tend to be long; thus the longer pronoun heightens the symmetry.

The structure of the triplet is *l*:b::*l*:b::*l*:b.

There is "internal" parallelism betwen the elements in the first bicolon, an "echo" parallelism, as well as the expected correspondence of the first and second bicola. On the other hand the correspondence between colon 3 and colon 4 is vague; colon 4 (b) is more closely linked semantically with colon 5 (*l*) with which it is in chiastic tension.

Elements of auditory correspondence are not dramatic, but note *-â* / *-â* ending the first two words of colon 1 and colon 3 echoed in *–â* in colon 2 (*ʿbdh*) and colon 4 (*mṣʾh*). The repetition of the nasal *m* may be observed: *mʿny*, *mrb*, *mṣʾh*, *mnwḥ*, and the (unusual) *hmṣrym*.

Long range structure appears in the sequence, "the city, the mistress" (v 1), "Judah (as a maiden)" v 3 (cf. *bt yhwdh*, "Maiden Judah," v 15), "Zion" or "Maiden Zion" (*bt ṣywn*) vv 4, 6, and "Jerusalem" (as a maiden) vv 7, 8. Compare v 17 where "Zion" and "Jerusalem" stand in the same triplet in parallelism.

Verse 4 ד

The ways of Zion mourn	דרכי ציון אבלות	[8]	*l*	1.
Because none comes to the sacral assembly.	מבלי באי מועד	[7]	b	2.

All her gates are desolate;	כל שעריה שממים	[8] *l* 3.
Her priests sigh.	כהניה נאנחים	[7] b 4.
Her virgins are led away,	בתולתיה נהוגות	[8] *l* 5.
And she is bitter.	והיאה מר לה	[5] b 6.

This triplet like the last is composed of long bicola.[9] Its structure is *l*:b::*l*:b::*l*:b. Binary parallels and contrasts are complex in the verse, and generally misunderstood. Colon 1 (Zion's streets mourn), colon 4 (Her priests sigh), and colon 6 (She [Zion] is bitter) are strictly parallel, colon 6 returning to colon 1 as an *inclusio*. Colon 2 (none enters the assembly [in the sanctuary]) and colon 5 (her virgins are led out) correspond (no men enter—virgins go out—*bʾy-nhwgwt*)[10] in a second cyclic device. At another level there is parallelism between elements in colon 1 (Zion's streets), colon 3 ([Zion's] gates), and less strictly *ʾblwt* (colon 1) and *šmmym* (colon 3), which belong in the same semantic field, and contrast in gender. Grammatical parallelism also obtains between *nʾnḥym* and *nhwgwt*, passive participles, beginning with *nun*, contrasting in gender.

The reading *nhwgwt*, MT *nwgwt* requires discussion. Generally *nwgwt* has been taken as an anomalous *Nipʿal* participle of a root *ygy*, "to suffer" (cf. *hwgh* v 5), appearing only here and in Zeph 3:18, in the expression *nwgy mmwʿd*. The latter is most difficult and has also been analyzed as from *ygy* II "to thrust away, exclude." The Greek here translated *ʾagomenai*, obviously for *n(h)wgwt*, Aquila *diōkomenai*, probably on the basis of *nwgy* in Zeph 3: 18 (*ygy* II); Symmachus has (inexactly) *aichmalōtoi*, "prisoners." To complicate matters, Hebrew furnishes a *nhg* II "to mourn"; cf. Syriac *yhg*. There is no problem in taking the reading of MT, *nwgwt*, as standing for *nhwgwt*. The syncope of intervocalic *he* in speech and writing is evidenced already in pre-Exilic Hebrew inscriptions, and is frequent, not to say ubiquitous, in the manuscripts of Qumrân and contemporary material (e.g., the Nash Papyrus). The structures of the poem must be determinative. Our analysis above suggests strongly that *nhwgwt*, "led out," rather than a meaning "mourn" from *ygy* (I), is to be preferred. I should add, negatively, that reading "mourn" makes for a mechanical, unvaried, even wearisome, parallelism.

In the case of *šwmmyn* of the Massoretic Text, we have corrected to *šwmmym* on the assumption that this is simply one of many instances, well documented at Qumrân, of a scribal slip with later (or dialectal) ending—*-în* replacing classical *-îm*. Cf. *šwmmym* (v 16) and *šmmh* (v 13).

The expression *bʾy mwʿd* is to be compared with *bʾw mqdšh* and *lwʾ ybwʾw* [*mwʿdyh*] (4QLam, see below), said of the nations in v 10. This is another instance of "long-range structure," the extension of the parallelistic principle beyond the units of verse or triplet. And again, in v 18 the theme of virgins (and striplings) going captive, and in v 19 priests (and elders) expiring, recall the themes here in v 4.

Verse 5 ה

Her adversaries have become head;	היו צריה לראש	[7] *l* 1.
Her enemies are at ease.	איביה שלו	[6] b 2.

But Yahweh had made her suffer	כי יהוה הוגה	[5] b 3.
For the multitude of her transgressions.	על רב פשעיה	[6] *l* 4.
Her children have gone—	עלליה הלכו	[7] *l* 5.
Captives before the adversary.	שבי לפני צר	[6] b 6.

The structure of the triplet is *l*:b::b:*l*::*l*:b. The first bicolon has internal parallelism, the formulaic pair *ṣr* / *ʾyb* in evidence. At the same time colon 2 (enemies at ease) corresponds by contrast with colon 3 (Zion made to suffer). Colon 1 *ṣryh lrʾš* also stands in contrast with colon 6 *lpny ṣr*, the elements *rʾš* and *pny* consciously chosen, *ṣr* in each forming an *inclusio*, victors and vanquished, juxtaposed in position.

At longer range, colon 2, "her enemies are at ease," recalls v 3, colon 4, "she finds no rest," and *mrb pšʿym* colon 4 echoes *mrb ʿbdh*, v 3, colon 2. The final bicolon also has parallelistic links with v 6, the final bicolon:

עלליה הלכו	שבי לפני צר
וילכו בלי כח	לפני רדף

Verse 6 ו

And there went forth from Daughter Zion	ויצא מבת ציון	[7] *l* 1.
All her splendor.	כל הדרה	[4] b 2.
Her princes became like stags	היו שריה כאילים	[9] *l* 3.
That find no pasturage.	לא מצאו מרעה	[6] b 4.
And they went on without strength,	וילכו בלי כח	[7] *l* 5.
Before the chaser.	לפני רודף	[5] b 6.

The Hebrew *ʾylym* was read *ʾēlîm* by the Greek translator and by Jerome. Ehrlich is probably correct, however, in arguing that *ʾayyālîm* of MT is better. The figure seems to be that of the chase in the final bicolon, and *rdp* is used of hunting (1 Sam 26:20).

In colon 4, the text of 4QLam is corrupt. *lwʾ lwʾ* is an obvious dittography, and the sequence *mṣʾ wmrʿh* is wrongly divided—a sleepy scribe. On the other hand 4QLam *bly kwḥ* is perhaps to be preferred over MT *blʾ kwḥ*. *blʾ* arises easily from misreading *bly* as *blw* corrected orthographically to *blʾ*. It is not easy to see how an original *blʾ* would have been corrupted to *bly*.

The structure of the triplet is *l*:b::*l*:b::*l*:b. The cola of the second bicolon are both long, in contrast to the first and third bicola, which are comparatively short. The triplet is rather devoid of artifice. The unusual *waw*-consecutive *wyṣʾ* beginning colon 1 is decreed by the acrostic form but is inelegant judged by older poetic norms.[11] The repetition of the grammatical form beginning colon 5, *wylkw*, accents a faint parallelism. Stronger synonymous parallelism is found actually between the third bicolon of the verse and the final bicolon of verse 5 (see above).

Verse 7 ז

Remember, Yahweh, her troubles,	זכרה יהוה מרודיה	[8]	*l*	1.
Which are from the days of old.	אשר מימי קדם	[6]	b	2.
When her people fell into the adversary's hand,	בנפל עמה ביד צר	[8]	*l*	3.
And she had no helper,	ואין עוזר לה	[5]	b	4.
The adversaries looked on her, gloating,	ראוה צרים	[5]	b	5.
They mocked at her ruins.	שחקו על משבריה	[8]	*l*	6.

As long recognized, the Massoretic Text of v 7 is corrupt, and, as often is the case when corruption has occurred, it has spread like a cancer. 4QLam presents us with a badly corrupt text also, but the corruptions are not identical. By tracing the history of the readings, we believe progress can be made toward establishing a text which gave rise to the variant corrupt forms of the text.

There appear to be two primary sources of corruption. Most serious is the development by misreading of an original *mrwdyh* (variant *kl mrwdyh*) as *kl mḥm(w)dyh*. *mḥmdyh* (v 11 4QLam) and *kl mḥmdyh* (v 10) are presumably the cause of the "assimilation" or anticipation triggering the error. MT in its present form preserves a doublet: *wmrwdyh kl mḥmdyh*. The inappropriateness of *mḥmdyh* "her delights" in this context is evident. MT has suffered yet another expansion, by conflation with the parallel readings: *zkr ʿnyy wmrwdy* from Lam 3:19.

4QLam for original *mrwdyh* reads *mkʾwbnw* (for *mkʾwbyh*), either as a revision of the rare word under the influence of *mkʾwb* / *mkʾby* later in the lament (vv 12, 18), or much more likely, as a correction, conscious or unconscious, of the impossible *mḥm(w)dyh* in its manuscript tradition: *kl mḥmwdyh* > *kl mkʾwbyh*.

The second point of infection is the form *zkrh*; MT reads the 3.f.s. perfect, 4QLam the emphatic imperative, *zkwrh* (equivalent to Tiberian *zokrâ*). The alternate readings *yrwšlm* MT, *yhwh* 4Q, are triggered by the interpretation of the verb. To be preferred is *yhwh*. The reading *yrwšlm* is easily explained as an assimilation to *yrwšlm* (4QLam *yrwšlym*), the subject in the first colon of the next verse. Further, the imperative *zkrh yhwh* begins a long-range sequence of addresses to the deity: *rʾh yhwh ʾt ʿnyh* (v 9c), and *rʾh yhwh whbyṭh* (v 11c), in the structure of Part I (vv 1–11) of the lament. Finally, the reading with *yhwh* produces a colon of normal length, *yrwšlm* a colon of abnormal length.

Once corrupt, the corruption spread in such a fashion as to produce what appears to be a four-line verse in the otherwise invariable sequence of triplets.

Other readings require comment. *ymy* in MT (v 7a) is a secondary intrusion under the influence of *mymy* in colon 2; it perhaps arose from a text with the sequence:

ירושלימםרודיה

in a script in which *y*, *w*, and *r* were easily confused (for example, in third century B.C.E. scripts of the type of 4QSam[b]), and in which medial and final *mem* were not distinguished. In any case, there is no trace of it in 4QLam, or in the reconstructed early stages of the corruption of the verse. In colon 5, there is a haplogaphy in 4QLam, caused no doubt by homoioteleuton: *ʿwzr* < *lh rʾwh* > *ṣryh*. And finally, 4QLam reads *mšbryh* for *mšbth*. One might be tempted to choose *mšbth* as *lectio difficilior*, were not the graphic confusion of *t* and *ry* simple in the Jewish script (before the reduction of the size of *yod*), and *mšbt* a *hapax legomenon* of dubious meaning in this context.

The structure of the reconstructed triplet is *l*:b::*l*:b::b:*l*. There is "internal" parallelism between colon 5 (b) and colon 6 (*l*). The expression *rʾwh* carries the connotation of "gloat over, look with pleasure on," as often in Biblical Hebrew and in the Mešaʿ Inscription.[12] Indeed *rʾy* and *śḥq* are strictly parallel grammatically and semantically. The second and third bicola are bound together syntactically, and together recount the troubles mentioned in the first bicolon. This is an unusual structure in early poetry. Minor correspondences may be noted: the repetition of the element *ṣr* (s./pl.) in the final element of colon 3 and colon 5, and the formal and semantic parallelism of *mrwdyh* and *mšbryh*, the final elements in colon 1 and colon 6, a cyclic feature.

We have referred above to the correspondence of *zkrh yhwh* to other addresses to deity in alternating triplets: v 7, v 9, and v 11. Mention should be made also of *ʾyn ʿwzr lh*, echoing in variant form the sequence *ʾyn lh mnḥm* (v 2), *ʾyn mnḥm lh* (v 9), *ʾyn mnḥm lh* (v 17), and *ʾyn mnḥm ly* (v 21).

Verse 8 ח

Jerusalem has sinned grievously;	חטא חטאה ירושלם	[9]	*l* 1.
Therefore she has become an object of derision.	על כן לנוד היתה	[7]	b 2.
All who honored her have come to despise her,	כל מכבדיה הזילוה	[10]	*l* 3.
For they have seen her nakedness.	כי ראו ערותה	[6]	b 4.
Also she herself groans,	גם היאה נאנחה	[6]	*l* 5.
And turns back (defeated).	ותשב אחור	[5]	b 6.

4QLam takes *ḥṭʾ* to be an infinitive absolute (*ḥṭwʾ*) adding weight to Ehrlich's argument (1914: 31) for reading the infinitive rather than a noun. More dramatic is the reading *lnwd* in 4QLam. The material reading is certain in the manuscript, and is reflected in the G *eis salon*. *lnydh* of MT (read also by Aquila *eis kechōrismenēn* and Syr *ndtʾ*) arose in assimilation to *lndh* v 17 (cf. Zech 13: 1 *lḥṭʾt wlndh*). The *he* of *lnydh* is a dittograph of the following *he* of *hyth*, and *waw* is confused with *yod*, as persistently in Late Hasmonean and Herodian Jewish scripts. That the meaning "object of (head-) wagging" was required by the context was recognized as early as Ibn Ezra.

The structure of the triplet is *l*:b::*l*:b::*l*:b. There is parallelism between cola 2 and 3, and internal parallelism of sorts in cola 5 and 6. The concentration (repetition) of the phonemes ʾ and *ḥ* in colon 1, and again in cola 5 and 6 may be observed. The triplet in v 7 and the triplet in v 8 are bound together by corresponding themes: *rʾwh*, *śḥqw* (v 7), and *hzylwh*, *rʾw* (v 8).

Verse 9 ט

Filthiness is in her skirts,	טמאה בשוליה	[6] b 1.
She was not mindful of her fate.	לא זכרה אחריתה	[7] *l* 2.
And she has fallen wonderfully,	ותרד פלאים	[6] *l* 3.
There is none to comfort her.	אין מנחם לה	[5] b 4.
Look, Yahweh, on my affliction,	ראה יהוה את עניי	[7] *l* 5.
For the enemy has magnified himself.	כי הגדיל אויב	[5] b 6.

We have emended the text at one point: *ṭmʾh* for *ṭmʾth*. The repetition of the pronoun offends, or at least is unnecessary, and colon 1 appears to be the "b"-colon. For *plʾym* (colon 3), 4QLam reads *plʾwt*.

Colon 5, a cry to the deity in the first person is surprising. Part I (vv 1–11) of the poem thus far has maintained a consistent point of view: observing Zion in the third person. In Part II (vv 12–22) the point of view is that of Zion, speaking in the first person. However, the third-person stance reappears twice in Part II, in v 15c and v 17. It appears then that the present shift in v 9c and the shift to first person in v 11c point ahead, structurally, to the stance of Part II in conscious artifice. It may also be observed that both the exceptional bicola in Part I (v 9c and v 11c) are parallel, the first colon of each beginning *rʾh yhwh*, a cry to the deity, the second colon of each commencing with *ky*.

The structure of the triplet is b:*l*::*l*:b::*l*:b. It is not particularly rich in binary parallels and contrasts—unlike the better triplets in the lament, and quite unlike the classical verse form.

Verse 10 י

The adversary has grasped	ידו פרש צר	[5] b 1.
After all her treasures.	על כל מחמדיה	[6] *l* 2.
Indeed she looked on the heathen:	כי ראתה גוים	[6] *l* 3.
They entered her sanctuary,	באו מקדשה	[5] b 4.
Concerning whom you commanded:	אשר צויתה	[5] b 5.
"They shall not enter her assemblies."	לא יבאו מועדיה	[6] *l* 6.

We have reconstructed *mwʿdyh* in colon 6 on the basis of the indirect evidence of 4QLam. 4QLam has suffered haplography as follows: *lwʾ ybwʾw* < *mmwʿdy . . .* > *mḥmdyh*. The text of MT gives no basis for the haplography. The reconstructed *mwʿdyh* provides this basis. The reading *bqhl lk* conforms to the usual form of the commandment in Deut 23: 2ff. *(bqhl yhwh)*; Neh 13: 1 (*bqhl hʾlhym*); etc. The variant expression may be compared with *bbwʾ . . . lpny yhwh bmwʿdym* (Ezek 46: 9), and, indeed, *bʾy mwʿd* in Lam 1: 4. While my reconstruction entails speculation, it has the advantage of providing an explanation of the haplography in the text of 4QLam, and binds the text in thematic and verbal correspondence (both likeness and contrast) to colon 2 in Lam 1: 4. We prefer also to read *ybʾw mwʿdyh* to a more usual *(ybʾw) bmwʿdyh* to parallel *bʾw mqdšh*.

The structures of the triplet is b:*l*::*l*:b::b:*l*, a chiastic pattern of long and short cola, or it may be described as a cyclic pattern of bicola, the reverse of the pattern *l*:b::b:*l*::*l*:b found in triplets in v 2 and v 5. Each of the bicola in this triplet is quite short—but of the same length.

The parallelism between *bʾw* in colon 5 and *lʾ ybʾw* is rather flat; more interesting is the set *mḥmdyh* (colon 2), *mqdšh* (colon 4), and *mwʿdyh* (colon 6) with their phonetic (*m . . .d. . .h*) and morphological correspondences.

Verse 11 כ

All her people sigh;	כל עמה נאנחים	[6] *l* 1.
They seek bread.	מבקשים לחם	[5] b 2.
They have given her treasures for food	נתנו מחמדיה באכל	[9] *l* 3.
To keep alive.	להשיב נפש	[4] b 4.
Look, Yahweh, and behold,	ראה יהוה והביטה	[8] *l* 5.
Yea, I have become of no account.	כי הייתי זוללה	[7] b 6.

4QLam and the Greek read *mḥmdyh*, with the f.s. suffix, probably correctly. There is no reason, I believe, to repoint *mē-ḥămudêhem* (Ehrlich), which may or may not be the *Kĕtîb*, and interpret the expression to mean "some of their darling (children)." Rather, Zion's treasures are meant, and *mḥmdyh* (or *mḥmdyhm*) is meant to recall the treasures after which the enemy grasped in v 10a. Such repetition is characteristic of the poetic structure of the lament.

4QLam has the variant *npšh* for *npš* in MT, "her (i.e., Zion's) life." This strikes me as an "explicating plus." The picture of the people selling Zion's treasure to revivify Zion is, however, an appealing one, and not to be dismissed automatically, at least in the interpretation of the poet's meaning. In this case the children feed the mother rather than the mother eating the children, the more usual image in famine or siege.

In the final colon, 4QLam provides the reading *zwll*. In v 13c similarly 4QLam has the variant *šwmm* (for *šmmh*). Evidently in the textual tradition it represents, the "I" of personified Zion has been incorrectly taken as the "I" of the poet in these passages.

The structure of the triplet is *l*:b::*l*:b::*l*:b. The first and second bicola are in parallelistic correspondence, with the formulaic pair *lḥm* (colon 2 [b]) and *ʾkl* (colon 3 [*l*]) in chiastic order. In colon 6 *zwllh* "worthless" stands in subtle contrast to *mḥmdyh* "treasures" in colon 3.

In colon 1 *nʾnḥym* links with *nʾnḥym* in v 4b (priests sigh), *nʾnḥh* in v 8c (she [Jerusalem] sighs), *nʾnḥh* in v 21a (I [Zion] sigh).[13] To be sure "sighing" in a lament is not unexpected. It must be observed, howver, that *nʾnḥ* is a relatively rare word, found nowhere else in the poems of the Book of Lamentations, and not once in the laments of the Psalter.

The final colon *ky hyyty zwllh*, which brings to a close Part I of the lament, at the half point in the acrostic, is strongly reminiscent of the paired cola of v 1 beginning the section: *hyth kʾlmnh* and *hyth lms*. There is thus a return to the beginning, and with the shift of person, at the same time an anticipation of the second part of the lament.

Verse 12 ל

Would that on me all who pass by the way	לוא אלי כל עברי דרך	[8]	*l*	1.
Gaze and see:	הביטו וראו	[6]	b	2.
If there has been any pain like my pain	אם יש מכאב כמכאבי	[8]	*l*	3.
Which He has dealt out to me—	אשר עולל לי	[5]	b	4.
Wherewith Yahweh has terrified me	אשר הוגירני יהוה	[8]	*l*	5.
In the day of His wrath.	ביום חרונו	[5]	b	6.

The text of colon 1 is corrupted both in the received text and in 4QLam. The reading of the latter is uncertain in part, a break in the leather and surface damage obscuring the letter following *k* and before *h*. Little space is found in the break (note the stretching apart of the split above in the first line of the column). I do not believe that there is room for the letter *mêm*; *yod* (for archaizing *ʾlyky*) conforms best, perhaps, to the traces of ink on the leather.

I am inclined to read *lûʾ ʾēlay . . .hbyṭw*, "Would that they look closely at me."

As has been observed (Budde), *lwʾ* in MT is easily pointed *lûʾ*, and *hbyṭ* regularly takes *ʾl* with its object.[14] The placement of *ʾly* may arise from poetic artifice—in a chiastic structure with *ly* at the end of colon 4. The reading *ʾlykm kl* may have arisen in an initial dittography, later wrongly corrected: *ʾly kl* > *ʾlyk kl* > *ʾlykm kl*; the reading of 4QLam may be explained similarly: *ʾly kl* > *ʾlyk kwl* > *ʾlykh kwl* > *ʾlyk hkwl* > *ʾlyky hkwl*.

4QLam has the variant reading *hwgyrny* for *hwgh* in colon 5. It is a unique form, an otherwise unattested *Hipʿil* of *ygr*. The root itself (in *Qal*) occurs in similar contexts in Deut 9: 19 (where the divine wrath is the source of terror), and in Deut 28: 60 (where disease is the cause of fear). The reading in MT, *hwgh yhwh*, immediately recalls *yhwh hwgh* in v 5. One must ask, is the repetition of *hwgh* an artifice of the poet or a corruption of an original *hwg(y)rny* by reminiscence of *hwgh* in v 5? I am inclined to choose *hwgyrny* provisionally on the basis of the principle of *lectio difficilior praeferenda est*. This choice is reinforced by the reading of the pronominal suffix in the Greek and in the Pešiṭta.

In colon 4 we find in 4QLam the variant *ʿwllw ly* corresponding to *ʿwll ly* in MT. The former reflects late usage, the indefinite 3.m.pl. passive with *l*-, a slight modernizing of the passive indefinite construction marked by the Massoretic pointing. The text I believe should be read *ʿōlēl ly* "(which He [Yahweh]) dealt out to me," the active form with *l*- found twice in v 22. Both the Syriac and Vulgate versions so read, and parallelism with *hwgyrny* (or *hwgh*) *yhwh* demands it.

We have chosen the variant *bywm ḥrwnw* (4QLam) in colon 6, preferring the shorter reading. The longer reading *bywm ḥrwn ʾpw* is easily explained as an expansion to a familiar cliché.

The structure of the triplet is *l*:b::*l*:b::*l*:b. We noted above the parallelism between *ʾšr ʿwll ly* (colon 4), and *ʾšr hwgyrny yhwh* (colon 5). The cola, one b, one *l*, are in chiastic order. The theme of "harsh treatment dealt out by Yahweh" begins Part II of the lament here in v 12, and in v 22, ending the lament, we find the *inclusio*: *wʿwll lmw* / *kʾšr ʿwllt ly* (cola 2 and 3).

Verse 13 מ

From on high he sent fire,	ממרום שלח אש	[6]	b	1.
Into my bones he made it sink.	בעצמתי יורידנה	[8]	*l*	2.
He spread a snare for my feet,	פרש רשת לרגלי	[6]	*l*	3.
He turned me back.	השיבני אחור	[6]	b	4.
He made me desolate,	נתנני שממה	[7]	*l*	5.
Ill all the day long.	כל היום דוה	[5]	b	6.

In colon 2, MT reads *wyrdnh*, 4QLam *wywrydnw* or *wywrydny*. The Greek translates *ywrydnh* or *ywrydnw* (*katēgagen auto*). These variants provide a basis of reconstructing an original *ywrdnh* (*ʾēš* taken as feminine). The variant *ywrydnw* is possible, especially later with *ʾēš* often treated as masculine; presumably this is the reading of 4QLam (or stands behind a corruption to *wywrydny*).[15]

In colon 5 and 6 4QLam has the variants *šwmm* and *dwy*, masculines, according to its tendency, recognized above, to take the first person on occasion as the poet.

The structure of the triplet is b:*l*::*l*:b::*l*:b.[16] Binary correspondence in chiastic patterns is frequent in the triplet: *mmrwm* (first element of colon 1) contrasts with *lrgly* (last element of colon 3), *šlḥ ʾš* (last element of colon 1) correspond to *prś ršt* (first elements of colon 3), reinforced with the repetition of sibilants. In colon 4 and 5, chiastically positioned, *hšybny* corresponds to *ntnny* grammatically and semantically, each initiating its colon. At the same time, there is some internal parallelism within the first bicolon: *šlḥ ʾš* stands parallel to *ywrdnh* as well as to *prś ršt*. Also *lrgly* is parallel to *bʿṣmty* as well as contrasting with *mmrwm*. At longer range, *hšybny ʾḥwr* echoes *wtšb ʾḥwr* (v 8c), and *ntnny šmmh* faintly recalls *šʿryh šwmmym* (v 4b).

Verse 14 נ

The yoke of my rebellion is bound on,	נקשר על פשעי	[5]	b	1.
By his hand it is tied together.	בידו ישתרג	[6]	*l*	2.
His yoke is on my neck.	עלו על צוארי	[6]	*l*	3.
He has made my strength ebb.	הכשיל כוחי	[4]	b	4.
Yahweh has delivered me	נתנני יהוה	[6]	b	5.
Into the hands of those I am unable to resist.	בידי לא אוכל קום	[7]	*l*	6.

In colon 1, 4QLam reads *nqšrh* for the *hapax legomenon nśqd*. Evidently this tradition takes the subject to be the speaker: "Bound (am I [f.])."[17]

The subject, however, is "the yoke of my rebellion," i.e., the yoke due a captured rebel, and the better reading is *niqšar* which also stands behind MT, *nśqd* arising from metathesis and the confusion of *reš* and *dalet*. The evidence of 4QLam justifies the emendations of Oettli (*nqšr*) and (in part) Ehrlich (*nqšrw*). For *yśtrgw*, 4QLam reads *wyśtrg*; the structure of the bicolon requires that we read *yśtrg* as original, partly with MT, partly with 4QLam. The plural form arose out of attraction to *pšʿy* taken as a plural, the reading *wyśtrg* out of wrong division of the colon. In colon 3, 4QLam reads *ʿwlw* (for MT *ʿlw*), certainly reflecting the original reading *ʿullô*. Symmachus interestingly has *ho zygos autou*, reflecting the same text. In colon 5, 4QLam has the reading *yhwh*, to be preferred over *ʾdny* of the received text. The final colon is read in 4QLam *byd lwʾ ʾwkl lqwm* which has nothing to be recommended over the text of MT. The construction *byd/bydy lʾ ʾwkl qwm* is, of course, unusual in its elliptical use of a bound construction as a surrogate for a relative clause, but is not without parallel, at least in Massoretic Hebrew.

The reconstructed text of the triplet gives a coherent picture of Zion, punished for her rebellion by being bound by Yahweh's own hand in the yoke symbolic of captivity, and delivered by Yahweh into the hands of her adversaries. Bowed under the yoke, she is spent in strength and unable to resist her foes.

The structure of the triplet as reconstructed is b:*l*::*l*:b::b:*l*. There is "internal" parallelism in the first bicolon, *nqšr*, the first word, corresponding to *yśtrg*, the last word. At the same time there is linkage between colon 1 and colon 3 with the repetition of the element *ʿōl*. Cola 3 and 4 also correspond and link with the final bicolon, as they recount parallel actions of Yahweh bringing low captive Zion. Worthy of note also is the juxtaposition of *bydw* in the first bicolon, and *bydy* in the last colon: the hand of God and the hands of the enemy.

Verse 15 ס

He has made an offering of all my mighty ones,	סלה כל אבירי	[6] *l* 1.
Yahweh in my midst.	יהוה בקרבי	[5] b 2.
He has proclaimed against me a solemn assembly,	קרא עלי מועד	[6] *l* 3.
To break (the bones of) my warriors.	לשבר בחורי	[5] b 4.
Yahweh has trodden the winepress,	גת דרך יהוה	[5] b 5.
Of the maiden Judah.	לבתולת בת יהודה	[8] *l* 6.

The triplet is made up of images taken from the language of holy war. The last bicolon, Yahweh treading out the vintage, recalls Isa 63: 1–6, with its combination of vintage festival, slaughter, and the celebration of the rites of holy war. The first two cola recall Isa 34: 1–8, also a song of holy war, with its combination of the images of animal sacrifice and of the *ḥerem*. Especially important is the play on animal names which are at the same time titles of military leaders. In colon 1 of Lam 1: 15 we find a similar play: *ʾbyry*, lit. "my bulls," parallel to *bḥwry*, "my young warriors."[18] The first word, *slh*, must be taken as the *Piʿel* of the root *slh* / *slʾ*, "to weight, pay," and in Old South Arabic, "to pay tribute, dedicate as an offering, devote to a deity." Thus we find in the triplet the images of animals/warriors set aside as an offering or booty (the first bicolon), the festival of victory with its slaughter (the second bicolon), and the treading out of the vintage/blood of warriors (the third bicolon).

In colon 1 4QLam appears to read *ʾbydy*; if so, it is a simple lapse for *ʾbyry*. In colon 5 4QLam reads *yhwh* correctly for the *ʾdny* of MT, and *yhwh* is evidently to be restored in colon 2 where both 4QLam and MT have *ʾădōnay*.

The structure of the triplet is *l*:b::*l*:b::b:*l*. The general semantic parallelism between the three bicola has been described above, as well as the correspondence of *ʾbyry* (colon 1) and *bḥwry* (colon 4). One notes also the sequence of *bqrby* (colon 2), *ʿly* (colon 3), and *lbtwlt* (colon 6), which are positioned chiastically, as are *yhwh* (colon 2, first element) and *yhwh* (colon 5, last element). The shift to the third person in colon 5 has been discussed above in v 9 and v 11. The following triplet, v 17 MT, continues that reprise of the point of view of Part I, before reverting to the first person for the remainder of the poem. The calling of a *mwʿd* by Yahweh in this triplet, a *mwʿd* to which the enemy is invited, stands in interesting tension with v 10 (as reconstructed) with its allusion to Yahweh's command that the nations shall not enter *mwʿdyh*, as well as with *mbly bʾy mwʿd* in v 4.

Verse 17 MT פ

Zion reaches out with her hands,	פרשה ציון בידיה	[9]	*l*	1.
There was none to comfort her.	אין מנחם לה	[5]	b	2.
Yahweh kept watch on Jacob:	צפה יהוה ליעקב	[7]	*l*	3.
His enemies have surrounded him;	סביביו צריו	[5]	b	4.
Jerusalem has become	היתה ירושלם	[7]	*l*	5.
As an unclean thing among them.	לנדה ביניהם	[6]	b	6.

In colon 3, 4QLam has the reading *ṣph* for *ṣwh* of MT. The reading of MT is extremely awkward, if not impossible: "Yahweh commanded as to Jacob those around him (to be) his adversaries." On the contrary, *ṣph*, "to keep watch," makes admirable sense. The root may be used of the judge or witness who keeps watch to see that justice is done, a covenant kept, wrongdoers punished, etc. (cf. Gen 31: 49; Ps 66: 7; Prov. 15: 3), as well one who keeps military watch. *ṣph* with *l* appears in one context where evil intent is meant: *ṣwph ršʿ lṣdyq* (Ps 37: 32). The ease with which *ṣph* could be misread as *ṣwh* can be seen by glancing at the reading in 4QLam, and *ṣwyth* in v 10 may have triggered the error (reminiscence).

Elsewhere in the verse the text of 4QLam is complete: after *ʾyn mnḥm lh*, 4Q adds *mkwl ʾwhbyh*, expanded from v 2, *ʾyn lh mnḥm mkwl ʾwhbyh*, and a variant of colon 1 of v 18 has intruded, presumably the insertion of the text of a marginal reading: *ṣdyq ʾth yhwh*. In colon 3, 4QLam reads *ʾdwny* for the superior reading *yhwh* in MT. In colon 6 4QLam preserves a reading, *lndwḥ bnyhmh*, obviously inferior, arising initially in a graphic confusion of *he* and *ḥet* and confounded by orthographic revision.

In 4QLam, the verse beginning with *pe* precedes the verse beginning *ʿayin* in the acrostic sequence. Thus it conforms to the rare alphabetic order found in Lamentations chapters 2, 3, and 4.[19] One finds a parallel textual variation in Prov 31: 25–26, where MT has the order *ʿayin-pe*, the Greek text of Proverbs the order *pe-ʿayin*.

The existence of two alphabetic orders in the textual transmission of Lamentations 1 raises the question of the original order. I do not believe the question can be answered. If one posits a single anonymous author for the book, he could well argue that the order of chapters 2–4 reflects the author's preference, and that Lamentations 1 has been secondarily conformed to the standard order. However, we are not sure that the laments come from a single hand. Again, if we assume that Lamentations is the collection of a systematic editor, we might argue that the *pe-ʿayin* order is original at least in the principal edition of the book. But we do not know that the putative editor was systematic; he may have included Lamentations 1 in his collection in the form it came to him, in which case it has been secondarily conformed to the order of Lamentations 2–4 in the textual tradition preserved in 4QLam (and so on).

The structure of the triplet is *l*:b::*l*:b::*l*:b. The verse is rich with long-range parallelism. In colon 1 *prśh ṣywn bydyh* corresponds to *ydw prś ṣr* in the first colon of v 10. Colon 2, *ʾyn mnḥm lh*, repeats a theme which persists throughout the lament in delicate variations: v 2 *ʾyn lh mnḥm*, v 7 *ʾyn ʿwzr lh*, v 9 *ʾyn mnḥm lh*, v 17 *ʾyn mnḥm lh*, v 21 *ʾyn mnḥm ly*. In the final bicolon there is a similar repetition of a theme in a grammatically fixed pattern: *hyth . . . ndh*, which is to be compared to *hyth kʾlmnh* and *hyth lms* (v 1), *lnwd hyth* (v 8), and *hyyty zwllh* (v 11).

Verse 16 MT ע

My eye weeps,	עיני בכיה	[5] b	1.
My eye runs with tears.	עיני ירדה מים	[6] *l*	2.
A comforter is far from me,	רחק ממני מנחם	[8] *l*	3.
One who would restore my soul.	משיב נפשי	[4] b	4.
My children are desolate,	היו בני שממים	[7] *l*	5.
But the enemy is mighty.	כי גבר אויב	[5] b	6.

The text of MT in the first bicolon is corrupt, as is generally recognized. Behind the received text are probably two variants in colon 1: *ʿyny bkyh* and *bkyh ʿyny*, and 4QLam adds a third variant, *bkw ʿyny*. *ʾny* is not found in 4QLam, and its absence in a conflate text like 4QLam requires an explanation. We should argue, therefore, that *ʾny* in the textual tradition behind MT is a simple misreading of *ʿyny*. The combination of two variants has produced the conflate reading *ʾny bkyh ʿyny* in MT. The reading of 4QLam is a revision of *bkyh ʿyny*, which takes *ʿyny* as a plural. The second colon also probably existed at one time in two variants: *ʿyny yrdh mym* (MT) and *ʿyny yrdh dmʿty*. Compare Lam 3: 48, *plgy mym trd ʿyny*, and Jer 13: 17, *wtrd ʿyny dmʿh*. Since both variants are formulaic, it is difficult to choose between them. The versions omit one of the occurrences of *ʿyny* following *bkyh* further suggesting that the first colon read *ʾny/ʿyny bkyh*. In the second colon the versions read *mym* with the possible exception of Symmachus, who has *dakrua*, the usual translation of *dmʿh*, but this may be interpretive.

The first colon may be reconstructed as a whole either to read *ʿl ʾlh ʿyny bkyh*, which would make a suitable long colon, or to read *ʿyny bkyh*, a short colon. *ʿl ʾlh* is suspect in good poetry and may be secondary, introduced to head the *ʿayin* triplet when initial *ʿyny* had been corrupted to *ʾny*.[20]

The structure of the triplet as reconstructed is b:*l*::*l*:b::*l*:b. The first bicolon exhibits "internal" parallelism between its members, with the repetition of *ʿyny* beginning each colon reminiscent of archaic repetitive parallelism, and the participles *bkyh* and *yrdh* parallel grammatically and semantically. Zion's weeping and the absence of a comforter in the first and second bicola correspond to the themes of the first and second bicola of v 2. *mšyb npšy* (colon 4) echoes *lhšyb npš* of v 11 (colon 4), and *šmmym* (colon 5) continues a sequence in v 4 (*šmmym*) and v 13 (*šmmh*). Finally *ky gbr ʾwyb* repeats with minor variation *ky hgdyl ʾwyb*.

In the second bicolon *mšyb npšy* may be described fairly as a "ballast variant" of *mnḥm*, lending an element of "internal" parallelism. In the third bicolon there is strong antithetic parallelism between the members.

Verse 18 צ

Yahweh is just,	צדיק הוא יהוה	[5]	b	1.
For I defied his command.	כי פיהו מריתי	[6]	*l*	2.
Hear, pray, all you peoples,	שמעו נא כל עמים	[6]	*l*	3.
And behold my pain.	וראו מכאבי	[5]	b	4.
My maidens and young men,	בתולותי ובחורי	[8]	*l*	5.
Have gone into captivity.	הלכו בשבי	[6]	b	6.

The variant misplaced in line 8 of Column III of 4QLam, *ṣdyq ʾth yhwh*, can be filled out to read, presumably, *ky pyk mryty*. However, at the proper place (III, line 10) the manuscript stands with MT save for the substitution of *ʾ{dwny}* for *yhwh*. Unfortunately 4QLam breaks off here.

The structure of the triplet is b:*l*::*l*:b::*l*:b. It is poor in internal parallelistic devices, but brings new variations on persistent themes. In the second bicolon, there is the call on the nations to observe the pain of Zion, a theme we have heard in v 12, where wayfarers are asked to observe her pain. The third bicolon recalls v 4 (colon 5) *btwltyh nhwgwt*. In colon 2 *mryty* anticipates *mrh mryty* in v 20b.

Verse 19 ק

I appealed to my lovers;	קראתי למאהבי	[8]	*l*	1.
They betrayed me.	המה רמוני	[5]	b	2.
My priests and my elders	כהני וזקני	[7]	*l*	3.
Expire in the city.	בעיר גועו	[5]	b	4.
For they sought food for themselves,	כי בקשו אכל למו	[7]	*l*	5.
And found none.	ולא מצאו	[5]	b	6.

For colon 6 the Greek and Syriac preserve two variants (conflated): *wyšybw ʾt npšm* (with MT), and *wlʾ mṣʾw* (*kai ouk euron* / *wlʾ ʾškḥw*). I am inclined to take *wlʾ mṣʾw* as original. The reading of MT is long, prosaic (using both the *waw*-consecutive and the particle *ʾt*), and appears to be an expanded parallel reading introduced from v 11: (*bʾkl*) *lhšyb npš*. Such expansion is well attested in the transmission of Lamentations by the 4QLam manuscript.

The structure of the triplet as reconstructed is *l*:b::*l*:b::*l*:b. Antithetical parallelism between cola is found in the first and last bicolon. *bqš* and *mṣʾ* are a formulaic pair. Zion's faithless lovers, first mentioned in v 2, return in this verse.[21] The priests who sighed in v 4 reappear to expire. The theme of famine—the search for food, struck first in the figure of v 6, more explicitly in parallel language in v 11 (giving rise to the parallel reading discussed above), returns powerfully in this verse.

Verse 20 ר

Behold, Yahweh, for I am in anguish	ראה יהוה כי צר לי	[7] *l* 1.
My bowels churn.	מעי חמרמרו	[6] b 2.
My heart is turned over within me,	נהפך לבי בקרבי	[7] *l* 3.
For I have grievously rebelled.	כי מרה מריתי	[6] b 4.
Outside the sword has bereaved,	מחוץ שכלה חרב	[6] *l* 5.
Inside there was terror.	בבית אימות	[5] b 6.

There is a textual difficulty in colon 6. The bicolon is a traditional one. Often *ḥrb* and *rʿb* are the formulaic pair. Cf. Ezek 7: 15 and Jer 14: 18. Hillers (1972: 14) has for this reason suggested the rare term *kāpān*, "hunger, famine" as an emendation for *kmwt*. An emendation is desiderated, but I much prefer to turn to the closest alloform of this traditional bicolon for help: *mḥwṣ tškl ḥrb, wmḥdrym ʾymh* (Deut 32: 25). This verse suggests that an alternate pair is available in old poetic tradition: *ḥrb*/*ʾymh*. We propose, therefore, to read *ʾymwt* for *kmwt*. It may be observed further that in another close parallel to cola 3 and 6 in Psalm 55: 5, *mwt* occurs as a dittograph of *ʾymwt*: *lby yḥyl bqrby*/*wʾymwt mwt nplw ʿly*.

The structure of the triplet is *l*:b::*l*:b::*l*:b. In the first bicolon there is internal parallelism, *mʿy ḥmrmrw* acting as a ballast variant of *ṣr ly*. However, the strongest set of correspondences is between colon 2 and colon 3, cola (b/*l*) positioned chiastically with chiastic patterning also in the cola *-ḥmrmrw*/*nhpk-*, *mʿy-*/*-bqrby*.[22] The final bicolon also reveals internal parallelism: *mḥwṣ-*/*bbyt-* and *-ḥrb*/*-ʾymwt*.

Verse 21 ש

They heard that I sigh,	שמעו כי נאנחה אני	[9] *l* 1.
(That) there was none to comfort me.	אין מנחם לי	[5] b 2.
They heard of my evil; they rejoice	שמעו רעתי ששו	[8] *l* 3.
That you have done it.	כי אתה עשית	[6] b 4.

May you bring the day that you proclaimed	הבאת יום קראת	[7] *l* 5.
When they will become as I.	ויהיו כמוני	[6] b 6.

In colon 1 we prefer to read with MT *šmʿw*, with the subject—enemies—understood, in view of the structure of the triplet. Colon 2, however, has been expanded by a parallel reading and is impossibly long. We have noted above that the bicolon in v 2, *ʾyn lh mnḥm mkl ʾhbyh*, has triggered in v 17 an expansion in 4QLam: *ʾyn mnḥm lh mkwl ʾwhbyh*; we believe that the same expansion by insertion of the parallel reading occurred here: *ʾyn mnḥm ly mkl ʾwhby*. This expanded reading then was further altered to provide a subject for *šmʿw*, producing the variant in MT (*ʾyn mnḥm ly) kl ʾ(w)yby šmʿw rʿty śśw*.

The structure of the triplet as reconstructed is *l*:b::*l*:b::*l*:b. The repetition of *šmʿw* in colon 1 and colon 2, beginning each cola, is studied. So also is the frequency of sibilants in cola 1, 3, and 4. The themes of "sighing" and "failure of a comforter" have been discussed above; they find their final expression here.

Verse 22 ת

Let all their wickedness come before you,	תבא כל רעתם לפניך	[10] *l* 1.
And deal with them	ועולל למו	[5] b 2.
As you have dealt with me,	כאשר עללת לי	[7] *l* 3.
For all my acts of rebellion.	על כל פשעי	[5] b 4.
For many are my sighs,	כי רבות אנחתי	[6] *l* 5.
And my heart is sick.	ולבי דוי	[5] b 6.

This triplet has some striking parallels with the preceding triplet, notably the last two bicola of v 21, and the first two bicola of v 22. Note the correspondence of *rʿty* in colon 3 of v 21 and *rʿtm* in colon 1 of v 22, and the general semantic correspondence between *ʿśyt* (colon 4, v 21), and *ʿll/ʿllt* (cola 2 and 3, v 22). Both verses appeal to Yahweh to reverse the roles of Zion and the enemy, the enemy punished by Yahweh for his sins, as Zion has been punished for her sins. One perceives also an envelope construction in the correspondence of *nʾnḥh ʾny* (colon 1, v 21), and *ʾnḥty* (colon 5, v 22).

In the final triplet colon 2 is bound to colon 3 by enjambment and repetition (*ʿwll lmw/ʿllt ly*), an unexpected structure. The phase *ʿl kl pšʿy* (colon 4) recalls *ʿl rb pšʿyh* (v 5, colon 4).

4. The structures of the acrostic poem as a whole may be summarized as follows:

Part I

1.	א	*l*:b::*l*:b::*l*:b
2.	ב	*l*:b::b:*l*::*l*:b
3.	ג	*l*:b::*l*:b::*l*:b

4. ד *l*:b::*l*:b::*l*:b
5. ה *l*:b::b:*l*::*l*:b
6. ו *l*:b::*l*:b::*l*:b
7. ז *l*:b::*l*:b::b:*l*
8. ח *l*:b::*l*:b::*l*:b
9. ט b:*l*::*l*:b::*l*:b
10. י b:*l*::*l*:b::b:*l*
11. כ *l*:b::*l*:b::*l*:b

Part II

12. ל *l*:b::*l*:b::*l*:b
13. מ b:*l*::*l*:b::*l*:b
14. נ b:*l*::*l*:b::b:*l*
15. ס *l*:b::*l*:b::b:*l*
17. פ *l*:b::*l*:b::*l*:b
16. ע b:*l*::*l*:b::*l*:b
18. צ b:*l*::*l*:b::*l*:b
19. ק *l*:b::*l*:b::*l*:b
20. ר *l*:b::*l*:b::*l*:b
21. ש *l*:b::*l*:b::*l*:b
22. ת *l*:b::*l*:b::*l*:b

The compound verse form found in this lament is built up fundamentally of cola of traditional length, the long colon we have labeled *l̲* and the short colon we have labeled b̲, which are the stuff of the traditional oral poetry represented in Ugaritic poetry and especially in the corpus of Israel's most ancient poetry. This is evident from the regularity of the caesural pause and especially in the frequent occurrence of "internal" parallelism, i.e., correspondence at multiple levels between the cola of a bicolon. The long colon is most often seven syllables, but also counts of eight and six are quite common. Nine-syllable cola are rare.[33] A short colon of five syllables is much the most common, but six is frequent, seven or four, rare. Since syllable counts overlap, it seems doubtful that the poet was counting syllables. Cola are long or short within a range, but most important is the relative length of each in a bicolon *l*:b or b:*l*, the contrast between unbalanced units.

The *dominant* parallel structures are found in corresponding couplets and triplets of bicola. The verse form is thus best described as *l*:b::*l*:b (::*l*:b), with variants b:*l*::*l*:b (::b:*l*), etc. There is here a powerful cyclic or chiastic impulse, and this impulse is reflected as well in chiastic and cyclic positioning of parallel grammatical and semantic units at every level of the verse. This lament from Lamentations is not the best example of the full potentiality of the verse form. The lament in Jonah, especially in its archaic section, shows a much higher density (*Dichtung*) of such artifice, and will be studied elsewhere.

The origin of the verse form *l*:b::*l*:b (to use its dominant pattern) must be looked for in archaic "mixed meters" of the type *l*:*l*(:*l*) alternating with series of verses b:b::b:b (see above). Such mixed verse was chosen for the earliest Hebrew lament extant, the "Lament of David." In fact, the verse *l*:b::*l*:b is legitimately described as a variety of "mixed meter" of even more complex structure.

The recurrence of corresponding words, phrases, cola, and themes at "long range," throughout the poem, often in significant cyclic structures, has occupied our attention in analyzing the lament. We may appropriately end our paper, as we began it, with a quotation from Roman Jakobson. "We have learned the suggestive etymology of the terms *prose* and *verse*—the former, oratio prosa < prorsa < proversa 'speech turned straightforward', and the latter, versus 'return.' Hence, we must consistently draw all inferences from the obvious fact that on every level of language, the essence of poetic artifice consists in recurrent returns" (1966: 399).

Notes

1. See the important but unpublished study of Ehlen (1970).

2. See especially the important if difficult monograph of Geller, *Parallelism in Early Hebrew Poetry* (1979) and his forthcoming "The Dynamics of Parallel Verse." Ehlen's volume (cited above, n. 1) also builds heavily on Jakobson's insights, as does my own paper "Prose and Poetry in the Mythic and Epic Texts from Ugaritic" (Cross 1974). Remarkably, certain other recent studies appear innocent of the implications of Jakobson's work including Kugel (1981).

3. The term is not a happy one since, as is well known, this verse form has far wider distribution among the genres of Hebrew poetry.

4. It may be noted that if we scan in stress meter, the bicola cited give the following: 4: 3, 4: 4, 2: 2, 2: 2, 4: 3, and 3: 3. Such an analysis veils even the binary symmetry of the verses.

5. See, for example, my treatments of Hebrew poetry in Cross 1973: 115f.; 122; 126–131; 152–155; 170–173, and *passim*; and Cross 1968: 4, n. 12, and *passim*.

6. Contrast Hillers (1972: 5–6).

7. This suggestion is not new but goes back at least as far as Budde.

8. Cross and Freedman 1975: 126–28, and esp. the Table, pp. 161–68.

9. Note that the syllable county of *drky* is three, *darakê*, of which a trace is found in the spirant *kap*, assimilated to the second *a*, later lost.

10. Cf. Isa 60: 11 where *lhby*ʾ and *nh(w)gym* are parallel.

11. See the discussion of Hillers (1972: 7–8).

12. See, e.g., Pss 54: 9; 112: 8; 118: 7; Mešaʿ lines 4, 7; in Judg 16: 27 there is the combination *hrʾym bśḥwq šmšwn*.

13. Cf. *ʾnḥty* in v 22c.

14. On *lwʾ* with the imperative, see Gen 23: 13 (where *ʾm* also appears in the context), and Cross 1978: 69, n. 1.

15. The last letter in 4QLam is more easily read *yod*, perhaps, but in ligatured forms *yod* and *waw* are all but interchangeable.

16. In fact colon 3 and 4 are balanced in syllable count, the single instance in this poem. Such license seems to have been allowed even in older, more traditional exemplars of this verse form, to judge from its rare appearance elsewhere, for example, in the Song of Jonah.

17. Cf. *nqšrh*, "bound," in 1 Sam 18: 1, etc.

18. See especially Miller 1970: 180–81.

19. This order of the alphabet is now known outside biblical acrostics in the texts from Kuntillet ʿAjrūd, and in the abecedary from ʿIzbet Ṣarṭah. See most recently Cross 1980.

20. In colon 3 we have omitted *ky* (found both in MT and 4QLam [*kyʾ*]) This line is rather long, and the tendency of the particle to multiply at the beginning of cola in textual transmission, especially in proximity to other occurrences of *ky* (cf. colon 6), is well documented.

21. On the meaning of the figure, see the excellent discussion of Hillers (1972: 19).

22. Dashes are used here to indicate position of an element in a colon.

23. Twice we find long cola of ten syllables, in v 8, colon 3, and in v 22, colon 1. Both cola contain a suspicious occurrence of *kl*. We have left them in the text above, but in view of the rarity of cola of such length, it may be better to excise them. The tendency of *kl* to multiply in the process of textual transmission is notorious.

References

Barthélemy, D.
1963 *Les devanciers d'Aquila*. Supplements to Vetus Testamentum 10. Leiden: Brill.

Cross, F. M.
1961 The Development of the Jewish Scripts. Pp. 133–202 in *The Bible and the Ancient Near East: Essays in Honor of William Foxwell Albright*, ed. G. E. Wright. New York: Doubleday. Rpt. 1979. Winona Lake, Indiana: Eisenbrauns.
1966 The Contribution of the Qumrân Discoveries to the Study of the Biblical Text. *Israel Exploration Journal* 16: 81–95. Rpt. as pp. 278–92 in Cross and Talmon 1975.
1968 The Song of the Sea and Canaanite Myth. *Journal for Theology and the Church* 5: 1–25.
1973 *Canaanite Myth and Hebrew Epic*. Cambridge: Harvard University Press.
1974 Prose and Poetry in the Mythic and Epic Texts from Ugarit. *Harvard Theological Review* 67: 1–15.
1978 David, Orpheus, and Psalm 151: 3–4. *Bulletin of the American Schools of Oriental Research* 231: 69–71.
1980 Newly Found Inscriptions in Old Canaanite and Early Phoenician Scripts. *Bulletin of the American Schools of Oriental Research* 238: 8–30.

Cross, F. M., and Freedman, D. N.
1975 *Studies in Ancient Yahwistic Poetry*. Society for Biblical Literature Dissertation Series 21. Missoula: Scholars Press. Originally 1950.

Cross, F. M., and Talmon, S.
1975 *Qumran and the History of the Biblical Text*. Cambridge: Harvard University Press.

Ehlen, A. J.
1970 *The Poetic Structure of a Hodayah from Qumran: An Analysis of Grammatical, Semantic, and Auditory Correspondence in 1QH 3: 19–36*. Harvard Dissertation.

Ehrlich, A. B.
1914 *Randglossen zur hebräischen Bibel. VII*. Leipzig: J. C. Hinrichs.

Freedman, D. N.
1972a Prolegomenon. Pp. vii-lvi in Gray 1972. Rpt. as pp. 23–50 in Freedman 1980.
1972b Acrostics and Metrics in Hebrew Poetry. *Harvard Theological Review* 65: 367–92. Rpt. as pp. 51–76 in Freedman 1980.
1980 *Pottery, Poetry, and Prophecy: Studies in Early Hebrew Poetry*. Winona Lake, Indiana: Eisenbrauns.

Geller, S. A.
1979 *Parallelism in Early Hebrew Poetry*. Harvard Semitic Monographs 20. Missoula: Scholars Press.

Gray, G. B.
1972 *The Forms of Hebrew Poetry*. New York: Ktav. Originally 1915.

Hillers, D. R.
1972 *Lamentations*. Anchor Bible 7A. Garden City: Doubleday.

Jakobson, R.
1966 Grammatical Parallelism and its Russian Facet. *Language* 42: 399–429.

Kugel, J. L.
1981 *The Idea of Biblical Poetry: Parallelism and Its History*. New Haven: Yale University Press.

McDaniel, T. F.
1968 Philological Studies in Lamentations I, II. *Biblica* 49: 27–53, 199–220.

Miller, P.
1970 Animal Names as Designations in Ugaritic and Hebrew. *Ugaritic-Forschung* 2: 177–86.

Sirach 10: 19–11: 6: Textual Criticism, Poetic Analysis, and Exegesis

Alexander A. Di Lella, O.F.M.
The Catholic University of America, Washington, D.C.

There is little agreement among scholars as to the limits of our passage or its strophic structure. N. Peters and M. H. Segal, for example, end the unit at 11: 9. For Peters, the strophic structure is 2 (10: 19) + 2 (10: 20.22) + 3 (10: 23–25) + 2 (10: 26–27) + 2 (10: 28–29) + 3 (10: 30–11: 1) + 2 (11: 2–3) + 2 (11: 4) + 2 (11: 5–6) + 3 (11: 7–9) bicola (1913: 91–92); for Segal, 2 (10: 19) + 5 (10: 20.22–25) + 2 (10: 26–27) + 2 (10: 28–29) + 2 (10: 30–31) + 4 (11: 1–4ab) + 3 (11: 4cd-6) + 3 (11: 7–9) (1958: 64–65). G. H. Box and W. O. E. Oesterley do not consider the passage as a unit but rather as a series of poems, and they give each poem a separate title: 10: 19–20.22–25; 10: 26–29; 10: 30–11: 1; 11: 2–13 (1913: 350–54). H. Duesberg and I. Fransen hold a similar view but divide the passage differently and append their own titles to the poems: 10: 19–20.22–24; 10: 25–27; 10: 28–29; 10: 30–11: 1; 11: 2–6 (1966: 138–40). The *NAB* prints the poem as a discrete unit, entitled "True Glory," containing three stanzas: 9 (10: 19–20.22–27) + 4 (10: 28–31) + 7 (11: 1–6).

What I offer in this study is the poem's strophic structure as I see it and the justification thereof, textual criticism, and poetic analysis and exegesis of the individual strophes. The poem is found in MSS A and B from the Cairo Geniza.[1] In the margin I have indicated the manuscript(s) forming the basis of each colon, though in some cases I have made emendations (cf. notes on the text below). When these manuscripts differ from each other, I shall give reasons for my choice of reading. I shall also discuss other matters of textual criticism.[2]

In this analysis, the poem has five symmetrical stanzas: 5 (10: 19–20.22–23) + 4 (10: 24–27) + 2 (10: 28–29) + 4 (10: 30–11: 2) + 5 (11: 3–6) bicola, for a total of 20 bicola. The rhetorical device of *inclusio* formed by the verbs *nikbād*/*niqleh* (10: 19) and *niqlû*/*nikbādîm* (11: 6), in chiastic order, is skillfully employed by Ben Sira to indicate the precise limits of the poem. A second indicator may be seen in the last word of the poem, *zĕʿērîm* (11: 6b), which reverses the *reš* and *ʿayin* of the first word, *zeraʿ* (10: 19a).

I

זרע נכבד מה זרע לאנוש	A	10: 19a
זרע נכבד ירא ייי		b
זרע נקלה מה זרע לאנוש	B	c
זרע נקלה עובר מצוה	AB	d
בין אחים ראשם נכבד	AB	20a
וירא אלהים בעמו	A	b
גר זר נכרי ורש	B	22a
תפארתם יראת ייי	B	b
אין לבזות דל משכיל	AB	23a
ואין לכבד כל איש חמס	B	b

II

שר שופט ומושל נכבדו	B	24a
ואין גדול מירא אלהים	A	b
עבד משכיל חורים יעבדוהו	B[3]	25a
וגבר משכיל לא יתאונן	B[3]	b
אל תתחכם לעשות חפצך	B	26a
ואל תתכבד במועד צרכך	A	b
טוב עובד ויותר הון	AB	27a
ממתכבד וחסר מזון	B	b

III

בני בענוה כבד נפשך	AB	28a
ותן לה טעם כיוצא בה	B	b
מרשיע נפשו מי יצדיקנו	A	29a
ומי יכבד מקלה נפשו	AB	b

IV

דל נכבד בגלל שכלו	B	30a
ועשיר נכבד בגלל עשרו	B	b
הנכבד בעוניו בעשרו איככה	B[1]	31a
ונקלה בעשרו בעוניו איככה	B[1]	b
חכמת דל תשא ראשו	AB	11: 1a
ובין נדיבים תשיבנו	AB	b
אל תהלל אדם בתארו	AB	2a
ואל תתעב אדם משבר במראהו	B	b

V

קטנה בעוף דבורה	B[1]	3a
וראש תנובות פריה	B[1]	b
בעוטה אזור אל תהתל	B[2]	4a
ואל תקלס במרירי יום	B[2]	b
כי פלאות מעשי ייי	A	c
ונעלם מאדם פעלו	A	d
רבים נדכאים ישבו על כסא	A	5a
ובל עלים על לב עטו צניף	AB[1]	b
רבים נשאים נקלו מאד	AB[1]	6a
ונכבדים נתנו ביד זעירים	B[1]	b

I

10: 19a What can be an honorable seed? The seed of man.
b The honorable seed is the one that fears Yahweh.
c What can be a dishonorable seed? The seed of man.
d The dishonorable seed is the one that transgresses the Commandment.
20a Among brothers their leader is honored;
b but he who fears God (is honored) among his [God's] people.
22a Resident alien, stranger, foreigner, and pauper—
b their glory is the fear of Yahweh.
23a It is not right to despise the wise poor man,
b nor is it right to honor any violent [or lawless] man.

II

24a Prince, judge, and ruler are honored;
b but none is greater than the one who fears God.
25a The wise slave nobles serve,
b and the wise man will not complain.
26a Make not a display of wisdom in doing your work,
b nor boast in your time of need.
27a Better the worker who has goods in plenty
b than the boaster who is without sustenance.

III

28a My son, with humility honor yourself,
b and give yourself the esteem you deserve.
29a Who will acquit him who condemns himself?
b and who will honor him who dishonors himself?

IV

30a The poor man is honored on account of his wisdom,
b but the rich man is honored on account of his wealth.
31a Honored in poverty, in wealth how much more so!
b But dishonored in wealth, in poverty how much more so!
11: 1a The wisdom of the poor man lifts up his head
b and makes him sit among princes.
2a Praise not a man for his looks,
b nor abhor a man broken in his appearance.

V

3a Least among flying things is the bee,
b but the best of produce is her fruit.
4a The one who wears a loincloth mock not,
b and scoff not at a man's bitter day.
c For strange are the deeds of Yahweh,
d and hidden from man is his work.
5a Many oppressed have sat on a throne,
b and those that none would consider have worn a crown.
6a Many exalted have been dishonored completely.
b and the honored have been given into the power of the few.

Strophe I (10: 19–20.22–23)

The Text. The words of 10: 19b I restore on the basis of the Syriac and Syrohexaplar as well as the parallelism to 10: 19d (found in both A and B). A omits 10: 19bc because of homoioarchton. B has 10: 19cd at the beginning of a folio (T.-S. 12.871a); the preceding folio, which most likely contained 10: 19ab, is no longer extant.[3] In 10: 20b, the third word in A has extant only the letters *bᶜ*; with Smend, I restore the word to read *bĕᶜammô,* which suits the context well (1906a: 97); others prefer the reading *bĕᶜênāyw* on the basis of Greek (cf. Rüger 1970: 56). But Greek probably misread *bĕᶜammô* as *bĕᶜênāyw*. B has instead *mimmennû* (the basis of Syriac), which is a later reading. 10: 21 is found only in a few of the Greek witnesses (Syh *L*–694–743) and does not belong to the original poem. In 10: 22a, A has the erroneous *wĕzēd* for the correct *zār* of B. In 10: 22b, A reads *ʾĕlōhîm* for *yyy* (Yahweh) in B. In 10: 22b, B^{mg} reads *byr,* an abbreviation for *bĕyirʾat* (cf. Syriac), a reading influenced by 9: 16b. In 10: 23b, A has *[ḥā]kām* instead of *ḥāmās;* it is often stated that *ḥākām* is a mistake for *ḥāmās*.[4] It is more probable, however, that *ḥākām* here and in 32: 17a (B^{txt}), 18a.c (B^{txt}) is an early substitution for *ḥāmās,* based on Prov 11: 30 where *ḥākām* has a similar meaning, "an arrogant, deviously cunning man," or, to use the slang expression, "a wise guy."

Poetic Analysis and Exegesis. The opening stanza contrasts the God-fearing wise man, who is often poor or disadvantaged (10: 22a.23a), with the lawless man (10: 23b), who transgresses the Law (10: 19d). The expression "fear of Yahweh/God" occurs three times (10: 19b.20b.22b) to emphasize the centrality of this concept in the poem.

Note the striking antithetic parallelism between 10: 19b and d: *zeraᶜ nikbād* (19b) vs. *zeraᶜ niqleh* (19d), and *yĕrêʾ yyy* (19b) vs. *ᶜôbēr miṣwâ* (19d). The participles *nikbād* and *niqleh* occur together also in Isa 3: 5. The verse, like Sir 1: 25–27 and 32: 23–24, alludes to the great Deuteronomic equation: to fear the Lord = to keep the Law, summarized in "the Commandment," i.e., Deut 6: 4–5; cf. Mark 12: 28–30; Matt 22: 36–38; Luke 10: 26–28. Sir 10: 19 gives the principal idea of the poem: people are honorable only when they fear the Lord; they are dishonorable when they transgress the Law. In 10: 20a, "brothers," or "kinsmen," refers to members of the same social, religious, or political community (cf. 7: 17). The point of v 20 is that the one who fears God has among God's own people honor equal to that which earthly leaders receive because of their office. B and Syriac go even further: the God-fearing person receives more honor than the earthly leader (cf. 25: 10). V 20 may be an allusion to the Joseph story (Gen 42: 1–47: 12); indeed, Joseph says of himself early on "*I fear God*" (Gen 42: 18), in words Ben Sira uses here.

In 10: 22a, note the *r*–alliteration in the four words, with the two velars (*g* and *k*), and the two sibilants (*z* and *š*). The nouns *zār* and *rāš* reverse the order of the *r* and the sibilant. Interestingly, Ben Sira places together four social groups, all of whom are disadvantaged. The *gēr* (a *hapax* in Sirach), who was not even an Israelite but a resident alien, had no inherited rights. He was, however, granted certain rights by the Law (cf. Exod 20: 10; 23: 12; Deut 5: 14) and was obliged to observe its prescriptions (cf. Exod 12: 19, 48, 49; Lev 16: 29; 17: 8, 10, 12, 13, 15; 18: 26). The *zār* and *nokrî* occur together in Prov 20: 16 and 27: 13. Though these four groups have social, economic, and political disadvantages, "their glory is the fear of Yahweh." Cf. Jer 9: 22–23. In 10: 23, Ben Sira employs antithetic parallelism (cf. 10: 19): note the contrasts between *libzôt* and *lĕkabbēd* and between *dal maśkîl* and *kol ʾîš ḥāmās*. In Gen 6: 13(P), *ḥāmās,* "violence, lawlessness," is the reason for the Flood. The *ʾîš ḥāmās,* in synonymous parallelism with *ᶜôbēr miṣwâ* (10: 19d), is featured also in Pss 18: 49; 140: 12; Prov 3: 31; 16: 29. The idea of "the wise poor man" being "despised" (10: 23a) is found also in Qoh 9: 15–16; cf. Jas 2: 1–6. The verb *kbd* occurs in the opening colon (10: 19a) and closing colon (10: 23b), thus forming an *inclusio* to signal the end of the stanza.

Strophe II (10: 24–27)

The Text. In 10: 24a, A has about a four-letter lacuna at the beginning, and then the words *môšēl wĕšôpēṭ*. Smend is probably correct in restoring *nādîb* because of the size of the lacuna and Greek *megistan* (1906a: 98). Syriac has the word order of A. But B is the original form of the colon (cf. below). In B, 10: 24b is fragmentary but probably read the same as A. In 10: 25a, B gives four cola; since the left side of the folio is damaged, only a few letters of the second, third, and fourth corresponding cola (as 10: 25b) are extant. Only the third form of 10: 25a is the correct one; A is corrupt (Di Lella 1964: 156 and Tab. I). By combining the evidence of Greek and fragmentary A and B, we may now reconstruct 10: 25b: *wĕgeber maś[kîl]* (from B) [*l*]*ō*ʾ *yitʾōnān* (from A). In 10: 26a, A reads *lāʿăbōd* instead of *laʿăśôt,* which is a preferred reading because the phrase occurs in Isa 58: 13. Instead of *ḥepṣekā* (10: 26a) in both A and B, B^{mg} has [*da*]*rkekā.* B is lacking part of 10: 26b, and A also has some lacunae; but the restoration seems certain. Both A and B are fragmentary in 10: 27b; instead of my restored *māzôn,* suggested by Greek, Latin, and Syriac, A has *mattān,* which receives no support from the versions.

Poetic Analysis and Exegesis. This stanza describes different classes of people— prince, judge, ruler (10: 24a), the one who fears God (10: 24b), the wise slave (10: 25a), the conscientious worker (10: 26–27a), and the idle boaster (10: 27b). Note that the *Nipʿal* of *kbd* and the expression "the one who fears Yahweh/God" occur in the opening bicola of the first (10: 19ab) and second stanzas (10: 24). In 10: 24a, there is alliteration and assonance in *śar, šôpēṭ, ûmôšēl:* 3 sibilants (*ś, š, š*), 2 liquids (*r, l*), 2 labials (*p, m*), 2 *ô*'s, and 2 *ē*'s. Also *śar* corresponds to the last syllable of *môšēl*, i.e., sibilant + liquid. The nouns *śar* and *šôpēṭ* are found together in the plural in Prov 8: 16. For the thought of 10: 24b, cf. 40: 25–27. The phrase *ʿebed maśkîl* (10: 25a) occurs also in Prov 17: 2. As the *dal maśkîl* should not be despised (10: 23a), so the *ʿebed maśkîl* will be served by *ḥôrîm,* "free men," or "nobles" (10: 25a); and the *geber maśkîl* will not complain (10: 25b) because his wisdom enables him to judge rightly. The nouns *ḥôrîm* and *śārîm* (cf. 10: 24a) form a pair in Isa 34: 12. The final words of each colon in 10: 26 rhyme: *ḥepṣekā* and *ṣorkekā.* The point of 10: 26b is: make no extravagant claims about what you might have done "in your time of need." Note the remarkable antithesis in 10: 27 between the energetic worker and the idle boaster; cf. Prov 12: 9. There is an *ô*–assonance in 10: 27a. The final words of 10: 27a and b rhyme: *hôn* and *māzôn* (cf. also 10: 26 above)—a good way to indicate the conclusion of a stanza.

Strophe III (10: 28–29)

The Text. In 10: 28b, A reads *wĕyitten lĕkā* instead of *wĕtēn lâ* (B), which is surely original; cf. Greek and Syriac. Before *maršîaʿ* (10: 29a) B adds *bĕnî,* a dittograph from 10: 28a. B is missing the end of 10: 29b, but it most likely read the same as A.

Poetic Analysis and Exegesis. The opening of this stanza is clearly indicated by *bĕnî.* The stanza, which contains the two middle bicola of the poem, has as subject matter the need for proper self-esteem. On the importance and religious value of humility, cf. 3: 17. The noun *ʿănāwâ* occurs only 4 times in the MT: Zeph 2: 3; Prov 15: 33; 18: 12; and 22: 4. In the Hebrew fragments of Sirach, the word occurs 5 times: 3: 17a; 4: 8b; 10: 28a; 13: 20a; and 45: 4a. For the thought of 10: 28a, cf. 7: 17; 10: 14; and 13: 20. One can achieve proper self-esteem only when one thinks of oneself with humility, and not with pride. The late idiom *kayyôṣēʾ bĕ-* (10: 28b) is found also in 38: 17b. In 10: 29, Ben Sira excoriates self-depreciation, which, contrary to popular opinion then and now, is not what humility is all about. A striking *a:b::b:a* chiastic pattern underscores his thought: *(maršîaʿ) napšô:mî (yaṣdîqennû)::ûmî (yĕkabbēd): (maqleh) napšô.* Note also the two sets of antithetic verbs (one set in each colon): *ršʿ* and *ṣdq*; and *kbd* and *qly* (found also in the opening couplet of the poem, 10: 19).

Strophe IV (10: 30–11: 2)

The Text. In 10: 30a, A adds *yēš* before *dal.* In 10: 30b, A reads: *wĕyēš nikbād biglal ʿošrô* (a reading which, curiously, is reflected in the Old Latin); B: *wĕyēš ʾîš ʿāšîr nikbād biglal* [*ʿošrô*]. A does not balance well with the first colon. B has too many words; hence, my deletion, on the basis of Greek, of the first two words. A and B give two forms of 10: 31; only the first form as found in B is the original, except that in the word *bʿynyw* in both cola (and in the second colon of A) read *waw* instead of the first *yod: bĕʿonyô* (cf. Greek and Syriac). Some scribe in the tradition confused *waw* and *yod* in the text he was copying.[5] In Ben Sira's time, it was not uncommon to use *waw* as a *mater lectionis* for a simple *o*–vowel; cf. also 13: 24b where *ʿŏnî* is written *ʿwny*. A omits *bĕʿonyô* in the first colon and *bĕʿošrô* in the second. The second form of 10: 31 in both A and B is: *hammitkabbēd bĕdallûtô bĕʿošrô mitkabbēd yōtēr; wĕhanniqleh bĕʿôšrô bĕdallûtô niqleh yōtēr*. This doublet is clearly a retroversion from Syriac.[6] In 11: 2b, A and B^{mg} read *mĕkōʿār* instead of *mošbār* of B.[7] Cf. Jer 8: 21 for another example of the *Hopʿal* of *šbr*.

Poetic Analysis and Exegesis. This stanza contrasts the poor man and rich man and gives the reason why each is honored (10: 30–31). It also describes the happy fate of the wise poor man (11: 1) and urges against reacting to a man solely on the basis of his appearance (11: 2). The opening verse (10: 30) has the verb *kbd* in both cola, as do the opening verses of the first three stanzas (10: 19, 24, 28). Note the balance and rhythm in the strong sentiment expressed in 10: 30: the poor man—honored—for wisdom (cf. 10: 25); the rich man—honored—for wealth. Cf. 13: 21–23. The last words of 10: 30a and b rhyme: *śiklô* and *ʿošrô*. 10: 31, which contains the verbs *kbd* and *qly* found also in 10: 19, restates and develops the thought of 10: 30. Note the *a:b::b:a* chiastic pattern in 10: 31: *bĕʿonyô:bĕʿošrô::bĕʿošrô:bĕʿonyô*. The subject of the wise poor man continues in 11: 1. The expression *nśʾ rōʾš* (11: 1a) occurs also in Gen 40: 13 and 2 Kgs 25: 27, in which it means, in effect, "to release from prison, set free." Thus, Ben Sira implies that "the wisdom of the poor man" frees him from the (apparent) confinement of his economic condition; cf. Prov 15: 33. The thought of 11: 1b derives from 1 Sam 2: 8a = Ps 113: 8a, in which the *Hipʿil* of *yšb* and the noun *nĕdîbîm* occur; cf. also 2 Kgs 25: 28. Note the dental- and sibilant-alliteration in 11: 1a: *ḥokmat dal tiśśāʾ rōʾšô;* and the pleasing rhythm created by the labial- and *n*-alliteration in 11: 1b: *ûbên nĕdîbîm tôšîbennû*. The injunctions of 11: 2 are based on the conviction that appearances can be misleading, as Yahweh taught Samuel in not choosing Eliab (1 Sam 16: 6–7). Wisdom, which resides within to motivate a person to fear the Lord by observing the Law, is all that really matters; looks do not count in God's sight (cf. 1 Chr 28: 9; Jer 17: 10). Note the labial-, liquid-, and dental-alliteration in 11: 2b: *wĕʾal tĕtaʿēb ʾādām mošbār bĕmarʾēhû*.

Strophe V (11: 3–6)

The Text. Instead of *qĕṭannâ* (11: 3a), A reads *ʾĕlîl* (B^2: *ʾlwl* because of the confusion of *waw* for *yod*); I agree with Segal that the former is the better reading (1959–60: 316). In 11: 4ab, B gives two forms, of which the second seems better. The first is *bimĕʿûtap bĕgādîm ʾal titpāʾēr* (cf. Greek), *wĕʾal tĕqallēs kimĕrîrî yôm*. A agrees with B^2, though there is a hole in the middle of the second word: ʾ[ ]*r*, which probably read *ʾēzôr*, as in B. In 11: 4d, B reads *mēʾĕnôš* instead of *mēʾādām*. B gives two forms of 11: 5; in both, several words are missing at the beginning of 5a. In 11: 5b, AB^1 omit before *ʿal* the participle *ʿōlîm* (cf. Syriac) because of homoioarchton. In 5b, B^2 reads: *wĕšiplê lēb yaʿăṭû ṣānîp;* cf. Isa 57: 15. The idiom *ʿly ʿal lēb* is found also in Jer 3: 16. B gives two forms of 11: 6, but the opening words of 6a are missing in each. B^1 ends 6a with [*mĕ*]*ʾōd*, most likely reading the same as A in the earlier words. A and B^2 add after *mĕʾōd: wĕhošpālû yaḥad* (cf. 1 Sam 2: 7b). In 6b, A reads *wĕgam nikbādîm* instead of *wĕnikbādîm* and together with B^2 omits *zĕʿērîm* after *bĕyād*. Although *ntn bĕyād* (of A and B^2) is idiomatic (cf. 1 Sam 26: 23 and 2 Chr 25: 20), I now prefer the reading of B^1 (cf. Di Lella 1964: 159^{q-q}). Greek *heterōn* (most MSS) or *echthrōn* (L^{-248}) points to Heb. *zārîm*, which in turn gives support to *zĕʿērîm* of B^1. For other reasons, cf. below.

Poetic Analysis and Exegesis. The final stanza has as its theme how mysterious are God's ways and how God can reverse human expectations. Note how the stanza begins with *qĕṭannâ*, "least," and ends with *zĕʿērîm*, "few." There is a labial-alliteration in 11: 3 and an *ô*/*ō*-assonance in the middle four words (*bāʿôp dĕbôrâ wĕrōʾš tĕnûbôt*) and end-rhyme in the first, third, and sixth words (*qĕṭannâ, dĕbôrâ, piryâ*). Note the antithetic parallelism between *qĕṭannâ* and *rōʾš*. In 11: 4ab, the *a:b::b':a'* chiastic pattern emphasizes Ben Sira's negative injunction: *bĕʿôṭeh ʾēzôr: ʾal tĕhattēl:: wĕʾal tĕqallēs: bimĕrîrî yôm*. Note also the dental- and liquid-alliteration. The noun *ʾēzôr* (found also in 45: 10c), "loincloth, waistcloth," occurs twice in Isa 11: 5 as a metaphor for *ṣedeq* and *ʾĕmûnâ*. It is a relatively rare word: 2 Kgs 1: 8 (= part of Elijah's apparel); Jer 13: 1, 2, 4, 6, 7 *(bis)*, 10, 11 (= symbol of the closeness which Israel and Judah were intended to have with Yahweh); Job 12: 18 (= a sign that a king is reduced to the condition of a slave wearing a waistcloth). For the background of the expression *bimĕrîrî yôm*, cf. Amos 8: 10. The adjective *mĕrîrî* (so also in Deut 32: 24) here means "the bitter man." The reason why one should not mock the poor man (11: 4a) or scoff at a man's troubles (11: 4b) is given in 11: 4cd and amplified in 11: 5–6; cf. Isa 55: 8–9.

In 11: 4cd, another *a:b::b′:a′* chiastic pattern is obvious: *maʿăśê: yyy:: mēʾādām: poʿŏlô*. Note also the labial-alliteration in the bicolon: 4 *m*'s, 2 *p*'s, and 2 *w*'s (the first being in *yhwh*, though the word is abbreviated, as usual in B, *yyy*). In the three words of 4d, there is also a beautiful rhyme and rhythm: *wĕneʿlām mēʾādām poʿŏlô*. Note the reversal of the labials in *ʿl+m* in *neʿlām* and the *p+ʿl* in *poʿŏlô*. As regards 11: 5a, cf. Isa 57: 15. 11: 5b is in synthetic parallelism with 5a. Note the remarkable labial-, *ʿayin-*, and *lamed*-alliteration in 5b, as well as the reversal of consonants in *bal* and *lēb*. For the sentiments expressed in 11: 5–6, cf. 10: 14; 1 Sam 2: 7–8; Ps 113: 7–8; Luke 1: 52. The thought and vocabulary of 11: 6, including *zĕʿērîm* (which A and B^2 omit), derive from Isa 16: 14: "The glory [*kābôd*] of Moab shall be dishonored [*wĕniqleh*] in all its great [*rab*] multitude; there shall be a remnant, a little, a few [*mizʿār*], not much." In the context of the poem, the verse implies that the "many exalted" (11: 6a) and "the honored" (11: 6b) do not fear the Lord (10: 19; cf. 10: 20, 22, 24); hence, their fate is to become "dishonored completely" (11: 6a) and to be "given into the power of the few," i.e., the Jewish remnant who remain steadfast in their service of the Lord (11: 6b). There is end rhyme in the first, second, fifth, and eighth words of 11: 6. Note the sharp contrast developed in an *a:b::b′:a′* chiastic pattern: *rabbîm: niqlû: wĕnikbādîm:zĕʾērîm*. As I indicated above, this verse also contains the same two verbs, *kbd* and *qly*, found in the opening verse (10: 19).

Notes

1. For MS A, I used the editions especially of Smend (1906b), the most reliable of all, and Segal (1958). For MS B, I used my own edition (Di Lella 1964).

2. For the Greek of Sirach I used the definitive edition of Ziegler (1965); for the Old Latin, the splendid critical edition in the *Biblia sacra* (1964); for the Syriac, the editions of Walton (1657), de Lagarde (1861), Ceriani (1876–83), and Mosul (1951); for the Syrohexaplar, the sumptuous photofacsimile of Ceriani (1874).

3. Cf. Di Lella 1964: Tab. I. For a full discussion of what the versions do with this verse, cf. Di Lella 1966: 60–63.

4. Smend 1906a: 98; Peters 1913: 93; Rüger 1970: 93.

5. For a discussion and other examples of this phenomenon in the Geniza fragments, cf. Di Lella 1966: 97–101.

6. For proof of retroversion, cf. Di Lella 1966: 115–19.

7. Schirmann (1959–60: 125–34) reads *mʿzb* for my reading of *mšbr*. Rüger (1970: 64, 94, n. 52) follows Schirmann.

References

Biblia sacra iuxta latinam vulgatam versionem, 12: *Sapientia Salomonis, Liber Hiesu filii Sirach.*
1964 Rome: Vatican Press.

Biblia sacra iuxta versionem simplicem quae dicitur Pschitta, 2 (referred to as the Mosul edition).
1951 Beirut: Catholic Press (Sirach pp. 204–55).

Box, G. H., and Oesterley, W. O. E.
1913 Sirach. In *The Apocrypha and Pseudepigrapha of the Old Testament,* 1, ed. R. H. Charles. Oxford: Clarendon.

Ceriani, A. M.
1874 *Codex syro-hexaplaris Ambrosianus photolithographice editus.* Milan: J. B. Pogliani.
1876–83 *Translatio Syra Pescitto veteris testamenti ex codice Ambrosiano sec. fere VI photolithographice edita.* Milan: J. B. Pogliani.

Di Lella, A. A.
1964 The Recently Identified Leaves of Sirach in Hebrew. *Biblica* 45: 153–67.
1966 *The Hebrew Text of Sirach: A Text-Critical and Historical Study.* Studies in Classical Literature 1. The Hague: Mouton.

Duesberg, H., and Fransen, I.
1966 *Ecclesiastico.* La Sacra Bibbia . . . di S. Garofalo: Antico Testamento, ed. G. Rinaldi. Turin: Marietti.

de Lagarde, P. A.
1861 *Libri veteris testamenti apocryphi syriace.* Leipzig—London: F. A. Brockhaus—Williams & Norgate.

Peters, N.
1913 *Das Buch Jesus Sirach oder Ecclesiasticus.* Exegetisches Handbuch zum Alten Testament 25. Münster i. W.: Aschendorffsche Verlagsbuchhandlung.

Rüger, H. P.
1970 *Text und Textform im hebräischen Sirach: Untersuchung zur Textgeschichte und Textkritik der hebräischen Sirachfragmente aus der Kairoer Geniza.* Beihefte zur Zeitschrift für die Alttestamentliche Wissenschaft 112. Berlin: de Gruyter.

Schirmann, J.
1959–60 *Dappîm nôsĕpîm mittôk sēper 'ben-Sîrā>'.* *Tarbız* 29: 125–34.

Segal, M. H.
1958 *Sēper ben-Sîrā> ha-šālēm*[2]. Jerusalem: Bialik Institute.
1959–60 *Dappîm nôsĕpîm mittôk sēper ben-Sîrā>. . . Tarbiz* 29: 313–23.

Smend, R.
1906a *Die Weisheit des Jesus Sirach erklärt.* Berlin: G. Reimer.
1906b *Die Weisheit des Jesus Sirach, hebräisch und deutsch.* Berlin: G. Reimer.

Walton, B.
1657 *Biblia sacra polyglotta,* 4. London: Thomas Roycroft. (Variants are contained in vol. 6, pp. 46–47.)

Ziegler, J.
1965 *Sapientia Jesu Filii Sirach.* Septuaginta 12/2. Göttingen: Vandenhoeck & Ruprecht.

"Prose Particle" Counts of the Hebrew Bible

Francis I. Andersen
The University of Queensland, Brisbane, Queensland
and
A. Dean Forbes
Palo Alto, California

The definite article *(h-),* the relative pronoun *(ʾăšer),* and the sign of the definite object *(ʾet)* are among the commonest vocabulary items in Biblical Hebrew. They seem so pivotal in the realization of even the simplest grammatical constructions that it is hard to imagine any passage of Biblical Hebrew without at least a few. Yet twenty-four chapters of Hebrew in the Bible contain none of these particles; with the single notable exception of Hosea 11, all are in the poetic books, namely Psalms 4, 17, 23, 39, 43, 75, 76, 91, 93, 110, 111, 141, 143, 149, Job 16, 17, 21, 24, and Proverbs 11, 12, 14, 15, 28.

1. The overall frequency of occurrence of the three particles ranges from zero in these chapters up to the amazing 36.55% of Leviticus 3. (For eight other chapters the score exceeds 30%.) Different genres clump together at different parts of the range.

2. A separate examination of each particle is informative. In the following we recognize 900 chapters of Hebrew in the Bible. Nine chapters consisting wholly or largely of Aramaic are left aside. We also omit Qohelet and the Song of Songs (20 chapters total), which are written in a distinct dialect, out of the mainstream.

2.1. There are 56 chapters that never use the consonantal article, all in Isaiah, Hosea, Psalms, Job, and Proverbs. The highest concentration of consonantal articles occurs in Ezekiel 42, in which the frequency of occurrence is 26.67%. (By "consonantal article" we mean the article represented by the consonant *h.* The masoretic vowel that rides on a one-consonant preposition has a different history and less weight, and is often dubious.)

2.2. There are 169 chapters in which *ʾăšer* is never used. Most of these chapters are in the poetic books: 94 psalms (the tally would be higher if we disregarded the prose titles), 21 chapters of Proverbs and 18 of Job; runners-up are Isaiah (12 chapters) and Hosea (6 chapters). (The highest score for *ʾăšer* is 7.12% in Qohelet 8.)

2.3. There are 153 chapters in which the *nota accusativi* is never used, and these chapters are mainly in the books with chapters having neither definite article nor relative: Psalms (81 psalms), Proverbs (14 chapters), Job (26), Isaiah (9), and Hosea

(3). The chapter with the highest concentration of *ʾet* is Joshua 21, with a relative frequency of 19.38%.

3. Each of the three particles deserves more detailed individual attention; indeed, the distribution of other prepositions and conjunctions should be studied along the same lines. Since this is only a preliminary report, we shall concentrate on the scores for the sum of the occurrences of the three particles. There are good historical reasons for so doing, since *ha-*, *ʾăšer,* and *ʾet* are known to be innovations in Hebrew. It has long been realized that they are characteristic of prose but often lacking in poetry. This lack calls for an explanation. It is not enough to say that these particles are often "left out" of poetry, as if they were to be "understood." It would be quite different if biblical poetry were written in an archaic dialect in which these "particles" did not exist or were not "needed."

3.1. In Table 0 we analyze 900 chapters of Biblical Hebrew. Each book as a whole is classified into one of four general categories: Poetry, Prophecy, Torah, or History. This is a rough classification, since many books have portions falling into various categories; only Poetry is more or less homogeneous. The individual prophetic books are quite diverse, and some include chapters of history. There are poems in the Pentateuch and in the historical books. The four categories are of roughly the same size. The Poetry category (Psalms, Proverbs, Job [minus three narrative chapters], and Lamentations) has 225 chapters; Prophecy (excluding Jonah) has 235; Pentateuch has 187, and History (including three chapters of Job, and Jonah and Esther) has 253.

3.2. Chapters with a score of less than 5% for the three particles under investigation are wisdom (Proverbs and Job), lyrical—mainly cultic—poetry (Psalms and Lamentations), and oracular prophecy (mainly in Hosea and Isaiah). Similar low scores characterize a number of archaic poems in the Pentateuch and the historical books.

3.3. Most chapters with a score of 5-10% are poetic, the majority embedded in prophetic books. There are as well quite a few chapters of prose with a score of less than 10%, mainly old narrative in Genesis and Samuel.

3.4. Chapters in the middle range (10-20%) are mixed in character. The handful of psalms with such scores attract attention. Prophecy, Pentateuch, and History are well represented. The intermediate scores, especially those in the lower half of the range (where there is more prophecy), can be accounted for in three ways: 1) some chapters contain (low-score) cultic or oracular poetry embedded in (high-score) narrative prose, and the two average out; 2) some chapters of narrative contain much dialogue, the lower score of which is due either to its vernacular background or its quasi-poetic form; and 3) there are homogeneous chapters of prose in which the incidence of the particles happens to be low for reasons yet to be examined.

3.5. The 122 chapters with scores above 20% are virtually pure prose. Such chapters in the prophetic books (mainly Jeremiah and Ezekiel) are historical narrative of the same kind as found in Kings and Chronicles. At the top of the range is the literary prose of Deuteronomy and Leviticus.

4. The crudity of our measure must be emphasized. The individual chapters vary enormously in size, so the probability of a chapter's containing any specified item is not invariant. That is, two chapters with the same score do not necessarily represent a similar population. Since statistical inferences are not being made in the present study, more rigorous calculations of levels of confidence in comparing similar samples are not necessary. Even so, such raw results based on the conventional chapter divisions, many of which are arbitrary, show that the particle frequency is a powerful discriminator between poetry and prose. When the score fluctuates within the same chapter, portions with extreme values (e.g., the poems in Exodus 15, Genesis 49, and Deuteronomy 32) can be segregated.

4.1. The score has less utility for determining dates. The fact that Lamentations has scores as low as most cultic poetry shows that the poetic tradition still held up strongly in the sixth century. The few psalms with high scores attract the suspicion of being late. The scores for all post-exilic prophecies (Haggai, Zephaniah, Malachi, and Daniel) appear significantly higher than the rest.

4.2. It is not possible to chart a systematic rise in the score for prose from early to late. Certainly a prose passage with a low score can be rightly suspected of being ancient. But just as a poem with a low score is not necessarily ancient, so a prose passage with a high score is not necessarily late. The inscriptions prove that: they are written in the same kind of prose as we find in historical narrative, with normal incidences of the three particles.

5. Segregation of different kinds of prose, by both genre and date, using such criteria, will require more delicate work. This will need to be done on a broader front, looking at grammatical constructions and other "particles" as well as the three "prose particles."

6. The fact that Hebrew poetry makes sparse use of the "prose particles" is generally known, but the reason for this fact is not understood except in general terms (e.g., cult poetry tends to be archaic). The distribution of the phenomenon and its significance for the history of Hebrew language and literature await attention. Traditional interest in etymology has produced discussion of the possible origins of these particles. Notwithstanding the hesitation of BDB (p. 81), the derivation of *ʾăšer* from Proto-Semitic **ʾaṯru(m)* may be taken as certain. The origin of the article is debatable. (See the challenging discussion by Lambdin 1971, though the evidence of Berber, Diakonoff 1965: 61, suggests a possible pronominal origin.) While a nominal ancestry for *ʾet/ʾōt* is suspected, its cognativity with *ʾōt,* "sign," is not established; an equally good (but equally unconvincing) case can be made for existential **yat,* etc. The philological significance of the non-use of these particles has not been deliberately studied (see the few lines on *ha-* in BDB: 208b), since grammarians prefer to talk about attested usage. For *ʾăšer* the entry in BDB is unsurpassed. For *ʾet* see Hoftijzer 1965.

6.1. The significance of the article as a discriminator between prose and poetry was used by Radday and Shore (1976). Their prime measure was the fraction of "potential carriers of the article" that actually used it. Although based only on broad sampling of larger books, their results resemble ours in the main. The relative and the *nota accusativi* figured in the investigation of word frequencies and vocabulary richness in the "Five Scrolls" by Radday and Pollatschek (1978) and in the study of Zechariah by Radday and Wickmann (1975), though the method followed in the latter failed to detect the incredibly low score of Zechariah 9. All three particles figured in a battery of thirty-eight criteria used by Radday *et al.* (1977) in a study of Judges; but Judges 5 was disregarded, and the sampling was based on a source critical analysis of the text. Working with big chunks as samples blurs the results when small portions of prose and poetry occur in the same passage. Our study of individual chapters overcomes this difficulty to some extent, but even then there are some chapters which are a mixture. And the small sample size puts a limitation on the validity of statistical inference.

6.2. Andersen and Freedman (1980: 61-66) did a hand count of the "prose particles" in Hosea. The results are confirmed by the computer counts; comparison with the rest of the Bible now brings out the unique position of Hosea among the prophets in this respect.

APPENDIX

Tables 1-3 present counts and scores for the three "prose particles," individually and in aggregate, for every chapter in the Hebrew Bible. Table 1 lists the chapters in canonical order and includes the word count for each chapter. The ratio of particle count to total word count per chapter is expressed as a percentage. The total for all three does not include the count of "dubious" (or non-"consonantal") articles. In Table 2 the total scores for the three, as percentages, are arranged in increasing order. (The Aramaic chapters head the list.) Table 3 does the same for the relative, Table 4 for the article, Table 5 for the *nota accusativi.* Thanks are expressed to Belinda Foletta, who wrote and executed the programs and prepared the tables, and to Ann Eyland for continued assistance and advice.

References

Andersen, F. I., and Freedman, D. N.
1980 *Hosea.* The Anchor Bible 24. Garden City, NY: Doubleday.

Diakonoff, I. M.
1965 *Semito-Hamitic Languages: An Essay in Classification.* Moscow: Nauka Publishing House.

Hoftijzer, J.
1965 Remarks concerning the use of the particle *ʾt* in classical Hebrew. *Oudtestamentische Studien* 14:1-99.

Lambdin, T. O.
1971 The Junctural Origin of the West Semitic Definite Article. Pp. 315-33 in *Near Eastern Studies in Honor of William Foxwell Albright,* ed. Hans Goedicke. Baltimore: Johns Hopkins University Press.

Radday, Y. T., and Pollatschek, M. A.
1978 Frequency Profiles and the Five Scrolls. *Revue de l'Organisation internationale pour l'étude des langues anciennes par l'ordinateur* 2: 1-30.

Radday, Y. T., and Shore, H.
1976 The Definite Article: A Type- and/or Author-Specifying Discriminant in the Hebrew Bible. *Association for Literary and Linguistic Computing Bulletin* 4: 23-31.

Radday, Y. T., and Wickmann, D.
1975 The Unity of Zechariah Examined in the Light of Statistical Linguistics. *Zeitschrift für die Alttestamentliche Wissenschaft* 87: 30-55.

Radday, Y. T.; Leb, G.; and Wickmann, D.
1977 The Book of Judges Examined by Statistical Linguistics. *Biblica* 58: 469-99.

TABLE 0: NUMBER OF CHAPTERS WITH GIVEN RANGES OF PARTICLE FREQUENCIES ARRANGED AS A FUNCTION OF GENRE

Range of % Frequencies[1]	Number of Chapters in Range				
	Poetry	Prophecy	Torah	History	Total
0.00– 1.00	50[2]	4[3]	0	0	54
1.01– 2.00	55[4]	6[5]	0	0	61
2.01– 3.00[6]	47[7]	12[8]	0	0	59
3.01– 4.00	22[9]	17[10]	1[11]	2[12]	42
4.01– 5.00	12	13	4	0	29[13]
0.00– 5.00	186	52	5	2	245
5.01– 6.00	5	10	2[14]	2[15]	19
6.01– 7.00	3	19[16]	2[17]	2	26
7.01– 8.00	12	17	4	7[18]	40
8.01– 9.00	4	14	8[19]	2	28
9.01–10.00	6	12	6	10	34
5.01–10.00[20]	30	72	22	23	147
10.01–11.00	1[21]	10	6	13	30
11.01–12.00	3[22]	17	5	19	44
12.01–13.00	0	10	12	21	43
13.01–14.00	0	10	15	20	45
14.01–15.00	1[23]	7	10	20	38
10.01–15.00[24]	5	54	48	93	200
15.01–16.00	2[25]	8	14	18	42
16.01–17.00	1[26]	8	16	21	46
17.01–18.00	1[27]	4	10	24	39
18.01–19.00	0	8	14	9	31
19.01–20.00	0	6	14	8	28
15.01–20.00[28]	4	34	68	80	186
20.01–25.00[29]	0	21	30	42	93
25.01–30.00	0	0	8	12	20
30.01–35.00	0	1[30]	5[31]	2	8
35.01–40.00	0	0	1[32]	0	1

Particle frequency ("score") is defined as the number of consonantal articles, relatives, and *notae accusativi* divided by the number of words in the chapter.

Notes to Table 0

1. The total number of occurrences of nouns etc., with the consonantal definite article, *ʾăšer,* and *ʾet,* as a percentage of the number of words in the chapter.
2. 22 psalms, 15 chapters of Job, and 13 chapters of Proverbs.
3. Hosea 8, 11, 14, and Ezekiel 19.
4. 34 psalms, 10 chapters of Job, 10 of Proverbs, and Lamentations 5.
5. Hosea 6, 13; Habakkuk 3; Isaiah 44, 58; Zechariah 9. The last, at 1.35%, is astonishing in a post-exilic prophet.
6. Of the 174 chapters with 3% or less, 152 are in poetry books—84 psalms, 36 chapters of Job (out of 39 that are poetry), 28 of Proverbs (out of 31), four of Lamentations (out of five). The other 22 chapters with total frequency of prose particles in the range 1–3% are all in the prophets: 7 chapters of Hosea (out of 11 chapters of prophecy), 11 of Isaiah (mainly Deutero-), and one each in Habakkuk, Nahum, Ezekiel, and Zechariah. No chapter of Torah or History has such a low score.
7. 28 psalms, 11 chapters of Job, 5 of Proverbs, and 3 of Lamentations. Proverbs is the leanest book of all; 23 of its 31 chapters have a score less than 2.00%, 28 less than 3.00%.
8. Nine of these are in Isaiah.
9. All of Proverbs, 37 chapters of Job, and 102 psalms have totals less than 4%. Of the remaining chapters of Job, 32 scores 5.08% because of the prose introduction. Job 3 stands alone with 7.84%.
10. Of the 39 chapters of prophecy with less than 4%, 20 are in Isaiah, 9 in Hosea.
11. Deuteronomy 33, which contains an ancient poem.
12. Judges 5 and 2 Samuel 22, both poetic at least in part.
13. The number of chapters in this range is smaller; there is more prophecy than poetry. 27 chapters of Isaiah score less than 5%. For the first time we have low-scoring prose from the Pentateuch (Genesis 16; Leviticus 12; Numbers 2, 23 [contains poetry]). Leviticus thus contains the chapter with the lowest score for prose in the Pentateuch (Leviticus 12 at 4.27%), as well as the highest (Leviticus 3 at 36.55%).
14. Exodus 15 (the poem itself has no particles at all) and Deuteronomy 23.
15. Includes Ruth 1.
16. 40 of Isaiah's 66 chapters have a score of less than 7%.
17. Deuteronomy 32 (the poem has a very low score), Numbers 24 (includes old poetry).
18. Includes the poem in Jonah 2.
19. Seven in Genesis.
20. The range of up to 10% is dominated by poetry (216 of the 225 chapters in the four poetic books) and by oracular prophecy (more than half the chapters in the prophetic books). Quite a few of the low-scoring chapters in the Pentateuch and the historical books contain archaic poetry.
21. Psalm 148.
22. Psalms 117, 127, and 137.
23. Psalm 123.
24. In this range nearly half of the chapters come from "History." The old style of prophetic prose or folk narrative, also found in the Pentateuch (especially Genesis) and in the prophetic books themselves, is a major ingredient.
25. Psalms 114 and 134.
26. Psalm 125.
27. Psalm 133.
28. Since the histories have more chapters than the Pentateuch, the proportions are similar. Both corpora have a wide range of prose styles; the same styles are also well represented in narrative chapters of prophetic books, mainly Jeremiah and Ezekiel.
29. There are fewer prophetic chapters in this range. Deuteronomy and Leviticus contribute most of the high-density chapters from the Pentateuch.
30. Ezekiel 42.
31. Four chapters in Leviticus.
32. Leviticus 3.

TABLE ONE: Listing of the Particles for each chapter (in canonical order) Page 1

Book and Chapter		Word Count	Relative Count	Relative Percentage	Article Count	Article Percentage	Nota Accusativi Count	Nota Accusativi Percentage	Total of Three Count	Total of Three Percentage	Dubious Article Count	Dubious Article Percentage
Genesis	1	434	9	2.074	68	15.668	26	5.991	103	23.733	10	2.304
Genesis	2	328	7	2.134	59	17.988	14	4.268	80	24.390	3	.915
Genesis	3	347	6	1.729	42	12.104	8	2.305	56	16.138	4	1.153
Genesis	4	341	1	.293	10	2.933	21	6.158	32	9.384	4	1.173
Genesis	5	365	2	.548	3	.822	27	7.397	32	8.767	0	.000
Genesis	6	305	9	2.951	36	11.803	16	5.246	61	20.000	7	2.295
Genesis	7	332	13	3.916	68	20.482	6	1.807	87	26.205	9	2.711
Genesis	8	308	4	1.299	59	19.156	13	4.221	76	24.675	13	4.221
Genesis	9	353	10	2.833	32	9.065	15	4.249	57	16.147	8	2.266
Genesis	10	288	1	.347	23	7.986	38	13.194	62	21.528	2	.694
Genesis	11	392	3	.765	12	3.061	29	7.398	44	11.224	2	.510
Genesis	12	268	6	2.239	15	5.597	17	6.343	38	14.179	4	1.493
Genesis	13	241	7	2.905	18	7.469	9	3.734	34	14.108	7	2.905
Genesis	14	342	8	2.339	25	7.310	19	5.556	52	15.205	0	.000
Genesis	15	259	4	1.544	31	11.969	22	8.494	57	22.008	3	1.158
Genesis	16	223	1	.448	5	2.242	4	1.794	10	4.484	3	1.345
Genesis	17	355	5	1.408	9	2.535	23	6.479	37	10.423	2	.563
Genesis	18	437	7	1.602	26	5.950	5	1.144	38	8.696	11	2.517
Genesis	19	563	8	1.421	67	11.901	25	4.440	100	17.762	15	2.664
Genesis	20	282	7	2.482	13	4.610	9	3.191	29	10.284	3	1.064
Genesis	21	436	13	2.982	35	8.028	24	5.505	72	16.514	6	1.376
Genesis	22	367	8	2.180	38	10.354	41	11.172	87	23.706	5	1.362
Genesis	23	275	10	3.636	15	5.455	12	4.364	37	13.455	3	1.091
Genesis	24	918	24	2.614	81	8.824	30	3.268	135	14.706	12	1.307
Genesis	25	405	7	1.728	15	3.704	20	4.938	42	10.370	2	.494
Genesis	26	466	10	2.146	33	7.082	13	2.790	56	12.017	12	2.575
Genesis	27	638	14	2.194	22	3.448	19	2.978	55	8.621	1	.157
Genesis	28	323	9	2.786	21	6.502	13	4.025	43	13.313	6	1.858
Genesis	29	471	4	.849	32	6.794	28	5.945	64	13.588	4	.849
Genesis	30	560	13	2.321	33	5.893	28	5.000	74	13.214	12	2.143
Genesis	31	768	16	2.083	53	6.901	40	5.208	109	14.193	6	.781
Genesis	32	453	7	1.545	38	8.389	23	5.077	68	15.011	7	1.545
Genesis	33	268	9	3.358	20	7.463	13	4.851	42	15.672	1	.373
Genesis	34	421	10	2.375	24	5.701	36	8.551	70	16.627	8	1.900
Genesis	35	378	15	3.968	17	4.497	12	3.175	44	11.640	7	1.852
Genesis	36	487	4	.821	13	2.669	24	4.928	41	8.419	1	.205
Genesis	37	494	5	1.012	26	5.263	31	6.275	62	12.551	7	1.417
Genesis	38	405	6	1.481	22	5.432	6	1.975	36	8.889	3	.741
Genesis	39	347	15	4.323	31	8.934	10	2.882	56	16.138	7	2.017
Genesis	40	312	7	2.244	33	10.577	22	7.051	62	19.872	6	1.923
Genesis	41	776	15	1.933	88	11.340	43	5.541	146	18.814	10	1.289
Genesis	42	528	4	.758	32	6.061	31	5.871	67	12.689	5	.947
Genesis	43	485	9	1.856	44	9.072	21	4.330	74	15.258	8	1.649
Genesis	44	455	14	3.077	32	7.033	17	3.736	63	13.846	5	1.099
Genesis	45	397	7	1.763	8	2.015	19	4.786	34	8.564	5	1.259
Genesis	46	414	11	2.657	10	2.415	13	3.140	34	8.213	1	.242
Genesis	47	512	7	1.367	33	6.445	25	4.883	65	12.695	12	2.344
Genesis	48	350	4	1.143	22	6.286	23	6.571	49	14.000	2	.571
Genesis	49	368	8	2.174	13	3.533	15	4.076	36	9.783	7	1.902
Genesis	50	375	8	2.133	20	5.333	25	6.667	53	14.133	2	.533
Exodus	1	240	5	2.083	27	11.250	14	5.833	46	19.167	6	2.500
Exodus	2	340	1	.294	39	11.471	27	7.941	67	19.706	8	2.353
Exodus	3	395	5	1.266	39	9.873	23	5.823	67	16.962	2	.506
Exodus	4	453	9	1.987	29	6.402	22	4.857	60	13.245	6	1.325
Exodus	5	318	6	1.887	17	5.346	14	4.403	37	11.635	10	3.145
Exodus	6	404	6	1.485	7	1.733	29	7.178	42	10.396	0	.000
Exodus	7	418	13	3.110	20	4.785	19	4.545	52	12.440	14	3.349
Exodus	8	422	6	1.422	41	9.716	23	5.450	70	16.588	12	2.844
Exodus	9	521	10	1.919	55	10.557	29	5.566	94	18.042	18	3.455
Exodus	10	497	6	1.207	36	7.243	36	7.243	78	15.694	3	.604
Exodus	11	174	4	2.299	11	6.322	6	3.448	21	12.069	0	.000
Exodus	12	751	15	1.997	78	10.386	29	3.862	122	16.245	22	2.929
Exodus	13	325	4	1.231	30	9.231	13	4.000	47	14.462	5	1.538
Exodus	14	474	4	.844	44	9.283	29	6.118	77	16.245	9	1.899
Exodus	15	321	1	.312	13	4.050	4	1.246	18	5.607	12	3.738
Exodus	16	548	14	2.555	50	9.124	22	4.015	86	15.693	26	4.745
Exodus	17	246	4	1.626	15	6.098	9	3.659	28	11.382	5	2.033
Exodus	18	418	16	3.828	46	11.005	24	5.742	86	20.574	5	1.196
Exodus	19	375	6	1.600	49	13.067	10	2.667	65	17.333	12	3.200
Exodus	20	312	12	3.846	23	7.372	23	7.372	58	18.590	7	2.244
Exodus	21	451	6	1.330	25	5.543	17	3.769	48	10.643	9	1.996
Exodus	22	361	3	.831	18	4.986	7	1.939	28	7.756	5	1.385
Exodus	23	398	7	1.759	30	7.538	23	5.779	60	15.075	5	1.256
Exodus	24	252	5	1.984	33	13.095	9	3.571	47	18.651	5	1.984
Exodus	25	440	10	2.273	51	11.591	25	5.682	86	19.545	8	1.818
Exodus	26	480	2	.417	101	21.042	23	4.792	126	26.250	23	4.792
Exodus	27	262	2	.763	21	8.015	11	4.198	34	12.977	12	4.580
Exodus	28	595	5	.840	59	9.916	37	6.218	101	16.975	1	.168

TABLE ONE: Listing of the Particles for each chapter (in canonical order) Page 2

Book and Chapter		Word Count	Relative Count	Relative Percentage	Article Count	Article Percentage	Nota Accusativi Count	Nota Accusativi Percentage	Total of Three Count	Total of Three Percentage	Dubious Article Count	Dubious Article Percentage
Exodus	29	649	18	2.773	96	14.792	74	11.402	188	28.968	14	2.157
Exodus	30	468	8	1.709	33	7.051	37	7.906	78	16.667	4	.855
Exodus	31	229	3	1.310	27	11.790	27	11.790	57	24.891	7	3.057
Exodus	32	544	22	4.044	47	8.640	21	3.860	90	16.544	6	1.103
Exodus	33	354	9	2.542	37	10.452	15	4.237	61	17.232	4	1.130
Exodus	34	538	11	2.045	42	7.807	23	4.275	76	14.126	14	2.602
Exodus	35	440	12	2.727	49	11.136	61	13.864	122	27.727	13	2.955
Exodus	36	514	8	1.556	85	16.537	25	4.864	118	22.957	20	3.891
Exodus	37	366	3	.820	41	11.202	33	9.016	77	21.038	4	1.093
Exodus	38	412	4	.971	59	14.320	30	7.282	93	22.573	16	3.883
Exodus	39	568	14	2.465	87	15.317	66	11.620	167	29.401	2	.352
Exodus	40	440	10	2.273	65	14.773	71	16.136	146	33.182	10	2.273
Leviticus	1	252	6	2.381	52	20.635	24	.524	82	32.540	2	.794
Leviticus	2	200	2	1.000	17	8.500	7	3.500	26	13.000	6	3.000
Leviticus	3	249	11	4.418	52	20.884	28	11.245	91	36.546	0	.000
Leviticus	4	542	26	4.797	90	16.605	41	7.565	157	28.967	5	.923
Leviticus	5	430	21	4.884	31	7.209	18	4.186	70	16.279	7	1.628
Leviticus	6	303	10	3.300	35	11.551	13	4.290	58	19.142	12	3.960
Leviticus	7	480	15	3.125	65	13.542	34	7.083	114	23.750	24	5.000
Leviticus	8	570	16	2.807	89	15.614	87	15.263	192	33.684	9	1.579
Leviticus	9	318	8	2.516	65	20.440	34	10.692	107	33.648	9	2.830
Leviticus	10	327	7	2.141	26	7.951	19	5.810	52	15.902	4	1.223
Leviticus	11	593	21	3.541	100	16.863	41	6.914	162	27.319	12	2.024
Leviticus	12	117	0	.000	5	4.274	0	.000	5	4.274	3	2.564
Leviticus	13	893	7	.784	155	17.357	37	4.143	199	22.284	50	5.599
Leviticus	14	818	17	2.078	192	23.472	70	8.557	279	34.108	35	4.279
Leviticus	15	456	20	4.386	54	11.842	12	2.632	86	18.860	19	4.167
Leviticus	16	552	15	2.717	72	13.043	50	9.058	137	24.819	19	3.442
Leviticus	17	274	12	4.380	24	8.759	8	2.920	44	16.058	10	3.650
Leviticus	18	344	9	2.616	20	5.814	18	5.233	47	13.663	1	.291
Leviticus	19	440	3	.682	18	4.091	22	5.000	43	9.773	12	2.727
Leviticus	20	428	20	4.673	28	6.542	50	11.682	98	22.897	13	3.037
Leviticus	21	305	6	1.967	14	4.590	11	3.607	31	10.164	1	.328
Leviticus	22	439	13	2.961	15	3.417	14	3.189	42	9.567	9	2.050
Leviticus	23	593	7	1.180	51	8.600	22	3.710	80	13.491	30	5.059
Leviticus	24	277	3	1.083	22	7.942	13	4.693	38	13.718	10	3.610
Leviticus	25	710	14	1.972	46	6.479	28	3.944	88	12.394	21	2.958
Leviticus	26	582	6	1.031	22	3.780	54	9.278	82	14.089	8	1.375
Leviticus	27	458	14	3.057	46	10.044	17	3.712	77	16.812	7	1.528
Numbers	1	588	6	1.020	24	4.082	14	2.381	44	7.483	5	.850
Numbers	2	342	3	.877	12	3.509	2	.585	17	4.971	1	.292
Numbers	3	599	7	1.169	72	12.020	30	5.008	109	18.197	2	.334
Numbers	4	668	12	1.796	61	9.132	50	7.485	123	18.413	9	1.347
Numbers	5	462	9	1.948	69	14.935	36	7.792	114	24.675	7	1.515
Numbers	6	360	7	1.944	28	7.778	16	4.444	51	14.167	6	1.667
Numbers	7	1072	1	.093	74	6.903	27	2.519	102	9.515	26	2.425
Numbers	8	361	5	1.385	27	7.479	31	8.587	63	17.452	8	2.216
Numbers	9	354	7	1.977	44	12.429	12	3.390	63	17.797	11	3.107
Numbers	10	382	2	.524	29	7.592	7	1.832	38	9.948	9	2.356
Numbers	11	549	10	1.821	71	12.933	21	3.825	102	18.579	10	1.821
Numbers	12	196	5	2.551	10	5.102	0	.000	15	7.653	5	2.551
Numbers	13	394	9	2.284	42	10.660	17	4.315	68	17.259	6	1.523
Numbers	14	635	21	3.307	78	12.283	31	4.882	130	20.472	21	3.307
Numbers	15	511	12	2.348	47	9.198	20	3.914	79	15.460	28	5.479
Numbers	16	493	9	1.826	38	7.708	23	4.665	70	14.199	1	.203
Numbers	17	395	9	2.278	37	9.367	17	4.304	63	15.949	4	1.013
Numbers	18	521	10	1.919	30	5.758	28	5.374	68	13.052	7	1.344
Numbers	19	346	10	2.890	51	14.740	13	3.757	74	21.387	22	6.358
Numbers	20	418	8	1.914	38	9.091	26	6.220	72	17.225	4	.957
Numbers	21	472	10	2.119	50	10.593	31	6.568	91	19.280	8	1.695
Numbers	22	652	14	2.147	45	6.902	31	4.755	90	13.804	13	1.994
Numbers	23	389	5	1.285	6	1.542	6	1.542	17	4.370	6	1.542
Numbers	24	306	4	1.307	9	2.941	8	2.614	21	6.863	1	.327
Numbers	25	232	3	1.293	22	9.483	13	5.603	38	16.379	4	1.724
Numbers	26	674	5	.742	82	12.166	20	2.967	107	15.875	3	.445
Numbers	27	319	12	3.762	19	5.956	17	5.329	48	15.047	3	.940
Numbers	28	348	2	.575	39	11.207	6	1.724	47	13.506	28	8.046
Numbers	29	420	0	.000	32	7.619	1	.238	33	7.857	51	12.143
Numbers	30	263	13	4.943	4	1.521	15	5.703	32	12.167	0	.000
Numbers	31	677	16	2.363	91	13.442	44	6.499	151	22.304	32	4.727
Numbers	32	555	11	1.982	44	7.928	42	7.568	97	17.477	9	1.622
Numbers	33	464	8	1.724	30	6.466	15	3.233	53	11.422	9	1.940
Numbers	34	303	5	1.650	31	10.231	6	1.980	42	13.861	1	.330
Numbers	35	482	18	3.734	56	11.618	24	4.979	98	20.332	20	4.149
Numbers	36	212	5	2.358	9	4.245	5	2.358	19	8.962	1	.472
Deuteronomy	1	654	30	4.587	62	9.480	38	5.810	130	19.878	25	3.823
Deuteronomy	2	532	18	3.383	49	9.211	28	5.263	95	17.857	13	2.444
Deuteronomy	3	461	16	3.471	70	15.184	27	5.857	113	24.512	17	3.688

TABLE ONE: Listing of the Particles for each chapter (in canonical order) Page 3

Book and Chapter		Word Count	Relative Count	Relative Percentage	Article Count	Article Percentage	Nota Accusativi Count	Nota Accusativi Percentage	Total of Three Count	Total of Three Percentage	Dubious Article Count	Dubious Article Percentage
Deuteronomy	4	813	43	5.289	92	11.316	47	5.781	182	22.386	24	2.952
Deuteronomy	5	472	21	4.449	36	7.627	28	5.932	85	18.008	13	2.754
Deuteronomy	6	318	21	6.604	24	7.547	18	5.660	63	19.811	3	.943
Deuteronomy	7	412	12	2.913	49	11.893	19	4.612	80	19.417	2	.485
Deuteronomy	8	293	15	5.119	23	7.850	14	4.778	52	17.747	7	2.389
Deuteronomy	9	499	21	4.208	53	10.621	31	6.212	105	21.042	10	2.004
Deuteronomy	10	324	12	3.704	42	12.963	18	5.556	72	22.222	12	3.704
Deuteronomy	11	508	32	6.299	59	11.614	39	7.677	130	25.591	3	.591
Deuteronomy	12	520	31	5.962	48	9.231	24	4.615	103	19.808	9	1.731
Deuteronomy	13	328	12	3.659	33	10.061	18	5.488	63	19.207	6	1.829
Deuteronomy	14	351	15	4.274	45	12.821	20	5.698	80	22.792	10	2.849
Deuteronomy	15	354	11	3.107	24	6.780	14	3.955	49	13.842	7	1.977
Deuteronomy	16	334	18	5.389	26	7.784	9	2.695	53	15.868	13	3.892
Deuteronomy	17	368	18	4.891	51	13.859	13	3.533	82	22.283	8	2.174
Deuteronomy	18	304	16	5.263	34	11.184	7	2.303	57	18.750	3	.987
Deuteronomy	19	332	17	5.120	33	9.940	12	3.614	62	18.675	5	1.506
Deuteronomy	20	316	12	3.797	39	12.342	8	2.532	59	16.671	7	2.215
Deuteronomy	21	354	10	2.825	39	11.017	17	4.802	66	18.644	10	2.825
Deuteronomy	22	437	9	2.059	53	12.128	19	4.348	81	18.535	12	2.746
Deuteronomy	23	339	10	2.950	5	1.475	5	1.475	20	5.900	9	2.655
Deuteronomy	24	327	10	3.058	22	6.728	9	2.752	41	12.538	13	3.976
Deuteronomy	25	260	6	2.308	18	6.923	8	3.077	32	12.308	4	1.538
Deuteronomy	26	319	16	5.016	32	10.031	15	4.702	63	19.749	11	3.448
Deuteronomy	27	326	10	3.067	41	12.577	19	5.828	70	21.472	7	2.147
Deuteronomy	28	994	49	4.930	69	6.942	34	3.421	152	15.292	24	2.414
Deuteronomy	29	439	21	4.784	59	13.440	23	5.239	103	23.462	10	2.278
Deuteronomy	30	326	13	3.988	38	11.656	17	5.215	68	20.859	4	1.227
Deuteronomy	31	553	18	3.255	72	13.020	41	7.414	131	23.689	7	1.266
Deuteronomy	32	615	12	1.951	22	3.577	8	1.301	42	6.829	5	.813
Deuteronomy	33	336	3	.893	5	1.488	3	.893	11	3.274	1	.298
Deuteronomy	34	176	6	3.409	17	9.659	12	6.818	35	19.886	1	.568
Joshua	1	320	20	6.250	36	11.250	17	5.312	73	22.812	3	.937
Joshua	2	403	12	2.978	52	12.903	27	6.700	91	22.581	8	1.985
Joshua	3	293	6	2.048	58	19.795	15	5.119	79	26.962	8	2.730
Joshua	4	390	16	4.103	56	14.359	18	4.615	90	23.077	9	2.308
Joshua	5	288	9	3.125	35	12.153	10	3.472	54	18.750	12	4.167
Joshua	6	474	11	2.321	83	17.511	39	8.228	133	28.059	18	3.797
Joshua	7	494	8	1.619	49	9.919	35	7.085	92	18.623	16	3.239
Joshua	8	616	20	3.247	92	14.935	34	5.519	146	23.701	31	5.032
Joshua	9	414	12	2.899	40	9.662	14	3.382	66	15.942	9	2.174
Joshua	10	766	20	2.611	73	9.530	46	6.005	139	18.146	9	1.175
Joshua	11	409	10	2.445	46	11.247	32	7.824	88	21.516	13	3.178
Joshua	12	240	4	1.613	35	14.113	1	.403	40	16.129	10	4.032
Joshua	13	439	19	4.328	65	14.806	11	2.506	95	21.640	10	2.278
Joshua	14	278	14	5.036	28	10.072	14	5.036	56	20.144	11	3.957
Joshua	15	553	6	1.085	50	9.042	12	2.170	68	12.297	5	.904
Joshua	16	123	0	.000	19	15.447	2	1.626	21	17.073	1	.813
Joshua	17	337	5	1.484	33	9.792	6	1.780	44	13.056	4	1.187
Joshua	18	405	8	1.975	40	9.877	11	2.716	59	14.568	8	1.975
Joshua	19	485	4	.825	58	11.959	9	1.856	71	14.639	1	.206
Joshua	20	172	3	1.744	21	12.209	11	6.395	35	20.349	9	5.233
Joshua	21	583	5	.858	47	8.062	113	19.383	165	28.302	10	1.715
Joshua	22	688	17	2.471	47	6.831	25	3.634	89	12.936	7	1.017
Joshua	23	299	13	4.348	43	14.381	11	3.679	67	22.408	3	1.003
Joshua	24	574	23	4.007	51	8.885	60	10.453	134	23.345	3	.523
Judges	1	529	4	.756	55	10.397	65	12.287	124	23.440	5	.945
Judges	2	363	15	4.132	32	8.815	24	6.612	71	19.559	2	.551
Judges	3	481	7	1.455	52	10.811	40	8.316	99	20.582	4	.832
Judges	4	422	7	1.659	26	6.161	23	5.450	56	13.270	6	1.422
Judges	5	364	1	.275	10	2.747	0	.000	11	3.022	8	2.198
Judges	6	679	18	2.651	70	10.309	37	5.449	125	18.409	16	2.356
Judges	7	504	12	2.381	49	9.722	25	4.960	86	17.063	16	3.175
Judges	8	527	11	2.087	38	7.211	35	6.641	84	15.939	4	.759
Judges	9	875	19	2.171	70	8.000	42	4.800	131	14.971	12	1.371
Judges	10	249	5	2.008	20	8.032	19	7.631	44	17.671	4	1.606
Judges	11	663	10	1.508	26	3.922	34	5.128	70	10.558	5	.754
Judges	12	223	0	.000	14	6.278	14	6.278	28	12.556	2	.897
Judges	13	394	6	1.523	32	8.122	7	1.777	45	11.421	4	1.015
Judges	14	336	3	.893	26	7.738	11	3.274	40	11.905	4	1.190
Judges	15	321	6	1.869	19	5.919	9	2.804	34	10.592	9	2.804
Judges	16	553	12	2.170	46	8.318	24	4.340	82	14.828	9	1.627
Judges	17	192	3	1.563	17	8.854	6	3.125	26	13.542	3	1.563
Judges	18	548	14	2.555	61	11.131	31	5.657	106	19.343	9	1.642
Judges	19	529	5	.945	74	13.989	12	2.268	91	17.202	14	2.647
Judges	20	747	9	1.205	87	11.647	10	1.339	106	14.190	34	4.552
Judges	21	375	10	2.667	32	8.533	6	1.600	48	12.800	11	2.933
1 Samuel	1	415	4	.964	23	5.542	19	4.578	46	11.084	1	.241
1 Samuel	2	556	11	1.978	35	6.295	21	3.777	67	12.050	11	1.978

TABLE ONE: Listing of the Particles for each chapter (in canonical order) Page 4

Book and Chapter		Word Count	Relative Count	Relative Percentage	Article Count	Article Percentage	Nota Accusativi Count	Nota Accusativi Percentage	Total of Three Count	Total of Three Percentage	Dubious Article Count	Dubious Article Percentage
1 Samuel	3	304	6	1.974	10	3.289	8	2.632	24	7.895	5	1.645
1 Samuel	4	370	1	.270	52	14.054	8	2.162	61	16.486	9	2.432
1 Samuel	5	218	1	.459	17	7.798	20	9.174	38	17.431	4	1.835
1 Samuel	6	395	9	2.278	36	9.114	26	6.582	71	17.975	12	3.038
1 Samuel	7	287	1	.348	24	8.362	18	6.272	43	14.983	6	2.091
1 Samuel	8	271	7	2.583	20	7.380	16	5.904	43	15.867	2	.738
1 Samuel	9	495	8	1.616	56	11.313	22	4.444	86	17.374	15	3.030
1 Samuel	10	442	8	1.810	38	8.597	14	3.167	60	13.575	4	.905
1 Samuel	11	257	1	.389	31	12.062	7	2.724	39	15.175	4	1.556
1 Samuel	12	425	12	2.824	25	5.882	36	8.471	73	17.176	2	.471
1 Samuel	13	355	6	1.690	39	10.986	12	3.380	57	16.056	12	3.380
1 Samuel	14	845	19	2.249	105	12.426	18	2.130	142	16.805	16	1.893
1 Samuel	15	529	10	1.890	32	6.049	31	5.860	73	13.800	7	1.323
1 Samuel	16	373	5	1.340	12	3.217	10	2.681	27	7.239	8	2.145
1 Samuel	17	914	10	1.094	124	13.567	40	4.376	174	19.037	17	1.860
1 Samuel	18	433	3	.693	34	7.852	16	3.695	53	12.240	12	2.771
1 Samuel	19	395	3	.759	23	5.823	19	4.810	45	11.392	17	4.304
1 Samuel	20	703	8	1.138	59	8.393	27	3.841	94	13.371	9	1.280
1 Samuel	21	282	4	1.418	28	9.929	9	3.191	41	14.539	5	1.773
1 Samuel	22	419	5	1.193	25	5.967	15	3.580	45	10.740	11	2.625
1 Samuel	23	436	5	1.147	20	4.587	13	2.982	38	8.716	15	3.440
1 Samuel	24	374	11	2.941	23	6.150	20	5.348	54	14.439	4	1.070
1 Samuel	25	750	18	2.400	47	6.267	31	4.133	96	12.800	12	1.600
1 Samuel	26	475	11	2.316	44	9.263	14	2.947	69	14.526	9	1.895
1 Samuel	27	209	4	1.914	17	8.134	2	.957	23	11.005	1	.478
1 Samuel	28	431	7	1.624	30	6.961	17	3.944	54	12.529	14	3.248
1 Samuel	29	218	6	2.752	13	5.963	2	.917	21	9.633	10	4.587
1 Samuel	30	487	30	6.160	55	11.294	17	3.491	102	20.945	7	1.437
1 Samuel	31	202	3	1.485	16	7.921	20	9.901	39	19.307	2	.990
2 Samuel	1	367	4	1.090	31	8.447	4	1.090	39	10.627	4	1.090
2 Samuel	2	515	11	2.136	38	7.379	9	1.748	58	11.262	7	1.359
2 Samuel	3	655	11	1.679	43	6.565	24	3.664	78	11.908	5	.763
2 Samuel	4	237	3	1.266	23	9.705	15	6.329	41	17.300	0	.000
2 Samuel	5	351	1	.285	20	5.698	14	3.989	35	9.972	3	.855
2 Samuel	6	376	10	2.660	32	8.511	18	4.787	60	15.957	5	1.330
2 Samuel	7	461	16	3.471	28	6.074	18	3.905	62	13.449	4	.868
2 Samuel	8	262	6	2.290	13	4.962	13	4.962	32	12.214	3	1.145
2 Samuel	9	222	4	1.802	14	6.306	3	1.351	21	9.459	0	.000
2 Samuel	10	314	3	.955	15	4.777	18	5.732	36	11.465	3	.955
2 Samuel	11	442	4	.905	53	11.991	18	4.072	75	16.968	5	1.131
2 Samuel	12	527	7	1.328	52	9.867	28	5.313	87	16.509	10	1.898
2 Samuel	13	648	9	1.389	55	8.488	27	4.167	91	14.043	6	.926
2 Samuel	14	598	10	1.672	83	13.880	31	5.184	124	20.736	8	1.338
2 Samuel	15	603	15	2.488	67	11.111	23	3.814	105	17.413	5	.829
2 Samuel	16	388	11	2.835	45	11.598	11	2.835	67	17.268	6	1.546
2 Samuel	17	521	16	3.071	55	10.557	18	3.455	89	17.083	12	2.303
2 Samuel	18	589	9	1.528	86	14.601	23	3.905	118	20.034	18	3.056
2 Samuel	19	806	12	1.489	119	14.764	37	4.591	168	20.844	10	1.241
2 Samuel	20	443	9	2.032	39	8.804	8	1.806	56	12.641	7	1.580
2 Samuel	21	424	12	2.830	30	7.075	28	6.604	70	16.509	7	1.651
2 Samuel	22	374	0	.000	9	2.406	3	.802	12	3.209	6	1.604
2 Samuel	23	444	3	.676	53	11.937	7	1.577	63	14.189	15	3.378
2 Samuel	24	455	4	.879	55	12.088	19	4.176	78	17.143	11	2.418
1 Kings	1	800	9	1.125	108	13.500	33	4.125	150	18.750	12	1.500
1 Kings	2	806	21	2.605	49	6.079	37	4.591	107	13.275	7	.868
1 Kings	3	472	12	2.542	63	13.347	22	4.661	97	20.551	10	2.119
1 Kings	4	200	6	3.000	14	7.000	3	1.500	23	11.500	6	3.000
1 Kings	5	503	14	2.783	48	9.543	13	2.584	75	14.911	12	2.386
1 Kings	6	510	4	.784	94	18.431	24	4.706	122	23.922	22	4.314
1 Kings	7	793	17	2.144	159	20.050	50	6.305	226	28.499	31	3.909
1 Kings	8	1147	57	4.969	130	11.334	54	4.708	241	21.011	17	1.482
1 Kings	9	472	26	5.508	50	10.593	37	7.839	113	23.941	13	2.754
1 Kings	10	464	16	3.448	45	9.698	13	2.802	74	15.948	12	2.586
1 Kings	11	690	21	3.043	38	5.507	30	4.348	89	12.899	7	1.014
1 Kings	12	584	21	3.596	65	11.130	31	5.308	117	20.034	17	2.911
1 Kings	13	592	25	4.223	78	13.176	24	4.054	127	21.453	18	3.041
1 Kings	14	519	21	4.046	42	8.092	18	3.468	81	15.607	10	1.927
1 Kings	15	523	18	3.442	26	4.971	30	5.736	74	14.149	3	.574
1 Kings	16	545	24	4.404	33	6.055	23	4.220	80	14.679	8	1.468
1 Kings	17	356	8	2.247	31	8.708	6	1.685	45	12.640	8	2.247
1 Kings	18	730	10	1.370	79	10.822	31	4.247	120	16.438	10	1.370
1 Kings	19	371	5	1.348	19	5.121	18	4.852	42	11.321	10	2.695
1 Kings	20	746	9	1.206	67	8.981	24	3.217	100	13.405	16	2.145
1 Kings	21	480	16	3.333	36	7.500	19	3.958	71	14.792	7	1.458
1 Kings	22	810	15	1.852	51	6.296	29	3.580	95	11.728	16	1.975
2 Kings	1	359	9	2.507	32	8.914	14	3.900	55	15.320	0	.000
2 Kings	2	427	7	1.639	29	6.792	12	2.810	48	11.241	5	1.171
2 Kings	3	435	6	1.379	31	7.126	17	3.908	54	12.414	11	2.529

TABLE ONE: Listing of the Particles for each chapter (in canonical order) Page 5

Book and Chapter		Word Count	Relative		Article		Nota Accusativi		Total of Three		Dubious Article	
			Count	Percentage	Count	Percentage	Count	Percentage	Count	Percentage	Count	Percentage
2 Kings	4	671	1	.149	69	10.283	10	1.490	80	11.923	17	2.534
2 Kings	5	489	5	1.022	26	5.317	8	1.636	39	7.975	6	1.227
2 Kings	6	528	8	1.515	58	10.985	24	4.545	90	17.045	4	.758
2 Kings	7	408	11	2.696	44	10.784	12	2.941	67	16.422	13	3.186
2 Kings	8	516	12	2.326	40	7.752	20	3.876	72	13.953	8	1.550
2 Kings	9	611	4	.655	55	9.002	22	3.601	81	13.257	6	.982
2 Kings	10	621	21	3.382	67	10.789	26	4.187	114	18.357	10	1.610
2 Kings	11	358	4	1.117	80	22.346	34	9.497	118	32.961	12	3.352
2 Kings	12	362	8	2.210	49	13.536	17	4.696	74	20.442	7	1.934
2 Kings	13	416	8	1.923	15	3.606	17	4.087	40	9.615	3	.721
2 Kings	14	479	15	3.132	31	6.472	23	4.802	69	14.405	6	1.253
2 Kings	15	587	15	2.555	34	5.792	24	4.089	73	12.436	4	.681
2 Kings	16	363	9	2.479	56	15.427	30	8.264	95	26.171	5	1.377
2 Kings	17	689	32	4.644	47	6.821	51	7.402	130	18.868	5	.726
2 Kings	18	668	17	2.545	57	8.533	34	5.090	108	16.168	5	.749
2 Kings	19	571	14	2.452	35	6.130	21	3.678	70	12.259	13	2.277
2 Kings	20	363	13	3.581	34	9.366	18	4.959	65	17.906	6	1.653
2 Kings	21	397	26	6.549	32	8.060	24	6.045	82	20.655	4	1.008
2 Kings	22	370	10	2.703	59	15.946	21	5.676	90	24.324	9	2.432
2 Kings	23	773	41	5.304	112	14.489	69	8.926	222	28.719	18	2.329
2 Kings	24	313	9	2.875	22	7.029	20	6.390	51	16.294	2	.639
2 Kings	25	508	14	2.756	72	14.173	41	8.071	127	25.000	20	3.937
Isaiah	1	360	4	1.111	6	1.667	3	.833	13	3.611	9	2.500
Isaiah	2	253	4	1.581	25	9.881	2	.791	31	12.253	7	2.767
Isaiah	3	249	0	.000	31	12.450	1	.402	32	12.851	7	2.811
Isaiah	4	89	0	.000	6	6.742	2	2.247	8	8.989	3	3.371
Isaiah	5	384	2	.521	12	3.125	5	1.302	19	4.948	15	3.906
Isaiah	6	188	2	1.064	16	8.511	6	3.191	24	12.766	3	1.596
Isaiah	7	345	6	1.739	24	6.957	8	2.319	38	11.014	16	4.638
Isaiah	8	299	4	1.338	30	10.033	12	4.013	46	15.385	2	.669
Isaiah	9	267	1	.375	16	5.993	11	4.120	28	10.487	3	1.124
Isaiah	10	406	2	.493	21	5.172	3	.739	26	6.404	6	1.478
Isaiah	11	219	4	1.826	7	3.196	6	2.740	17	7.763	7	3.196
Isaiah	12	62	0	.000	4	6.452	0	.000	4	6.452	3	4.839
Isaiah	13	253	2	.791	8	3.162	3	1.186	13	5.138	3	1.186
Isaiah	14	376	3	.798	20	5.319	1	.266	24	6.383	4	1.064
Isaiah	15	125	0	.000	5	4.000	1	.800	6	4.800	1	.800
Isaiah	16	192	1	.521	8	4.167	0	.000	9	4.687	5	2.604
Isaiah	17	178	2	1.124	9	5.056	0	.000	11	6.180	4	2.247
Isaiah	18	124	3	2.419	7	5.645	1	.806	11	8.871	3	2.419
Isaiah	19	327	5	1.529	15	4.587	8	2.446	28	8.563	8	2.446
Isaiah	20	96	2	2.083	5	5.208	4	4.167	11	11.458	2	2.083
Isaiah	21	201	2	.995	7	3.483	1	.498	10	4.975	3	1.493
Isaiah	22	308	2	.649	28	9.091	4	1.299	34	11.039	8	2.597
Isaiah	23	217	2	.922	9	4.147	2	.922	13	5.991	3	1.382
Isaiah	24	256	1	.391	26	10.156	1	.391	28	10.938	20	7.813
Isaiah	25	161	1	.621	14	8.696	0	.000	15	9.317	9	5.590
Isaiah	26	233	1	.429	5	2.146	1	.429	7	3.004	6	2.575
Isaiah	27	174	1	.575	14	8.046	2	1.149	17	9.770	7	4.023
Isaiah	28	381	5	1.312	17	4.462	7	1.837	29	7.612	17	4.462
Isaiah	29	326	5	1.534	22	6.748	9	2.761	36	11.043	7	2.147
Isaiah	30	492	5	1.016	19	3.862	7	1.423	31	6.301	11	2.236
Isaiah	31	156	5	3.205	4	2.564	2	1.282	11	7.051	1	.641
Isaiah	32	203	0	.000	7	3.448	0	.000	7	3.448	4	1.970
Isaiah	33	275	1	.364	5	1.818	2	.727	8	2.909	4	1.455
Isaiah	34	220	0	.000	4	1.818	1	.455	5	2.273	4	1.818
Isaiah	35	126	0	.000	5	3.968	0	.000	5	3.968	3	2.381
Isaiah	36	385	7	1.818	43	11.169	19	4.935	69	17.922	2	.519
Isaiah	37	566	14	2.473	34	6.007	21	3.710	69	12.191	12	2.120
Isaiah	38	281	5	1.779	16	5.694	8	2.847	29	10.320	7	2.491
Isaiah	39	146	9	6.164	12	8.219	8	5.479	29	19.863	1	.685
Isaiah	40	357	0	.000	16	4.482	2	.560	18	5.042	16	4.482
Isaiah	41	351	3	.855	10	2.849	6	1.709	19	5.413	7	1.994
Isaiah	42	288	0	.000	11	3.819	1	.347	12	4.167	11	3.819
Isaiah	43	314	2	.637	7	2.229	1	.318	10	3.185	10	3.185
Isaiah	44	389	1	.257	4	1.028	1	.257	6	1.542	8	2.057
Isaiah	45	360	1	.278	8	2.222	3	.833	12	3.333	3	.833
Isaiah	46	150	1	.667	4	2.667	0	.000	5	3.333	5	3.333
Isaiah	47	213	3	1.408	3	1.408	1	.469	7	3.286	4	1.878
Isaiah	48	265	0	.000	6	2.264	1	.377	7	2.642	5	1.887
Isaiah	49	363	4	1.102	2	.551	8	2.204	14	3.857	4	1.102
Isaiah	50	176	3	1.705	0	.000	2	1.136	5	2.841	6	3.409
Isaiah	51	334	3	.898	16	4.790	4	1.198	23	6.886	9	2.695
Isaiah	52	202	3	1.485	6	2.970	2	.990	11	5.446	2	.990
Isaiah	53	166	1	.602	0	.000	6	3.614	7	4.217	9	5.422
Isaiah	54	221	1	.452	4	1.810	0	.000	5	2.262	3	1.357
Isaiah	55	185	5	2.703	10	5.405	3	1.622	18	9.730	4	2.162
Isaiah	56	179	3	1.676	7	3.911	2	1.117	12	6.704	3	1.676

TABLE ONE: Listing of the Particles for each chapter (in canonical order) Page 6

Book and Chapter		Word Count	Relative		Article		Nota Accusativi		Total of Three		Dubious Article	
			Count	Percentage	Count	Percentage	Count	Percentage	Count	Percentage	Count	Percentage
Isaiah	57	260	0	.000	10	3.846	6	2.308	16	6.154	8	3.077
Isaiah	58	222	2	.901	0	.000	1	.450	3	1.351	9	4.054
Isaiah	59	284	2	.704	3	1.056	2	.704	7	2.465	16	5.634
Isaiah	60	295	1	.339	13	4.407	0	.000	14	4.746	4	1.356
Isaiah	61	165	0	.000	3	1.818	1	.606	4	2.424	4	2.424
Isaiah	62	178	2	1.124	8	4.494	4	2.247	14	7.865	3	1.685
Isaiah	63	239	2	.837	2	.837	3	1.255	7	2.929	6	2.510
Isaiah	64	128	1	.781	1	.781	1	.781	3	2.344	3	2.344
Isaiah	65	361	7	1.939	28	7.756	5	1.385	40	11.080	13	3.601
Isaiah	66	386	7	1.813	27	6.995	14	3.627	48	12.435	14	3.627
Jeremiah	1	266	6	2.256	11	4.135	4	1.504	21	7.895	3	1.128
Jeremiah	2	512	3	.586	13	2.539	12	2.344	28	5.469	10	1.953
Jeremiah	3	410	3	.732	18	4.390	19	4.634	40	9.756	8	1.951
Jeremiah	4	423	0	.000	25	5.910	4	.946	29	6.856	13	3.073
Jeremiah	5	431	5	1.160	14	3.248	8	1.856	27	6.265	7	1.624
Jeremiah	6	415	1	.241	15	3.614	7	1.687	23	5.542	11	2.651
Jeremiah	7	540	19	3.519	51	9.444	29	5.370	99	18.333	13	2.407
Jeremiah	8	348	7	2.011	17	4.885	11	3.161	35	10.057	10	2.874
Jeremiah	9	375	5	1.333	17	4.533	12	3.200	34	9.067	7	1.867
Jeremiah	10	320	3	.937	14	4.375	8	2.500	25	7.812	6	1.875
Jeremiah	11	385	11	2.857	27	7.013	18	4.675	56	14.545	6	1.558
Jeremiah	12	263	2	.760	11	4.183	16	6.084	29	11.027	4	1.521
Jeremiah	13	378	8	2.116	28	7.407	18	4.762	54	14.286	8	2.116
Jeremiah	14	356	2	.562	22	6.180	5	1.404	29	8.146	14	3.933
Jeremiah	15	316	5	1.582	12	3.797	9	2.848	26	8.228	11	3.481
Jeremiah	16	367	8	2.180	31	8.447	20	5.450	59	16.076	8	2.180
Jeremiah	17	404	7	1.733	23	5.693	8	1.980	38	9.406	9	2.228
Jeremiah	18	319	6	1.881	16	5.016	5	1.567	27	8.464	9	2.821
Jeremiah	19	284	12	4.225	39	13.732	18	6.338	69	24.296	6	2.113
Jeremiah	20	294	8	2.721	15	5.102	15	5.102	38	12.925	5	1.701
Jeremiah	21	248	3	1.210	31	12.500	17	6.855	51	20.565	10	4.032
Jeremiah	22	468	8	1.709	39	8.333	12	2.564	59	12.607	14	2.991
Jeremiah	23	609	14	2.299	39	6.404	30	4.926	83	13.629	9	1.478
Jeremiah	24	185	6	3.243	24	12.973	12	6.486	42	22.703	3	1.622
Jeremiah	25	615	13	2.114	65	10.569	51	8.2 3	129	20.976	9	1.463
Jeremiah	26	434	9	2.074	70	16.129	18	4.147	97	22.350	5	1.152
Jeremiah	27	421	9	2.138	43	10.214	27	6.413	79	18.765	8	1.900
Jeremiah	28	304	7	2.303	51	16.776	12	3.947	70	23.026	5	1.645
Jeremiah	29	537	24	4.469	53	9.870	26	4.842	103	19.181	8	1.490
Jeremiah	30	342	6	1.754	9	2.632	8	2.339	23	6.725	4	1.170
Jeremiah	31	623	5	.803	27	4.334	15	2.408	47	7.544	8	1.284
Jeremiah	32	748	24	3.209	104	13.904	44	5.882	172	22.995	17	2.273
Jeremiah	33	419	13	3.103	40	9.547	18	4.296	71	16.945	9	2.148
Jeremiah	34	426	12	2.817	40	9.390	27	6.338	79	18.545	5	1.174
Jeremiah	35	368	12	3.261	21	5.707	16	4.348	49	13.315	0	.000
Jeremiah	36	620	15	2.419	92	14.839	37	5.968	144	23.226	17	2.742
Jeremiah	37	331	3	.906	46	13.897	12	3.625	61	18.429	5	1.511
Jeremiah	38	548	14	2.555	84	15.328	26	4.745	124	22.628	18	3.285
Jeremiah	39	304	5	1.645	31	10.197	15	4.934	51	16.776	11	3.618
Jeremiah	40	366	12	3.279	35	9.563	10	2.732	57	15.574	8	2.186
Jeremiah	41	361	21	5.817	32	8.864	22	6.094	75	20.776	10	2.770
Jeremiah	42	408	20	4.902	23	5.637	16	3.922	59	14.461	10	2.451
Jeremiah	43	237	11	4.641	18	7.595	22	9.283	51	21.519	10	4.219
Jeremiah	44	623	22	3.531	48	7.705	23	3.692	93	14.928	14	2.247
Jeremiah	45	93	4	4.301	7	7.527	4	4.301	15	16.129	1	1.075
Jeremiah	46	403	5	1.241	22	5.459	3	.744	30	7.444	10	2.481
Jeremiah	47	107	1	.935	6	5.607	3	2.804	10	9.346	0	.000
Jeremiah	48	580	2	.345	19	3.276	1	.172	22	3.793	12	2.069
Jeremiah	49	584	7	1.199	18	3.082	14	2.397	39	6.678	16	2.740
Jeremiah	50	693	11	1.587	21	3.030	14	2.020	46	6.638	15	2.165
Jeremiah	51	890	6	.674	42	4.719	30	3.371	78	8.764	16	1.798
Jeremiah	52	567	15	2.646	75	13.228	44	7.760	134	23.633	20	3.527
Ezekiel	1	382	6	1.571	43	11.257	3	.785	52	13.613	11	2.880
Ezekiel	2	156	4	2.564	5	3.205	9	5.769	18	11.538	0	.000
Ezekiel	3	411	6	1.460	17	4.136	16	3.893	39	9.489	2	.487
Ezekiel	4	264	4	1.515	9	3.409	15	5.682	28	10.606	5	1.894
Ezekiel	5	287	9	3.136	16	5.575	13	4.530	38	13.240	9	3.136
Ezekiel	6	212	6	2.830	13	6.132	7	3.302	26	12.264	13	6.132
Ezekiel	7	343	2	.583	33	9.621	6	1.749	41	11.953	8	2.332
Ezekiel	8	319	8	2.508	26	8.150	13	4.075	47	14.734	12	3.762
Ezekiel	9	199	7	3.518	27	13.568	5	2.513	39	19.598	3	1.508
Ezekiel	10	310	7	2.258	56	18.065	9	[illegible]	72	23.226	10	3.226
Ezekiel	11	349	9	2.579	26	7.450	19	5.444	54	15.473	8	2.292
Ezekiel	12	399	11	2.757	21	5.263	11	2.757	43	10.777	15	3.759
Ezekiel	13	358	7	1.955	21	5.866	14	3.911	42	11.732	4	1.117
Ezekiel	14	391	6	1.535	26	6.650	13	3.325	45	11.509	3	.767
Ezekiel	15	103	3	2.913	9	8.738	5	4.854	17	16.505	2	1.942
Ezekiel	16	833	19	2.281	18	2.161	48	5.762	85	10.204	7	.840

TABLE ONE: Listing of the Particles for each chapter (in canonical order) Page 7

Book and Chapter		Word	Relative		Article		Nota Accusativi		Total of Three		Dubious Article	
		Count	Count	Percentage	Count	Percentage	Count	Percentage	Count	Percentage	Count	Percentage
Ezekiel	17	382	6	1.571	22	5.759	17	4.450	45	11.780	2	.524
Ezekiel	18	474	13	2.743	30	6.329	13	2.743	56	11.814	2	.422
Ezekiel	19	156	0	.000	1	.641	0	.000	1	.641	7	4.487
Ezekiel	20	734	20	2.725	34	4.632	59	8.038	113	15.395	17	2.316
Ezekiel	21	530	5	.943	14	2.642	7	1.321	26	4.906	7	1.321
Ezekiel	22	390	5	1.282	13	3.333	13	3.333	31	7.949	7	1.795
Ezekiel	23	621	12	1.932	9	1.449	32	5.153	53	8.535	9	1.449
Ezekiel	24	375	5	1.333	26	6.933	10	2.667	41	10.933	10	2.667
Ezekiel	25	259	0	.000	6	2.317	9	3.475	15	5.792	4	1.544
Ezekiel	26	307	6	1.954	13	4.235	8	2.606	27	8.795	11	3.583
Ezekiel	27	407	2	.491	9	2.211	2	.491	13	3.194	2	.491
Ezekiel	28	352	2	.568	7	1.989	4	1.136	13	3.693	2	.568
Ezekiel	29	344	5	1.453	13	3.779	12	3.488	30	8.721	10	2.907
Ezekiel	30	342	0	.000	10	2.924	20	5.848	30	8.772	14	4.094
Ezekiel	31	312	3	.962	11	3.526	8	2.564	22	7.051	4	1.282
Ezekiel	32	482	8	1.660	10	2.075	28	5.809	46	9.544	13	2.697
Ezekiel	33	517	6	1.161	34	6.576	19	3.675	59	11.412	16	3.095
Ezekiel	34	458	3	.655	39	8.515	31	6.769	73	15.939	10	2.183
Ezekiel	35	194	4	2.062	3	1.546	6	3.093	13	6.701	0	.000
Ezekiel	36	565	17	3.009	40	7.080	23	4.071	80	14.159	18	3.186
Ezekiel	37	446	9	2.018	20	4.484	21	4.709	50	11.211	2	.448
Ezekiel	38	370	4	1.081	25	6.757	6	1.622	35	9.459	9	2.432
Ezekiel	39	433	9	2.079	28	6.467	22	5.081	59	13.626	6	1.386
Ezekiel	40	724	12	1.657	124	17.127	18	2.486	154	21.271	31	4.282
Ezekiel	41	370	8	2.162	70	18.919	3	.811	81	21.892	25	6.757
Ezekiel	42	285	14	4.912	76	26.667	2	.702	92	32.281	7	2.456
Ezekiel	43	415	10	2.410	57	13.735	26	6.265	93	22.410	8	1.928
Ezekiel	44	501	11	2.196	43	8.583	23	4.591	77	15.369	5	.998
Ezekiel	45	396	1	.253	68	17.172	9	2.273	78	19.697	28	7.071
Ezekiel	46	381	9	2.362	66	17.323	17	4.462	92	24.147	26	6.824
Ezekiel	47	366	11	3.005	53	14.481	8	2.186	72	19.672	6	1.639
Ezekiel	48	527	7	1.328	39	7.400	1	.190	47	8.918	11	2.087
Hosea	1	137	1	.730	2	1.460	6	4.380	9	6.569	1	.730
Hosea	2	339	5	1.475	23	6.785	20	5.900	48	14.159	8	2.360
Hosea	3	81	0	.000	1	1.235	3	3.704	4	4.938	0	.000
Hosea	4	223	0	.000	13	5.830	2	.897	15	6.726	4	1.794
Hosea	5	179	1	.559	3	1.676	5	2.793	9	5.028	8	4.469
Hosea	6	104	0	.000	1	.962	1	.962	2	1.923	4	3.846
Hosea	7	189	1	.529	2	1.058	1	.529	4	2.116	5	2.646
Hosea	8	154	0	.000	0	.000	1	.649	1	.649	3	1.948
Hosea	9	216	1	.463	5	2.315	1	.463	7	3.241	6	2.778
Hosea	10	201	0	.000	2	.995	3	1.493	5	2.488	6	2.985
Hosea	11	123	0	.000	0	.000	0	.000	0	.000	2	1.626
Hosea	12	160	1	.625	4	2.500	1	.625	6	3.750	2	1.250
Hosea	13	163	1	.613	1	.613	0	.000	2	1.227	3	1.840
Hosea	14	116	1	.862	0	.000	0	.000	1	.862	8	6.897
Joel	1	235	1	.426	17	7.234	0	.000	18	7.660	2	.851
Joel	2	385	3	.779	27	7.013	8	2.078	38	9.870	8	2.078
Joel	3	67	3	4.478	7	10.448	2	2.985	12	17.910	4	5.970
Joel	4	271	5	1.845	22	8.118	8	2.952	35	12.915	7	2.583
Amos	1	212	2	.943	6	2.830	2	.943	10	4.717	3	1.415
Amos	2	215	3	1.395	12	5.581	7	3.256	22	10.233	6	2.791
Amos	3	207	3	1.449	17	8.213	3	1.449	23	11.111	2	.966
Amos	4	215	2	.930	10	4.651	5	2.326	17	7.907	5	2.326
Amos	5	322	4	1.242	20	6.211	7	2.174	31	9.627	9	2.795
Amos	6	178	1	.562	20	11.236	2	1.124	23	12.921	2	1.124
Amos	7	257	0	.000	6	2.335	4	1.556	10	3.891	6	2.335
Amos	8	190	0	.000	14	7.368	2	1.053	16	8.421	11	5.789
Amos	9	251	3	1.195	25	9.960	13	5.179	41	16.335	10	3.984
Obadiah	1	291	4	1.375	12	4.124	9	3.093	25	8.591	5	1.718
Jonah	1	254	4	1.575	35	13.780	6	2.362	45	17.717	2	.787
Jonah	2	112	1	.893	4	3.571	3	2.679	8	7.143	1	.893
Jonah	3	140	3	2.143	19	13.571	2	1.429	24	17.143	1	.714
Jonah	4	183	4	2.186	12	6.557	3	1.639	19	10.383	4	2.186
Micah	1	212	2	.943	7	3.302	0	.000	9	4.245	6	2.830
Micah	2	176	1	.568	10	5.682	0	.000	11	6.250	3	1.705
Micah	3	166	4	2.410	13	7.831	6	3.614	23	13.855	2	1.205
Micah	4	222	1	.450	13	5.856	2	.901	16	7.207	6	2.703
Micah	5	171	3	1.754	2	1.170	3	1.754	8	4.678	3	1.754
Micah	6	203	3	1.478	5	2.463	5	2.463	13	6.404	2	.985
Micah	7	244	2	.820	9	3.689	1	.410	12	4.918	5	2.049
Nahum	1	154	0	.000	5	3.247	0	.000	5	3.247	2	1.299
Nahum	2	173	1	.578	7	4.046	1	.578	9	5.202	7	4.046
Nahum	3	232	1	.431	5	2.155	0	.000	6	2.586	12	5.172
Habakkuk	1	197	1	.508	9	4.569	2	1.015	12	6.091	3	1.523
Habakkuk	2	262	1	.382	7	2.672	1	.382	9	3.435	5	1.908
Habakkuk	3	212	1	.472	2	.943	1	.472	4	1.887	8	3.774
Zephaniah	1	269	2	.743	44	16.357	11	4.089	57	21.190	8	2.974

TABLE ONE: Listing of the Particles for each chapter (in canonical order) Page 8

Book and Chapter		Word	Relative		Article		Nota Accusativi		Total of Three		Dubious Article	
		Count	Count	Percentage	Count	Percentage	Count	Percentage	Count	Percentage	Count	Percentage
Zephaniah	2	222	2	.901	10	4.505	5	2.252	17	7.658	6	2.701
Zephaniah	3	276	2	.725	11	3.986	7	2.536	20	7.246	9	3.26.
Haggai	1	238	3	1.261	32	13.445	3	1.261	38	15.966	5	2.101
Haggai	2	362	4	1.105	55	15.193	15	4.144	74	20.442	12	3.315
Zechariah	1	273	7	2.564	25	9.158	6	2.198	38	13.919	4	1.465
Zechariah	2	220	2	.909	16	7.273	11	5.000	29	13.182	1	.455
Zechariah	3	164	1	.610	21	12.805	7	4.268	29	17.683	1	.610
Zechariah	4	187	3	1.604	25	13.369	2	1.070	30	16.043	1	.535
Zechariah	5	155	0	.000	25	16.129	6	3.871	31	20.000	3	1.935
Zechariah	6	203	2	.985	23	11.330	7	3.448	32	15.764	8	3.941
Zechariah	7	187	6	3.209	20	10.695	5	2.674	31	16.578	4	2.139
Zechariah	8	356	7	1.966	38	10.674	18	5.056	63	17.697	8	2.247
Zechariah	9	222	0	.000	3	1.351	0	.000	3	1.351	8	3.604
Zechariah	10	166	1	.602	5	3.012	6	3.614	12	7.229	7	4.217
Zechariah	11	254	4	1.575	32	12.598	19	7.480	55	21.654	2	.787
Zechariah	12	227	1	.441	22	9.692	8	3.524	31	13.656	12	5.286
Zechariah	13	152	1	.658	19	12.500	8	5.263	28	18.421	4	2.632
Zechariah	14	362	9	2.486	53	14.641	6	1.657	68	18.785	16	4.420
Malachi	1	239	1	.418	5	2.092	12	5.021	18	7.531	3	1.255
Malachi	2	269	4	1.487	15	5.576	9	3.346	28	10.409	3	1.115
Malachi	3	368	8	2.174	20	5.435	15	4.076	43	11.685	13	3.533
Psalms	1	67	4	5.970	2	2.985	0	.000	6	8.955	2	2.985
Psalms	2	92	0	.000	1	1.087	2	2.174	3	3.261	1	1.087
Psalms	3	70	1	1.429	1	1.429	1	1.429	3	4.286	0	.000
Psalms	4	77	0	.000	0	.000	0	.000	0	.000	2	2.597
Psalms	5	111	0	.000	2	1.802	0	.000	2	1.802	2	1.802
Psalms	6	84	0	.000	1	1.190	0	.000	1	1.190	2	2.381
Psalms	7	142	1	.704	0	.000	0	.000	1	.704	3	2.113
Psalms	8	77	2	2.597	5	6.494	0	.000	7	9.091	1	1.299
Psalms	9	165	0	.000	1	.606	1	.606	2	1.212	6	3.636
Psalms	10	162	1	.617	1	.617	0	.000	2	1.235	3	1.852
Psalms	11	68	0	.000	2	2.941	0	.000	2	2.941	2	2.941
Psalms	12	79	1	1.266	2	2.532	0	.000	3	3.797	2	2.532
Psalms	13	55	0	.000	1	1.818	1	1.818	2	3.636	1	1.818
Psalms	14	73	0	.000	1	1.370	1	1.370	2	2.740	1	1.370
Psalms	15	55	0	.000	1	1.818	1	1.818	2	3.636	0	.000
Psalms	16	97	2	2.062	0	.000	2	2.062	4	4.124	2	2.062
Psalms	17	124	0	.000	0	.000	0	.000	0	.000	2	1.613
Psalms	18	397	1	.252	9	2.267	2	.504	12	3.023	8	2.015
Psalms	19	126	0	.000	5	3.968	0	.000	5	3.968	2	1.587
Psalms	20	70	0	.000	1	1.429	0	.000	1	1.429	3	4.286
Psalms	21	104	0	.000	1	.962	1	.962	2	1.923	1	.962
Psalms	22	253	0	.000	2	.791	0	.000	2	.791	7	2.767
Psalms	23	57	0	.000	0	.000	0	.000	0	.000	1	1.754
Psalms	24	89	1	1.124	6	6.742	0	.000	7	7.865	1	1.124
Psalms	25	159	0	.000	3	1.887	2	1.258	5	3.145	2	1.258
Psalms	26	85	1	1.176	0	.000	1	1.176	2	2.353	0	.000
Psalms	27	149	0	.000	0	.000	3	2.013	3	2.013	0	.000
Psalms	28	96	0	.000	1	1.042	2	2.083	3	3.125	0	.000
Psalms	29	91	0	.000	3	3.297	2	2.198	5	5.495	4	4.396
Psalms	30	97	0	.000	1	1.031	0	.000	1	1.031	2	2.062
Psalms	31	220	2	.909	3	1.364	3	1.364	8	3.636	4	1.818
Psalms	32	110	0	.000	2	1.818	0	.000	2	1.818	1	.909
Psalms	33	161	2	1.242	11	6.832	1	.621	14	8.696	4	2.484
Psalms	34	165	0	.000	4	2.424	5	3.030	9	5.455	0	.000
Psalms	35	229	2	.873	3	1.310	2	.873	7	3.057	1	.437
Psalms	36	100	0	.000	1	1.000	0	.000	1	1.000	2	2.000
Psalms	37	298	0	.000	1	.336	1	.336	2	.671	8	2.685
Psalms	38	168	1	.595	2	1.190	0	.000	3	1.786	0	.000
Psalms	39	129	0	.000	0	.000	0	.000	0	.000	2	1.550
Psalms	40	185	1	.541	3	1.622	0	.000	4	2.162	1	.541
Psalms	41	119	2	1.681	2	1.681	0	.000	4	3.361	3	2.521
Psalms	42	132	0	.000	2	1.515	0	.000	2	1.515	3	2.273
Psalms	43	59	0	.000	0	.000	0	.000	0	.000	0	.000
Psalms	44	197	0	.000	3	1.523	0	.000	3	1.523	6	3.046
Psalms	45	160	0	.000	3	1.875	0	.000	3	1.875	2	1.250
Psalms	46	100	1	1.000	1	1.000	0	.000	2	2.000	5	5.000
Psalms	47	77	1	1.299	3	3.896	2	2.597	6	7.792	1	1.299
Psalms	48	111	1	.901	2	1.802	0	.000	3	2.703	1	.901
Psalms	49	167	0	.000	4	2.395	0	.000	4	2.395	5	2.994
Psalms	50	178	0	.000	2	1.124	0	.000	2	1.124	1	.562
Psalms	51	153	1	.654	2	1.307	1	.654	4	2.614	2	1.307
Psalms	52	90	0	.000	4	4.444	0	.000	4	4.444	1	1.111
Psalms	53	77	0	.000	0	.000	1	1.299	1	1.299	1	1.299
Psalms	54	62	0	.000	2	3.226	0	.000	2	3.226	1	1.613
Psalms	55	192	2	1.042	0	.000	0	.000	2	1.042	5	2.604
Psalms	56	120	1	.833	4	3.333	1	.833	6	5.000	2	1.667
Psalms	57	105	0	.000	4	3.810	0	.000	4	3.810	5	4.762

TABLE ONE: Listing of the Particles for each chapter (in canonical order) Page 9

Book and Chapter		Word	Relative		Article		Nota Accusativi		Total of Three		Dubious Article	
		Count	Count	Percentage	Count	Percentage	Count	Percentage	Count	Percentage	Count	Percentage
Psalms	58	100	1	1.000	1	1.000	0	.000	2	2.000	4	4.000
Psalms	59	156	0	.000	3	1.923	1	.641	4	2.564	6	3.846
Psalms	60	113	0	.000	0	.000	3	2.655	3	2.655	1	.885
Psalms	61	68	0	.000	1	1.471	0	.000	1	1.471	1	1.471
Psalms	62	117	0	.000	1	.855	0	.000	1	.855	1	.855
Psalms	63	93	0	.000	3	3.226	0	.000	3	3.226	1	1.075
Psalms	64	82	1	1.220	0	.000	0	.000	1	1.220	3	3.659
Psalms	65	109	0	.000	2	1.835	0	.000	2	1.835	1	.917
Psalms	66	154	3	1.948	4	2.597	0	.000	7	4.545	9	5.844
Psalms	67	53	0	.000	0	.000	1	1.887	1	1.887	3	5.660
Psalms	68	310	0	.000	5	1.613	0	.000	5	1.613	13	4.194
Psalms	69	291	2	.687	0	.000	1	.344	3	1.031	3	1.031
Psalms	70	47	0	.000	1	2.128	0	.000	1	2.128	1	2.128
Psalms	71	203	3	1.478	4	1.970	0	.000	7	3.448	0	.000
Psalms	72	162	0	.000	3	1.852	1	.617	4	2.469	3	1.852
Psalms	73	193	0	.000	1	.518	0	.000	1	.518	7	3.627
Psalms	74	196	0	.000	3	1.531	0	.000	3	1.531	4	2.041
Psalms	75	87	0	.000	0	.000	0	.000	0	.000	4	4.598
Psalms	76	90	0	.000	0	.000	0	.000	0	.000	3	3.333
Psalms	77	154	0	.000	2	1.299	0	.000	2	1.299	7	4.545
Psalms	78	530	7	1.321	2	.377	6	1.132	15	2.830	23	4.340
Psalms	79	132	3	2.273	4	3.030	5	3.788	12	9.091	2	1.515
Psalms	80	141	1	.709	1	.709	1	.709	3	2.128	2	1.418
Psalms	81	125	0	.000	2	1.600	0	.000	2	1.600	4	3.200
Psalms	82	61	0	.000	3	4.918	0	.000	3	4.918	0	.000
Psalms	83	130	1	.769	1	.769	1	.769	3	2.308	2	1.538
Psalms	84	115	1	.870	2	1.739	0	.000	3	2.609	2	1.739
Psalms	85	96	0	.000	2	2.083	0	.000	2	2.083	1	1.042
Psalms	86	147	1	.680	2	1.361	1	.680	4	2.721	1	.680
Psalms	87	54	0	.000	1	1.852	0	.000	1	1.852	0	.000
Psalms	88	142	1	.704	2	1.408	0	.000	3	2.113	9	6.338
Psalms	89	384	3	.781	5	1.302	0	.000	8	2.083	9	2.344
Psalms	90	140	0	.000	1	.714	0	.000	1	.714	6	4.286
Psalms	91	112	0	.000	0	.000	0	.000	0	.000	2	1.786
Psalms	92	112	0	.000	1	.893	1	.893	2	1.786	5	4.464
Psalms	93	45	0	.000	0	.000	0	.000	0	.000	1	2.222
Psalms	94	169	1	.592	3	1.775	1	.592	5	2.959	2	1.183
Psalms	95	89	4	4.494	2	2.247	0	.000	6	6.742	1	1.124
Psalms	96	112	1	.893	8	7.143	0	.000	9	8.036	2	1.786
Psalms	97	95	0	.000	7	7.368	0	.000	7	7.368	3	3.158
Psalms	98	75	0	.000	5	6.667	1	1.333	6	8.000	1	1.333
Psalms	99	83	0	.000	2	2.410	0	.000	2	2.410	0	.000
Psalms	100	43	0	.000	1	2.326	1	2.326	2	4.651	0	.000
Psalms	101	83	0	.000	0	.000	2	2.410	2	2.410	2	2.410
Psalms	102	212	0	.000	4	1.887	6	2.830	10	4.717	6	2.830
Psalms	103	167	0	.000	6	3.593	5	2.994	11	6.587	6	3.593
Psalms	104	271	2	.738	16	5.904	2	.738	20	7.380	11	4.059
Psalms	105	294	3	1.020	2	.680	8	2.721	13	4.422	3	1.020
Psalms	106	330	2	.606	7	2.121	12	3.636	21	6.364	12	3.636
Psalms	107	278	1	.360	1	.360	0	.000	2	.719	8	2.878
Psalms	108	98	0	.000	2	2.041	0	.000	2	2.041	2	2.041
Psalms	109	227	2	.881	1	.441	0	.000	3	1.322	6	2.643
Psalms	110	65	0	.000	0	.000	0	.000	0	.000	2	3.077
Psalms	111	74	0	.000	0	.000	0	.000	0	.000	0	.000
Psalms	112	79	1	1.266	0	.000	1	1.266	2	2.532	4	5.063
Psalms	113	60	0	.000	5	8.333	1	1.667	6	10.000	2	3.333
Psalms	114	52	0	.000	8	15.385	0	.000	8	15.385	0	.000
Psalms	115	135	2	1.481	6	4.444	2	1.481	10	7.407	1	.741
Psalms	116	131	0	.000	3	2.290	3	2.290	6	4.580	0	.000
Psalms	117	17	0	.000	1	5.882	1	5.882	2	11.765	0	.000
Psalms	118	198	0	.000	6	3.030	0	.000	6	3.030	3	1.515
Psalms	119	1065	8	.751	6	.563	3	.282	17	1.596	9	.845
Psalms	120	51	0	.000	1	1.961	0	.000	1	1.961	2	3.922
Psalms	121	56	0	.000	2	3.571	1	1.786	3	5.357	3	5.357
Psalms	122	62	0	.000	2	3.226	0	.000	2	3.226	0	.000
Psalms	123	41	0	.000	5	12.195	1	2.439	6	14.634	1	2.439
Psalms	124	57	0	.000	5	8.772	0	.000	5	8.772	0	.000
Psalms	125	49	0	.000	7	14.286	1	2.041	8	16.327	1	2.041
Psalms	126	50	0	.000	3	6.000	2	4.000	5	10.000	2	4.000
Psalms	127	60	1	1.667	5	8.333	1	1.667	7	11.667	1	1.667
Psalms	128	47	0	.000	2	4.255	0	.000	2	4.255	0	.000
Psalms	129	54	0	.000	2	3.704	1	1.852	3	5.556	0	.000
Psalms	130	54	0	.000	3	5.556	1	1.852	4	7.407	2	3.704
Psalms	131	33	0	.000	1	3.030	0	.000	1	3.030	1	3.030
Psalms	132	131	1	.763	1	.763	1	.763	3	2.290	0	.000
Psalms	133	40	0	.000	6	15.000	1	2.500	7	17.500	1	2.500
Psalms	134	25	0	.000	2	8.000	2	8.000	4	16.000	1	4.000
Psalms	135	167	2	1.198	5	2.994	5	2.994	12	7.186	4	2.395

TABLE ONE: Listing of the Particles for each chapter (in canonical order) Page 10

Book and Chapter		Word	Relative		Article		Nota Accusativi		Total of Three		Dubious Article	
		Count	Count	Percentage	Count	Percentage	Count	Percentage	Count	Percentage	Count	Percentage
Psalms	136	166	0	.000	10	6.024	2	1.205	12	7.229	3	1.807
Psalms	137	84	0	.000	4	4.762	6	7.143	10	11.905	0	.000
Psalms	138	76	0	.000	0	.000	1	1.316	1	1.316	0	.000
Psalms	139	177	2	1.130	0	.000	0	.000	2	1.130	5	2.825
Psalms	140	116	2	1.724	0	.000	0	.000	2	1.724	3	2.586
Psalms	141	95	0	.000	0	.000	0	.000	0	.000	2	2.105
Psalms	142	75	0	.000	1	1.333	1	1.333	2	2.667	1	1.333
Psalms	143	117	0	.000	0	.000	0	.000	0	.000	2	1.709
Psalms	144	130	3	2.308	6	4.615	1	.769	10	7.692	4	3.077
Psalms	145	152	1	.658	5	3.289	5	3.289	11	7.237	1	.658
Psalms	146	85	1	1.176	3	3.529	4	4.706	8	9.412	3	3.529
Psalms	147	141	1	.709	10	7.092	3	2.128	14	9.929	4	2.837
Psalms	148	111	1	.901	7	6.306	4	3.604	12	10.811	1	.901
Psalms	149	63	0	.000	0	.000	0	.000	0	.000	2	3.175
Psalms	150	37	0	.000	1	2.703	0	.000	1	2.703	0	.000
Job	1	345	3	.870	27	7.826	6	1.739	36	10.435	6	1.739
Job	2	209	1	.478	22	10.526	8	3.828	31	14.833	4	1.914
Job	3	204	2	.980	12	5.882	2	.980	16	7.843	2	.980
Job	4	149	2	1.342	1	.671	0	.000	3	2.013	1	.671
Job	5	207	1	.483	5	2.415	0	.000	6	2.899	4	1.932
Job	6	220	1	.455	1	.455	0	.000	2	.909	2	.909
Job	7	172	0	.000	1	.581	1	.581	2	1.163	1	.581
Job	8	166	1	.602	1	.602	0	.000	2	1.205	0	.000
Job	9	259	3	1.158	3	1.158	0	.000	6	2.317	2	.772
Job	10	169	1	.592	0	.000	0	.000	1	.592	5	2.959
Job	11	148	0	.000	1	.676	0	.000	1	.676	1	.676
Job	12	183	2	1.093	3	1.639	0	.000	5	2.732	6	3.279
Job	13	203	0	.000	0	.000	4	1.970	4	1.970	2	.985
Job	14	177	0	.000	0	.000	1	.565	1	.565	3	1.695
Job	15	261	2	.766	2	.766	0	.000	4	1.533	8	3.065
Job	16	172	0	.000	0	.000	0	.000	0	.000	4	2.326
Job	17	112	0	.000	0	.000	0	.000	0	.000	4	3.571
Job	18	143	0	.000	1	.699	0	.000	1	.699	2	1.399
Job	19	213	1	.469	0	.000	0	.000	1	.469	3	1.408
Job	20	208	0	.000	1	.481	0	.000	1	.481	2	.962
Job	21	240	0	.000	0	.000	0	.000	0	.000	3	1.250
Job	22	210	2	.952	3	1.429	0	.000	5	2.381	1	.476
Job	23	118	0	.000	1	.847	0	.000	1	.847	1	.847
Job	24	203	0	.000	0	.000	0	.000	0	.000	12	5.911
Job	25	43	0	.000	1	2.326	0	.000	1	2.326	0	.000
Job	26	100	0	.000	2	2.000	1	1.000	3	3.000	0	.000
Job	27	169	1	.592	0	.000	2	1.183	3	1.775	5	2.959
Job	28	207	0	.000	7	3.382	1	.483	8	3.865	7	3.382
Job	29	169	2	1.183	0	.000	0	.000	2	1.183	7	4.142
Job	30	227	1	.441	3	1.322	0	.000	4	1.762	5	2.203
Job	31	310	0	.000	1	.323	0	.000	1	.323	8	2.581
Job	32	197	1	.508	5	2.538	4	2.030	10	5.076	0	.000
Job	33	246	0	.000	1	.407	0	.000	1	.407	6	2.439
Job	34	297	2	.673	0	.000	0	.000	2	.673	2	.673
Job	35	116	0	.000	1	.862	1	.862	2	1.724	2	1.724
Job	36	240	2	.833	2	.833	1	.417	5	2.083	8	3.333
Job	37	188	2	1.064	3	1.596	0	.000	5	2.660	2	1.064
Job	38	299	1	.334	6	2.007	1	.334	8	2.676	11	3.679
Job	39	213	2	.939	1	.469	0	.000	3	1.408	9	4.225
Job	40	215	1	.465	2	.930	3	1.395	6	2.791	4	1.860
Job	41	177	0	.000	2	1.130	1	.565	3	1.695	2	1.130
Job	42	241	3	1.245	11	4.564	9	3.734	23	9.544	0	.000
Proverbs	1	237	0	.000	1	.422	2	.844	3	1.266	3	1.266
Proverbs	2	143	1	.699	3	2.098	1	.699	5	3.497	7	4.895
Proverbs	3	259	1	.386	0	.000	4	1.544	5	1.931	3	1.158
Proverbs	4	200	0	.000	1	.500	0	.000	1	.500	2	1.000
Proverbs	5	160	0	.000	1	.625	1	.625	2	1.250	2	1.250
Proverbs	6	272	1	.368	3	1.103	2	.735	6	2.206	5	1.838
Proverbs	7	193	0	.000	5	2.591	0	.000	5	2.591	7	3.627
Proverbs	8	258	0	.000	0	.000	1	.388	1	.388	2	.775
Proverbs	9	127	0	.000	1	.787	0	.000	1	.787	0	.000
Proverbs	10	234	0	.000	1	.427	0	.000	1	.427	8	3.419
Proverbs	11	223	0	.000	0	.000	0	.000	0	.000	2	.897
Proverbs	12	202	0	.000	0	.000	0	.000	0	.000	2	.990
Proverbs	13	183	0	.000	0	.000	2	1.093	2	1.093	1	.546
Proverbs	14	248	0	.000	0	.000	0	.000	0	.000	0	.000
Proverbs	15	252	0	.000	0	.000	0	.000	0	.000	1	.397
Proverbs	16	252	0	.000	1	.397	3	1.190	4	1.587	4	1.587
Proverbs	17	227	1	.441	3	1.322	1	.441	5	2.203	4	1.762
Proverbs	18	175	0	.000	2	1.143	0	.000	2	1.143	1	.571
Proverbs	19	230	0	.000	1	.435	0	.000	1	.435	3	1.304
Proverbs	20	226	0	.000	2	.985	0	.000	2	.885	7	3.097
Proverbs	21	233	1	.429	2	.858	0	.000	3	1.288	5	2.146

TABLE ONE: Listing of the Particles for each chapter (in canonical order) Page 11

Book and Chapter		Word Count	Relative		Article		Nota Accusativi		Total of Three		Dubious Article	
			Count	Percentage	Count	Percentage	Count	Percentage	Count	Percentage	Count	Percentage
Proverbs	22	225	1	.444	1	.444	3	1.333	5	2.222	4	1.778
Proverbs	23	274	1	.365	4	1.460	4	1.460	9	3.285	9	3.285
Proverbs	24	269	1	.372	0	.000	1	.372	2	.743	11	4.089
Proverbs	25	239	3	1.255	0	.000	2	.837	5	2.092	5	2.092
Proverbs	26	211	0	.000	3	1.422	1	.474	4	1.896	10	4.739
Proverbs	27	212	0	.000	6	2.830	1	.472	7	3.302	7	3.302
Proverbs	28	229	0	.000	0	.000	0	.000	0	.000	1	.437
Proverbs	29	204	0	.000	1	.490	1	.490	2	.980	0	.000
Proverbs	30	301	0	.000	4	1.329	1	.332	5	1.661	7	2.326
Proverbs	31	219	1	.457	2	.913	0	.000	3	1.370	11	5.023
Ruth	1	325	6	1.846	12	3.692	1	.308	19	5.846	2	.615
Ruth	2	378	15	3.968	36	9.524	7	1.852	58	15.344	7	1.852
Ruth	3	258	10	3.876	24	9.302	4	1.550	38	14.729	3	1.163
Ruth	4	335	11	3.284	32	9.552	19	5.672	62	18.507	3	.896
Song	1	150	1	.667	11	7.333	2	1.333	14	9.333	4	2.667
Song	2	177	0	.000	26	14.689	4	2.260	30	16.949	4	2.260
Song	3	133	0	.000	7	5.263	6	4.511	13	9.774	8	6.015
Song	4	178	0	.000	12	6.742	0	.000	12	6.742	1	.562
Song	5	185	0	.000	7	3.784	5	2.703	12	6.486	7	3.784
Song	6	114	0	.000	12	10.526	0	.000	12	10.526	7	6.140
Song	7	139	0	.000	13	9.353	1	.719	14	10.072	10	7.194
Song	8	174	0	.000	9	5.172	6	3.448	15	8.621	9	5.172
Qohelet	1	215	3	1.395	18	8.372	2	.930	23	10.698	5	2.326
Qohelet	2	381	4	1.050	31	8.136	8	2.100	43	11.286	11	2.887
Qohelet	3	273	7	2.564	39	14.286	7	2.564	53	19.414	2	.733
Qohelet	4	237	10	4.219	29	12.236	11	4.641	50	21.097	0	.000
Qohelet	5	266	8	3.008	19	7.143	7	2.632	34	12.782	7	2.632
Qohelet	6	170	5	2.941	12	7.059	0	.000	17	10.000	9	5.294
Qohelet	7	330	11	3.333	24	7.273	10	3.030	45	13.636	4	1.212
Qohelet	8	281	20	7.117	24	8.541	9	3.203	53	18.861	8	2.847
Qohelet	9	309	12	3.883	31	10.032	8	2.589	51	16.505	19	6.149
Qohelet	10	196	2	1.020	17	8.673	2	1.020	21	10.714	7	3.571
Qohelet	11	143	2	1.399	17	11.888	5	3.497	24	16.783	8	5.594
Qohelet	12	186	5	2.688	35	18.817	5	2.688	45	24.194	6	3.226
Lamentations	1	377	5	1.326	4	1.061	2	.531	11	2.918	9	2.387
Lamentations	2	382	3	.785	5	1.309	2	.524	10	2.618	11	2.880
Lamentations	3	381	0	.000	9	2.362	1	.262	10	2.625	13	3.412
Lamentations	4	260	1	.385	9	3.462	1	.385	11	4.231	11	4.231
Lamentations	5	145	0	.000	1	.690	1	.690	2	1.379	1	.690
Esther	1	371	8	2.156	65	17.520	8	2.156	81	21.833	8	2.156
Esther	2	438	12	2.740	59	13.470	18	4.110	89	20.320	9	2.055
Esther	3	303	7	2.310	43	14.191	8	2.640	58	19.142	7	2.310
Esther	4	285	14	4.912	26	9.123	11	3.860	51	17.895	7	2.456
Esther	5	265	8	3.019	45	16.981	15	5.660	68	25.660	5	1.887
Esther	6	263	16	6.084	45	17.110	10	3.802	71	26.996	8	3.042
Esther	7	187	5	2.674	39	20.856	2	1.070	46	24.599	2	1.070
Esther	8	343	12	3.499	60	17.493	12	3.499	84	24.490	10	2.915
Esther	9	546	16	2.930	83	15.201	32	5.861	131	23.993	11	2.015
Esther	10	46	1	2.174	6	13.043	0	.000	7	15.217	2	4.348
Daniel	1	309	12	3.883	40	12.945	12	3.883	64	20.712	2	.647
Daniel	2	843	0	.000	5	.593	1	.119	6	.712	6	.712
Daniel	3	631	0	.000	0	.000	0	.000	0	.000	0	.000
Daniel	4	599	0	.000	0	.000	0	.000	0	.000	0	.000
Daniel	5	524	0	.000	0	.000	0	.000	0	.000	0	.000
Daniel	6	551	0	.000	0	.000	0	.000	0	.000	0	.000
Daniel	7	492	0	.000	0	.000	0	.000	0	.000	0	.000
Daniel	8	383	6	1.567	57	14.883	7	1.828	70	18.277	8	2.089
Daniel	9	462	17	3.680	39	8.442	6	1.299	62	13.420	10	2.165
Daniel	10	342	5	1.462	22	6.433	11	3.216	38	11.111	7	2.047
Daniel	11	611	4	.655	42	6.874	1	.164	47	7.692	12	1.964
Daniel	12	177	3	1.695	29	16.384	1	.565	33	18.644	6	3.390
Ezra	1	186	7	3.763	16	8.602	5	2.688	28	15.054	6	3.226
Ezra	2	542	5	.923	31	5.720	0	.000	36	6.642	0	.000
Ezra	3	250	1	.400	38	15.200	6	2.400	45	18.000	15	6.000
Ezra	4	403	1	.248	7	1.737	2	.496	10	2.481	0	.000
Ezra	5	329	0	.000	0	.000	0	.000	0	.000	0	.000
Ezra	6	393	0	.000	13	3.308	1	.254	14	3.562	1	.254
Ezra	7	436	4	.917	25	5.734	2	.459	31	7.110	4	.917
Ezra	8	463	0	.000	63	13.607	8	1.728	71	15.335	9	1.944
Ezra	9	286	3	1.049	38	13.287	5	1.748	46	16.084	6	2.098
Ezra	10	465	3	.645	46	9.892	1	.215	50	10.753	8	1.720
Nehemiah	1	202	8	3.960	27	13.366	11	5.446	46	22.772	3	1.485
Nehemiah	2	371	16	4.313	43	11.590	6	1.617	65	17.520	14	3.774
Nehemiah	3	555	3	.541	79	14.234	11	1.982	93	16.757	5	.901
Nehemiah	4	250	7	2.800	43	17.200	5	2.000	55	22.000	13	5.200
Nehemiah	5	328	13	3.963	46	14.024	14	4.268	73	22.256	4	1.220
Nehemiah	6	305	8	2.623	26	8.525	7	2.295	41	13.443	11	3.607
Nehemiah	7	626	5	.799	51	8.147	6	.958	62	9.904	3	.479

TABLE ONE: Listing of the Particles for each chapter (in canonical order) Page 12

Book and Chapter		Word Count	Relative		Article		Nota Accusativi		Total of Three		Dubious Article	
			Count	Percentage	Count	Percentage	Count	Percentage	Count	Percentage	Count	Percentage
Nehemiah	8	357	8	2.241	67	18.768	7	1.961	82	22.969	15	4.202
Nehemiah	9	656	17	2.591	59	8.994	31	4.726	107	16.311	5	.762
Nehemiah	10	341	2	.587	55	16.129	11	3.226	68	19.941	12	3.519
Nehemiah	11	378	1	.265	44	11.640	0	.000	45	11.905	6	1.587
Nehemiah	12	471	1	.212	69	14.650	10	2.123	80	16.985	16	3.397
Nehemiah	13	473	7	1.480	77	16.279	15	3.171	99	20.930	15	3.171
1 Chronicles	1	422	2	.474	15	3.555	37	8.768	54	12.796	1	.237
1 Chronicles	2	535	2	.374	22	4.112	50	9.346	74	13.832	1	.187
1 Chronicles	3	195	1	.513	11	5.641	0	.000	12	6.154	0	.000
1 Chronicles	4	474	5	1.055	24	5.063	26	5.485	55	11.603	0	.000
1 Chronicles	5	451	4	.887	16	3.548	24	5.322	44	9.756	12	2.661
1 Chronicles	6	629	3	.477	27	4.293	93	14.785	123	19.555	10	1.590
1 Chronicles	7	426	1	.235	9	2.113	13	3.052	23	5.399	7	1.643
1 Chronicles	8	301	0	.000	8	2.658	31	10.299	39	12.957	0	.000
1 Chronicles	9	473	1	.211	52	10.994	13	2.748	66	13.953	8	1.691
1 Chronicles	10	192	4	2.083	10	5.208	18	9.375	32	16.667	3	1.563
1 Chronicles	11	520	4	.769	71	13.654	14	2.692	89	17.115	13	2.500
1 Chronicles	12	494	3	.607	42	8.502	6	1.215	51	10.324	21	4.251
1 Chronicles	13	212	4	1.887	26	12.264	12	5.660	42	19.811	4	1.887
1 Chronicles	14	194	2	1.031	12	6.186	7	3.608	21	10.825	3	1.546
1 Chronicles	15	363	2	.551	39	10.744	16	4.408	57	15.702	9	2.479
1 Chronicles	16	409	7	1.711	34	8.313	8	1.956	49	11.980	11	2.689
1 Chronicles	17	408	17	4.167	27	6.618	15	3.676	59	14.461	4	.980
1 Chronicles	18	243	5	2.058	16	6.584	14	5.761	35	14.403	0	.000
1 Chronicles	19	318	4	1.258	17	5.346	12	3.774	33	10.377	4	1.258
1 Chronicles	20	143	1	.699	12	8.392	10	6.993	23	16.084	2	1.399
1 Chronicles	21	492	5	1.016	38	7.724	14	2.846	57	11.585	15	3.049
1 Chronicles	22	298	2	.671	14	4.698	7	2.349	23	7.718	9	3.020
1 Chronicles	23	333	1	.300	28	8.408	6	1.802	35	10.511	10	3.003
1 Chronicles	24	270	1	.370	32	11.852	0	.000	33	12.222	5	1.852
1 Chronicles	25	287	0	.000	23	8.014	0	.000	23	8.014	5	1.742
1 Chronicles	26	355	1	.282	57	16.056	0	.000	58	16.338	27	7.606
1 Chronicles	27	407	2	.491	83	20.393	2	.491	87	21.376	27	6.634
1 Chronicles	28	381	1	.262	42	11.024	8	2.100	51	13.386	9	2.362
1 Chronicles	29	480	5	1.042	57	11.875	3	.625	65	13.542	16	3.333
2 Chronicles	1	284	12	4.225	26	9.155	6	2.113	44	15.493	9	3.169
2 Chronicles	2	327	14	4.281	20	6.116	5	1.529	39	11.927	22	6.728
2 Chronicles	3	238	4	1.681	47	19.748	9	3.782	60	25.210	6	2.521
2 Chronicles	4	311	4	1.286	60	19.293	26	8.360	90	28.939	13	4.180
2 Chronicles	5	246	5	2.033	46	18.699	14	5.691	65	26.423	7	2.846
2 Chronicles	6	741	38	5.128	66	8.907	22	2.969	126	17.004	13	1.754
2 Chronicles	7	395	14	3.544	56	14.177	21	5.316	91	23.038	7	1.772
2 Chronicles	8	291	13	4.467	33	11.340	15	5.155	61	20.962	11	3.780
2 Chronicles	9	486	15	3.086	45	9.259	13	2.675	73	15.021	11	2.263
2 Chronicles	10	311	12	3.859	38	12.219	14	4.502	64	20.579	9	2.894
2 Chronicles	11	293	3	1.024	11	3.754	35	11.945	49	16.724	4	1.365
2 Chronicles	12	253	5	1.976	24	9.486	10	3.953	39	15.415	4	1.581
2 Chronicles	13	363	2	.551	18	4.959	13	3.581	33	9.091	11	3.030
2 Chronicles	14	217	1	.461	24	11.060	11	5.069	36	16.590	1	.461
2 Chronicles	15	252	4	1.587	16	6.349	6	2.381	26	10.317	6	2.381
2 Chronicles	16	259	4	1.544	21	8.108	15	5.792	40	15.444	3	1.158
2 Chronicles	17	239	3	1.255	17	7.113	4	1.674	24	10.042	2	.837
2 Chronicles	18	558	7	1.254	36	6.452	20	3.584	63	11.290	13	2.330
2 Chronicles	19	182	1	.549	16	8.791	1	.549	18	9.890	3	1.648
2 Chronicles	20	578	3	.519	40	6.920	10	1.730	53	9.170	7	1.211
2 Chronicles	21	321	5	1.558	21	6.542	13	4.050	39	12.150	2	.623
2 Chronicles	22	243	3	1.235	16	6.584	14	5.761	33	13.580	4	1.646
2 Chronicles	23	385	6	1.558	87	22.597	30	7.792	123	31.948	12	3.117
2 Chronicles	24	454	1	.220	48	10.573	22	4.846	71	15.639	7	1.542
2 Chronicles	25	493	11	2.231	35	7.099	19	3.854	65	13.185	8	1.623
2 Chronicles	26	369	2	.542	40	10.840	9	2.439	51	13.821	12	3.252
2 Chronicles	27	129	1	.775	7	5.426	2	1.550	10	7.752	3	2.326
2 Chronicles	28	450	3	.667	35	7.778	24	5.333	62	13.778	9	2.000
2 Chronicles	29	540	5	.926	85	15.741	21	3.889	111	20.556	12	2.222
2 Chronicles	30	432	5	1.157	60	13.889	10	2.315	75	17.361	13	3.009
2 Chronicles	31	332	2	.602	50	15.060	10	3.012	62	18.675	17	5.120
2 Chronicles	32	549	8	1.457	39	7.104	19	3.461	66	12.022	7	1.275
2 Chronicles	33	380	14	3.684	34	8.947	17	4.474	65	17.105	9	2.368
2 Chronicles	34	614	15	2.443	97	15.798	43	7.003	155	25.244	7	1.140
2 Chronicles	35	431	5	1.160	60	13.921	6	1.392	71	16.473	28	6.497
2 Chronicles	36	366	4	1.093	26	7.104	14	3.825	44	12.022	5	1.366

TABLE TWO: Total of Three

Book and Chapter		Count	Percentage
Daniel	3	0	.000
Daniel	4	0	.000
Daniel	5	0	.000
Daniel	6	0	.000
Daniel	7	0	.000
Ezra	5	0	.000
Hosea	11	0	.000
Job	16	0	.000
Job	17	0	.000
Job	21	0	.000
Job	24	0	.000
Proverbs	11	0	.000
Proverbs	12	0	.000
Proverbs	14	0	.000
Proverbs	15	0	.000
Proverbs	28	0	.000
Psalms	4	0	.000
Psalms	17	0	.000
Psalms	23	0	.000
Psalms	39	0	.000
Psalms	43	0	.000
Psalms	75	0	.000
Psalms	76	0	.000
Psalms	91	0	.000
Psalms	93	0	.000
Psalms	110	0	.000
Psalms	111	0	.000
Psalms	141	0	.000
Psalms	143	0	.000
Psalms	149	0	.000
Job	31	1	.323
Proverbs	8	1	.388
Job	33	1	.407
Proverbs	10	1	.427
Proverbs	19	1	.435
Job	19	1	.469
Job	20	1	.481
Proverbs	4	1	.500
Psalms	73	1	.518
Job	14	1	.565
Job	10	1	.592
Ezekiel	19	1	.641
Hosea	8	1	.649
Psalms	37	2	.671
Job	34	2	.673
Job	11	1	.676
Job	18	1	.699
Psalms	7	1	.704
Daniel	2	6	.712
Psalms	90	1	.714
Psalms	107	2	.719
Proverbs	24	2	.743
Proverbs	9	1	.787
Psalms	22	2	.791
Job	23	1	.847
Psalms	62	1	.855
Hosea	14	1	.862
Proverbs	20	2	.885
Job	6	2	.909
Proverbs	29	2	.980
Psalms	36	1	1.000
Psalms	30	1	1.031
Psalms	69	3	1.031
Psalms	55	2	1.042
Proverbs	13	2	1.093
Psalms	50	2	1.124
Psalms	139	2	1.130
Proverbs	18	2	1.143
Job	7	2	1.163
Job	29	2	1.183
Psalms	6	1	1.190
Job	8	2	1.205
Psalms	9	2	1.212
Psalms	64	1	1.220
Hosea	13	2	1.227
Psalms	10	2	1.235
Proverbs	5	2	1.250
Proverbs	1	3	1.266

TABLE THREE: Relative Page 1

Book and Chapter		Count	Percentage
1 Chronicles	8	0	.000
1 Chronicles	25	0	.000
2 Samuel	22	0	.000
Amos	7	0	.000
Amos	8	0	.000
Daniel	2	0	.000
Daniel	3	0	.000
Daniel	4	0	.000
Daniel	5	0	.000
Daniel	6	0	.000
Daniel	7	0	.000
Ezekiel	19	0	.000
Ezekiel	25	0	.000
Ezekiel	30	0	.000
Ezra	5	0	.000
Ezra	6	0	.000
Ezra	8	0	.000
Hosea	3	0	.000
Hosea	4	0	.000
Hosea	6	0	.000
Hosea	8	0	.000
Hosea	10	0	.000
Hosea	11	0	.000
Isaiah	3	0	.000
Isaiah	4	0	.000
Isaiah	12	0	.000
Isaiah	15	0	.000
Isaiah	32	0	.000
Isaiah	34	0	.000
Isaiah	35	0	.000
Isaiah	40	0	.000
Isaiah	42	0	.000
Isaiah	48	0	.000
Isaiah	57	0	.000
Isaiah	61	0	.000
Jeremiah	4	0	.000
Job	7	0	.000
Job	11	0	.000
Job	13	0	.000
Job	14	0	.000
Job	16	0	.000
Job	17	0	.000
Job	18	0	.000
Job	20	0	.000
Job	21	0	.000
Job	23	0	.000
Job	24	0	.000
Job	25	0	.000
Job	26	0	.000
Job	28	0	.000
Job	31	0	.000
Job	33	0	.000
Job	35	0	.000
Job	41	0	.000
Joshua	16	0	.000
Judges	12	0	.000
Lamentations	3	0	.000
Lamentations	5	0	.000
Leviticus	12	0	.000
Nahum	1	0	.000
Numbers	29	0	.000
Proverbs	1	0	.000
Proverbs	4	0	.000
Proverbs	5	0	.000
Proverbs	7	0	.000
Proverbs	8	0	.000
Proverbs	9	0	.000
Proverbs	10	0	.000
Proverbs	11	0	.000
Proverbs	12	0	.000
Proverbs	13	0	.000
Proverbs	14	0	.000
Proverbs	15	0	.000
Proverbs	16	0	.000
Proverbs	18	0	.000
Proverbs	19	0	.000
Proverbs	20	0	.000
Proverbs	26	0	.000

TABLE TWO: Total of Three

Book and Chapter		Count	Percentage
Proverbs	21	3	1.288
Psalms	53	1	1.299
Psalms	77	2	1.299
Psalms	138	1	1.316
Psalms	109	3	1.322
Isaiah	58	3	1.351
Zechariah	9	3	1.351
Proverbs	31	3	1.370
Lamentations	5	2	1.379
Job	39	3	1.408
Psalms	20	1	1.429
Psalms	61	1	1.471
Psalms	42	2	1.515
Psalms	44	3	1.523
Psalms	74	3	1.531
Job	15	4	1.533
Isaiah	44	6	1.542
Proverbs	16	4	1.587
Psalms	119	17	1.596
Psalms	81	2	1.600
Psalms	68	5	1.613
Proverbs	30	5	1.661
Job	41	3	1.695
Job	35	2	1.724
Psalms	140	2	1.724
Job	30	4	1.762
Job	27	3	1.775
Psalms	38	3	1.786
Psalms	92	2	1.786
Psalms	5	2	1.802
Psalms	32	2	1.818
Psalms	65	2	1.835
Psalms	87	1	1.852
Psalms	45	3	1.875
Habakkuk	3	4	1.887
Psalms	67	1	1.887
Proverbs	26	4	1.896
Hosea	6	2	1.923
Psalms	21	2	1.923
Proverbs	3	5	1.931
Psalms	120	1	1.961
Job	13	4	1.970
Psalms	46	2	2.000
Psalms	58	2	2.000
Job	4	3	2.013
Psalms	27	3	2.013
Psalms	108	2	2.041
Job	36	5	2.083
Psalms	85	2	2.083
Psalms	89	8	2.083
Proverbs	25	5	2.092
Psalms	88	3	2.113
Hosea	7	4	2.116
Psalms	70	1	2.128
Psalms	80	3	2.128
Psalms	40	4	2.162
Proverbs	17	5	2.203
Proverbs	6	6	2.206
Proverbs	22	5	2.222
Isaiah	54	5	2.262
Isaiah	34	5	2.273
Psalms	132	3	2.290
Psalms	83	3	2.308
Job	9	6	2.317
Job	25	1	2.326
Isaiah	64	3	2.344
Psalms	26	2	2.353
Job	22	3	2.381
Psalms	49	4	2.395
Psalms	99	2	2.410
Psalms	101	2	2.410
Isaiah	61	4	2.424
Isaiah	59	7	2.465
Psalms	72	4	2.469
Ezra	4	10	2.481
Hosea	10	5	2.488
Psalms	112	2	2.532
Psalms	59	4	2.564

TABLE THREE: Relative Page 2

Book and Chapter		Count	Percentage
Proverbs	27	0	.000
Proverbs	28	0	.000
Proverbs	29	0	.000
Proverbs	30	0	.000
Psalms	2	0	.000
Psalms	4	0	.000
Psalms	5	0	.000
Psalms	6	0	.000
Psalms	9	0	.000
Psalms	11	0	.000
Psalms	13	0	.000
Psalms	14	0	.000
Psalms	15	0	.000
Psalms	17	0	.000
Psalms	19	0	.000
Psalms	20	0	.000
Psalms	21	0	.000
Psalms	22	0	.000
Psalms	23	0	.000
Psalms	25	0	.000
Psalms	27	0	.000
Psalms	28	0	.000
Psalms	29	0	.000
Psalms	30	0	.000
Psalms	32	0	.000
Psalms	34	0	.000
Psalms	36	0	.000
Psalms	37	0	.000
Psalms	39	0	.000
Psalms	42	0	.000
Psalms	43	0	.000
Psalms	44	0	.000
Psalms	45	0	.000
Psalms	49	0	.000
Psalms	50	0	.000
Psalms	52	0	.000
Psalms	53	0	.000
Psalms	54	0	.000
Psalms	57	0	.000
Psalms	59	0	.000
Psalms	60	0	.000
Psalms	61	0	.000
Psalms	62	0	.000
Psalms	63	0	.000
Psalms	65	0	.000
Psalms	67	0	.000
Psalms	68	0	.000
Psalms	70	0	.000
Psalms	72	0	.000
Psalms	73	0	.000
Psalms	74	0	.000
Psalms	75	0	.000
Psalms	76	0	.000
Psalms	77	0	.000
Psalms	81	0	.000
Psalms	82	0	.000
Psalms	85	0	.000
Psalms	87	0	.000
Psalms	90	0	.000
Psalms	91	0	.000
Psalms	92	0	.000
Psalms	93	0	.000
Psalms	97	0	.000
Psalms	98	0	.000
Psalms	99	0	.000
Psalms	100	0	.000
Psalms	101	0	.000
Psalms	102	0	.000
Psalms	103	0	.000
Psalms	108	0	.000
Psalms	110	0	.000
Psalms	111	0	.000
Psalms	113	0	.000
Psalms	114	0	.000
Psalms	116	0	.000
Psalms	117	0	.000
Psalms	118	0	.000
Psalms	120	0	.000

TABLE TWO: Total of Three

Book and Chapter		Count	Percentage
Nahum	3	6	2.586
Proverbs	7	5	2.591
Psalms	84	3	2.609
Psalms	51	4	2.614
Lamentations	2	10	2.618
Lamentations	3	10	2.625
Isaiah	48	7	2.642
Psalms	60	3	2.655
Job	37	5	2.660
Psalms	142	2	2.667
Job	38	8	2.676
Psalms	48	3	2.703
Psalms	150	1	2.703
Psalms	86	4	2.721
Job	12	5	2.732
Psalms	14	2	2.740
Job	40	6	2.791
Psalms	78	15	2.830
Isaiah	50	5	2.841
Job	5	6	2.899
Isaiah	33	8	2.909
Lamentations	1	11	2.918
Isaiah	63	7	2.929
Psalms	11	2	2.941
Psalms	94	5	2.959
Job	26	3	3.000
Isaiah	26	7	3.004
Judges	5	11	3.022
Psalms	18	12	3.023
Psalms	118	6	3.030
Psalms	131	1	3.030
Psalms	35	7	3.057
Psalms	28	3	3.125
Psalms	25	5	3.145
Isaiah	43	10	3.185
Ezekiel	27	13	3.194
2 Samuel	22	12	3.209
Psalms	54	2	3.226
Psalms	63	3	3.226
Psalms	122	2	3.226
Hosea	9	7	3.241
Nahum	1	5	3.247
Psalms	2	3	3.261
Deuteronomy	33	11	3.274
Proverbs	23	9	3.285
Isaiah	47	7	3.286
Proverbs	27	7	3.302
Isaiah	45	12	3.333
Isaiah	46	5	3.333
Psalms	41	4	3.361
Habakkuk	2	9	3.435
Isaiah	32	7	3.448
Psalms	71	7	3.448
Proverbs	2	5	3.497
Ezra	6	14	3.562
Isaiah	1	13	3.611
Psalms	13	2	3.636
Psalms	15	2	3.636
Psalms	31	8	3.636
Ezekiel	28	13	3.693
Hosea	12	6	3.750
Jeremiah	48	22	3.793
Psalms	12	3	3.797
Psalms	57	4	3.810
Isaiah	49	14	3.857
Job	28	8	3.865
Amos	7	10	3.891
Isaiah	35	5	3.968
Psalms	19	5	3.968
Psalms	16	4	4.124
Isaiah	42	12	4.167
Isaiah	53	7	4.217
Lamentations	4	11	4.231
Micah	1	9	4.245
Psalms	128	2	4.255
Leviticus	12	5	4.274
Psalms	3	3	4.286
Numbers	23	17	4.370

TABLE THREE: Relative Page 3

Book and Chapter		Count	Percentage
Psalms	121	0	.000
Psalms	122	0	.000
Psalms	123	0	.000
Psalms	124	0	.000
Psalms	125	0	.000
Psalms	126	0	.000
Psalms	128	0	.000
Psalms	129	0	.000
Psalms	130	0	.000
Psalms	131	0	.000
Psalms	133	0	.000
Psalms	134	0	.000
Psalms	136	0	.000
Psalms	137	0	.000
Psalms	138	0	.000
Psalms	141	0	.000
Psalms	142	0	.000
Psalms	143	0	.000
Psalms	149	0	.000
Psalms	150	0	.000
Song	2	0	.000
Song	3	0	.000
Song	4	0	.000
Song	5	0	.000
Song	6	0	.000
Song	7	0	.000
Song	8	0	.000
Zechariah	5	0	.000
Zechariah	9	0	.000
Numbers	7	1	.093
2 Kings	4	1	.149
1 Chronicles	9	1	.211
Nehemiah	12	1	.212
2 Chronicles	24	1	.220
1 Chronicles	7	1	.235
Jeremiah	6	1	.241
Ezra	4	1	.248
Psalms	18	1	.252
Ezekiel	45	1	.253
Isaiah	44	1	.257
1 Chronicles	28	1	.262
Nehemiah	11	1	.265
1 Samuel	4	1	.270
Judges	5	1	.275
Isaiah	45	1	.278
1 Chronicles	26	1	.282
2 Samuel	5	1	.285
Genesis	4	1	.293
Exodus	2	1	.294
1 Chronicles	23	1	.300
Exodus	15	1	.312
Job	38	1	.334
Isaiah	60	1	.339
Jeremiah	48	2	.345
Genesis	10	1	.347
1 Samuel	7	1	.348
Psalms	107	1	.360
Isaiah	33	1	.364
Proverbs	23	1	.365
Proverbs	6	1	.368
1 Chronicles	24	1	.370
Proverbs	24	1	.372
1 Chronicles	2	2	.374
Isaiah	9	1	.375
Habakkuk	2	1	.382
Lamentations	4	1	.385
Proverbs	3	1	.386
1 Samuel	11	1	.389
Isaiah	24	1	.391
Ezra	3	1	.400
Exodus	26	2	.417
Malachi	1	1	.418
Joel	1	1	.426
Isaiah	26	1	.429
Proverbs	21	1	.429
Nahum	3	1	.431
Job	30	1	.441
Proverbs	17	1	.441

TABLE TWO: Total of Three

Book and Chapter		Count	Percentage
Psalms	105	13	4.422
Psalms	52	4	4.444
Genesis	16	10	4.484
Psalms	66	7	4.545
Psalms	116	6	4.580
Psalms	100	2	4.651
Micah	5	8	4.678
Isaiah	16	9	4.687
Amos	1	10	4.717
Psalms	102	10	4.717
Isaiah	60	14	4.746
Isaiah	15	6	4.800
Ezekiel	21	26	4.906
Micah	7	12	4.918
Psalms	82	3	4.918
Hosea	3	4	4.938
Isaiah	5	19	4.948
Numbers	2	17	4.971
Isaiah	21	10	4.975
Psalms	56	6	5.000
Hosea	5	9	5.028
Isaiah	40	18	5.042
Job	32	10	5.076
Isaiah	13	13	5.138
Nahum	2	9	5.202
Psalms	121	3	5.357
1 Chronicles	7	23	5.399
Isaiah	41	19	5.413
Isaiah	52	11	5.446
Psalms	34	9	5.455
Jeremiah	2	28	5.469
Psalms	29	5	5.495
Jeremiah	6	23	5.542
Psalms	129	3	5.556
Exodus	15	18	5.607
Ezekiel	25	15	5.792
Ruth	1	19	5.846
Deuteronomy	23	20	5.900
Isaiah	23	13	5.991
Habakkuk	1	12	6.091
1 Chronicles	3	12	6.154
Isaiah	57	16	6.154
Isaiah	17	11	6.180
Micah	2	11	6.250
Jeremiah	5	27	6.265
Isaiah	30	31	6.301
Psalms	106	21	6.364
Isaiah	14	24	6.383
Isaiah	10	26	6.404
Micah	6	13	6.404
Isaiah	12	4	6.452
Song	5	12	6.486
Hosea	1	9	6.569
Psalms	103	11	6.587
Jeremiah	50	46	6.638
Ezra	2	36	6.642
Jeremiah	49	39	6.678
Ezekiel	35	13	6.701
Isaiah	56	12	6.704
Jeremiah	30	23	6.725
Hosea	4	15	6.726
Psalms	95	6	6.742
Song	4	12	6.742
Deuteronomy	32	42	6.829
Jeremiah	4	29	6.856
Numbers	24	21	6.863
Isaiah	51	23	6.886
Ezekiel	31	22	7.051
Isaiah	31	11	7.051
Ezra	7	31	7.110
Jonah	2	8	7.143
Psalms	135	12	7.186
Micah	4	16	7.207
Psalms	136	12	7.229
Zechariah	10	12	7.229
Psalms	145	11	7.237
1 Samuel	16	27	7.239
Zephaniah	3	20	7.246

TABLE THREE: Relative Page 4

Book and Chapter		Count	Percentage
Zechariah	12	1	.441
Proverbs	22	1	.444
Genesis	16	1	.448
Micah	4	1	.450
Isaiah	54	1	.452
Job	6	1	.455
Proverbs	31	1	.457
1 Samuel	5	1	.459
2 Chronicles	14	1	.461
Hosea	9	1	.463
Job	40	1	.465
Job	19	1	.469
Habakkuk	3	1	.472
1 Chronicles	1	2	.474
1 Chronicles	6	3	.477
Job	2	1	.478
Job	5	1	.483
1 Chronicles	27	2	.491
Ezekiel	27	2	.491
Isaiah	10	2	.493
Habakkuk	1	1	.508
Job	32	1	.508
1 Chronicles	3	1	.513
2 Chronicles	20	3	.519
Isaiah	5	2	.521
Isaiah	16	1	.521
Numbers	10	2	.524
Hosea	7	1	.529
Nehemiah	3	3	.541
Psalms	40	1	.541
2 Chronicles	26	2	.542
Genesis	5	2	.548
2 Chronicles	19	1	.549
1 Chronicles	15	2	.551
2 Chronicles	13	2	.551
Hosea	5	1	.559
Amos	6	1	.562
Jeremiah	14	2	.562
Ezekiel	28	2	.568
Micah	2	1	.568
Isaiah	27	1	.575
Numbers	28	2	.575
Nahum	2	1	.578
Ezekiel	7	2	.583
Jeremiah	2	3	.586
Nehemiah	10	2	.587
Job	10	1	.592
Job	27	1	.592
Psalms	94	1	.592
Psalms	38	1	.595
2 Chronicles	31	2	.602
Isaiah	53	1	.602
Job	8	1	.602
Zechariah	10	1	.602
Psalms	106	2	.606
1 Chronicles	12	3	.607
Zechariah	3	1	.610
Hosea	13	1	.613
Psalms	10	1	.617
Isaiah	25	1	.621
Hosea	12	1	.625
Isaiah	43	2	.637
Ezra	10	3	.645
Isaiah	22	2	.649
Psalms	51	1	.654
2 Kings	9	4	.655
Daniel	11	4	.655
Ezekiel	34	3	.655
Psalms	145	1	.658
Zechariah	13	1	.658
2 Chronicles	28	3	.667
Isaiah	46	1	.667
Song	1	1	.667
1 Chronicles	22	2	.671
Job	34	2	.673
Jeremiah	51	6	.674
2 Samuel	23	3	.676
Psalms	86	1	.680

TABLE TWO: Total of Three

Book and Chapter		Count	Percentage
Psalms	97	7	7.368
Psalms	104	20	7.380
Psalms	115	10	7.407
Psalms	130	4	7.407
Jeremiah	46	30	7.444
Numbers	1	44	7.483
Malachi	1	18	7.531
Jeremiah	31	47	7.544
Isaiah	28	29	7.612
Numbers	12	15	7.653
Zephaniah	2	17	7.658
Joel	1	18	7.660
Daniel	11	47	7.692
Psalms	144	10	7.692
1 Chronicles	22	23	7.718
2 Chronicles	27	10	7.752
Exodus	22	28	7.756
Isaiah	11	17	7.763
Psalms	47	6	7.792
Jeremiah	10	25	7.812
Job	3	16	7.843
Numbers	29	33	7.857
Isaiah	62	14	7.865
Psalms	24	7	7.865
1 Samuel	3	24	7.895
Jeremiah	1	21	7.895
Amos	4	17	7.907
Ezekiel	22	31	7.949
2 Kings	5	39	7.975
Psalms	98	6	8.000
1 Chronicles	25	23	8.014
Psalms	96	9	8.036
Jeremiah	14	29	8.146
Genesis	46	34	8.213
Jeremiah	15	26	8.228
Genesis	36	41	8.419
Amos	8	16	8.421
Jeremiah	18	27	8.464
Ezekiel	23	53	8.535
Isaiah	19	28	8.563
Genesis	45	34	8.564
Obadiah	1	25	8.591
Genesis	27	55	8.621
Song	8	15	8.621
Genesis	18	38	8.696
Psalms	33	14	8.696
1 Samuel	23	38	8.716
Ezekiel	29	30	8.721
Jeremiah	51	78	8.764
Genesis	5	32	8.767
Ezekiel	30	30	8.772
Psalms	124	5	".772
Ezekiel	26	27	8.795
Isaiah	18	11	8.871
Genesis	38	36	8.889
Ezekiel	48	47	8.918
Psalms	1	5	8.955
Numbers	36	19	8.962
Isaiah	4	8	8.989
Jeremiah	9	34	9.067
2 Chronicles	13	33	9.091
Psalms	8	7	9.091
Psalms	79	12	9.091
2 Chronicles	20	53	9.170
Isaiah	25	15	9.317
Song	1	14	9.333
Jeremiah	47	10	9.346
Genesis	4	32	9.384
Jeremiah	17	38	9.406
Psalms	146	8	9.412
2 Samuel	9	21	9.459
Ezekiel	38	35	9.459
Ezekiel	3	39	9.489
Numbers	7	102	9.515
Ezekiel	32	46	9.544
Job	42	23	9.544
Leviticus	22	42	9.567
2 Kings	13	40	9.615

TABLE THREE: Relative Page 5

Book and Chapter		Count	Percentage
Leviticus	19	3	.682
Psalms	69	2	.687
1 Samuel	18	3	.693
1 Chronicles	20	1	.699
Proverbs	2	1	.699
Isaiah	59	2	.704
Psalms	7	1	.704
Psalms	88	1	.704
Psalms	80	1	.709
Psalms	147	1	.709
Zephaniah	3	2	.725
Hosea	1	1	.730
Jeremiah	3	3	.732
Psalms	104	2	.738
Numbers	26	5	.742
Zephaniah	1	2	.743
Psalms	119	8	.751
Judges	1	4	.756
Genesis	42	4	.758
1 Samuel	19	3	.759
Jeremiah	12	2	.760
Exodus	27	2	.763
Psalms	132	1	.763
Genesis	11	3	.765
Job	15	2	.766
1 Chronicles	11	4	.769
Psalms	83	1	.769
2 Chronicles	27	1	.775
Joel	2	3	.779
Isaiah	64	1	.781
Psalms	89	3	.781
1 Kings	6	4	.784
Leviticus	13	7	.784
Lamentations	2	3	.785
Isaiah	13	2	.791
Isaiah	14	3	.798
Nehemiah	7	5	.799
Jeremiah	31	5	.803
Exodus	37	3	.820
Micah	7	2	.820
Genesis	36	4	.821
Joshua	19	4	.825
Exodus	22	3	.831
Job	36	2	.833
Psalms	56	1	.833
Isaiah	63	2	.837
Exodus	28	5	.840
Exodus	14	4	.844
Genesis	29	4	.849
Isaiah	41	3	.855
Joshua	21	5	.858
Hosea	14	1	.862
Job	1	3	.870
Psalms	84	1	.870
Psalms	35	2	.873
Numbers	2	3	.877
2 Samuel	24	4	.879
Psalms	109	2	.881
1 Chronicles	5	4	.887
Deuteronomy	33	3	.893
Jonah	2	1	.893
Judges	14	3	.893
Psalms	96	1	.893
Isaiah	51	3	.898
Isaiah	58	2	.901
Psalms	48	1	.901
Psalms	148	1	.901
Zephaniah	2	2	.901
2 Samuel	11	4	.905
Jeremiah	37	3	.906
Psalms	31	2	.909
Zechariah	2	2	.909
Ezra	7	4	.917
Isaiah	23	2	.922
Ezra	2	5	.923
2 Chronicles	29	5	.926
Amos	4	2	.930
Jeremiah	47	1	.935

TABLE TWO: Total of Three

Book and Chapter		Count	Percentage
Amos	5	31	9.627
1 Samuel	29	21	9.633
Isaiah	55	18	9.730
1 Chronicles	5	44	9.756
Jeremiah	3	40	9.756
Isaiah	27	17	9.770
Leviticus	19	43	9.773
Song	3	13	9.774
Genesis	49	36	9.783
Joel	2	38	9.870
2 Chronicles	19	18	9.890
Nehemiah	7	62	9.904
Psalms	147	14	9.929
Numbers	10	38	9.948
2 Samuel	5	35	9.972
Psalms	113	6	10.000
Psalms	126	5	10.000
Qohelet	6	17	10.000
2 Chronicles	17	24	10.042
Jeremiah	8	35	10.057
Song	7	14	10.072
Leviticus	21	31	10.164
Ezekiel	16	85	10.204
Amos	2	22	10.233
Genesis	20	29	10.284
2 Chronicles	15	26	10.317
Isaiah	38	29	10.320
1 Chronicles	12	51	10.324
Genesis	25	42	10.370
1 Chronicles	19	33	10.377
Jonah	4	19	10.383
Exodus	6	42	10.396
Malachi	2	28	10.409
Genesis	17	37	10.423
Job	1	36	10.435
Isaiah	9	28	10.487
1 Chronicles	23	35	10.511
Song	6	12	10.526
Judges	11	70	10.558
Judges	15	34	10.592
Ezekiel	4	28	10.606
2 Samuel	1	39	10.627
Exodus	21	48	10.643
Qohelet	1	23	10.698
Qohelet	10	21	10.714
1 Samuel	22	45	10.740
Ezra	10	50	10.753
Ezekiel	12	43	10.777
Psalms	148	12	10.811
1 Chronicles	14	21	10.825
Ezekiel	24	41	10.933
Isaiah	24	28	10.938
1 Samuel	27	23	11.005
Isaiah	7	30	11.014
Jeremiah	12	29	11.027
Isaiah	22	34	11.039
Isaiah	29	36	11.043
Isaiah	65	40	11.080
1 Samuel	1	46	11.094
Amos	3	23	11.111
Daniel	10	38	11.111
Ezekiel	37	50	11.211
Genesis	11	44	11.224
2 Kings	2	48	11.241
2 Samuel	2	58	11.262
Qohelet	2	43	11.286
2 Chronicles	18	63	11.290
1 Kings	19	42	11.321
Exodus	17	28	11.382
1 Samuel	19	45	11.392
Ezekiel	33	59	11.412
Judges	13	45	11.421
Numbers	33	53	11.422
Isaiah	20	11	11.458
2 Samuel	10	36	11.465
1 Kings	4	23	11.500
Ezekiel	14	45	11.509
Ezekiel	2	18	11.539

TABLE THREE: Relative Page 6

Book and Chapter		Count	Percentage
Jeremiah	10	3	.937
Job	39	2	.939
Amos	1	2	.943
Ezekiel	21	5	.943
Micah	1	2	.943
Judges	19	5	.945
Job	22	2	.952
2 Samuel	10	3	.955
Ezekiel	31	3	.962
1 Samuel	1	4	.964
Exodus	38	4	.971
Job	3	2	.980
Zechariah	6	2	.985
Isaiah	21	2	.995
Leviticus	2	2	1.000
Psalms	46	1	1.000
Psalms	58	1	1.000
Genesis	37	5	1.012
1 Chronicles	21	5	1.016
Isaiah	30	5	1.016
Numbers	1	6	1.020
Psalms	105	3	1.020
Qohelet	10	2	1.020
2 Kings	5	5	1.022
2 Chronicles	11	3	1.024
1 Chronicles	14	2	1.031
Leviticus	26	6	1.031
1 Chronicles	29	5	1.042
Psalms	55	2	1.042
Ezra	9	3	1.049
Qohelet	2	4	1.050
1 Chronicles	4	5	1.055
Isaiah	6	2	1.064
Job	37	2	1.064
Ezekiel	38	4	1.081
Leviticus	24	3	1.083
Joshua	15	6	1.085
2 Samuel	1	4	1.090
2 Chronicles	36	4	1.093
Job	12	2	1.093
1 Samuel	17	10	1.094
Isaiah	49	4	1.102
Haggai	2	4	1.105
Isaiah	1	4	1.111
2 Kings	11	4	1.117
Isaiah	17	2	1.124
Isaiah	62	2	1.124
Psalms	24	1	1.124
1 Kings	1	9	1.125
Psalms	139	2	1.130
1 Samuel	20	8	1.138
Genesis	48	4	1.143
1 Samuel	23	5	1.147
2 Chronicles	30	5	1.157
Job	9	3	1.158
2 Chronicles	35	5	1.160
Jeremiah	5	5	1.160
Ezekiel	33	6	1.161
Numbers	3	7	1.169
Psalms	26	1	1.176
Psalms	146	1	1.176
Leviticus	23	7	1.180
Job	29	2	1.183
1 Samuel	22	5	1.193
Amos	9	3	1.195
Psalms	135	2	1.198
Jeremiah	49	7	1.199
Judges	20	9	1.205
1 Kings	20	9	1.206
Exodus	10	6	1.207
Jeremiah	21	3	1.210
Psalms	64	1	1.220
Exodus	13	4	1.231
2 Chronicles	22	3	1.235
Jeremiah	46	5	1.241
Amos	5	4	1.242
Psalms	33	2	1.242
Job	42	3	1.245

TABLE TWO: Total of Three

Book and Chapter		Count	Percentage
1 Chronicles	21	57	11.585
1 Chronicles	4	55	11.603
Exodus	5	37	11.635
Genesis	35	44	11.640
Psalms	127	7	11.667
Malachi	3	43	11.685
1 Kings	22	95	11.728
Ezekiel	13	42	11.732
Psalms	117	2	11.765
Ezekiel	17	45	11.780
Ezekiel	18	56	11.814
Judges	14	40	11.905
Nehemiah	11	45	11.905
Psalms	137	10	11.905
2 Samuel	3	78	11.908
2 Kings	4	80	11.923
2 Chronicles	2	39	11.927
Ezekiel	7	41	11.953
1 Chronicles	16	49	11.980
Genesis	26	56	12.017
2 Chronicles	32	66	12.022
2 Chronicles	36	44	12.022
1 Samuel	2	67	12.050
Exodus	11	21	12.069
2 Chronicles	21	39	12.150
Numbers	30	32	12.167
Isaiah	37	69	12.191
2 Samuel	8	32	12.214
1 Chronicles	24	33	12.222
1 Samuel	18	53	12.240
Isaiah	2	31	12.253
2 Kings	19	70	12.259
Ezekiel	6	26	12.264
Joshua	15	68	12.297
Deuteronomy	25	32	12.308
Leviticus	25	88	12.394
2 Kings	1	54	12.414
Isaiah	66	48	12.435
2 Kings	15	73	12.436
Exodus	7	52	12.440
1 Samuel	28	54	12.529
Deuteronomy	24	41	12.538
Genesis	37	62	12.551
Judges	12	28	12.556
Jeremiah	22	59	12.607
1 Kings	17	45	12.640
2 Samuel	20	56	12.641
Genesis	42	67	12.689
Genesis	47	65	12.695
Isaiah	6	24	12.766
Qohelet	5	34	12.782
1 Chronicles	1	54	12.796
1 Samuel	25	96	12.800
Judges	21	48	12.800
Isaiah	3	32	12.851
1 Kings	11	89	12.899
Joel	4	35	12.915
Amos	6	23	12.921
Jeremiah	20	38	12.925
Joshua	22	89	12.936
1 Chronicles	8	39	12.957
Exodus	27	34	12.977
Leviticus	2	26	13.000
Numbers	18	68	13.052
Joshua	17	44	13.056
Zechariah	2	29	13.182
2 Chronicles	25	65	13.185
Genesis	30	74	13.214
Ezekiel	5	38	13.240
Exodus	4	60	13.245
2 Kings	9	81	13.257
Judges	4	56	13.270
1 Kings	2	107	13.275
Genesis	28	43	13.313
Jeremiah	35	49	13.315
1 Samuel	20	94	13.371
1 Chronicles	28	51	13.386
1 Kings	20	100	13.405

TABLE THREE: Relative Page 7

Book and Chapter		Count	Percentage
2 Chronicles	18	7	1.254
2 Chronicles	17	3	1.255
Proverbs	25	3	1.255
1 Chronicles	19	4	1.258
Haggai	1	3	1.261
2 Samuel	4	1	1.266
Exodus	3	5	1.266
Psalms	12	1	1.266
Psalms	112	1	1.266
Ezekiel	22	5	1.282
Numbers	23	5	1.285
2 Chronicles	4	4	1.286
Numbers	25	3	1.293
Genesis	8	4	1.299
Psalms	47	1	1.299
Numbers	24	4	1.307
Exodus	31	3	1.310
Isaiah	28	5	1.312
Psalms	78	7	1.321
Lamentations	1	5	1.326
2 Samuel	12	7	1.328
Ezekiel	48	7	1.328
Exodus	21	6	1.330
Ezekiel	24	5	1.333
Jeremiah	9	5	1.333
Isaiah	8	4	1.338
1 Samuel	16	5	1.340
Job	4	2	1.342
1 Kings	19	5	1.348
Genesis	47	7	1.367
1 Kings	18	10	1.370
Obadiah	1	4	1.375
2 Kings	3	6	1.379
Numbers	8	5	1.385
2 Samuel	13	9	1.389
Amos	2	3	1.395
Qohelet	1	3	1.395
Qohelet	11	2	1.399
Genesis	17	5	1.408
Isaiah	47	3	1.408
1 Samuel	21	4	1.418
Genesis	19	8	1.421
Exodus	8	6	1.422
Psalms	3	1	1.429
Amos	3	3	1.449
Ezekiel	29	5	1.453
Judges	3	7	1.455
2 Chronicles	32	8	1.457
Ezekiel	3	6	1.460
Daniel	10	5	1.462
Hosea	2	5	1.475
Micah	6	3	1.478
Psalms	71	3	1.478
Nehemiah	13	7	1.480
Genesis	38	6	1.481
Psalms	115	2	1.481
Joshua	17	5	1.484
1 Samuel	31	3	1.485
Exodus	6	6	1.485
Isaiah	52	3	1.485
Malachi	2	4	1.487
2 Samuel	19	12	1.489
Judges	11	10	1.508
2 Kings	6	8	1.515
Ezekiel	4	4	1.515
Judges	13	6	1.523
2 Samuel	18	9	1.528
Isaiah	19	5	1.529
Isaiah	29	5	1.534
Ezekiel	14	6	1.535
2 Chronicles	16	4	1.544
Genesis	15	4	1.544
Genesis	32	7	1.545
Exodus	36	8	1.556
2 Chronicles	21	5	1.558
2 Chronicles	23	6	1.558
Judges	17	3	1.563
Daniel	8	6	1.567

TABLE TWO: Total of Three

Book and Chapter		Count	Percentage
Daniel	9	62	13.420
Nehemiah	6	41	13.443
2 Samuel	7	62	13.449
Genesis	23	37	13.455
Leviticus	23	80	13.491
Numbers	28	47	13.506
1 Chronicles	29	65	13.542
Judges	17	26	13.542
1 Samuel	10	60	13.575
2 Chronicles	22	33	13.580
Genesis	29	64	13.588
Ezekiel	1	52	13.613
Ezekiel	39	59	13.626
Jeremiah	23	83	13.629
Qohelet	7	45	13.636
Zechariah	12	31	13.656
Leviticus	18	47	13.663
Leviticus	24	38	13.718
2 Chronicles	28	62	13.778
1 Samuel	15	73	13.800
Numbers	22	90	13.804
2 Chronicles	26	51	13.821
1 Chronicles	2	74	13.832
Deuteronomy	15	49	13.842
Genesis	44	63	13.846
Micah	3	23	13.855
Numbers	34	42	13.861
Zechariah	1	38	13.919
1 Chronicles	9	66	13.953
2 Kings	8	72	13.953
Genesis	48	49	14.000
2 Samuel	13	91	14.043
Leviticus	26	82	14.089
Genesis	13	34	14.108
Exodus	34	76	14.126
Genesis	50	53	14.133
1 Kings	15	74	14.149
Ezekiel	36	80	14.159
Hosea	2	48	14.159
Numbers	6	51	14.167
Genesis	12	38	14.179
2 Samuel	23	63	14.189
Judges	20	106	14.190
Genesis	31	109	14.193
Numbers	16	70	14.199
Jeremiah	13	54	14.286
1 Chronicles	18	35	14.403
2 Kings	14	69	14.405
1 Samuel	24	54	14.439
1 Chronicles	17	59	14.461
Jeremiah	42	59	14.461
Exodus	13	47	14.462
1 Samuel	26	69	14.526
1 Samuel	21	41	14.539
Jeremiah	11	56	14.545
Joshua	18	59	14.568
Psalms	123	6	14.634
Joshua	19	71	14.639
1 Kings	16	80	14.679
Genesis	24	135	14.706
Ruth	3	38	14.729
Ezekiel	8	47	14.734
1 Kings	21	71	14.792
Judges	16	82	14.828
Job	2	31	14.833
1 Kings	5	75	14.911
Jeremiah	44	93	14.928
Judges	9	131	14.971
1 Samuel	7	43	14.983
Genesis	32	68	15.011
2 Chronicles	9	73	15.021
Numbers	27	48	15.047
Ezra	1	28	15.054
Exodus	23	60	15.075
1 Samuel	11	39	15.175
Genesis	14	52	15.205
Esther	10	7	15.217
Genesis	43	74	15.258

TABLE THREE: Relative Page 8

Book and Chapter		Count	Percentage
Ezekiel	1	6	1.571
Ezekiel	17	6	1.571
Jonah	1	4	1.575
Zechariah	11	4	1.575
Isaiah	2	4	1.581
Jeremiah	15	5	1.582
2 Chronicles	15	4	1.587
Jeremiah	50	11	1.587
Exodus	19	6	1.600
Genesis	18	7	1.602
Zechariah	4	3	1.604
Joshua	12	4	1.613
1 Samuel	9	8	1.616
Joshua	7	8	1.619
1 Samuel	28	7	1.624
Exodus	17	4	1.626
2 Kings	2	7	1.639
Jeremiah	39	5	1.645
Numbers	[illegible]	5	1.650
Ezekiel	40	12	1.657
Judges	4	7	1.659
Ezekiel	32	8	1.660
Psalms	127	1	1.667
2 Samuel	14	10	1.672
Isaiah	56	3	1.676
2 Samuel	3	11	1.679
2 Chronicles	3	4	1.681
Psalms	41	2	1.681
1 Samuel	13	6	1.690
Daniel	12	3	1.695
Isaiah	50	3	1.705
Exodus	30	8	1.709
Jeremiah	22	8	1.709
1 Chronicles	16	7	1.711
Numbers	33	8	1.724
Psalms	140	2	1.724
Genesis	25	7	1.728
Genesis	3	6	1.729
Jeremiah	17	7	1.733
Isaiah	7	6	1.739
Joshua	20	3	1.744
Jeremiah	30	6	1.754
Micah	5	3	1.754
Exodus	23	7	1.759
Genesis	45	7	1.763
Isaiah	38	5	1.779
Numbers	4	12	1.796
2 Samuel	9	4	1.802
1 Samuel	10	8	1.810
Isaiah	66	7	1.813
Isaiah	36	7	1.818
Numbers	11	10	1.821
Isaiah	11	4	1.826
Numbers	16	9	1.826
Joel	4	5	1.845
Ruth	1	6	1.846
1 Kings	22	15	1.852
Genesis	43	9	1.856
Judges	15	6	1.869
Jeremiah	18	6	1.881
1 Chronicles	13	4	1.887
Exodus	5	6	1.887
1 Samuel	15	10	1.890
1 Samuel	27	4	1.914
Numbers	20	8	1.914
Exodus	9	10	1.919
Numbers	18	10	1.919
2 Kings	13	8	1.923
Ezekiel	23	12	1.932
Genesis	41	15	1.933
Isaiah	65	7	1.939
Numbers	6	7	1.944
Numbers	5	9	1.948
Psalms	66	3	1.948
Deuteronomy	32	12	1.951
Ezekiel	26	6	1.954
Ezekiel	13	7	1.955
Zechariah	8	7	1.966

TABLE TWO: Total of Three

Book and Chapter		Count	Percentage
Deuteronomy	28	152	15.292
2 Kings	1	55	15.320
Ezra	8	71	15.335
Ruth	2	58	15.344
Ezekiel	44	77	15.369
Isaiah	8	46	15.385
Psalms	114	8	15.385
Ezekiel	20	113	15.395
2 Chronicles	12	39	15.415
2 Chronicles	16	40	15.444
Numbers	15	79	15.460
Ezekiel	11	54	15.473
2 Chronicles	1	44	15.493
Jeremiah	40	57	15.574
1 Kings	14	81	15.607
2 Chronicles	24	71	15.639
Genesis	33	42	15.672
Exodus	16	86	15.693
Exodus	10	78	15.694
1 Chronicles	15	57	15.702
Zechariah	6	32	15.764
1 Samuel	8	43	15.867
Deuteronomy	16	53	15.868
Numbers	26	107	15.875
Leviticus	10	52	15.902
Ezekiel	34	73	15.939
Judges	8	84	15.939
Joshua	9	66	15.942
1 Kings	10	74	15.948
Numbers	17	63	15.949
2 Samuel	6	60	15.957
Haggai	1	38	15.966
Psalms	134	4	16.000
Zechariah	4	30	16.043
1 Samuel	13	57	16.056
Leviticus	17	44	16.058
Jeremiah	16	59	16.076
1 Chronicles	20	23	16.084
Ezra	9	46	16.084
Jeremiah	45	15	16.129
Joshua	12	40	16.129
Genesis	3	56	16.138
Genesis	39	56	16.138
Geresis	9	57	16.147
2 Kings	18	108	16.168
Exodus	12	122	16.245
Exodus	14	77	16.245
Leviticus	5	70	16.279
2 Kings	24	51	16.294
Nehemiah	9	107	16.311
Psalms	125	8	16.327
Amos	9	41	16.335
1 Chronicles	26	58	16.338
Numbers	25	38	16.379
2 Kings	7	67	16.422
1 Kings	18	120	16.438
2 Chronicles	35	71	16.473
1 Samuel	4	61	16.486
Ezekiel	15	17	16.505
Qohelet	9	51	16.505
2 Samuel	12	87	16.509
2 Samuel	21	70	16.509
Genesis	21	72	16.514
Exodus	32	90	16.544
Zechariah	7	31	16.578
Exodus	8	70	16.588
2 Chronicles	14	36	16.590
Genesis	34	70	16.627
1 Chronicles	10	32	16.667
Exodus	30	78	16.667
2 Chronicles	11	49	16.724
Nehemiah	3	93	16.757
Jeremiah	39	51	16.776
Qohelet	11	24	16.783
. Samuel	14	142	16.805
Leviticus	27	77	16.812
Jeremiah	33	71	16.945
Song	2	30	16.949

TABLE THREE: Relative Page 9

Book and Chapter		Count	Percentage
Leviticus	21	6	1.967
Leviticus	25	14	1.972
1 Samuel	3	6	1.974
Joshua	18	8	1.975
2 Chronicles	12	5	1.976
Numbers	9	7	1.977
1 Samuel	2	11	1.978
Numbers	32	11	1.982
Exodus	24	5	1.984
Exodus	4	9	1.987
Exodus	12	15	1.997
Judges	10	5	2.008
Jeremiah	8	7	2.011
Ezekiel	37	9	2.018
2 Samuel	20	9	2.032
2 Chronicles	5	5	2.033
Exodus	34	11	2.045
Joshua	3	6	2.048
1 Chronicles	18	5	2.058
Deuteronomy	22	9	2.059
Ezekiel	35	4	2.062
Psalms	16	2	2.062
Genesis	1	9	2.074
Jeremiah	26	9	2.074
Leviticus	14	17	2.078
Ezekiel	39	9	2.079
1 Chronicles	10	4	2.083
Exodus	1	5	2.083
Genesis	31	16	2.083
Isaiah	20	2	2.083
Judges	8	11	2.087
Jeremiah	25	13	2.114
Jeremiah	13	8	2.116
Numbers	21	10	2.119
Genesis	50	8	2.133
Genesis	2	7	2.134
2 Samuel	2	11	2.136
Jeremiah	27	9	2.138
Leviticus	10	7	2.141
Jonah	3	3	2.143
1 Kings	7	17	2.144
Genesis	26	10	2.146
Numbers	22	14	2.147
Esther	1	8	2.156
Ezekiel	41	8	2.162
Judges	16	12	2.170
Judges	9	19	2.171
Esther	10	1	2.174
Genesis	49	8	2.174
Malachi	3	8	2.174
Genesis	22	8	2.180
Jeremiah	16	8	2.180
Jonah	4	4	2.186
Genesis	27	14	2.194
Ezekiel	44	11	2.196
2 Kings	12	8	2.210
2 Chronicles	25	11	2.231
Genesis	12	6	2.239
Nehemiah	8	8	2.241
Genesis	40	7	2.244
1 Kings	17	8	2.247
1 Samuel	14	19	2.249
Jeremiah	1	6	2.256
Ezekiel	10	7	2.258
Exodus	25	10	2.273
Exodus	40	10	2.273
Psalms	79	3	2.273
1 Samuel	6	9	2.278
Numbers	17	9	2.278
Ezekiel	16	19	2.281
Numbers	13	9	2.284
2 Samuel	8	6	2.290
Exodus	11	4	2.299
Jeremiah	23	14	2.299
Jeremiah	28	7	2.303
Deuteronomy	25	6	2.308
Psalms	144	3	2.308
Esther	3	7	2.310

TABLE TWO: Total of Three

Book and Chapter		Count	Percentage
Exodus	3	67	16.962
2 Samuel	11	75	16.968
Exodus	28	101	16.975
Nehemiah	12	80	16.985
2 Chronicles	6	126	17.004
2 Kings	6	90	17.045
Judges	7	86	17.063
Joshua	16	21	17.073
2 Samuel	17	89	17.083
2 Chronicles	33	65	17.105
1 Chronicles	11	89	17.115
2 Samuel	24	78	17.143
Jonah	3	24	17.143
1 Samuel	12	73	17.176
Judges	19	91	17.202
Numbers	20	72	17.225
Exodus	33	61	17.232
Numbers	13	68	17.259
2 Samuel	16	67	17.268
2 Samuel	4	41	17.300
Exodus	19	65	17.333
2 Chronicles	30	75	17.361
1 Samuel	9	86	17.374
2 Samuel	15	105	17.413
1 Samuel	5	38	17.431
Numbers	8	63	17.452
Numbers	32	97	17.477
Psalms	133	7	17.500
Nehemiah	2	65	17.520
Judges	10	44	17.671
Zechariah	3	29	17.683
Zechariah	8	63	17.697
Jonah	1	45	17.717
Deuteronomy	8	52	17.747
Genesis	19	100	17.762
Numbers	9	63	17.797
Deuteronomy	2	95	17.857
Esther	4	51	17.895
2 Kings	20	65	17.906
Joel	3	12	17.910
Isaiah	36	69	17.922
1 Samuel	6	71	17.975
Ezra	3	45	18.000
Deuteronomy	5	85	18.008
Exodus	9	94	18.042
Joshua	10	139	18.146
Numbers	3	109	18.197
Daniel	8	70	18.277
Jeremiah	7	99	18.333
2 Kings	10	114	18.357
Judges	6	125	18.409
Numbers	4	123	18.413
Zechariah	13	28	18.421
Jeremiah	37	61	18.429
Ruth	4	62	18.507
Deuteronomy	22	81	18.535
Jeremiah	34	79	18.545
Numbers	11	102	18.579
Exodus	20	58	18.590
Joshua	7	92	18.623
Daniel	12	33	18.644
Deuteronomy	21	66	18.644
Exodus	24	47	18.651
Deuteronomy	20	59	18.671
2 Chronicles	31	62	18.675
Deuteronomy	19	62	18.675
1 Kings	1	150	18.750
Deuteronomy	18	57	18.750
Joshua	5	54	18.750
Jeremiah	27	79	18.765
Zechariah	14	69	18.785
Genesis	41	146	18.814
Leviticus	15	85	18.850
Qohelet	8	53	18.861
2 Kings	17	130	18.868
1 Samuel	17	174	19.037
Esther	3	58	19.142
Leviticus	6	58	19.142

TABLE THREE: Relative Page 10

Book and Chapter		Count	Percentage
1 Samuel	26	11	2.316
Genesis	30	13	2.321
Joshua	6	11	2.321
2 Kings	8	12	2.326
Genesis	14	8	2.339
Numbers	15	12	2.348
Numbers	36	5	2.358
Ezekiel	46	9	2.362
Numbers	31	16	2.363
Genesis	34	10	2.375
Judges	7	12	2.381
Leviticus	1	6	2.381
1 Samuel	25	18	2.400
Ezekiel	43	10	2.410
Micah	3	4	2.410
Isaiah	18	3	2.419
Jeremiah	36	15	2.419
2 Chronicles	34	15	2.443
Joshua	11	10	2.445
2 Kings	19	14	2.452
Exodus	39	14	2.465
Joshua	22	17	2.471
Isaiah	37	14	2.473
2 Kings	16	9	2.479
Genesis	20	7	2.482
Zechariah	14	9	2.486
2 Samuel	15	15	2.488
2 Kings	1	9	2.507
Ezekiel	8	8	2.508
Leviticus	9	8	2.516
1 Kings	3	12	2.542
Exodus	33	9	2.542
2 Kings	18	17	2.545
Numbers	12	5	2.551
2 Kings	15	15	2.555
Exodus	16	14	2.555
Jeremiah	38	14	2.555
Judges	18	14	2.555
Ezekiel	2	4	2.564
Qohelet	3	7	2.564
Zechariah	1	7	2.564
Ezekiel	11	9	2.579
1 Samuel	8	7	2.583
Nehemiah	9	17	2.591
Psalms	8	2	2.597
1 Kings	2	21	2.605
Joshua	10	20	2.611
Genesis	24	24	2.614
Leviticus	18	9	2.616
Nehemiah	6	8	2.623
Jeremiah	52	15	2.646
Judges	6	18	2.651
Genesis	46	11	2.657
2 Samuel	6	10	2.660
Judges	21	10	2.667
Esther	7	5	2.674
Qohelet	12	5	2.688
2 Kings	7	11	2.696
2 Kings	22	10	2.703
Isaiah	55	5	2.703
Leviticus	16	15	2.717
Jeremiah	20	8	2.721
Ezekiel	20	20	2.725
Exodus	35	12	2.727
Esther	2	12	2.740
Ezekiel	18	13	2.743
1 Samuel	29	6	2.752
2 Kings	25	14	2.756
Ezekiel	12	11	2.757
Exodus	29	18	2.773
1 Kings	5	14	2.783
Genesis	28	9	2.786
Nehemiah	4	7	2.800
Leviticus	8	16	2.807
Jeremiah	34	12	2.817
1 Samuel	12	12	2.824
Deuteronomy	21	10	2.825
2 Samuel	21	12	2.830

TABLE TWO: Total of Three

Book and Chapter		Count	Percentage
Exodus	1	46	19.167
Jeremiah	29	103	19.181
Deuteronomy	13	63	19.207
Numbers	21	91	19.280
1 Samuel	31	39	19.307
Judges	18	106	19.343
Qohelet	3	53	19.414
Deuteronomy	7	80	19.417
Exodus	25	86	19.545
1 Chronicles	6	123	19.555
Judges	2	71	19.559
Ezekiel	9	39	19.598
Ezekiel	47	72	19.672
Ezekiel	45	78	19.697
Exodus	2	67	19.706
Deuteronomy	26	63	19.749
Deuteronomy	12	103	19.808
1 Chronicles	13	42	19.811
Deuteronomy	6	63	19.811
Isaiah	39	29	19.863
Genesis	40	62	19.872
Deuteronomy	1	130	19.878
Deuteronomy	34	35	19.886
Nehemiah	10	68	19.941
Genesis	6	61	20.000
Zechariah	5	31	20.000
1 Kings	12	117	20.034
2 Samuel	18	118	20.034
Joshua	14	56	20.144
Esther	2	89	20.320
Numbers	35	98	20.332
Joshua	20	35	20.349
2 Kings	12	74	20.442
Haggai	2	74	20.442
Numbers	14	130	20.472
1 Kings	3	97	20.551
2 Chronicles	29	111	20.556
Jeremiah	21	51	20.565
Exodus	18	86	20.574
2 Chronicles	10	64	20.579
Judges	3	99	20.582
2 Kings	21	82	20.655
Daniel	1	64	20.712
2 Samuel	14	124	20.736
Jeremiah	41	75	20.776
2 Samuel	19	168	20.844
Deuteronomy	30	68	20.859
Nehemiah	13	99	20.930
1 Samuel	30	102	20.945
2 Chronicles	8	61	20.962
Jeremiah	25	129	20.976
1 Kings	8	241	21.011
Exodus	37	77	21.038
Deuteronomy	9	105	21.042
Qohelet	4	50	21.097
Zephaniah	1	57	21.190
Ezekiel	40	154	21.271
1 Chronicles	27	87	21.376
Numbers	19	74	21.387
1 Kings	13	127	21.453
Deuteronomy	27	70	21.472
Joshua	11	88	21.516
Jeremiah	43	51	21.519
Genesis	10	62	21.528
Joshua	13	95	21.640
Zechariah	11	55	21.654
Esther	1	81	21.833
Ezekiel	41	81	21.892
Nehemiah	4	55	22.000
Genesis	15	57	22.008
Deuteronomy	10	72	22.222
Nehemiah	5	73	22.256
Deuteronomy	17	82	22.283
Leviticus	13	199	22.284
Numbers	31	151	22.304
Jeremiah	26	97	22.350
Deuteronomy	4	182	22.386
Joshua	23	67	22.408

TABLE THREE: Relative Page 11

Book and Chapter		Count	Percentage
Ezekiel	6	6	2.830
Genesis	9	10	2.833
2 Samuel	16	11	2.835
Jeremiah	11	11	2.857
2 Kings	24	9	2.875
Numbers	19	10	2.890
Joshua	9	12	2.899
Genesis	13	7	2.905
Deuteronomy	7	12	2.913
Ezekiel	15	3	2.913
Esther	9	16	2.930
1 Samuel	24	11	2.941
Qohelet	6	5	2.941
Deuteronomy	23	10	2.950
Genesis	6	9	2.951
Leviticus	22	13	2.961
Joshua	2	12	2.978
Genesis	21	13	2.982
1 Kings	4	6	3.000
Ezekiel	47	11	3.005
Qohelet	5	8	3.008
Ezekiel	36	17	3.009
Esther	5	8	3.019
1 Kings	11	21	3.043
Leviticus	27	14	3.057
Deuteronomy	24	10	3.058
Deuteronomy	27	10	3.067
2 Samuel	17	16	3.071
Genesis	44	14	3.077
2 Chronicles	9	15	3.086
Jeremiah	33	13	3.103
Deuteronomy	15	11	3.107
Exodus	7	13	3.110
Joshua	5	9	3.125
Leviticus	7	15	3.125
2 Kings	14	15	3.132
Ezekiel	5	9	3.136
Isaiah	[illegible]	5	3.225
Jeremiah	32	24	3.229
Zechariah	7	6	3.229
Jeremiah	24	6	3.243
Joshua	9	[illegible]	3.247
Deuteronomy	[illegible]	19	3.255
Jeremiah	35	12	3.261
Jeremiah	[illegible]	12	3.279
Ruth	4	[illegible]	3.294
Leviticus	6	[illegible]	[illegible]
Numbers	14	[illegible]	[illegible]
1 Kings	[illegible]	16	3.333
Qohelet	[illegible]	[illegible]	3.333
Genesis	33	9	3.358
2 Kings	[illegible]	[illegible]	3.392
Deuteronomy	[illegible]	[illegible]	3.393
Deuteronomy	34	6	3.429
1 Kings	15	19	3.442
1 Kings	[illegible]	16	3.448
2 Samuel	[illegible]	16	[illegible]
Deuteronomy	3	16	[illegible]
Esther	[illegible]	12	3.499
Ezekiel	9	[illegible]	3.519
Jeremiah	[illegible]	19	3.529
Jeremiah	44	[illegible]	[illegible]
Leviticus	[illegible]	[illegible]	[illegible]
2 Chronicles	[illegible]	14	3.544
2 Kings	[illegible]	[illegible]	[illegible]
1 Kings	[illegible]	[illegible]	3.596
Genesis	[illegible]	[illegible]	3.636
Deuteronomy	[illegible]	[illegible]	3.659
Daniel	4	[illegible]	[illegible]
2 Chronicles	33	14	3.684
Deuteronomy	[illegible]	[illegible]	3.704
Numbers	35	[illegible]	3.734
Numbers	[illegible]	[illegible]	3.762
Ezra	[illegible]	[illegible]	3.763
Deuteronomy	[illegible]	[illegible]	[illegible]
Exodus	18	16	3.828
Exodus	[illegible]	[illegible]	3.846
2 Chronicles	[illegible]	[illegible]	3.859

TABLE TWO: Total of Three

Book and Chapter		Count	Percentage
Ezekiel	43	93	22.410
Exodus	38	93	22.573
Joshua	2	91	22.581
Jeremiah	38	124	22.628
Jeremiah	24	42	22.703
Nehemiah	1	46	22.772
Deuteronomy	14	80	22.792
Joshua	1	73	22.812
Leviticus	20	98	22.897
Exodus	36	118	22.957
Nehemiah	8	82	22.969
Jeremiah	32	172	22.995
Jeremiah	28	70	23.026
2 Chronicles	7	91	23.038
Joshua	4	90	23.077
Ezekiel	10	72	23.226
Jeremiah	36	144	23.226
Joshua	24	134	23.345
Judges	1	124	23.440
Deuteronomy	29	103	23.462
Jeremiah	52	134	23.633
Deuteronomy	31	131	23.689
Joshua	8	146	23.701
Genesis	22	87	23.706
Genesis	1	103	23.733
Leviticus	7	114	23.750
1 Kings	6	122	23.922
1 Kings	9	113	23.941
Esther	9	131	23.993
Ezekiel	46	92	24.147
Qohelet	12	45	24.194
Jeremiah	19	69	24.296
2 Kings	22	90	24.324
Genesis	2	80	24.390
Esther	8	84	24.490
Deuteronomy	3	113	24.512
Esther	7	46	24.599
Genesis	8	76	24.675
Numbers	5	114	24.675
Leviticus	16	137	24.819
Exodus	31	57	24.891
2 Kings	25	127	25.000
2 Chronicles	3	60	25.210
2 Chronicles	34	155	25.244
Deuteronomy	11	130	25.591
Esther	5	68	25.660
2 Kings	16	95	26.171
Genesis	7	87	26.205
Exodus	26	126	26.250
2 Chronicles	5	65	26.423
Joshua	3	79	26.962
Esther	6	71	26.996
Leviticus	11	162	27.319
Exodus	35	122	27.727
Joshua	6	133	28.059
Joshua	21	165	28.302
1 Kings	7	226	28.499
2 Kings	23	222	28.719
2 Chronicles	4	90	28.939
Leviticus	4	157	28.967
Exodus	29	188	28.968
Exodus	39	167	29.401
2 Chronicles	23	123	31.948
Ezekiel	42	92	32.281
Leviticus	1	82	32.540
2 Kings	11	118	32.961
Exodus	40	146	33.182
Leviticus	9	107	33.648
Leviticus	8	192	33.684
Leviticus	14	279	34.108
Leviticus	3	91	36.546

TABLE THREE: Relative Page

Book and Chapter		Count	Percentage
Ruth	3	10	3.876
Daniel	1	12	3.883
Qohelet	9	12	3.883
Genesis	7	13	3.916
Nehemiah	1	8	3.960
Nehemiah	5	13	3.963
Genesis	35	15	3.968
Ruth	2	15	3.968
Deuteronomy	30	13	3.988
Joshua	24	23	4.007
Exodus	32	22	4.044
1 Kings	14	21	4.046
Joshua	4	16	4.103
Judges	2	15	4.132
1 Chronicles	17	17	4.167
Deuteronomy	9	21	4.208
Qohelet	4	10	4.219
1 Kings	13	25	4.223
2 Chronicles	1	12	4.225
Jeremiah	19	12	4.225
Deuteronomy	14	15	4.274
2 Chronicles	2	14	4.281
Jeremiah	45	4	4.301
Nehemiah	2	16	4.313
Genesis	39	15	4.323
Joshua	13	19	4.328
Joshua	23	13	4.348
Leviticus	17	12	4.380
Leviticus	15	20	4.386
1 Kings	16	24	4.404
Leviticus	3	11	4.418
Deuteronomy	5	21	4.449
2 Chronicles	8	13	4.467
Jeremiah	29	24	4.469
Joel	3	3	4.478
Psalms	95	4	4.494
Deuteronomy	1	30	4.587
Jeremiah	43	11	4.641
2 Kings	17	32	4.644
Leviticus	20	20	4.673
Deuteronomy	29	21	4.784
Leviticus	4	26	4.797
Leviticus	5	21	4.884
Deuteronomy	17	18	4.891
Jeremiah	42	20	4.902
Esther	4	14	4.912
Ezekiel	42	14	4.912
Deuteronomy	28	49	4.930
Numbers	30	13	4.943
1 Kings	8	57	4.969
Deuteronomy	26	16	5.016
Joshua	14	14	5.036
Deuteronomy	8	15	5.119
Deuteronomy	19	17	5.120
2 Chronicles	6	38	5.128
Deuteronomy	18	16	5.263
Deuteronomy	4	43	5.289
2 Kings	23	41	5.304
Deuteronomy	16	18	5.389
1 Kings	9	26	5.508
Jeremiah	41	21	5.817
Deuteronomy	12	31	5.962
Psalms	1	4	5.970
Esther	6	16	6.084
1 Samuel	30	30	6.160
Isaiah	39	9	6.164
Joshua	1	20	6.250
Deuteronomy	11	32	6.299
2 Kings	21	26	6.549
Deuteronomy	6	21	6.604
Qohelet	8	20	7.117

TABLE FOUR: Article

Book and Chapter		Count	Percentage
Daniel	3	0	.000
Daniel	4	0	.000
Daniel	5	0	.000
Daniel	6	0	.000
Daniel	7	0	.000
Ezra	5	0	.000
Hosea	8	0	.000
Hosea	11	0	.000
Hosea	14	0	.000
Isaiah	50	0	.000
Isaiah	53	0	.000
Isaiah	58	0	.000
Job	10	0	.000
Job	13	0	.000
Job	14	0	.000
Job	16	0	.000
Job	17	0	.000
Job	19	0	.000
Job	21	0	.000
Job	24	0	.000
Job	27	0	.000
Job	29	0	.000
Job	34	0	.000
Proverbs	3	0	.000
Proverbs	8	0	.000
Proverbs	11	0	.000
Proverbs	12	0	.000
Proverbs	13	0	.000
Proverbs	14	0	.000
Proverbs	15	0	.000
Proverbs	24	0	.000
Proverbs	25	0	.000
Proverbs	28	0	.000
Psalms	4	0	.000
Psalms	7	0	.000
Psalms	16	0	.000
Psalms	17	0	.000
Psalms	23	0	.000
Psalms	26	0	.000
Psalms	27	0	.000
Psalms	39	0	.000
Psalms	43	0	.000
Psalms	53	0	.000
Psalms	55	0	.000
Psalms	60	0	.000
Psalms	64	0	.000
Psalms	67	0	.000
Psalms	69	0	.000
Psalms	75	0	.000
Psalms	76	0	.000
Psalms	91	0	.000
Psalms	93	0	.000
Psalms	101	0	.000
Psalms	110	0	.000
Psalms	111	0	.000
Psalms	112	0	.000
Psalms	138	0	.000
Psalms	139	0	.000
Psalms	140	0	.000
Psalms	141	0	.000
Psalms	143	0	.000
Psalms	149	0	.000
Job	31	1	.323
Psalms	37	1	.336
Psalms	107	1	.360
Psalms	78	2	.377
Proverbs	16	1	.397
Job	33	1	.407
Proverbs	1	1	.422
Proverbs	10	1	.427
Proverbs	19	1	.435
Psalms	109	1	.441
Proverbs	22	1	.444
Job	6	1	.455
Job	39	1	.469
Job	20	1	.481
Proverbs	29	1	.490
Proverbs	4	1	.500

TABLE FIVE: Nota Accusativi Page 1

Book and Chapter		Count	Percentage
1 Chronicles	3	0	.000
1 Chronicles	24	0	.000
1 Chronicles	25	0	.000
1 Chronicles	26	0	.000
Daniel	3	0	.000
Daniel	4	0	.000
Daniel	5	0	.000
Daniel	6	0	.000
Daniel	7	0	.000
Esther	10	0	.000
Ezekiel	19	0	.000
Ezra	2	0	.000
Ezra	5	0	.000
Hosea	11	0	.000
Hosea	13	0	.000
Hosea	14	0	.000
Isaiah	12	0	.000
Isaiah	16	0	.000
Isaiah	17	0	.000
Isaiah	25	0	.000
Isaiah	32	0	.000
Isaiah	35	0	.000
Isaiah	46	0	.000
Isaiah	54	0	.000
Isaiah	60	0	.000
Job	4	0	.000
Job	5	0	.000
Job	6	0	.000
Job	8	0	.000
Job	9	0	.000
Job	10	0	.000
Job	11	0	.000
Job	12	0	.000
Job	15	0	.000
Job	16	0	.000
Job	17	0	.000
Job	18	0	.000
Job	19	0	.000
Job	20	0	.000
Job	21	0	.000
Job	22	0	.000
Job	23	0	.000
Job	24	0	.000
Job	25	0	.000
Job	29	0	.000
Job	30	0	.000
Job	31	0	.000
Job	33	0	.000
Job	34	0	.000
Job	37	0	.000
Job	39	0	.000
Joel	1	0	.000
Judges	5	0	.000
Leviticus	12	0	.000
Micah	1	0	.000
Micah	2	0	.000
Nahum	1	0	.000
Nahum	3	0	.000
Nehemiah	11	0	.000
Numbers	12	0	.000
Proverbs	4	0	.000
Proverbs	7	0	.000
Proverbs	9	0	.000
Proverbs	10	0	.000
Proverbs	11	0	.000
Proverbs	12	0	.000
Proverbs	14	0	.000
Proverbs	15	0	.000
Proverbs	18	0	.000
Proverbs	19	0	.000
Proverbs	20	0	.000
Proverbs	21	0	.000
Proverbs	28	0	.000
Proverbs	31	0	.000
Psalms	1	0	.000
Psalms	4	0	.000
Psalms	5	0	.000
Psalms	6	0	.000

TABLE FOUR: Article

Book and Chapter		Count	Percentage
Psalms	73	1	.518
Isaiah	49	2	.551
Psalms	119	6	.563
Job	7	1	.581
Daniel	2	5	.593
Job	8	1	.602
Psalms	9	1	.606
Hosea	13	1	.613
Psalms	10	1	.617
Proverbs	5	1	.625
Ezekiel	19	1	.641
Job	4	1	.671
Job	11	1	.676
Psalms	105	2	.680
Lamentations	5	1	.690
Job	18	1	.699
Psalms	80	1	.709
Psalms	90	1	.714
Psalms	132	1	.763
Job	15	2	.766
Psalms	83	1	.769
Isaiah	64	1	.781
Proverbs	9	1	.787
Psalms	22	2	.791
Genesis	5	3	.822
Job	36	2	.833
Isaiah	63	2	.837
Job	23	1	.847
Psalms	62	1	.855
Proverbs	21	2	.858
Job	35	1	.862
Proverbs	20	2	.885
Psalms	92	1	.893
Proverbs	31	2	.913
Job	40	2	.930
Habakkuk	3	2	.943
Hosea	6	1	.962
Psalms	21	1	.962
Hosea	10	2	.995
Psalms	36	1	1.000
Psalms	46	1	1.000
Psalms	58	1	1.000
Isaiah	44	4	1.028
Psalms	30	1	1.031
Psalms	28	1	1.042
Isaiah	59	3	1.056
Hosea	7	2	1.058
Lamentations	1	4	1.061
Psalms	2	1	1.087
Proverbs	6	3	1.103
Psalms	50	2	1.124
Job	41	2	1.130
Proverbs	18	2	1.143
Job	9	3	1.158
Micah	5	2	1.170
Psalms	6	1	1.190
Psalms	38	2	1.190
Hosea	3	1	1.235
Psalms	77	2	1.299
Psalms	89	5	1.302
Psalms	51	2	1.307
Lamentations	2	5	1.309
Psalms	35	3	1.310
Job	30	3	1.322
Proverbs	17	3	1.322
Proverbs	30	4	1.329
Psalms	142	1	1.333
Zechariah	9	3	1.351
Psalms	86	2	1.361
Psalms	31	3	1.364
Psalms	14	1	1.370
Isaiah	47	3	1.408
Psalms	88	2	1.408
Proverbs	26	3	1.422
Job	22	3	1.429
Psalms	3	1	1.429
Psalms	20	1	1.429
Ezekiel	23	9	1.449

TABLE FIVE: Nota Accusativi Page 2

Book and Chapter		Count	Percentage
Psalms	7	0	.000
Psalms	8	0	.000
Psalms	10	0	.000
Psalms	11	0	.000
Psalms	12	0	.000
Psalms	17	0	.000
Psalms	19	0	.000
Psalms	20	0	.000
Psalms	22	0	.000
Psalms	23	0	.000
Psalms	24	0	.000
Psalms	30	0	.000
Psalms	32	0	.000
Psalms	36	0	.000
Psalms	38	0	.000
Psalms	39	0	.000
Psalms	40	0	.000
Psalms	41	0	.000
Psalms	42	0	.000
Psalms	43	0	.000
Psalms	44	0	.000
Psalms	45	0	.000
Psalms	46	0	.000
Psalms	48	0	.000
Psalms	49	0	.000
Psalms	50	0	.000
Psalms	52	0	.000
Psalms	54	0	.000
Psalms	55	0	.000
Psalms	57	0	.000
Psalms	58	0	.000
Psalms	61	0	.000
Psalms	62	0	.000
Psalms	63	0	.000
Psalms	64	0	.000
Psalms	65	0	.000
Psalms	66	0	.000
Psalms	68	0	.000
Psalms	70	0	.000
Psalms	71	0	.000
Psalms	73	0	.000
Psalms	74	0	.000
Psalms	75	0	.000
Psalms	76	0	.000
Psalms	77	0	.000
Psalms	81	0	.000
Psalms	82	0	.000
Psalms	84	0	.000
Psalms	85	0	.000
Psalms	87	0	.000
Psalms	88	0	.000
Psalms	89	0	.000
Psalms	90	0	.000
Psalms	91	0	.000
Psalms	93	0	.000
Psalms	95	0	.000
Psalms	96	0	.000
Psalms	97	0	.000
Psalms	99	0	.000
Psalms	107	0	.000
Psalms	108	0	.000
Psalms	109	0	.000
Psalms	110	0	.000
Psalms	111	0	.000
Psalms	114	0	.000
Psalms	118	0	.000
Psalms	120	0	.000
Psalms	122	0	.000
Psalms	124	0	.000
Psalms	128	0	.000
Psalms	131	0	.000
Psalms	139	0	.000
Psalms	140	0	.000
Psalms	141	0	.000
Psalms	143	0	.000
Psalms	149	0	.000
Psalms	150	0	.000
Qohelet	6	0	.000

TABLE FOUR: Article

Book and Chapter		Count	Percentage
Hosea	1	2	1.460
Proverbs	23	4	1.460
Psalms	61	1	1.471
Deuteronomy	23	5	1.475
Deuteronomy	33	5	1.488
Psalms	42	2	1.515
Numbers	30	4	1.521
Psalms	44	3	1.523
Psalms	74	3	1.531
Numbers	23	6	1.542
Ezekiel	35	3	1.546
Job	37	3	1.596
Psalms	81	2	1.600
Psalms	68	5	1.613
Psalms	40	3	1.622
Job	12	3	1.639
Isaiah	1	6	1.667
Hosea	5	3	1.676
Psalms	41	2	1.681
Exodus	6	7	1.733
Ezra	4	7	1.737
Psalms	84	2	1.739
Psalms	94	3	1.775
Psalms	5	2	1.802
Psalms	48	2	1.802
Isaiah	54	4	1.810
Isaiah	33	5	1.818
Isaiah	34	4	1.818
Isaiah	61	3	1.818
Psalms	13	1	1.818
Psalms	15	1	1.818
Psalms	32	2	1.818
Psalms	65	2	1.835
Psalms	72	3	1.852
Psalms	87	1	1.852
Psalms	45	3	1.875
Psalms	25	3	1.887
Psalms	102	4	1.887
Psalms	59	3	1.923
Psalms	120	1	1.961
Psalms	71	4	1.970
Ezekiel	28	7	1.989
Job	26	2	2.000
Job	38	6	2.007
Genesis	45	8	2.015
Psalms	108	2	2.041
Ezekiel	32	10	2.075
Psalms	85	2	2.083
Malachi	1	5	2.092
Proverbs	2	3	2.098
1 Chronicles	7	9	2.113
Psalms	106	7	2.121
Psalms	70	1	2.128
Isaiah	26	5	2.146
Nahum	3	5	2.155
Ezekiel	16	18	2.161
Ezekiel	27	9	2.211
Isaiah	45	8	2.222
Isaiah	43	7	2.229
Genesis	16	5	2.242
Psalms	95	2	2.247
Isaiah	48	6	2.264
Psalms	18	9	2.267
Psalms	116	3	2.290
Hosea	9	5	2.315
Ezekiel	25	6	2.317
Job	25	1	2.326
Psalms	100	1	2.326
Amos	7	6	2.335
Lamentations	3	9	2.362
Psalms	49	4	2.395
2 Samuel	22	9	2.406
Psalms	99	2	2.410
Genesis	46	10	2.415
Job	5	5	2.415
Psalms	34	4	2.424
Micah	6	5	2.463
Hosea	12	4	2.500

TABLE FIVE: Nota Accusativi Page 3

Book and Chapter		Count	Percentage
Song	4	0	.000
Song	6	0	.000
Zechariah	9	0	.000
Daniel	2	1	.119
Daniel	11	1	.164
Jeremiah	48	1	.172
Ezekiel	48	1	.190
Ezra	10	1	.215
Numbers	29	1	.238
Ezra	6	1	.254
Isaiah	44	1	.257
Lamentations	3	1	.262
Isaiah	14	1	.266
Psalms	119	3	.282
Ruth	1	1	.308
Isaiah	43	1	.318
Proverbs	30	1	.332
Job	38	1	.334
Psalms	37	1	.336
Psalms	69	1	.344
Isaiah	42	1	.347
Proverbs	24	1	.372
Isaiah	48	1	.377
Habakkuk	2	1	.382
Lamentations	4	1	.385
Proverbs	8	1	.388
Isaiah	24	1	.391
Isaiah	3	1	.402
Joshua	12	1	.403
Micah	7	1	.410
Job	36	1	.417
Isaiah	26	1	.429
Proverbs	17	1	.441
Isaiah	58	1	.450
Isaiah	34	1	.455
Ezra	7	2	.459
Hosea	9	1	.463
Isaiah	47	1	.469
Habakkuk	3	1	.472
Proverbs	27	1	.472
Proverbs	26	1	.474
Job	28	1	.483
Proverbs	29	1	.490
1 Chronicles	27	2	.491
Ezekiel	27	2	.491
Ezra	4	2	.496
Isaiah	21	1	.498
Psalms	18	2	.504
Lamentations	2	2	.524
Hosea	7	1	.529
Lamentations	1	2	.531
2 Chronicles	19	1	.549
Isaiah	40	2	.560
Daniel	12	1	.565
Job	14	1	.565
Job	41	1	.565
Nahum	2	1	.578
Job	7	1	.581
Numbers	2	2	.585
Psalms	94	1	.592
Isaiah	61	1	.606
Psalms	9	1	.606
Psalms	72	1	.617
Psalms	33	1	.621
1 Chronicles	29	3	.625
Hosea	12	1	.625
Proverbs	5	1	.625
Psalms	59	1	.641
Hosea	8	1	.649
Psalms	51	1	.654
Psalms	86	1	.680
Lamentations	5	1	.690
Proverbs	2	1	.699
Ezekiel	42	2	.702
Isaiah	59	2	.704
Psalms	80	1	.709
Song	7	1	.719
Isaiah	33	2	.727

TABLE FOUR: Article

Book and Chapter		Count	Percentage
Psalms	12	2	2.532
Genesis	17	9	2.535
Job	32	5	2.538
Jeremiah	2	13	2.539
Isaiah	31	4	2.564
Proverbs	7	5	2.591
Psalms	66	4	2.597
Jeremiah	30	9	2.632
Ezekiel	21	14	2.642
1 Chronicles	8	8	2.658
Isaiah	46	4	2.667
Genesis	36	13	2.669
Habakkuk	2	7	2.672
Psalms	150	1	2.703
Judges	5	10	2.747
Amos	1	6	2.830
Proverbs	27	6	2.830
Isaiah	41	10	2.849
Ezekiel	30	10	2.924
Genesis	4	10	2.933
Numbers	24		2.941
Psalms	11	2	2.941
Isaiah	52	6	2.970
Psalms	1	2	2.985
Psalms	135	5	2.994
Zechariah	10	5	3.012
Jeremiah	50	21	3.030
Psalms	79	4	3.030
Psalms	118	6	3.030
Psalms	131	1	3.030
Genesis	11	12	3.061
Jeremiah	49	18	3.082
Isaiah	5	12	3.125
Isaiah	13	8	3.162
Isaiah	11	7	3.196
Ezekiel	2	5	3.205
1 Samuel	16	12	3.217
Psalms	54	2	3.226
Psalms	63	3	3.226
Psalms	122	2	3.226
Nahum	1	5	3.247
Jeremiah	5	14	3.248
Jeremiah	48	19	3.276
1 Samuel	3	10	3.289
Psalms	145	5	3.289
Psalms	29	3	3.297
Micah	1	7	3.302
Ezra	6	13	3.308
Ezekiel	22	13	3.333
Psalms	56	4	3.333
Job	28	7	3.382
Ezekiel	4	9	3.409
Leviticus	22	15	3.417
Genesis	27	22	3.448
Isaiah	32	7	3.448
Lamentations	4	9	3.462
Isaiah	21	7	3.483
Numbers	2	12	3.509
Ezekiel	31	11	3.526
Psalms	146	3	3.529
Genesis	49	13	3.533
1 Chronicles	5	16	3.548
1 Chronicles	1	15	3.555
Jonah	2	4	3.571
Psalms	121	2	3.571
Deuteronomy	32	22	3.577
Psalms	103	6	3.593
2 Kings	13	15	3.606
Jeremiah	6	15	3.614
Micah	7	9	3.689
Ruth	1	12	3.692
Genesis	25	15	3.704
Psalms	129	2	3.704
2 Chronicles	11	11	3.754
Ezekiel	29	13	3.779
Leviticus	26	22	3.780
Song	5	7	3.784
Jeremiah	15	12	3.797

TABLE FIVE: Nota Accusativi Page 4

Book and Chapter		Count	Percentage
Proverbs	6	2	.735
Psalms	104	2	.738
Isaiah	10	3	.739
Jeremiah	46	3	.744
Psalms	132	1	.763
Psalms	83	1	.769
Psalms	144	1	.769
Isaiah	64	1	.781
Ezekiel	1	3	.785
Isaiah	2	2	.791
Isaiah	15	1	.800
2 Samuel	22	3	.802
Isaiah	18	1	.806
Ezekiel	41	3	.811
Isaiah	1	3	.833
Isaiah	45	3	.833
Psalms	56	1	.833
Proverbs	25	2	.837
Proverbs	1	2	.844
Job	35	1	.862
Psalms	35	2	.873
Deuteronomy	33	3	.893
Psalms	92	1	.893
Hosea	4	2	.897
Micah	4	2	.901
1 Samuel	29	2	.917
Isaiah	23	2	.922
Qohelet	1	2	.930
Amos	1	2	.943
Jeremiah	4	4	.946
1 Samuel	27	2	.957
Nehemiah	7	6	.958
Hosea	6	1	.962
Psalms	21	1	.962
Job	3	2	.980
Isaiah	52	2	.990
Job	26	1	1.000
Habakkuk	1	2	1.015
Qohelet	10	2	1.020
Amos	8	2	1.053
Esther	7	2	1.070
Zechariah	4	2	1.070
2 Samuel	1	4	1.090
Proverbs	13	2	1.093
Isaiah	56	2	1.117
Amos	6	2	1.124
Psalms	78	6	1.132
Ezekiel	28	4	1.136
Isaiah	50	2	1.136
Genesis	18	5	1.144
Isaiah	27	2	1.149
Psalms	26	1	1.176
Job	27	2	1.183
Isaiah	13	3	1.186
Proverbs	16	3	1.190
Isaiah	51	4	1.198
Psalms	136	2	1.205
1 Chronicles	12	6	1.215
Exodus	15	4	1.246
Isaiah	63	3	1.255
Psalms	25	2	1.258
Haggai	1	3	1.261
Psalms	112	1	1.266
Isaiah	31	2	1.282
Daniel	9	6	1.299
Isaiah	22	4	1.299
Psalms	53	1	1.299
Deuteronomy	32	8	1.301
Isaiah	5	5	1.302
Psalms	138	1	1.316
Ezekiel	21	7	1.321
Proverbs	22	3	1.333
Psalms	98	1	1.333
Psalms	142	1	1.333
Song	1	2	1.333
Judges	20	10	1.339
2 Samuel	9	3	1.351
Psalms	31	3	1.364

TABLE FOUR: Article

Book and Chapter		Count	Percentage
Psalms	57	4	3.810
Isaiah	42	11	3.819
Isaiah	57	10	3.846
Isaiah	30	19	3.862
Psalms	47	3	3.896
Isaiah	56	7	3.911
Judges	11	26	3.922
Isaiah	35	5	3.968
Psalms	19	5	3.968
Zephaniah	3	11	3.986
Isaiah	15	5	4.000
Nahum	2	7	4.046
Exodus	15	13	4.050
Numbers	1	24	4.082
Leviticus	19	18	4.091
1 Chronicles	2	22	4.112
Obadiah	1	12	4.124
Jeremiah	1	11	4.135
Ezekiel	3	17	4.136
Isaiah	23	9	4.147
Isaiah	16	8	4.167
Jeremiah	12	11	4.183
Ezekiel	26	13	4.235
Numbers	36	9	4.245
Psalms	128	2	4.255
Leviticus	12	5	4.274
1 Chronicles	6	27	4.293
Jeremiah	31	27	4.334
Jeremiah	10	14	4.375
Jeremiah	3	18	4.390
Isaiah	60	13	4.407
Psalms	52	4	4.444
Psalms	115	6	4.444
Isaiah	28	17	4.462
Isaiah	40	16	4.482
Ezekiel	37	20	4.484
Isaiah	62	8	4.494
Genesis	35	17	4.497
Zephaniah	2	10	4.505
Jeremiah	9	17	4.533
Job	42	11	4.564
Habakkuk	1	9	4.569
1 Samuel	23	20	4.587
Isaiah	19	15	4.587
Leviticus	21	14	4.590
Genesis	20	13	4.610
Psalms	144	6	4.615
Ezekiel	20	34	4.632
Amos	4	10	4.651
1 Chronicles	22	14	4.698
Jeremiah	51	42	4.719
Psalms	137	4	4.762
2 Samuel	10	15	4.777
Exodus	7	20	4.785
Isaiah	51	16	4.790
Jeremiah	8	17	4.885
Psalms	82	3	4.918
2 Chronicles	13	18	4.959
2 Samuel	8	13	4.962
1 Kings	15	26	4.971
Exodus	22	18	4.986
Jeremiah	18	16	5.016
Isaiah	17	9	5.056
1 Chronicles	4	24	5.063
Jeremiah	20	15	5.102
Numbers	12	10	5.102
1 Kings	19	19	5.121
Isaiah	10	21	5.172
Song	8	9	5.172
1 Chronicles	10	10	5.208
Isaiah	20	5	5.208
Ezekiel	12	21	5.263
Genesis	37	26	5.263
Song	3	7	5.263
2 Kings	5	26	5.317
Isaiah	14	20	5.319
Genesis	50	20	5.333
1 Chronicles	19	17	5.346

TABLE FIVE: Nota Accusativi Page 5

Book and Chapter		Count	Percentage
Psalms	14	1	1.370
Isaiah	65	5	1.385
2 Chronicles	35	6	1.392
Job	40	3	1.395
Jeremiah	14	5	1.404
Isaiah	30	7	1.423
Jonah	3	2	1.429
Psalms	3	1	1.429
Amos	3	3	1.449
Proverbs	23	4	1.460
Deuteronomy	23	5	1.475
Psalms	115	2	1.481
2 Kings	4	10	1.490
Hosea	10	3	1.493
1 Kings	4	3	1.500
Jeremiah	1	4	1.504
2 Chronicles	2	5	1.529
Numbers	23	6	1.542
Proverbs	3	4	1.544
2 Chronicles	27	2	1.550
Ruth	3	4	1.550
Amos	7	4	1.556
Jeremiah	18	5	1.567
2 Samuel	23	7	1.577
Judges	21	6	1.600
Nehemiah	2	6	1.617
Ezekiel	38	6	1.622
Isaiah	55	3	1.622
Joshua	16	2	1.626
2 Kings	5	8	1.636
Jonah	4	3	1.639
Zechariah	14	6	1.657
Psalms	113	1	1.667
Psalms	127	1	1.667
2 Chronicles	17	4	1.674
1 Kings	17	6	1.685
Jeremiah	6	7	1.687
Isaiah	41	6	1.709
Numbers	28	6	1.724
Ezra	8	8	1.728
2 Chronicles	20	10	1.730
Job	1	6	1.739
2 Samuel	2	9	1.748
Ezra	9	5	1.748
Ezekiel	7	6	1.749
Micah	5	3	1.754
Judges	13	7	1.777
Joshua	17	6	1.780
Psalms	121	1	1.786
Genesis	16	4	1.794
1 Chronicles	23	6	1.802
2 Samuel	20	8	1.806
Genesis	7	6	1.807
Psalms	13	1	1.818
Psalms	15	1	1.818
Daniel	8	7	1.828
Numbers	10	7	1.832
Isaiah	28	7	1.837
Psalms	129	1	1.852
Psalms	130	1	1.852
Ruth	2	7	1.852
Jeremiah	5	8	1.856
Joshua	19	9	1.856
Psalms	67	1	1.887
Exodus	22	7	1.939
1 Chronicles	16	8	1.956
Nehemiah	8	7	1.961
Job	13	4	1.970
Genesis	38	8	1.975
Jeremiah	17	8	1.980
Numbers	34	6	1.980
Nehemiah	3	11	1.982
Nehemiah	4	5	2.000
Psalms	27	3	2.013
Jeremiah	50	14	2.020
Job	32	4	2.030
Psalms	125	1	2.041
Psalms	16	2	2.062

TABLE FOUR: Article

Book and Chapter		Count	Percentage
Exodus	5	17	5.346
Isaiah	55	10	5.405
2 Chronicles	27	7	5.426
Genesis	38	22	5.432
Malachi	3	20	5.435
Genesis	23	15	5.455
Jeremiah	46	22	5.459
1 Kings	11	38	5.507
1 Samuel	1	23	5.542
Exodus	21	25	5.543
Psalms	130	3	5.556
Ezekiel	5	16	5.575
Malachi	2	15	5.576
Amos	2	12	5.581
Genesis	12	15	5.597
Jeremiah	47	6	5.607
Jeremiah	42	23	5.637
1 Chronicles	3	11	5.641
Isaiah	18	7	5.645
Micah	2	10	5.682
Jeremiah	17	23	5.693
Isaiah	38	16	5.694
2 Samuel	5	20	5.698
Genesis	34	24	5.701
Jeremiah	35	21	5.707
Ezra	2	31	5.720
Ezra	7	25	5.734
Numbers	18	30	5.758
Ezekiel	17	22	5.759
2 Kings	15	34	5.792
Leviticus	18	20	5.814
1 Samuel	19	23	5.823
Hosea	4	13	5.830
Micah	4	13	5.856
Ezekiel	13	21	5.866
1 Samuel	12	25	5.882
Job	3	12	5.882
Psalms	117	1	5.882
Genesis	30	33	5.893
Psalms	104	16	5.904
Jeremiah	4	25	5.910
Judges	15	19	5.919
Genesis	18	26	5.950
Numbers	27	19	5.956
1 Samuel	29	13	5.963
1 Samuel	22	25	5.967
Isaiah	9	16	5.993
Psalms	126	3	6.000
Isaiah	37	34	6.007
Psalms	136	10	6.024
1 Samuel	15	32	6.049
1 Kings	16	33	6.055
Genesis	42	32	6.061
2 Samuel	7	28	6.074
1 Kings	2	49	6.079
Exodus	17	15	6.098
2 Chronicles	2	20	6.116
2 Kings	19	35	6.130
Ezekiel	6	13	6.132
1 Samuel	24	23	6.150
Judges	4	26	6.161
Jeremiah	14	22	6.180
1 Chronicles	14	12	6.186
Amos	5	20	6.211
1 Samuel	25	47	6.267
Judges	12	14	6.278
Genesis	48	22	6.286
1 Samuel	2	35	6.295
1 Kings	22	51	6.296
2 Samuel	9	14	6.306
Psalms	148	7	6.306
Exodus	11	11	6.322
Ezekiel	18	30	6.329
2 Chronicles	15	16	6.349
Exodus	4	29	6.402
Jeremiah	23	39	6.404
Daniel	10	22	6.433
Genesis	47	33	6.445

TABLE FIVE: Nota Accusativi Page 6

Book and Chapter		Count	Percentage
Joel	2	8	2.078
Psalms	28	2	2.083
1 Chronicles	28	8	2.100
Qohelet	2	8	2.100
2 Chronicles	1	6	2.113
Nehemiah	12	10	2.123
Psalms	147	3	2.128
1 Samuel	14	18	2.130
Esther	1	8	2.156
1 Samuel	4	8	2.162
Joshua	15	12	2.170
Amos	5	7	2.174
Psalms	2	2	2.174
Ezekiel	47	8	2.186
Psalms	29	2	2.198
Zechariah	1	6	2.198
Isaiah	49	8	2.204
Isaiah	4	2	2.247
Isaiah	62	4	2.247
Zephaniah	2	5	2.252
Song	2	4	2.260
Judges	19	12	2.268
Ezekiel	45	9	2.273
Psalms	116	3	2.290
Nehemiah	6	7	2.295
Deuteronomy	18	7	2.303
Genesis	3	8	2.305
Isaiah	57	6	2.308
2 Chronicles	30	10	2.315
Isaiah	7	8	2.319
Amos	4	5	2.326
Psalms	100	1	2.326
Jeremiah	30	8	2.339
Jeremiah	2	12	2.344
1 Chronicles	22	7	2.349
Numbers	36	5	2.358
Jonah	1	6	2.362
2 Chronicles	15	6	2.381
Numbers	1	14	2.381
Jeremiah	49	14	2.397
Ezra	3	6	2.400
Jeremiah	31	15	2.408
Psalms	101	2	2.410
2 Chronicles	26	9	2.439
Psalms	123	1	2.439
Isaiah	19	8	2.446
Micah	6	5	2.463
Ezekiel	40	18	2.486
Jeremiah	10	8	2.500
Psalms	133	1	2.500
Joshua	13	11	2.506
Ezekiel	9	5	2.513
Numbers	7	27	2.519
Deuteronomy	20	8	2.532
Zephaniah	3	7	2.536
Ezekiel	31	8	2.564
Jeremiah	22	12	2.564
Qohelet	3	7	2.564
1 Kings	5	13	2.584
Qohelet	9	8	2.589
Psalms	47	2	2.597
Ezekiel	26	8	2.606
Numbers	24	8	2.614
1 Samuel	3	8	2.632
Leviticus	15	12	2.632
Qohelet	5	7	2.632
Esther	3	8	2.640
Psalms	60	3	2.655
Exodus	19	10	2.667
Ezekiel	24	10	2.667
Zechariah	7	5	2.674
2 Chronicles	9	13	2.675
Jonah	2	3	2.679
1 Samuel	16	10	2.681
Ezra	1	5	2.688
Qohelet	12	5	2.688
1 Chronicles	11	14	2.692
Deuteronomy	16	9	2.695

TABLE FOUR: Article

Book and Chapter		Count	Percentage
2 Chronicles	18	36	6.452
Isaiah	12	4	6.452
Numbers	33	30	6.466
Ezekiel	39	28	6.467
2 Kings	14	31	6.472
Leviticus	25	46	6.479
Psalms	8	5	6.494
Genesis	28	21	6.502
2 Chronicles	21	21	6.542
Leviticus	20	28	6.542
Jonah	4	12	6.557
2 Samuel	3	43	6.565
Ezekiel	33	34	6.576
1 Chronicles	18	16	6.584
2 Chronicles	22	16	6.584
1 Chronicles	17	27	6.618
Ezekiel	14	26	6.650
Psalms	98	5	6.667
Deuteronomy	24	22	6.728
Isaiah	4	6	6.742
Psalms	24	6	6.742
Song	4	12	6.742
Isaiah	29	22	6.748
Ezekiel	38	25	6.757
Deuteronomy	15	24	6.780
Hosea	2	23	6.785
2 Kings	2	29	6.792
Genesis	29	32	6.794
2 Kings	17	47	6.821
Joshua	22	47	6.831
Psalms	33	11	6.832
Daniel	11	42	6.874
Genesis	31	53	6.901
Numbers	22	45	6.902
Numbers	7	74	6.903
2 Chronicles	20	40	6.920
Deuteronomy	25	18	6.923
Ezekiel	24	26	6.933
Deuteronomy	28	69	6.942
Isaiah	7	24	6.957
1 Samuel	28	30	6.961
Isaiah	66	27	6.995
1 Kings	4	14	7.000
Jeremiah	11	27	7.013
Joel	2	27	7.013
2 Kings	24	22	7.029
Genesis	44	32	7.033
Exodus	30	33	7.051
Qohelet	6	12	7.059
2 Samuel	21	30	7.075
Ezekiel	36	40	7.080
Genesis	26	33	7.082
Psalms	147	10	7.092
2 Chronicles	25	35	7.099
2 Chronicles	32	39	7.104
2 Chronicles	36	26	7.104
2 Chronicles	17	17	7.113
2 Kings	3	31	7.126
Psalms	96	8	7.143
Qohelet	5	19	7.143
Leviticus	5	31	7.209
Judges	8	38	7.211
Joel	1	17	7.234
Exodus	10	36	7.243
Qohelet	7	24	7.273
Zechariah	2	16	7.273
Genesis	14	25	7.310
Song	1	11	7.333
Amos	8	14	7.368
Psalms	97	7	7.368
Exodus	20	23	7.372
2 Samuel	2	38	7.379
1 Samuel	8	20	7.380
Ezekiel	48	39	7.400
Jeremiah	13	28	7.407
Ezekiel	11	26	7.450
Genesis	33	20	7.463
Genesis	13	18	7.469

TABLE FIVE: Nota Accusativi Page 7

Book and Chapter		Count	Percentage
Song	5	5	2.703
Joshua	18	11	2.716
Psalms	105	8	2.721
1 Samuel	11	7	2.724
Jeremiah	40	10	2.732
Isaiah	11	6	2.740
Ezekiel	18	13	2.743
1 Chronicles	9	13	2.748
Deuteronomy	24	9	2.752
Ezekiel	12	11	2.757
Isaiah	29	9	2.761
Genesis	26	13	2.790
Hosea	5	5	2.793
1 Kings	10	13	2.802
Jeremiah	47	3	2.804
Judges	15	9	2.804
2 Kings	2	12	2.810
Psalms	102	6	2.830
2 Samuel	16	11	2.835
1 Chronicles	21	14	2.846
Isaiah	38	8	2.847
Jeremiah	15	9	2.848
Genesis	39	10	2.882
Ezekiel	10	9	2.903
Leviticus	17	8	2.920
2 Kings	7	12	2.941
1 Samuel	26	14	2.947
Joel	4	8	2.952
Numbers	26	20	2.967
2 Chronicles	6	22	2.969
Genesis	27	19	2.978
1 Samuel	23	13	2.982
Joel	3	2	2.985
Psalms	103	5	2.994
Psalms	135	5	2.994
2 Chronicles	31	10	3.012
Psalms	34	5	3.030
Qohelet	7	10	3.030
1 Chronicles	7	13	3.052
Deuteronomy	25	8	3.077
Ezekiel	35	6	3.093
Obadiah	1	9	3.093
Judges	17	6	3.125
Genesis	46	13	3.140
Jeremiah	8	11	3.161
1 Samuel	10	14	3.167
Nehemiah	13	15	3.171
Genesis	35	12	3.175
Leviticus	22	14	3.189
1 Samuel	21	9	3.191
Genesis	20	9	3.191
Isaiah	6	6	3.191
Jeremiah	9	12	3.200
Qohelet	8	9	3.203
Daniel	10	11	3.216
1 Kings	20	24	3.217
Nehemiah	10	11	3.226
Numbers	33	15	3.233
Amos	2	7	3.256
Genesis	24	30	3.268
Judges	14	11	3.274
Psalms	145	5	3.289
Ezekiel	6	7	3.302
Ezekiel	14	13	3.325
Ezekiel	22	13	3.333
Malachi	2	9	3.346
Jeremiah	51	30	3.371
1 Samuel	13	12	3.380
Joshua	9	14	3.382
Numbers	9	12	3.390
Deuteronomy	28	34	3.421
Exodus	11	6	3.448
Song	8	6	3.448
Zechariah	6	7	3.448
2 Samuel	17	18	3.455
2 Chronicles	32	19	3.461
1 Kings	14	18	3.468
Joshua	5	10	3.472

TABLE FOUR: Article

Book and Chapter		Count	Percentage
Numbers	8	27	7.479
1 Kings	21	36	7.500
Jeremiah	45	7	7.527
Exodus	23	30	7.538
Deuteronomy	6	24	7.547
Numbers	10	29	7.592
Jeremiah	43	18	7.595
Numbers	29	32	7.619
Deuteronomy	5	36	7.627
Jeremiah	44	48	7.705
Numbers	16	38	7.708
1 Chronicles	21	38	7.724
Judges	14	26	7.738
2 Kings	8	40	7.752
Isaiah	65	28	7.756
2 Chronicles	28	35	7.778
Numbers	6	28	7.778
Deuteronomy	16	26	7.784
1 Samuel	5	17	7.798
Exodus	34	42	7.807
Job	1	27	7.826
Micah	3	13	7.831
Deuteronomy	8	23	7.850
1 Samuel	18	34	7.852
1 Samuel	31	16	7.921
Numbers	32	44	7.928
Leviticus	24	22	7.942
Leviticus	10	26	7.951
Genesis	10	23	7.986
Judges	9	70	8.000
Psalms	134	2	8.000
1 Chronicles	25	23	8.014
Exodus	27	21	8.015
Genesis	21	35	8.028
Judges	10	20	8.032
Isaiah	27	14	8.046
2 Kings	21	32	8.060
Joshua	21	47	8.062
1 Kings	14	42	8.092
2 Chronicles	16	21	8.108
Joel	4	22	8.118
Judges	13	32	8.122
1 Samuel	27	17	8.134
Qohelet	2	31	8.136
Nehemiah	7	51	8.147
Ezekiel	8	26	8.150
Amos	3	17	8.213
Isaiah	39	12	8.219
1 Chronicles	16	34	8.313
Judges	16	46	8.318
Jeremiah	22	39	8.333
Psalms	113	5	8.333
Psalms	127	5	8.333
1 Samuel	7	24	8.362
Qohelet	1	18	8.372
Genesis	32	38	8.389
1 Chronicles	20	12	8.392
1 Samuel	20	59	8.393
1 Chronicles	23	28	8.408
Daniel	9	39	8.442
2 Samuel	1	31	8.447
Jeremiah	16	31	8.447
2 Samuel	13	55	8.488
Leviticus	2	17	8.500
1 Chronicles	12	42	8.502
2 Samuel	6	32	8.511
Isaiah	6	16	8.511
Ezekiel	34	39	8.515
Nehemiah	6	26	8.525
2 Kings	18	57	8.533
Judges	21	32	8.533
Qohelet	8	24	8.541
Ezekiel	44	43	8.583
1 Samuel	10	38	8.597
Leviticus	23	51	8.600
Ezra	1	16	8.602
Exodus	32	47	8.640
Qohelet	10	17	8.673

TABLE FIVE: Nota Accusativi Page

Book and Chapter		Count	Percentage
Ezekiel	25	9	3.475
Ezekiel	29	12	3.488
1 Samuel	30	17	3.491
Qohelet	11	5	3.497
Esther	8	12	3.499
Leviticus	2	7	3.500
Zechariah	12	8	3.524
Deuteronomy	17	13	3.533
Exodus	24	9	3.571
1 Kings	22	29	3.580
1 Samuel	22	15	3.580
2 Chronicles	13	13	3.581
2 Chronicles	18	20	3.584
2 Kings	9	22	3.601
Psalms	148	4	3.604
Leviticus	21	11	3.607
1 Chronicles	14	7	3.608
Deuteronomy	19	12	3.614
Isaiah	53	6	3.614
Micah	3	6	3.614
Zechariah	10	6	3.614
Jeremiah	37	12	3.625
Isaiah	66	14	3.627
Joshua	22	25	3.634
Psalms	106	12	3.636
Exodus	17	9	3.659
2 Samuel	3	24	3.664
Ezekiel	33	19	3.675
1 Chronicles	17	15	3.676
2 Kings	19	21	3.678
Joshua	23	11	3.679
Jeremiah	44	23	3.692
1 Samuel	18	16	3.695
Hosea	3	3	3.704
Isaiah	37	21	3.710
Leviticus	23	22	3.710
Leviticus	27	17	3.712
Genesis	13	9	3.734
Job	42	9	3.734
Genesis	44	17	3.736
Numbers	19	13	3.757
Exodus	21	17	3.769
1 Chronicles	19	12	3.774
1 Samuel	2	21	3.777
2 Chronicles	3	9	3.782
Psalms	79	5	3.788
Esther	6	10	3.802
2 Samuel	15	23	3.814
2 Chronicles	36	14	3.825
Numbers	11	21	3.825
Job	2	8	3.828
1 Samuel	20	27	3.841
2 Chronicles	25	19	3.854
Esther	4	11	3.860
Exodus	32	21	3.860
Exodus	12	29	3.862
Zechariah	5	6	3.871
2 Kings	8	20	3.876
Daniel	1	12	3.883
2 Chronicles	29	21	3.889
Ezekiel	3	16	3.893
2 Kings	1	14	3.900
2 Samuel	7	18	3.905
2 Samuel	18	23	3.905
2 Kings	3	17	3.908
Ezekiel	13	14	3.911
Numbers	15	20	3.914
Jeremiah	42	16	3.922
1 Samuel	28	17	3.944
Leviticus	25	28	3.944
Jeremiah	28	12	3.947
2 Chronicles	12	10	3.953
Deuteronomy	15	14	3.955
1 Kings	21	19	3.958
2 Samuel	5	14	3.989
Exodus	13	13	4.000
Psalms	126	2	4.000
Isaiah	8	12	4.013

TABLE FOUR: Article

Book and Chapter		Count	Percentage
Isaiah	25	14	8.696
1 Kings	17	31	8.708
Ezekiel	15	9	8.738
Leviticus	17	24	8.759
Psalms	124	5	8.772
2 Chronicles	19	16	8.791
2 Samuel	20	39	8.804
Judges	2	32	8.815
Genesis	24	81	8.824
Judges	17	17	8.854
Jeremiah	41	32	8.864
Joshua	24	51	8.885
2 Chronicles	6	66	8.907
2 Kings	1	32	8.914
Genesis	39	31	8.934
2 Chronicles	33	34	8.947
1 Kings	20	67	8.981
Nehemiah	9	59	8.994
2 Kings	9	55	9.002
Joshua	15	50	9.042
Genesis	9	32	9.065
Genesis	43	44	9.072
Isaiah	22	28	9.091
Numbers	20	38	9.091
1 Samuel	6	36	9.114
Esther	4	26	9.123
Exodus	16	50	9.124
Numbers	4	61	9.132
2 Chronicles	1	26	9.155
Zechariah	1	25	9.158
Numbers	15	47	9.198
Deuteronomy	2	49	9.211
Deuteronomy	12	48	9.231
Exodus	13	30	9.231
2 Chronicles	9	45	9.259
1 Samuel	26	44	9.263
Exodus	14	44	9.283
Ruth	3	24	9.302
Song	7	13	9.353
2 Kings	20	34	9.366
Numbers	17	37	9.367
Jeremiah	34	40	9.390
Jeremiah	7	51	9.444
Deuteronomy	1	62	9.480
Numbers	25	22	9.483
2 Chronicles	12	24	9.406
Ruth	2	36	9.524
Joshua	10	73	9.530
1 Kings	5	48	9.543
Jeremiah	33	40	9.547
Ruth	4	32	9.552
Jeremiah	40	35	9.563
Ezekiel	7	33	9.621
Deuteronomy	34	17	9.659
Joshua	9	40	9.662
Zechariah	12	22	9.692
1 Kings	10	45	9.698
2 Samuel	4	73	9.705
Exodus	8	41	9.716
Judges	7	49	9.722
Joshua	17	33	9.792
2 Samuel	12	52	9.867
Jeremiah	29	53	9.870
Exodus	3	39	9.873
Joshua	18	40	9.877
Isaiah	2	25	9.881
Ezra	10	46	9.892
Exodus	28	59	9.916
Joshua	7	49	9.919
1 Samuel	21	28	9.929
Deuteronomy	19	33	9.940
Amos	9	25	9.960
Deuteronomy	26	32	10.031
Qohelet	9	31	10.032
Isaiah	8	30	10.033
Leviticus	27	46	10.044
Deuteronomy	13	33	10.061
Joshua	14	28	10.072

TABLE FIVE: Nota Accusativi Page 9

Book and Chapter		Count	Percentage
Exodus	16	22	4.015
Genesis	28	13	4.025
2 Chronicles	21	13	4.050
1 Kings	13	24	4.054
Ezekiel	36	23	4.071
2 Samuel	11	18	4.072
Ezekiel	8	13	4.075
Genesis	49	15	4.076
Malachi	3	15	4.076
2 Kings	13	17	4.087
2 Kings	15	24	4.089
Zephaniah	1	11	4.089
Esther	2	18	4.110
Isaiah	9	11	4.120
1 Kings	1	33	4.125
1 Samuel	25	31	4.133
Leviticus	13	37	4.143
Haggai	2	15	4.144
Jeremiah	26	18	4.147
2 Samuel	13	27	4.167
Isaiah	20	4	4.167
2 Samuel	24	19	4.176
Leviticus	5	18	4.186
2 Kings	10	26	4.187
Exodus	27	11	4.198
1 Kings	16	23	4.220
Genesis	8	13	4.221
Exodus	33	15	4.237
1 Kings	18	31	4.247
Genesis	9	15	4.249
Genesis	2	14	4.268
Nehemiah	5	14	4.268
Zechariah	3	7	4.268
Exodus	34	23	4.275
Leviticus	6	13	4.290
Jeremiah	33	18	4.296
Jeremiah	45	4	4.301
Numbers	17	17	4.304
Numbers	13	17	4.315
Genesis	43	21	4.330
Judges	16	24	4.340
1 Kings	11	30	4.348
Deuteronomy	22	19	4.348
Jeremiah	35	16	4.348
Genesis	23	12	4.364
1 Samuel	17	40	4.376
Hosea	1	6	4.380
Exodus	5	14	4.403
1 Chronicles	15	16	4.408
Genesis	19	25	4.440
1 Samuel	9	22	4.444
Numbers	6	16	4.444
Ezekiel	17	17	4.450
Ezekiel	46	17	4.462
2 Chronicles	33	17	4.474
2 Chronicles	10	14	4.502
Song	3	6	4.511
Ezekiel	5	13	4.530
2 Kings	6	24	4.545
Exodus	7	19	4.545
1 Samuel	1	19	4.578
1 Kings	2	37	4.591
2 Samuel	19	37	4.591
Ezekiel	44	23	4.591
Deuteronomy	7	19	4.612
Deuteronomy	12	24	4.615
Joshua	4	18	4.615
Jeremiah	3	19	4.634
Qohelet	4	11	4.641
1 Kings	3	22	4.661
Numbers	16	23	4.665
Jeremiah	11	18	4.675
Leviticus	24	13	4.693
2 Kings	12	17	4.696
Deuteronomy	26	15	4.702
1 Kings	6	24	4.706
Psalms	146	4	4.706
1 Kings	8	54	4.708

TABLE FOUR: Article

Book and Chapter		Count	Percentage
Isaiah	24	26	10.156
Jeremiah	39	31	10.197
Jeremiah	27	43	10.214
Numbers	34	31	10.231
2 Kings	4	69	10.283
Judges	6	70	10.309
Genesis	22	38	10.354
Exodus	12	78	10.386
Judges	1	55	10.397
Joel	3	7	10.448
Exodus	33	37	10.452
Job	2	22	10.526
Song	6	12	10.526
2 Samuel	17	55	10.557
Exodus	9	55	10.557
Jeremiah	25	65	10.569
2 Chronicles	24	48	10.573
Genesis	40	33	10.577
1 Kings	9	50	10.593
Numbers	21	50	10.593
Deuteronomy	9	53	10.621
Numbers	13	42	10.660
Zechariah	8	38	10.674
Zechariah	7	20	10.695
1 Chronicles	15	39	10.744
2 Kings	7	44	10.784
2 Kings	10	67	10.789
Judges	3	52	10.811
1 Kings	18	79	10.822
2 Chronicles	26	40	10.840
2 Kings	6	58	10.985
1 Samuel	13	39	10.986
1 Chronicles	9	52	10.994
Exodus	18	46	11.005
Deuteronomy	21	39	11.017
1 Chronicles	28	42	11.024
2 Chronicles	14	24	11.060
2 Samuel	15	67	11.111
1 Kings	12	65	11.130
Judges	18	61	11.131
Exodus	35	49	11.136
Isaiah	36	43	11.169
Deuteronomy	18	34	11.184
Exodus	37	41	11.202
Numbers	28	39	11.207
Amos	6	20	11.236
Joshua	11	46	11.247
Exodus	1	27	11.250
Joshua	1	36	11.250
Ezekiel	1	43	11.257
1 Samuel	30	55	11.294
1 Samuel	9	56	11.313
Deuteronomy	4	92	11.316
Zechariah	6	23	11.330
1 Kings	8	130	11.334
2 Chronicles	8	33	11.340
Genesis	41	88	11.340
Exodus	2	39	11.471
Leviticus	6	35	11.551
Nehemiah	2	43	11.590
Exodus	25	51	11.591
2 Samuel	16	45	11.598
Deuteronomy	11	59	11.614
Numbers	35	56	11.618
Nehemiah	11	44	11.640
Judges	20	87	11.647
Deuteronomy	30	38	11.656
Exodus	31	27	11.790
Genesis	6	36	11.803
Leviticus	15	54	11.842
1 Chronicles	24	32	11.852
1 Chronicles	29	57	11.875
Qohelet	11	17	11.888
Deuteronomy	7	49	11.893
Genesis	19	67	11.901
2 Samuel	23	53	11.937
Joshua	19	58	11.959
Genesis	15	31	11.969

TABLE FIVE: Nota Accusativi Page 10

Book and Chapter		Count	Percentage
Ezekiel	37	21	4.709
Nehemiah	9	31	4.726
Jeremiah	38	26	4.745
Numbers	22	31	4.755
Jeremiah	13	19	4.762
Deuteronomy	8	14	4.778
Genesis	45	19	4.786
2 Samuel	6	18	4.787
Exodus	26	23	4.792
Judges	9	42	4.800
2 Kings	14	23	4.802
Deuteronomy	21	17	4.802
1 Samuel	19	19	4.810
Jeremiah	29	26	4.842
2 Chronicles	24	22	4.846
Genesis	33	13	4.851
1 Kings	19	18	4.852
Ezekiel	15	5	4.854
Exodus	4	22	4.857
Exodus	36	25	4.864
Numbers	14	31	4.882
Genesis	47	25	4.883
Jeremiah	23	30	4.926
Genesis	36	24	4.928
Jeremiah	39	15	4.934
Isaiah	36	19	4.935
Genesis	25	20	4.938
2 Kings	20	18	4.959
Judges	7	25	4.960
2 Samuel	8	13	4.962
Numbers	35	24	4.979
Genesis	30	28	5.000
Leviticus	19	22	5.000
Zechariah	2	11	5.000
Numbers	3	30	5.008
Malachi	1	12	5.021
Joshua	14	14	5.036
Zechariah	8	18	5.056
2 Chronicles	14	11	5.069
Genesis	32	23	5.077
Ezekiel	39	22	5.081
2 Kings	18	34	5.090
Jeremiah	20	15	5.102
Joshua	3	15	5.119
Judges	11	34	5.128
Ezekiel	23	32	5.153
2 Chronicles	8	15	5.155
Amos	9	13	5.179
2 Samuel	14	31	5.184
Genesis	31	40	5.208
Deuteronomy	30	17	5.215
Leviticus	18	18	5.233
Deuteronomy	29	23	5.239
Genesis	6	16	5.246
Deuteronomy	2	28	5.263
Zechariah	13	8	5.263
1 Kings	12	31	5.308
Joshua	1	17	5.312
2 Samuel	12	28	5.313
2 Chronicles	7	21	5.316
1 Chronicles	5	24	5.322
Numbers	27	17	5.329
2 Chronicles	28	24	5.333
1 Samuel	24	20	5.348
Jeremiah	7	29	5.370
Numbers	18	28	5.374
Ezekiel	11	19	5.444
Nehemiah	1	11	5.446
Judges	6	37	5.449
Exodus	8	23	5.450
Jeremiah	16	20	5.450
Judges	4	23	5.450
Isaiah	39	8	5.479
1 Chronicles	4	26	5.485
Deuteronomy	13	18	5.488
Genesis	21	24	5.505
Joshua	8	34	5.519
Genesis	41	43	5.541

TABLE FOUR: Article

Book and Chapter		Count	Percentage
2 Samuel	11	53	11.991
Numbers	3	72	12.020
1 Samuel	11	31	12.062
2 Samuel	24	55	12.088
Genesis	3	42	12.104
Deuteronomy	22	53	12.128
Joshua	5	35	12.153
Numbers	26	82	12.166
Psalms	123	5	12.195
Joshua	20	21	12.209
2 Chronicles	10	38	12.219
Qohelet	4	29	12.236
1 Chronicles	13	26	12.264
Numbers	14	78	12.283
Deuteronomy	20	39	12.342
1 Samuel	14	105	12.426
Numbers	9	44	12.429
Isaiah	3	31	12.450
Jeremiah	21	31	12.500
Zechariah	13	19	12.500
Deuteronomy	27	41	12.577
Zechariah	11	32	12.598
Zechariah	3	21	12.805
Deuteronomy	14	45	12.821
Joshua	2	52	12.903
Numbers	11	71	12.933
Daniel	1	40	12.945
Deuteronomy	10	42	12.963
Jeremiah	24	24	12.973
Deuteronomy	31	72	13.020
Esther	10	6	13.043
Leviticus	16	72	13.043
Exodus	19	49	13.067
Exodus	24	33	13.095
1 Kings	13	78	13.176
Jeremiah	52	75	13.228
Ezra	9	38	13.287
1 Kings	3	63	13.347
Nehemiah	1	27	13.366
Zechariah	4	25	13.369
Deuteronomy	29	59	13.440
Numbers	31	91	13.442
Haggai	1	32	13.445
Esther	2	59	13.470
1 Kings	1	108	13.500
2 Kings	12	49	13.536
Leviticus	7	65	13.542
1 Samuel	17	124	13.567
Ezekiel	9	27	13.568
Jonah	3	19	13.571
Ezra	8	63	13.607
1 Chronicles	11	71	13.654
Jeremiah	19	39	13.732
Ezekiel	43	57	13.735
Jonah	1	35	13.780
Deuteronomy	17	51	13.859
2 Samuel	14	83	13.880
2 Chronicles	30	60	13.889
Jeremiah	37	46	13.897
Jeremiah	32	104	13.904
2 Chronicles	35	60	13.921
Judges	19	74	13.989
Nehemiah	5	46	14.024
1 Samuel	4	52	14.054
Joshua	12	35	14.113
2 Kings	25	72	14.173
2 Chronicles	7	56	14.177
Esther	3	43	14.191
Nehemiah	3	79	14.234
Psalms	125	7	14.286
Qohelet	3	39	14.286
Exodus	38	59	14.320
Joshua	4	56	14.359
Joshua	23	43	14.381
Ezekiel	47	53	14.481
2 Kings	23	112	14.489
2 Samuel	18	86	14.601
Zechariah	14	53	14.641

TABLE FIVE: Nota Accusativi Page 11

Book and Chapter		Count	Percentage
Deuteronomy	10	18	5.556
Genesis	14	19	5.556
Exodus	9	29	5.566
Numbers	25	13	5.603
Judges	18	31	5.657
1 Chronicles	13	12	5.660
Deuteronomy	6	18	5.660
Esther	5	15	5.660
Ruth	4	19	5.672
2 Kings	22	21	5.676
Exodus	25	25	5.682
Ezekiel	4	15	5.682
2 Chronicles	5	14	5.691
Deuteronomy	14	20	5.698
Numbers	30	15	5.703
2 Samuel	10	18	5.732
1 Kings	15	30	5.736
Exodus	18	24	5.742
1 Chronicles	18	14	5.761
2 Chronicles	22	14	5.761
Ezekiel	16	48	5.762
Ezekiel	2	9	5.769
Exodus	23	23	5.779
Deuteronomy	4	47	5.781
2 Chronicles	16	15	5.792
Ezekiel	32	28	5.809
Deuteronomy	1	38	5.810
Leviticus	10	19	5.810
Exodus	3	23	5.823
Deuteronomy	27	19	5.828
Exodus	1	14	5.833
Ezekiel	30	20	5.848
Deuteronomy	3	27	5.857
1 Samuel	15	31	5.860
Esther	9	32	5.861
Genesis	42	31	5.871
Jeremiah	32	44	5.882
Psalms	117	1	5.882
Hosea	2	20	5.900
1 Samuel	8	16	5.904
Deuteronomy	5	28	5.932
Genesis	29	28	5.945
Jeremiah	36	37	5.968
Genesis	1	26	5.991
Joshua	10	46	6.005
2 Kings	21	24	6.043
Jeremiah	12	16	6.084
Jeremiah	41	22	6.094
Exodus	14	29	6.118
Genesis	4	21	6.158
Deuteronomy	9	31	6.212
Exodus	28	37	6.218
Numbers	20	26	6.220
Ezekiel	43	26	6.265
1 Samuel	7	18	6.272
Genesis	37	31	6.275
Judges	12	14	6.278
1 Kings	7	50	6.305
2 Samuel	4	15	6.329
Jeremiah	19	18	6.338
Jeremiah	34	27	6.338
Genesis	12	17	6.343
2 Kings	24	20	6.390
Joshua	20	11	6.395
Jeremiah	27	27	6.413
Genesis	17	23	6.479
Jeremiah	24	12	6.486
Numbers	31	44	6.499
Numbers	21	31	6.568
Genesis	48	23	6.571
1 Samuel	6	26	6.582
2 Samuel	21	28	6.604
Judges	2	24	6.612
Judges	8	35	6.641
Genesis	50	25	6.667
Joshua	2	27	6.700
Ezekiel	34	31	6.769
Deuteronomy	34	12	6.818

TABLE FOUR: Article

Book and Chapter		Count	Percentage
Nehemiah	12	69	14.650
Song	2	26	14.689
Numbers	19	51	14.740
2 Samuel	19	119	14.764
Exodus	40	65	14.773
Exodus	29	96	14.792
Joshua	13	65	14.806
Jeremiah	36	92	14.839
Daniel	8	57	14.883
Joshua	8	92	14.935
Numbers	5	69	14.935
Psalms	133	6	15.000
2 Chronicles	31	50	15.060
Deuteronomy	3	70	15.184
Haggai	2	55	15.193
Ezra	3	38	15.200
Esther	9	83	15.201
Exodus	39	87	15.317
Jeremiah	38	84	15.328
Psalms	114	8	15.385
2 Kings	16	56	15.427
Joshua	16	19	15.447
Leviticus	8	89	15.614
Genesis	1	68	15.668
2 Chronicles	29	85	15.741
2 Chronicles	34	97	15.798
2 Kings	22	59	15.946
1 Chronicles	26	57	16.056
Jeremiah	26	70	16.129
Nehemiah	10	55	16.129
Zechariah	5	25	16.129
Nehemiah	13	77	16.279
Zephaniah	1	44	16.357
Daniel	12	29	16.384
Exodus	36	85	16.537
Leviticus	4	90	16.605
Jeremiah	28	51	16.776
Leviticus	11	100	16.863
Esther	5	45	16.981
Esther	6	45	17.110
Ezekiel	40	124	17.127
Ezekiel	45	68	17.172
Nehemiah	4	43	17.200
Ezekiel	46	66	17.323
Leviticus	13	155	17.357
Esther	8	60	17.493
Joshua	6	83	17.511
Esther	1	65	17.520
Genesis	2	59	17.988
Ezekiel	10	56	18.065
1 Kings	6	94	18.431
2 Chronicles	5	46	18.699
Nehemiah	8	67	18.768
Qohelet	12	35	18.817
Ezekiel	41	70	18.919
Genesis	8	59	19.156
2 Chronicles	4	60	19.293
2 Chronicles	3	47	19.748
Joshua	3	58	19.795
1 Kings	7	159	20.050
1 Chronicles	27	83	20.393
Leviticus	9	65	20.440
Genesis	7	68	20.482
Leviticus	1	52	20.635
Esther	7	39	20.856
Leviticus	3	52	20.884
Exodus	26	101	21.042
2 Kings	11	80	22.346
2 Chronicles	23	87	22.597
Leviticus	14	192	23.472
Ezekiel	42	76	26.667

TABLE FIVE: Nota Accusativi Page 12

Book and Chapter		Count	Percentage
Jeremiah	21	17	6.855
Leviticus	11	41	6.914
1 Chronicles	20	10	6.993
2 Chronicles	34	43	7.003
Genesis	40	22	7.051
Leviticus	7	34	7.083
Joshua	7	35	7.085
Psalms	137	6	7.143
Exodus	6	29	7.178
Exodus	10	36	7.243
Exodus	38	30	7.282
Exodus	20	23	7.372
Genesis	5	27	7.397
Genesis	11	29	7.398
2 Kings	17	51	7.402
Deuteronomy	31	41	7.414
Zechariah	11	19	7.480
Numbers	4	50	7.485
Leviticus	4	41	7.565
Numbers	32	42	7.568
Judges	10	19	7.631
Deuteronomy	11	39	7.677
Jeremiah	52	44	7.760
2 Chronicles	23	30	7.792
Numbers	5	36	7.792
Joshua	11	32	7.824
1 Kings	9	37	7.839
Exodus	30	37	7.906
Exodus	2	27	7.941
Psalms	134	2	8.000
Ezekiel	20	59	8.038
2 Kings	25	41	8.071
Joshua	6	39	8.228
2 Kings	16	30	8.264
Jeremiah	25	51	8.293
Judges	3	40	8.316
2 Chronicles	4	26	8.360
1 Samuel	12	36	8.471
Genesis	15	22	8.494
Genesis	34	36	8.551
Leviticus	14	70	8.557
Numbers	8	31	8.587
1 Chronicles	1	37	8.768
2 Kings	23	69	8.926
Exodus	37	33	9.016
Leviticus	16	50	9.058
1 Samuel	5	20	9.174
Leviticus	26	54	9.278
Jeremiah	43	22	9.283
1 Chronicles	2	50	9.346
1 Chronicles	10	18	9.375
2 Kings	11	34	9.497
Leviticus	1	24	9.524
1 Samuel	31	20	9.901
1 Chronicles	8	31	10.299
Joshua	24	60	10.453
Leviticus	9	34	10.692
Genesis	22	41	11.172
Leviticus	3	28	11.245
Exodus	29	74	11.402
Exodus	39	66	11.620
Leviticus	20	50	11.682
Exodus	31	27	11.790
2 Chronicles	11	35	11.945
Judges	1	65	12.287
Genesis	10	38	13.194
Exodus	35	61	13.864
1 Chronicles	6	93	14.785
Leviticus	8	87	15.263
Exodus	40	71	16.136
Joshua	21	113	19.383

Hôy and *Hôy*-Oracles: A Neglected Syntactic Aspect

Delbert R. Hillers
The Johns Hopkins University, Baltimore, Maryland

The particle *hôy*, which occurs about fifty times in Biblical Hebrew, has been the subject of much recent discussion, including one monograph, Janzen 1972, yet many aspects of its meaning and usage still remain debated. Readers may consult Janzen for an extended review of the literature; that given below is meant only to illustrate the variety of opinions on one point: the presence or absence of a vocative element after the particle *hôy*.

In an influential article, E. Gerstenberger (1962) associated what he called the "Woe Oracles of the Prophets" with popular ethos or popular wisdom, and just as he found in wisdom an impersonal pronouncement of disapproval on evildoers, so he noted the participles which often follow on *hôy* and suggested they be translated: "Woe (comes upon) one who is doing such and such." He referred to "the impersonal classification and enumeration of misdeeds introduced by the woe-formula. . . ." Direct address is lacking, in his opinion; where the initial third person is followed by second person, this has resulted from the juxtaposition of two disparate forms. This point of view influenced Wolff, who wrote: "The person threatened with the woe is never addressed; he is never characterized by a name, but always only by his deed" (1964: 14).

Gunther Wanke (1966) offered sharp criticism of Gerstenberger's view that *hôy*-speeches are at home in wisdom literature, by separating *ʾôy* and *hôy* sharply and by showing that *hôy* never occurs in wisdom literature. Yet on the matter of direct address he is of one mind with Gerstenberger; he stresses the impersonality and indirectness of the *hôy*-speeches in the prophets.

The main contention of Clifford (1966), that *hôy* was originally a cry associated with the funeral lament, is picked up and elaborated by Janzen in a treatment which surpasses all others in completeness (1972). Aside from the connection to funeral laments, which is much elaborated, Janzen's work brings a turn away from others' stress of the impersonal, indirect nature of prophetic *hôy*-speeches. In his view, *hôy* is often followed by the vocative, a view he grounds (a) comparatively, with an attempt to identify similar particles in other languages, especially Ugaritic; (b) grammatically, identifying the definite article on participles following *hôy* as a vocative marker; and especially (c) form-critically: the funeral lament contained an element of address to the dead, and this direct address is carried over elsewhere (Janzen 1972: 13, 19, 21–23).

Janzen's main contention has won some followers. Zobel (1977) and Kraus (1973) accept the notion that *hôy* originally had to do with funerals. Yet Kraus disagrees sharply with Janzen over the idea of direct address following *hôy*: ". . . in *hôy*–speeches precisely an addressee is lacking" (Kraus 1973: 46).

Those experienced in biblical and Hebrew studies will doubtless feel that this is one of those problems where a clear solution is lacking, not for want of industry or skill on the part of scholars, but because of the nature of our evidence. Yet perhaps some gain may be made by studying the *hôy*-passages in the light of the syntax of the vocative in Semitic, especially the syntax of relative clauses modifying the vocative.

In Classical Arabic, in relative clauses referring to a first or second person element, the retrospective pronoun is usually in the first or second person, though fairly often the third person occurs, e.g., *ʾinnī mruʾun fī hudhaylīn nāṣiruhu* 'I am a man whose helper is among the Hudhaylites' (Reckendorf 1921: 424). In relative clauses after a vocative, it is this construction with the third person which dominates (Reckendorf 1921: 444). According to Brockelmann (1913: 589), in the older language this usage is the only one followed, thus: *yā ʾayyuhā ʾlladhīna ʾamanū* 'O you believers.'

Hebrew grammarians have noted the same construction in Biblical Hebrew: pronominal elements referring back to a vocative are in the third person. Micah 1: 2, quoted in part in 1 Kgs 22: 28 (cf. 2 Chr 18: 27), contains two examples: *šimʿû ʿammîm kullām haqšîbî ʾereṣ ûmĕlōʾāh.* Compare also Isa 44: 23, *yaʿar wĕkol ʿēṣ bô* 'O forests with all your trees' (JPS); and Isa 54: 1, *ronnî ʿăqārâ lōʾ yālādâ.*

The last example to be quoted here, Isa 22: 16–17a, is especially instructive.

> *mah-llĕkā pōh ûmî lĕkā pōh*
> *kî ḥāṣabtā llĕkā pōh qāber*
> *ḥōṣĕbî mārôm qibrô*
> *ḥōqĕqî bassela' miškān lô*
> *hinnêh yhwh mĕṭalṭelkā*
>
> What have you here, and whom have you here,
> That you have hewn out a tomb for youself here?—
> O you who have hewn your tomb on high;
> O you who have hollowed out for yourself an abode in the cliff!
> The Lord is about to shake you. . . (after JPS).

This passage has been quoted to show 1) the unmistakable vocative elements; 2) the switch to modifiers with third-person pronominal elements; 3) a reversion to second-person pronouns.

Some other biblical verses showing this peculiarity of the vocative are Ezek 21: 30; Isa 47: 8a; and possibly 2 Kgs 9: 31. Somewhat longer examples are rather common, thus Ps 18: 50–51 (note *malkô* etc.); Ps 104: 3, 4, 6, 7, 13; and, from the prophets (not including *hôy*–oracles), Amos 4: 1–3; Obad 3–4; Mic 3: 9–12; 7: 18–20; Isa 44: 1; 65: 11; Jer 5: 21–22; 49: 4–5.

In the light of this usage, some *hôy*-oracles appear in a new light. The second-person elements which come in sooner or later in many of them have been thought to be secondary. In many cases it seems altogether more plausible to suppose that a vocative element comes right after the *hôy* and pronouns referring back to this are for a time in third person in keeping with ancient usage; explicitly second-person forms reassert themselves later. In other words, the pattern is like that of Isa 22: 16–17, cited above. A fair example, of some length, is Isa 10: 1–3.

> *hôy haḥōqĕqîm ḥiqqê ʾāwen*
> *ûmĕkattĕbim ʿāmāl kittēbû*

lĕhaṭṭôt middîn dallîm
wĕligzōl mišpaṭ ʿănîyê ʿammî
lihyôt ʾalmānôt šĕlālām
wĕʾet yĕtômîm yābōzzû
ûmāh taʿăśû lĕyôm pĕquddâ

Ha! You who write out evil writs
And compose iniquitous documents,
To subvert the cause of the poor,
To rob of their rights the needy of my people;
That widows may be your spoil,
And fatherless children your booty!
What will you do on the day of punishment . . . ? (after JPS)

Several shorter examples showing a similar switch from third person, following what may be regarded as a vocative, to second person (or vice versa) may be quoted.

hôy maggîʿê bayit bĕbayit
śādeh bĕśādeh yaqrîbû
ʿad ʾepes māqôm
wĕhûšabtem lĕbaddĕkem bĕqereb hāʾāreṣ Isa 5: 8
hôy šôdēd wĕʾattāh lōʾ šādûd
ûbôgēd wĕlōʾ bāgĕdû bô Isa 33: 1
hôy kol ṣāmēʾ lĕkû lammayim
waʾăšer ʾên lô kasep lĕkû
šibrû etc. Isa 55: 1

For other examples see Isa 1: 4–5; 30: 1–3; Jer 22: 13–15; 23: 1–2; Ezek 34: 2–3; Amos 6: 1–2; Mic 2: 1–3; Hab 2: 6–7, 9–10, 15–16.

Several conclusions may be offered. First, it seems possible to understand the syntax of a significant number of *hôy*-oracles in a rather new way, with a vocative at the beginning and direct address continued throughout. As noted above, a form-critical or source-critical way of explaining the syntax of these oracles is available. The present writer does not claim to have refuted that explanation but does propose that the present view is preferable, as being based on a known feature of Hebrew (and Arabic) syntax and as simpler. If the view presented here is correct, a good deal of what has been written about the "impersonal" character of these oracles must be abandoned, of course.

Second, questions as to the life-situation of *hôy* and *hôy*-speeches are affected. If a good many of these speeches contain direct address, it is difficult to connect them with a supposedly impersonal wisdom. Furthermore, recognition of a prominent vocative element would seem to tie these speeches more closely to other elements of address in the prophets such as *šimʿû* 'hear ye' and to loosen any special tie to funeral laments.

Complexities and problems remain: the relation to *ʾôy* and the construction *hôy ʿal;* the number of cases where a *hôy*-speech is continued in third-person without any direct address being present (Isa 17: 12–14; 31: 1–3); or where a *hôy*-passage could contain direct address, but no threat to the evildoers follows (Isa 5: 11–12; 5: 18–23). Some of these complexities and problems might yield to further study, but it seems clear that usage of *hôy* is not simple and uniform.

References

Brockelmann, C.
1913 *Grundriss der vergleichenden Grammatik der semitischen Sprachen. II. Syntax.* Berlin: Töpelmann. Rpt., 1961, Hildesheim: Olms.

Clifford, R. J.
1966 The Use of HÔY in the Prophets. *Catholic Biblical Quarterly* 28: 458–64.
1974 Review of Janzen 1962. *Biblica* 55: 98–100.

Crenshaw, J. L.
1967 The Influence of the Wise upon Amos. *Zeitschrift für die Alttestamentliche Wissenschaft* 79: 42–52.

Gerstenberger, E.
1962 The Woe-Oracles of the Prophets. *Journal of Biblical Literature* 81: 249–63.

Hermisson, H. J.
1968 *Studien zur altisraelitischen Spruchweisheit.* Wissenschaftliche Monographien zum Alten und Neuen Testament 28. Neukirchen: Neukirchener.

Janzen, W.
1972 *Mourning Cry and Woe Oracle.* Beihefte zur Zeitschrift für die Alttestamentliche Wissenschaft 125. Berlin: De Gruyter.

Kraus, H.-J.
1973 *hôj* als profetische Leichenklage über das eigene Volk im 8. Jahrhundert. *Zeitschrift für die Alttestamentliche Wissenschaft* 85: 15–46 [Krause *falso*].

Reckendorf, H.
1921 *Arabische Syntax.* Heidelberg: Carl Winter.

Wanke, G.
1966 *ʾwy* und *hwy*. *Zeitschrift für die Alttestamentliche Wissenschaft* 78: 15–18.

Westermann, C.
1960 *Grundformen prophetischer Rede.* Munich: Kaiser.

Williams, J. G.
1967 The Alas-Oracles of the Eighth Century Prophets. *Hebrew Union College Annual* 38: 75–91.

Wolff, H. W.
1964 Amos' geistige Heimat. Pp. 232–50 in his *Gesammelte Studien zum Alten Testament.* Theologische Bücherei 22. Munich: Kaiser.
1969 *Dodekapropheton 2, Joel und Amos.* Biblischer Kommentar Altes Testament 14/2. Neukirchen-Vluyn: Neukirchener.

Zobel, H. J.
1977 *hôy*. Bd. II, Sp. 382–88 in *Theologisches Wörterbuch zum Alten Testament,* ed. G. J. Botterweck and Helmer Ringgren. Suttgart: Kohlhammer. Trans. 1978. Vol. III, pp. 359–64 in *Theological Dictionary of the Old Testament*, trans. D. Green et al. Grand Rapids: Eerdmans.

II. The Prose of the Hebrew Bible

A Syllable-Word Structure Analysis of Genesis 12–23

Cornelius B. Houk
Waukesha, Wisconsin

Relatively recent applications of statistical linguistics to Biblical Hebrew have uncovered new dimensions of the language.[1] Two useful statistics are mean word length and the frequencies of words of various lengths, measured by syllables (Houk 1978; 1979; 1981). Using these syllable-word statistics, sections of Genesis 12–23 which are significantly different from each other can be distinguished by the application of inferential statistical tests such as the chi square test. Such syllable-word structure analysis offers new information concerning the formation of Genesis 12–23.

The analysis assumes that the narratives are homogeneous as written, i.e., that the underlying structures of syllables and words exhibit consistent, regular patterns of choice and chance (Radday 1973: 23–48). Working from this assumption of unity we can apply inferential statistical tests to give information concerning the extent of difference between two sections of material which are compared. In this study significant difference is recognized at the $p \leq 1.05$ level. Unless otherwise specifically stated the p values are all dependent on chi square tests. Occasionally analysis of variance and Fisher's exact test are used, as noted.

The Abraham narratives offer a key starting point for syllable-word structure analysis because supposed doublet stories in Gen 16: 1–16; 21: 8–21 and in Gen 12: 10–20; 20: 1–18 are offered as essential evidence for the separate contributions of J and E (Noth 1972: 22; Van Seters 1975: 127; Jenks 1977: 21–24). These passages will be analyzed in detail. To this is added Gen 22: 1–19, an example of an E passage which occurs without a parallel.[2] In order to provide a context for the interpretation of these results the JEP materials as a whole in this section of Genesis will be examined. The observations and interpretations must be held as preliminary; it is essential to move to a knowledge of the syllable-word structures underlying all of Genesis.

The analysis begins with calculations of mean word length and of frequencies of words of various lengths measured by syllables. The following conventions were adopted for counting syllables in the unemended MT: vocal *shewa* was counted as forming a syllable (including *shewa* following all long and changeable long vowels), *maqqep* and furtive *pataḥ* were ignored, and final diphthongs were counted as one syllable. Because syllable counts are compared in the statistical tests, absolute counts are not necessary, and disagreements about segholates, *shewa*, etc., may be set aside.

Genesis 12–23

The first step in the analysis of Genesis 12–23 takes each chapter as a set of

TABLE 1 GENESIS 12–23

Chap.	Words	Mean	SD	Word Frequencies (syl.)					
				1	2	3	4	5	6
12	268	2.38	.985	51	101	89	20	5	2
13	241	2.24	.980	59	91	70	16	4	1
14	342	2.34	.920	56	157	93	29	7	0
15	258	2.33	.914	46	113	70	27	2	0
16	223	2.24	.823	43	95	75	9	1	0
17	355	2.44	.935	46	163	97	41	8	0
18	437	2.44	.911	71	151	170	41	3	1
19	563	2.39	.989	117	195	172	73	6	0
20	282	2.30	.986	71	90	89	30	2	0
21	436	2.30	.910	97	144	164	28	3	0
22	367	2.39	.942	69	130	132	29	7	0
23	275	2.33	.942	54	110	80	28	3	0

observed values. The data are given in Table 1. Whether variations in mean word lengths from chapter to chapter are significant is tested with an analysis of variance (ANOVA), a common statistical procedure. The null hypothesis is rejected ($F = 2.37$, $p = .01$). There is significant variation among the chapter means. Genesis 12–23 is not homogeneous.

Variation within Genesis 12–23 can be demonstrated in another way by dividing the material approximately in half. If frequencies of 1, 2, 3, 4–6 syllable words are compared for Genesis 12–17 and Genesis 18–23, significant difference is found (df 3, $p \leq .001$). To discover, however, the syllable-word structures which make chaps. 12–17 different from chaps. 18–23 requires further analysis.

Next the frequencies of 1, 2, 3, 4–6 syllable words are compared for J12–23/E12–23/P12–23, the individual source materials (Noth 1972: 263–64), each taken as a set of observed values (see Table 2). Significant difference between the three kinds of material is found (df 6, $p \leq .001$). Secondly, the following pairwise comparisons all indicate significant difference: J12–23/P12–23 (df 3, $p \leq .05$), P12–23/E12–23 (df 3, $p \leq .001$), and J12–23/E12–23 (df 1; 2 syllable words, $p \leq .02$). (The notation "2 syllable words" means that the chi square test cited compares the frequencies of two syllable words alone and of all other words grouped. Unless such a qualifying notation is given for succeeding chi square tests, the comparison is reported for the frequencies of 1, 2, 3 syllable words separately and 4–6 syllable words grouped.)

The sets of observed values, however, may be drawn in another way, comparing approximately the first half with the second of each of the JEP strands (see Table 2). Significant difference between the halves is demonstrated for the following compari-

TABLE 2 JEP NARRATIVES

Source	Words	Word Frequencies (syl.)			
		1	2	3	4–6
J12–17	783	160	312	236	75
J18–23	1059	195	376	361	127
E12–20	345	86	114	106	39
E21–22	678	143	221	256	58
P12–17	468	63	213	139	53
P18–23	346	70	135	106	35

sons: J12–17/J18–23 (df 3, $p \leqslant .05$), E12–20/E21–22 (df 1; 3 syllable words, $p \leqslant .05$), and P12–17/P18–23 (df 2; 1,2,3–6 syllable words, $p \leqslant .05$). The disunity evidenced goes against any large scale unity of composition in the final formulations of JEP such as that proposed by Noth, who suggests that single authors put the oral sources into writing in "their own speech and idiom," each source having its own "particular individual linguistic and stylistic form" (1972: 228–31). Speiser similarly speaks of E and J as individual authors, J being "not only the most gifted biblical writer, but one of the greatest figures in world literature" (1964: xxvii, xxxiv). According to syllable-word structure analysis this thesis does not hold, at least for larger blocks of material.

Because there is significant difference between the approximate halves of each of the JEP materials, the question arises as to which section of J is to be compared with which section of E, etc. For example, J12–17/P12–17 differs significantly (df 3, $p \leqslant .02$), but J18–23/P18–23 does not (df 3, $p \leqslant .50$). In order to move beyond the problems of these generalizations, chaps. 12, 16, 20, 21: 1–21, and 22 are each analyzed in detail. Because syllable counts are easily made for individual verses and brief texts, and out of consideration for space, only data for the major sections of the chapters are given (see Table 3). The principal narratives which are homogeneous are separated from those sections of the text which differ significantly. Then these narratives are compared to one another, providing an initial appraisal of the formation of several of the Abraham JE stories.

Genesis 12

That Gen 12: 1–20 is not a unity is concluded from the comparison of 12: 1–3/4–6/7–9/10–13/14–16/17–20 (df 12, $p \leqslant .005$). Furthermore, v 16, according to Fisher's exact test comparing four syllable words, differs from its context (12: 16/17–20, $p \leqslant .001$ and 12: 10–15/16, $p \leqslant .001$). Vv 2–3 are also a different element according to the comparison of 12: 2–3/1, 4–15, 17–20 (df 1; 1–2, 3–6 syllable words, $p \leqslant .02$). The two

TABLE 3 CHAPTER ANALYSES

Section		Words	Mean	Word Frequencies (syl.)			
				1	2	3	4–6
12:	1, 4–15, 17–20	239	2.29	48	95	83	13
	2–3	17	3.41	1	4	4	8
	16	12	3.08	2	2	1	7
16:	1–9, 15–16	155	2.36	28	55	62	10
	10–14	68	1.97	15	40	13	0
20:	1–14	230	2.27	62	66	81	21
	15–17, 18	52	2.40	9	24	8	11
21:	1–16, 19–21	238	2.30	49	83	94	12
	17–18	40	2.03	17	9	11	3
22:	1–19	307	2.40	60	101	114	32
	20–24	60	2.28	9	29	18	4

narratives within chap. 12 do not differ according to a comparison of 12: 1, 4–9/10–15, 17–20 (df 3, $p \leqslant .50$).[3] The consecutive stories of Abram's migration and of Abram and Sarai in Egypt form a homogeneous whole, with the exception of vv 2–3, 16.

Von Rad describes vv 1–3 as "a free composition of the J writer" (1966: 67) of key importance in integrating the patriarchal history as a whole with the idea of the settlement (1966: 60; cf. Westermann 1976: 123). A comparison of vv 1–3 with 6–9 does show significant difference (df 1; 4 syllable words, $p \leqslant .005$). Nevertheless, a comparison of vv 1/2–3, according to Fisher's exact test for four syllable words, also demonstrates difference ($p \leqslant .05$). These results go against taking 12: 1–3 as a unit, whether as a composition by the J writer or as a poem (Speiser 1964: 85; Muilenberg 1965: 391). Instead vv 2–3 form an independent unit,[4] reflecting an idea which does not appear elsewhere until Deutero-Isaiah (Winnett 1965: 11).

Furthermore, a comparison of 12: 4b–5/6–9 indicates no difference (df 3, $p \leqslant .98$) and offers no support for separating out vv 4b–5 as P material (Skinner 1910: 242). Noth's analysis of 12: 1–4a, 6–20 as J (1972: 13) cannot be sustained because the comparison 12: 1–4a/6–20 shows significant difference (df 3, $p \leqslant .005$). Noth's J in chap. 12 is not a continuous composition. The first story has a theophany and promise concerning land and descendants (v 7) which appropriately relate to the story's opening (v 1); this promise does not differ from its context (so Wagner 1977: 23), according to the comparison vv 7/6, 8–9 (df 2; 1, 2, 3–6 syllable words, $p \leqslant .80$). According to the syllable-word structure analysis the basic narrative is 12:1, 4–15, 17–20; it contains two complete stories, each with an introduction and a conclusion.

Genesis 16

Noth assigns 16: 1b, 2, 4–8, 11–14 to J and 16: 1a, 3, 15–16 to P, with vv 9, 10 as additions (1972: 17, 28; cf. Skinner 1910: 285). A comparison of 16: 1b, 2, 4– 8/11–14 shows a significant difference (df 3, $p \leqslant .005$). The results go against the unified J narrative in the chapter described by Noth's analysis. Moreover, a comparison of 16: 1–9/10–14/15–16 demonstrates significant difference (df 4; 1, 2, 3–6 syllable words, $p \leqslant .01$). Genesis 16 is not homogeneous. Vv 10–14 are different from vv 1–9 (df 3, $p \leqslant .005$) and from vv 15–16 (df 1; 1–2, 3–6 syllable words, $p \leqslant .05$). The final composition of the story of Hagar has at least two different parts, 16: 1–9, 15–16 and 16: 10–14.

The argument could be made that vv 10–14 are different from the rest of the chapter because vv 11–12 may be a poetic composition within a narrative setting (see, e.g., Speiser's translation 1964: 117). A comparison of vv 10,13–14/11–12 shows no significant difference (df 2; 1, 2, 3–6 syllable words, $p \leqslant .50$). The promise to Hagar as a whole (vv 10–14) stands out in contrast to the rest of the chapter according to the syllable-word structure.[5]

When 16: 10–14 is removed from the Hagar narrative, the original no longer has the threefold repetition of "the angel of the Lord said to her" (16: 9, 10, 11) which had led Van Seters to cut 16: 10 as secondary (1975: 194). In identifying vv 9, 10 as redactional additions Skinner speaks of the threefold repetition as "a fault of style which is in striking contrast to the exquisite artistic form of the original narrative" (1910: 285). The comparison, however, of 16: 1–8/11–14 still shows significant difference (df 3, $p \leqslant .01$). The discontinuity in the narrative at vv 10–14 is not the result simply of either v 9 or v 10.

The conclusion in 16: 15–16 is commonly assigned to P because, as Speiser notes, "vital statistics" are given (1964: 119). Skinner assumes that Hagar never returned but remained in the desert and bore her child there (1910: 285). On the other hand von Rad theorizes that Hagar had meantime returned to Abraham, but that the "ancient unusable conclusion" to the story was lost (1961: 190). Simpson holds that the original J at this point was dropped by Rje because of 21: 8ff (1948: 72). Nevertheless a comparison of 16: 1–9/15–16 indicates no difference (df 3, $p \leqslant .70$). Moreover the usual assignment of vv 1a, 3, 15–16 to P is not corroborated by the comparison of 16: 1a, 3, 15–16/1b, 2, 4–8 in which no difference may be concluded (df 3, $p \leqslant .20$). The assumption of continuity of the narratives is to be maintained: Hagar heeded the angel's instruction to return to her mistress (v 9), as she was able to do because she had not been sent away. Then Hagar bore Abram a son, who named him Ishmael (vv 15–16).

Genesis 20

The supposed doublet of 12: 10–20 appears in Gen 20: 1–18. The story, however, ends with v 14, according to the conclusion of significant difference from the comparison of 20: 1–14/15–18 (df 3, $p \leqslant .005$). Although v 18 is not infrequently designated as secondary, the comparison of 20: 1–14/15–17 still shows significant difference (df 3, $p \leqslant .001$). This result is not contrary to the special information about infertility in vv 17–18, information which does not follow from the death threat to Abimelech in v 7. For example, Simpson assigns 20: 17 to E2 as secondary and finds v 18 to be a gloss on v 17. He also cuts out "for he is a prophet, and he will pray for you" in v 7 as secondary (1948: 80). The syllable-word structure analysis, however, separates vv 15–17, 18 as different. The principal narrative in 20: 1–14 is homogeneous according to the comparison 20: 1–5/6–9/10–14 (df 6, $p \leqslant .90$).

Genesis 21: 1–21

The second story of Hagar is found in 21: 6, 8–20 (Noth 1972: 35). A comparison, however, of vv 6, 8–16/17–18/19–20 indicates significant internal difference (df 2; 1 syllable words, $p \leqslant .02$). Subsequent analysis shows that vv 17–18 are different[6] from vv 6, 8–16 (df 2; 1, 2, 3–6 syllable words, $p \leqslant .05$) and from vv 19–21 (df 1; 1 syllable words, $p \leqslant .01$). Moreover, there is no indication that the introduction to the story in vv 1–5, 7 is at all different, according to the comparison of vv 1–5, 7/6, 8–16 (df 3, $p \leqslant .90$). Thus when vv

17–18 are omitted in an analysis of the whole Hagar narrative, the text is homogeneous: 21: 1–4/5–8/9–12/13–16/19–21 (df 4; 1 syllable words, $p \leqslant .80$). The promise to make the lad a great nation (vv 17–18) differs from the homogeneous narrative of 21: 1–16, 19–21.

Genesis 22

The testing of Abraham in chap. 22 is a continuous narrative according to the comparison of 22: 1–3/4–7/8–11/12–15/16–19 (df 12, $p \leqslant .90$). On the other hand, 22: 1–19/20–24 shows a significant difference (df 1; 2 syllable words, $p \leqslant .025$). The details of Nahor's children are not integral to the preceding story, and may be separated, following a common source division (e.g., Noth 1972: 29).

A major critical question concerning the unity of the testing narrative centers on vv 15–18, commonly held to be secondary (e.g., Noth 1972: 35). A comparison of 22: 1–14/15–18 indicates no difference (df 3, $p \leqslant .80$). The narrative is homogeneous, which is to be expected according to arguments proposed by Coats for the unity of the story (1973: 395–98). Van Seters also finds vv 15–18 integral to the narrative: without them the story comes to no real consequence. The ultimate aim of the test of Abraham is that because of his obedience his children will be blessed (1975: 239). The principal narrative unit is 22: 1–19.

Chapter Comparisons

When Gen 12: 1, 4–15, 17–20 is compared to 20: 1–14, significant difference is evident (df 3, $p \leqslant .02$). This result is not unexpected and corroborates the existence of a doublet where the role of J and E has long been postulated.[7] Since the particular features of language under study here must be assumed to be the result of unconscious choice, the syllable-word structure analysis is independent evidence for the thesis of differences between the parallel stories. Syllable-word patterns operate at a lower level in the language than such phenomena as word choices, patterns of rhetoric, and styles of composition and narrative flow, which are among the usual criteria for literary analysis. Thus syllable-word structure analysis using inferential statistics would seem to be a prior task in the complex effort to describe the formation of the Genesis narratives.

Because Genesis 12 and 16 are commonly considered J material, they are compared. There is no significant difference for 12: 1, 4–15, 17–20/16: 1–9, 15–16 (df 3, $p \leqslant .70$). Although the statistical tests used cannot show common origin, the lack of difference and the assumption of narrative unity allow for a continuous J narrative, an expected result. Whether or not, however, this longer narrative piece is the product of the traditional J as an author cannot be asserted from this limited view of Genesis. Even Genesis 12–23, let alone all of Genesis, must be further analyzed.

Unexpectedly the other proposed doublet story being examined does not receive confirmation as a doublet. The comparison 16: 1–9, 15–16/21: 1–16, 19–21 indicates no difference (df 3, $p \leqslant .95$). Similarly the multiple comparison 12: 1, 4– 15, 17–20/16: 1–9, 15–16/21: 1–16, 19–21 shows no difference (df 6, $p \leqslant .80$). The assumption of unity is not denied by the tests based on syllable-word data. Let us examine the Hagar stories from the point of view of their having been written by one author.

Contrary to Noth's judgment that the two Hagar stories are "the most striking examples of duplicate narratives" (1972: 249 n. 646), the stories differ (Van Seters 1975: 199). The first story concerns Hagar's flight to avoid Sarai's jealousy and the harsh treatment precipitated by Hagar's pregnancy. The second story describes the conflict concerning an heir which arises after Isaac's weaning. Hagar and Ishmael are expelled to the wilderness. The two stories follow one another in the chronology of the story line. Scholars seem to have assumed the stories are doublets too easily, perhaps because of the prior decision that the stories are from two sources according to the divine name criterion and the use of *ʾamâ*.

If the decision is made that the two stories are doublets, then 16: 9 is problematic in relation to the second story (Simpson 1948: 71). If, however, the two stories are seen as parts of one Hagar-Ishmael narrative, then there is no problem with 16: 9. In a similar way the prior decision to designate 16: 15–16 as P raises the question of what the outcome of the first story was, as noted above. Syllable-word structure analysis suggests a homogeneous, continuous narrative.

Van Seters holds that because chap. 21 shows a knowledge of chap. 16 (the son of a slave girl could never challenge the rights of the son of the principal wife), chap. 21 is a dependent variant of chap. 16 (1975: 197). He also has the second author placing chap. 21 at a point of time later than chap. 16 (1975: 198). Hence an independent variant. The arguments, however, work just as well for a continuous narrative, which is allowed by the homogeneity of the syllable-word structure of 12: 1, 4–15, 17–20; 16: 1–9, 15–16; 21: 1–16, 19–21. Chap. 21 knows chap. 16 because it is the continuation of chap. 16. Chap. 21 comes after chap. 16 in time because that is the actual story line.

Two difficulties seem to stand in the way of recognizing a continuous narrative in chaps. 12, 16, and 21: patterns of the divine names, and the use of *ʾamâ* and *šipḥâ*. Uncertainties over the divine name criterion are not unusual. For example, in chap. 22 the use of both Elohim (vv 1, 3, 8, 9, 12) and Jahweh (vv 11,14,15) should encourage seeking alternatives to the criterion. Speiser argues that "it is possible that a hand which had nothing to do with E (conceivably even from the P school) miswrote Elohim for Jahweh in the few instances involved, sometime in the long course of written transmission" (1964: 166). Also the use of *ʾamâ* and *šipḥâ* is not clearcut, as Jenks cautions (1977: 69–70; against Jepsen 1958). For example, *ʾamâ* is used at 20: 17 and *šipḥâ* at 20: 14. Van Seters points also to the mixed usage in Genesis 30 where the source division is doubtful (1975: 202). The terms are also mixed in the Book of the Covenant, *ʾamâ* at Exod 21: 7, 27, 32 and *šipḥâ* at Exod 21: 20, 26.

Perhaps the mixing of divine names and of *ʾamâ* and *šipḥâ* had its beginnings in the several additions to the primary narratives. For example, 12: 16, an addition, has *šipḥâ*. Perhaps the redactor changed the term also in chap. 16 when the two parts of the narrative once stood in closer proximity, although he did not do so in chap. 21, which may have already become separated from the other parts of the narrative. In chap. 21 the addition at vv 17–18 uses Elohim three times. Did the redactor who made the addition also change to Elohim elsewhere in chap. 21? Later redactors and transmitters would then tend to cluster Elohim in that section of the growing collection of narratives.

Still another suggestion is that the writer of the homogeneous narratives in chaps. 12, 16, 21 actually wrote the material as we have it in a thoroughgoing way, since the material exhibits the unconscious syllable-word choices of an author. The narrative is actually written in an author's own 'style,' as it can be viewed by syllables and words. This author, however, was not creating new stories; in the writing of each story the author reflected some of the overt stylistic peculiarities of the different sources of the stories. At the surface level, moving from story to story, the writer could not abandon the sources' stylistics of divine names and other word choices, etc., but at the unconscious level the writer wrote in the individual pattern of choices uncovered by syllable-word structure analysis. The question is admittedly a difficult one. Perhaps the extension of syllable-word structure analysis to the rest of Genesis will give further assistance.

If the materials usually designated as E are considered as a group, each is found to be different from the other as the following comparisons demonstrate: 20: 1–14/21: 1–16, 19–21 (df 2; 1, 2–3, 4–6 syllable words, $p \leq .05$), 20: 1–14/22: 1–19 (df 1; 1 syllable words, $p \leq .05$) and 21: 1–16, 19–21/22: 1–19 (df 1; 4 syllable words, $p \leq .05$). These stories, if an E supplement (Winnett 1965: 6), are in reality a collection, each story written in its present form by a different author.

If, as Jenks holds, these chapters are the product of a school, the "carefully unified and systematic presentations of Israel's patriarchal traditions" (1977: 19, 26; against Noth 1972: 228 n. 601), then the syllable-word structure analysis shows different authors within the school. The unconscious choices of syllables and words are personal, not related to the geographical or cultural provenance of the school or to the date of composition. The individual independent units can be separated from each other even if there is a similarity of overt literary style and a common theological orientation.

If, as discussed above, the stories in chaps. 12, 16, 21 form a continuous narrative, they may be compared to the independent narratives of Genesis 20, 22. Significant difference is demonstrated for the following comparisons: narrative/20: 1–14/22: 1–19 (df 6, $p \leq .02$), narrative/20: 1–14 (df 3, $p \leq .02$), and narrative/22: 1–19 (df 1; 4 syllable word, $p \leq .01$).

Because Genesis 12–23 is principally narrative, changes in the character of the material cannot be held to be the cause of the variations in statistics. Radday has suggested, however, that there are differences between narration and direct discourse in large blocks of material in Genesis.[8] Attention to the three speeches in Gen 12: 1–3, 11–13, 18–19 shows that the first speech differs from the other two (df 1; 1–2, 3–6 syllable words, $p \leq .05$). In the same way the two speeches in 16: 5–6, 8–12 differ from each other (df 1; 1–2, 3–6 syllable words, $p \leq .005$). Thus direct discourse does not seem to provide in itself a type of configuration of words of various lengths. Each speech must be examined for homogeneity and then compared to its own narrative context. The studies above show that some discourse is different from and some is homogeneous with the narrative context.

Freedman has long urged the importance of syllable counts for describing the meter of poetry, more recently as providing a guide to the poetic structure.[9] Syllable counts are also useful for syllable-word structure analyses which uncover a homogeneous narrative in 12: 1, 4–15, 17–20; 16: 1–9, 15–16; 21: 1–16, 19–21, with two mutually independent stories in 20: 1–14 and 22: 1–19. To these principal narratives a number of fragmentary additions were made: 12: 2–3; 12: 16; 16: 10–14; 20: 15–17, 18; 21: 17–18; and 22: 20–24. These analyses, a first step, elucidate the shape of the final, written compositions in Genesis 12–23.

Notes

1. For example, see Radday (1973), Radday and Wickman (1975), Radday and Shore (1977), Radday et al. (1977), Andersen (1976), Bee (1973; 1978; 1979), Deist (1977), and Parunak (1978; 1979; 1980).

2. For the debate over chap. 22, see Coats (1973: 396 n.7). Additional positions include Noth, special E (1972: 114); Speiser, J (1964: 166); Van Seters, J (1975: 230); and Jenks, E (1977: 26).

3. Koch argues against dividing 12: 1–9, 10–20 into two sources because such a division "does not take into consideration J's custom of gathering together and combining different material" (1969: 130).

4. So Kilian 1966: 1–15. Simpson assigns vv 2–3a to his J2 because the material anticipates the "concrete promise" of v 7 and is an elaboration of the simpler narrative of J1 (1948: 69).

5. Wagner finds that 16: 10–14 represents a recasting, utilizing material from chap. 21, by a pro-Yahwist. For example, the well in 16: 14 makes perfect sense if chap. 21 is known (1967: 232; 1977: 24).

6. See Dion's discussion of a later literary form (1967).

7. See the extended form critical discussion by Koch (1969: 111–32).

8. Personal communication, 3/17/81. Specification of details must await the publication of Radday's extensive statistical linguistic analysis of Genesis after the model of his earlier studies.

9. Andersen and Freedman (1980: 77); Freedman (1977: 11–15). See also Cross and Freedman (1975), Freedman (1972). Freedman (1977: 11 n.14, 13 n.16–17) lists additional articles.

References

Andersen, F. I.
1976 Style and Authorship. *Tyndale Paper* 21/2: 1–44.

Andersen, F. I., and Freedman, D. N.
1980 *Hosea*. Anchor Bible 24. Garden City: Doubleday.

Bee, R.
1973 The Use of Statistical Methods in Old Testament Studies. *Vetus Testamentum* 23: 257–72.
1978 The Mode of Composition and Statistical Scansion. *Journal for the Study of the Old Testament* 6: 58–68.
1979 An Empirical Dating Procedure for Old Testament Prophecy. *Journal for the Study of the Old Testament* 11: 23–35.

Coats, G. W.
1973 Abraham's Sacrifice of Faith. *Interpretation* 27: 389–400.

Craghan, J. F.
1977 The Elohist in Recent Literature. *Biblical Theology Bulletin* 7: 23–35.

Cross, F. M., Jr., and Freedman, D. N.
1975 *Studies in Ancient Yahwistic Poetry*. SBL Dissertation Series 21. Missoula: Scholars. Originally 1950.

Deist, F.
1977 Stilvergleichung als literarkritisches Verfahren. *Zeitschrift für die Alttestamentliche Wissenschaft* 89: 325–57.

Dion, H. M.
1967 The Patriarchal Traditions and the Literary Form of the "Oracle of Salvation." *Catholic Biblical Quarterly* 29: 198–206.

Freedman, D. N.
1972 Prolegomenon. Pp. VII-LVI in G. B. Gray, *The Forms of Hebrew Poetry* New York: KTAV.
1977 Pottery, Poetry, and Prophecy: An Essay on Biblical Poetry. *Journal of Biblical Literature* 96: 5–26.

Houk, C. B.

1978 Psalm 132, Literary Integrity, and Syllable-Word Structures. *Journal for the Study of the Old Testament* 6: 41–48, 54–57.

1979 Syllables and Psalms: A Statistical Linguistic Analysis. *Journal for the Study of the Old Testament* 14: 55–62.

1981 A Statistical Linguistic Study of Ezekiel 1: 4–3: 11. *Zeitschrift für die Alttestamentliche Wissenschaft* 93: 76–84.

Jenks, A. W.

1977 *The Elohist and North Israelite Traditions.* SBL Monograph Series 22. Missoula: Scholars.

Jepsen, A.

1958 Ama^h und Schiphcha^h. *Vetus Testamentum* 8: 293–97.

Kilian, R.

1966 *Die vorpriesterliche Abrahamsüberlieferungen, literarkritisch und traditionsgeschichtliche untersucht.* Bonn: Hanstein.

Koch, K.

1969 *The Growth of the Biblical Tradition.* Trans. S. Cupitt. New York: Scribner's. Originally 1967^2.

Muilenburg, J.

1965 Abraham and the Nations. *Interpretation* 19: 387–98.

Noth, M.

1972 *A History of Pentateuchal Traditions.* Trans. B. Anderson. Englewood Cliffs: Prentice Hall. Originally 1948.

Parunak, H. V. D.

1978 *Structural Studies in Ezekiel.* Harvard Dissertation.

1979 *Linguistic Density Plots in Zechariah.* The Computer Bible 20. Wooster: Biblical Research Associates.

1980 The Literary Architecture of Ezekiel's Marʾôt ʾĔlōhîm. *Journal of Biblical Literature* 99: 61–74.

von Rad, G.

1961 *Genesis.* Trans. J. Marks. Philadelphia: Westminster. Originally 1956.

1966 *The Problem of the Hexateuch.* Trans. E. Dicken. New York: McGraw-Hill. Originally 1938.

Radday, Y. T.

1973 *The Unity of Isaiah in the Light of Statistical Linguistics.* Gerstenberg: Hildesheim.

Radday, Y. T., and Wickman, D.

1975 The Unity of Zechariah Examined in the Light of Statistical Linguistics. *Zeitschrift für die Alttestamentliche Wissenschaft* 87: 30–55.

Radday, Y. T., and Shore, H.

1977 An Inquiry into the Homogeneity of the Book of Judges by Means of Discriminant Analysis. *Linguistica Biblica* 41/42: 21–34.

Radday, Y. T. et al.

1977 The Book of Judges Examined by Statistical Linguistics. *Biblica* 58: 469–99.

Simpson, C. A.

1948 *The Early Traditions of Israel.* Oxford: Blackwell.

Skinner, J.

1910 *Genesis.* International Critical Commentary. New York: Scribners'.

Speiser, E. A.

1964 *Genesis.* Anchor Bible 1. Garden City: Doubleday.

Van Seters, J.

1975 *Abraham in History and Tradition.* New Haven: Yale University.

Wagner, N. E.
1967 Pentateuchal Criticism: No Clear Future. *Canadian Journal of Theology* 13: 225–32.
1977 A Response of Professor Rolf Rendtorff. *Journal for the Study of the Old Testament* 3: 20–27.

Westermann, C.
1976 *The Promises to the Fathers*. Trans. D. Green. Philadelphia: Fortress. Originally 1976.

Winnett, F. V.
1965 Re-examining the Foundations. *Journal of Biblical Literature* 84: 1–19.

Abraham and David in the Theology of the Yahwist

Jack R. Lundbom
Yale Divinity School, New Haven, Connecticut

Just over a century ago Julius Wellhausen published his *Geschichte Israels* I (1878) which had such enormous influence upon Old Testament studies. This influence has of course waxed and waned, and Wellhausen's particular type of literary criticism (now "source criticism") has given way to other methods such as form criticism, traditio-historical criticism, and rhetorical criticism. Nevertheless, certain assumptions made by him about the composition of the Pentateuch and about how it relates to later material in the Old Testament, notably Samuel and Kings, are as valid today as they were a century ago and remain the foundation for all future work.

We are still committed, for example, to the idea that certain materials in the primeval and patriarchal histories of Genesis were written and edited by someone preferring the divine name Yahweh, for which reason we call him the Yahwist. This Yahwist adapts traditions from outside Israel (Genesis 2–11) and makes use also of indigenous traditions originating in northern Israel (Jacob and Joseph stories in Gen 25: 19–50: 26), but is himself oriented towards the south, where Abraham looms large in traditions surviving around Hebron (Gen 12: 1–25: 18) and David is the recent figure of prominence from Jerusalem. The Yahwist does his writing in Jerusalem from the perspective of the United Monarchy. His audience is Israel in the 10th century B.C., most probably the generation living during the early reign of Solomon (von Rad 1966a: 69; Wolff 1966: 135–36) which includes among its number some who retain a living memory of David. A date of 950 B.C. is about right. This is a time of high literary culture and international vision—an "enlightenment" to quote von Rad (1966b: 203). The current focus of the Yahwist, however, is not upon Solomon but upon David.

Wellhausen also argued that a literary work about antiquity is a primary source only for the historical situation out of which it arose. For the time about which it gives information it is but a secondary source. Wellhausen said the following about the patriarchal narratives in Genesis 12–50:

> It is true, we attain to no historical knowledge of the patriarchs, but only of the time when the stories about them arose in the Israelite people; this later age is here unconsciously projected, in its inner and its outward features, into hoar antiquity, and is reflected there like a glorified mirage (1965: 318–19).

Obviously this is an exaggeration. The patriarchal epics—and indeed also the primeval history in Genesis 2–11—are not merely idealized retrojections from the United Monarchy. Their *origins* lie somewhere in "hoar antiquity," though admittedly in much less focused and much less theological form. Having said this, however, we concede at the same time that Wellhausen expounds a valid principle. Yahwistic Genesis is a product of the 10th century and events of the 10th century—

including their interpretation—leave upon the work a decisive mark. The same can be said *mutatis mutandis* about certain modern writings. In George Mendenhall's *The Tenth Generation* (1973) and Norman Gottwald's *The Tribes of Yahweh* (1979) modern sociological and political theory—also social revolutions of the 20th century—control to a large extent the authors' interpretation of the Hebrew Conquest. They likewise become a primary source only for the age of their composition (20th century A.D.) and a secondary source for the period about which they give information (13th century B.C.).

From the early Solomonic era comes another important biblical document. I refer to the so-called Court History of David (2 Samuel 7, 9–20; 1 Kings 1–2), or as some prefer to call it, the Succession Document (Eissfeldt 1965: 137–39; Ellis 1968: 77–85). This work has been discussed thoroughly by von Rad (1966b) who builds on an earlier study by Rost. The Court History seems to have been composed shortly after the events themselves took place (Freedman 1962: 726), making it the earliest specimen of historical writing in ancient Israel (von Rad 1966b: 176; Jackson 1965: 183). This document in all likelihood was accessible to the Yahwist, in which case it could have influenced him in his writings about antiquity. Working from this assumption Walter Brueggemann (1968) attempted a few years ago to show that the Yahwist's compilation of Genesis 2–11 was dependent upon a sequence of events in the Court History. But this effort was in my opinion only partly successful.[1] What appears to be much clearer is that events described in the Court History served rather as a catalyst for the Yahwist in the recall, the shaping, and the preservation of traditions about the patriarchs (Genesis 12–50). That is, traditions we possess about Abraham were determined to some extent by things happening later to David, and the theological importance of both finds its common source in the mind of the Yahwist. Professor Freedman has shown very well how the unconditional covenant given to Abraham (Genesis 12: 1–3; 15) parallels the unconditional covenant given to David (2 Samuel 7; Freedman 1962: 714–15; 1964: 13).

In the present essay we shall narrow the focus to the two passages linking together the primeval and patriarchal histories, viz., the Tower of Babel story (Gen 11: 1–9) and the Call of Abraham (Gen 12: 1–3); and the chapter we believe to be the beginning of the Court History, viz., 2 Samuel 7.[2] Our thesis is that 2 Samuel 7—with its message about what kind of house Yahweh really wants—provides the Yahwist with just the inspiration he needs to complete the transition from primeval to patriarchal history. It leads him to juxtapose the Tower of Babel story and the Call of Abraham, and in doing so he is able to render a theological judgment about "hoar antiquity" that comes very close to being the same as one already contained in the Court History. The net result is to strengthen the link he intends between David and Abraham and to undergird at the same time those covenants given by Yahweh to each of them.

The Babel story and the Call of Abraham are both from the Yahwist's hand (Carpenter-Battersby 1900: 17–19). The former was at his disposal and the latter was perhaps composed by him *de novo* and not a piece of fixed tradition (von Rad 1966a: 67 following Gunkel; Zimmerli 1963: 91). The Yahwist is credited also with the basic editorial work, i.e., he juxtaposed the passages prior to the time when the Priestly genealogies of 11: 10–27 were inserted (von Rad 1961: 150).

It has long been recognized that the Yahwist's editorial work contributes greatly to his theological purpose. Von Rad has shown how the primeval history as a whole contains a sin / punishment / grace cycle which then makes 12: 1–3 its proper end. After sin and punishment at Babel Yahweh shows his grace anew to Abraham (von Rad 1962: 163–64; 1966a: 65). And the universal elements in each passage combine to give theological importance to all history. Whereas the judgment at Babel results in the scattering of people over the whole earth (11: 9), the blessing to Abraham is to be for "all the families of the earth" (12: 3). The Yahwist has yet another point to make. While the men of Babel seek for themselves a name, in Abraham's case Yahweh gives the name (von Rad 1961: 155; Wolff 1966: 141–42). In Gen 11: 4 the men say: "And let us *make* for ourselves a *name*." But in Gen 12: 2 Yahweh says to Abraham: "And I will *make* of you a great nation, and I will bless you, and I will make great your *name*."

The Yahwist here creates in his editorial work a dialectic similar to one contained in the Babel story itself. Rashi (1970: 38–39) and Herder (1833: 203–4) both observed long ago that at Babel Yahweh deliberately imitates the men's resolves. Whereas they say: "*Come let us* make bricks. . . . *Come let us* build ourselves a city and a tower . . . "(11: 3–4), Yahweh says: "*Come let us* go down and there confuse their language . . ." (11: 7). The purposed ascent of man and the descent of God are "placed silently side by side," says Herder. So we see here how the Yahwist in his editorial work duplicates theology contained in the very material he makes use of. This same technique is used in editorial work done within the book of Jeremiah (Lundbom 1975: 32).

But in the transition from primeval to patriarchal history the references to "making a name" function to contrast in a subtle way the hubris at Babel with God's graciousness to Abraham and subsequent humanity. Yahweh is also seen to be a God who seizes the initiative. But the real key to the Yahwist's mind is found by observing a play here on words. "Making a name" means one thing in 11: 4 but quite another in 12: 2. In the Babel story men seek a name by erecting a city within which there is a religious temple.[3] Some have thought the latter structure to be a ziggurat of the type built by Nabopolassar and Nebuchadnezzar in the 7th-6th centuries B.C., but Speiser (1964: 75–76) contends the reference is rather to a more ancient structure such as we have described for us in *Enuma elish* VI, 60–66 (cf. ANET 68–69). At any rate the word "tower," found in most English translations (RSV, NEB, JB, NAB), is misleading. The reference is to a religious temple. Abraham, however, will achieve his name by having a myriad of descendants. These will become a great nation which no doubt is what the men of Babel are also striving for as they set out to build their city.[4]

With this play on words the Yahwist makes his main point. He wants above all to contrast descendants on the one hand with imposing structures on the other. We can refine this a bit more. If we take 2 Samuel 7 as the passage providing primary inspiration for the Yahwist, we find out there that Yahweh is averse not to structures in general but to temples in particular, especially temples of a pretentious sort.

2 Samuel 7 in its present form betrays (in v 13 at least) work of a later editor who seeks to harmonize the original promise to David with 1 Kings 8. Solomon, after all, did finally build Yahweh a temple. Yet despite the editing there is in v 9 the promise of a "great name" to David; also in David's prayer we find a request for Yahweh's "blessing" (v 29). Both reinforce the connection between David and Abraham. David

is chosen for greatness just as Abraham was. Also, David fulfills the promise of Gen 12: 1–3, making him Abraham's spiritual son. More importantly, the editing does nothing to obscure the main point of the chapter: whereas David wants to build Yahweh a house, Yahweh says he will instead build a house for David (S. R. Driver 1966: 275–76; Hertzberg 1964: 283). Again Yahweh seizes the initiative. And here a word-play on *byt,* "house," brings home the basic theological affirmation. David has in mind a house of stone and cedar, i.e., a lavish temple, but Yahweh is thinking of a house of royal descendants.

So the Yahwist's thrust in Genesis 11–12 is basically the same as 2 Samuel 7. Yahweh rejects temples planned by ambitious individuals. Instead he initiates work on a structure of his own choosing, which in each case is a line of perpetual descendants.

Writing then in the early part of Solomon's reign the Yahwist intends, we believe, a quiet protest against the building of a temple. We know from his work elsewhere that he tends to be less than direct. Von Rad, writing about the patriarchal traditions, says:

> In these stories we are not confronted with an account of the history which furnishes the reader with explicit theological judgments, or which constantly allows him to participate in extensive theological reflexion upon the history, as the Deuteronomistic account does. In the stories of the patriarchs the reader will look in vain for any formulation of the narrator's own theological judgment. This being the case, there is more prospect of success in attempting to arrive at an indirect understanding of the narrator and his opinion (1962: 165).

We must not, however, attribute the Yahwist's indirectness only to his style. There are political reasons for what he does. The temple is perhaps already under construction and public sentiment is behind it. Thus he cannot be any more explicit in his criticism.

What we are saying then is that the Yahwist is anti-temple. This squares with von Rad's view that the Yahwist is not concerned about the cult but interested rather in Yahweh's activity in history (1966a: 71). But it challenges von Rad's notion that the Yahwist has sympathies with the Settlement tradition. According to him it was the Yahwist who integrated the patriarchal history with the idea of the Settlement (1966a: 60). Of course von Rad also believed that the Settlement recorded in Joshua constituted the "proper end" of what he thought was a "Hexateuch," but Noth (1972: 6) has convincingly shown that a Hexateuch as such never existed. Instead Deuteronomy begins a separate history which extends through the end of 2 Kings. It is the Deuteronomic School, as von Rad also knows well enough, that puts the emphasis on the Settlement (1966c). But even so the "rest" which the Settlement makes possible is controlled always by the Mosaic Covenant, which is conditional in nature. Israel must obey the commandments if this covenant is to remain in force (Freedman 1964). If it does not, the land will be lost (Deuteronomy 28).

Thus I am inclined to see in the Yahwist more of a "pilgrim mentality." This explains why he is so interested in recovering the traditions of the patriarchs. Also when the Yahwist looks at the Court History he can find ample evidence for his thesis that Abraham and David both journey like pilgrims through history. The Court History makes no attempt to hide the fact that rest in the land is a prelude to trouble, while salvation comes to the one who trusts the Lord of History. It was after Yahweh had given David rest from all his enemies round about (2 Sam 7: 1) that David decided to build Yahweh a permanent resting place, and as we know Yahweh turned that plan down. From the Court History we learn too that only after David is settled well enough in Jerusalem so he can remain there while Joab and others go out to fight the spring battle with the Ammonites (2 Sam 11: 1) is he led straightaway into trouble with Bathsheba, the wife of Uriah the Hittite. Finally, David is forced into being a pilgrim in the wilderness when his son Absalom moves to overthrow him (2 Samuel 15–18), which teaches him again that kingship—at least his—is tied not to settlement in the land but to Yahweh's deliverance in history.

The Yahwist then is not pro-Settlement nor is he even mildly concerned about Settlement traditions current in the 10th century. As far as he is concerned Yahweh would rather that revelation be kept in the sphere of historical events where people are the important thing and continuity through the generations counts for more than continuity with the land. It is in support of this theology that the Yahwist labors. He shows that both Abraham and David are brought into covenant after Yahweh rejects permanent places of worship. Temples signify divine settlement—indeed permanent divine settlement, as Jeremiah found out later to his utter dismay (Jer 7: 1–15).

Jeremiah in his famous Temple Sermon (Jeremiah 7; 26) is not the only prophet to speak in opposition to the temple. According to Hanson (1975: 161–86) that nameless prophet of the exile speaking for the disenfranchised in Second Isaiah is concerned not at all about a temple. The tradition lives on in Jesus, who, in speaking to his disciples (Mark 13: 1–2) and also to the Samaritan woman (John 4: 21–24), points beyond the temple to the true locus of worship. Elsewhere in the New Testament 1 Pet 2: 4–10 describes Jesus as a "living stone" and the church as more "living stones . . . built into a spiritual house." Finally, Rev 21: 22 teaches that the New Jerusalem will have no need of a temple, for its temple will be Yahweh God the Almighty and the Lamb.

Notes

1. Of the four parallels which Brueggemann sets up, only the first two, viz., David and Bathsheba // Adam and Eve; and Amnon and Absalom // Cain and Abel are likely to have been consciously made by the Yahwist. The rebellion of Absalom makes for a weak comparison with Noah and the Flood. And the fourth parallel of Solomon // Tower of Babel turns out to be no parallel at all because Solomon's building activities, his subsequent prosperity, and the final disintegration of his rule—all of which contribute to the alleged parallel—come not in the Court History but in 1 Kings 5ff. Brueggemann indicates early on (p. 159) that he is using only 1 Kings 1–2, but before he is through he has gone far beyond that point. According to von Rad (1962: 164) and Fohrer (1968: 88) the Yahwist inherited a fixed cosmological scheme long in existence. At the same time he may well have fashioned his superb account of the Fall (Genesis 3) with David and Bathsheba in mind. The Cain and Abel story has affinities with the story of Amnon and Absalom because both recount brotherly rivalries, yet the almost opposite characters of Amnon and Abel argue more for discontinuity than continuity in this parallel.

2. The beginning of the Court History is, of course, much in dispute. For the various views see Eissfeldt (1965: 137–38). The inclusion of chap. 7 is essential, in my opinion, because without the promise about David's house of royal descendants the whole struggle of succession—which is what the Court History is all about—loses all significance and 1 Kings 1–2 has no climactic value whatsoever.

3. Gunkel's source analysis of the passage (1966: 92ff), in which he proposed two original accounts, a city recension (*Stadtrezension*) and a tower recension (*Turmbaurezension*), is no longer taken seriously. One of the most obvious problems with this view is that the phrase "Let us make for ourselves a name" is placed in the city recension. Even von Rad, who is sympathetic to this view (1961: 146), recognizes that the tower (not the city) is what symbolizes the men's will to fame (1961: 144). Cassuto (1964: 235–38) is no doubt correct when he says that the city and the tower were meant to be together from the beginning.

4. Professor Freedman is to be given credit for this observation.

References

Brueggemann, W.
1968 David and His Theologian. *Catholic Biblical Quarterly* 30: 156–81.

Carpenter, J. E., and Harford-Battersby, G.
1900 *The Hexateuch.* Vol. II. London: Longmans, Green & Co.

Cassuto, U.
1964 *A Commentary on the Book of Genesis.* Vol. II. Jerusalem: Magnes.

Driver, S. R.
1966 *Notes on the Hebrew Text and the Topography of the Books of Samuel*[2]. Oxford: Clarendon. Originally 1913.

Eissfeldt, O.
1965 *The Old Testament: An Introduction.* Trans. P. R. Ackroyd. New York: Harper & Row.

Ellis, P. F.
1968 *The Yahwist: The Bible's First Theologian.* Notre Dame, Indiana: Fides.

Fohrer, G.
1968 *Introduction to the Old Testament.* Trans. David E. Green. New York: Abingdon.

Freedman, D. N.
1962 Pentateuch. Vol. 3, pp. 711–27 in *Interpreter's Dictionary of the Bible,* ed. George A. Buttrick. New York: Abingdon.
1964 Divine Commitment and Human Obligation. *Interpretation* 18: 3–15.

Gottwald, N. K.
1979 *The Tribes of Yahweh.* Maryknoll, New York: Orbis.

Gunkel, H.
1966 *Genesis*[7]. Göttingen: Vandenhoeck & Ruprecht.

Hanson, P. D.
1975 *The Dawn of Apocalyptic.* Philadelphia: Fortress.

Herder, J. G.
1833 *The Spirit of Hebrew Poetry.* Vol. I. Trans. James Marsh. Burlington: Edward Smith.

Hertzberg, H. W.
1964 *I & II Samuel.* Trans. J. S. Bowden. Philadelphia: Westminster.

Jackson, J. J.
1965 David's Throne: Patterns in the Succession Story. *Canadian Journal of Theology* 11: 183–95.

Lundbom, J. R.
1975 *Jeremiah: A Study in Ancient Hebrew Rhetoric.* SBL Dissertation Series, 18. Missoula: Society of Biblical Literature and Scholars Press.

Mendenhall, G. E.
1973 *The Tenth Generation.* Baltimore: Johns Hopkins.

Noth, M.
1972 *A History of Pentateuchal Traditions.* Trans. Bernhard W. Anderson. Englewood Cliffs, New Jersey: Prentice-Hall.

von Rad, G.
1961 *Genesis.* Trans. John H. Marks. Philadelphia: Westminster.
1962 *Old Testament Theology.* Vol. I. Trans. D. M. G. Stalker. London: Oliver & Boyd.
1966a The Form-Critical Problem of the Hexateuch. Pp. 1–78 in *The Problem of the Hexateuch and Other Essays.* Trans. E. W. Trueman-Dicken. New York: McGraw-Hill.
1966b The Beginnings of Historical Writing in Ancient Israel. Pp. 166–204 in *The Problem of the Hexateuch and Other Essays.*
1966c There Remains Still a Rest for the People of God. Pp. 94–102 in *The Problem of the Hexateuch and Other Essays.*

Rashi
1970 *Rashi—Commentaries on the Pentateuch.* Sel. and trans. Chaim Pearl. New York: Viking.

Speiser, E. A.
1964 *Genesis.* Anchor Bible 1. Garden City, New York: Doubleday & Co.

Wellhausen, J.
1965 *Prolegomena to the History of Ancient Israel.* Trans. J. S. Black and A. Menzies. New York: World. Originally 1883.

Wolff, H. W.
1966 The Kerygma of the Yahwist. Trans. Wilbur A. Benware. *Interpretation* 20: 131–58.

Zimmerli, W.
1963 Promise and Fulfillment. Trans. James Wharton. Pp. 89–122 in *Essays on Old Testament Hermeneutics,* ed. Claus Westermann. Richmond: John Knox.

The Two Pericopes on the Purification Offering

Jacob Milgrom
University of California, Berkeley, California

Lev 4: 13–21 and Num 15: 22–31 seem to deal with the same issue: the inadvertent wrong of the entire community which is expiable by sacrifice. However, they are not identical. On the one hand, the sacrifices are not the same: Leviticus 4 requires a bull for a *ḥaṭṭā't*, purification offering (Milgrom 1971), whereas Numbers 15 requires a bull for an *ʿōlâ*, whole offering, and a male goat for a purification offering (and appropriate supplements for the whole offering). On the other hand, the nature of the sin is not the same: in Leviticus 4 the sin is the inadvertent violation of a prohibitive commandment (v 13, cf. vv 2, 22, 27), whereas in Numbers 15 the sin is the inadvertent violation of any commandment (vv 22–23). These differences lead Ibn Ezra (on Num 15: 27) to postulate that these ostensibly similar laws are in reality dealing with two different sins: Leviticus 4 with violation of a prohibitive commandment (*lō' taʿăśeh*) and Numbers 15 with violation of a performative commandment (*ʿăśēh*); for this reason, different expiatory sacrifices are required. Thus if the community inadvertently violated the Passover by mistakenly celebrating it on the wrong day, they would have brought the purification offering of Leviticus 4 for violating the prohibition against eating leaven during the festival (Exod 12: 15) and would have brought the required sacrifices of Numbers 15 for neglecting to perform the Passover sacrifice on the proper day (Num 9: 13).

This solution, however, was faulted by Ramban (on Num 15: 22), who noted that the Numbers passage cannot be limited to performative sins alone since the verb *ʿāśâ*, "to do, act," in "If this was done inadvertently" (v 24), "anyone who acts in error" (v 29) and "who acts defiantly" (v 30), predicates an active violation, one that involves actually doing rather than passively neglecting.

Indeed, as noted by *Sepher Hammivḥar* (ad loc.), the language of Numbers 15, *kol hammiṣwot . . . kol 'ăšer ṣiwwâ*, "any of the commandments . . . anything that [the Lord] has enjoined" (vv 22, 23), must be understood literally: the word *kol* embraces all the commandments, positive and negative, performative and prohibitive. Abetting this insight is the recognition that not only this section but indeed the entire chapter emphasizes the totality of the commandments. First, it should be noted that v 22aβ-b, clearly an editorial interpolation, has been added to underscore the fact that all the commandments are involved. It says in effect that sacrificial expiation is required for the violation not only of prohibitive commandments (Leviticus 4) but of all commandments, including performative ones. Second, this section (vv 22–31) contains no heading, thus connecting it with the previous section on *ḥallâ* (vv 17–21). The intent is clear: *ḥallâ* and the sacrificial supplements (in the preceding section, vv 1–16) are positive, performative commandments and are therefore also subject to the prescribed penalties. Finally, the last unit in Numbers 15, on the *ṣîṣit* (vv 37–41), contains the identical emphasis: "you will keep in mind all the commandments of the Lord and observe them" (v 39); "observe all My commandments" (v 40). Here we find the same usage of *ʿāśâ* and *kol miṣwot* as in vv 22, 23. The reason for the inclusion of the *ṣîṣit* ritual in this chapter is now clear: the wearing of the *ṣîṣit*, itself a performative commandment, will be a constant reminder to its wearers of the totality of *all* the commandments, performative as well as prohibitive, thus preventing or at least lessening the chance of inadvertent neglect or violation.

In sum, Num 15: 22–31 emphasizes that all inadvertencies are subject to sacrificial expiation, and the attachment of these verses to other performative commandments which make up this chapter, i.e., sacrificial supplements (vv 1–16), *ḥallâ* (vv 17–21) and *ṣîṣit* (vv 37–41), points to a polemic against the position taken in Leviticus 4: not only prohibitive commandments require sacrificial expiation but also performative ones. Thus one cannot say that Leviticus 4 and Numbers 15 speak of discrete sins which warrant discrete sacrificial solutions. Both require sacrificial expiation for inadvertent violation of prohibitive commandments, and Numbers 15 also requires it for inadvertent violation of performative ones. Clearly, the solution suggesting that the two sections describe different sins does not work. There is an overlap: both speak of the violation of prohibitive commandments; hence, another solution must be sought.

Recently, A. Toeg (1973/4) has proposed that Numbers 15 is in reality a reworking of Leviticus 4. His position, briefly stated, is that the text of Leviticus 4 was shortened by eliminating the sacrificial procedure, then lengthened in order to emphasize elements of inadvertency (vv 25b, 26), the stranger (e.g., v 29), and presumptuousness (vv 30–31) while, at the same time, subjected to a major change: the purification-offering bull became the whole-offering bull, to which the purification goat and the whole-offering bull's supplementary meal and wine were added. Thus "a bull of the herd as a purification offering" (Lev 4: 14) was expanded to "a bull of the herd [as a whole offering of pleasing odor to the Lord, with its proper meal offering and to libation, and one he-goat] as a purification offering" (Num 15: 24).

I would add one important bit of evidence that would support his theory: the sacrificial requirement is governed by the verb *ʿāśâ* "(the community shall) sacrifice" (v 24). The verb *ʿāśâ* is a technical term in the cult which means "to sacrifice," i.e., perform the entire sacrificial ritual (cf. Lev 4: 20; 9: 7; 14: 19, 30; 15: 15, 30; 16: 9, 24; 17: 9; 23: 19; Num 6: 11, 16, 17; 8: 12; 9: 5; etc.). It is therefore a descriptive term; it tells exactly how and in what order the sacrificial ritual is to be performed. Now in all rituals calling for the use of both the whole offering and the purification offering, the latter is invariably offered first (Milgrom 1976, nn. 251, 295). As exemplified in the law of the Nazirite, even though the prescriptive ritual lists the whole offering ahead of the purification offering (Num 6: 10, 14), the descriptive ritual puts the latter offering first (vv 11, 16–17). It is important to realize that the descriptive ritual always uses the verb *ʿāśâ* and the prescriptive ritual uses a different verb. Thus in the induction of the Levites, the prescriptive text lists the whole offering first (Num 8: 8) but the descriptive text puts the purification offering first—and uses the verb *ʿāśâ* (v 12). Indeed, a descriptive ritual can be identified simply by its use of *ʿāśâ* and, conversely, a prescriptive ritual will be characterized by the use of some other verb. For example, the sacrificial order for the parturient (Lev 12: 6, 8), which ostensibly violates the rule by listing the whole offering before the purification offering, is in fact only a prescriptive text because it employs the verbs *hēbî*ʾ and *lāqaḥ* but not the verb *ʿāśâ*.[1]

Thus Leviticus 4 must be a prescriptive ritual since it does not use the verb *ʿāśâ*, whereas Numbers 15 can only be descriptive since it does use the verb *ʿāśâ*. However, here we encounter an exception to the rule: though the verb is *ʿāśâ*, the whole offering is listed first! The solution therefore suggests itself that originally only one sacrifice was listed. And when one compares Numbers 15 with Leviticus 4, what that sacrifice was is clear: the purification offering. The writer of Numbers 15, not wanting to detail the complex procedure of Lev 4: 15–20, changed the verb to *ʿāśâ*, thereby telescoping the entire ritual. Thus "the congregation shall offer (*wĕhiqrîbû*) a bull of the herd for a purification offering" became "the whole community shall sacrifice *wĕʿāśû* one bull of the herd for a purification offering." In other words, the verb *ʿāśâ* was correctly applied to one sacrifice. However, an interpolation was later inserted, adding the whole offering and its accompaniments before the purification offering (above); the verb *ʿāśâ* was no longer correct, but it was not changed, thereby betraying the development of the text.

This solution, despite its virtues, is subject to two serious objections. (1) It does not explain why other cases of the purification offering found in Leviticus 4 are missing in Numbers 15. It might be suggested that the author of Numbers 15 had no interest in the cases of the high priest (Lev 4: 1–12) or of the chieftain (Lev 4: 22–26). But why would he have omitted the option of offering a ewe by the individual (Lev 4: 32–35)? By selecting the she-goat as the exclusive offering for the individual (Num 15: 27), he picked the animal that appears in no other specific case as a purification offering, whereas the ewe—the animal he rejected—is attested elsewhere as the individual's purification offering (e.g., the leper, Lev 14: 10; the Nazirite, Num 6: 14). (2) In the alleged reworking of the text of Leviticus 4 the author would have introduced yet another perplexing change. Instead of referring to the community as *qāhāl* (Lev 4: 14–21) he consistently uses *ʿēdâ* (Num 15: 24 [2x], 25, 26). It has already been shown that *ʿēdâ* is the old technical term for the Israelite community (Milgrom 1978), and it is hardly likely that he would have replaced *qāhāl* by this more archaic term.

Thus the attempt to find literary dependency between the two purification offering pericopes must be abandoned. There is no alternative but to assume that we are dealing with two independent traditions concerning the purification offering. But what of the term *ʿāśâ*, which strongly suggests that only one sacrifice was originally stipulated by Num 15: 24?

The probability rests with R. Rendtorff (1967: 22) who, on other grounds, suggests that v 24 originally stipulated only the whole offering and that the purification offering was added later. He correctly points to the whole offering as initially being the sole expiatory sacrifice both for the nation (e.g., Judg 20: 26; 21: 2–4; 1 Sam 7: 6, 9–10; 13: 12; 2 Sam 24: 25) and for individuals (Jer 7: 21–22; 14: 12 and esp. Job 1: 15; 42: 7–9). The evidence from this non-cultic literature is confirmed by the Priestly Code, which continues to permit the use of the whole offering as the individual's sole expiatory sacrifice (e.g., in Lev 1: 4). The rabbis express a similar view: originally "the open altars (*bāmôt*) were permitted and only the whole offering was sacrificed" (*t. Zebaḥ.* 13: 1). However, Priestly Legislators made this alteration: they added the purification offering to the whole offering for all fixed, public sacrifices. That even here the precedence of the whole offering can still be detected is shown by the fact that all the public sacrifices require male animals, even the purification offering which, everywhere else, is limited to females (e.g., in Leviticus 4). That the whole offering must be a male, therefore, can only mean that originally it was the only public sacrifice; and when other sacrifices were added to the public cult, they were made to conform to the standard of the whole offering.[2]

Thus Num 15: 22–31 represents a tradition of communal expiation other than Leviticus 4. In its earlier stage it required only the bull of a whole offering but when the purification offering was added it was made to conform to the male requirement for sacrificial animals used in public, expiatory sacrifices; thus the sacrificial animals became a bull and a he-goat.[3] Regarding the individual's inadvertency, whereas Leviticus 4 allows either a female goat or sheep, Numbers 15 mandates only the female goat.[4] Moreover, important innovations were added to Numbers passage. Foremost among them is the ordinance, found nowhere else, that presumptuous, unrepented sins are not eligible for sacrificial expiation but are punished by *kārēt* (vv 30–31) (Milgrom 1976: 108–10). Other important additions were the inclusion of the resident alien and the special emphasis on the factor of inadvertency (Milgrom forthcoming). Of equal significance, as noted, is the inclusion of all the commandments—performative as well as prohibitive—under the rule of sacrificial expiation and *kārēt*.

Finally, once it is accepted that we are dealing with two independent traditions, the possibility must be left open that Numbers 15, like Leviticus 4, speaks only of prohibitive commandments; that *ʿāśâ bišĕgāgâ,* "do . . . inadvertently" (v 29) implies an act of commission, i.e., that a prohibitive commandment has been violated, and is the equivalent of the wording of Leviticus 4, "doing (*wĕʿāśâ*) inadvertently (*bišĕgāgâ*) . . . one of the commandments . . . which should not be done" (Lev 4: 22). If this be the case, then "these commandments" (Num 15: 22) cannot refer to the previous performative commandments (vv 1–21) and the entire pericope (vv 22–31) may have to be considered as the displaced conclusion of another legal section.[5] This problem cannot be resolved as yet.

Notes

1. Lev 23: 18–19 is also not an exception, even though, in this case, *ʿāśâ* is used and the whole offering precedes the purification offering, since *ʿāśâ* refers solely to the purification offering whereas the whole offering has its own verb and it is a different one.

2. Parenthetically, it should be stated that other claims made by Rendtorff (1967: 83) must be rejected: Num 15: 24a does not refer to an individual whose sin has harmed the community; such a case is only predicated of the high priest (Lev 4: 3), not of the commoner; and the purification offering described in Num 15: 25b is not a later interpolation: since the purification offering is not an *ʾiššê,* it had to be listed separately.

3. The combination of a whole-offering bovine and the purification-offering he-goat is found in Lev 9: 3 and in the cultic calendar, Lev 23: 18–19 and Numbers 28–29.

4. Even in this common case of the female goat, the language is not the same: e.g., *śĕ ʿîrat ʿizzîm,* Lev 4: 28; *ʿēz bat šĕnātāh,* Num 15: 27.

5. For other solutions, see K. Koch (1959: 57–58); D. Kellermann (1973).

References

Kellermann, D.
1973 Bemerkungen zum Sündopfergesetz in Num. 15, 22ff. Pp. 107–14 in *Wort und Geschichte* (Festschrift K. Elliger), ed. H. Gese, H. T. Rüger, et al. Kevelaer: Butzon und Bercker.

Koch, K.
1959 *Die Priesterschrift von Exodus 25 bis Leviticus 16*. Göttingen: Vandenhoeck und Ruprecht.

Milgrom, J.
1971 Sin-offering or Purification-offering? *Vetus Testamentum* 21: 149–56.
1976 *Cult and Conscience. The Asham and the Priestly Doctrine of Repentance.* Leiden: Brill.
1978 Priestly Terminology and the Political and Social Structure of Pre-monarchic Israel. *Jewish Quarterly Review* 69: 65–81.
forthcoming *Commentary on the Book of Numbers.* Philadelphia: Jewish Publication Society.

Rendtorff, R.
1967 *Studien zum Geschichte des Opfers in alten Israel.* Neukirchen-Vluyn: Neukirchener Verlag.

Toeg, A.
1973/4 A Halakhic Midrash in Num. xv: 22–31. *Tarbiz* 43: 1–20 (Hebrew).

The Composition of Deuteronomy 5–11

Brian Peckham
Regis College, Toronto, Ontario

Martin Noth's theory of a Deuteronomistic history is generally accepted (cf. Eissfeldt 1964: 321–30; Fohrer 1968: 192–95). According to his theory, the Deuteronomist (DTR) is the author of an historical work (Deuteronomy–2 Kings). DTR is not just a redactor who combined and organized traditional materials. DTR is an author and historian, acquainted with tradition through literary sources, giving tradition a particular form in the structure, arrangement and composition of a history (Noth 1943: 11; 1948: 2). On this theory DTR should be the author of Deuteronomy. But Noth sustains his theory of a DTR history by relying on a subsidiary theory which excludes DTR authorship of Deuteronomy. This subsidiary theory is that Deuteronomy contains original and independent traditions, with their own history and their own literary development. Deuteronomy 1–3 (4), 31: 1–13, and 34* introduce the DTR history. Deut 4: 44–30: 20 is a separate and independent complex of traditions whose entire literary development was pre-DTR (Noth 1943: 14–16). DTR wrote the introduction and the history but is not the author of Deuteronomy.

Noth's theory of an original and independent DT tradition is not explained but is sustained by a correlative literary theory (Noth 1943: 16–18). Supposing that DT began with Deut 4: 44, the simplest explanation of the book's present form is that it was elaborated from a basic text (*Grundlage*) by a process of literary accretion. Supposing, further, that the original text of Deut 4: 44–11: 32 and of Deut 27: 1–30: 20 is composed in the singular, it can be assumed that the disparate plural sections, with their origin in the practice of preaching on the law, were added in successive stages. This literary process ended when DTR incorporated DT into a history by affixing framework texts. The evidence that DTR received the DT tradition (4: 44–30: 20) and incorporated it unchanged is that even the latest accretion to the DT tradition (Deut 27: 1–8) is presupposed by the DTR history (Josh 8: 30–35).

These subsidiary theories of text and tradition were mutually sustaining. The literary theory was used to corroborate the notion of an original DT tradition and to make it an independent literary source of the DTR history. The theory of an original DT tradition allowed the literary theory to function randomly and without regard for the theory of a DTR history. The framework texts seem to contain duplicate introductions (Deut 1–3 [4] and Deut 4: 44–11: 32) and conclusions (Deut 27: 1–30: 20 and Deut 31: 1–13; 34*). Since duplication indicates literary stratification, the framework texts seem to contradict the theory of a unified DTR history. The difficulty was not handled by that theory. Instead, the literary theory solved the problem by distributing the introductions and conclusions arbitrarily between the DTR history (Deut 1–3 [4]; 31: 1–13; 34*) and the DT tradition (Deut 4: 44–11: 32; 27: 1–30: 20).

The literary theory is an alternative to the theory of a DTR history. In Noth's work the literary theory seems plausible only by association with the correlative theory of an original DT tradition. Neither is supported by or compatible with the theory that DTR is the author of a history. The literary theory isolates DT and renders it intrusive in a DTR text. The theory of an original tradition excludes DT as a source of the DTR history and leaves it a separate and unassimilated resource. Together they contradict the theory that DTR was the author of a history using authentic historical sources. DTR becomes the final editor of a DT text, putting a stop to an anonymous process of literary accretion by composing an unrelated and circumscribing literary framework. DTR is an editor who incorporates the text but ignores the tradition. It was Noth's insight that DT is inexplicable apart from the DTR history. His mistake was to maintain and justify the perennial quest for an Urdeuteronomium with subsidiary and incompatible theories which obscured this insight.

Nicholson (1967) tried to settle the theoretical conflict by developing an exact parallel between DTR and the authors of DT. They share a common heritage, language, tradition and interpretation. All that divides DTR and DT is separate and consecutive authorship in distinct geographical locations. But this is a presupposition and not a necessary conclusion of his study. He has abandoned the literary theory and admits (p. 120) that the DT text does not preserve the tradition intact. But he retains the notion of a separate DT tradition and, although the tradition is not a text, separate DT authorship. This position is illogical but it allows Nicholson to sustain Noth's contention that DTR used sources and so to preserve the authenticity and credibility of the DTR history (p. 121). His attempt to reconcile Noth's conflicting theories has obscured the logical alternative that DTR is the author of DT and used authentic sources in its composition.

This is the position approached by Minette de Tillesse (1962). He contends that DTR is the author of DT, but combines this idea with Noth's subsidary theories. DTR's source was the DT code written in the singular. DTR rewrote this source as an introduction to a history by composing the plural sections. In elaborating the complex of Noth's theories, Minette de Tillesse has demonstrated their incompatibility. DTR is the author of a history which included only the plural sections of DT. The theory of an original DT tradition is retained as an assumption, but the tradition is restricted and excluded from the history. The literary theory is adapted to the purposes of a DTR history, but DTR ceases to be an author and becomes an editor, while DT ceases to be a tradition and becomes a residual text.

Nicholson and Minette de Tillesse are alone in attempting to integrate DT into the DTR history and in maintaining Noth's theory of DTR authorship. Seitz (1971) concentrated on the original tradition and proposed that a primary collection underwent first a deuteronomic and then a DTR revision. DTR composed most of the framework (Deuteronomy 1–4, 27–34*), but the DTR revision of DT itself was confined to a new system of headings (1: 1; 4: 44; 28: 69; 33: 1) and scattered editorial comments. Similarly, García López (1977, 1978a, b, 1979) dedicated his studies of Deuteronomy 5–11 to the quest for a DT tradition. Deploying all the theories and assumptions of the quest, and working with a flexible method of literary affinity, he discovered original units, a proto-DT redaction, a DT and post-DT redaction, and a final DTR edition. The first four phases are unrelated to the DTR history, but are distinguished and distributed chronologically with reference to Hosea and pentateuchal themes. The DTR phase comprises the historical sections (Deut 5: 1–6: 3; 9: 7b-10: 11) and developed in complex stages. There is no intrinsic connection between this phase and the earlier parenetic development of the tradition. The DTR texts are connectives and sutures attributable neither to an author nor to an editor but to a series of redactors with similar interests. The theory of an original DT tradition has become a license to pursue the correlative literary theory beyond the restraints of a text. Inevitably, the theory of a DTR history must be abandoned.

This becomes more obvious in Mittmann's study of Deut 1: 1–6: 3 (Mittmann 1975; cf.

Braulik 1978). From the distinction of singular and plural sections (cf. Begg 1979, 1980) Mittmann develops a stratigraphy of the text in six levels: an original level (*Grundschicht*), two plural editions, a pre-singular, a singular and a post-singular redaction. None of these is DTR. The theory of an original DT tradition is retained and elaborated in every detail. The theory of a DTR history is discarded. But Mittmann retains Noth's insight that the correlative of a tradition is not a text but a history. The gradual accumulation of the DT tradition which he reconstructs is sustained by an implicit history of pentateuchal development. But under the tyranny of the correlative literary theory he has inherited, Mittmann is led to believe that the chronology and structure of this history is identifiable in a sequence of fragmented texts. He rejects the notion of framework which had correlated the DTR history and the DT tradition, but instead of reconstructing a history, he reconstitutes a text.

The absolute priority and autonomy of theory is illustrated in Merendino's treatment of Deuteronomy 6 (1977). The theory of an original DT tradition and the correlative literary theory are combined with every assumption of critical method. The applicability of the theories implies a fragmentation of the text, while the logical coherence of the methods suggests its integrity: Merendino is struck by the astonishing unity of the text (p. 206) but supposes that its composition was as difficult and complex as its analysis. Assuming the distinctiveness of the *Wir-Stil* (von Rad 1966: 38), he isolates the first person plural texts at the beginning (5: 2–3), in the middle (6: 4) and at the end (6: 20b, 24). Relying on a postulate of redaction criticism (Richter 1971: 32, 71, 167), Merendino finds that these framework texts (5: 2–3; 6: 4–9; 6: 20, 21, 23b, 24ab[b]) are secondary. Since the history of traditions prescribes an *Urschicht* and secondary expansions, and since the parenetic has priority over the historical, Deut 6: 10–13 is designated the core text. Then the text is assembled by rigorous and repeated application of the same logical procedures. The core text was elaborated in three successive stages: first, it was given an introduction and a conclusion; then it was interpreted by the addition of the decalog with its own introduction and conclusion; finally, it was incorporated into the framework. The dismantling of the text proves the literary theory; the coherence of the reassembled text proves that an original tradition was transmitted in stages.

Merendino attributes these four stages of tradition to a pre-DT phase. In the time of Hezekiah this parenetic phase was historicized. It was made the prologue to a collection of laws by the addition of an introduction and conclusion. This phase of the tradition may be designated "Deuteronomy." In the time of Josiah, the law book was elaborated at the beginning, in the middle, and at the end. During the Exile, further additions were made.

Merendino's analysis is perfectly logical. He makes no reference to the theory of a DTR history since the literary theory excludes it. But since the notion of a DT tradition involves historical reconstruction, he justifies his multiple stages by reference to his own version of the DTR history.

Noth's theory of a DTR history allowed for one author. Later additions were made to the work (Noth 1943: 6–9) and the division into books is secondary (Noth 1943: 4, 10), but there is no evidence for a theory of duplicate redaction. Freedman (1962: 716; 1976b) differs with Noth in proposing a pre-exilic and an exilic edition of the DTR history. The earlier version was inspired by the restoration of the empire and of the Mosaic covenant under Josiah. During the Exile, when its theology became essentially untenable, it was revised by an editor who was also responsible for the final compilation of the books Genesis—2 Kings. Cross (1973) adheres to Noth's position of a single author, but also finds evidence in Deuteronomy and Kings of a later edition. DTR I wrote the history in the time of Josiah "as a programmatic document of his reform and of his revival of the Davidic state" (p. 287). DTR II revised the history during the exile (ca. 550 B.C.E.) and explained the catastrophe with reference to the reign of Manasseh.

Levenson (1979) applied Cross's theory to the composition of DT. He maintains the originality of the DT tradition and, as that theory requires, concludes that the DTR I history simply did not include DT. DTR I may have been motivated indirectly by DT theology, but on some fundamental issues the two are contradictory. It was DTR II who found DT pertinent and incorporated it into the history. DTR II wrote a new introduction (3: 29; 4: 1–40) and conclusion (29: 16, 21–28; 30: 1–20; 31: 16–22, 24–29; 31: 30–32: 44*) and inserted DT with this framework between DTR I's notices on the installation of Joshua (3: 28; 31: 1ff).

DTR II is an editor, as the theory of an independent DT tradition requires.

Levenson's study systematizes the error that can be traced to Noth. It is impossible to hold the theory of a DTR history and the contradictory theory of an original and independent DT tradition. The DTR theory was verified by Noth in his study of Joshua–Kings and has been corroborated and corrected by subsequent studies. The DT theory cannot be verified. As a tradition, DT is inconceivable apart from the DTR history, but as literature DT excludes a history composed by DTR. Since the theory of an original and independent DT tradition is both useless and redundant, it must be discarded.

Noth's theory of the DTR history, in the version proposed by Cross, is sufficient by itself to explain Deuteronomy (cf. Polzin 1980: 15–16). When the prejudices introduced by the subsidiary theories are eliminated, this theory states that DTR I composed DT on the evidence of reliable sources as part of an historical work, and that the history was revised and interpreted by DTR II. This theory can be verified in Deuteronomy 5–11). One of the prejudices eliminated by the theory of a DTR history is the notion of "framework," a correlative of the theories of an autonomous tradition and an intrusive text. The DTR I history is continuous from the beginning of DT. It was DTR II, as Levenson (1979) perceived, who segmented the book with the addition of interpretative texts. DTR II establishes legitimate succession from Moses to Joshua (1: 9–18, 37–39; 3: 18–20, 23–28; 31: 2b, 3b, 7–8; [33: 1–29]; 34: 10–11) to insure transmission of the "Book of the Law" (Deut 28: 58, 61; 29: 20; 30: 10; 31: 26; Josh 1: 8; 8: 34; 23: 6; 2 Kgs 14: 6; 22: 8, 11, 13). This Book of the Law is the work of DTR II, constructed from the DTR I history by the insertion of an introductory (1: 31a, 35a^b; 3: 29; 4: 1–40, 41–43) and concluding (29: 1b-3, 5, 15–28; 30: 1–20; 31: 9–13, 16–22, 24–30; 32: 1–47) commentary. The "book" of DT (Noth 1943: 4, 10) is the product of DTR II's revision of the DTR I history.

DTR I wrote the "Book of the Covenant" (2 Kgs 23: 2–3, 21). To emphasize its interpretative significance in the history (Noth 1943: 5, 13–14), DTR I composed it as a speech of Moses with a superscription (1: 1a, 4–5) and a colophon (28: 69; 29: 1a, 4, 6–14). When the Book of the Covenant is concluded, the DTR I history continues with a preview of the conquest (31: 1, 2a, 3a, 4–6), the succession of Joshua (31: 14–15, 23), and the death of Moses (34: 1a^b-6).

The DTR I Narrative

The DTR narrative documents the covenant "in the land of Moab" (28: 69) and its antecedent in the covenant at Horeb. The covenant is anticipated in the superscription (1: 5) but is delayed by the scout narrative (1: 6–8, 19–30, 31b-35a^ab, 36, 40–46; Lohfink 1960), the account of the destruction of the wilderness generation (2: 1–15; Moran 1963), and the history of the wars with Sihon and Og (2: 16–3: 17, 21–22). There are two covenants distributed in chronological sequence before the departure from Horeb (1: 6–8) and, as the superscription relates (1: 4), after the defeat of Sihon and Og. In DTR I's narrative sequence, however, the covenants coalesce and pertain proleptically (1: 4–5) to the history of rebellion in the wilderness.

The first part of the narrative (1) relates the events at Horeb (4: 44; 5: 1a, 2–4, 6–7, 9b-11, 17–21, 23–25, 27–28; 6: 4–9), (2) situates the covenant at Horeb between the Exodus and the entrance into the land (6: 10–13, 20–21, 23b-24), and (3) explains how Israel will take possession of the land (7: 1–3, 5, 17–18, 21, 23–24). It is an account of what happened before the first address of Moses (1: 6–8) and refers to it explicitly. The opening words of the address (1: 6a, *yhwh ʾĕlohênû dibbēr ʾēlênû bĕḥoreb lēʾmor*) are repeated at the beginning of the covenant narrative (5: 2, 4, 5*, *yhwh ʾĕlohênû kārat ʿimmānû bĕrît bĕḥoreb . . . dibbēr . . . lēʾmor*). The address of Moses concludes (1: 8b[b]) with the oath to the patriarchs concerning the land; the account of the Exodus and the entry into the land begins (6: 10) and ends (6: 23b) the same way. The address contains a command to take possession of the land (1: 7–8b[a]) which the conquest narrative repeats and elaborates: Yahweh has ceded the land to Israel (*ntn lpny,* 1: 8a; 7: 2a, 23a), and Israel must go in and take possession of it (*bʾ* + *yrš*, 1: 8b[a]; 7: 1, 17).

The second part recounts the events in the wilderness following the departure from Horeb (1: 19) and after the defeat of Sihon and Og. It narrates (4) how Israel was led through the wilderness toward the good land (8: 1, 7–12, 14b, 15–16a[a]), (5) how Israel rebelled at Horeb as it had in the wilderness (9: 1–3, 7–8a, 9, 11–12, 15–17, 21–24), and (6) how at last they entered into a covenant concerning the land (10: 12–14, 17–18, 20–21; 11: 4–8, 10–15). It ends with a summary of the impending conquest (11: 22–25) and a transition to the laws (11: 31–32). It is linked systematically to the beginning of the history. The account of the wilderness opens (8: 1) with a reference to the command to go in and take possession of the land sworn to the fathers (1: 7–8). The history of rebellion in the wilderness begins (9: 1–3 = 1: 21, 28, 30) and ends (9: 23 = 1: 21, 26, 43) with quotations from the scout narrative. The covenant in the land of Moab is new, but the summary of the impending conquest rephrases (11: 24) the initial description of the land (1: 7; Josh 1: 3–4) and quotes the promise of victory made before the battle with Sihon and Og (11: 25 = 2: 25).

In this narrative DTR I refers to known texts, and interprets and combines accepted traditions in developing a covenant theory of history (Polzin 1980: 9–12). The elimination of the wilderness generation allows the Horeb covenant to be made with the present generation (5: 2–3; 6: 24) and provides the evidence for a theory of the conquest (1: 29 = 7: 18a + 21a). The defeat of Sihon and Og rehabilitates Israel for the covenant at Horeb, becomes a paradigm of victory (*ntn byd*, 2: 24, 30; 3: 2, 3, 21; 7: 24), and, with the scout narrative, provides the context (9: 1–3; 11: 22–25) for the covenant in the land. The Horeb covenant integrates the Exodus and the conquest and confirms Yahweh as God of Israel. The covenant in the land of Moab narrates the Exodus and the wilderness and constitutes Israel as the people of Yahweh in the land he has given them.

The DTR I text is: 1: 1a, 4–8, 19–30, 31b–35a[a]b, 36, 40–46; 2: 1–3: 17, 21–22; 4: 44; 5: 1a, 2–4, 6–7, 9b–11, 17–21, 23–25, 27, 28; 6: 4–13, 20–21, 23b–24; 7: 1–3, 5, 17–18, 21, 23–24; 8: 1, 7–12, 14b–16a[a]; 9: 1–3, 7, 8a, 9, 11–12, 15–17, 21–24; 10: 12–14, 17–18, 20–21; 11: 4–7, 8, 10–15, 22–25, 31–32.

The introduction to the narrative (4: 44–5: 1a) has the same style as the superscription (1: 1a, 4–5), which it resumes and from which it derives the title "this law" (1: 5b; 4: 44a). Its form and substance are repeated in the colophon (28: 69–29: 1a).

1. The covenant on Horeb is incorporated into an address by Moses (5: 2–4, 23, 28a; 6: 4–9). It is in direct discourse and comprises a declaration of Yahweh (5: 6–7, 9b–11, 17–21), the response of the people (5: 24–25, 27), and confirmation by Yahweh (5: 28b). The introduction (5: 2–4), the conclusion (6: 4–9), and the transitions between the parts (5: 23, 28a) are narrated by Moses.

The address begins and ends with the summons, "Hear, Israel" (5: 1a; 6: 4). The announced topic, the "statutes and ordinances" (5: 1a), is the Book of the Covenant: the same formula is repeated at the end of the covenant narrative (11: 32) and at the beginning (12: 1) and end (26: 16) of the laws. The address is a solemn declaration (5: 1a, *dbr bʾzn*; cf. 31: 11, 28) comparable to Josiah's proclamation of the covenant (*qrʾ bʾzn*, 2 Kgs 23: 2).

The first part of the address (5: 2–4) explains the covenant and introduces the declaration of Yahweh. The form of the covenant is direct address and reciprocal affirmation (cf. 26: 17–19; 29: 9–14). Reciprocity is expressed in the first person plural: the covenant is between "Yahweh our God" and "us" (5: 2–3; cf. 29: 13–14). Yahweh makes the covenant (*krt bryt*, 5: 2; cf. 28: 69; 29: 11, 13) by speaking directly to the people (5: 4). DTR I affirms the direct address of Yahweh by relying on a variety of sources and traditions. That Yahweh spoke to the people "face to face" is derived from the traditions concerning the access of Moses to Yahweh (Exod 33: 11; Num 12: 6; cf. Num 14: 14; Deut 34: 10). That Yahweh spoke on the mountain and out of the fire is taken from the first encounter of Moses with Yahweh (Exod 3: 1–6). This episode of the burning bush provides the location on Horeb (5: 2; Exod 3: 1). Its reference to the bush burning (*hassĕneh boʿēr bāʾēš*) and not being consumed (Exod 3: 2b) is the source of the mountain burning (5: 23a[b], *hāhār boʿēr bāʾēš*; cf. 9: 15). Combined with the Taberah tradition of Yahweh's destructive fire (Num 11: 1–3: *ʾš, bʿr, ʾkl*), it is the source of the people's fear of being consumed (5: 25a). In DTR I's sources, Yahweh descended in fire on Sinai (Exod 19: 18a), but the notion that Yahweh spoke out of the fire (*mittôk hāʾēš*, 5: 4, 24) is an interpretation of Yahweh's summons to Moses out of the burning bush (Exod 3: 4b, *mittôk hassĕneh*). Since there is no precedent for Yahweh speaking directly to the people, the covenant adopts the language of the direct address of Yahweh to Moses.

This convention is maintained in the declaration of Yahweh (5: 6–7, 9b–11, 17–21), which comprises a protocol (5: 6–7, 9b–11) and a series of prohibitions (5: 17–21). The protocol contains an historical prologue (5: 6b) summarizing the Exodus. It identifies Yahweh as the God of Israel (5: 6a) to the exclusion of all other gods (5: 7). It specifies Yahweh as lord of the covenant (5: 9b–10) and prohibits violation of the covenant oath (5: 11).

DTR I composed this protocol from sources in which Yahweh is revealed to Moses and not directly to the people. The proclamation of the divine name (5: 6a) is an amalgam of declarations made to Moses at the burning bush (Exod 3: 6, 15). The historical prologue (5: 6b) is derived from the same context (Exod 3: 10, 12) but is expressed in traditional confessional language (Exod 13: 4, 14). The rest of the protocol is drawn from a parallel self-proclamation and the associated covenant (Exodus 34). The prohibition of other gods (5: 7) depends on an earlier form of the prohibition in that covenant (Exod 34: 14a). The self-proclamation (5: 6a) is repeated (5: 9b[a]) and is specified by the designation "a jealous God" drawn from the same source (Exod 34: 14b). This is followed (5: 9b[b]) by a version of the divine self-proclamation found in the earlier covenant (Exod 34: 7; cf. Num 14: 18) with the addition of the terminology of love and hate peculiar to covenant. The prohibition of false oaths (5: 11a) belongs in this covenant context (Fishbane 1980: 352–53). It is enforced by a clause (5: 11b[a], "because Yahweh does not forgive") taken from the earlier text (Exod 34: 7b[a]), and is applied specifically to the name that has been revealed (5: 11b[b]).

The prohibitions (5: 17–21) cover personal injury (5: 17–19) and damage to property (5: 20–21). They are designed for the protection of the covenant partners and are drawn, at least in part, from standard lists (Moran 1967).

Yahweh's declaration is composed from traditional sources. It proclaims Yahweh as lord of the covenant and stipulates the obligations to which Israel must agree. The response of the people (5: 24–25, 27) is introduced by Moses (5: 23). The report combines the theophany at the bush ("the mountain was burning") and the theophany at Sinai ("the voice," Exod 19: 19). It also alludes to the scout narrative. When they hear the voice out of the fire (MT "darkness"; cf. 4: 11; Exod 14: 20), the heads of the tribes and the elders (cf. 29: 9) approach Moses, as the people had approached him to reject Yahweh's command to take the land (1: 22).

The response of the people (5: 24–25, 27) combines elements of the theophany on Sinai and of the special revelation to Moses (Exod 33: 17–23) with the general setting of theophany at the burning bush. The last is represented in the voice heard out of the fire (5: 24–25). References to the Sinai theophany are the "voice" (5: 24–25) and the fear of dying (5: 25; Exod 20: 20). But allusions to both texts are subsumed in a commentary on the special theophany of Moses. Moses asks Yahweh to show him his glory (Exod 33: 18, *har'ēnî-nā' 'et kĕbodekā*): the people profess Yahweh has shown them his glory (5: 24, *her'ānû yhwh 'ĕlohênû 'et kĕbodô'*). Yahweh objects that no one can see him and live (Exod 33: 20b, *kî lo' yir'anî hā'ādām wāḥāy*): the people have seen that it is possible to hear him and live (5: 24 *kî yĕdabbēr 'ĕlohîm 'et 'hā'ādām wāḥāy.*)

The combination of sources is typical of DTR I. It is also characteristic of this covenant to apply to the people what the tradition affirms of Moses. The response confirms the covenant. The people make Moses their spokesman (5: 27b) in the language used to make prophets of the people (Num 11: 16–17, 24–25, especially 24a). They agree to the covenant (5: 27) with the response to hear-and-do peculiar to the Sinai theophany (Exod 19: 8, 9; 20: 19). Their response cancels the refusal of the wilderness generation, who saw the glory of Yahweh but refused to obey and perished without seeing the land (Num 14: 22–23). The covenant, by contrast, gives life (5: 3; 6: 24).

With the affirmative response of the people, the covenant is confirmed by Yahweh (5: 28b). The words of Yahweh are bound with a remark by Moses (5: 28a) which quotes the sequel to the refusal of the land (1: 34a, *wayyišma' yhwh 'et qôl dibrêkem*). Yahweh's confirmation consists in approving what the people have said (cf. 1: 23).

By inserting the covenant into a speech of Moses, DTR I has made Moses its witness and spokesman. By attributing to the people the characteristics of Moses, DTR I gives them the same function. The covenant is affirmed in a formal proclamation (6: 4–9) which declares the sovereignty of Yahweh (6: 4) and perfect allegiance (6: 5). It is witnessed in the equivalent of the deposit of the covenant text (6: 6), the provision for periodic reading of the covenant (6: 7), and the preparation of authentic copies of the covenant text (6: 8–9).

2. DTR I's narrative of the Horeb covenant incorporates elements proper to state treaties (Weinfeld 1972: 61–65). These include a preamble (5: 6a, 7, 9b–11), an historical prologue (5: 6b), stipulations (5: 17–21), an oath of allegiance (5: 23–25, 27–28), witnesses (6: 4–5), and provisions regarding the covenant text (6: 6–9). The historical prologue usually concludes with a grant of land which contains a description of the land and provides for its tenure in perpetuity (Weinfeld 1972: 71–81). The enduring validity of the treaty requires its provisions to be related to succeeding generations (Weinfeld 1972: 104). DTR I's narrative of the Horeb covenant continues with an historical prologue (6: 10–13, 20–21, 23b–24) which combines these elements and is modeled on traditional sources (Exod 13: 5–10, 11–16).

Yahweh's grant of the land in accordance with the oath to the patriarchs (6: 10a; cf. 1: 8) is substantiated by a description of its resources (6: 10b-11). It is a description of a settled land (cf. 20: 5–6, 10–14) expressed in the adversative style typical of futility curses (cf. 28: 30, 39–40). Since the land is given in accordance with the terms of the covenant, the description is followed by a version of the divine protocol (6: 12; cf. 5: 6) and a repetition of the covenant obligation (6: 13; cf. 6: 5).

The permanence of the covenant is expressed in its pertinence to succeeding generations (6: 20–21, 23b-24). A son's question concerning the stipulations (6: 20) is answered by a summary of the covenant's historical antecedents: slavery in Egypt (6: 21a; cf. 6: 12), the Exodus (6: 21b; cf. 5: 6b; 6: 12) and the gift of the land (6: 23b; cf. 6: 10) urge Israel to the service of Yahweh (6: 24a; cf. 6: 13). The blessing of the covenant, as Moses proclaimed (5: 3), is life (6: 24b).

3. The covenant on Horeb concludes with stipulations concerning the conquest (7: 1–3, 5) and assurance of divine assistance (7: 17–18, 21, 23–24). Like the historical prologue, its structure is derived from the narrative transmission of the covenant from generation to generation, and comprises: an entrance formula ("when Yahweh your God brings you into the land," 7: 1a; 6: 10; Exod 13: 5, 11); a description of the land (cf. 6: 10–11) listing the nations inhabiting it (7: 1b–2a; Exod 13: 5, 11); the law to be observed in the land (7: 2b–3, 5; 6: 12–13; Exod 13: 5–7, 12–13); a question (7: 17; 6: 20; Exod 13: 14); a reply recounting the Exodus (7: 18, 21; 6: 21, 23b; Exod 13: 8, 14); and a sign (7: 23–24; 6: 6–9; Exod 13: 9, 16).

DTR I composed the introduction (7: 1–2b[a]) with formulaics and with reference to the defeat of Sihon and Og. The entrance formula (7: 1a[a]) is combined with the conquest formula (7: 1a[b], *b'* + *yrš*; cf. 1: 8, 39; 8: 1; 11: 8, 10, 31; Num 14: 24) and specified by a list of seven nations greater and mightier than Israel (7: 1b; Exod 1: 9, 20). Victory is assured by Yahweh

(7: 2a = 7: 23a; cf. 1: 8, 21; 2: 31, 33, 36). When the nations have been defeated (*nkh*, 7: 2a; cf. 1: 4; 20: 13), they will be subject to the ban (7: 2b[a]) like Sihon and Og (2: 34) and will receive no mercy (7: 2b[b]; Josh 11: 20).

The remaining stipulations are not formulaic. The prohibition of covenant (7: 2b[b]) is taken from DTR I's covenant source (Exod 34: 12, 15; cf. Exod 23: 32). The prohibition of foreign marriages (7: 3) depends on the same source (Exod 34: 16), but the exact formulation is derived from the covenant with Hamor (Gen 34: 9, 16, 21). The treatment of religious installations (7: 5) quotes the source (Exod 34: 13; cf. Exod 23: 24) and adds "You shall burn their images" (12: 3; 2 Kgs 23: 12–15). These stipulations confirm the covenant with Yahweh by excluding alliances that would jeopardize his unique sovereignty (5: 7).

The objection and the assurance of victory are written from the perspective of the scout narrative. The question (7: 17) does not concern the stipulations but the conquest formula (7: 1a[b], *yrš* + *gôyim rabbîm*). It contrasts with the objection of the wilderness generation (1: 28), which is answered (7: 18a, 21a) with the assurance Moses gave them (1: 29, "Do not dread them or fear them"). In both instances (1: 30; 7: 18) the Exodus is the paradigm of Yahweh's war. He is the great and terrible God (7: 21b) who is in the midst of his people (Num 14: 14), as he was not in the midst of those who rejected the land (1: 42; Num 14: 42).

As the conquest generation is contrasted with the wilderness generation, so the fate of the conquered is compared to the punishment of that rebellious generation. The nations will be routed and destroyed (7: 23, *hmm* + *šmd*) as the wilderness generation was routed and perished (2: 15, *hmm* + *tmm*). The model for both texts (Moran 1963) is the rout of the Egyptians at the Red Sea (Exod 14: 24), the Exodus which is Israel's assurance (7: 18). In a similar manner, Sihon and Og represent the fate of kings (7: 24a, *ntn byd*; cf. 2: 24, 30; 3: 2, 3). Their name is to be obliterated (7: 24a[b]) like the name of their gods (2: 25; 12: 3). The people are assured, as Joshua is assured (Josh 1: 5), that no one will prevail against them (7: 24b; 11: 25).

This section is connected by its form to the preceding grant of the land. It is composed of *stipulations* which combine the jargon of war with the provisions of DTR I's covenant source, and of *assurances* which draw on the scout narrative, the annihilation of the wilderness generation, and the defeat of Sihon and Og. It elaborates the covenant with Yahweh (5: 6) and the exclusion of other gods (5: 7) and illustrates what Yahweh does to those who hate him and for those who love him (5: 9b-10).

4. The account of the covenant in the land of Moab begins with an historical prologue (8: 1, 7–12, 14b-16a[a]). It comprises a declaration of intent (8: 1), a description of the land (8: 7–10), and a summary of the Horeb covenant (8: 11–12, 14b, 15–16a[a]). It repeats the earlier prologue by reconfirming the gift of the land (8: 1b[b], 7a = 6: 10a) and by emphasizing the command not to forget Yahweh in the prosperity of the land (8: 10a, 11a, 12a, 14b = 6: 11b-12). It differs from the earlier text in its description of a fertile but uninhabited land (8: 7–10) contrasted with the barren wilderness where Yahweh led Israel (8: 15–16a[a]).

The declaration of intent (8: 1) refers to the command of Yahweh at Horeb (1: 8) to take possession of the land. It introduces the concept of commandment (*kol hammiṣwâ*, 8: 1a) to define the covenant in the land of Moab (11: 8, 22) and, like the Horeb covenant (5: 3; 6: 24), promises life in the land (8: 1b).

Like the land seen by the scouts (1: 25) and denied to the wilderness generation (1: 35), it is a good land (*ʾereṣ ṭôbâ*, 8: 7, 10) where they will lack nothing (8: 9a) as the wilderness generation had lacked nothing (2: 7). In contrast to the wilderness (8: 15), it is a land with plenty of water (8: 7b) and rain (8: 9b; cf. 28: 23) and crops throughout the year (8: 8).

The historical prologue summarizes the Horeb covenant by citing its stipulation not to forget Yahweh (8: 11a, 12a, 14b[a] = 6: 11b–12a), by alluding to its description of the land (8: 12b; cf. 6: 10b–11a[a]), and by quoting the divine protocol (8: 14b[b] = 6: 12b = 5: 6). Horeb is included in a narrative of Yahweh's benefits in the wilderness (8: 15 – 16a[a]) which is constructed from sources pertaining to the history of rebellion. Israel's journey through the great and terrible wilderness (8: 15a) is an allusion to the scout narrative (1: 19) and the rejection of the land. The fiery serpents in the wilderness (8: 15a) evoke Israel's rebellion in the Nehushtan episode (Num 21: 5–9), and the scorpions (8: 15a) suggest a time of punishment (cf. 1 Kgs 12: 11, 14). The parched land (8: 15a) and water from the rock (8: 15b; 32: 13) refer to the tradition of Massah and Meribah (Exod 17: 1–7), and the manna (8: 16a[a]) brackets the entire history of rebellion (Exod 16: 35b; Num 11: 4–9).

5. The prologue continues with the history of the Horeb covenant (9: 1–3, 7–8a, 9, 11–12, 15–17, 21–24). It begins (9: 1–3, 7) and ends (9: 22–24) with a summary of Israel's rebellions. The first has the form of an argument from historical evidence (Lohfink 1963: 125–31) which includes a narrative version of the order to take the land (9: 1–2), a summary statement of Yahweh's role in the conquest (9: 3, *yd*ʿ), and a recollection of the history of rebellion (9: 7, *zkr*). The argument is constructed by allusion to other DTR I texts. The imminent conquest (9: 1–2a) is described in terms taken from Israel's rejection of the land: the command to go in and take possession of the land (*b*ʾ + *yrš*, 1: 8, 21); the scouts' report that "the people are bigger and taller than we are, the cities huge and fortified to the sky" (1: 28a); the presence of the Anakim (1: 28b) whose size is proverbial (2: 10, 21); the size and might of the nations (Num 14: 12; cf. Deut 7: 1, 17). Reference to these texts is explicit (9: 2b): Israel knows these facts and has heard of them in the texts DTR I has used (Num 13: 28) and written (1: 28); it knows that the saying "Who can withstand the Anakim?" is a parody of the usual conviction that no one can withstand Israel (7: 24; 11: 25).

The summary statement affirms (9: 3a) that Yahweh will go before Israel (= 1: 30) and will be a raging fire against the nations, as he was against Sihon (Num 21: 28). The nations will be destroyed (9: 3b), as Yahweh promised in the Horeb covenant (7: 24; Skweres 1979: 31–34).

The recollection of the history of rebellion (9: 7) alludes to the same complex of texts. The admonition not to forget (9:7a[a]) is taken from the preceding account of the wilderness (8: 11, 14 = 6: 12a). The wilderness is described, in terms taken from the scout narrative (1: 31b[b]), as the time from the Exodus "until you came to this place" (9: 7b[a]; 11: 5). It is summarized in the language of the same narrative as a time of rebellion (9: 7b[b] = 1: 26, 43) when Israel provoked Yahweh to rage (9: 7a[b] = 1: 34).

The Horeb covenant belongs to this time (9: 8a). Its history includes the making of the covenant (9: 9, 11), the abrogation of the covenant (9: 12, 15–17), and the removal of Israel's sin (9: 21). The account of the making of the covenant combines texts from the Sinai tradition: Moses' ascent of the mountain to receive the tablets (9: 9a[a]) refers to a command of Yahweh at Sinai (Exod 24: 12–13); Moses' remaining there forty days and nights without food or water (9: 9b) is taken from the conclusion of the Sinai covenant (Exod 34: 28); instead of the tablets inscribed with the law and commandment (Exod 24: 12b) Moses receives the tablets of the covenant (9: 9a, 11, 15). This is an account of events omitted in the earlier narrative of the Horeb covenant, as DTR I explicitly states (9: 9a[b] = 5: 2).

The account of the abrogation of the covenant (9: 12, 15–17) is constructed from the episode of the golden calf. Yahweh's command to Moses to witness the rebellion of the people (9: 12) is quoted from that episode (Exod 32: 7–8). The compliance of Moses (9: 15) combines a quotation from the source text (Exod 32: 15a), the tablets of the covenant, and a reference to the blazing mountain of the first Horeb account (5: 23). What Moses sees is described (9: 16) by summarizing the golden calf source: Moses sees (Exod 32: 19a) that Israel has sinned against Yahweh (Exod 32: 31) by making the statue of a calf (Exod 32: 4a) and by turning from the way Yahweh had commanded it (Exod 32: 8a). The abrogation of the covenant consists in breaking the tablets (9: 17; Exod 32: 19b), no longer called the tablets of the covenant, in the sight of the people.

The removal of Israel's sin (9: 21) interprets the destruction of the golden calf (Exod 32: 10). In the source text Moses burns, grinds, and scatters the calf. In the DTR I version Moses rids the people of their sin (9: 21a). In the golden calf episode the powdered calf is sprinkled on water and drunk by the people (Exod 32: 20b). The DTR I interpretation is taken from the account of Josiah's reform. The calf is crushed into dust (*lĕʿāpār*) and its dust is thrown into the brook that flowed down the mountain. The account of Josiah's reform records that he burned the Asherah at the brook Kidron, ground it into dust (*lĕʿāpār*) and threw its dust on graves (2 Kgs 23: 6); that he tore down the altars Ahaz and Manasseh had made and threw their dust into the brook Kidron (2 Kgs 23: 12); that at Bethel, where Jeroboam had made Israel sin, Josiah burned the high place, ground it into dust (*lĕʿāpār*), and destroyed the Asherah (2 Kgs 23: 15).

The account closes (9: 22–24) as it began (9: 1–3, 7), with a summary of Israel's rebellions constructed from the text of the scout narrative. It begins (9: 22a) by listing places (Exod 17: 1–7; Numbers 11) alluded to earlier (5: 23, 25; 8: 15b-16a[a]) where Israel provoked Yahweh to anger (1: 34). It refers to the original command to take the land (9: 23a = 1: 21), the rebellion of the people (9: 23b[a] = 1: 26), and their refusal to believe (9: 23b[b] = 1: 32b) or obey (= Num 14: 22b). It sums up the history of Israel as a series of rebellions against Yahweh (9: 24a = 9: 7) from the time he made a covenant with them (9: 24b).

6. The history of the Horeb covenant is a prologue to the covenant in the land of Moab (10: 12–14, 17–18, 20–21; 11: 4–8, 10–15, 22–25, 31–32). The transition is effected by the appeal for an appropriate response (10: 12a). The response (10: 12b-13) is that demanded in the covenant at Horeb: fear (6: 13), love (6: 5a), wholehearted service (6: 5b, 13), walking in the way of Yahweh (cf. 9: 12b), and fidelity to the covenant stipulations (cf. 6: 24). The covenant document comprises a preamble (10: 14, 17–18, 21), an historical prologue (11: 4–7), and a description of the land (11: 10–12), stipulations (10: 12–13, 20; 11: 8, 13), and blessings (11: 13–15).

The preamble formulates the divine protocol: Yahweh is God (10: 14), lord (10: 17a), warrior (10: 17b[a]), judge (10: 17b[b]-18), and benefactor (10: 21).

The historical prologue narrates the crossing of the Reed Sea (11: 4), the wilderness (11: 5) and the fate of Dathan and Abiram (11: 6). It begins (10: 21b[b]) and ends (11: 7) by insisting that Israel is the witness of these events (cf. 1: 19, 30, 31; 3: 21; 9: 17). The account of the Reed Sea alludes to the Song of the Sea (Exod 15: 1, 4) and to the pursuit by the Egyptians recounted in the prose parallel (Exod 14: 9a; cf. Exod 15: 9). The wilderness is described as the interval between Egypt and this place (11: 5; cf. 1: 31b; 9: 7). The story of Dathan and Abiram summarizes the earlier narrative source (Num 16: 1, 30). It is connected with the crossing of the Reed Sea in the source texts by a clause common to both ("The earth swallowed them," Exod 15: 12; Num 16: 30). The two are connected in the DTR I text by additions which DTR I makes to each from a single source. The Reed Sea account ends (11: 4b): "And Yahweh destroyed them to this day" (*yĕʾabbĕdēm yhwh ʿad hayyôm hazzeh*). The Dathan and Abiram account notes that the earth swallowed "every living thing (*ʾet kol hayĕqûm*) in their train" (11: 6b[a]). The source of these two clauses is a summary statement in the flood narrative where they are combined (Gen 7: 4, 23): Yahweh destroyed every living thing (*yimaḥ ʾet kol hayĕqûm*) on the face of the earth.

The description of the land is preceded (11: 8) by the reminder that obedience to the commandment (8: 1; 11: 22) will guarantee possession of the land. The usual conquest formula (*bʾ* + *yrš*) is combined with a battle admonition (*ḥzq*, Josh 1: 6). The land, in contrast to Egypt (11: 10), is a land of hills and valleys, with plenty of water and crops throughout the year (11: 11–12; cf. 8: 7–10). Egypt is a royal garden (11: 10; Gen 13: 10): the land is Yahweh's domain, watered with rain from heaven (11: 11; cf. 10: 14), governed by his emissaries (11: 12; Oppenheim 1968).

The blessings are introduced by the precepts of the Horeb covenant (11: 13; cf. 6: 4, 13). The blessings are rain in its season (cf. 28: 12) on the land, now designated "your land" (11: 14a), the crops according to their season (11: 14b), crops for the cattle (11: 15a; cf. Gen 3: 18), and complete satisfaction (11: 15b = 6: 11b = 8: 10a, 12a).

The covenant in the land of Moab begins with a discussion of the conquest (9: 1–3, 7) and concludes on the same theme (11: 22–25). The conclusion repeats the basic stipulation of the covenant (11: 22; cf. 6: 5; 10: 20), summarizes the assurance of the conquest (11: 23; cf. 7: 1, 17; 9: 1), quotes the assurance given to Joshua (11: 24a, 25a = Josh 1: 3a, 5a), and fixes the boundaries of the land (11: 24b = 34: 2 + Josh 1: 4). It ends with a quotation of the promise made to Israel before the conquest of Sihon and Og (11: 25b = 2: 25). The text of the covenant continues with a transition to the laws (11: 31–32). It combines the conquest formula and the grant of land (11: 31a; cf. 1: 8, 20) with an allusion to settlement in the land (11: 31b; cf. 3: 20), and contains an admonition to maintain the covenant (11: 32; cf. 5: 1a; 12: 1; 26: 16).

The stipulations of the Book of the Covenant regulate centralization (12: 1–7), sacrifice (12: 13–15a, 16–18a[a]b, 21, 26; 14: 4–5, 11–12, 13a[a]*, 16*, 17*, 18b–19), the economy (14: 22–23a, 24–26; 15: 1–3, 7–8, 11–18), festivals (15: 19–20; 16: 1–2, 5–6a, 7a,

10–11a[a]b), homicide (19: 1–6, 11–12), war (20: 1–14, 19–20; 21: 10–14), primogeniture (21: 15–17) and other matters that pertain to brothers (22: 1–4; 23: 20–21), and the affairs of neighbors (23: 25–26; 24: 10–13a), sojourners, and widows and orphans (24: 14–15a, 17–22). The stipulations are followed by the covenant oath (26: 16–19), blessings (28: 1–13), curses (28: 15–20a, 21, 22a, 23, 24a, 25a, 26–35, 38–45), and a colophon (28: 69–29: 1a, 4, 6–14).

The Book of the Covenant is the work of DTR I. It is a history depending on written sources and on a theory of history derived from covenant. The history of Israel is governed by a covenant with Yahweh established in the beginning, abrogated by Israel, and restored at the end. Its variables are the infidelity of the people and punishment to the third and fourth generation. Its constants are the land and the fidelity of Yahweh.

The DTR II Edition

DTR II revised the DTR I narrative and wrote the Book of the Law. The revision affected the substance of DTR I's history by reinterpreting the covenant between Yahweh and Israel. In the DTR I history the covenant is reciprocal, made by Yahweh, confirmed by the people, and witnessed by Moses and the tradition (5: 1a, 6–7, 9b–11, 17–21, 23–25, 27–28; 6: 4–9). The covenant gives Israel the land promised to the fathers and is valid from generation to generation (6: 10–13, 20, 21, 23b–24). It voids aboriginal claims of gods and nations and assures Israel's possession of the land (7: 1–3, 5, 17–18, 21, 23–24). It is as irrevocable as Yahweh's suzerainty in the land (10: 12–14, 17–18, 20–21; 11: 4–8, 10–15, 22–25, 31–32) and is not invalidated by Israel's rebellion and sin (8: 1, 7–12, 14b–16a[a]; 9: 1–3, 7, 8a, 9, 11–12, 15–17, 21–24).

In DTR II's interpretation the covenant is univocal (Polzin 1980: 205–6). It is the decalog (4: 13) revealed by Yahweh and interpreted by Moses (5: 1b, 5, 8–9a, 12–16, 22, 26, 29–33). The decalog does not include the land; the land and the conquest were promised to the fathers; disregard of the decalog by worshipping other gods entails the anger of Yahweh and destruction (6: 14–19, 22–23a, 25). The land has not been conquered, and worship of the gods of the nations left in the land is a constant threat: Israel is separated from the nations by the oath to the fathers and must distinguish itself from the nations by abolishing the worship of their gods (7: 4, 6–16, 19–20, 22, 25–26). Israel is distinguished by obedience to the decalog even in a time of affliction by Yahweh; the worship of other gods is disobedience and assimilates Israel to the nations and their fate (8: 1*, 2–6, 13, 14a, 16a[b]–20). At Horeb Israel rejected the decalog, made an image, and incurred the anger of Yahweh. Through the intercession of Moses and by appeal to the oath to the fathers the decalog was restored and confided to the tribe of Levi (9: 4–6, 8b, 10, 13–14, 18–20, 25–29; 10: 1–5, 8–11). Now if Israel considers the lessons of history and takes the decalog to heart, it will receive blessing in the land promised to the fathers; if it worships other gods, it will perish from the land (10: 15–16, 19, 22; 11: 1–3, 9, 16–21, 26–29).

The DTR II revision consisted in substituting the decalog for the covenant between Yahweh and the people, and the promise to the patriarchs for the gift of the land (Freedman 1976b: 227). Yahweh's fidelity to the promise is the alternative to

Israel's violation of the decalog, the anger of Yahweh, destruction and exile (4: 25–31).

This correction of the DTR I history depends on both reinterpretation of sources and use of variant texts and traditions. It is done by inserting brief additions (e.g., 5: 1b, 5) which anticipate extended explanation (e.g., 5: 29–6: 3). It comments on each part of the DTR I covenant, homogenizes the text, and produces a segmented and repetitive structure. The effect of the DTR II structure is to suppress the covenant in the land of Moab and to valorize the decalog at Horeb. DTR I's historical prologue and grant of the land (6: 10–13, 20, 21, 23b–24) are assimilated into a commentary on the decalog and the promise to the patriarchs (5: 1–6: 25). The conquest and wilderness are combined in DTR II's explanation of Israel's distinctiveness from the nations (7: 1–8: 20). DTR I's history of rebellion is changed into a repetition of the Horeb covenant which reinstitutes the decalog (9: 1–10: 11). The covenant in the land of Moab, the objective of the DTR I history, is revised by DTR II into a commentary on the decalog and the promise (10: 12–11: 32), parallel and carefully linked (11: 18–21 = 6: 4–9) to the first commentary.

The DTR II text is: 1: 9–18, 31a, 35a[b], 37–39; 3: 18–20, 23–29; 4: 1–40, 41–43, 45–49; 5: 1b, 5, 8–9a, 12–16, 22, 26, 29–33; 6: 1–3, 14–19, 22–23a, 25; 7: 4, 6–16, 19–20, 22, 25–26; 8: 1b*, 2–6, 13, 14a, 16a[b]b–20; 9: 4–6, 8b, 10, 13–14, 18–20, 25–29; 10: 1–5, 8–11, 15–16, 19, 22; 11: 1–3, 9, 16–21, 26–29.

The DTR II introduction (4: 45–49) is a resumptive summary required by the insertion of DTR II's main commentary (4: 1–40, 41–43). It combines DTR I expressions (4: 45–46a[a]; cf. 1: 1a; 4: 44b; 6: 20b[a]), localizes the address of Moses near Beth Peor (cf. 3: 29), and summarizes the wars with Sihon and Og (4: 46–49; cf. 1: 4; 2: 33, 36; 3: 2, 3, 8, 12, 17). It omits reference to the scout narrative or the destruction of the wilderness generation and insists (4: 45b[b], 46b[b]) that Moses addressed Israel "when they came out of Egypt" (= Josh 5: 4, 5; 1 Kgs 8: 9; cf. Deut 29: 24; 1 Kgs 8: 21; Jer 11: 3; 31: 32; 34: 13). This is faithful to the tradition (Exod 19: 1, P) but contradicts DTR I's contention that the covenant was made with those present after the destruction of the wilderness generation (5: 2–3).

1. DTR II composed the decalog, the set of ten words, by adding to DTR I's covenant text a prohibition of images (5: 8–9a), the sabbath law (5: 12–15), and the command to honor parents (5: 16). The decalog is confided to Moses (5: 5, 22) and included in a commentary which urges instruction (5: 1b) and makes Moses the interpreter of the law (5: 26, 29–33; 6: 1–3).

The prohibition of images (5: 8–9a) interrupts the sequence in the protocol (Zimmerli 1950) between the exclusion of other gods (5: 7) and the declaration of Yahweh (5: 9b–10). Its source is a DTR II affirmation (Josh 2: 11; 1 Kgs 8: 23) which is integral (4: 39) to DTR II's theological synthesis (4: 32–40). The prohibition is unknown to DTR I but is programmatic for DTR II (7: 25–26) and is the substance of DTR II's interpretation of the decalog (4: 15–24). The worship of images is excluded (5: 9a) on the basis of a tradition (Exod 23: 24a) which DTR II uses here and in the conquest narrative (7: 4, 16, 20, 22) to correct DTR I's reliance on a parallel covenant source (Exodus 34). The terminology of worship and service is typical of DTR II (*ḥwh* + *ʿbd*, 4: 19; 30: 17; 1 Kgs 9: 9; 2 Kgs 17: 16, 35; Jer 22: 9; *ʿbd* + *ḥwh*, 8: 19; 11: 16; 17: 3; 29: 25; Josh 23: 7, 16; Judg 2: 19; 1 Kgs 9: 6; 16: 31; 22: 54; 2 Kgs 21: 21; Jer 13: 10; 16: 11; 25: 6).

The sabbath command (5: 12–15) interrupts a sequence of prohibitives. Its use of the promulgation formula (5: 12b, 15b) defies the convention of direct address by Yahweh and makes the command part of the teaching of Moses, as DTR II's insertions (5: 5, 22) and interpretation (5: 26, 29–33; 6: 1–3) insist. The command is bound by DTR II's obedience formula (*šmr*, 5: 12 + *laʿăśôt*, 5: 15; cf. 5: 1b, 32; 6: 3, 25; 7: 11 . . .) and combines elements of an early sabbath law with elements from the later P formulation: the phrases "Six days you shall labor . . . but the seventh . . ." (5: 13a + 14a) correspond to the law in Exod 34: 21a; the phrases "and do all your work . . . you shall not do any work" (5: 13b + 14b[a]) use the language of P (Gen 2: 2–3; Exod 31: 15). The holiness of the sabbath (5: 12a) and its observance "for Yahweh" (5: 14a) are P conceptions (Gen 2: 3; Exod 31: 15). The list (5: 14b) corresponds in part to the lists of festival participants (16: 11, 14): the addition of "your ox and your ass" (= Exod 23: 12b[a]) makes the list conform to the final catalog (5: 21); "the sojourner in your towns" (cf. 14: 21; 24: 14; 31: 12) is a variant of "the Levite in your towns" (12: 12, 18; 14: 27; 16: 11) but, together with the final motivation (5: 14b[b]), is taken from earlier sabbath legislation (Exod 23: 12b[b]). A concluding exhortation (5: 15) legitimates the insertion of this command by paraphrasing the first commandment (5: 6b).

In conjunction with the sabbath law DTR II added the command to honor parents (5: 16). Like the sabbath law it is distinguished by the promulgation formula (5: 16a). It is enforced (5: 16b) by clauses peculiar to DTR II: length of days (6: 2; 25: 15) and prosperity (5: 29; 6: 3, 18; 12: 25, 28; 22: 7) in the land (*ʾădāmâ*) Yahweh gives them (4: 40; 25: 15).

DTR II suppresses DTR I's covenant between Yahweh and the people by inserting the decalog, which is declared by Yahweh (4: 13, *yaggēd*) and interpreted by Moses (5: 5, *lĕhaggîd*). The interposition of Moses (5: 5) breaks up the fixed expression *dibbēr* (5: 4) *lēʾmor* (5: 5b[b]). Since DTR II insists that the people saw no form (4: 12, 15), it is essential to correct the DTR I statement that Yahweh spoke to the people "face to face" (5: 4). The correction combines elements of the Sinai tradition (5: 5a[a]b) with the tradition of Moses as prophet (5: 5a[b]). It is integral to the Sinai tradition that the people did not ascend the mountain (Exod 19: 12, 23, 24; 24: 12–14), but, because they were afraid, stayed far away and let Moses approach God (Exod 20: 18–21). The original sense of the expression "face to face" is that Moses is a prophet (Exod 33: 11; Num 12: 6; Deut 34: 10), and DTR II returns to it: Moses declares the word of Yahweh (cf. 18: 15–22) as the judge interprets the law (1: 17; 17: 11).

DTR II's conclusion to the decalog (5: 22) canonizes the ten commandments and confirms Moses as their interpreter. From the Sinai tradition DTR II concludes that they were written on tablets of stone and given to Moses (5: 22b; Exod 24: 12; 34: 1). It is DTR II's own interpretation (5: 22a) that they are the words of Yahweh (4: 10, 36; 9: 10; 10: 2), spoken in a loud voice (4: 12, 33) from the fire (4: 12, 33; 5: 26), the cloud and the darkness (4: 11), addressed to the assembly (4: 10; 9: 10; 10: 4; 18: 16; 23: 2, 3, 4, 9; 31: 12, 28, 30), and finished (4: 2; 13: 1).

Before giving an extended interpretation of the role of Moses, DTR II emphasizes that the decalog is Yahweh's declaration to the people (5: 26). The saying duplicates the DTR I text (5: 24) and interrupts the consent of the people (5: 25, 27). It is expressed in a style used by DTR II (cf. 4: 7–8) but in language typical of P (*kol bāśār*); it attributes to God (*ʾĕlohîm ḥayyîm*, 1 Sam 17: 26, 36; Jer 10: 10; 23: 36) the life which the covenant gave to the people (5: 3; 6: 24).

In accordance with the Sinai tradition (Exod 19: 7; 24: 3), DTR II interprets the consent of the people (5: 27) as willingness to obey the decalog. Yahweh's confirmation of the covenant (5: 28) is changed by a reflection on obedience and blessing (5: 29; cf. 5: 16; 6: 2, 18; 8: 6; 28: 58) into a confirmation of Moses as interpreter of the law. The people are dismissed (5: 30; cf. Josh 22: 8), Moses is ordered to remain (*ʿmd*, cf. 5: 5) and is given the law to teach (5: 31). The reciprocity of the covenant becomes the teaching authority of Moses (cf. 4: 1, 5, 14; 6: 1; 31: 19, 22) and the corresponding obligation of the people to learn the law (5: 1b; cf. 4: 10; 17: 19; 31: 12). With the confirmation of Moses, the address of Yahweh ends; Moses then elaborates Yahweh's reflection on obedience and blessing (5: 32–33). It is a DTR II conviction that unswerving obedience to the decalog (5: 32b; cf. 17: 11, 20; 28: 14; Josh 1: 7; 23: 6; 2 Kgs 22: 2) brings life (5: 33b[a]; cf. 4: 1; 30: 16, 19), blessing (5: 33b[a]; cf. 19: 13; and DTR I, 6: 24; 10: 13), and continued existence in the land (5: 33b[b], cf. 4: 26, 40; 6: 2; 11: 9; 17: 20; 30: 18, 20; 32: 47).

The installation of Moses is a substantial correction of the DTR I history. It suppresses the covenant between Yahweh and the people and makes DTR II's Book of the Law a commentary on the decalog (Lohfink 1963; Kaufman 1979). The commentary begins by repeating the appointment of Moses (6: 1 = 5: 31) and the obligation of teaching and learning (6: 2; cf. 4: 9–10; 14: 23; 17: 19; 31: 12). Its first part will convert DTR I's historical prologue (6: 4–13, 20, 21, 23b–24) into an analysis of the first commandment (6: 14–19, 22–23a, 25). It is anticipated in a transition which duplicates the summons to Israel (6: 3 = 6: 4a) and introduces the patriarchal covenant (6: 3) in the promise of numerous descendants (cf. 1: 10; 7: 13; 8: 1; 11: 21; 13: 18; 28: 63; 30: 5, 16) in a land flowing with milk and honey (cf. 11: 9; 26: 9, 15; 27: 3; 31: 20).

2. In revising the historical prologue and grant of the land DTR II adds two prohibitions (6: 14, 16) with their motivating clauses (6: 15, 17–19), an emphasis on the Exodus (6: 22–23a) and a conclusion on justification (6: 25). The revision cancels the gift of the land by substituting the promise to the fathers.

The prologue repeats and develops (6: 12–13) the divine protocol (5: 6). On the basis of the protocol (5: 7) DTR II prohibits (6: 14) the worship of other gods. This anticipates the covenant's exclusion of foreign alliances (7: 1–3, 5) but is a constant in the interpretation of the decalog (7: 4; 8: 19; 11: 28; 13: 3, 7, 14; 17: 3; 28: 14; 29: 25). Since DTR II is convinced that Israel's apostasy is occasioned by the nations (Smend 1971), the other gods are specified as the gods of the surrounding nations (6: 14b; 13: 8; Judg 2: 12).

The first motivation (6: 15a) is taken from the protocol (5: 9b) and is traditionally bound with the prohibition of alien worship (Exod 34: 14; Deut 4: 24; Josh 24: 19; cf. Deut 29: 19). The second motivation (6: 15b) introduces a theme peculiar to DTR II's edition of the history (McCarthy 1974). The consequence of disobedience to the decalog is the anger of Yahweh (9: 8b; 29: 19, 22, 23, 26, 27; 31: 17; Josh 23: 16; 1 Kgs 8: 46; 11: 9). It explains the loss of Israel (2 Kgs 17: 18) and the downfall of Judah and Jerusalem (2 Kgs 23: 26; 24: 20); neither Moses (1: 37; 4: 21) nor Aaron (9: 20) is exempt. The effect of Yahweh's anger is annihilation and banishment from the land (4: 26; 7: 4; 9: 8b, 19; 11: 17; Josh 23: 15–16; Weinfeld 1972: 133).

The affirmation that Yahweh is "among you" (6: 15) recalls the plaint of Israel at Massah (Exod 17: 7) and leads to the second prohibition (6: 16; Exod 17: 1–7). Since the tradition connects Massah and Horeb (Exod 17: 6) the prohibition is contrasted with a command to observe the law (6: 17). The law is balanced by the promise to the patriarchs (6: 18–19). In the DTR I covenant the agreement of the people brought the gift of the land. For DTR II obedience to the law brings the blessings promised to the fathers. Relying on an earlier conquest tradition (Exod 23: 27–33; Skweres 1979: 192), DTR II includes expulsion of the enemy (*hdp,* 6: 19; 9: 4; Josh 23: 5) among the promises. Disobedience to the decalog will lead to loss of the land (6: 15), but it is the promise to the patriarchs, and not obedience, which assures its possession.

DTR II shifts the emphasis from Israel to Yahweh. The law explains the decalog. The decalog affirms that Yahweh alone is God. The people have not entered into a reciprocal covenant which transfers the land, but have agreed to observe the decalog. Obedience does not entail the land, which depends on Yahweh's fidelity, but sustains the decalog affirmation. This is emphasized in DTR II's addition to the Exodus account (6: 22–23a). The stereotyped list of punishments (cf. 7: 19; 29: 2; 34: 11) assumes that Egypt is the model enemy (6: 19; 7: 19) but is used by DTR II to argue that Yahweh alone is God (4: 34–35). It is in this affirmation, and not in possession of the land (9: 4–6), that Israel is justified (6: 25).

3. DTR II revised the conquest narrative by inserting a warning against false worship (7: 4), motivated by an argument on the distinctiveness of Israel (7: 6–15) and explained by reference to the threat from the nations left in the land (7: 16, 19–20, 22, 25–26). The revision comments on the first commandment (7: 4, 16, 25–26); it depends on a variant conquest tradition (Exod 23: 20–33) to correct DTR I's reliance on a covenant tradition (Exodus 34), and interprets DTR I's covenant declaration (26: 17–19) in terms of the decalog (7: 9–10) and the promise to the patriarchs.

The warning (7: 4) interrupts a series of commands and prohibitions (7: 2–3, 5). It describes apostasy (7: 4a[a]) in terms used to evaluate the fidelity or defection of the monarchy (2 Kgs 18: 6; etc), and reiterates (7: 4b = 6: 15b) that the consequence of apostasy is the anger of Yahweh and banishment. The warning against serving other gods (7:4a[b]), standard in the DTR II edition (11: 16; Josh 24: 2, 16; Judg 10: 13; 1 Sam 8: 8), is derived from the conquest tradition (Exod 23: 24, 33): the DTR I narrative (7: 2–3, 5) interprets Exod 34: 12–13, 15–16, omitting 34: 14; DTR II corrects the narrative by quoting the parallel to 34: 14 (*ḥwh*) in Exod 23: 24, 33 (*ʿbd*).

The warning is motivated by reference to Israel's distinctiveness (7: 6–11) and to the blessings consequent on obedience (7: 12–15). The motivation is stated (7: 6) and then argued by appeal to the historical facts (7: 7–8), in a summary of the decalog (7: 9–10), and in an exhortation to obey (7: 11). It is a pastiche of known texts. The declaration of Israel's special status (7: 6) combines clauses from DTR I's covenant declaration (26: 18–19, *ʿam qādôš . . . ʿam sĕgullâ*) with a phrase from the parallel in the Sinai tradition (Exod 19: 5b[a], *mikkol hāʿammîm*). The historical summary (7: 7–8) interprets the covenant declaration as the oath to the patriarchs. It is connected to the initial statement by the repetition of *mikkol hāʿammîm* (7: 6, 7, 14, 16, 19; cf. 4: 19; 28: 37, 64; 30: 3; 1 Kgs 9: 7) and is constructed antithetically (*loʾ . . . kî*, cf. 9: 5). The choice of Israel (7: 7; cf. 4: 37; 10: 15; 14: 2) is combined with the Exodus (7: 7, *rb . . . mʿṭ* = 26: 5; cf. 10: 22) but the Exodus is ascribed to the promise to the fathers (7: 8; Genesis 15; Skweres 1979: 110–18) and is often described in the language of the decalog (7: 8b = 5: 6). The summary statement (7: 9–10) combines the decalog and the patriarchal promise. The first commandment (5: 6a) is rephrased in the affirmation that Yahweh alone is God (7: 9a = 4: 35, 39). Yahweh's fidelity to the covenant (5: 10) is interpreted (7: 9b) as his fidelity to the patriarchal promises, but in language familiar from DTR I's interpretation of the Davidic covenant (*hbryt whḥsd*, 1 Kgs 3: 6; 8: 23; Weinfeld 1972: 193–95). Reference to disobedience to the decalog (7: 10a) uses the language of the protocol (5: 9, *lĕśonʾay*), but its punishment is immediate annihilation, as DTR II has warned (7: 10b = 7: 4b[b]; Fishbane 1980: 353). Since the argument reinterprets DTR I's covenant as the covenant with the patriarchs and defines the distinctiveness of Israel as its obedience to the decalog, the final exhortation (7: 11) urges adherence to the commandments, statutes, and ordinances declared by Yahweh (5: 31) and taught by Moses (6: 1).

The blessings of the patriarchal covenant (7: 12–15) are linked to the argument by verbatim repetitions: both contain an exhortation (7: 11, 12a), the patriarchal covenant (7: 9b[b] = 7: 12b[a]), and oath (7: 8a[a] = 7: 12b[b]), the terminology of love (7: 8a[a], 13a[a]) and hate (7: 10a[a], 15b[b]), and reference to other nations (7: 6–7, 14; *mikkol hāʿammîm*) and to Egypt (7: 8, 15). The blessings emphasize the distinctiveness of Israel: as Israel is chosen (7: 6), so it will be blessed (7: 14a), above all people; as Yahweh punishes those who hate him (7: 10), so all the curses will be inflicted on those who hate Israel (7: 15).

The blessings combine elements of the patriarchal tradition with materials in DTR II's conquest source (Exodus 23). Israel's numerical insignificance (7: 7) is contrasted with the promise of multiplication (7: 13a; cf. 1: 10; 8: 1; 13: 18; 30: 5) made to the patriarchs (Gen 16: 10; 22: 17; 26: 4, 24). The blessing is amplified (7: 13b) with quotations from the DTR I covenant (28: 4, 11), and then restated in terms of the conquest source (7: 14b = Exod 23: 26a). In agreement with this source, Israel is relieved of sickness and of the diseases of Egypt (7: 15ab[a] = Exod 23: 25b, 26b; cf. Deut 28: 59–61). But since Egypt is the paradigm of the surrounding nations (6: 22; 7: 19), those who hate Israel will be afflicted with its diseases (7: 15b[b]).

The warning which DTR II inserted (7: 4) is explained in part by the distinctiveness of Israel (7: 6–15) and in part by the threat from the nations left in the land (7: 16, 19–20, 22, 25–26). The warning is resumed (7: 16) in a command and in prohibitions. The command (7: 16a[a]) to destroy (*ʾkl*, cf. 31: 17) all the nations is attached to the preceding argument by *mikkol hāʿammîm* (7: 6, 7, 14). Since not all the peoples will be conquered (7: 20, 22), DTR I's conquest formulas (7: 23–24) are not used, and the destruction of the people is assimilated to the promise of the land with the formula "which Yahweh your God is giving you." The first prohibition (7: 16a[b], "Your eye shall not pity them") is derived from the purge laws (13: 1; 19: 13, 21). The second prohibition (7: 16b) resumes the warning against worship of foreign gods (7: 4) but is a literal quotation from the conquest source (Exod 23: 33b).

The command and prohibitions introduce DTR II's revision of DTR I's program for the conquest (7: 17–18, 21, 23–24). The revision contains three related segments: Pharaoh and Egypt as paradigm of the nations (7: 19); the tradition of an incomplete and gradual destruction of the nations (7: 20, 22); and precepts for the abolition of alien cults (7: 25–26).

The first interpolation (7: 19) is smoothed out by its concluding clause (7: 19b[b], "whom you fear") which resumes DTR I's command (7: 18a, "Do not fear them"). It amasses synonyms for the affliction of Egypt (cf. 4: 34; 6: 22; 29: 2) and makes this the model of what Yahweh will do to all the people (7: 19b, *kol hāʿammîm*).

The second segment (7: 20, 22) quotes the conquest source (Exod 23: 28–30) to correct DTR I's narrative. For DTR II the conquest is a gradual process (7: 22 = Exod 23: 29–30). As the Exodus proves (7: 19), it is Yahweh who will destroy the nations left in the land (7: 20b). As the blessings have anticipated (7: 15b), they will be destroyed by a destructive pestilence (7: 20a = Exod 23: 28). An incomplete and ineffectual conquest explains Israel's apostasy: worship of other gods (7: 4, 16) is occasioned by the nations left in the land (7: 20, 22; Smend 1971).

The third segment (7: 25–26) derides the worship of other gods and implicitly affirms that Yahweh alone is God. The command to burn the images of their gods (7: 25a) repeats DTR I's command (7: 5) but changes the exclusion of foreign alliances into the rejection of idols (cf. 29: 16). This change becomes explicit in the following prohibition (7: $25b^a$) of coveting the silver and gold on the images. Two reasons are given for the prohibition (7: $25b^b$): the first repeats the warning (7: 16^b = Exod 23: 33b) that serving other gods would be a snare; the second is derived from the abomination laws (16: 21–17: 1; 18: 10–12; 22: 5; 23: 18–19; 25: 13–16). The next prohibition (7: $26a^a$) identifies idols and abominations (= 27: 15). The final command (7: 26b) urges contempt for the silver and gold in language (cf. 29: 16; 2 Kgs 23: 13) that implies the rejection of idols. The prohibition and command are motivated by reference to the ban which is legislated in DTR I's narrative (7: 2) and illustrated in the story of Achan (Joshua 7).

4. DTR II's revision of the prologue to the covenant in the land of Moab (8: 1, 7–12, $14b–16a^a$) comprises a lesson from the wilderness (8: 2–6, $16a^bb$), a reminder on the patriarchal covenant (8: $1b^a$, *ûrĕbîtem*, 17–18), a warning (8: 13–14a) and a concluding threat (8: 19–20). The revision stresses Israel's distinctiveness in knowledge of the law (8: 2–6, $16a^bb$; cf. 4: 5–8) and the promise to the patriarchs (8: $1b^a$, *ûrĕbîtem*, 17–18), and warns against assimilation to the nations (8: 13–14a, 19–20). For DTR I's contrast between the wilderness and the gift of the land, DTR II substitutes a contrast between obedience in the wilderness and apotasy in the land.

The lesson recalls (*zkr*) the wilderness events (8: 2–4), summarizes them in a theological statement (8: 5, *ydʿ*), and concludes with the practical implications (8: 6). The beginning (8: 2a) and end (8: 4) of the historical section are marked by the same phrase (*zeh ʾarbāʿîm šānâ* [*bammidbār*]) which DTR II borrowed from DTR I (= 2: 7; cf. 29: 4a) together with the description of the wilderness (8: 4 = 29: 4b). These borrowed texts (8: 2a, 4 = 2: 7 + 29: 4) articulate the tradition of leading in the wilderness (cf. 8: 15), which DTR II's argument (8: 2b-3) supplements and corrects.

The argument minimizes leading in the wilderness by substituting two variant wilderness traditions. The first part of the lesson (8: 2b, 16b) describes the wilderness as a time of affliction (cf. 1 Kgs 8: 35; 11: 9; 2 Kgs 17: 20) and testing (cf. 4: 34; 6: 16; 7: 19; 8: $16b^a$; 13: 4; 29: 2; 33: 8) and refers to an isolated tradition in the manna story (Exod 16: $4b^b$ + 28; Noth 1948: 32, n. 109). The second part (8: 3) describes the wilderness as a time of affliction, famine, and feeding with the manna and is derived from the final edition of the same source (Exod 16: 3, 35a, P). By combining the traditions DTR II includes the manna among the afflictions in the wilderness and describes it as the worship of other gods (cf. 4: 28; 28: 36, 64) "whom you do not know and whom your fathers did not know" (8: 3a, $16a^b$; 11: 28; 13: 3, 7, 14; 29: 25; 32: 17). The lesson of the manna is that the wilderness is a test of Israel's obedience to the decalog (8: 2b; cf. 30: 11–14) from which Israel learned that Yahweh alone is God (8: $3b^a$; cf. Exod 16: 6, 12, P) and that obedience is life (8: 3b; cf. 5: 33; 8: 1b; 30: 15–20). The summary (8: 5) is derived from another manna tradition (1: 31a; Num 11: 10–15) and emphasizes that Israel learned this lesson from Yahweh (cf. 4: 36a; 11: 2a). The lesson concludes (8: 6) with an exhortation to observe the law (cf. 8: 1), to walk in the ways of Yahweh (cf. 8: 2a) and to fear him (cf. 4: 10; 31: 13).

The alternative to obedience (cf. 8: 2b) is apostasy (8: 13–14a). DTR II includes among the blessings of obedience the promise of increase (8: 1b; *ûrĕbîtem*; cf. 1: 10; 6: 3; 7: 13; 11: 21; 13: 18; 30: 16) made to the patriarchs (Gen 22: 17; 26: 4, 24). The blessing is exaggerated in DTR II's description of prosperity in the land (8: 13) to include the increase of flocks and herds appropriate to the patriarchs (cf. Gen 13: 2) as well as the multiplication of silver and gold which is forbidden to the king (17: 17b) and proper to the worship of idols

(7: 25b). Israel is warned (8: 14a), as the king is warned (17: 20), against arrogance. The time of affliction will be followed by a time of prosperity (8: 16b). The presumption that prosperity is an achievement (8: 17) is corrected by an appeal to observance of the decalog (8: 18a) and by the reminder that prosperity confirms the validity (*kayyôm hazzeh*, 4: 20, 38; 10: 15; 29: 17) of Yahweh's covenant with the patriarchs.

DTR II changed the description of the land in order to include the elements of apostasy (8: 13–14a), and suppressed the tradition of leading in the wilderness as a prelude to possession of the land in order to stress the lesson of obedience which Israel learned in the wilderness. If Israel forgets its lesson and worships other gods (8: 19a), Yahweh is witness (cf. 4: 26; 30: 19; 31: 19, 21, 26, 28; 32: 46) that it will be annihilated like the nations (8: 19b–20a; cf. 7: 20). Obedience (*ʿēqeb tišmĕʿûn*, 7: 12) separates Israel from the nations and elicits the blessings promised to the patriarchs. Disobedience (*ʿēqeb loʾ tišmĕʿûn*, 8: 20b) assimilates Israel to the nations and their fate.

5. DTR II's revision of the Horeb narrative includes an argument on the law, the promise and the conquest (9: 4–6; 10: 11), an account of Yahweh's anger and threatened destruction of Israel (9: 8b, 13–14), reflection on the sin of Israel (9: 18–19) and the fidelity of Yahweh (9: 25–29; 10: 10), a description of the presentation and restoration of the decalog (9: 10; 10: 1–5), mention of Yahweh's anger at Aaron (9: 20), and an explanation of his choice of the tribe of Levi (10: 8–9).

The argument (9: 4–6) reflects on the legal basis for the possession of the land. The proposition (9: 4) contrasts the innocence (*ṣdqh*, cf. 6: 25) of Israel with the guilt of the nations expelled (*hdp*, cf. 6: 19; Josh 23: 5) from the land. Yahweh's retort (9: 5) dismisses the innocence and rectitude (*yošer lēb*, cf. 1 Kgs 3: 6; 9: 4) of Israel, affirms the guilt of the nations, and bases possession of the land on Yahweh's oath to the patriarchs. The point of the argument (9: 6a) is that it is not Israel's obedience to the decalog but Yahweh's fidelity to his promise that assures possession of the land. The proof is (9: 6b) that Israel will possess the land despite its intransigence (*qšh ʿrp*, 9: 6, 13, 27; 10: 16; 31: 27; 2 Kgs 17: 14). The contrast is not that proposed by Israel (9: 4) between its innocence and the guilt of the nations. Israel is as guilty as the nations (9: 27). The contrast is between the fidelity of Yahweh (9: 25–29; 10: 11) and the sin of Israel.

DTR II borrows the theme of Israel's intransigence (9: 6) from the Sinai traditions (Exod 32: 9; 33: 3, 5; 34: 9) and comments on DTR I's introduction to the Horeb account (9: 8a) by explaining that the worship of other gods angers Yahweh and leads to annihilation (9: 8b; cf. Exod 32: 10). This anticipates an accusation (9: 13) and a threat (9: 14). The accusation repeats DTR II's argument on Israel's intransigence, but it is a quotation from the Sinai source (Exod 32: 9). The threat paraphrases the same source (Exod 32: 10) in language borrowed from other texts: the threat to Israel (9: 14a[b], *mḥh šm*) is derived from a curse against the idolater (29: 19); the benefit to Moses (9: 14b, *gôy ʿaṣûm wārab mimmennû*) is taken from DTR I's description of the nations to be conquered (7: 1, 17). By using this language, DTR II implies that destruction (*šmd*, 9: 14a[a]; cf. 9: 8b, 19, 20, 25) is a punishment for idolatry occasioned by the nations left in the land.

The threat and accusation are followed by a reflection on sin (9: 18–20). It is linked to the DTR I narrative (*ḥaṭṭaʾtkem*, 9: 21; *ḥaṭaʾtem*, 9: 16) by verbatim repetition (9: 18b[a], *kol ḥaṭṭaʾtkem ʾăšer ḥaṭaʾtem*). It is represented (9: 18a[a]) as the intercession of Moses and, contradicting DTR I (9: 15) but in accord with the Sinai tradition (Exod 32: 11–14), as taking place when the decalog was first given (9: 18a[b] = 9: 9b). However, it is not the intercession of Moses, which is recounted in 9: 25–29, but a reflection on the giving of the decalog (9: 10) and the sin of Israel (9: 18b-20).

DTR II's incise on the tablets of stone (9: 10) corrects DTR I's narrative on the Horeb covenant (9: 9, 11, 15). It is taken from DTR II's first account (5: 22) with the addition, derived from P (Exod 31: 18b; cf. Exod 32: 16), that they were inscribed by God, and with the notation peculiar to DTR II that the words were spoken "on the day of assembly" (9: 10, MT; 10: 4; 18: 16; cf. 31: 9–13). The insertion emphasizes that the decalog was addressed directly to Israel. The sin of Israel is the rejection of the decalog by making the golden calf (9: 18b[a]). This is how Israel did what was wrong in the eyes of Yahweh (9: 18b; cf. 4: 25; 17: 2; 31: 29; 2 Kgs 17: 17; 21: 2, 6, 9, 15, 16; 23: 37; 24: 9, 19) and how Israel provoked

Yahweh (9: 18b; cf. 4: 25; 31: 29; 2 Kgs 21: 6, 15, 17). The consequence of sin (9: 19a) is Yahweh's anger (6: 15; 7: 4; 11: 17; 29: 19, 23, 26, 27; 31: 17; 2 Kgs 23: 26) and rage (29: 22, 27; 2 Kgs 22: 17) and the imminent destruction of Israel (= 9: 8b, 14). Since Aaron is to blame for the sin of the people (Exod 32: 21–26), the same threat is applied specifically to him (9: 20a = 9: 8b).

Destruction is averted (9: 19b, 20b) by the intercession of Moses (9: 25–29). It is presented (9: 25) as the continuation of the first intervention of Moses (9: 18–20) and refers to the same circumstances ("I prostrated myself before Yahweh"), to the same time ("the forty days and nights that I prostrated myself"), and to the same predicament ("because Yahweh meant to destroy you") as the reflection on sin. The prayer (9: 26–29) is a paraphrase of the intercession of Moses in the golden calf episode (Exod 32: 11–14) intricately combined with the prayer of Moses in the spy narrative (Num 14: 13–19). The appeal to the Exodus and the patriarchs (9: $26a^b$–27a) is drawn from the Sinai source (Exod 32: 11, 13). Egypt's taunt (9: 28; cf. 29: 23–27; 1 Kgs 9: 8–9) is found in the Sinai account (Exod 32: 12) but its formulation is derived from the taunt of the nations in the spy narrative (Num 14: 16) with an addition (9: $28b^a$, *ûmiśśinʾatô ʾôtām*) from the DTR I version of the same narrative (1: $27a^b$, *bĕśinʾat yhwh ʾotanû*).

The intercession consists in turning attention (9: 27b) from Israel's intransigence (9: 6, 13), sin (9: 18–19), and guilt (9: 4–6), to Yahweh's promise to the patriarchs (9: 27a). It is DTR II's argument that Yahweh brought Israel out of Egypt and make it his people to fulfill his oath to the patriarchs (7: 6–11). The intercession of Moses appeals to this oath (9: 27a) and to the fact that Israel is Yahweh's "people and inheritance" (9: $26a^a$, 29a; cf. 1 Kgs 8: 51, 53; 2 Kgs 21: 14), whom he brought out of Egypt (9: $26a^b$) by his great power and outstretched arm (9: 29b = 2 Kgs 17: 36). It is because Yahweh remembers his covenant with the patriarchs that he will not destroy Israel (9: 27a; cf. 4: 31).

Yahweh's response to the intercession of Moses has been anticipated (9: 19b) but is reserved (10: 11) until the decalog is restored (10: 1–5) and the ark is confided to the tribe of Levi (10: 8–9). DTR II's account of the restoration of the decalog combines elements of the Sinai tradition (Exod 34: 1–2, 4, 27–29) with the ark tradition peculiar to P (Exod 25: 16, 21; 31: 7; 40: 20). The decalog is restored in its original form (10: $4a^b$ = 5: 22), written by Yahweh (10: $4a^a$; cf. Exod 34: 1b, 27–28) and given to Moses. Moses descends the mountain (10: $5a^a$ = 9: $15a^a$) and the tablets are placed in an ark of acacia wood (10: $3a^a$ = Exod 25: 10, P) where they remain (10: 5b; 1 Kgs 8: 9).

The chief function of the Levites is to carry the ark of the covenant (10: 8a; 31: 9, 25). They are priests (17: 9, 18; 18: 1; 21: 5; 24: 8; 27: 9; 31: 9) who stand and serve (10: 8b; 17: 12; 18: 5; cf. 1 Kgs 8: 11) and bless in the name of Yahweh (10: 8b; 18: 5; 21: 5). They were set apart (*hibdîl*; cf. Num 8: 14; 16: 9, P) as Israel was set apart from all the peoples of the earth to be Yahweh's heritage (1 Kgs 8: 53). They are priests (cf. Exod 32: 26–29; Deut 33: 8–11; Cross 1973: 199–200) in accordance with the promise of Yahweh (10: $9b^b$; cf. Josh 13: 33; 18: 7) to Aaron (10: 9 = Num 18: 20, P; cf. Skweres 1979: 188–91).

After Yahweh's favorable answer to the intercession of Moses (10: 10; cf. 9: 9b, 18, 25) the DTR II account concludes with Yahweh's command to set out (10: 11a; cf. Exod 32: 34; Num 10: $33b^a$) and to take possession of the promised land (10: 11b = 1: $8b^a$).

The DTR I narrative included the Horeb covenant (9: 8a, 9, 11–12, 15–17, 21) in a history of Israel's rebellion (9: 1–3, 7, 22–24). DTR II changed the narrative into a consideration of sin (9: 8b, 13–14, 18–20; 10: 10), the law (9: 10; 10: 1–5, 8–9), and the promise (9: 4–6, 25–29; 10: 11) in order to contrast the recalcitrance of Israel and the fidelity of Yahweh. The sin of Israel is rejection of the decalog and leads to destruction. The decalog (9: 10), guaranteed by the institutions of the law (10: 1–5, 8–9), declares that Yahweh is the God of Israel. Israel is the people of Yahweh according to the promise (9: 25–29), and will possess the land which Yahweh swore to give them (9: 4–6; 10: 11).

In DTR I's narrative, the Horeb account is a prelude to the covenant in the land of Moab. DTR II's revision suppresses the covenant and makes the DTR I narrative conform to the pentateuchal account. From this source DTR II added and interpreted Yahweh's predilection for Moses (9: 13–14; Exod 32: 9–10; Num 14: 12), the prayer of Moses (9: 25–29; Exod 32: 11–14; Num 14: 13–19), the sin of Aaron (9: 18–20; Exod 32: 21–26), the renewal of covenant (10: 1–5; Exod 34: 1–2, 4, 27–29), and the choice of Levi (10: 8–9; Exod 32: 26–29). Clear affinities with P (9: 10; 10: 1–5, 8–9) indicate that DTR II knew that source.

6. DTR II's revision of the covenant in the land of Moab consists of expansions concerning the patriarchs (10: 15, 16, 22; 11: 1, 9), the Exodus (10: 19; 11: 2–3) and the law (11: 16–17, 18–21), and a prolepsis (11: 26–29) to the ceremony on Ebal and Gerizim (27: 11–26).

The patriarchal references substitute the traditional promises to the patriarchs for DTR I's covenant between Yahweh and the people. The choice of the patriarchs and their descendants (10: 15) confirms DTR I's statement (10: 14) on the sovereignty of Yahweh. DTR II has used the same argument and identical wording (4: 37–39; 7: 7–9) to affirm that Yahweh alone is God, and to urge obedience to the law (4: 40; 7: 11). In conformity with the patriarchal covenant (cf. Genesis 17) the exhortation to obedience (10: 16a) is expressed as circumcision of the heart (cf. 30: 6; Lev 26: 41; Jer 4: 4; 9: 25; Ezek 44: 7, 9), the obverse of the intransigence (10: 16b) manifested at Horeb (9: 6, 13, 27).

The same pattern is repeated in DTR II's commentary on the historical prologue. DTR I's account of the Exodus begins (10: 21) with a general statement which is developed (11: 4–7) in a detailed summary of historical traditions. DTR II comments on the statement with a synthesis of patriarchal traditions (10: 22a) and another exhortation to fidelity (11: 1). The synthesis begins (10: 22a) with Jacob's descent into Egypt in small numbers. The tradition is preserved in other DTR II summaries (7: 7; 26: 5; cf. 4: 27) but the specific reference to seventy persons is peculiar to P (Gen 46: 27; Exod 1: 5). The growth of Israel (10: 22b = 1: 10 = 28: 62) is also traditional (26: 5) but its formulation is a DTR II conflation of two promises of a multitude of descendants: like the sand on the seashore which cannot be counted *lārob* (Gen 32: 12); or like the stars in the sky (Gen 22: 17; 26: 4; Exod 32: 13). The exhortation to fidelity begins (11: 1a) with the theme of love proper to DTR I's covenant (10: 12; 11: 13, 22), but the command to obey the law (11: 1b) repeats, with some variation, the summary of Abraham's obedience (Gen 26: 5) and David's exhortation to Solomon (1 Kgs 2: 3).

The third patriarchal reference (11: 9) is also a motive for obedience. The promise of long life in the land (*ʾădāmâ*) is intrusive in DTR I's description of the cultivated land (*ʾereṣ*, 11: 8, 10–12) but is typical of DTR II (cf. 4: 40; 25: 15; 30: 18, 20; 32: 47). The promise of the land (cf. Gen 13: 15; 15: 18; 26: 3; Exod 32: 13) corrects the DTR I narrative in which the land is given to Israel in accordance with the terms of the covenant in the land of Moab.

The first reference to the Exodus (10: 19) disrupts the preamble with a command to love the sojourner "because you were sojourners in the land of Egypt." The command (10: 19a) expands on the preamble's affirmation that Yahweh loves the sojourner (10: 18b), and in conjunction with the motivation attests Yahweh's love for Israel (7: 8, 13; 23: 6). The motivation (10: 19b) differs from the decalog motivation ("You shall remember you were a slave in Egypt," 5: 15; 15: 15; 24: 18, 22) and is derived from earlier legislation (Exod 22: 20; 23: 9). DTR II's reliance on these texts was determined by the correspondence between their context and the preamble on which DTR II was commenting: the first law is followed (Exod 22: 21–23) by legislation concerning orphans and widows; the second is preceded (Exod 23: 8) by a prohibition against taking a bribe; the preamble combines both elements (10: $17b^{b}$–18a) in its description of Yahweh as judge.

The second reference to the Exodus (11: 2–3) comments on DTR I's narrative of the crossing of the Reed Sea (11: 4). It begins (11: 2a) as an appeal for understanding (*wîdaʿtem*, 4: 39; 7: 9; 8: 5; 9: 6) of the Exodus as a lesson (cf. 4: 36; 8: 5). The appeal is emphasized by excluding children who have not been witnesses to the Exodus and cannot understand it (11: 2a). DTR II describes the familiar stereotyped Exodus (11: 2b–3; cf. 4: 34; 6: 22; 7: 19; 29: 2; 34: 11), whose lesson is that Yahweh alone is God (4: 35).

DTR II comments on the law (11: 13) with the usual warning against apostasy (11: 16; cf. 7: 4), the prospect of Yahweh's anger (11: 17a = 6: $15b^{a}$), and the threat of annihilation (11: 17b = 6: $15b^{b}$). The variants are determined by their immediate context (11: 14–15) but have been borrowed from other sources: the closing of the heavens and the lack of rain (11: $17a^{a}$) is a situation envisaged in the prayer of Solomon (1 Kgs 8: 35–36); lack of rain and failure of the crops (11: $17a^{b}$) is one of the curses in the Holiness Code (Lev 26: 19–20; cf. Deut 28: 23–24).

DTR II's argument progresses from the patriarchal covenant and the choice of Israel as the people of Yahweh (10: 15–16, 19) to the affirmation that Yahweh alone is God (11: 2–3). The blessings are those promised to the fathers (10: 22; 11: 9); the curse is banishment from the land (11: 16–17). Israel is encouraged to love Yahweh its God, observe the law (11: 1), and abandon the recalcitrance it demonstrated at Horeb (10: 16).

The argument concludes with an exhortation (11: 18–21). The exhortation belongs with the command to love Yahweh (11: 1a), as its model (6: 6–9) is linked to the identical command (6: 5a). It is a copy of the original: the beginning adds (11: 8a; cf. 6: 6) "and on yourselves" which is derived from the original command to love (6: 5b); it is plural at the beginning and the end (11: 18–19a, 21) where it differs from the original, but is singular (11: 19b-20) where the original is quoted verbatim. By repeating the original, DTR II closes the commentary on the first commandment as it began. It is this commentary by Moses (11: 18a, *ʾet dĕbāray ʾēlleh*) which must be taken to heart. It is to be "placed" (*wĕśamtem*, 11: 18a; cf. *wĕhāyû* 6: 6), and "taught" (*wĕlimmadtem*, 11: 19a; cf. *wĕšinnantem*, 6: 7), as the song of Moses is to be placed in the mouths of Israel and taught to them (31: 9) or as the Book of the Law is to be placed beside the ark (31: 26) and learned (31: 12). The motivation (11: 21a[a], *lĕmaʿan yirbû yĕmêkem wîmê bĕnêkem*) combines the blessing of a long life (*ʾrk ymm*, 11: 9) and the patriarchal blessing of a multitude of descendants (*rbh*, 10: 22). The blessing and the patriarchal promise of the land (11: 21a[b]) are confirmed by the invocation of heaven and earth (11: 21b; cf. 11: 17; cf. 4: 26; 30: 19).

The commentary is separated from the rest of the Book of the Law by a prolepsis (11: 26–29) to the ceremony on Ebal and Gerizim (27: 11–26). It is attached to the exhortation by the theme of blessing (11: 21, 26–27), and to the commentary by the warning against worshipping other gods (11: 16–17, 28). It states the options which Israel has with regard to the Book of the Law (11: 26 = 30: 15) and lets the conquest hinge on Israel's choice (11: 29; cf. 30: 15–20).

In composing the Book of the Law DTR II revised and expanded the stipulations in DTR I's Book of the Covenant. The laws are distinguished from the rest of the book by a ceremonial introduction (11: 26–29) and conclusion (27: 1–26). They are ordered in the sequence of the decalog (Kaufman 1978–1979); they interpret the commandments from the sabbath law onward (5: 12–21) and manifest DTR II's concern with false worship, legal procedures and the performance of the courts, holiness and purity, the Levitical priesthood, and the maintenance of the law. The expansions reflect the development of legislation which is preserved in Leviticus and Numbers. The revisions include interpretations of DTR I texts, the inclusion of purge and abomination laws, a reflection on the law and the promise to the patriarchs (26: 1–15), and threats of destruction (28: 14, 20b, 22b, 24b, 25b), of siege (28: 47–57), and of exile (28: 36–37, 46–48).

The DTR II edition of the laws includes: the sabbath, worship, the calendar and festivals, 12: 8–12, 15b, 18a[b], 19, 20, 22–25, 27–31; 13: 1–19; 14: 1–3, 6–10, 13*, 14–15, 16*, 17*, 18a, 20, 21, 23b, 27–29; 15: 4–6, 9–10, 21–23; 16: 3–4, 6b, 7b–9, 11a[b], 12–17; parents and institutions of the law, 16: 18–18: 22; homicide, bloodshed, and the death penalty, 19: 7–10, 13–21; 20: 15–18; 21: 1–9, 18–23; adultery, generation, and prostitution, 22: 5–23: 19; theft and property, 23: 22–24; 24: 1–7; false witness and oppression, 24: 8–9, 13b, 15b, 16; 25: 1–4; covetousness and complicity, 25: 5–19; and the patriarchs and the blessing of the land, 26: 1–15.

Conclusion

The DTR I narrative is the history of the covenant in the land of Moab. The history recounts the fulfillment of the promise of the land despite Israel's repeated disbelief and disobedience. Israel refused to believe the promise and rejected the land. It was left to wander in the wilderness until the rebellious generation had been destroyed. The next generation began the conquest and made a covenant with Yahweh that granted them the land and victory over their enemies. In the land Israel forgot Yahweh and rejected the covenant. But when its sin was removed, Israel reconfirmed the covenant and praised Yahweh in the land he had given them.

The narrative is constructed from literary sources preserved in Genesis, Exodus, and Numbers. It is written in the style of state treaties and contains the original duplicates of the treaty document. The treaty form allows DTR I to synthesize the traditions of the Exodus, Sinai, the wilderness, and the conquest in the reciprocal declarations of Yahweh and Israel (cf. 26: 17–19). Composition in duplicate distributes the treaty documents chronologically in the history of Israel. The DTR I history of Israel is the history of a treaty from its promulgation to its ratification, from the Exodus to the conquest and the gift of the land. The intervening period, from Sinai to the wilderness, is the history of Yahweh's fidelity and the rebellions of Israel.

The account of the covenant in the land of Moab is the narrative of Israel's origins. But it is also the theory of history which DTR I used to construct the history of Israel from Moses to Josiah (Polzin 1980: 9, 19). The history begins with the covenant at Horeb narrated by Moses, and ends with the covenant in the land of Moab proclaimed by Josiah. Each incorporates and transmits the traditions of Israel united in a covenant with Yahweh. The history from Joshua–2 Kings repeats and illustrates DTR I's interpretation of these traditions in the conquest under Joshua, the rebellions of the era of the judges, the gift of the land in the covenant with David, and the rejection of the covenant by the sin of Jeroboam. Josiah removed the sin of Jeroboam, and the DTR I theory of history is verified when the Book of the Covenant becomes the covenant between Yahweh and the king and the people (Freedman 1962: 716).

The DTR II revision changed the history into a theology. At Horeb Yahweh gave the decalog to Israel and the law to Moses. The decalog declares that Yahweh alone is God, as the victory over Pharaoh and Egypt has shown. If Israel learns the law and observes the decalog, Yahweh will drive out the nations, as he promised the patriarchs, and Israel will possess the land. If they do not learn that Yahweh alone is God but go and worship the gods of the nations, Yahweh will be angry and banish them from the land. Because some of the nations will be left in the land, Israel will be lured to worship their gods. But Israel should know that it is the people of Yahweh, as he promised its fathers, and that the gods of the nations are idols. If Israel forgets the law and the promise it will become like the nations whose gods it worships and like them will be banished from the land. But even this affliction and the worship of gods they do not know is a lesson from Yahweh that he alone is God and is faithful to his oath to the patriarchs. Similarly, when Israel sinned at Horeb by worshipping an idol and was almost destroyed, it learned that sin does not abrogate the law or the promise. The law is still in force, confided to Moses and the tribe of Levi. The decalog is intact, sealed in an ark of acacia wood, and observable. Israel is still the people of Yahweh according to the promise and will possess the land sworn to the patriarchs. So Israel should take the decalog to heart, learn that Yahweh alone is God, and receive the blessings promised to the fathers in the land that Yahweh swore he would give them.

Like DTR I's interpretation of tradition, the DTR II theology is applicable to every phase of Israel's history. It is expressed in monotonous, stereotyped, and easily identifiable language (Noth 1943: 4), and makes the history which it interprets the same and homogeneous throughout. The predictability of sin and punishment substantiates the absolute uniqueness of Yahweh, the indefectibility of the promise, and the incorruptibility of the law. Repeatedly, but most clearly as the history closes, the Book of the Law reveals the sin of Israel, the holiness of Yahweh, and the expectation of the promise (Freedman 1963: 258).

The assumption that DT is an original tradition which developed through a process of literary accretion is promoted by DTR II's editorial policy. DTR I wrote the Book of the Covenant from texts and traditions in Genesis, Exodus, and Numbers. DTR II wrote the Book of the Law and revised DTR I's theory of history with additions, corrections and a running commentary derived from sources preserved in the P edition of Genesis–Numbers. The result is a mixture of original ideas and ancient traditions in an artificially constructed text. The product of the DTR II revision is the book of Deuteronomy, separated from the DTR I history by a system of introductions and conclusions, and attached to the P edition of the Pentateuch as a commentary on history and the law (Freedman 1976a: 131; 1976b).

Noth's insight was that DT belonged with the DTR history. His mistake was to consider it a source instead of a creation of the DTR history. It was an error induced by his attempt to maintain the prevailing theory of an Urdeuteronomium. This theory resolved the literary and historical problems of the Pentateuch, but could be valid only if DT were part of the Pentateuch. If, as Noth proved, DT is not part of the Pentateuch but belongs to the DTR history, the theory of an Urdeuteronomium is both useless and contradictory. The contradiction was perceptible in Noth's work and has been verified in subsequent studies. Disentangled from this error, and revised by Cross, Noth's theory of the DTR history is sufficient to explain the composition of DT and the ultimate development of the Pentateuch.

References

Begg, C. T.

1979 The Significance of the *Numeruswechsel* in Deuteronomy. The "Pre-History" of the Question. *Ephemerides Theologicae Lovanienses* 55: 116–24.

1980 The Literary Criticism of Deut 4, 1–40. Contributions to a Continuing Discussion. *Ephemerides Theologicae Lovanienses* 56: 10–55.

Braulik, G.

1978 Literarkritik und archäologische Stratigraphie. Zu S. Mittmanns Analyse von Deuteronomium 4, 1–40. *Biblica* 59: 351–83.

Cross, F. M.

1973 *Canaanite Myth and Hebrew Epic. Essays in the History of the Religion of Israel.* Cambridge, MA: Harvard University Press.

Eissfeldt, O.

1964 *Einleitung in das Alte Testament.* Tübingen: J. C. B. Mohr (Paul Siebeck).

Fishbane, M.

1980 Revelation and Tradition: Aspects of Inner-Biblical Exegesis. *Journal of Biblical Literature* 99: 343–61.

Fohrer, G.

1968 *Introduction to the Old Testament.* Trans. D. E. Green. Nashville: Abingdon Press.

Freedman, D. N.

1962 Pentateuch. Pp. 711–27 in *The Interpreter's Dictionary of the Bible*, ed. G. A. Buttrick et al. Nashville: Abingdon.

1963 The Law and the Prophets. *Supplements to Vetus Testamentum* 9: 250–65.

1976a Canon of the OT. Pp. 130–36 in *The Interpreter's Dictionary of the Bible. Supplementary Volume*, ed. K. A. Crim et al. Nashville: Abingdon.

1976b The Deuteronomic History. Pp. 226–28 in *The Interpreter's Dictionary of the Bible. Supplementary Volume*, ed. K. A. Crim et al. Nashville: Abingdon.

García López, F.

1977 Analyse littéraire de Deutéronome, V-XI. *Revue biblique* 84: 481–522.

1978a Analyse littéraire de Deutéronome, V-XI (fin). *Revue biblique* 85: 5–49.

1978b Deut., VI et la Tradition-Rédaction du Deutéronome. *Revue biblique* 85: 161–200.

1979 Deut., VI et la Tradition-Rédaction du Deutéronome (fin). *Revue Biblique* 86: 59–91.

Kaufman, S. A.

1978–1979 The Structure of the Deuteronomic Law. *Maarav* 1/2: 105–58.

Levenson, J. D.

1979 Who Inserted the Book of the Torah? *Harvard Theological Review* 68: 203–33.

Lohfink, N.

1960 Darstellungskunst und Theologie in Dtn 1, 6–3, 29. *Biblica* 41: 105–34.

1963 *Das Hauptgebot. Eine Untersuchung literarischer Einleitungsfragen zu Dtn 5–11.* Analecta Biblica 20. Rome: Pontificio Istituto Biblico.

McCarthy, D. J.

1974 The Wrath of Yahweh and the Structural Unity of the Deuteronomistic History. Pp. 97–110 in *Essays in Old Testament Ethics. J. P. Hyatt in Memoriam*, ed. J. L. Crenshaw and J. T. Willis. New York: KTAV.

Meredino, R. P.

1977 Die Zeugnisse, die Satzungen und die Rechte. Überlieferungsgeschichtliche Erwägungen zu Deut 6. Pp. 185–208 in *Bausteine biblischer Theologie. Festgabe für G. Johannes Botterweck zum 60. Geburtstag*, ed. H.-J. Fabry. Bonner Biblische Beiträge 50. Bonn: Peter Hanstein.

Minette de Tillesse, G.

1962 Sections "tu" et sections "vous" dans le Deutéronome. *Vetus Testamentum* 12: 29–87.

Mittmann, S.

1975 *Deuteronomium 1, 1–6, 3 literarkritisch und traditionsgeschichtlich untersucht.* Beihefte zur Zeitschrift für die Alttestamentliche Wissenschaft 139. Berlin: Walter de Gruyter.

Moran, W. L.

1963 The End of the Unholy War and the Anti-Exodus. *Biblica* 44: 333–42.

1967 The Conclusion of the Decalogue (Ex 20, 17 = Dt 5, 21). *The Catholic Biblical Quarterly* 29: 543–54.

Nicholson, E. W.

1967 *Deuteronomy and Tradition.* Philadelphia: Fortress Press.

Noth, M.

1943 *Überlieferungsgeschichtliche Studien I. Die sammelnden und bearbeitenden Geschichtswerke im Alten Testament.* Tübingen: Niemeyer.

1948 *Überlieferungsgeschichte des Pentateuch.* Stuttgart: W. Kohlhammer.

Oppenheim, A. L.

1968 The Eyes of the Lord. *Journal of the American Oriental Society* 88:

173–80.

Polzin, R.
1980 *Moses and the Deuteronomist. A Literary Study of the Deuteronomic History. Part One: Deuteronomy, Joshua, Judges*. New York: The Seabury Press.

von Rad, G.
1966 *Deuteronomy. A Commentary*. Trans. D. Barton. The Old Testament Library. Philadelphia: The Westminster Press.

Richter, W.
1971 *Exegese als Literaturwissenschaft. Entwurf einer alttestamentlichen Literaturtheorie und Methodologie*. Göttingen: Vandenhoeck & Ruprecht.

Seitz, G.
1971 *Redaktionsgeschichtliche Studien zum Deuteronomium*. Stuttgart: W. Kolhammer.

Skweres, D. E.
1979 *Die Rückverweise im Buch Deuteronomium*. Analecta Biblica 79. Rome: Biblical Institute Press.

Smend, R.
1971 Das Gesetz und die Völker. Ein Beitrag zur deuteronomistischen Redaktionsgeschichte. Pp. 494–509 in *Probleme biblischer Theologie. Gerhard von Rad zum 70. Geburtstag*, ed. H. W. Wolff. München: Chr. Kaiser.

Weinfeld, M.
1972 *Deuteronomy and the Deuteronomic School*. Oxford: Clarendon Press.

Zimmerli, W.
1950 Das Zweite Gebot. Pp. 550–63 in *Festschrift für Alfred Bertholet*, ed. W. Baumgartner. Tübingen: J. C. B. Mohr (Paul Siebeck). Rpt., 1963, as pp. 234–248 in his *Gottes Offenbarung. Gesammelte Aufsätze zum Alten Testament*. Theologische Bücherei 19. München: Chr. Kaiser.

Levitical History and the Role of Joshua

Robert G. Boling
McCormick Theological Seminary, Chicago, Illinois

In a poignant essay on the literature from the period of the Babylonian Exile, David Noel Freedman summarized "The Final Response: Second Isaiah" in one unforgettable sentence: "What everyone else thought was the question (Why do the innocent suffer?) was in fact the answer to a larger question, How does history work?" (Freedman 1975a: 186).[1] In the same essay Freedman gave relatively low marks to "Deuteronomism," especially as represented by the final contributor to the Books of Kings: that writer "is only faintly conscious of his situation; he scarcely seems to be linked to the world around him, he feels the pain in it too slightly even to move us" (*ibid,* 177).

However, it has become increasingly difficult to describe anything like a uniform "Deuteronomic" phenomenon. We hope to show that the final contributors to the historical corpus (Deuteronomy–2 Kings) do in fact have much in common with the major poets of the exile. We begin with the canonical portrait of Joshua, which might not seem to be a promising point of entry to the poetic vision. What were the role and achievements of Joshua?

For at least one very influential circle in ancient Jerusalem and Judah, Joshua was the military ideal, field commander *par excellence*. It is in the Book of Joshua, and only there, that offensive warfare by the Israelites is shown to be both divinely legitimated and properly executed—almost to perfection. As noted by scholars on all hands, the narrative in Joshua is highly stylized so as to present the three-way relationship of Yahweh, Joshua, and Israel as exemplary.

Except in the reconnaisance and initial defeat at The Ruin (Ha-Ai) in Joshua 7, Joshua does nothing on his own initiative in the battle stories; Israel proceeds only at Yahweh's command.[2] In sharp contrast to the unpredictable and variable leadership (and its following) in the subsequent era of the Judges, the performance of Israel under Joshua's leadership appears nearly flawless. But the one lapse was serious indeed. Two whole chapters are taken up with the sequel to one man's violation of the *ḥerem*, so as to make the point that it didn't happen twice, not in the era of Joshua! After the humiliating defeat at The Ruin, Yahweh took direct command, ordering an ambush and a sign to be given by Joshua. Thus it is only upon closer critical scrutiny that there begin to appear certain cracks in the portrait of the leader of the conquest. The cracks become much clearer in the light of a redaction-history.

Dtn, Dtr 1, Dtr 2

In the books of Joshua and Judges we must distinguish the work of at least two major "editors," each making use of older stories, for which we use the following shorthand (as recommended by Cross 1973: 274 n).

The symbol Dtr 1 stands for the major portion of the books of the Former Prophets (Joshua–2 Kings). They represent a late pre-exilic enterprise coming from the time of King Josiah (640–609). The work was clearly designed to be supportive of life in a reformed Davidic monarchy. The symbol Dtr 2 stands for a subsequent, and perhaps penultimate, edition; it is addressed to a drastically altered situation. The bulk of the later editing may be exilic, but it need only be post-Josiah to make sense.[3] The symbols Dtr 1 and Dtr 2 thus correspond to the terms "Deuteronomic" and "Deuteronomistic" respectively, in our earlier studies (Boling 1974 and 1975). There is an unresolved tension running throughout the corpus of Dtr materials.

The symbol Dtn stands for the bulk of Deut 4: 44–28: 68, comprising an old Book of the Law which so effectively accounted for the demise of the Northern Kingdom that it became in Josiah's day the theological preface to the southern version of the whole story from Moses to the era of revival in the late seventh century. This old book stems from no royal sanctuary; the regulation of kingship in Deut 17: 14–20 is probably secondary (Fohrer 1965: 170). Without those verses the book is neither pro-monarchical nor anti-monarchical; it is simply a-monarchical. So why not trace it to an older circle of Levites claiming Mosaic legitimacy, concentrated mainly in the north, and calling for a renewal of the Sinai/Moab/Shechem covenant pattern? (For the earliest form of the proposal see von Rad 1953 and 1962: 834–37; Wright 1953: 323–26 and 1954).

It is a reasonable working hypothesis that this tradition is ultimately rooted in the religious conversion of Levitical families (Deut 33: 8–11) left stranded in Egypt after events that are reflected, however obscurely, in stories such as Genesis 34 and in other poetic fragments such as Gen 49: 5–7. (On the archaic poetry and historical reconstruction, see Freedman 1975b, 1976, 1979.) Sociologically the Levites in Israel may be understood as "a quasi-guild structure or professional caste into which one might gain entrance by choice and appointment *or* by heredity" (Polk 1979: 4; see also the analysis of Gottwald 1979). Dispersal of the Levitical carriers of militant Yahwism throughout the territory of the people was institutionalized in the designation of Levitical towns (Mazar 1960); but a uniformly monarchical-administrative approach to the institution is inadequate in that it fails to account for subsequent Levitical history, which was very different in the north and in the south.

For the alienation of many northern Levites we can look to developments as early as Solomon's reign, with its exploitative fiscal policies rapidly draining the north, to the economic and military advantage of the south. For example, it is clear that the list of Levitical towns assigned by the league leaders in Joshua 21 also reflects a series of monarchical adaptations. One of the earliest of these adaptations concerned the Gershonites, who were very early consigned *en masse* to the distant north (Josh 21: 27–33). The name Gershom—first son of Levi in the standard genealogy of Exod 6: 16–19—also appears as a patronymic of Moses' grandson Jonathan, founder of the priesthood at Dan (Judg 18: 30, cf. Boling 1975: 266). It is therefore probable that Gershom was the name of a major division of Levi alternatively called Mushites in the fragmentary genealogy of Num 26: 58a (Cross 1973: 197–98). The Gershonites/Mushites claiming Moses rather than Aaron as their priestly founder exercised their priesthood in the northern cities, a number of which first became "Israelite" thanks to David's conquests. This distribution might plausibly reflect "an attempt to remove them as far as possible from Jerusalem" (Halpern 1974: 519). After the banishment of the Shilonite (and Mushite) Abiathar, early in Solomon's reign, priesthood in Jerusalem became the exclusive prerogative of the Zadoqites, whose Aaronite legitimacy was most likely rooted in David's earlier power base at Hebron (Cross 1973: 207–15).

It is families such as these northern Levites, in contrast to those close to the Jerusalem throne, that we have in view as candidates for the producers of the nuclear Dtn. We may cite next the sale, in Solomon's twenty-fourth year, of the Cabul district to Hiram of Tyre for one hundred and twenty talents of gold (1 Kgs 9: 10–14). The Cabul district included three or four Gershonite towns: Abdon, Rehob, Mishal, and possibly Helqath. It may be argued that "the displaced Levites must have relocated farther south, dispersing through much of the north and carrying with them their cult objects and the wind of revolution" (Halpern 1974: 523).

There is no indication that the northern administration did anything to heal the breach, but precisely the reverse. The early Deuteronomic movement was doubtless spurred on by such actions as the early relocation of the capital away from Shechem (1 Kgs 12: 25b?; 15: 21; cf. 14: 17), and Jeroboam's priestly appointments at Bethel (originally Aaronite, as is clear from Judg 20: 26–28) and at the high places (non-Levitical appointments, 1 Kgs 12: 31). The Chronicler's History reports that Rehoboam was able, for three years, to exploit a new-found support among the victims of Jeroboam's priestly assignments (2 Chr 11:13–14, 17). Out of such a milieu, then, Dtn probably took documentary shape in relation to the late eighth century reforms of Hezekiah (2 Kings 18//2 Chronicles 29). There is much new archeological evidence to suggest that in matters military, as well as civil and administrative, Hezekiah's power was actually superior to that of Josiah a century later (Rosenbaum 1979). There must have been a major exodus of northerners to the south precipitated by events culminating in the fall of the north in 721. As shown by excavations since 1967, the area of Jerusalem increased enormously around 700 B.C.E., exploding onto the western ridge of the city.

With Dtn we are in any case involved in a complex Levitical history. Since the priestly arrangements in Deuteronomy cannot be derived from anything post-exilic, G. Ernest Wright sought to explain the contrasting ways of referring to Levitical persons in Deuteronomy as truly reflecting the pre-exilic situation (Wright 1954). The formulae are not strictly synonymous, Wright argued. There are "the priests the Levites" (RSV "the Levitical priests"; Deut 18: 1); and there is "the Levite" or "all the tribe of Levi" (12: 12, 18; 16: 11, 14; 26: 11, 13).

"The priests the Levites," Wright argued, were the altar clergy. In narratives of the early period they are the ones who carry and guard the ark of Yahweh's covenant (Josh 3: 3; 8: 33), a most prestigious and highly responsible function. But when Deuteronomy refers to "the Levite" or "all the tribe of Levi" (a group of persons in need of special benevolence, along with other unlanded persons, aliens, widows, and orphans), context generally indicates client priests in much larger numbers. Wright sought to understand them as the teachers, rural torah-givers, dispersed throughout north and south. It was for them that provision had once been made in the institution of Levitical towns where they were provided residential space and pasture rights. Dtn was careful to stipulate that every Levite had the same prerogative to priesthood at the most prestigious of all the sanctuaries, the one especially distinguished by Yahweh's choice (Deut 18: 6).

The distinction between altar clergy and teaching Levites in Deuteronomy has been challenged, most seriously perhaps on the basis of Deut 18: 1, where "the priests the Levites" is immediately explained appositionally as "all the tribe of Levi" (Emerton 1962). However, there is no conjunction between the phrases in MT; the second and more inclusive formula may very possibly be a gloss claiming for all Levitical persons the prerogatives of "the priests the Levites."

The problem nonetheless remains how to account for the origin of the formulae which first evoked Wright's study, formulae yielding a clear impression of contrast between the prestigious character and high responsibility of "the priests the Levites" and the poverty of "the Levite." In an unpublished paper presented at the AAR/SBL meetings (St. Louis, 1976), Merlin Rehm reviewed the matter once again and proposed the theory that "the two names do not represent two different groups living and working at the same time, but they represent (essentially) the same group working at two different times." That is, "the situation of the poor country Levite who is to be helped by the Israelites (coming to the central sanctuary) reflects the time of the monarchy—between Jeroboam I and Josiah." It probably also reflects, we would add, the collapse or suppression of the system of Levitical towns, especially in the north. Regarding the other formula, "the priests the Levites," since the term cannot be derived from anything later, Rehm concluded that this usage must be even older, stemming from the heyday of Levitical prestige and high responsibility in the premonarchy period.

Levites Elsewhere in Dtr

A possibly serious objection to Levitical sponsorship, of any sort, for the historical corpus (Dtr 1 > Dtr 2) is the near total lack of any direct reference to Levites in all of the books of Samuel and Kings—two occurrences at most. The abrupt reference formulated in disjunctive syntax in 1 Sam 6: 15 may well be secondary. Elsewhere the Levites are mentioned only in 2 Sam 15: 24, a verse firmly embedded in a major pre-Deuteronomic source, the old Court History of David.

We suggest that the reason for this low Levitical profile is bound up in the relation of Dtn to the Dtr corpus and the relation of both to Josiah's reform. While Dtn comes out of the north and only secondarily allows for a monarchy, Dtr 1 has learned lessons from the disaster of 721 and would use the authority of Moses to reform the nation while keeping the monarchy intact. In other words, the first edition (Dtr 1) would stem from the Levitical-priestly circles which had attained preeminence close to the southern throne. And on this view, the post-Josiah edition (Dtr 2) would derive from families of the old movement for covenant renewal who had fled south in 721 and later, only to find that the promise of service and livelihood at the central sanctuary (now clearly Jerusalem) would there be unfulfilled. On the non-fulfillment of Deut 18: 6, the statement in 2 Kgs 23: 8 is ambiguous, but v 9 of the same chapter is clear. These were the circles that had the last word in the formation of the "Deuteronomic" Corpus; both the southern Priestly tradition, as represented by the Tetrateuch source "P," and Ezekiel the exiled Jerusalem priest explicitly consigned all the formerly provincial Levites to second-class status.

In other words, we suggest that Dtr 1 and Dtr 2 reflect opposite sides of a rift in the ranks of the Levites, a rift created by political manipulation and/or repudiation of militant priestly houses. The result is an unresolved dialectic within the material which brings into clear focus the contrasting stories of two very different Levites at the end of the premonarchy period (Judges 17–18 and 19–20). It also explains the momentary eruption of interest in Levites at several points in Joshua. And finally it helps to understand the problem of the shifting locations of the ark and covenant sanctuary, from the murkier background of the premonarchy period to the clear foreground of Josiah's day. The question at issue was the corporate identity of Israel.

People and Nation

If the great historical work was assembled first in a sympathetic relation to Josiah's policy and program, it will explain some puzzling alternations in vocabulary. In the old Book of Torah (Dtn), Israel is Yahweh's *ʿam* "people," and never a *gôy* "nation." In fact, as Yahweh's *ʿam*, Israel is repeatedly promised some sort of superiority to the *gôyyîm*. On the other hand, Israel in the historical corpus (Dtr) is sometimes an *ʿam*, sometimes a *gôy*. But Israel in Dtn is never clearly referred to as a *gôy*, not once.

Three texts might seem to challenge the claim. The first passage is Deut 9: 14 where, after the Horeb rebellion of the "stiff-necked *ʿam*," Yahweh wills to make Moses into a *gôy* that is mightier and greater than they. The context is a distinctive unit which compares form-critically to Deuteronomy 1–3; it is "historical narrative by Moses in the first Person" (von Rad 1966: 77). Those opening three chapters comprise the introduction to Dtr (Noth 1957). Thus we may suspect that in 9: 14 we have another bit of Dtr; in certain circles the tension had been resolved.

The second passage is Deut 26: 5 (the "historical credo"), which recalls that in Egypt your fathers became a great *gôy*. But the outcome of the covenant renewal in which one recites the credo is that "you will become an *ʿam* consecrated to Yahweh, as promised" (Deut 26: 18). The credo chapter seems to prefer the same distinction as Dtn.

The third passage is Deut 32: 28, the archaic Song of Moses, where the poetic usage is sarcastic; Israel is indeed a *gôy*—"without understanding."

These are the only exceptions in all of Deut 4: 44ff. In the old Book of Torah (Dtn), Yahweh's solution to the problem of the *gôyyîm* is precisely the formation of Israel, his *ʿam*. The explanation for this must be that Dtn stems rather directly from carriers of a value system rooted in premonarchy reality. But the distinction is blurred in the historical corpus, where there is no reservation about referring to Israel as a *gôy* (Josh 3: 17; 4: 1; 5: 6, 8; Judg 2: 20; and most significantly Deut 4: 6, 34). In the one remaining example, Josh 10: 13, an archaic poetic piece celebrating the defense of Gibeon "when the sun stood still . . . till a *gôy* defeated its enemies," the *gôy* may well be Gibeon (possibly render "until he defeated the forces of his enemies," Mendenhall 1973: 84).

In any case, we may be reasonably sure that for Josiah's historian (our Dtr 1), who uses both words, what had begun as a divinely constituted *ʿam* had become a divinely legitimated *gôy*, and on that point there could be no turning back; the authority of Moses should now be established by the power of the throne.

Congregation and Assembly

In Joshua and Judges there is yet another way of referring to Israel that is not found in the old Book of Torah (Dtn), Israel as *ʿēdâ* "congregation." This is usually taken as a sign of either a "priestly" source or a "priestly" redaction. But with one or two exceptions, there is nothing in the *ʿēdâ* contexts that is formally archival or catechetical and little that is at first blush edifying or characteristically priestly. Moreover, the distribution of *ʿēdâ* in Joshua and Judges collates with another old Dtn-word which seems also to be carefully *avoided in the first edition* of the historical work: Israel as *qāhāl* "tribal assembly" (Deut 5: 22; 9: 10; 10: 4; 18: 16). In all of Samuel and Kings this noun is used only once, where David in a sweeping generalization includes Philistines as well as Israelites (1 Sam 17: 47). Likewise the verb *qhl* is used but once, with Solomon in control of the action (1 Kgs 8: 2). The clustering in Joshua and Judges must therefore be significant.

Israel the *ʿedâ* (Judg 20: 1; 21: 10, 13, 16) and *qāhāl* (Judg 21: 5) at the end of the premonarchy period is presented in a most unpriestly perspective. After the disastrous civil war with Benjamin in Judges 20, this "congregation/assembly" finds it necessary to wage one more small civil war against Jabesh-gilead, in order to secure wives for the survivors of Benjamin. After the expedition to Jabesh-gilead they are still two hundred short, and so the elders of the congregation send the remnant of the wifeless Benjaminites to the Yahweh festival at Shiloh, where each one is to seize one for himself. It is presented as a theologically foolproof plan: when their fathers or brothers come to complain, the elders will be able to say: "We did them a gracious deed . . ." (Judg 21: 22; Boling 1975: 290–94).

This is Israel? Yes, this skillfully crafted story of do-it-yourself salvation presents Israel in comic perspective. It is a way of dealing with the painful memory of civil war on the one hand, while facing the reality of impending exile on the other. It is comic in the sense of Christopher Fry—"an escape, not from truth but from despair, a narrow escape into faith" (Fry 1964: 286). This picture of Israel at the end of the Judges era may be read as a designedly dialectical complement to the irrelevance of Dtr 1, which was apparent at the end of the monarchy, after the death of Josiah and the collapse of the reform, and with the escalating political and diplomatic chaos and the impending terror of 598 and 587. It was time for a new beginning, with Yahweh alone as king. That is, the post-monarchy *ʿedâ* is presented as the true and proper successor to the old *qāhāl* of Dtn, thus bracketing the entire history of the *gôy*.

The presentation of Israel as comic congregation, Yahweh's true tribal assembly, can be correlated with other indicators to trace out Dtr 2. Here we may turn to the portrayal of Levites. The civil war with Benjamin in Judges 20 was triggered by a certain Levite from the north. He is a prosperous and well-established Levite; he has a servant and a couple of asses. Trouble begins when his concubine walks out and returns to her father's house in Bethlehem of Judah. Here is one northern Levite who enjoyed southern hospitality. It is thanks precisely to the exaggeration (at Bethlehem) and perversion (at Gibeah) of the obligation of hospitality that this Levite at last sets himself up as judge and rallies the entire militia of Israel to avenge the gangstyle rape and murder of his concubine. This only compounds the tragedy, for in the warfare the tribe of Benjamin is nearly wiped out. Without twelve tribes, of course, it would not be possible to be Israel any longer! Hence the expedition to Jabesh-gilead and its sequel. Surely for this to be taken seriously, the absurdity must be there by narrative design. We suggest that Judges 19–20 comprises a memory retold in such a way as to evoke comparison with events leading up to the final tragedy of 587, for which Judges 21 is the intentionally comic resolution. Gottwald also observes that the unified activity of the tribes makes this story relevant to the final editing; the story was "apparently placed here to show that, in extremity, the unified action of all Israel could still be elicited" (1979: 186).

The two clusters of Levite stories at the end of Judges (chapters 17–18 and 19–21) point explicitly to rival sanctuary towns of years gone by and presuppose distinctly different priestly circles. The story of the well-heeled Levite from the north is told in obvious contrast to the preceding stories in Judges 17–18; narrative inversion stands out boldly. Judges 17–18 tells of an aspiring young client Levite from the south (Bethlehem to be precise) who finds employment at Micah's free-lance northern sanctuary (probably Bethel). This young man, grandson of Moses, starts out doing what is right in his eyes (and everyone else's too)—the only one doing so in all of Judges 17–18. But he is tragically exploited, first by Micah and then by the migrating Danites, who hire him away from Micah and install him at the far northern sanctuary (Dan), while all that time the one *legitimate* Mushite sanctuary (from the *southern* point of view) was at Shiloh (18: 31). Scholars regularly take Judg 18: 31 as a Dtr ending. It must be Dtr 1, for whom a number of Jerusalem priests were, prior to the banishment of Abiathar, heirs of the old Mushite house in Shiloh.

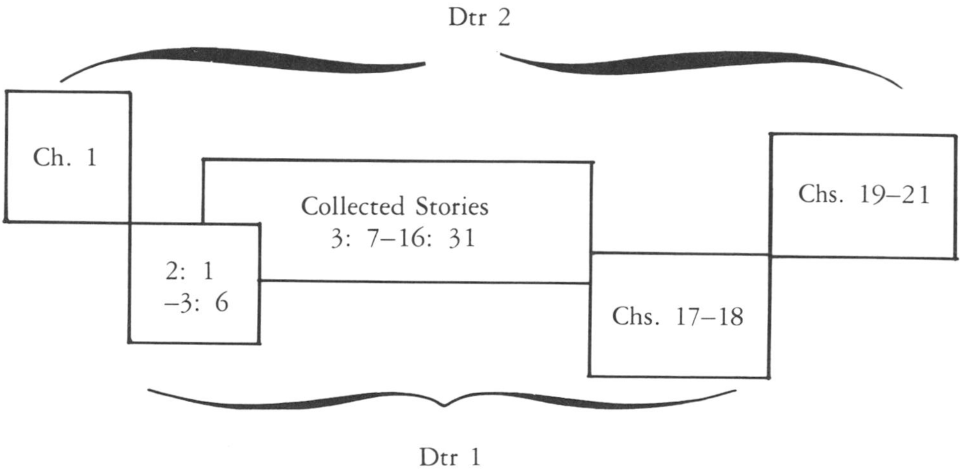

Figure 1. Structure of the Book of Judges.

In the larger framework to the Book of Judges (Dtr 1 edition), this concluding polemic against Bethel and Dan in chapters 17–18 balances introductory polemic in 2: 1–5 also directed against Bethel, which is there called "(Place of) Weeping." These relationships are shown schematically in Figure 1.

We suggest that Judges 2: 1–3: 6 and 17–18 are the Dtr 1 limits, which framed a collection of Judges stories that centered in the destruction of Shechem's covenant temple (ch. 9), thus removing all possible contenders to Jerusalem's Aaronite supremacy in Josiah's day. It was known in this period that Yahweh had himself destroyed Shiloh (Jer 7: 12, 14; 26: 6, 9).

If the first edition is recognizable as belonging to the Josianic era, then Dtr 2 will be known for displaying a broader view but without a lot of rhetoric, settling mostly for argument by supplementation. The tragic story of Micah's Levite and the atrocity of Dan's conquest of Laish (chs. 17–18) was intended to show us how *not* to be Israel in the time of Josiah. But in chs. 19–21 the story of an equally tragic civil war, triggered by the action of one Levite from the north, nevertheless leads to a positive conclusion in the reconstitution of Israel. The final pericopes affirm how it is possible to continue to be Israel in an era when the monarchical state and its temple were being dismantled. After "going by the book" in Judges 20, and nearly wiping out an entire tribe, the people spend the day weeping before God at the outset of ch. 21 and enquiring: Why? But there is no answer, and so the Jabesh-gilead expedition is launched. But it does not suffice. The elders at last begin to think theologically, as they struggle to recall the precise location of the venerable Mushite sanctuary at Shiloh; and Israel is at last reconstituted—not the monarchical nation-state, but the old Mosaic ideal, where there is no king but Yahweh, and each one does what is right on internal ethical control.

In these stories it is not the specific behavior but the decision-making process that is commended. And in these stories, which offer the last word on the Judges era, it is precisely the northern Aaronite sanctuary at Bethel that has the higher reliability (Judg 20: 26), while the significance of Shiloh is caricatured. We think it is very plausible that the later redactor (Dtr 2)—at the brink of exile—is drawing upon material preserved among formerly northern families, thus offsetting the Jerusalem bias of the first edition.

It is impossible to miss the structural inversion of chapters 1 and 20–21. If in 20–21 Israel starts out fully mobilized for *civil* war but is *theologically* united at the end, it is just the reverse in Judges 1. There at the outset of the period Israel is initially "united" for offensive warfare, but by the end of chapter 1 Israel is in complete disarray, as noted above. The question "Which of us shall go first?" in 1: 1 and 20: 18, with identical answer in both, "Judah first," is a sure redactional and rhetorical inclusio. Therefore in chapter 1 the capture of Bethel, against which the first edition polemicizes in chapters 2 and 18, is presented as a parade example of keeping treaty-faith (*ḥesed*[4])! This balances the scene where Bethel at last becomes the place to go for a reliable oracle, in 20: 26–28.

Deuteronomy

If our analysis of the "Deuteronomic/Deuteronomistic" editions of Judges (where major redactional seams are relatively clear) is accurate, what can be said about the finished Book of Deuteronomy? That the opening chapters of Deuteronomy comprise an introduction to the larger historical corpus seems clear enough: the bulk of these chapters have thus been recognized ever since the work of Noth. But chapters 1–3 are mainly pre-exilic, in our terms Dtr 1, leaving 4: 1–40 as a discrete unit belonging to the later redaction.[5]

We suggest, moreover, that Dtr 2 signals its presence right at the outset, in retouched verses of Deuteronomy 1 and 2. There, as has recently been shown, the rebellion at Kadesh now unfolds with inverted use of the Holy War language (Moran 1963). It is Yahweh versus Israel, until the entire generation of warriors is dead. Only then is it time for Yahweh's conquest! At this point Dtr 2 has simply rewritten the first edition. Presumably Dtr 2 could do this because the *recent* writing of Dtr 1 was well known; chapters 1–3 formed no part of the original Book of the Torah of Moses, rediscovered in the reign of Josiah. For the post-monarchy situation, however, the old Dtn would be as valuable as ever, describing what Israel in the promised land was supposed to have been and introducing a history which in its first edition had presented Joshua as the ideal field commander.

The Book of Joshua

Therefore it is different in the Book of Joshua, where the very composition of stories is much more specifically "Deuteronomic," as scholars have long observed. In the Book of Judges, the Dtr evidence is found only in the larger framework and, here and there, scantily in the seams between stories; in Judges the stories were clearly not recast to produce a uniform image. In other words, it appears that Dtr 1 in Judges tells it as it was (in the old stories handed down from the past), but Dtr 1 in Joshua tells it as it is supposed to be (and is going to be thanks to Josiah). Joshua, like Josiah, goes by the book (Deut 17: 18–20; Josh 1: 7–8; 23: 6; 2 Kings 22–23). Joshua is a model for the Jerusalem king. It is small wonder that scholars have recently been recognizing kingly features in the portrayal of Joshua (Widengren 1957).

Dtr 2 let the portrayal stand. The final redactor had no quarrel with the idea that the military offensives under Moses and Joshua were the holiest wars in Israel's history. They were in fact, supposed to be recognized as the last such, sealed off in the past by the message of the angel in Judges 2 and by the events which followed the collapse of Josiah's realm. Dtr 2 did not need to rewrite much of anything in Joshua, but could confine itself to clarification by way of supplements. How much did the Dtr 2 people contribute to the Book of Joshua? We may list six possible criteria for tracking Dtr 2.

1. Northern Levitical bias.
2. Critical treatment of private vengeance.
3. Negative expectation for the future of military enterprise.
4. Interest in a full definition of "Israel," frequently expressed in terms of the east-west axis, Transjordan and Cisjordan.
5. Israel as *ʿēdâ/qāhāl*, "congregation"/"tribal assembly."
6. Comic perspective, characteristically expressed in portrayal of the ironic and the absurd.

These characteristics are not listed here in any order of priority; the presence of one or more of them will suggest (obviously not prove) that we are on Dtr 2 terrain in the Book of Joshua. We shall scout that terrain first in the latter half of the book.

The story of the altar near the Jordan is a good place to begin the tracking. In Joshua 22, with the conquest in the past and all allotments determined, all is in readiness for Israel's enjoyment of life in the land. Whereupon Israel as the *ʿedâ* moves directly to the brink of civil war on the east-west axis (cf. Israel as *ʿēdâ* at last surviving the civil war at the end of Judges). Here we have the *threat* of civil war over an altar at the Jordan, though which side of the river is intended by the narrative has never been determined. Probably, we should now say, it is left intentionally vague. The potential civil war is only headed off by protracted theological discussion, thanks to the priest Phinehas ben Eleazar[6] (two names favored by the Aaronites of Bethel, as indicated by Judg 20: 26–28, which belongs to the companion piece). If in Judges 21 the rationale for the theft of the Shiloh maidens is clear and theologically foolproof ("We did them a gracious deed"), here in the laborious deliberations of Joshua 22 it is not at all clear who wins what points. But the point of the story is abundantly clear: in order to be Israel, it is better to talk than to fight!

It is impossible to miss the structural inversion of narrative elements. In Josh 22: 9 the Transjordan tribes go from "Shiloh which is in the land of Canaan" to settle down in "the land of Gilead." In Judg 21: 12, the expedition returns with the four hundred maidens captured at Jabesh-gilead to "Shiloh which is in the land of Canaan." This way of locating Shiloh occurs only once again in Scripture, Josh 21: 2 (a variation of the formula), which is the setting for the assignment of Levitical towns.

In Joshua this end-of-the-book interest in the east-west axis helps to explain the abrupt references to the Transjordan tribes in Josh 1: 12–18 and 4: 12–13. Outside of the description of territorial allotments and special assignments (chapters 13–21) and the discovery of Achan, another lot procedure (7: 16–21), these are the only passages where specific tribes are mentioned by name anywhere in the book! Scholars have in fact often suggested that these verses in chapters 1 and 4 are secondary. They make good sense as representing Dtr 2's interest in a fuller definition of Israel, something much larger than Josiah's kingdom west of the Jordan.

Joshua's farewell address in chapter 23, spiralling down to its devastatingly stern warning, may also be recognized as a contribution of Dtr 2. Based upon an old source, it was adapted and put in place about the time that its prophecy was being fulfilled. To understand the redaction of this chapter as secondary helps to make sense of a marked redundancy at the end of the book.

Concerning chapter 21, the assignment of Levitical towns "at Shiloh in the land of Canaan," scholars frequently note how easily the list can be removed without leaving any signs of a gap. The institution of the Levitical towns is probably prior to monarchy in origin, the Yahweh league's adaptation of an Egyptian administrative model (as first pointed out by Mazar), an adaptation designed to capitalize on the militancy of the early Levites. The actual list seems to reflect in part the late Davidic or Solomonic arrangements (with concentration at the borders and in newly incorporated areas) and in part a later attempt by certain Levitical families (eighth century, perhaps) to transcend the political schism between north and south (Peterson 1977). Alienation of a major priestly house had begun with Solomon, and by Josiah's day the institution of the Levitical towns was probably defunct. In any case the list presupposes an era where there was a viable Transjordan claim; it was used at last to expand upon the limited definition of Josiah's realm.

Other "Levitical" references in the Book of Joshua provide a redactional clue. In 13: 14 and 13: 33 we read "To the Levite tribe he/Moses gave no fief" (our translation). Verse 14 continues: "Offerings by fire to Yahweh God of Israel are its fief, exactly as he promised it." Verse 33 has a variation: "Yahweh the God of Israel is himself their 'fief,' as he promised them." The pattern displays a classic framing device, consisting of repetition with slight variation. The bracket thus formed encloses an ancient supplement to the sketchy Transjordan description in verses 8–12.

Finally in Josh 14: 4b we have the fullest statement on Levites outside of chapter 21: ". . .they gave no division to the Levites in the land, except to live in certain towns, with pasture rights providing for their cattle and their substance." This reference to Levitical towns and Levitical substance anticipates chapter 21. And like chapter 21, the entire block of chapters 12–14 separates cleanly, framed in 11: 23 and 14: 15 by another bracketing formula: "And the land had rest from war" (LXX reflects a slight variation). The statement occurs nowhere else in exactly this form but it must be related to the famous redactional formula in Judges. The first occurrence in Josh 11: 23, where it indeed makes sense, must be Dtr 1, but the repetition in 14: 15, where it serves no smooth transitional function, must be Dtr 2. The two occurrences frame a block of material in chapters 12–14 that reflects other interests, in addition to the Levitical concern, that are characteristic of the later redactor: east-west definition of Israel and the incompleteness of Joshua's conquest (as also in Judges 1).

Thus chapter 13 describes, as we have seen, the "irrelevant" Transjordan allotments. There is no clear evidence that Josiah ever exerted himself with any lasting effects in Transjordan. If Dtr 1 was interested in precedents for the current or recent revival of the nation under Josiah, there would be no reason to include a description of the Transjordan allotments, where Josiah staked no very successful claim.[7]

The list of defeated kings in chapter 12 similarly directs attention to the east-west axis: territory and kings conquered east of the river under Moses, west of the river under Joshua. Following this summary list, chapter 13 begins with Yahweh taking special notice of how Joshua has grown old, while there is much land yet to be taken—not a very bright picture. This whole block of material ends in 14: 6–15 with the story of elderly Caleb (not Joshua) still capable of taking Hebron from the Anaqim. This is the fuller statement on Caleb which Dtr 2 will echo, though briefly, in Judges 1: 20, after including in the same chapter a longer Caleb unit taken over unaltered from Dtr 1—the Achsah story of Joshua 15. We note its comic implications in introducing the first major judge (Judg 1: 11–15).

There is thus a lot to be said for the recognition of Joshua 12–14 as a lengthy Dtr insertion, calling attention to the larger definition of Israel and preparing the way for insertion of the Levitical cities list in Joshua 21, as well as the story of the prosperous Levite from the north at the end of the era (Judges 19–20).

With chapters 12–14 bracketed out, it is clear that the Book of Joshua uses the prestigious old title "the priests the Levites" in 3: 3 and 8: 33 to refer to the bearers of the ark. This leaves only 18: 7, where the Levites specifically have "the priesthood," as the one remaining reference to Levites in Dtr 1 until the story appended in Judges 17–18 tells how one famous client Levite from the south (a grandson of Moses) had been tragically exploited on his way to the top, an incident that had happened at two old northern sanctuaries. This is clearly southern polemic.

In other words, for the Josianic historian (Dtr 1) the old prestigious title "the priests the Levites" expressed self-understanding, whereas the great majority of impoverished Levites doubtless seemed to him a radical nuisance. The Levitical towns were already defunct as such (if not suppressed). The seventh-century historian need not mention them.

This is not the last time in history that a reformation historian would make conservative political use of radical religious sources. Indeed this use of the Book of the Torah of Moses is like the same historian's use of the old "Court History of David," which despite its ironically critical Yahwism was rather clumsily turned into a "Succession Document" (Flanagan 1972). In the case of Dtn the Levitical background was too well known; Josiah's historian might supplement but could not subtract from Dtn. That historian was content to say as little as possible about the poor provincial Levites who must have been making their way to Jerusalem in sizable numbers ever since 721.

Dtr 2 noticed the omission and used the list of Levitical towns which had been assigned at "Shiloh in the land of Canaan" to correct an imbalance. This list would also help to understand how in the early days there could have been Levites from the north who, like the one in Judges 19, already appear to be quite prosperous. According to the list, the Levites had been given residences and pasturage in some of the choicest towns.

Probably from the same redactional hand comes the list of asylum towns in chapter 20. Again, the institution is very old, originally an attempt to curb the blood feud in the time before the establishment of the monarchy with its agencies of military and civil service. This institution was also surely long since passé by Josiah's day; and the list includes the Transjordan territory. Using this list the Dtr 2 redactor could show an *ʿedâ* with elders and the priest doing what they were supposed to do: putting an end to private vengeance. This story is, however, offset by the tragic companion piece at the end of the era, where the civil war in Judges 20 is presented as one Levite's massive resort to private vengeance.

Thus, in its finished Dtr 2 form, the account of the land division begins in chapter 12 by calling attention to the larger dimensions of the "conquest," focussing especially on the east-west axis, and emphasizes finally the special situation and potential significance of the Levites.

The Conquest Stories: Joshua 1–11

The signs of supplementation are differently distributed in the stories of the warfare for Yahweh's control of Canaan. In this section one very abrupt transition is the splice with the Rahab story in 6: 22–25. Scholars have long agreed that the spy story in Joshua 2 is stylistically distinct from the bulk of the conquest stories, reflecting a prehistory of its own. In this account of reconnaissance of the land, which gets no farther than Rahab's house, the only protagonist to use Deuteronomic rhetoric is Rahab (2: 9–11). We may suspect that it was a contribution by Dtr 2 that saved her story from oblivion.

A key to the story of Ha-Ai "The Ruin" in Joshua 7–8 is provided by the clarification of one word. The word *'lp* is not always "1,000" (*'elep*) but often the village unit (*'ālep*) for the military muster, consisting of seven to twelve men where the size can be checked (Mendenhall 1958). The latter meaning was lost to Massoretes and later translators, who have thought that Joshua sent three thousand warriors for the first battle at The Ruin. Yet the Israelites considered a total loss of thirty-six dead or disabled to be a disastrous defeat. Joshua must have sent three units, which possibly totalled about thirty-six—a disastrous day indeed.

The story of The Ruin is etiological, but with an uncharacteristic twist. What Joshua 7 does is to explain away the fact that somewhere in Benjamin the great leader of Yahweh's guerrilla force once suffered a resounding and thoroughly embarrassing setback. The defeat is blamed on Achan, who is mentioned elsewhere in scripture only in the Dtr 2 altar-story (Josh 22: 20). We may conclude that a true story was thus originally told in the form of an etiological diversion; the smaller units totalling about thirty-six for the first assault force brings the story into very credible focus alongside the unwalled Iron I village (slightly later) of 2.75 acres recently excavated by Callaway, nested amidst the large-proportioned rubble of a great Early Bronze Age metropolis (Callaway 1976). A local population mustering at The Ruin in the late thirteenth century would not have been large.

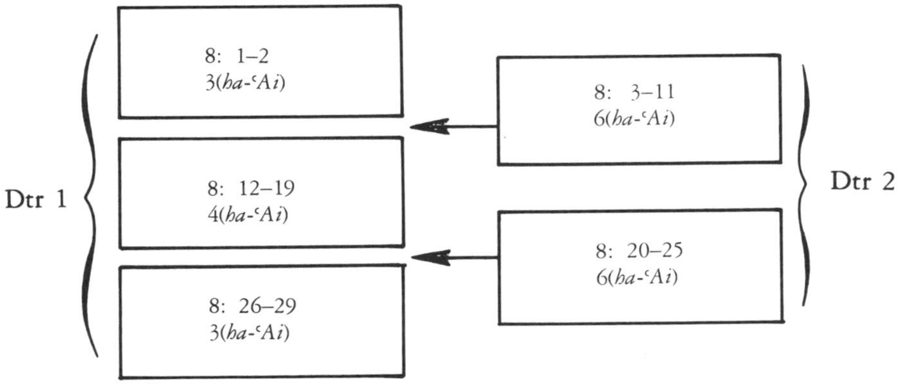

Figure 2. Second attack on The Ruin

The story of the victory at The Ruin has had a complex history. There are twenty-two occurrences of Ha–Ai in chapter 8, which separate into two distinct patterns, as shown in Figure 2. Three segments mention The Ruin a total of ten times (3–4–3), alternating with two units in each of which The Ruin occurs six times. In this lineup the group of three passages makes continuous narrative. On the other hand, the two additional units swarm with words, phrases, sentences, motifs, and overall organization which make the story of Ha–Ai a redactional companion to the final victory at Gibeah (also told thanks to Dtr 2) in Judges 20.

In other words, if the first edition told the story etiologically, the final edition exploited its comic potential. The key to the victory in the first edition is that Joshua obediently gives a sign. It has been argued persuasively that the rare word *kîdôn* in this chapter is Israel's word for the old sicklesword, a weapon already obsolete by

Joshua's day but which continued throughout the second millennium and on into the first millennium to have high symbolic status in representations of divine sovereignty in human affairs (Keel 1974: 11–82). On this reading, the victory was *entirely* Yahweh's doing and we are given scant details of Israel's participation. To be sure, the narrative in final form seems to interpret Joshua's flashing of the *kîdôn* not as a sign but as a signal to the men in ambush. Geography, however, makes it improbable in the extreme that one man's raising of a weapon, among all those retreating downhill to the east, would have been visible to the ambush stationed behind The Ruin somewhere to the west. We are reminded of the geographical imprecision in the story (also Dtr 2) of the Jordan-altar crisis (Joshua 22), as noted above.

We conclude, therefore, that in the beginning Joshua 8 recounted a Divine Warrior story, in which Joshua was privileged to flash the symbol of divine imperium while Yahweh went into action. Dtr 1 told it simply as another story about Joshua as ideal field commander, directly responsible to the word of Yahweh, a point which Dtr 2 was ready to reinforce.

The Mount Ebal pericope (Josh 8: 30–35) is another corrective supplied by the same redactor, to which we shall return. Here it will suffice to note the fluidity in the textual tradition. LXX has this unit following the panicked reaction of the kings reported in 9: 2 (MT), rather than preceding it. No doubt the two rallies were nearly concurrent and closely related.

Gibeon: Problematical Treaty

In the unit which begins "three days after" the Gibeonite ruse (9: 16), Israel is the *ʿēdâ*, "congregation," repeatedly. The section 9: 16–27 separates cleanly, leaving a smooth transition from 9: 15a to 10: 1. But the addition of verses 16–27 makes clear what is only hinted in 9: 1–15, another crack in the portrait of Joshua. This time he was apparently caught off guard and found himself in the position of having to ratify a defense treaty negotiated in effect by other Israelites. Without the inclusion of verses 16–27 the story gives primacy in the negotiations, from Israel's side, to some anonymous representatives of the Bene Israel (9: 7, 14). In the bracketed verses, however, both the treaty and the solution which will make Gibeonites "hewers of wood and drawers of water" are proposed by "the leaders of the congregation," *nĕśîʾê hā-ʿēdâ*. The "congregation" is mentioned six times in the unit (vv 18 bis, 19, 21 bis LXX, 27), seven if we include the transitional half-verse.[8] The result is rhetorical inversion with the story in Judges 21 where the elders of the *ʿēdâ* at last devise a solution to the problem of wives for Benjamin.

In all of Joshua, outside the seven occurrences of *ʿēdâ* here, six more in Dtr 2's altar story (22: 12, 16, 17, 18, 20, 30), and two more at the selection of asylum-towns (at 20: 6, 9, also supplied by Dtr 2), the word occurs elsewhere only in 18: 1, "all the congregation of the people of Israel." The latter verse is very possibly a conflation. It is in any case one of the latest texts in the book, an editorial transition to the long account of land survey for unallocated tribal estates.

In the entire Book of Judges, *ʿēdâ* occurs outside the Dtr 2 conclusion only at 14: 8, where Samson discovers a "congregation" of honey bees; he seems to have missed there a sign about the meaning of his own prodigious strength (Boling 1975: 230).

Surely the status of "hewers of wood and drawers of water" was not supposed to be understood as an entirely admirable implementation of treaty obligation. Rather it stands as part of the tragicomic past in the final edition.

Sun and Moon at Gibeon

Within the warfare section of the Joshua book, yet another point where redaction history brings things into sharper focus is the performance of Sun and Moon in the defense of Gibeon (10: 12–14). This flashback unit is highly mythic in content and strictly Yahwistic. We have argued (in Boling 1982) that Sun and Moon are here addressed by Yahweh, in immediate response to Joshua's plea. Joshua is only mentioned in verse 12, not quoted, thus highlighting the immediate salvific response. In this flashback pericope, that is, Sun and Moon are commanded by Yahweh to guard the exits at opposite ends of the Beth-horon pass, apparently flashing the sign in a manner imitating Joshua at The Ruin in the first edition of chapter 8. Sun and Moon seem to be functioning thus in Hab 3: 11 (as rendered by Cross 1973: 71 after Albright):

> On high Sun raised his arms,
> Moon stood < on > his lordly dais.
> They march by the gleam of thy darts,
> By the (lightning) flash of thy spear.

And the next verse of Habakkuk's Divine Warrior hymn speaks of Yahweh's earthly victory.

The idea, in the final form of Joshua 10, seems to be that while Sun and Moon thus inhibited retreat, Yahweh threw down the previously mentioned hailstones. "Never has there been a day like that before or since—God's heeding of a human voice! Surely Yahweh fought for Israel!" (10: 14, our translation).

Mobilization and Invasion

There remain two major contributions of Dtr 2 to the Book of Joshua. The first describes the establishment of the memorial shrine at Gilgal (3: 17–4: 8). Having reviewed many attempts to disentangle the text as a composite of narrative sources, we suggest that the simplest and best solution is to suspect that this *formerly* important sanctuary was not mentioned by Josiah's historian. After the ringing prophetic denunciations of the place (in Hos 4: 15; 9: 15; 12: 11; Amos 4: 4; 5: 5; cf. Mic 6: 5), Josiah the Deuteronomic reformer appears to have had no positive interest in the Gilgal sanctuary. We suggest that the first edition told only of twelve stones carried into the river so as to provide a firm footing for the priestly bearers of the ark (3: 1–16; 4: 10–11, 14–18). With the addition of the Gilgal foundation story by Dtr 2 (3: 17–4: 8), some explanation was necessary and is best preserved in the Greek: "Twelve other stones" are still there in the river "to this day" (4: 9 LXX).

Finally there is Dtr 2's account of what happened at Gilgal. The picture of the entire militia undergoing ritual surgery just three days before the Passover (5: 2–10) is not given adequate space by the description of the kings' panicky reaction upon hearing what Yahweh had done at the Jordan River (5: 1). But if the unit belongs to a subsequent redaction which was in fact an attempt to prepare for life in exile, then the high didactic value of these units, placed just here, becomes very clear. Without Yahweh, Israel is utterly defenseless.

The Conquest: What Actually Happened?

When the rhetoric of Dtr 1 is recognized and allowance is made for the dialectical method of Dtr 2, the actual claims for military conquest in the nuclear materials of the Book of Joshua are extremely modest. One or two treaties plus two or three unexpected "divine" interventions touched off a surprising chain of victories beginning with a relatively small force.

A medical approach to the Jericho tradition now commends itself, in light of the overall decline of the Jericho oasis in the Late Bronze Age, together with the archeological evidence for the snail (*Bulinus truncatus*) which is the intermediate carrier of Schistosomiasis in Late Bronze Age Jericho and the biblical curse formulated precisely in terms of infant mortality (Hulse 1971; for a similar sense of disease crisis with respect to *ḥerem*, see Meyers 1978: 97). Prophylactic clamor by a small force surrounding a dilapidated fort (not a ritual "conquest" but just the reverse), might, for example, combine with a timely earthquake along a notoriously unstable rift to produce a very impressive experience of saving grace. Jericho alone would be placed off limits for settlement because it was known to be especially unhealthy. The entire oasis had in fact fallen on hard times, so that not even Gilgal can be located with confidence.

If it is allowed that some such interpretation is within the realm of possibility, and with the credibility of a nuclear Ruin-story now archeologically and philologically established, the subsequent Shechem Valley and Gibeon units appear in a new light. It is surely significant that Joshua makes covenants only where we are told in one source or another that there was an important Hivite (that is, of Anatolian background) ingredient in the populace: Shechem and Gibeon (see Halpern 1975). In the first case (Josh 8: 30–35; cf. 24: 1–28) Joshua was initiating negotiations; in the other he was responding (9: 1–15). Joshua's own allotment at Timnath-heres is only a bit closer to Gibeon than to Shechem; these three together with Shiloh (which likewise has no conquest tradition) form a large diamond-shaped segment of the central hill country. It is precisely within this area that an impressive number of new unwalled villages appear in Iron I, making extensive use of upland agricultural terracing for the first time. A major difference between Gibeon and Shechem was the latter's heritage of the *ʾēl-bĕrît/baʿal-bĕrît* sanctuary and the safer quality of life in the area of the Shechem city-state. This security stemmed from the earlier Late Bronze period and is reflected both in the Amarna correspondence of Labayu, who reigned early in the 14th century, and in the archeological record of an increase in the number of towns and unwalled villages (Campbell 1968).

Labayu's achievement as administrator and Joshua's success as negotiator will come more to the fore in theology. Joshua's diplomatic achievement was played down by Dtr 1, a historian who favored the approach of royal militancy and who emphasized Joshua's negotiating only at the end of the fighting and land division (Joshua 24, put in place by Dtr 1). It must have been a successor to the compiler of the militant first edition who recalled the old Dtn teaching that Moses had said, in effect:

as soon as you get to the land, go to Shechem (Deuteronomy 27). And so the final redactor reports that the Israelites did so (Josh 8: 30–35).

According to the received tradition, a surprising successful southern campaign followed on the heels of the Shechem and Gibeon events. It is there in the southern hills that the archeological evidence for turn-of-the-era chaos is mostly concentrated. Yet if Khirbet Rabûd is biblical Debir (with no major destruction in evidence) then there may be a southern parallel for the Shechem pattern (Campbell 1975: 153).

Turning to the far north: if it was Israel that destroyed Hazor, there was nevertheless a rapid Canaanite revival that is archeologically clear. It must have been in the new village settlements of Upper Galilee that Yahwism was most effectively rooted (Aharoni 1976).

It is a cramped chronological sequence. The rapid consolidation of Israel in late thirteenth to early twelfth-century Canaan requires a leader with great organizational ability. And we may therefore suspect that Dtr 2 was using reliable tradition. After initial events which would establish Gilgal as a small rural sanctuary specializing in celebration of Yahweh's Holy War, and after the experience in the neighborhood of The Ruin, the small guerrilla force from across the river went soon to Shechem, where negotiations were so successful that counter-coalitions hastily formed, while at least one "Tetrapolis" succeeded in securing special status, perhaps because it already had no monarchy.

Thanks to Albright's final reading of Gen 49: 22–24, we can be sure that Joseph belongs originally to the "Sons of the North," flanked by Benjamin on the south; Benjaminite clans still further south would at last be absorbed in Judah (Albright 1973).

Taking our bearings from Amarna, we can see that what was needed two centuries after Labayu was a catalyst for reform. It arrived in the person of Joshua at the head of an expeditionary force from the movement that had swept over much of Transjordan in one generation. On this view, Joshua 24 illustrates Josh 8: 30–35 (not the other way around), and the Shechem covenant came early. Given the tradition's clear implications that Gideon behaved like a king (Judges 8), and with the archeological evidence for Abimelech's early destruction of Shechem (Judges 9, an event to be dated roughly between 1150 and 1120; see Wright 1965: 101–2, 122), it is in fact possible that Shiloh became the place of the muster within Joshua's lifetime (Josh 18: 1). Thus we might account for the two-phase allotment of tribal estates west of the Jordan in the Book of Joshua. Phase 1 was based at Shechem, with allotments for the Sons of the North and the earlier Sons of the South. Phase 2 was based at Shiloh, which added finally four allotments in the far north (Zebulun, Issachar, Asher, Naphtali) and which saw the consolidation of Judah (at last absorbing Simeon and sharply restricting Benjamin and Dan). This leaves Joshua 24 as a separate pre-Deuteronomic liturgical source, based ultimately on the Shechem phase but misplaced by Dtr 1 who assumed that it covered all tribal allotments west of the Jordan. To that historian, Joshua was the military hero whose story properly told would provide the standard for a great reforming king, the restorer of the Davidic empire.

And yet, for a truly satisfactory conclusion to the quest for the historical Joshua, the persons to interview would not be Dtr 1 or Dtr 2; better would be persons such as the family of Rahab, the citizens of Hivite Gibeon, and the participants in Joshua 24,

BOOK OF JOSHUA

I. Mobilization and Invasion

Dtr 1		Dtr 2
Yahweh, Joshua, and Israel	1: 1–11	
	1: 12–18	East Jordan tribes
	2: 1–24	Rahab's house
Opening the river	3: 1–16	
	3: 17–4: 8	Twelve stones
	(4: 9)	Twelve other (LXX) stones
Crossing the river	4: 10–11	
	4: 12–13	East Jordan tribes
Closing the river	4: 14–18	
	4: 19–5: 12	Cultic encampment

II. Warfare

Dtr 1		Dtr 2
The commander	5: 13–15	
Intervention I: Jericho	6: 1–21	
	6: 22–25	The Rahab splice
The curse on Jericho	6: 26–27	
Defeat at The Ruin	7: 1–26	
Second attack on The Ruin	8: 1–2	
	8: 3–11	Judges 20 prefigured: part I
Intervention II: The Ruin	8: 12–19	
	8: 20–25	Judges 20 prefigured: part II
The sign	8: 26–29	
	8: 30–35	Shechem: chronological corrective
Gibeon treaty	9: 1–15	
	9: 16–27	Judges 21 prefigured
Intervention III: Keeping faith	10: 1–11	
	10: 12–15	Sun and Moon (cf. Joshua at The Ruin)
Sequel	10: 16–43	
A northern coalition	11: 1–15	
Concluding summary	11: 16–23	

III. Land Division

	Dtr 1		Dtr 2
SHECHEM phase		**12: 1–21**	Former lords
		13: 1–23	Transjordan flashback
		14: 1–15	Special introduction to Judah
	Judah and Ephraim	15: 1–16: 10	
		17: 1–6	Daughters of Zelophehad
	Western Manasseh	17: 7–13	
	Joshua as judge	17: 14–18	
SHILOH phase	Seven more estates	18: 1–19: 50	
	Conclusion to Part III	19: 51	

IV. Two Key Institutions

Dtr 1		Dtr 2
	20: 1–9	Asylum towns
	21: 1–42	Levitical towns
Conclusion to Parts I-III	21: 43–45	

V. How to Avoid Civil War

Dtr 1		Dtr 2
	22: 1–34	Phinehas ben Eleazar
	23: 1–16	Final warning
Shechem covenant	24: 1–28	

the event which is most likely to be the close sequel to the victory near The Ruin and the prelude to all that follows. At the risk of over-simplification, we may summarize the clearest indications of redactional emphases and the unresolved tension in the finished book of Joshua in the accompanying figure.

The unresolved tension in the finished corpus shows such a rare capacity for self-criticism that it surely deserves to be called inspired, and all the more so in view of its final exilic shaping among the sufferers. The two poles of the corpus represented by King Josiah's "Heyday History" (Dtr 1) and the exiles' "Book of Hard Times" (Dtr 2) are an imperishable reminder of how difficult if not impossible it is for any one historian to know and tell all of the truth. Between the two of them the central message of the Books of Joshua and Judges comes clear and wears well. The conquest of Canaan was a settlement; the settlement of Canaan was a conquest. The movement led by Joshua established a new peace of God for multitudes, a peace which seems to have lasted just about as long as Joshua was alive.

Notes

1. This essay is presented to David Noel Freedman with unbounded appreciation for his unlimited sharing of insights and criticism, over the ten years and more that have gone into the making of two books on Joshua and Judges (Boling 1975 and 1982).

2. Consultation of the oracle before battle was standard practice in Israel as elsewhere. The practice is essential to the rhetorical framework in the Book of Judges (1: 1 and 20: 18); cf. Boling 1975: 53–67, 285–86. The practice is notably not even hinted in Josh 7: 2–5.

3. The last words appended to the corpus describe the Babylonians' benevolent treatment of the exiled Judean king Jehoiachin; this forms a final ironic inclusio with the very first story of Israel versus a Canaanite king in the post-Joshua era, that is, the defeat, mutilation, and under-the-table treatment of Adonibezeq in Judg 1: 5–7. However, we see no reason to bring the entirety of the Dtr 2 enterprise down into the exilic period.

4. This term cannot be contained within merely covenantal parameters. At the semantic core is something like "responsible caring." See the dissertation by Katherine Doob Sakenfeld, 1978.

5. See now Jon D. Levenson, 1975. His attempt to track Dtr 1 and Dtr 2 in the framework of the Book of Deuteronomy appears to be largely successful. However, we are not persuaded by his conclusion that it was Dtr 2 who "inserted the Book of the Torah." Such a radical dissection would leave the Book of the Law of Moses in 2 Kings 22–23 without recognizable referent and would resolve the tension between threat and promise which have been shown to be characteristic of Dtr. (See Cross 1973: 278–84.)

6. This is apparently the same Eleazar who is named ahead of Joshua in the appeal made by the daughters of Zelophehad in another land inheritance question that poses a problem on the east–west axis (Josh 17: 3–6).

7. Any success of Josiah in extending his sway beyond the Jordan (Ginsberg 1950) was so shortlived that it left no reflex in Dtr. Moreover, Bethel seems to have experienced a revival. Excavations at Beitin found no evidence for a Babylonian destruction. Instead Bethel became quite prosperous during the sixth century (Albright 1942: 172–73).

References

Aharoni, Y.
1976 Upper Galilee. Vol. 2, pp. 406–8 in *Encyclopedia of Archaeological Excavations in the Holy Land*, ed. M. Avi-Yonah. Jerusalem: Israel Exploration Society and Massada Press.

Albright, W.F.
1942 *Archaeology and the Religion of Israel*. Baltimore: Johns Hopkins Press.
1973 From the Patriarchs to Moses: I, From Abraham to Joseph. *The Biblical Archaeologist* 36: 5–33.

Boling, R. G.
1974 In Those Days There Was No King in Israel. Pp. 33–48 in *A Light Unto My Path*, eds. H. N. Bream, R. D. Heim, and C. A. Moore. Philadelphia: Temple University Press.
1975 *Judges*. Anchor Bible 6A. Garden City, NY: Doubleday.
1982 *Joshua*. Anchor Bible 6. Garden City, NY: Doubleday.

Callaway, J. A.
1976 Excavating Ai (et–Tell): 1964–72. *Biblical Archeologist* 39: 18–30.

Campbell, E. F., Jr.
1968 The Shechem Area Survey. *Bulletin of the American Schools of Oriental Research* 190: 19–41.
1975 Moses and the Foundations of Israel. *Interpretation* 29: 141–54.

Cross, F. M.
1973 *Canaanite Myth and Hebrew Epic*. Cambridge, MA: Harvard University Press.

Emerton, J. A.
1962 Priests and Levites in Deuteronomy. An Examination of Dr. G. E. Wright's Theory. *Vetus Testamentum* 12: 129–38.

Flanagan, J.
1972 Court History or Succession Document? A Study of 2 Samuel 9–20 and 1 Kings 1–2. *Journal of Biblical Literature* 91: 172–81.

Fohrer, G.
1965 *Introduction to the Old Testament*. Trans. D. E. Green. Nashville: Abingdon.

Freedman, D. N.
1975a "Son of Man, Can These Bones Live?": The Exile. *Interpretation* 29: 171–86.
1975b Early Israelite History in the Light of Early Israelite Poetry. Pp. 3–35 in *Unity and Diversity: Essays in the History, Literature and Religion of the Ancient Near East*, ed. H. Goedicke and J. J. M. Roberts. Baltimore: Johns Hopkins University.
1976 Divine Names and Titles in Early Hebrew Poetry. Pp. 55–107 in *Magnalia Dei: The Mighty Acts of God*, eds. F. M. Cross, W. L. Lemke, and P. D. Miller, Jr. Garden City, NY: Doubleday.
1979 Early Poetry and Historical Reconstructions. Pp. 85–96 in *Symposia*, ed. F. M. Cross. Cambridge, MA: American Schools of Oriental Research.

Fry, C.
1964 Comedy. In *The New Orpheus*, ed. N. A. Scott. New York: Sheed and Ward.

Ginsberg, H. L.
1950 Judah and the Transjordan States from 734 to 582 B.C.E. Pp. 347–68 in *Alexander Marx Jubilee Volume: English Section*, ed. S. Lieberman. New York: Jewish Theological Seminary.

Gottwald, N.
1979 *The Tribes of Yahweh*. Maryknoll, New York: Orbis.

Halpern, B.
1974 Sectionalism and the Schism. *Journal of Biblical Literature* 93: 519–32.
1975 Gibeon: Israelite Diplomacy in the Conquest Era. *Catholic Biblical Quarterly* 37: 303–16.

Hulse, E. V.
1971 Joshua's Curse and the Abandonment of Ancient Jericho: Schistosomiasis as a Possible Medical Explanation. *Medical History* 15: 376–86.

Keel, O.
1974 *Wirkmächtige Siegeszeichen im Alten Testament*. Freiburg: Universitätsverlag.

Levenson, J. D.
1975 Who Inserted the Book of the Torah? *Harvard Theological Review* 68: 203–33.

Mazar, B.
1960 The Cities of the Priests and the Levites. *Supplements to Vetus Testamentum* 7: 193–205.

Mendenhall, G. E.
1958 The Census Lists of Numbers 1 and 26. *Journal of Biblical Literature* 77: 52–66.
1973 *The Tenth Generation*. Baltimore: Johns Hopkins University Press.

Meyers, C.
1978 The Roots of Restriction: Women in Early Israel. *Biblical Archeologist* 41: 91–103.

Moran, W. L.
1963 The End of the Unholy War and the Anti-Exodus. *Biblica* 4: 333–42.

Noth, M.
1957 *Überlieferungsgeschichtliche Studien*[2]. Tübingen: Niemeyer.

Peterson, J.
1977 *A Topographical Surface Survey of the Levitical "Cities" of Joshua 21 and 1 Chronicles 6: Studies on the Levites in Israelite Life and Religion*. Seabury–Western Theological Seminary Dissertation.

Polk, T.
1979 The Levites in the Davidic–Solomonic Empire. *Studia Biblica et Theologica* 9: 3–22.

von Rad, G.
1953 *Studies in Deuteronomy*. London: SCM.
1962 Deuteronomy. Vol. 1, pp. 831–38 in *The Interpreter's Dictionary of the Bible*. New York and Nashville: Abingdon.
1966 *Deuteronomy*. London: SCM.

Rosenbaum, J.
1979 Hezekiah's Reform and the Deuteronomistic Tradition. *Harvard Theological Review* 72: 23–44.

Sakenfeld, K. D.
1978 *The Meaning of Ḥesed in the Hebrew Bible*. Missoula, Montana: Scholars Press.

Widengren, G.
1957 King and Covenant. *Journal of Semitic Studies* 2: 1–32.

Wright, G. E.
1953 Deuteronomy, Introduction and Exegesis. *The Interpreter's Bible* 2: 311–537.
1954 The Levites in Deuteronomy. *Vetus Testamentum* 4: 325–30.
1965 *Shechem: The Biography of a Biblical City*. New York: McGraw-Hill.

Judges 9 and Biblical Archeology

Edward F. Campbell, Jr.
McCormick Theological Seminary, Chicago, Illinois

Throughout recent discussions of the pertinence and validity of the term "biblical archeology," David Noel Freedman has kept a steady hand on the helm of ASOR's journal given to that endeavor. Independent-minded, resilient, and creative, he has been clear in his own mind that an interpretive enterprise called biblical archeology must go forward. It is a source of satisfaction to travel a road close to Freedman's own, and to have him as ally, supporter, and editor. And it is a joy to join in honoring him on an occasion celebrating his manifold contributions to biblical scholarship.

Few chapters in the Bible invite so readily the interpretive task of biblical archeology as does Judges 9, the story of Abimelek, son of Jerubbaal (Gideon), his rise to power in and around Shechem, and the events that bring him to his death. The chapter uses nearly a dozen designations for topographic and architectural features of the city and its immediate vicinity, some of which are probably duplicate names for the same feature. In addition, several locations in the larger region play a part in the story. Then there is a whole range of information about the social structure of the Shechem "municipality," upon which archeology in the broadest sense may have bearing.

Seventeen years ago, G. Ernest Wright presented a picture of the information bearing on Judges 9 as it had developed from the excavation at Shechem by the Joint Expedition which he directed, through its 1962 campaign (1965: 123–38). More recently, J. Alberto Soggin, a member of the expedition staff in 1962, produced a rather different portrayal (1967), and then brought it up to date for his newly-published Judges commentary (1981: 162–94). In the interim, there appeared Robert G. Boling's Anchor Bible volume on Judges (1975b), which incorporates dozens of excellent suggestions from Noel Freedman; Boling's treatment of Judges 9 has a number of new proposals. In 1976, an article by Hartmut Rösel on the "topography of war" in Joshua and Judges included a fresh review of the data (1976: 24–31); in that same year Karl Jaroš's book on Shechem appeared, with yet another review of the information (1976: 76–83, 112–21). Then, in 1979, Norman Gottwald (esp. pp. 563–7) made some new suggestions growing out of his large program of portraying early Israel's sociological character.

I shall limit my attention here to three problems in Judges 9 (one touching on Joshua 24) on which archeology has something to say, as arbiter among alternative possibilities for understanding. As always, the evidence is not conclusive, but it affects the balance of likelihood.

I

Judg 9: 6 and Josh 24: 26 each give sparse descriptions of sanctuaries at (or near)

Shechem. Are the two the same? Does Judges 9 portray a defection back to Canaanite worship, at a sanctuary which was originally Canaanite but had become Yahwist (for Joshua 24)? What relationship is there between the population of Shechem in the twelfth century B.C. and the Israelite federation now at least partially established in the land?

Let's begin with Judg 9: 6. Having removed all but one of his seventy "brothers" as claimants to rule over Shechem, Abimelek is made king by "the lords of Shechem and all Beth-millo . . . near the sacred tree *muṣṣāb* which is in Shechem." The troublesome word *muṣṣāb* has been regularly emended to *maṣṣēbâ,* "standing, memorial stone," by commentators (Wright 1965: 135, 257 note 22); Soggin and Jaroš among the recent studies cited above accept the change (but see the reservations of Soggin, 1967: 189 and 1981: 169). The result is expressed by the RSV: "by the oak of the pillar at Shechem."

At Freedman's suggestion, Boling (1975b: 171–72) stays with *muṣṣāb* and translates "palisade," in accord with Isa 29: 3. Boling then adopts the LXX[B] variant of this sentence and reads: ". . . beside the oak which survives (*hnmṣ*ʾ) at the palisade in Shechem." The reading dispenses with the stone pillar and presents another designation for what almost all would agree is the court around the temple building at the west edge of excavated Shechem, the so-called temenos area. Most commentators would find this court on its elevated platform to be referred to also in the term *millô*ʾ, "fill," of the designation Beth-millo, also used in Judg 9: 6.

Norman Gottwald (1979: 563–67) has also concluded that "palisade" or "embankment" is the correct meaning for *muṣṣāb,* but he builds a good bit more on his decision. He makes it the conclusive piece of evidence for the claim that the holy place inside Shechem in Judg 9: 6 is different from the holy places mentioned in all the other biblical passages about sanctuaries at Shechem. This includes Gen 12: 6; 33: 18–20; 35: 4; Deut 11: 29–30; Josh 24: 26; Judg 9: 37 (and assuredly Josh 8: 30).

The important passage in that group for our purposes is Josh 24: 26. Gottwald wants to place Joshua's "great stone . . . under the oak in the sanctuary of Yahweh" outside Shechem, and thus to maintain a clear distinction between the Canaanite inhabitants of Shechem and the Yahwist Israelites, who gathered at a Yahweh sanctuary at some distance outside town. Logically, the Yahwist sanctuary would be related to the altar of Jacob in Gen 33: 20 (clearly outside the city), and probably to the sacred trees of Gen 12: 6, 35: 4, and Deut 11: 30, as well as to the Diviners' Oak visible from the city gate of Shechem in Judg 9: 37.

If I understand Gottwald's reasoning, there would be then an outside sanctuary which consisted of a tree, a stone, and a sacred building or precinct. The inside, Canaanite, sanctuary of Judg 9: 6 would have a tree, but no stone. The outside sanctuary, at least in Joshua 24, was Yahwist, while the inside one was dedicated to Baʿal-berith, Baal of the Covenant (Judg 9: 4), and was wholly Canaanite. The inside one had not at one point been Yahwist (for Joshua 24) and then reverted to Baal worship (as the redactorial piece in Judg 8: 33–35 might suggest).

The archeologist raises an important consideration at this point. In the forecourt of the Shechem temple precinct, dated to 1450–1100 B.C., is a great standing-stone and its socket. That is, we may be able to keep the *maṣṣēbâ* out of the text of Judg 9: 6, but it is nevertheless there at the inside-Shechem sanctuary in the twelfth century B.C., almost certainly the time of the Abimelek story. Put another way, if Josh 24: 26 and Judg 9: 6 describe different sanctuaries, they each have both a tree and a stone along with the structures or precincts called respectively "the house of Baᶜal-berith" and "the sanctuary of Yahweh." It is not impossible that two sanctuaries would be so similar—the features are common enough as religious furnishings; but it seems to me quite unlikely. In any case, the degree of similarity between the two sanctuary descriptions (when archeology and text are taken together) must be kept in the picture.

In my judgment, this tips the balance back in favor of keeping Joshua 24 related to the sacred precinct inside Shechem. (We shall return later to some of the other biblical passages about sanctuaries outside.) I am then more attracted to Boling's conclusion (1975b: 183) that Shechem and Israel were interlocked prior to the Abimelek adventure, and that Judges 9 represents "a nearly disastrous departure" by Shechemites and Israelites from participation in the Israelite theocratic league. This position requires that one take seriously 9: 16b-19a, 22, and 55, verses which Wolfgang Richter in his masterly literary and traditio-historical analysis assigned to a late "Israelitizing" hand and dismissed as non-historical (1963: 250–52, 313–14). These passages link Jerubbaal (Gideon) with Shechem in unspecified acts of rescue and protection; place Abimelek as commander, *not king,* in Israel for a three-year period; and picture disillusioned Israelites, after Abimelek's death, going home, apparently to places other than Shechem in the Manassite countryside.

There is another consideration. Gottwald does not tackle the question of "the house of El-berith" in Judg 9: 46, and its relation to the house of Baᶜal-berith in 9: 4. We shall come back to this issue below, in section III. But let me assert anew Wright's conclusion (1965: 141), that El-berith, a known manifestation of the old high god El (Cross 1973: 79), is more conducive to syncretism with Yahweh, lord of Israel's covenant at the onset of the theocratic league, than would be Baᶜal-berith, manifesting the deity whom biblical Israel is regularly told to abhor.

II

Gottwald's proposal would call for spotting possible locations for a sanctuary or sanctuaries in the Shechem plain or on the adjacent mountains. Even if Gottwald is mistaken about the location of the Joshua 24 sanctuary, Judges 9 itself would call for such a search. In 9: 37, Gaal stands at the city gate of Shechem and sees Abimelek's men "descending from the navel of the land, and one division coming from the direction of the Soothsayers' Oak."

Soggin (1967: 190, 194–95; 1981: 189–90) has raised the question of the whereabouts of these sites in connection with asking in what direction Gaal is looking. Excavation at Shechem has revealed two city gates, at the east and the northwest; Soggin is confident that the gate in question is the one at the northwest, and is encouraged by a plus in the LXX which reads "from (*or* toward) the sea," suggesting a westward vista. He also observes that the vista from the east gate at Shechem is out into the plain and lacks heights from which the men might be descending.

On the basis of the probing done at the northwest gate, fully cleared by the earlier German excavation, the American Shechem expedition at first judged that the northwest gate belonged to the Middle Bronze IIC period (roughly 1650–1540 B.C.) and was not reused later. That would seem to settle the issue, assuming the episode in Judg 9: 26–41 is historical or at least plausible; Gaal could only have been at the east gate.

In 1966, further work at the northwest gate reopened the bare possibility that there was a reuse in Late Bronze and Iron I times; the evidence involves architectural alterations but is not buttressed by pottery of the later periods *in situ* in soil layers. Not far inside the gate, meanwhile, Field XIII produced, in 1966, 1968, and 1969, the well-preserved remains of fine LB homes, in a lay-out which persisted into the twelfth century. The quality of this segment of urban housing suggests that this was the right part of town in which to live. Indirectly it supports the likelihood that there was a means of access on the western perimeter of town which would serve the upper city residents. Soggin's proposal is, then, more plausible than it appeared to be when it could be claimed Shechem had no northwest gate in LB-Iron I.

What about the two landmarks mentioned by Gaal? It is not all certain, of course, that these two locales would any longer be identifiable in the Shechem neighborhood. Indeed, Talmon has made a strong case against concluding that the "navel of the land" is a sanctuary at all (1977: 243–68), rather than simply a topographic feature. In what follows, I am going to assume that some vestige of the two landmarks will have survived, even perhaps evidence of Iron Age use in the form of surface pottery.

We turn, then, to the sites of twelfth century occupation near Shechem. Figure 1 presents a map of the Shechem region showing locations of ancient occupation of all periods, as explored by the American Joint Expedition, by German colleagues, and by the Israeli survey of 1967–68 (sites newly contributed by this survey are marked by triangles and numbers prefixed with IS). A word about several of these sites is in order.

Above Shechem, on Jebel eṭ-Ṭûr (Mt. Gerizim) lies Tell er-Râs, site 42, where Robert J. Bull and his colleagues have located a Zeus temple of Hadrian's time on top of what is almost certainly the Samaritan sanctuary of the Hellenistic period. Excavation has reached bedrock at several places on the knoll. In the lowest layers of fill against the Hellenistic structure, there were regularly found a few sherds of Late Bronze and Iron Age pottery. Pottery likely to date from the thirteenth or twelfth century has also been found on the east-facing slopes of Mt. Gerizim, at site 39. This, along with evidence that some of the building stone in the Hellenistic construction on Tell er-Râs is reused from an earlier building, holds out the possibility that something dating back to the time of the early Israelite theocratic league occupied the heights above Shechem to the south. By way of contrast, no evidence of comparable date has come from Mt. Ebal—where biblical tradition would locate at least an altar (Josh 8: 30, cf. Deut 11: 29–30). The Iron Age pottery reported from site 3, Askar (Schenke 1968), seems likely to have come from tombs belonging to the Shechem cemetery on the low flanks of Mt. Ebal.

In passing, it should be observed that the sanctuary site of Tananir (300 meters south of Shechem, not shown on Figure 1), where lies the Middle Bronze IIC structure re-excavated in 1968 by Robert Boling (1975a; 1969; Campbell and Wright 1969), may also pertain to the designation of the mountain above Shechem as the navel of the land. Boling, by the way, sees Tananir as perhaps the place from

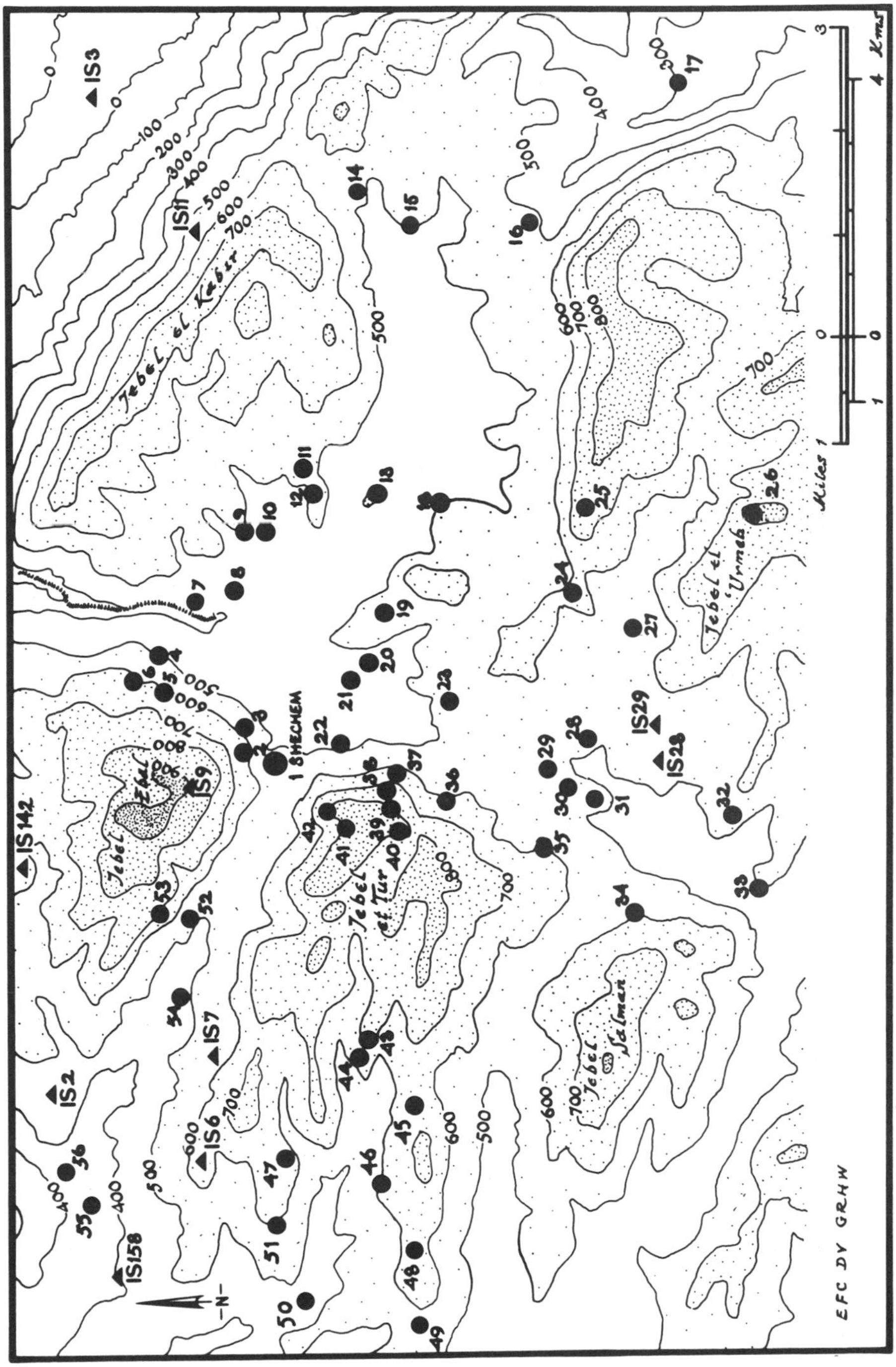

Figure 1. Contour Map of the Shechem region, showing locations of sites explored by recent surface surveys. Numbers preceded by IS were discovered by the Israeli survey in 1967–68. Prepared by G. R. H. Wright.

which Jotham intones his fable (Judg 9: 7) (1975b: 172).

Soggin's proposal that Gaal looked westward into the pass toward modern Nablus would mean that slopes of Mt. Gerizim and Mt. Ebal loomed to either side. No location suggesting the "navel" of the land is identified on Mt. Gerizim in this direction, but perhaps, after all, we are to think of the entire mountain under this term. On Mt. Ebal, a *weli* dedicated to Sheikh ʿAmād ed-Dîn occupies a knoll at site 53; exploration throughout its vicinity has yielded no artifacts earlier than the Ottoman period. In short, assuming that the locales of the two places named in 9: 37 would have accumlated some material evidence of their presence, the surveys fail to support Soggin's proposal—at least within the line of vision of the northwest gate. There are, as we shall see later, other Iron Age sites farther west but out of sight.

If instead Gaal looked eastward from the east gate, the shoulder of Mt. Gerizim which Tell er-Râs caps is far enough out into the line of sight to serve as one direction from which Abimelek's men were coming. East and southeast, sites 11, 14, 15, 19 and 26 on the map all attest twelfth-century occupation and are visible from Shechem's east gate.

The most plausible site for the location of the Soothsayers' Oak is site 19; it is now a small walled orchard with little depth of soil on an outlying summit of the main mountain and bears the name Khirbet Ibn Naṣir (Bull and Campbell 1968: 29; Kallai 1972: 166). It is Elliger's (and my own) candidate as the location for Michmetat of Josh 16: 6 and 17: 7 (Elliger 1970: 91–100). Its plausibility would be significantly enhanced if we could be sure that Judg 9: 41 means that Arumah was Abimelek's base of operations before the Gaal episode as well as afterwards (contra Boling 1975b: 178–79). Arumah, all agree, is at site 26, Khirbet el-ʿUrmeh, a striking mountain-top fortress replete with massive water-storage facilities. Some of Abimelek's men would have moved westward across the plain and come up from the south along the flanks of Mt. Gerizim out of sight until almost upon Shechem. Others would have moved north across the flattish uplands of the massive mountain of which Khirbet Ibn Naṣir is a forward salient, to drop to the plain about one mile just south of due east from Shechem, "on the way from the Soothsayers' Oak." As for men coming down from the mountain top, in Judg 9: 36, it is unclear whether a third group is meant, or this is a general description covering the two in 9: 37.

All in all, placing Gaal and Zebul at the east gate, and spreading the early morning advance from "ambush" positions out to the east and south, seems much more plausible than Soggin's suggestion. Rösel (1976: 29–30) is of the same feeling, after a careful review of all the circumstances, including the question of what perspective would let Zebul scoff at Gaal for seeing "the shadows of the mountains as if they were men"—a perspective placing the sun in front of him, casting shadows toward him.

III

Judg 9: 46–49, an episode about the Migdal (Fortress) of Shechem, presents an event in the exploits of Abimelek which is not easily squared with the other episodes in the overall narrative. If verses 46–49 describe events in the city of Shechem, there is a distinct tension with verses 42–45, which have already brought the destruction of the city to its conclusion. If as well this episode pertains to the same city as does the portrayal in 9: 1–6, it presents us with a quite different set of designations for features of the city of Shechem. These tensions have long been recognized and have served as the basis for division of the text into sources, or have urged the assignment of 9: 1–6 and 42–45 to a group of non-historical additions to a basic story in 9: 26–40, 46–49 (Richter 1963).

It is Soggin who has reopened the question of the places and structures mentioned in verses 46–49. He tends to the conclusion that Judges 9 forms an overall unity, however complex its composition (1981: 165–66). For that reason, he expects vv 46–49 to make sense with reference to both the immediately preceding report and 9: 1–6. He takes verse 46 to mean, by its report that the lords of the Migdal of Shechem *heard*, that the Migdal of Shechem must lie outside Shechem proper, far enough away for a report of the fall of Shechem to reach it and give time for defensive preparation. This location also contained the Temple of El-berith, distinct from the Temple of Baʿal-berith at Shechem (9: 4). And nearby must be Mt. Ṣalmon, from which Abimelek gathers his firewood for the devastation of the Migdal of Shechem. In 1967, Soggin (p. 197) proposed Tell Ṣōfar, site 54 on Figure 1, as the site for this episode, and made Mt. Ṣalmon into Mt. Ebal.

Soggin's effort here is properly motivated. As respect for the literary craft of redactors of biblical narrative and of biblical story-tellers grows in contemporary research, it becomes more and more difficult to rest content with explanations that leave jarring inconsistencies in otherwise coherent texts. Furthermore, Tell Ṣōfar makes a good candidate for a Shechem outrider at the western end of the pass between Ebal and Gerizim. Surface survey found pottery covering Late Bronze II (1350–1225 B.C.), Iron I of the twelfth century, and later Iron age material (Bull and Campbell 1968: 36). Salvage excavation at the site in 1972 found strata reaching back from Hellenistic times to the ninth century B.C.; the excavation had to be discontinued well before reaching bedrock (Yeivin 1973: 12–13). An even better candidate, if large size is advantageous to Soggin's proposal, would be Kûmeh, site 56 on the map, a rather extensive tell still within the pass but nearly five miles west of Shechem.

Plausible as all of this may sound, however, there are major problems with it. When verse 46 uses the verb "heard," it is not at all clear that distance and lapse of time are involved. Our story has a verb it uses several times to convey just the idea of a report reaching someone by messenger across a distance: *wayyugad/wayyagīdû,* "it was made known/they made known" (9: 25, 42, and 47). As for "heard" in 9:46, it can readily be taken to mean that the sound of fighting on the lower east side of Shechem could reach people in the western precinct and send them running for safety (Wright 1965: 128).

It is also difficult to believe that the temple of El-berith is not indeed equivalent to the temple of Baʿal-berith in 9: 4, and that the Migdal of Shechem is not the same as the Beth-millo of 9: 6 (cf. also the fire in v 46 and the fire to devour Beth-millo in Jotham's curse in 9: 20).

Rejecting Soggin's proposal for 9: 46–49 leaves us, however, with the curious change in terminology for the features of Shechem's western precinct. I suspect there is an as-yet-undiscerned reason for this shift. We should not be content, I think, with the explanation that vv 46–49 must be from another source, material which the redactor was not at liberty to revise in order to conform it to its context (so Boling 1975b: 180).

We have a good bit more to learn about narrative composition in the Bible. I am content, then, to leave some of these questions open. It should be noted, however, that there are a considerable number of devices knitting the story together; Richter has noted a group of these within 9: 26–45 (1963: 256–59), for some of which he has no good explanation when he seeks to separate verses 41–45 from 26–40. Observe the use of the making-known-to-Abimelek motif already mentioned; the designation *baʿălê* for the leading citizens or lords of Shechem (9: 2, 20, 23), of the Migdal of Shechem (9: 46), and of Tebeṣ (9: 51); the "brothers" of Abimelek in 9: 3 beside Gaal's "brothers" in 9: 26; and the sequence of ambushes in 9: 25, 32, 34, 35, and 43. That Judges 9 is a unity and that it presents an overall plausible face seems to me more and more likely.

Biblical scholarship for the eighties needs to practice bringing together all of its variety of means of access to the text. Noel Freedman has practiced such eclecticism throughout his career. May the number of scholars like him increase!

References

Boling, R. G.
1969 Bronze Age Buildings at the Shechem High Place. *Biblical Archeologist* 32: 81–103.
1975a Excavations at Tananir, 1968. Pp. 24–85 in *Report on Archaeological Work at Ṣuwwānnet eth-Thanīya, Tananir, and Khirbet Minḥa (Munḥata),* ed. G. M. Landes. Missoula, MT: Scholars Press for ASOR.
1975b *Judges.* Anchor Bible 7. Garden City, NY: Doubleday.

Bull, R. J., and Campbell, E. F., Jr.
1968 The Sixth Campaign at Balâṭah (Shechem). *Bulletin of the American Schools of Oriental Research* 190: 2–41.

Campbell, E. F., Jr., and Wright, G. E.
1969 Tribal League Shrines in Amman and Shechem. *Biblical Archeologist* 32: 104–16.

Cross, F. M.
1973 *Canaanite Myth and Hebrew Epic.* Cambridge, MA: Harvard.

Elliger, K.
1970 Michmethath. Pp. 91–100 in *Archäologie und Altes Testament,* ed. A. Kuschke and E. Kutsch. Tübingen: J. C. B. Mohr.

Gottwald, N.
1979 *The Tribes of Yahweh.* Maryknoll, NY: Orbis.

Jaroš, K.
1976 *Sichem.* Orbis Biblicus et Orientalis 11. Göttingen: Vandenhoeck & Ruprecht.

Kallai, Z.
1972 The Surveys: The Land of Benjamin and Mt. Ephraim. Pp. 151–93 in *Judaea, Samaria and the Golan: Archaeological Survey, 1967–1968,* ed. M. Kochavi. Jerusalem: Carta (Hebrew).

Richter, W.
1963 *Traditionsgeschichtliche Untersuchungen zum Richterbuch.* Bonner Biblische Beiträge 18. Bonn: Peter Hanstein.

Rösel, H.
1976 Studie zur Topographie der Kriege in den Büchern Josua und Richter. *Zeitschrift des Deutschen Palästina-Vereins* 92: 11–46.

Schenke, H.-M.
1968 Jakobsbrunnen—Josephsgrab—Sychar: Topographische Untersuchungen und Erwagungen in der Perspektive von Joh. 4,5.6. *Zeitschrift des Deutschen Palästina-Vereins* 84: 159–86.

Soggin, J. A.
1967 Bemerkungen zur alttestamentlichen Topographie Sichems mit besonderem Bezug auf Jdc. 9. *Zeitschrift des Deutschen Palästina-Vereins* 83: 183–98.
1981 *Judges: A Commentary.* Philadelphia: Westminster.

Talmon, S.
1977 The 'Navel of the Earth' and the Comparative Method. Pp. 243–68 in *Scripture in History and Theology: Essays in Honor of J. Coert Rylaarsdam,* ed. A. L. Merrill and T. W. Overholt. Pittsburgh, PA: The Pickwick Press.

Wright, G. E.
1965 *Shechem: The Biography of a Biblical City.* New York: McGraw-Hill.

Yeivin, Z.
1973 Tel Ṣophar. *Ḥadashot Arkiologiot* 47: 12–13 (Hebrew).

The Ritual Dedication of the City of David in 2 Samuel 6

P. Kyle McCarter, Jr.
The University of Virginia, Charlottesville, Virginia

Second Samuel 6 describes the arrival of Yahweh's ark in Jerusalem. The holy object is conducted into the city by a team of priests (vv 3–4) in a formal procession escorted by David and "all the elite troops (*kol-bāḥûr*) of Israel" (v 1). The accompanying ceremony is described in considerable detail. As the ark bearers advance, the king sacrifices a bull and a fatling every six paces (v 13).[1] The Israelites, led by David, dance and sing and play a long catalogue of musical instruments (vv 5, 14–15). When the ark has been deposited "inside the tent[2] David pitched for it" (v 17), sacrifices are again offered, and the king blesses the people "by the name of Yahweh" (v 18). Finally, David distributes a banquet of breads and cakes to "the whole multitude of Israel, both men and women" (v 19).

It is the prevailing view of scholars that this chapter was composed under the influence of an annual festival of the monarchical period reenacting the ark's entry into Jerusalem. The significance of this festival is understood in one of two ways. According to S. Mowinckel (1967 I: 128–30, 175–76), it was an agricultural festival of harvest and new year—the "feast of Yahweh's enthronement" that Mowinckel reconstructs from certain psalms (1967 I: 106–92). This festival, though it had absorbed historical elements, remained primarily a celebration of the mythic event of Yahweh's victory over the powers of chaos. H.-J. Kraus, on the other hand, argues that it was a celebration of purely historical events, a "royal Zion festival," commemorating the choice of Zion and the election of David (1951: 27–35; 1966: 183–85). The details of these two positions are well known (cf. Porter 1954), and we need not rehearse them here. Our concern is with an assumption they have in common, viz., that the author of 2 Samuel 6 "had no contemporary reports about the festival from the time of David, so he described it on the model of the celebration of his own day" (Mowinckel 1967 I: 175, cf. 237–39). If this is true, the description of the procession of the ark and the accompanying rites can be used for the reconstruction of a "feast of Yahweh's enthronement" or a "royal Zion festival," but it provides no reliable information about the historically unique event it purports to describe.

P. D. Miller, Jr. and J. J. M. Roberts have recently challenged this assumption. In their study of the so-called "ark narrative" of First Samuel (1977), which they compare to Mesopotamian accounts of the capture and return of divine images in battle, they touch on the problem of 2 Samuel 6, challenging "the widespread tendency to regard [it] as the reflex of a regular temple liturgy. Such an interpretation," they say (1977: 16), "runs counter to the parallels where the similar, historical return of an image to its sanctuary is accompanied by ritual practices analogous to those mentioned in the ark narrative." One especially striking parallel is Assurbanipal's account of his return of Marduk's image to his shrine in Babylon after a generation of captivity in Assur (Luckenbill 1926/27 II: §§988–89). "Just as Assurbanipal's army participated in the return of Marduk to his new sanctuary, so David's army participated in the return of the ark of Yahweh. Just as Marduk's journey was accompanied by music and rejoicing, so was the ark's. Moreover, just as the Assyrians offered sacrifices every double mile from the quay of Assur to the quay of Babylon, so David offered an ox and a fatling every six steps" (Miller and Roberts 1977: 16–17). In view of these points of contact Miller and Roberts prefer to think of 2 Samuel 6 as a direct witness to a single, historically unique event, viz., David's transfer of the ark to Jerusalem.

As a by-product of their assessment of the ark narrative, then, Miller and Roberts have made an impressive case for the need for a reassessment of 2 Samuel 6 as well. One might maintain the case for seeing the reflex of an annual ceremony here on the grounds that reenactment implies repetition of the original event in its various details; but as far as present evidence is concerned, it must be said that the most impressive parallels refer to rites accompanying historically unique events. Moreover, the particular form of the processional rites reinforces this impression. The offering of sacrifices "every six paces" (2 Sam 6: 13) suggests the progressive sanctification of a previously profane district and thus the preparation of a new sacred precinct. The ark must not cross unholy ground as it proceeds from its sanctified (cf. 1 Sam 7: 1) resting place in Kiriath-jearim[3] to its new tent shrine in the City of David; thus the way is gradually prepared with sacrifices until a new holy place has been established. In the Assyrian parallels drawn by Miller and Roberts the sanctuary toward which the procession moves is not, strictly speaking, new, but it has been previously defiled, and the god has been absent for some time. Therefore the same kind of preparation is necessary: sacrifices are offered "every double mile," and the sacred precinct is (re)sanctified.

With regard to the issue of the newness of the holy district, however, it seems possible to question the adequacy of the parallels Miller and Roberts cite. Is it sufficient to compare 2 Samuel 6 to accounts of "the return of an image to its sanctuary"? We can accept the analogy of the ark and a divine image and grant to "the tent David pitched" the status of a sanctuary, but there remains the difficulty of the notion of "return." It can hardly be said that the ark is returning to Jerusalem in 2 Samuel 6 in the way that Marduk is returning to Babylon in the Neo-Assyrian texts mentioned above. On the contrary, Yahweh is entering Jerusalem for the first time; our account is concerned with the inauguration, not reestablishment, of his cult there. The validity of comparison to accounts of the return of images lies in the fact that the ark is brought back to a "genuine national sanctuary" (Cross 1973: 96) from a temporary stopping place[4] after a period of exile. The light shed on the ritual procedures by which a sanctuary was prepared—by sanctification or resanctification—for the reception of a divine image or emblem is considerable. But the particular circumstance of the introduction of the ark to the City of David invites us also to consider other parallels.

Throughout 2 Samuel 6 the destination of the ark is referred to as "the City of David" (vv 10,12,16), i.e., the fortified hilltop called "the stronghold of Zion" in 2 Sam 5: 7 and renamed after its capture by David (5: 9). The ark is on its way to David's city, and David is everywhere the central human figure in the account, organizing the expedition (vv 1–2), leading the procession (v 5), dancing before the ark (vv 14–16), offering sacrifices (vv 13,18), blessing the people (v 18), and distributing the feast (v 19). Thus the new royal city is David's City, and David is the center of interest in the account. The introduction of Yahweh's ark represents the sanction of the national deity for David's kingship and his new capital.

Comparison with other ancient Near Eastern accounts of the introduction of national deities to new royal cities is instructive. The records of Sargon II of Assyria and his successors provide a series of examples. Sargon, progenitor of a new ruling branch of the royal family, built a new royal city and, like David named it for himself. When Dur-sharrukin (*dūr šarrukīn*, "Sargonsburg" [modern Khorsabad]) was completed, Sargon invited the national god, Assur, and the other great gods of Assyria into the city where he honored them with sacrifices (Luckenbill 1926/27 II: §§94, 98, 101). Afterwards there was a banquet for the people and "a feast of music" (§98). When Sennacherib, Sargon's son and successor, established a new capital of his own at Nineveh, he conducted a similar ceremony of dedication (Luckenbill 1926/27 II: §§370, 403, 416). Long revered as the seat of the worship of the great Ishtar of Nineveh, the city was now resanctified, befitting its new status as residence of the ruling gods of the state. Assur and the other gods were invited into the newly completed royal palace and honored with sacrifices. There followed a great feast: "I drenched the foreheads of my people with wine," boasts Sennacherib (§§403, 416), "with mead I sprinkled their hearts." Esarhaddon, Sennacherib's successor, did not build a new capital city, but he did replace the palace in Nineveh with a much larger complex—in effect a new seat of government as he saw it (Luckenbill 1926/27 II: §§689–95, 697–700)—and he dedicated it according to the celebratory pattern of his predecessors, inviting into the palace Assur and the other state gods, offering them sacrifices, and providing the people with "feasts and banquets of choice dishes" (§699). The most elaborate Assyrian example of this pattern, however, is reported not in the annals of the Sargonid kings but in a text describing the dedication of the palace of Assurnasirpal II in his new royal city, Calah (modern Nimrud). Again Assur and the other Assyrian gods are invited and presented with sacrifices, listed in a very long catalogue; then food and drink are provided to Assurnasirpal's guests from Assyria and abroad, who number an extraordinary 69,574 (ANET 558–60).

This ceremonial pattern—the invitation of the national god into a new capital city, the presentation of sacrifices, and the provision of a banquet for the people of the land—is also present in 2 Samuel 6, where the ark of Yahweh, the god of Israel, is conducted into the new capital city, the City of David, and honored with sacrifices, after which a feast is served to the people of the land. The significance of this pattern is not difficult to identify. As noted above, the account of the ark's arrival in Jerusalem centers on the figure of the king, and the same is true of the Assyrian parallels. The ceremony has two facets corresponding to two aspects of an ideology of kingship that Mesopotamia and Israel shared. There is, in the first place, a concern for the national god's sanction of the rule of the king, as exhibited by the invitation of Assur or Yahweh into a new seat of government closely identified with the king ("Sargonsburg," "the City of David"). The sacrifices mentioned in the Assyrian texts and in 2 Sam 6: 17–18 are offered in the hope that the deity will be willing to reside in the new shrine, as the Assyrian texts make clear, and make his presence actively felt there—that is (to use the biblical expression), in the hope that he will "arise" there (cf. the petition in v 8 of Psalm 132, the subject of which is the ceremony described in 2 Samuel 6[5]). Secondly, the pattern points to the king's responsibility for the welfare of his people. The joyful celebration and the distribution of food to the people effectually symbolize the prosperity the people may expect from the king ruling in his new seat of government. Thus in 2 Sam 6: 19 it is "the whole multitude of Israel, both men and women," who participate in the feast of breads and cakes, and in the Assyrian records the banquet is served to "the people of [the king's] land" (Luckenbill 1926/27 II: §403, etc.), to whom are sometimes added guests from foreign countries that have "submitted to the yoke of [the king's] rule" (§98; cf. ANET 599: "47,074 persons, men and women, who were bid to come from across [the king's] entire country, [also] 5,000 important persons, delegates from" a list of tributary states). In short, the ceremonial pattern reflected in 2 Samuel 6 and the Assyrian texts cited concerns both the national god's regard for the king and the king's ability to provide for the welfare of his people; both of these things are demonstrated in the course of a ritual involving the introduction of the national god to a new royal city.

A king would conduct a ceremony of this kind, therefore, in the hope of securing the blessing of the national god for himself and his people in a new seat of government. This is made explicit in the case of David. According to 2 Sam 6: 12, David, having learned of the blessing of the house of Obed-edom the Gittite that has resulted from the ark's sojourn there (cf. 6:10–11), says to himself, "I'll bring the blessing back to my own house!"[6] and indeed the chapter that follows is principally concerned with the blessing of David's house (cf. especially 2 Sam 7: 29). In 6: 18 the people receive their blessing. The Assyrian records, too, show that the kings were motivated by a desire to secure a blessing for themselves, their people, and their new royal cities (cf. Luckenbill 1926/27 II: §699, etc.). Another parallel comes to mind at this point. The Phoenician inscription of Azitawadda, the eighth-century B.C. king of a small state in eastern Cilicia (KAI 26; ANET 653–54), records the building of a new royal city (modern Karatepe), which was again named after the king who built it. "When I had built this city and assigned it the name Azitawaddiya," says Azitawadda, "I caused Baal-*krntryš* to take up residence in it and brought sacrifice at all the appointed times[7]..." (II: 17–III: 1). At this point he invokes the following blessing: "May Baal-*krntryš* bless Azitawadda with life and peace and glorious power over every other king, so that Baal-*krntryš* and all the other gods of the city might give Azitawadda length of days, a multitude of years, a pleasant term of office, and glorious power over every other king! And may this city possess grain and wine! And may this people, who dwell within it, possess herds, flocks, grain, and wine! In their abundance may they sire children! In their abundance may they gain glory! In their abundance may they serve Azitawadda and the house of Mupsh, by the grace of Baal and the other gods!" (III: 2–11).

In light of the Akkadian and Phoenician parallels cited, therefore, we are in a position to understand 2 Samuel 6 as the record of a historically unique cultic event, viz., the ritual dedication of the City of David as the new religious and political capital of the Israelites, the people of Yahweh. The purpose of the ceremony was the sanctification of the City of David for the installation of the ark in the hope that Yahweh's presence would assure the success of David's government and the welfare of the people. The specific features of the rites reported here—the procession of sanctification, the musical celebration, the banquet of the people, and the blessing of the king and his subjects—correspond to practices known from accounts of comparable dedications elsewhere. Indeed the correspondence of 2 Samuel 6 to these accounts, each of which also records a historically unique event, is so close that appeal to subsequent cultic reenactment of the event in explanation of the ritual dimension of the chapter seems gratuitous. On the contrary, the concerns signified by the rites—the recovery of the ark, the sanctification of the new city, the divine sanction of the rule of David—are peculiarly those of the time of David and invite comparison with the older documents underlying the adjacent materials—the report of David's expulsion of the Philistines from Israelite territory (2 Sam 5: 17–25), the account of the capture of the stronghold of Zion (2 Sam 5: 6–10), and the oldest components of 2 Samuel 7.[8]

Notes

1. For this interpretation, which is rejected by Hertzberg (1964: 279), see Arnold (1917: 41) and Miller and Roberts (1977: 96 n. 157). The syntax of the verbs in MT (*wyhy . . . wyzbḥ*) suggests a different meaning, viz., "When the ark bearers had advanced six paces, he sacrificed a bull and a fatling.' The meaning we prefer, "Whenever the ark bearers advanced six paces, he would sacrifice a bull and a fatling," would be more naturally expressed by *whyh . . . wzbḥ* (Driver 1890: 207). The reading *wzbḥ* is supported by LXX *kai thyma*. In my opinion the repeated sacrifices in the Assyrian parallels cited by Miller and Roberts and the pattern of progressive sanctification of a new sacred precinct that is evident here are decisive (see below).

2. MT and LXX have "*in its place* inside the tent, etc." We omit *bmqwmw* with the Peshiṭta and, as space considerations indicate, a fragmentary manuscript from Qumran (4QSam[a]). The shorter reading is preserved in the synoptic passage in 1 Chr 16: 1, and Josephus' text seems also to have had it (*Ant.* 7.86). The source of the expansion is probably 1 Kgs 8: 6.

3. Called "Baalah" in 2 Sam 6: 2 as in the description of the northern border of Judah in Josh 15: 9, 10. On the textual problems of the present reference, see Ulrich 1978: 198–99.

4. While in Kiriath-jearim the ark was technically on Israelite soil, but it may have remained inaccessible until David's explusion of the Philistine army of occupation (2 Sam 5: 25). See the discussion of Ishida 1977: 140–43.

5. See Cross 1973: 94–97. In vv 8 and 10 we read: "Arise, O Yahweh at [or "from," but not "to"; cf. Hillers 1968: 49, 50] your resting place, you and your mighty ark . . . for the sake of your servant David! Do not rebuff your anointed one!"

6. The long plus appears only in the so-called Lucianic manuscripts of LXX (*kai eipen daueid epistrepsō tēn eulogian eis ton oikon mou*) and in OL (*et dīxit david revocābō benedictionem in domum meam*), from which we can reconstruct *wy*ʾ*mr dwd* ʾ*šyb* ʾ*t hbrkh* ʾ*l byty,* "And David said, 'I'll bring the blessing back to my own house!'" Though there is no apparent mechanism for the loss of this material from the text, it is highly unlikely that a scribe would add a sentence assigning a selfish motive to David's pious deeds. It was probably excised from the witnesses that lack it in protection of David.

7. Or "for all the molten images" (*lmskt*). In view of the short sacrificial calendar that follows in the text I prefer to associate the noun with Biblical Hebrew *nāsak,* "appoint" (Ps 2: 6 and Prov 8: 23; cf. *nāsîk*, "appointed officer"), and interpret it to mean "appointed times" or perhaps "stipulations."

8. On this and related topics see the excellent discussion in Mann 1977: 213–30.

References

Arnold, W. R.
1917 *Ephod and Ark. A Study in the Records and Religion of the Ancient Hebrews.* Harvard Theological Studies 3. Cambridge: Harvard University.

Cross, F. M.
1973 *Canaanite Myth and Hebrew Epic.* Cambridge: Harvard University.

Driver, S. R.
1890 *Notes on the Hebrew Text of the Books of Samuel.* Oxford: Clarendon.

Hertzberg, H. W.
1964 *I & II Samuel. A Commentary.* Trans. J. S. Bowden. The Old Testament Library. Philadelphia: Westminster.

Hillers, D. R.
1968 Ritual Procession of the Ark and Ps 132. *Catholic Biblical Quarterly* 30: 48–55.

Ishida, T.
1977 *The Royal Dynasties in Ancient Israel. A Study on the Formation and Development of Royal-Dynastic Ideology.* Beiheft zur Zeitschrift für die Alttestamentliche Wissenschaft 142. Berlin: W. de Gruyter.

Kraus, H.-J.
1951 *Die Königherrschaft Gottes im Alten Testament.* Beiträge zur Historischen Theologie 13. Tübingen: J. C. B. Mohr.
1966 *Worship in Israel. A Cultic History of the Old Testament.* Trans. G. Buswell from German, 1962. Richmond, VA: John Knox.

Luckenbill, D. D.
1926/27 *Ancient Records of Assyria and Babylonia.* 2 vols. Chicago: University of Chicago.

Mann, T. W.
1977 *Divine Presence and Guidance in Israelite Traditions. The Typology of Exaltation.* Johns Hopkins Near Eastern Studies. Baltimore: The John Hopkins University.

Miller, P. D., Jr., and Roberts, J. J. M.
1977 *The Hand of the Lord. A Reassessment of the "Ark Narrative" of I Samuel.* Johns Hopkin Near Eastern Studies. Baltimore: The John Hopkins University.

Mowinckel, S.
1967 *The Psalms in Israel's Worship.* 2 vols. Trans. D. R. Ap-Thomas from Norwegian, 1951. New York: Abingdon.

Porter, J. R.
1954 The Interpretation of 2 Samuel vi and Psalm cxxxii. *Journal of Theological Studies* 5: 161–73.

Ulrich, E. C., Jr.
1978 *The Qumran Text of Samuel and Josephus.* Harvard Semitic Monograph 19. Missoula, MT: Scholars.

Rab-saris and Rab-shakeh in 2 Kings 18

Hayim Tadmor
The Hebrew University of Jerusalem

The titles of two of the three envoys of Sennacherib who appeared before the gates of Jerusalem in 701 (2 Kgs 18: 17ff.) have been a subject of scholarly debate, both Assyriological and biblical, for over a century—a curious case of mistaken lexical equations and circular argumentation.

Whereas the identity of the Tartan with the Assyrian *turtānu*, "Commander-in-Chief" (lit., "the second-in-command"), was apparent even after the first stages of the decipherment of the Assyrian royal inscriptions, the question of the cuneiform counterpart of the other two Assyrian titles in Hebrew guise could not easily be resolved. But even before the decipherment of the cuneiform, when Assyriology was still in its infancy, Semitists and biblical scholars had surmised that "Rab-saris" (KJV Rabsaris) must mean "Chief of the Eunuchs"/"Chief Eunuch." This title was compared to *rāb sārîsîm* (Dan 1: 3), "Master of (Nebuchadnezzar's) eunuchs," and was related to *sārîs, sārîsîm* in Isa 53: 3 and to *sârîsāʾ/sarsāʾ* in Aramaic and Syriac.

Similarly, "Rab-shakeh" (KJV Rabshakeh) was understood to be Sennacherib's "Chief Cupbearer" (RSV: Chief of the Butlers, Luther: *Erzschenke*) and was compared to *śar hammašqîm* in Gen 40: 2, 9, etc.[1]

A few years later, the early Assyriologists concluded—rather unfortunately—that Rab-shakeh corresponds to LÚ.GAL.SAG, a logogram believed to be pronounced *rab šaq* or *rab šaqu* (from *šaqû*, high), a title of a high ranking dignitary occasionally dispatched by the kings of Assyria on military missions. Hence this title was no longer rendered as "Chief Cupbearer" but as "General," "General Staff-officer," or the like.[2]

As no cuneiform counterpart could be provided at that time for the "Rab-saris," Schrader stated that it was "probably the translation of a corresponding Assyrian title. But it has not been possible to say anything more definite hitherto. The [Biblical Hebrew] word *sārîs*, 'eunuch,' has not yet been found in the inscriptions" (1883: 319 = 1888: 2: 3). Schrader's disciple Hugo Winckler was much less cautious. He suggested that the "Rab-saris" of 2 Kgs 18: 17 was merely a wrong explanatory gloss to the rab-SAG (1889: 138). A learned glossator, knowing that SAG = *rēšu*, had "retranslated" *rab-šaq* (Rab-shakeh) with the non-existent Assyrian title *rab ša rīš* and then hebraized it into *rab-sārîs*! As supporting evidence for this argument, Winckler pointed out that in Isa 36: 2, the parallel to 2 Kgs 18: 17, only one Assyrian envoy appears, the Rabshakeh.[3]

At about the same time, sounder suggestions were brought forth, mainly from the Leipzig school, headed by Zimmern (1899: 116; 1905: 651). The latter, followed by Klauber's penetrating study (1910: 70–72), adduced ample evidence that the Chief Cupbearer in Assyria was not the GAL.SAG, but the GAL.BI.LUL (or

GAL.KAŠ.LUL), pronounced *rab-šaqê*, another high ranking dignitary also mentioned in the eponym lists and in royal correspondence. Consequently, *rab šaqû/šaqê* was taken as the original of the Rab-shakeh of the biblical narrative. As for the LÚ.GAL.SAG, this title was either transcribed, rather cautiously as *amêlrab*-SAG (Klauber 1910: 73–77; 89) or transliterated as *amêlrab-rešu*, and translated "General" (Streck 1916: 682). It was further suggested that LÚ.SAG by itself was pronounced *ša-rēši* and, like the *šūt-rēšu* of the Assyrian royal inscriptions, denoted a (royal) eunuch, often employed in various imperial-administrative posts.[4]

Convincing as they might have seemed, these renderings were not universally accepted. The entirely incorrect equation of Rab-shakeh with LÚ.GAL.SAG and the transcription of the latter as *rab-šaq* were not abandoned. Several leading Assyriological publications,[5] collections of ancient Near Eastern texts in translation,[6] as well as several recent translations of the Old Testament have followed the old error.[7]

More recently, the equation of LÚ.SAG with *ša ri-šu* in a lexical text published by Landsberger and Gurney (1957: 83: 232) has finally settled the century-old dispute. Yet, the question of how the title LÚ.GAL.SAG in the royal inscriptions should be read still remains a matter of debate. Some continue to normalize it as *rab-rēši*,[8] while others prefer *rab-ša-reši*, which thus corresponds to *rab-sārîs* of 2 Kgs 18: 17.[9] The issue is not merely one of lexicographical conventions; it relates to the question whether the *ša-rēši* and consequently the *rab ša-rēsi* were or were not eunuchs—a cardinal problem of the Assyrian imperial administration.

Curiously enough, the proof that LÚ.GAL.SAG was indeed pronounced *rab ša-rēši* in Assyria has been close at hand all these years. A bilingual "heart-shaped" docket from the Kuyunjik collection at the British Museum (81–2–4, 147), bearing an Aramaic superscription with the title *rbsrs*, was published almost a century ago.[11] The editors of that text in *CIS* recognized that *rbsrs* corresponds to Rab-saris in 2 Kgs 18: 17 and hence rendered the date *l'm Nbsrṣr rbsrs* as "Anno eunochorum principis Nabosaruṣur" (*CIS* 2/I: 145). It was rather unfortunate that in the cuneiform text the date-formula had been shortened to *limmu Nabu-šar-uṣur* and his title omitted. Subsequently, this eponym was identified with Nabu-šar-uṣur the governor of Marqasi and the eponym for 682,[12] and not with one of his two name-sakes,[13] both post-canonical eponyms (i.e., after 648).[13] That identification has never been questioned, nor has the resulting strange situation that a provincial governor would at the same time have held the high rank of Chief Eunuch.

The long awaited clue to the correct identity of the Nabu-šar-uṣur of the bilingual docket and to his title has been provided by three economic documents, one—unpublished—from Assur (Weidner 1941: 316) and two from Nimrud, ND 3423 (Wiseman 1953: 140; Deller 1966: 193) and ND 5465 (Parker 1957: 134, pl. 21). In all three texts Nabu-šar-uṣur carries the title of GAL.SAG. Weidner, when referring to the date in the Assur document (*lim-mu Nabu-šar-uṣur rab*-SAG), noted its relation to that of the *rbsrs* of the Aramaic superscription (CIS no. 38) but did not draw the prosopographic and chronological inference. This was performed, very convincingly, by Margarete Falkner, who has shown that Nabu-šar-uṣur, the LÚ.GAL.SAG of the Nimrud and Assur tablets, should be placed in the early post-canonical period, i.e., in the fifth decade of the seventh century (1956: 114). Our bilingual docket was also assigned by her to the same post-canonical eponym and not to that for 682. She made no reference, however, to the Aramaic superscription.[14]

More recent prosopographic examination of our docket and of another bilingual docket, K. 3784, closed relately to it,[15] has revealed that both must belong to the mid-seventh century or somewhat later and not to 682.[16] Thus, the identification of the Nabu-šar-uṣur of the bilingual docket with the early post-canonical Nabu-šar-uṣur the LÚ.GAL.SAG has once and for all been established.[17] It eliminates any possible doubt that the logographically written title LÚ.GAL.SAG (or, occasionally, LÚ.GAL.LÚ.SAG[18]) was indeed rendered in Aramaic *rbsrs*, i.e., *rab ša-rēši* in Akkadian or *Rab-sārîs* in Biblical Hebrew. Thus oddly enough, proper analysis of the Assyriological evidence has returned us to the answers offered in the pre-cuneiform stage of inquiry.

Notes

1. Thus, e.g., Thenius 1849: 383; Eddrup 1875: 2858; Berger 1886: 201. But already Jerome did not doubt that "Rabsaris" was "princeps eunuchus sive magister aut major eunuchus" and "Rabsace" was "princeps deosculans sive multus osculo" (*Liber de Nominibus Hebraicis*, ad loc.).

2. Delitzsch 1883: 13; 1896: 685; Schrader 1888: 319–20; Knudtzon 1893: 317; Muss-Arnolt 1905: 1099; Winckler 1903: 273; Manitius 1910: 199–209.

3. Before Winckler's ingenious speculation Klosterman (1887: 459) had suggested that the shorter version in Isa 36: 2 should be preferred. Influenced by these opinions, Stade and Schwally (1904: 271) excised the "Tartan" and the "Rab-saris" from 2 Kgs 18: 17, considering them marginal glosses. (In modern scholarship, this hyper-critical approach has been followed by Gray 1970: 675 and by the JB.) Several years after his short note of 1899 Winckler offered yet another, but no less far-fetched, speculation. He suggested that the original text in 2 Kgs 18: 17 read "and he sent the Tartan" etc., but the "Tartan" was later supplanted by "Rab-shakeh" (1903: 273, n. 3). Haupt's tacit objection (*apud* Stade and Schwally 1904: 271) must have salvaged the "Rab-shakeh" but not the other two titles in the English edition of the *Polychrome Bible*.

4. Ungnad 1917/18: 56; Zimmern 1923: 31; Weidner 1956: 264. By that time it had been widely recognized that Hebrew *sārîs*, Aramaic *srs*ʾ, *srys*ʾ, and Syriac *sārîsāʾ*, "eunuch," were loan words from Assyro-Babylonian *ša rēši* (lit., "he who is at head"). Thus already, Delitzsch 1896: 694; Zimmern 1899: 116; 1903: 649; and BDB: 710.

5. Cf., e.g., Smith 1921: 60: 20; Waterman 1930–31: no. 283: 1 and vol. 3, p. 111; Piepkorn 1933: 12: 9. This error, reiterated recently by Henshaw, 1969: 15, goes back to the parallel passage in Streck 1916: 160: 25.

6. See, e.g., Luckenbill 1926: ¶717; ¶802; ¶803; Oppenheim 1950: 282^{b}; Wiseman 1958: 56. Cf. also Wiseman 1962: 1072.

7. "Rab-shakeh" was translated as "field-marshall" in Waterman (1947), as "the commander" in NAB, and as "chief officer" in NEB. NJPS left this and the other two Assyrian titles untranslated, as in KJV and RSV.

8. So, e.g., AHW: 938b; Kinnier Wilson 1972: 35; Garelli 1974: 135. Borger (1978: 91) renders LÚ.SAG as *ša*$_{11}$*-rēši*. As for LÚ.GAL.SAG, he cautiously noted: "Lesung unsicher, etwa *ráb-rēši*." Only in those few cases when it is written as LÚ.GAL.LÚ.SAG does he read it as ^{lú}*rab-ša*$_{11}$*-rēši*. Cf. below, note 18.

9. So Oppenheim 1963: 3; Fenton 1968: 1127; Henshaw 1969: 14; Parpola 1976: 171; Tadmor 1976: 323.

10. For the Neo-Assyrian material see most recently Brinkman 1968: 309; Reade 1972: 91; Oppenheim 1973: 330–34 (with survey of previous literature); Garelli 1974: 133–36; Parpola 1979: 33; Henshaw 1980: 293. In a paper presented at the 27th *Rencontre Assyriologique internationale* in Paris (July 1980), I adduced some evidence for the political role of the influential *ša-rēši*'s in the Assyrian Empire of the late 9th and the early 8th centuries. It is not our purpose here to discuss the controversial question whether all these high royal courtiers were castrates or whether the appellation *šut-rēši*/*ša-rēši*/*sārîs* could also denote non-castrated personnel. In all brevity, I would like to draw attention to two crucial but generally overlooked passages: (a) CT 23 10: 14 (quoted—as far as I know—for the first time by Jensen *apud* Manitius 1910: 109): *kima šūt rēši la ālidi nīlka lībal*, "May your semen dry up like that of a eunuch

who cannot beget" (CAD N 234[a]); (b) Isa 56: 3–5: *wĕʾal yʾômar hassārîs hēn ʾănî ʿēṣ yābēš*," "And let not the eunuch say 'I am a withered tree'" (NJPS). The eunuchs are consoled that they will have "a monument and a name better than sons and daughters" (v 5). Both passages, I believe, speak for themselves and require no further comment.

11. Berger 1886: 220; Brünnow 1888: 238–42; *CIS* no. 38. The Akkadian text was republished in Johns 1889: no. 129 and edited by Kohler and Ungnad 1913: no. 313, where the Aramaic text is also quoted and translated. The Aramaic text is discussed in full by Delaporte 1912: 39–41.

12. Bezold 1896: 1765; Pinches 1902: 181; Kohler and Ungnad 1913: no. 313; Ungnad 1938: 452.

13. Cf. Johns 1901: 3: 223, Ungnad 1938: 452.

14. Falkner (1956: 104 no. 124) rendered LÚ.GAL.SAG as *[amêl]rab-rēši*, and translated 'General.'

15. Johns 1898: no. 130; Kohler and Ungnad 1913: no. 327; Delaporte 1912: no. 22.

16. [m]*Taquni*, [m]*Hamaṭuṭu*, and [uru]*Ḫanduate* (probably in the West) are mentioned in both dockets but do not occur in other documents from Nineveh. However, [m]*Apladdu-ḫutin*, son of one [m]*Ḫa-ma-ṭù-ṭù*/[m]*Ḫamadudu* (most likely identical with [m]*Ḫa-ma-ṭu-ṭu* of the two dockets), appears in a document from Kannu'; see VAT 5399 = Kohler and Ungnad 1913: no. 209, dated to the *limmu* of Nabu-šar-uṣur the Palace Scribe (A.BA.KUR). To judge by the prosopography, this eponym, the third of the same name, belongs to the latest group of the post-canonical *limmu*'s: Falkner (1956: 114–15; 119). For the personal names in that document from Kannuʾ, cf. Lipiński 1976: 58; Zadok 1977: 137; for the location of Kannuʾ see Fales 1973: 105 and Lipiński 1976: 53–63.

17. This Chief Eunuch, like the earlier bearers of that title, was in reality the Commander-in-Chief. He is known to have been dispatched by Ashurbanipal on military missions against the Manneans and the Gambulu; see Knudtzon 1893: nos. 150; 153. If he is identical with Nabu-šar-uṣur the LÚ.GAL-*mu-gi* of Knudtzon 1893: nos. 66, 67, texts which derive from the time when Ashurbanipal was still a crown prince, it would seem that he had a long military career, becoming finally the 'Chief Eunuch' no later than 658 (Knudtzon 1893: no. 153). Already as the *rab-ša-rēši* he received a land-grant from Ashurbanipal; see Postgate 1969: no. 10. Falkner (1956: 118) placed his eponymy in 645 but that was the year of Nabu-šar-ahhešu and 646 was that of Nabu-nadin-ahi; see Tadmor 1964: 240–41 and Cogan and Tadmor 1981: 238–39. The earliest dates for his tenure as *limmu* would thus be either 647 or 644.

Nabu-šar-uṣur was the first of the three post-canonical eponyms who bore the title of *rab-ša-rēši*: see Falkner 1956: 102, no. 38; 105, nos. 133 and 137 (from the time of Sin-šar-iškun). The last, and perhaps the most famous of these high potentates, was Sin-šum-lišir, who not only placed another son of Ashurbanipal on the throne (Postgate 1969: nos. 13–14) but also seized the throne for a short while during the bleak period which followed Ashurbanipal's death; see Borger 1969: 237–39.

18. This writing is attested for Ša-Nabu-šu, Esarhaddon's Chief Eunuch and Commander-in-Chief: Knudtzon 1893: no. 57; Klauber 1913: no. 37. However, the same person is referred to as LÚ.GAL.SAG. in Klauber 1913: no. 36: 2 and in Johns 1901: no. 890: 5. He was the eponym for 658, when Nabu-šar-uṣur served as Ashurbanipal's Chief Eunuch: Johns 1898: no. 48 = Kohler and Ungnad 1913: no. 299. Note that his title in this document is no more *rab ša-rēši* but *ša-rēši*.

References

Berger, P.

1886 — Rapport sur quelques inscriptions araméennes inedites ou imparfaitement traduites du British Museum. *Comptes rendus de l'Académie des Inscriptions et Belles-Lettres* 1886: 198–223.

Bezold, C.

1896 — *Catalogue of the Cuneiform Tablets on the Kouyunjik Collection of the British Museum*. Vol. 4. London: British Museum.

Borger, R.

1969 — Zur Datierung des Assyrischen Königs Sinšumulišir. *Orientalia* 38: 237–39.

1978 — *Assyrisch-babylonische Zeichenliste*. Alter Orient und Altes Testament Sonderreihe 33. Neukirchen-Vluyn: Neukirchener Verlag.

Brinkman, J. A.
1968 *A Political History of Post-Kassite Babylonia.* Analecta Orientalia 43. Roma: Pontifical Biblical Institute.

Brünnow, R. E.
1888 Eine assyrisch-aramäische Bilinguis. *Zeitschrift für Assyriologie* 3: 238–242.

Cogan, M., and Tadmor, H.
1981 Ashurbanipal's Conquest of Babylon: The First Official Report—Prism K. *Orientalia* 50: 229–40.

CIS *Corpus Inscriptionum Semiticarum*, Pars 2 inscriptiones aramaicas continens. 1, ed. M. de Vogüé, et al. Paris: Klincksieck, 1889.

Delaporte, L.
1912 *Épigraphes araméens.* Paris: Geuthner.

Delitzsch, Friedrich
1883 *The Hebrew Language Viewed in the Light of Assyrian Research.* Edinburgh: Williams and Norgate.
1896 *Assyrisches Handwörterbuch.* Leipzig: Pfeiffer.

Deller, K.
1966 Review of M. Mallowan. *Nimrud and its Remains.* London: British School of Archaeology in Iraq. *Orientalia* 35: 179–94.

Eddrup, E. P.
1875 *Rab-saris; Rab-shakeh.* Vol. 3, p. 2658–59 in *W. Smith's Dictionary of the Bible*, ed. H. B. Hackett. Cambridge: Riverside Press.

Fales, F. M.
1973 *Censimenti e cadasti di Epoca Neo-Assira.* Studi economici e technologici No. 2. Roma: Centro per le Antichità e la Storia dell'Arte del Vicino Oriente.

Falkner, M.
1956 Die Eponymen der spätassyrischen Zeit. *Archiv für Orientforschung* 17: 100–19.

Fenton, T.
1968 Saris, Rab-saris. Vol. 5, cols. 1126–27 in *Encyclopaedia Miqraʾit.* Jerusalem: Mosad Bialik (Hebrew).

Garelli, P.
1974 Remarques sur l'Administration de l'Empire Assyrien. *Revue d'Assyriologie* 68: 129–40.

Gray, J.
1970 *I and II Kings. A Commentary*[2]. Old Testament Library. Philadelphia: Westminster.

Henshaw, R. A.
1969 The Assyrian Army and its Soldiers, 9th–7th c. B.C. *Paleologa* 16: 1–24.
1980 Review of Kinnier Wilson 1972. *Journal of the American Oriental Society* 100: 283–305.

Johns, C. H. W.
1898–1901 *Assyrian Deeds and Documents.* Vols. 1–3. Cambridge: Bell.

Kinnier Wilson, J. V.
1972 *The Nimrud Wine Lists.* Cuneiform Texts from Nimrud 1. London: British School of Archaeology in Iraq.

Klauber, E. G.
1910 *Assyrisches Beamtentum nach Briefen aus der Sargonidenzeit.* Leipzig: Hinrichs.
1913 *Politisch-religiöse Text aus der Sargonidenzeit.* Leipzig: Pfeiffer.

Klostermann, A.
1887 *Die Bücher Samuelis und der Könige.* Nordlingen: Beck.

Knudtzon, J. A.
1893 *Assyrische Gebete an den Sonnengott*. Vol. 2. Einleitung, Umschrift und Erklärung, Verzeichnisse. Leipzig: Pfeiffer.

Kohler, J., and Ungnad, A.
1913 *Assyrische Rechtsurkunden*. Leipzig: Pfeiffer.

Landsberger, B., and Gurney, O. R.
1957 igi-duḫ-a = *tāmartu*, short version. *Archiv für Orientforschung* 18: 81–88.

Lipiński, E.
1976 Apladad. *Orientalia* 45: 53–74.

Luckenbill, D. D.
1926–27 *Ancient Records of Assyria and Babylonia*. Vols. 1–2. Chicago: University of Chicago.

Manitius, W.
1910 Das stehende Heer der Assyrierkönige und seine Organisation. *Zeitschrift für Assyriologie* 24: 97–149, 185–224.

Meissner, B.
1920 *Babylonien und Assyrien*. Vol. 1. Heidelberg: Winter.

Muss-Arnolt, W.
1905 *Assyrisch-englisch-deutsches Handwörterbuch*. Vol. 2. Berlin: Reuther und Reichard.

Oppenheim, A. L.
1950 Babylonian and Assyrian Historical Texts. Pp. 265–317 in ANET.
1963 Rab-saris; Reb-shakeh. Vol. 4, p. 3 in *The Interpreter's Dictionary of the Bible*, ed. G. A. Buttrick et al. Nashville: Abingdon.
1973 A Note on *Ša Rēši*. *The Journal of the Ancient Near Eastern Society of Columbia University* 5 [The Gaster Festschrift]: 267–79.

Parker, B.
1957 The Nimrud Tablets, 1956. *Iraq* 19: 125–38.

Parpola, S.
1976 Review of Kinnier Wilson 1972. *Journal of Semitic Studies* 21: 165–74.
1979 Review of AHW II/3. *Orientalische Literaturzeitung* 74: 24–36.

Piepkorn, A. C.
1933 *Historical Prism Inscriptions of Ashurbanipal. I.* The Oriental Institute of The University of Chicago Assyriological Studies, No. 5. Chicago: University of Chicago Press.

Pinches, T. G.
1902 Rab-saris; Reb-shakeh. Vol. 4, p. 181 in *A Dictionary of the Bible*, ed. by J. Hastings. Edinburgh: T. and T. Clark.

Postgate, J. H.
1969 *Neo-Assyrian Royal Grants and Decrees*. Studia Pohl Series Maior 1. Rome: Pontifical Biblical Institute.

Reade, J. E.
1972 The Neo-Assyrian Court and Army: Evidence from the Sculptures. *Iraq* 34: 87–112.

Schrader, E.
1883 *Die Keilinschriften und das Alte Testament*^{2}. Giessen: Ricker.
1888 *The Cuneiform Inscriptions and the Old Testament*, trans. O. C. Whitehouse. Vols. 1–2. Edinburgh: Williams and Norgate.

Smith, S.
1921 *The First Campaign of Sennacherib, King of Assyria*. The Eothen Series 2. London: Luzac.

Stade, B., and Schwally, F.
1904 *The Books of Kings*. Sacred Books of The Old Testament 9, ed. P. Haupt. English translation of the notes by R. E. Brünnow and P. Haupt. Leipzig: Hinrichs.

Streck, M.
1916 *Assurbanipal und die letzten Assyrische Könige bis zum Untergang Nineveh's*. Vols. 1–3. Vorderasiatische Bibliothek 7. Leipzig: Heinrichs.

Tadmor, H.
1964 Three Last Decades of Assyria. Vol. 1, pp. 240–41 in *The Proceedings of 25th International Congress of Orientalists* (1960). Moscow: Izdatelstvo Vostočnoy Literatury (Russian).
1976 Rabshakeh. Vol. 7, cols. 326–29, *Encyclopaedia Miqra*ʾ*it*. Jerusalem: Mosad Bialik (Hebrew).

Thenius, O.
1849 *Die Bücher der Könige*. Leipzig: Weidmann.

Ungnad, A.
1917/18 Lexikalisches. *Zeitschrift für Assyriologie* 31: 38–57.
1938 Eponymen. Vol. 2, pp. 415–57 in *Reallexikon der Assyriologie*, ed. E. Ebeling-B. Meissner [D. O. Edzard et al]. Berlin: de Gruyter.

Waterman, L.
1930–36 *Royal Correspondence of the Assyrian Empire*. Vols. 1–4. Ann Arbor: University of Michigan.
1947 I and II Kings. Pp. 310–372 in *The Old Testament, An American Translation*, ed. J. M. Powis Smith. Chicago: University of Chicago.

Weidner, E.
1941 Die assyrischen Eponymen. *Archiv für Orientforschung* 13: 308–18.
1956 Hof- und Harems-Erlasse assyrischer Könige aus dem 2. Jahrtausend v. Chr. *Archiv für Orientforschung* 17: 257–93.

Winckler, H.
1889 *Untersuchungen zur altorientalischen Geschichte*. Leipzig: Pfeiffer.
1903 Geschichte und Geographie. Pp. 1–342 in E. Schrader, *Die Keilinschriften und das Alte Testament*³. Berlin: Reuther und Reichart.

Wiseman, D. J.
1953 The Nimrud Tablets, 1953. *Iraq* 15: 135–60.
1958 Historical Records of Assyria and Babylonia. Pp. 46–83 in *Documents from Old Testament Times*, ed. D. Winton Thomas. London: Nelson.
1962 Rab-saris; Rab-shakeh. Pp. 1072–73 in *The New Bible Dictionary*, ed. J. D. Douglas. London: Inter-Varsity Fellowship.

Zadok, R.
1977 *On West Semites in Babylonia during the Chaldean and Achaemenian Periods: An Onomastic Study*. Jerusalem: Wanaarta and Tel Aviv University.

Zimmern, H.
1899 Über Bäcker und Mundschenk im Altsemitischen. *Zeitschrift der Deutschen Morgenländischen Gesellschaft* 53: 115–19.
1903 Religion und Sprache. Pp. 343–653 in E. Schrader, *Die Keilinschriften und das Alte Testament*³. Berlin: Reuther und Reichard.
1923 Zur Etymologie von *sārîs*, Eunuch. *Zeitschrift für Assyriologie* 34: 91–92.

Dareios, der Meder

Klaus Koch
Universität Hamburg

1. Der falsche Mederkönig

Nirgends setzt sich das Danielbuch mit dem tatsächlichen Verlauf der Geschichte des Altertums so sehr in Widerspruch wie bei der Gestalt des medischen Königs Dareios. Nach Dan 6: 1 und 9: 1 soll *dārĕjāweš mādājjā* das neubabylonische Reich gestürzt und danach das Königtum über die Kaldäer ausgeübt haben, bis er von Kyros, dem Perser, abgelöst wurde. Da jedoch nicht nur griechische (Herodot), sondern auch keilschriftliche (ANET 315–16) und selbst alttestamentliche Quellen (Esra 1) die Eroberung Babels dem Perserkönig Kyros zuschreiben und die achaimenidischen Grosskönige von da an über Vorderasien herrschten, gilt der medische Dareios als "un personnage purement fictif" (Delcor 1971: 133, vgl. Porteous 1962: 71), enstanden aus "a conflation of confused traditions" (Rowley 1935: 54). Für manche Exegeten liefert gerade der medische Dareios den Beweis dafür, dass der apokalyptische Verfasser des Danielbuches am tatsächlichen Verlauf der Geschichte nicht interessiert ist, sondern geschichtliche Figuren nur als Bilder für überzeitliche Ideen benutzt. Ob ihm jedoch an den geschichtlichen Fakten liegt oder nicht (Hartman-Di Lella 1978: 31), er knüpft in vielen Fällen an der seinen Lesern bekannten Geschichte der Exilszeit an. Warum hat er ausgerechnet an der Stelle, die für die Wende der Geschichte Israels hochbedeutsam war, bei der Beendigung des Exils durch die Niederlage der neubabylonischen Macht, entgegen klarem profetischen Wort (Jes 45: 1 z.B.) und entgegen der geschichtlichen Überlieferung seines eigenen (Esra 1) wie der anderen Völker eine so obskure Gestalt in den Ablauf der Geschehnisse eingeflochten? Auch eine Fiktion bedarf der Erklärung.

Die modernen Exegeten geben zwei Begründungen für die seltsame Geschichtsklitterung des Danielbuches. Einmal verweisen sie auf profetische Weissagungen, die einen Zusammenbruch Babels durch einen Angriff der Meder künden: Jes 13: 17–18; 21: 2; Jer 51: 11, 27–28. Der Danielverfasser "seems to have been misled by the earlier hopes" (Rowley 1935: 58, vgl. Porteous 1962: 71). Jedoch, angesichts der geläufigen Zusammenstellung von Medern und Persern im Altertum überhaupt wie der tatsächlichen Dualität beider Reichsvölker im Achaimenidenreich reichen solche Hinweise zur Erklärung nicht aus. Die profetischen Stellen lassen sich ohne weiteres auf medische Truppen unter dem Oberbefehl des Perserkönigs beziehen, zumal Jes 21: 2 ausdrücklich unter den Eroberern Babels Elam vorangeht, was ganz sicher auf Persien bezogen wurde.

Da also die erste Erklärung, für sich genommen, kaum tragfähig ist, bieten die Gelehrten noch eine zweite. Danach soll Daniel die erste persische Eroberung Babels durch Kyros 539 v.Chr. mit einer zweiten durch Dareios I. 520, die geschichtlich hinreichend belegt ist, verwechselt haben und diesen Dareios, der aus einer achaimenidischen Nebenlinie stammt, fälschlich als Meder angesehen haben (Montgomery 1927: 65; Rowley 1935: 54; Porteous 1962: 71; Delcor 1971: 90; Hartman-Di Lella 1978: 36; Lacocque 1979: 109). Doch mit solcher Erklärung geraten die Exegeten in einen Widerspruch zu ihrer Interpretation einer anderen Danielstelle, nämlich 9: 25. Dort nämlich wird vermeldet, dass es 49 Jahre währt vom Untergang Jerusalems bis zum Auftauchen eines Messias-Nagid. Die modernen Exegeten beziehen das auf den Zeitraum von 587/6 bis 538 v.Chr., also bis zu dem Jahr, in dem das Kyros-Edikt ergeht. Der V 25 genannte Messias wird entweder auf Kyros selbst bezogen (Delcor 1971: 144) oder auf den von ihm eingesetzten Hohenpriester Jeschua (Montgomery 1927: 379; Hartman-Di Lella 1978: 251; Lacocque 1979: 195). An dieser Stelle wird also dem Danielbuch eine bis auf die Jahreszahlen genaue Kenntnis der Vorgänge bei der Wende des Exils zugeschrieben! Weist sich aber der Autor in 9: 25 als gut informiert aus, wie kann man ihm dann für dem Anfang desselben Kapitels, für 9: 1–2, horrende Unkenntnis im Blick auf dieselbe Epoche zuschreiben? Die angeführten Exegeten geraten in Gefahr, ihrerseits eine Verschmelzung von "confused traditions" zu produzieren, also genau das zu tun, was sie dem Autor des Danielbuches vorwerfen! Die Frage, wieso Daniel auf eine sonst unbekannte Figur des medischen Königs Dareios als Herr über Babylonien zwischen der neubabylonischen und der persischen Herrschaft verfallen ist, ist durch die bisherigen Erklärungen nicht erledigt, sondern harrt noch auf eine überzeugende Antwort.

2. Gaubaruwa/Gubaru als medischer Dareios

Konservative Gelehrte haben seit langem die Reputation Daniels dadurch zu retten versucht, dass sie den medischen Dareios mit einer anderen, aus historischen Quellen bekannten Persönlichkeit des 6. Jh. v.Chr. gleichgesetzt haben, entweder mit Kambyses, dem Sohn des Kyros und zeitweiligen Vizekönig über Babylonien, oder Gubaru, dem Heerführer bei der Einnahme Babylons, oder Angehörigen des früheren medischen Königshauses wie Astyages oder Kyaxares. Rowley hat diese Versuche gesammelt, die Argumentationen geprüft, und sie allesamt als wertlos befunden. Seine Widerlegung überzeugt in allen Fällen ausser einem: Gubaru. Ausgangspunkt der Diskussion ist die zuverlässigste historische Quelle, die wir für den Zusammenbruch des neubabylonischen Reiches besitzen, die sogenannte Nabunid-Chronik (Smith 1924: 98ff.; Grayson 1975: 104–11; AOAT 367–68; ANET 306–7; TGI 81). Sie berichtet III 15–28.

- Am 17. Tišri (539) hat *Ugbaru,* der Statthalter von Gutium, ohne Schwertstreich mit der Armee des Kyros Babel eingenommen und fortan mit den "Schilden von Gutium" den Haupttempel Esagil geschützt.
- Kyros selbst trifft 14 Tage später in Babel ein. Gubaru, sein Statthalter, setzt (Unter-)Statthalter über Babylonien ein (anders übersetzt: Kyros ernennt *Gubaru* zum Statthalter über alle Statthalter in Babylonien; Grayson 1975: 110 A.). Danach zieht Kyros wieder ab (wie nicht ausdrücklich vermerkt wird). In den folgenden Monaten werden die Götterbilder, die Nabunid nach Babel verschleppt hat, wieder in die angestammten Heiligtümer zurückgebracht, so dass bis zum Neujahrsfest im Nisan 538 die kultische Ordnung im Lande Akkad wieder hergestellt ist.
- 8 Monate später stirbt *Ugbaru* und danach die Frau des Königs. Das hat eine allgemeine Landestrauer in Babylonien zur Folge.

– Um die Zeit des Neujahrsfestes (537) taucht der Kronprinz Kambyses in Babel auf und wird anscheinend feierlich installiert.

Der persische König Kyros tritt im Abschnitt zurück hinter den Aktionen eines Mannes, dessen Name dreimal verschieden geschrieben wird (Shea 1972: 156), dessen Identität aber "wohl mit Sicherheit anzunehmen" ist (RLA III 671); die abweichenden Schreibungen erklären sich vielleicht daraus, dass es sich um einen fremdländischen Namen handelt. Vom gleichen Mann, griechisch Gobryas genannt, berichtet Xenophon in seiner *Kyrupaideia* (IV 6: 1–9; VII 5: 7–34; VIII 4: 1–27). Xenophon schildert ihn als einen Überläufer, der vorher dem babylonischen König dienstbar gewesen sei. Daraus hat sich in der modernen Geschichtsschreibung die These gebildet, Gubaru sei als Statthalter von Gutium dem neubabylonischen König Nabunid untertan gewesen (z.B. Albright 1921: 112 A.; so noch Meuleau 1965: 331). Doch die neubabylonische Herrschaft hat sich, nach allem was wir wissen, nie bis in jene Gegenden nördlich des Tigris, die als Gutium gelten, erstreckt. Also war Gubaru kein Babylonier. Als historischer Vorgang schält sich demnach heraus, dass Kyros nicht nur die Eroberung Babels, sondern auch die Verwaltung des eroberten neubabylonischen Landesteiles für ein Jahr seinem Satrapen Gubaru übertragen hatte. Dieser hatte auch die dem König zukommende Fürsorge für die babylonischen Kulte zu übernehmen, ohne dass man ihn deshalb zum "Kommissar für die Kultrestitution" erniedrigen darf (so Galling 1964: 27). Zwar wird Gubaru nicht ausdrücklich König genannt. Da jedoch die Frau des Königs (*aššat šarri*), nach dem Kontext aller Wahrscheinlichkeit nach seine Gemahlin gewesen ist, liefert die Nabunid-Chronik den indirekten Hinweis, dass dieser Mann tatsächlich einige Monate lang (nach dem Neujahrsfest 538 bis zu seinem Tod im Herbst desselben Jahres) den Titel *šarru* als persischer Vizekönig getragen hat (zum Einzelnachweis Shea 1971/2 und Calmeyer 1977).

In der Frühzeit der persischen Herrschaft tauchen mehrere einflussreiche Würdenträger mit dem iranischen Namen Gaubaruwa "cattle-possessor" (Kent 1953: 182) auf, die nicht miteinander verwechselt werden dürfen. So regiert vom 4. Jahr des Kyros an über das ehemalige Gebiet des neubabylonischen Reiches ein "Herr der Statthalter" (*bel piḫati*) Gubaru und das mindestens 10 Jahre lang. Zu den Getreuen, die später Dareios I. ab 522 zum Sieg über seinen Nebenbuhler verhelfen, gehört ein Gaubaruwa, Sohn des Mardonios. Auf dem Grabdenkmal desselben Königs in Naqš-i-ruštam wird der königliche Lanzenträger "Gaubaruwa, der Partischorier" abgebildet. Alle diese Gestalten haben mit dem Eroberer Babyloniens und dem nachmaligen Vizekönig nichts zu tun (anders Rowley 1935: 19ff.; vgl. jedoch RLA III 670–71).

In den letzten Jahren haben Shea und Calmeyer die Gleichsetzung Gubarus von Gutium mit Dareios, dem Meder, wieder aufgegriffen und sie durch neue Argumente untermauert (vgl. schon Albright 1921: 112 A.). In der Tat ergeben sich frappante Übereinstimmungen:

a) Gaubaruwa hat tatsächlich Babel erobert und das ehemals neubabylonische Gebiet als Vizekönig verwaltet, was Dan 6: 1; 9: 1–2 entspricht.

b) Er setzte Statthalter ein, wie Dan 6: 2 berichtet, wenn auch kaum 120 Satrapen, wie es das biblische Buch will.

c) Xenophon nennt ihn einen Alten (*presbys*) als er Babylon erobert. Das passt zum hohen Alter von 62 Jahren Dan 6: 1.

d) Die seltsame Ausdrucksweise Dan 9: 1 "Dareios . . . , der sich als König hatte einsetzen lassen" oder "als König eingesetzt wurde" (*mlk, Hopʿal*) "über das Königreich der Chaldäer" weist nach dem masoretischen Text auf eine untergeordnete Stellung, die nicht die Königsherrschaft überhaupt betrifft (*malkûtāʾ* absolut, so 2: 37), sondern nur diejenige über Chaldäa (gegen Rowley 1935: 52f.).

e) Die Zusammenstellung des medischen und persischen Königs Dan 6: 29 fällt auf: "Daniel hatte Erfolg unter der Königsherrschaft des Dareios und unter der Königsherrschaft Kyros, des Persers," dies setzt vielleicht ein Nebeneinander beider Regierungen voraus, wobei Kyros als "König der Länder" ausserhalb Babels regiert, während sein Vizekönig Gaubaruwa als "König von Babel" amtiert. Auch anderswo lässt Daniel die medische und persische Herrschaft gleichzeitig auftreten 8: 20, wie denn auch Belschazzar 5: 28 geweissagt wird: "Geteilt wird dein Königtum und den Medern und Persern gegeben."

Ein wichtiges Indiz für die Gleichsetzung der beiden Gestalten, das in der bisherigen Diskussion, soweit ich sehe, noch nicht berücksichtigt worden ist, bietet der enge Bezug des Namens Gutium zu dem Volk der Meder. Die Landschaft Gutium liegt in altbabylonischer Zeit östlich/nordöstlich des Tigris. Später verliert der Name seine regionale Begrenzung und wird in der Omen-Literatur für das nordöstliche Himmelsviertel gebraucht (neben Akkad, Elam und Amurru; Meissner 1925: 248, 253, 258; RLA III 708ff.). In der Nabunid-Chronik wird der Ausdruck wohl archaisierend aufgegriffen und vermutlich ebenso weit ausgreifend verstanden wie im etwa gleichzeitigen Kyros-Zylinder. Dort wird Kyros gerühmt als der, den der Gott Marduk "zum Königtum über die Gesamtheit" berufen hat. Danach heisst es: "Das Land Gutium (^{kur}*Quti*), die Gesamtheit der Umman-Manda beugte er unter seine Füsse" (Eilers 1971: 156ff.; ANET 315). Der Sieg des Persers über die Umman-Manda, zweifellos die Meder, wird als erster Akt eines Aufstieges zum Weltherrn nach dem Willen Marduks gerühmt. Dabei gilt Gutium aller Wahrscheinlichkeit nach als das "Weltviertel," in dem die Meder zu Hause sind. Auch Berossos setzt später Gutäer und Meder gleich (Schnabel 1925: 193). Nach der Eroberung des Mederlandes hat Kyros Gubaru/Gabaru zum Statthalter von Gutium eingesetzt, entweder über Medien insgesamt oder aber über ein Teilgebiet (das Land der Sagartier?, Hinz 1976: 104). Die Bezeichnung eines Mannes, der über Gutium geherrscht hat, als Meder ist in der späteren Überlieferung also vollauf begreiflich.

Woher rührt aber der Name Dareios? Er stellt einen Thronnamen dar, den nur designierte oder tatsächliche Herrscher getragen haben, wie Kent nachgewiesen hat (iran. *Dārayava^{h}u,* "der das Gute festhält," Kent 1953: 189).

Die Daniellegenden gehen von der Voraussetzung aus, dass dem Gaubaruwa ein solcher Thronname (von Kyros verliehen) war, dies mag ein Irrtum sein. Doch die historische Wahrscheinlichkeit, dass der vorher in Medien beheimatete babylonische Vizekönig Gaubaruwa das Vorbild für Dareios den Meder in den Daniellegenden abgegeben hat, hat viel für sich. Demnach verfügt aber das Danielbuch oder zumindest dessen älterer Teil, die Daniellegenden, über eine relativ gute Kenntnis der babylonischen Geschichte des 6. Jahrhunderts.

3. Die vorherbestimmte Sukzession von vier Monarchien

Warum greift "Daniel" auf einen medischen Vizekönig zurück, der nur ein knappes Jahr über das Königtum der Chaldäer geherrscht und in dessen Erinnerung bei den Völkern des Altertums kaum eine Spur hinterlassen hat? Den apokalyptischen Verfasser interessiert nicht der Mann, sondern sein Volkstum, die Meder. Das ganze Danielbuch durchzieht das Bestreben, die Geschichte der Menschheit in den 490 Jahren (9: 25) zwischen dem Untergang des judäischen Königtums (1: 1) und dem Anbruch eines ewigen Gottesreiches (2: 45; 7: 13) als Epoche einer Monarchie im strengen Sinne, also einer zentralistischen einzigen (*mon-*) Herrschaft (*archē*) über den Erdkreis darzustellen, die nacheinander von vier nichtisraelitischen Völkern wahrgenommen wird. Die Vierteilung des irdischen Grossreichs (*malkûtāʾ*), das zu dem derzeit noch verborgenen Gottesreich in einer spannungsvollen Beziehung steht, und zwar so, dass Königtum, Reichtum, Macht, und Herrlichkeit von Gott dem jeweiligen König übertragen sind (2: 36), dessen Hybris aber frevelhafte Schuld ist (Kap. 4–5), bildet das Thema der Visionen in Kap. 2 und 7 und in abgewandelter Form, nämlich auf die drei letzten Reiche beschränkt, auch das Thema von Kap. 8 und 10–11. Die gottgewollte Abfolge der irdischen Monarchie durch verschiedene Völker spiegelt sich auch in den Über- und Unterschriften, die sowohl im Legendenkranz 2: 1; 5: 1; 6: 1, 29, vgl. 1: 21 wie im Visionskranz 7: 1; 8: 1; 9: 1; 10: 1 die Offenbarungen an Daniel mit den ersten drei Reichsbildungen verbinden, mit Babyloniern, Medern und Persern. Das letzte, vierte, hellenistische Reich (*jawan*) wird von einer Tätigkeit Daniels nicht mehr begleitet, da es, grundsätzlich "verschieden" von den vorhergehenden (7: 19), sich dem Einfluss des durch Daniel repräsentierten göttlichen Geistes (4: 5–6, 15; 5: 11–12, 14; 6: 4) entzogen hat. (S. Appendix A).

Für diese Sukzession sind die Meder und damit Dareios–Gaubaruwa ein wichtiges Glied, sonst wäre die Vierzahl als Symbol der Ganzheit (Sach 2: 1–4) nicht erreicht. Deshalb also wird auf einen Vizekönig zurückgegriffen, obwohl seine kurze Regierungszeit und sein beschränkter Machtbereich in einem schreienden Missverhältnis zu den langen Epochen babylonischer, persischer oder hellenistischer Grosskönige stehen. Ein historisch gebildeter Betrachter fragt sich freilich, warum das Danielbuch nicht zu anderen Lösungen greift, um die Vierzahl zu erfüllen. Warum schaltet der Autor nicht z.B. die Ägypter in die Sukzession ein, entweder mit der immerhin vier Jahre währenden Oberherrschaft des Pharao Necho über Palästina (609–605 v.Chr.) oder mit dem Regiment ptolemäischer Könige über Palästina im 3. Jh. v.Chr.? Der Rückgriff auf die Meder hangt gewiss mit den oben angeführten profetischen Hinweisen zusammen, nach denen dieses Volk Babel zerstören soll, während Weissagungen betreffs einer ägyptischen Vormacht über andere Völker bei den Profeten fehlen. Aber mindestens ebenso wichtig ist für den Autor des Danielbuches und seine Leser, dass die Vierer-Sukzession der Monarchien, einschliesslich der Meder, nicht nur in der internationalen "Geschichtswissenschaft" der Zeit weithin als selbstverständlich gilt, sondern vermutlich auch im Rahmen hellenistischer Herrschaftsideologie eine entscheidende Rolle spielt.

Seit Swain's epochemachender Studie 1940 gilt als ausgemacht, dass das Danielbuch ein im ausserisraelitischen Nahen Osten längst umlaufendes Vier-Reiche-Schema mit der Sukzession

Assyrien
Medien
Persien
Griechenland-Makedonien

aufgegriffen und es so umgebogen hat, dass es sich nahtlos an die Geschichte der Königreiche Israel und Juda anschliesst. Zu diesem Zweck soll der Autor des Danielbuches die assyrische Herrschaft durch die babylonische ersetzt haben, die ihrerseits erst mit Nebukadnezzar II. und dessen Eroberung von Jerusalem 587/586 anhebt. Demnach hätte das Danielbuch das überkommene, historisch zutreffende Sukzessionsschema in eine Zwangsjacke gepresst, die allen zuverlässigen Nachrichten über jenes Zeitalter widerspricht. Denn nach der Sicht des Danielbuches folgt nun ein medisches Grossreich dem babylonischen nach; chronologisch gesehen verhielt es sich genau umgekehrt. Nicht nur hatten die Meder längst ein eigenständiges Reich geschaffen, ehe die Babylonier sich von assyrischer Oberherrschaft befreiten, das medische Königreich fiel auch dem Angriff der Perser, also der dritten Macht innerhalb der Sukzession, ein Dutzend Jahre früher zum Opfer als die chaldäische Dynastie in Babylonien. Demnach hätte also das Danielbuch eine sachgemässe historische Theorie aus Unkenntnis und israelitischem Nationalstolz gründlich verfälscht, so die einhellige Deutung der neueren Kommentatoren.

Besteht jedoch die Meinung zu recht, dass Dareios mit Gaubaruwa identisch und dieser nicht nur der Eroberer von Babel, sondern dort für einige Monate der Vizekönig war und Gubaru von Gutium leicht als Meder eingereiht werden konnte, dann lässt sich der Darstellung des Danielbuchs eine historische Berechtigung nicht absprechen. Doch ein genauerer Vergleich des danielischen Geschichtsbildes mit ausserisraelitischen Geschichtstheorien des Altertums bietet weitere Aufschlüsse über die Metahistorie, die dem Verfasser vorschwebt. Die Vier-Monarchien-Sukzession ist damals in (iranischen und) hellenistischen Kreisen weithin anerkannt, aber keineswegs allgemein gültig. Daniel scheint alternative Theorien zu kennen und kritisch Stellung zu beziehen.

4. Auseinandersetzung mit hellenistischen Geschichts- und Staatstheorien

Während der Wirren des Makkabäeraufstandes entstanden, setzt sich das Danielbuch mit dem Hellenismus auseinander. Hellenismus bedeutet aber im 2. Jh. v.Chr. nicht vornehmlich griechische Philosophie und Geistesart, nicht die Nachwirkungen von Plato und Aristoteles, wie der Begriff gemeinhin heute angewendet wird, sondern vor allem Eigenart und religiöse Begründung hellenistischer Herrschaft über die Völker des Orients. Um den Legitimationsansprüchen seiner Gegner entgegenzutreten, bemüht sich "Daniel" um die Einordnung der Nachfolger Alexander des Grossen in die vom Gott Israels seit uran festgelegte Ordnung der Zeiten. Sie eilen ihrem Ende entgegen, weil die hellenistischen Könige die verruchtesten sind, welche die Erde je gesehen hat, und ihr Verhalten gegenüber Menschen und Gottheit (11: 36–37) allem guten Brauch und jeder Vernunft Hohn spricht.

Die Diadochenkönige haben, nachdem ihnen der Nahe Osten als Herrschaftsbereich zugefallen war, sich vor der Notwendigkeit gesehen, gegenüber Griechen wie Nichtgriechen ihr Regiment zu legitimieren. Dafür bietet sich die Theorie von einer durch die Gottheit bestimmten Sukzession der Monarchien an, die sie aller Wahrscheinlichkeit nach der iranischen Reichsidee entnahmen. Monarchie gilt hier als die Herrschaft eines einzigen Grosskönigs, die sich kraft göttlicher Setzung auf alle Länder und Völker erstreckt. Die entsprechende Idee wird in vielen achaimenidischen Inschriften verkündet. Als eine davon sei die Grabinschrift Dareios I. zitiert.

> Ein grosser Gott (ist) Ahuramazda, der diese Erde schuf, der jenen Himmel schuf, der den Menschen schuf, der die Segensfülle schuf für den Menschen, der den Darius zum König machte, den einen zum König von vielen, den einen zum Gebieter von vielen (Weissbach 1911: 87; vgl. die Xerxesinschrift, ANET 316–17).

Die persischen Grosskönige haben sich dabei anscheinend als Nachfolger medischer und assyrischer Vorgänger gefühlt (Swain 1940). Bereits Herodot berichtete deshalb, die Herrschaft über Asien (*basileia tēs ʾAsias*) habe 520 Jahre den Assyrern gehört, dann 128 Jahre (unterbrochen von 28 Jahren Skytheneinfall) den Medern und schliesslich den Persern (I.95, 102, 106, 130, 178). Und Ktesias, der sich ausdrücklich auf persische Geschichtswerke beruft, schreibt den Assyrern, angefangen bei Ninos (bzw. seinem Vorgänger Bel?; dazu jedoch König 1972: 34) und seiner Frau Semiramis, bereits 1300 (1306) Jahre Königsherrschaft über Asien zu, danach den Medern 284 (319) Jahre, bis dann die Perser die Macht an sich reissen (König 1972: 126f., 161f.). Die Überzeugung, dass ein Grosskönig zentrale Herrschaft über die gesamte Erde oder zumindest über einen ihrer massgeblichen Teile, nämlich über Asien oder/und Europa, ausgeübt hätte, haben hellenistische Autoren sich früh zu eigen gemacht. Schon Theopomp versucht um 300 v.Chr. in seiner *Philippika* den Nachweis, dass das makedonische Königtum (in Europa) gleichzeitig mit dem medopersischen sich an das assyrische (in Asien) angeschlossen habe. In Rom bemüht sich bereits um 170 v.Chr. ein gewisser Aemilius Sura, den Übergang der höchsten Herrschaft (*summum imperium*) über alle Völker an das römische Volk als 5. Nation zu rechtfertigen, nachdem nun 1995 Jahre vergangen sind, in denen zuerst die Assyrer, danach Meder, Perser und Makedonen geherrscht haben. Um die gleiche Zeit will der Geschichtsschreiber Ennius nachweisen, dass die Gründung der Stadt Roms mit der Entstehung der assyrischen Grossmacht zeitlich zusammengefallen ist, zwischen beiden also eine providentielle Beziehung waltet. Wenige Jahrzehnte später weist Polybios (38.22) um 140 v.Chr. auf diese von der Schicksalsmacht der Tyche gewollte Abfolge hin. Von da an reisst die Kette griechisch-römischer Autoren nicht ab, welche die Sukzession Assyrer—Meder—Perser—Römer als ebenso evident wie göttlich vorherbestimmt ansehen; sie setzt sich im christlichen Europa bis ins 18. Jh. n.Chr. hinein fort und bildet in dieser Zeit das Rückgrat jeder Weltgeschichtsschreibung. Dabei wird das medopersische Reich gelegentlich als zwei, meistens aber als eine Epoche gezählt.

Aufgrund der iranischen Apokalypse *bahman-yašt* lässt sich vermuten, dass die Iraner hellenistische Könige als viertes Reich in die Reihe der Monarchien eingestellt haben, mit Ausblick auf ein fünftes, wieder iranisches Reich. Doch geht Eddy (1961) zu weit, wenn er darin nur das Geschichtsbild antihellenistischer Oppositionsgruppen sieht (ähnlich Swain 1940). Auch die offizielle Geschichtsschau hellenistischer Staaten hat die Vier-Monarchien-Sukzession offensichtlich zugrunde gelegt.

Die Sukzession von vier Monarchien in der Menschheitsgeschichte hat historische Evidenz für sich. Denn mit dem assyrischen Imperialismus des 9./8. Jh. v.Chr. beginnt tatsächlich eine Ära von Grossreichen, die vorher ihresgleichen nicht hatte, und die sich nach dem Untergang Ninives unter anderen Herrenvölkern fortsetzt. Das gilt wenigstens unter dem Gesichtswinkel der Meder und Perser, wie der Kleinasiaten und Griechen, weniger aber in der Erfahrung babylonischer und syropalästinischer Völker, welche eine medische Oberherrschaft nie erlebt haben.

Dieses Geschichtsbild setzt mit Ninos ein, von Haus aus wohl der sagenhafte Gründer Ninives. Ninos wird ursprünglich eine Gestalt des 8. Jh. v.Chr. gewesen sein; König (1972: 36) denkt an Sargon II., auch Sanherib lässt sich erwägen, weil er Ninive zur Hauptstadt erhoben und ausgebaut hat. Allenfalls lässt sich noch an einen assyrischen König des 9. Jahrhunderts denken, worauf Semiramis = Sammurat als seine Gemahlin deuten könnte. Die Gestalt und damit der Anfang assyrischer Weltherrschaft wird im Laufe der Jahrhunderte in immer fernere Vergangenheit zurückdatiert. Setzt Herodot 520 Jahre für die assyrische Machtentfaltung an, so werden es bei Ktesias schon 1300, bis schliesslich bei den Kirchenvätern Euseb und Hieronymus (vgl. 4 *Sib. Or.* 49–54) Ninos mit dem biblischen Nimrod Gen 10: 9f. identifiziert wird. Das israelitische 1. Henochbuch erweist sich demgegenüber sehr viel stärker dem historischen Tatbestand verhaftet. Es lässt die Zeit der vier Weltreiche, die 70 Hirten (= 23 + 12 + 12 + 23 Völkerengel) unterstehen, mit der Assyrerherrschaft über Nordisrael und Juda beginnen (1 Hen 89: 59ff.; zum Anfang vgl. die oben vermutete älteren Tradition, die Ninos mit Sargon II. identifiziert).

Die Theorie von einer chronologisch nachweisbaren Sukzession der vier Monarchien weist allerdings einen Schönheitsfehler auf: Sie vermag die neubabylonische Herrschaft nicht einzuordnen. Der Glanz der Stadt Babylon überstrahlt im Altertum den jeder anderen; sie liess sich dadurch notdürftig in das Monarchienschema einzeichnen, dass man Babylon zur Hauptstadt Assyriens erklärte (schon Herodot 1. 178ff.) Grössere Schwierigkeiten bereitete dann aber die Erinnerung an den mächtigen König Nebukadnezzar II. Nach dem, was der Grieche Megasthenes um 280 v.Chr. im Orient vernommen hatte, war er ein Herrscher gewesen, der selbst Herakles übertraf und grosse Teile von Libyen und Iberien beherrschte (Josephus, *Ant* 10 § 227). Er war offensichtlich kein Untertan medischer Grosskönige, die doch jene Zeit geprägt haben sollten—nach der Monarchien-Theorie. An dieser Stelle verstrickt sich bereits Herodot in Widersprüche. Er weiss nur von einem König aus jener Zeit, die wir neubabylonisch zu nennen pflegen, nämlich Labynetos (= Nabunid?), schreibt ihm die Herrschaft über die Assyrer zu und lässt den Perser Kyros gegen ihn ziehen und ihn besiegen (1.188). Wie aber kann es noch zu Kyros' Zeiten eine assyrische Herrschaft geben, wenn diese längst durch die Meder beseitigt war? Aber die neubabylonischen Könige lassen sich nicht anders in das Sukzessionsschema einordnen. So wird es weithin selbstverständlich, Nebukadnezzar als einen assyrischen König anzusehen. Selbst der Babylonier Berossos sieht in Nebukadnezzar einen Nachfolger des Assyrers Sardanapal = Assurbanipal (RLA II 12), auch in die israelitische Überlieferung findet die Anschauung Eingang (Judit 1: 1). Bei solcher Auffassung bleibt aber kein Raum für eine medische Mon-archie über Asien vor dem Aufkommen der Perser und die Sukzessionstheorie wird gesprengt.

Noch eine weitere Erschwerung kommt hinzu. Die babylonische Literatur lässt nicht nur die Theorie von einer Sukzession der Weltmonarchien vermissen, dieser wird sogar eine andere Geschichtsauffassung entgegen gesetzt. Die babylonischen Chroniken (Grayson 1975) setzen ein mit dem babylonischen König Nabonassar (Nabu-naṣir) um 747 v.Chr. als dem Anfang einer der Erwähnung werten, zuverlässigen Chronographie und lassen den assyrischen Grosskönig Tiglatpileser III., der unter seinem babylonischen Namen Phul geführt wird, als Könige von Babel folgen. Auch die späteren persischen und hellenistischen Herren über Babylonien werden in solcher Weise eingereiht, ohne dass der Übergang zu Grosskönigen anderer Nationalität als eine Zäsur in der Geschichte Babylons empfunden wird. In gleicher Weise verfahren die babylonischen Königslisten (z.B., ANET 566) und die davon abhängige hellenistische Literatur, so der berühmte Kanon des Ptolemäus (Schmidtke 1952: 98–99; RLA VI 101). Wo ein Babylonier wie Berossos eine medische Herrschaft mit solcher Tradition seines Landes vereinen will oder vereinen muss, tut er das, indem er die Mederkönige weit zurück datiert und ihre Herrschaft mit der von Gutium im 3. Jt. v.Chr. gleichsetzt; die 21 medischen Könige entsprechen bei Berossos den 21 Gutäerkönigen der assyrischen Königslisten (Schnabel 1923: 191–93). Auch hier wird also bemerkenswerterweise Gutium und Medien gleichgesetzt.

Erst auf dem Hintergrund der divergierenden Geschichtsdeutungen seiner Zeit wird die Leistung des Danielbuches erkennbar. Mit seiner Umprägung der Theorie der Vier-Monarchien-Sukzession schaltet es sich in die internationale Diskussion ein und legt eine originelle Lösung vor, die derjenigen des berühmten Babyloniers Berossos überlegen ist. Den modernen Historiker mag sie nicht befriedigen, im spätbabylonisch-seleukidischen Kontext erscheint sie diskutabel. Die iranischen und hellenistischen Kreisen als selbstverständlich geltende Strukturierung der Menschheitsgeschichte durch eine von der Tyche geprägte Abfolge der Weltmonarchien wird übernommen; sie wird aber mit dem tatsächlichen Verlauf der neubabylonischen Geschichte wie auch mit der babylonischen Überzeugung ausgeglichen, dass nur der "König von Babel" zugleich "Herr der Welt" sei (vgl. die Titel Antiochos I. Soter, ANET 317). Das hat einige wesentliche Korrekturen zur Folge.

a) Unter Rückgriff auf die bekannte jahrhundertelange Symbiose von Assyrern und Babyloniern wird die erste Monarchie nicht als assyrisch, sondern als babylonisch bestimmt.
b) An die Stelle des Nabonassar der babylonischen und des Ninos der griechischen Überlieferung als Anfangsfigur einer Grossreichsgeschichte tritt der Chaldäer Nebukadnezzar II. Zum Ersatz von Ninos durch Nebukadnezzar lässt sich eine Parallele aufweisen, die zufällig sein mag, aber nicht zufällig sein muss. Jener Nebukadnezzar, der bei Berossos dem assyrischen Sardanapal folgt, wird bei Kastor von Rhodos um 50 v.Chr. zum (jüngeren) Ninos (der allerdings von einem älteren Ninos abgehoben wird [König 1972: 120], doch dies mag eine Kompilation zweier unterschiedlicher Überlieferungen sein).
c) Der aus babylonischen Texten bekannte, aus Medien kommende und durch Kyros eingesetzte Satrap Gaubaruwa ersetzt die Serie medischer Könige, die vor Kyros regiert haben. Aus babylonischer wie palästinischer Sicht geschieht das durchaus zu recht, da die zuerst von Herodot gelisteten Mederkönige nie über diese Teile Vorderasiens geherrscht haben, wohl aber eine Zeit lang jener Gaubaruwa.

Das Danielbuch reduziert dadurch die Zeit der ersten beiden Grossreiche gegenüber allen früheren Darstellungen um ein Erhebliches. Statt der 520 Jahre allein für die assyrische Grossmacht bei Herodot oder gar der astronomischen Zahlen bei Berossos—36000 Jahre nach sintflutlicher Könige bis Alexander dem Grossen (RLA II 10)—bleiben nur 490 Jahre für alle vier Monarchien übrig! Dies kommt der tatsächlichen Geschichte von Grossreichen im Nahen Osten erheblich näher! Doch das ist nicht das eigentliche Ziel. Vielmehr geht es dem Danielbuch darum, die vorangehende Epoche mit der vorexilischen Geschichte Jerusalems aus dem Monarchienschema herauszuhalten, um es als Zeit eines freien, autonomen Israel zu erfassen (s. Appendix B).

Nicht Historie, sondern Metahistorie interessiert letztlich den Verfasser des Buches. Nicht die vordergründigen Verläufe gelten ihm als entscheidend, sondern die hintergründigen Wirkungsmächte, die allein der Geschichte ihr Gefälle und ihren Sinn geben. So lange Israel seinen Tempel besass und dort ungestört seinem Gott begegnen konnte, hatten fremde Mächte keine wirkliche Gewalt über das Volk Gottes. Doch die Schuld Israels (Dan 9: 4–14) hatte den Untergang von Königtum und Selbständigkeit notwendig zur Folge. Aber auch in der Zeit der Verwüstung (9: 24) steht Israel nicht ausserhalb göttlicher Geschichtslenkung, ebensowenig wie die übrigen Völker der Erde und sogar die Tierwelt (4: 18) ausserhalb des Waltens jenes einzigen Urgrundes alles Wirklichen stehen. Die Grosskönige, welchen Völkern sie auch immer angehören und welchen Göttern sie anhängen, sie erhalten ihr Mandat einzig von dem in Jerusalem anwesenden Gott. Zu ihm können sie sogar in ein bewusstes Verhältnis treten und dadurch nicht nur den Bestand ihres Reiches, sondern auch die Gerechtigkeit ihrer Regierung sichern (2: 47; 3: 28-30; 4: 31-34; 6: 27-28; 4: 24), bis dass jenes Reich in Erscheinung treten wird, welches ewige Gerechtigkeit auf Erden für immer heraufführt und Grosskönige überflüssig macht (9: 24).

Appendix A
Die vier Monarchien im Danielbuch, ihre Symbole und Identifikationen

		Über- und Unterschriften				
Legenden	**Visionen**	**Kap. 2**	**Kap. 5**	**Kap. 7**	**Kap. 8**	**Kap. 10–12**
(1:1 Juda)	——	——	——	——	——	——
2:1; 5:1 Babylon	7:1; 8:1 Babylon	1. Gold = Babylon (V 38)	Babylon	1. Löwengreif	——	——
6:1 Meder	9:1 Meder	2. Silber	Meder +	2. Bär	Zweigehörnter Widder } Meder + Perser	11:1 Meder
6:29 (Meder-) Perser	10:1 Perser	3. Bronze	Perser	3. Leopard		11:2 Perser
——	——	4. Eisen (+ Ton)	——	4. Untier	Ziegenbock = Jawan	11:2ff Jawan
——	——	Stein = Ewiges Reich (V 44)	——	Ewiges Reich = Menschensohn (V 13f)	Reines Heiligtum (V14)	Michael 12:1

APPENDIX B
Monarchien vor Alexander dem Großen in historischen Werken des Altertums

Herodot um 450	Ktesias um 390	Alex. Polyhist. um 50 (nach Berossos 280)	1. Henoch 89f um 165	Daniel um 165	Absolute moderne Chronologie
		Sintflut [36300] Chaldäer			
		[3200] Meder [2970] Chaldäer und Araber			
	[2123] Assyrer ab (Bel) Ninos und Semiramis	[1255] Assyrer ab Semiramis			
Fall Trojas [1215] Assyrer ab Semiramis					
					900–612 *Neuassyrisches Reich*
	[823] Meder ab Arbaces	- - - - - [729] Chaldäer ab Phul	*Königtum Israels* [722] 23 Hirten = Assyrer und Chaldäer		745–727 *Tiglat Pileser III*
[695] Meder ab Deiokes				*Königtum Judas* [601] Babylonier ab Nebukadnezzar bis Belschazzar	626(612)-539 Neubabyl. Reich 625–585 Kyaxares v. Medien 604–562 Nebukadn. II 585–550 Astyages v. Medien
[539] Perser ab Kyros	[539] Perser ab Kyros	[539] Perser ab Kyros	[539] 12 Hirten = Perser	[539] Meder Dareios [537] Perser ab Kyros	539 Gaubaruwa v. Gutium verwaltet Babel unter Kyros 537 Kambyses Vizekönig v. Babel unter Kyros dem Perser

(Hypothetisches Ausgangsdatum nach Jahreszählung vor Christus in eckigen Klammern [ ].)

Bibliographie

W. F. Albright
1921 The Date and Personality of the Chronicler. *Journal of Biblical Literature* 40: 104–24.

AOAT H. Gressman, hrsg. 1926. *Altorientalische Texte zum Alten Testament.* Berlin: De Gruyter.

P. Calmeyer
1977 Zur Genese altiranischer Motive. V. Synarchie. *Archäologische Mitteilungen aus dem Iran* N.F. 10: 191–92.

M. Delcor
1971 *Le livre de Daniel.* Sources bibliques. Paris: Gabalda.

S. K. Eddy
1961 *The King is Dead. Studies in the Near Eastern Resistance to Hellenism 334–31 B.C.* Lincoln: University of Nebraska Press.

W. Eilers
1971 Der Keilschrifttext des Kyros-Zylinders. Pp. 156–68 in *Festgabe deutscher Iranisten zur 2500–Jahrfeier Irans,* hrsg. W. Eilers. Stuttgart: Hochwacht Druck *pro* der Deutsche Iranistenkreis *et al.*

K. Galling
1964 *Studien zur Geschichte Israels im persischen Zeitalter.* Tübingen: Mohr.

A. K. Grayson
1975 *Assyrian and Babylonian Chronicles.* Texts from Cuneiform Sources. Locust Valley: J. J. Augustin.

L. F. Hartman and A. A. Di Lella
1978 *The Book of Daniel.* Anchor Bible 23. Garden City: Doubleday & Co.

W. Hinz
1976 *Darius und die Perser.* Baden-Baden: Holle.

R. G. Kent
1953 *Old Persian*². American Oriental Series 33. New Haven: American Oriental Society.

K. Koch
1980 *Das Buch Daniel.* Erträge der Forschung 144. Darmstadt: Wissenschaftliche Buchgesellschaft.

F. W. König
1972 *Die Persika des Ktesias von Knidos.* Archiv für Orientforschung, Beiheft 18. Graz: E. Weidner.

A. Lacocque
1979 *The Book of Daniel.* Trans. D. Pellauer. London: SPCK. Original 1976.

B. Meissner
1925 *Babylonien und Assyrien.* 2. Band. Heidelberg: C. Winter.

M. Meuleau
1965 Mesopotamien in der Perserzeit. Kap. 17 in *Fischer-Weltgeschichte* 5. Frankfurt-Hamburg: Fischer-Bücherei.

J. A. Montgomery
1927 *A Critical and Exegetical Commentary on the Book of Daniel.* International Critical Commentary. Edinburgh: T. & T. Clark.

N. W. Porteous
1962 *Das Danielbuch.* Das Alte Testament Deutsch 23. Göttingen: Vandenhoek & Ruprecht.

RLA E. Ebeling, D. O. Edzard et al., hrsg. 1932. *Reallexicon der Assyriologie.* Berlin: De Gruyter.

H. H. Rowley
1935 *Darius the Mede and the Four World Empires in the Book of Daniel.* Cardiff: University of Wales Press.

V. Scheil
1912 Le Gobryas de la *Cyropédie. Revue d'Assyriologie* 9: 164–74.

F. Schmidtke
1952 *Der Aufbau der Babylonischen Chronologie.* Orbis Antiquus 7. Münster: Aschendorff.

P. Schnabel
1923 *Berossos und die babylonisch-hellenistische Literatur.* Leipzig-Berlin: Teubner. Hildesheim: Olms. Nachdruck, 1968.

W. H. Shea
1971/72 An Unrecognized Vassal King of Babylon in the Early Achaemenid Period I–IV. *Andrews University Seminary Studies* 9: 51–57; 99–128; 10: 88–117, 147–178.

S. Smith
1924 *Babylonian Historical Texts Relating to the Capture and Downfall of Babylon.* London: Methuen & Co.

J. W. Swain
1940 The Theory of the Four Monarchies. *Classical Philology* 35: 1–21.

TGI K. Galling et al., hrsg. 1968. *Textbuch zur Geschichte Israel*². Tübingen: Mohr.

F. H. Weissbach
1911 Die Keilinschriften der Achämeniden. Vorderasiatische Bibliothek 3. Leipzig: J. C. Hinrichs.

III. History and Institutions of Israel

The Proto-History of Israel: A Study in Method

Abraham Malamat
The Hebrew University of Jerusalem

Proto-History Versus History

In considering the study of the proto-history of Israel in all its complexity—as against the study of the historical period of biblical Israel—let us begin by defining this "proto-history" and its chronological boundaries.[1] "Proto-history" must be differentiated from both "pre-history" and "history." Despite its popularity among students of the Bible, the term "the pre-history of Israel" should be avoided, since by definition it implies a time prior to Israel's existence. "Proto-history," on the other hand, describes the span of time during which an embryonic Israel took shape, the span culminating in its emergence as an ethnic/territorial entity in Canaan. In conventional terms this would encompass the so-called Patriarchal Age, the descent to Egypt, the Exodus from the "house of bondage," the subsequent wanderings in the wilderness (including the events at Mount Sinai), the eventual conquest of the land of Canaan, and finally the settlement of the Israelite tribes.

It should be pointed out that this "standard" sequence, and indeed the very division into these particular stages, may be nothing more than a reflection of the Bible's own highly schematic division of the Israelite past: the Five Books of Moses, the Book of Joshua, and (to some extent) the Book of Judges. Thus the conventional stages listed above are in fact problematic as conceptualizations of historical reality. This applies to the very first stage of Israelite proto-history, the "Patriarchal Age," an expression presupposing a specific, well-defined period in time. This avoidable term ignores the possibility that the "Age" may be an artificial construct telescoping a prolonged historical process (see below). An even more radical approach contends that the Patriarchs are pure fable and thus have no particular time of their own at all (e.g., Mazar 1969; Thompson 1974, 1978, 1979; Van Seters 1975).

Questions of chronology and content naturally obscure the upper limits of Israelite proto-history, but the lower limit—the line dividing it from "history"—is more accessible. A given scholar's placement of this dividing line generally hinges on just where he sees real historiography beginning to appear in the flow of biblical narrative—a matter subject to argument. Two contradictory views have recently been advanced in this regard.

W. W. Hallo, for one, sees a more or less credible and coherent record beginning with the opening chapter of Exodus (1: 8), and so he fixes the beginning of the historical period in the time of the Israelites' oppression in Egypt, when an "awareness of a 'group identity' . . . first dawned on" them (Hallo 1980: 16ff.). Hallo's view seems to coincide with that of the biblical historiographer, who in Exod

1: 9 first uses the expression "the People of the Children of Israel" (*ʿam bĕnê Yiśrāʾēl*). Prior to that, in the introductory verses of Exodus and in all of Genesis, the common term is "Children of Israel" (*bĕnê Yiśrāʾēl*)—limited in meaning to the actual offspring of the Patriarch Jacob (i.e., Israel) as individuals. (Of course, here one has to exclude general statements or anachronisms, such as Gen 32: 33: "That is why the children of Israel to this day do not eat the thigh muscle that is on the socket of the hip . . ."; 34: 7: ". . . an outrage in Israel . . ."; 36: 31: ". . . before any king reigned over the children of Israel"; 48: 20: ". . . by you shall Israel invoke blessings . . ."; or, for that matter, 49: 7: ". . . scatter them in Israel"; 16, 28: . . . "at one with the tribes of Israel," "All these were the tribes of Israel . . . .") On the other hand, the shorter term "People of Israel" (*ʿam Yiśrāʾēl*) first occurs in the Book of Samuel (2 Sam 18: 7; 19: 41; but cf. Josh 8: 33, though the usage there is awkward).[2] Significantly, this parallels the occurrence of the geographical descriptions, "land of the Children of Israel" (*ʾereṣ bĕnê Yiśrāʾēl*), first appearing in Josh 11: 22, and "Land of Israel" (*ʾereṣ Yiśrāʾēl*), the shorter term again making its first appearance only in the Book of Samuel (1 Sam 13: 19). Thus what emerges from the textual evidence is a progression of terms: first "Children of Israel," then "People of the Children of Israel," and finally "People of Israel." These are likely to reflect critical junctures in the formation of the People of Israel or, in any event, stages in the developing consciousness of a national identity. The last term, "People of Israel," is clearly more national and political in character than the designation "People of the Children of Israel" (which still smacks of tribalism), and its first use coincides with the beginning of the period of the monarchy. The same applies to the geographical term "Land of Israel."[3]

The second view, recently adopted by J. A. Soggin, fixes the starting point of the historical era in the early monarchy—when there arose conditions conducive to true historiography, in the time of David and Solomon (Soggin 1978). But, as Hallo has shown, Soggin's reasoning leads to a circular argument: "History begins where historiography begins, and historiography begins . . . where history is said to have its datum point" (Hallo 1980: 9–10).

The truth probably lies somewhere between these two views. As noted, I see the transition from Israelite proto-history as occurring when the Israelite tribes crystallized within Canaan, becoming the dominant, sovereign force there. Thus the dividing line between proto-history and history proper would fall at the time when the migratory movements of the Israelites had effectively come to a close, the tribes having consolidated what were to be their hereditary holdings for hundreds of years to come. This situation[4] emerged apparently in the first half of or around the middle of the 12th century B.C.E.—in biblical terms, at some point in the period of the Judges—and the tribal territories remained stable "for the duration." It is this historical-territorial zygote which set the stage for the subsequent narrative of events in the Bible.

The biblical record retains only vague recollections and indirect evidence of the primary, dynamic stage in the process of Israelite settlement (except for the removal of the tribe of Dan to Laish) (Kallai 1967; Malamat 1970; 1976a: 60ff.). Though a more advanced stage is described in Judges, the book's schematic structure and arbitrary chronological framework do not reflect the actual unfolding of historical events (Malamat 1976b: especially pp. 152–56). Therefore, in our quest for this dividing line we must shake free from a characteristic short-coming—sole dependence upon the reliability of biblical historiography. We must take into account additional factors, such as the ongoing formation of Israelite society and the molding of national solidarity—the establishment of inter-tribal and supra-tribal structures, and the narrowing of the gap between tribal and national identity. Moreover, in considering the extra-biblical data, too, we must take into account their particular character, and especially the fact that different methodologies apply to the study of proto-history and of historical periods, respectively. To a great extent this difference stems from the special quality and scope of the data available, both extra-biblical and biblical.

Admittedly, biblical sources are also problematical in regard to the period of the monarchy (Van Seters 1981). Not only are they selective (as is all historiography); they are tendentious and have undergone various stages of editing. Yet for all their shortcomings, the biblical sources for the monarchical period are decidedly more reliable than the stories which describe Israelite proto-history. Moreover, they enable us to trace with some precision the actual, historical-chronological sequence of events, as distinct from the "evidence" of epic depictions of Israel's distant past. Even so, the Bible does not present authentic documents contemporary to events described, as are to be found in quantity for many of the peoples of the Ancient Near East. By contrast, significant contemporaneous evidence directly relating to the history of the Israelite and Judean monarchies is available from outside the Bible: the epigraphic sources from Assyria, Babylonia, and Egypt, as well as numerous Hebrew inscriptions. Two astonishing examples relate to the same period: the Babylonian Chronicle from the reign of Nebuchadnezzar II, mentioning the precise date of the surrender of Jerusalem during Jehoiachin's reign (the second of Adar of the seventh year of the Babylonian king, i.e., 16 March 597 B.C.E.) (Wiseman 1956: 33, 72f.); and, on a different plane, a seal-impression (bulla) reading "Belonging to Berachiahu, son of Neriahu, the scribe"—apparently the biblical figure Baruch, Jeremiah's amanuensis (Avigad 1978).

Alas, such fortunate discoveries are not to be expected in conjunction with Israelite proto-history; both the internal and the external data simply do not allow for such analysis on the micro-level of history. Explicit, external references to biblical events and personalities are utterly lacking for this remote period. Even the pharaohs mentioned in the Joseph and Moses cycles are anonymous. The first king of Egypt mentioned by name in the Bible is Shishak, contemporary with Solomon. Thus precisely those data which would be of the essence to the historian's craft are lacking: synchronisms and correlates which would link the biblical text to events in the broader world.

The earliest extra-biblical use of the collective name "Israel" for an entity clearly within the land of Canaan occurs in the well-known "Israel Stele" of Merneptah (ca. 1220 B.C.E.) (see, comprehensively, Engel 1979). The exact nature of this entity is elusive; it may be a pan-Israelite league of twelve tribes, or a more limited group such as the "House of Joseph" (more probable in light of the geographical sequence of toponyms in the stele). Whatever its nature, the fact remains: "Israel" is mentioned in an early historical, historiographical document—heralding the threshold of Israelite history.

Despite the general absence of directly related external sources for the early period of Israel's past, we do have a wealth of indirect sources. These shed circumstantial light on the geographical and ethno-cultural milieu of Israel's formative period. But the asymmetry in the historical documentation—between the extreme paucity of directly related material and the vast body of indirect, external evidence, and especially between it and the abundant biblical source material—dictates *a priori* the parameters of historical research and the limits of plausible conclusions. A multitude of unknowns are encountered in comparison to research into later periods. The historian must weave a complex but loose fabric from the threads of internal and external sources, and he must risk putting forth much bolder hypotheses than those tolerated for later historical periods. .But it is doubtful whether research into the proto-history of Israel will ever exceed the bounds of speculation.

Israel was the only people amongst those of the ancient Near East to preserve a comprehensive national tradition of its origins. That Israel's neighbors did have similar traditions seems to be reflected in several oblique biblical references, such as one in the book of Amos: "True, I brought Israel up from the land of Egypt, but also the Philistines from Caphtor and the Arameans from Kir" (9: 7). In Amos' time (mid-8th century B.C.E.), some 400 years after the appearance of the Philistines and the Arameans in their historical domains, traditions were still circulating regarding migrations in their distant pasts: the Philistines from Caphtor (Crete or, more likely, the Aegean world in general), and the Arameans from somewhere called Kir.[5] These two nations seem to have transmitted traditions, over many generations, concerning their removal from their original homes—much as the Patriarchal, Exodus and Conquest narratives were maintained in Israel within a broad, multifaceted tradition.

The Nature of the Biblical Tradition

The historian studying the origins of Israel is thus obviously not confronted by any lack of biblical source material, but rather by the question of the historical reliability of that material. It need hardly be added that the intention here is not to claim that biblical folktales be taken at face value, nor that historicity is to be conferred upon myriad independent details, many of which no doubt reflect merely literary artifice. Rather, the tradition should be considered in a broader focus, appraising the historicity of its basic elements—what Goethe calls *die grossen Züge*, "the broad sweep of matters," forming the historical picture. In the Patriarchal narratives, for instance, these principal features can be outlined as follows: (a) the Patriarchal migration from Mesopotamia to Canaan; (b) residence as aliens (Hebrew *gērîm*) in their new habitat (and not indigenous to Canaan, *contra* much current scholarly conjecture; e.g., de Geus 1976; Gottwald 1979); (c) maintenance of ties ith their erstwhile homeland (e.g., the marriages of Isaac and Jacob); (d) restriction of migratory movements within Canaan to the central hill country and the Negev; (e) existence as semi-nomadic herdsmen, in close relationship with various Canaanite cities (*contra* Gordon 1958; Albright 1961; 1968: 56ff.); (f) practice of monolatry, their god being the patron-deity of the Patriarchal clan (the name Yahweh, and the monotheism attached to it, are an anachronistic legacy from the time of Moses; cf. Exod 3: 6; 6: 3).

But do such features reveal an accurate reflection of the historical events? When the historian attempts to derive history from the biblical tradition, he is confronted by several hazards in method (see, e.g., Smend 1977 and references there; also see Tsevat 1980). One of these is that all the available direct evidence is self-testimony—internal evidence, both subjective and ethnocentric. The distant past is idealized and romanticized, and cut to fit later ideological exigencies (see, e.g., most recently Herion 1981). To use an intriguing example, some scholars have assumed that Abraham, Father of the Nation, or alternately, Melchizedek, king and priest, find a simple prototype in King David, the "earlier" figures initially contrived as it were, to lend legitimacy to David's kingdom (e.g., Mazar 1969: 74).

These deficiencies are, of course, somewhat offset by the intrinsic value of having a record of a nation's own perception of its past (Dinur 1968; Harrelson 1977 and cf. for general questions of method Gadamer 1979). Israel's self-portrait of its singularity is painted on several levels. (a) Israel's position on the *ethnic* map of the family of man—its descent from Shem and Eber, basing its specific lineage on Abraham, Isaac, and Jacob and his twelve sons. An elaborate genealogy of this sort (based on both vertical and horizontal lines) has no counterpart in the literature of the ancient Near East (Malamat 1968; Wilson 1977). (b) Israel's *religious* distinctiveness, the divine revelation to the Patriarchs (with the attendant promise of land and progeny), and the later revelation through Moses of a revolutionary, monotheistic doctrine, having no antecedents in the surrounding world. (c) On the *societal* level, growth from a basic domestic unit (Hebrew *bêt ʾāb*), eventually expanding into clans and tribes, and culminating in a nation. (d) On the *territorial* plane, an acute consciousness of a national home—not merely a geographical domain but sacred soil. (e) *Destiny,* the signal bond between the Chosen People and the Promised Land.

In this connection a further stumbling block confronting us in the biblical tradition, from the historical point of view, is the fact that the received text underwent complex literary reworking for hundreds of years after the events it relates (see references in Weippert 1973: 415–17; and recently Buss 1979). Only two of the processes affecting biblical historiography and blurring historical reality need be noted here.

The first process is known in scholarship as "reflection." Rudimentary ancient descriptions were recontemplated in the current intellectual and theological terms, yielding new appraisals and motivations for past events. Thus, for example, why did the Israelites conquer Canaan? Because—by way of *contemplation*—the land had been promised to the Patriarchs long before. And how was Canaan conquered? By the God of Israel (rather than by the human actors in the drama)—*in contemplation* (Seeligmann 1969–74: 273ff.).

The second process is "telescoping," the compression of a chain of historical events into a simplified, artificial account. Later redactors would, in retrospect, compress a complex of events into a severely curtailed time-span. A signal example is the attribution of the protracted process of the Conquest to a single national hero, Joshua. I would also impute to telescoping the compression of a centuries-long "Patriarchal" experience into a literary précis: the brief, three-generation scheme of Abraham-Isaac-Jacob. The Patriarchal narrative cycles may preserve isolated reminiscences of a dim past, perhaps harking back as far as the West Semitic movements westward from the end of the third millennium B.C.E. on. The literary result thus resembles a closed accordion, and the full extent of the original events can be reconstituted by opening it out accordingly. This is why the sensational Ebla discoveries should not overly unsettle our historical cool: if the material there indeed proves at all relevant to the Patriarchal tradition, the accordion can simply be stretched out to accommodate another few centuries or so.

All these hazards notwithstanding, there is no cause for the degree of skepticism, occasionally extreme, to which scholars often fall prey. The received tradition can indeed be utilized in reconstructing early events, but criteria must first be established by which the historical kernel may be identified and distinguished from later accretions. This task can be accomplished only by careful critique of the biblical texts themselves, and of the relevant extra-biblical sources, and subsequent meaningful comparison of them (similarly Hallo 1980), undertaken in a controlled manner which eschews all superficiality and romanticism (for support of the comparative method in general, see Gelb 1980). In other words, "typological" or "phenomenological" links must be sought out, focussing upon parallel features essentially typical to both the biblical and the extra-biblical sources.

A prime means for such comparison is provided by the large royal archive of the 18th century B.C.E. found at Mari, the unusually broad spectrum of which—probably more than any other extra-biblical source—has put the proto-history of Israel into a new perspective (Malamat 1971). Some scholars have been inclined to link the Mari evidence directly to the roots of Israel, supposing a primary, genetic relationship between the tribal elements reflected in the Mari texts and the Patriarchs (e.g., Albright 1961, 1973; Parrot 1962). Though we should not altogether discount the possibility of a direct relationship, the external data currently available are certainly inadequate to demonstrate such a tie.

The likelihood is that the milieu of Israel's formative period as described in the Bible is reliable and "authentic"—given the assumptions and qualifications noted above—if the overall historical reality of the first two-thirds of the second millennium B.C.E. tallies with it in various realms. This likelihood increases particularly when extra-biblical circumstances and their biblical counterparts conflict with norms of the later Israelite period, or when these common elements are entirely void of meaning in a first millennium B.C.E. context.

There are several aspects of the Mari material which can serve as points of departure for fertile comparison.

CHRONOLOGY. For those who place the Patriarchal period in the first third of the second millennium B.C.E. (e.g., Albright 1961; de Vaux 1978: 257ff.), the Mari archives represent a nearly contemporaneous picture, and thus a "genetic" approach would be suitable for them. But my attitude toward the "Patriarchal Age," clearly stated above, would deprive such a direct comparison of much of its validity, though the Mari material could well lie *within* the span of the "un-telescoped" proto-history of Israel.

GEOGRAPHY. The relevant Mari data is on several levels: the region encompassed by the Mari documents includes "Aram Naharaim," whence, according to the Bible, the Patriarchs came to Canaan. Haran and Nahor, home-towns of the Patriarchs, are frequently mentioned at Mari as focal points of nomadic tribes. The documents also reveal extensive diplomatic and commercial caravan activities, as well as tribal migrations, between the Middle Euphrates region and Canaan—providing a realistic background for the Patriarchal movements, which proceed roughly between the same regions. On a different level, the Mari documents make specific mention of two cities within what later became the Land of Israel—Hazor and Laish (later called Dan). A recently published document even mentions "Canaan" or "Canaanites," though it is not clear whether the use here is ethnic or geographical (Dossin 1973; Rainey 1979: 161).

SOCIETAL ASPECT. The clearest and most extensive picture of tribal society in all the extra-biblical literature of the ancient Near East is revealed in the Mari documents: the various patterns and mechanisms of tribal structure and organization, and a variegated spectrum of settlement (ranging from wholly nomadic to permanently settled) are attested. Significantly, Mari reveals a synchronic cross-section of the various stages of settlement, whereas the Bible provides a diachronic view, with the earliest Israelites progressing through a multi-stage settlement process. These two sources together can produce a "stereoscopic" view of the phenomena. A specific facet common to both sources is the fascinating confrontation between tribal and urban societies, the symbiotic process eventually leading to interdependence. Many and various institutions and rituals can also be clarified, for example, such vestiges of tribal heritage as the covenant-making ritual (Malamat 1971: 18).

ETHNO-LINGUISTIC AFFINITIES. Like the Patriarchs, most of the peoples associated with the Mari documents were of West Semitic stock, as revealed by their personal names and their idiom. Personal names were a sort of ethnic calling-card in antiquity, and such names as Abram, Ishmael, Laban, Leah, and Jacob were current at Mari. The name Jacob is to be found in Akkadian documents from other sites as well, from the 19th to the 17th centuries B.C.E., although always with an additional theophoric element: *Yaḫqub-el, -aḫ, - ʿam,* or the like; the name *Yaʿqob-har* (or *-el*) was even borne by one of the Hyksos rulers of Egypt (Albright 1968: index, s.v. Jacob; Giveon 1981). On another plane, the Babylonian language of the Mari documents displays intrusive West Semitic idioms. The Mari scribes seem occasionally to have found themselves at a loss for the right word or phrase, and would use typical West Semitic expressions. Some of these usages have no Babylonian equivalents, and others are standard Babylonian used in a modified manner. Significantly, some such terms appear in early Biblical Hebrew as well: in the realm of tribal organization, *gōy/gâʾum, ḥeber/ḫibrum* and *ummâ/ummatum;* concepts of settlement, *naḥălâ/niḫlatum* and *nāweh/nawûm* (in the sense of a pastoral encampment cum flock and pasturage; cf. *nĕwēh midbār*); tribal leadership, *šōpeṭ/šāpiṭum;* the cardinal points of the compass, *qedem/aqdamātum, ʾāḥōr/aḫarātum, yāmîn/*yamīna* and *śĕmôl/*simʾal* (for further examples, see Malamat 1971: 13ff.).

All in all, however, and despite the body and substance of the Mari material, it does not constitute any more than circumstantial evidence: Abrams and Jacobs were indeed doing much the same things at Mari as Abraham and Jacob were doing in the Patriarchal narratives. So, too, with the other extra-biblical sources; it is doubtful that even the material from Ebla will be able to contribute significantly beyond this.

A Note on Method

Given these circumstances, as well as others not treated here, recent scholarship has taken up a broad variety of approaches in grappling with the problems of Israelite proto-history, ranging from the neo-fundamentalistic to the hypercritical (altogether denying validity to the biblical tradition, e.g., Thompson 1974 especially pp. 324–26; still more extreme 1979; 1978; Van Seters 1975; de Geus 1976). The general outline of my own position within this spectrum will emerge more clearly from the following. It has become fashionable to borrow models from such fields as sociology and anthropology (Mendenhall 1962; 1978; Gottwald 1979)—as indeed I do, too (Malamat 1976b)—but these must not be imposed arbitrarily upon Israelite proto-history *per se*. Such misapplications often lead to disqualification of the biblical text, distortion of it, or simply disregard for it. We could all do well to give heed to Wellhausen's dictum, astounding for him: "If it [the Israelite tradition] is at all feasible, it would be utter folly (*Torheit*) to give preference to any other feasibility" (Wellhausen 1899: 347, albeit limited in context; for the general issue of tradition, see now Shils 1981).

Let us regard the biblical account itself as a conceptual model of Israel's genesis. It is as if the Israelites themselves formulated an articulate portrayal of their distant past, much as modern scholarship does. Such a paradigm for a description of Israel's emergence is feasible. This projection embedded within the biblical text has certain clear advantages over modern speculation: being much closer to the actual events—by thousands of years—and being a product of the locale itself, it inherently draws upon a much greater intimacy with the land, its topography, demography, military situation, ecology, and the like.[6]

Such a working hypothesis enables us to avoid the extremes which have all too often left their imprint upon modern historiography in our field. By conceding that the biblical tradition could be a reflective, "theorizing" account—rather than strictly factual, "Wie es eigentlich gewesen" (Ranke)—we sidestep the pitfall of neofundamentalism. And by spurning the view of Israel's proto-history as a deliberately fabricated tradition, we keep from being swept into the other, radical—and now more fashionable—extreme. This paves the way, on an operative plane, to a dialectical approach to the biblical text, one which retains the option that the tradition represents an admixture of ancient, reliable, historical components and late, untrustworthy, anachronistic elements.

Notes

1. This is an English version of part of the introductory chapter to a forthcoming collection of Hebrew essays by the author. The archeological aspects of the subject treated, though of relevance in themselves, fall outside the scope of our discussion of historiography.

2. This issue is, of course, more complex and calls for further elucidation. Note that already in the "early" books, the following expressions are found: *ʿădat/qĕhal Yiśrāʾēl*, "Congregation/Assembly of Israel" (Exod 12: 3; Josh 8: 35); *bēt Yiśrāʾēl*, "House of Israel" (Exod 16: 31; 40: 38); and, above all, the name "Israel" itself, referring to the nation or to a group of tribes (especially in the Book of Judges; and see Danell 1946).

3. But note the "early" terms: *gĕbûl Yiśrāʾēl*, "Territory of Israel" (Judg 19: 29; 1 Sam 7: 13); *naḥălat Yiśrāʾēl*, "Inheritance of Israel" (Judg 20: 6); *har Yiśrāʾēl*, "hill country of Israel" (Josh 11: 16, 21).

4. This view basically resembles that of Noth in his various studies (e.g., 1958: 85ff.), though arrived at by an entirely different path. Noth regarded the nation's emergence as a gradual federation of tribes, culminating in an amphictyonic league.

5. It has been brought to my attention that Professor C. H. Gordon has orally cited this passage in a similar context.

6. For application to specific episodes, see Malamat 1976a: 40–46 (concerning the Exodus from Egypt) and, in particular, Malamat 1979 (concerning the Conquest of Canaan).

References

Albright, W. F.
1961 Abram the Hebrew. *Bulletin of the American Schools of Oriental Research* 163: 36–54.
1968 *Yahweh and the Gods of Canaan.* London: Athlone.
1973 From the Patriarchs to Moses. *Biblical Archaeologist* 36: 5–33.

Avigad, N.
1978 Baruch the Scribe and Jerahmeel the King's Son. *Israel Exploration Journal* 28: 52–56.

Buss, M. J., ed.
1979 *Encounter with the Text. Form and History in the Hebrew Bible.* Philadelphia: Fortress. Especially Willis 1979.

Danell, G. A.
1946 *Studies in the Name Israel in the Old Testament.* Uppsala: Appelbergs.

Dinur, B. Z.
1968 Jewish History—Its Uniqueness and Continuity. *Journal of World History* 11: 15–29.

Dossin, G.
1973 Une mention de Cananéens dans une lettre de Mari. *Syria* 50: 277–82.

Engel, H.
1979 Die Siegesstele des Merenptah. *Biblica* 60: 373–99.

Gadamer, H. G.
1979 The Problem of Historical Consciousness. Pp. 103–60 in *Interpretive Social Science. A Reader,* ed. P. Rabinow and W. M. Sullivan. Berkeley: University of California Press.

Gelb, I. J.
1980 Comparative Method in the Study of the Society and Economy of the Ancient Near East. *Rocznik Orientalistyczny* 41: 29–36.

de Geus, C. H. J.
1976 *The Tribes of Israel.* Assen/Amsterdam: Van Gorcum.

Giveon, R.
1981 Ya^cqob-har. *Göttinger Miszellen* 44: 17–19.

Gordon, C. H.
1958 Abraham and Merchants of Ura. *Journal of Near Eastern Studies* 17: 28–31.

Gottwald, N. K.
1979 *The Tribes of Yahweh.* Maryknoll, NY: Orbis.

Hallo, W. W.
1980 Biblical History in its Near Eastern Setting: The Contextual Approach. Pp. 1–26 in *Scripture in Context. Essays on the Comparative Method,* ed. C. D. Evans, W. W. Hallo, and J. B. White. Pittsburgh: Pickwick.

Harrelson, W.
1977 Life, Faith and the Emergence of Tradition. Pp. 11–30 in *Tradition and Theology in the Old Testament,* ed. D. A. Knight. Philadelphia: Fortress.

Herion, G. A.
1981 The Role of Historical Narrative in Biblical Thought: The Tendencies Underlying Old Testament Historiography. *Journal for the Study of the Old Testament* 21: 25–57

Kallai, Z.
1967 *The Tribes of Israel.* Jerusalem: Bialik Institute (Hebrew).

Malamat, A.
1968 King Lists of the Old Babylonian Period and Biblical Genealogies. *Journal of the American Oriental Society* 88: 163–73.
1970 The Danite Migration and the Pan-Israelite Exodus-Conquest. A Biblical Narrative Pattern. *Biblia* 51: 1–16.
1971 Mari. *Biblical Archaeologist* 34: 2–22.
1976a Origins and the Formative Period. Pp. 3–87 in *A History of the Jewish People,* ed. H. H. Ben-Sasson. Cambridge, MA: Harvard University.
1976b Charismatic Leadership in the Book of Judges. Pp. 152–168 in *Magnalia Dei: The Mighty Acts of God. Studies . . . G. E. Wright,* ed. F. M. Cross et al. Garden City, NY: Doubleday.
1979 Conquest of Canaan: Israelite Conduct of War according to Biblical Tradition. *Revue internationale d'histoire militaire* (Tel Aviv) 42: 25–52.

Mazar, B.
1969 The Historical Background of the Book of Genesis. *Journal of Near Eastern Studies* 28: 73–83.

Mendenhall, G.
1962 The Hebrew Conquest of Palestine. *Biblical Archaeologist* 25: 66–87.
1978 Between Theology and Archaeology. *Journal for the Study of the Old Testament* 7: 28–34.

Noth, M.
1958 *The History of Israel.* Trans. P. Ackroyd. New York: Harper.

Parrot, A.
1962 *Abraham et son temps.* Neuchatel: Delachaux & Niestlé.

Rainey, A. F.
1979 Toponymic Problems. *Tel-Aviv* 6: 158–61.

Seeligmann, A. L.
1969–74 From Historical Reality to Historiographical Conception in the Bible. *P'raqim* 2: 273–313 (Hebrew).

Shils, E.
1981 *Tradition.* Chicago: University of Chicago Press.

Smend, R.
1977 Tradition and History: A Complex Relation. Pp. 49–68 in *Tradition and Theology in the Old Testament,* ed. D. A. Knight. Philadelphia: Fortress.

Soggin, J. A.
1978 The History of Ancient Israel—A Study in Some Questions of Method. *Eretz-Israel* 14 (H. L. Ginsberg Volume): 44*–51*.

Thompson, L. T.
1974 *The Historicity of the Patriarchal Narratives: The Quest for the Historical Abraham.* Beihefte zur Zeitschrift für die Alttestamentliche Wissenschaft 133. Berlin: de Gruyter.
1978 The Background of the Patriarchs: A Reply to W. Dever and M. Clark. *Journal for the Study of the Old Testament* 9: 2–43.
1979 Conflict Themes in the Jacob Narratives. *Semeia* 15: 5–26.

Tsevat, M.
1980 Israelite History and the Historical Books of The Old Testament. Pp. 177–87 in M. Tsevat, *The Meaning of The Book of Job and other Biblical Studies.* New York: KTAV.

Van Seters, J.
1975 *Abraham in History and Tradition.* New Haven: Yale University.
1981 Histories and Historians of the Ancient Near East: The Israelites. *Orientalia* 50: 137–85.

de Vaux, R.
1978 *The Early History of Israel.* London: Darton, Longman & Todd.

Weippert, M.
1973 Fragen des israelitischen Bewusstseins. *Vetus Testamentum* 23: 415–42.

Wellhausen, J.
1899 *Die Composition des Hexateuch*[3]. Berlin: Reimer.

Willis, J. T.
1979 Redaction Criticism and Historical Reconstruction. Pp. 83–89 in Buss 1979.

Wilson, R. R.
1977 *Genealogy and History in the Biblical World.* New Haven: Yale University Press.

Wiseman, D. J.
1956 *Chronicles of the Chaldaean Kings (626–556 B.C.) in the British Museum.* London: British Museum.

The Identity of the Biblical *ṣirʿâ*

Oded Borowski
Emory University, Atlanta, Georgia

Several times in the Hexateuch it is mentioned that the conquest of Canaan by the Israelites was a result of divine intervention rather than of Israelite might. Three times this intervention is attributed to Yahweh's agent the *ṣirʿâ* in speeches describing events during the conquest (Exod 23: 28; Deut 7: 20; Josh 24: 12). The basic idea expressed in all three references is that Yahweh sent the *ṣirʿâ* ahead of the Israelites, and the appearance of this agent caused the land to fall into the hands of the incoming Israelites.

Commentators and scholars have tried for many centuries to identify the *ṣirʿâ*. The Mishnah, the Talmud, the various ancient translations, and most of the Medieval commentators tend to see in the *ṣirʿâ* a wasp or hornet sent down from heaven, one of the series of miracles which had started in Egypt before the Exodus (Kasowski 1940: 395; Rosenbaum and Silberman 1960: 44; Chavel 1962: 444–46). This trend is maintained by modern traditional commentators, who rely heavily on their predecessors (Patsanovski n.d.: 225; Bonfils 1911 II: 272; Epstein 1957: 80). Most other modern scholars also regard the *ṣirʿâ* as an insect (Gesenius 1854: 906; Sigfield and Stade 1893: 638; Driver 1895: 104; Post 1899: 416; Jastrow 1950: 1303; Cohen 1959: 416; Frerichs 1962: 645; *Encyclopedia Miqraʾit* 1971 VI: 773–74; BDB, p. 864; Davidson n.d.: dcli), while a few interpret it as a reference to a terrible disease, depression, or discouragement (Koehler 1936: 291; Koehler and Baumgartner 1953: 817; cf. Rabbi Sa'adya Ga'on [Rasag] and Jonah Ibn Janah, cited in *Encyclopedia Miqraʾit* 1971 VI: 773).

Those who gloss *ṣirʿâ* as a great fear or terrible disease connect the word with the root *ṣrʾ* and the noun *ṣāraʿat*, "leprosy," respectively. However, most scholars agree with the ancient translations (Onkelos: *ʿarʿîtā*; LXX: *sphēkia*; Vulgate: *crabro*) that the *ṣirʿâ* is "an insect of the order Hymnoptera; actually a Wasp, but larger and more dangerous" (Frerichs 1962: 645), and try to identify it with the species *Vespa orientalis*. Some scholars accept the literal sense of the passages and believe that the Israelites were aided by a natural phenomenon of swarms of wasps. It has been recently suggested by Neufeld (1980) that the biblical references to the wasp/hornet are descriptions of biological warfare, but attractive as this suggestion is the author fails to produce any concrete evidence to support it.

Several scholars who identify the *ṣirʿâ* as a hornet maintain that it is used metaphorically "as a symbol of *terror, panic*, sent from God upon the enemy . . ., by which they are agitated and put to flight as if stung to madness" (Gesenius 1854: 906), and "that the hornet represents the terror that the Lord sent to paralyze the land" (Wright 1953: 669).

John Garstang suggested the identification of the hornet with Egypt. According to him the Egyptians conducted against the Canaanite cities a policy "of tyranny and spoliation, calculated in the issue to break their individual strength," a policy which seems "to have removed one by one various . . . obstacles which beset the pathway of the tribes" (Garstang 1931: 259–60). Garstang assumed that the continuous campaigns of Egypt against Canaan from the time of Thutmoses III (ca. 1475 B.C.E.) on prepared the ground for rebellion against Egyptian rule and a reorientation of the Canaanite cities toward the Israelites. The constant removal of raw materials, objects, and people from Canaan to Egypt by the victorious Egyptians had impoverished the country and forced the Canaanites to look for an alternative, which appeared to be the incoming Israelites.

Garstang's theory is based on the fact that he identifies the symbol of Lower Egypt with the hornet rather than the bee, as most scholars do; he discusses this matter at some length (Garstang 1931: 258–61). The theory has been rejected by many scholars as "ingenious but far-fetched" (Cohen 1959: 146). Recently, this hypothesis has been revived by Yadin, who has claimed that "the 'hornet' could refer to the Egyptian Pharaohs, whose title, denoting the kingship of Lower Egypt, was probably the hornet, commonly taken for a bee" (1979: 68). Yadin notes that whatever the force of *ṣirʿâ*, "Canaan of the 13th century was ripe politically, economically, and militarily for a conquest of the type described in Joshua" (68), and this is the context of study.

The Garstang theory, I believe, cannot be lightly dismissed; furthermore, the references to the *ṣirʿâ* should be considered seriously because they contain vital information for understanding the Israelite conquest. Neufeld, in his linguistic treatment of this topic, has demonstrated successfully that the biblical *ṣirʿâ* is a hornet (1980: 34–36). That a country or a people can be symbolized in the Bible by an animal or insect is well known. Egypt was referred to as *tanîm* = *tanîn*, "crocodile" (Ezek 29: 3; 32: 2) and as *zĕbûb*, "fly" (Isa 7: 18), while Assyria was called *dĕbôrâ*, "bee" (Isa 7: 18). Thus, it is possible that references to the hornet are also allusions to a people.

The hieroglyphic sign denoting Lower Egypt is, in Garstang's opinion, "probably a hornet though commonly taken for a bee" (Garstang 1931: 260); "when drawn out pictorially . . . the insect is seen to possess features which in the opinion of zoologists are peculiar to wasps" (ibid.). This interpretation of the hieroglyphic sign is supported by other scholars (see Yadin 1979: 68).

Another reason for the use of *ṣirʿâ*, the hornet, to symbolize Egypt in these speeches is the similarity between the words *ṣirʿâ* and *miṣrayim*, "Egypt." Both words contain the consonants *ṣ* and *r* and sound a great deal alike. There are several other examples of wordplay in the three relevant speeches, a fact which suggests that the choice of words was made carefully. In Exod 23: 27 note *ʾêmâ* and the root *hmm*: "I will send my terror (*ʾêmātî*) before you and will throw into confusion (*wĕhammotî*) all the people against whom you shall come." The wordplay here is obvious, and it appears in the verse immediately preceding mention of the hornet. Another case of wordplay can be observed in Deut 7: 21, in the verse after the hornet is mentioned: "You shall not be in dread (*taʿărōṣ*) of them"; here the wordplay involves *ṣirʿâ* and a form of the root *ʿrṣ*; the latter could have been replaced by a form of the more common root *ḥtt*.

Although Garstang dated the appearance of the Israelites at Jericho to 1406 B.C.E. (1931: 115), which is too early a date for today's consensus, in Yadin's opinion (1979: 68), the hornet reference to Egypt would also have been appropriate in the 13th century because of continued Egyptian military campaigns into Canaan during the latter part of the Late Bronze Age. There are, however, several questions that still have to be answered. (1) Why would the biblical text use a code-name for Egypt to describe an historical event? (2) Is the reference to Egypt a general one or can we identify a specific Pharaoh? (3) By what means did the Israelites overtake Canaan?

The basic reason for the code-name was noted by Garstang.

> The religion of the Israelites, and in particular the ideals of those who set down and arranged these records, could not tolerate the notion that any power other than that of the God of Israel might influence their destinies (Garstang 1931: 259).

In addition, it should be remembered that Egypt was always considered Israel's enemy. The fact that Egyptian activities in Canaan had paved the way for the Israelite conquest had to be concealed but could not be denied; therefore Egypt appears under a code-name as an agent of Yahweh. Israelite ideology recognized that foreign powers could serve as Yahweh's agents, as in, e.g., Isa 7: 18; 10: 5–12, but in these instances the foreign powers were charged with the mission of punishing Israel and there was no reason to conceal their identity. In the *ṣirᶜâ* references, credit is given to Egypt for its "help" to Israel, though it is given in a way recognizable only by those familiar with the details of the conquest.

On the basis of archeological information available today, scholars believe that the Israelite takeover of Canaan occurred in the latter part of the 13th century B.C.E. By that time Canaan had been weakened by continuous Egyptian military activities, city-state quarrels, and the invasion of the Sea People. It seems that the Israelites, who were at the time building their power base in the hill-country (Borowski 1979: 28–29), were waiting for an opportunity which would enable them to take over the cities of the plains and the fertile agricultural lands of the valleys. This takeover could have been accomplished by the slow process of a peasant rebellion, as suggested by G. E. Mendenhall (1962: 66–87).

The biblical record states that after the appearance of the hornet the Israelites inherited the land and that when the land was transferred to them it was suitable for immediate occupation: "I gave you a land on which you had not labored, and cities which you had not built, and you dwell therein; you eat the fruit of vineyards and oliveyards which you did not plant" (Josh 24: 13; see also Exod 23: 29–30; Deut 7: 22). This transfer must have occurred following an impressive event which convinced a large number of Canaanites that they should throw in their lot with the Israelites. Those who did not join peacefully were subdued by force; their defeat is also recorded in the Bible.

What was the event later disguised by the code-name "hornet"? The hornet speeches suggest that the reference is indeed to a particular event which influenced the outcome of the Israelite occupation: first the hornet appeared; its appearance caused terror among the Canaanites, and as a result the Israelites inherited the land. It is possible that the hornet references to Egyptian military presence in Canaan before the Israelite takeover are to be associated with Merneptah's campaign in ca. 1220 B.C.E., celebrated in the "Israel Stele." As described in that stele, Merneptah's campaign involved destroying several cities in Canaan and annihilating Israel, which is mentioned as consisting of unsettled people. Merneptah's activities in the hill-country are commemorated in the name of the well Me-nephtoah (Josh 15: 9; 18: 15; see Aharoni 1979: 184). During this campaign Merneptah must have encountered in the hill-country groups of Israelites, some of which he destroyed. Being dispersed throughout the hill-country, not all the Israelites could have been involved. Those Israelites who survived the Egyptian campaign were ready to reap its consequences; they were joined by Canaanites who, for many reasons, ideological or otherwise, decided to make a covenant with them, as exemplified by the Gibeonites (Joshua 9). The Canaanites who did not join the Israelites were defeated by the newly-formed Yahwistic alliance.

References

Aharoni, Y.
1979 *The Land of the Bible*[2]. Philadelphia: Westminster Press.

Bonfils, J.
1911 *Tsofnat Pa'aneach I–II*. Heidelberg: Carl Winters Universitätsbuchhandlung (Hebrew).

Borowski, O.
1979 *Agriculture in Iron Age Israel*. Michigan Dissertation.

Chavel, C. B.
1962 *Commentary on the Torah by Moshe ben Nachman {Nachmanides}*. Jerusalem: Talmudic Research Institute (Hebrew).

Cohen, A.
1959 *Joshua and Judges*. London: Soncino Press.

Davidson, B.
n.d. *The Analytical Hebrew and Chaldee Lexicon*. London: Samuel Bagster.

Driver, S. R.
1895 *A Critical and Exegetical Commentary on Deuteronomy*. New York: Scribners'.

Encyclopedia Miqra'it
1971 Jerusalem: Mosad Bialik (Hebrew).

Epstein, B. H.
1957 *Torah Tmimah II*. Tel Aviv: Am Olam (Hebrew).

Frerichs, W. W.
1962 Hornet. Vol. 2, p. 645 in *The Interpreter's Dictionary of the Bible*, ed. G. A. Buttrick et al. Nashville: Abingdon Press.

Garstang, J.
1931 *Joshua and Judges*. London: Constable.

Gesenius, W.
1854 *Hebrew-English Lexicon*. Trans. E. Robinson. Boston: Crocker and Brewster.

Jastrow, M.
1950 *A Dictionary of Targumim, the Talmud Babli and Yerushalmi, and the Midrashic Literature*. New York: Pardes Publishing Press.

Kasowski, J.
1940 *Thesaurus Aquilae Versionis, Concordantiae Verborum I*. Jerusalem (Hebrew).

Koehler, L.
1939 Hebräische Vokabeln I. *Zeitschrift für die Alttestamentliche Wissenschaft* 54: 287–93.

Koehler, L., and Baumgartner, W.
1953 *Lexicon in Veteris Testamenti Libros*. Leiden: E. J. Brill.

Mendenhall, G. E.
1962 The Hebrew Conquest of Palestine. *Biblical Archaeologist* 25: 66–87.

Neufeld, E.
1980 Insects as Warfare Agents in the Ancient Near East (Ex. 23: 28; Deut. 7: 20; Josh 24: 12; Isa 7: 18–20). *Orientalia* 49: 30–57.

Patsanovski, J.
n.d. *Pardes Yoseph II.* Tel Aviv (Hebrew).

Post, G. E.
1899 Hornet. *A Dictionary of the Bible,* ed. J. Hastings. New York: Scribners'.

Rosenbaum, M., and Silberman, A. M.
1960 *Pentateuch, with Targum Onkelos, Haphtaroth and Rashi's Commentary: Deuteronomy.* New York: Hebrew Publishing Co.

Sigfield, C., and Stade, B.
1893 *Hebräische Wörterbuch zum alten Testamente.* Leipzig: Verlag von Veit.

Tregelles, S. P.
1890 *Gesenius's Hebrew and Chaldee Lexicon to the Old Testament Scriptures.* New York: John Wiley and Sons.

Wright, G. E.
1953 Deuteronomy. Vol. 2, pp. 311–533 in *The Interpreter's Bible,* ed. G. A. Buttrick et al. New York: Abingdon-Cokesbury Press.

Yadin, Y.
1979 The Transition from a Semi-Nomadic to a Sedentary Society in the Twelfth Century B.C.E. Pp. 57–68 in *Symposia Celebrating the Seventy-fifth Anniversary of the Founding of the American Schools of Oriental Research,* ed. F. M. Cross. Cambridge: American Schools of Oriental Research.

Israelites as *gērîm*, 'Sojourners,' in Social and Historical Context

Frank Anthony Spina
Seattle Pacific University, Seattle, Washington

Throughout the Hebrew Bible there are scattered references to the fact that prior to settlement in Canaan Israel had been *gērîm*, which has usually been rendered "sojourners" and understood as "resident aliens" (Kellerman 1977: 439–49). For example, Abraham is called a *gēr* in Gen 23: 4, where he is depicted as having to purchase a burial plot for his deceased wife, since he owned no property in the land in which he was temporarily residing. In Exod 6: 4 the patriarchs are referred to collectively as *gērîm* when Yahweh declares to Moses that he had promised to give the fathers the land in which they were then dwelling as outsiders. Ps 105: 12 refers to Abraham, Isaac and Jacob (vv 8–11) as *gērîm* who wandered about Canaan (v 13) before their descendants took possession of the land at a later time. And in two other cases, Ps 39: 13 and 1 Chr 29: 15, Israel's fathers are called *gērîm*; the temporal reference is not explicit in these instances, but the designation "fathers" most likely is to be taken as meaning the patriarchal ancestors. In addition, there are several places in the patriarchal stories where the verbal form is used to indicate that this patriarch or that "sojourned" (Gen 12: 10; 19: 9; 20: 1b; 21: 23, 34; 26: 3; 32: 5; 35: 27; 47: 4).

Besides these references, there are also those which indicate that Israel had been *gērîm* during the Egyptian bondage. Gen 15: 13 has Yahweh saying to Abram that his descendants would one day be *gērîm* in a land not their own and that they would also be enslaved and oppressed there. There are a cluster of references in Deuteronomy which recall the experience of having been *gērîm* in Egypt in order to admonish Israel to treat fairly those now related to them as *gērîm* (Deut 10: 19; 16: 11–12; 23: 8; 24: 17–18, 19–22). Similar references are to be found in the Book of the Covenant (Exod 22: 20; 23: 9) and the Holiness Code (Lev 19: 33–34). Ps 105: 23 and Isa 52: 4 employ the verbal form to describe the time Israel spent in Egypt. The verbal form is likewise used in the important passage which von Rad regarded as an ancient creed, Deut 26: 5ff. (von Rad 1962: 166). In this text is the notation that Jacob, who is the "father" cited, was an *ʾărammī ʾōbēd,* a "fugitive Aramean," who traveled to Egypt and whose descendants, after having become numerous, were badly mistreated (see Albright 1957: 238; Mendenhall 1973: 137; Millard 1980: 155).

There are many other occurrences of *gēr* in the Hebrew Bible, but these refer almost exclusively to non-Israelites. For example, there are instances in which *gērîm* are to be treated on a par with Israelites (Deut 1: 16; 10: 18–19; 16: 11, 14; 24: 14, 17; 26: 11–13; 27: 19) or in which *gērîm* are to be subject to the same laws as Israelites (Exod 12: 19, 48–49; Lev 16: 29; Num 9: 14; 15: 14–16, 26, 29–30; 19: 10). Israel itself, however, is regarded as *gērîm* only prior to the settlement.[1] Once Israel had been established in Canaan and had become a "host" people, it was no longer possible for Israel *as a whole* to have *gēr*-status. By this time an individual Israelite or group of Israelites could have been *gērîm* outside of Israelite territory, as could a member of one tribe/state traveling within the borders of another tribal district/state boundary (Deut 18: 6; Judg 17: 7–9; 19: 1, 16 [verbal form]; 2 Chr 15: 9). But the only other time when Israel as a people could be said to have been *gērîm* was during the Exile, though there is only a single reference to this (Ezra 1: 4, verbal form).[2] Thus, for the most part the biblical tradition is remarkably consistent in portraying Israel as *gērîm* only prior to the settlement in Canaan.[3]

It is the purpose of the present essay to argue that this tradition preserves a genuine historical memory. While it can hardly be doubted that much in the pre-settlement literature is merely a retrojection of later experiences, I shall try to show that this does not account for the tradition in question. What is most probably a retrojection, however, is the depiction of Israel as a cohesive socio-ethnic entity all the members of which shared in the same history from the very beginning. This schematized portrayal of Israel's pre-settlement history needs to be re-evaluated in light of evidence which suggests that before the settlement Israel was not a single social organism. In spite of the Bible's editorial framework, it is possible to find allusions to the existence of diverse groups. The members of these groups had had different historical experiences and thus had quite different recollections of the past. It is therefore more appropriate to think of the "Israel" of the pre-settlement tradition as various groups of "proto-Israelites" who had participated in different events and who would only later become part of Israel in the sense of a total social organism. The fact that the discrete traditions of these various groups were later fused under the impulse of the "all Israel" ideology should not detract us from seeing the socio-historical complexity of the pre-settlement period (Gottwald 1979: 63, 84, 106).

Partial evidence for the diversity just mentioned may be found in the following: 1) Exod 12: 38, where Israel is called a "mixed multitude"; 2) the ethnic diversity of early Israelite names, such as Jerubbaal (Judg 9: 1); 3) the Amorite taunt song against Heshbon in Num 21: 27b–30; 4) the eclectic assembly pictured in Joshua 24; 5) the dialectical differences reflected in Judg 12: 6; 6) Deut 26: 5, where Jacob is called a "fugitive Aramean"; 7) non-Israelite elements becoming part of Israel, as suggested by Josh 6: 22–25, Judg 1: 22–26 and Genesis 38; 8) the diversity of divine names in Israelite tradition (see Mendenhall 1973: 22, 26, 105–21; Cross 1973: 1–75; Freedman 1976: 55–107; Gottwald 1979: 215ff.). Thus, even if the *gēr*-tradition has been applied artificially to Israel as a whole, this does not mean that it cannot be a bona fide recollection of the past. In no way, however, does the present argument depend on the absolute historicity of the canonical account in the way it portrays Israel in either the patriarchal era or the time of the Exodus. Indeed, it seems to be a naive historical method to ask simply whether a given canonical tradition is historical or not. What is instead at issue here is the essential validity of the memory (or memories) that *some* of the groups which eventually comprised Israel had in fact been *gērîm* in one circumstance or another prior to their inclusion in Israel proper, when their individual histories and traditions began to undergo the process of transformation into a single "history" and tradition.

A further aspect of the argument undertaken here is that the concept of *gēr* involves social unrest or conflict, especially in those circumstances in which people initially become *gērîm*. This is indicated by the descriptions of *gērîm* in the sources, as well as by semantic and etymological considerations in Hebrew and other languages, especially Akkadian. The nuance of social conflict may also be connected in some way to the tradition that Israel's antecedents [=*some* of Israel's antecedents] were *ʿibrîm,* or "Hebrews." If so, it is possible that in the *gēr*- and *ʿibrî*-traditions there was a "bonding" agent which facilitated the coalescence of heterogeneous peoples and fusion of discrete traditions that took place when Israel *as Israel* was born.

I

It is generally acknowledged that *gēr* in the Hebrew Bible refers to people who are no longer directly related to their original social setting and who have therefore entered into dependent relationships with various groups or officials in a new social setting (Bertholet 1896: 21ff.). The *gēr* was of another tribe, city, district, or country who was without customary social protection or privilege and of necessity had to place himself under the jurisdiction of someone else (Smith 1956: 75). This justifies the designation "resident alien," indicating persons with rights and legal standing but whose status was nevertheless distinguishable from that of the "native born." In the biblical accounts *gērîm* have many of the same advantages and are subject to the same civic or ritual regulations as Israelites themselves. Indeed, there seems to be little or no disadvantage in having *gēr*-status, though the emphasis in the legal corpus on treating *gērîm* equitably may mean that the general citizenry sometimes did otherwise. Still, *gērîm* do not have all the rights and privileges of regular members of the society; for example, Deut 28: 43 hints that *gērîm* were borrowers rather than lenders, suggesting a slightly inferior financial position. Moreover, *gērîm* are often mentioned along with typically disenfranchised or powerless persons, such as slaves, the poor, widows, strangers, and orphans. But these types too are protected by civil and religious laws, making mistreatment a violation of official policy. This seems to be analogous to much of American history where there are many laws designed to protect aliens or minorities but because of the stigma attached to being "foreign" or "underclassed" unofficial discrimination is commonplace.

In this light "immigrant" may be proposed as an acceptable translation for *gēr*. This term is richer in nuance and less awkward than "resident alien." Likewise, it seems preferable to the somewhat archaic "sojourner," which also has the disadvantage of reflecting only one social feature involved in being a *gēr,* namely, the roles, functions and relationships in the new host society. Not only does "immigrant" contain the nuances inherent in "resident alien" and "sojourner," but it also calls attention to the original circumstances of social conflict which are inevitably responsible for large-scale withdrawal of people. It is my contention that *gēr* should be translated by a word that underscores not simply the outsider status in the adopted social setting, but in addition those factors and conditions related to the emigration in the first place. Rather than concentrating on the plight of persons after they have become *gērîm*/immigrants, as important as that dimension of the problem is, it is equally instructive to give attention to why people became *gērîm* initially. Why leave tribe, city, district, or country, with the protection and privileges they afford, to move to a new social setting in which one will be, theoretically at least, more vulnerable? What are the reasons for becoming a *gēr*/immigrant? *Gērîm* are obviously pictured "on the move"; the question is, what motivates this movement?

Given the widespread assumption that nomadism or seminomadism lies behind much of the movement in the ancient Near East, it is curious that this has only infrequently been appealed to in answer to the above questions.[4] Instead, social conflict of one kind or another has been suggested. De Vaux connects the term *gēr* to Arabic *jār,* which may denote a "refugee" who has fled his original home due to unfortunate or intolerable circumstances, or because he was compelled to leave (de Vaux 1961: 74). Mauch cites among reasons for becoming *gērîm* escape from famine or military attack, or to search for sanctuary after a land has been destroyed by conquest (Mauch 1962: 398). And Selbie points out that one may become a *gēr* because of a blood feud or simply out of a desire to improve one's lot in life (Selbie 1903: 156). But what is most important to keep in mind about all these suggestions is that they involve situations of social conflict, and they are all in one way or another appropriate to the phenomenon of emigration.

While it is true that most of the biblical references speak of *gērîm* in their new setting, a few allude to the reasons for becoming *gērîm* initially. Exod 2: 22 (cf. 18: 3) says that Moses was a *gēr* in Midian. According to the story, Moses had to flee Egypt because his murder of the Egyptian overseer had become common knowledge (2: 14). 2 Sam 4: 3 notes that the Beerothites fled to Gittaim where they remained *gērîm* "to this day." Why they fled is not made explicit in the passage, but verses 1–2 intimate military activity and social unrest. According to 2 Kgs 8: 1–2 and Ruth 1: 1 one becomes a *gēr* in response to famine or the threat of famine. Intense social conflict is obvious in Isa 16: 1–5, which is part of the prophet's oracle against Moab. When destruction is visited upon Moab, Israel is to hide the outcasts (*niddāḥîm*) and refuse to betray the fugitives (*nôdēd*) who will flee Moab and try to "sojourn" [verbal form] in Israel. The verbal form of the root is used several times in Jeremiah (Jer 42: 15, 17, 22; 43: 2, 5; 44: 8, 12, 14, 28) where the prophet warns Israel not to try to escape the pending military destruction, which he assumes will be the natural reaction. There is a cryptic reference in 2 Chr 15: 9 [verbal form] to the fact that citizens of the northern kingdom had "deserted" (*nāpĕlû*) in order to "sojourn" with King Asa of Judah. A theological reason for the emigration is given: "when they saw that the Lord his God was with him"; still, there is a suggestion at least of social and political upheaval here. Finally, Deut 26: 5 connects Jacob's being a "fugitive Aramean" (or a "fugitive from Aram"?) with "sojourning" [verbal form].

It seems to be clear, then, that *gēr*-status could be attained voluntarily or involuntarily, depending on whether the original social setting was abandoned on account of dissatisfaction, or because of severe political, social or economic pressures. In either case, however, the "wandering" of *gērîm* is not necessarily a function of a regular occupation, such as pastoralism (which could itself be a response to conflict), but rather a function of the desire for or necessity of seeking out a new and potentially more favorable social setting elsewhere. It was social and political upheaval due to war, famine, economic and social troubles, oppression, plague and other misfortunes that produced *gērîm*. About the only time one might become a *gēr* in relatively tranquil circumstances is when there was actual evidence or the hope that a significantly better life was available elsewhere. Otherwise, *gērîm* had chosen or been forced to that status because of adverse conditions. This is why it is so important not to make the error of concentrating on what happens to *gērîm* *after* their relocation. The matter of reasons for becoming *gērîm* is simply a separate issue from that of the social roles and functions of *gērîm* already established in a new setting.[5]

This way of conceiving the problem seems to make the correlation between "immigrant" and *gēr* at least as reasonable as the alternatives usually suggested. All of the reasons cited for becoming *gērîm* may also be posited for emigration. Similarly, what transpires after emigration, whether for good or ill, will depend entirely on the social and political make-up of the new setting, and to some degree the impact of the immigrants on it. Sometimes immigrants look back on voluntary departure as a sound choice, or come to regard a forced emigration as a "blessing in disguise." At other times, immigrants are tragically subjected to equally harsh or even harsher treatment in the new land. Or the conditions in the adopted country may turn out to be more unfortunate, adding to rather than relieving the human misery that the immigrants hoped to leave behind. Still, it must be reiterated that what happened subsequently to immigrants has little if anything to do with what triggered the departure. To be sure, in some instances there could be a degree of correlation, as when immigrants are viewed as dissidents who will likely make trouble wherever they end up, or when because of unrealistic or frustrated expectations the immigrants breed social turmoil in the new setting. But even in these cases there is no *necessary* correlation between the original and the adopted social context. In any case, the validity of the immigrant terminology is underscored by the underlying nuance of social unrest or conflict, mostly in reference to the conditions which foster emigration initially, but also on occasion in reference to the new social situation in which the immigrants have settled down (cf. OED s. v. "immigrant" 3.).

II

The semantic range of Hebrew *GWR* and its probable etymology fits in rather well with the above analysis, especially with respect to the verbal form of the root. Standard lexica provide three *gûr* roots: 1) *gûr* I "to sojourn"; 2) *gûr* II "to stir up strife, create confusion, quarrel"; 3) *gûr* III "to dread, be afraid" (KB: 175–76; BDB: 157–58). While these seem to be more or less adequate translations, is it plausible to suppose that there are actually three different roots in question? On the one hand, *gûr* II may be a byform of *gārâ,* "to attack, strive," and *gûr* III a byform of *yāgōr,* "to be afraid, fear." On the other hand, there may be an original connection between the words so that the various meanings represent special meanings of a single root (see Kellerman 1977: 439–40). It is certainly possible for an identical term to have several different and apparently unrelated meanings. Thus, the supposition that *GWR,* whether it connotes "to sojourn," "to stir up strife," or "to dread," is in fact the same word is as or perhaps more likely than that these are all separate words with coincidentally identical spellings. This contention would surely be strengthened if a case could be made for a semantic "common denominator." While the nature of the evidence is such that the argument is unlikely to be proven, it is plausible that emigration, with its connotation of social conflict and unrest, underlies the basic meaning of Hebrew *GWR*. The different nuances of *gûr*, in my opinion, support such an interpretation.

The most extensive use of *gûr* is in instances where "to sojourn" is the obvious meaning. I asserted above that *gēr* is best understood as "immigrant," in which case to be consistent *gûr* I should be translated "to emigrate" or "to be an immigrant." This rendering emphasizes both the initial departure as well as the subsequent settlement. "To sojourn," which otherwise might be suitable, unfortunately calls attention too exclusively to the new situation in which the aliens find themselves. However, whatever word is used to translate *gēr* or *gûr* I, it is imperative to keep in mind the complex sociological background reflected in the terms. The "sojourning" or "emigrating" suggested by *gûr* I cannot be adequately explained simply by appealing to regular occupational migrations. Much of the movement implied by *gûr* I had to do with social conflict and unrest, not the carrying out of normal occupational duties. But even if one were to cite pastoralism as a primary explanation for the mobility connoted by the verb, and doubtless some varieties of pastoralism may be adduced, it cannot be forgotten that often pastoralism in the ancient Near East was in fact a form of emigration. Not a few pastoralists adopted that occupation as a means of protesting against and withdrawing from urban centers of power (Gottwald 1974: 240–41; Mendenhall 1976: 133–34). There is nothing about *gûr* I that requires one to posit pastoralism, but even in those cases where pastoralism might be involved, the underlying sense of social unrest and conflict is not thereby eliminated.

It is this understanding of *gûr* I that makes its correlation with *gûr* II feasible. At least four times the word means something like "to cause trouble," or "to attack": Pss 56: 7; 59: 4; 140: 3; Isa 54: 15. The MT of the three Psalms passages is as follows.

Ps 56: 7
yāgûrû yiṣp{y}ônû {?} hēmmâ
ʿăqēbay yišmōrû kaʾăšer qiwwû napšî

Ps 59: 4
kî hinnēh ʾārĕbû lĕnapšî
yāgûrû ʿālay ʿazzîm

Ps 140: 3
ʾăšer ḥāšĕbū rāʿōt bĕlēb
kol-yôm yāgûrû milḥāmôt

For Ps 56: 7 Dahood suggests "evilly they conspire," because elsewhere *gûr* II is parallel to terms signifying "to plot." According to Dahood, Jerome's translation *congregabuntur* supports this rendering (Dahood 1968: 43). It is not implausible that a word which means in general "to stir up strife" may imply "plotting" or "conspiring"—that is simply one very effective way of bringing about disorder. However, while "conspire" may be applicable here, in my view it is a derived meaning, so that Dahood's attempt to locate the etymology in terms such as *gārôn* or *gargĕrôt,* which have to do with "throat," is unnecessary. Besides, there seems to be a much more obvious etymology in Akkadian, to which we shall shortly turn. This derived sense may also be present in Ps 140: 3, though Ps 59: 4 appears to be more straightforward. The following translations are suggested:

Ps 56: 7
They stir up strife [by plotting], concealing themselves [?],
my assailers watch, who wait for me.

Ps 59: 4
Indeed, they lie in wait for me,
strong men rage against me.

Ps 140: 3
Who devise evil in their heart,
all day long they plot battles.[6]

The MT of Isa 54: 15 is as follows.

hēn gôr yāgûr ᵓepes mēᵓôtî
mî-gār ᵓittāk ʿālayik yippôl

McKenzie (1968: 139) translates:

If anyone assails you, it is not from me;
whoever attacks you will fall on your account.

Isa 54: 14, 16–17 would seem to support McKenzie's rendering, in that aggression in general is the context of the passage. The thrust of the entire oracle is that Zion's enemies will no longer harass her. The RSV also takes the root in this way, but translates with the more conventional "stir up strife." Unfortunately, the sample is not as large as one would prefer, but with these four examples there is a modicum of evidence that the above interpretation of *gēr* and *gūr* I is possible.

However, if my supposition about the relationship between *gûr* and *gārâ* is correct, there is even more reason for seeing Hebrew *GWR* in this manner. Sometimes *gārā* takes a direct object, such as *mādôn,* "strife, contention" (e.g., Prov 15: 18; 28: 25; 29: 22) and sometimes it occurs without one (e.g., Deut 2: 5, 9, 19, 24). In either case, the range of meaning is between the expression of personal anger (e.g., Prov 15: 18) and the manifestation of anger in a social or political setting (e.g., Deut 2: 5). Again, it appears to be the case that a word related to *GWR* conveys the idea of disharmony on both personal and social levels. This in turn is related to *gēr* and *gûr* I in the sense that "immigrant" and "to emigrate" are concepts suggestive of anger, contention, strife, protest, bitterness, and so forth. A correct understanding of the social background of *gēr*/*gûr* I does not make it at all surprising that byforms of the root connote such things.

It is somewhat more difficult to tie in the meaning of *gûr* III, "to fear" or "to dread" (Num 22: 3; Deut 1: 17; 18: 22; 32: 27; 1 Sam 18: 15; Hos 10: 5; Ps 22: 24; 33: 8; Job 19: 29; 41: 17). Perhaps all that can be said is that fear may be related to the emotional and psychological state of persons who have chosen or been forced to emigrate. A combination of fear and anger or contentiousness is a priori probable in such social contexts. Besides, there are other Semitic terms which display a similarly perplexing range of seemingly unrelated meanings. Arabic *jāra* may mean "to depart from, commit a crime, III to be a neighbor, IV to put under someone's protection" (Kellerman 1977: 442). There is at least some evidence that all these nuances are contained in Hebrew *GWR,* so that the idea that "to sojourn," "to stir up strife" and "to be afraid" are interrelated may not be as unlikely as it at first appears.

Before turning to the question of the etymology of *GWR,* a few comments about the nouns *gôr*/*gûr,* "whelp, young lion," are in order.[7] These particular terms are interesting in that in ancient sources it is not uncommon for animal names to be used in reference to social antagonists. It was apparently believed by those employing such terminology that these pejorative epithets called attention to the "uncivilized" behavior and attitudes of people dissatisfied with the status quo. This phenomenon may be observed in a couple of psalms (Pss 59 and 140) in which the enemies enumerated are called "dogs" and "serpents."[8] And in two old poems, which deal with the character of the Israelites, animal names, including *gôr* and *gûr,* are used (Gen 49: 9; Deut 33: 22). Rather than seeing in this a reference to the *natural* disposition of early Israelites, it may be understood as a reflection of the socially troubled situations in which many early proto-Israelites found themselves. In this light, it is interesting that there is an Akkadian text which describes a dog's [= enemy's] behavior with a word related to *GWR: kalba maṣi libbišu ugira jaši,* "Behold the dog, he has turned against me according to his whim" (CAD G: 61; see generally Thomas 1960: 410–27; Miller 1970: 177–86; Mendenhall 1973: 130, 137). Though this is largely conjectural, it is tempting to see in such animal names appellations designed to denigrate those seen to be at odds with established authority and social systems.

A reasonable case can be made that *GWR* is related etymologically to Akkadian *giaru* and *gērû/garû*.[9] The former is medially weak and semantically close to *gûr* II—*giaru* means "to provoke, challenge or defy" (AHw 287)—so its correlation with the Hebrew root is fairly straightforward. But *gērû/garû* are somewhat more problematic in that they are finally weak. However, the Semitic root system is of such a nature that this does not pose an insurmountable problem. As is well known, Semitic words are based on a triradical root system, though perhaps a few words originally had only two root consonants. In the course of time many of these evolved into triradical roots by analogy with genuine triradical words, which accounts for the existence of a number of weak stems that appear in both medial and final weak forms, but with two radicals in common and a common base of meaning (Moscati 1964: 159). There is therefore no intrinsic reason why a West Semitic middle weak root and an Eastern Semitic final weak root could not be etymologically related, just as medial weak *gûr* and finally weak *gārâ* are almost certainly related. Of course, if semantic equivalency can be demonstrated as well, then the connection becomes even more credible.

The noun *gērû* means "enemy" (both personal and military) or, in a legal context, "adversary." The verb *garû* means either "to be hostile" or, again in a legal context, "to start a lawsuit" (CAD G: 62–63; AHw 286). It is fairly easy to see a connection between "enemy/adversary/to be hostile" and the various nuances of Hebrew *GWR* pointed out above. Immigrants were often viewed as "enemies" or "outlaws" in the sense that their attitudes and actions were construed as or in fact constituted an explicit denunciation of the social and political order. Seldom would emigration, especially if it involved a significant number of people, be looked upon neutrally by authorities (Renger 1972: 167–82). Further, though immigrants saw themselves as reacting to social difficulties, officials and rulers often saw them as the *cause* of turmoil. "To bring a lawsuit" seems to be some semantic distance from *GWR* or, for that matter, the other meanings of the Akkadian root. However, what happens in a lawsuit is that one party "complains" about another in order to obtain redress of grievance. It is still necessary to sign a "complaint" form in contemporary legal process. By this means one becomes a legal enemy-adversary or, at least, formally identifies his enemy-adversary. In a legal setting "hostility" is still being expressed, but in a controlled and socially regulated manner. Thus, being hostile and suing someone are not as unrelated as one might think. In support of this argument, there is a virtual semantic equivalent in Hebrew. The term *rîb* means on the one hand "to agitate, dispute, quarrel noisily, strive against" and on the other "to conduct a legal case" (BDB: 936). *Gērû/garû,* then, describe the hostility of a military or personal enemy, and the hostility that one expresses in a court of law. Both socio-political and legal conflict underlie the Akkadian root. Certainly the semantic range of Hebrew *GWR* and Akkadian *gērû/garû* are not identical, nor would one expect them to be. But the various nuances are similar enough to make the supposition of etymological association reasonable.

Given a probable relationship between Hebrew *GWR* and the Akkadian (and Arabic) root, there is little doubt about the underlying connotation of social conflict and its several derivatives.

III

At this juncture the issue of date must be broached. What is the evidence that the tradition of Israel's [= some proto-Israelites'] having been *gērîm* before the settlement is an early one? Does this tradition preserve a genuine memory of the pre-settlement era? If the above arguments about the etymology of *GWR* are valid, then it can be established that the root in question was used in texts prior to the date of the settlement. In the case of Israelite sources the root likewise occurs in some relatively early texts. The pertinent Akkadian terms occur in texts which antedate the relevant Israelite events.[10] The Hebrew root is found in three early poems: Gen 49: 9; Judg 5: 17; Deut 33: 22. The terms *gēr* and *gûr* refer to Israelites and the sojourning tradition in several instances in the JE corpus (Gen 12: 10; 15: 13; 19: 9; 20: 1b; 21: 23, 34; 26: 3; 32: 5; 47: 4), which has traditionally been dated in the ninth or eighth centuries B.C.E. (but see Van Seters 1975). Some of the references in the Book of the Covenant, the Holiness Code and the D Corpus could conceivably be early, but there is no way to be certain. Deut 26: 5ff., even if not as old as von Rad maintained, may nevertheless be a fairly early tradition.

But perhaps the most compelling evidence for the authenticity of this tradition lies elsewhere than in genuinely early references. The use of *gēr* throughout the Hebrew Bible is most instructive. We have already seen that only a few times are Israelites said to have been *gērîm*, and this is only for the time prior to the settlement (except Ezra 1: 4). Most of the time *gērîm* in Deuteronomistic and Priestly materials, and in some other later materials, refers to non-Israelites. Now, if *gērîm* first applied to non-Israelites, it is difficult to figure out how the term would later be applied to Israelites. Except for the presettlement era, there was no time when Israel, conceived as a totality, could have been called *gērîm*. What experience in the life of Israel after the settlement would have led to the invention of the *gēr*-tradition? It seems that the only possible answer to this question is the Exile, when Israel in a sense did become *gērîm*. As a matter of fact, this setting would appear to explain the invention of the tradition, but looking more closely suggests otherwise. If the *gēr*-tradition were invented in this period, then one is hard pressed to ascertain a reason as to why the exilic literature is so silent on the subject. Were an analogy between Israel's "original" sojourn and the exilic sojourn to be drawn—on the pattern, say, of the original Exodus from Egypt and the later one from Babylon—it would be reasonable to expect more than a single reference to Israel's deportation to and stay in Babylon as a "sojourn." But that is all there is. The Bible is otherwise steadfastly consistent in citing only the pre-settlement era as the time when Israelites were *gērîm*. The point is simply that if the tradition is pre-exilic, then it also must be pre-settlement, since there is no other time when the tradition would be appropriate to Israel's pre-exilic history or which could explain adequately the invention of the tradition.

At the very least, this should place the burden of proof on any who would argue that the tradition was invented as a response to the Exile. But such a view seems to strain at a number of key points. The composition of the JE Corpus would have to be redated to the exilic period, a position for which the evidence is in my opinion less than compelling (but see Van Seters 1975). Some explanation for the silence of the sources on Israel's being *gērîm* in Babylon is required. Arguments from silence are often problematic, but in this instance it is rather hard to see how Israel's "sojourn" in

Egypt could have been connected to the "sojourn" in Babylon without more explicit reference than we have. This viewpoint in addition disregards the consistency with which the Deuteronomist portrays *gērîm* as indigenous Palestinians, and the Priestly editors portray them as proselytes (Meek 1930: 172–73). And, given the connection between the *gēr*-tradition and the traditions of the patriarchal wanderings and the Exodus, if one were to postulate that the *gēr*-tradition had been invented then, these other traditions would logically have to be considered exilic as well. But the tradition of the Exodus, at least, is surely pre-exilic, as a reading of the eighth-century prophets shows.

Finally, there is a possibility that the *gēr*-tradition should be considered along with another tradition which almost certainly reflects the pre-settlement (and settlement) periods. I refer here to the tradition that Israelites were once *ʿibrîm,* "Hebrews," to a discussion of which we now turn.

IV

It is beyond the scope of this essay to provide an exhaustive analysis of the *ʿapiru/ʿibrîm* problem. The issues are well known and they need not be rehearsed here (see the bibliography). However, it is necessary to underscore those dimensions of the problem which are most pertinent to the above analysis of *gēr.*

It is generally recognized that those who are described as SA.GAZ or *ʿapiru (Ḫap/biru)* in ancient texts are characterized by considerable diversity. Their ethnic make-up is heterogeneous, their places of origin are scattered throughout the Near East, their occupations and social roles are vastly different, and their secondary places of residence range over wide areas (Greenberg 1955: 87). This is one of the main reasons why the *ʿapiru* problem has been so difficult—how are we to account for the fact that the same term can apply to such diverse groups of people? However, it has been argued in recent years that the problem will not be solved as long as attention is paid exclusively to *ʿapiru after* they attain that status rather than to the *origins* of *ʿapiru.* What can be learned about *ʿapiru* once they are *ʿapiru* is a worthwhile topic of study, but still a quite different subject. It must not be forgotten that the same term has been used for people who not only transcend ethnic, linguistic, cultural, political, and geographical boundaries, but who are depicted as engaging in activity ranging from piracy or inciting revolution on the one hand to perfectly normal, peaceful occupations (e.g., trading, pastoralism) on the other. If there is anything common to *ʿapiru,* it must be sought elsewhere than in these obviously diverse characteristics. This is what lends cogency to the argument that the commonality which *ʿapiru* share should be sought in their origins rather than in their experiences subsequent to becoming *ʿapiru.* As was noted with respect to the *gēr,* what happens after becoming an *ʿapiru* may have little or nothing to do with why one became an *ʿapiru* in the first place (Mendenhall 1973: 136, n. 64; Gottwald 1979: 401; Chaney 1978).

Putting the accent on the origins of *ʿapiru* is warranted by the fact that it is either demonstrable or possible in virtually every case to conclude that *ʿapiru* are alienated from the original social context—they are "outsiders." This observation is underlined by the etymology of *ʿapiru.* Mendenhall cites *ʿBR,* "to cross" [especially a boundary], as the etymology of both *ʿapiru* and *ʿibrī.* An *ʿapiru* is one who crosses "illegally" a political boundary.[11] Arabic *ʿābir*, "transient, wayfarer," is also instructive (Mendenhall 1973: 140–41). A possible etymology of SA.GAZ is equally suggestive. It has been proposed that SA.GAZ is a pseudo-logogram for Akkadian *sāggāšu,* which is related to West Semitic *ŠGŠ,* "disturber, one who is restive" (Greenberg 1955: 88–90). Thus, one becomes an *ʿapiru* by rejecting the legitimacy of the political authority in a particular social setting, a rejection which is signalled by departure [= "crossing the boundary"]. This makes the *ʿapiru* an "outlaw" from the state's perspective. However, an *ʿapiru* could also be a "fugitive" (*emigré?*) if for any reason he had been driven out of his original social setting. Being driven out might follow, for example, any behavior which the government was convinced undercut either its claim to legitimacy or ability to exercise control.

This understanding of the *ʿapiru* phenomenon makes the correlation with biblical *ʿibrî* intriguing. There is little difficulty in showing that *ʿapiru* and *ʿibrî* may be linguistically related, as both Mendenhall and Weippert have demonstrated (Mendenhall 1973: 138; Weippert 1971b: 63ff.). But it is equally significant that there are sociological parallels between the two terms—both seem to refer to the same social "type." One of the interesting parallels is that there is little evidence that *ʿapiru* or *ʿibrîm* used these epithets to refer to themselves. They had a pejorative connotation and were usually applied by the "insiders" in the original or new social setting. For example, in the Hebrew Bible *ʿibrî* is most often used by others rather than the "Hebrews" themselves, except when the term is used as an ethnicon or when the "Hebrews" are talking to foreigners. When one compares the typical view of *ʿapiru* and *ʿibrîm* by the "insiders," who were by and large authorities, the similarities are striking. Gottwald's summary of these similarities, which he bases on a study of Philistine attitudes toward Hebrews as found in the Bible, is revealing. According to Gottwald, Israelites were *ʿapiru/ʿibrîm* in the sense that they could be viewed as subordinates in the overall imperialistic system (e.g., 1 Sam 4: 9; 13: 19–20). Israelites were *ʿapiru/ʿibrîm* in that they gave promise of being good auxiliary troops in the best *ʿapiru* tradition (e.g., 1 Sam 14: 21–23a). Israelites were *ʿapiru/ʿibrîm* in that they had been successful rebels against an imperial feudal system (e.g., 1 Sam 13: 3). And Israelites were *ʿapiru/ʿibrîm* in that with enough force they could be reduced to state slaves, as the Egyptians had done to many of their *ʿapiru/ʿibrî* captives (Gottwald 1979: 417–25, esp. 422). Of course, not all Israelites were *ʿapiru/ʿibrîm,* or vice versa, a fact that has been obscured by the Deuteronomist's use of the term as an ethnicon. But 1 Sam 14: 21 should leave no doubt that some *ʿapiru/ʿibrî* groups were not identified with Israel. But the point is not that all Israelites were *ʿapiru/ʿibrîm*; rather, the point is that the tradition(s) which says that *some* Israelites [= proto-Israelites] were *ʿapiru/ʿibrîm* is a reliable one. Later on, after groups of proto-Israelites, some of whom had been *ʿapiru/ʿibrîm,* united to become *bĕnê Yiśrāʾēl,* other *ʿapiru/ʿibrîm* joined them (1 Sam 14: 21).

By now it should be clear that I am suggesting that the *ʿibrî*-tradition and the *gēr*-tradition constitute similar though not necessarily identical memories of the past which were preserved by some of the groups which eventually made up Israel. Both terms refer to people away from their original homes. Both have to do with situations of social unrest, conflict or instability. And both have to do with the status of "outlaws, fugitives and immigrants." To be sure, in both cases the exact social nuances and precise historical circumstances have been lost or obscured by artificial literary designs or theological/ideological "tampering." Nevertheless, the various editors and redactors were not completely successful in hiding the socio-political realities underlying the terms *ʿibrî* and *gēr*, as I have tried to point out.

The relevance of this approach is heightened in the light of the revolt model of the Israelite conquest which Mendenhall advanced some twenty years ago and which has been most recently elaborated on by Gottwald (Mendenhall 1962: 66–87; Gottwald 1979: 191–233). According to their reconstruction, Israel emerged in Canaan when (1) a sizeable number of indigenous Canaanite peasants were joined by (2) various groups of *ʿapiru/ʿibrîm,* some of whom had probably been involved in the escape from Egypt and others of whom had been on the fringes of Canaanite cities inciting rebellion or taking advantage of social unrest, and by (3) pastoralists who had been in the process of withdrawing from urban centers. Disparate elements of one description or another, including some "Sea Peoples," may also have taken part in this complex process (Spina 1977: 60–71). These groups together made common cause against the interlocking Canaanite political system and succeeded in breaking its grip on the society (see Josh 12: 7–24). In place of the Canaanite hierarchy and political structure, an entirely new kind of religio-social system was established. Thus, Israel's birth *as Israel* resulted from a coalescence of peoples with widely differing backgrounds and experiences and a fusion of their discrete traditions. The basis for this unification was the common rejection of a hierarchical, centralized political control system and the concomitant embracing of the cult of Yahweh and decentralized, non-hierarchical social forms.

The tradition that pre-settlement Israel had been *gērîm* fits in well with this view of the genesis of Israel. Proto-Israelite *ʿibrîm,* dissenting and withdrawing pastoralists, Sea Peoples trying to escape one form of hegemony or another, and rebelling Canaanite peasants were by definition *gērîm*. Other groups of *gērîm* would have readily added to and benefitted from this social ferment. No matter how diverse the people who made up Israel were, most of them had in common their status as "outlaws, fugitives and immigrants." They, in addition, had in common a commitment to a deity, Yahweh, who was believed to be uniquely concerned with the array of human problems reflected by such epithets. Indeed, this may represent the first time in human history in which the divine world was seen to side with "outlaws, fugitives and immigrants" rather than with the political structures whose policies and use of power made such social types inevitable.

Notes

1. It was observed almost fifty years ago that references to Israelites as *gērîm* were to be found in the earlier strata of the Pentateuch. Later on *gēr* meant foreigners in Israelite territory and then finally proselytes. See Meek 1930: 172–73. Is it possible that the Phoenician-Punic personal names made up of *gr* + DN mean "proselyte/convert of DN"? See the names *grʾšmn; grmlqrt; grʿštrt; grṣd.* See KAI III. 47; cf. Benz 1972: 298–99. Note also the biblical toponym *gûr-bāʿal* (2 Chr 26: 7).

2. Isa 14: 1 says that *gērîm* will join Israel in the return from exile.

3. There are two places where *gēr* is used to refer to a particular relationship to Yahweh and to the land. In Lev 25: 23 Israelites are forbidden in perpetuity to sell any of the land since it belongs to Yahweh. In this context Israel is a *gēr* in relationship to Yahweh's land, that is, Israel does not own the land. In 1 Chr 29: 15 David calls Israel "strangers" (*tôšābîm*) and *gērîm* "before" Yahweh, alluding to the transitory nature of Israel's life.

The reference to Moses' having been a *gēr* may also be mentioned here. It is found in the story where Moses names his son Gershom: Exod 2: 22 [J]; 18: 3 [E]. Moses explains the name with the phrase: *gēr hāyîtî bĕʾereṣ nokriyyâh*, "I was a *gēr* in a foreign land." However, in this case Moses, who at this point in the story is unaware of his ties with the Hebrew slaves, is a *gēr* in relation to Midian, not Egypt. Strictly speaking, then, this does not refer to an Israelite experience.

4. For a summary and critique of views regarding nomadism in Israel and the ancient Near East, see Gottwald 1974: 223–55; 1979: 435–63. Not only has the role of nomadism been greatly overestimated, its multi-faceted character has been poorly understood. For example, nomadism often constituted a movement *away* from urban settlements rather than toward them, which is exactly the opposite of what has been commonly suggested.

5. This fact has been misunderstood by Heaton. Because the legal material in the Bible admonishes Israel to treat *gērîm* fairly since that was Israel's status in Egypt, he concludes that the memory preserved in these traditions involves a "beneficial" sojourn. In part this is based on Heaton's a priori rejection of a "love thy enemy" ethic in this section of the Old Testament. More importantly, he confuses the issues involved in becoming *gērîm* with those involved subsequently. In either case, however, it does not seem to me that Heaton has successfully argued for the tradition of a beneficial sojourn, though I would agree that it is certainly possible that some proto-Israelites had been in Egypt without being subject to slavery or oppression. See Heaton 1946: 80–82.

6. In this reference *milḥāmôt* is the object of *yāgûrû*. While *gûr* does not seem to take an object, in the light of the byform *gārâ*, "to stir up," which often does, it may be best to retain *milḥāmôt* rather than eliminating it as a gloss or conflation.

7. Gen 49: 9; Deut 33: 22; Jer 51: 38; Ezr 19: 2, 3, 5; Nah 2: 12–13; Lam 4: 3.

8. A monograph is currently being prepared which argues the thesis that the enemies mentioned in many of the psalms of lament are actually political dissidents.

9. In addition to Arabic *jāra* and *jarwᵘⁿ*, "whelp," *GWR* is probably related to Ugaritic *gr* as well. See Aisleitner 1963: 68–69.

10. The root in Ugaritic occurs in texts in which social conflict of one sort or another is indicated, but the contexts are in general too difficult to be helpful in the present discussion. See Aisleitner 1963: 68, for example.

11. The semantic shift from crossing a political boundary to crossing a moral/ethical one may be seen in Num 22: 18; Judg 9: 18; 11: 29; Exod 32: 27; 2 Sam 3: 10. See Mendenhall 1973: 140–41.

References

Aisleitner, J.
1963 *Wörterbuch der Ugaritischen Sprache*. Berlin: Academie-Verlag.

Albright, W. F.
1957 *From the Stone Age to Christianity: Monotheism and the Historical Process*[2]. Garden City, New York: Doubleday.
1961 Abram the Hebrew: A New Archaeological Interpretation. *Bulletin of the American Schools of Oriental Research* 163: 36–54.

Bertholet, A.
1896 *Die Stellung der Israeliten und der Juden zu der Fremden*. Freiberg und Leipzig: Mohr.

Borger, R.
1958 Das Problem der *ʿapiru ('Ḫabiru'). Zeitschrift des Deutschen Palästina-vereins* 74: 121–32.

Bottéro, J.
1954 *Le Problem des Ḫabiru*. Cahiers de la Société Asiatique 12. Paris: Imprimerie Nationale.

Cazelles, H.
1973 The Hebrews. Pp. 1–28 in *Peoples of Old Testament Times,* ed. D. J. Wiseman. Oxford: Clarendon Press.

Chaney, M.
1978 Social Unrest in Late Bronze Syro-Palestine and the Formation of Pre-monarchic Israel: Some Modes of Analysis from the Comparative Social Sciences. Paper read to Social World of Ancient Israel Group, the Society of Biblical Literature, New Orleans, 1978.

Cross, F. M.
1973 *Canaanite Myth and Hebrew Epic.* Cambridge: Harvard University Press.

Dahood, M.
1968 *Psalms II: 51–100.* The Anchor Bible 17. Garden City, New York: Doubleday.

Freedman, D. N.
1976 Divine Names and Titles in Early Hebrew Poetry. Pp. 55–107 in *Magnalia Dei* [G. E. Wright *Festschrift*], ed. F. M. Cross, W. E. Lemke and P. D. Miller, Jr. Garden City, New York: Doubleday.

Gottwald, N. K.
1974 Were the Early Israelites Pastoral Nomads? Pp. 223–55 in *Rhetorical Criticism: Essays in Honor of James Muilenburg,* ed. J. J. Jackson. Pittsburgh Theological Monograph Series 1. Pittsburgh: Pickwick Press.
1979 *The Tribes of Yahweh: A Sociology of the Religion of Liberated Israel, 1250–1050 B.C.E.* Maryknoll: Orbis.

Greenberg, M.
1955 *The Ḫab/piru.* American Oriental Series 39. New Haven: Yale University Press.

Heaton, E. W.
1946 Sojourners in Egypt. *Expository Times* 58: 80–82.
KB
1958 *Lexicon in Veteris Testamenti Libros,* eds. L. Koehler and W. Baumgartner. Leiden: E. J. Brill.

Kellerman, D.
1977 *gûr; gēr; gērûth; mĕghûrîm.* Vol. 2, pp. 439–49 of *Theological Dictionary of the Old Testament.* Rev. ed. Ed. G. J. Botterweck and H. Ringgren. Trans. J. T. Willis. Grand Rapids, Michigan: Eerdmans.

Kline, M. G.
1956, 1957 The ḪA-BI-RU—Kin or Foe of Israel? *Westminster Theological Journal* 19: 1–24; 20: 46–70.

Koch, Klaus
1969 Die Hebraer vom Auszug aus Ägypten bis zum Grossreich Davids. *Vetus Testamentum* 19: 37–81.

McKenzie, J.
1968 *Second Isaiah.* The Anchor Bible 20. Garden City, New York: Doubleday.

Mauch, T. M.
1962 Sojourner. *Interpreter's Dictionary of the Bible.* Vol. 4: 397–99.
Meek, T. J.
1930 The Translation of *Gēr* in the Hexateuch and Its Bearing on the Documentary Hypothesis. *Journal of Biblical Literature* 49: 172–80.

Mendenhall, G. E.
1962 The Hebrew Conquest of Palestine. *The Biblical Archaeologist* 35: 66–87.
1973 *The Tenth Generation: The Origins of the Biblical Tradition.* Baltimore: Johns Hopkins University Press.

1976 Social Organization in Early Israel. Pp. 132–51 in *Magnalia Dei* [G. E. Wright *Festschrift*], ed. F. M. Cross, W. E. Lemke and P. D. Miller, Jr. Garden City, New York: Doubleday.

Millard, A. R.
1980 A Wandering Aramean. *Journal of Near Eastern Studies* 39: 153–55.

Miller, P. D.
1970 Animal Names as Designations in Ugaritic and Hebrew. *Ugarit Forschungen* 2: 177–86.

Moscati, S.
1964 *An Introduction to the Comparative Grammar of the Semitic Languages.* Wiesbaden: Harrassowitz.

von Rad, G.
1962 *Old Testament Theology.* Vol. I. Trans. D. M. G. Stalker. Edinburgh: Oliver and Boyd.

Renger, J.
1972 Flucht als soziales Problem in der altbabylonischen Gesellschaft. Pp. 167–82 in *Gesellschaftsklassen im Alten Zweistromland und in den angrenzenden Gebieten. XVIII. Rencontre assyriologique internationale, München, 29. Juni bis 3. Juli 1970.* München: Verlag der Bayerischen Akademie der Wissenschaften.

Selbie, J. A.
1903 *Gēr.* Vol. 2, pp. 156–157 in *Hastings Dictionary of the Bible,* ed. James Hastings. New York: Scribner.

Smith, W. R.
1956 *The Religion of the Semites.* New York: Meridian.

Spina, F. A.
1977 The Dan Story Historically Reconsidered. *Journal for the Study of the Old Testament* 4: 60–71.

Thomas, D. W.
1960 *Kelebh* 'Dog': Its Origin and Some Usages of it in the Old Testament. *Vetus Testamentum* 10: 410–27.

Van Seters, J.
1975 *Abraham in History and Tradition.* New Haven: Yale University Press.

de Vaux, R.
1961 *Ancient Israel: Social Institutions.* New York and Toronto: McGraw-Hill.

1968 Le Problème des *Ḫapiru* après quinze années. *Journal of Near Eastern Studies* 27: 221–28.

Weippert, M
1971a Abraham der Hebraer? Bemerkungen zu W. F. Albrights Deutung der Väter Israels. *Biblica* 52: 407–32.

1971b *The Settlement of the Israelite Tribes in Palestine.* Studies in Biblical Theology, 2nd. ser., 21. Trans. J. D. Martin. London: SCM.

Gender Roles and Genesis 3: 16 Revisited

Carol L. Meyers
Duke University, Durham, North Carolina

The investigation of sex roles in ancient Israel is never an easy task because of the imbalance of information in the major source of knowledge about this community, the Hebrew Bible.[1] The asymmetrical legal and public authority of men over women in Israelite society is apparent in many of the legal and narrative portions of the biblical text. The nature of formal transactions such as marriage and property ownership and the male domination of public roles and offices such as the priesthood and court bureaucracy point to a patriarchal society. Biblical materials dealing with such matters constitute the bulk of our information about sex roles in ancient Israel. Yet these kinds of data are incomplete; and the biblical record provides little material that offers direct comment upon the role and status of the female within this patriarchal system.

Nonetheless, the task is not impossible. An optimistic view of the potential for studying ancient gender roles derives from the availability of methodological assistance from the social sciences. Examination of oft-studied biblical texts, such as the one that will be considered here, can provide fresh insights when set against concepts of human behavior in appropriate and analogous societal contexts. Our return to Genesis 3 will thus be preceded first by a methodological statement and then by an identification of the relevant variables in pre-monarchic Israelite society.

Methodological Statement

During the past several decades, the value of using social scientific concepts in dealing with ancient Israel has become increasingly understood. The people of the Book should not be limited by that Book but rather need to be recognized as a living community which produced that literary testimony to various aspects of its societal dynamics and religious beliefs. Comprehending the ideology-bearing narratives and formulations that constitute the canonical record cannot be divorced from comprehending the community, in its formation and ongoing vitality, that produced the biblical corpus.

With the emergence of social history as a fundamental key to Israelite history and character, the renewed focus on methodology has been reasonably productive in finding appropriate procedures and strategies for analyzing an ancient society. As biblical scholars have become more comfortable with the disciplines of sociology and anthropology, there has been a decrease in the tendency to identify phenomena cross-culturally at the superficial level without thorough consideration of the validity of the analogy. At the same time, the social sciences themselves have progressed in statistical analyses of data and in the ability to identify correlative sets of societal variables. This aspect of social scientific research is critical, since correlations provide the core of the usefulness of social scientific methodology in studying an ancient population for which the full range of desired information can never be obtained. Sociology and anthropology thus allow at least some of the gaps in our knowledge to be filled inferentially. This process depends on the extent to which the variables can be supplied on the basis of all possible materials: biblical, archeological, and extra-Israelite ancient literary sources.

Despite the overall productive results which have emerged from critical appraisal of social history in biblical studies, there remains an additional kind of concern about the probability of events having occurred in the way that social reconstruction recreates. For example, a typical response of the critic or skeptic—who may not be one and the same—of the peasant revolt model of the Conquest (e.g., Mendenhall 1976, and Gottwald 1979) as ways to probe Israelite beginnings is directed towards the seeming failure of the biblical materials themselves to record such events or circumstances. If there were a large uprising of indigenous Palestinians (Canaanites) against the oppression of their elitist overlords, "it is a curious anomaly," goes the argument (e.g., Hauser 1978: 10), "that there is no trace in the biblical traditions of a massive conversion and uprising" such as is proposed.

This criticism needs to be taken seriously. It can be answered in two complementary ways. First, on theoretical grounds the validity of such an objection can be met by taking into account the nature of the biblical sources and learning to "translate" the religious and symbolic language of the biblical writers into the historical realities which underlay and prompted the religious response. Second, specific examples of the existence of evidence in the Bible and other historical documents, such as the El-Amarna letters, for the reconstructions proposed by social scientific analysis need to be educed.

It is the latter task which will be involved here. A presupposition of this task is that the requisite data can in fact be located in some fashion or to some degree in the biblical text. The problem lies not in their existence but rather in their availability. Since the purpose of the ancient literature is so different from the modern techniques and structures we seek to superimpose, the possibility that the data are present in forms that are not readily recognizable must be entertained. We have not yet learned to ask all the right questions; we have not yet become sensitive enough to the subtle ways in which social values and structures are communicated. That the Bible is an extremely complex body of literature is beyond dispute. Within that rich complexity, then, must surely lie the potential for answering new sets of questions.

Models formulated by the social sciences have been extremely useful in providing direction to the quest for information about the ways in which men and women related to each other within the family structure of tribal Israel. This quest is one which is openly predicated upon concerns generated in the sixties and seventies by the women's movement. The models, particularly those derived from anthropology, are likewise the products of recent research carried out by scholars with sensitivity toward feminist issues. In other words, relevant anthropological studies which can inform an inquiry into gender roles and status in an ancient society have not been available until the past few years.

Descriptions of sex role behaviors have long been a part of the anthropologist's field work. The contributions of Margaret Mead (e.g., 1953) to this aspect of ethnographic pursuits are indeed noteworthy. But the theoretical analyses and correlations that can make sense of this fundamental dimension of human social behavior are just now entering the literature. Personal interest or political concern may have sparked this development, but the intellectual and functional challenge of exploring gender status as a fundamental factor in human society cannot be gainsaid. The proliferation of publications in this field can only be understood by taking into account both kinds of stimuli.

Some sense of the variety and relative success of these recent works can be found in Quinn's excellent review article (1977), "Anthropological Studies on Women's Status." Quinn catalogues the treatments of cross-cultural case studies of women's status and also evaluates the various hypotheses which have been offered to deal with observed similarities and differences in the relative status of men and women in various societies. Another review article is particularly helpful in dealing with ancient societies, for which data cannot be retrieved from empirical studies. Conkey and Spector are preparing an essay on "Archaeology and the Study of Gender" which, in addition to surveying research questions and findings, is concerned with developments in archeological methods and theory that can foster investigation of sex roles through the archeological record.

Relevant Variables in Tribal Israel

In another article (Meyers forthcoming) this author has presented a series of concepts that anthropologists have formulated in order, first, to account for the universal disparity in the roles and statuses of the two sexes, and second, to comprehend the variety of cultural patterns of relative sex roles and status that have been identified in cross-cultural studies. Without repeating the discussion of these concepts, a brief summary of their salient features can be made.[2]

Within any society, there exists a division of labor whereby contributive and interlocking roles are assumed by different members of a group. Usually there is a stable and traditional pattern of responsibilities divided along gender lines. This pattern, however, varies enormously from society to society. In some societies the relative contributions of men and women are strikingly askew, with one sex seeming to carry the burden of essential tasks; in others, there is something approaching a balance of labor.

The continuum of possible relative contributions of males and females to societal chores can be correlated with the status of women. While women are never valued as a class more than men, their status can vary a great deal cross-culturally. The societal conditions which tend to produce the least sexual stratification are those in which women make significant contributions in supplying the basic needs of the community. Within certain parameters, societies in which women enjoy relatively high status are those in which women bear a quantitatively large portion of the roles which comprise the productive labor of the community.

These statements about gender roles and sexual status lead to two important questions. First, is there a maximum level at which females can operate and enjoy a high status? Or, stated another way, what is the balance in the division of labor that produces optimal valuation of both males and females? Second, what are the variables in a societal configuration that can produce such an optimum balance?

We have dealt in our other essay with both those questions. Again, a brief summation will further this discussion. Answers to both queries revolve around an analysis of the three major spheres of activity which determine the allocation of energies of a group's members and upon which the survival and development of the group depend. Those three activities are protection (through defensive or offensive military actions), production (subsistence: foodstuffs, shelter, clothing), and procreation (child-bearing and child-rearing). The balance of labor in the central area is the critical factor, for therein lies the greatest potential for gender asymmetry on the one hand or near balance on the other hand. Similarly, that is the area in which shifting external factors can exert powerful enough pressure to rearrange traditional sex roles.

The most balanced societies with respect to division of labor along gender lines are those in which subsistence tasks are divided about 60%-40%, male-female. When women contribute about 40% of the subsistence effort, sexual stratification within the society tends to be least marked. This ratio is a reasonable deviation from an equal 50%-50% since it takes into account the fact that some portion of female energy is absorbed in the fixed roles of childbearing and early nurturing. Male involvement in warfare, while nearly as universal as female involvement in procreation, is far less consistent and demanding and is often non-existent. There is some evidence that in ancient Israel such a 40%-60% balance of labor, with a concomitant high status for women, did exist. The redemption valuations of Leviticus 27 can be viewed as such a pattern. If so, the seeming anomalies in patriarchal Israelite society, with both idealized texts and male dominant materials appearing in the Bible, are thereby comprehensible. At least at some point in Israel's history, a high status existed for women and left its mark in the biblical record.

The variables which tend to produce such a balance of labor are those in which the efforts required of females in the subsistence area are appreciable. A variety of exogenous factors can produce such a situation. The absence of a significant number of males due to military service or conscription is an obvious example. The move to a new environment with a concomitant increase in pioneer tasks (land clearing, water procurement and storage, initial horticultural planting, house building) is another typical circumstance that affects the contributive labor of the group's members.

Both of these factors can be shown to have been operative in tribal Israel, in the early Iron Age. The demands of the latter variable are particularly relevant in that the new environment—the central mountainous core of Palestine—constitutes an ecosystem which is less hospitable to agrarian production than are the nearby coastal areas and broad valleys, to say nothing of the great riverine areas of the Near East. In other words, even without pioneer tasks added to the list of jobs to be done, eking out a livelihood in the rocky, dry hilly country has never been a particularly easy or pleasant task. Self-sufficiency is not easily attained since the soils and terrains most suited to essential grain staples are lacking; extraordinary technological efforts must be made to terrace hillsides and secure water. Furthermore, the delicate timing in the succession of rainy and dry seasons with respect to the growing cycle of basic foodstuffs, grains and olives in particular, causes an inherent insecurity to permeate the subsistence effort.

The earliest Iron Age villages in the hill country could have been established only through the performance of pioneer tasks. An increase of female participation in subsistence activities is a normal correlate of such a situation. We can therefore propose a reconstruction in which women entered the subsistence sphere in a major way.

Furthermore, on the basis of ethnographic analyses of such situations (Brown 1970), the specific and appropriate tasks within that sphere can be delineated along gender lines. When women participate as fully as possible in the agrarian efforts, they typically take on tasks related to hoe agriculture. They tend gardens and orchards and vineyards, which are usually contiguous to their domestic base. Child-care responsibilities can thus be sustained along with subsistence chores, particularly since the rhythm of hoe agriculture can be easily interrupted. In contrast, plow agriculture and the growing of field crops (notably grain) are often carried out at a distance from the domicile, often require some sustained and time-bound periods of toil, and thus tend to be male responsibilities. Thus the division of labor in the realm of food production under the circumstances of life in early pre-monarchic Israel would have meant an identification of field labor and thus grain production as an exclusively male task. Horticulture and viticulture would have proceeded through the efforts of men along with women (and children), with seasonal variations related to times of sowing and reaping.

The reproductive role of women has already been noted as a factor in determining the assignment of agrarian tasks when increased female participation in production must be achieved. That role, too, is somewhat flexible in response to the demands in the subsistence realm. For example, wide spacing of children and low fertility is a typical adaptation (Friedl 1975: 137) in societies where women must spend considerable energy and time removed from direct domestic chores and/or child care. In general, the average spacing of children and the number of children per family in any society stands in a dependent relationship to the involvement of women in subsistence tasks, and not vice versa.

This last point is important because it seems that the reproductive role for women in early Israel could not have tolerated such an adaptation to economic exigencies. On the contrary, as we have discussed elsewhere (Meyers 1978: 96–109), there is evidence that the beginnings of Israel coincided with a population decrease of serious proportions. Just when the tasks facing the nascent community increased in volume, the cumulative effects of the famines, wars, and plagues of the end of the Late Bronze Age left Canaan relatively underpopulated. Further, pioneer efforts are typically augmented not only by increased female participation but also by large families, by the contributions of children to certain agricultural chores.

Thus the normal decrease in fertility which is an adjustment to economic demands would not have been feasible for early Israel. The biblical record shows the channeling of sexual energy into the reproductive processes. There are a variety of religious sanctions for fertility ("Be fruitful and multiply"); patriarchal and other narratives contain strong themes of overcoming barrenness. These models and exhortations for the parenting of many children can be seen as a function of population needs in much the same way that a contrasting situation existed in Mesopotamia. There, mythographic reinforcement of the acceptance of miscarriages, of infant (and adult) mortality, and of non-sexuality for women (Frymer-Kensky 1977: 149–50; Kilmer 1972: 171–72) arose from and aided adaptation to the problems of overpopulation.

In sum, the variables at work in the highlands of early Iron Age Palestine were such that strenuous efforts would have been required to meet the pioneer demands. A near balance of labor would have ensued. The labor division can likewise be suggested. Men's roles would have involved occasional militia duty, initial settlement tasks such as land-clearing and cistern digging, plow agriculture, and as many additional horticultural tasks as time and energy required. Women's roles included the maternal ones, probably to a heightened degree insofar as bearing many children was essential, domestic or household chores, and considerable contributions to the subsistence chores involved in tending trees, vines, and gardens in contrast to the usual tendency for maximized female economic productivity to be accompanied by a reduced biological productivity. Thus, for at least a brief period of time, the female population of early Israel rose to the simultaneous demands of a high birth rate and a large role in the productive tasks.

Genesis 3—A Reconsideration

There is hardly a chapter in the biblical corpus the interpretation of which has been more rooted in traditional Judeo-Christian interpretations than has the Eden episode. The centrality of the matter of sin, its origins and its meaning for humanity, has consistently figured prominently in discussions of the Garden narrative. This kind of interpretation, which can be traced at least as far back as the first century in the New Testament (Rom 5: 12–14) and in the various versions of the life of Adam and Eve, has tended to permeate all modern scholarly treatments of the narratives of Genesis 2 and 3.

To cite just one example, von Rad's treatment of Genesis 3 (1961: 83–99) is entitled "The Story of the Fall." This notion of a fall is not found in the story itself but rather derives from Orphic thought, influential throughout the eastern Mediterranean world in late antiquity; Plato's *Phaedrus* is perhaps the best-known exposition of Orphic ideas (Hanson 1972: 41–42). Working from such a designation at the outset, von Rad's conclusion (p. 98) that Genesis 3 "asserts that all sorrow comes from sin" is nearly foregone. The assumption that Genesis 3 is about the origins of sin dominates nearly all treatments of primeval history.

While the role of disobedience and its consequences clearly figure in the story of the first human pair, it is an oversimplification of a rich and powerful narrative to allow that theme to obliterate other, perhaps equally important features. For several reasons, the focus upon sin and punishment may be a distortion caused by two millennia of traditional midrash and theology. A few of those reasons will be enumerated briefly here. Then we will present our own analysis of part of the Genesis 3 text. This analysis in our opinion constitutes additional evidence that, at the least, a variety of levels of meaning are operating in Genesis 3, and perhaps also that the centrality of the sin/punishment theme should be reconsidered.

First, there is no explicit reference to sin in the narrative (see Naidoff 1978: 2–3). None of the Hebrew words that refer to "sin" are present in the text of either Genesis 2 or 3. It is not until Cain and Abel, the first naturally-born humans, are involved in the act of murder in Genesis 4, that sin (*ḥaṭṭā᾿t*) comes knocking—or couching—at the door (4: 7). This may be an argument from silence, but it may speak audibly when one holds it in juxtaposition with the fact that the Adam and Eve story essentially disappears thereafter. Adam and Eve are not mentioned in Genesis 4, when sin is introduced. Nor are they mentioned again in the Hebrew Bible despite the fact that the frequent prophetic concern with sin, judgment, punishment, and banishment would provide many suitable instances in which the primeval sin could be cogently cited.

Second, the strong etiological flavor of the Eden story creates many problems for a systematic focus on the supposed cause-effect relationship between the sin and the punishment. The very fact that the serpent is held accountable along with the people diminishes the truly human theme of obedience to God's word. Similarly, the act in question, eating of a taboo food source, seems insignificant. While this may in some ways provide emphasis for the concept of disobedience itself, it can in other ways make the causality seem weak so that the etiological force dominates.

Third, if the absence of the vocabulary of sin is to be taken seriously, then the nature of the lexical emphases that are present must also be noted. In particular, the use of the verb *ʾkl*, "to eat," stands out, both by its frequency and also by the way in which it establishes structural correspondences (Walsh 1977; Trible 1978: 82–87, 128–132). Its repetition is striking and should tell us that the beginning of human existence coincides with a concern for food. In the Eden story, the first verbal message directed towards the first human explains this food source. Original human consciousness and the need to know about one's food supply are interrelated. In the anthropological language that has been introduced above, the Eden story is a strong testimony to the essential human task of subsistence, particularly in a less than ideal ecosystem. "Eating" is not simply or only a symbolic vehicle for the concept of disobedience. It is a central issue. One can sense the profound anxiety about life, about food necessary to sustain life, in the pivotal usage of *ʾkl*. What else would have been the central, daily, interminable concern of the Palestinian peasant?

A fourth reason for reconsidering the emphasis on sin as the major if not only meaning of the Eden narrative is related to this key motif of food, or subsistence, as a reflection of the life situation in ancient Israel. What genre is it that speaks to the realities, the difficulties in particular, of daily living and of accepting one's lot in life? The answer to this question appears in several recent scholarly works which have independently placed Genesis 3 within the context of wisdom literature. Almost without exception, literary critics have considered this chapter part of the J tradition of Pentateuchal literature. Yet even within the context of the Yahwistic source, it has been identified as a special and an individual type of a document, a one-of-a-kind literary unit (Wright 1960: 24–25; von Rad 1961: 98). Recently, however, its wisdom background in terms of literary motifs and structures and also its existential concern has been convincingly recognized (Lieberman 1975: 153–170; Mendenhall 1974: 320–26; Scott 1965: XXII).

In terms of format, technique (vocabulary and use of puns and *double entendres*), setting, characterizations, and even "plot," Genesis 3 follows the form of a parable or, perhaps more accurately, a "wisdom tale" (Lieberman 1975: 156–157). While it is fascinating to explore the formal and literary characteristics that place this chapter within the wisdom tradition, its thematic expression of problems of human existence is what makes it relevant to our investgation. In contradistinction to the pragmatic instructional kind of wisdom epitomized in Proverbs, the third chapter of Genesis and in particular its poetic addresses belong, like Job and Ecclesiastes and certain Psalms, to the speculative type of wisdom which deals with a questioning of the paradoxes and harsh realities of life.

As a *māšāl*, the story in Genesis 3 must be approached in terms of the real world in which it operated. The purpose of such a literary form was to address reality and help the audience accept an aspect of reality in a way that could not effectively be conveyed by more direct means (cf. Mendenhall 1974: 320). Understanding the social function of Genesis 3 as wisdom tale is thus central to interpreting its original message and focus. Unfortunately, this segment has been lifted from its literary and social context and hence has been subject to thousands of years of misinterpretation and consequently misuse. Scholarly exposition (e.g., Mendenhall 1974: 319–20) of this exploitation is justifiably irate and long overdue; from late biblical times to the present day, citation of Genesis 3, in particular verse 16, has been the authoritative glue sealing the document of divinely-ordained female subordination, if not inferiority.

Genesis 3: 16 Analyzed

The function of God's address to woman within its Genesis 3 narrative context can be removed from the domination of the sin/disobedience theme only with consideration of this passage in its social setting, in awareness of its wisdom formulation, and with openness to the possibility that an exposition of primal sin is not its only, and perhaps not even its major, function. Literary analysis has provided a major breakthrough in understanding the first half of Genesis 3 (Trible 1978: 72–105). Now sociological sensitivity must be added to the scholarly effort to recover the context and hence the meaning of this valuable portion of ancient Israel's intellectual tradition. A careful line-by-line treatment of the divine address to the woman in 3: 16 is the most effective way to present here the lexical nuances of this biblical text.

3: 16b *harĕbâ ʾarĕbeh ʿiṣṣĕbônēk wĕhērōnēk*
bĕʿeṣeb tēldî bānîm
3: 16c *wĕʾel- ʾîšēk tĕšûqâtēk*
wĕhûʾ yimĕšāl-bāk

3: 16b I will greatly increase your work and your pregnancies;
(Along) with toil you shall give birth to children.
3: 16c To your man is your desire,
And he shall predominate over you.

In the first half of the bicolon 3: 16b, the verbal form consists of an infinitive absolute along with the verb. The use of the infinitive absolute before the verb has the effect of emphasizing or strengthening the verb (GKC: 122–123, 340). The absolute certainty of the occurrence of the verbal action is thus expressed. In this case, the simple notion of quantitative "increase" in the verb alone is intensified, thus implying even greater quantity. That intensification is conveyed in English by the addition of an adverb, thus putting greater stress on the verb: "greatly increase" (multiply).

The object of this verb is twofold. Although there has been a tendency to regard the two terms as a model example of hendiadys (Speiser 1964: 24), a lexical study of the first of the terms dictates against such an interpretation (Cassuto 1961: 165). *ʿiṣṣābôn*, "work," derives from the root *ʿṣb*. Three times does a form of this root appear in Genesis 3, twice in verse 16 (in the form just mentioned and in *ʿeṣeb* in the second part of 16b) and once in verse 17b in God's address to the man (*ʿiṣṣābôn* again).

In its usage in verse 17, "work" clearly refers to the physical labor involved in the man's daily struggle to earn a livelihood. Elsewhere in the Hebrew Bible, the root is used consistently to convey this same idea of hard work and in particular the unremitting work of one's hands necessary to achieve the bare necessities in life. For example, the etymological explanation of Noah's name in Gen 5: 29 plays upon the description of man's lot in Gen 3: 17–18, conveying the difficulty in eking out a living, expressed by "what we do: the work (*ʿiṣṣĕbôn*) of our hands". Similarly another word derived from this root is used in Ps 127: 2 to link long hours of work with the procurement of the "bread of labors (*ʿăṣṣābîm*)." Thus it is not only physical work that is involved but also the notion of unabating difficulty accompanying this toil.

This terminology, however, is nowhere associated with the description of childbirth. The Bible does preserve a vocabulary (Cassuto 1961: 165) associating the birth process with pain or suffering, but none of those words is present in this passage. As a matter of fact, it would hardly be appropriate to use a word for the pain or anguish of childbirth in this first part of v 16b, even were an argument for hendiadys to be sustained, since the second object of this clause is "pregnancy" or "conception," not "birth." That is, even if pain were an appropriate description of the birth process, it is not an accurate or suitable description of pregnancy. Actually, unremitting toil would likewise be an inept way to describe either conception or gestation. Consequently, the possibility of seeing hendiadys in this instance can be eliminated.

To reiterate, the two objects of the verbal construct are independent concepts. On the one hand, the woman's productive work is mentioned and on the other hand reference is made to her procreative role. In both cases a substantial if not exponential increase is to take place. The female contribution to society is intensified as *both* the woman's contributive labor and her pregnancies are quantitatively increased. The translation offered above gives a plural in the latter case, although the Hebrew uses the singular. A collective plurality, however, is implicit in the verbal form, and a simple English plural seems to best convey that.

The second stichos of verse 16b stands in parallelism with the first half-line. As part of a poetic insertion into the narrative sequence, this verse along with others in this section of Genesis 3 exhibits many of the features associated with the metrical rhythm and internal structure of Hebrew poetry (Gray 1915: 216–17; Cassuto 1961: 72–73); the attribution of this passge to the wisdom tradition does not affect such a judgment (Eissfeldt 1965: 82–83).

Again, the root *ʿṣb* is used, this time in the form *ʿeṣeb*, as noted above. It is introduced with the particle *b*, generally "with" or "in". In this case *b* is comitative rather than instrumental. The force of the preposition is conveyed by the suggested translation "(along) with." Just as pregnancy or conception in the first stichos is presented as an entity separate from toil, the parallel member here deals with labor—again *not* the labor of the birth process but rather the labor of the subsistence realm—distinct from childbirth. "Toil" is used to translate *ʿeṣeb* rather than the more frequently used "labor" because the latter carries too much of the notion of parturition pains. The pain of labor may simultaneously be conveyed here, but not by a lexical choice that ties it specifically with childbirth.

The second portion of this member refers to the childbirth process itself, not to be identified with the event of conception or the period of gestation. The parallelism here is of the complementary rather than of the synonymous type (Freedman 1972: XXVII). Pregnancy and parturition together, along with the subsequent nurturing, constitute the reproductive function of women in society. The increase in performance of that function prescribed in the previous colon cannot be accompanied by a decrease in women's participation in the labor force, i.e., in the subsistence sphere, to use terminology suitable to the agrarian framework of early Israel. The call for a rise in the birth rate does not obviate the expansion of woman's contributive role to production tasks.

The translation of verse 16c requires fewer corrections of previous lexical notions. However the organic connection between the two parts of this line and the two separate but related concepts of the preceding line must be recognized. Both members of this bicolon are introduced by the conjunction *waw*, in what may be a somewhat unusual form of the construction normally formed with *gam . . . gam*; if this is so, the bicolon has not been properly understood. Were there a *waw* only between the two members of this verse or only before the first, then the suggested translations must be justified which understand the second half to be consequent on the first or which take the whole line to contrast with or be consequent to the line before it. The variety and combination of particles found in translations—*but, and, since, yet, for*—reflect the ambiguity sensed by the translators.

This ambiguity is perhaps dispelled by seeing in the double *waw* construction a separating of the two members of the line and a connecting of each of them to the separate concepts expressed in each of the parallel segments of the line above. In cumbersome English this arrangement would be expressed by something like "on the one hand . . . and on the other hand" or better "in the first instance . . . and in the second instance." Since such phrases would badly distort the poetic structure, simple "and" best conveys the way in which the two parts of this line are distinct and are related to the two distinct ideas of the beginning of this verse.

The first stichos of verse 16c picks up thematically on the second concept of 16b, so that there is chiastic relationship between the two lines. The use of *ʾîš* for man here is a gender-marked word, as demanded by the relational context of this member to the pregnancy and childbirth of the corresponding position of 16b. This does not necessarily limit the meaning, however, to sexuality, although that sort of sexual connotation is present in that conception and birth are clearly the desired outcome.

The use of *tĕšûqâ*, which at first glance appears to support a sexual nuance, actually broadens sexuality into a depiction of a fuller female-male relationship. This word is found twice elsewhere in the Hebrew Bible. In the Song of Songs, where the reciprocal nature of human love is the keynote (Trible 1973: 42–47 and 1978: 144–65), *tĕšûqâ* appears at the beginning (Gordis 1974: 70–71) of a song (Cant 7: 11–14) and refers to the man's "desire" for the woman. The consequence of their mutual love-attraction is not simply a sexual meeting; it is spelled out in the following verses. The man and woman rise early, first to make their way through both field (normally the male's sphere of activity) and vineyard (more likely to be associated with the female's contribution in the division of labor) to check on the crops; only then do they make love. Their desire for each other as stated at the outset of this song is fulfilled by their sharing in all agricultural tasks and also in sexual love. "Desire" therefore is an attraction which includes sexuality but is not limited to that. The use of *tĕšûqă* in Genesis 4: 7, where it can hardly mean sexual urge but rather conveys the intensity and scope of sin's attraction, reaffirms the broader aspects of "desire." The strength of the woman's feeling for the man and also the extension of those feelings to include more than the sexuality needed for reproduction are conveyed in this half-line, thus elaborating upon the reproductive imperative of the preceding line. While somewhat awkward, "to" is used, rather than the more customary "for," to translate *lĕ* before *ʾîš*; the nuance of "(directed) towards" seems more appropriate.

The last half-line to be considered here is perhaps the most difficult of all, since it has provided the locus for so many broad generalizations about the subservience of woman to man. Yet within the context of the literary structure of 3: 16 as a whole and the description of the female role as it is now understood in the foregoing analysis, many of the difficulties—which are perhaps only emotional difficulties caused by the results of misinterpretation—fall away.

The man's relationship to the woman is herein described but it is not a general statement. This half-line comments on or offers more information about the first concept of the preceding line, the increase of female responsibilities in the realm of the toil and labor of an agrarian society. Just as the woman's attraction for the man and thus her full involvement with the man allows for the success of the second (reproductive) imperative, the increase in subsistence work in the first imperative can succeed because the woman will not bear that burden alone. As a matter of fact, in absolute terms the involvement in unremitting toil, in the *ʿiṣṣābôn* with which both man (Gen 3: 17) and woman have been charged, will not be more than what the woman can handle, given the portion of her energy needed for her other role, procreation. She will not have to carry too large a share of the work load; her man's contribution in that sphere, even allowing for her increased role, will still be greater.

The use of the verb *mšl* here bears out this understanding. Unlike other words for dominion or authority used in the Bible, this root often refers to the unnatural exercise of the power or authority of one person or group over another person or group, or alternately to control attained with difficulty. Of the Davidides, *mšl* is only used of Solomon and Hezekiah, two wise men both of whom ruled territory not part of the Israelite inheritances. For Solomon, at least, this word play on Solomon's reputation as wise man and source of 3000 parables or proverbs (1 Kgs 4: 32) could not be resisted. Otherwise the divinely-ordained rule of the Davidic house or even of the northern kingdom is rarely if ever expressed by *mšl*.

In other words, whatever the particular nature of the dominion in Gen 3: 16 may be, it does not come about by inherent right. It is a conditional and sometimes a temporary authority, and it often requires considerable effort to attain in that the object of the authority resists. This aspect of *mšl*, however, in which clear rule or dominion as in the political realm is conveyed, is not the only dimension of that word. Especially in wisdom sources, it can operate in a more figurative rather than in a technical sense, in which case the nuance is one of prevailing or overcoming or taking precedence. This can be found in Gen 4: 7, in the verse in which *tĕšûqâ*, "desire," also appears, as well as in several other places specifically classified as wisdom literature (e.g., Prov 16: 32, 17: 2; Eccl 9: 17).

The rendering given above, "predominate," conveys the "dominion" notion of the Hebrew and yet preserves the relative nature of the verb, unlike words such as "rule" which tend to imply some sort of monarchic or legal control. Even more important, "predominate" circumvents to some extent the whole power/authority connotation and allows for the specific context of this verse. In terms of the labor imperative, the woman will need to increase her contribution; but given the simultaneous fact of the procreation imperative, she will not be put into a position of doing more than her mate in the subsistence sphere. She may contribute nearly as much as he does, but his share will remain larger than hers. No matter what other demands there may be on his energies, they are not equivalent to the demands of pregnancy and childbirth, and hence he must provide more of the subsistence labor than does the female.

This explication of Genesis 3: 16 has been rather extensive because it differs so fundamentally from the traditional or even more recent scholarly interpretations. Yet in each segment of this passage, the lexical analysis and poetic arrangements have mandated the translation proposed at the outset and the understanding of that translation put forth in the above discussion. It remains to set this text against the societal conditions to which it speaks and then to the larger issue of the female-male balance which is the overriding concern of this discussion.

Without entering into a detailed discussion of the address to the man in verses 17–19 of Genesis 3, a few comments about that passage and its information about the male role are in order. Enormous effort on the part of the male is depicted. Work and sweat, day in and day out, are entailed in order to produce a livelihood. The purpose of the unceasing labor is the harvest of field crops, cereals; the phrase *ʿēśeb haśśādeh*, "grains of the fields," in v 18 and the world *leḥem*, "bread," in v 19 both relate to the production of grains (Cassuto 1961: 169). If the vocabulary used to describe the male role conveys an image of constant and laborious toil, this notion is intensified in the image of the environment with which he must work. The soil is inhospitable in the extreme, suited only for thorns and thistles. It is indeed cursed, and a cursed land lacks rainfall and fertility: there will be no increase and yield when God makes the "heavens like iron" and the "earth like brass" (Lev 26: 19; cf. Deut 28: 23). Under such conditions only a greatly increased effort can provide a grain crop.

Gen 3: 16–19 addresses the situation faced by people living in the Levant and especially in the central hill country of Palestine as a territory isolated from the contiguous plains. Life under such conditions was more difficult and more fragile than in most other areas of agrarian existence in the Near East. This would have been especially true if normal concerns of daily existence were augmented with the need for performing additional subsistence tasks. The elementary questions about life and its hardships, about the endless and excessive efforts to survive—these are the human enigmas of existence to which this passage speaks. The gnawing WHY—why is life so hard for both men and women, why is there so much to be done for survival alone—is dealt with here (Davidson 1973: 43; von Rad 1961: 89).

This question is of the same order though perhaps even more fundamental than the question of Job and Ecclesiastes (Scott 1965: xx). The Bible answers this question with a parable or tale in much the way other mythographic categories respond to the human predicament in other ancient cultures (Mendenhall 1974: 327). The answer turns out to be comparable, whether in the Bible or in pagan literature: the human condition is ordained by God and must be accepted as such. Compare some Akkadian wisdom texts, such as those from Ugarit, which were evidently well-remembered and oft-repeated (Khanjian 1974: 182, 187–90): each happy day is followed by many days of scarcity and evil; such was the plan of Ea in establishing the universe. Biblical wisdom does, however, include the dimension whereby the knowledge of this God who so ordained life can, in and of itself, remove the futility and emptiness of the situation. The unending tasks will not be alleviated but the possibility for happiness within that context exists when God's sovereignty is accepted. Although Genesis 3 itself does not deal directly with this, the two wisdom psalms (127 and 128) related to Genesis 3 make this ideological dimension explicit (see Dahood 1970: 224–27).

Because the actual Genesis description of the human condition does not present the positive possibilities involved in God's imperative, it has been repeatedly given an inherent connection with the disobedience of the primordial couple in the first part of the chapter. Yet there is a strong case to be made for the discreteness of the poetic section in verses 14–19. It does indeed, on literary criteria alone, stand separate from the first half of the chapter. While it continues the characters and the setting of the Edenic scene, at the very least it is an Act Two of the full drama (cf. Trible 1978: 123). The pronouncements themselves have an independent etiological force (Bailey 1970: 149) that has been recognized even by those who adhere to the notion of a single framework for the entire chapter (Westermann 1974: 98; von Rad 1961: 89). The prose framework contains its own punishment, expulsion from the Garden, in verses 20–24. Thus God's poetic pronouncements, involving a curse for serpents and soil and an establishment of life roles for man and woman, are separate from the Edenic acts and are penalties only in terms of their etiological inclusion in the prose framework (cf. Naidoff 1978: 10).

Further, it may be that the only section of the poetic address that has not yet been considered here may contain an indirect presentation of the wisdom response in which human wisdom, beginning with the acknowledgment of God's control, provides the positive dimension to the human struggle for survival. The serpent in verses 14–15 is deprived of its power. As a symbol of wisdom and/or fertility common in ancient Near Eastern cultures and persisting in the Israelite world (Hvidberg 1960: 207–80; Joines 1974), its status is completely reversed in the divine curse. Its previously superior position, crafty and able to speak and to influence, has been transformed into that of the lowliest and most despised creature. Implied in the reversal of the serpent's status is a total eclipse of its powers. The serpent is no longer a mediator or representative of wisdom. The powers it exhibited are now confined to the God-human continuum and are solely in the realm of human existence. If this is so, then wisdom is securely within the grasp of mankind and thus it becomes possible to give meaning to life's exigencies.

Genesis 3: 16 and Earliest Israel

In general, then, the societal conditions to which Genesis 3: 14–19 speaks are those which demand maximum output on the part of both men and women. The question as to whether this situation can be directly related to the earliest period of Israelite corporate existence described above cannot be evaded. Removing the Genesis 3 passage considered here from its supposed Yahwist context reopens the question of its original emergence into Israelite literary tradition. The matter of its specific date in the literary form in which it now appears probably cannot be resolved without further linguistic and poetic studies of the entire passage.

It can be argued that the life situation which evoked the Genesis 3 response was the situation which prevailed in Israel during the Iron I period. The settlement of Palestinian hill country was a one-time event demanding an output of human energy that would have represented a significant increase over levels of male and female endeavor in preceding periods, whether among the serfs of the Canaanite city states or the pastoralists of the steppes or the Semitic survivors of Egyptian imperialism (the Moses or Exodus group). With the recognition that this passage speaks directly to that situation, calling for a multiplication of the female's contribution in the areas of subsistence and child-bearing and for an unremitting dedication on the part of the male to the hardships of cereal agriculture, a pre-monarchic setting appears likely indeed. This is not to say that existence was not always difficult and that the "whys" to which wisdom responded did not arise at other critical moments (Mendenhall 1974: 327–30). Rather, the early Iron Age stands out as the period in which the historical and environmental features provide the most suitable background for the blunt and inescapable imperative concerning the use of human energy that Gen 3: 16–19 contains. In the pioneer period of Israelite history, the demands for participation in basic societal tasks were critical in a way which perhaps was never quite duplicated. Never again would the need for a powerful and direct religious sanction of "work ethic" for both males and females and also a high fertility rate be so strong.

In terms of thematic content and also, to a lesser extent, in terms of language, the relationship of Genesis 3 to several poetic passages may lend support to an early context for the Genesis 3 poetic addresses. Psalm 127 as well as its companion piece Psalm 128 (Dahood 1970: 227), as has been pointed out, are Wisdom psalms which together portray acknowledgment of God as the way for humanity to derive fulfillment from its constant toil. The three areas of human activity each appear—reproduction, subsistence, and defense—and the persistence in carrying out each in the knowledge of God removes the futility from the struggle involved. The language of these psalms has an archaic quality and also a syntactic and lexical connection with Ugaritic texts that suggest they belong to the Davidic stage of Israelite psalmody (cf. Dahood 1965: xxx).

Similarly, the Song of Hannah (1 Sam 2: 1–10) conveys the message of Yahweh's unlimited authority and wisdom in human affairs, regardless of what empirical observation may suggest, i.e., difficulties of life do not gainsay God's power or dominion. God's involvement with and interest in the struggles of human existence are portrayed in a series of reversals dealing with God's unexpected assistance in each of the three basic activities of human society: the battle is won, the barren conceive many, the impoverished receive bread. Thematically this song deals with the same questions as Genesis 3. It dates as a whole from the early monarchy; and precisely at the point where the reversals proclaim God's supreme wisdom and power in human affairs (vv 4–5), it depends on the language of Psalm 113, which can be dated to the twelfth century (Freedman 1978: 65*–66*).

Thus the life situation of the pre-monarchic period and thematic and linguistic connections with certain early poems present converging lines of evidence testifying to the connection of Genesis 3: 14–19 with the early experience of Israel. Israel at its outset—and whether one dates Genesis 3 to within that period or not does not affect this conclusion—undertook a way of life which demanded the cooperation and participation of all members of society. Genesis 3 portrays this situation whether or not its final literary formulation derives from that moment. The life situation required a shift of energies such that women increased their procreative role and also made large contributions to the subsistence sphere.

Clearly the second conclusion reached above, regarding an intensification in the use of human energy in all areas of basic societal need, has been illuminated by this analysis of Genesis 3. That the female share in the division of labor nearly balances that of the male is indicated by the assurance that she will not in fact be on a par with him in her cultural as opposed to her natural contributions. His role in the non-domestic life activities is to be greater. Therefore, while a pair of individuals appears in which each member is working to ultimate capacity, the male share in the critical subsistence sphere is presented as larger.

This fits the conceptual model of a near-equal division of labor. It also reflects part of the complex configuration of factors which ultimately leads to the lesser valuation placed on female modalities, a goodly portion of which are natural or biological (having to do with child bearing) as opposed to the fully cultural and thus creative and potentially transcendent functions of males in society (Ortner 1974). The greater valuation given males in the cultic and legal portions of the Pentateuch derives to some extent from this formulation. Yet the basic pattern here of increased female participation in food-producing tasks would nonetheless have created a relative increase in female status and power, as we have pointed out above. Genesis 3 presents only the cause of such increase, not the effects; the latter must be sought in other texts.

The specific types of contributions of male and female, i.e., the gender roles, to societal survival, in early Israel, are partially reflected in Genesis 3. Pregnancies along with unspecified kinds of physical toil comprise the woman's portion. The social scientific perspectives we have presented, however, can provide specificity: horticultural and viticultural tasks would have been included in the spectrum of a woman's tasks. The man's labor is clearly specified in the reiteration of the unending efforts he must make so that the cursed earth will bring forth bread. The difficult but essential tasks of using plow agriculture for growing grain in the uplands is the man's lot.

While these basic conclusions can be reached concerning gender roles in earliest Israel, they represent only a broad, or rather a basic, kind of outline. One would hope to be able to take them further, to provide more nuanced delineations of male and female roles, responsibilities, and interactions. For example, the relationship of man and woman to children, i.e., their relative parenting roles, should be pursued in a full study of gender roles. Similarly, the distinctions made between male and female with respect to behavior in the public domain must be examined. While such other aspects of sexual dimorphism need to be addressed, they remain secondary to the roles of male and female in the basic life activities. That is, the issues we have considered here will perhaps lay the groundwork for a more comprehensive treatment of sex roles in earliest Israel and also in subsequent periods of Israelite existence.

Notes

1. This article is offered to David Noel Freedman in deep gratitude for his encouragement of the author's work in this area and in humble indebtedness to his scholarship in his many areas of expertise.

2. An excellent resource for the social scientific study of gender roles is the anthology *Women, Culture, and Society*, edited by M. Z. Rosaldo and L. Lamphere (1974). In that volume, contributions by M. Z. Rosaldo, M. Z. Rosaldo and L. Lamphere, S. B. Ortner, and P. R. Sanday are particularly relevant to the concepts presented in this paper. In addition, Hamburg (1974), which is published in the useful anthology Freidl (1975), and Nerlove (1974) have been helpful to our understanding of social scientific information that can be used in examining gender roles in biblical Israel.

References

Bailey, J. A.
1970 Initiation and the Primal Woman in Gilgamesh and Genesis 2–3. *Journal of Biblical Literature* 89: 137–50.

Brown, J.
1970 A Note on the Division of Labor. *American Anthropologist* 72: 1073–78.

Cassuto, U.
1961 *A Commentary on the Book of Genesis. Part I, From Adam to Noah.* Jerusalem: Magnes Press.

Conkey, M., and Spector, J.
forthcoming Archaeology and the Study of Gender. *Advances in Archaeological Method and Theory* VI.

Dahood, M.
1966 *Psalms I* (1–50). Anchor Bible 16. New York: Doubleday.
1970 *Psalms III* (101–150). Anchor Bible 17A. New York: Doubleday.

Davidson, R.
1973 *Genesis 1–11*. N. E. B. Commentary. Cambridge: University Press.

Eissfeldt, O.
1965 *The Old Testament*, trans. P. R. Ackroyd. New York: Harper & Row.

Freedman, D. N.
1972 Prolegomenon to G. B. Gray's *The Forms of Hebrew Poetry*. New York: KTAV.
1978 Psalm 113 and The Song of Hannah. *Eretz Israel* 14: 56*–69*.

Freidl, E.
1975 *Women & Men: An Anthropologist's View*. New York: Rinehart & Winston.

Frymer-Kensky, T.
1977 The Atrahasis Epic and Its Significance for Our Understanding of Genesis 1–9. *Biblical Archeologist* 40: 147–55.

Gordis, R.
1974 *The Song of Songs and Lamentations*. New York: KTAV.

Gottwald, N. K.
1979 *Tribes of Yahweh*. Maryknoll, New York: Orbis.

Gottwald, N. K., and Frick, F. S.
1976 The Social World of Ancient Israel. Pp. 110–19 in *The Bible and Liberation*, coord. by N. K. Gottwald and A. C. Wise. Berkeley: Community for Religious Research and Education.

Gray, G. B.
1915 *The Forms of Hebrew Poetry*. London: Hodder and Stoughton.

Hamburg, B. A.
1974 The Psychobiology of Sex Differences: An Evolutionary Perspective. Pp. 373–390 in *Sex Differences in Behavior*, ed. R. C. Friedman *et al.* New York: Wiley.

Hanson, R. S.
1972 *The Serpent Was Wiser.* Minneapolis: Augsburg Publishing House.

Hauser, A. J.
1978 Israel's Conquest of Palestine: A Peasant's Rebellion? *Journal for the Study of the Old Testament* 7: 2–19.

Hvidberg, F.
1960 The Canaanite Background of Genesis I-III. *Vetus Testamentum* 10: 285–294.

Joines, K. R.
1974 *Serpent Symbolism in the Old Testament.* Haddenfield, N. J.: Haddenfield Press.

Khanjian, J.
1974 *Wisdom in Ugarit and in the Ancient Near East with Particular Emphasis on Old Testament Wisdom Literature.* Claremont Dissertation.

Kilmer, A.
1972 The Mespotamian Concept of Overpopulation and Its Solution as Represented in the Mythology. *Orientalia* 41: 160–77.

Lieberman, S. R.
1975 *The Eve Motif in Ancient Near Eastern and Classical Greek Sources.* Boston University Dissertation.

Mead, M.
1953 *Male and Female.* New York: Morrow.

Mendenhall, G. E.
1974 The Shady Side of Wisdom: The Date and Purpose of Genesis 3. Pp. 319–334 in *Light Unto My Path* (Myers Festschrift), ed. H. N. Bream, R. D. Heim, C. A. Moore. Philadelphia: Temple University Press.

1976 Social Organization in Early Israel. Pp. 132–51 in *Magnalia Dei*, ed. F. M. Cross, W. E. Lemke, P. D. Miller, Jr. New York: Doubleday.

Meyers, C.
1978 Roots of Restriction: Women in Early Israel. *Biblical Archeologist* 41: 91–103.

forthcoming Procreation, Production, and Protection: Male-Female Balance in Early Israel. *Journal of the American Academy of Religion..*

Naidoff, B. D.
1978 A Man to Work the Soil: A New Interpretation of Genesis 2–3. *Journal for the Study of the Old Testament* 5 (1978): 2–14.

Nerlove, S.
1974 Women's Workload and Infant Feeding Practices: A Relationship with Demographic Implications. *Ethnology* 13: 207–214.

Ortner, S. B.
1974 Is Male to Female as Nature is to Culture? Pp. 67–80 in *Women, Culture, and Society*, ed. M. Z. Rosaldo and L. Lamphere. Stanford: Stanford University Press.

Quinn, N.
1977 Anthropological Studies on Women's Status. *Annual Review of Anthropology* 6: 181–225.

von Rad, G.
1961 *Genesis*, trans. John H. Marks. Philadelphia: Westminster Press. (German edition 1956).

Rosaldo, M. Z.

1974 Women, Culture, and Society: A Theoretical Overview. Pp. 17–42 in *Women, Culture, and Society*, ed. M. Z. Rosaldo and L. Lamphere. Stanford: Stanford University Press.

Rosaldo, M. Z., and Lamphere, L.
1974 Introduction. Pp. 1–16 in *Women, Culture, and Society*, ed. M. Z. Rosaldo and L. Lamphere. Stanford: Stanford University Press.

Sanday, P. R.
1974 Female Status in the Public Domain. Pp. 189–206 in *Women, Culture, and Society*, ed. M. Z. Rosaldo and L. Lamphere. Stanford: Stanford University Press.

Scott, R. B. Y.
1965 *Proverbs/Ecclesiastes*. Anchor Bible 18. New York: Doubleday.

Speiser, E. A.
1964 *Genesis*. Anchor Bible 1. New York: Doubleday.

Trible, P.
1973 Depatriarchalizing in Biblical Interpretation. *Journal of the American Academy of Religion* 41: 30–48.

1978 *God and the Rhetoric of Sexuality*. Philadelphia: Fortress Press.

Walsh, J. T.
1977 Genesis 2: 46–3: 24: A Synchronic Approach. *Journal of Biblical Literature* 96: 161–77.

Westermann, C.
1974 *Creation*, trans. J. Scullion. Philadelphia: Fortress Press.

Wright, G. E.
1960 The Nature of Man: An Exposition of Genesis 3. Pp. 21–34 in *The Rule of God*. New York: Doubleday.

Priestly Divination in Israel

Herbert B. Huffmon
Drew University, Madison, New Jersey

Priestly divination in Israel represents a simple, unsophisticated type of technical divination. It does not involve the techniques of the elaborate, learned divination so familiar from Mesopotamia nor the utilization of numerous archetypal symbols or patterns familiar from Yoruba or Ndembu divination. Israel's official divination involves the simple technique of designated lots. Although the lots are drawn or cast, as far as the evidence goes, by priests or comparable persons, the biblical texts provide no information about the conditions of purity or place that presumably were prerequisite for successful divination. The texts do inform us about the occasions for divination, the results, and, to some extent, the procedure. The texts do not provide any overall interpretation of the meaning and function of divination.

Various studies by social anthropologists who have had opportunity to observe closely the role and character of divination as practiced among various contemporary societies can be helpful in interpreting the nature and function of priestly divination. Here we may draw particularly on the analyses of Yoruba (Bascom 1969; Gleason 1973), Bunyoro (Beattie 1964), and Ndembu divination (V. Turner 1975), as well as theoretical interpretations by scholars such as George K. Park (1963). A fundamental conclusion from these closely observed practices is that the divination procedures do not typically give solutions to problems on a random or chance basis—i.e., like merely flipping a coin—even though the *apparent* random character of divination is important to the community's perception of the process as unbiased or, indeed, as divine in origin. Commonly the situation really allows only one answer, and the role of divination is to declare that answer and, in the process, provide both reassurance to the client and public (divine) legitimation of the plan of action proposed. Since only questions of importance are presented for such divination, the procedure serves to allow the integration of important and even dangerous actions into a traditional religious system.

Priestly divination in Israel appears to reflect a similar purpose. The answers supplied are the admittedly appropriate answers, representing manipulation of the results at some level. An interesting parallel is provided by Greek divination, for which Amandry (1966: 173) notes that apart from the advice given Nicias, which went contrary to the advice of the generals and led to the Athenian disaster in Sicily, there is no well-attested example of a diviner's advice going contrary to the intentions of a political or military chief.

For illustration of the issues involved in the typical priestly divination by means of the Urim and Thummim lots, the most illuminating text is 1 Sam 14: 23–46, preserved in its full form only in the LXX *Vorlage*.[1] In the course of a prolonged and extensive battle with the Philistines, Saul put the people under oath not to eat that day. But his son, Jonathan, was unaware of the oath and, coming across some honey, ate and felt energized. The people saw Jonathan eating, and one of them spoke up and informed him of the ban. Jonathan responded that the ban was unwise; it limited the effectiveness of the army.

In spite of Jonathan's violation of the ban, Israel did have success against the Philistines, so much so that Saul wanted to continue the pursuit of the Philistines during the night as well. He proposed such pursuit to the army, and they replied as one was supposed to respond to a request by the king, "Do whatever seems good to you." However, the problem of the violation of the oath remained, and even if the army spokesmen were unwilling to inform the king of the violation of what they also perhaps regarded as an unwise ban, the priest could not let it pass. So the priest said, "Let us consult God." Accordingly, Saul, by means of priestly divination, asked, "Shall I go down after the Philistines? Will you give them into Israel's power?" That is, Saul posed a binary question, to be answered yes or no; presumably one of the Urim and Thummim lots would be designated "Yes," the other "No." But there was no answer that day. In the context no answer was possible, because the relationship between God and the people had been disturbed by the violation—a public violation—of the oath. To judge from parallel situations elsewhere, the failure to answer was probably indicated either when a confirming question was put and the two answers disagreed or when the priest stopped the consultation on some unspecified ground, though there are other possibilities. The outcome of the failed process is that the priest thereby discreetly informed Saul of the violation of the ban.

Saul now understood that something was wrong and undertook to discover the source of the breakdown. His suspicions led him first to set up a choice between himself and Jonathan, on the one side, and the army officers on the other side; Urim was designated for one side, Thummim for the other. But in spite of the reminder about the death–demanding oath, no one was willing to speak up except to say the conventional, "Do whatever seems good to you." Divination would have to reveal the hidden matter. So Jonathan and Saul were chosen by lot and the choice had to be between them. (At this point the people finally intervened to try to stop the process, but Saul insisted on carrying out the full procedure.) The second lot specified Jonathan, and there was no longer any doubt as to what had gone wrong. Saul now understood fully and drew forth the details from Jonathan. Divination had provided a means for telling Saul indirectly what the people were unwilling to say directly.

In this procedure the outcome of the divination had to be Jonathan, as perhaps everyone but Saul knew. It is publicly seen as a discovery or uncovering of the truth by resort to divinely directed divination, but actually the outcome was controlled by the priest, responding to public opinion. It is like the occasion when the Greeks at Troy were selecting by lot one of nine warriors to fight Hector. They agreed among themselves that the best choice would be Aias, though two others are mentioned. To no one's surprise, when Nestor cast the lots, Aias' lot leapt forth (*Iliad* 7. 161–83).

As a further illustration of the point that the situation normally dictates the divinatory answer, note Judges 20, which tells of the Israel's response to the frightful outrage at Gibeah of Benjamin, with the violation of the Levite's concubine and his invoking of the covenant curses by sending the cut-up body of his concubine throughout the territory of Israel. Benjamin supported the people of its city, Gibeah, and Israel assembled at Bethel for warfare. There they sought God's guidance. Presumably they inquired as to the battle generally, but the only question preserved in the tradition is, "Who shall go up first to fight with Benjamin?" The priests, who must have assisted in the consultation—perhaps with lots having the various tribes named—are not specifically mentioned at this point. Instead, the text merely states, "God said, 'Judah first.'" That Judah was chosen must have seemed right to everyone; not only was Judah preeminent among the tribes (cf. Judg 1: 1–2), but the concubine was from Bethlehem of Judah. Could a different tribe have been chosen?

In the continuation of the divinatory questioning that followed upon the stiff resistance Israel encountered from Benjamin, the issue was, "Shall I continue to do battle with my brother, Benjamin?" God replied, "Go up against him." Was there any alternative? And when Israel again suffered heavily and retreated to Bethel to weep and to inquire of the Lord, the Lord said, "Go up, for tomorrow I will give him into your power." Could Israel have stopped before Benjamin had been defeated for its support of the outrage of Gibeah? The purpose of the oracles was to offer reassurance, to give divine legitimation of the obvious choice, and to incorporate a dangerous and unpleasant task into the religious schema.

Consider further the process of selecting Saul as king (1 Sam 10: 17–24). The people being assembled in the Lord's presence at Mizpah, the tribes are presented to God, presumably for priestly divination by Urim and Thummim or designated lot. The sorting proceeds through the tribes to Benjamin, then to the clan of the Matrites, to the house of Qish—a prominent family—and specifically to Saul, son of Qish, a man already known for his commanding height and appearance (1 Sam 9: 2; 10: 23). That Saul was not immediately at hand indicates that the sorting did not require physical presence and that written lots may have been used. Saul's absence led to further questioning of the Lord: "Is he here?" Presumably other questions—not specified—followed, until the divination indicated that Saul was concealed among the baggage,[2] thereby offering a kind of confirmation of the earlier choice. This procedure of uncovering by lot what the people recognized as an appropriate choice included divine determination throughout the process and incorporated the traditional reluctance of the person selected. The appearance of randomness is a means of affirming divine choice.

The case of the selection of Achan as the one who violated the ban (Joshua 7) provides an interesting parallel to witchcraft accusations in which a diviner is the medium for the expression of the community sense as to the suspected violator. The diviner senses from the people assembled for the occasion, usually by means of careful questioning, the identity of the chief suspect and lets that judgment express itself through the divination results. The discovery can then be attributed to divine guidance (Wilson 1973: 80; Park 1963: 236, 238).

Many other texts could be discussed. As a summary of the features of priestly divination in Israel, note the following points.

1) Priestly divination is normally passive, responding to a request from others. Only on rare occasions would a priest take the initiative to suggest divination, as in 1 Sam 14: 36–37.

2) The answer is by a prearranged code, using written lots or designating Urim and Thummim for binary questions. Although the lots are identified as Urim and Thummim only in connection with binary divination, the plural forms may refer to using the lots in cases of sorting larger groups, with the possibility, for example, that eleven lots might be Urim and one lot Thummim. Written lots may have been used in instances such as the choice of a city for David's new center (2 Sam 2: 1).

3) There are instances when the divine choice could appropriately be indicated at random, as in the designation of the two different goats on the Day of Atonement (Lev 16: 8ff), apparently the only occasion for priestly divination that survived the early monarchy. Normally, though, the choice was dictated by the circumstances. The answer was controlled by priestly manipulation of the lots, unseen by the people. The role of divination was to provide the correct answer without any obvious bias, so as to involve clearly divine sanction for the choice and to do so publicly. To judge by parallels in contemporary cultures, the diviner may well be quite unconscious of controlling the outcome and may even insist that the answer is fully independent (V. Turner 1967: 361, 366–67, 372–73). Somehow the answer turns out to be the proper one, the one that reflects the leader's viewpoint or the consensus of the community.[3]

4) The failure of the divination process to yield an answer is due to a situation that is not yet ready for an answer because of prior interference with communication (1 Sam 14: 37) or a situation that does not allow an answer acceptable to the consulter, as in the case of Saul's search for reassurance on the eve of virtually certain defeat by the Philistines (1 Sam 28: 6). The technique for no answer is not indicated, but one can speculate about various possibilities (see above).

5) From a form-critical perspective, many of the consultations follow a clear form, with the binary question put to the deity and the answer coming as a positive restatement of the question. A typical example of the form is 1 Sam 23: 2, "David asked the Lord, 'Shall I go and attack these Philistines?' The Lord said (to David), 'Go and attack (these) Philistines and rescue Keilah.'" However, the consultation reports often give an abbreviated account; the question may not be explicitly stated and the answer may merely be introduced with "God said" (note Judg 20: 18; 1 Sam 23: 2, 4, 11, 12; 2 Sam 5: 23–24 // 1 Chr 14: 14–15; etc., for variations).

6) Priestly divination in Israel, using an apparently unbiased procedure, provides divine reassurance, gives public divine legitimation to the option selected, and allows the integration of anomalous, dangerous ventures into the traditional religious schema.

Notes

1. The passage is textually and redactionally complex. For an excellent recent discussion of the problems, especially concerning the text, see McCarter 1980: 243–48, and the literature there cited.

2. Lindblom, 1962: 165 n.l, argues that "the answer . . . cannot have been given by lot-casting. Here a seer or a cult prophet is speaking," referring to the first *ʿôd* in v 22. But on the text see now McCarter 1980: 190. The form, even in the MT, is easily paralleled by priestly divination texts; see 2 Sam 2: 1 in particular and note the recurring "the Lord said" (e.g., Judg 20: 23, 28; 1 Sam 23: 2, 11, 12).

3. Note that in 1 Kings 22 (// 2 Chronicles 18) the question is put to Zedekiah and the 400 prophets in the same style as that of priestly divination, and the desired answer is similarly declared. The introduction into the process of the prophet Micaiah, who knows the divine secrets and who gives a contrary answer, shows the danger of putting important questions to unprogrammed specialists. One result of this danger was the increased reluctance to pose such questions. The answer was no longer safe.

References

Amandry, P.
1966 La divination en Grèce: État actuel de quelques problèmes. Pp. 171–78 in *La divination en Mésopotamie ancienne et dans les régions voisines.* Rencontre assyriologique internationale XIV. Paris: Presses universitaires de France.

Bascom, W.
1969 *Ifa Divination.* Bloomington: Indiana University Press.

Beattie, J.
1964 Divination in Bunyoro, Uganda. *Sociologus* 14/1: 44–61. Reprinted as pp. 211–31 in *Magic, Witchcraft, and Curing,* ed. J. Middleton. Garden City: Natural History Press, 1967.

Gleason, J., with Aworinde, A., and Ogundipe, J. O.
1973 *A Recitation of Ifa, Oracle of the Yoruba.* New York: Grossman.

Lindblom, J.
1962 Lot-casting in the Old Testament. *Vetus Testamentum* 12: 164–78.

McCarter, P. K., Jr.
1980 *I Samuel.* Anchor Bible 8. Garden City: Doubleday.

Park, G. K.
1963 Divination and Its Social Contexts. *Journal of the Royal Anthropological Institute* 93/2: 159–209. Reprinted as pp. 233–54 in *Magic, Witchcraft, and Curing,* ed J. Middleton. Garden City: Natural History Press, 1967.

Turner, V.
1967 *The Forest of Symbols: Aspects of Ndembu Ritual.* Ithaca: Cornell University Press.

1975 *Revelation and Divination in Ndembu Ritual.* Ithaca: Cornell University Press. Reprint of two studies that originally appeared as Rhodes-Livingstone Papers Nos. 31 and 33 (1961, 1962).

Wilson, B. R.
1973 *Magic and the Millennium.* New York: Harper & Row.

Social Transformation and Ritual in 2 Samuel 6

James W. Flanagan
University of Montana, Missoula, Montana

> It is of the first importance to realize clearly from the outset that ritual and practical usage were, strictly speaking, the sum-total of ancient religions.
> —William Robertson Smith
> *Lectures on the Religion of the Semites*

The ancient literary records depicting Iron Age I Israel describe a society in the throes of social, political, economic, and religious transformation. The segmental tribal organization of the Yahwistic community was rapidly giving way to centralized territorial governance. The northern leadership of the house of Saul was being displaced by the southern Judahite family of Jesse and house of David. And competition for trade, agriculturally productive land, and natural resources was causing increased hostility between the Yahwists and their neighbors.[1]

The purpose of this essay is to describe the turbulence and uncertainty that characterized the transitional period connecting Saul's with David's reign and to demonstrate that the ritual transfer of the ark of the covenant to Jerusalem constituted a rite of passage which mediated and legitimated the temporal, spatial, and social transformations occurring at that time, especially the shift in power whereby the house of Saul grew weaker and the house of David stronger (2 Sam 3: 1).

In the narrative of the Books of Samuel, the immediate setting for the report of the ark's transfer is 2 Sam 5: 13–8: 18, now a single literary unit woven together by content and structure from originally separate sources. The section includes (a) a list of the children born to David in Jerusalem (5: 13–16); (b) accounts of the Philistine wars (5: 17–25); (c) a description of the transfer of the ark (6: 1–20a) and of Michal's objection to David's behavior (6: 16, 20b–23); (d) the dynastic oracle of Nathan with David's response (7: 1–29); (e) reports of a series of battles with peoples who were subdued in order to form the Davidic empire (8: 1–14); and (f) a list of David's court officers (8: 15–18), which concludes both chap. 8 and the unit.

Several literary devices have been used by the compilers to join the episodes in a continuous narrative. First was the artificial, contracted and telescoped, consecutive order that has been imposed upon events (Flanagan 1979: 238; Mazar 1963: 239). A chronological sequence has been created which makes David's tasks during his early days in Jerusalem appear orderly and progressive: first, fighting the Philistines, then relocating the ark, and then planning a temple (but having to be satisfied with a promise of dynasty!), and finally conquering enemies all around. As a result, David is portrayed as having moved swiftly, decisively, and systematically to secure Jerusalem's preeminence.

The compilers' second device was to arrange David's actions in stages which portray the process of displacement as one of ascending dominance. Not only did events unfold along the horizontal plane of time, but they also evolved vertically in step by step fashion so that David's hold on the affairs of administration seems to have increased steadily and at the expense of those he formerly served. David's cause was advanced and he rose, but his enemies were subdued and, more importantly perhaps, Saul's house was displaced, giving David dominance over his foes, who were internal as well as external to the Yahwistic community. The compilers linked the enemies with Saul in terms of common opposition to David, so that the long struggle between the two houses (2 Sam 3: 1) emerged as an obstacle to the Davidic dynasty just as the hostility of Israel's enemies. As we shall see, Michal's barrenness assured that no eligible male heirs could be born to Saul's family through her, so that the way was open for David to establish his own dynasty. But we must postpone discussion of Michal's role until after the binary oppositions within 2 Sam 5: 13–8: 18 have been examined.[2]

The compilers' skill in weaving the horizontal and vertical transitions into a single fabric has not erased the inconsistencies within the narrative (e.g., compare 7: 1 with 8: 1–14 and 5: 17–25 with 8: 1). The irregularities are due in part to a successor/supplanter theme that the scribes had to contend with. David was a relative by marriage and an accomplice of Saul, but he was also one of his strongest, most detested opponents.

The compilers played upon this paradox in structuring the narrative so that events and personalities were transformed and inverted as the story progressed. Former circumstances were set opposite and were balanced by others, displacing or transforming them. Three sets of such parallels are immediately apparent. First, a list of David's children has been balanced by a list of court officers. Together these bracket the entire section 5: 13–8: 18 and indicate the socio-political change which had taken place in between. Second, the battles against the Philistines have been set over against battles with enemies (including the Philistines again) who formed the empire. And finally, the ark, the symbol of the old tribal confederation headed by Saul, has been balanced by the oracle establishing the Jerusalemite, Davidic dynasty.

The contrasts within each pair occur on several planes of classification simultaneously so that the opposition between old and new, tribal and monarchical, Saulide and Davidide coincide to form poles in the same fundamental opposition (see V. Turner 1977c: 41). This is a complex set of values and feelings which had separated Saul and David and was now at stake in the choice of Israel's leader. In the case of the lists, however, the tension was not so much between Saulide and Davidide as between conflicting values and administrative manners, which after all were at the base of Israel's concerns. As in other tribal societies, inheritance and succession depended greatly upon kinship and were measured and controlled by genealogies. In centralized, stratified communities these play a lesser role (Goody 1966: 43; 1970: 637). Of the several lists of David's family recorded in the Books of Samuel, the one in chap. 5 is the last. It has been placed at the beginning of David's Jerusalem years, where the number of children credited to him since the move from Hebron seems excessive for the time allowed. Its position, therefore, was artificial and intentional. In addition, the omission of mothers' names from the list where they had been included in earlier lists indicates that factors other than the order of birth had already begun to influence inheritance and succession. Since wives in polygamous marriages are often ranked as a way of determining sons' priority (Goody 1966: 32), the absence of mothers here reveals that the sons' administrative skills and personal traits had already come into play in David's administration. This contrasts with the situation in the North where the weak and incompetent Ishbosheth had succeeded solely on the basis of primogeniture. Solomon's succession at the end of David's reign, however, demonstrates that the son of a favorite wife still enjoyed an advantage.

The officers' names at the close of the section indicate that the importance of kinship had declined during the Jerusalem years and was becoming restricted to the upper echelons of David's administration. By the time of this list, specializations had been institutionalized in offices which could be filled, by kin or non-kin, according to an individual's talent (see Goody 1966: 43). Therefore, a list of sons gave way to a list of officers as the compilers explained the political transitions which had occurred.

In the second contrast, the Philistines, who had been the principal opponents of Saul, have been set opposite all Israel's enemies in Palestine, Syria, and Transjordan, the peoples who were subdued to form the empire. As usual, the Philistines played a paradoxical role. In the social drama that brought David to power, they always opposed Saul, but were at different times David's refuge, the benefactors of his raids, his suzerains, and his enemies. When they seized the ark, they forced Israel to unite under Saul, and a battle between them and Israel had brought David to Saul's attention. But they had also been responsible for the deaths of Saul and three of his sons. Thus, David's victories over them reported in chap. 5 ended the paradox and distinguished him from Saul. Where Saul had failed, David succeeded.

Israel was released from subservience by the events described in 2 Sam 5: 13–8: 18. Under David's leadership, the Yahwists moved from defense to offense, trading status as beleaguered prey for that of empire founders. The Yahwists' subjugation of enemies in chap. 8 paralleled the wars in chap. 5 so that narrative poles were again established. Continuity was attested by the fact that the earlier successes paved the way for the later ones, but discontinuity was also stressed by using the latter state to reverse the former. Within a short time after David's move to Jerusalem, the Philistine dominance had been overcome, so that in the compilers' view, David had moved history forward, leaving the Philistine age behind (Flanagan 1979: 235), while he simultaneously inverted the territory's pattern of relationships, including those within Israel as well as the ones outside.

Before taking up the third set of parallels associated with the ark and the oracle, we must consider the circumstances that led David to decide upon transferring the ark. His move from Hebron to Jerusalem took place within a matrix of events and shifts in power that accompanied his rise to leadership (Flanagan 1979: 239). The relocating included not only the obvious geographical, religious, and political transitions, but also the transferring of the capital from an orthogenetic center which housed Yahwists to a heterogenetic city which, because it harbored no previous Yahwistic traditions, brought these into conflict with foreign and pagan elements (Flanagan 1979: 225, 239). This meant moving it to an environment that was threatening to the isolation and integrity of the Yahwists' traditional cultural values (compare Redfield and Singer 1954/55: 58). The transition toward centralized, supra- and extra-tribal administration signaled class and social distinctions which would inevitably bestow economic and political advantage upon a core of elite specialists. Such innovations were looked upon with disfavor by the conservative, egalitarian-minded Yahwists who were justly suspicious of paganizing tendencies. David's moves, therefore, brought to a head the critical issue of Israelite social structure and leadership which had not been addressed while he ruled from Yahwistic Hebron.

For David, or at least for the biblical scribes who were writing for a Yahwistic audience, the most problematic aspect of his struggle was his desire to displace Saul's family as the ruling house in Israel. We would expect this to be the case in tribal society where rivalry and intrigue constitute the daily routine for those who lead or seek to do so. The rebellions first of Absalom and then of Sheba a few years later stand as evidence that David's problems were not drastically different from those in other societies (Flanagan 1981). Social scientists have in fact singled out legitimacy as the primary, indispensable stabilizer for new authority structures and have noted that the need to legitimate is especially pressing when the new structures do not rest easily upon traditional values (Eisenstadt 1963: 19). Weber, for example, argued that without legitimacy a ruler or government could not manage conflicts or sustain stability (Weber 1947: 124–26). Fried identified legitimacy as "the means by which ideology is blended with power" and went on to describe its functions as explaining and justifying the existence of concentrated social power (Fried 1967: 26). Stable support for such a concentration derives from community members' conviction that they are correct in obeying the authorities and in abiding by the requirements of the regime (Easton 1965: 278; Richards 1969: 24). Hudson (1977: 2) summarized the importance of legitimacy by noting, "It is the extent to which leadership and regimes are perceived by elites and masses as congruent and compatible with the society's fundamental myths . . . that hold[s] society together." Therefore, it is not surprising that David, like other innovative leaders in history, would have to demonstrate the legitimacy of his regime and make his case in terms that were either enforceable or acceptable to the dominant factions within his empire.

The death of the incumbent Saul no doubt rendered David's task somewhat easier, as did the incompetence of Saul's son and successor, Ishbosheth. Still, the air of uncertainty and opportunism that pervaded the atmosphere did not assure David's triumph. He could expect potential heirs and successors to vie relentlessly, even after his own accession. They could be expected to raise any claim they might have for paramountcy. Continuity in office is always a problem, especially in societies evolving toward a permanent, centralized monopoly of force because of the intense competition for high office (Goody 1966: 24–25). Conspiracy, rivalry, and violence, the hallmarks of transitional periods, are intensified by indeterminate succession patterns, expanding pools of eligible contenders, and fewer high offices to be shared. Then, even more than at other times, allegiances become shallow and commitments superficial because shifts in power, or in the mere perception of power, influence tribal leaders to follow their instincts when judging who the ultimate winners will be. In an effort to protect themselves and to gain the advantage for their followers, leaders repeatedly abandon former allies and hasten to join those whom they think will finally hold the stronger position and thus bestow the greater reward.

In such circumstances, preventing cleavages and maintaining solidarity requires a shrewd leader who plays his cards well. He must be able to parlay his successes into greater support which in turn will win even more followers. He must create, in a sense, an expanding economy of relationships in which growth begets growth and stability, stability. To miscalculate or to withdraw from competition even temporarily —unless the withdrawal is timed and calculated for its long-term advantages—is to surrender opportunities and to risk failure (Almana 1980: 25). To survive in such an environment, the successful leader must establish a network of coalitions, hold them in place by a system of balances and counter-balances, and prevail, because ironically prevailing is itself sometimes a sufficient indicator of strength which can be recalled during subsequent crises of authority. More often, however, the stable leader must be personally astute, his views and policies must be congruent with those of his people, and he must establish the structures which support the continuation of his leadership. All types of legitimacy must be combined to insure that individuals and groups will continue to depend upon the leader and benefit from his authority (Hudson 1977: 18–23). Therefore, a successful candidate will often appeal to close-in marriage with the ruling house, allegiances with other strong men and skilled warriors, control and redistribution of booty, a shrewd sense of timing, and personal charism. David claimed them all (Flanagan 1981).

Calling attention to the problems of legitimation is not done in order to exaggerate the traumas of social evolution and succession in tribal societies. Rather, it serves to indicate that periods of accelerated change, wherein major structural transformations and indeterminate succession patterns coexist, are simultaneously less predictable and more complex than the hindsight of several thousand years may at first suggest. To appreciate the fragileness of the coalitions and structures that are only beginning to be formed is to recognize the importance of personal and symbolic resources employed during transitional periods. In the short term, people's perceptions of matters may be as important as the actual state of affairs. Symbolic gestures, therefore, strongly affect the legitimacy of a ruler, and communal symbols such as rituals express, control, and regularize the allegiances of groups and individuals (Moore 1976: 237; V. Turner 1977a: 64).

The records of events immediately following Saul's death are meagre. However, they do indicate several events which concern us here. First, David's lament over the deaths of Saul and Jonathan and his concern for their burial did more than extol the virtues of the deceased and protect the rights of the dead (2 Samuel 1–2). It fulfilled David's ritual, tribal responsibilities toward his wife's paternal kin (see Fortes 1962: 63–64), even though Saul had taken his daughter from David without restitution of her bride price. In other words, even though Saul neglected his duty toward David, David continued to fulfill his. Second, when the hostility between Saul and David continued to erupt among their followers they attempted to settle the dispute by duel (2 Samuel 2). This technique suggests a ritual resolution of hostility which is often practiced in tribal societies. And third, when Ishbosheth became leader with the help of his strong man and cousin, Abner, he was forced to establish his capital at Mahanaim, east of the Jordan. The site, as yet unidentified, was the same place David chose later when he was forced into exile by his son, Absalom. It must have afforded greater security than the hills of Israel, but the need to go there indicates the tenuous hold Ishbosheth had on his office. His succession appears to have been uncontested in the North where primogeniture was the deciding factor, but in the South where David was chosen the case was different. It would lead us too far afield to discuss the relationship between Judah and Israel, but these circumstances show that the prevailing social patterns were still tribal, and that ritual played a major role in David's conduct. They indicate also that David was favorably positioned for the struggle for paramountcy. He had a power base which was not dependent upon his affinity to Saul, one which he could use as he saw fit when challenged by northern contenders.

David's tactics also included maneuvers which were typical of a chief who has lost in earlier competition for paramountcy. After he was forced to withdraw from Saul's court, he moved from the center to the periphery of Yahwistic territory and eventually to the territory of the Philistines where he turned exile into advantage by allying himself with Saul's enemies and by befriending the Judahites while he waited for a chance to compete again for leadership of the North. In this way, he created dependents and became a popular source for gifts and booty accumulated on his raids. He seized the opportunity to move to Hebron where distance from Saul's house and Israel did not prohibit contact with Yahwistic traditions (Flanagan 1981). Peaceful, profitable relations with Israel's religious brothers, as well as with her enemies, stood David in good stead when the house of Saul failed.

But David's association with Saul was a two-edged sword. On the one hand, his position within Saul's entourage, his allegiance to Jonathan, and his marriage to Michal had established a basis upon which Israelites could claim him as one of their own, if they were disposed to do so. On the other hand, however, all these relationships had been ended by death or decree. Saul had driven David from Israel, had tracked him through the hills of Judah, and had purposely cut his ties to the family by reclaiming Michal in order to give her to Paltiel as wife (McCarter 1980: 400). Jonathan had been killed, and conflict had erupted between Israel and Judah. The chasm between David and Saul's house had to be bridged if David was to convince the family-oriented, tribal factions in the North that he was a truly legitimate candidate for leadership of their people.

Michal provided the necessary link in the broken chain of relationships. Therefore, David demanded her return as a condition for beginning the treasonous negotiations with Abner, who as a cousin of Saul may have been a candidate himself. After she had been returned, a deal was struck, and soon the deaths of Abner and Ishbosheth removed the incumbent and reduced the pool of eligible contenders David had rejoined. As husband of Michal, he could be considered an adopted son (compare Num 27: 1–11; 36: 1–2), and through optative affiliation, a custom which allowed a couple to affiliate with either the husband's or wife's family, he could enjoy succession rights as a stand-in or regent for his wife (see Goody 1966: 10; Service 1962: 153, 162). Before long the elders of Israel were moved by the pressure of circumstances, the absence of viable alternatives, and David's personal attractiveness to choose the Judahite as their leader. His marriage to Michal gave them a successor who was of the house of Saul.

Against the background of these events, the transfer of the ark and the dynastic oracle take on added significance. As with the other parallels in 2 Sam 5: 13–8: 18, the ark and oracle formed a paradoxical balance which includes continuity and discontinuity, fulfillment and inversion. David had built upon the base he sought to displace, but his election as husband of Michal had left critical issues unresolved. Did he rule in his own right, as he did in Judah, or was he only a stand-in for Michal? And what about his successor? Would he be a son of Michal and David, not yet born, or

Mica son of Jonathan's son Meribaal, or a son of David by another wife?

The answers to these questions were quick in coming. Michal's childless state, which 2 Sam 6: 23 testifies was perpetual, and Meribaal's and Mica's house arrest (2 Samuel 9), gave David the opportunity to pass the leadership on to his sons by other wives (compare Goody 1973: 18–20). The return of Michal and her barrenness serve as the pivot upon which the transition of ruling houses turned.

In the compilers' view, by transferring the ark to Jerusalem, David symbolically linked himself to and laid claim to the ancient northern traditions associated with the tribal league and Saul, while the pronouncement of the dynastic oracle transferred perpetual custody of those traditions to David and his house in Jerusalem. Through it the city became the legitimate center for Yahwism, and David won the personal, ideological, and structural legitimacy he needed in order to lead the Yahwists.

Here, the ritual aspects of the transfer scene are especially evident. In fact, the drama in chaps. 6 and 7 unfolds in three phases which correspond to those identified by van Gennep in 1909 as constituting a rite of passage (van Gennep 1960).

Van Gennep's concept and description of the ritual process has had exceptional influence upon more recent studies of the change process and of human transitional experiences (Gluckman 1962; V. Turner 1974, 1977a, 1977b, 1977c; Moore 1976; T. Turner 1976). According to his hypothesis, humans often face transitions wherein the stability of a former state has to be abandoned (separation phase) before the routines of a later state can be established (reaggregation). In the midst of such changes is a period when people feel insecure and adrift, as if betwixt and between, on a threshold where they are at one and the same time "no longer" and "not yet" (liminality). Their uncertainty is often manifested in beliefs that doorways, mid-points, pilgrimages, processions, and the like are charged with extraordinary power and are spatially and conceptually sacred zones (V. Turner 1974: 166). Birth, puberty, betrothal, marriage, death, and other dramatic human experiences wherein status or place is upset fall into this category. Fortes (1962: 55) has in fact claimed that entry into or exit from critical stages in life is always marked by ritual and ceremony which mediate the transitions occurring at that time.

Fortes therefore agrees with van Gennep and others in their belief that persons and groups confronting spatial, temporal, and structural changes experience complex, ambiguous, and contradictory roles which are often acted in ritual (see Gluckman 1962: 42). The rites "homogenize" the various levels of existence so that distinctions between planes of classification, as between sacred and profane or religious and secular, lose their meaning. But, political, social, and religious are fused in ways which manifest them as facets of the same experience. The rites of passage not only symbolize the transitions they are expressing; they also mediate, regulate, and effect the change from one state to the next (V. Turner 1977b: 96; Rappaport 1979: 41). The structure of the ritual is therefore a model of the structure of its society, and the hierarchy of relationships manifested in the ritual accurately represents those operating in other spheres in the same society (T. Turner 1977: 68).

Although van Gennep distinguished three phases in rites of passage, most human transitions emphasize one stage more than the other two, depending upon the nature of the transformation. Each transition has a period of separation, followed by a time of liminality or marginality, and then a period of aggregation where new relationships are made routine. It is the second phase, however, which is often the most complex and confusing because that is where the actual threshold of change is crossed. It is in it, in a rite of passage, that role reversals, ritual dance, exceptional garb (or nudity), and ecstatic behavior are often employed as ways of manifesting the anti-structure and dialectical quality of the transitions that are taking place personally, socially, and religiously (V. Turner 1974: 272–73; 1977c: 36–40). It is the middle phase which also assists in understanding Michal and David in 2 Samuel 6.

The rite of passage in the section we are discussing has a separation phase and a reaggregation phase as well. The former was manifested when David claimed the ark and removed it from its resting place to begin the procession toward Jerusalem. That signalled the break with the past and asserted his claim upon the Yahwistic traditions. The aggregation was evident in the dynastic oracle which confirmed David's claims and established the new matrix of relationships between the ruling houses and within Israel. The first and second pairs of parallels described above, that is, the lists and the battles, fall conveniently into place around these poles.

Between the separation and aggregation was the procession which took David from humble shepherd to exalted leader by way of a ritual dance, transient humility, exceptional attire, and unusual conduct which Michal deemed unseemly and indecorous for the successor to her father (2 Sam 6: 16–22). The scene was staged in what Rappaport (1979: 214, 232) has called the arena of confrontation between order and disorder, during what is described by V. Turner (1977a: 68) as a period of release from usual constraints and an occasion for creative response. It was here that the structures of the former state no longer held sway and the new state of Davidic dynasty had not yet been fully established. The dialogue between Michal and David made explicit that the issue was the legitimacy of his house as leaders in Israel.

Set in the midst of the procession and the David/Michal exchange is a description of a cultic scene in which David made offerings, shared their fruits, and blessed his people (2 Sam 6: 16–19). Levine (1974: 28–46) had identified the episode as a *šĕlāmîm* sacrifice, one of three recorded in inauguration scenes associated with the United Monarchy. In the other instances, peace offerings were made on the occasion of Saul's accession in Gilgal (1 Sam 11: 14–15) and of Solomon's dedication of the temple (1 Kgs 8: 63–64). David's episode combined aspects of accession and dedication.

The two Mesopotamian parallels cited by Levine (pp. 28–32) can aid our understanding of the scene in 2 Samuel 6. The first is a brief reference in the fourth tablet of the *Enuma eliš* which reports that the Mesopotamian *šulmānû* peace offerings were made by the hero god, Marduk, after his victory over Tiamat. However brief, the scene associates the sacrifice with a change in dominance and authority as in 2 Samuel 6.

The second parallel, a *Königsritual* dating from the end of Tukulti-Ninurta's reign (c. 1220–1150 B.C.E.), is a long account of a king's investiture at a temple ceremony. In it, the ritual officers are both king and priests, representing dual channels of authority. As the ceremony progresses, the king and his subordinates are divested of their royal insignia. The monarch then appears before the god Assur as a humble supplicant proclaiming the god's sovereignty and presenting gifts of precious materials. Afterwards, the king is reinvested with the symbols of office, is crowned, and is extolled with praises and wishes for a long reign. A procession within the temple follows and is succeeded by an offer of obeisance given by the high officials, then the king's procession to his throne, and officials offering him gifts, *šulmānû*.

The officials are reinvested, and the reign of the city gods proclaimed.

The use of parallel cultic terminology, the ritual humiliation, and the proclamation of the leader's divine election in 2 Samuel 6 leaves little doubt that the investiture of David and the relocation of the ark in Jerusalem took place within a ritual setting. Throughout the scene, divine power was manifested in event (e.g., Uzziah's death, 6: 7) and word (dialogues, 6: 12; 7: 5). So, even without asserting direct historical influence from Mesopotamia, we can recognize that a ritual displacement and reaggregation of power similar to that found by Levine in other scenes accompanied the transfer and David's inauguration in Jerusalem.

In the Yahwistic rite of passage, religious attributes combined with social, political, and geographical aspects of the time in a way that stresses the liminality of the event, but which also makes it difficult for us to separate the planes of classification in David's social drama. This is what we should expect. However, Michal's misplaced concern for propriety, another in the long list of miscalculations by members of Saul's house, allowed David to reprimand her severely, and it gave the scribes a chance to state finally that he had excelled where Saul had failed. The ark, Saul's house, tribal traditions and religious centers, and northern predominance were all displaced as David overturned the course of history by humbling himself in order to be exalted (6: 21–23; 7). Fortes (1962: 86) has described the dynamics at work in such situations.

> The burden of my thesis is that societies distinguish between the individual and his offices, statuses or roles. It is because the individual is more than the offices or statuses or roles he may have, because he stands over against them, that ritual is needed in order to confer them upon him or, alternatively, to deprive him of them. In this way office is entrusted to the holder in a binding manner, or again, conversely, legitimately stripped from him. Ritual presents office to the individual as the creation and possession of society or a part of society into which he is to be incorporated through the office. Ritual mobilizes incontrovertible authority behind the granting of office and status and thus guarantees its legitimacy and imposes accountability for its proper exercise.

From the Jerusalemite perspective, the transitions in 2 Samuel 6 established a new matrix of relationships that would remain perpetually intact regardless of future circumstances. Although the efficacy of the dynastic oracle was to be tested repeatedly almost from the beginning (e.g., Sheba), in the minds of the scribes, the social, political, economic, and religious center of Israel's world had shifted. They believed, as we have already stressed, that David had raised himself to a new state and had done so at Michal's expense.

Since we have described the changes taking place in Israel as moving simultaneously along horizontal and vertical planes, it is important to appreciate the manner whereby the dynamic and iconic elements in ritual are identified with the intersection of these planes. Leach (1954: 11–16) and Fortes (1980: ix) have addressed the issue, but it is Terrence Turner (1977) who has raised questions passed over in van Gennep's analysis. Turner has asked why there should be an iconic relationship between the structure of rituals and that of the social transitions they mediate, why the three-phase pattern should be the appropriate iconic pattern, and why the liminal phase has distinctive qualities not found in the other two?

Turner's answers are complex and somewhat convoluted. He insists that the social context of a situation expresses itself in the symbolic form and content of ritual (rather than ritual creating the social context as Gluckman suggests), and that there is a reciprocal relationship between the social context and the ritual situation whereby ritual behavior constitutes a "controllable, unambiguous, orderly pattern of action" which is an effective mechanism for "reordering the uncontrollable, ambiguous, or otherwise dangerous aspects of the situation" (1977: 60). He claims also that social transitions have both a vertical or hierarchical dimension which van Gennep did not understand, and a horizontal one which he did discuss. Rather than a simple triadic sequence, for Turner, rites of passage are composed of a pair of cross-cutting binary contrasts. Using the example of a boy becoming a man, he demonstrates that the process is not only horizontal, i.e., a young male moving toward adulthood, becoming older and larger, but also a transformation of role categories in which jural dependence gives rise to (and way to) independence. Such transformations occur even though other roles played simultaneously may remain intact, such as the male's status as son and brother.

Turner identifies the first and third phases of rites of passage with the horizontal transitions, but he also finds these phases at work in the hierarchical movement. The liminal phase, it seems to me, he limits to the "pivot of the sacred" of which van Gennep spoke. There the changes, inversions, and reversals take place. It is there that ritual elevates the various levels of classification to a single plane where the social context and the ritual situation become one and the same.

He states (1977: 68):

> The point is that the structure of *rites de passage* models both of these axes simultaneously, in a way that defines each as a function of the other. The rites of separation and aggregation, in other words, mark the vertical (interlevel) separation between the level at which the initial and final social status or status-identities of the transition are defined and the higher level comprised by the principle of transformation between them, as well as the horizontal (intra-level) separation from the first of the two statuses and aggregation with the second.
>
> The liminal phase of the ritual, as this implies, is the direct expression of the higher level of transcendent, transformational principles which form the ground and mechanism of the social transition in question. It is the hierarchical relation between the liminal phase and the profane social states or categories that form the terminal points of the ritual process which in turn accounts for the peculiar properties of the rites associated with this phase (1977: 68).

Biblical scholars have long recognized the role which the transfer of the ark played in Jerusalem's legitimation. However, understanding 2 Samuel 6 as the liminal phase in a rite of passage, situated within a literary context that is divided into fore- and after-states, exposes the trauma that Israel experienced when establishing the Davidic, Jerusalemite dynasty. Recognizing this also helps us appreciate the complexity of the Books of Samuel, where the transitions modeled in the transfer scene are described at length and the persons and places whose lives were affected by the relocation are exposed. The course of their history was being upset and realigned. The rite of passage makes clear what was at stake and who was paying the greatest price. The house of Saul had indeed grown weaker and the house of David stronger.

Notes

1. It is a pleasure to dedicate this article to David Noel Freedman who has contributed so much to our knowledge of Hebrew poetry, often associated with ritual settings, and Israelite history. With gratitude and appreciation, I wish him health and long life. Research for this article was supported in part by a Fellowship from the National Endowment for the Humanities, Centers Program, 1981.

2. The text does not state whether Michal had no children because David put her away or because she was infertile (2 Sam 6: 23). Because no children are credited to her from her earlier marriages to David or Paltiel, it seems likely that the compilers' interest was in recording the state of affairs rather than in determining David's intention. In any case, Bright's suggestion (1972: 193) that David hoped to produce male issue by Michal in order to unite the claims of their houses overlooks David's immediate concern with legitimating himself and his capital.

References

Almana, Mohammed
1980 *Arabia Unified. A Portrait of Ibn Saud.* London: Hutchinson and Benham.

Bright, John
1972 *A History of Israel*[2]. Philadelphia: Westminster.

Easton, David
1965 *A Systems Analysis of Political Life.* New York: Wiley.

Eisenstadt, S. N.
1963 *The Political Systems of Empires.* London: Collier-Macmillan.

Flanagan, James W.
1979 The Relocation of the Davidic Capital. *Journal of the American Academy of Religion* 47: 223–44.
1981 Chiefs in Israel. *Journal for the Study of the Old Testament* 20: 47–73.

Fortes, Meyer
1962 Ritual and Office in Tribal Society. Pp. 53–88 in *Essays on the Ritual of Social Relations,* ed. Max Gluckman. Manchester: University Press.
1980 Preface. Anthropologists and Theologians: Common Interests and Divergent Approaches. Pp. v-xix in *Sacrifice,* ed. M. F. C. Bourdillon and Meyer Fortes. London: Academic Press.

Fried, Morton H.
1967 *The Evolution of Political Society.* New York: Random House.

Gluckman, Max
1962 Les rites de passage. Pp. 1–52 in *Essays on the Ritual of Social Relations,* ed. Max Gluckman. Manchester: University Press.

Goody, Jack
1961 Religion and Ritual: the Definitional Problem. *British Journal of Sociology* 12: 142–64.
1966 Introduction. Pp. 1–56 in *Succession to High Office,* ed. Jack Goody. Cambridge: Cambridge University.
1970 Sideways or Downwards? Lateral and Vertical Succession, Inheritance and Descent in Africa and Eurasia. *Man* N.S. 5: 627–38.
1973 Strategies of Heirship. *Comparative Studies in Society and History* 15: 3–20.

Hudson, Michael C.
1977 *Arab Politics. The Search for Legitimacy.* New Haven: Yale University.

Leach, Edmund R.
1954 *Political Systems of Highland Burma.* London: Athlone.

Levine, Baruch
1974 *In the Presence of the Lord.* Leiden: E. J. Brill.

McCarter, P. Kyle, Jr.
1980 *I Samuel.* Anchor Bible 8. Garden City: Doubleday.

Mazar, Benjamin
1963 David's Reign in Hebron and the Conquest of Jerusalem. Pp. 237–44 in *In the Time of Harvest. Essays in Honor of A. H. Silver,* ed. D. J. Silver. New York: Macmillan.

Moore, Sally Falk
1976 Epilogue. Pp. 210–39 in *Symbols and Politics in Communal Ideology,* ed. Sally Falk Moore and Barbara G. Meyerhoff. Ithaca: Cornell.

Rappaport, Roy A.
1979 *Ecology, Meaning, and Religion.* Richmond: North Atlantic Books.

Redfield, Robert, and Singer, Milton B.
1954/55 The Cultural Role of Cities. *Economic Development and Cultural Change* 3: 53–73.

Richards, Audrey I.
1969 Keeping the King Divine. *Proceedings of the Royal Anthropological Institute for 1968:* 23–35.

Robertson, A. F.
1976 Ousting the Chief: Deposition Changes in Ashanti. *Man* N.S. 11: 410–27.

Service, Elman R.
1962 *Primitive Social Organization*^{2}. New York: Random House.

Turner, Terence S.
1977 Transformation, Hierarchy and Transcendence: A Reformulation of Van Gennep's Model of the Structure of *Rites de Passage.* Pp. 53–70 in *Secular Ritual,* ed. Sally F. Moore and Barbara G. Meyerhoff. Amsterdam: van Gorcum.

Turner, Victor
1974 *Dramas, Fields, and Metaphors.* Ithaca: Cornell.
1977a Process, System, and Symbol: A New Anthropological Synthesis. *Daedalus* 106: 61–80.
1977b *The Ritual Process.* Ithaca: Cornell (published 1969, Chicago: Aldine).
1977c Variations on a Theme of Liminality. Pp. 36–52 in *Secular Ritual,* ed. Sally F. Moore and Barbara G. Meyerhoff. Amsterdam: van Gorcum.

van Gennep, Arnold
1960 *The Rites of Passage.* Trans. Monika B. Vizedom and Gabrielle L. Caffee. London: Routledge and Kegan Paul. Originally 1909.

Weber, Max
1947 *The Theory of Social and Economic Organization.* Trans. A. M. Henderson and Talcott Parsons. New York: Oxford University.

David's Relations with Hiram: Biblical and Josephan Evidence for Tyrian Chronology

Alberto R. Green
Rutgers College, New Brunswick, New Jersey

There is a paucity of epigraphic extra-biblical sources bearing upon the foreign contacts of David and Solomon. Egypt and Assyria were relatively weak during the reigns of these Hebrew kings; hence, the kings of those lands conducted no major military expeditions to Palestine. As a consequence, references to that region in inscriptions from such sources are scarce. Following the reign of Tiglat-Pileser I (1115–1077), the power of Assyria was on the wane due in part to pressure from the Arameans; it did not wax strong again to any great extent until the time of Adad-Nirari (911–891).[1] At the same time, Egypt was divided between the kings of the 21st Dynasty, who ruled Lower Egypt from Tanis, and the high priests of Amun, who controlled Upper Egypt from Thebes. Five pharoahs and four high priests were contemporaries of David and Solomon; what fragmentary evidence there is suggests that only one of them, Siamun from Tanis, ever participated actively in Palestinian affairs.[2]

Another reason for the difficulty in illuminating this period from extra-biblical sources is that historically significant inscriptions relating to it have not been recovered from the territory of ancient Israel or her immediate neighbors. David's campaigns ranged far and wide through Syro-Palestine (2 Samuel 5, 8, 10–12) and Solomon's commercial contacts reached even farther (1 Kgs 9: 26–10: 29); so far, however, no inscriptions referring to these matters have turned up. As a result, the Old Testament remains virtually the sole source for information on such activities.

The late exception to this general absence of extra-biblical evidence relating directly to the United Monarchy comes from Josephus' reference to Hiram of Tyre. Hiram appears there at the head of the Tyrian king-list which Josephus obtained from Menander of Ephesus (*AgAp* 1.117-125), and Josephus identified him clearly as the ruler whose relations with Solomon are referred to in 1 Kings and 2 Chronicles (*AgAp* 1.108, 126; *Ant* 8.50).[3] Solomon's contacts with Hiram will not be dealt with; our concern here is primarily with Hiram's less commonly considered relations with David.

I. The Old Testament

The biblical reference to relations between David and Hiram is brief. The description of David's conquest of Jerusalem is followed in 2 Sam 5: 11 by the simple statement that "Hiram king of Tyre sent messengers to David, and cedar trees, also carpenters and masons who built David's house." Josephus makes a similar statement in this regard, adding only that Hiram wrote to David proposing friendship and an alliance (*Ant* 7.66). Josephus does not refer to Menander in this connection. He goes on to say that David enclosed the lower city with a wall at that time, apparently transferring the essence of 2 Sam 5: 9 to follow the reference to Hiram. This passage of Josephus closes with the observation that David conquered Jerusalem 515 years after Joshua conquered Canaan (*Ant* 7.68).

Even without Josephus' comments on Hiram, the biblical reference to the Tyrian king raises a question about his reign. The Deuteronomist in 2 Sam 5: 5 states that David reigned over Judah from Hebron 7 years and 6 months and subsequently reigned over all Israel from Jerusalem for 33 years. The latter datum constitutes a preface to the verses that tell of David's conquest of Jerusalem, and they in turn are followed by the notice of Hiram's embassy to David. Taken at face value, the location of this embassy in the text implies, as John Gray has observed, that "Hiram had entered into friendly relations with David soon after his establishment in Jerusalem as king over all Israel" (1970: 151).

In 1 Kgs 9: 10–14 the Deuteronomist locates the transfer of twenty Galilean towns to Hiram near the end of Hiram's reign, around Solomon's 24th regnal year.[4] Even if specific dates are not applied in 2 Sam 5: 11 and 1 Kgs 9: 10–14, the passages still imply that Hiram reigned half a century at the minimum, three decades or so contemporary with David and at least two decades with Solomon. Half a century is a rather lengthy reign, but it is not impossible. It should be noted that this figure represents merely the *minimum* number of years required by these two synchronisms. In view of this problem, observations that have been made on these texts warrant review before turning to Josephus' references to Hiram. Suggestions about how to reduce the distance between these two biblical events for Hiram's reign fall into three categories: 1) change the chronology of the kings of Tyre or Israel, 2) alter the name of the king of Tyre involved, and 3) change the location in the text of the event referred to in 2 Sam 5: 11.

In his discussion of the first of these proposals, H. P. Smith observed that the embassy came soon after David's occupation of Jerusalem, following the reading of the text; however, he has argued that Hiram could not have come to the throne that early, hence the chronology is at fault (1899: 289). Smith did not specify whether he felt this fault lay with Hiram's dates derived from Josephus or with David's dates determined by the Deuteronomist. It seems more likely that he referred to the former, but he did not elaborate further upon this point, perhaps because he had no specific suggestions to make about where the chronological fault should be corrected. E. Lipiński regards the 40 regnal years attributed to Solomon in 1 Kgs 11: 42 as artificial and excessive; hence he reduces the length of Solomon's reign to synchronize his accession with dates for Hiram based on an interpretation of the Tyrian king-list (1970: 65). This procedure has the effect of lowering the Julian date B.C.E. for David's accession, but it does not bring the references to Hiram in 2 Sam 5: 11 and 1 Kgs 9: 10–14 any closer together in terms of relative chronology.

With regard to the second category of suggestions, the name and identity of the king of Tyre who sent his embassy to David have received much attention in efforts to explain these references. Several suggestions have been made along this line. J. R. Lumby proposed that there were two kings of Tyre in succession whose names were the same, a view which he says is confirmed by 2 Chr 2: 13 (1890: 47). There are several problems with that proposal. On the basis of the commonly practiced principle of papponymy one would expect grandfather and grandson to have borne the same name, not father and son.[5] If this principle was in use in Tyre in the 10th century, then another king should have reigned between Lumby's two assumed

Hirams. According to this interpretation, the name of his first Hiram assimilated to his second Hiram; if another king ruled between them, his name had fallen out of the king-list. Lumby also appears to have misunderstood the reference to Huram-abî in 2 Chr 2: 13.[6]

The strongest objection to this arrangement of kings stems from the clear implication of 1 Kgs 5: 15 that the Hiram who helped Solomon build the temple was the same Hiram that sent assistance to David since he "always loved David." The Chronicler concurred with this identification when he cited Solomon's request to Hiram: "As you dealt with David my father and sent him cedar to build himself a house to dwell in, so deal with me" (2 Chr 2: 2). The implication of these verses was not lost upon Lumby, and, in commenting upon the passage from Kings, he proposed to surmount this difficulty by stating that Hiram must be taken here merely as a synonym for the king of Tyre, just as Pharoah is often used for the king of Egypt (1890: 48). "Hiram" may well have been a throne name and not the name given the king at birth, but there is no evidence from either inscriptional or classical sources that "Hiram" ever served as a title among Tyrian kings.

A. F. Kirkpatrick has offered similar suggestions, adding that if the statements of Josephus are correct, Hiram was either the father or grandfather of Solomon's ally (1930: 203). The problems connected with identifying David's Hiram as the grandfather of Solomon's Hiram have already been discussed above. In assuming, as Kirkpatrick does, that Abi-Baal, Hiram's father according to Josephus, also bore the name of Hiram, and that it was he who sent ambassadors to David, Kirkpatrick needs to explain why Hiram's name appears in the text instead of Abi-Baal's. His first explanation is that Hiram was another name for Abi-Baal. Regardless of whether Abi-Baal was his personal name and Hiram was his throne name or vice-versa, this interpretation still results in one Hiram following another. Such a situation is not only unattested but also runs contrary to the aforementioned practice of papponymy.

Kirkpatrick's alternate explanation is that Hiram's name replaced Abi-Baal's because Hiram was the more familiar of the two. Undoubtedly, it must be assumed that Hiram was well known to the Israelites of that era for his relations with Solomon. Given the statement from these records that were kept in David's court, however, if Abi-Baal sent an embassy to David, that event should have been noted in these court records. The fact that 2 Samuel drew upon such sources suggests that the name of Hiram in 5: 11 could well have been transferred from those texts correctly.[7] As far as subsequent transmission is concerned, there is no textual or other evidence to indicate that a later scribe substituted Hiram's name for Abi-Baal's.

Because of David's military activities, more names of foreign kings are connected with him in the Books of Samuel than are connected with Solomon in 1 and 2 Kings; even the transition from Nahash to Hanun on the throne of Ammon was noted in 2 Sam 10: 2. In general, the use of such names elsewhere in Samuel tends to parallel and thus support the authenticity of the reference to Hiram in Samuel and his recognition of the transition from David to Solomon in 1 Kings 5. On the basis of the latter text, supplemented by 2 Chr 2: 3, there is little reason to doubt that Hiram was king of Tyre during the time that David ruled from Jerusalem. The question is, for how long? Of the suggestion that Abi-Baal preceded Hiram, Bright says, "Although it is possible that David had earlier made a treaty with Hiram's father Abi-Baal, we have no information of it" (1974: 199, n. 49; 183, 191).

R. W. Corney considered the possibility that David's embassy from Tyre came from Abi-Baal rather than from Hiram but argues rather that either the Old Testament has mistakenly named Hiram instead of his father Abi-Baal, or, if not, that the Old Testament has placed the contact with Hiram too early (1962: 607).

This brings up the third and probably the most common approach to the problem, the proposal that the reference to Hiram should be placed later in the course of the events described in 2 Samuel. If Hiram did not send his embassy to David soon after he conquered Jerusalem, when was the embassy sent to the Israelite king? Three occasions have been suggested: 1) after the battle with the Philistines recorded in 2 Sam 5: 17–25, 2) after the subsequent wars of 2 Samuel 8–12, and 3) towards the end of David's reign.

A number of commentators and historians have adopted the interpretation that David's battles with the Philistines described in 2 Sam 5: 17–25 preceded his conquest of Jerusalem referred to in 2 Sam 5: 6–8 (Caird 1953: 1073; Katzenstein 1973: 74, 94–96; Maly 1965: 125; Noth 1960: 187–90; Smith 1899: 286–87); hence Hiram's embassy to David occurred after the battles with the Philistines, since it is connected in the text with the conquest of Jerusalem. There is little doubt that David's victory over the Philistines enhanced his prestige in Hiram's eyes and could well have been a strong reason for Hiram's interest in cementing relations with him. This could have been a later development in Tyrian history, for it is apparent that Tyrian policy on the eve of the establishment of the Kingdom of Israel was hostile towards the Israelites.[8] Hiram's interest in the fall of the Philistines, however, could fit either order for these events; that is, after the fall of Jerusalem or after the defeat of the Philistines. He might have provided David with moral or even economic support for his showdown with the Philistines in order to eliminate any threat to or competition with Tyrian shipping from the Philistines.[9] The difference between these two arrangements for the events of 2 Samuel 5 is peripheral to our main interest here, since the absolute date that Hiram sent his embassy to David differs little between them—they both locate it around the time that David began to rule from Jerusalem.

The same cannot be said of the proposal to locate David's relations with Hiram after the wars with Syria and Transjordan (Noth 1960: 197, n. 2). This later location could shorten Hiram's reign and would depend to a significant degree upon what period of time elapsed between David's defeat of the Philistines in 2 Sam 5: 25 and the end of the Transjordanian wars in 2 Sam 12: 31. At least two problems arise from this arrangement.

First, there is the problem presented by 2 Sam 7: 1. This verse sets the stage for Nathan's oracle, which follows, by referring to the fact that at the time that oracle was given David "dwelt in his house" in Jerusalem. The following verse adds the information that cedar was used in the construction of that house. In all likelihood, therefore, this was the house that Hiram helped David build. The way the text of 2 Samuel is arranged, the brief narrative about David dwelling in his house of cedar and the preceding narrative about transporting the ark to Jerusalem occupy the interval between the records of David's victories over the Philistines and the commencement of the Transjordanian wars. It could reasonably be concluded from the location of this reference in the text that David's new residence in Jerusalem was completed before the Transjordanian wars began. It follows, therefore, that if Hiram sent his embassy to David following the conclusion of the Transjordanian wars, Nathan's oracle to David should be transferred to follow that event also. Noth is consistent in treating this point, as he is in the way in which he has arranged these materials in the course of his exposition (Noth 1960: 194–97).

The second problem with the location of Hiram's embassy after the Transjordanian wars comes from references to David's palace in 2 Samuel 6 and 11. It is evident from the contents of 2 Samuel 11–12 that David's affair with Bathsheba was intimately connected with the Ammonite war. The problem arose when David was strolling "upon the roof of the king's palace" and observed Bathsheba bathing (11: 2). Later, after her husband Uriah delivered his report to David on the progress of the siege at the Ammonite capital, "he left the palace" and subsequently "slept by the palace door" (vv 7–9).

Earlier, David had returned to his palace after bringing the ark to Jerusalem (2 Sam 6: 19–20) and through a window of that palace Michal saw David dancing before the Lord (v 16). Noth did not specifically comment on this point, but his application of 2 Sam 5: 11 requires that all of these references to David's palace be applied to "temporary housing" in old Jebusite quarters, used before Hiram helped him build his new residence. From another point of view, however, 2 Sam 5: 11 fits well as a preface to and explanation for the references to David's palace in 2 Samuel 6, 7 and 11.

The third location for Hiram's embassy to David is late in the latter's reign. This location has been specifically adopted by most scholars because of 1) the chronological statements of Josephus and Timaeus that lead to a synchronization of the reign of Hiram with that of Solomon, and 2) the dates derived from the Tyrian king list. Since the time of Eduard Meyer the tendency has been to date Hiram's reign from 969–936 (Meyer 1931: 125–27). This school of thought has located David's accession around 1000 B.C.E., and his death around 962/61 B.C.E. (Albright 1942: 119–31; 1955: 1–9; Bright 1974: 190–91). According to this scheme, Hiram ruled contemporaneously with David for from 7 to 9 years. In aligning these kings in this way, Albright, for example, has observed that he was influenced by the fact that there should be a considerable overlap between the reigns of David and his friend and ally (2 Sam 5: 11; 1 Kgs 5: 15), Hiram of Tyre. "In my system there is an overlap of some eight years, but according to most recent systems there would be no overlap at all" (Albright 1955: 8).

J. Liver, on the other hand, accepted an 8-year overlap as a satisfactory solution to this problem but recognized the dilemma in doing so. Against Meyer, who only overlapped the reigns of David and Hiram one year, he pointed out that "the biblical narrative suggests that Hiram was king somewhat earlier in David's reign" (Liver 1953:1 116–17). Against Kittel, who held that David built his new residence at the beginning of his reign in Jerusalem (Kittel 1922: 155), however, Liver objected that 2 Sam 5: 11 was "an incidental passage which does not stand in proper chronological sequence," and that it was placed there "without implying any chronological sequence" (Liver 1953: 116–17; also Myers 1965: 106).

The Tyrian king-list and Josephus' statements synchronizing Hiram's reign with Solomon's will be discussed in detail below; our purpose at this point is to examine the problems created by such an understanding for the biblical text. These problems appear to be considerable, and the later in David's reign that embassy is dated, the more problems that late date appears to create with the text of 2 Samuel. In addition to inheriting the problems with Noth's proposal discussed above, this view creates some new ones of its own. Even the problems already mentioned become more acute in Bright's case, for he is more specific than Noth about when the events of 2 Samuel occurred.

The narrative of 2 Samuel 7 presupposes two conditions, 1) that the ark had been brought to Jerusalem, and 2) that David had built his new residence there. Bright raises and answers the logical question that stems from these two presuppositions: "One might, indeed, wonder why David, who so soon built a palace for himself in Jerusalem (2 Sam 5: 11; 7: 1), never built an appropriate temple to house the ark. The writer gives an explanation for this: David was deterred from building one by prophetic oracle" (Bright 1974: 196). According to Bright then, David built this palace soon after he established Jerusalem as the new capital of his kingdom. This palace was the same one Hiram helped David construct, according to 2 Sam 5: 11, cited by Bright. There is, therefore, an internal contradiction in Bright's reconstruction of these events when he locates Hiram's embassy of workmen to build David's new residence in Jerusalem a quarter of a century after he conquered that city.

There are several other statements in 2 Samuel which, when taken together, make dating Hiram's embassy this late in David's reign somewhat difficult. The chronological references in 13: 23, 38; 14: 28; and 15: 7 put ten to a dozen years between Absalom's appearance on the scene of action in 13: 1 and his overt break with David in 15: 10; and the balance of the book, in conjunction with the events described in 1 Kings 1–2, could easily add half a dozen years to that.[10] At the time when Amnon abused Tamar, the initial incident in the Absalom cycle, Amnon was living in his own house in Jerusalem (13: 8). If David had taken sufficient interest to assign a house to Amnon, even if it was an old Jebusite residence, one might estimate that he could also have paid attention to building a new residence for himself, the one in which Tamar lived (v 7). If the chronological statements cited above are anywhere near correct, and if Tamar's home was the one that Hiram helped David build, it could not have been built so late as the last 7 or 8 years of David's reign.

Jacob Myers objects to an early date for Hiram's embassy because "it is difficult to see how all of this building activity could have taken place at the early stages of his reign when he was occupied with war on many sides" (Myers 1965: 106). Do the last years of David's reign offer any better opportunity for the construction of this residence, when he was beset with internal revolts, a famine, and renewed fighting with the Philistines? Dating Hiram's embassy late in David's reign also requires that Nathan's oracle in 2 Samuel 7 be located there, since it was given in response to David's proposal to build a temple for Yahweh because the former had taken up residence in his new cedar palace.

In addition, the objection to the dating of Hiram's embassy late in the king's reign makes no allowance for a lull in the fighting between David's victories over the Philistines and the commencement of the Transjordanian wars. These two military encounters were of a somewhat different nature. David defeated the Philistines to liberate the Israelites from the yoke of their oppression. In a sense then, this was a "defensive" war. No specific reason is given in 2 Samuel 8 for the inception of the Moabite war, the first of the Transjordanian wars: in a general sense it might be labelled an "offensive" war. If this analysis is correct, there was a shift in David's policy from a defensive war of consolidation to offensive operations when he embarked on a series of wars in Transjordan and Syria between 2 Samuel 5 and 8.[11]

How long did it take for David to adopt this new policy? The text does not tell us, but given the weakness of both Egypt and Assyria at the time, such a change of policy is understandable. One such example might be cited from elsewhere and earlier in the history of the Near East. Ahmose of the 18th Dynasty of Egypt completed the "liberation" of Lower Egypt by defeating the Hyksos in what might be called a "defensive" war from the Egyptian point of view. However, it was his successor Thutmose I, two generations later, who started Egypt on the "offensive" campaigns that put an empire together (Steindorff and Seele 1968: 30–66; Gardiner 1969: 165–210). If the Egyptians can be allowed two generations to arrive at such a change in policy, it is not too much to suggest that it took David a few years to come around to this point of view. If David waited a while before returning to the battlefield, he could have consolidated his situation during that interval by converting Jerusalem into the political and religious capital of his new kingdom. Fortifying Jerusalem further, building a new royal residence in it for himself, along with bringing the ark there (2 Samuel 6), would have fit well with such a program (2 Sam 5: 9–11).

II. Josephus

The factors examined thus far bear upon David's relations with Hiram from the biblical point of view. Before any conclusions can be drawn from this avenue of investigation, however, the references to Hiram in the writings of Josephus need to be examined more closely. The statement of Josephus that bears upon this problem most directly is his explicit synchronism that dates the commencement of Solomon's construction of the temple in Hiram's 11th (*Ant* 8.62) or his 12th year (*AgAp* 1.126). 1 Kgs 6:1 dates the same event in Solomon's 4th year; thus Hiram came to the throne of Tyre 7 for 8 years before Solomon succeeded David in Jerusalem, if this synchronism from Josephus is correct. Since a date for Hiram's embassy that late in David's reign creates problems with the biblical text, as discussed above, the question arises as to how firm this synchronism is.

Even if Hiram did come to the throne 7 or 8 years before the beginning of Solomon's reign, Josephus still supplies us with four different dates for Hiram, according to different chronological statements in his writings. He dated David's death 1300 years before Antiochus VII beseiged John Hyrcanus in Jerusalem, in 134/33 (*Ant* 7.392), or 1435, which would date Hiram's accession in 1442 or 1443. *Antiquities* 9.280–82 states that 240 years elapsed from Jeroboam's revolt to the fall of Samaria, and the sum of the regnal years he gives for the individual kings of Israel approximates that figure closely.[12] Since Samaria fell in 722 according to Assyrian sources, that dates the division of the monarchy in 962 according to Josephus. Josephus gives 80 years, not 40, as the length of Solomon's reign (*Ant* 8.211), which dates his accession to 1042 and Hiram's in 1049 or 1050, 7 or 8 years earlier.

Josephus' other dates for Hiram come from calculations based upon classical sources. His statements that apply in this direction come from the same passages that date the construction of the temple in terms of Hiram's reign. In the first case, the commencement of the temple construction is dated 240 years after the founding of Tyre (*Ant* 8.62). According to Justin's Epitome of Pompeius Trogus (18.3.5), Tyre was founded the year before Troy fell. Classical sources supply at least seven dates for the fall of Troy.[13] Excluding Duris' date of 1334 as exceptional, the other six dates for the fall of Troy are distributed between 1270 (Herodotus) and 1135 (Epherus) in terms of Julian years B.C.E., and they average out to around 1190.

These differences appear to stem from the different estimates employed by the various writers for the number of years per generation which they used to figure back to the fall of Troy. Of the dates near the average, Eratosthenes' date of 1183 is now most generally accepted, while Eusebius' date of 1171 has received the least acceptance. Timaeus' date of 1194/3 and the date of 1209/8 from the Parian Chronicle follow Eratosthenes' date in order of favor. These three most favored and central dates yield accession dates for Hiram of 981/0, 966/5, and 956/5 respectively.

Working from the other direction, Josephus dated the building of Solomon's temple 143 years before the founding of Carthage (*AgAp* 1.121–25).[14] The date for the latter event most commonly indicated by chronological statements in classical sources is 814.[15] Pompeius Trogus is the only classical writer who has given 825 B.C.E. for the founding of that city.[16] Adding Josephus' 143 years to 814 dates the commencement of the work on Solomon's temple to 957 and Hiram's accession in 968 or 969, Albright's date for him. This date is not too far from the middle figure obtained above by subtracting from the date for the founding of Tyre.

Pompeius Trogus dated the founding of Carthage 72 years before the founding of Rome, instead of the 60 years more commonly indicated. The absolute date assigned to this reference depends in turn upon the assumption that, like the other classical writers, he has adopted 753 B.C.E. for the founding of Rome. Interpreting this statement as referring to 825 dates the temple-building to 968 and Hiram's accession in 979 or 980, a figure which comes reasonably close to the dates obtained above from the higher date for the founding of Tyre.

Only two of the accession dates for Hiram discussed thus far fall within the range of those generally accepted for him by modern scholarship. This series of dates for Hiram's accession derived from Josephus has been cited not so much in the interest of selecting one of them as correct, as to demonstrate how difficult it is to use Josephus' statements to develop a precise chronology.

The context of Josephus' statement that dates the commencement of the temple construction to Hiram's 11th year (*Ant* 8.62) contains chronological problems similar to those discussed above, and these need to be taken into account in evaluating the significance of that statement. This datum occurs at the juncture where Josephus elaborated upon the reference in 1 Kgs 6: 1 that dates the commencement of Solomon's construction of the temple in his 4th year, 480 (LXX, 440) years after the Exodus. Josephus' comment here serves as an introduction to his description of the temple and its construction. He dated the commencement of that construction by aligning it with a number of important events that preceded it; the creation of Adam 3102 years before, Noah's flood 1440 years before, Abraham's arrival in Canaan 1000 years before, the Exodus 592 years before, the founding of Tyre 240 years before, Hiram's accession 11 years before, and Solomon's accession 4 years before.

Among the various problems with these statements none is more obvious than that of the date given for the Exodus, which contrasts directly with the 480 years of the MT and the 440 of the LXX. In addition, Josephus did not employ this figure of 592 years consistently. It agrees with his 515 years from Joshua to David (*Ant* 7.68), but disagrees with his 504½ total years for the judges and rules between Joshua and Solomon, and two other passages give this figure as 612 years (*Ant* 20.230; *AgAp* 2.19). Combining his 2262 years from the creation to the deluge (*Ant* 1.82) with the 1440 from the deluge to the temple in this passage yields 3702 years from Adam to the temple, not 3102. There is also a contradiction with regard to the interval between the flood and the temple; he gave 1067 years between the flood and Abraham (*Ant* 1.148), instead of the 420 obtained here by subtraction. Aside from the historical questions involved in these references, it is obvious from these observations that Josephus was far from consistent in his use of chronological data, which could cast some doubt on his date for Hiram in the same context.

The date for the construction of the temple in Hiram's 12th year might be more significant, since it follows the list of the kings of Tyre. Although Josephus quoted a lengthy passage from Menander about Hiram (*AgAp* 1.117–20), and he quoted a similar passage from Dius about him twice (*AgAp* 1.113–15; *Ant* 8.144), he only paraphrased Menander's king-list. To the end of that paraphrase he added a summary consisting of three points: 1) "The whole period from the accession of Hirom to the foundation of Carthage thus amounts to 155 years and eight months;" 2) "The temple at Jerusalem was built in the twelfth year of King Hirom's reign;" 3) "(Therefore) 143 years and eight months elapsed between the erection of the temple and the foundation of Carthage" (*AgAp* 1.126).

The first point to be noted about this summary is that the first and third items in it originated with Josephus and not with Menander. One might assume that the total of 155 years came to Josephus with the king-list, but this assumption seems unlikely since that total splits up the reign of one of the kings in that list, Pygmalion (Peñuela 1954: 41–42). This makes no chronological difference, however, since Josephus' total matched the sum of the individual figures he copied down originally unless he added them incorrectly. It is even more obvious that the third item in the summary, the 143 years from the building of the temple to the founding of Carthage, resulted from Josephus' calculations (see below).

If the first and third items in this summary originated with Josephus, it seems unlikely that Menander supplied Hiram's 12th year as the date for the building of the temple (*AgAp* 1.126). Josephus also states that when the building of the temple in Jerusalem had started, "Eiromos was already in the eleventh year of his reign at

Tyre" (*Ant* 7.62), a number more readily accepted than the round number of 12 years (Meyer 1931: 2, 79, n. 2; Liver 1953: 155, n. 6). Menander and Dius had both recorded that Hiram was engaged in various building activities during the first years of his reign, pulling down the temples of Heracles and Astarte in Tyre and later rebuilding them (*AgAp* 1.113, 118 = *Ant* 8.146–47; Gutschmidt 1890: 63; 1893: 488–89). No date, however, is given in Menander or Dius for the rebuilding of the Tyrian temples.

A negative argument can be made that, though Josephus had ample opportunity, to attribute this datum to Menander when he quoted and paraphrased him, he did not do so. Citing such a reference for this synchronism would have strengthened Josephus' case against Apion, whose arguments provided the occasion for citing Phoenician sources here in the first place. Thackeray said of this statement, "The source for this statement is unknown" (Thackeray 1926: 213). Albright originally concurred with this viewpoint (Albright 1950: 68); later, however, he lent his support to the former interpretation, observing that "there is no trace of secondary calculation" (Albright 1955: 8) in this synchronism from Josephus, despite his suspicion of the author's statements.

It has also been felt that Josephus attributed the construction of the temple to Hiram's 12th year on the basis of an original Phoenician source because he felt that the part Hiram played in that building was sufficiently important to have been recorded in the Tyrian annals (Rowton 1950: 20–22). Undoubtedly, Tyrian scribes kept track of the number of workmen and the amount of lumber used by Solomon (1 Kgs 5: 6–11), but since such trade went on for 20 years (1 Kgs 9: 10–11), would the inception of such commerce have been sufficiently significant to be included and dated in Tyre's royal annals?

Even if that event and its date were to have been recorded in the Tyrian annals, it is doubtful that the date could have reached Josephus through his secondary sources. This is evident from the passage Josephus quoted from Menander about Hiram's activities. As is usual with such sources, the principal events of Hiram's reign recorded there are five building projects, mainly temples, and his one military campaign by sea against Utica (*AgAp* 1.117–20). Not one of these events is dated to a specific regnal year of Hiram. If Menander did not hand down dates for these activities of Hiram, is it conceivable that he conveyed the date when the construction of a temple was begun in a neighboring country?

Josephus purports to present some correspondence that passed between Hiram and Solomon (*AgAp* 1.111; *Ant* 8.50–54), and he stated that such correspondence was still on file in the archives of Tyre (*AgAp* 1.107). It is of interest to note in this connection that Josephus never claimed to have read the letters there personally. In addition, our credulity is strained if we take literally Josephus' statement that "it is there recorded that the Temple at Jerusalem was built by King Solomon 143 years and eight months before the foundation of Carthage by Tyrians" (*AgAp* 1.108).

If the Tyrians recorded any date for the construction of Solomon's temple it would have been in terms of Hiram's contemporary regnal years, not 143 years before the founding of Carthage, since such a date is anachronistic. This is where Josephus should have given a date for Hiram's reign; instead he gave a calculated date. What he meant, obviously was that his calculated date could be obtained from the materials that were on deposit in Tyre. Again, since he never wrote that he consulted these materials personally, it may reasonably be assumed that Josephus was entirely dependent upon secondary sources for the figures from which these dates were obtained.

Our personal estimate from these considerations is that Josephus obtained his date for the construction of Solomon's temple in Hiram's 12th year by attempting to synchronize Israelite and Phoenician history. His calculations were apparently based on Tyrian annals which recorded the rebuilding of the temples of Heracles and Astarte in Tyre, presumably in the 11th and 12th years, which numbers he transferred to the construction of the temple in Jerusalem on the assumption that all these constructions took place in the 11th and 12th years of Hiram. We suggest that there is no historical basis for Josephus' synchronism between the 11th and 12th year of Hiram and the 4th year of Solomon. That this attempted synchronism is solely Josephus' is evident by his attempted justification in these words: "*There was good reason* why the erection of our temple should be mentioned in their records, for Hirom, King of Tyre, was a friend of our King Solomon, a friendship which he inherited from his father" (*AgAp* 1.109). This hypothesis cannot be proved, however, due to the bewildering variety of chronological schemes that Josephus offers us. At any rate, it is reasonable to conclude that this synchronism should not be accepted uncritically without examining the other data in Josephus relating to this matter.

The king-list of Tyre that Josephus paraphrased from Menander is the other passage from his writings that needs to be examined here. This list contains the names of eleven kings of Tyre from Hiram to Pygmalion, along with the numbers of years each of them reigned. From Josephus' total of these regnal years it should be possible to date Hiram's accession, if a fixed point can be found later in the list from which to figure back. This starting point can be taken either from the date for the founding of Carthage discussed above, or from an Assyrian synchronism with the next to the last king in the list before Pygmalion.

Respect for and interest in this king-list have increased since Fuad Safar published a previously unknown passage from the annals of Shalmaneser III of Assyria in 1951. This text identifies Baal-mazzer as the king of Tyre who paid tribute to Shalmaneser during his western campaign of 841 B.C.E. (Safar 1951: 3–21; Liver 1953: 113–20; Lipiński 1970: 59–65). Since this Baal-mazzer appears in the Tyrian king-list as Balezoros (cf. Albright 1955: 1–9; 1956: 23–27), the next to last king before Pygmalion, Shalmaneser's annals provide an additional link between Josephus' list and the history and chronology of the ancient Near East. Such a synchronism also raises the question of how reliable an historical source the Tyrian king-list is.

In order to arrive at a reasonable answer to this question, a number of problems with the Tyrian king-list should be examined: 1) there are variants for the lengths of reign for the kings in the different manuscripts of *Against Apion*; 2) Josephus' total for the list does not match the sum of the figures given for the individual kings in any of the manuscripts; 3) the number, names, and order of the kings vary in the early part of the list; 4) the starting point for the list is rather problematic and could be clarified further; and 5) the period of time over which no external synchronism is available for cross checking, correlation, and calibration in the king-list extends for more than a century.

The first of these problems focuses on the matter of textual criticism. The textual evidence in the manuscripts of *Against Apion* relating to the king-list divides into two categories that are referred to here as Text Family A and Text Family B. The most important witness in Text Family A is the Greek Codex Laurentianus (L. hereafter) of Josephus.[17] The Latin version of Josephus and another Greek fragment of lesser importance (Peñuela 1954: 40)[18] also belong to this group. Josephus' list has also come to us through the works of Theophilius of Antioch,[19] and through Eusebius in the *ʾEklogē historiōn* and the Armenian version of his *Chronicorum libri*,[20] which belong to Text Family B.[21] The list that appears in Georgius Syncellus' *Chronographia* also belongs in this group. The regnal years for the kings in these textual traditions are these (cf. Peñuela 1954: 40–43).

Text Family A	King	Text Family B
34	Eirōmos/Ḥīrōm I	34
7	Balbazeros/Baʿl-mazzer I	17
9	Abdastartos/ʿAbd-ʿAštart	9
12	Eldest Usurper	–
12	Astartos/ʿAštart (Usurper)	12
9	Astharumos/ʿAštart-ram (Usurper)	9
2/3	Phellēs/Pillēs (Usurper)	2/3
32	Ithōbalos/ʾIttō-baʿl	32
6	Balezeros/Baʿl-mazzer II	6
9	Mattēnos/Mattēn	29
7(+40)	Pugmalion/Pummay-ʿelyôn	7 (+40)
137 2/3	from 1 Hiram to 7 Pygmalion	155 2/3

The differences involved in some of these variants should be noted. In Family A the Latin version assigns Pygmalion 40 years. The period beyond his 7th year lies outside Josephus' calculations and, therefore, is not of great importance here; it may be incorrect since all other MSS. in both families give him a total of 47 years. More important is the fact that the period of 12 years the first usurper reigned after ʿAbd-ʿAštart according to the Codex L. is missing from the Latin text.

Variants are multiplied many more times in Text Family B. Theophilus of Antioch omitted ʿAbd-ʿAštart, omitted the years of Hiram, and gave ʾItto-Baal only 12 years. The figures 9, 34, and 32 are assured, however, because there are no other variants for them in either text family. For Baal-mazzer II, Family B actually has 7 (Theophilus) and 8 (Armenian Eusebius, Syncellus) instead of the 6 listed above with Family A. The 18 listed for him in *ʾEklogē historiōn* is obviously incorrect even for Family B. Textual evidence for the years of Mattēn is evenly divided in Family B. *ʾEklogē historiōn* and Syncellus give him 25 while Theophilus and Armenian Eusebius give him 29, which seems more likely when compared with his 9 in Family A.

To summarize the situation briefly, the larger number of variants in Family B makes this source look a bit more dubious than Family A, although the evidence from more manuscripts might change this picture. For the present at least, Lipiński's esteem for Codex L. as "the prototype of all the Greek manuscripts of Josephus" (Lipiński 1970: 62–64) appears justified. The significant differences from it in Family B (10 more years for Baal-mazzer I, 20 more for Mattēn, omission of the first usurper) may have been made by ancient copyists to harmonize the list, as modern scholars do, with the total of 155 years given for it in the manuscripts. The curious aspect of this sum is that, in spite of the fact that it is attested in all MSS. without exception, none of the lists in the individual MSS. add up to that many years.[22]

A brief survey of the editions and studies of the Tyrian king-list both before and after the publication of the new text from Shalmaneser's annals is sufficient to demonstrate the great influence Niese's critical edition of Josephus, published in 1889, has had upon these investigations. For the basic text of this passage, Niese adopted the three significant features of Family B listed above that differ from Family A, thereby justifying the total of 155 years and 8 months for the period.[23] In this he was followed by Gutschmidt (1890), Ruhl (1893), Thackeray (1926), Reinach-Blum (1930), Meyer (1931), and Delaporte (1948); virtually all of the editors and commentators on this passage from the time of Niese's publication followed him with regard to Baal-Mazzer, Matten, and the first usurper, until the new text of Shalmaneser's annals was published.

With the publication of this new text, however, a change has taken place. A number of studies on this subject have appeared since that publication, by Liver (1953), Peñuela (1954), Albright (1955), Lipiński (1970), Cross (1972) and Katzenstein (1973). The factor common to all of these studies except Albright's is the adoption of 825 as the date for the founding of Carthage in place of 814, commonly held before.[24] This computation has been arrived at by taking the 9 years of Mattēn from the Codex L. instead of the 29 that Niese *et al.* utilized from Text Family B. Adding the first 7 years of Pygmalion to this gives 16 years to subtract from 841 (assumed to be Baal-Mazzer II's last year), which yields 825 for the founding of Carthage. This date correlates well with that of Pompeius Trogus discussed above. Using Josephus' 155 years to work back from 825, three of these studies agree on dates of 980 (Cross and Peñuela) or 979 (Liver) for Hiram's accession. Using the synchronisms between Hiram and Solomon in Josephus as a basis, this also results in the dates for Solomon of 971–932 (Cross), 971/970–931/930 (Liver), or 970–931 (Peñuela), and for his commencement of temple construction in 968 (Liver and Cross).

It is apparent that Liver did not work his way back through the problems of the king-list but merely utilized Josephus' total of 155 years to arrive at his dates for Hiram and Solomon. Recent studies on the list have attempted to reconcile the figures in the list with that total by means of different solutions and with varying degrees of success.[25] One point at issue is how many years should be assigned to Baal-Mazzer I, who follows Hiram in the list. Peñuela, Albright, Cross, and Katzenstein agree in giving him the 17 years of Text Family B, while Lipiński retains his 7 years from Codex L. Lipiński's argument here is that since Baal-Mazzer II's appearance in Shalmaneser's annals supports the 9 years for Mattēn in Codex L. against his 29 in Text Family B, the 7 years of Baal-Mazzer I in Codex L. should be accepted (Lipiński 1970: 60–61).

The difference between these two points of view is that whereas one school of thought (Albright, Peñuela and Cross) attempts to reconcile the figures in the list with Josephus' total for them, the other does not. This results in lower dates for Hiram and Solomon in Lipiński's and Katzenstein's chronology. If one wishes to reconcile the list with its total, some years have to be added to the list someplace. In accordance with the new dates from Baal-Mazzer II, Liver, Peñuela and Cross have added them before his time instead of after him as was done by the other interpreters of the list.

In addition to the problem of determining the original number of regnal years for each king in the list, the part of the list that deals with the four brother usurpers presents special difficulties. Peñuela and Lipiński utilized Codex L. to organize the names and dates of the rulers of this period. According to that source an unnamed usurper of the family ruled before ʿAštart and was on the throne for 12 years. The comparison between the following two lines indicates Niese's adaptation of the basic text here; Codex L. has *hōn ho presbytatos ebasileusen etē dekaduo methʾ hous Astartos*,[26] while Niese reads *hōn ho presbyteros ebasileusen Methousastartos* (Niese 1889: 22). In adopting *Methous* as the first portion of ʿAštart's name Niese followed only Theophilus of Antioch, the poorest Greek textual witness to this passage, and the Latin version of Josephus. Both versions through Eusebius agree with Codex L. in separating this prepositional phrase from ʿAštart's name. The reduplication of the verb before and after Methousastartos is clearly redundant (Thackeray 1926: 211), and a number of regnal years would ordinarily be expected with the former, as attested in Codex L.

The manuscripts witness that four brothers ruled in succession at this juncture.[27] Regardless of the order in which they ruled or what their names were, the only chronological difference involved here is whether the 12 years from Codex L. are accepted for the unnamed brother or the number of regnal years is supplied from other considerations. Peñuela, Lipiński, and Katzenstein retained his 12 years while Albright rejected them as a scribal error related to the 12 years of ʿAštart who followed him. The alternative is that the 12 years belonged to this brother and that ʿAštart's 12 years originated in a dittography from them. If the unnamed brother did not reign 12 years, how long did he reign? Albright estimated that in all probability the eldest of the brothers reigned so briefly that his name was not recorded in the lists (Albright 1955: 6); consequently, he did not assign any significant amount of time to him in his interpretation of the list. Peñuela suggested that this brother's name was omitted because of the reprehensible nature of his crime. A more likely explanation could simply be that the text of Menander from which Josephus worked was defective where his name occurred: this could also explain the absence of his age.

Cross has struck out in a new direction to resolve this problematic juncture: "We presume a haplography in the Josephan text between ʿAštart, the oldest brother of the four usurpers, and Dalay-ʿAštart his successor" (Cross 1972: 17–18). Thackeray's translation of this passage follows Niese's text: "The four sons of his (ʿAbd-ʿAštart's) nurse conspired against him and slew him. The eldest of these, Methusastartus, son of Deleastartus, mounted the throne and lived fifty-four years and reigned twelve" (Thackeray 1926: 211). Restoring the haplography that Cross has proposed, the text would read, *hōn ho presbyteros (Methous)astartos {hos biōsas etē n + ?ʾ ebasileusen etē kʾ. meta touton ho adelphos autou} Delaiastartos hos biōsas etē ndʾ ebasileusen etē ibʾ.*, "The eldest of these, (Methus-?)Astartos [lived fifty + x years and reigned twenty. He was followed by his brother] Dalay-Astartos who lived fifty-four years and reigned twelve."[28]

A favourable aspect of Cross's proposal is the fact that at least he has a personal name in the text for the fourth brother: "In the present corrupt text Dalay-ʿAštart has been made the name of ʿAštart's father: *Astartos ho Delaiastartou*. We do not expect the second brother's patronymic. None are given for other usurpers or founders of new dynasties in the entire king-list" (Cross 1972: 18). Regardless of what this brother's name was, his regnal formula did not survive in any manuscript tradition; therefore the number of years necessary to make up Josephus' total must be supplied. Since this is a case of a brother-to-brother succession here and not a father-to-son, the higher the number supplied the more unlikely it becomes. Cross's total of 42 years for the 4 brothers lies within the limits of possibility. If this situation is correct, it is surprising that this datum did not survive in any manuscript. Since Josephus calculated the 155 years from the figures in the list he had, in all probability the loss must have occurred between Josephus' original text and our later manuscripts of it and not between Menander and Josephus. On the other hand, the regnal phrase is formulaic in character and recurs often in this passage, so it would have been as easy for a haplography to have occurred here as elsewhere in the list.

Either of two starting points can be employed to work back to Hiram using the king-list. The founding of Carthage is one event that serves as such a point of reference, and the difficulties in determining its precise date from classical sources have already been discussed. The other point from which to start is the text of Shalmaneser III's annals, which indicate that Baal-Mazzer was on the throne of Tyre in 841. That text, however, does not tell us how long he reigned or when he came to the throne. Those details can only be determined from the Tyrian king-list. The various MSS. of *Against Apion* give 6, 7, 8, or 18 years for the length of his reign. The 18 years can be discarded on text-critical grounds and the other figures are sufficiently close that they make little chronological difference.[29]

Four interpretations of Baal-mazzer's reign have been advanced since 1951. Peñuela assigned him a reign of 14 years but cited no textual evidence in support of such an interpretation. Albright held that this Baal-mazzer was distinct from Balezoros and that his name had fallen out of the king-list. He inserted him in the list after Balezoros and estimated the length of his reign as 20 years. Albright arrived at this figure by subtracting the regnal years in the list from its total, but in doing so he noted: "The duration of this reign is naturally dependent on the accuracy of the transmitted numbers" (Albright 1955: 5). Katzenstein has ascribed 26 years to Baal-mazzer by reducing Mattēn's reign by 20 years (Katzenstein 1973: 349).

Liver, Lipiński, and Cross make 841 Baal-mazzer's 6th and last year, but that interpretation depends upon the number of years Mattēn reigned between Baal-mazzer and Pygmalion, in whose reign Carthage was founded. To fit the gap between 841 and 825, these scholars have adopted a reign of 9 years for Mattēn from Codex L., in place of his 29 in Text Family B. The difference involved here is not great, since it depends only upon whether Baal-mazzer's short reign is exended before, after, or on both sides of 841.

The other problem with the Tyrian king-list is that virtually no external evidence is extant by which it can be checked or calibrated over the century between Hiram and Baal-mazzer II. The only king from this portion of the list who is known from external sources is Ithobalos, Ethbaal of the Old Testament, who was the father of Jezebel (1 Kgs 16: 31). This reference to ʾItto-Baal is quite general as far as chronological significance is concerned, but it does assist with one minor problem in the king list. Codex L. indicates that ʾItto-Baal died at the age of 68 after a reign of 32 years, whereas the other MSS. give his age at death as 48. Codex L. appears to provide the preferable reading in this case also, according to the information about

Jezebel in the Old Testament.

If ᵓItto-Baal was 16 when he came to the throne instead of 36, Jezebel would have been almost as old as he was, since she was a mature woman when she married Ahab, who came to the throne soon after her father died.[30] A detail added to the king-list concerning ᵓItto-Baal supports this interpretation of ᵓItto-Baal's age by stating that he usurped the throne by assassinating Pilles when he was a priest of Aštarte. While ᵓItto-Baal might have been a priest of Aštarte at 16, it seems unlikely that he would have been able to carry out a successful assassination and usurpation at that age without considerable assistance. Thus the biblical reference to ᵓItto-Baal sheds some light on the minor matter of his age, but it does not provide much assistance in dealing with the larger problem of the Tyrian king-list.

III. Conclusions

The topics treated above will be dealt with in reverse order, which puts the Tyrian king-list first in line for evaluation. The first feature for observation in this list is the names of the kings preserved in it. In a general way, the eleven names listed comprise a reasonable number of kings to reign for the two centuries covered (including Pygmalion's 47 years), since this averages out to just under twenty years of rule for each king. This figure is relatively close to that employed in classical sources for such rough calculations. Allowing for some distortion during the process of their transmission into Greek, if the four instances in which they can be checked by external evidence are any indication, the names themselves Hiram, ᵓItto-Baal, Baal-mazzer and Pygmalion have been transmitted with a reasonable degree of accuracy.

Albright's suggestion that Baal-mazzer II's name fell out of the list is unacceptable: it is difficult to disconnect Baal-mazzer from Balezoros who occupies the same chronological position in the list. If such an omission did occur, it probably would have to be attributed to Menander and the state of transmission of the list from the archives of Tyre, since there is no trace of Albright's Baal-mazzer II in any extant copy of Josephus' writings. On the other hand, a similar line of reasoning would indicate that the name of the eldest usurper fell out of the list between Menander and Josephus, since Josephus preserved his place in line even though he did not provide his name.

While the names of the Tyrian king-list appear to have been handed down relatively well, the figures for their regnal years are open to serious question. Since Josephus' total of 155 years for the period from Hiram to the founding of Carthage is attested by every known manuscript of *Against Apion*, it seems reasonable to accept that figure as his original sum. This total cannot be attributed to Menander for the reasons discussed above. The curious feature of this figure, as mentioned above, is that it is not yielded by the sum of the regnal years in any of the lists in the manuscripts. The total from the best witness (Codex L.), for example, falls almost 20 years short of it. Thus some adjustments must be made in the figures for the regnal years which the various copies of the list present, in order to arrive at Josephus' original total for them. As can be seen from the various studies and interpretations of this list, a considerable amount of scholarly ingenuity has gone into such efforts. It should be remembered, however, that such work has dealt mainly with the final stage in the transmission of this list, from the extant manuscripts of *Against Apion* back to

Josephus' original text.

During this phase of their transmission the variant readings for the regnal years of these kings in the various MSS. of *Against Apion* have indicated that in general the names were transmitted more accurately than the numbers. This observation casts some doubt upon the regnal years from which Josephus computed his 155 years, but not upon his calculations *per se*. Unfortunately, no source materials are available whereby the early stages in the course of this transmission might be checked, but the process they went through can be described.

Before any such list could be compiled the kings listed in it had to reign, and if the practice in Tyre was the same as elsewhere in the ancient Near East, their annals had to be composed during the course of their reigns.[31] At some later date these individual annals were combined into a composite document, like the Babylonian Chronicle.[32] We cannot be certain whether Menander copied from such a text or composed his own from the annals of the individual kings on deposit in the Tyrian archives; while neither possibility can be ruled out, the former alternative seems considerably more likely. In that case the "Tyrian Chronicle" probably went through a number of editions and copies during the five centuries between Pygmalion and Menander. Menander's work may also have gone through the hands of copyists during the three centuries between his original writing and the manuscript from which Josephus paraphrased his copy of the Tyrian king-list. Each stage in this process over the millennium from Hiram to Josephus offered opportunities for errors to creep into the number of years attributed to the eleven kings in the list.

As far as the individual figures are concerned, according to the various manuscripts of *Against Apion,* problems occur in connection with at least two of the seven kings who reigned between Hiram and Baal-mazzer II. In order to harmonize the sum of the individual reigns with the total given, Baal-mazzer I's 17-year reign has been adopted from Text Family B in place of his 7 years in the generally better textual witness of Codex L. The length of the reign of the first and unnamed usurper appears only in Codex L. Four solutions for this problem has been proposed: 1) his 12 years were copied from Aštart's; 2) Aštart's 12 years were copied from his; 3) he did not reign a full year; or 4) the years missing at this point must be supplied, possibly with Dalay-Aštart, if he is accepted as a king in the list. In addition, if there is some merit to Albright's suggestion of supplying the number of regnal years for Baal-mazzer II, then there is a problem with three out of eight of the kings in this part of the list.

If there is some doubt about the accuracy of the year totals attributed to the kings in the list, then there is no reason why Josephus' sum of 155 years, which was computed from them, should be considered sacrosanct. Some scholars have broken away from that figure and have arrived at 167 years for the period from Hiram's accession to the founding of Carthage. The additional years involved have been attributed to Hiram, giving him a reign of 45 and 46 years respectively (Delaporte 1948: 41–42; Vogelstein 1944: 81). Such a procedure should be adopted only if there is external evidence to indicate that it is preferable to do so: since the data relating to Hiram reported by the Deuteronomist point in that direction, that possibility should be left open.

Next there is the matter of Josephus' date for the founding of Solomon's temple in Hiram's 11th or 12th year. The former reference is found in the context of several inaccurate chronological statements (*Ant* 8.62) and the latter is located between two of Josephus' own calculations (*AgAp* 1.126). Josephus had ample opportunity to cite Menander as the source for this statement, especially in the instance where he supposedly dated Solomon's temple by the Tyrian archives (*AgAp* 1.108), but he did not do so. Citing such a reference from Menander would have strengthened Josephus' case against Apion, but he did not attribute it to him. Several important actions undertaken by Hiram on behalf of Tyre are mentioned in Josephus' quotations about Hiram taken from Menander, but none of them is dated. If Menander did not date these events, which were of considerable importance to Tyre, it seems unlikely that he, or the annals he depended on, would have dated Hiram's contribution to Solomon's temple construction in neighboring Israel. As indicated above, it is more likely that Josephus found it recorded in the annals of Tyre that, in the 11th and 12th years of Hiram's reign, the king rebuilt the temples of Heracles and Aštarte in Tyre, and that Josephus transferred these dates to the construction of Solomon's temple. This line of reasoning does not prove that this datum originated from Josephus' own calculations, but it lends some support to that idea.

Turning to 2 Sam 5: 11, the context of this reference implies that no great amount of time elapsed between David's conquest of Jerusalem and the time when Hiram sent his embassy to him there. The question then is whether there is any indication elsewhere in 2 Samuel that points to a later date for Hiram's embassy, i.e., after the Transjordanian wars or during the last years of David's reign. It is difficult, in the first place, to locate Hiram's embassy after the Transjordanian wars, since the references to David's palace during the Ammonite war (2 Samuel 11) imply that David had occupied his new residence by that time, unless he still was living in temporary quarters taken from the Jebusites.

Both of these later locations for 2 Sam 5: 11 also require that 2 Samuel 6 and 7 be transferred there too, since the oracle of 2 Samuel 7 presupposes both David's residence in his new cedar palace and the ark's having been moved to Jerusalem. Locating 2 Samuel 5: 11, 6 and 7 late in David's reign poses the problem of fitting them into the framework of the events and chronology of the last half of 2 Samuel. This interpretation would suggest that the Court History (2 Samuel 7–20, 1 Kings 1) is more disorganized and less reliable than has generally been accepted. Such an interpretation also raises the question of why David would wait a quarter of a century after his capture of Jerusalem to build his new royal residence there, when his aim was to make that previously neutral city the new base from which to govern both the northern and southern parts of his kingdom.

If David did wait until that late in his reign to *begin* construction of his new residence, then he was not able to enjoy it very long. In such a situation one could almost see Solomon's construction of his palace (1 Kgs 7: 1–12) as a continuation of what David had recently started. Not only would he have been unable to enjoy it very long, but also he would not have been able to enjoy it very much, according to the description of his physical condition by that time in 1 Kings 1. In summary, no valid reason has been raised from the Old Testament text to indicate why Hiram's embassy should be located later in David's reign than the context of 2 Samuel 5 implies, and there are several good reasons why it should not be.

This conclusion carries with it the chronological corollary that Hiram was on the throne of Tyre by around 1000 B.C.E., since David took Jerusalem at about that time, if the 33 years of 2 Sam 5: 5 be added to Solomon's accession in 972 or 971 B.C.E. Such a conclusion is at odds with 1) Josephus' date for Hiram's accession; 2) Josephus's total number of years for the Tyrian king-list: and 3) current interpretations of that king-list. The question then is, Which source does the weight of historical probability favor, *Against Apion* 1.116–26 or 2 Sam 5: 11?

At this point we may refer back to a previously discussed problem with the Tyrian king-list, the lack of any specific external synchronism by which the regnal years in that list can be checked between the middle of the 10th century and the middle of the 9th century. 1 Kgs 9: 10 indicates that Hiram ruled as late as Solomon's 24th year, or 947 B.C.E., but ʾItto-Baal, who is mentioned in 1 Kgs 16: 31 as Jezebel's father, is the only king of Tyre known from any external source between that point and the Assyrian reference to Baal-mazzer II in 841. Over the same century there are eleven kings in Israel and seven in Judah, including Solomon. Besides supplying the number of years they reigned, the text of 1 Kings provides synchronisms for the accession of eight kings in the north starting with Nadab, excluding only Tibni, and for all five kings who ruled Judah starting with Abijam.

Interpretations of these data differ, and there was also opportunity enough for errors to creep in amongst them. Nevertheless, the synchronisms involved served as a check upon the development of wide divergences between the regnal years of contemporaneous kings. The side-by-side existence of Israel and Judah provided an intricate and interlocking set of historical and chronological data the likes of which do not exist for the Tyrian king-list. The Old Testament is also the sole source for the early synchronisms with the kings of Tyre, i.e., David with Hiram, Solomon with Hiram, and Ahab with ʾItto-Baal. From these two factors it seems more reasonable to check the chronology of the kings of Tyre by means of the chronology taken from the Old Testament than the reverse. Such a course of interpretation indicates, as discussed above, that David's neighbor Hiram succeeded his father Abi-Baal on the throne of Tyre by around 1000 B.C.E.

One objection that might be raised against this interpretation is that the same type of text-critical work performed on *Against Apion* above needs to be done on the relevant biblical text before such a conclusion can be reached. Text-critical work is of little assistance in this instance, however, as it only accentuates the disparity between biblical chronology and that of the Tyrian king-list. In a recent text-critical study of Kings, J. D. Shenkel has demonstrated that the Old Greek chronology taken from LXX MSS. boc_2e_2 is at least a decade longer for the early period of the Hebrew kings than that of the MT for the same period (Shenkel 1968: 32–40; App. A). Working from the Assyrian synchronisms with the kings of Israel in the middle 9th century, the Old Greek chronology would push Solomon's accession back before 980 B.C.E., and Hiram's accession correspondingly earlier. Since the Old Greek chronology puts even more years between Hiram and the foundation of Carthage than the MT does, on the basis of comparison with the Tyrian king-list, the MT appears to provide the better chronological system of the two.

There is, finally, the matter of how long Hiram ruled. The biblical synchronisms of David and Solomon with Hiram point to a reign of half a century at the minimum. That is a long time to reign, but such a long reign is not unknown in the ancient Near East. Among Hiram's contemporaries, Amenemope of the 21st Dynasty of Egypt ruled for 52 years (1033–981), and Menkheperre was Theban high priest of

Amun for 49 years (1035–986) (Kitchen 1973: 1–16, 466). Forty years falls somewhat short of 50, but David, Solomon, and Asa of Judah reigned that long, as did Ashur-rabi II (1013–973) of Assyria (Brinkman 1964: 335–52). A little later Azariah of Judah and Sheshonk III of the 22nd Dynasty of Egypt ruled for 52 years, while earlier, Thutmose III of the 18th Dynasty fell only two months short of his 54th year and Ramesses II of the 19th Dynasty reached his 67th (Thiele 1965: 134; Kitchen 1973: 100–5, 567; Steindorff and Seele 1968: 53–64; Gardiner 1969: 188–98, 443, 252–70, 445). Thus such a long reign for Hiram of Tyre does not exceed the limits of possibility, and one suggestion related to this matter might be that his age of 53 years in the king-list was taken over from the number of his regnal years during the course of its transmission. In round figures, then, we may suggest that the long reign of David and Solomon's contemporary, Hiram, spanned the first half of the 10th century B.C.E.

Appendix

COMPARATIVE CHRONOLOGICAL CHART

	Peñuela		*Lipiński*		*Cross*	
Kings	**Years**	**Dates**	**Years**	**Dates**	**Years**	**Dates**
Hiram I	34	980–947	34	962–929	34	980–947
Baᶜal-mazzer I	17	946–930	7	928–922	17	946–930
ᶜAbd-ᶜAštart	9	929–921	9	921–913	9	929–921
(1st Usurper)	12	920–909	12	912–901	–	– –
ᶜAštart	12	908–897	12	900–889	20	920–901
(Dalay-ᶜAštart)	–	– –	–	– –	12	900–889
ᶜAštart-ram	9	896–888	9	888–880	9	888–880
Pillēs	2/3	887	2/3	879	2/3	879
ʾItto-Baᶜal	32	886–885	32	878–847	32	878–847
Baᶜal-mazzer II	14	854–841	6	846–841	6	846–841
Mattēn	9	840–832	9	840–832	9	840–832
Pygmalion	47	831–785	47	831–785	47	831–785

	Albright		*Katzenstein*	
Kings	**Years**	**Dates**	**Years**	**Dates**
Hiram I	34	969–936	34	969–936
Baᶜal-mazzer I	17	935–919	17	935–919
ᶜAbd-ᶜAštart	9	918–910	9	918–910
(1st Usurper)	–	– –	–	– –
ᶜAštart	12	909–898	12	909–898
ᶜAštart-ram	9	897–889	9	897–889
Pillēs	2/3	888	2/3	888
ʾItto-Baᶜal	32	887–856	32	887–856
(Baᶜal-ᶜazor)	6	855–850	–	– –
Baᶜal-mazzer II	20	849–830	26	855–830
Mattēn	9	829–821	9	829–821
Pygmalion	47	820–774	47	820–774

Notes

1. For this period in Mesopotamian history see D. J. Wiseman (1975). More brief statements on this subject may be found in Saggs (1962: 88–92), Roux (1969: 47–61), and Olmstead (1923: 70–80).

2. The standard work for this period of Egyptian history now is Kitchen (1973); see especially ¶220–240 and Table I. Note also Redford (1973), Lance (1976), and Green (1978).

3. Unless otherwise indicated, all quotations and references from Greek and Roman sources are taken from volumes in the Loeb Classical Library.

4. 1 Kgs 9: 10 states that this transaction followed the completion of the temple and palace after the 20 years of construction which, according to 1 Kgs 6: 1, began in Solomon's 4th year.

5. For the practice of papponymy by Ammonite kings in the 7th century see Cross (1973). The

same principle was practiced by the Samaritans of the 4th century according to Cross' studies of the Wâdī Dâliyeh texts (1963: 19–21; 1969: 55–56, nn. 35, 36) and aspects of Samaritan and Jewish history (1966: 203–4). For papponymy among the Tobiads see B. Mazar (1957: 137–145, 229–38 n. 73). Based on his studies Cross has suggested that this practice started in the 7th century. The same feature is found, however, among the pharaohs of the New and Middle Kingdoms in Egypt; it would be even more evident there if we possessed full family genealogies. See also Redford on the coregency of Thutmose III and Amenophis II (1965: 113–15).

6. Lumby appears to believe that, since the man's name is given as Hiram and Huram elsewhere (1 Kgs 7: 13, 40, 45; 2 Chr 4: 11), his name was the same as his father's. Most likely this was simply the short form of his name. The other possibility suggested by commentators is that the "father" part of his name was honorific meaning "master workman" or "counselor." In either case there is no indication here that both a father and his son bore precisely the same name.

7. 1 Sam 14: 2–2 Sam 5: 10 and 1 Kings 1–2 comprise what is known as the "Court History of David." In quality, this masterpiece is possibly the oldest piece of interpretive and descriptive history written against the background of the political sophistication of the United Monarchy.

8. "Philistia and the inhabitants of Tyre" (Ps 83: 8) may allude to the earlier historical events of this period if we follow B. Mazar and date this Psalm to the period between the Report of Wen-Amun and the Kingdom of Saul, i.e., late in the period of the Judges, when there may have been cooperation between Tyre and the Philistines (cf. Judg 10: 11–12). In this connection Josephus' statement that the nations of Syria and Phoenicia fought alongside the Philistines (*Ant* 7.74) may be of significance. See Mazar (1963: 47–48) and Katzenstein (1973: 73–74). A counter opinion, however, maintains that in general, the relations between Israel and the cities of Tyre and Sidon were amicable (Eissfeldt 1936: 7).

9. It was the defeat of the Philistines on land that opened up the possibilities for the establishment of Tyre as a maritime power (Albright 1975: 525; Katzenstein 1973: 75).

10. Hiram's embassy to David during the last 7 to 9 years of the latter's reign would imply that this important development occurred during the final waning years of his monarchy.

11. The annalistic presentation in 2 Sam 8: 1–14 could suggest that David did have imperial designs from the beginning. On the other hand, 2 Sam 10: 1–5 advances the idea that his foreign wars began more or less unexpectedly with the incident involving David's ambassadors to the Ammonite royal court.

12. The actual figure given on the basis of the stated totals of all the kings is 240 years 7 months and 7 days.

13. See pertinent discussion on the fall of Troy (Hayes 1970: 246–47; Katzenstein 1973: 61–62).

14. The whole period from the accession of Hiram to the foundation of Carthage amounts to 155 years and 8 months, and, since the temple at Jerusalem was built in the 12th year of Hiram's reign, 143 years and 8 months elapsed between the building of the Temple and the foundation of Carthage.

15. According to Timaeus, Carthage was founded thirty-eight years before the first Olympiad, that is 814/813 B.C.E. (Dion. Halic., *Ant. Rom.* 1.74). Cicero speaks of 38 years (*Rep.* 2.23). Velleius Peterculus states that Carthage was in existence for 667 years before it was demolished (*Hist. Rom.* 1.21–22) = 667 + 114 = 814 B.C.E. Another calculation according to Aristotle is based on the founding of Utica 287 years before the founding of Carthage (*Op. Min.* 844). Pliny wrote that the original beams installed in the temple of Apollo at the foundation of the city of Utica lasted for 1178 years (*HN* 16.216). Pliny's work was written in 77/78, hence (1178/77 - 77/78 =) 1101/1100 - 287 = 814/813. There is the likelihood that a number of these writers relied to some degree on Timaeus. See additional discussion on the relative importance of each proposed date for the founding of Carthage by Picard (Picard and Picard 1968: 28–35; Picard 1965: 15–27).

16. According to Justinus, Pompius Trogus states that Carthage was founded 72 years before the founding of Rome (753 + 72 = 825 B.C.E.) (*Epit.* 18.6.9). See additional discussion in Harden (1962: 66–75).

17. There were seven editions between 1544 and 1930. Four of the editions were the *princeps graeca* (1544) and those by Havercamp (1726), Dindorf (1847) and Naber (1896). Three other editions of a more critical nature incorporated variants from other MSS., Niese (1889), Thackeray (1926) and Reinach (1930). Blum's French translation is based on Reinach's text. For references see Peñuela (1954: 40–42).

18. *Editio latina Basileae* (1524), J. Frobenium, 2d ed. by C. Boysen (1898) and Peñuela (1954: 40).

19. Scaliger's *Veterum graecorum fragmenta selecta, Quibus loci aliquot obscurissimi chronologiae sacrae et*

Bibliorum illustrantur, published as an appendix to Scaliger (1598). The chronological data tabulated from this source by Peñuela agree with the Codex Laurentianus in all respects (Peñuela 1954: 42).

20. The original Greek text of Eusebius of Caesarea's *Chronicorum Libri* is lost, but paragraphs 106–27 are found in the XIth century *ʾEklogē historiōn* and reprinted by A. Schöne (1875: 114–20). Note additional discussion in Lipiński (1970: 59).

21. G. Syncelli (1652: 183c), and Peñuela (1953: 225, n. 38).

22. See, for example, the total of each list in the individual MSS. in Peñuela (1954: 40–42).

23. So, for Baal-mazzer I 17 years instead of 7, Mattēn 29 instead of 9 years, and 0 years for the first usurper instead of the 12 years accredited in A. If this is done, the total is 155 years and 8 months up to the 7th year of Pygmalion, rather than 137 years 8 months, which represents the combined total reign of all the kings given in family A or B.

24. Albright (1955: 1–9) argues for a 814/813 date.

25. See Comparative Chronological Chart below.

26. Translated, "The eldest of these reigned 12 years. After this ʿAštart."

27. Only Syncellus disagrees and says there were three sons (Niese 1889: 22). The four brothers were the unnamed eldest or Dalay-ʿAštart, ʿAštart, ʿAštart-ram, and Pillēs (Peñuela 1954: 16–18; Katzenstein 1973: 126–28).

28. Based on the Greek text in Thackeray (1926: 210) and Niese (1889: 22). According to Cross, if the haplography is restored the entire bracketed section would be inserted between the names Astartos and Dalay-ʿAštartos, his successor.

29. See discussion above.

30. Her marriage to Ahab is the first event mentioned in his reign (1 Kgs 16: 31). The religious crisis she was instrumental in precipitating seems to have come to a head at least 6 or 7 years before the end of Ahab's reign (1 Kgs 18: 1; 22: 1) and must have taken some time to develop before that. Her son Joram (2 Kgs 9: 22) was old enough to exercise his kingly powers when he came to the throne 23 or 24 years after the accession of his father.

31. See discussions on the importance of the king-lists in Western Asia: Rowton 1970: 193–200; Lewy 1971: 740–52; and Katzenstein 1973: 77–78.

32. Comprehensive works on the Assyrian and Babylonian Chronicles are Wiseman (1956) and Grayson (1975).

References

Albright, W. F.

1942 *Archaeology and Religion of Israel*. Baltimore: Johns Hopkins University.

1950 The Judicial Reform of Jehosaphat. Pp. 61–82 in *Alexander Marx Jubilee Volume*. New York: Jewish Publication Society.

1955 The New Assyro-Tyrian Synchronism and the Chronology of Tyre. *Annuaire de l'Institut de Philologie et d'Histoire Orientales et Slaves* 13: 1–9.

1956 Further Light on Synchronisms between Egypt and Asia in the Period 935–685 B.C. *Bulletin of the American Schools of Oriental Research* 141: 23–27.

1975 Syria, the Philistines, and Phoenicia. CAH³ II/2, pp. 507–605.

Boysen, C., ed.

1898 *Flavii Iosephi Opera, Pars VI. Ex Versione Latina Antiqua*. Prague: F. Tempsky.

Bright, John

1974 *A History of Israel²*. Philadelphia: Westminster.

Brinkman, J. A.

1964 Appendix: Mesopotamian Chronology of the Historical Period. Pp. 335–52 in A. L. Oppenheim, *Ancient Mesopotamia: Portrait of a Dead Civilization*. Chicago: University of Chicago.

Caird, G. B.
1953 I and II Samuel. Vol. 2, pp. 853–1176 in *The Interpreter's Bible*, ed. G. A. Buttrick et al. Nashville: Abingdon.

Croney, R. W.
1962 Hiram. Vol. 2, pp. 606–7 in *The Interpreter's Dictionary of the Bible*, ed. G. A. Buttrick et al. Nashville: Abingdon.

Cross, F. M.
1963 The Discovery of the Samaria Papyri. Pp. 227–39 in *The Biblical Archaeologist Reader III*, ed. D. N. Freedman and E. F. Campbell. Garden City, New York: Doubleday.
1966 Aspects of Samaritan and Jewish History in Late Persian and Hellenistic Times. *Harvard Theological Review* 59: 203–11.
1969 Papyri of the Fourth Century B.C. from Dâliyeh. Pp. 41–62 in *New Directions in Biblical Archaeology*, ed. D. N. Freedman and J. C. Greenfield. Garden City, New York: Doubleday.
1972 An Interpretation of the Nora Stone. *Bulletin of the American Schools of Oriental Research* 208: 13–19.
1973 Notes on the Ammonite Inscription from Tell Siran. *Bulletin of the American Schools of Oriental Research* 212: 12–15.

Delaporte, L.
1948 *Le Proche-Orient asiatique*. Vol. I. Paris: Renaissance du livre.

Eissfeldt, O.
1936 *Der Alte Orient*. Tübingen: J. C. B. Mohr.

Flavius, Josephus
1926 *Against Apion*. Trans. H. St. James Thackeray. Loeb Classical Library. Cambridge: Harvard University Press.
1927–32 *Jewish Antiquities I-XI*. Trans. H. St. J. Thackeray and R. Marcus. Loeb Classical Library. Cambridge: Harvard University Press.

Freedman, D. N.
1965 The Chronology of Israel and the Ancient Near East. Pp. 265–81 in *The Bible and the Ancient Near East*, ed. G. E. Wright. Garden City, New York: Doubleday.
1979 The Age of David and Solomon. Vol. 4, Part 1, pp. 101–25 in *The World History of the Jewish People: The Age of the Monarchies, Political History*, ed. Abraham Malamat. Jerusalem: Massada.

Gardiner, A. H.
1969 *Egypt of the Pharaohs*. New York: Oxford University Press.

Gray, John
1970 *I and II Kings*. Old Testament Library. Philadelphia: Westminster.

Grayson, A. K.
1975 *Assyrian and Babylonian Chronicles*. Texts from Cuneiform Sources 5. Locust Valley, New York: J. J. Augustin.

Green, A. R.
1978 Solomon and Siamun: A Synchronism between Early Dynastic Israel and the Twenty-First Dynasty of Egypt. *Journal of Biblical Literature* 97: 353–67.

Gutschmidt, A.
1889–93 *Kleine Schriften*. Bd. I, 1889; Bd. II, 1890; Bd. III, 1893. Leipzig: Teubner.

Harden, D.
1962 *The Phoenicians*. London: Thames and Hudson.

Harris, Z. S.
1936 *A Grammar of the Phoenician Language*. American Oriental Series 8. New Haven: Yale University.

Hayes, W. C.
1970 Chronology. CAH^3 I/1, pp. 173–247.

Justinus
1872 Trogi Pompei. In *Historiarum Philippicarum Epitoma*. Trans. Justus Ieep. Lipsiae: B. G. Teubner.

Katzenstein, H. J.
1973 *The History of Tyre*. Jerusalem: Goldberg.

Kirkpatrick, A. F.
1930 *The First and Second Books of Samuel*. Cambridge Bible for Schools and Colleges. Cambridge: Cambridge University.

Kitchen, K. A.
1973 *The Third Intermediate Period in Egypt (1100–650 B.C.E.)*. Warminster: Aris and Phillips.

Kittel, R.
1922 *Geschichte des Volkes Israel*[5]. Vol. 1. Gotha: F. A. Perthes.

Lance, H. D.
1976 Solomon, Siamun, and the Double Ax. Pp. 209–23 in *Magnalia Dei . . .Essays . . . G. E. Wright*, ed. F. M. Cross et al. Garden City: Doubleday.

Lewy, H.
1971 King-list and Chronology. CAH[3] I/2, pp. 740–52.

Lipiński, E.
1970 Baʿli-Maʿzer II and the Chronology of Tyre. *Rivisti degli studi orientali* 45: 59–65.

Liver, J.
1953 The Chronology of Tyre at the Beginning of the First Millennium B.C. *Israel Exploration Journal* 3: 113–20.

Lumby, J. R.
1890 *The First Book of Kings*. Cambridge Bible for Schools and Colleges. Cambridge: Cambridge University Press.

Maly, E. H.
1965 *The World of David and Solomon*. Englewood Cliffs, N. J.: Prentice Hall.

Mazar, B.
1957 The Tobiads. *Israel Exploration Journal* 7: 137–45.
1963 David's Reign in Hebron and the Conquest of Jerusalem. *Bulletin of the Jewish Palestine Exploration Society* 4: 47–48 (Hebrew).

Meyer, Eduard
1931 *Geschichte des Altertums*[2]. Vol. 2. Stuttgart: J. G. Gotta'sche.

Myers, J.
1965 *I Chronicles*. Anchor Bible 12. Garden City, New York: Doubleday.

Niese, B.
1889 *Flavius Josephus*. Berolini: Apud Weidmannos.

Noth, M.
1960 *The History of Israel*[2]. New York: Harper and Row.

Olmstead, A. T.
1923 *History of Assyria*. New York: Charles Scribners Sons.

Paterculus, V.
1724 *Historiae Romanae I*. Trans. Thomas Newcomb. London: John Pemberton.

Peñuela, J. N.
1953 La Inscripcíon Asiria IM 55644 y la Cronologia de los reyes Tiro. *Sefarad* 13: 217–37.
1954 La Inscripcíon Asiria IM 55644 y la Cronologia de los reyes Tiro. *Sefarad* 14: 3–42.

Picard, C.
1965 Notes de Chronologie Punique: Le problème du Ve Siècle. *Karthago* 12: 15–27.

Picard, G. C., and Picard, C.
1968 *The Life and Death of Carthage*. New York: Taplinger.

Redford, D. B.
1965 The Coregency of Thutmose III and Amenophis II. *Journal of Egyptian Archaeology* 51: 107–22.
1973 Studies in Relations between Palestine and Egypt during the First Millennium B.C. II: The Twenty-Second Dynasty. *Journal of the American Oriental Society* 96: 3–17.

Roux, G.
1969 *Ancient Iraq*. Harmondsworth: Penguin.

Rowton, M. B.
1950 The Date of the Founding of Solomon's Temple. *Bulletin of the American Schools of Oriental Research* 119: 20–22.
1970 Ancient Western Asia. CAH[3] I/1, pp. 193–247.

Safar, F.
1951 A Further Text of Shalmaneser III from Assur. *Sumer* 7: 3–21.

Saggs, H. W. F.
1962 *The Greatness that was Babylon*. New York: Mentor.

Scaligeri, Iosephi
1598 *Opus de emendatione temporum*[2]. Batavorum Lugduni.

Schöne, A. K. I.
1875 *Eusebi Chronicorum libri duo I*. Berlin: Wiedmann.

Shenkel, J. D.
1968 *Chronology and Recensional Development in the Greek Text of Kings*. Harvard Semitic Monographs 1. Cambridge: Harvard University.

Smith, H. P.
1899 *The Books of Samuel*. International Critical Commentary. New York: Charles Scribners Sons.

Steindorff, G., and Seele, K. C.
1968 *When Egypt Ruled the East*. Chicago: University of Chicago.

Syncelli, G.
1652 *Chronographia ab Adamo usque ad Diocletianum*. Paris: P. I. Goar.

Thiele, E. R.
1965 *The Mysterious Numbers of the Hebrew Kings: A Reconstruction of the Kingdoms of Israel and Judah*[2]. Grand Rapids: Zondervan.

Ulrich, E.
1978 *Qumran Texts of Samuel and Josephus*. Harvard Semitic Studies 19. Missoula, Montana: Scholars Press.

Vogelstein, M.
1944 *Biblical Chronology*. Cincinnati: Hebrew Union College.

Wiseman, D. J.
1975 Assyria and Babylonia c. 1200–1000. CAH[3] II/2, pp. 443–81.

Pollution, Purification, and Purgation in Biblical Israel

Tikva Frymer-Kensky
Ann Arbor, Michigan

Major and Minor Pollutions

The ideas of pollution, purity, and purification were fundamental concepts of biblical Israel. The desire for purity was so intense that a major social class, the priesthood, was entrusted with the task of determining and giving instruction about purity and impurity. Pollution, the lack of purity, could affect individuals, the temple, the collectivity of Israel, and the land of Israel itself. Some forms of pollution could be eradicated by rituals; the performance of these purifications and expiations was a major function of the priesthood. The pollution caused by the performance of certain deeds, however, could not be eradicated by rituals; Israel believed that the person intentionally committing these acts would suffer catastrophic retribution. Wrongful acts could cause the pollution of the nation and of the land of Israel, which could also not be "cured" by ritual. There was therefore an ultimate expectation of catastrophic results for the whole people, the "purging" of the land by destruction and exile. Pollution was thus thought to be one of the determinants of Israel's history, and the concepts of pollution and purgation provided a paradigm by which Israel could understand and survive the destruction of the Temple. The idea of pollution was such an important part of Israel's world-view that its Primeval History, its story of origins, was also seen as a story of cosmic pollution and purgation.

The simplest type of impurity is the impure state of the levitical laws. If an individual comes into contact with a polluting substance, that person becomes impure for seven days or more, in the case of major pollutions, or until the evening, for minor pollutions. During the period of his impurity, the polluted individual is highly contagious. He must avoid contact with others and must take care to avoid coming into contact with the sacred.

External causes (things) normally cause only minor contamination. The chief exception to this is death. Corpse-contamination is a most virulent pollution. Contamination for seven days results not only from contact with a corpse but from being in a tent when someone dies, and even from contact with the human bones or graves of a corpse-defiled person (Num 19: 11, 14, 16); everyone involved in purification rituals suffers minor contamination. In the ideal camp of the desert, therefore, corpse-defiled people were to stay outside the camp for seven days (Num 31: 19). The other major external pollutant is the disease of leprosy (Leviticus 13–14). The leper's contamination is considered so intense that he must dwell outside the camp, alone, and he must indicate his condition by tearing his clothes, growing a mustache, leaving his hair disheveled, and calling out, "Unclean, unclean"

(Lev 13: 45–46). He remains impure for seven days after the leprosy is pronounced healed. We are not informed what happens to an individual who comes into contact with a "leper" (assuming of course that he does not contract the disease from casual contact); we might speculate that he would become impure, perhaps for the major period of seven days. Other external causes of pollution (see chart below) cause only minor pollution.

The extremely defiling nature of corpses has been explained as an attempt to avoid a cult of the dead (Wold 1979: 18). However, there may be a more fundamental reason: in Israelite cosmology it was considered vitally important to maintain the structure of the universe by keeping all distinctions (boundaries) firm (Douglas 1966: 53). The boundaries between life and death are crucial and no individual who has had contact with the world of death can be part of life. He must therefore stay in limbo—outside the camp—for seven days and undergo a special ritual (sprinkling with the "waters of impurity," Numbers 19) to enable him to rejoin the life-group. Before he has spent his time in limbo and been readmitted to the group he belongs at least partially to the world of death. The severe isolation of the leper may also be related to this distinction between life and death (in addition to its value as a medical quarantine). If the disease was at all similar to modern leprosy, its effect in an advanced state was similar to the decomposition of a corpse; the biblical association of leprosy and corpses is expressed in Num 12: 12, where the leprous Miriam is compared to one born dead and half decomposed. The afflicted individual, like one who has been in contact with a corpse, might have been considered to be in a no-man's land between two realms which must be kept rigidly apart. It may be relevant that disheveled hair and rent clothes are a sign of mourning (Lev 10: 6); the leper may be mourning his own "death." The ritual that the healed leper undergoes before he can reenter the camp (Lev 14: 4–7) may also indicate that this blurring of the demarcation between life and death lies behind the virulence of the contamination of leprosy. Two clean birds are taken, one of which is killed over a bowl with running water. The living bird is dipped in the blood of the dead bird, the leper is sprinkled with the blood of the slain bird, and the living bird is let loose in the field. The formal similarity between this ritual and the ritual of the Day of Atonement is apparent: both involve two creatures, one of which is killed and the other set free. In the case of the leper, the symbolism focuses on the living bird who has been in contact with death (dipped in the blood of the killed bird) and is then set free; so too the leper has been set free from his brush with death. The leper may then return to the camp, although he is still impure and must remain outside his tent seven days before undergoing a ritual of readmission and resuming normal life (Lev 14: 10–32).

The other major pollutions are caused by emissions from the human body. The most enduring is that of childbirth (Leviticus 12). Birth of a male child renders a woman impure for seven days, birth of a female for fourteen days. After this period, although no longer impure, the mother is not totally pure and must avoid the realm of the holy for an additional 33 days for a male and 66 days for a female. This additional semi-impure period is known as the period of blood-purification (*dmy ṭhrh* Lev 12: 4, also *ymy ṭhrh* 12: 4). No reason is given why a male pollutes his mother only half as long as a female pollutes hers: one might speculate that the necessity of having the circumcision on the eighth day made it impossible for the period of full impurity to last more than seven days after the birth of a male child, but why should the birth of a female contaminate for fourteen? The lengthy transitional period ("purification") after childbirth is unique. Although childbirth involves emissions of blood and other fluids, and therefore could be expected to contaminate, like menstruation, for at least seven days, this does not explain why the contamination of childbirth lingers on, at least partially, after the seven- or fourteen- day period has elapsed. It may be that, like the person who has touched death, the person who has experienced birth has been at the boundaries of life/non-life and therefore cannot directly reenter the community. She therefore must undergo a long period of transition before she can reapproach the sacred.

The other two causes of major pollution are menstruation, and genital discharge for males and females (Leviticus 15). Menstruation pollutes a woman and any man who has intercourse with her for seven days after (apparently from the onset of menstruation); genital discharge pollutes for seven days after the discharge has disappeared. The reason for the severity of this pollution, or for its cause, is not quite clear. In her pioneering study of impurity, Douglas suggested that the human body served as the symbol for the body politic. Since Israel, as a hard-pressed minority, was careful to maintain its boundaries, that which entered the body was carefully regulated, and that which left was a polluting agent (1966: 124, see 1975: 269). Douglas explicitly assumes (1966: 51, 124), that all bodily emissions were considered polluting. This, however, is not indicated in the Bible. On the contrary, only emissions from the genitalia were considered polluting agents. Despite the fact that food (entry into the body) was carefully regulated, the excreta involved in the digestive process—saliva, urine, feces—are not mentioned as polluting. Defecation is supposed to take place outside the ideal camp (Deut 23: 13 15) but individuals excreting or even touching feces are not considered defiled until evening nor is it prescribed that they must bathe. Even those emissions that might be considered somewhat diseased—nasal discharge, sputum, pus—are not mentioned as polluting agents. The most conspicuous human emission absent from the list of polluting agents is human blood (or, for that matter, any blood). Blood, of course, may not be eaten. However, despite the fact that menstrual blood is a major contaminant, and that (innocent) bloodshed is the most important pollutant of the land (see below), ordinary blood is not mentioned as a contaminant. Bleeding or touching blood is not considered polluting, and people who are wounded and bleeding are not defiled and are not forbidden to come to the temple or to partake of sacrifices. The only bodily emissions that pollute are those involved with sex: menstrual blood and discharges as major pollutants, ejaculation (with or without intercourse) until the evening. The reason that these are considered polluting must lie in the social relations between men and women and in the culture's attitude towards sex.

Minor pollutions are generally contracted from external causes: contact with impure things, such as the carcasses of unclean animals, or contact with something that has become unclean through contact with someone under a major pollution, or contact with someone who is polluted with a major pollution. The only internally-caused minor pollution mentioned is caused by seminal discharge through ejaculation or fornication. For convenience, I include a chart of the minor pollutions mentioned in the levitical laws.[1]

The prime characteristic of the major pollutions is their contagion. People who have a major pollution can defile others, making them impure for the duration of the

	verse	source of uncleanness	action of a person	wait till evening	wash clothes	bathe
Lev	11:24,27	carcass of unclean animal	touching	X	—	—
	11:25,28	carcass of unclean animal	carrying	X	X	—
	11:31	carcass of creepy-crawly	touching	X	—	—
	11:39	carcass of clean animal	touching	X	—	—
	11:40	carcass of clean animal	carrying	X	X	—
	11:40	carcass of clean animal	eating	X	X	—
	14:46	leprous house	entering while sealed before examination	X	—	—
	14:47	leprous house	eating, sleeping in	(X)[2]	X	—
	15:5	man with discharge	touching bedding of	X	X	X
	15:6	man with discharge	sitting on seat of	X	X	X
	15:7	man with discharge	touching person of	X	X	X
	15:10	man with discharge	touching something that has been under (e.g., saddle)	X	—	—
	15:10	man with discharge	carrying something that has been under	X	X	X
	15:11	man with discharge	being touched by with unwashed hands	X	X	X
	15:16	ejaculation		X	—	X
	15:18	fornication (for m and f)		X	—	X
	15:19	menstruant	touching	X	—	—
	15:21	menstruant	touching bedding of	X	X	X
	15:22	menstruant	touching seat of	X	X	X
	15:26-27	woman with discharge	touching bedding or seat of	X	X	X
	17:15	carrion	eating	X	X	X
			action of a priest			
	22:4-7	impure person	touching	X	—	X
	22:4-7	ejaculation	having; possibly touching	X	—	X
	22:5	unclean animal	touching	X	—	X
	22:5	unclean person who can make unclean	touching	X	—	X
Num	19:6-7	red cow	putting hyssop, cedar and crimson into fire of	X	X	X
			action of a person			
	19:8	red cow	burning	X	X	X
	19:10	red cow	gathering ashes of	X	X	—
	19:21	waters of impurity	touching	X	—	—
	19:21	waters of impurity	sprinkling	(X)[2]	X	—
	19:22	corpse-defiled person	touching	X	—	—

day. People with a major pollution can also defile things which, in turn, can defile other people for the day. The levitical laws do not indicate whether a person under a minor pollution can himself defile during the day that he is impure. Our assumption would be that a person with a minor pollution cannot defile, because otherwise there would be no end,[3] and because we would expect some warning if minor defilement was contagious. This is indeed the way later Jewish law understood the issue of contagion.

These pollutions are contagious, but they are not dangerous. No harm is expected to come to the individual who has become impure in any of these ways, nor is there a hint that a man who, e.g., touches his menstruating wife would suffer harm or fail in his crops, only that he himself will become impure for the day. The only characteristic of *ṭm*ʾ*h*, "pollution," is contagion; the only misfortune associated with the condition is isolation from the people and alienation from all things holy. The condition of impurity becomes actively dangerous to the individual only when it comes into contact with the sacred. Since the impure can defile the sacred, the sacred must be protected. This goal may be accomplished by direct means such as posting guards to prevent the visibly impure from approaching the Temple (2 Chr 23: 19). It is also achieved by a belief that catastrophe will strike whoever approaches the sacred while impure: an impure priest who eats the sacred portions (Lev 22: 3–9), an impure person who eats a sacrifice of well-being (Lev 7: 20–21),[4] and anyone who comes to the Temple while impure. As long as the polluted individual avoids the realm of the sacred he is not expected to suffer any harm: he waits out his period of pollution, performs appropriate purification and readmission rituals, and returns to ordinary membership in the community. There is only one threat inherent in these pollutions. Since they are contagious, there is a danger that the contagion will spread throughout the community, thus effectively isolating the entire community from contact with God. Since the community believes its well-being to be dependent on its relationship to God, alienation from God could present impossible danger.

There is no onus attached to these pollutions, no idea that they result from forbidden or improper actions, no "guilt" attributed to the impure. Acts which are prohibited are not said to result in an impure state. On the contrary, many of the acts which result in the polluted state are natural functions which cannot be avoided. Without childbirth (a major pollutant) and sexual intercourse (a minor pollutant) society would cease to exist. Avoidance of intercourse and childbirth is, moreover, an avoidance of the explicit command to procreate. Similarly, corpses must be disposed of properly even though contact with the corpse results in major pollution. The world must come into contact with the dead—only the Holy has to be kept separate from it. Even priests may attend the deceased of their immediate family, and then remain in limbo until their corpse-contamination is over (Lev 21: 1–6). Only the High Priest (Lev 21: 10–11) and the Nazirite (Num 6: 6–7) must avoid all corpses. If someone falls down dead right next to the Nazirite, the contamination of the death disrupts the vow and terminates his period as a Nazirite (Num 6: 9–12). There is, however, no question of moral culpability for such inadvertent contact with death.

The only instance in which there was any moral opprobrium attached to a polluted state is the case of the leper. In narrative portions of the Bible, leprosy (like premature death or *karet*) is a divine sanction imposed for the commission of certain wrongs: on Miriam for her affrontery against Moses (Num 12: 10–15), Gehazi for wrongfully taking money from Naaman (2 Kgs 5: 27), and Uzziah for presuming to offer incense by himself (2 Chr 26: 19–21). Since the tradition records instances in which leprosy was a divine punishment, there may have been a tendency to suspect lepers of wrongdoing. This, however, is simply folk suspicion, much as in nineteenth-century social philosophy the poor may have been suspected of being "shiftless." The formal tradition of Israel attached no blame to lepers, only impurity. Ritual pollution, even in the case of lepers, was not a moral issue.

The lack of wrong-doing involved in these pollutions distinguishes them from other forms of pollution which do convey a moral message. Biblical Israel had two separate sets of what anthropologists would consider "pollution beliefs": a set discussed extensively as pollutions in the Priestly laws, since the priests were responsible for preventing the contamination of the pure and the Holy; and a set of beliefs that we might term "danger beliefs." The deeds that involve these danger beliefs differ fundamentally from the deeds that result in ritual impurity. There is a clear implication of wrong-doing, for the individual has placed himself in danger by doing something that he and the people have been expressly forbidden to do; the danger is seen as a divine sanction for the deed. Unlike the ritual pollutions, which last a set period, the danger caused by these deeds is permanent (until the catastrophe strikes). The ritual pollutions may have accompanying rituals of purification and readmission; the danger pollutions cannot be ameliorated in this way, although there is a sense that repentance and sacrifice can avert some if not all of the calamity. The state induced by committing one of these infractions is also not contagious. No one can become impure by contact with someone who has committed one of these wrongful acts. One does not share the danger of an adulterer or of someone who has eaten blood by touching him. There is no immediate danger to others in allowing these people to walk around, and therefore there are no prescribed patterns of avoidance. There is, however, an ultimate danger to the people, for if too many individuals commit these deeds, then the whole society might be considered polluted and might thus be in danger of a collective catastrophe.

When an individual commits one of these wrongful catastrophe-deeds, the catastrophe may not be specified, but rather indicated by the phrase *nś᾽ ᾽t ʿwnw*, "he shall bear his penalty," a phrase which always indicates divine punishment (Zimmerli 1954: 8–11; Frymer-Kensky forthcoming). More often, the individual may be set to be *nkrt*, "cut off", a phrase which may appear alone (e.g., Lev 20: 18) or with the *nś᾽ ᾽t ʿwnw* warning (e.g., Lev 20: 17). This *karet* provision is an integral part of the priestly understanding of purity and was probably understood to mean the extirpation of one's lineage.[5]

The deeds that entail the *karet* sanction are acts against the fundamental principles of Israelite cosmology; in particular, acts that blur the most vital distinction in the Israelite classificatory system, the separation of sacred and profane. The protection of the realm of the sacred is of prime importance in Israelite thought in view of the belief that God dwells among the children of Israel. Since he is holy, they must be holy (Lev 11: 44, 45; 19: 2; 20: 7, 26) and must not contaminate the camp, temple, or land in which he lives. The protection of the realm of the sacred is a categorical imperative in Israel: it must be differentiated, not only from the impure, but also from the pure, which serves almost as a buffer zone between the sacred and the defiling. Violating the distinctions between sacred and profane disrupts the entire system. The violator is therefore expected to incur the *karet* penalty; in other words, his deed is expected to result in calamity to his entire lineage through the direct intervention of God ("automatically") and without necessitating societal action. This belief in automatic retribution protects the realm of the sacred by deterring acts which would encroach upon it.

The protection of the sacred was the prime purpose of the *karet* penalty. Israel considered itself a holy nation which was to keep itself distinct from other nations: failure to keep this distinction by not performing circumcision would result in *karet* (Gen 17: 14). The direct contamination of the sacred by approaching sacred things while impure, as in the case of eating sacred offerings while impure, results in *karet* (Lev 7: 20–21; 22: 3–9). The spread of impurity threatens the sacred by eliminating the "buffer-zone"; thus failure to be cleansed from corpse contamination results in *karet* (Num 19: 13, 20), while failure to be cleansed from the lesser contamination caused by eating carrion results in the doer "bearing his punishment" (*nś*ʾ ʾ*t* ʿ*wnw*, Lev 17: 15–16). Unauthorized contact with the sacred is believed to result in death (Num 4: 18–20, cf. 1 Sam 6: 19; 2 Sam 6: 6–7). Holy objects must not be subverted: lay persons, though pure, may not eat the holy offerings. The blood (Lev 7: 27; 17: 10, 14), the sacrificial suet (Lev 7: 25), the oil of installation (Exod 30: 33), and the sanctuary incense (Exod 30: 38) are all protected from profane consumption by the *karet* belief; the holy altar is thus maintained as the only proper place for slaughter (Lev 17: 4) and sacrifice (Lev 17: 9). Even the prohibition against eating sacrificial offerings on the third day (Lev 7: 18; 19: 8), which seems to us to be an excellent hygiene measure, is explicitly understood to be a matter of profaning God's holy offering (Lev 19: 8) and is therefore believed to incur the *karet* sanction. Similarly, the distinctions between sacred and profane time are a crucial part of the structure of Israelite thought and failure to maintain the characteristic distinctions of holy time results in *karet*: eating *ḥāmeṣ* on the Feast of Unleavened Bread (Exod 12: 15–19); working on the Sabbath (Exod 31: 14); working and eating on the Day of Atonement (Lev 23: 29–30); not performing the Passover sacrifice at its appointed time (Num 9: 13).

In all of these instances the function of the *karet* belief is clear: it serves as a divine reinforcement of the boundaries between sacred and profane by providing a sanction for acts which violate these boundaries but which are not normally provided with legal sanctions. This is also its function in the two instances of *karet*-belief which do not ostensibly involve sacred/profane distinctions, the prohibition against sleeping with one's sisters (Lev 20: 17) and the prohibition against sleeping with a menstruating woman (Lev 20: 18, the only instance in which a deed is believed to result both in a temporary pollution and in *karet*). The two provisions are part of a group of sexual laws establishing the limits of permitted sexual contact. One subset (Lev 20: 10–16) consists of relationships which society acts to punish with the death penalty. The other subset (Lev 20: 17–21) of relations which society apparently will not punish, but which it seeks to prevent by threat of supernatural sanction, i.e., danger beliefs: sexual intercourse with a sister or menstruant by *karet*, with one's aunt by unspecified danger (*nś*ʾ ʾ*t* ʿ*wnw*), with one's uncle's wife or brother's wife by childlessness. In Lev 18: 29, in what seems to be a general statement, all forbidden sexual relations are sanctioned by *karet*.

Pollution of the Temple

Fundamental to the function of the *karet*-belief is the idea that the sacred can be defiled and that there is a needs to protect it from such contamination. The temple in particular, as the site of God's presence, needs such protection. It could be defiled by enemies (Ps 79: 1), corpses (Ezek 9: 7), and idols or idolatrous practices (Jer 7: 30; 32: 34; Ezek 5: 11). It could also be defiled by impure people: by those who came to the temple while ritually impure (Lev 15: 31), and those who indulged in Molech worship and then came to the temple (Ezek 23: 38–39). Moreover, those who have not purified themselves of corpse-contamination (Num 19: 13, 20) or who have indulged in the abominations of the Gentiles (2 Chr 36: 14) are said to have defiled the temple, either because they came in an impure state or simply because they spread impurity.

The temple may also be defiled indirectly, from a distance. As Jacob Milgrom has explained (Milgrom 1976a), the Priestly image of the temple is that of a "Picture of Dorian Gray." The sanctuary can become polluted without direct contact with impurity. All misdeeds pollute the outer altar, misdeeds of the whole people or of the High Priest pollute the shrine, and wanton sin pollutes the adytum. This pollution of the temple would result in alienation from God, for God will not tolerate the pollution of his home: this alienation would have serious historical consequences.

There is, however, a cure for such pollution. The temple cult is meant to expiate and atone for misdeeds. On an individual level, there is a danger-belief that inadvertently committing an infraction results in the doer "bearing his punishment"; if, however, he brings an offering, the danger will be lifted ("it shall be forgiven him," Lev 5: 17–18). Individual and national sacrifices, particularly the *ḥaṭṭāʾt* sacrifice, purify the temple from the pollution caused by misdeeds (Milgrom 1971a, 1971b, 1976a, 1976b). And the Day of Atonement rituals were intended both to purify the people (the Azazel Goat) and to cleanse the temple from the pollution caused by the people (Milgrom 1971c). Within limits, therefore, the pollution of the temple could be rectified by ritual means.

Pollution of the People and the Land

Karet is usually mentioned alone or together with *nś*ʾ *ʾt* *ʿwnw*: specific legal sanctions are not mentioned. The exception to this is the "gruesome threesome" of apostasy: idolatry, child-Molech service and necromancy. All three of these acts constitute serious apostasy from God and are thus sanctioned by *karet*, in each instance by the unusual formula *hkrty(w)*, "I (God) will cut (him) off," in which the divine nature of the sanction is manifest (Molech-service, Lev 20: 5; necromancy, Lev 20: 6; idolatry, Ezek 14: 8). These offenses, moreover, are particularly grave in that they strike at the very basis of Israel, its relationship with God. The society cannot wait passively for divine action, but is commanded to punish the offender actively. The punishment meted out in all three cases is stoning (Molech-service, Lev 20: 2–6; necromancy, Lev 20: 27; idolatry, Deut 13: 7–12; 17: 2–7). This is a form of execution without an executioner, i.e., one in which the whole people act as the executioner since the people as a whole and the world-order on which they depend have been endangered (Finkelstein 1981: 26–27). Stoning is limited in the laws to these three instances of apostasy, to the disobedient son (Deut 21: 18–21), the non-virgin bride (Deut 22: 20–21), and both partners in the seduction of an engaged girl (Deut 22: 23–24). The corporate execution of the offender indicates the collective responsibility of the people for the act. It is extended to the protection of the sacred by three cautionary tales that are included in the narrative portions of the Hexateuch; the tales of the blasphemer (Lev 24: 10–16), of the man who violated the Sabbath (Num 15: 32–36), and of the man who took from the *ḥērem* (Joshua 7). In all three stories the violator was stoned; whether these stories had the force of law, and whether there was any intent to prescribe stoning for violating the Sabbath or blasphemy, is unknown.

The provision for stoning in Deuteronomy is accompanied by the phrase "you shall exterminate the evil from your midst" (*wbʿrt hrʿ mqrbk*), which implies that should society not act to punish the offender, the evil would in some way be imputed to it. This phrase is not limited to cases which demand stoning: ignoring a divine judgment (Deut 17: 12), murder (Deut 19: 11–13), false witness (Deut 19: 16–21), adultery (Deut 22: 22), and kidnap-and-sale (Deut 24: 7) must all be punished by society in order to exterminate the evil from its midst. These provisions (and the concept of exterminating evil from the midst of the people) may pre-date the book of Deuteronomy and may be part of an ancient criminal corpus (L'Hour 1963).

The concern about collective responsibility indicated by the stoning laws and the *biʿartā* provisions can also be expressed in the language of pollution. Necromancy is considered polluting (Lev 19: 31), as are Molech-worship (Ezek 20: 26, 30–31) and idolatry (Ezek 14: 11; 20: 31; cf. 22: 3–4; 23: 7–38). All forms of apostasy pollute the people, and this pollution does not disappear with time (Josh 22: 17). Sexual immorality is also a polluting agent: rape (Gen 34: 5, 13, 27), incest with one's daughter-in-law (Ezek 22: 11), and adultery (Num 5: 11–31; Ezek 18: 6, 11, 15). Adultery, moreover, results in the pollution of both parties (Lev 18: 20), as does bestiality (Lev 18: 23). All the improper sexual acts of Leviticus 18 are considered defiling to both the people and the land (Lev 18: 24). Murder, which is explicitly described as polluting the land, is not said to "pollute" the people in this terminology. It is clearly contaminating (McKeating 1975), but its contamination is expressed by the phrases *dām nāqî*, "innocent blood" (Deut 19: 13; 21: 8), and *dammîm*. General misdeeds and sins are also categorized as polluting the people (Ps 106: 39; Ezek 14: 11; 20: 43), though this may be a late extension of the pollution concept as it refers to the people. Ultimately, the people are considered as having become polluted; at the Restoration, according to Ezekiel, they will be purified by God (Ezek 36: 25; 37: 23).

There is no "cure" for the pollution engendered by these immoral acts, no ritual purification that can be performed until the sprinkling of pure water by God at the Restoration. The progressive pollution of the people by these deeds is thus like the most catastrophic pollution, that is, the pollution of the land.[6] The crimes of the people are considered to pollute the very earth of Israel (Jer 2: 7; Ezek 36: 17), and certain acts are explicitly termed contaminants. Bloodshed (Ps 106: 38) is a major pollutant, as is everything connected with it, such as leaving the body of an executed murderer exposed (Deut 21: 22–23), accepting composition for murder (Num 35: 31–34), or letting accidental murderers go free from the city of refuge (Num 35: 32). Idolatry pollutes (Ezek 36: 18), and so do such wrongful sex acts as the illicit sexual relations proscribed by Leviticus 18, whoredom (of the individual, Lev 19: 29; of the nation-as-female, Jer 3: 9; Ezek 23: 17), and adultery and remarriage to a previous wife who has been married in the interim (Deut 24: 1–4). These three classes of pollutants—murder, sexual abominations, and idolatry—pollute both the people and the land. In later theology, they are the cardinal sins that a Jew must die rather than commit and from which (according to James in Acts 15) it is incumbent on all nations to refrain. The results of performance of these sins are catastrophic, for, as Rabbinic sources recognized, they (together with unfulfilled public promises) bring drought (*y. Taʿan.* 3: 3 = 66C), and they (together with the nonobservance of the Sabbath and the Sabbath and Jubilee years) bring exile to the world (*b. Šabb.* 33a).

These acts have catastrophic results because they pollute the land that God protects as his own. Israel based its right of possession of its land on the idea that God dispossessed the original inhabitants because of their misdeeds. This concept is found in both the Deuteronomic and Priestly traditions. According to Deuteronomy, it was not the goodness of Israel that caused God to give it the land, but the evil of the nations living there (Deut 9: 4–5). Its right of occupation is therefore contingent on its actions. Israel is warned against performing the abominations of the nations that God dispossessed: passing children through fire, and engaging in magic, divination, and necromancy (Deut 18: 9–12). The Priestly tradition is also quite explicit that the abominations of the nations made them lose the land. Leviticus 18 lists the sexual abominations practised by the dispossessed nations, warns the people not to become polluted by them as the nations did, and explains that the land had become polluted by its inhabitants, that God had exacted the land's punishment[7] and that the land had thereupon vomited out its inhabitants. Israel is warned not to do these actions lest the land become polluted and vomit it out; people who engage in these abominations are "cut off" from the people (*karet*). In Leviticus 20, some of these sexual abominations are reiterated, Molech-service and necromancy are added to the list, and the people are again reminded that they are inheriting the land, that the previous inhabitants who did these abominations are being expelled, and that the land might vomit Israel out, too (Lev 20: 22–25).

Israel thus considered the non-pollution of the land a matter of national survival. The people are warned not to pollute the land by letting murderers go free or allowing accidental murderers to leave the city of refuge (Numbers 35: 31–34), by leaving the corpses of the executed unburied (Deut 21: 22–23), or even by permitting a man to remarry his divorced and since remarried wife (Deut 24: 1–4, cf. Jer 3: 1–4).

The pollution of the land cannot be rectified by ritual purification. In the case of murder, the law explicitly states that the blood of the slain cannot be expiated except by the blood of the shedder. The only ritual at all connected with the pollution of the land is the ritual of the decapitated heifer, the *ʿeglâ ʿarûpâ* (Deut 21: 1–9; see Patai 1939–40, Roifer 1961, Zevit 1976). This is clearly designed to avert the contamination of the land and the people by a murder whose perpetrator cannot be found. Although the people cannot properly expiate the blood of the slain, by performing this action they may eradicate (*bʿr*) the blood-contamination.

The pollution of the land may build up and ultimately reach a point beyond the level of tolerance, when a cataclysm becomes inevitable. There can be no "repentance" in the face of such pollution; it should be noted that repentance is seen as a privilege that is not automatically available. The concept of pollution was thus understood as one of the motive principles of Israelite history: the pollution of the land cleared the way for Israel to enter it; its pollution during their occupation presents a major danger. The idea of pollution was a major theoretical paradigm which enabled Israel to absorb and survive the eventual destruction of the state. It existed alongside, but is not identical to, the better known theoretical explanation of the destruction, the legal paradigm of misdeed and punishment.

By the time of the prophets, Israel is seen as a land which has become polluted. In the Deuteronomic historian, there is a stress on the abominations performed by the disinherited peoples set into the record that the people or their kings performed these abominations (1 Kgs 14: 24; 2 Kgs 16: 3; 21: 2); the destruction of Samaria is attributed to its having acted like the dispossessed nations (2 Kgs 17: 7–8). At the time of the Assyrian threat, Hosea viewed Israel as a contaminated people and land (Hos 5: 3; 6: 10); the term used, *nṭmʾ*, is later applied to Judah (Ezek 36: 18; Ps 106: 38). The land is seen as defiled, *ḥnp* (Isa 24: 5; Ps 106: 38). The people have polluted the land (Jer 2: 7; Ezek 36: 4), they have defiled it (Jer 3: 9). The land of Israel is described as full of blood (Hos 6: 8). Judah is described as full of *ḥāmās*, "unlawfulness" (Ezek 8: 17; 12: 19, see discussion below) and bloodshed (Ezek 7: 23; 9: 9), murderers (Hos 6: 8), gods (Isa 2: 8), and adulterers (Jer 23: 10); the city is full of *ḥāmas* (Ezek 7: 23) and blood (Ezekiel 22; Nah 3: 1). Judah and Jerusalem are described as whores (Hos 1: 2; Isa 1: 21; Jer 2: 20; 3: 3; Ezekiel 16: 30–35; chap. 23; Mic 1: 7; Nah 3: 4). By the time of the destruction the nation is portrayed in the image of the ultimate defiled woman, the menstruant (Ezek 36: 17; probably Lam 1: 8, *nydh*, and Ezra 9: 11) and, even more, the menstruant whose skirts have become soiled with blood (Jer 13: 22, reading *nĕgōʾălû šûlayik*; cf. Lam 4: 14). Even the ultimate image of defilement, the image of the leper, is applied to the nation, who sits alone (Lam 1: 1; cf. Lev 13: 46) and before whose priests one must call "Impure, impure" (Lam 4: 15; cf. Lev 13: 45). In the face of such pollution, the temple and its cult could not be enough to save Israel, and this necessitated the land being destroyed and the people sent into exile. The Exile is thus seen as a necessary result of the pollution of Israel.

The Exile and the Flood

The Exile was necessitated by the polluted state of the land. It was not, according to this paradigm, an act of vengeance or even a result of anger. It was also not intended to be a final destruction of the people. The prophesies of doom are frequently accompanied by mention of the remnant which is to be saved and restored to the land. In this respect the Exile resembles the Flood, which also allowed a remnant—Noah—to be rescued and restored. The connection between the Exile and the Flood, moreover, is not simply a matter of destruction and restoration. As narrated in Genesis, the Flood is the grand cosmic paradigm of the Exile. Genesis has taken the ancient flood story and the old structure of a "primeval history" (now Genesis 1–9) and retold it in the light of Israel's ideas about pollution. According to the Genesis story, the prerequisites of human existence are laws. Man has inherently evil impulses and man without law polluted the world to such an extent that the Lord had to bring the flood to erase the pollution that man had brought (Frymer-Kensky 1977).

With this reinterpretation of the flood story, the Flood was seen as a cosmic paradigm of the Exile, and the retelling of the story of the Flood became a way for Israel to assimilate its own fate. We must, of course, ask when Israel looked at the Flood in this light. There is no reason to look for a late postexilic date for this. Source analysis cannot provide a solution. Genesis 9 is conventionally assigned to P, but I would not like to venture to date the material in P, nor do I believe it likely that the J version of the flood did not conclude with a remedy for the cause of the flood, although J's remedy, which may also have been laws, is lost to us. Pollution ideas are certainly not new to Israel, and there is no reason to suggest that the purity laws are late, even though they are preserved primarily in P. The characteristic Israelite notion that the pollution of the land leads to its desolation is already attested in Hosea. Hosea describes Gilead as defiled with blood (6: 8), defiled by the doing of perversion and by "whoredom" (6: 9–10). Furthermore Hosea states that because Israel has become defiled it will be desolated (5: 3, 9, note the key words *hznyt, nṭmʾ* and *šmh*). The concept of pollution as a historical force is thus attested long before the Exile: it may be an innovation of Hosea, or it may already have been part of Israelite cosmology.

The idea that misdeeds pollute the land is also attested in Isa 24: 5–6, part of the "Isaian apocalypse": "And the land was defiled under its inhabitants for they transgressed the teachings, violated the laws, and broke the ancient covenant. Therefore the curse[8] consumes the land and the inhabitants pay the penalty." There is some question about the dating of this passage; despite the conventional wisdom it should probably not be taken as postexilic since Jer 23: 10 appears to be dependent on it. Certainly the idea of the pollution of the land is well established by the time of Jer 3: 1–9. We therefore do not have to look for a postexilic date for the understanding of pollution as a motive force in Israel's history or for the retelling of the Flood story as a case of cosmic pollution. It is possible that the anticipation and/or experience of the Assyrian threat and the experience of the destruction of the northern kingdom led to a profound awareness of the pollution problem and occasioned a retelling of the Flood story in light of it. The belief in the corruptibility of the land of Israel and the catastrophic consequences of such corruption may even be earlier than the Assyrian period, for all we know.

There is also no reason to think that the midrashic perception of the Flood and the Exile as parallel events is an exilic innovation. I am tempted to take Hos 6: 7 as evidence that Hosea, who clearly believes that the pollution of Israel will lead to its desolation, also saw a connection between this destruction and the primeval cataclysm. The translation of 6: 7a, *whmh kʾdm ʿbrw bryt,* as "They like men have transgressed the covenant" seems needlessly weak and obscure. In the context of the pollution described in 6: 8–10 it may be more proper to translate, "They like Adam have transgressed the covenant" and see an indirect allusion to antediluvian events. Jeremiah, who is so conscious of the pollution of the land (Jer 3: 1–9), also uses cosmic parallels. A cosmic paradigm, i.e., the Flood, seems to underlie the so-called "Jeremian apocalypse" in Jer 4: 23–27. Jeremiah here describes the coming military destruction of Israel (cf. 4: 20–21) in terms that are clearly reminiscent of Genesis 1; he depicts the event as a reversal of creation: the world is returned to chaos (*tohû wābohû*), there is no more light in the skies, the mountains are quaking and there are no more people. In this vision, however—as at the original, cosmic undoing of creation (the Flood)—the destruction will not be final: "All the land will be made desolate, but I will not finish it off completely" (Jer 4: 27). This passage has been understood—or misunderstood—as an apocalyptic vision, but to understand it this way it was necessary to posit later accretions to the passage (Eppstein 1968). The context, however, makes it clear that we are dealing with the imminent destruction of Israel rather than a future cosmic upheaval. It may be that the use of the cosmic symbolism of the primeval parallel in such passages as this and the "Isaian apocalypse" of Isaiah 24 laid the groundwork and provided the symbolic imagery for the later development of universal apocalyptic.

The parallelism between the Flood and the destruction is well developed by Ezekiel, and the early chapters of Ezekiel are replete with flood imagery, particularly with the repetitive statement that the land is full of *ḥāmās* (Ezek 7: 23; 8: 17; and cf. 12: 19; 45: 9; for the Flood story, Gen 6: 11) and with the emphatic use of the term *qēṣ* (Ezek 7: 2–7, esp. vv 2–3: "Thus says the Lord to the land [or (?) ground?] of Israel, The *qēṣ* is come, the *qēṣ* on the four corners of the earth; now the *qēṣ* is upon you and I send my anger against you and judge you as your ways"; and cf. v 6; for Genesis, see 6: 13). Another allusion to the primeval story may be the marking on the forehead of those not to be killed (Ezek 9: 4–5), possibly an allusion to the mark of Cain.

The parallelism between the Flood and the Exile does not involve only pollution and destruction, but also additional themes which are an inherent part of the parallel. The Flood and the Exile were necessary purgations; they were not ultimate, permanent destructions. Just as mankind was saved from permanent destruction by Noah's survival, so too God will not exterminate the people, but will rescue a remnant to begin again. The Flood and the Exile are also not viewed as repeatable acts. The Flood is immediately followed by God's promise not to bring a flood again (Gen 9: 11). It is significant that the one explicit reference to the Flood outside of Genesis 1–9 occurs in a passage dealing with the Restoration of Israel. In this passage (chosen by Jewish tradition as the prophetic reading to accompany the liturgical recitation of the Genesis Flood story), the Flood paradigm is taken as assurance that, just as the Flood was to be a unique occurrence, so too God will not again punish the people of Israel: "As the waters of Noah this is to me, about which I swore that the waters of Noah would not (again) pass over the earth; so too I swear that I will not get angry at you and rebuke you" (Isa 54: 9).

The Flood was not to be repeated because it was followed, not only by the restoration of mankind, but by the establishment of a new order, the "reign of law." Jeremiah and Ezekiel (possibly anticipated by Hosea) develop the concept of the Exile in line with this cosmic parallel. They consider the destruction the result of the pollution of the land, and see it as followed, not only by the restoration of the remnant, but by the inauguration of a new order. The Flood inaugurated the rule of law: mankind's evil impulses were recognized, and therefore laws were given to educate and restrain it. This would prevent the pollution of the earth and eliminate the need for a future flood. This reliance on law culminated in the covenant of Sinai, in which one people (Israel) was given a more elaborate and demanding set of laws, with the expectation that this would enable it to be a holy people entitled to live in God's country. However, the covenant of Sinai was "broken." The misdeeds of the people polluted Israel, and God had to exile the people. The land had to rest; after the purgation (evacuation of the land) it needed time to recuperate. As the impure individual becomes pure after a set period of time even without purification rituals, so too time can eliminate the impurity of the land.[9] After the land has "fulfilled its Sabbaths" (2 Chr 36: 21; cf. Lev 26: 32–45; see Ackroyd 1968: 153, 242) God will restore the people. He will purify them (Jer 33: 8; Ezek 36: 25, 33) and reestablish relations with them; he will be their god and they will be his people (Jer 31: 32–33; Ezek 36: 28).

There will be fundamental changes at the restoration, for the world after the Exile is to be different from the world before it, just as the world after the Flood was different from the antediluvian world. There is a radical change in the mechanism of sin, for the new stress on individual retribution (Jer 31: 29–30; Ezekiel 11: 16–21; 14: 12–23; chap. 18; 33: 12–20) represents a reversal of the concept of the national responsibility of Israel for the sins of its members (see Weinfeld 1976), and a removal of the idea of the build-up of pollution across generational lines. In this context it may be significant that Ezekiel's formulation of this change refers to the proverb which is spoken about the "land/ground of Israel."

The renewed relationship with restored Israel is to be established by a covenant which is called a "new covenant" (Jer 31: 31), an eternal covenant (Jer 32: 40), and a "covenant of peace" (Ezek 34: 25). This covenant is fundamentally different from the Noahide covenant and from its typological extension, the Sinai covenant (see Jer 31: 32 for its differences from Sinai). The Covenant of Noah and even more the Covenant of Sinai were covenants of law to be studied and obeyed. At the time of the "new covenant," however, no one will have to study the laws anymore; everyone will know the law (Jer 31: 33–34). The law of God will be engraved on the heart (Jer 31: 33); everyone will have a "new heart and a new spirit" (Ezek 36: 26). Internal law is not "law." This radical change is projected for the Restoration after the Exile. After the Flood, God instituted the rule of law to cope with man's evil instincts. These instincts, part of the nature of man, would continue to exist, but they would be held in check by an increasingly detailed set of laws. To Jeremiah and Ezekiel, this approach to the problem of evil and the pollution of the world has failed.[10] Man's evil instincts were not effectively restrained by law, even by the Law of Sinai and God's ongoing instruction by history and the prophets. Israel continued to do evil and ultimately, as in the time before law, the microcosm of Israel became so polluted that another cataclysm, the Exile, became necessary to destroy that polluted world. In the restored Israel, therefore, the attempt to control man's instincts will be abandoned. Instead, God will effect a fundamental change in the nature of man: his evil impulses are to be eradicated, the "law" internalized, and he is to receive a "new heart and a new spirit."

It should be noted as a postscript that this search for an alteration of man's spirit, with the concomitant abandonment of the Law as the agent of God's instruction, was later developed in the early Christian Church. Israel, however, ultimately rejected this vision of Jeremiah and Ezekiel in that it never abandoned its belief in the ability of the Law to control man's evil instincts. The Law in all its ramifications became the defining characteristic of the Judaism that emerged after the biblical period.

Notes

1. This is not a complete picture, for the laws do not mention all cases. An example is the status of the person who eats impure food. In the case of carrion we know that the ordinary people (unlike the priests) were not forbidden to eat it; however, they would become impure until evening and must bathe and wash their clothes (Lev 17: 15–16). In the case of impure animals we know that lay people were not to eat them (Lev 20: 25), and we therefore do not hear of the pollution of such people (as discussed below, pollution terminology is not applied to those who do forbidden acts). The question is the status of the person who eats food that has been tainted by contact with an impure person, given especially that meat rendered impure should be burned (Lev 7: 19). From Hosea we know that whoever eats impure food will himself become impure (Hos 9: 3–4). The laws, however, do not discuss what happens to the person who eats impure food. We can only assume that the resultant pollution would be minor, like that from eating carrion.

2. Assumed but not explicitly mentioned.

3. There is clearly a desire to prevent infinite contagion in the provision in Lev 14: 36 that all things in a house suspected of "leprosy" be removed before the house is examined, so that they will not be "made unclean": the contagion does not start until the declaration, rather than with exposure prior to the determination of impurity.

4. From Num 9: 10 it is clear that impure people (here, specifically from corpse-contamination) may not perform the Passover sacrifice; calamity is not explicitly mentioned.

5. The major study of *karet* is that of Wold (1979), who realizes that *karet* should be seen in the context of the purity laws, and who argues convincingly that it means extirpation of one's lineage. The analysis of *karet* presented here does not always agree with Wold's.

6. Although the emphasis in Deuteronomy is on the pollution of the people and that of the Priestly sections on the pollution of the land, this may simply be a question of style; one should note that Lev 18: 24 mentions the pollution of the people and Deut 21: 1–9 is concerned with the pollution of the land as well as the people; Deut 21: 22–23 is clearly concerned with the pollution of the land. See also the discussions by Weinfeld 1973 and Milgrom 1973.

7. This punishment is probably drought, infertility and famine. According to Israel, rain, so necessary to Israel's agriculture (Deut 11: 11) is to be withdrawn in case of apostasy (Deut 11: 13–17). Drought is a clear indication of chastisement (1 Kings 17–19; Amos 4: 7; Isa 5: 6; Jeremiah 14; Ezek 22: 24). Even after the Restoration, the infertility and drought prevalent are attributed to Israel's failure to rebuild the temple (Hag 1: 6–11). See also Ackroyd 1968: 157, Roifer 1961: 136 and Patai 1939.

8. The "curse" probably also refers to drought and famine. See n. 7.

9. It may be particularly relevant that women do not have fixed purification rituals. Although both men and women are to bathe after intercourse, women become pure after their set period of impurity for menstruation and childbirth: there is no mention of bathing. In light of the feminine conception of the land, one would expect that the land too would have to wait out its impure period, and that time alone would make it pure.

10. It is difficult to say whether the idea of the new covenant originated with Hosea. Hosea clearly anticipated a Restoration, with a covenant and God betrothing Israel forever (Hos 2: 20–21); nothing, however, is said about fundamental changes in the covenant or in the people.

References

Ackroyd, Peter
1968 *Exile and Restoration: A Study of Hebrew Thought in the Sixth Century* B.C. Old Testament Library. London: SCM Press.

Douglas, Mary
1966 *Purity and Danger: An Analysis of Concepts of Pollution and Taboo*. New York: Praeger.
1975 *Implicit Meanings*. London: Routledge and Kegan Paul.

Eppstein, Victor
1968 The Day of Judgement in Jeremiah 4: 23–28. *Journal of Biblical Literature* 87: 93–97.

Finkelstein, J. J.
1981 *The Ox that Gored*. Transactions of the American Philosophical Society 71/2. Philadelphia: The American Philosophical Society.

Frymer-Kensky, Tikva
1977 The Atrahasis Epic and its Significance for our Understanding of Genesis 1–9. *Biblical Archeologist* 40: 147–154.
forthcoming The Strange Case of the Suspected Soṭah: Numbers 5: 11–31. *Vetus Testamentum.*

L'Hour, J.
1963 Une législation criminelle dans le Deutéronome. *Biblica* 44: 1–28.

McKeating, H.
1975 The Development of the Law of Homicide in Ancient Israel. *Vetus Testamentum* 25: 46–68.

Milgrom, Jacob
1971a Sin Offering or Purification Offering. *Vetus Testamentum* 21: 237–239.
1971b Kipper. *Encyclopaedia Judaica* 10: 1039–1043.
1971c Day of Atonement. *Encyclopaedia Judaica* 5: 1383–87.
1973 The Alleged "Demythologization" and Secularization in Deuteronomy. *Israel Explorational Journal* 23: 156–161.
1976a Israel's Sanctuary: the Priestly "Picture of Dorian Gray." *Revue biblique* 33: 390–99.
1976b Two Kinds of Ḥaṭṭa'ṭ. *Vetus Testamentum* 26: 333–337.

Patai, Raphael
1939 The "Control of Rain" in Ancient Palestine. *Hebrew Union College Annual* 14: 251–286.
1939–40 The ʿEglā ʿArufa or the Expiation of the Polluted Land. *Jewish Quarterly Review* 30: 59–69.

Roifer, A.
1961 The Breaking of the Heifer's Neck. *Tarbiz* 31: 129–43 (Hebrew).

Weinfeld, Moshe
1973 On "Demythologization" and Secularization in Deuteronomy. *Israel Exploration Journal* 23: 230–33.
1976 Jeremiah and the Spiritual Metamorphosis of Israel. *Zeitschrift für die Alttestamentliche Wissenschaft* 88: 17–56.

Wold, Donald
1979 The *Kareth* Penalty in P: Rationale and Cases. Vol. 1, pp. 1–46 in *Society of Biblical Literature 1979 Seminar Papers*, ed. P. J. Achtemeier. Missoula: Scholars Press.

Zevit, Ziony
1976 The ʿEglā Ritual of Deuteronomy 21: 1–9. *Journal of Biblical Literature* 95: 377–90.

Zimmerli, W.
1954 Die Eigenart der prophetischen Rede des Ezechiel. *Zeitschrift für die Alttestamentliche Wissenschaft* 66: 1–27.

Jerusalem in der Sicht des Ezechielbuches

Walther Zimmerli
Georg August Universität Göttingen

I.

David Noel Freedman, der Herausgeber des *Biblical Archeologist,* dem diese Zeilen als Gruss zu seinem 60. Geburtstag zugedacht sind, hat dem Herbstheft des 43. Bandes seiner Zeitschrift eine wertvolle Ergänzungskarte (aus dem Wide Screen Project) beigegeben. Diese bietet nicht nur Pläne des Jerusalem des 1. und 2. Tempels und der byzantinischen Zeit, sondern erlaubt auch, die wichtigeren archäologischen Reste in der gegenwärtigen Stadtlage zu orten.

Der hier vorgelegte Beitrag möchte der kleinen Detailfrage nachgehen, ob auch das Buch Ezechiel etwas zur Kenntnis des Jerusalem der Königszeit beizutragen vermag.

Ezechiel gehört nach den Angaben seines Buches, an denen m.E. nicht zu zweifeln ist, zur Gruppe der 597 deportierten, in der Siedlung *tēl ābîb* nahe beim "grossen Kanal" (in der Nähe von Nippur) angesiedelten Judäer. Hier erreicht ihn nach 33: 21 etwa 10 Jahre später die Kunde vom endgültigen Fall Jerusalems. Dass er nach der nachträglich eingefügten Überschrift des Buches (1: 3) als Priester (oder Sohn eines Priesters) bezeichnet wird, bestätigt, dass er zur Schicht der 597 deportierten "oberen Zehntausend," von denen 2 Kgs 24: 14 redet, gehört hat. Es erklärt auch die Intensität, in der sein Denken und Reden auf Jerusalem und zumal dessen Heiligtum gerichtet bleibt. Da von einer Deportation ganzer Familien in 2 Könige 24 nichts gesagt ist und Ezek 24: 21 ganz ausdrücklich "eure Söhne und Töchter, die ihr zurückgelassen habt," erwähnt, wird man annehmen dürfen, dass Ezechiel als erwachsener Mann deportiert worden ist. Er hat möglicherweise schon selber im Tempel Dienst getan. Das Jerusalem der ausgehenden Königszeit wird ihm noch deutlich vor Augen stehen. Da die Deportierten von 597 anders als die Deportierten des Nordreiches zur Assyrerzeit (2 Kgs 17: 6) nicht als Oberschicht in einem von den Babyloniern unterworfenen Gebiet angesiedelt worden sind, sondern ihre Ansiedlung im babylonischen Kernland, wie auch Jeremia 28–29 verraten, als ein Provisorium verstanden haben dürften (Alt 1953: 316–37), lässt sich das gespannte Interesse für das noch bestehende Jerusalem, das Ezechiel mit den übrigen Deportierten teilt, auch von daher voll verstehen.

Nun bietet das Buch Ezechiel keine Berichte über des Propheten Leben in Jerusalem vor seiner Deportation. Es ist auch nirgends eine nostalgische Schilderung seiner Heimatstadt in seine Worte eingeflochten. So reichlich die theologischen Urteile über die "Blutstadt" (22: 2), über ihre von den Anfängen her verderbte Geschichte (16), über ihre Wertlosigkeit nach dem Geschehen von 597, die durch die Wertlosigkeit eines schon angebrannten Stückes Rebenholz illustriert wird (15), sind, so deutlich in Zeichenhandlungen die anhebende Belagerung (4: 1–3), die Aushungerung der belagerten Stadt (4: 9–11), die Vernichtung (5:1-3), die Deportation ihrer Bewohnerschaft (12), die Zerstörung alles dessen, was Zier und Kostbarkeit in ihren Augen war (24: 21), ausgesagt ist, so wenig wird all dieses mit konkreter Anschauung aus des Propheten eigener Erinnerung genährt.

Eine Ausnahme ist nur in zwei Komplexen zu erkennen. In den eigentümlichen Entrückungsvisionen Ezechiel 8–11 und 40–48 gewinnt etwas von konkreter Anschauung Jerusalems Raum. Die Visionen sind inhaltlich von sehr verschiedener Bedeutsamkeit. Die ins 6. Jahr datierte Vision 8–11 lässt den Propheten vor dem endgültigen Fall der Stadt den Stand der Dinge in Jerusalem und das daraufhin von Jahwe veranstaltete Gericht schauen. Die ins 25. Jahr nach der Deportation, das nach 40: 1 ausdrücklich mit dem 14. Jahr nach dem Fall der Stadt gleichgesetzt wird, datierte Vision 40–48 lässt den Propheten dagegen in einem Zeitpunkt, zu dem die Stadt in Trümmern liegt, visionär das Neue erschauen, das sich infolge des göttlichen Neubeginns Jahwes mit seinem Volke im "Land Israels" erhebt. Kann man von 8–11 erwarten, dass hier noch echte Erinnerung des Verbannten an seine Heimatstadt lebendig ist, so lässt sich auch bei 40–48 fragen, ob nicht in das veränderte Neue, das ihm am Ort dieser Stadt von Gott gezeigt wird, Elemente alter Erinnerung eingedrungen sind.

II.

Das Entrückungserlebnis von 8–11 ist gerahmt. In einer konkreten, für Ezechiel nach Ausweis von 14: 1 und 20: 1 typischen Situation, die aber schon in der Vor-Schriftprophetie ihr Analogon hat (Elisa, 2 Kgs 6: 32, vgl. 4: 38; 6: 1), fällt die Hand Jahwes auf ihn, wie er in seinem Hause sitzt, Älteste des Volkes vor ihm, und versetzt ihn in den Zustand visionärer Schau. In der Schau wird er durch eine Männergestalt von überirdischem Aussehen (Greenberg 1980: 153f. glaubt in ihr die "majesty" Gottes selber vermuten zu können) an den Haaren gefasst. Durch den "Geist" wird er "zwischen Himmel und Erde" nach Jerusalem, das mit Namen genannt ist, entrückt. Ganz entsprechend hebt ihn nach 11: 24–25 der "Geist" hinterher wieder hoch und bringt ihn "zu den Verbannten nach Chaldäa im Gesicht durch den Geist Gottes" (so MT) zurück, wo sich dann das "Gesicht," das er erschaut hat, von ihm weghebt (*wayyaʿal*), sodass er alles den Verbannten erzählen kann, was Jahwe ihn schauen liess.

Mit der bei Ezechiel beliebten Vierzahl der Totalität (Zimmerli 1979: 53 zu 1: 5, ET 120) wird der Prophet in Jerusalem zunächst auf seinem Weg durch die Schau von 4 "Greueln" geführt. In Frageform leitet jeweils eine göttliche Stimme von einem Greuel zu einem noch grösseren Greuel über (8: 6, 12–13, 15). Die Absicht der steigernden Hinführung zu einem Allerschlimmsten ist in 8: 15 deutlich ausgesprochen. Der Weg führt den Propheten in der Schau von Norden nach Süden, vom Nordtor (8: 3) ins Innerste des heiligen Bezirkes (8: 16). In der Entrückungsschau Ezechiel 40–48 wird der Weg von Osten her ans Allerheiligste heranführen. Man mag sich fragen, ob bei der starken Stilisierung des Ganzen schon durch diesen Weg von Norden nach Süden ein Unheilsakzent zu Gehör gebracht werden will. In der Schilderung des Gerichtes in Ezechiel 9, das dann ganz so in der Gestalt der göttlichen Gerichtshelfer von Norden her in den Tempelbereich einbricht

(9: 2), ist dieser Akzent deutlich zu vernehmen.

Hinter der Schilderung der vier Wegstationen, über die der Prophet in der Schau vom Nordtor her geführt wird, scheint nun aber eine deutliche Anschauung der Stadt, wie sie der Prophet in der Erinnerung gegenwärtig hat, vorzuliegen. Was ist über diese zu sagen? Es empfiehlt sich dabei, den Weg vom Ende her zu verfolgen.

Eindeutig ist die innerste Station zu lokalisieren: Im inneren Hof des Tempelbezirkes (*bêt yhwh*), beim Eingang zum Tempelgebäude (*hêkāl yhwh*), zwischen Vorhalle und Altar, stehen 25 Männer (Priester?). Ihr Gesicht gegen Osten, zur (aufgehenden) Sonne hin gewendet erweisen sie die verehrende Proskynese nach Osten hin (8: 16). Sie wenden damit Jahwe, der westwärts im Hause in der Cella des Allerheiligsten wohnt, den Rücken zu. Ein in seiner Deutung nicht mehr mit Sicherheit aufzuhellendes Wort Gottes bringt in 8: 17 die unerhörte Entehrung des im Heiligtum Wohnenden zum Ausdruck. Zur Bedeutung der Stelle "zwischen Tempelhaus und Altar" sind Joel 2: 17 und Matt 23: 35 zu vergleichen.

Die vorhergehende Station des Weges, auf dem der Prophet geführt wird, beschreibt 8: 14. "Bei der Öffnung des Tores zum Tempelbereich (*bêt yhwh*), das gegen Norden hin liegt," sieht der Prophet "Frauen sitzen, die den Tammuz beweinen." Von Norden her tritt der Prophet also in den innersten Heiligkeitsbereich. Ein Tor führt durch die Nordmauer dieses Bereichs.

Ist die örtliche Festlegung dieser beiden inneren Stationen des Weges des Propheten und dessen Nord-Südrichtung mühelos zu bestimmen, so ist das bei den beiden ersten Stationen und der Lokalisierung des hier Erschauten schwieriger. Von der zweiten Station sagen 8: 7–9 nach MT: "Und er brachte mich zum Eingang des Vorhofes. Und als ich hinschaute, siehe, da war ein Loch in der Wand. Und er sprach zu mir: Menschensohn, grabe durch die Wand. Und ich grub durch die Wand. Und siehe, da war ein Eingang. Und er sprach zu mir: Geh hinein und schau die bösen Greuel, die sie hier begehen."

Der Prophet wird offenbar von Norden her an den Toreingang eines (anderen) Hofes geführt. Im Weiteren ist das von MT Ausgesagte nur mühsam vorstellbar. Hat man an eine Höhlung (*ḥor*) zu denken, die sich im Toreingang selber in einer Seitenwand befindet, oder an eine solche, die der Prophet an der Aussenwand des Torbaus wahrnimmt? Ist dann an einen ersten Raum gedacht, in den er durch Erweiterung dieser Öffnung hineingelangt? Führt von diesem eine weitere Öffnung (*petaḥ*) in den Raum hinein, in dem die 70 Ältesten den Greuelbildern an der Wand räuchern? Der Verdacht, dass hier nachträgliche Erweiterungen zur Unklarheit des vorliegenden Textes geführt haben, ist gross. Offenbar soll das zweifache Hineingehen (oder -kriechen?) in verborgene Räume den Eindruck, dass hier Dinge im Verborgenen getan werden, verstärken. Die Aussage der 70 Männer, "Jahwe sieht uns nicht, Jahwe hat das Land verlassen" (8: 12), kann zu solcher Ausmalung auch tiefster räumlicher Verborgenheit des Ortes, an dem der Greueldienst geschieht, angeregt haben. Es sprechen starke Gründe dafür, dass hier ursprünglich von einfacher Heranführung an die Toröffnung des Hofes (8: 7a) die Rede war und daran unmittelbar die Aufforderung von 8: 9 anschloss: "Geh hinein und schaue. . . ." Man ist dann auch von dem Zwang befreit, sich vorstellen zu müssen, wie in einem verborgenen, offenbar nicht allzugrossen Raum gleich 70 Älteste beisammen sind, welche das gottlose Räuchern vollziehen.

Man wird immerhin die Frage stellen, wie sich wohl der Ergänzer diese Frage beantwortet hat. Hat er das Phänomen einer kasemattenartigen Mauer vor Augen, in der sich seitlich vom Toreingang der Mauer einzelne Gemächer befanden?

Wichtiger aber ist für den vorliegenden Zusammenhang die Frage, welche Örtlichkeit der Prophet vor Augen hat, wenn er vom Hineintreten in den "Hof" redet, in dem die 70 Ältesten, offenbar die "Laienvertretung Israels" (Zimmerli 1979: 216, ET 240), vor den Ritz-Zeichnungen an der Innenseite der Hofmauer ihren Räucherdienst vollziehen. Dem "inneren Vorhof des Hauses Jahwes" (8: 16), dem die "Toröffnung des Hauses Jahwes, die gegen Norden ging" (8: 14) zuzuordnen ist, tritt hier eine nördlich davon zu suchende "(Tor)Öffnung" des Hofes gegenüber. Sie wird den Eingang in einen umfassenderen Hofbereich meinen. Auf eine umgreifende äussere Hofanlage weist indirekt auch die in 8: 16 ausdrücklich beigefügte Bezeichnung "innerer Hof" zurück. Das Fehlen jeder Qualifikation des "Hofes" von 8: 7 in diesem von einem Priester verfassten Text kann verraten, dass nach dessen (viz., Ezechiels) Empfinden diesem Hof mindere Heiligkeit eignet als dem inneren Hof, der ausdrücklich durch den zugefügten Genitiv "des Hauses Jahwes" gekennzeichnet war. So dürfte es sich um den alten Palastvorhof handeln, der den salomonischen Palastbezirk, in den auch der engere Tempelbezirk eingeordnet war, rings umgibt. Andere, weniger streng in priesterlicher Akribie formulierte spätvorexilische Texte reden unbekümmerter von den "zwei Vorhöfen des Hauses Jahwes" (2 Kgs 21: 5; 23: 12). Im Baubericht von 1 Kgs 7: 12 wird noch ohne diese Bewertung vom "grossen Hof," neben dem man den eigentlichen Tempelhof als "kleinen Hof" bezeichnet haben wird, geredet.

8: 3 redet von der äussersten Station auf dem Wege des Propheten von Norden nach Süden. "Er [d.h. der Geist] brachte mich nach Jerusalem in Gottesgesichten zum Eingang des Tores [die Beifügung "inneren" fehlt in LXX und ist kaum ursprünglich], das nach Norden geht, wo sich der Standort des Eiferbildes, das zum Zorneifer reizt, befand." Die Beschreibung wird in 8: 5 fortgesetzt: "Und er sprach zu mir: Menschensohn, erhebe deine Augen gegen Norden. Und ich erhob meine Augen gegen Norden, und siehe, im Norden des Tores stand ein Altar—das Eiferbild aber stand im Eingang." Es legt sich nahe, hier das äussere Stadttor erwähnt zu finden, durch welches der Prophet in den Stadtbereich gelangt. In Anlehnung an Albright (1956: 183f.) ist bei dem "Eiferbild" an eine (wohl gegen Albright als Vollskulptur gestaltete) Toreingangs-Figur zu denken. Dass dieser hier auf einem nördlich ausserhalb des Tores errichteten, wohl kleinen, Altar Verehrung dargebracht wird, liegt ganz auf der Linie der Verehrung der Wanddarstellungen des äusseren (Palast-)Hofes von 8: 10 und ist wie jenes mit der Aussage des zeitgenössischen Jeremia (11: 13) zu verbinden: "So viele Städte, so viele Götter hast du, Juda, und so viele Strassen, Jerusalem, so viele Altäre habt ihr errichtet." Es kennzeichnet die offenbar in der Spätphase des vorexilischen Jerusalem hektisch übersteigerte Devotionsgeschäftigkeit, die in orthodoxerer Weise auch in der Tempelrede Jeremias (7: 4, 10) erkennbar wird.

Für den vorliegenden Zusammenhang, der sich mit dem Aussehen des Jerusalem der Tage Ezechiels beschäftigt, ist bedeutsam, dass zwischen dem Stadttor (8: 3) und dem Tor der Palastmauer, das in den äusseren Hof führt (8: 7a), eine erste Wegstrecke liegt. Darin liegt eine Aussage, die mir in der Diskussion um das vorexilische Jerusalem nicht genug bewertet zu sein scheint. Sie belegt die Existenz einer Nordstadt nördlich der Umwallung der Palastanlagen. Das in 8: 3 des MT sich findende *happĕnîmît* ist wohl schuld daran gewesen, dass man den Propheten in seiner Entrückung gleich in das Innere des Palast-Tempelbereichs versetzt sah. So etwa Cooke (1936: 91): "Probably we are to understand that Ez. was set down within the inner court and south of the entrance to the N. gateway"; Rothstein (1922: 887 Anm. b): "Gemeint ist wohl das Nordtor, das zum inneren Vorhof führte, dasselbe wie Jer 20, 2.26, 10.36, 10; 2 Kg 15, 35." Etwas anders Bertholet (1936: 32): "Er kommt zuerst . . . an das Nordtor der grossen Umfassungsmauer der königlichen Bauten, und zwar wohl an dessen Aussenseite; dann durch den Torweg hindurchgehend zu dessen Innenseite (7), die in den 'grossen Vorhof' . . . führt." Fast wörtlich gleich Fohrer (1955: 50). Der Blick auf 40: 3–19, wo der Prophet in der grossen Entrückungs-Schlussvision direkt von der Ostseite her an den Tempelbereich herangeführt wird, mag das Verständnis von 8: 3ff. irregeleitet haben. Auf der Grundlage dieses Verständnisses vermutet Donner (1977: 161), dass die Neustadt Jerusalems im Laufe der Königszeit nach Nordwesten "das Stadttal hinauf, vielleicht bis auf die Höhe der nördl. Begrenzung des salomonischen *ḥaram*" gewachsen sei. Das von Donner mit dem Schaftor (Neh 3: 1; 12: 39) = Wachtor (Neh 3: 31; 12: 39) gleichgesetzte Benjamintor ist danach "in der Nordmauer des salomonischen *ḥaram*" lokalisiert. Ezechiel 8 dürfte demgegenüber deutlich machen: Das Stadttor (8: 3), das nur durch das irreführende *happenîmît* mit einem Tempeltor gleichgesetzt worden ist, muss von dem "Eingang in den Hof" (8: 7), der vom Priester Ezechiel noch nicht eigentlich als "Tempelvorhof" betrachtet wird, abgerückt werden. Stadtbefestigung und Stadtumwallung fallen in den Tagen Ezechiels keineswegs zusammen. So ist denn auch richtig in der Jerusalemkarte, die dem *Biblical Archeologist* beiliegt, für die Zeit des 1. Tempels im Norden des Tempel- und Palastbereichs noch ein Nordstadtbereich ausserhalb der Palastummauerung angenommen. Im *Bibelatlas* von Guthe ist auf Nebenkarte II von Blatt 3 die Annahme gemacht, dass Nordrand von "Tempel und Residenz Salomos" mit der Stadtgrenze zusammenfallen. Auf der Nebenkarte II von Blatt 4 dagegen, wo das Jerusalem des 7. Jahrhunderts dargestellt wird, ist mit einer "Vorstadt" gerechnet, die nicht nur im Westen (so Donner), sondern auch im Norden und sogar im Osten die Salomostadt im engeren Sinne überschiessend erweitert. Die neuere Karte des Wide Screen Project rechnet demgegenüber bei der Salomostadt im engeren Sinne nicht mit einem Überschiessen nach Osten hin, sondern nimmt einen solchen Überschuss nach Osten nur für den Ophelbezirk an.

Der Blick auf die beiden Darstellungen von Guthe führt auf die Frage, ob der Nordteil der "Neustadt," der von Ezechiel 8 vorausgesetzt ist, erst eine Erweiterung der nachsalomonischen Zeit darstellt, oder schon für die Zeit Salomos anzunehmen ist. Biblische Nachrichten über diese Erweiterung fehlen. Die "Neustadt" (*mišneh*) ist nur spärlich im spätvorexilischen Schrifttum erwähnt (2 Kgs 22: 14 = 2 Chr 34: 22; Zeph 1: 10). Zur Zephanjastelle gilt wohl, was Alt (1959: 323 Anm. 1) feststellt: "Sowohl er [d.h. der Stadtteil "Neustadt"] als auch die anderen Quartiere die in Zeph. 1, 10f. zusammen mit ihm genannt werden, müssen nach dem Sachgehalt dieser Stelle auf der Angriffsseite von Jerusalem, also im Norden gesucht werden." Über den Zeitpunkt der Ausweitung Jerusalems durch diese "Neustadt" im Norden vermag allerdings keine der Belegstellen für diese Bezeichnung etwas auszusagen. So kann man nur indirekte Wahrscheinlichkeitserwägungen anstellen.

Für die Zeit Salomos könnte einmal sprechen, dass man für jenen Zeitpunkt angesicht der anschwellenden Verwaltungsaufgaben des von ihm neu strukturierten Grossreichgebildes (Alt 1953: 76–89) erheblich mehr Wohnmöglichkeiten in Jerusalem benötigte, als die kleine Davidstadt sie bot und die wohl auch durch den Ausbau des Ophel, des Zwischenstückes zwischen David- und Salomostadt, noch nicht befriedigt waren. Man wird sich zudem, gerade im Gedanken an das von Alt zur Zephanjastelle Gesagte, fragen, ob denn Salomo bei seiner Stadtplanung es wirklich unterlassen haben sollte, die exponierteste Stelle seiner Stadt durch ein Vorgelände vor seiner Palastumwallung abzuschirmen. Wenn 2 Kgs 14: 13 sagt, dass Jerusalem nach dem unglücklichen Feldzug Amazjas gegen Joas von Israel durch Schleifung seiner Mauer "vom Ephraimtor bis zum Ecktor" entfestigt worden sei, so ist auf diese bei jedem Angriff am stärksten exponierte und darum vor allem zu befestigende Nordmauer gewiesen. Da hier nicht von der Mauer des "äusseren Hofes," bzw. des "Palasthofes" geredet wird, führt diese Stelle auf das Bestehen einer Mauer mit zwei Toren, die nördlich vom Palastbereich gelegen war und dort den Schutz der Stadt besorgte. Sie wurde nach dem verlorenen Krieg geschleift. Die Stelle führt ins 8. Jahrhundert zurück. Aber sie lässt es als wahrscheinlich erscheinen, dass schon Salomo bei seiner bewusst geplanten Stadterweiterung diesen Gesichtspunkt bedacht hat. Im Rahmen seines Vergleichs der ebenfalls bewusst geplant angelegten Stadtgründung Samarias durch Omri (und ihrer Erweiterung durch Ahab) mit der Salomostadt kommt Alt (1959: 321 Anm. 2) zur Folgerung: "Nach der Analogie von Samaria wird man mit einer erheblichen Ausdehnung der Salomostadt nördlich des Palast- und Tempelkomplexes zu rechnen haben." Dafür spricht abgesehen von der Analogie Samarias auch alle innere Wahrscheinlichkeit. Die in Ezechiel 8 erkennbare "Nordstadt" dürfte danach aller Wahrscheinlichkeit nach schon aus Salomos Zeit stammen.

Die Weiterführung der Entrückungsvision Ezechiels berichtet in Ezek 9: 2, dass 6 Verderbergestalten und ein "Linnengekleideter" in ihrer Mitte "vom oberen Tor her, das gegen Norden schaut," in den innersten Tempelbereich, in dem sich der Prophet am Ende der Schau von Ezechiel 8 befindet, hereintreten. Die Bezeichnung des Tores, in dem nach 8: 14 eben noch die den Tammuz beweinenden Frauen zu sitzen schienen, als "oberes Tor" vermag deutlich zu machen, dass der innerste Tempelbereich gegenüber dem äusseren Hof etwas erhöht ist. In Jer 20: 2 bekommt dieses dort als "Benjaminstor" bezeichnete "obere Tor" den ausdrücklichen Zusatz, dass es "im Hause Jahwes," d.h. wohl dem inneren Tempelbereich, gelegen sei. Das in 2 Chr 23: 20 erwähnte "obere Tor" muss dagegen auf der Südseite des Innenhofes gegen den Palastbereich zu gesucht werden. Die Angabe 2 Kgs 15: 35, dass Jotham "das obere Tor des Hauses Jahwes" gebaut habe, lässt nicht erkennen, welches der beiden "oberen Tore" hier gemeint ist.

So wie Ezechiel 9 keine weiteren Erkenntnisse über die Staffelung der Nordtore von Tempel-, Palast- und Stadtbereich gegen Norden hin ermöglicht, so ist auch aus Ezechiel 10f., welche den Wegzug der Jahweherrlichkeit über das "Osttor des Hauses Jahwes" (10: 19), "mitten aus der Stadt" zum "Berg, der im Osten der Stadt liegt" (11: 23) schildern, nichts mehr über eine Staffelung von Toren auf der Ostseite des Tempelbereichs zu entnehmen. Einzig die Erwähnung des in 11: 23 wohl gemeinten Ölberges verrät noch ein Element der Anschauung der Lage Jerusalems.

III.

Der Blick auf die Entrückungsvision Ezechiel 40–48 zeigt eine sehr andere Welt. Zwar sind da Elemente, die an Ezechiel 8–11 erinnern. Aber stärker drängt sich dem Betrachter die grosse Verschiedenheit der Aussagen auf. Es wird im Folgenden, da auch hier lediglich die Aussagen über die Gestalt Jerusalems nach den Aussagen des Ezechielbuches zur Sprache kommen sollen, darum gehen müssen, Kontinuität und Diskontinuität der Aussagen in dieser Richtung festzustellen und damit einer Fragerichtung zu folgen, mit der sich in einem weiteren Horizont in besonderer Intensität P. Ackroyd befasst hat. In der Beachtung von Kontinuität ganz so wie von Diskontinuität kann sich auch etwas für die gestellte Themafrage ergeben. Polemische Diskontinuität kann im negativen Spiegelbild etwas von dem verraten, von dem man sich abgrenzt. Kontinuität dagegen macht sichtbar, inwiefern sich Elemente zäh durchhalten, die auch durch die Absicht, Neues zu zeigen, nicht zu verdrängen sind.

Auch die Vision 40–48 ist datiert. Neben die Angabe: "Im 25. Jahr unserer Verbannung, am Jahresanfang . . .," die sich an der gewohnten Ära des Ezechielbuches orientiert, tritt hier erst- und einmalig die Angabe: "Im 14. Jahr nach dem Fall der Stadt." Damit ist der grosse Einschnitt markiert, der auch die Elemente der Diskontinuität zum Früheren rechtfertigt. Mit dem Fall Jerusalems und dem Ende des ersten Tempels ist der Abschluss eines Alten gekennzeichnet, das unter das Gericht gefallen ist. Ihm wird nun, bis in die architektonische Gestaltung hinein, ein völlig Neues entgegengesetzt.

Die Entrückung ist mit analogem Vokabular, wenn auch knapper geschildert als in 8: 1–3. An die Stelle des Mannes von überirdischem Glanz, der den Propheten nach Jerusalem entrafft, tritt am Ort der Schau des Neuen eine ohne jede überirdischen Züge beschriebene Gestalt eines "Mannes." Als Begleiter führt er den Propheten durch die neuartigen Gebäude und misst mit dem Messtab ihre Masse. Erst am Ziel der Wanderung durch das Neue öffnet er nach dem von Gese (1957) herausgearbeiteten Grundtext von 40:1–41: 4 erstmals seinen Mund, um das Ziel der Wanderung zu benennen (41: 4). Es fällt auf, dass der Name Jerusalem, der in 8:3 unbefangen als Ziel der Entrückung genannt war, fehlt. Er taucht auch durch die ganze Visionsschilderung 40–48 hin nie auf. Daran, dass es sich beim Ziel der Entrückung nur um Jerusalem handeln kann, besteht (gegen Mackay 1934/35) kein Zweifel. Man möchte diesen auffälligen Tatbestand mit der Wahrnehmung in Verbindung bringen, dass 40–48 abschliessend in eine neue Namengebung ausmünden: "Der Name der Stadt heisst von nun an: Jahwe ist dort" (48: 35). So fehlt denn anders als in 8–11 auch eine Rückkehraussage in die bedrängte Situation der Exulanten (11: 24f.). Die neue herrliche Namengebung als Abschluss könnte ein bewusstes Element der Komposition von 40–48 sein. Allerdings wird sich zeigen, dass dieser Abschluss 48: 30–35 inhaltlich ein Überraschungselement enthält, welches darauf führt, dass ursprünglich ganz andere Momente zur Vermeidung des Jerusalemnamens geführt haben dürften.

Der Prophet wird in seiner Schau "ins Land Israels . . . auf einen sehr hohen Berg" entrückt. Vom "hohen Berg" ist bei der Verheissung eines neuen (königlichen?) Schosses in 17: 22 die Rede, von "meinem heiligen Berg, dem hohen Berg Israels" in

20: 40, wo vom Ziel der neuen Herausführung aus der Gefangenschaft in der Völkerwelt geredet wird. In dieser Erhöhung des neuen Tempelberges über das Jerusalem der geschichtlichen Tage Jerusalems tritt das Element endzeitlicher Überhöhung der gottfernen Gegenwart, das in Isa 2: 2 = Mic 4: 1 seine eindrücklichste Ausgestaltung erfahren hat, als Element der Diskontinuität besonders stark heraus. Es ist ein auch geographisch verwandelter Ort der Gottes-(Tempel-)-Stadt.

Auf dem hohen Berge im Lande Israels sieht sich der Prophet einem Gebilde "gleich dem Bauwerk einer Stadt" gegenüber. (Zum Problem des *minnegeb* des MT in 40: 2 vgl. Zimmerli 1979: 983 Anm. g, zur Stelle). Eine Mauer, die durch grosse Torbauten Einlass gewährt, umgibt dieses. Der Weg, auf dem der begleitende Mann mit dem Propheten geht, führt zum Tempelhaus, in das nur der Mann selber hineingeht um es zu vermessen. Erstmals hier öffnet er nach dem Grundtext den Mund zur deklaratorischen Bestimmung: "Das ist das Hochheilige (Allerheiligste)." Dieser Weg vom Tor bis zum Tempelhaus, in dem das Allerheiligste liegt, entspricht grundsätzlich dem Führungsweg von Ezechiel 8. Allerdings mit zwei bedeutsamen Abweichungen. Nicht in der Unheilsrichtung von Norden nach Süden wird er gegangen, sondern von Osten nach Westen. Und er führt nicht gradlinig über 4 Stationen, sondern auf Umwegen über 6 geschilderte Vorbauten (Tore) hin zum Zentrum des Heiligen. Die Stilisierung nach dem Vorbild des Weges der Woche, auf welchem die 6 Wochentage hinführen zum geheiligten 7. Tag des Sabbats, nach welcher der priesterliche Erzähler der Anfangsgeschichte den Schöpfungsvorgang stilisiert hat, ist nicht zu übersehen. Es ist nicht die einzige Stelle, an der ein neues, geheiligtes Mass die Diskontinuität des Neuen zum Alten ausdrückt und Zahlberechnungen Verkündigungsgehalte zu Gehör bringen. (Vgl. Zimmerli 1970.)

Durch zwei Höfe hin führt der Weg in 40: 1–41: 4 zum Tempelhaus, in dem das Allerheiligste liegt. Darin besteht Kontinuität zur Vision von 8 und dem historischen Zustand der Zeit Ezechiels, dass auch hier von zwei Höfen die Rede ist. Aber Diskontinuität darin, dass der ganze Bereich der 2 Höfe nach 42: 20 durch seine Mauer als Heiliges von Profanen geschieden ist, ja, nach 43: 12 gar als "Hochheilig" bezeichnet wird.

Im Vergleich mit Ezechiel 8 wird weiter auffallen, dass in der Führung von 40f. ein Äquivalent zu der ersten Wegstrecke vom Stadttor zum Eingang der Palasthofumgrenzung und ihrem Eingang (8: 7) völlig fehlt. Der Weg führt hier unmittelbar in den geheiligten Tempelbereich hinein. Das lässt einem schärfer auf die Formulierung der Einleitung 40: 2 achten: Nicht zur einer Stadt wird der Prophet entrückt, sondern zu einem Bauwerk auf dem hohen Berg Israels, das aussah "wie eine Stadt." Dieses ist nicht die Stadt Jerusalem, sondern, wie alles Folgende zeigt, allein die Tempelanlage mit ihren zwei Höfen. "Wie ein stadtartiger Bau" sieht sie aus, weil man durch einen grossangelegten Torbau mit der Ausmessung von 50: 25 Ellen in sie hineintritt. Dieser Torbau kehrt dann auch beim Übergang vom äusseren in den inneren Hof in gleichen Ausmessungen wieder. In dem Artikel "Ezechielstadt und Salomostadt" (1967) habe ich zu zeigen gesucht, wie diese Toranlagen mit ihren drei Nischen auf jeder Seite des Tordurchganges ihre Entsprechung in den wohl aus der Salomozeit stammenden Torbauten von Megiddo, Hazor und Gezer haben, die dort eindeutig Stadttore sind. Man wird nicht ausschliessen können, dass das Nordtor, durch das der Prophet nach 8: 3 die Stadt betritt, ebendiese Gestalt hatte und ev. wie die genannten Tore der anderen, von

Salomo ausgebauten Städte, in die Salomozeit zu datieren ist. Kontinuität und Diskontinuität in Einem: Die Stadttorbauten sind in ihrer alten Gestalt hier zu Tempeltorbauten geworden. Dabei ist aus dem Ganzen deutlich zu entnehmen, dass nicht mehr die politische Grösse der Stadt durch diese starken Wehrbauten geschützt werden soll, sondern der heilige Bereich, der durch seine Umwallungsmauer streng abgesondert worden ist vom Profanen (42: 20). Der polemische Akzent ist in alledem nicht zu überhören. Diskontinuität gegenüber dem Greuelzustand von Ezechiel 8.

Nicht zu übersehen ist weiter die Tatsache, dass jeder Hof nur drei Tore hat, nach Osten, Norden und Süden. Auf der Westseite, auf der heute die eigentlich wichtigen Zugänge zum *ḥaram-* Bezirk liegen, auf der Rückseite des Tempelhauses mit seinem Allerheiligsten im Westteil des Hauses von Ezechiel 40f., ist kein Tempelzugang, auch nicht zum äusseren Tempelvorhof, denkbar. Hatte in 8: 16 die vierte, grösste Verfehlung darin bestanden dass die Männer "zwischen Tempel und Altar" auf der Ostseite des Tempelhauses bei ihrer Verehrung der aufgehenden Sonne dem Tempelhaus, dem Wohnbereich Jahwes, den Rücken zuwandten, so will hier in etwas modifizierter Weise jeder Zugang zum Heiligen von der Rückseite aus strikte verwehrt bleiben. Das ungefüge Gebilde des *binyān* (Baues), das nach 41: 12 die ganze Westseite des Tempelhauses (bis auf einen schmalen Durchgang unmittelbar hinter dem Haus) zur äusseren Tempelmauer hin abdeckt, ohne dass ein Verwendungszwecke dieses Baues angegeben würde, verstellt einem Westtor des Tempelbereiches den Weg.

In der strengen Heiligerklärung der beiden Tempelvorhöfe ist für den "grossen," als Hof der Palastanlage zu interpretierenden Hof von 1 Kgs 7: 12, der den Tempelbereich um fasst haben dürfte, kein Raum mehr. Das ist in 43: 1ff. denn auch ganz deutlich zum Ausdruck gebracht. Hier ist geschildert, wie die Herrlichkeit Jahwes in diesen neuen, in geheilten und geheiligten Massen erbauten Tempelbereich und sein Allerheiligstes einzieht. Daran ist das Versprechen geknüpft, dass Jahwe im Allerheiligsten, dem "Ort seines Thrones und dem Ort seiner Fussohlen" nun für alle Zeiten inmitten der Israeliten wohnen werde. Ausdrücklich ist dabei verordnet: "Das Haus Israel soll meinen heiligen Namen nicht mehr unrein machen—weder sie noch ihre Könige—durch ihre Buhlerei und durch die Denksteine ihrer Könige bei ihrem Tode [vgl. Komm. z.St.], dadurch, dass sie ihre Schwelle neben meine Schwelle setzten und ihren Türpfosten neben meinen Türpfosten, sodass nur eine Wand zwischen mir und ihnen lag. . . . Nun mögen sie ihre Buhlerei und die Denksteine ihrer Könige von mir fernhalten, so will ich für alle Zeiten in ihrer Mitte wohnen" (43: 7–9). Gerne wüssten wir, ob die stelae pro memoria ihrer Könige, die hier gemeint sein dürften (Neiman 1948, Galling 1959) in der vorexilischen Zeit an der Wand des eigentlichen (inneren) Tempelvorhofes aufgerichtet waren oder an einer Zwischenmauer, die schon in der spätvorexilischen Zeit ev. den eigentlichen Palastvorhof gegen den zum Tempel geschlagenen Teil des "grossen Hofes" (1 Kgs 7: 12) im Süden abgrenzte. Die Angaben reichen zu einer sicheren Entscheidung der Frage nicht aus. Unüberhörbar aber ist die Forderung, dass keine Berührung mehr zwischen den früheren Elementen des Palastes und des heiligen Tempelbereichs bestehen dürfe.

Das führt zu der Frage, wo denn überhaupt der Palast des "Fürsten" (*nāśîʾ*) von dem in 40–48 die Rede ist, seinen Ort haben könne. Die Baubeschreibung schweigt sich darüber im Unterschied zu 1 Kgs 6f. völlig aus. Aber aus einer wohl als spätere Ergänzung zugefügten, noch ganz im Sinne der Tempelbeschreibung gehaltenen Erweiterung in 48: 1–29 ist auf diese Frage eine Antwort zu entnehmen. Vom Königspalast ist dort zwar ausdrücklich nicht geredet. Aber es darf wohl angenommen werden, dass dieser Palast im Bereich der nicht unter der strengen Heiligtumsordnung stehenden Stadt zu suchen ist. Über die Lage der Stadt ist hier geredet—freilich so, dass sich dabei eine neue Überraschung ergibt. Bei der neuen Landverteilung soll ein Landstreifen von 25000 Ellen Breite zwischen den 7 nördlichen und den 5 südlichen Stammanteilen als "heilige Weihegabe (*tĕrûmâ*)" ausgesondert werden. Während die Randstücke dieses Teiles dem Fürsten zugewiesen werden, ist ein Quadrat von je 25000 Ellen Seitenlänge in seiner Mitte für Leviten, Priester und Stadt reserviert. Der Tempel wird in der Mitte dieses Quadrates im Priesteranteil zu suchen sein, der wie der Levitenanteil 10000 Ellen Breite hat. Für die Stadt verbleibt somit ein Streifen von 5000 Ellen Breite im Süden, der sich mit dem Tempelbezirk in der Mitte des Priesterlandes gar nicht berühren dürfte. Diskontinuität im strengen Sinne. Umklammerte früher die Stadt den Tempelbereich in nordsüdlicher Abfolge: Nordstadt, Palastvorhof, Tempelvorhof, südlicher Teil des Palastvorhofes, von Salomo ausgebauter Ophel, Davidsstadt, so ist hier der Tempel räumlich völlig vom Stadtbereich getrennt. Die Stadt ist in den Süden verbannt, in den Bereich der früheren Davidsstadt, ohne das Zwischenstück des von Salomo überbauten Ophel, der Davidsstadt und Salomopalast und -tempel verbinden sollte. Wenn der Verfasser von Ezechiel 48 überhaupt Reflexionen über die Lage des Palastes im Blick auf das vorexilische, historische Jerusalem angestellt haben sollte, so wird er ihn im Stadtbereich, wenn nicht gar im Fürstenland draussen angesetzt haben.

Wieweit aber für den Verfasser konkrete geographische Überlegungen eine Rolle gespielt haben, ist schon bei den Ausmessungen für das gesamte Tempelareal fraglich. Dieses übergreift mit seinen 500: 500 Ellen ohne Zweifel das für den salomonischen Tempel zur Verfügung stehende Mass an Landfläche und reicht schon nahe an die Dimensionen des herodianischen Tempelareals mit seinen gewaltigen Substruktionen heran. Wie kühn der Verfasser von 40–48 Kontinuität verleugnet, wird weiter besonders krass an der geographischen Verteilung der künftigen Stämmeanteile erkennbar. Nicht nur werden da die Nordstämme Issachar und Sebulon zusammen mit dem ostjordanischen Gad ganz in den Süden hinunter verlegt, sondern auch die zentralen Stämme Juda und Benjamin vertauschen ihren Platz: Benjamin wird in den Süden des Heiligtumszentrums verlegt, Juda in den Norden desselben. Für die Begründung dieser letzten seltsamen Vertauschung könnte höchstens die etymologische Erwägung beigebracht werden, dass Benjamin als "Sohn der Rechten," d.h. bei Ostorientierung der Himmelsrichtungen, als "Sohn des Südens" auf die Südseite verlegt wird. Für die weiteren Umstellungen war vielleicht die Überlegung massgebend, dass die heilige Mitte der "Weihegabe" auch räumlich ungefähr in die Mitte des 12-Stämmevolkes gelegt werden musste, wobei nur in dem leichten Übergewicht der Zahl der Nordstämme (7 gegenüber 5 im Süden) ein schwacher Hinweis auf Kontinuität zu erkennen sein dürfte.

Am überraschendsten macht sich dann allerdings der Wille zur Kontinuität in dem zweifellos aus anderer Hand stammenden Abschluss 48: 30–35 bemerkbar. Von der "Stadt," nicht vom Tempelbereich, der im Vorhergehenden säuberlich von der Stadt getrennt worden war, heisst es nun, dass sie den Namen "Jahwe ist dort" bekommen solle, wo doch 43:1ff. den Einzug der Herrlichkeit Jahwes nicht in die

Stadt, sondern in das Innerste des Tempelbereichs geschildert und angesagt hatte dass Jahwe für alle Zeiten dort in der Mitte seines Volkes wohnen wolle. Tore auf allen vier Seiten der Stadt sind nach den Namen der 12 Stämme benannt, wobei von der Aussparung der Westseite, welche die Tempelanlage von 40–42 kennzeichnete, nichts mehr zu erkennen ist und offensichtlich auch das Element von Heils- und Unheilsrichtung, das im Nebeneinander von Ezechiel 8 und 40ff. wahrgenommen werden konnte, völlig verschwunden ist. Die Tore von Ruben, Juda (dem Königsstamm) und Levi (dem Priesterstamm) sind im Norden, Joseph, Benjamin und Dan an der Ostseite angeordnet.

In dieser, gegenüber dem Vorausgehenden völlig konträren Schilderung der Stadt als Ort der Gegenwart Jahwes und der Stadttore schlägt mit Macht die Kontinuitätsabsicht durch: Jahwe wohnt in seiner heiligen Stadt, so wie es dann bei Deutero- und Tritojesaja ganz selbstverständlich vorausgesetzt ist.

So vermag die zweite Entrückungsvision des Propheten, was immer die verschiedenen Hände gewesen sein mögen, die an ihrer Gestaltung gearbeitet haben, im Unterschied zu Ezechiel 8 nur sehr indirekt einen Beitrag zur wirklichen Erkenntnis des Jerusalem der Tage Ezechiels zu geben. Wohl aber führt sie mitten hinein in den theologisch erregenden Vorgang der Auseinandersetzung mit vorgegebenem Gut und den Widerstreit von kontinuierlicher Übernahme und radikaler Neuerwartung.

References

Ackroyd, P. R.
1962 *Continuity. A Contribution to the Study of the Old Testament Religious Tradition.* Inaugural Lecture in the Samuel Davidson Chair of Old Testament Studies delivered at King's College London. Oxford: Blackwell.

Albright, W. F.
1956 *Die Religion Israels im Lichte der archäologischen Ausgrabungen.* München: Reinhardt.

Alt, A.
1953 *Kleine Schriften zur Geschichte des Volkes Israel II.* Pp. 76–89, Israels Gaue unter Salomo (Erstpublikation 1913); pp. 316–37, Die Rolle Samarias bei der Entstehung des Judentums (Erstpublikation 1934). München: Beck.
1959 *Kleine Schriften zur Geschichte Israels III.* Pp. 303–25, Archäologische Fragen zur Baugeschichte von Jerusalem und Samaria in der israelitischen Königszeit (Erstpublikation 1955/6). München: Beck.

Bertholet, A.
1936 *Hesekiel.* Handbuch zum Alten Testament I/13. Tübingen: Mohr (Siebeck).

Cooke, G. A.
1936 *The Book of Ezekiel.* The International Critical Commentary. Edinburgh: Clark.

Donner, H.
1977 *Jerusalem.* Pp. 165–79 in K. Galling, *Biblisches Reallexikon.* 2. Aufl. Tübingen: Mohr (Siebeck).

Fohrer, G.
1955 *Ezechiel.* Handbuch zum Alten Testament I/13. Tübingen: Mohr (Siebeck).

Galling, K.
1959 Erwägungen zum Stelenheiligtum von Hazor. *Zeitschrift des Deutschen Palästinavereins* 75: 1–13.

Gese, H.
1957 *Der Verfassungsentwurf des Ezechiel (Kap. 40–48) Traditionsgeschichtlich untersucht.* Beiträge zur historischen Theologie 2. Tübingen: Mohr (Siebeck).

Greenberg, M.
1980 The Vision of Jerusalem in Ezekiel 8–11: A Holistic Interpretation. Pp. 143–64 in *The Divine Helmsman. Studies on God's Control of Human Events, Presented to Lou H. Silberman.* New York: Ktav Publishing House.

Guthe, H.
1936 *Bibelatlas.* 2. Auflage. Leipzig: Wagner und Debes.

Mackay, C.
1934/35 The Key of the Old Testament (Ezek. 40–48). *The Church Quarterly Review* 119: 173–96.

Neiman, D.
1948 *PGR.* A Canaanite Cult-Object in the Old Testament. *Journal of Biblical Literature and Exegesis* 67: 55–60.

Rothstein, W.
1922 Das Buch Ezechiel (Hesekiel). Bd 1, pp. 868–1000 in Kautzsch-Bertholet, *Die Heilige Schrift des Alten Testaments,* 4 Aufl. Tübingen: Mohr (Siebeck).

Zimmerli, W.
1967 Ezechieltempel und Salomostadt. Pp. 398–414 in *Hebräische Wortforschung. Festschrift zum 80. Geburstag von W. Baumgartner.* Supplement to Vetus Testamentum 16. Leiden: Brill (= Theologische Bücherei 51, 1974, 148–64, München: Kaiser).

1970 Das "Gnadenjahr des Herrn." Pp. 321–332 in *Archäologie und Altes Testament: Festschrift für K. Galling.* Tübingen: Mohr (Siebeck) (= Theologische Bücherei 51, 1974, 222–34).

1979 *Ezechiel.* Biblischer Kommentar XIII/1 und 2. 2. Auflage. Neukirchen: Neukirchener Verlag. English Translation (ET), Vol. 1, 1979. Philadelphia: Fortress Press.

587 ou 586?

Henri Cazelles, S. S.
École des Hautes Études, Paris

Il s'agit évidemment de la prise de Jérusalem par Nabuchodonosor II et de la destruction du premier Temple. Comme beaucoup, j'ai admis longtemps[1] que cette destruction avait eu lieu en 586 av JC.[2] Mais la date de 587 a gardé de nombreux adhérents.[3] Et certains restent indécis.[4] Le débat a été profondément renouvelé depuis la publication de la Chronique Babylonienne de D. Wiseman en 1956[5] et il s'est surtout concentré sur le problème du début de l'année dans le Juda préexilique: l'année commençait-elle au printemps comme en Mésopotamie? Ou en automne comme en Egypte, du moins en principe, et en Canaan? Mais il y a d'autres approches du problème.

Grâce à ce que l'on appelle le canon de Ptolémée, cet astronome grec du 2ème siècle, qui donne des dates astronomiques en fonction des règnes perses et babyloniens à partir de Nabonassar (daté 747),[6] Parker et Dubberstein ont pu donner des dates précises aux règnes en calendrier julien.[7] Nous admettrons, en les suivant, que l'an 1 de Nabuchodonosor va de Nisan 604 à Nisan 603. Les mois qui s'écoulent entre la mort de son père Nabopolassar (8 du mois de Ab = 15 ou 16 Août 605) et la fête de Nisan où commence son année 1 s'appelle l'année d'accession: en accadien, *rēš šarrūti,* début du règne. L'an 7 de Nabuchodonosor va donc de Nisan 598 à Nisan 597. Cette 7ème année comprend, selon la Chronique de Wiseman, la prise de Jérusalem et le changement de règne qui a lieu pendant son dernier mois, le 2 de Adar, 15 ou 16 Mars 597, année julienne.

Sur ce point il y a accord. Mais le désaccord apparaît quand on passe des données babyloniennes aux données bibliques. Or celles-ci sont divergentes et ne peuvent s'expliquer que par une pluralité de sources, sources qui ont été respectées dans leurs divergences par les rédacteurs des livres de Jérémie, d'Ezéchiel, et des Rois.

a) Jér 52: 28–29 est en plein accord avec la Chronique babylonienne et date de la 7ème année de Nabuchodonosor une déportation de 3023 Judéens. Dans une comptabilité sobre et précise, elle enregistre ensuite une déportation de 832 habitants de Jérusalem. Cette différence correspond bien à celle qui existe entre 597 où Jérusalem s'est soumise sans siège, et la seconde campagne de Nabuchodonosor où la ville fut isolée de la province par un long siège. Cette seconde captivité date de la 18ème année de Nabuchodonosor et est à dater de l'année Nisan 587–Nisan 586; la chronique babylonienne est brisée après 594/3 et ignore donc cette seconde prise. Elle l'aurait certainement enregistrée à l'année 18, également, car nous allons retrouver ce même écart de 11 années entre les deux captivités dans l'autre système chronologique du livre de Jérémie. Ce parallèle 7/8 et 18/19 ne nous permet pas d'accepter deux captivités distinctes en 587 et 586.

b) En Jér 52: 12, ce serait en l'an 19 de Nabuchodonosor qu'aurait eu l'incendie de Jérusalem par Nabuzaradan après la capture du roi Sédécias, alors en sa 11ème année de règne. C'est le texte même de II Reg 25: 8 avec la seule différence du jour du mois (10 au lieu de 7). Or II Reg 24: 12 garde ainsi le même laps de temps entre les deux campagnes du roi babylonien et donne pour la première, non plus l'année 7, mais l'année 8 de Nabuchodonosor. Le même système chronologique qui date l'incendie de l'été de l'an 11 de Sédécias et de la 19ème année de Nabuchodonosor, date un évènement de l'an 10 de Sédécias et de la 18ème année du roi babylonien (Jér 32: 1), ce qui suggère que l'année judéenne commence en Tishri ou en Nisan.

C'est aussi selon ce système que nous est donnée la date du début du siège: le 10 de la 10ème de l'année 9 de Sédécias selon Jér 52: 4; Jér 39: 1 (sans quantième du mois); II Reg 25: 1; et Ezéch 24: 1. Selon ce comput, si rien ne vient le contredire, le siège a duré 18 mois jusqu'à la brèche (4ème mois Jér 52: 6; II Reg 25: 3) ou 19 mois jusqu'à l'incendie (5ème mois Jér 52: 12; II Reg 25: 8).[8]

c) Mais, selon Ezéch 33: 21, l'annonce de la destruction n'arrive aux exilés que le 5 du 10ème mois de l'an 12 de la *gālût*. Cette *gālût* dans le livre d'Ezéchiel est la captivité de 597 identifiée avec la captivité de Joyakin en Ezéch 1: 2, cf. Jér 52: 31. Tous les commentateurs remarquent combien il est invraisemblable que la nouvelle de l'incendie de Jérusalem ait mis 17 mois pour atteindre les rives de l'Euphrate (du 7 ou 10,5,9 au 5,10,12).[9] 5 mois sont bien suffisants, comme le suggèrent certains copistes. N'aurions-nous pas ici une dualité de sources et de chronologie comme dans le livre de Jérémie? En fait nous en avons une autre trace dans le livre d'Ezéchiel en 40: 1. On nous y donne d'une manière embarrassée l'équivalence entre le 10 du mois du début de l'année[10] 25 de la *gālût* et l'année 14 de l'incendie de Jérusalem.

Nous n'avons pas à privilégier un système sur l'autre. En fait, toutes les rédactions actuelles des livres de Jérémie, Ezéchiel, Rois, plus encore Chroniques, sont postexiliques.[11] Mais ces rédactions ont eu souvent à transcrire dans un calendrier postexilique, commençant au printemps, des sources judéennes où la datation reposait sur d'autres bases, d'où les divergences.

a) Il est sûr que sous la monarchie, d'après les calendriers anciens (Exod 23: 16, cf. 34: 22)[12] et la pratique (I Reg 8: 2) confirmée par la tablette de Gezer,[13] la liturgie d'Emar,[14] et des expressions de Mari,[15] c'est à l'automne que l'année commençait, "sortait," "entrait," "se recyclait," avec une grande fête. Je reste persuadé que le changement de calendrier qui bouleversait les habitudes de la population ne s'est fait à Jérusalem qu'avec l'établissement d'une administration babylonienne.

b) Mais il n'est pas sûr que l'année royale et l'année civile coincidaient.

1. L'année d'accession, *rēš šarrūti* en accadien, n'est pas une expression hébraïque. Elle apparaît quatre fois dans le livre de Jérémie, mais dans ses rédactions en prose, et sous des formes diverses; ce n'est donc que l'adaptation d'une forme étrangère babylonienne: *rēšît malkût* (49: 34), *rēšît mamlĕkût* (26: 1), *rēšît mamleket* (27: 1; 28: 1). Il n'est pas sûr qu'elle ait toujours sa valeur technique d' "année d'accession," surtout en 28: 1 où il est question d'une 4ème année, et 49: 34 sur l'Elam: selon la chronique babylonienne l'Elam est à l'horizon, non lors de l'avènement de Sédécias (an 7 de Nabuchodonosor), mais en l'an 9 du roi babylonien.

2. De la 18ème dynastie à la 20ème, selon l'*Egyptian Grammar* de A. Gardiner[16] mais plus probablement jusqu'à la 24ème dynastie[17] comprise, l'année royale diffère de l'année civile et commence avec la mort du prédécesseur et l'accession. Or on sait l'influence des pratiques égyptiennes sur l'administration de Jérusalem et de Juda. Ce ne sont pas seulement les titres des fonctionnaires,[18] les écrits de sagesse comme

Amenemope,[19] mais aussi la manière d'écrire les chiffres.[20] Le plus probable est que la cour de Jérusalem a pris le système de la 20ème dynastie.

Dans ce cas, il n'y a plus aucune difficulté à admettre que la captivité de Joyakin ait lieu dans les premiers jours de Adar an 7 de Nabuchodonosor comme le dit la Chronique de Wiseman. C'est la date officielle babylonienne et on n'a pas à supposer des retards dans l'exécution. Les années de Sédécias ne se comptent pas à partir de Tishri ou de Nisan, mais à partir de Adar[21] et l'an 11 de Sédécias va de Adar 587 à Adar 586, la chute de Jérusalem ayant lieu dans l'intervalle, mois 4 ou 5 de l'an 11 (587).

C'est donc par Jér 52: 28 et la médiation de la chronique babylonienne que nous pouvons dater en calendrier julien la chute de Jérusalem. Le siège commence le 10ème mois de l'an 9 de Sédécias, donc fin 588 ou début 587, et cela convient bien à la nouvelle date proposée par R. Parker pour la mort de Psammétique II et l'avènement d'Hophra.[22] C'est le changement de règne en Egypte qui pousse Jérusalem à la révolte contre Babylone. Si l'an 10 de Sédécias commence en Adar, et l'an 18 de Nabuchodonosor en Nisan, il n'y a pas difficulté à trouver une date commune pour Jér 32: 1. De même si la bataille de Carkémish a lieu en Juin-Juillet 605 selon la chronique babylonienne, et pendant la 4ème année de Joyaqim selon Jér 46: 2, cela convient à une année "royale" de Joyaqim. L'an 1 de Joyaqim commence vers Septembre 609 (après Megiddo et les trois mois de règne de Joachaz) et se termine en Septembre 608; sa 4ème année va de Septembre 606 à Septembre 605 et englobe la bataille de Carkémish. Cette année 4 de Joyaqim est dite (en Jér 25: 1) contemporaine de l'an 1 de Nabuchodonosor qui, en calendrier babylonien, ne commence qu'en Nisan 604. Mais Jér 46: 2 donne le titre de roi à Nabuchodonosor lors de la bataille alors qu'il n'est encore que prince héritier. Il ne sera roi que le 8 de Ab (Août), après la mort de Nabopolassar. Un rédacteur judéen pouvait considérer que Août//Septembre étaient déjà dans sa 1ère année de règne, mais non la bataille qui précède. Il y a donc là certainement un élément rédactionnel.

c) Cette rédaction est faite en fonction du changement de calendrier qui, sous l'influence de l'administration babylonienne, fait commencer l'année civile au printemps et non plus en automne (Tishri). Dans ce cas l'année de l'incendie de Jérusalem (étant de l'été de l'année "royale" 11 de Sédécias) est traduite comme étant non plus l'année 18 mais l'année 19 de Nabuchodonosor, évidemment en se basant sur des sources judéennes et non babyloniennes. L'année 10 de Sédécias devient l'année 18 de Nabuchodonosor, l'année de l'accession de Sédécias l'année 8 et non plus 7 de Nabuchodonosor. C'est aussi sous l'influence du système babylonien que le rédacteur parle de "l'année d'accession," de Sédécias ou de Joyaqim, et que Jér 25: 2 parle d'un évènement qui est à la fois de la 1ère année de Nabuchodonosor et de la 4ème de Joyaqim. Le 10ème mois de la 5ème année de Joyaqim est en effet certainement un mois d'hiver (Jér 36: 9), lors du jeûne consécutif à la prise d'Ascalon[23] supposant une année commençant au printemps 604. Selon les calculs de cette rédaction, la 4ème année de Joyaqim va de Nisan 605 à Nisan 604. Enfin l'arrivée de l'annonce de la prise de Jérusalem a bien lieu de 5 du 10ème mois d'une 12ème année d'une *gālût* commençant en Adar 597. Le rédacteur ajoute une année au comput réel. Joyaqim est censé avoir commencé non plus en Automne 609, mais en Mars, avec une année 4 commençant en Mars puisqu'elle met la bataille de Carkémish *dans* l'an 4 de Joyaqim; l'an 1 de Nabuchodonosor commençerait en Mars 605 et non plus Mars 604.

En reconnaissant cette dualité de chronologie venant de l'utilisation de sources différentes, on peut aussi expliquer la dualité des dates de la prise de Jérusalem. La date traditionnelle est le 9 de Ab. Or cette date n'est pas biblique. La Bible parle soit du 7 de Ab (II Reg 25: 8), soit du 10 (Jér 52: 12). Or Nabopolassar est mort le 8 de Ab d'après la chronique babylonienne. Du point de vue judéen, qui ignorait avant l'exil l'année d'accession, le 7 de Ab 587 serait dans l'an 18 de Nabuchodonosor et le 10 dans sa 19ème année. Le 9 pourrait donc bien être la date exacte que les deux rédactions bibliques ont transcrites en fonction de leurs deux systèmes. Certes le "9 du mois" est connu des textes bibliques, mais il s'agit du 4ème mois qui n'est pas Ab, mais Tammuz. On a remarqué depuis longtemps ce qu'il y a d'étrange dans ce délai d'un mois entre la brèche faite dans la muraille et l'entrée de Nabuzaradan dans la ville. Si la Bible et ses rédactions dépendent de deux calendriers différents, il se peut qu'il s'agisse du même mois. Toutefois il s'agirait du mois de Tammuz, 5ème après Adar, 4ème après Nisan. Il faudrait supposer que la tradition ait réinterprété le 5ème mois après Adar comme étant après Nisan.

Ceci n'est pas impossible, car ce n'est que tardivement que les mois chiffrés du système postexilique ont reçu les noms des mois babyloniens.[24] Le calendrier aux mois "chiffrés" est en effet le calendrier où l'année dure 364 jours de 52 sabbats revenant toujours à la même date de l'année. C'est le calendrier auquel restèrent fidèles les Esséniens et le livre des Jubilés. Mais il allait se trouver en discordance avec l'année civile réelle. Or, dès le début, il était d'environ dix jours plus long que l'année lunaire des Babyloniens qui comprend approximativement 354 jours de moyenne. On sait que ces 10 jours supplémentaires apparaissent dans le récit du Déluge (Gen 8: 14 et 7: 11; Lév 25: 9). Il est probable qu'ils expliquent aussi la discordance entre II Reg 24: 8 qui n'attribue que 3 mois de règne à Joyakin, alors que II Chr 36: 9 lui donne 3 mois et 10 jours. C'est en effet au dernier mois de l'année, en Adar, qu'il a été déposé par Nabuchodonosor. Plus important pour notre sujet, le fait qu'en Ezéch 40: 1 le *rôš haššānâ* est également identifié au 10ème jour du mois. Ceci confirme que le rédacteur d'Ezéchiel a eu à unir deux systèmes.

Il ne faut donc pas considérer Jér 52: 28–30 comme une insertion tardive dans le livre de Jérémie. Si, en 52: 1–27, nous sommes en présence d'une insertion massive venant du Livre des Rois (II Reg 24: 18–25, sauf 52: 11b), on observe le même phénomène au Jérémie 39. Les vv 39: 1–2, 4–10 sont une addition du livre des Rois interpolée dans 39: 3 et 14 qui concernaient la faveur faite à Jérémie. K.F. Pohlmann[25] a montré que le Livre des Rois en II Reg 25: 22–26 dépendait de Jérémie 40 en évitant de parler de Jérémie. C'est très probablement parce que l'auteur du Livre des Rois mettait son espérance dans Joyakin tandis que Jérémie lui avait été très hostile (Jér 22: 30) et avait soutenu Sédécias. L'éditeur définitif du livre de Jérémie adopta le point de vue du Livre des Rois sur Joyakin (Jér 52: 31–34), son système chronologique (19ème année de Nabuchodonosor pour l'incendie de Jérusalem), certains de ses textes (39: 1–2; 39: 4–10; 52: 1–27) mais sans détruire le texte plus ancien qui célébrait les faveurs de Nabuchodonosor pour Jérémie. Ce dernier datait la prise de la ville de l'an 18, la captivité de Joyakin et l'avènement de Sédécias de l'an 7, ce qui nous oblige à adopter en calendrier julien 597 pour cet avènement et 587 pour la destruction de la ville et du Temple.

Notes

1. Cazelles 1974: 64 n. 2, cf. Cazelles 1958: 325.

2. Sans être exhaustif et pour nous en tenir aux travaux postérieurs à la publication de la Chronique de Wiseman (1956), sont favorables à cette date: Arnaud 1970: 174; Auerbach 1961: 128; Freedy & Redford 1970: 468; Gray 1970: 764; Horn 1968: 43; K. Kenyon 1974: 169; Malamat 1968: 154–55, 1975: 123, 1979b: 220; Mazar 1976: 591; Meuleau 1971: 244; Rainey 1975: 51; Schedl 1962: 211; Spalinger 1977: 221–45, esp.233; Stern 1975; Tadmor 1979: 55; Thiele 1956: 26; Vogt 1975.

3. Freedman 1956, 1961: 121–22; Albright 1956: 32; K. T. Andersen 1969: 109; Briend & Seux 1977: 141; Bright 1972: 329; Burrows 1958: 191; Eissfeldt 1967: 195; Garelli & Nikiprovetzki 1974: 254; Katzenstein 1973: 319; Kutsch 1974; Noth 1958: 150; Orlinsky 1974: 159; Pohlmann 1978: 205; de Vaux 1966: 494; Zimmerli 1969: 564, 1976: 500.

4. Clines 1974; Greenberg 1957; Herrmann 1973: 345; Larrson 1967: 417–18; Oded 1979: 273; Weinberg 1971: 78 n. 1, plutôt favorable à 586. M. Weippert (1971: 364 et n. 1237) distingue la déportation de 587 et l'incendie de 586.

5. Wiseman 1956, où la première prise de Jérusalem par Nabuchodonosor et le changement de règne (de Joyakin à Sédécias, non nommés dans la Chronique) eut lieu de 2 Adar de la 7ème année du règne. Voir maintenant Grayson 1975. Le calcul astronomique donne pour cette date en calendrier julien les 15 ou 16 Mars (Parker & Dubberstein 1956: 33).

6. Bickerman 1980: 110. Les équivalences entre 1er Nisan et les dates juliennes de Kugler (1924) et de Sidersky (1933) ne commencent qu'en 573/0 av JC.

7. Parker & Dubberstein 1956: 10ss; pour Nabuchodonosor tableau pp. 27s.

8. Voir l'utile tableau de Malamat 1979b: 145. Entre le début et la fin du siège, il y a deux changements d'années, mais entre le 10, 10, 9 (Jér 52: 6) et le 7 (ou 10), 5, 11 il y a moins de deux ans.

9. Cf. Zimmerli 1969: 813. On compte 8 manuscrits hébreux, ainsi que la recension lucianique grecque, quelques minuscules grecs, et la Syriaque qui ont senti la difficulté et corrigé 12 en 11.

10. Début de l'année, *rôš haššānâ* en hébreu. On pense aussitôt au *rôš haššānâ* traditionnel. C'est certainement un jour précis (*bĕʿeṣem hayyôm*), mais il est fort possible que le rédacteur, qui commence l'année au printemps (cf. 45: 18), pense à un premier de l'an de printemps; de même que Exod 12: 2 insiste pour affirmer que le premier mois de l'année est au printemps. Sur ce dernier point, voir de Vaux 1961: 291.

11. Sur ce point je suis entièrement d'accord avec H. Tadmor 1979: 50. "Tous les passages de l'Ancien Testament où les mois sont désignés par un chiffre ordinal s'expliquent sans difficulté dans une année commençant au printemps" (de Vaux 1961: 291). Mais aucun texte n'est preéxilique (cf. Cazelles 1958: 325). Les objections faites par J.M. Baumgarten (1962) and R. T. Beckwith (1981) ne s'opposent pas à ce que le calendrier des Jubilés ait été une tentative de l'École "sacerdotale" faite aux 6ème/5ème siècle av JC, pour maintenir la spécificité des fêtes juives traditionnelles et du sabbat lorsque le début de l'année fut transféré au printemps sous la pression de l'administration babylonienne.

12. "Sortie de l'année," "recyclage de l'année" (*tĕqûpat,* cf. le *nqp* ugaritique et Isa 29: 1; Caquot, Sznycer, & Herdner 1974: 558).

13. La liste des mois commence avec l'engrangement, *'sp,* H. Tadmor 1979: 50.

14. D. Arnaud 1977: 254, n. 50.

15. Birot 1964: 58; AHw 236a. Sur le début de l'année civile en Tishri sous la monarchie je suis d'accord avec A. Malamat dont les études restent les plus documentées sur les dernières années de Juda.

16. Gardiner 1957: 204; esp. n. 1.

17. Communication de J. v. Beckerath, cité par Barta 1979: 40, n. 17.

18. Après les travaux de Begrich et de de Vaux, voir Mettinger (1971) et sa bibliographie; Cazelles (1973a, b).

19. Texte et références dans ANET[3] 421–24.

20. Ce qui était pressenti est certain depuis la publication des ostraca d'Arad. Avec les travaux d'Aharoni (Arad), I. T. Kaufman et Y. Yadin, et Cohen (à Qedeirat), voir Lemaire 1977: 277–82.

21. Parker & Dubberstein, tenant compte dans leur seconde édition de la documentation de Goetze (1944), ne signalent pas de mois intercalaire Addar II dans le 7/8 et 18/19èmes années de Nabuchodonosor. Il y a seulement un Ullul II pour l'an 7.

22. Parker 1957, suivi par Gardiner 1961: 451 et Malamat 1968: 141.

23. J.D. Quinn 1961 avec sa bibliographie.

24. R. de Vaux 1961: 281ss.

25. K.F. Pohlmann (1978: 93–107, 1979) qui insiste sur la perspective de dévastation totale de Juda du Deutéronomiste. C'est aussi cette source qui parle de 10.000 déportés en 597 (II Reg 25: 14) tandis que Jér 52: 28 n'en connaît que 3023.

Références

W. F. Albright
1956 The Nebuchadnezzar and Neriglissar Chronicles. *Bulletin of the American Schools of Oriental Research* 143: 28–33.

K. T. Andersen
1969 Die Chronologie der Könige von Israel und Juda. *Studia Theologica* (Oslo) 23: 69–119.

D. Arnaud
1970 *Le Proche Orient ancien, de l'invention de l'écriture à l'hellénisation.* Collection études supérieures 102. Paris: Bordas.
1977 Traditions urbaines et influences semi-nomades à Emar, à l'âge du bronze récent. Pp. 245–64 dans *Le Moyen Euphrate, Zone de contacts et d'échanges,* ed. J. Cl. Margueron. Strasbourg: Université des sciences humaines de Strasbourg.

E. Auerbach
1961 Wann eroberte Nebuchadnezar [si.] Jerusalem? *Vetus Testamentum* 11: 128–36.

W. Barta
1979 Das Jahr in Datumsangeben und seine Bezeichnungen. Pp. 35–42 dans *Aegypten und Altes Testament. Festschrift Elmar Edel. (12 März 1979),* ed. M. Görg et E. Pusch. Bamberg.

J. M. Baumgarten
1962 The Calendar of the Book of Jubilees. *Tarbiz* 34: 317–28. Dans *Studies on Qumran Law* [1977], pp. 101–14.

R. T. Beckwith
1981 Enoch Literature and its Calendar. *Revue de Qumran* 39: 379–81.

E. J. Bickerman
1980 *Chronology of the Ancient World*[2]. London: Thames and Hudson.

M. Birot
1964 Les Lettres de Iasîm-Sumû. *Syria* 41: 25–65.

J. Briend et M.-J. Seux
1977 *Textes du Proche Orient ancien et histoire d'Israël.* Paris: Editions du Cerf.

J. Bright
1972 *A History of Israel*[2]. Philadelphia: Westminster.

M. Burrows
1958 *More Light on the Dead Sea Scrolls.* New York: Viking Press.

A. Caquot; A. Sznycer; et A. Herdner
1974 *Textes Ougaritiques. I. Mythes et Légendes.* Litteratures anciennes du Proche-Orient. Paris: Editions du Cerf.

H. Cazelles
1958 Compte-rendu de Vaux 1958. *Vetus Testamentum* 8: 321–26.
1973a Administration salomonienne et terminologie administrative égyptienne. *Comptes rendu du Groupe Linguistique d'Études Chamito-Sémitiques* 17: 23–25.
1973b Compte-rendu Mettinger 1971. *Theologische Revue* 69: 276–77.
1974 *Introduction Critique à l'Ancien Testament.* Paris: Tournai.

D. J. A. Clines
1974 The Evidence for an Autumnal New Year in Pre-exilic Israel Reconsidered. *Journal of Biblical Literature* 93: 22–30.

D. N. Freedman
1956 The Babylonian Chronicle. *Biblical Archaeologist* 19: 50–60. Cf. Freedman 1961.
1961 The Babylonian Chronicle. Pp. 113–27 dans *The Biblical Archaeologist Reader 1*, ed. G.E. Wright et D.N. Freedman. Garden City, New York: Doubleday.

K. S. Freedy et D.B. Redford
1970 The Dates in Ezekiel in Relation to Biblical, Babylonian, and Egyptian Sources. *Journal of the American Oriental Society* 90: 462–85.

A. Gardiner
1950 *Egyptian Grammar*[3]. London: Oxford University Press.
1961 *Egypt of the Pharoahs*. London: Oxford University Press.

D. Garelli et V. Nikiprovetzki
1974 *Le Proche Orient asiatique: Les empires Mésopotamiens. Israel.* Paris: Presses universitaires de France.

A. Goetze
1944 Additions to Parker and Dubberstein's Babylonian Chronology. *Journal of Near Eastern Studies* 3: 43–46.

J. Gray
1970 *I and II Kings*[2]. Old Testament Library. London: S. C. M.

A. K. Grayson
1975 *Assyrian and Babylonian Chronicles.* Texts from Cuneiform Sources 5. Locust Valley, New York: J.J. Augustin.

M. Greenberg
1957 Ezekiel 17 and the Policy of Psammetichus II. *Journal of Biblical Literature* 76: 304–9.

S. Herrmann
1973 *Geschichte Israels in alttestamentlicher Zeit.* München: Kaiser.

S. H. Horn
1968 Where and When Was the Aramaic Saqqara Papyrus Written? *Andrews University Seminary Studies* 6: 29–45.

H. J. Katzenstein
1973 *The History of Tyre.* Jerusalem: The Schocken Institute for Jewish Research.

K. Kenyon
1974 *Digging Up Jerusalem.* London: Benn.

K. Kugler
1924 *Sternkunde und Sterndienst in Babel: assyriologische, astronomische und astralmythologische Untersuchungen. II. Natur, Mythus, und Geschichte als Grundlagen babylonischer Zeitordnung. II/2.* Münster: Aschendorf.

E. Kutsch
1974 Das Jahr der Katastrophe: 587 v. Chr. Kritische Erwägungen zu neueren chronologischen Versuchen. *Biblica* 55: 520–45.

G. Larrson
1967 When did the Babylonian Captivity begin? *Journal of Theological Studies* 18: 417–23.

A. Lemaire
1977 *Inscriptions hébraïques. I. Les Ostraca.* Litteratures anciennes du Proche-Orient. Paris: Editions du Cerf.

A. Malamat
1968 The Last Kings of Judah and the Fall of Jerusalem. *Israel Exploration Journal* 18: 137–55.
1975 The Twilight of Judah: In the Egyptian-Babylonian Maelstrom.

Supplements to Vetus Testamentum 28: 123–35.

1979a
ed., *The World History of the Jewish People. First Series: Ancient Times. Volume 4: The Age of the Monarchies. Part I. Political History.* Massada: Jerusalem.

1979b
The Last Years of the Kingdom of Judah. Pp. 205–21 dans Malamat 1979a.

B. Mazar

1976
Jerusalem in The Biblical Period. Vol. II, pp. 580–91 dans *Encyclopedia of Archaeological Excavations in the Holy Land,* ed. M. Avi Yonah et E. Stern. Jerusalem: Massada Press.

T. N. D. Mettinger

1971
Solomonic State Officials. A Study of the Civil Government Officials of the Israelite Monarchy. Coniectanea Biblica Old Testament Series 5. Gleerup: Lund.

J. Meuleau

1971
Le Monde et son histoire. Bordas: Paris.

M. Noth

1958
Die Einnahme von Jerusalem in Jahre 597 v. Chr. *Zeitschrift des Deutschen Palästina-Vereins* 74: 137–57.

B. Oded

1979
Neighbors on the East. Pp. 247–75 dans Malamat 1979a.

H. M. Orlinsky

1974
Essays in Biblical Culture and Biblical Translation. Ktav: New York.

R. Parker

1957
The Length of the Reign of Amasis and the Beginning of the 26th Dynasty. *Mitteilungen des Deutschen Archäologischen Instituts in Kairo Abteilung* 15 [Junker Festschrift]: 208–12.

R. Parker et W. H. Dubberstein

1942
Babylonian Chronology 626 B.C.–A.D. 45. Studies in Ancient Oriental Civilization 24. The Oriental Institute of the University of Chicago: Chicago.

1956
Babylonian Chronology 626 B.C.–A.D. 75. Brown University Studies 19. Providence: Brown University Press.

K. F. Pohlmann

1978
Studien zu Jeremiabuch: Ein Beitrag zur Frage der Entstehung des Jeremiasbuches. Forschungen zur Religion und Literatur des Alten und Neuen Testaments 118. Göttingen: Vandenhoeck und Ruprecht.

1979
Erwägungen zum Schlusskapitel des deuteronomischen Geschichtswerkes. Oder: Warum wird der Prophet Jeremia in 2 Kön 22–25 nicht erwähnt? Pp. 94–109 dans *Textgemäss: Aufsätze und Beiträge zur Hermeneutik des Alten Testaments: Festschrift für Ernst Würthwein zum 70 Geburtstag.* Göttingen: Vandenhoeck und Ruprecht.

J. D. Quinn

1961
Alcaeus 48 (B16) and the Fall of Ascalon. *Bulletin of the American Schools of Oriental Research* 164: 19–20.

A. F. Rainey

1975
The Fate of Lachish During the Campaigns of Sennacherib and Nebuchadrezzar. Pp. 47–60 dans *Investigations at Lachish,* ed. Y. Aharoni. Tel Aviv: Institute of Archaeology, Tel Aviv University.

C. Schedl

1962
Nochmals das Jahr der Zerstörung Jerusalems: 587 oder 586 v. Chr. *Zeitschrift für die Alttestamentliche Wissenschaft* 74: 209–13.

D. Sidersky

1933
Contribution à l'étude de la chronologie néo-babylonienne. *Revue d'Assyriologie* 30: 57–70.

A. Spalinger
1977 *Egypt and Babylon, A Survey Circa 620 B.C.–550 B.C.* Studien zur Altägyptischen Kultur 5. Hamburg: Helmut Buske Verlag.

E. Stern
1975 Israel at the Close of the Period of the Monarchy—An Archeological Survey. *Biblical Archeologist* 38: 26–56.

H. Tadmor
1979 The Chronology of the First Temple Period. Pp. 44–60 dans Malamat 1979a.

E. R. Thiele
1956 New Evidence on the Chronology of the Last Kings of Juda. *Bulletin of the American Schools of Oriental Research* 145: 22–72.

R. deVaux
1961 *Les Institutions de l'Ancien Testament I*[2]. Paris: Éditions du Cerf.
1966 Jérusalem et les prophètes. *Revue biblique* 83: 481–509.

E. Vogt
1975 Bermerkungen über das Jahr der Eroberung Jerusalems. *Biblica* 56: 223–30.

S. Weinberg
1975 *Post-exilic Palestine.* Proceedings of the Israel Academy of Sciences and Humanities 5.4. Jerusalem: The Academy.

M. Weippert
1971 *Edom. Studien und Materialen zur Geschichte der Edomiter auf Grund schriftlicher und archäologischer Quellen.* Tübingen Habilitationsschrift.

D. J. Wiseman
1956 *Chronicles of the Chaldean Kings (626–556 B.C.) in the British Museum.* London: The British Museum.

W. Zimmerli
1969 *Ezechiel.* Biblischer Kommentar Altes Testament 13. Neukirchen-Vluyn: Neukirchener Verlag.
1976 *Ezekiel 1.* Trans. R.E. Clements. Hermeneia. Philadelphia: Fortress.

IV. Northwest Semitic Epigraphy

Writing Systems, Native Speaker Analyses, and the Earliest Stages of Northwest Semitic Orthography

M. O'Connor
Ann Arbor, Michigan

1. Writing and the Language Sciences

It is often alleged that the modern complex of language sciences, in removing writing from the privileged position it once enjoyed in the study of communication, has gone too far, and that writing is unwisely and unjustly neglected.[1] A glance at recent work suggests that is not true. Psycholinguists and educators, for example, have attended to the proper relation of speech and writing, with special emphasis on the immense differences in the acquisition of speaking and reading abilities (see the papers in Kavanagh and Mattingly 1972 and the new journal *Applied Psycholinguistics*).

Neurolinguists, further, have paid close attention to agraphia and alexia as frequent concomitants of aphasia and related disorders, and to the general problems of language ability loss (see Albert and Obler 1978, especially pp. 224–25, 251–53, and the papers in Obler and Albert 1980). Some examples from this field may be cited; I hope their anecdotal character is not misleading. The student of writing systems is struck, for instance, by the case reported by Hinshelwood (1902), of "a highly-educated man" who "suffered a stroke at age 34. The patient had difficulties with comprehension and naming, but his most striking deficit was an alexia in English. His reading in Greek, on the other hand, was perfect" (Albert and Obler 1978: 98). Mixed writing systems interact remarkably with brain damage: "monolingual Japanese aphasics may lose one or the other of the two writing systems," the syllabographic *kana* or the logographic *kanji*, generally the former (Albert and Obler 1978: 99, cf. 112; Jakobson and Waugh 1979: 71). Pretrauma bilinguals who were literate in both sinistro- and dextrograde writing systems may produce mirror writing for one or both of their languages after trauma (Albert and Obler 1978: 124, 131). An interesting case of dysgraphia in an aphasic speaker of Modern Hebrew is described in Barkai (1980). This speaker, though he pronounced *Hitpaʿel* forms correctly, wrote them in underlying structure, ignoring the rules metathesizing dental-sibilant clusters and harmonizing voicing in the prefix for I'*z* roots (and, in terms of historical spelling, harmonizing emphasis in the prefix for I'*ṣ* roots). Similarly, the speaker correctly pronounced definite nouns with monographic prepositions, but always wrote *bh* . . ., *kh* . . ., *lh* . . . .

In another area of language study, communication engineers have focused steadily on written forms of language in their search for devices to perform mechanical translation, non-tag information retrieval, speech recognition, and other forms of automatic language analysis. All these efforts have ended in failure, as is well known. Evidently, though some children and aphasics can be taught to read and write, computers cannot.

The language sciences have not, it seems, neglected writing. What, then, do the three bodies of research mentioned suggest about writing? The work of psycho- and neurolinguists hints that writing is involved in cognition in complex ways; the fact of such research work suggests that script has special pragmatic importance, to which the cognitive abilities pertain. The labors of communication engineers, having attained a definitive failure, provide a crucial, not to say definitive, insight into language. Computer study of language (aside from the trivial application of information management) has failed, it is now evident, because speech is much closer to being a code than a cipher; the information conveyed in speech is not decomposable (Cooper 1972). "The difficulty or even the impossibility of a consistent segmentation of a [sound] sequence into phonemes has again and again been confirmed by instrumental studies both on the motor and on the acoustic level" (Jakobson and Waugh 1979: 26). The contrary is true of writing: it is close to being a cipher proper, from which information can be mapped more or less directly. This feature of writing has been evident since the time of the great decipherments and is still evident in the work of modern heirs of those labors.[2]

The special features of writing revealed by these disparate lines of inquiry are among the reasons that writing is more aptly considered not in the framework of linguistics but in the framework of semiotics, the science of sign systems. (I do not wish to suggest that semiotics is a science properly superordinate to linguistics, an epistemologically dubious proposition). Writing is not part of language proper; it is rather a delinguistic sign system, one in which linguistic units are replaced by units proper to other productional and perceptual channels (cf. whistle "languages" and drum "languages"; see Umiker 1974 and Nketia 1971). The replacement process necessarily involves analysis; my concern here is with some features of such analyses.

Two qualifications of this separation of speech and writing must be noted. The first is motivated by scientific considerations. The basic structural parallels of the two systems, crucial reliance on signans: signatum relations (for writing, graph: sound) as they are played out over a continuity (for writing, the continuity is space, as for speech, it is time), cannot be denied. In many respects the delinguistic character of writing is not as crucial as these parallels are; thus efforts to discover universals of writing similar to those studied in language proceed admirably in the work of Justeson (1976), despite his neo-Praguian insistence on writing as an integral form of language. The second qualification is similar at base but quite other in focus. Writing is often regarded as continuous with speech in communities with writing systems, and writing therefore plays a special role in the maintenance and development of language in those communities. The character of this role will be elucidated most successfully in the framework of Silverstein's neo-Whorfian notion that a language functions and changes in terms of the categories with which its speakers regard it (Silverstein 1979). With the second qualification, I have adumbrated my central concern in its most complex form. Let me backtrack.

2. Writing as a Native Speaker Analysis of Language

Speakers of a language, no matter how apparently innocent of linguistic knowledge, know its structure in many ways and derive information about its structure from many sources, among them writing. The knowledge possessed by a native speaker is reflected in the ways in which (a) a writing system is developed, (b) a writing system is adapted, and these in turn influence (c) the way native speaker knowledge is formalized. The evaluation of these reflections is difficult; the usual tendency is to note the defects of a writing system and not its strengths. Given that writing is a delinguistic system, it is clearly not reasonable (though it is comprehensible) to evaluate it as a linguistic system rather than in relation to the linguistic system it represents. It will prove easiest to move backwards through the ways of knowing just listed, with careful attention to theoretical considerations.

Let us begin by looking at how native speaker knowledge, reflected in writing, is formalized, particularly in the great linguistic systems of South Asia (Bugarski 1970). One of the insights of the Sanskrit grammarians most highly prized by Euroamerican linguists of the last century is the notion that the basic unit of speech is not a single sound or word, but a single clause; one of the most complex set of phonological phenomena explained by those grammarians involves the rules of *sandhi*, word fusion. The Devanagari script used for Sanskrit is distinctive in running words within an utterance together if the appropriate signs are available in the syllabary. This means that *sandhi* phenomena are more likely to be evident in Devanagari than in other scripts, and that an utterance can seem to be more primary as a linguistic unit than a word. Note that there is no question of strict implication here. It is not the case, for example, that syllabic scripts encourage *sandhi* writings or utterance-level parsings. Akkadian written in syllabic cuneiform signs, for example, shows *sandhi* rather rarely (Reiner 1973b) and utterance-level parsing never.

The Sanskrit example might suggest a strong hypothesis about speech and writing, and Bugarski offers one, contending that a writing system must represent a linguistic analysis of a language performed at a specifiable linguistic level (cf. Walker 1974). He attempts to support this hypothesis by arguing that Chinese writing reflects an essentially morphemic analysis of the language; his failure to show this, most evident in his reliance on crucial evidence from the most modern stages of the language, suggests the error of the strong hypothesis. This error involves taking writing as a linguistic rather than a delinguistic system.[3]

Before we discuss the ways in which native speaker knowledge interacts with writing systems, I want to mention a few corollaries of the fact that language and writing belong to different semiotic orders. First, this notion helps in explaining the stimulus-diffusion spread of writing (Mendenhall 1971, 1978). If writing represents a variety of delinguistic behavior, rather than a special variety of linguistic activity, it is at least as likely for *the notion* of a writing system to be borrowed as for *the system itself* to be taken over. This has been shown repeatedly despite the historical dominance of borrowed scripts. These facts belong to the relatively unexplored field of the ethnography of writing (see the papers in Fishman 1977). The best-known cases of script spread involve the North American Indian writing systems invented from the end of the eighteenth century on, most notably the Cherokee syllabary invented by Sequoya, and the West African writing systems, which first appeared in the 1830's (Tucker 1971). (See further Excursus A.) For a case of recent script innovation in a Cushitic language, see Hayward and Hassan (1981).

Another important corollary of the recognition of writing as a delinguistic system helps to define a linguistically crucial facet of the ethnography of writing. The only area of language which is radically affected by writing is the lexicon, notably the specialized lexicon (this is a little discussed area; see Holenstein 1976: 38–39). I would suggest roughly that as writing systems privilege more and more people with the ability to approach or even control certain realms of knowledge, other barriers must be created to safeguard those realms. To put it still more crudely, where reading cannot hide knowledge, language is made to. My thesis would affect phenomena other than the specialized lexicon, notably the loan lexicon and professional pseudobilingualism. These phenomena are the counterparts for historical study of anthropological inquiry into code-switching, code-mixing, pidginization, and creolization, and may prove to be of comparable importance.

It may not be otiose to record one final advantage of acknowledging writing as a delinguistic system: it is thereby possible to be explicit about why linguists tend intuitively to mistrust writing as a source for linguistic study. Writing is at least a focus for, if not the prime stimulus to, the great linguistic fallacies of atomism and emergence, the beliefs (in Hockett's elegant formulations) that "utterances . . . are composed . . . of unmistakably identifiable unmistakably minimal elements" and that "the meaning of an utterance . . . is a determinant function of the meanings of the minimal elements and of how they are assembled" (Hockett 1977: 81).

Having seen linguistic and semiotic consequences of our approach to writing systems, we can return to a weak hypothesis about speech and writing, namely, that writing will reflect some features of speech as they are grasped by native speakers. Consider the analyses implicit in two borrowed scripts. The Icelandic language was inadequately recorded in its earliest reduction to writing because the thirty-six distinctive vowels could not be notated in Latin script. A twelfth-century anonymous grammarian, in what must be the first graphological treatise, proposed to solve the problem with diacritics (Haugen 1972; Jakobson and Waugh 1979: 12–13, 21). He wrote nasal vowels with a superlinear dot and long vowels with a macron; combined with digraphs, the diacritics served to solve the problem. A diacritic modification was also crucial to Czech use of the Latin alphabet; the reformer Jan Hus introduced the use of a *haček* (inverted circumflex) on a dental consonant to show the corresponding palatal (Jakobson and Waugh 1979: 21), though it was not for his graphic innovations that the Council of Constance ordered him burned. These simple and elegant adaptations of scripts represent analyses of isolated features in the languages being recorded, the features of nasality, length, and palatal articulation.

The extreme case of putting native speaker analysis to work is script innovation, the situation when a language is represented for the first time in a new variety of writing. This situation is vastly more common than might be imagined because of the dominance, mentioned earlier, of borrowed scripts; it is not obvious that script innovation has any special connection with the invention of writing except in the trivial sense that the invention of writing and of each of the major modalities of writing (logographic, syllabographic, and alphabetic) are cases of script innovation.

One of the most graphemically sophisticated scripts ever invented, the Enmun script of Early Modern Korea (Cho 1967), presents no different a *situational* profile than, say, Sequoya's Cherokee syllabary. This feature of script innovation is in contrast to another aspect of the process. When a script is designed for a language, it fits; this is not to say that it is a complete representation of the language but merely that it is free of "errors" (Gelb 1975: 65 gives a weaker formulation). That discrepancies between script and sound develop historically because of the immensely greater flexibility of speech is well-understood; the theoretical implications of this fact have been ignored.[4]

One of the foundations of modern language study has been the uniformitarian axiom which, like its counterpart in geology, stipulates that everything in the records of the past must be explained by recourse to phenomena attested today. Linguistic research, that is, must assume that the object of study is more or less homogeneous; we cannot suppose that language change is merely degenerative, for example, or that the organs of speech have altered during the history of the species. (Interestingly, it has recently been observed that the patterns of brain lateralization associated with humans and especially with our capacity for speech can also be found in early hominid cranial casts; LeMay 1976, 1980.) Writing is not liable to the uniformitarian axiom: each script began once and exhibited a language fit, which, if the script perdured over any length of time, it lost. Script change is largely degenerative, despite the efforts of reformers. The fact that writing is anti-uniformitarian offers further support for the contention that it is a delinguistic, rather than a linguistic, system.

3. The Earliest Stages of Northwest Semitic Alphabetic Orthography

Let us consider the earliest forms of the alphabet to see what native speaker analyses are reflected in them. (The term alphabet is used here to comprehend both systems which do not represent vowels and those which do, *pace* Gelb 1963: 136–53, 166–76 and, following him, Gibson 1979: 429, who contend that the former are not truly alphabetic.)

3.1. Consonantism

The first and most noteworthy feature is one almost universally ignored: consonantism represents an expression of "the higher informativeness of consonants" (Jakobson and Waugh 1979: 85); this feature is reflected elsewhere in language (cf. Blache 1978: 131). The class of vowels, for example, is almost always smaller than that of consonants (cf. Hockett 1966: 24–28; Crothers 1978).

> [Further,] in children's language, the sense-discriminative role of consonants as a rule antedates that of vowels (i.e., oppositions within the consonantal system appear before those in the vocalic system) (Jakobson and Waugh 1979: 85).

Although children begin vowel discriminations after consonantal ones, because the vowel system is smaller, it is acquired completely before the consonantal system is; it is consistently the source of fewer speech errors than consonants afford (Blache 1978: 205–7, 215–25).

The foundation of alphabetic writing, then, is the set of distinctions among the classes of sounds marked by the presence of noise or radical midsagittal obstruction (consonantal sounds in the broad sense) and those marked by maximal sonority or radical oral constriction (vowels and liquids), as opposed to the class marked by neither of these features (glides). The distinction is not a unitary one, in that sounds which are consonantal are notated even if they are also characterized by full sonority, as liquids are. The distinction is further mediated by the concept of syllabicity since, along with the true consonants and liquids, the glides, the members of the small sound class which is nonconsonantal and nonvocalic but the members of which behave nonsyllabically, are also notated.

3.2. The Historical Context of Early Alphabets

The fundamental character of consonantism can be established in a relatively ahistorical context, but further commentary on early alphabetic systems and the language analyses behind them requires some historical background. The alphabet developed in the Middle and Late Bronze Age Levant in the context of the two great mixed syllabo- and logographic writing systems of the ancient world, cuneiform and hieroglyphic, a context that also included various purely syllabic writing systems (Mendenhall forthcoming). The earliest attested alphabetic writing, found in the Proto-Sinaitic inscriptions, presumably represents a purely consonantal system, as would other early experimental alphabets.

In the Middle and Late Bronze Age three formal alphabetic traditions are attested, although only one is well-represented. The linear alphabet, proper to the stemma of traditions that yielded the Proto-Sinaitic system, is the least known of these three (examples at Hazor, Megiddo, Shechem, Gezer, Beth-Shemesh, Lachish; McCarter 1975: 104–8, 1976: 18). The other two traditions are both wedge alphabets.[6]

The northern wedge alphabet, attested now not only at Ugarit but also at Rās ibn-Ḥāni and Tell Sukas, is a dextrograde system that preserves an inventory of sounds of about the same size as Arabic. The central-southern wedge alphabet group represents a sound system close to that of the first-millennium Canaanite dialects. It is attested in a few texts from Ugarit, in the Beth-Shemesh Clay Plaque (found in 1933), the Mount Tabor Bronze Dagger (found in 1944), and in the Tell Taanach Tablet (found in 1970); and more recently it has been found in texts (mostly on jar handles) from Sarepta in the Phoenician homeland, Kumidi (Kamid el-Loz) to the west, and Qadesh-on-the-Orontes (Tell Nebi Mend) further north (Bordreuil 1979; Millard 1976, 1979; Dietrich, Loretz, and Sanmartín 1974, 1975a, 1975b). The unique texts from Sarepta and Tell Taanach are dextrograde, as is one of the Kumidu texts; the other Kumidu text and the unique Beth Shemesh, Mount Tabor, and Tell Nebi Mend texts are sinistrograde. The Late Bronze Age linear and central-southern wedge alphabets apparently share the presumed consonantism of the Proto-Sinaitic inscriptions. The northern wedge alphabet deviates in notating some vowels.

3.3. Ugaritic Vowel Notation

The basic system of vowel notation in Ugaritic is syllabographic: syllables beginning with any sound other than the *spiritus lenis* show no vowel; syllables beginning with the lax, wide-slit (i.e., non-flat) glide are written with the syllabographs *ʾa, ʾi, ʾu*. This pattern is essentially atavistic, pointing back to the syllabary scripts whence the alphabet is typologically derived. Whether the usage is historically atavistic is a separate question, though one of general interest given the standard explanation for this feature of Ugaritic, namely that the city was a focal point for language contact.

The linguistic analysis represented by the Ugaritic *ʾaleph*s is straightforward, given the odd requirement that of 27 or so nonsyllabic sounds only one be represented by syllabographs. That one sound should be unmarked. That is, it should be made without major buccal constriction or obstruction (and thus be both nonvocalic and nonconsonantal); and it should be unmarked for the two features for which such extra-buccal sounds can be marked, tenseness and flatness, i.e., it should be non-flat and lax. The sound must be ʾ. (The oddity of this requirement is paralleled by the status of *ʾalif* in Arabic script.) From the properly syllabographic notation of ʾ*V* is derived a secondary, pseudo-syllabic notation of *V*ʾ, though the extent of this notation is not clear.

It has been alleged (systematically at least from the time of Fronzaroli 1955) that there are non-syllabographic vowel notations in Ugaritic. Those first noted were the three cases of words written with two vowelled *ʾaleph*s in a row; surely this alleged usage is derived from the syllabic pattern. This extension of syllabic notation to purely vocalic notation has been conjoined, generally without qualification, to other alleged vowel-letter uses, included these.

1. final *yod* for *ī*, as a 1 c. s. suffix (three times, according to Blau and Loewenstamm 1970: 25–26, cf. Pardee 1973: 233 and Dietrich and Loretz 1974)
2. final *waw* for *ô*, as a 3 m. s. suffix (once, according to Dahood, cited apud Halpern 1979–80; see further below; all *mater* uses of *w* [and ʿ!] are denied by Blau and Loewenstamm 1970: 27; cf. Dietrich and Loretz 1973, 1974)
3. final *he* for *ē* (in at least one word, *ʿšrh*, according to Kutscher, followed by Blau and Loewenstamm 1970: 28)
4. medial *yod* for *ē* or *ī* (in perhaps seven cases, according to Blau and Loewenstamm 1970: 28–29; Blau 1979: 58; Dietrich and Loretz 1967: 541 and 1977a: 53; cf. Dietrich and Loretz 1973 and deMoor 1969: 181)
5. medial *waw* for *ū* (or *u*!, *s. v. l.*) (once, according to Dietrich and Loretz 1977b and perhaps on another occasion, according to Dietrich, Loretz, and Sanmartín 1975c) and for *ō* (or *o*!, *s. v. l.*) (once, according to Dietrich, Loretz, and Sanmartín 1975c; cf. deMoor 1970: 321)
6. medial *he* for *ā*(!) (once, according to Dietrich, Loretz, and Sanmartín 1975c; cf. Dietrich and Loretz 1973)

Most of the writings in questions are either not contextually clear enough to qualify for serious scrutiny, or can be alleged to be vocalic only on the basis of rearrangements of Ugaritic morphology, generally de-Arabizing and Canaanizing rearrangements (*pace* Blau's anti-"Canaanite" *tendenz*). I do not take account of other, marginal references to vowel letters such as Margalit's recognition of vowel letters as dictational errors in student written texts (Margalit 1979–80: 105).

There are two points to be made in treating the dozen and a half alleged cases of vowel letters listed above: (a) if these are vowel letters, they must be treated as the weak end of a continuum of Ugaritic vowel notations, ranging from the systematic syllabographs through the pseudo-syllabographs to the double *ʾaleph* writings and beyond, i. e., they must be assessed in the context of Ugaritic writing and not merely as flashforwards to the first millennium; the notion of error must incidentally be reckoned with; and (b) if these are vowel letters, the clear morphological determinants of many examples so far recognized needs some explicit treatment, since it is not (for reasons which will be evident below) what would be expected.

3.4. Consonantism in Iron Age Scripts

The overall picture of vowel notation in the northern wedge alphabet involves a clear and atavistic syllabographic writing of *ʾV* syllables, with alleged sporadic uses of other forms of notation. The wedge alphabets did not survive the Bronze Age, and it is the linear forms of the alphabet that have later descendants. One class of these, the South Arabian scripts, remained purely consonantal, and another class, the Greek scripts, developed into fully voweled alphabets (McCarter 1975, 1976; Cross 1980). The geographically intermediate group of scripts, the early Iron Age Northwest Semitic scripts (the so-called Phoenician script and its congeners throughout the Levant), present a history of developing vowel notation which reflects several interesting stages of linguistic analysis. (On the most recent evidence for the Iron I scripts themselves, see Cross 1980).

The pattern of the development in the use of vowel letters was first noted by Albright and worked out in detail by his students Freedman and Cross in their monograph *Early Hebrew Orthography* (Cross and Freedman 1952). The pattern elaborated there has been modified by them slightly since, in light of recent finds (see Cross and Freedman 1975: 181–87, cf. Freedman 1969, Jackson 1980), but in large measure it has held good. The extensive criticism directed at *Early Hebrew Orthography*, of which Zevit (1980) is only the latest example, is more interesting from the point of view of the sociology of knowledge than from that of a language science.[8]

The first stage of Iron Age Northwest Semitic orthography, from the twelfth to the tenth centuries, was entirely consonantal. The evidence is just abundant enough to indicate that there was no continuity with the Ugaritic practice of vowel notation. This pattern remained characteristic of the script used for Phoenician, both in Asia and in many colonies, though Punic and especially Neo-Punic orthographies came to diverge violently.

3.5. Final Vowel Notation in Iron Age Scripts

The next stage of Iron Age orthographic development emerged during the ninth century and seems to have spread through all non-littoral scripts, perhaps beginning with Aramaic but in any case coming to involve as well the southern scripts, Moabite, Ammonite, Edomite, and Hebrew. The system of vowel notation is used only for final (and therefore long) vowels: *waw* is used for *ū*, *yod* for *ī*, and *he* for *ā*, *ē* (and congeners, if there were such), and *ō*. This form of notation represents a phonological analysis of the languages' vowel systems, and of their consonant systems, and a match between the two. In part, I suspect, this three-pronged basis of the vowel notation system has been ignored because it is intuitively obvious to associate the primary *potestas* of the graph *waw, w*, with *ū* and that of the graph *yod*, *y*, with *ī*. Intuition in this case is good for two-thirds of the system; the use of *he* has remained unexplained. Zevit, for example, has remarked on the point:

> The origin of *hē* as a *m[ater] l[ectionis]* [in Hebrew] is uncertain. . . . The internal Hebrew evidence evaluated independently is incapable of yielding a definite solution. This usage may represent an innovation by Hebrew scribes who arbitrarily assigned a vocalic value to *hē* in word final position where there was little danger of mistaking it for a consonant. A second possibility is that Hebrew scribes were influenced by the conventions of Aramaic scribes who used *hē* for *ā* in word final position (1980: 12, cf. 4).

The source of Zevit's confusions is clear. There is no *independent* explanation for the *mater* use of *he* because it is part of the final vowel *system* of the ninth century. It makes little difference to the usage whether it originated with one of the scripts or another, given the similarity of the languages involved. Arbitrariness is not in question, though a degree of arbitrariness may be said to be. The system demands that a single *litera* or graph under certain circumstances be given a double *potestas*; the association of *he* with, say, *ā* may be slightly more arbitrary than that of *waw* with *ū*, but both are somewhat arbitrary in deforming the system which basically matches one *litera* with one *potestas*. (I here prescind from discussing the problems of Old Aramaic phonology.)

It may be well to note that the Northwest Semitic ninth-century pattern is not an obvious one. Justeson, in his important review of the spelling conventions of a wide range of scripts, predicts as a universal of writing systems that "no long vowels are represented distinctly unless some short vowels are" (1976: 68). The pattern at hand diverges from this predicted universal. Whether there is any historical importance to this divergence, I cannot say; it seems unlikely.

Let us return to the three parts of the phonological analysis I suggested that the ninth-century innovation represented. First, the vowel system is implicitly analyzed. We can visualize this analysis by referring to a vowel triangle of the type first described just two centuries ago by Christopher Friedrich Hellwag (1754–1835) in his 1781 Tübingen dissertation, *De Formatione Loquelae* (see Jakobson and Waugh 1979: 126–27 for an illustration). The three points of the triangle are provided by the upper front of the mouth, the upper back and the lower central portion (the oral cavity is longer on top than it is below), and the points of the triangle refer to the position of the body of the tongue when the sound noted is pronounced.[9] This triangle shows the Classical Arabic and Ugaritic vowel systems, one of the commonest vowel systems in the languages of the world. (See further Excursus B.)

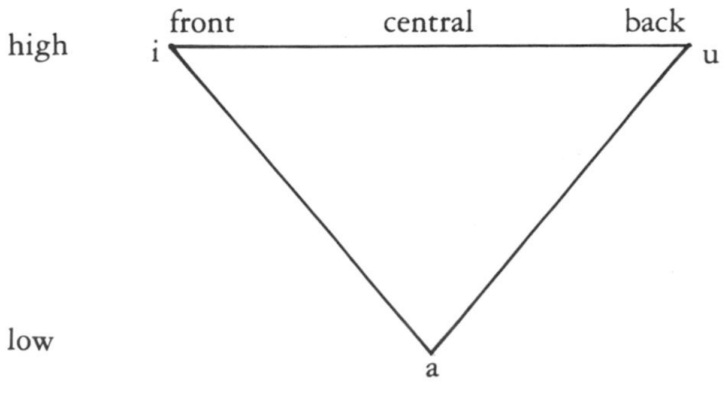

A five-vowel system can be represented in this way.

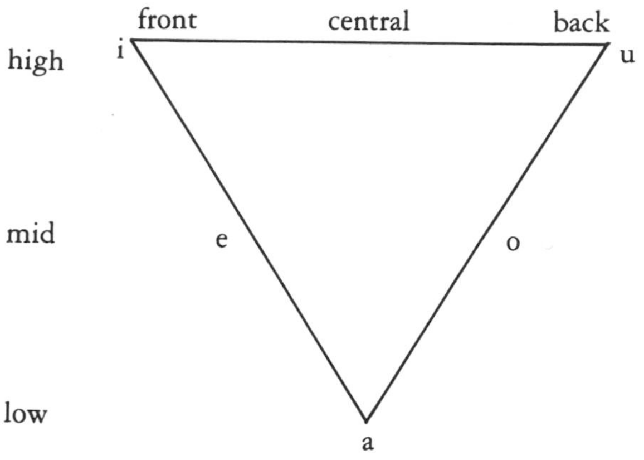

This system is roughly the system of the Northwest Semitic dialects under consideration. If we examine the final-vowel notation system, the correlation with the vowel triangle is evident. The vowels have been analyzed into high and nonhigh groups; the high vowels have been further analyzed into front and back groups.

This description is articulatory, i.e., it refers to the position of the major articulator, but the differentiation of these vowel groups has other phonetic correlates. The nonhigh vowels are acoustically saturated or compact: energy used in producing them is concentrated in the mid-frequencies of the sound spectrum. The high vowels are diffuse: their energy is spread away from the center of the sound spectrum. The opposition of back and front vowels, functional here for the high vowels, also has acoustic consequences. Back vowels are grave and have lower tonality; they are produced with a larger and less divided oral cavity. Front vowels are acute (German *hell*); their higher tonality issues from a smaller and more divided cavity.[10]

The analysis of the consonant system implicit in the orthography is based on the facts of the prior, consonantal stage of orthography. In particular, it is based on the separation of speech sounds into a category of those which are both vocalic and nonconsonantal, the vowels, which are not represented, and all others, consonants in the broadest sense, or nonsyllabic sounds. This same analysis will support a division of the last into three groups: (a) the true consonants (which are consonantal and nonvocalic), (b), the liquids (which are both vocalic and consonantal), and (c) the glides (which are neither vocalic nor consonantal). In seeking to find signs to use in representing vowels, thereby introducing polyphony into the system, the most favored signs would be those which represent the least complex sounds, the glides, which are articulated with neither the possibility of spontaneous voicing nor a major constriction in the oral cavity (thus they are nonvocalic) nor a midsagittal obstruction of the vocal tract (thus they are nonconsonantal).

Let us turn our attention to the six glides of the languages: the buccal glides *y*, *w*; the extrabuccal plain glides, ʾ, *h*; and the extrabuccal flat glides, ʿ, *ḥ*. It seems clear that the feature of flatness, or pharyngeal constriction, makes ʿ and *ḥ* unlikely candidates for polyphonous use. The remaining four glides can be characterized in terms of the articulatory and acoustic features already noted and one other, the feature of tenseness (more traditionally, the quality fortis, as opposed to laxness or the quality lenis). Tense sounds require more force or more flow in pronunciation than lax sounds do.

Buccal Glides		**Extrabuccal Glides**	
y	*w*	ʾ	*h*
diffuse	diffuse	compact	compact
acute	grave	acute	acute
lax	lax	lax	tense

The features used to classify these four glides phonologically are features we noted earlier in connection with the vowels. The two buccal glides *y, w* are diffuse and lax; one of them is acute and the other grave. The two extrabuccal glides differ in the feature of tenseness (see further Jakobson and Waugh 1979: 150–53).

The mapping of the two phonological analyses into the writing systems remains to be considered. It is easy to array diffuse vowels with diffuse glides (*i, u* with *y, w*), and, within these groups, to put together acute segments and grave segments. How do we accomplish the rest of the mapping? The crucial fact is this: the tonal feature of gravity grows less marked as the sound in question becomes more compact; a sound pronounced with a burst of energy is less likely to reveal tonality. The extrabuccal nonflat glides are thus both acute; the feature of tenseness becomes the functional discriminator.

The system of orthography is to be deformed by the admission of polyphony and that deformity must be as restrained as possible. The greatest restraint will follow from the greatest economy, and that economy demands parsimonious use of the distinctive features of the segments. Compare these two matrices.

	y	*w*	*h*	*y*	*w*	ʾ
diffuse	+	+	−	+	+	−
acute	+	−	+	+	−	+
lax	+	+	−	+	+	+

It is evident that ʾ, in being, like the buccal glides, lax, is more similar to them than *h* is, and its use (viz., the use of the corresponding *litera*) is therefore less parsimonious. The glide of preference for the nonhigh vowels is therefore *h*.

Thus it is possible to account for the first stage in the development of Northwest Semitic orthography away from consonantism. The accounting is based on phonetic and phonological facts and turns crucially on a systemic approach to the case, leaving aside the mere satisfactions of unconsidered intuition.

4. Later Developments and Relevant Extensions

The linguistic analyses implicit in the earliest stages of Northwest Semitic orthography are phonological. Let us briefly consider some facets of the stages that followed; since they are more complex, the treatment will necessarily be schematic.

Sometime after 750 B.C.E., vowel letters began to appear medially, *waw* used for *ū* and *yod* for *ī*. This development is an extension of the earlier system and of no special linguistic interest. Somewhat later than this, medial vowel letters appeared which marked the mid vowels *ē* and *ō* where they were derived from the diphthongs *ay* and *aw*. Again, these spellings, initially morphological and eventually historical, are of no special linguistic interest. The next two developments (though rigid chronological ordering is not to be looked for) are of interest, however, since they attest to a reanalysis of the original system of vowel letter usage. The use of the vowel letters *waw* and *yod* was extended from marking medial derived *ē* and *ō* (traditionally, *ê* and *ô*) to marking all medial *ē* and *ō*. At about the same time, *waw* and *yod* were extended to marking the mid vowels, as well as the high vowels, finally.

To widely varying degrees, all four of these orthographic changes are underway in texts of the Bible found at Qumran and in Massoretic texts. Freedman (1962) and others have enumerated some Qumranic features. Some facts about Massoretic spellings are well known, but speculation on the dynamics of orthographic development and scribal revision must await the findings of F. I. Andersen and Dean Forbes, based on their mechanical study of Leningradensis and the concomitant linguistic reanalysis.

A second phase of development I want to treat is later than the phases just mentioned and illustrates not a linguistic analysis but a pragmatic feature of writing systems. It concerns a special feature of the use of *ʾaleph* in late-first-millennium B.C.E. Hebrew orthography. First, however, the status of ʾ in earlier orthography must be clarified. There is no evidence that in the first half of the first millennium, ʾ had quiesced, i.e., was regularly realized as Ø.[11] Despite the contrary assertions of a number of scholars, the position of Cross and Freedman (1952: 24, 33–34, 59) and Fitzmyer (1967: 147–48, cf. 1971: 196–98, 1981: 227–28) need not be doubted (*pace* most recently Blau 1979–80: 148–50 and Zevit 1980: 4, 8, 18, 21, 22, 28, 29).[12] The major development in the orthographic use of ʾ as a vowel letter parallels exactly that of the medial use of *yod* and *waw*: the earliest usage reflects the loss of consonantal signification (diphthongs with *y* and *w* contract, ʾ quiesces), coupled with the maintenance of traditional spellings. This is followed by a stage in which the traditional spelling pattern is generalized. This happened most crucially in the case of *ʾaleph* as a vowel letter for *ā* in Aramaic, though the use of *ʾaleph* for other vowels occurs, and *ʾaleph* is used as a vowel letter in other Northwest Semitic languages. This, however, is not the use of *ʾaleph* with which I am concerned.

There is another use of *ʾaleph* that is pertinent: in the Hebrew orthography used at Qumran, *ʾaleph* functions as an *avia lectionis*, a "grandmother of reading," a sign that the letter preceding the *ʾaleph* is to be read as a vowel letter and not as a consonant, e.g., *kyʾ* for Massoretic *kî*.[13] This usage is sporadic, and the conditioning factors for it are not clear. The choice of the consonantal sign used is guided by the preference for glides noted above and by the other vowel-letter uses of *ʾaleph*. It is the principle of repeating a sign type to show special signification that I want to draw attention to. Similar repetition is basic to adult-child interaction, as Jakobson and Waugh remark, though their allusions to intention might be better qualified; their description is apparently sound, even if not verifiable.

> By repetition of the same syllable, children signal that their phonation is not babbling but a verbal message to their adult interlocutor, and through reduplication the child recognizes a message addressed to him and is helped by the repetition to decode it. The process of reduplication is similar here to the iteration of verbal and other acoustic signals in long-distance navigational communication. As noted by Lévi-Strauss . . ., such a reduplication "a pour fonction de signifier la signification" (Jakobson and Waugh 1979: 196).

This pragmatic use of repetition is paralleled in the marking of *aviae lectionis*.

More complex linguistic and language-related analyses are embedded in various features of writing systems. The first great Orientalist, Sir William Jones (1746–1794), in his "Dissertation on the Orthography of Asiatick Words in Roman Letters," contended that the vowels of the Latin alphabet are ordered to mirror the progression from low to high in front vowels (*a, e, i*) and then in back (*o, u*) (in Lehmann 1967: 8–9). How secondary this ordering is, he never had adequate material to know.[14] I have elsewhere suggested that similar phonological determinants are partially responsible for the order of the Northwest Semitic and Arabic alphabets (1977: 16–17, cf. 1980: 9–10). The regularities of writing systems as systems of delinguistic signs remain on the whole neglected sources of native speaker analyses of speech and as such of linguistic and semiotic insights, though Cho (1967) and Walker (1974) offer important exceptions. No theoretical considerations obviously privilege the early alphabets of the Levant, but semiotic scrutiny may make evident linguistic correlates of their historical import.

Excursus A: Some Historical Notes

1. *Speech and Writing in Culture Myths*. Some support for the differentiation of the modalities of script and speech may be derived from myths of cultural attainments, which treat writing and in contrast do not refer to language as a whole. I limit myself to a few examples.
1.1. *Mesopotamian*. The Sumerian myth of "Inannna and Enki" includes a list of over one hundred great functions and components of world order (*mes*); the *mes* are variously called "the arts of civilization" (Kramer 1963: 116), "the powers of office" (Jacobsen 1976: 114), and "divine powers" (Farber-Flügge 1973: 197, after Falkenstein; I follow her edition below; cf. Cavigneaux 1978: 183, who also deals with the full range of the evidence and offers a carefully nuanced range of glosses). They are the bases of culture, in particular priestly culture, and the group of *mes* in the text, though it refers to some language capabilities, never marks out language as such. The list of professional abilities, on the other hand, does include n a m - d u b - s a r, 'scribal art' (#67). The other language-marked entries are a diverse lot; the following is a rough survey.

41.	n a m - e m e - d i	Loud Cry
42.	n a m - e m e - s i g	Slander
43.	n a m - š e - e r - k a - a n	Flattery
58.	i - s i - i š - g á - g á	Lamentation tunes
60.	l u l - d a	Mendacity
73.	g e š t ú	Understanding
74.	g i z - z a l	Knowledge
75.	š u - l u ḫ - k ù - g a	Pure washing rituals
90.	ù - m a	Victory cry

Numbers 58, 75, and perhaps 90 may refer to literary genres, though their relative positions in the list show that no emphasis should be placed on that connection. Of all the general human qualities included in the list, #60, 73 and 74 are most notably language-bound. These six entries occur in portions of the list that show no large-scale theme. The first three *mes* listed above occur in the *Liebesleben* section (#37–49; Farber-Flügge 1973: 107), along with kissing, intercourse, and prostitution. The first two, #41 and 42 are the only *mes* that are called forms of *eme* 'language.' Their placement in the list shows the specialized light in which they are regarded.

Cavigneaux's suggestion (1978: 182–83), that the things listed in the myth are not *mes*, is not relevant here; she calls the list rather "une explication . . . de ce que peut être [*me*], dans la réalité discursive du recit." The bilingual lexical material on *me*, also cited by Cavigneaux, does use three Akkadian words for language among the many, many glosses given for *me*, but these reflect paronomasia based on Sumerian terms: *qabû* 'to speak' (= Sum *im-me*) in Proto-Ea, and *atmû* 'to say' (also = Sum *im-me*) and *lišānu* (= Sum *eme*) in canonical Izi.

Another Mesopotamian story crucially involves writing among the arts of civilization. In the *Babyloniaca* of the Hellenistic chronographer Berossus, the people in Babylonia lived originally "without laws just as wild animals" do (*ataktōs hōsper ta thēria*). Then a quasi-divine revelation came to them.

> A beast named Oannes [earlier Adapa] appeared from the Erythraean Sea [probably the Persian-Arabian Gulf]. . . . Its entire body was that of a fish, but a human head had grown beneath the head of the fish and human feet likewise had grown from the fish's tail. It also had a human voice (*einai de autōi phōnēn anthrōpou*) . . . .

A shared capacity for language is, at least in this late text, an absolute prerequisite.

> This beast spent the days with the men but ate no food. It [a] gave to the men the knowledge of [1] letters (*paradidonai te tois anthrōpois grammatōn*)
> [2] and sciences
> [3] and crafts of all types.
> It also [b] taught them how to [1] found cities,
> [2] establish temples,
> [3] introduce law,
> [4] and measure land (*geōmetrian*).
> It also [c] revealed to them [1] seeds
> [2] and the gathering of fruit.
> And in general it gave men everything which is connected with the civilized life. . . . When the sun set this beast Oannes plunged back into the sea and spent the nights in the deep. (Text after Jacoby 1958: 369, translation after Burstein 1978: 155–56).

Full treatment of this latter-day form of a myth at base doubtless similar to "Inanna and Enki" would take us far afield. The primacy of learning to write is neatly coupled with the presupposition of speech; that point needs no exposition.

1.2. *Chinese*. There are two Chinese traditions about the invention of writing. One associates it with the distant past of the early third millennium and the world of the quasi-human, quasi-divine *huang*-emperors. The three or four *huang* are linked to the bases of civilization: habitation, cooking, animal husbandry, fishing, and agriculture. The middle *huang*, Fu Hsi (traditionally 2852–2738), is the originator of human affairs, as opposed to his predecessor Sui Huang (heavenly affairs; the use of fire) and his successor Sheng Nung (earthly affairs; agriculture). Fu Hsi one day saw a turtle (or a dragon-horse) emerge from the water and was inspired by the markings on its back to devise the *pa kuai*, 'eight trigrams,' of the mystical system of divination later canonized in the *I Ching (Book of Changes)*. From this system (originally, it is claimed, used for record keeping rather than divination), Fu Hsi devised writing.

(This legend has later echoes, perhaps the most notable involving the culture hero Chu Hsi, the twelfth century C.E. Neo-Confucian polymath whose thought dominated Chinese life for seven centuries after his death. A basic apocryphal legend about Chu's labors has him reinventing the trigrams and then writing itself, as if to furnish a pseudo-precedent for his reinvention of Chinese culture. See Shirokauer 1962: 185 and references).

The second myth of writing's origin, given its basic form by the Later Han lexicographer Hsü Shen, has a later and more secular setting. The first of the five *ti*-emperors was Huang Ti, the "Yellow Emperor," who reigned in the second quarter of the third millennium, a contemporary of Gilgamesh and Cheops. Huang Ti is an aggressively human figure, noted for military prowess; the invention of writing is attributed not to him but to his archivist minister Tsʾang Chieh, who got the idea from studying the footprints of animals and birds. (The association of writing with the eight trigrams is not made here).

Both these legends associate writing with the emperors of highest antiquity. It is only with the last two of the five *ti*, Yao and Shun, and their successor Yü, the Flood Controller and founder of the Hsia Dynasty, that the Confucian line of sage emperors (and thus the Golden Age of imperial proto-history) begins.

2. *The Gender of Writing Terms*. The secondary cultural role of phenomena which are treated as feminine is generally recognized. The use of strongly feminine vocabulary for elements of writing may reflect some aspects of native speaker analyses; I mention two cases. The Chinese term *tzu mu*, first used in the Six Dynasties Period (or Northern and Southern Dynasties, 420–589 C.E.), means literally 'word (= character) mother.' It was used first to designate initials (effectively, consonants) and now means 'alphabet.' In logographic Chinese writing, the first level is that of the character (*tzu*), and the next level of abstraction is the breakdown of the word (*tzu*) into initial + rhyme; designating initial sounds as the mothers of words thus shows the primacy, in the second order, of consonants, and eventually (after further refinement of the underlying analysis) of sounds. Similarly, the Hebrew term *ʾimmôt haqqĕrîʾâ*, *matres lectionis*, "mothers of reading," associates mothers with the first level of abstraction (in its graphic form) away from a purely consonantal script.

3. *Stimulus-Response: India-China-Japan-China*.
3.1. *India-China*. Early in the first millennium C.E. (around the end of the Later Han Dynasty), the Chinese, under Sanskrit influence (Bugarski 1970), developed a system of phonetic notation, *fan chʾieh*, in which a character is glossed with two other characters, one to show the initial, the other to show the syllable peak, the final (if any), and the tone (these last three elements constitute the rhyme). Thus the analysis implicit in a syllabic writing system *and* analyses drawn from such a system combined to prompt a syllable analysis of a language written logographically.
3.2. *China-Japan*. Somewhat later in the first millennium the process of spreading the notion of writing throughout China's cultural dependencies began, resulting most notably in the mixed syllabo- and logographic system of Japanese writing. It seems likely that *fan chʾieh* played a role in the growth of *kana* notation.
3.3. *Japan-China*. The *kana* notation played a crucial role in the growth, well over a millennium after Japanese writing began, of Chinese phonetic alphabets. Experimentation with these began in the 1860's and flourished in the late imperial period. The system which emerged is called *Chü-yin tzu-mu*, 'sound notation alphabet,' or more popularly, *po pʾo mo fo*; it uses a system of simplified characters as syllabic signs to gloss logographs. The system was drafted in response to the government-sponsored "Conference on the Standardization of Pronunication" in 1913 and promulgated on 23 November 1918.
3.4. *Consequent to 3.1*. The adoption of *fan chʾieh* stimulated the development of phonological analyses of syllable initials and finals; see Section 2. This continued through the Ch'ing dynasty and an important stage in the process is accessible in a quaint format. The Ch'ing polymath eccentric Li Ju-Chen (1763–ca. 1830) incorporated his insights into sound systems into a chapter of his romance *Flowers in the Mirror* (Li 1965). In the Country of Split-Tongued (or branching-tongued) People, a group of travellers acquire knowledge of the natives' phonological insights (codified in a rhyme scheme), which are reputed to enable people to acquire knowledge of all

languages effortlessly (Li 1965: 95–106). (Curiously, the phonological insights fit Chinese better than any other language).

3.5. *Consequent to 3.3.* The feedback from Japan occurred in a context that had also included efforts by Westerners to romanize Chinese since the Jesuit advent late in the Ming dynasty. These efforts achieved a firm basis through the labors of the late Yuen Ren Chao, an American- and European-trained linguist who combined formal linguistic study with the native speaker tradition in drafting the system of *Kuo-yü lo-ma tzu*, "Mandarin Romanization," promulgated on 26 September 1928.

Excursus B: The Akkadian Series *tu-ta-ti*

A native speaker analysis of a three-vowel system is reflected in an obscure corner of the greatest gathering of linguistic information in the ancient world, the Mesopotamian scholarly tradition, in the sign lists called *tu-ta-ti*. Scribal training in Old Babylonian Nippur, Landsberger has suggested, began with study of three elementary textbooks, Proto-*Ea* = *nâqu, tu-ta-ti*, and Silbenalphabet B (apud Çiğ and Kızılyay 1959: 114), perhaps in that order. The group of texts called *tu-ta-ti* are lists of signs ordered by vowels in four-line units like this one:

line 1 *tu*
line 2 *ta*
line 3 *ti*
line 4 *tu-ta-ti*

The vowels in these groups proceed from high back to low to high front positions; then the positions are recapitulated in the last line of the group.

Bayan Hatice Kızılyay, working in collaboration with Bayan Muazzez Çiğ, has edited the series on the basis of the Istanbul Nippur texts, with reference to some of the published Nippur texts of the University Museum; no definitive edition will be possible until all relevant texts have been inspected, a task that promises more tedium than insight since the school-"children" wrote "in einer sehr hässlichen, unleserlichen und vielfach ausradierten Schrift" (Çiğ and Kızılyay 1959: 5). Hatice Bayan and her collaborator offer two main texts, Format a (based chiefly on 27 Istanbul texts and 2 Pennsylvania texts) and Format b (based chiefly on 3 texts, all in Istanbul).

Format a, reconstructed to include 102 lines, covers 26 syllable types (the final entry is incomplete; we would expect 104 lines). The first 17 types are CV syllables and the following 9 are CVC syllables. The CV syllables begin with *t*, a voiceless dental stop. Entry #2 is *n*, a dental stop but with nasal articulation, and so on. Here is a brief and crude sketch of the text.

	voice	place	manner	
t	–	dental	stop	
n	+	dental	nasal stop	
b	+	bilabial	stop	
z	+	dental	fricative	
s	–	dental	fricative	
ḫ	–	post-palatal	fricative	
d	+	dental	stop	
r	+	dental	continuant	
w	+	buccal	glide	
k	–	palatal	stop	
l	+	dental	continuant	
Ø	–	extrabuccal	glide	
m	+	bilabial	nasal stop	
š	–	palatal	fricative	
g	+	palatal	stop	
m*	+	bilabial	nasal stop	* bis !
p	–	bilabial	stop	

Crudely simplifying, we can say that the sounds are listed in groups of six (perhaps better, three) and that within each group the list proceeds roughly by varying one or two features at a time; the matrix laid out above is an ad hoc approximation. All features change only between the first two entries in the third group, *m* and *š*.

The CVC syllables are largely of the form Ø—final, but *t—m* and *p—r* occur as frames. The syllables are these. As above, the lines separating the groups are supplied.

Ø–r	Ø–continuant
t–m	stop–nasal
Ø–š	Ø–continuant

p–r	stop–continuant
Ø–b	Ø–bilabial
Ø–l	Ø–continuant

Ø–z	Ø–continuant
Ø–g	Ø–stop
Ø–m	Ø–nasal

The groups of three we have set off are indeed only faint reflections of an underlying analysis of the consonant system.

Two-thirds of the Format a entries are devoted to CV syllables and Format b is curiously just two-thirds the length of Format a, 17 entries, in 67 lines (we would expect 68 lines but the last entry is again broken). There are eight CV syllable types (the single solidus separates consecutive entries and the double solidus separates groups of entries interspersed with CVC entries: *d/m/s/Ø//p//š//t/n*). The intercutting of CV and CVC syllable types is weird. In the list of CVC syllable types, some patterns noted above recur (nine CVC types, for example, are used and only a few do not have an initial Ø) but on the whole the list is both fresh and bizarre: *Ø-l//Ø-n//Ø-š/Ø-r/t-m/Ø-d//g-l/Ø-ḫ/l-m*.

More interesting than the analyses of the Akkadian consonant system is the implicit vowel analysis. It is a three-vowel system, although every Semitist has known since 1887 that Akkadian has a four-vowel system with three vowels on the front axis and only two on the back. Paul Haupt said it was so and so it has seemed since. I want to submit that this native speaker analysis is a real datum to be considered in evaluating the vowel system of Akkadian. I do not seek to shortcircuit the process of inquiry begun with Erica Reiner's crucial paper "How We Read Cuneiform Texts" (1973). It is, at any rate, Reiner's phonological canniness that is wanted and not the sort of philological muscleboundedness exhibited in Lieberman's recent attempt (1979) to provide Sumerian and Akkadian with five-vowel systems.

Another question to be considered is, What good was *tu-ta-ti* as an intrument of instruction? The series is apparently strictly Old Babylonian; no later versions have come to light. A bastard form does emerge later, in the West, combining a short form of *tu-ta-ti* with an acrostic name list (differing from the *Silbenalphabeten* in using Akkadian rather than Sumerian personal names and thus apparently representing a truly Western scholarly format, just as the great Ugaritic quadrilinguals do.) A handful of Ras Shamra texts, edited by Nougayrol (1965), witness this form; though a comparable El-Amarna text (no. 350) is badly preserved, Nougayrol argues plausibly that it corresponds in type to the Ugarit texts. (Another native speaker analysis may be reflected in the Ethiopic syllabary, which arranges its seven orders in this progression: I–*ä*—low; II–*u*— high back; III–*i*— high front; IV– *ā*— low; V–*ē*— mid-front; VII–*o*— mid-back, setting aside VI—*ĕ*/Ø. This feature is taken over in the Oromo syllabary; see Hayward and Hassan 1981: 563–64.)

Notes

1. An abbreviated form of this paper was delivered at the joint meeting of the Middle West Branch of the American Oriental Society and the Midwest Region of the Society for Biblical Literature in Ann Arbor on 24 February 1981. Comments on an early draft of the whole from Li Chi, Carol Meyers, and L. K. Obler were received with thanks and used with the mixture of enthusiasm and stubbornness usually called advisement.

2. Whether theoretical (Gelb 1963, 1973, 1975; Trager 1974), or areal, in Southwestern Asia (Mendenhall 1971, 1978) and Oceania and "pre-contact" American (Arutiunov 1977; Barthel 1968, 1971; Justeson 1976 and references; Taack 1976, 1977; but cf. Gelb 1975 on the whole matter).

3. The further problem that writing is simply not important in the cultural scheme of South Asia is not proper to our argument; in fact, Bugarski is exaggerating on both cultural and strictly semiotic grounds. I owe this observation to Paul Kiparsky.

4. Indeed, Justeson is thereby misled in looking to script usage for the sort of typological clustering associated with language universal typology, though mystified when he correctly does not find it, 1976: 67, cf. p. 78. In general, however, his data and work are revealing for a conceptualization of fit.

5. On the uniformitarian axiom in linguistics and historical poetics, see O'Connor 1980: 21–24. The historical context of the notion's introduction, by Wilhelm Scherer in his 1868 *Zur Geschichte der deutschen Sprache*, is one determined by Lyell's *Principles of Geology* (1830–1833); see Sampson 1980: 13–33, especially 24–25, on this material. On related issues in the history of linguistics, see Kiparsky 1974. Some relevant currents in the broader stream of nineteenth-century European intellectual history are vetted by Said in *Orientalism* (1978) and more briefly in *Covering Islam* (1981: 127–53).

6. On the mechanism of borrowing behind the wedge alphabets' creation, see Hodge 1969, Windfuhr 1970, and Millard 1979. It is confusing, even if correct, to call either of these wedge systems a cuneiform alphabet, and it is coming to be anachronistic to call both Ugaritic.

7. The prize for oddity goes to the case in #2, the form *b.btw* in RS 1957.702, a much-studied *marziḫu* text. The final *w*, which Dahood takes as a *mater* for final *ô*, is taken by R. E. Friedman as a writing for the 3 m. s. suffix *-ew* in a dialect of Ugaritic with intervocalic *h* syncope (1979–80: 192–94), a possibility first adumbrated by Miller. Miller also allowed that the form might be an error, and Halpern has recently sought to clarify the situation by calling the form "obscure" (see Halpern 1979–80: 126–27, 128–30, 138 for references).

8. Note, for example, the great solemnity with which the now-discomfitted Neo-grammarian postulate formulated by Brugmann in 1875 is cited from a misunderstood passage in Bloomfield (Zevit 1980: 21 n. 21) and entirely ignored in its implications. Note, too, the disingenuousness of Zevit's concern with text-critical questions in the framework of Cross's and Freedman's essentially pre-Qumranic work, a concern which needs some qualification thirty years after the discovery of Qumran. Zevit's confusions regarding the form of the tetragrammaton, for which see 1980: 12, 13, 14, etc., can be examined in light of Freedman and O'Connor (1980), a necessarily sketchy and tentative survey for which we claim at least the virtue of trying to be systematic.

9. On other forms of the vowel triangle, see Blache 1978: 119, 146–49, 171–77. The only major innovation in graphic representation of vowel space was provided by Lotz (1962); the innovation is not relevant here.

10. For phonological background, see Harris 1942; Jakobson 1957; Jakobson and Waugh 1979; Blache 1978; Chomsky and Halle 1968.

11. On the *Ø*/ʾ alternation in the extrabuccal glide system of a number of languages, see Jakobson and Waugh 1979: 150–53.

12. The canny sociologist of science will not overlook the writing systems of the native languages of the scholars quoted in reckoning up the structure of this debate; I do not mean to imply that these scholars should be jumbled together.

13. The most recently published examples are those of 4QSam^{c}, in Ulrich 1979. The term *avia lectionis* was first used in Mathews 1980.

A related usage is characteristic of Neo-Babylonian Akkadian cuneiform (after ca. 1200 B.C.E.) and consequent to a major reanalysis of the system (Hyatt 1941). *CV* signs used word-finally have only the *C* value after the reanalysis; though other features of the reanalysis affect *CV* (and *VC*) signs (Reiner 1964: 168 n. 2), they need not concern us. To indicate a final vowel (there were few such in the dialect), either a *V* sign or the ʾ*V*/*V*ʾ sign (the ÚMUN sign) is used. If a *V* sign is used, it follows a sign ending in the same vowel; if ÚMUN is used, it "takes on" the value of the vowel ending the previous sign. Thus both final *V* signs and final ÚMUN signs are *aviae lectionis*, the former determined, the latter undetermined.

Hyatt's description of the system treats final *V* signs as only incidentally *aviae*, but in fact writings with a final *V* sign after a *CVC* sign are extremely rare; of all the "long vowel" writings he treats, there are few -*CVC-V* spellings, e.g., *iṣ-bat-ú* (p. 44), and of all the "circumflected vowel" writings, only one, *a-ga-nu-til-e* (so in the third syllable with AHw 15, CAD A/I 144; indeed CAD takes this writing as a unique Sumerographic writing, transliterating A.GA.NU.TÌL-*e*), cf. *a-ga-nu-til-la-a* (pp. 51, 55); note also *ta-aṣ-bat-a*ʾ. Such writings may be set aside.

For further references, see Borger 1978: 181. On the indifference of signs in ʾ, *y*, and *w* to vowel quality and their syllabic reversibility in Akkadian cuneiform generally, see Reiner 1964. On the patterning of glides there, see Reiner 1966: 35–38, 47–49, 90–92. The differentiation in post-Old Babylonian orthography of ÚMUN from the *aḫ* sign (which is indifferent to vowel quality but not reversible) raises problems of an entirely different order.

Because of the undetermined character of ÚMUN when it is used as an *avia lectionis*, there has arisen the convention of transliterating the sign as simply ʾ. This is a transliterational convention and should not prejudice the analysis of the system; one recent statement of the convention may be cited: "The ÚMUN sign is given a specific vocalic value only when it is the last sign [of a unit, here a name] and follows a *(C)VC* sign or a Sumerogram ending in a consonant" (Zadok 1978: 353).

14. James Joyce was not so naive, and so in *Ulysses* uses AEIOU not only as "the minimally literate prophylactic retort to the Devil," but also, in "an awful pun," as an acknowledgment of his debt to George Russell (AE). On this and on the role of the 18-letter Irish alphabet as one of the many structural frames for *Ulysses*, see Davenport (1981: 290–93).

References

M. L. Albert and L. K. Obler
1978 — *The Bilingual Brain: Neuropsychological and Neurolinguistic Aspects of Bilingualism.* New York: Academic.

F. I. Andersen
1970 — Orthography in Repetitive Parallelism. *Journal of Biblical Literature* 89: 343–44.

S. Arutiunov
1977 — Rev. Sebeok 1974. *Current Anthropology* 18: 77–78.

M. Barkai
1980 — Aphasic Evidence for Lexical and Phonological Representations. *Afroasiatic Linguistics* 7: 163–87.

T. S. Barthel

1968 [Non-Ibero-American] Writing Systems. Pp. 275–301 in Sebeok et al. 1968.

1971 Pre-contact Writings in Oceania. Pp. 1165–1187 in Sebeok et al. 1971b.

S. E. Blache

1978 *The Acquisition of Distinctive Features*. Baltimore: University Park Press.

J. Blau

1979 Zu Lautlehre und Vokalismus des Ugaritischen. *Ugarit-Forschungen* 11: 55–62.

1979–80 Short Philological Notes on the Inscriptions of Mešaᶜ. *MAARAV* 2: 143–57.

———and S. E. Loewenstamm

1970 Zur Frage der Scriptio Plena im Ugaritischen und Verwandtes. *Ugarit-Forschungen* 2: 19–33.

R. Borger

1978 *Assyrisch-babylonische Zeichenliste*. Alter Orient und Altes Testament 33. Kevelaer and Neukirchen-Vluyn: Verlag Butzon und Bercker and Neukirchener Verlag.

P. Bordreuil

1979 L'inscription phénicienne de Sarafand en cunéiformes alphabétiques. *Ugarit-Forschungen* 11: 63–68.

R. Bugarski

1970 Writing Systems and Phonological Insights. Pp. 453–58 in *Papers from the Sixth Regional Meeting*. Chicago: Chicago Linguistic Society.

S. M. Burstein

1978 The *Babyloniaca* of Berossus. *Sources from the Ancient Near East* 1 [5]: 141–80.

A. Cavigneaux

1978 L'essence divine. *Journal of Cuneiform Studies* 30: 177–85.

S.-B. Cho

1967 *A Phonological Study of Korean*. Studia Uralica et Altaica Upsaliensia 2. Uppsala: Almqvist & Wiksells.

N. Chomsky and M. Halle

1968 *The Sound Pattern of English*. New York: Harper and Row.

M. Çiğ and H. Kızılyay with B. Landsberger

1959 *Zwei altbabylonische Schulbücher aus Nippur*. Türk Tarih Kurumu Yayinlarindan 7/35. Ankara: Türk Tarih Kurumu Basimevi.

F. S. Cooper

1972 How is Language Conveyed by Speech? Pp. 25–45 in Kavanagh and Mattingly 1972.

F. M. Cross

1980 Newly Found Inscriptions in Old Canaanite and Early Phoenician Scripts. *Bulletin of the American Schools of Oriental Research* 238: 1–20.

———and D. N. Freedman

1952 *Early Hebrew Orthography: A Study of the Epigraphic Evidence*. American Oriental Society Monograph 36. New Haven: American Oriental Society.

1975 *Studies in Ancient Yahwistic Poetry*. Society of Biblical Literature Dissertation 21. Missoula: Scholars Press.

J. Crothers

1978 Typological Universals of Vowel Systems. Pp. 93–152 in *Universals of Human Language. 2. Phonology*, ed. J. H. Greenberg et al. Stanford: Stanford University Press.

G. Davenport

1981 Joyce's Forest of Symbols. Pp. 286–99 in his *The Geography of the Imagination: Forty Essays*. San Francisco: North Point Press.

John DeFrancis

1967 Language and Script Reform [in China]. Pp. 130–50 in Sebeok et al. 1967.

M. Dietrich and O. Loretz

1967 Zur Ugaritische Lexicographie II. *Orientalistische Literaturzeitung* 62: 533–51.

1973 Untersuchungen zur Schrift- und Lautlehre des Ugaritischen II. Lesehilfen in der ugaritischen Orthographie. *Ugarit-Forschungen* 5: 71–77.

1974 Der Eilbrief PRU 2, 20 (= RS 15.07). *Ugarit-Forschungen* 6: 471–72.

1977a *gzr* "abschneiden, abkneifen" in Ugar. and Hebr. *Ugarit-Forschungen* 9: 51–56.

1977b Die ug. Gewandbezeichungen *pǵndr, knd, kndpnṯ*. *Ugarit-Forschungen* 9: 340.

M. Dietrich, O. Loretz, and J. Sanmartín

1974 Das reduzierte Keilalphabet. *Ugarit-Forschungen* 6: 15–18.

1975a Entzifferung und Transkription von RS 22.03. *Ugarit-Forschungen* 7: 548–49.

1975b Die Zählung der Alphabet-Sénestrogyre-Texte aus Ugarit. *Ugarit-Forschungen* 7: 550.

1975c Untersuchungen zur Schrift- and Lautlehre des Ugaritischen IV. *w* als Mater lectionis in *bwtm* and *kwt*. *Ugarit-Forschungen* 7: 559–60.

G. Farber-Flügge

1973 *Der Mythos "Inanna und Enki" unter besonder Berücksichtigung der Liste der me*. Studia Pohl 10. Rome: Biblical Institute Press.

J. A. Fishman, ed.

1977 *Advances in the Creation and Revision of Writing Systems*. Contributions to the Sociology of Linguistics 8. The Hague: Mouton.

J. A. Fitzmyer

1967 *The Aramaic Inscriptions of Sefîre*. Biblica et Orientalia 19. Rome: Pontifical Biblical Institute

1971 *The Genesis Apocryphon of Qumran Cave I*. Biblica et Orientalia 18A. Rome: Pontifical Biblical Institute.

1981 New Testament *Kyrios* and *Maranatha* and Their Aramaic Background. Pp. 218–35 in his *To Advance the Gospel: New Testament Studies*. New York: Crossroad.

D. N. Freedman

1962 The Massoretic Text and the Qumran Scrolls: A Study in Orthography. *Textus* 2: 87–102. Rpt. in *Qumran and the History of the Biblical Text*. Ed. F. M. Cross and S. Talmon. Cambridge: Harvard University Press.

1969 The Orthography of the Arad Ostraca. *Israel Exploration Journal* 19: 52–56.

———and M. O'Connor

1980 JHWH. Bd. 3, Lf. 4/5, Sp. 533–54 in *Theologisches Wörterbuch zum Alten Testament*, ed. G. J. Botterweck and H. Ringgren. Stuttgart: Kohlhammer.

R. E. Friedman

1979–80 The *MRZḤ* Tablet from Ugarit. *MAARAV* 2: 187–206.

P. Fronzaroli

1955 *La Fonetica Ugaritica*. Sussidi Eruditi 7. Rome: Edizioni di Storia e

Letteratura.

I. J. Gelb
1963 *A Study of Writing*. Chicago: University of Chicago Press.
1973 Written Records and Decipherment. Pp. 253–85 in Sebeok et al. 1973.
1975 Records, Writing, and Decipherment. Pp. 61–86 in *Languages and Texts: The Nature of Linguistic Evidence*. Ed. H. H. Paper. Ann Arbor: Center for Coordination of Ancient and Modern Studies, The University of Michigan.

J. C. L. Gibson
1976 Semitic Inscriptions. Pp. 429–36 in *The Interpreter's Dictionary of the Bible: Supplementary Volume*. Ed. K. Crim et al. Nashville: Abingdon.

B. Halpern
1979–80 A Landlord-Tenant Dispute at Ugarit? *MAARAV* 2: 121–40.

Z. S. Harris
1942 The Phonemes of Moroccan Arabic. *Journal of the American Oriental Society* 62: 309–18. Rpt. as pp. 161–76 in his *Papers in Structural and Transformational Linguistics*. Formal Linguistics Series 1. Dordrecht: Reidel.

E. Haugen
1972 *First Grammatical Treatise: The Earliest Germanic Phonology—An Edition, Translation and Commentary*. London: Longman.

R. J. Hayward and M. Hassan
1981 The Oromo Orthography of Shaykh Bakri Sápalō. *Bulletin of the School of Oriental and African Studies* 44: 550–56.

J. Hinshelwood
1902 Four cases of word-blindness. *Lancet* 1: 358–63.

C. F. Hockett
1966 The Problem of Universals in Language. Pp. 1–29 in *Universals of Language*, ed. J. H. Greenberg. Cambridge: MIT Press.
1977 Rev. Sebeok 1974. *Current Anthropology* 18: 78–82.

C. T. Hodge
1969 The Hieratic Origin of the Ugaritic Alphabet. *Anthropological Linguistics* 11: 277–89.

E. Holenstein
1976 *Roman Jakobson's Approach to Language: Phenomenological Structuralism*. Trans. C. Schelbert and T. Schelbert. Bloomington: Indiana University Press.

J. P. Hyatt
1941 *The Treatment of Final Vowels in Early Neo-Babylonian*. Yale Oriental Series Researches 23. New Haven: Yale University Press.

K. P. Jackson
1980 *The Ammonite Language of the Iron Age*. Michigan Dissertation.

T. Jacobsen
1976 *The Treasures of Darkness*. New Haven: Yale University Press.

F. Jacoby
1958 *Die Fragmente der Griechischen Historiker. Dritter Teil. Geschichte von Städten und Völkern (Horographie und Ethnographie). C. Autoren über einzelne Länder. Nr. 608a-856. I. Aegypten-Geten. Nr. 608a-708.* Leiden: Brill.

R. Jakobson
1957 Mufaxxama: The 'Emphatic' Phonemes in Arabic. Pp. 105–15 in *Studies Presented to Joshua Whatmough*, ed. E. Pulgram. 's-Gravenhage: Mouton.

——and L. Waugh
1979 *The Sound Shape of Language*. Bloomington: Indiana University Press.

J. S. Justeson
1976 Universals of Language and Universals of Writing. Vol. 1, pp. 57–94 in *Linguistic Studies Offered to Joseph Greenberg,* ed. Alphonse Juilland et al. Studia Linguistica et Philologica 4. Saratoga, California: Anma Libri.

J. F. Kavanagh and I. G. Mattingly, eds.
1972 *Language by Ear and by Eye: The Relationships Between Speech and Reading*. Cambridge: MIT Press.

Paul Kiparsky
1974 From Paleogrammarians to Neogrammarians. Pp. 331–45 in *Studies in the History of Linguistics: Traditions and Paradigms*, ed. Dell Hymes. Bloomington: Indiana University Press.

S. N. Kramer
1963 *The Sumerians*. Chicago: University of Chicago Press.

W. P. Lehmann
1967 *A Reader in Nineteenth-Century Historical Indo-European Linguistics*. Bloomington: Indiana University Press.

M. J. LeMay
1976 Morphological Cerebral Asymmetries of Modern Men, Fossil Man, and Nonhuman Primates. *Annals of the New York Academy of Science* 280: 349–66.
1980 Neurological Aspects of Language Disorders in the Elderly: An Anatomical Overview. Pp. 107–19 in Obler and Albert 1980.

S. J. Lieberman
1979 The Phoneme /o/ in Sumerian. Pp. 21–28 in *Studies in Honor of Tom B. Jones*, ed. M. A. Powell and R. H. Sacks. AOAT 203. Kevelaer and Neukirchen: Verlag Butzon & Bercker and Neukirchener Verlag.

Li Ju-chen
1965 *Flowers in the Mirror*. Trans. Lin Tai-yi. Berkeley: University of California Press.

J. Lotz
1962 Thoughts on Phonology as Applied to the Turkish Vowels. Pp. 343–51 in *American Studies in Altaic Linguistics*. Ed. N. Poppe. Indiana University Publications Uralic and Altaic Series 13. Bloomington/The Hague: Indiana University Press/Mouton.

P. K. McCarter
1975 *The Antiquity of the Greek Alphabet and the Early Phoenician Scripts*. Harvard Semitic Monographs 9. Missoula: Scholars Press.
1976 Alphabet. Pp. 17–19 in *The Interpreter's Dictionary of the Bible: Supplementary Volume*. Ed. K. Crim et al. Nashville: Abingdon.

B. Margalit
1979–80 The Ugaritic Feast of the Drunken Gods: Another Look at RS 24.258 (KTU 1.114). *MAARAV* 2: 65–120.

K. Mathews
1980 *The Paleo-Hebrew Leviticus Scroll from Qumran Cave 11*. Michigan Dissertation.

G. E. Mendenhall
1971 A New Chapter in the History of the Alphabet. *Bulletin du Musée de Beyrouth* 24: 13–18.
1978 On the History of Writing. *Biblical Archeologist* 41: 134–45.
forthcoming The Byblos Syllabic Texts. *Berytus*.

A. R. Millard
1976 A Text in a Shorter Cuneiform Alphabet from Tell Nebi Mend (TNM 022). *Ugarit-Forschungen* 8: 459–60.
1979 The Ugaritic and Canaanite Alphabets—Some Notes. *Ugarit-Forschungen* 11: 613–16.

J. C. deMoor
1969 Studies in the New Alphabetic Texts from Ras Shamra I. *Ugarit-Forschungen* 1: 167–88.
1970 Studies . . . II. *Ugarit-Forschungen* 2: 303–34.

J. H. Kwabena Nketia
1971 Surrogate Languages in Africa. Pp. 699–732 in Sebeok et al. 1971a.

J. Nougayrol
1965 "Vocalisés" et "syllables en liberté" à Ugarit. Pp. 29–39 in *Studies in Honor of Benno Landsberger*, ed. H. G. Güterbock and T. Jacobsen. Assyriological Studies 16. Chicago: The Oriental Institute.

L. K. Obler and M. L. Albert, eds.
1980 *Language and Communication in the Elderly*. Lexington: D. C. Heath/Lexington Books.

M. O'Connor
1977 The Rhetoric of the Kilamuwa Inscription. *Bulletin of the American Schools of Oriental Research* 226: 15–29.
1980 *Hebrew Verse Structure*. Winona Lake, Indiana: Eisenbrauns.

D. Pardee
1973 A Note on the Root *ʿtq* in CTA 16 I 2,5 (UT 125, KRT II). *Ugarit-Forschungen* 5: 229–34.

E. Reiner
1964 The Phonological Interpretation of a Subsystem in the Akkadian Syllabary. Pp. 167–80 in R. D. Biggs et al., *Studies presented to A. Leo Oppenheim*. Chicago: The Oriental Institute.
1966 *A Linguistic Analysis of Akkadian*. Janua Linguarum Series Practica 21. The Hague: Mouton.
1973a How We Read Cuneiform Texts. *Journal of Cuneiform Studies* 25: 3–58.
1973b New Cases of Morphophonemic Spellings. *Orientalia* 42: 35–38.

E. W. Said
1978 *Orientalism*. New York: Pantheon.
1981 *Covering Islam*. New York: Pantheon.

T. A. Sebeok et al., eds.
1967 *Current Trends in Linguistics 2. Linguistics in East Asia and South East Asia*. The Hague: Mouton.
1968 *Current . . . 4. Ibero-American and Caribbean Linguistics*. The Hague: Mouton.
1971a *Current . . . 7. Linguistics in Sub-Saharan Africa*. The Hague: Mouton.
1971b *Current . . . 8. Linguistics in Oceania*. The Hague: Mouton.
1973 *Current . . . 11. Diachronic, Areal, and Typological Linguistics*. The Hague: Mouton.
1974 *Current . . . 12. Linguistics and Adjacent Arts and Sciences*. The Hague: Mouton.

C. M. Shirokauer
1962 Chu Hsi's Political Career: A Study in Ambivalence. Pp. 162–88 in *Confucian Personalities*, ed. A. F. Wright and D. Twichett. Stanford: Stanford University Press.

M. Silverstein
1979 Language Structure and Linguistic Ideology. Pp. 193–247 in *The Elements: A Parasession on Linguistic Units and Levels*, ed. P. R. Clyne, W. F. Hanks, and C. L. Hofbauer. Chicago: The Chicago Linguistic Society.

G. H. Taack
1976 Accession Glyphs on Maya Monuments: A Linguistic Approach. *Anthropological Linguistics* 18: 29–52.
1977 Maya Script and Maya Language: New Data with Regard to the Phoneme /Hʾ/. *Anthropological Linguistics* 19: 280–302.

Y. Toshio
1967 The Writing System [of Japan]: Historical Research and Modern Development. Pp. 693–732 in Sebeok et al. 1967.

G. L. Trager
1974 Writing and Writing Systems. Pp. 373–496 in Sebeok et al. 1974.

A. N. Tucker
1971 Orthographic Systems and Conventions in Sub-Saharan Africa. Pp. 619–53 in Sebeok et al. 1971a.

E. C. Ulrich
1979 4QSam[c]: A Fragmentary Manuscript of 2 Samuel 14–15 from the Scribe of the *Serek Hay-yaḥad* (1QS). *Bulletin of the American Schools of Oriental Research* 235: 1–25.

D. J. Umiker
1974 Speech Surrogates: Drum and Whistle Systems. Pp. 497–536 in Sebeok et al. 1974.

W. Walker
1974 The Winnebago Syllabary and the Generative Model. *Anthopological Linguistics* 16: 393–414.

G. Windfuhr
1970 The Cuneiform Signs of Ugarit. *Journal of Near Eastern Studies* 29: 48–51.

R. Zadok
1978 *On West Semites in Babylonian During the Chaldean and Achaemenian Period.* Jerusalem: Wanaarta.

Z. Zevit
1980 *Matres Lectionis in Ancient Hebrew Epigraphs.* American Schools of Oriental Research Monograph 2. Cambridge: American Schools of Oriental Research.

The Descriptive Ritual Texts from Ugarit: Some Formal and Functional Features of the *Genre*

Baruch A. Levine
New York University, New York City

The term "descriptive ritual" was first proposed as a way of identifying what was, in the early 1960's, a small group of texts and fragments from Ugarit, containing unusual formulas, and employing terms of reference largely unknown from other types of material written in alphabetic cuneiform.[1] Since that time, many new finds from Ugarit, and from Ras Ibn-Hani in the vicinity of Ugarit, have lent substance to the identity of this *genre*. It is now possible to classify, on the basis of formal criteria, more than forty examples—in Ugaritic, Hurrian, and in mixtures of the two languages—as descriptive rituals. This classification is valid whether or not one is entirely satisfied with the adjective "descriptive," which has been problematic since the outset (see further below).

These ritual texts have not received as much scholarly attention as has been showered on other types of texts, especially Ugaritic poetry. And yet the realization is growing that they are an indispensable source of knowledge about the operative cult at Ugarit, despite perplexing problems of interpretation.[2]

In a volume of studies dedicated to David Noel Freedman, who has enriched our formal understanding of ancient Near Eastern poetry in particular, and of literary creativity generally, it is certainly appropriate to engage the problem of *engenrement* with respect to the descriptive rituals in alphabetic cuneiform.[3]

Preliminary to a complete edition of the descriptive rituals, now in preparation, it might be of value to re-examine certain features of their structure and archival character, showing just how these texts cohere as a *genre*, and how they relate to other types of preserved materials.

The descriptive rituals from Ugarit and from Ras Ibn-Hani are written in alphabetic cuneiform, mostly in the Ugaritic language, but also in Hurrian, and even in mixtures of both languages. As Laroche has shown in his valuable study of the Hurrian texts from Ugarit, the Hurrian rituals, and Hurrian sections of rituals, parallel their Ugaritic counterparts in most aspects of composition and formulation.[4]

In terms of content, the descriptive ritual records or describes a coherent rite, or more often, a complex of rites. It provides detailed information on the following subjects: 1) sacrificial offerings to specific deities, 2) dates, occasions, and sites where rites are performed, 3) ritual acts, such as purifications and processionals, which compose overall celebrations, and 4) officiants, quite often the king, who had a significant role in the cult.

This definition may be sharpened by showing how the descriptive ritual differs, strictly speaking, from the administrative list or temple record. The descriptive ritual purports to describe a coherent rite or complex of rites, and this is its organizing principle. What it describes is unified by time-frames and centers around certain localities. In its totality, the descriptive ritual includes at least most of what constituted the rite(s) as a whole, after which it is entitled or designated. This distinction may be illustrated by reference to KTU 1.104, a text of the contrasting, administrative list type. Entitled *iršt*, "requisition,"[5] this text lists several commodities as "used up" (*d ykl*) and "delivered" (*ytn*) to various cult sites on particular occasions.[6] It does not, however, record the overall rituals to which it is related functionally, and it cannot be said to "describe" the performance of a temple ritual as such.

A similar case is represented by KTU 1.91, a text entitled *yn d ykl b dbḥ mlk*, "Wine that is 'used up' in the sacral celebration[7] by the king." This record pertains to a single commodity, wine of several varieties, to be supplied for a series of elaborate occasions. In fact, two of these occasions are known from another ritual text, KTU 1.148. Thus *dbḥ ṣpn*, "The sacral celebration in honor of *Ṣapān*" (line 3), is a rite described in KTU 1.148 lines 1f.; this phrase is actually the main title of the text as a whole. Also related to KTU 1.148 is the reference in line 10 of KTU 1.91 (cf. KTU 1.148 lines 18f.).

> *k tʿrb ʿṯtrt šd bt mlk*
> As '*ʿ*Athtart of the Field' enters the temple of Mulku.

Administrative records such as KTU 1.91 and 1.104 thus have a direct bearing on the compilation of the descriptive rituals, and they shed light on the relationship between the temple record *per se* and the more coherent structure of the descriptive ritual. The temple records were, in reality, the sources upon which the scribes drew for their data.

KTU 1.91 is suggestive in yet another way. Most of KTU 1.148 deals with sacrifices of animals and fowl, but lines 18–22 list other commodities as well, including oil and spices, honey, etc. Now, parts of this section are difficult to understand and there are sizable breaks; it is conceivable that *yn*, "wine," might have been listed originally and not been preserved. It is more likely, however, that KTU 1.91, in this instance, provides information relevant to one of the occasions described by KTU 1.148, *but not included in that text*. This method is reminiscent of certain priestly codes in the Pentateuch of the Hebrew Bible which are limited to ancillary commodities, such as wine for libations, spices, etc.[8] If this analysis of the relationship between KTU 1.91 and 1.148, as examples, is correct, we may suggest that the descriptive rituals focused on the major components of the coherent rites—largely but not exclusively on animal sacrifices—but did not exhaust all of the accompanying ritual acts involved.

It is now relevant to discuss the adjective "descriptive" which I have used to characterize these and similar ritual texts in Hebrew and other languages. This characterization has met with the objection that such texts were clearly intended to serve as manuals for priests and other officiants, and that they had, consequently, more of a *prescriptive* than a *descriptive* function. This objection actually confuses *form* with *function*. The adjective "descriptive" is meant primarily to reflect the formulation and detailed structure of these texts, not their operative function.

An ambiguity exists regarding the formulation of the ritual texts, one which derives ultimately from the alphabetic cuneiform writing system itself. In the case of strong verbs, it is impossible to determine from the orthography whether *yqtl* forms are *indicative* or *modal* in force. For example, the recurrent clause *yrtḥṣ mlk brr* could be translated in either of two ways: a) "The king, the purifier (?), *washes* himself," or b) "The king, the purifier (?), *shall wash* himself." In my earlier studies, I opted for the former alternative, taking such *yqtl* forms as indicatives. This interpretation has seemed to be borne out by the growing number of verbal clauses appearing in these texts wherein *yqtl* forms are preceded by adverbial indicators, for example, *id ydbḥ mlk*, "When the king performs a sacral celebration" (KTU 1.41 line 50).[9]

In the light of more recent discoveries, one could argue that modal forms occur in the ritual texts, thus demonstrating that they are not consistently descriptive. For example, in KTU 1.119 lines 13–14 we read *l ydbḥ mlk*, "Let the king perform a sacral celebration." What are we to conclude from this occurrence, which will inevitably be replicated in further discoveries? Actually it illustrates the process by which descriptive rituals gradually appropriate prescriptive formulations as their functional role comes to determine their formal structure to an ever greater extent. There appears to be only one case of a modal form in this text, which, for the rest, lists sacrifices in pretty much the usual manner. The fact that, in this instance, the *yqtl* form of the verb is introduced by *l* (= *lû*) strongly implies that where modal force was intended, it was clearly indicated, and that elsewhere, *yqtl* forms were intended to have indicative force.

It seems that KTU 1.119 represents a transitional form, helping us to trace a development from a) archival records, to b) descriptions of coherent rites, to c) prescriptions, and actual codes. That development was the context in which the contrast was originally drawn between "descriptive" and "prescriptive" rituals; special reference was made to the *archival* derivation of the priestly codes of the Pentateuch in the Hebrew Bible. Such a development is not inevitably chronological, although there is evidence to suggest that the temple record is the oldest source of information on the operation of temple cults in the ancient Near East.

The relationship between form and function, relevant to the descriptive rituals, can be approached in another way. There can be little doubt that these texts, though formulated descriptively, were virtually canonical or, at the least, fixed in structure and formulation. This is indicated, first of all, by the retrieval of duplicates, as, for instance, KTU 1.41 and 1.87, and by the overlapping of, for example, KTU 1.46 and 1.109. What is more, a close comparison of KTU 1.46 and 1.109 reveals a clear instance of scribal variation, and a probable instance of a copyist's error.

A) KTU 1.46, lines 10f.
10) *{b ar}bʿt ʿ{š}rt yrtḥṣ mlk brr*
11) *{b ym ml}at y{qln} ṯn alpm yrḫ . . ʿšrt*
12) *{l bʿl ṣ}pn d{q}tm w{yn}t qrt*
13) *{w mtntm š} l rm{š} kbd w š*
14) *{l šlm}* etc.

B) KTU 1.109, line 1f.
1) *b arbʿt ʿšr{t}*
2) *yrtḥṣ mlk b{rr}*
3) *b ym mlat*
4) *tqln alpm*

5) *yrḫ ʿšrt l bʿ{l ṣpn}*
6) *dqtm w ynt qr{t}*
7) *w mtntm š l rmš*
8) *w kbd w š l šlm* etc.

When the two copies are compared, one notes that in KTU 1.46 line 11, we have *y{qln}*, as restored, followed by *ṯn alpm yrḫ*, literally, "They shall 'fall,' two male heads of large cattle, (before) *Yariḫ*." Note that KTU 1.109 line 4 has *tqln alpm yrḫ*, with the dual form of the noun, and the 3rd person plural imperfect with *t*-preformative, instead of *y*-preformative. This is a clear scribal variant.

The probable copyist's error concerns the word *ʿšrt* in KTU 1.46 line 11 (// 1.109 line 5). This word, which means "ten," cannot indicate the number of large cattle offered to *bʿl ṣpn* because such an interpretation would upset the formulation of the sacrifices, which follows:

l bʿl ṣpn dqtm w ynt qrt w mtntm
š l rmš
w kbd w š l šlm, etc.
For Baal-Ṣāpān—2 female head of small cattle and a domestic dove (?) and two gifts (?);
A male head of small cattle for Remeš;
And a liver, and a male head of small cattle for Šalām, etc.

If we look at KTU 1.46, with its longer lines, we can surmise that the word *ʿšrt* was erroneously copied from the line above, from the day-formula *b arbʿt ʿšrt*, "on the fourteenth day." Note the brief space left before this word in line 11 of KTU 1.46, which does not show up on KTU 1.109 line 5. If this word is an error, it was undoubtedly copied from KTU 1.46 into 1.109 and not *vice versa*, since in the latter tablet the shorter lines created a greater distance between the day-formula and the subsequent *ʿšrt*, making the error less likely.

When we compare KTU 1.41 with the duplicate KTU 1.87 we see a different situation. In KTU 1.41, lines 1–49 are almost identical with 1.87 lines 1–53. But, here, too, there is a slight variation, hardly significant in terms of meaning, but informative in terms of scribal practice.

A) KTU 1.41 lines 17–19
17) *{w b urm lb}*
18) *rmṣt ilhm {bʿlm dṯt w}*
19) *ksm ṯlṯm {mlu}*

B) KTU 1.87 lines 19–21
19) *w b urm l{b rmṣt ilhm}*
20) *bʿlm w mlu {dṯt w ksm}*
21) *ṯlṯm*

The adjective *mlu* is simply located at different syntactic points in the two copies, as can be learned from KTU 1.39 lines 9–10, where the order is the same as that in KTU 1.41 lines 9–10.

More important, perhaps, is the fact that in KTU 1.41 a brief descriptive ritual, opening with a verbal clause, has been appended to or combined with the larger description (lines 50–55), whereas in 1.87, we find two *addenda*, 1) a brief descriptive ritual, opening with a day formula (lines 54–57), and 2) a list of persons, according to the *bn X* formula (lines 58–61).[10] This means that scribes could combine different ritual texts for preservation in the temple archives.

The fixed structure of the descriptive rituals is also demonstrated by the order in which deities, the recipients of the sacrificial offerings, are listed. Virolleaud long ago noted that the divine name *kṯr* could be restored in KTU 1.39 line 14, on the basis of the list of gods in KTU 1.102, because the order in 1.39 lines 13–19 was identical with that in 1.102 obverse.[11] Now, one can add the same correspondence between the order of deities in KTU 1.148 lines 1ff. and that in the list of gods KTU 1.118 lines 1ff. There were several lists of deities, which were variously utilized by scribes in compiling the descriptive rituals.

The characterization of the descriptive rituals as non-poetic, which is valid generally, also requires further comment and some qualification. First of all, there are several ritual texts which actually contain poetic excerpts. In KTU 1.119, discussed above in another connection, we find a hymn to Baal (lines 24–36). This is topically logical, because the text had been describing rites performed on various occasions in the temple of Baal of Ugarit. A brief poetic excerpt also occurs in KTU 1.43 lines 22–26; it relates to the appearance of the king before the gods. Finally, in KTU 1.148 there is a Hurrian section, which, although not fully interpreted, seems to be a hymn (lines 13–17).[12]

The relationship between on the one hand the descriptive rituals and on the other hymns and liturgical recitations is further demonstrated by recurrent references in the descriptive ritual texts to poetic recitations. The most frequent formula is *rgm yṯṯb*, "He responds with a recitation," or variations of the same. Usually this introductory formula is followed by the identifying first lines of the intended liturgical recitation or hymn:

> *ṣbu špš w ḥl ym*
> *ʿrb špš w ḥl mlk*
> "The going-forth of Shapsh (= the East),
> "And the rampart of Yamm;
> "The setting of Shapsh (= the West),
> "And the rampart of Mulku."[13]

Often, this couplet is abbreviated, after the introductory formula; in other instances, it appears, in full or abbreviated, without any formulaic introduction! Similarly, in KTU 1.106 line 15f., we find another reference to a poetic recitation:

> *w šr yšr šr (= ʿšr) pamt l pn mlk*:
> *"ptḥ yd mlk!"*
> And he truly recites(= sings) ten times before Mulku:
> "Open (your) hand, O Mulku!"[14]

This excerpt is reminiscent of KTU 1.112 line 20:

> *wrgm yṯṯb w qdš yšr*
> And he responds with a recitation,
> And he sings in the sanctuary (?).

These references to well-known liturgical poems suggest that the descriptive rituals belong to the widespread tradition of the *Ritualtafel*, a type of canonical text, best known from the magical literature of Mesopotamia, which specifies details of praxis, while making reference, at special points, to known recitations of a magical or ritual character.

There are two observations that can be made about another structural feature of the descriptive rituals, i.e., chronological designations. One pertains to different times of the twenty-four day cycle, and the other to the practice of recapitulation, whereby the text may revert to earlier days in the month in order to specify additional rituals.

The former subject relates to the enigmatic sub-title *w b urm*, which occurs several times in some of the more elaborate rituals. Most interpreters have taken *urm* as reflecting *ʾur*, "fire," and have suggested that it indicates the manner in which the sacrifices which follow it were to be disposed of.[15] And yet in KTU 1.39 we have an uninterrupted sequence of *w b urm* and *w l ll* (cf. line 8 with line 12). The meaning of Ugaritic *ll* is established independently as "evening, night." In KTU 1.132 we find *l pn ll* "before evening/night" (line 22), and *pn ll*, with the same meaning, later on (line 25). The structure of KTU 1.132 is quite clear. On the nineteenth day of an unnamed month, a complex of rituals was performed, which involved the offering of certain sacrifices (lines 1–16). Subsequently, on the same day, before evening, two birds were to be offered (lines 16–17). This sequence is repeated further on in the text: line 22 records that on the third day (*b ṯlṯ*) certain sacrifices were offered, and further *pn ll* another ritual took place in addition (lines 35–36).

This suggests that in the sequence *w b urm*/ *w l ll*, the word *urm* should yield a meaning such as "day, morning," or the like. Indeed Akkadian supplies a probable cognate: *urru(m)*, "light, the brightness of day," etc., is related to *urra(m)*, a form with adverbial force "in the morning, in day-time." This form frequently occurs in the idiom *urram šēram*, "morning and evening," and it is also used in contrast to *mūšu(m)*, "night." We could, therefore, read *b urm* as *be urri-ma*, "in the light of day," referring, perhaps, to the morning, in contrast to *w l ll* "and in the evening/night."[16] This interpretation also makes sense out of KTU 1.119 lines 12–13:

> *b ṯmnt ʿšrt ibʿlt alp l mgdl bʿl ugrt b urm*
> On the eighteenth of *ibʿlt*, a male head of large cattle to the watch-tower of Baal of Ugarit, in the morning.

As for the custom of recapitulation, we had best return for a moment to KTU 1.132, where we just noted that the text opens with a reference to the nineteenth of the month and then reverts to rites performed on the third day of the month. A close examination of several of the more complex rituals reveals that such recapitulation was a fairly common practice among the scribes at Ugarit. Thus KTU 1.41 (//1.87) begins with the New Moon, and proceeds to the thirteenth and fourteenth of the month. Later on in the text (lines 37–38) we read of rites performed on the fifth day of the month, and in line 45, on the sixth day. In line 47, we read of a recitation scheduled for the seventh of the month. Finally, in line 48 we again find a reference to the New Moon. This final reference may, of course, indicate the New Moon of the following month, but this is unlikely. In any event, we see how this text focuses on major features of the ritual complex, carrying us up to the middle of the month, and then reverts to earlier days of the month.

It is likely that this recapitulation reflects a change of locale, because it is introduced as follows: *w bt bʿlt btm rmm w ʿly mdbḥt* "And in the temple of Baalat of the Exalted Temples: And for the ascent onto the altar(s)."[17] This, of course, also leaves open the possibility that the reversion to earlier days of the month had something to do with a shift to another category of sacrificial offerings. In KTU

1.132, where we also noted a recapitulation, it is difficult to explain it as clearly. In another text, KTU 1.119, the text begins with the seventh day of *ibʿlt*, and proceeds to the seventeenth and eighteenth days of the month. But later on, in line 20, a new sequence is begun, referring to the fourth, fifth, and seventh days of the month. The preceding lines of the text are broken, and do not allow us to speculate on the reason for the reversion.

As new finds become available for study, it will be possible to venture resolutions to other enigmatic terms and formulas occurring in the descriptive ritual texts. What we have learned thus far is that this *genre* allowed for considerable adaptation in its structure and content, and that it bore a direct, functional relationship to other *genres* of texts, especially to the hymns and poetic recitations of the Ugaritic cult. The ritual texts were essentially descriptive in style, but functionally speaking were quasi-canonical models, or manuals for the operation of the temple cults at Ugarit and vicinity. Copies were made of the same text and deposited. The deities were listed according to several accepted or canonical lists of the pantheon.

As a whole this *genre* exhibits a high degree of tradition and conventionality, so that it should be possible, bit by bit, to arrive at a proper apparatus for the study and analysis of the descriptive rituals.

Notes

1. See Levine 1963 and 1965. See also Levine and Hallo 1967 for a discussion of the descriptive character of temple records in the ancient Near East and the historical implications of this type of archival material. Also see Levine 1974: 8–9 for further comment on some Ugaritic descriptive rituals.

2. See the recent monograph by J.-M. de Tarragon (1980) which utilizes extensive data furnished by the ritual texts and my review of de Tarragon's study, Levine 1981.

3. All textual references and citations are from KTU (= Dietrich, Loretz, and Sanmartín 1976). This was considered convenient since KTU is the first publication to incorporate the more recently discovered texts, along with those previously available, in a systematic way. For Ras Ibn-Hani, see Bordreuil and Caquot 1979.

4. See Laroche 1968: 497–99.

5. See Herdner (1978: 39), who translates in a more religious or personal sense. Ugaritic *iršt* and the cognate verb *arš* can, of course, have many specific connotations, but it seems that administrative and legal contexts are primary. This primacy also emerges among the Akkadian usages of *erēšu* A and nominal *erištu*; see CAD s.v. *erištu*. It is a fairly widespread phenomenon to have cultic and religious terminology that originates in the administrative vocabulary, and it is crucial, in interpreting temple records, not to read piety into the accounting system!

6. In KTU 1.104 see line 3 for *d ykl*, and note forms of the verb *ytn* in line 12 and line 16, where *tpnn* is erroneously written for *ttnn*.

7. Ugaritic *dbḥ* (substantive) in titles of elaborate rituals should be understood in a generic sense, as designating the overall celebration. On the etymology of *dbḥ*, Hebrew *zebaḥ*, see Levine (1974: 115 f.); see Xella (1979) on KTU 1.91 as a whole.

8. As an example, see Num 15: 1–16, which specifies the ingredients used for the grain-offering (Hebrew *minḥa*), and the libation (Hebrew *nesek*). These offerings normally accompanied the major sacrifices.

9. Cf. the same clause in KTU 1.115 line 1. Also note the following examples of temporal clauses: a) KTU 1.43 line 1: *k tʿrb ʿṯtrt ḫr*, "As *ʿAthtart Ḫr* enters"; b) KTU 1.90 line 1: *id yph mlk*, "When the king 'sees'" (cf. KTU 1.151 line 12); c) KTU 1.91 line 10: *k tʿrb ʿṯtrt šd*, "When 'Athtart of the Field' enters," and in line 11: *k tʿrbn ršpm*, "When the Reshep-gods enter," and in line 14: *k tdd bʿlt bhtm*, "When 'Baalat of the Temples' marches (in the processional)."

On the sense of the verb *ndd*, see Xella (1979: 834); cf. Psalm 42: 5: *kî ʾeʿebōr bassāk ʾeddaddēm (read: ʾeddad-ma) ʿad-bêt ʾĕlōhîm*, "as I pass in the processional, I *march* toward the Temple of God." (I remember hearing H. L. Ginsberg suggest that Massoretic *ʾddm* reflects a 1st person singular imperfect of the verb *nādad*, with enclitic *mem*). Perhaps cf. Psalm 68: 13.

Similar verbal clauses in the Ras Ibn-Hani texts are: 1) Hani 77/2B: *id ydbḥ mlk* (lines 1, 3); 2) Hani 77/10B: *id yph mlk* (lines 1, 8). See Bordreuil and Caquot (1979).

10. On the anonymous *bn X* formula for listing names, see Levine 1962.

11. See Virolleaud 1968: 594.

12. See Laroche 1968: 517. Also note, in KTU 1.43 lines 7–8, a trace of poetic parallelism:

šbʿ pamt l ilm
šb[ʿ] l kṯr
Seven times to the gods;
Seven—to Kothar.

13. This is my proposed translation, argued for in Levine (1981).

14. Biblical hymnody offers numerous expressions of the notion that "opening the hand" is as much a sign of divine blessing and the granting of abundance as it is of human generosity. See Pss 104: 28; 145: 16, and, on the human level, Deut 15: 8, 11.

15. Thus, for instance, de Moor 1970: 115 and note 21, and also Dietrich-Loretz-Sanmartín 1975: 142.

16. See AHw s.v. *urra(m)* and *urru(m)*.

17. On the spelling *btm*, instead of *bhtm* (or *bwtm*), see KTU 1.48 line 3. For a discussion of what is known from the ritual texts about this goddess, see de Tarragon 1980: 163ff.

References

P. Bordreuil and A. Caquot
1979 — Les Textes en cunéiformes alphabétiques découverts en 1977 à Ibn Hani. *Syria* 56: 295–315.

M. Dietrich, O. Loretz, and J. Sanmartín
1975 — Die Texteinheiten in *RS* 1.2 = *CTA* 32 und *RS* 17.100 = *CTA* Appendice I. *Ugarit Forschungen* 7: 141–46.

A. Herdner
1978 — Nouveaux Textes Alphabétiques de Ras Shamra - XXIVᵉ Campagne, 1961. Pp. 1–78 in *Ugaritica VII*. Paris: Geuthner.

E. Laroche
1968 — Documents en langue hourrite provenant de Ras Shamra. Pp. 447–544 in *Ugaritica V*. Paris: Geuthner.

B. A. Levine
1962 — The *Netînîm*. *Journal of Biblical Literature* 82: 207–12.
1963 — Ugaritic Descriptive Rituals. *Journal of Cuneiform Studies* 17: 105–11.
1965 — The Descriptive Tabernacle Texts of the Pentateuch. *Journal of the American Oriental Society* 85: 307–18.
1974 — *In the Presence of Lord*. Leiden: Brill.
1981 — Review de Tarragon 1980. *Revue biblique* 88: 245–50.

B. A. Levine and W. W. Hallo
1967 — Offerings to the Temple Gates at Ur. *Hebrew Union College Annual* 38: 17–58.

J. C. de Moor
1970 — The Peace Offering in Ugarit and Israel. Pp. 113–17 in *Schrift en Uitleg W. H. Gispen*. Kampen.

J.-M. de Tarragon
1980 — *Le Culte à Ugarit*. Cahiers de la Revue Biblique 19. Paris: Geuthner.

Ch. Virolleaud
1968 Les Nouveaux Textes Mythologiques et Liturgiques de Ras Shamra. Pp. 544–604 in *Ugaritica V*. Paris: Geuthner.

P. Xella
1979 *KTU* 1.91 (*RS* 19.15) Ei Sacrifici del Re. *Ugarit-Forschungen* 11: 833–38.

The Gezer Jar Signs: New Evidence of the Earliest Alphabet

Joe D. Seger
Omaha, Nebraska

Until recently it could still be claimed that the oldest known specimens of writing which with certainty belong among the direct ancestors of our alphabet are the so-called Proto-Sinaitic inscriptions, the group of rock-cut graffiti from the ancient turquois mining community of Serābîṭ el-Khâdem in the Sinai peninsula.* These Sinai materials, reclaimed for modern research through the explorations of Sir Flinders Petrie in 1905 and deciphered through the pioneering study of Sir Alan Gardiner in 1916, provided the key to unlocking the origins of the alphabetic writing system.[1] As the Sinai mines date from the beginning of the Egyptian New Kingdom Period, a late 16th/early 15th century B.C.E. chronology for alphabetic beginnings has been proposed.[2]

To date, all other clearly datable Proto-Canaanite materials have come from the subsequent, Late Bronze II period.[3] The small collection of 14th- and 13th- century inscriptions has been supplemented in recent years by several additions, including a four-letter inscription from the LB II B levels of our excavations at Tell Halif, north of Beersheva[4]; a longer, early Iron I inscription was found at Izbet Sarteh, near Tell Aphek.[5] However, apart from a few uncertain fragments found early in this century,[6] no clear parallels definitely prior to or contemporary with the Sinai materials had been forthcoming.

This situation has been changed by new discoveries from Gezer. Work during Phase II of the Hebrew Union College excavations between 1972 and 1974 inherited the major problem of reinvestigating the city's Southern Gate system of the Middle Bronze Age. During these seasons the efforts in the gate area, designated Field IV, produced extensive new information concerning these impressive fortifications and their history. (Pending publication of the final report on these seasons, see the map in Seger 1976: 134.) As finally exposed the complex included a huge 50-foot-wide Wall/Tower (5017) on the west, a massive mudbrick three-entryway gate on the east, and a sizeable stretch of the connecting wall and its outlying *glacis*, all elements that were in use during the final phase of the city's Middle Bronze age history. Principal stratigraphic efforts during these final seasons were concentrated on the investigation of the domestic complex along the inside of the connector wall (Locus 13004). Remains at this point were sealed by a heavy cover of mud-brick debris left from the MB city's final destruction. Several of the rooms along this line proved to be storage units with numerous storage vessels *in situ*.

The pottery and artifacts collected from these rooms all belong to the transitional MB II C/LB I horizon. The ceramic repertoire provided a variety of interesting late-16th century forms including typical jars, cooking pots, bowls, and juglets, all of local manufacture, as well as a few samples of Cypriot monochrome ware. This pottery, along with other artifactual evidence, confirms a date for the final destruction of the MB city toward the close of the 16th century, probably at the hands of Tuthmosis I just after 1525 B.C.E.[7]

With the close of the excavation season in 1973, the ceramic materials recovered from the complex were moved to the workrooms of the Hebrew Union College, Nelson Glueck School of Biblical Archaeology, in Jerusalem. There the masses of collected pottery were worked on by Gezer staff formator Moshe Ben Arie. This restoration work produced a large corpus of whole reconstructed vessels. Among these were a special group of storage jars, on the shoulders of which appeared a series of letter signs, signs which provide us with the earliest group of securely dated, Proto-Canaanite letters as yet discovered in Palestine.

By the time reconstruction work was completed the corpus had grown to include 18 clear signs and several uncertain fragments (Pls. I-IV).† All of these signs had been etched in the wet clay of the jars with a reed or some other crude stylus prior to firing. They are thus clearly associated in date with the manufacture of the vessels. The signs appear high on the shoulders of the vessels, with the exception of number 23 (Pl. IV).

On two jars signs are found in pairs (Pls. III, No. 11 and 12; IV, No. 17 and 18). On these jars an additional horizontal stroke is found circling the vessel around the shoulder. One other jar with a sign (Pl. II, No. 7) also carries a similar stroke, as do two vessels which otherwise have no further signs or markings (Pl. IV, No. 19 and No. 22).

Within the group, the jar with sign No. 6 (Pl. II) is distinctive in several ways. The sign it bears (*kap*) is placed very low on the shoulder, between the vessel's handles. Moreover, the tips of the sign's fingers intersect with a previously etched horizontal stroke around the shoulder. Unlike the strokes on the other jars, however, this stroke is not made with a stylus, but with a brush or crude comb. A short vertical stroke made with the same tool also appears on the upper shoulder. A similar brush tool was also used to etch sign No. 21 (pl. IV). One might conjecture that the strokes on the jar of sign No. 6 reflect a false start, corrected by the subsequent etching of *kap* using a normal stylus.

The total corpus includes twelve different signs, seven of which can be immediately and unambiguously identified with known letters of the Proto-Canaanite alphabet. A strong case can also be made in favor of a similar association for each of the remaining forms. The fragmentary signs, No. 15 and 16 (Pl. III) and No. 20 (Pl. IV) are here published without comment.

The certain letters include:

bet	1 example	No. 14 Pl. III
dag/dalet	2 examples	No. 3 and No. 4 Pl. I
kap	1 example	No. 6 Pl. II
lamed	2 examples	No. 7 and No. 8 Pl. II
mem	4 examples	No. 9-12 Pl. III
nun	1 example	No. 17 Pl. IV
taw	1 example	No. 18 Pl. IV

Comparisons for each of these signs are easily found in the inscriptions from Sinai. For example, all are included in the well-known Proto-Sinaitic Inscription No. 357

which still remains *in situ* in Mine L at Serabit, and most are also found on Proto-Sinaitic Inscription No. 349; these are given in the figure and parallels can be readily identified. The letter designations in the notes that follow correspond to those indicated to the left of P. S. No. 357.

A. *bet* — The Gezer sign (Pl. III No. 14), like those on P.S. No. 357 and 349, is the more archaic closed-box form. Later examples, e.g., on the Goetze Seal and the Lachish Bowl, show a developed open-sided form.

B. *dag* — While on P. S. No. 357 the fish is drawn with only one dorsal and one ventral fin stroke, Gezer Signs No. 3 and No. 4 (Pl. I) are more elaborate, with three dorsal and two ventral fins. However, double fin strokes are also simulated in the *dag* which appears in column 2 of the Gerster No. 1 inscription from the Wadi Naṣb in eastern Sinai. Albright has argued that this may be the oldest Proto-Canaanite inscription yet found.[8]

C. *kap* — Again, unlike the somewhat stylized forms in P. S. No. 357 and No. 349 (with 3 or 4 finger strokes and no apparent thumb),[9] Gezer sign No. 6 is clearly more pictographic. Even the relative lengths of the several fingers are accurately represented.

D. *lamed* — While both the upright stance and more open curl of the Gezer signs No. 7 and No. 8 (Pl. II) differentiate them from the *lamed* on P. S. No. 357,[10] they are very similar to the *lamed* forms as they appear in lines 3 and (less obviously) 7 of P.S. No. 349. Another close parallel, though with the curl turned to the right rather than the left is found in column 4 of Gerster No. 1.[11]

E. *mem* — Apart from their apparently vertical stance all four Gezer *mems* (No. 9-12, Pl. III) have close parallels in P.S. No. 357 and 349. Vertical *mem* forms become more normative in later Proto-Canaanite inscriptions, e.g., on the Lachish Ewer.[12]

F. *nun* — The Gezer *nun* (No. 17, Pl. IV) is an obvious picture form of a snake, though without a distinct head as in P.S. No. 357. However, the early attrition of this feature is also clearly witnessed in the disparity of *nun* forms on P.S. No. 349.

G. *taw* — Again parallels are obvious and further commentary is not warranted.

The remaining signs may also plausibly be identified with Proto-Canaanite letters as follows.

gimel	1 example	No. 13 Pl. III
gimel (variant)	1 example	No. 21 Pl. IV
yod	1 example	No. 5 Pl. II
ḥet	1 example	No. 23 Pl. IV
pe	2 examples	No. 1 and 2 Pl. I

Of these the most certain is No. 5 (Pl. II), quite clearly a *yod*. Not only is this form similar to the hieroglyph for the *yad* body part, viz., the hand and the forearm, but it compares well with the two other (howbeit later) known Proto-Canaanite *yods*—those on the 13th century B.C.E Lachish Ewer and on the more recent fragment from Tell Nagila.[13] Already in 1954 Frank Cross had predicted the appearance of an early Proto-Canaanite *yod* almost exactly like this Gezer form.[14]

Most suspect within this group is sign No. 23 (Pl. IV) posited here as a *ḥet*. The position of this mark low on the side of the vessel and the general nature of the almost punctate etching raise questions as to whether it was intended to be a letter or sign at all. However, assuming that it is an intentional marking, the best comparison is with the double or triple loop form of *ḥet* found in the Sinaitic script. Once again a clear example for comparison is found in Gerster No. 1.[15]

The rest of the signs, identified as *gimel*s (No. 13, Pl. III and No. 21, Pl. IV) and *pe*s (No. 1 and No. 2, Pl. I) are similar enough to warrant discussion together. The identification of sign No. 13 as a *gimel* or "throwstick" is perhaps the most secure. The stance of the form, for example, agrees (howbeit with a tilt to the left rather than the right) with the *gimel* on P.S. No. 357 (Figure, above *nun* at F). Less certain is sign No. 21, which is larger and has a different stance. Its execution also differs, the sign having been formed in the wet clay with a comb or brush. However, it does conform in shape to the sign for *gimel* identified on later Proto-Canaanite inscriptions, e.g., on the Goetze Seal.

At the same time, however, some clear similarity can be noted between sign No. 21 and signs No. 1 and 2. The latter are identified as *pe*s. Originally signs No. 1 and 2 were viewed as variants of the *lamed*. Comparisons with short-tailed *lamed* forms from Sinai, as well as on the Beth Shemesh Ostracon and the Goetze Seal, give support to this suggestion. However, inasmuch as there are clear long-tailed *lamed* forms in the Gezer corpus, and because the variant represented by No. 1 and 2 is very consistent, an alternative identification seems to be in order. Presently the identification of these signs as forms of the letter *pe*, "mouth," seems most defensible. This identification is based both on the very close correspondences provided by later Phoenician forms of *pe* and, now that the "throw stick" formerly considered the sign for *pe* has been unequivocally identified with *gimel* by the Ugaritic ABCderies,[16] by the absence of alternative shapes for the letter within the larger Proto-Canaanite corpus. Considering the relative similarity between the forms for *lamed* and *pe* throughout the subsequent development of the alphabet, it is not unreasonable to expect close correspondences also in these early materials. In any event such an identification is a consideration to be weighed in subsequent review and restudy of the Proto-Sinaitic texts and of other early alphabetic inscriptions. Finally, however, the further possibility that these forms may reflect yet a third variant of the *gimel* cannot be ignored.

As noted previously, most of the Gezer signs are found individually on the shoulders of single jars. Accordingly, were it not for the close Proto-Sinaitic comparisons it would be presumptuous to conclude that they are in fact evidences of alphabetic origins at all.[17] Happily, such suspicions are still further allayed by the two instances where jars carry a pair of signs. These include jar G72 IV.5.162 No. 1 (signs No. 11 and 12) with two *mem*s and jar G73 IV.5.265 No. 1 (signs No. 17 and 18) with a *nun-taw* or *taw-nun* sequence. While neither of these pairs can unequivocally be identified as words, it can be proposed that *mayim* "water" may be intended in one case (recognizing that this will revolutionize all current theories on the contraction of diphthongs in early Canaanite) and suggested, a bit more seriously, that in the other we are perhaps dealing with a variant of the root *ntn* "to give." However speculative these suggestions may be (and they are avowedly so), I do believe that these paired signs provide some modest additional evidence to show that those using the signs at Gezer did in fact recognize them to be part of a linguistic orthography, i.e., an alphabet, and that they were not simply using random picture signs. Significantly it can also be noted that such jar signs are not wholly idiosyncratic to Gezer. Bronze Age jars with signs very comparable to the *mems* and to the *gimel* or *pe* signs at Gezer have been reported by J. Kaplan from a cemetery near Tel Aviv.[18]

What exactly these letters meant to those applying them to the Gezer jars will from this point doubtless produce numerous additional speculations, but these we leave for later discussions. Our purpose in presenting these materials here is rather more restricted. It is specifically to emphasize that this new corpus not only modestly expands our knowledge of early Proto-Canaanite paleography, but that it in fact provides us with the very earliest alphabetic forms from the Palestinian area itself which can be securely dated via ceramic and stratigraphic controls.

A final note will reaffirm and underscore this point. Most of these jar inscriptions were recovered from the final, late 16th-century, Stratum XVIII city levels during work completed in the summer of 1973. However, a modest additional effort was also carried out in Field IV again in the spring of 1974. At that time probes were dug at various points to investigate occupation prior to the Stratum XVIII floors. One such probe was located at the juncture of the city wall and the western gate tower in Area 6. Though of very limited scope, excavations at this point found good evidence of the earlier, Stratum XIX occupation, including another group of storage vessels *in situ*. Significantly it was on the shoulder of one of these earlier MB jars, jar G74 IV.6.150 No. 1, that sign No. 21 was found. The earlier date of this jar is also reflected in its rim form. It is a flat-topped variety of the profiled type quite typical of the 17th-century MB II B and early MB II C horizons.

Thus the new Gezer materials not only confirm the use of Proto-Canaanite letters just before the end of the Middle Bronze occupation in the mid to late 1500's, but in fact push back the dating to as early as perhaps the beginning of the MB II C period, in the late 17th century B.C.E. This establishes a new, more secure chronological threshold for the introduction and use of the alphabetic system in Palestine.

*This paper is doubly appropriate for a volume honoring David Noel Freedman. Not only does it deal with subject matter very much within his field of interest and expertise, but it also satisfies a scholarly demand for which he crusades, that being to publish new data as rapidly as possible so that it may be fodder for the grist of the larger research community—so be it!

†Field IV MB storejars and signs. Scale: signs, 1:2; jar rims, 1:5; jars and fragments with sign placements, 1:10; reproduced at 10% reduction.

Notes

1. These early discoveries are summarized in Albright's treatment *The Proto-Sinaitic Inscriptions and Their Decipherment* (1969).

2. While discussion continues with respect to the more precise dating of specific inscriptions and inscription groups, the 16th-15th century range originally proposed by Petrie and Gardiner still pertains. Cf. Albright 1969 and, e.g., Rainey 1975.

3. The catalogue includes

Lachish Bowl No. 1	Diringer 1958: 129, Pls. 43-44
the Lachish Ewer	Gaster 1940: 47-54, frontispiece
the Beth Shemesh Ostracon	Grant 1931: Pl. 10
the Lachish Prism	Diringer 1958: 128, Pls. 37-38
the Lachish Censer Lid	Diringer 1958: 128-29, Pls. 44-45
the Tell Nagila Sherd	Leibovitch 1965
the Goetze Seal	Goetze 1953
the Hazor Dipinto	Yadin et al. 1958: Pls. 99, 160
the Megiddo Gold Ring	Irwin and Bowman 1938: 173-76
the ʿAjjūl Handle	Petrie 1932: Pl. 40.

In dispute as to an LB or Iron I date is the Raddana Jar Handle. See Cross and Freedman 1971 and Aharoni 1971.For a current summary of the field, see McCarter 1975: 104-13.

4. See Seger 1977: 45 and Pl. 5B.

5. See Kochavi 1977 and Demsky 1977.

6. Included are

the Gezer Sherd	Taylor 1930: 17, Pl. 1
the Lachish Dagger	Diringer 1958: 128, Pls. 22, 42
the Shechem Plaque	de Liagre Böhl 1938: 21-25
the Shechem Potsherds	de Liagre Böhl 1938: 24-25.

Readings for all these fragments are enigmatic and none of them comes from a secure stratigraphic provenance. Dating in all cases remains questionable.

7. The storage jars shown on Plates I-IV all display typical MB II C profiled rims and are otherwise standard late-17th to 16th-century jar forms. On this evidence alone the corpus could be considered securely dated. For further discussion of the stratigraphy and date, see Seger 1975.

8. Cf. Albright 1969: 28-29 and Fig. 11; also Rainey 1975: 107, Fig. No. 1, and Pl. 11A.

9. While identification of the sign on P.S. No. 357 (Figure, at C) as *kap* is not disputed, its detail is not well preserved. Rainey (1975: 113, Fig. No. 2 and Pls. 11B and 12A) reconstructs a five-fingered form. At the same time he identifies the series of strokes at the inscription's lower left (shown in the figure here is a block of 10 short vertical lines) as another *kap*. From my own *in situ* examination of the inscription in August 1973, and study of slides taken at that time, I would agree with this latter reading. However, this lower form can be reconstructed as a four-fingered sign and a similar four-fingered reconstruction would also be more appropriate for the upper *kap*. Similar four-fingered forms are standard elsewhere in the Proto-Sinaitic corpus as, e.g., in line 3 of P.S. No. 349. An apparent exception again comes from Gerster No. 1 which seems to provide a more truly pictographic *kap* with five fingers. See Rainey 1975: 107, Fig. No. 1, column No. 1.

10. A point of confusion that has haunted this inscription from its first publication involves the apparent intersection at this point of the tail of the *lamed* and the *alep* sign below it. As first drawn and published (Figure) the *lamed* was at times interpreted as a circular form. However, my examination of the inscription in 1973 indicated that the *lamed* form extends only laterally and that the right horn of the *alep* in fact does not cross over the long tail of the *lamed* into the space above. Unfortunately the stroke shown above the intersection erroneously copies an otherwise natural nick in the rock face which has no connection with the etchings of the inscription. In his reinterpretation and redrawing of the inscription Rainey fails to correct this error, though his accompanying photograph clearly shows that the change is warranted. Cf. 1975: 113, Fig. No. 2 and especially Pl. 11B.

11. Rainey, 1975: 107, Fig. No. 2, p. 110, and pl. 11A.

12. For a more complete discussion of stance rotation in early alphabetic forms see Cross (1954) and his updated study (1967).

13. See n. 3 above.

14. Cross (1954: 21).

15. Rainey 1975: 107, Fig. No. 1, column No. 4.

16. See Cross and Lambdin 1960: 25-26.

17. The question of differentiating clusters of scratches from samples of writing is complex. F. M. Cross, after repeated attempts to read the Goetze Seal, now denies that it is a sample of Proto-Canaanite writing, suggesting rather that it is an "imitation of script" (1979: 100 n. 19). The status of other clusters of scratches is even vaguer. The McClelland Sherd, from Tell Jiṣr (in the Biqaʿ of Lebanon), which Mendenhall (1971) has interpreted as containing text in a Middle Bronze age syllabary, is described by Cross as "a most dubious witness to a writing system." Nonetheless continued study of these and other conjectured traces of early written communication is mandatory, lest scholars be guilty of overlooking significant data.

18. Kaplan 1955: 8, Fig. No. 1, see items No. 3 and No. 7/8.

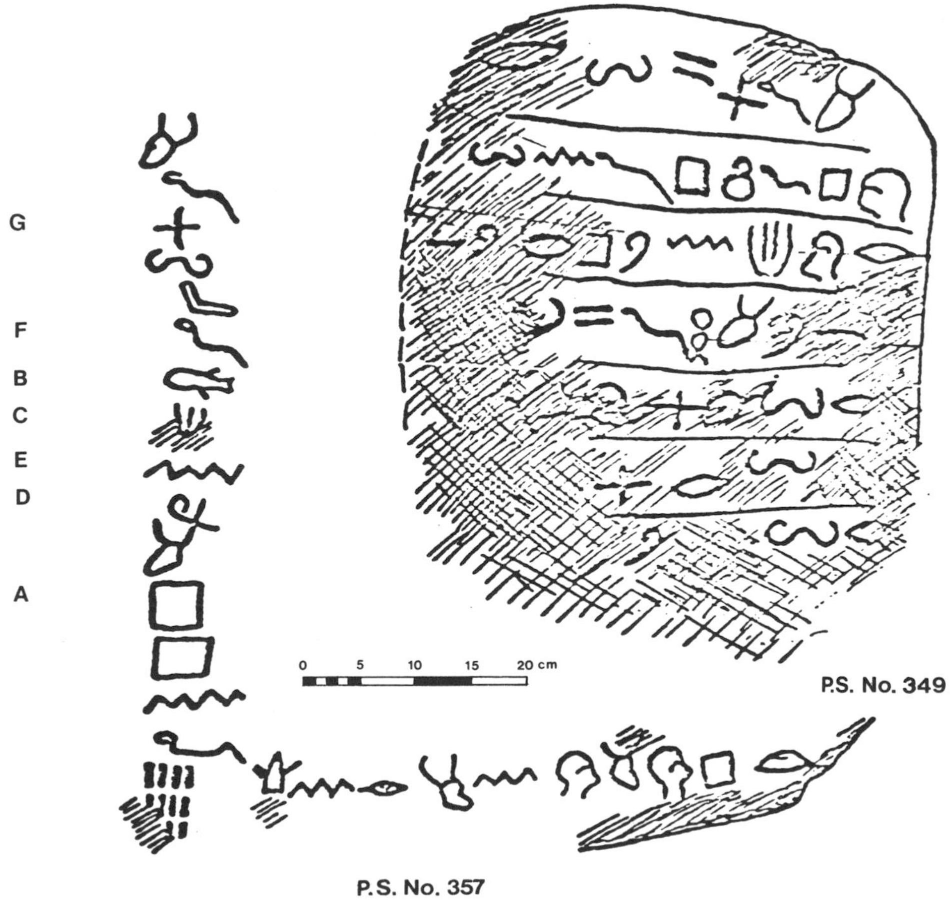

Figure Proto-Sinaitic Inscriptions No. 357 and No. 349.

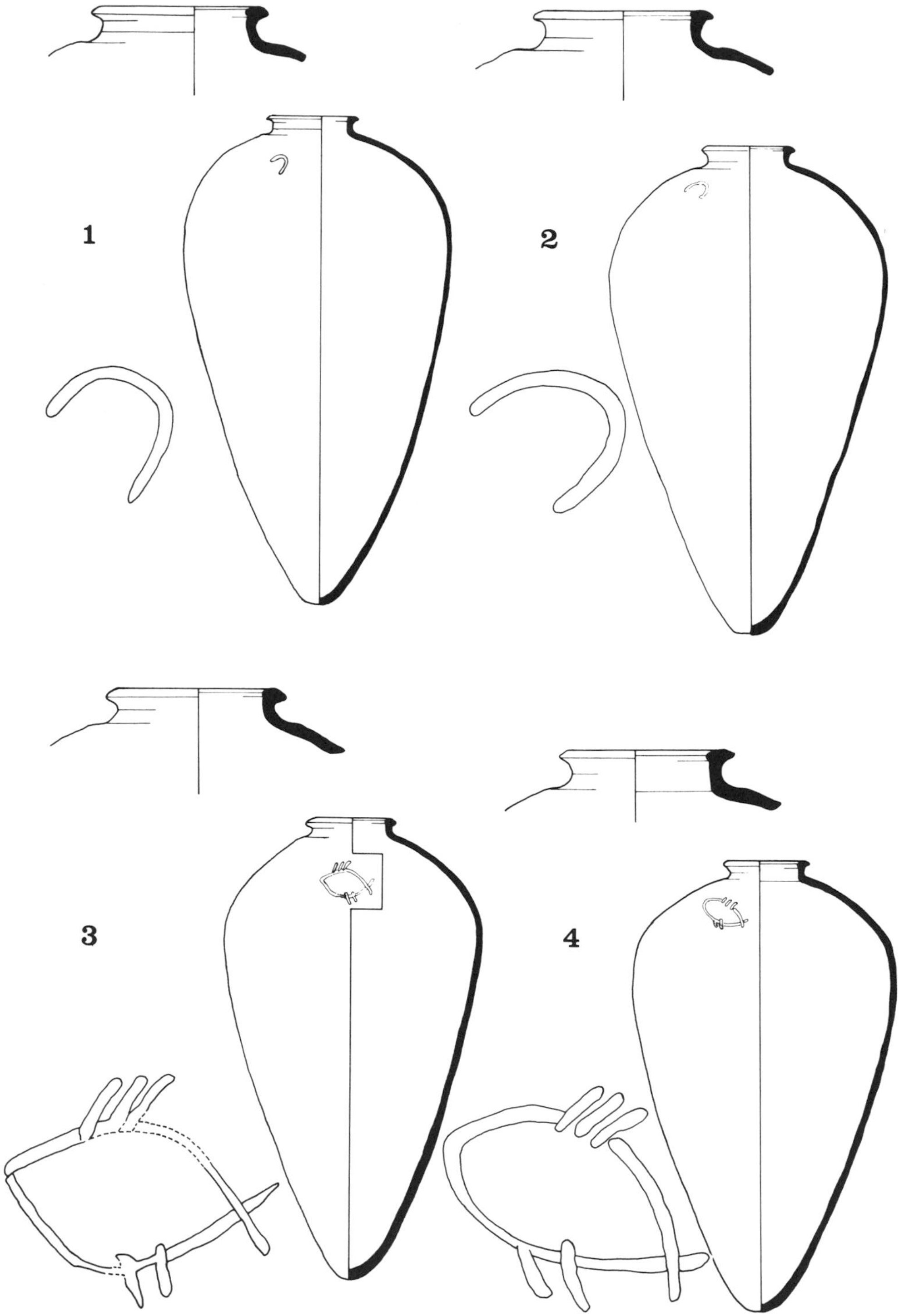
1
2
3
4

Plate I

1. G72 IV.5.70 #1

FORM: Storejar		
TECHNIQUE: Wheelmade		
WARE PASTE:		
Color:	5 YR "Reddish Yellow" 6/6	
Inclusions:	Many large wadi gravel, some medium to large lime	
Firing:	No core	
Hardness:	Hard	
WARE SURFACE:	*Interior*	*Exterior*
Color:	As paste	5 YR "Reddish Yellow" 7/6
Treatment:	None	Sign on shoulder

2. G72 IV.5.98 #1

FORM: Storejar		
TECHNIQUE: Wheelmade		
WARE PASTE:		
Color:	5 YR "Reddish Yellow" 6/6	
Inclusions:	Many medium to large wadi gravel, some large lime	
Firing:	No core	
Hardness:	Hard	
WARE SURFACE:	*Interior*	*Exterior*
Color:	As paste	5 YR "Reddish Yellow" 7/8
Treatment:	None	Sign on shoulder

3. G72 IV.5.265 #1

FORM: Storejar		
TECHNIQUE: Wheelmade		
WARE PASTE:		
Color:	10 YR "Light Yellowish Brown" 6/4	
Inclusions:	Very many medium to large wadi gravel; some large lime	
Firing:	No core	
Hardness:	Hard	
WARE SURFACE:	*Interior*	*Exterior*
Color:	As paste	7.5 YR "Pink" 7/4
Treatment:	None	Sign on shoulder

4. G72 IV.5.95 #1

FORM: Storejar		
TECHNIQUE: Wheelmade		
WARE PASTE:		
Color:	5 YR "Pink" 7/4	
Inclusions:	Many large wadi gravel; some medium to large lime; few medium ceramic	
Firing:	No core	
Hardness:	Hard	
WARE SURFACE:	*Interior*	*Exterior*
Color:	As paste	As paste
Treatment:	None	Sign on shoulder

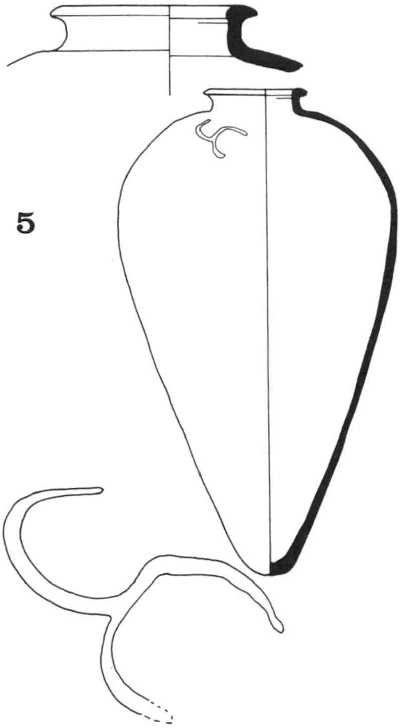

5

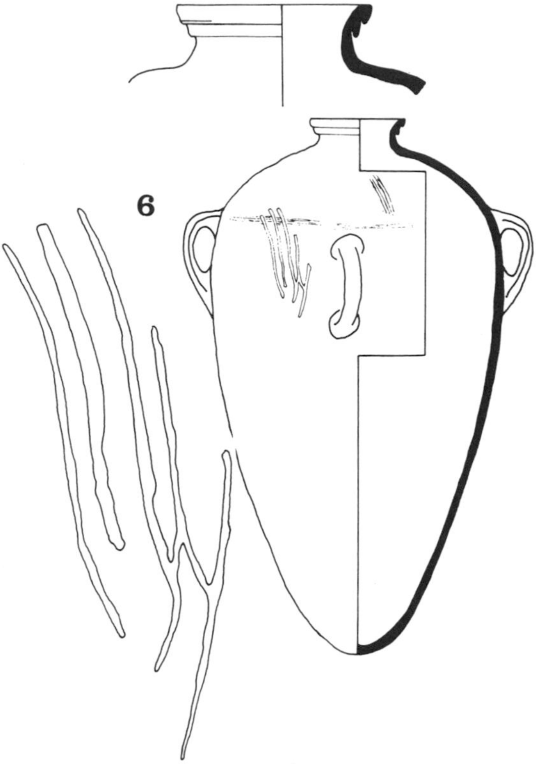

6

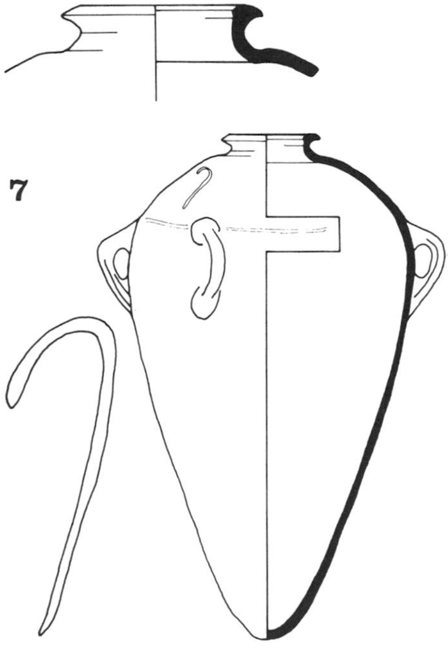

7

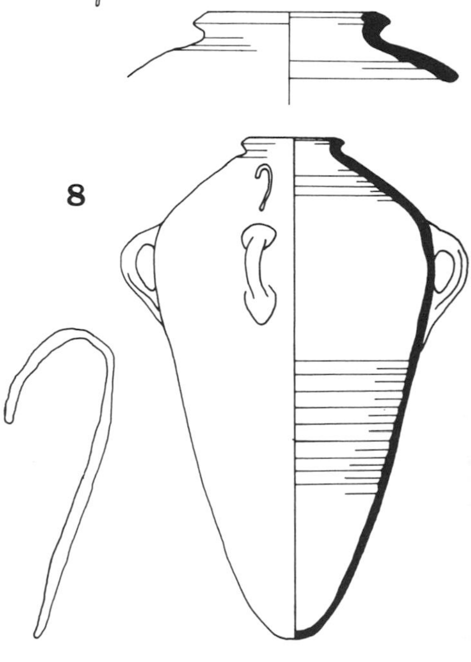

8

Plate II

5. G73 IV.5.239 #1

FORM: Storejar
TECHNIQUE: Wheelmade
WARE PASTE:

Color:	2.5 YR "Light Red" 6/6	
Inclusions:	Many medium to large wadi gravel; some medium lime, few small ceramic	
Firing:	No core	
Hardness:	Hard	
WARE SURFACE:	*Interior*	*Exterior*
Color:	As exterior	7.5 YR "Reddish Yellow" 8/6
Treatment:	None	Sign on shoulder

6. G73 IV.5.249 #1

FORM: Storejar
TECHNIQUE: Wheelmade
WARE PASTE:

Color:	7.5 YR "Pink" 8/4	
Inclusions:	Some large organic; few large wadi gravel and lime; few small ceramic	
Firing:	No core	
Hardness:	Hard	
WARE SURFACE:	*Interior*	*Exterior*
Color:	As paste	As paste
Treatment:	None	Sign on shoulder: horizontal combing around shoulder

7. G73 IV.5.315 #1

FORM: Storejar
TECHNIQUE: Wheelmade
WARE PASTE:

Color:	7.5 YR "Pinkish Gray" 7/2	
Inclusions:	Some small lime, few medium wadi gravel, few medium ceramic	
Firing:	No core	
Hardness:	Hard	
WARE SURFACE:	*Interior*	*Exterior*
Color:	As paste	5 YR "Reddish Yellow" 7/8
Treatment:	None	Sign on shoulder, groove around shoulder

Plate II ***(continued)***

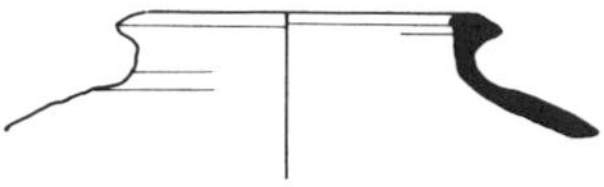

9

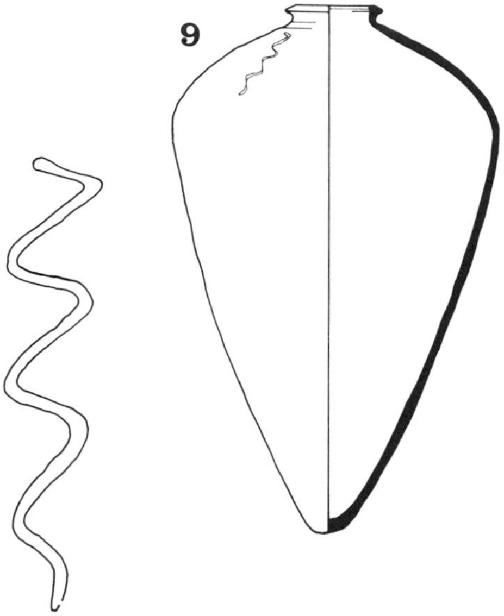

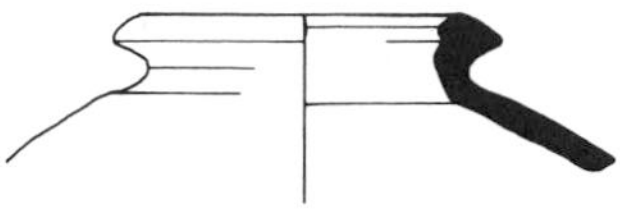

10

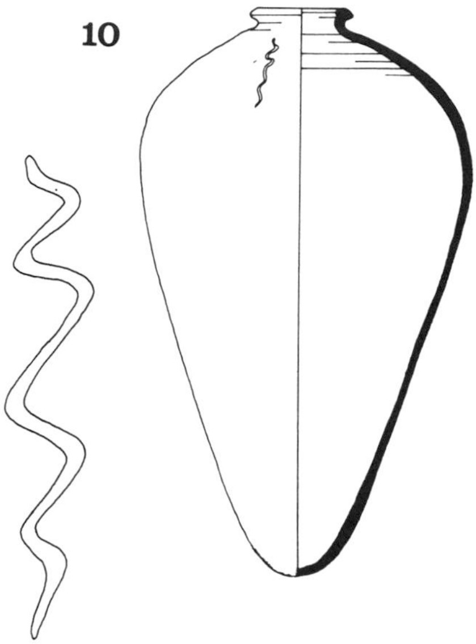

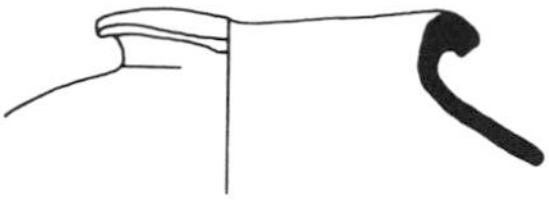

11 12

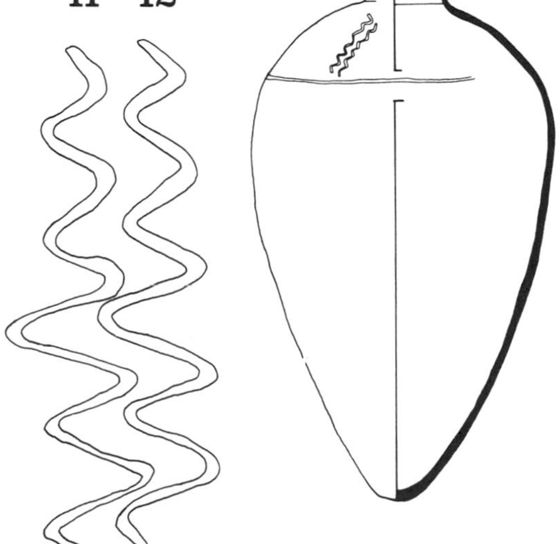

13

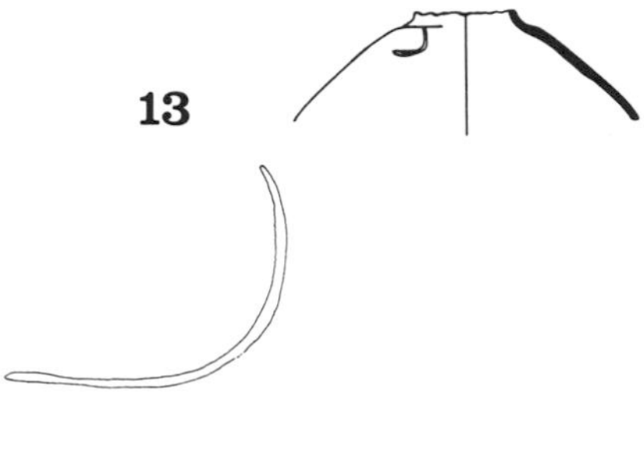

14

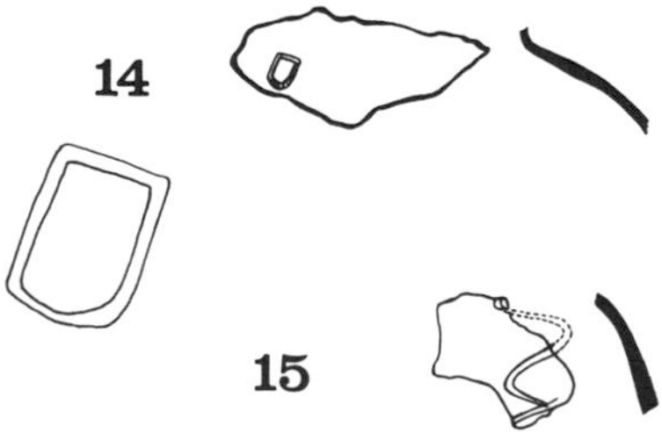

15

16

Plate II *(continued)*

8. G73 IV.5.314 #1

FORM: Storejar		
TECHNIQUE: Wheelmade		
WARE PASTE:		
Color:	5 YR "Reddish Yellow" 7/6	
Inclusions:	Some medium to large wadi gravel and lime; few large organic	
Firing:	No core	
Hardness:	Hard	
WARE SURFACE:	*Interior*	*Exterior*
Color:	As paste	As paste
Treatment:	None	Sign on shoulder

Plate III

9. G72 IV.5.48 #1

FORM: Storejar		
TECHNIQUE: Wheelmade		
WARE PASTE:		
Color:	5 YR "Pink" 8/4	
Inclusions:	Many medium to large wadi gravel	
Firing:	No core	
Hardness:	Hard	
WARE SURFACE:	*Interior*	*Exterior*
Color:	As paste	As paste
Treatment:	None	Sign on shoulder

10. G72 IV.5.70, 63-65 #1

FORM: Storejar		
TECHNIQUE: Wheelmade		
WARE PASTE:		
Color:	5 YR "Pink" 7/4	
Inclusions:	Many medium to large wadi gravel; some medium to large lime; few medium ceramic	
Firing:	No core	
Hardness:	Hard	
WARE SURFACE:	*Interior*	*Exterior*
Color:	As paste	As paste
Treatment:	None	Sign on shoulder: horizontal combing around shoulder

Plate III *(c*

Plate III *(continued)*

11.-12. G72 IV.5.162 #1

FORM: Storejar

TECHNIQUE: Wheelmade

WARE PASTE:

Color:	5 YR "Pink" 7/4	
Inclusions:	Many medium to large wadi gravel and lime	
Firing:	No core	
Hardness:	Hard	
WARE SURFACE:	*Interior*	*Exterior*
Color:	As paste	7.5 YR "Pink" 7/4
Treatment:	None	Signs on shoulder, groove around shoulder

13. G72 IV.5.184 #1

FORM: Storejar

TECHNIQUE: Wheelmade

WARE PASTE:

Color:	5 YR "Reddish Yellow" 7/6	
Inclusions:	Many large wadi gravel; many medium to large lime	
Firing:	Light grey core	
Hardness:	Hard	
WARE SURFACE:	*Interior*	*Exterior*
Color:	7.5 YR "Pink" 8/4	As paste
Treatment:	None	Sign on shoulder

14. G73 IV.6.134 #3

FORM: Storejar

TECHNIQUE: Wheelmade

WARE PASTE:

Color:	7.5 YR "Reddish Yellow" 6/6	
Inclusions:	Very many medium, some small and large wadi gravel, few small to medium crystal	
Firing:	No core	
Hardness:	Hard	
WARE SURFACE:	*Interior*	*Exterior*
Color:	As paste	7.5 YR "Reddish Yellow" 7/6
Treatment:	None	Sign on shoulder

15. G73 IV.6.134 #1

FORM: Jar

TECHNIQUE: Wheelmade

WARE PASTE:

Color:	7.5 YR "Light Brown" 6/4	
Inclusions:	Very many small wadi gravel, lime and organic; some medium to large wadi gravel and lime; few very small ceramic	
Firing:	Light grey core	
Hardness:	Hard	
WARE SURFACE:	*Interior*	*Exterior*
Color:	7.5 YR "Reddish Yellow" 6/6	As paste
Treatment:	None	Sign?

16. G73 IV.6.144 #1

FORM: Jar
TECHNIQUE: Wheelmade
WARE PASTE:

Color:	5 YR "Reddish Yellow" 6/6	
Inclusions:	Few medium to large lime; many very small, some medium to large crystal; few small ceramic	
Firing:	Light grey core	
Hardness:	Hard	
WARE SURFACE:	*Interior*	*Exterior*
Color:	As paste	7.5 YR "Pink" 7/4
Treatment:	None	Sign?

Plate IV

17.-18. G73 IV.5.265 #1

FORM: Storejar
TECHNIQUE: Wheelmade
WARE PASTE:

Color:	7.5 YR "Pinkish White" 8/2	
Inclusions:	Many small to large wadi gravel and lime	
Firing:	No core	
Hardness:	Hard	
WARE SURFACE:	*Interior*	*Exterior*
Color:	As paste	5 YR "Pink" 7/4
Treatment:	None	Signs on shoulder, groove around shoulder

19. G73 IV.5.312 #1

FORM: Storejar
TECHNIQUE: Wheelmade
WARE PASTE:

Color:	7.5 YR "Reddish Yellow" 8/6	
Inclusions:	Few medium to large wadi lime; some small wadi gravel and ceramic; some small organic	
Firing:	No core	
Hardness:	Hard	
WARE SURFACE:	*Interior*	*Exterior*
Color:	7.5 YR "Pink" 8/4	As paste
Treatment:	None	Groove around shoulder

Plate IV *(continued)*

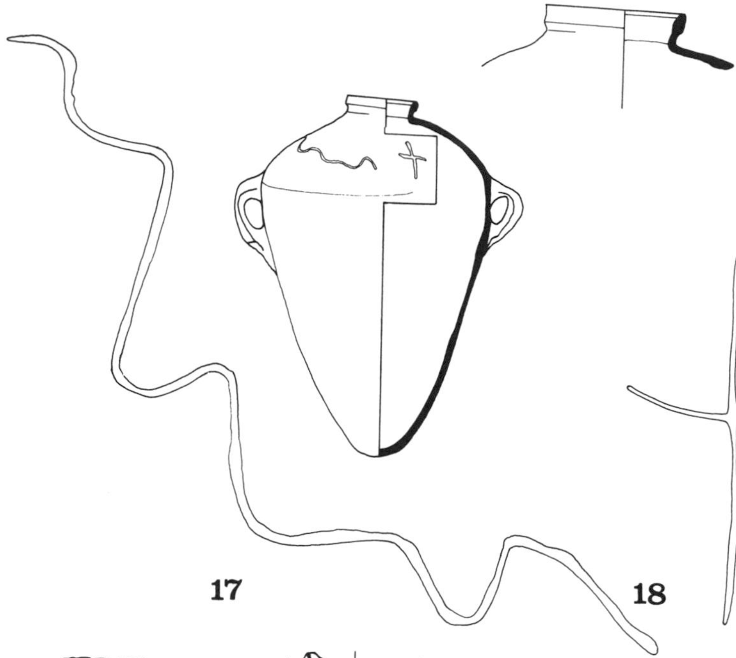

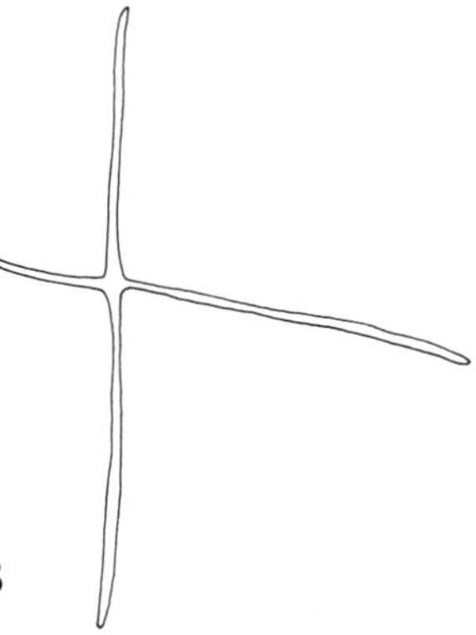

17

18

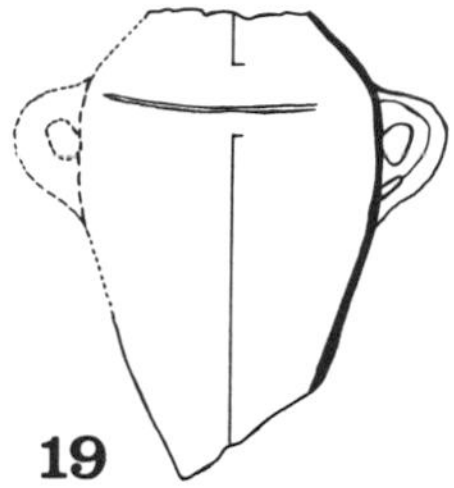

19

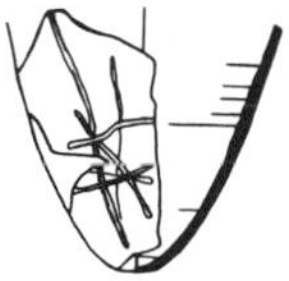

20

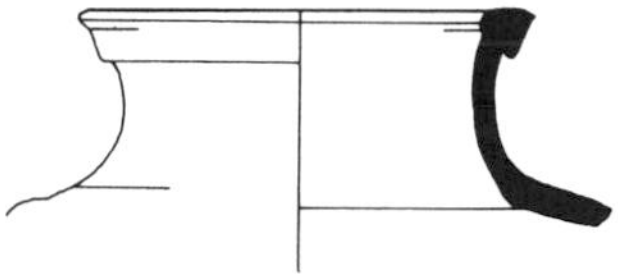

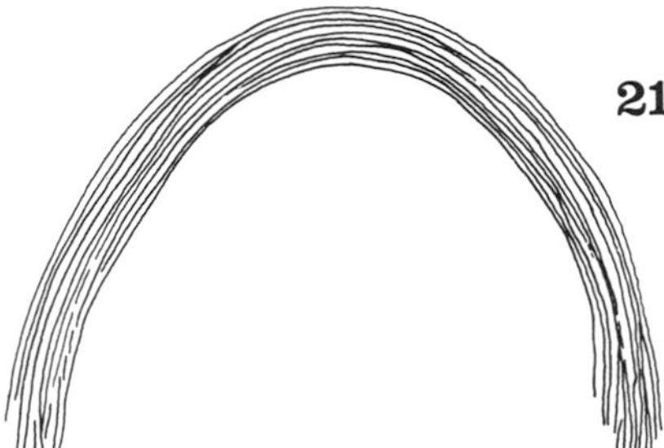

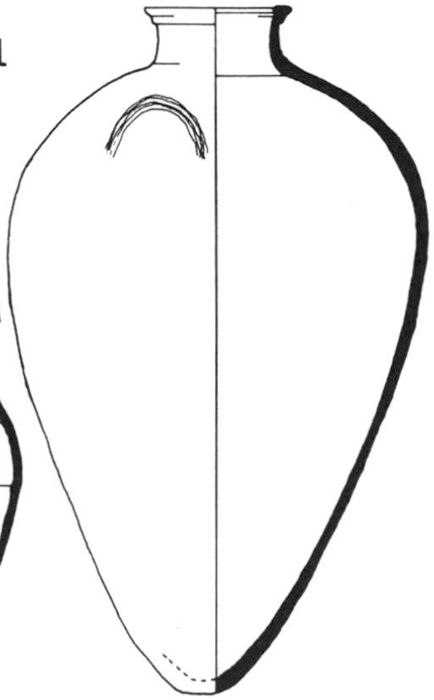

21

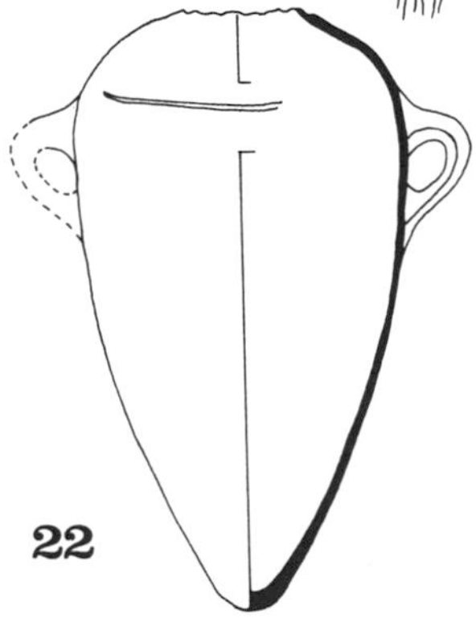

22

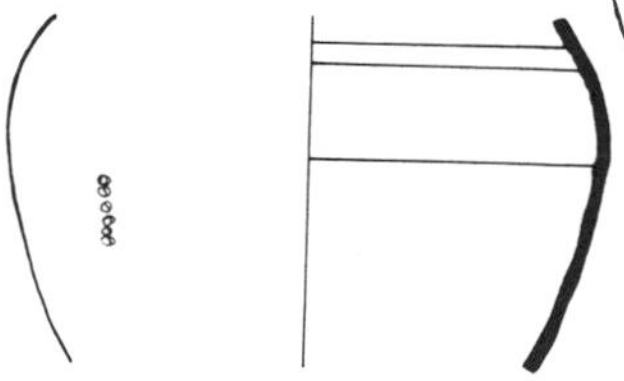

23

Plate IV *(continued)*

20. G73 IV.6.50 #8

FORM: Jar Base
TECHNIQUE: Wheelmade
WARE PASTE:

Color:	10 YR "Dark Grey" 4/1	
Inclusions:	Very many small lime; some medium wadi gravel and lime; few small ceramic	
Firing:	No core	
Hardness:	Hard	
WARE SURFACE:	*Interior*	*Exterior*
Color:	10 YR "Grayish Brown" 5/2	5 YR "Reddish Brown" 5/3
Treatment:	None	Signs?

21. G74 IV.6.150 #1

FORM: Storejar
TECHNIQUE: Wheelmade
WARE PASTE:

Color:	2.5 YR "Pink" 8/4	
Inclusions:	Many medium to large wade gravel and lime; some small ceramic and medium organic	
Firing:	No core	
Hardness:	Hard	
WARE SURFACE:	*Interior*	*Exterior*
Color:	5 YR "Reddish Yellow" 7/8	As interior
Treatment:	None	Sign on shoulder

22. G72 IV.5.122 #1

FORM: Storejar
TECHNIQUE: Wheelmade
WARE PASTE:

Color:	5 YR "Pinkish White" 8/2	
Inclusions:	Some medium to large wadi gravel; some large lime	
Firing:	Dark gray core	
Hardness:	Hard	
WARE SURFACE:	*Interior*	*Exterior*
Color:	5 YR "Light Gray" 7/1	7.5 YR "Reddish Yellow" 8/6
Treatment:	None	Groove around shoulder

23. G72 IV.5.90 #1

FORM: Storejar
TECHNIQUE: Wheelmade
WARE PASTE:

Color:	5 YR "Pink" 7/3	
Inclusions:	Some large wadi gravel, lime and ceramic	
Firing:	No core	
Hardness:	Hard	
WARE SURFACE:	*Interior*	*Exterior*
Color:	As paste	5 YR "Pink" 7/4
Treatment:	None	Sign?

References

Aharoni, Y.
1971 Khirbet Raddana and Its Inscription. *Israel Exploration Journal* 21: 130–35.

Albright, W. F.
1948 The Early Alphabetic Inscriptions from Sinai and Their Decipherment. *Bulletin of the American Schools of Oriental Research* 110: 6–22.
1969 *The Proto-Sinaitic Inscriptions and Their Decipherment*[2]. Harvard Theological Studies 22. Cambridge: Harvard University Press.

de Liagre Böhl, F. M. Th.
1938 Die Sichem-Plakette. *Zeitschrift des Deutschen Palästina-Vereins* 61: 1–25.

Cross, F. M.
1954 The Evolution of the Proto-Canaanite Alphabet. *Bulletin of the American Schools of Oriental Research* 134: 15–24.
1967 The Origin and Early Evolution of the Alphabet. *Eretz Israel* 8: 8*-24*.
1979 Early Alphabetic Scripts. Pp. 97–123 in *Symposia Celebrating the Seventy-Fifth Anniversary of the Founding of the American Schools of Oriental Research*, ed. F. M. Cross. Zion Research Foundation Occasional Publications. Cambridge: American Schools of Oriental Research.

Cross, F. M., and Freedman, D. N.
1971 An Inscribed Jar Handle from Raddana. *Bulletin of the American Schools of Oriental Research* 201: 19–22.

Cross, F. M., and Lambdin, T. O.
1960 A Ugaritic Abecedary and the Origins of the Proto-Canaanite Alphabet. *Bulletin of the American Schools of Oriental Research* 160: 21–26.

Demsky, A.
1977 A Proto-Canaanite Abecedary Dating from the Period of the Judges and Its Implications for the History of the Alphabet. *Tel Aviv* 4: 14–27.

Diringer, D.
1958 Inscriptions. In O. Tufnell et al., *Lachish IV (Tell ed-Duweir): The Bronze Age*. London: Oxford.

Gaster, T. H.
1940 Inscriptions. In O. Tufnell et al., *Lachish II (Tell ed-Duweir): The Fosse Temple*. London: Oxford.

Goetze, A.
1953 A Seal Cylinder with an Early Alphabetic Inscription. *Bulletin of the American Schools of Oriental Research* 129: 8–11.

Grant, E.
1931 *Ain Shems Excavations I*. Haverford College Biblical and Kindred Studies 3. Haverford: Haverford College.

Irwin, W. A., and Bowman, R. A.
1938 Inscriptions. In P.L.O. Guy with R. M. Engberg. *Megiddo Tombs*. Chicago: University of Chicago Press.

Kaplan, J.
1955 A Cemetery of the Bronze Age Discovered Near Tel Aviv Harbor. *Atiqot* 1: 1–12.

Kochavi, M.
1977 An Ostracon of the Period of the Judges from Izbet Sarteh. *Tel Aviv* 4: 1–13.

Leibovitch, J.
1965 Le tesson de Tell Nagila. *Le Museon* 78: 229–30.

McCarter, P. K.
1975 *The Antiquity of the Greek Alphabet and the Early Phoenician Scripts*. Harvard Semitic Monographs 9. Missoula: Scholars Press.

Mendenhall, G. E.
1971 A New Chapter in the History of the Alphabet. *Bulletin du Musée de Beyrouth* 24: 13–18.

Petrie, W. M. F.
1932 *Ancient Gaza II*. London: British School of Archaeology in Egypt.

Rainey, A. F.
1975 Notes on Some Proto-Sinaitic Inscriptions. *Israel Exploration Journal* 25: 106–16.

Seger, J. D.
1975 The MB II Fortifications at Shechem and Gezer. *Eretz Israel* 12: 34*-45*.
1976 Reflections on the Gold Hoard from Gezer. *Bulletin of the American Schools of Oriental Research* 221: 133–40.
1977 Notes and News: Tell Halif (Lahav). *Israel Exploration Journal* 27: 45–47.

Taylor, W. R.
1930 Recent Epigraphic Discoveries in Palestine. *Journal of the Palestine Oriental Society* 10: 16–22.

Yadin, Y., et al.
1958 *Hazor I*. Jerusalem: Magnes.

The Discovery of the Moabite Stone

Siegfried H. Horn
Pleasant Hill, California

The Moabite Stone, discovered in 1868, remains to the present day the longest monumental stone inscription written both in the Phoenician script and in a West Semitic Language ever found in Palestine, east or west of the Jordan River (KAI 181). Since its text was executed at the order of Mesha, a king of Moab mentioned in the Bible, and since it also refers to events recorded in the Bible, this ancient monument has been discussed in nearly every work that deals either with Old Testament history or biblical archeology.

Nearly all modern discussions of the inscription are introduced by a brief statement relating to the stone's discovery, subsequent destruction, and the retrieval of its surviving fragments. Most of these statements are true to fact in the essentials. They usually state correctly that the monument was discovered in 1868 by F. A. Klein at *Dhibān*, biblical Dibon, and was broken up by local people into many fragments before the stone in its reassembled state found a permanent home at the Louvre in Paris. Aside from these facts, correctly stated, the stories usually contain many inaccurate items of detail, probably due to two facts: first, that no authoritative and exhaustive work on the Moabite Stone has ever been published, although innumerable articles and books dealing with this monument saw the light of day during the first decade after its discovery; second, that few modern scholars go to the trouble of reading the original reports about the discovery of the stone, reports published more than a century ago.

Before pointing out some of the contradictions and inaccuracies of modern writers with regard to the events surrounding the discovery of the Moabite Stone, let me give one example of a small detail that is often inaccurately presented, namely the nationality and profession of the discoverer, F. A. Klein. Some modern authors call him a "German missionary" (Kittel 1927: 72; Sayce 1929; Noortzij 1931: 36; Keller 1956: 235; Price *et al.* 1958: 241; Owen 1961: 261). Others say he was a "German minister or clergyman" (Bentzinger 1903: 611; Barton 1944: 460). Some call him a "Prussian missionary" (Muir 1937: 159; Williams 1962), or "Prussian traveler" (Finegan 1946: 157). Only Hugo Gressman (1927: 41) and Yehoshua Ben-Arieh (1979: 209), among the modern authors consulted by me, correctly identify him, the former saying that Klein was an "Alsatian missionary" and the latter calling him "a French priest from Alsace." The inaccurate designations probably derive from the fact that modern writers do not realize that Klein's citizenship was changed involuntarily three years after he made his discovery and from the fact that they simply copy incorrect information, one from another. F. A. Klein came from Strasbourg, Alsace; in 1868, when he discovered the Moabite Stone, he was a French citizen, as he himself clearly states in one of his reports (1876), saying that he did not imagine at that time that he would ever become a German citizen. However, when as the result of the Franco-German War of 1870–1871 the French provinces of

Alsace and Lorraine were ceded to Germany, their citizens automatically became German citizens; among them was Klein. This may be the reason that he is almost universally referred to as German or even Prussian. As far as his profession is concerned, Klein was an Anglican minister employed by the English "Church Missionary Society" in Jerusalem, in which capacity he had served nearly twenty years when he made his discovery in 1868 (Klein 1876).

Conflicting Stories

First I want to present a few summaries of stories dealing with the discovery of the Moabite Stone. The attentive reader will easily notice that there are conflicting features in some of the details and that no two stories completely agree with each other. The consistent *Tendenzen* of the accounts will be evident. (Some spurious twentieth century material is treated in Albright 1945a,b.)

A. H. Sayce (1929) states that after Klein discovered the stone on 19 August 1868, unfortunately making neither a copy nor a squeeze of the inscription, the Berlin Museum entered into negotations for its purchase. While these proceeded slowly, Charles Clermont-Ganneau sent agents to make squeezes and tempt the Arabs to sell the stone for a large amount of money. This led to interference on the part of Turkish officials with the result that in 1869 it was broken up by the local people, who carried the fragments away as charms.

J. Benzinger (1903: 611) says that Klein succeeded in purchasing the stone for the Berlin Museum. However, because of French interference it never came into the possession of the purchasers. Rather it was demolished by the Bedouin, who hoped to find treasures in it, before it reached any European country.

James C. Muir (1937: 159) reports that Klein, recognizing the stone to be of historical value, started negotiations for its purchase which lasted for a year and resulted in an agreement to purchase the stone for $400. Meanwhile news of its existence had reached Jerusalem, and the noted French scholar Clermont-Ganneau made a bid for the stone. This led the wily Arabs to work up the price to about $1,500. Believing that the stone must have magic properties if it was of so much value to these foreigners, they reasoned that if one large charm was worth so much, a lot of small charms would bring much more money. Therefore they broke it up into many fragments.

George A. Barton (1944: 460) asserts that the French scholar Clermont-Ganneau had received reports of the stone's existence before Klein saw it. R. J. Williams (1962) makes the same claim, while G. Ernest Wright (1957: 156) even reports that the young French archeologist Clermont-Ganneau discovered the monument.

Ira M. Price, Ovid R. Sellers, and E. Leslie Carlson (1958: 241) claim that French residents in Jerusalem, including Mr. Clermont-Ganneau, learned of the stone's existence and then sent an Arab to *Dhibān* to make a squeeze of the inscription and to offer the Arabs $1,800 as purchasing price. Naturally, the owners suspected that the stone contained magical powers; when the governor of Nablus demanded it for himself, they destroyed it and distributed the fragments among themselves as amulets and charms.

G. Frederick Owen (1961: 261–62) says that Klein copied some words of the text and sent them to Berlin. However, the Turkish governor of Shechem, realizing the possible value of the stone and an opportunity for financial advancement, intervened and demanded that the stone be turned over to him.

The most fantastic story, which contains a great number of inaccuracies, is that told by Werner Keller in his "best seller" *The Bible as History*. It may be quoted in full.

> In 1868 a German missionary, F. A. Klein, was visiting Biblical sites in Palestine. The route he followed took him through Transjordan, through Edom, and eventually to Moab. As he was riding in the neighborhood of Diban, the ancient Dibon on the middle reaches of the Arnon, his attention was particularly aroused by a large smooth stone. The yellow sand had almost completely drifted over it. Klein jumped from his horse and bent over the stone curiously. It was unmistakably ancient Hebrew writing. He could hardly believe his eyes. It was as much as he could do in the heat of the midday sun to stand the heavy basalt stone upright. It was three feet high and rounded on top. Klein cleaned it carefully with a knife and a handkerchief. Thirty-four lines of writing appeared.
>
> He would have preferred to take the stone document away with him, then and there, but it was far too heavy. Besides, in no time a mob of armed Arabs was on the spot. With wild gesticulations they surrounded the missionary, maintaining that the stone was their property and demanding from him a fantastic price for it.
>
> Klein guessed that his discovery was an important one and was in despair. Missionaries never have much money. He tried in vain to make the natives change their minds. There was nothing for it but to mark the site carefully on his map. He then gave up the idea of continuing his journey, hurried back to Jerusalem and from there straight home to Germany to try to collect the necessary money for the Arabs.
>
> But in the meantime other people got busy, which was a good thing; otherwise an extremely valuable piece of evidence for Biblical history might well have been lost forever.
>
> A French scholar, Clermont-Ganneau, who was working in Jerusalem, had heard of the German missionary's discovery and had at once set out for Diban. It needed all his powers of persuasion to get the suspicious Arabs even to allow him to examine the writing on the basalt stone. Surrounded by the hostile eyes of the natives, Clermont-Ganneau took a squeeze of the surface. Months later when Parisian scholars had translated the text, the French government sanctioned the purchase without hesitation. But judge the Frenchman's disappointment when he reached Diban, equipped with a caravan and the neccessary sum of money, and found that the stone had disappeared. Only a patch of soot indicated the spot where it had been. The Arabs had blown it to pieces with gunpowder—from avarice. They hoped to do a more profitable trade with Europeans whose obsession with antiquity would make them willing to buy the individual pieces.
>
> What could Clermont-Ganneau do but set out on the trail of the individual pieces of the valuable document. After a great deal of trouble and searching, and after endless haggling he was successful in retrieving all the broken fragments. Two larger blocks and eighteen small pieces were reassembled in accordance with the squeeze, and before the German missionary had even collected the necessary money, the impressive stone from Diban was standing among the valuable recent acquisitions in the Louvre in Paris (1956: 235–37).

What Actually Happened

Having summarized briefly some of the various inconsistent and contradictory stories relating to the discovery of the Moabite Stone, I will now reconstruct the actual sequence of events, by gathering together the information given piecemeal by the principal actors involved in the discovery and acquisition of this famous monument.

F. A. Klein relates how in the course of a journey through the *Belqā*[1] in Transjordania he visited *Dhibān*, the ancient Dibon, on 19 August 1868. Westerners seldom dared to travel in the regions east of the Jordan River, where the Bedouin were a law to themselves and where the Turkish government, though officially in control of the countryside, could not guarantee the safety of any traveler. Klein was the first westerner in *Dhibān* since C. L. Irby and J. Mangles had visited it on 18 June 1818.[2] As a result of his many years of work in Palestine, Klein spoke Arabic fluently and had many friends among the Arabs of the region. On this trip he was accompanied by his friend *Zaṭam*, the son of *Findī al-Fāyiz*, the powerful sheikh of the *Banī Ṣakhr*.[3] The friendship of this sheikh guaranteed him a courteous reception wherever he traveled. Hence Klein was well received by the Bedouin of the *Banī Ḥamīdah*, who were encamped near *Dhibān*, when he arrived there.

It was during this visit that Klein learned that an inscribed stone lay in the ruins of *Dhibān*. He was anxious to see it. However, he did not get away from his friendly hosts until late afternoon and therefore had not much time to examine the stone when he finally reached the spot where it lay. Further, not being versed in ancient Oriental scripts, he could not determine whether the stone was of importance. He did measure the stone, make a sketch of it in his notebook, and copy "a few words from several lines [of the inscription] at random" (Klein 1870: 281, 382).

Before the end of August, Klein returned to Jerusalem and visited J. H. Petermann, who was consul of the North-German Federation and with whom he was well acquainted.[4] In the presence of three other friends of Petermann Klein gave a report of his trip around the Dead Sea and of his discovery of a stone at *Dhibān* containing a 33-line inscription.[5] Petermann, an expert in Oriental languages and scripts, recognized from the several words copied by Klein that the inscription was written in Phoenician characters and therefore was of importance.

On 29 August 1868 Petermann wrote to the Museum in Berlin and asked whether its directors were interested in purchasing this monument and whether they would be willing to spend about 100 Napoleons, worth about $400 at that time, for it. On 15 September 1868 Petermann received a telegram from K. R. Lepsius, director of the Berlin Museum, authorizing him to obtain the stone. Petermann then asked his three friends, who had heard Klein's story, to remain silent about it; he then learned that one of them had already told the news to Dr. J. Barclay of the Jewish Mission.

Klein then sent, at Petermann's request, a letter to Sheikh *Findī al-Fāyiz*, whose authority the Bedouin of *Dhibān* acknowledged, and asked him to lend his assistance in the acquisition of the stone. This letter was carried by *Beḥnam*, a teacher from *es-Salt*, whose name indicates that he must have been an "Assyrian" Christian. The first reply, received before the end of September, was noncommittal. Shortly thereafter the sheikh went to Damascus and after his return sent word to Petermann that he could do nothing in this matter. Hence Petermann made a second attempt in March 1869, by sending an Arab teacher from Jerusalem, *Sābā Qaʿwār*, to the

Bedouin in *Dhibān*, with whom this man was acquainted. *Qaʿwār* returned with the news that the Bedouin had now raised the price to 1,000 Napoleons (= ca. $4,000).

Thereupon Petermann reported to Berlin on 19 March 1869 that in his opinion the stone could be obtained only with the help of the Turkish authorities. Thus, with the help of the German ambassador in Constantinople, a letter was obtained from the Grand Vizier to the Pasha of Jerusalem in June 1869 authorizing him to have the stone removed at the expense of the Germans. However, Transjordania was subject to the Pasha of Nablus, and the Pasha of Jerusalem could not act in this matter. Before this confusion in authority was straightened out, Petermann left Jerusalem and handed over his duties to Oskar Meyer, the new chancellor of the North-German Consulate in Jerusalem. In the meantime further patient negotiations of *Sābā Qaʿwār* and the *Banī Ḥamīdah* succeeded in producing a written agreement to surrender the stone for 120 Napoleons (= ca. $480).

Another difficulty arose when the sheikh of a neighboring tribe, the *ʿAṭwān*, did not permit the stone to be transported through his territory. This forced *Sābā Qaʿwār* to return empty-handed to Jerusalem once more in early November 1869. By this time the Turkish authorities had finally straightened out the matter of responsibilities, and the Pasha of Nablus sent a demand to the Bedouin of *Dhibān* to surrender the stone. They, however, in their hatred of the Turkish governor, who had made a punitive foray into their territory a year earlier, broke the stone into many pieces by heating it in a fire and pouring cold water on the white-hot stone. The fragments were distributed among the local Bedouin to serve as talismans or amulets and guarantee fertility of the soil, for which reason their owners put them into their granaries.[6]

However, this is still not the whole story. It seems that the negotiations between the Germans and the Bedouin had also been complicated through the interference of Charles Clermont-Ganneau. This young Orientalist, who at the age of 21 had arrived in Jerusalem in 1867 as dragoman (interpreter) and chancellor of the French Consulate, seems to have received word of Klein's discovery, either through J. Barclay or someone else, soon after Klein's arrival in Jerusalem in August 1868. Clermont-Ganneau in his many publications on the Moabite Stone neither names the source of his information nor provides the date when he first learned of the existence of the stone. In his first published communication on the monument, a letter to the Count de Vogüé dated 16 January 1870, he said that he knew of the stone's existence "depuis longtemps" (1870a: 1). This first communication of Clermont-Ganneau was made nearly a year and a half after Klein had made his discovery. In addition, in a letter to the London *Times* of 22 March 1870, he says, "Il y a fort longtemps que j'avais connaissance de ce précieux monument, comme en fait foi une lettre datée du 20 Octobre, 1869 et adressée par moi à la *Revue de l'Instruction Publique* (17 Février, 1870)" (1870c). These somewhat ambiguous expressions evidently led several scholars to assume that Clermont-Ganneau had received some information about the existence of the Moabite Stone before Klein saw it on 19 August 1868.

Some light is shed on this affair by Captain Charles Warren, who from 1867 to 1870 carried out archeological surveys and excavations in the service of the British Palestine Exploration Fund. His first report on the Moabite Stone, sent to London on 21 January 1870, says that "a gentleman" had seen the stone in the summer of 1868 and that this had aroused the curiosity of the natives. Six weeks later Warren learned about it through a man from Kerak. After making inquiries and finding "that the

Prussian Consul was moving in that matter to get possession of it," Warren decided to do nothing about it. According to Warren, Clermont-Ganneau learned of the stone's existence through "the Rev. Dr. Barclay" in the spring of 1869. Warren also says in his report that Clermont-Ganneau "expressed surprise to hear" at that time "that no squeeze or copy of the stone had been taken" (1870a,b).

However, Clermont-Ganneau unlike Warren did not remain inactive in this matter. He tells us that on two occasions he brought the subject up in conversations with Petermann, who gave him to understand that he knew nothing about it (1870b). Therefore he felt free to act. First he obtained a hand copy of seven lines of the inscription, made in October 1869 by an Arab friend, *Salīm el-Qārī*.[7] Clermont-Ganneau at once recognized its extreme value and in early November sent another man, by the name of *Yaʿqūb Karavaca*,[8] to *Dhibān* to take a paper squeeze of the stone and to offer a purchasing sum much higher than the one agreed upon between *Sābā Qaʿwār* and the people of *Dhibān*. The local people granted Karavaca's request to take a squeeze, "but while the squeeze was still wet, a quarrel arose among the *Banī Ḥamīdah*, blows were exchanged, and Mr. Ganneau's messenger, tearing off the wet impression, had only time to spring upon his horse and escape by flight, bringing with him the squeeze in rags, and receiving a spear-wound in the leg" (Anonymous 1871).

The seven pieces of this extremely poor squeeze constituted the only copy of the complete inscription and later formed the basis for the reconstruction of the stone after its destruction. For many years this squeeze hung behind glass side by side with the original stone in the Louvre and gave scholars an opportunity to check Clermont-Ganneau's work of reconstruction.

It seems that the unfortunate destruction of the monument occurred right after the paper squeeze had been made. The exact date is not known. When Warren returned to Jerusalem from the Lebanon in November 1869, where he had been since July, a member of the *ʿAṭwān* tribe met him on his way from Jaffa to Jerusalem and told him of the destruction of the stone. He gave Warren a small fragment to prove the truth of his story (Warren 1870b).

In reading the various reports it is difficult to form an impartial judgment with regard to who must bear the blame for the misfortune. It may have been imprudent of the Germans to call upon the Turkish authorities, intensely hated by the Bedouin, to obtain the stone for them. With hindsight one might also criticize the secrecy with which the Germans tried to obtain it instead of consulting with British and French colleagues, although one should not forget that the political climate at that time was not conducive to fostering acts of friendship or courtesy between Germans and French; indeed, only a few months later the bitter Franco-German War of 1870–1871 broke out. It is inexcusable that the Germans seem to have made no effort to obtain a squeeze of the inscription in the course of the several months in which they negotiated for the purchase of the monument and during which time their agent was on friendly terms with the local people of *Dhibān*.

On the other hand the young French savant Clermont-Ganneau must also bear part of the blame, although the scholarly world owes him gratitude for having attempted to produce a copy of the stone, when more than a year after its discovery such a copy had not yet been obtained. That the young Frenchman was eager to acquire the stone for his country is understandable, although it is inexcusable that he offered a much higher amount of money than had been agreed upon contractually between the Bedouin and the Germans. This no doubt made the local people more intransigent. The added interest shown in the stone and the competition between the agents of the French and Germans to procure it also heightened their suspicion and caused them to wonder whether the stone contained either treasure or magical powers. The fact that Clermont-Ganneau in his early reports never, even with one word, mentions Klein as the discoverer but rather gives the impression that he was the discoverer, does not show the great man in the best light; he has since been castigated for this by some scholars (Schlottmann 1870, Ginsburg 1871: 13).

On the other hand, Clermont-Ganneau definitely put the scholarly world in his debt by making every effort to obtain the available fragments of the stone after its destruction. While the Germans seem to have lost all interest in the monument after it had been broken up, Warren and Clermont-Ganneau lost no time in obtaining squeezes of fragments of the demolished stone and purchasing those pieces that became available. In this way Clermont-Ganneau collected two large pieces and eighteen small fragments containing a total of 613 letters of the ca. 1,000 letters of the original inscription. Warren secured another eighteen fragments which contain 59 letters altogether; later K. Schlottmann purchased one more small fragment.

Clermont-Ganneau, having thus come into possession of about two-thirds of the original inscription, restored the monument with the help of the imperfect squeeze made before the stone's destruction. In 1873 the materials came into the possession of the Louvre. A year later the Palestine Exploration Fund ceded the eighteen fragments obtained by Warren to the Louvre, and in 1891 the Schlottmann fragment was ceded to the Louvre by Schlottmann's daughter Anna (Dussaud 1912: 17). These have all been incorporated into the reconstructed stone, of which about two-thirds is original and one-third consists of plaster. Although Freedman (1964) has observed that the tiny Moabite fragment found at *Dhibān* in the fifties may belong to another Mesha Stele, perhaps a duplicate, it is strange that in the century that has passed since it was destroyed no additional pieces of the great stele have ever come to light.

Notes

1. *Belqā* was the name of one of the two provinces into which Transjordania was divided under Turkish rule. It reached from the *Wadi ez-Zerqā* (the biblical Jabbok) in the north to the *Wadi el-Mōjib* (the biblical Arnon) in the south. The city of *es-Salt* was the *Belqā*'s capital, although the province was administered by the Pasha of Nablus in western Palestine. See Smith 1907: 535, 536. The term *Belqā* is still occasionally used as a geographical term covering approximately the same area as the Turkish administrative area described above. See Abel 1933 I: 277.

2. Irby and Mangels 1823: 462. Warren (1870c) incorrectly gives the date as 1809.

3. The Arabic names of individuals and tribes are presented in this study in modern spelling and not in the form in which they appear in the original publications. Some equivalents are modern *Zaṭam* for nineteenth century Zattam; *Findī al-Fāyiz* for Fendi-el-Faïz; *Banī Ṣakhr* for Beni Sachr; *Banī Ḥamīdah* for Beni Hamideh; *Beḥnam* for Behnam; *Sābā Qaʿwār* for Saba Cawar; *ʿAṭwān* for Adhwan; *Salīm el-Qārī* for Selîm el-Qâri; and *Yaʿqūb Karavaca* for Yaqoub Karavasa.

4. Neither Klein nor Petermann (1870) provides the exact date of this visit.

5. J. H. Petermann (1870) says that Klein reported to him that the stone contained an inscription of 33 lines. Klein (1870: 283), on the other hand, claims to have counted 34 lines.

6. This is a summary of Petermann's published report (1870), which is based on his own

experiences from August 1868 through the summer of 1869, when he left Jerusalem, and which incorporates a report of O. Meyer, Petermann's successor as consul in Jerusalem, dated 29 April 1870. My summary takes also into account a report of O. Meyer (1870).

7. This hand-copy was published eight years later, together with a facsimile reproduction, by Clermont-Ganneau (1887).

8. Since *Karavaca* is not an Arabic name, it is uncertain who this man was. His name may indicate that he was of Spanish (Moorish) descent, if it be derived from the name of the Spanish city Caravaca, or that he belonged to one of the Serbian families who lived in Jerusalem at that time.

References

F.-M. Abel
1933 *Géographie de la Palestine.* Paris: Gabalda.

W. F. Albright
1945a Is the Mesha Inscription a Forgery? *Jewish Quarterly Review* 35: 247–50.
1945b A Note on the Name of the Forger of the Moabite Antiquities. *Jewish Quarterly Review* 36: 177.

Anonymous
1871 The Moabite Stone. At p. 392 in C. Wilson and C. Warren, *The Recovery of Jerusalem.* New York: D. Appleton.

G. A. Barton
1944 *Archaeology and the Bible*[7]. Philadelphia: American Sunday School Union.

Y. Ben-Arieh
1979 *The Rediscovery of the Holy Land in the Nineteenth Century.* Jerusalem: Magnes.

J. Benzinger
1903 Researches in Palestine. In *Exploration in Bible Lands During the 19th Century*, ed. H. V. Hilprecht. Philadelphia: A. J. Holman.

C. Clermont-Ganneau
1870a *La stèle de Mésa roi de Moab 896 av. J. C. — Lettre à M. le Cte de Vogüé par Chr. Clermont-Ganneau drogman-chancelier du consulat de France à Jerusalem.* Paris: Baudry.
1870b The Moabite Stone. *The Athenaeum* #2219 for 7 May 1870 at p. 613.
1870c M. Ganneau's Letter to the 'Times.' *Quarterly Statement of the Palestine Exploration Fund* #5 for 1 April 1870 at pp. 175–76.
1887 La stèle de Mésa. *Journal Asiatique*, 8ième serie 9:72–86.

R. Dussaud
1912 *Les monuments palestiniens et judaïques.* Paris: Leroux.

J. Finegan
1946 *Light from the Ancient Past.* Princeton: Princeton University Press.

D. N. Freedman
1964 A Second Mesha Inscription. *Bulletin of the American Schools of Oriental Research* 175: 50–51.

C. D. Ginsburg
1871 *The Moabite Stone*[2]. London: Reeves and Turner.

H. Gressman
1927 *Altorientalische Bilder zum Alten Testament.* Berlin: De Gruyter.

C. L. Irby and J. Mangels
1823 *Travels in Egypt and Nubia, Syria and Asia Minor During the Years 1817 and 1818.* London: T. White.

W. Keller
1956 *The Bible as History.* New York: Morrow.

R. Kittel
1927 *Het Oude Testament in het licht der nieuwere onderzoekingen.* Zeist: J. Ploegsma.

F. A. Klein
1870 The Original Discovery of the Moabite Stone. *Quarterly Statement of the Palestine Exploration Fund* #6 for 30 June 1870 at pp. 281–83, 382.
1876 The Moabite Stone. *The Athenaeum* #2546 for 12 August 1876 at p. 210.

O. Meyer
1870 Bericht [16 March 1870]. *Zeitschrift der Deutschen Morgenländischen Gesellschaft* 24: 236–37.

J. C. Muir
1937 *His Truth Endureth.* Philadelphia: National Publishing Company.

A. Noordtzij
1931 *Gods woord en der eeuwen getuigenis*[2]. Kampen: J. H. Kok.

G. F. Owen
1961 *Archaeology and the Bible.* New York: Fleming H. Revell.

J. H. Petermann
1870 Über die Auffindung der moabitischen Inschrift des Königs Mesa. *Zeitschrift der Deutschen Morgenländischen Gesellschaft* 24 at p. 640.

I. M. Price; O. R. Sellers; and E. L. Carlson
1958 *The Monuments and the Old Testament.* Philadelphia: Judson Press.

A. H. Sayce
1929 Moabite Stone. Vol. 3, p. 2071 in *The International Standard Bible Encyclopaedia.* New York: Howard-Severance.

K. Schlottmann
1870 Additamenta über die Inschrift Mesas. *Zeitschrift der Deutschen Morgenländischen Gesellschaft* 24 at p. 647.

G. A. Smith
1907 *The Historical Geography of the Holy Land.* New York: A. C. Armstrong.

C. Warren
1870a Captain Warren's First Account of the Inscription from Moab. *Quarterly Statement of the Palestine Exploration Fund* #5 for 1 April 1870 at p. 169.
1870b Captain Warren's Fuller Account of the Moabite Stone, Received March 28, 1870. *Quarterly Statement of the Palestine Exploration Fund* #5 for 1 April 1870 at p. 180.
1870c Report. *Quarterly Statement of the Palestine Exploration Fund* #6 for 30 June 1870 at p. 346.

R. J. Williams
1962 Moabite Stone. Vol. 3, pp. 419–20 in *The Interpreter's Dictionary of the Bible,* ed. G. A. Buttrick et al. Nashville: Abingdon.

G. E. Wright
1957 *Biblical Archaeology.* Philadelphia: Westminster.

Ammonite Personal Names in the Context of the West Semitic Onomasticon

Kent P. Jackson
Brigham Young University, Provo, Utah

Introduction

Recent textual discoveries in Jordan have enabled scholars to identify the language of the Ammonites of the 1st millennium B.C.E. That language is now attested in about a dozen inscriptions of varying sizes and states of preservation and over sixty seals (cf. Jackson 1983 and references). Ammonite belongs to the Canaanite family of Northwest Semitic and demonstrates close affinities to Phoenician, Moabite, and Hebrew.

With the publication of an article dealing with the Amman Citadel Inscription, F. M. Cross (1969: 13–19) began a systematic analysis of the scripts used in the Ammonite texts. This analysis has found its most complete development in his work on some of the ostraca discovered in the 1970s at Tell Ḥisbān (e.g., Cross 1975; 1983) and in the work of his student L. G. Herr, whose doctoral dissertation included a paleographic study of the Ammonite seals (Herr 1978: 55–78 and figs. 34–45). Most of the larger texts and all of the seals identified by Herr fall within the period of time in which a national Ammonite script was used, ca. 700 to mid-6th century (cf. references cited above). It is now possible to distinguish the Ammonite script from all others and to trace devèlopments which took place during the period of its use. Thus with a certain degree of caution one can tentatively identify an inscription as Ammonite on the basis of the script type.

Unfortunately ancient seals, where most Canaanite names appear, provide little *linguistic* information which would enable scholars to identify the language in which they were written. Herr had to rely almost exclusively on script analysis in categorizing seals as proper to a given language. This is not a perfect system, but it simply is the best method available for such short texts. Since the great majority of the names in the following list are found on seals which, as mentioned, are identified as Ammonite solely on the basis of their script, it is to be recognized that there is a possibility of error in classification of the names.

The present study includes all of the personal names found in Ammonite texts. Each name is followed by references for all occurrences of the name, followed, wherever possible, by a suggested vocalization and translation. The dangers of translating and especially vocalizing ancient names in consonantal script are obvious. But supplying these reconstructions obviates the need to provide lengthy etymological discussions and explanations as to how I propose that the names should be understood. I must emphasize, however, that these data are suggested—and should be received—with utmost caution.

The emphasis in this study is on the distribution of names found in Ammonite texts among other Semitic languages. It will be shown that Ammonite names find their closest equivalents in the onomastica of the Northwest Semites and the pre-Islamic Arabic speakers. Each name is followed by a list of cognates and possible cognates, where available. The names listed first are those which appear to be exact consonantal equivalents of the given Ammonite names. These are followed by other possible cognates which are not identical but which show some (primarily lexical) similarities to the Ammonite examples. This list is not complete; some of the other languages have so many different names related to Ammonite names that it would be impractical to list them all. But representative cognates or possible cognates are cited for each of the languages for which onomastic information is available, along with one citation. (The transcription follows the authority cited.)

It is not my intention to suggest that all of the names listed are related to the Ammonite examples. Some of the lists in fact cite names which are mutually exclusive. For example, it is extremely unlikely that Ammonite *ḥṭš* is related to all three of the Safaitic names listed: *ḥṭš*, *ḥṭs*, and *ḫṭs*. But there is no reason to state that the Ammonite name cannot be cognate to any one of the three. Since the phonology of the pre-Islamic Arabic and Arabian dialects and much of their vocabulary are not understood fully, the cognates listed from those languages present the greatest possibility for error. I have chosen to list all of the names for which relationships with Ammonite examples are possible, based on our present understanding of the phonology and writing systems.

Other pitfalls in a study of this type also exist. In the absence of linguistic evidence to the contrary, one must assume that a name found in an inscription of a given language does in fact belong to the onomasticon of that language. Yet it is clear from this study and others like it that many names are found in several different Semitic languages and cannot be classified as part of one to the exclusion of another. Most Semitic peoples created names in the same ways (cf. Noth 1928; Tallqvist 1914; and any of the other Semitic name studies listed in the bibliography), and many of the divine elements found in personal names are common throughout much of the Semitic-speaking world. It is inevitable therefore to find names which are attested widely across language boundaries. The wisest method to follow in such cases is simply to call those which appear in Ammonite texts "Ammonite," those which appear in Ugaritic texts "Ugaritic," etc. A special problem of a similar nature is found in Aramaic texts from Egypt and Palestine. Many of the persons mentioned in the documents are Jewish, with names which undoubtedly are traceable to Hebrew. In keeping with the rationale described above, however, I have listed the names under Aramaic (cf. Kornfeld 1978: 19, who identifies the names simply as "semitisch"). I have only occasionally qualified a citation, in the line with the source, with an indication of "ethnic" origin or gender.

Abbreviations

In addition to the author references found in the bibliography, the name list contains the following abbreviations.

Languages
Akk (Akkadian), Amm (Ammonite), Amor (Amorite), Arab (Arabic), Aram (Aramaic), AWS (West Semitic found in first-millennium Akkadian sources), BH (Biblical Hebrew), BP (Byblian Phoenician), Eg (Egyptian), EH (Epigraphic Hebrew), Gk (Greek), H (Ḥaḍrami), Hat (Hatran Aramaic), L (Liḥyanite), M (Minean), Moab (Moabite), Nab (Nabatean), Pal (Palmyrene Aramaic), Phoen (Phoenician), PS (Proto-Semitic), Pun (Punic and Neo-Punic), Q (Qatabanian), S (Safaitic), Sa (Sabean), T (Thamudic), Ug (Ugaritic), WS (West Semitic).

Ammonite Texts
AS 1–61 (Ammonite seals in Jackson 1983), H 1–6 (Heshbon ostraca in Jackson 1983), NO (Nimrud ostracon; Naveh 1980; Jackson 1983), TS (Tell Siran inscription; Thompson and Zayadine 1973; Jackson 1983).

Other Texts
ArS (Aramaic seals in Herr 1978), Herod (Herodotus), HS (Hebrew seals in Herr 1978), *KAI*, Lach (Lachish ostraca; Diringer 1953), MS (Moabite seals in Herr 1978), Sam (Samaria ostraca; Reisner et al. 1924: 227–46).

Grammatical Abbreviations
DN (divine name), f (feminine), GN (geographical name), m (masculine), n (noun), NN (no name; generally the missing divine element in hypocoristica), obv (obverse), rev (reverse).

The Onomasticon

1. *ʾbyḥy* (f) (AS 40), **ʾabîḥay*, "My (Divine) Father lives."
Possible cognates: Aram *ʾbyḥy* (Kornfeld 1978: 37); Pal *ʾbyḥy* (Stark 1971: 1, 63). Cf. also BP *yḥmlk* (Benz 1972: 128); Ug *ḫa-ya-il*; *ḥyil* (Gröndahl 1967: 137).

2. *ʾbndb* (AS 49), **ʾabīnadab*, "My (Divine) Father is noble." Cf. *ʾyndb, ʾlndb, ndbʾl, ʿmndb*.
Possible cognates: BH *ʾăbînādāb* (1 Sam 7: 1); Phoen *ʾḥndb* (Benz 1972: 61); and sub #17, 68, 82.

3. *ʾdnnr* (AS 18), **ʾadonīnur*, "My Lord is light." Cf. *ʾlnr*.
Possible cognates: Cf. BH *nērîyāhû* (Jer 36: 14); EH *nryhw* (Lach 1.5); Pun *bʿlnr* (Benz 1972: 96); Ug *nûrī(NE)-^{d}ma-lik* (Gröndahl 1967: 166); *ʿmnr* (Gröndahl 1967: 109); and sub #18.

4. *ʾdnplṭ* (AS 19), **ʾadonīpillēṭ* (?), "My Lord has delivered." Cf. *plṭ, plṭw, plṭy*.
Possible cognates: Cf. sub # 89, 90, 91.

5. *ʾwʾ* (AS 47), "Refuge" (?).
Possible cognates: Cf. BH *ʾĕwî* (Num 31: 8); Pun *ʾwy* (Benz 1972: 60); S *ʾwy*; T *ʾwyt* (Harding 1971: 87).

6. *ʾyndb* (NO 13), **ʾaynadab*, "Where is nobility?" Cf. *ʾbndb, ʾlndb, ndbʾl, ʿmndb*.
Possible cognates: Cf. BH *ʾî-kābôd* (1 Sam 4: 21); *ʾîʿezer* (Num 26: 30); Phoen *ʾybʿl* (Benz 1972: 61); Amor *a-ya-da-du* (Huffmon 1965: 21); Ug *iybʿl* (Gordon 1965: 508); and sub #2, 17, 68, 82.

7. *ʾlʾ* (AS 14), **ʾilaʾ* (?).
Possible cognates: BH *ʾēlāʾ* (1 Kgs 4: 18); EH *ʾlʾ* (Sam 38.3). Cf. also Ug *ily* (Gröndahl 1967: 96); S *ʾlʾt* (Harding 1971: 63).

8. *ʾlʾwr* (H 3.5; AS 34); **ʾilīʾûr*, "My God is light."
Possible cognates: Cf. BH *ʾûrîʾēl* (1 Chr 6: 9); EH *ʾryhw* (HS 27); AWS *^{1}il-ur-ri* (Zadok 1978a: 59); Ug *uryy* (Gröndahl 1967: 103); Aram (?) *ʾwryw* (ArS 28); *ʾwry* (Kornfeld

1978: 39).

9. *ʾlʾmṣ* (AS 44), **ʾilʾamaṣ*, "ʾIl is strong."
Possible cognates: Cf. BH *ʾamṣî* (1 Chr 6: 31); *ʾămaṣyāhû* (2 Kgs 14: 1); Moab *ʾmṣ* (MS 1); Aram *ʾmṣ* (Kornfeld 1978: 41).

10. *ʾlʾmt* (AS 34), **ʾilīʾamt*, "My God is faithfulness."
Possible cognates: Cf. BH *ʾămitay* (2 Kgs 14: 25); Phoen *ʾlʾmn* (Benz 1972: 61).

11. *ʾlybr* (AS 38 obv and rev), **ʾilîbar*, "My God is pure."

12. *ʾlydn* (AS 11), **ʾilîdan* or **ʾilyadīn* (on the analogy of the AWS example cited below), "ʾIl will judge." Cf. *nnydn*.
Possible cognates: AWS [1]*DINGIR.MEŠ.ya-a-di-in* (Coogan 1976: 13). Cf. also BH *dānīʾēl* (Ezek 28: 3); Ug *dnil* (Gröndahl 1967: 96).

13. *ʾlyʿm* (AS 20), **ʾilîʿam*, "My God is a kinsman." Cf. *ʿmndb*.
Possible cognates: BH *ʾĕlîʿām* (2 Sam 11: 3); Pun *ʾlʿm* (Benz 1972: 61); L, Q *ʾlʿm* (Harding 1971: 68). Cf. also BH *ʿammîʾēl* (1 Chr 3: 5); and sub #82.

14. *ʾlyšʿ* (NO 11; AS 46; 54; 58), **ʾilyašaʿ* "ʾIl has delivered," or possibly **ʾilîšaʿ*, "My God is deliverance." Cf. *ʾlšʿ, yšʿ, yšʿʾl*.
Possible cognates: BH *ʾĕlîšāʿ* (1 Kgs 19: 16); EH *ʾlyšʿ* (Sam 1.4); L *ʾlyṯʿ* (Harding 1971: 73). Cf. also Amor *ì-lí-e-šu-uḫ* (Huffmon 1965: 24); and sub #53, 54.

15. *ʾlmg* (AS 61).

16. *ʾlmšl* (AS 42), **ʾilmašal*, "ʾIl has ruled."
Possible cognates: Cf. Phoen *mšl* (Benz 1972: 143); Pun *mlqrtmšl* (Benz 1972: 141).

17. *ʾlndb* (H 3.6; AS 11); **ʾilnadab*, "ʾIl is noble." Cf. *ʾbndb, ʾyndb, ndbʾl, ʿmndb*.
Possible cognates: Cf. BH *nādāb* (Exod 6: 23 and note *ʿammînādāb*, the name of this Nadab's maternal grandfather); AWS *kam-mu-su-na-ad-bi* (Moab; Benz 1972: 359); S, T, Sa *ndb* (Harding 1971: 584); and sub #2, 68, 82.

18. *ʾlnr* (NO 7, 8, 12), **ʾilīnur*, "My God is light." Cf. *ʾdnnr*.
Possible cognates: Cf. BH *ʾăbînēr* (1 Sam 14: 50); Aram *ʾl̊n̊ẘr̊ẙ* (ArS 46); and sub #3.

19. *ʾlntn* (AS 29), **ʾilnatan*, "ʾIl has given." Cf. *blntn, n]tnʾl*.
Possible cognates: BH *ʾelnātān* (2 Kgs 24: 8); EH *ʾlntn* (Lach 3.15); AWS [1]*DINGIR.MEŠ.na-*ta-nu (Coogan 1976: 13); Amor *ì-lí-na-tu-un* (Huffmon 1965: 25); Aram *ʾlntn* (ArS 110). Cf. also Phoen, Pun *ʾšmnytn* (Benz 1972: 71–72); and sub #31, 72.

20. *ʾlʿz* (AS 32; 55), **ʾilīʿuz*, "My God is strength." Cf. *ʿzʾ, ʿzyʾ[l*.
Possible cognates: H, M, Sa *ʾlʿz* (Harding 1971: 68). Cf. also BP *ʿzbʿl* (*KAI* 11); Pun *ʿštrtʿz* (Benz 1972: 175); Nab *ʾlʿzʾ* (DN) (Ingholt 1967: 42); and sub #77, 78.

21. *ʾlʿzr* (H 3.4; AS 37), **ʾilʿazar*, "ʾIl has helped." Cf. *ʿzrʾl*.
Possible cognates: BH *ʾelʿāzār* (Exod 6: 23); *ʾĕlîʿezer* (Gen 15: 2). Cf. also Phoen *ʾšmnʿzr* (*KAI* 13.2); *ʿzrbʿl* (*KAI* 49.28); Aram *ʿdr* (Kornfeld 1978: 66); and sub #79.

22. *ʾlrm* (H 3.2; AS 50), **ʾilīram*, "ʾIl is exalted."
Possible cognates: EH *ʾlrm* (HS 153); Amor *ì-lí-ra-am* (Huffmon 1965: 25); Ug *ilrm* (Gröndahl 1967: 95); *ilu-ra-mu* (Gröndahl 1967: 97); Aram *ʾlrm* (ArS 27); M, Q, Sa *ʾlrm* (Harding 1971: 66). Cf. also BH *yĕhôrām* (1 Kgs 22: 51); Phoen *bʿlrm* (Benz 1972: 98); BP *ʾḥrm* (*KAI* 1.1).

23. *ˀlšgb* (f) (AS 51), **ˀilśagab*, "ˀIl is exalted." Cf. *ḥmšgb*.
Possible cognate: Cf. BH *śĕgûb* (1 Chr 2: 21); and sub #47.

24. *ˀlšmʿ* (AS 5; 27 obv and rev; 33; 51), **ˀilšamaʿ*, "ˀIl has heard." Cf. *šmʿ*.
Possible cognates: BH *ˀĕlîšāmāʿ* (Num 1: 10); EH *ˀlšmʿ* (HS 148); H, M, Q, Sa *ˀlšmʿ* (Harding 1971: 67). Cf. also Phoen *bʿlšmʿ* (Benz 1972: 100); and sub #98.

25. *ˀlšʿ* (AS 44), **ˀilīšaʿ*, "My God is deliverance." Cf. *ˀlyšʿ*, *yšʿ*, *yšʿˀl*.
Possible cognates: Cf. sub #14, 53, 54.

26. *ˀltmk* (NO 14; AS 22), **ˀiltamak*, "ˀIl has supported." Cf. *tmk*[, *tmkˀ*, *tmkˀl*.
Possible cognates: Cf. sub #105.

27. *ˀmrˀl* (AS 45), **ˀamarˀil*, "ˀIl has commanded."
Possible cognates: Ug *amri*[*l*] (Gröndahl 1967: 99); S, T *ˀmrˀl* (Harding 1971: 75). Cf. also BH *ˀămaryāhû* (1 Chr 24: 23); *ˀimrî* (Neh 3: 2); EH *ˀmryhw* (HS 49); Ug *amrbʿl* (Gröndahl 1967: 99); Pal *ˀmry* (Stark 1971: 5); Nab *ˀmry* (Milik 1970: 159).

28. *bdˀl* (AS 7 obv and rev), **bōdˀil*. Cf. *bydˀl*.
Possible cognates: Ug *bdil* (Gröndahl 1967: 118); S *bdˀl* (Winnett and Harding 1978: 557). Cf. also EH *bdyw* (Sam 58.1); Phoen *bdbʿl* (*KAI* 17.2); *bdʿštrt* (*KAI* 15); Pun *bdmlqrt* (*KAI* 64.2); AWS [1]*ba-da-ya-a-ma* (Coogan 1976: 14); and sub #30.

29. *bṭš* (AS 53).

30. *bydˀl* (NO 3; AS 6; 60; 61), **bayadˀil*, "In/By the hand of ˀIl." Cf. *bdˀl*.
Possible cognates: Aram *bydˀl* (Kornfeld 1978: 43); Sa *bydˀl* (Harding 1971: 126). Cf. also Aram *bydyh* (Kornfeld 1978: 43); and sub #28.

31. *blntn* (NO 15), **bēlnatan*, "Bēl (< Akk < WS *baʿal*; cf. Albright 1958: 34) has given." Naveh (1980: 164) reads *bl ntn*, "a dissimilation of *bn ntn*." Cf. *ˀlntn*, *n*]*tnˀl*.
Possible cognates: AWS **bēlnatan* (Coogan 1976: 15). Cf. also Moab *bʿlntn* (MS 8); Phoen, Pun *bʿlytn* (Benz 1972: 94–96); Ug *bʿlytn* (Gordon 1965: 509); Aram *blhbh* (Kornfeld 1978: 43); Pal *blḥzy* (Stark 1971: 9); and sub #19, 72.

32. *bnny* (H 3.11), **binōnî* (so Cross 1983).
Possible cognates: Cf. BH *bĕnînû* (Neh 10: 14); *bunnî* (Neh 10: 16); EH *bn* (HS 81); Pun *bny* (Benz 1972: 89); Ug *bnn* (Gröndahl 1967: 119); Pal *bny* (Stark 1971: 10, 77); S *bny* (Winnett and Harding 1978: 561); S, M *bnn* (Harding 1971: 121).

33. *bʿrˀ* (AS 27 obv), **baʿaraˀ*.
Possible cognates: BH *baʿărāˀ* (f) (1 Chr 8: 8); EH *bʿrˀ* (Sam 47.1). Cf. also S *bʿr* (Harding 1971: 111).

34. *bʿš*[ˀ (H 1.6), **baʿšaˀ*.
Possible cognates: BH *baʿšāˀ* (1 Kgs 15: 16); S *bʿṯ* (Winnett and Harding 1978: 559). Cf. also Sa *bʿṯṯ* (Harding 1971: 109).

35. *bqš* (AS 41), **baqaš*, "NN has sought."
Possible cognates: Ug *bqš* (Gröndahl 1967: 120). Cf. also Phoen *bqšt* (f) (Benz 1972: 100); Sa *bqṯṯ* (Harding 1971: 113).

36. *brkˀl* (AS 53), **barakˀil*, "ˀIl has blessed."
Possible cognates: BH *bārakˀēl* (Job 32: 2); AWS **barīk-ˀil* (Zadok 1978b: 73); S *brkˀl* (Harding 1971: 102). Cf. also EH *brkyhw* (HS 8); Phoen, Pun *brkbʿl* (Benz 1972: 101); Pun *brkmlqrt* (*KAI* 77.1/2); AWS [1]*ba-rak-ku-ya-a-ma* (Coogan 1976: 16); Aram *brkyh* (Kornfeld

1978: 45).

37. *brq* (H 3.6), **baraq*, "Lightning."
Possible cognates: BH *bārāq* (Judg 4: 6); Ug *bu-ra-qu* (Gröndahl 1967: 120); *brq* (Gröndahl 1967: 121); Aram *brq* (ArS 78); Pal *brq* (Stark 1971: 12); L, S *brq* (Harding 1971: 102). Cf. also Pun *brqn* (Benz 1972: 101); Amor *bu-ur-qa-an* (Huffmon 1965: 28); S *brqt* (Winnett and Harding 1978: 558).

38. *gn*ʾ (NO 6).
Possible cognates: Cf. BH *gînat* (1 Kgs 16: 21); Phoen *gnn* (Benz 1972: 103); Aram *gnt* (ArS 85); S *jnʾt* (Harding 1971: 168).

39. *grgr* (AS 58).
Possible cognates: Perhaps reduplication of BH *gēr*, "sojourner." Cf. nouns: BH *gargar*, "berry" (Isa 17: 6); Arab *jirjīr*, "watercress"; Akk *gurgurru*, "craftsman" (*CAD* G: 138); names: EH *gr*ʾ (Sam 30.3); *gry* (HS 123); Phoen *gr*ʾ; Pun *gr* (Benz 1972: 103); S *jr* (Winnett and Harding 1978: 564).

40. *dblbs* (AS 57).

41. *h̊w*[. . .]*l* (H 3.2).

42. *hṣlʾl* (TS 2), **hiṣṣīlʾil*, "ʾIl has delivered."
Possible cognates: Cf. EH *hṣlyhw* (Lach 1.1); Aram *hṣwl* (Kornfeld 1978: 48).

43. *zkrʾl* (NO 9), **zakarʾil*, "ʾIl has remembered."
Possible cognates: T, H *d̲krʾl* (Harding 1971: 255). Cf. also BH *zikrî* (1 Chr 27: 16); *zĕkaryāhû* (2 Chr 29: 1); EH *zkr* (HS 89); *zkryw* (HS 138); Phoen *zkr* (Benz 1972: 109); Amor *za-ki-ru-um* (Huffmon 1965: 29); Aram *zkry* (ArS 39); Pal *dkry* (Stark 1971: 14, 83); L, S, M, Sa *d̲kr* (Harding 1971: 255).

44. *ḥgy* (NO 13), **ḥaggî*, "Festive."
Possible cognates: BH *ḥaggay* (Hag 1: 1); *ḥaggî* (Gen 46: 16); EH *ḥgy* (HS 41); Phoen *ḥgy* (Benz 1972: 109); AWS [1]*ḫa-ag-ga-a* (Coogan 1976: 23); Aram *ḥgy* (Kornfeld 1978: 49); Pal *ḥgy* (Stark 1971: 20); S, T, M, Sa *ḥjy* (Harding 1971: 178).

45. *ḥzʾl* (NO 5), **ḥazaʾil*, "ʾIl has seen."
Possible cognates: BH *ḥăzāʾēl* (Aram; 1 Kgs 19: 15); *ḥăzîʾēl* (1 Chr 23: 9); AWS *ḫa-za-ʾ-DINGIR.MEŠ* (Coogan 1976: 24).

46. *ḥṭš* (AS 8; 14), **ḥaṭṭūš*.
Possible cognates: BH *ḥaṭṭûš* (1 Chr 3: 22); S *ḥṭš* (Harding 1971: 175); S *ḥṭs* (Harding 1971: 193); S *ḥṭs* (Harding 1971: 223).

47. *ḥmšgb* (H 3.7), **ḥamīšagab*, "My (Divine) Father-in-Law is exalted." Cf. *ʾlšgb*.
Possible cognates: Cf. BH *ḥammûʾēl* (1 Chr 4: 26); Amor *ḫa-mi-i-ba-*[*a*]*l* (Huffmon 1965: 34); L, S *ḥmʾl* (Harding 1971: 199); and sub #23.

48. *ḥnʾ* (AS 60), **ḥanaʾ*, "Gracious." Cf. *ḥnn, ḥnnʾl*.
Possible cognates: Pun *ḥnʾ* (Benz 1972: 117–22); Aram *ḥnʾ* (Kornfeld 1978: 50); Pal *ḥnʾ* (f; Stark 1971: 23). Cf. also BH *ḥannâ* (1 Sam 1: 2); Pun *ḥnʾmlk* (Benz 1972: 122); AWS [1]*ḫi-in-ni-ʾ* (Coogan 1976: 25); Ug *ḥny* (Gordon 1965: 510); S, T *ḥny* (Harding 1971: 207); and sub #49, 50.

49. *ḥnn* (NO 10), **ḥanūn*, "Gracious." Cf. *ḥnʾ, ḥnnʾl*.
Possible cognates: BH *ḥānān* (1 Chr 11: 43); *ḥānûn* (Amm; 2 Sam 10: 1); EH *ḥnn* (HS 91; Sam

43.2); Phoen *ḥnn* (Benz 1972: 125); AWS [1]*ḫa-na-na;* [1]*ḫa-nun* (Coogan 1976: 24); Amor *ḫa-nu-nu* (Huffmon 1965: 35); Ug *ḥnn* (Gordon 1965: 510); Aram *ḥnn* (ArS 107); S, T, Sa *ḥnn* (Harding 1971: 206); and sub #48, 50.

50. *ḥnnʾl* (NO 2, 5; AS 52), **ḥananʾil*, "ʾIl is gracious." Cf. *ḥnʾ, ḥnn.*
Possible cognates: BH *ḥănanʾēl* (Jer 31: 38); Ug *ḥnnil* (Gröndahl 1967: 136); S *ḥnnʾl* (Harding 1971: 206). Cf. also EH *ḥnnyhw* (HS 44); Pun *ḥnbʿl* (*KAI* 68.2); AWS [1]*ḫa-na-ni-ya-a-ma* (Coogan 1976: 25); Aram *ḥnnyh* (Kornfeld 1978: 51); Pal *ḥnbl* (Stark 1971: 23); and sub #48, 49.

51. *ym̊n* (AS 1) **yamīn*, "Right hand."
Possible cognates: BH *yāmîn* (Num 26: 12); S *ymn* (Harding 1971: 684). Cf. also BH *yimnâ* (Gen 46: 17); Sa *ymnt* (Harding 1971: 685).

52. *ynḥm* (AS 40; 45), **yĕnaḥḥim*, "NN will comfort." Cf. *mnḥm, tnḥm.*
Possible cognates: Ug *ynḥm* (Gröndahl 1967: 165); Aram *ynḥm* (Kornfeld 1978: 54). Cf. also BH *naḥam* (1 Chr 4: 19); EH *nḥm* (HS 13); Amor *na-aḫ-ma-nu* (Huffmon 1965: 53); Ug *mnḥm* (Gröndahl 1967: 165); Aram *nḥm* (ArS 29); and sub #63, 106.

53. *yšʿ* (AS 56), **yašaʿ*, "NN has delivered." Cf. *ʾlyšʿ, ʾlšʿ, yšʿʾl* (cf. Sawyer 1975: 76–78).
Possible cognates: L, S, H, M, Sa *yṯʿ* (Harding 1971: 658); M *yšʿ* (Harding 1971: 669). Cf. also BH *yišʿî* (1 Chr 2: 31); Phoen *yšʿʾ* (Benz 1972: 129); Amor *ya-šu-ḫa* (f; Huffmon 1965: 48); Aram *yšʿʾ* (ArS 21).

54. *yšʿʾl* (AS 48), **yašaʿʾil*, "ʾIl has delivered." Cf. *ʾlyšʿ, ʾlšʿ, yšʿ.*
Possible cognates: Ug *yṯil* (?) (Gröndahl 1967: 147); M, Sa *yṯʿʾl* (Harding 1971: 658). Cf. BH *yĕšaʿyāhû* (Isa 1:1); EH *hwšʿyhw* (Lach 3.1); *yšʿyhw* (HS 49); Aram *yšʿyh* (Kornfeld 1978: 55); and sub #14, 53.

55. *ytb* (H 1.9)
Possible cognate: S, T *ytb* (Harding 1971: 657).

56. *ytyr* (AS 29).

57. *mgrʾl* (AS 28), **magarʾil*, "ʾIl has thrown."
Possible cognates: Cf. Pun *mgrbʿl* (Benz 1972: 137); Aram *mgr* (Kornfeld 1978: 57); S *mjr* (Harding 1971: 529).

58. *mḥm* (NO 7), probably *m<n>ḥm, q.v.*

59. *m]kʾl* (NO 12), **mīkaʾil*, "Who is like ʾIl?" Cf. *mkmʾl, mngʾnrt.*
Possible cognates: BH *mîkāʾēl* (Num 13: 13); cf. EH *mykyhẘ* (HS 119); AWS [1]*mi-ka-ya-a-ma* (Coogan 1976: 28); Aram *mykyh* (Kornfeld 1978: 57); Pal *mkbl* (Stark 1971: 31, 94); and sub #62.

60. *mkmʾl* (AS 35), **mī-kamō-ʾil*, "Who is like ʾIl?" Cf. *m]kʾl, mngʾnrt.*
Possible cognates: Cf. sub #59.

61. *m̊lkʾl* (H 3.4), **malkīʾil*, "My king is ʾIl."
Possible cognates: BH *malkîʾēl* (Gen 46: 17); Pal *mlkʾl* (Stark 1971: 32, 95); S, T *mlkʾl* (Harding 1971: 565). Cf. also Amm *mlkm* (AS 9); BH *malkîyāhû* (Jer 38: 6); EH *mlkyhw* (HS 112); Pun *mlky* (Benz 1972: 139); Amor *ì-lí-ma-lik* (Huffmon 1965: 25); Ug *ili-milku* (Gröndahl 1967: 157); *ilmlk* (Gröndahl 1967: 158); Aram *mlkyh* (Kornfeld 1978: 58); Nab *mlkw* (Ingholt 1967: 47).

62. *mngʾnrt* (AS 36), "Who is like Inurta?" Cf. *m]kʾl, mkmʾl.* From Akk *mannu-kī-inurta*

(Tadmor 1965). Cf. also Aram *mngʾsr* < Akk *mannu-kī-ašur* (*KAI* 234.Rs.4); and sub #59.

63. *mnḥm* (NO 3, 6, 11; AS 1; 3; 17; 28; 32; 38), **mĕnaḥḥim*, "Comforter." Cf. *ynḥm, tnḥm.*
Possible cognates: BH *mĕnaḥēm* (2 Kgs 15: 14); EH *mnḥm* (HS 30); Phoen, Pun *mnḥm* (Benz 1972: 141); AWS **minaḥḥem* (Zadok 1978b: 74); **munaḥḥim* (Zadok 1978a: 59); Ug *mnḥm* (Gröndahl 1967: 165); Aram *mnḥm* (ArS 55); T *mnḥm*; Q *mnḥm* (Harding 1971: 568); and sub #52, 106.

64. *mnr* (AS 30).
Possible cognates: Pun *mnr* (Benz 1972: 142); S, Sa *mnrt* (Harding 1971: 568).

65. *mqnmlk* (AS 10), **miqnēmilk*, "Property of the (Divine) King."
Possible cognates: Phoen *mqnmlk* (Benz 1972: 143). Cf. also BH *miqnēyāhû* (1 Chr 15: 18); EH *mqnyhw* (HS 116); Ug *qnmlk* (Gröndahl 1967: 176); Aram *qnyʾ* (Kornfeld 1978: 70).

66. *mrʾl* (AS 47).
Possible cognates: Ug *uruma-ra-el* (GN); *mril* (GN) (Gröndahl 1967: 160); S *mrʾl* (Harding 1971: 537). Cf. also EH *mrbʿl* (Sam 2.7); Pun *mrrbʿl* (Benz 1972: 143).

67. *mrʿ* (AS 21).

68. *ndbʾl* (H 1.3; NO 10; AS 7 obv and rev; 12; 25; 37; 41), **nadabʾil*, "ʾIl is noble." Cf. *ʾbndb, ʾyndb, ʾlndb, ʿmndb.*
Possible cognates: Pal *ndbʾl* (Stark 1971: 39). Cf. also BH *nādāb* (Exod 6: 23); *nĕdabyâ* (1 Chr 3: 18); Ug *ndbn* (Gröndahl 1967: 164); Aram *ndby* (Kornfeld 1978: 62); and sub #2, 17, 82.

69. *nnydn* (H 5.5), **nanaydan*, "Nanay has judged." Cf. *ʾlydn.*
Possible cognates: Cf. Aram *nnyḥm* (Kornfeld 1978: 62); Pal *nny* (DN) (Ingholt 1967: 48); Hat *brnny* (*KAI* 237.1); and sub #12.

70. *nʿmʾl* (H 1.3), **naʿīmʾil*, "ʾIl is pleasant."
Possible cognates: Phoen *nʿmʾl* (Benz 1972: 147); S *nʿmʾl* (Harding 1971: 594). Cf. also BH *nāʿam* (1 Chr 4: 15); *naʿămâ* (Amm; 1 Kgs 14: 21); Ug **naʿam-rašap* (Gröndahl 1967: 163); Pal *nʿm* (Stark 1971: 39).

71. *nqr* (H 3.5).
Possible cognate: S *nqr* (Harding 1971: 597).

72. *n]tnʾl* (H 6), **natanʾil*, "ʾIl has given." Cf. *ʾlntn, blntn.*
Possible cognates: BH *nĕtanʾēl* (Num 1: 8); AWS **natan-ʾil* (Zadok 1978b: 74). Cf. also EH *ntnyhw* (HS 120); Phoen *ytnbʿl* (*KAI* 43.2); Pun *ytnʾl* (Benz 1972: 129); L *ntnbʿl* (Harding 1971: 581); and sub #19, 31.

73. *smk* (AS 17), **samak*, "NN has supported."
Possible cognates: EH *smk* (HS 17); L, S, T *smk* (Harding 1971: 329). Cf. also BH *sĕmakyāhû* (1 Chr 26: 7); EH *smkyhw* (HS 78; Lach 4.6); Aram *smky* (Kornfeld 1978: 64).

74. *ʿbd* (AS 39), **ʿabd*, "Servant." Cf. *ʿbdʾ.*
Possible cognates: BH *ʿebed* (Judg 9: 26); *ʿōbēd* (Ruth 4: 22); Pun *ʿbd* (Benz 1972: 148); Aram *ʿbd* (*KAI* 207); L, S, T, M, Sa *ʿbd* (Harding 1971: 397); and sub #75.

75. *ʿbdʾ* (AS 50), **ʿabdaʾ*, "Servant." Cf. *ʿbd.*
Possible cognates: BH *ʿabdāʾ* (1 Kgs 4: 6); EH *ʿbdʾ* (Sam 57.1); BP *ʿbdʾ* (*KAI* 8); Pun *ʿbdʾ* (*KAI* 161.11); AWS *1ab-da-ʾ* (Coogan 1976: 31); Ug *ab-du* (Gröndahl 1967: 105); Aram *ʿbdʾ* (*KAI* 236.Rs.2); Pal *ʿbdʾ* (Stark 1971: 41, 102); S *ʿbdʾ* (Harding 1971: 397). Cf. also EH *ʿbdy* (HS 13); Ug *ʿbdy* (Gröndahl 1967: 106); Aram *ʿbdy* (Kornfeld 1978: 65); Nab

ʿbydw (Ingholt 1967: 48); and sub #74.

76. *ʿdʾl* (AS 56), **ʿadīʾil.*
Possible cognates: BH *ʿădîʾēl* (1 Chr 4: 36); S, Sa *ʿdʾl* (Harding 1971: 409). Cf. also BH *ʿădāyāhû* (2 Chr 23: 1); EH *ʿdyhw* (HS 55); Pun *ʿdbʿl* (Benz 1972: 165); Ug *ʿdmlk*; *ʿdršp* (Gröndahl 1967: 106); Aram *ʿdyh* (Kornfeld 1978: 65).

77. *ʿzʾ* (NO 4), **ʿuzzaʾ*, "Strength." Cf. *ʾlʿz, ʿzʾl.*
Possible cognates: BH *ʿuzzāʾ* (2 Sam 6: 3); EH *ʿzʾ* (HS 125); Phoen *ʿzʾ* (Benz 1972: 165); Aram *ʿzʾ* (ArS 99). Cf. also BH *ʿuzzâ* (1 Chr 6: 14); Pal *ʿzy* (Stark 1971: 44, 105); S *ʿz* (Harding 1971: 417); and sub #20, 78.

78. *ʿzyʾ[l* (H 5.2), **ʿuzzîʾil*, "My strength is ʾIl." Cf. *ʾlʿz, ʿzʾ.*
Possible cognates: BH *ʿuzzîʾēl* (Exod 6: 18); *ʿăzîʾēl* (1 Chr 15: 20); L, Sa *ʿzʾl* (Harding 1971: 417); H *ʿḏdʾl* (Harding 1971: 412). Cf. also EH *ʿzyw* (HS 4); BP *ʿzbʿl* (*KAI* 11); Ug *ʿzn* (Gröndahl 1967: 112); and sub #20, 77.

79. *ʿzrʾl* (H 3.3; AS 55), **ʿazarʾil*, "ʾIl has helped." Cf. *ʾlʿzr.*
Possible cognates: BH *ʿăzarʾēl* (1 Chr 12: 7); *ʿazrîʾēl* (Jer 36: 26); T *ʿzrʾl* (Harding 1971: 418); L, S *ʿḏrʾl* (Harding 1971: 412). Cf. also EH *ʿzryhw* (HS 10); Phoen *ʿzrbʿl* (*KAI* 49.28); Ug *a-zi-ru* (Gröndahl 1967: 113); Aram *ʿzryh* (Kornfeld 1978: 66; for the problem of PS *ḏ* > *d/z* in Eg Aram texts, cf. Silverman 1969: 694); Nab *ʿdrw* (Milik 1970: 148); and sub #21.

80. *ʿkbr* (NO 15), **ʿakbor*, "Mouse."
Possible cognates: BH *ʿakbôr* (Gen 36: 38); EH *ʿkbr* (HS 94); Phoen, Pun *ʿkbr* (Benz 1972: 171); Aram *ʿkbr* (Kornfeld 1978: 66); M *ʿkbr* (Harding 1971: 428).

81. *ʿlyh* (f) (AS 52), **ʿalīyah* (?).
Possible cognates: Aram *ʿlyh* (Kornfeld 1978: 66). Cf. also BH *ʿēlî* (1 Sam 1: 3); Ug *ʿly* (Gröndahl 1967: 108); Pal *ʿlyt* (f; Stark 1971: 45); L, S, T, Q *ʿly*; T, Q *ʿlyt* (Harding 1971: 433).

82. *ʿmndb* (TS 1, 3; AS 18; 19), **ʿammīnadab*, "My (Divine) Kinsman is noble." Cf. *ʾbndb, ʾyndb, ʾlyʿm, ʾlndb, ndbʾl.*
Possible cognates: BH *ʿammînādāb* (Exod 6: 23). Cf. also Ug *am-mu-ra-pi* (Gröndahl 1967: 109); and sub #2, 17, 68, for *ndb*; sub #13 for *ʿm*.

83. *ʿmsʾl* (AS 4; 12; 22), **ʿamasʾil*, "ʾIl has carried."
Possible cognates: Cf. BH *ʿāmôs* (Amos 1: 1); *ʿămasyâ* (2 Chr 17: 16); Phoen *ʿms* (Benz 1972: 172); Ug *ʿms* (Gröndahl 1967: 109); Aram *ʿms* (Kornfeld 1978: 67); S *ʿms* (Winnett and Harding 1978: 597).

84. *ʿnʾl* (NO 1, 2), **ʿanaʾil*, "ʾIl has answered."
Possible cognates: AWS *ˡa-na-ʾ-DINGIR.MEŠ* (Coogan 1976: 32); Ug *ʿnil* (Gordon 1965: 512); S *ʿnʾl* (Harding 1971: 444). Cf. also BH *ʿănāyâ* (Neh 8: 4); EH *ʿnnyhẘ* (HS 24); Pun *ʿnbʿl* (Benz 1972: 173).

85. *ʿnmwt* (f) (AS 57).
Possible cognates: Cf. Pal *ʿnmw* (Stark 1971: 45); Nab *ʿnmw* (Milik 1970: 142); T *ʿnm*; S, Sa *ʿnmt* (Harding 1971: 445); S, T, Q *ǵnm;* S, T *ǵnmt* (Harding 1971: 458).

86. *ʿqb* (H 3.10), **ʿaqūb* or **ʿaqab*, "NN has protected."
Possible cognates: BH *ʿaqqûb* (1 Chr 3: 24); AWS *ˡa-qu-bu* (Coogan 1976: 32); Aram *ʿqb* (Kornfeld 1978: 67); S, H, M, Sa *ʿqb* (Harding 1971: 426). Cf. also AWS *ˡaq-qab-bi-DINGIR.MEŠ* (Coogan 1976: 32); Amor *ḫa-aq-ba-an* (Huffmon 1965: 36); Pal *ʿqby* (Stark

1971: 45, 107); Hat *ʿqwbʾ* (*KAI* 241.1).

87. *ʿšnʾl* (AS 2), **ʿašanʾil*, "ʾIl is smoke" (?).

88. *pdʾl* (AS 6; 43), **padaʾil* or **padōʾil* (Cross 1974: 94), "ʾIl has redeemed."
Possible cognates: BH *pĕdahʾēl* (Num 34: 28); AWS [1]*pu-du-ilu* (Esarhaddon Nineveh A Text at V.62, in Borger 1956: 60); S *fdʾl* (Harding 1971: 463). Cf. also EH *pdyhw* (HS 132); Pun *pdʿ*, *pdy* (Benz 1972: 175); AWS [1]*pa-da-ʾ-ya-a-ma* (Coogan 1976: 33); Ug *pa-di-ya; pdy* (Gröndahl 1967: 171); Aram *pdh* (ArS 52); *pdyʾ* (Kornfeld 1978: 68).

89. *plṭ* (AS 26), **peleṭ*, "Deliverance." Cf. *ʾdnplṭ*, *plṭw*, *plṭy*.
Possible cognates: BH *peleṭ* (1 Chr 2: 47); Ug *plṭ* (Gröndahl 1967: 173); S *flt* (Harding 1971: 470); S, T *flṭ* (Harding 1971: 471). Cf. also BP *plṭbʿl* (*KAI* 11); AWS [1]*pa-la-ṭa-*[*a-a*] (Coogan 1967: 33); and sub #90, 91.

90. *plṭw* (AS 9), **palṭô*, "Deliverance." Cf. *ʾdnplṭ*, *plṭ*, *plṭy*.
Possible cognates: Aram *plṭw* (Kornfeld 1978: 68). Cf. also sub #89, 91.

91. *plṭy* (AS 16), **palṭî*, "Deliverance." Cf. *ʾdnplṭ*, *plṭ*, *plṭw*.
Possible cognates: BH *palṭî* (Num 13: 9). Cf. also sub # 89, 90.

92. *psmy* (H 5.4), **psammî*.
Possible cognates: Cf. Aram (< Eg) *psmy* (Kornfeld 1978: 91); note also Gk *Psammis* (Herod 2.160.1).

93. *pr̊š* (H 3.7), **paraš*, "Horseman"(?).
Possible cognates: BH *pereš* (1 Chr 7: 16); Ug *prṯ* (Gordon 1965: 471); S *frṯ*; L, S, Sa *frs*; T *frš* (Harding 1971: 465).

94. *ṣnr* (NO 9).
Possible cognates: Phoen, Pun *ṣnr* (Benz 1972: 177); Ug *ṣnr* (Gordon 1965: 512). Cf. also T *ṣnrt* (Harding 1971: 377), and perhaps BH nm *ṣinnôr* (2 Sam 5: 8).

95. *rpʾ* (H 5.3), **rapaʾ*, "NN has healed."
Possible cognates: BH *rāpāʾ* (1 Chr 8: 2); *rāpûʾ* (Num 13: 9); EH *rpʾ* (HS 63; Sam 24.2); Pun *rpʾ* (Benz 1972: 179); Pal *rpʾ* (Stark 1971: 50, 112); S, T, Sa *rfʾ* (Harding 1971: 283). Cf. also Ug *rpan* (Gröndahl 1967: 180); Aram *rpy* (Kornfeld 1978: 71).

96. *šbʾl* (NO 4; AS 15).
Possible cognates: BH *šĕbûʾēl* (1 Chr 23: 16); Ug *ṯbil* (Gröndahl 1967: 200); S *sbʾl* (Harding 1971: 308); S *šbʾl* (Harding 1971: 337); Sa *ṯbʾl* (Harding 1971: 142).

97. *šwḥr* (AS 59).
Possible cognates: EH *šḥr* (HS 32); Ug *sḫr* (Gröndahl 1967: 184); S *ṯḥr* (Harding 1971: 143); S, M, Sa *sḥr* (Harding 1971: 311); S, T, *sḫr* (Harding 1971: 312); M, Q *šḫr*; S *šḫr* (Harding 1971: 342). Cf. also BH *šĕḥaryāh* (1 Chr 8: 26); Pun *šḥrbʿl* (Benz 1972: 180); Ug *ilšḥr*; *ʿbdšḥr* (Gröndahl 1967: 192); Pal *šḥrʾ*; *šḥrw* (Stark 1971: 51); Hat *šḥrw* (DN) (Ingholt 1967: 50).

98. *šmʿ* (AS 13; 23), **šamaʿ*, "NN has heard." Cf. *ʾlšmʿ*.
Possible cognates: BH *šāmāʿ* (1 Chr 11: 44); EH *šmʿ* (HS 1); S, M, Sa *smʿ* (Harding 1971: 328). Cf. also Phoen *šmʿʾ* (Benz 1972: 181); AWS **šamʿōn* (Zadok 1978b: 74); Ug *šmʿy*; *šmʿn* (Gröndahl 1967: 194); Aram *šmʿy* (ArS 38); *šmʿn* (Kornfeld 1978: 74); and sub #24.

99. *šmʿl* (AS 9), **šamaʿ*<ʾ>*il*(?).

100. *šmš*ᵓ*l* (H 3.8), **šamšīᵓil*, "Šamš is God" or "ᵓIl is my sun."
Possible cognates: S *šmsᵓl* (Harding 1971: 358). Cf. also BH *šimšay* (Ezra 4: 8); *šimšôn* (Judg 13: 24); Phoen *ᵓdnšmš* (Benz 1972: 59); AWS **šamaš-naṭar* (Zadok 1978b: 74); Ug *špšmlk*; *ilšpš* (Gröndahl 1967: 195); Aram *šmšy* (Kornfeld 1978: 75); Nab *šmšw* (Milik 1970: 159).

101. *šʿl* (AS 46), **šūʿal*.
Possible cognates: BH *šûʿāl* (1 Chr 7: 36); EH *šʿl* (HS 140); Ug *ṯʿl* (Gröndahl 1967: 198); S, T *ṯʿl* (Harding 1971: 146); S *sʿl* (Harding 1971: 320); S *šʿl* (Harding 1971: 351).

102. *šql* (H 3.9), "Shekel."
Possible cognate: S *šqlt* (Harding 1971: 353).

103. *tmk*[(AS 10). Cf. *ᵓltmk, tmkᵓ, tmkᵓl*.

104. *tmkᵓ* (AS 25), **tamkaᵓ*, "Support." Cf. *ᵓltmk, tmk*[, *tmkᵓl*.
Possible cognates: Cf. sub #105.

105. *tmkᵓl* (H 4.3; AS 16; 24), **tamakᵓil*, "ᵓIl has supported." Cf. *ᵓltmk, tmk*[, *tmkᵓ*.
Possible cognates: Phoen *tmkᵓl* (Benz 1972: 186); Aram *tmkᵓl* (ArS 10).

106. *tnḥm* (AS 3), **tĕnaḥḥim*, "You will comfort." Cf. *ynḥm, mnḥm*.
Possible cognates: EH *tnḥm* (HS 12). Cf. also BH *tanḥūmet* (2 Kgs 25: 23); and sub # 52, 63.

Morphology of Ammonite Names

The Ammonite onomasticon exhibits many of the same patterns of construction found by Noth in Hebrew (1928: 11–41) and by other scholars dealing with different Semitic languages (cf. especially Gröndahl 1967: 24–85; Benz 1972: 206–39; Kornfeld 1978: 20–25; Huffmon 1965: 61–152). The Ammonite evidence presents nothing new in this regard.

Subject + adjective or perfect verb

In this category I have included names containing active and stative verbs as well as adjectives, since distinguishing between these in unvocalized names is not possible (cf. Kornfeld 1978: 22; Huffmon 1965: 87). Theophoric element (or equivalent) first: *ᵓbyḥy, ᵓbndb, ᵓdnplṭ, ᵓlᵓmṣ, ᵓlybr, ᵓlyšʿ, ᵓlmšl, ᵓlndb, ᵓlntn, ᵓlʿzr, ᵓlrm, ᵓlšgb, ᵓlšmʿ, ᵓltmk, blntn, ḥmšgb, nnydn, ʿmndb*. Theophoric element last: *ᵓmrᵓl, brkᵓl, hw*[. . .]*l (?), hṣlᵓl, zkrᵓl, ḥzᵓl, ḥnnᵓl, yšʿᵓl, mgrᵓl, ndbᵓl, nʿmᵓl, n*]*tnᵓl, ʿzrᵓl, ʿmsᵓl, ʿnᵓl, pdᵓl, šbᵓl, šmʿl (?), tmkᵓl*.

Subject + imperfect verb

Ammonite bears out the observation that names containing prefixing verbs are much less common than those with suffixing forms (Kornfeld 1978: 21). Our corpus includes only one: *ᵓlydn*. The verb in this name could also be read as a perfect, rendering the vocalization **ᵓilîdan*.

Subject + nominal predicate

Theophoric element (or equivalent) first: *ᵓdnnr, ᵓlᵓwr, ᵓlᵓmt, ᵓlyʿm, ᵓlnr, ᵓlʿz, ᵓlšʿ*. Theophoric element last: *mlkᵓl, mrᵓl, ʿdᵓl, ʿzyᵓ*[*l, ʿšnᵓl, šmšᵓl*.

Single element names and hypocristica

ʾwʾ, ʾlʾ, bṭš, bnny, bʿrʾ, bʿš[ʾ, bqš, brq, gnʾ, grgr, dblbs, ḥgy, ḥṭš, ḥnʾ, ḥnn, ym̊n, ynḥm, yšʿ, ytb, ytyr, mnḥm, mnr, mrʿ, nqr, smk, ʿbd, ʿbdʾ, ʿzʾ, ʿkbr, ʿlyh, ʿnmwt, ʿqb, plṭ, plṭw, plṭy, psmy, pr̊š, ṣnr, rpʾ, šwḥr, šmʿ, šʿl, šql, tmkʾ, tnḥm.

Construct phrase names

bdʾl, bydʾl, mqnmlk.

Question phrase names

ʾyndb, m]kʾl, mkmʾl, mngʾnrt.

Hypocoristic endings

ʾ (*ʾwʾ, ʾlʾ, bʿrʾ, gnʾ, ḥnʾ, ʿbdʾ, ʿzʾ, tmkʾ*)
w (*plṭw*)
y (*bnny* [?], *ḥgy, plṭy*)

Indices

1. *Ammonite names with multiple attestations*

#8, 11 (same seal), 14, 17, 18, 20, 21, 22, 24, 26, 28 (same seal), 30, 46, 50, 52, 63, 68, 79, 82, 83, 84, 88, 96, 98, 105

2. *Divine names and epithets* (used in first position unless otherwise indicated)

ʾb #1, 2
ʾdn #3, 4
ʾl #7?, 8, 9, 10, 11, 12, 13, 14, 15?, 16, 17, 18, 19, 20, 21, 22, 23, 24, 25, 26 second position: #27, 28, 30, 36, 42, 43, 45, 50, 54, 57, 59, 60, 61, 66?, 68, 70, 72, 76, 78, 79, 83, 84, 87, 88, 96, 99?, 100, 105
ʾnrt second position: #62
bl #31
ḥm #47
mlk #61 second position: #65
nny #69
ʿm #82 second position: #13
šmš #100

3. *Comparative onomastic material cited*

Bronze Age Material
Amorite #6, 14, 19, 22, 37, 43, 47, 49, 52, 53, 61, 86
Ugaritic #1, 3, 6, 7, 8, 12, 22, 27, 28, 31, 32, 35, 37, 48, 49, 50, 52, 54, 61, 63, 65, 66, 68, 70, 75, 76, 78, 79, 81, 82, 83, 84, 88, 89, 93, 94, 95, 96, 97, 98, 100, 101

Iron Age Material: Canaanite
Biblical Hebrew #2, 3, 5, 6, 7, 8, 9, 10, 12, 13, 14, 17, 18, 19, 21, 22, 23, 24, 27, 32, 33, 34, 36, 37, 38, 43, 44, 45, 46, 47, 48, 49, 50, 51, 52, 53, 54, 59, 61, 63, 65, 68, 70, 72, 73, 74, 75, 76, 77, 78, 79, 80, 81, 82, 83, 84, 86, 88, 89, 91, 93, 94, 95, 96, 97, 98, 100, 101, 106
Epigraphic Hebrew #3, 7, 8, 14, 19, 22, 24, 27, 28, 32, 33, 36, 39, 42, 43, 44, 49, 50, 52, 54, 59,

61, 63, 65, 66, 72, 73, 75, 76, 77, 78, 79, 80, 84, 88, 95, 97, 98, 101, 106
Byblian Phoenician #1, 20, 22, 75, 78, 89
Other Phoenician, Punic, and Neo-Punic #2, 3, 5, 6, 10, 13, 16, 19, 20, 21, 22, 24, 28, 31, 32, 35, 36, 37, 38, 39, 43, 44, 48, 49, 50, 53, 57, 61, 63, 64, 65, 66, 70, 72, 74, 75, 76, 77, 79, 80, 83, 84, 88, 94, 95, 97, 98, 100, 105
Moabite #9, 31

Iron Age Material: Aramaic
Hatran #69, 86, 97
Nabatean #20, 27, 61, 75, 79, 85, 100
Palmyrene #1, 27, 31, 32, 37, 43, 44, 48, 50, 59, 61, 68, 70, 75, 77, 81, 85, 86, 95, 97
Other Aramaic #1, 8, 9, 18, 19, 21, 22, 30, 31, 36, 37, 38, 42, 43, 44, 48, 49, 50, 52, 53, 54, 57, 59, 61, 62, 63, 65, 68, 69, 73, 74, 75, 76, 77, 79, 80, 81, 83, 86, 88, 90, 92, 95, 98, 100, 105

Iron Age Material: (North) Arabic
Liḥyanite #13, 14, 37, 43, 47, 53, 72, 73, 74, 78, 79, 81, 93
Safaitic #5, 7, 17, 27, 28, 32, 33, 34, 36, 37, 38, 39, 43, 44, 46, 47, 48, 49, 50, 51, 53, 55, 57, 61, 64, 66, 70, 71, 73, 74, 75, 76, 77, 79, 81, 83, 84, 85, 86, 88, 89, 93, 95, 96, 97, 98, 100, 101, 102
Thamudic #5, 17, 27, 43, 44, 48, 49, 55, 61, 63, 73, 74, 79, 81, 85, 89, 93, 94, 95, 97, 101

Iron Age Material: South Arabian
Ḥaḍrami #20, 24, 43, 53, 78, 86
Minean #20, 22, 24, 32, 43, 44, 53, 54, 74, 80, 86, 97, 98
Qatabanian #13, 22, 24, 63, 81, 85, 97
Sabean #17, 20, 22, 24, 30, 34, 35, 43, 44, 49, 51, 53, 54, 64, 74, 76, 78, 85, 86, 93, 95, 96, 97, 98

Iron Age Material: AWS
#8, 12, 17, 19, 28, 31, 36, 44, 45, 48, 49, 50, 59, 63, 72, 75, 84, 86, 88, 89, 98, 100

References

Albright, W. F.
1958 An Ostracon from Calah and the North-Israelite Diaspora. *Bulletin of the American Schools of Oriental Research* 149: 33–36.

Benz, F. L.
1972 *Personal Names in the Phoenician and Punic Inscriptions*. Studia Pohl 8. Rome: Pontifical Biblical Institute.

Borger, R.
1956 *Die Inschriften Asarhaddons Königs von Assyrien*. Archiv für Orientforschung Beiheft 9. Graz: Ernst Weidner.

Coogan, M. D.
1976 *West Semitic Personal Names in the Murašû Documents*. Harvard Semitic Monographs 7. Missoula, MT: Scholars Press.

Cross, F. M.
1969 Epigraphic Notes on the Ammān Citadel Inscription. *Bulletin of the American Schools of Oriental Research* 193: 13–19.
1974 Leaves from an Epigraphist's Notebook. *The Catholic Biblical Quarterly* 36: 486–94.
1975 Ammonite Ostraca from Heshbon. Heshbon Ostraca IV-VIII. *Andrews University Seminary Studies* 13: 1–20.
1983 An Unpublished Ammonite Ostracon from Ḥesbān. In *The Archaeology of Jordan and Other Studies*, ed. L. Geraty. Berrien Springs, MI: Andrews University.

Diringer, D.
1953 Early Hebrew Inscriptions. Pp. 331–59 in *Lachish III, The Iron Age*, by O. Tufnell, with contributions by M. A. Murray and D. Diringer. Oxford: Clarendon.

Gröndahl, F.
1967 *Die Personennamen der Texte aus Ugarit*. Studia Pohl 1. Rome: Pontifical Biblical Institute.

Harding, G. L.
1971 *An Index and Concordance of Pre-Islamic Arabian Names and Inscriptions*. Near and Middle East Series 8. Toronto: University of Toronto.

Herr, L. G.
1978 *The Scripts of Ancient Northwest Semitic Seals*. Harvard Semitic Monographs 18. Missoula, MT: Scholars Press.

Huffmon, H. B.
1965 *Amorite Personal Names in the Mari Texts*. Baltimore: Johns Hopkins Press.

Ingholt, H.
1967 IV. Palmyrene-Hatran-Nabataean. Pp. 42–51 in *An Aramaic Handbook, Part I/2 (Glossary)*. Porta Linguarum Orientalium N.S. 10. Wiesbaden: Otto Harrassowitz.

Jackson, K. P.
1983 *The Ammonite Language of the Iron Age*. Harvard Semitic Monographs 27. Chico, California: Scholars Press.

Kornfeld, W.
1978 *Onomastica Aramaica aus Ägypten*. Österreichische Akademie der Wissenschaften, Philosophisch-Historische Klasse Sitzungsberichte 333. Vienna: Österreichische Akademie der Wissenschaften.

Milik, J. T.
1970 Inscriptions nabatéennes. Pp. 141–60 in *Ancient Records from North Arabia*, by F. V. Winnett and W. L. Reed. Near and Middle East Series 6. Toronto: University of Toronto.

Naveh, J.
1980 The Ostracon from Nimrud: An Ammonite Name-List. *MAARAV* 2: 163–71.

Noth, M.
1928 *Die Israelitischen Personennamen im Rahmen der Gemeinsemitischen Namengebung*. Stuttgart: Kohlhammer. Reprint Georg Olms, 1966.

Reisner, G. A.; Fischer, C. S.; and Lyon, D. G.
1924 *Harvard Excavations at Samaria 1908–10*, vol. 1. Cambridge, MA: Harvard University.

Sawyer, John F. A.
1975 A Historical Description of the Hebrew Root YŠʿ. Pp. 75–84 in *Hamito-Semitica*, ed. J. and T. Bynon. Janua Linguarum 200. The Hague: Mouton.

Silverman, M. H.
1969 Aramean Name-types in the Elephantine Documents. *Journal of the American Oriental Society* 89: 691–709.

Stark, J. K.
1971 *Personal Names in Palmyrene Inscriptions*. Oxford: Clarendon.

Tadmor, H.
1965 A Note on the Seal of Mannu-ki-Inurta. *Israel Exploration Journal* 15: 233–34.

Tallqvist, K. L.
1914 *Assyrian Personal Names*. Acta Societatis Scientiarum Fennicae 43/1. Helsinki: Societas Scientiarum Fennicae.

Thompson, H. O., and Zayadine, F.
1973 The Tell Siran Inscription. *Bulletin of the American Schools of Oriental Research* 212: 5–11.

Winnett, F. V., and Harding, G. L.
1978 *Inscriptions from Fifty Safaitic Cairns*. Near and Middle East Series 9. Toronto: University of Toronto.

Leib 2nd Revision// GAL 2

Zadok, R.
1978a Phoenicians, Philistines, and Moabites in Mesopotamia. *Bulletin of the American Schools of Oriental Research* 230: 57–65.

1978b West Semitic Personal Names in the Murašû Documents [Rev. Coogan 1976]. *Bulletin of the American Schools of Oriental Research* 231: 73–78.

Social Organizations in Egyptian Military Settlements of the Sixth–Fourth Centuries B.C.E.: *dgl* and *m't*

Alexander Temerev
Moscow

In Persian-period military settlements in South Egypt, soldiers of local garrisons lived with their families, as did men not liable for call-up. The soldiers and their families were provided a certain living wage while doing garrison duty because the state guaranteed their economic condition. It is more difficult to understand the means of subsistence of the civilian non-Egyptian population and of the veterans who lived in Syene and Elephantine.

2. *Dgl*, 'a standard, a detachment,' is the commonest term for a garrison sub-unit in the Persian empire used in Aramaic materials of the fifth and fourth centuries B.C.E. from Upper Egypt, Memphis, and Arad (Palestine). The investigations of recent researchers (e.g., E. G. Kraeling 1953, Verger 1965, Porten 1972, Grelot 1972) have shown that belonging to a detachment, a group of several hundred people, entailed not only joining in the military duties of a certain part of the population of those settlements, but also receiving subsistence, for soldier and family, through rations (C24, K11) or the use of land plots (ploughed field, C16) as a temporary holder.* In other words, a *dgl* was an economic unit. Further, a *dgl* carried out certain administrative and legal functions. This is clearest from the requirement that a non-Egyptian soldier's detachment be mentioned in legal documents related to property-rights disputes (C5; 6; 8; 9; 13, etc.; K3; 5; 12, etc.). Unfortunately, lack of exhaustive information prevents us from ascertaining the *mechanism* of payment for service by a professional soldier who had lived in a military settlement; the role and size of military payments; the exact conditions of ownership of ploughed fields by members of the garrison detachment; techniques for the material maintenance of wives and daughters of soldiers who had lost their bread-winners, and so on.

3. Much more complicated is the role of the *m'ʾt*, 'a hundred,' in the life of South-Egyptian military settlements. Aramaic texts from Upper Egypt attest that members of 'hundreds' received various amounts of rations in Syene and Elephantine (C2; 3), revealing that these units served an economic function in the settlements. The so-called "Collection List," giving names of contributors to temple funds (C22), reveals certain administrative and legal functions of 'hundreds.' There are no direct references to garrison sub-units (*dglyn*) in texts which mention 'hundreds,' a fact which prevents us from affirming that 'a hundred' was part of the military organization of South Egypt.

4. It is known from the Elamite cuneiform tablets of the Persian period, the fifth-century Persepolis Treasury Tablets, that 'a hundred' was the usual term for collectives of civilians recruited to perform various economic jobs. Workers united in

professional 'hundreds' fulfilled certain jobs for which they received payment either by rations or by both rations and silver, depending on the season. We have an Aramaic papyrus (C26) recording the employment of some part of the Syenian and Elephantinian population at repair works in the Syenian shipyard. There are, further, references in some Aramaic texts to 'a builder/architect of the fortress of Syene' (*ʾrdybl lSwn byrtʾ*, C14: 2), 'a royal builder/architect' (*ʾrdkl zy mlkʾ*, C15: 2), 'carpenter' (*ngryʾ*, pl., C26: 9, 22; *ngrʾ*, sg., C2: 3; C63: 9), all of whom lived and worked in the region of Syene-Elephantine.

5. Herodotus (2.154) wrote, in the middle of the fifth century B.C.E., that remains of 'windlasses' (*holkoi*) were to be seen at the Camps (*Stratopeda*) where Saite mercenary veterans from Ionia and Caria had lived. The settlements seem to have been destroyed after the population was transferred to Memphis (2.30), and the shipyard and stop were restored near Memphis. A part of the archive of the Memphis armory has survived and some documents of the fifth century tell us that working brigades engaged there were paid with food rations (Aimé-Giron 1931: Nos. 5–75). This suggests that Saite, and later Persian, veterans living in settlements near Memphis worked at the Memphis shipyard and were paid in rations. The same situation seems to have existed in South Egypt, where the civilian population and veterans, united in 'hundreds,' worked at the local shipyard and in general attended to the trading station of Syene.

6. All this permits us to draw the following conclusions. There were two kinds of organization, one military and the other civilian, among the non-Egyptian population of Syene and Elephantine in the sixth–fourth centuries B.C.E. One part of the population constituted garrison detachments (soldiers and members of their families); the other formed civil 'hundreds.' Both types of organization were under the jurisdiction of local government bodies. The organizations enabled the population of Syene and Elephantine to get payments for its labor and to uphold its property interests in law-courts.

Note

**Abbreviations*

C texts in Cowley 1923

K texts in Kraeling 1953

This paper represents an abstract of a much longer Russian study of Egyptian social organizations during the Persian period.

References

Y. Aharoni
1975 *Arad Inscriptions.* Jerusalem: Bialik Institute (Hebrew).

N. Aimé-Giron
1931 *Textes araméens d'Égypte.* Le Caire: Imprimerie de l'Institut français d'archéologie orientale.

G. G. Cameron
1948 *Persepolis Treasury Tablets.* Oriental Institute Publications 65. Chicago: The University of Chicago Press.

G. Cardascia
1951 *Les archives des Murašû.* Paris: Adrien-Maisonneuve.

A. E. Cowley, ed.
1923 *Aramaic Papyri of the Fifth Century* B.C. Oxford: Oxford University Press. Rpt., 1967, Osnabrück: Otto Zeller.

M. A. Dandamayev
1973 Royal Estate Workers in Iran (End of VI, First Half of V Century B.C.). *Vestnik Drevnej Istorii* 3 (125): 3–26 (Russian).
1974 *Slavery in Babylonia in the 7th–4th Centuries* B.C. Moskva: Nauka (Russian).

M. A. Dandamayev and V. L. Lukonin
1980 *The Culture and Economics of Ancient Iran.* Moskva: Nauka (Russian).

G. Goossens
1949 Artistes et artisans étrangers en Perse sous les Achéménides. *La nouvelle Clio* 1/2: 32–44.

P. Grelot
1972 *Documents araméens d'Égypte.* Littératures anciens du Proche-Orient 5. Paris: Les éditions du Cerf.

R. T. Hallock
1969 *Persepolis Fortification Tablets.* Oriental Institute Publications 92. Chicago: The University of Chicago Press.

C.-F. Jean and J. Hoftijzer
1965 *Dictionnaire des inscriptions sémitiques de l'ouest.* Leiden: Brill.

E. G. Kraeling
1953 *The Brooklyn Museum Aramaic Papyri. New Documents of the Fifth Century* B.C. *from the Jewish Colony at Elephantine.* New Haven: Yale University Press for the Brooklyn Museum.

Y. Muffs
1969 *Studies in the Aramaic Legal Papyri from Elephantine.* Studia et Documenta ad Jura Orientis Antiqui Pertinentia 8. Leiden: Brill.

V. A. Livshitz
1979 The Neo-Babylonian *ḫaṭ(a)ru. Vestnik Drevnej Istorii* 4 (150): 95–100 (Russian).

B. Porten
1968 *Archives from Elephantine. The Life of an Ancient Jewish Military Colony.* Berkeley: University of California Press.

A. N. Temerev
1979 The Problematical Character of Literal Interpretations of Military Terms in Aramaic Papyri of the Fifth Century B.C. from Upper Egypt. Pp. 111–22 in *Problems in the History of the Countries of the Near and Middle East.* Moskva: Nauka (Russian).
1980 The Food-Supply System in Achaemenid Garrisons (According to Aramaic Texts from Upper Egypt and Arad). *Vestnik Drevnej Istorii* 1 (151): 124–31 (Russian).

A. Verger
1965 *Ricerche giuridiche sui papyri aramaici di Elefantina.* Studi semitici 16. Rome: Università di Roma/Centro di Studi Semitici.

R. Yaron
1961 *Introduction to the Law of the Aramaic Papyri.* Oxford: Oxford University Press.

Aramaic Papyri in the Egyptian Museum: The Missing Endorsements

Bezalel Porten
The Hebrew University of Jerusalem

With the aid of a grant from the American Research Center in Egypt, I visited the Egyptian Museum in Cairo on three separate occasions (October, December/January, March/April, 1980–81) to examine its collection of Aramaic papyri.* I am deeply indebted to Prof. David Noel Freedman for the encouragement he has given me in word and deed in pursuit of my research, and it is a pleasure to present these first fruits in his honor.

It is a truism that some of the best finds turn up on the antiquities market, and the two family archives of Elephantine Aramaic papyri were acquired by purchase. The first was bought in 1893 by Charles Edwin Wilbour but not published until 1953 by Emil G. Kraeling (=K); the second was bought in 1904 by Robert Mond and Lady William Cecil and by the Bodleian Library in Oxford and published shortly thereafter in 1906 by Archibald H. Sayce and Arthur Cowley. The Wilbour papyri are now in the Brooklyn Museum and the Mond-Cecil papyri, in the Egyptian Museum, Cairo. The twenty-two papyri in these two family archives are legal documents and most were acquired intact, i.e., folded, tied, and sealed with a one-or two-line endorsement, a docket written on the outer band.

The Brooklyn Museum has photographs of eight papyri intact (K 2–5, 9–12), and five are reproduced in the Kraeling volume (Pl. XXI—K 2, 9–12). The Bodleian papyrus roll (C 5) is reproduced at the beginning of the Sayce-Cowley publication.

In an unsuccessful attempt to open up some of the papyri, Wilbour caused considerable damage to three pieces (K 1, 6, 7 [Kraeling Pl. XXIII]) and their endorsements are missing from Kraeling's publication. One (K 7) has since been recovered: it turned out to have been a combination of the "endorsement of a lost papyrus" which Kraeling published separately (K 15) and another fragment (K 18:8) (cf. Porten 1979: 84–86).

The clay bulla of one papyrus (K 4) had completely disintegrated, and its cord was coming apart; the text was still intact. In another instance (K 8) the cord fell away and the upper third of the roll broke off. This third was originally mounted together with other fragments (January 1949) and only later (April 1949) was it discovered that it belonged to the right of two-thirds of a papyrus which had been mounted separately. One of the Egyptian Museum papyri (C 15) had similarly come apart—in this case the left third was separated from the right two-thirds. One of these portions had been acquired by Mr. Mond and another by Lady Cecil (see Porten 1979: 80). In the case of both texts (C 15; K 8) the endorsement is missing. The endorsement is likewise missing from another one of the Mond papyri (C 9). Unfortunately, there are no photographs of the Cecil-Mond papyrus rolls.

In the wake of the Sayce-Cowley publication, Germans under the direction of

Otto Rubensohn embarked upon an excavation of Elephantine which was essentially a papyrus hunt. In their second season, on 1 January 1907, close by the spot where the Mond-Cecil papyri were reportedly found by *sebakhīn,* they made their first discovery of Aramaic papyri. Fourteen of the texts eventually unearthed by them were legal contracts (C 1–3, 7, 10, 18, 29, 35, 43, 45–49), but only one (C 10) was fully preserved with seal and endorsement intact (Sachau 1911: Pls. 28–29). Two were fragmentary but the endorsement was partially preserved (C 2, 43). Thus, of 36 contracts sixteen lack endorsements (C 1, 3, 7, 9, 15, 18, 29, 35, 45–49; K 1, 6, 8). All these papyri were published by Eduard Sachau in 1911 and re-edited, along with the Sayce-Cowley papyri, by Cowley (=C) in 1923.

Can we solve the case of the missing endorsements? We shall treat here the five Egyptian Museum papyri whose endorsements may be restored with greatest plausibility (C 1, 3, 9, 15, 29).

The key to the deterioration of a papyrus is its preparation and redaction. I have elsewhere described this process (Porten 1979: 78–81). Here we have to consider three factors. 1) Where did the scribe tend to sever his papyrus from the scroll? 2) How much upper margin did he leave before writing his text? 3) How did he roll up and fold his document after it was written? Knowing these procedures, we can move from the preserved, fragmentary text to the complete original one.

1. As indicated, the scribe's supply of papyrus consisted not of individual sheets but of a scroll of sheets "joined" together by glue. When writing a contract the scribe first estimated its length and then cut away the appropriate size papyrus. When we measure the height of each sheet in a contract we should realize that the upper edge of the contract is where the scribe cut off the previous document from his scroll while the lower edge is where he cut off the present document. Examination of the upper and lower edges of seventeen contracts discovered intact with seal and endorsement reveals the scribal habit of severing the papyrus close to the join. Thus, a join visible just below the upper edge of the papyrus indicates that the scribe cut his previous document just above the join, while one visible just above the lower edge indicates that he severed the present document just below the join. Conversely, an upper sheet whose height is almost the same as that of the other sheets in the document indicates that the scribe severed the previous papyrus just below the join, while a lower sheet of such height would indicate that the present document was severed just above the join. Examination of the tops of these seventeen contracts shows nine cut below the join (C 6, 13; K 2, 3, 5, 9–12); three above (C 14, 20, 25); and four in the "middle" of the upper sheet (C 8, 10, 28; K 4). The upper sheet of one text (C 5) is the *protokollon* of the scroll, i.e., its first sheet (Turner 1978: 20). Statistics for the bottoms of these papyri reveal seven cut above the join (C 6, 10, 28; K 2, 5, 11, 12); six below (C 5, 13, 20; K 4, 9, 10); and four in the "middle" of the lower sheet (C 8, 14, 25; K 3) (See Table 1).

2. In ten contracts, the scribe began his document below the join of the second sheet, leaving an upper margin of between 8 and 18 cm. (C 5, 8, 10, 25, 28; K 3, 4, 10–12), while in six contracts the scribe began writing in the "middle" of the first sheet, leaving a margin of between 3 and ca. 8 cm. (C 6, 14, 20; K 2, 5, 9). The two texts that have the smallest upper margin (3 cm. [K 2] and 3.2 cm. [C 6]) also have a

tear in the first line which obliterated part of the date formula.

3. The scribe tended to leave such a wide margin at the top in order to create a protective envelope. Once written, most documents were rolled up from the bottom to just below the top; the top band (A) was then turned down and these two bands (A + B) turned down on the roll (Fig. 1, left: 1). The endorsement was then written on the penultimate band (B). While the lower part of a document was thus protected inside, the upper part was exposed to damage from the outside. The folds between outer band B and inner band C and between band C and folded-in band D were subject to tears (Fig. 1, left: 2). The lateral overlaps were particularly fragile (Fig. 1, left: 3). The extent of the repetitive tear pattern in the vertical folds of the opened roll depends upon the depth of damage to the overlaps in the closed roll. Since the left overlap covers a larger space than the right, the tear width of the right vertical fold will tend to be greater than that of the left (Fig. 1, left: 4). If the piece cracked along the horizontal edge of the bands, then two or three would be wholly or partially pried loose from the rest of the roll (C 6, 8, 20; K 11; Fig. 2).

One document appears to have been folded differently (C 13). It is not damaged at the top but at the bottom. Moreover, the endorsement, which would ordinarily appear at the top of the verso of the unrolled text, here appears at the bottom of the recto of the mounted papyrus (Fig. 3). The fibers on this fragment run parallel to the writing and so the endorsement was indeed written on the verso. (For fiber direction of recto and verso, cf. Porten 1979: 78). Because the last two bands of the contract had become completely separated from the document, whoever mounted the papyrus simply turned the fragments over so that recto and verso could be read together. He erred, however, in placement of the right and left fragments. If each is moved to its respective edge, we get the appropriate endorsement formula *spr by [zy ktb m]ḥsyh br ydnyh [lmptḥy]h brth,* "Document of a house [which Ma]hseiah son of Jedaniah [wrote for] his daughter [Miptahia]h." So this text was not rolled from the bottom up but from the top down. This is proven by the increasing height of the individual bands as one moves from the top to the bottom: 0.7–1.3–1.9–2–2.2–2.25–2.3–2.4–2.5–2.6–2.7–2.8–2.85–2.95–2.6 cm. Were the papyrus rolled bottoms-up the height would increase as one moved upward. The scribe of C 13 had left only a small 3.3 cm. top margin and after he finished writing his text, he had 10 cm. blank space left at the bottom. He must have assumed that this would give him a better protective envelope than the narrow top margin. As it turned out, the beginning of the text *was* preserved but the damage effecting the overlaps effaced the names of two witnesses and of the deity served by a priest who was neighbor to the house being transferred (C 13: 15, 18f). The Egyptian name of the priest himself, hitherto elusive, has now been restored by Ada Yardeni to read *ḥrwṣ,* Ḥarudj. The tops of the letters were written right across the join and at the right overlap and so were doubly damaged. Moreover, it is at least clear that only one deity (*ʾlhʾ* and not *ʾlhyʾ* as Cowley) was mentioned (Fig. 3).

In conclusion we see that documents (1) were usually cut close to the join, (2) begun in the middle of the top sheet or below the join of the second sheet, and (3) rolled bottoms up (with but one exception). We shall examine five documents with lost endorsements, spanning a period of almost ninety years (495 [C 1] to 408 B.C.E. [C 29]), and see how these may be reconstructed.

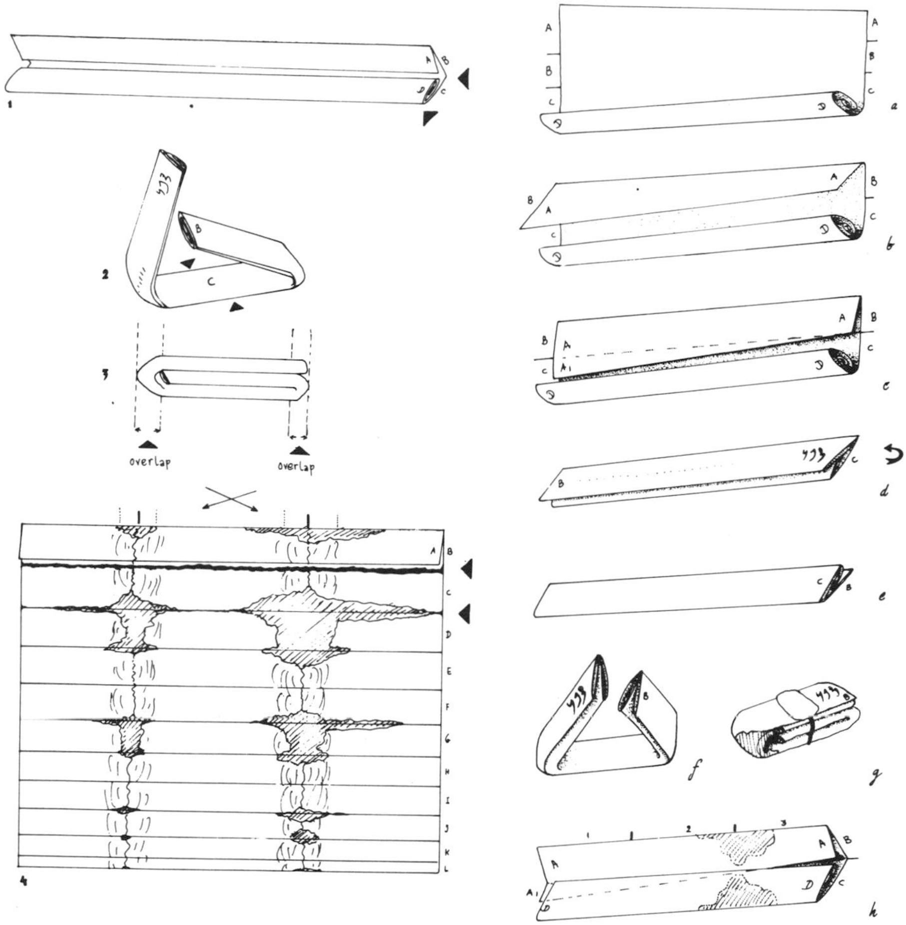

Figure 1. Folding of a contract into thirds. Left: sensitive spots in a roll and deterioration pattern. Right: folding and deterioration of C 9.

TABLE 1.
MEASUREMENT (IN CM.) OF UPPER AND LOWER JOIN DISTANCE AND MARGIN IN SEVENTEEN PAPYRUS CONTRACTS

	Upper Sheet		Lower Sheet	
	Join Distance	Margin	Join Distance	Margin
C5	*Protokollon*	12.7 bj	1.3 bj	2.4
6	1.3 bj	3.2	ca. 3 aj	9
8	8.2 (ht. of sheet)	18 bj (text begins mid-2nd sheet)	8.4 (ht. of sheet)	1.8
10	5 (ht. of sheet)	8	ca. 2 aj	4.5
13	ca. 3 bj	3.3	3.8 bj	10
14	1.8 aj	6.6	8 (ht. of sheet)	10.2–8.6
20	0.7 aj	8.2	0.3 bj	8.6
25	0.5 aj	17.3 bj	4.8 (ht. of sheet)	4
28	3.8 aj	15.7 bj	ca. 2 aj	8.2–7.5
K 2	ca. 3 bj	3	< 1 aj	1
3	< 1 bj	15–16.3 bj	6.3 (ht. of sheet)	10–10.2
4	ca. 5–6 bj	11.3–11.7 bj	0.4 bj	9.6
5	ca. 3 bj	5.2	< 1 aj	7.8
9	< 1 bj	6.5–7.9	0.3 bj	25.6
10	< 1 bj	13.3 bj	3.8 bj	8
11	< 1 bj	14–12 bj	ca. 3 aj	1.4
12	2–3	10.3–10.9 bj	< 1 aj	10.3

aj = cut above join. bj = cut or written below join. A height of < 4 cm. is considered not adjacent to join. The space above the join in the upper sheet and below the join in the lower sheet is measurable. The space below the join in the upper sheet and above the join in the lower sheet is estimated on the basis of the height of the other sheets in each respective papyrus.

1. The earliest Elephantine contract dates to 22 October 495 B.C.E. and is held by the Staatliche Museen zu Berlin (C 1 = P. 13489; Porten 1979: 81). In this case the damage is at the bottom of the text. Two bands of the right fold and its left adjacent overlap and part of two bands of the left fold are missing. If the document had been rolled bottoms-up it is hard to explain why the top, which would have been on the outside, is intact, while the bottom, though on the inside, is damaged. We must, conclude, therefore, that this document, unlike all the others except C 13, was rolled from the top down. This is borne out by the measurements of the individual folds which increase in size as we move from the top to the

bottom: 1.2–1.3–1.45– 1.55–1.65–1.8–1.85–1.9–2.05–2.1–2.2 cm. So, as with C 13, the endorsement would have been written at the bottom of the verso (if the document is turned from right to left) and not at the top, as in all the other contracts.

C 1 is mounted on cardboard and there is no photograph of the verso. One needs to assume that Sachau saw no trace of writing on the verso. Were there no bands missing at the bottom (= top of roll) and were our document attested by only four witnesses (as were C 10, 11, 14, 15 (?), 18, 20, 28, 43; K 3–5, 11–12), then we should have had the end of the dictation clause—*ktb* PN *br* PN *spr*ʾ *znh kpm* [or *ʿl pm*] *slwʾh brt qnyh wytwmh ʾḥth* or the like—on the last band of the recto and an endorsement on the penultimate band on the verso. But neither appears. We may thus assume that this was an eight witness document (like C 2, 5, 6, 25, 46; K 8–10) and three complete bands are missing. This would add 6.8 cm. to the bottom and yield 9.7 cm. from the join. Since the height between joins of the first and second sheets respectively is 11.2 and 11.7, this would mean that the piece was cut at the top just below the join and at the bottom ca. 2 cm. above the join. The dictation clause on the recto and the endorsement on the verso would both have been written on the penultimate band. Would the endorsement have been a *spr mnh*, "Share deed"? (Fig. 4)

2. C 2 is in the Staatliche Museen zu Berlin (P. 13493) while C 3 is in the Egyptian Museum (J. 43485; 3448). The left side of both texts is missing and the endorsement of C 3 has disappeared as well. The documents share many clauses in common; Sachau (1911: 107) thought that both concerned the same transaction but Cowley was sceptical. Though he restored most of C 2 on the basis of C 3, he refrained from restoring C 3. Grelot (1972) omitted C 3 from his collection. Since the documents were drawn up by the same scribe (as Sachau, contra Cowley), on the same day, and with the same witnesses (Yaron 1957: 47; read *psmšk*, "Psammetichus" for the patronymic [so Ada Yardeni] in C 2: 24), the presumption is great that they were also cut from the same scroll, one after the other. If we could establish that the original width of both contracts was identical we would have further support for this presumption.

The tear patterns and restoration of line 1 in both contracts enable us to arrive at a common width. Since the second line in both begins with the same word, the first line must have been identical. The preserved part ran as follows:

C 2 *b-28 lyrḥ pʾpy šnt 2 ḥsyrs mlkʾ*
C 3 *b-28 l*[*yrḥ*

Cowley restored *byb byrtʾ*, "in Elephantine the fortress" before the name [*hwšʿ*], "[Hosea]," while Grelot (1972: 267) restored only *ʾdyn*, "then." Examination of all known contracts shows that the term *ʾdyn* does not appear in that slot before 427 B.C.E. (K 5: 1) and recurs regularly thereafter (C 20, 25, 35, 43; K 6–12), while the place of redaction is found only after 420 B.C.E. (C 20), recurring frequently thereafter (C 20, 25, 28, 29, 43, 45; K 6–8, 11). Neither expression, therefore, should be restored in our texts, written in 484 B.C.E. The end of line 1 in C 2 need only be restored *ʾmr hwšʿ*, "said Hosea." This restoration accords fully with the presumption that one vertical fold is missing from C 2 and two folds are missing from C 3. The fold and tear patterns preserved in C 2 show that the right fold was 8 cm., the overlap 2.2 cm.; the center fold 7.3 cm. and its overlap 3 cm. A reasonable width of ca. 7 cm. for the left fold would bring the original width of our document up to 27.5 cm. This is likewise the width range of the two documents closest in time to C 2—27.4 cm. for C 5 (471 B.C.E.) and 27.7–28 cm. for C 1 (495 B.C.E.). The width of the right fold of C 3 is 8.5–9.5 cm. This includes ca. 1 cm. of overlap but the tear lines here are much less distinct than in C 2. The width of the two remaining folds would be comparable to those of C 2 but precise measurements for each fold are not possible.

It is possible, though, to determine which document was written first, by examining the height of the individual sheets between the joins. We are further aided in our task by the fact that the last sheet of C 2 must have been the last sheet in the scroll. This is clear not only from its measurement but also from the fact that the scribe had to write the names of the witnesses on the verso of his text. This was not standard procedure and occurs on only one other occasion (C 8). There the scribe had underestimated the length of papyrus necessary to write a 34-line document and cut off too short a piece. He therefore had to turn his papyrus over for the last three lines of witnesses. Here the scribe simply came to the end of the scroll. So C 3 must have been written prior to C 2. This is confirmed by the fact that the bottom sheet of C 3 measures 8.8 cm. and the top sheet of C 2, 2 cm.; total, 10.8 cm. The sequence of sheets that emerges would thus be 4.3–10–10.4–10.2–9.8–10.9–10.1–10.5–10.5. A deviation of 1+ cm. in the height of individual sheets in a scroll is not unusual.

The first sheet in C 3 measures only 4.3 cm. If we add another two bands at the top, measuring together 6 cm., we get an original 10.3 cm. with an upper margin of 6.9 cm. This would mean that C 3 was originally cut at the top by the join. The missing endorsement would thus have come on the penultimate band (B) and have read, like C 2 (contra Cowley), *ktb hwšʿ wʾḥyʾb lʾspmṭ*. Both documents were thus written by Hosea, and fragmentary line 21 in C 3 should be restored (contra Cowley), *ktb h⸢wšʿ⸣ bkpy n⸢pšh⸣*, "H[osea] wrote with [his] o[wn] hand" (cf. C 13: 17f ⸢*ktb mḥsyh bk<p>y npšh*⸣) (Fig. 5).

3. Like C 2 and 3, C 8 (J. 37114; 3652) and C 9 (J. 37106; 3467) were written on the same day, by the same scribe and with the same witnesses, twelve in all. One document (C 8) is a grant of a house by Mahseiah to his daughter Mibtahiah on the occasion of her marriage to Jezaniah, while the other (C 9) bestows building rights in that property upon the husband. While the first document is almost 80 cm. tall and consists of six papyrus sheets, the second one is under 20 cm. and covers only parts of three sheets. In preparing the first document, the scribe left the whole first sheet (actually a half sheet) blank and began to write toward the bottom of the second sheet (top margin of 18.5 cm.). As indicated, he had to write 34 lines in all and ran short of space at the bottom and so had to turn his papyrus bottoms-up and have the last three lines of witnesses written on the verso. The other document runs to 22 lines and is equally divided between both sides. This is the only extant contract where the scribe intended at the outset to write on both sides. The endorsement is intact in C 8, albeit slightly damaged, but is missing from C 9.

Which document was written first? Sayce and Cowley placed C 9 (Papyrus C) before C 8 (Papyrus D), and there might be a legal logic to such an order. Once the owner of the house had given his daughter full rights to it, he could not turn around and assign certain rights to her husband which would limit her rights. But he might reverse the order—assign his son-in-law certain building rights and bestow title on his daughter. Yet two factors counter this supposed logic—the statement in the document to Jezaniah that he had given the house to his daughter and written a document about it (C 9: 3f); and demonstration that C 9 was cut from the same scroll as C 8 and must have come below C 8 and not above.

C 8 measures 26.5 cm., while C 9 measures 26.2 cm. at the top but widens down to as much as 26.8 cm. The bottom of C 9 is thus wider than the top of C 8 and the two would not join together in the order C 9–C 8. Moreover the top sheet of C 8 is 8.2 cm. and the bottom of C 9 only 1.2 cm. Together this would give 9.4 cm. The height of the other sheets in C 8 is 15.2, 15.7, 15.5, 14.6 cm. and the first intact sheet in C 9 measures 15.1 cm. Such a 6 cm. disproportion also argues against a placement of C 9 over C 8. But the reverse order finds confirmation on the assumption that two bands fell away from the top of C 9. The last sheet in C 8 measures on the right edge 8.1 cm., and the top sheet in C 9 measures 3.5 cm. If we add 3.5 cm. for 1 3/4 missing bands we get 15.1 cm. On the left edge we have 8.4 for the bottom of C 8, 1.1 for the top of C 9 and an addition of 5.5 cm. for the 2 missing bands, giving a total of 15 cm. These figures of 15–15.1 cm. are compatible with the height of the other sheets in both contracts. Moreover the papyrus color of C 8 bottom matches well with that of C 9 top. The sheet height and color match thus confirm the assumption that C 8 and 9 were cut from the same scroll and that C 9 was written after C 8 (Fig. 6).

Having used up the equivalent of five sheets for Mibtahiah's contract, the scribe must have concluded that only 1 1/2 sheets could be spared for Jezaniah's and so he conserved papyrus by writing his second contract on both sides. For some reason, the scribe of C 8 had cut his previous document in the middle of a sheet and did the same for his present document. C 9, however, was cut just below the join. The scribe left a 5.4 cm. margin at the top and began writing just above the join. He folded his document in the usual manner, though band A was folded on an angle forming a secondary band A_1. The endorsement must have appeared on the penultimate band (B) as in C 8 (Fig. 1, right: a–d). Could C 9 like C 8 have been called a *spr by*, "House document," or would it have had some distinguishing title like *spr ʾrq lmbnh*,

"Document of land to build" (cf. *spr ʾgrʾ zy bnh,* "Document of the wall which was built" [C 5: 20])? After the roll was folded into thirds, tied and sealed, damage set in at the left overlap (Fig. 1, right: e–g). When the cord came loose and band A and 3/4 of band B fell away, there emerged the hole between vertical bands 2 and 3 in the opened papyrus (Fig. 1, right: h). The big hole in lost bands A + B was reduplicated in band D and the bottom half of band C and this explains the tear pattern in lines 1 and 2. This damage pattern at the fold of the first three (or four) bands is to be found also in the companion document (C 8), which has been here redrawn to indicate original position (Fig. 2d). The more severe the damage the more bands will be affected by reduplication of the tear pattern (as in C 28 [Sayce-Cowley 1906: Pl. K], or by a virtual break (as in C 20 [Sayce-Cowley 1906: Pl. H]).

4. The most damaged of the Mond-Cecil papyri is Mibtahiah's marriage contract (C 15=J. 37110; 3651). As indicated, the left fold had fallen away and the document was actually acquired by two separate purchasers. Though there is considerable damage to both overlaps, almost no word is uncertain because of the formulaic nature of the text. But the date formula in line 1 is severely damaged and the endorsement is missing. The document runs to 39 lines and for purposes of mounting was cut after line 20. The first half of the text was placed on the right side of the backing and the second half on the left. As preserved it consists of seven papyrus sheets measuring 3.8, 11.9, 12.6, 12.9, 12.8, 12.1, 12.6 cm. The bottom must have been cut just above the join. If we add 6.5 cm. for two+ bands at the top we will get a restored upper sheet of 10.3 cm. The scribe would thus have severed his previous document from this one ca. 2.5 cm. below the join and begun his present text just below the join, leaving an upper margin of (3.8 + 2.5 + 6.5 =) 12.8 cm. The endorsement would have been written on the penultimate band and have said something like *spr ʾntw zy ktb ʾsḥwr br ṣḥʾ lmbṭḥyh,* "Marriage document which Esḥor b. Ṣeḥo wrote for Mibtahiah." (Cf. the restored endorsements in K 2: 17, 7: 45 [Porten 1979: 82ff].)

The much more difficult problem is the restoration of the date formula in line 1. All scholars who have treated the chronology of the contracts have assumed that the first date was 25 Tishre. Close examination of the papyrus, however, reveals that we must restore *b*–20 + /// *[//]*/ = 26 Tishre. Similarly all scholars accepted the reading for the Egyptian month as 6 Epiphi. But there is a turned down piece of papyrus before the six strokes and it is not certain if any numeral preceded them. Paleographically we may say that a preceding "10" is not good because the required spacing would put the "10" sign too far from the numerals; it is usually written closer. Similarly, omission of a preceding numeral is no good because it leaves too much space. The best paleographic solution is a preceding "20," because it would be situated at a "reasonable" distance from the numeral strokes, as comparison with the date at the beginning of the line reveals. There are two dates in our period in which 26 Epiphi = 26 Tishre—8 November 451 and 5/6 October 440. The latter is 25 Artaxerxes and the former 14 Artaxerxes. Paleographically, the numeral "25" is less reasonable, since the "20" would have to stand too close to the numeral strokes. The combination "10" + "4," on the other hand, *is* reasonable. Paleographically, then, the most reasonable date for C 15 would be 8 November 451, though 5 October 440 (the document having been written after sundown) should not be excluded outright (Fig. 7).

This latter date would fit perfectly the accepted sequence and interpretation of C 14 and 15. C 14 was drawn up on 27 August 440 by Pia b. Paḥi renouncing claim upon "silver, grain, raiment, bronze, iron—all goods and property—and the marriage contract," after Mibtahiah had taken a judicial oath concerning them. According to the view first advanced by J. Halévy (1907: 111) and accepted by most scholars, Mibtahiah had been married to Pia, and this document was drawn up pursuant to divorce (Porten 1968: 245ff). But other interpretations of C 14 are equally plausible. We may assume, for example, that Mibtahiah had deposited goods with Pia, just as Shelomam b. Azariah later deposited with her husband Esḥor "wool and linen garments, bronze and iron vessels, wooden and palm-leaf vessels, grain and other things" (C 20: 5f). Among the objects of value deposited would have been Mibtahiah's "marriage contract."

It is noteworthy that the word "marriage" (*ʾntw,* originally misread *ʾntn* by Sayce-Cowley) was written in by the scribe above the line. He had come to the end of his sentence with *spr,* "a document" and dipped his pen to begin the new sentence, *ʾdyn,* "then." Only after he had written on, perhaps not until he reread the document after writing it, did he dip his pen afresh and add *ʾntw,* "marriage." Were the marriage contract of the essence to the transaction it is hard to imagine that the scribe would have failed to write this grammatical construct at the outset. More likely is it that he wrote the word initially as an absolute form, perhaps even intended to be collective as all the other absolute forms in the list of objects. Only when rereading the document (aloud?) was it called to his attention, or he himself noticed, that what was at hand was not just a document, or documents in general, but a "marriage contract." He obligingly converted the absolute form of *spr* into a construct by the supralinear addition of *ʾntw.*

If C 15 were thus indeed drawn up on 8 November 451, then it would have been the "marriage contract" listed among Mibtahiah's goods in her suit with Pia in August 440. Perhaps its imperfect state of preservation is due to its transfer and handling. In any event, the sequence of documents and events now has to be altered. Esḥor was Mibtahiah's second and not her third husband, while Pia was no husband at all but simply a colleague of her husband's with whom she had a disagreement regarding (deposited?) property. Married to her first husband in 460 or 459 (C 8–9), she would have been widowed or separated from him not too many years thereafter. A brief marriage would readily explain the absence of any children from Jezaniah. Her sons from Esḥor would be in their mid- or late twenties in 420 (C 20). The order of the Mibtahiah documents would thus be

C 5	–	471	
C 6	–	464	
C 8, 9	–	460/59	marriage to Jezaniah
C 15	–	451	marriage to Esḥor
C 13	–	446	
C 14	–	440	
C 20	–	420	
C 25	–	416	
C 28	–	410	

5. Cowley 29 (J. 43487; 3459) not only lacks endorsement; the papyrus has come apart at the two vertical folds. Sachau reports the width as 26.5 cm.; his Pl. 15 has the pieces arranged so that the width measures 26.1 cm., but subsequent rearrangement of the pieces by the Berlin Museum, before the piece was transferred to Cairo, yielded a width of 28.5 cm. This seems to be close to the original width. This can be fixed firmly by the restoration of the name and verb *{ʾmr ntn br}* in line 1 and the name *ys{lḥ}* in line 2. The resultant width accords better with two numeral strokes in the restored date formula in line 1 and eight in line 5. The deed of obligation was thus drawn up in November 408 and the debt was to be paid by August 407. The amount of 14 shekels is also given in Greek staters and the number in line 3 should be restored to 7 (cf. C 35: 3f, 7; K 12: 5f, 14). The debt was perhaps for *byt bnyk,* "(the) house of your sons," followed after the break in the papyrus by *ʾmk,* "your mother" and not *ʾmr* (line 3). Cowley's hunch that the fragment at the beginning of line 6 was misplaced is correct. It should be moved down to the next line. Nathan had undertaken to pay his obligation by the month of Pachons. The last two lines of the fragmentary papyrus would thus read

whn {ʾnh} ksp' znh krš ḥd šqln ʾrb{ʿh lʾ} šlmt yhbt byn yrḥ{

"And if {I} do {not} repay (and) give you this money—one karsh, fo[ur} shekels— within the month {of Pachons (?) . . .}."

As the contract stands the upper margin is 3.7 cm. and the height of the piece from the join to the upper edge is 9.5 cm. If we assume the loss of two bands, each of ca. 2 cm., this would give an upper margin of 7.7 cm. and bring the upper sheet to ca. 13.5 cm. This latter is a median height for individual sheets and would indicate that our document was cut close to the join. We may assume that the endorsement was written on the penultimate band and would read something like *spr ksp zy ktb ntn br hwšʿ lyslḥ br gdwl,* "Document of money which

Nathan b. Hosea wrote for Islaḥ b. Gaddul" (cf. C 10: 23f). (Fig. 8 top)

It is tempting to speculate how C 29 fell apart. Given its current state of preservation and tear pattern, we may conjecture the following four stages:

1. After the piece became untied, the outer bands AB fell away.
2. The piece became unrolled and the bottom fell off and became lost.
3. The vertical bands fell away at their folds.
4. The distinct and separate tear pattern of the left vertical band may be explained if we assume that it was refolded AB over CD, E over AD, BC over EAD (Fig. 8 bot.). The who, when, and why of this independent, secondary fold remains a mystery.

In conclusion, then, we have examined five contracts, from the earliest to among the latest, both fragmentary (C 3, 29) and intact (C 9) or virtually so (C 1, 15), whose common feature is the absence of endorsement. In two cases the upper margin was less than that in any of the documents with endorsement intact—0.9 cm. (C 3) and 1.9 cm. (C 9). In two cases the upper margin was comparable to that found in documents where the first line began in the "middle" of the upper sheet—3.7 cm. (C 29) and 4.1 (C 1). In the fifth case (C 15), with the largest upper margin (5.3 cm.), the text began just below the join. In one case (C 1), we saw that the document must have been rolled from the top down. The restoration of three bands at the bottom would yield the missing endorsement (cf. C 13). In the other four cases, the missing endorsement could be "restored" by the addition of two bands at the top. This brought the upper margins more in line with most of those found in the other texts which began in the "middle" of the sheet (5.2–8.2 cm. [K 5, 9; C 14, 20]); contrast 3–3.2 [K 2; C 6] – 5.4 (C 9), 6.9 (C 3), 7.7 (C 29), 11.8 (C 15). In three cases it also yielded an upper sheet which was cut at the join—10.3 cm. (C 15), 10.3 cm. (C 3), 13.5 cm. (C 29); in one of these cases (C 15), it can be verified that the cut was ca. 2.5 cm. below the join. In the fourth case, the papyrus was cut in the middle of the sheet—7 cm. (C 9). In the fifth instance, where the papyrus was rolled down, the restored height of the bottom sheet would be 9.7 cm., and it would have been cut ca. 2 cm. above the join.

Texture influences text. Careful attention to cuts, joins, folds, and tears enables the investigator to visualize how much has been lost from a fragmentary text. These physical features thus provide a controlling framework for textual restoration.

Note

*All the drawings are by Ada Yardeni. Her diligent work was part of the creative process which made this study possible.

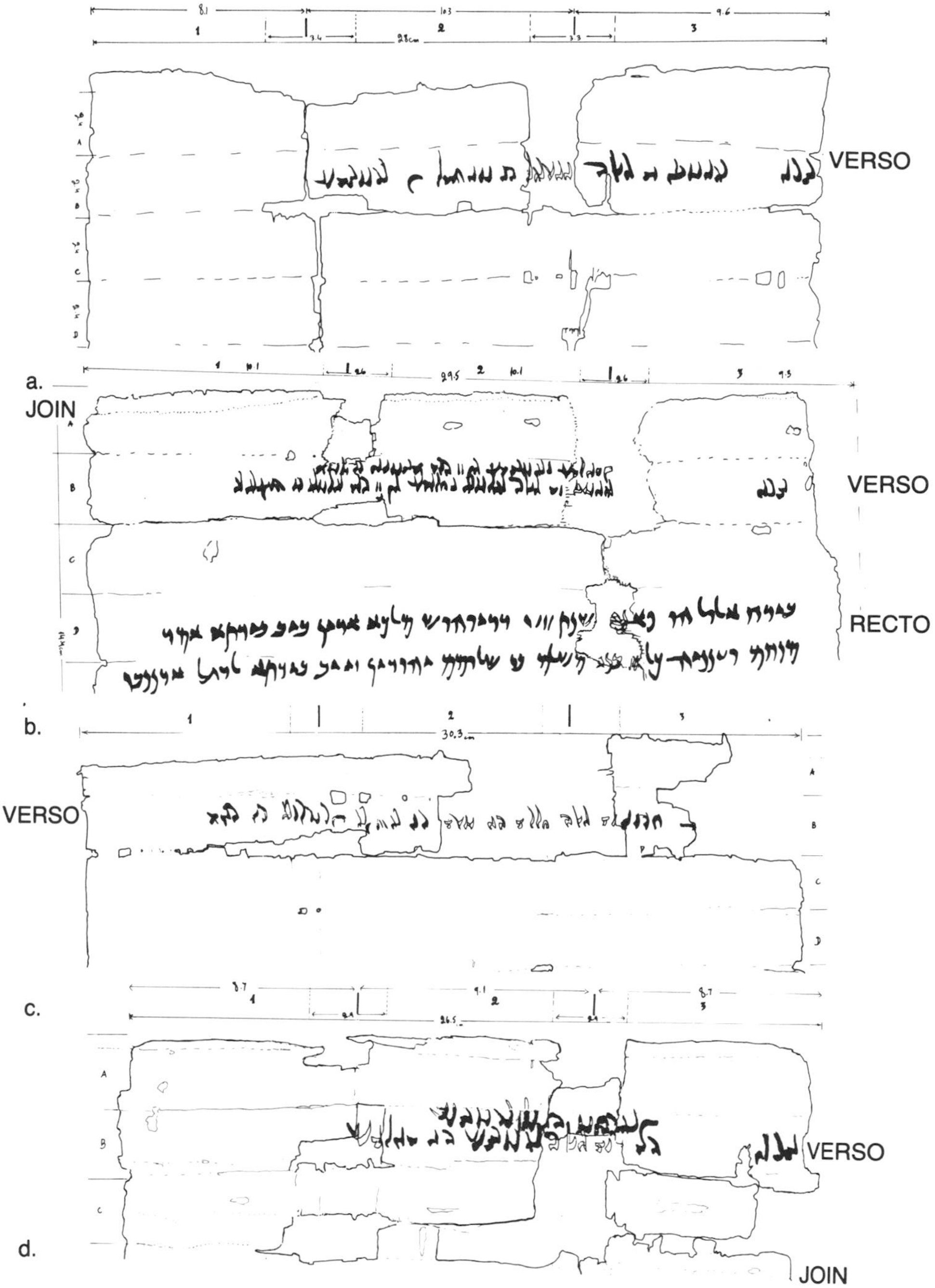

a.

b.

c.

d.

Figure 2. Four documents showing two or three bands damaged; arranged in descending order of deterioration (C 6, 20; K 11; C 8). Endorsement on verso appears upside-down in relation to recto.

a. C 6 Document of Withdrawal which [Dargamana] son of Ḥarshaina wrote for Mahseiah.

b. C 20 Document of [Withdrawal] which Menahem and Ananiah, all [2], sons of Menahem son of Sheloman wrote [for Jedania]h and Mahseiah, all 2, sons of Esḥor son of Ṣeḥọ.

c. K 11 [Document of?] Grain [which Anani son of Haggai] son of Meshullam [wrote] for Pakhnum son of Besa.

d. C 8 Document of a House [which] Mahseh son of Jedan[iah wrote] for Mibtah daughter of Mahseh.

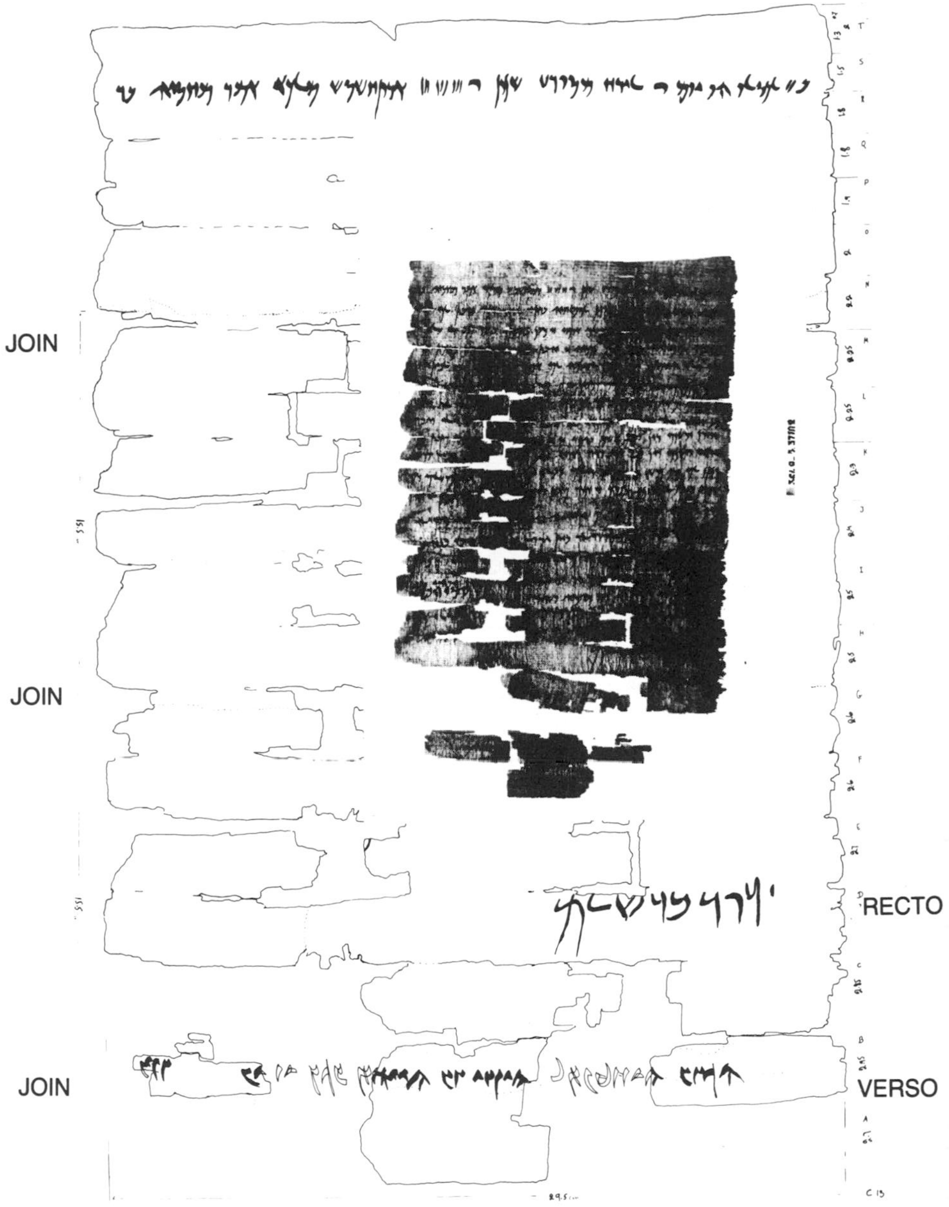

Figure 3. Photo inset shows fallen-away endorsement reversed and mounted at the bottom of the text (C 13). In drawing, endorsement restored and correctly positioned. Contract rolled from top (band T) to bottom (band A)

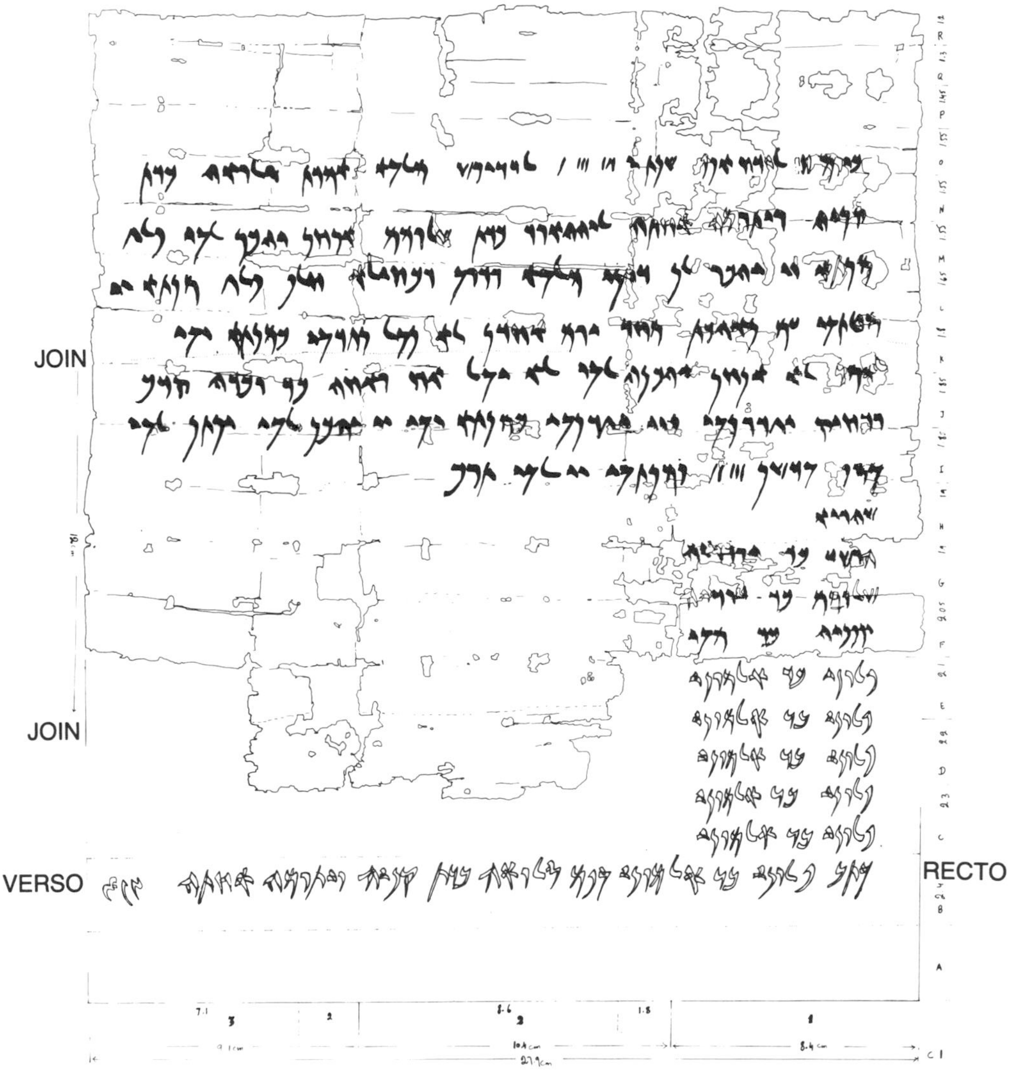

Figure 4. Contract rolled from top (band R) to bottom (band A). Reconstruction of three lost bands at bottom (CBA) yields eight witnesses, dictation clause and (on verso) endorsement (band B) (C 1).

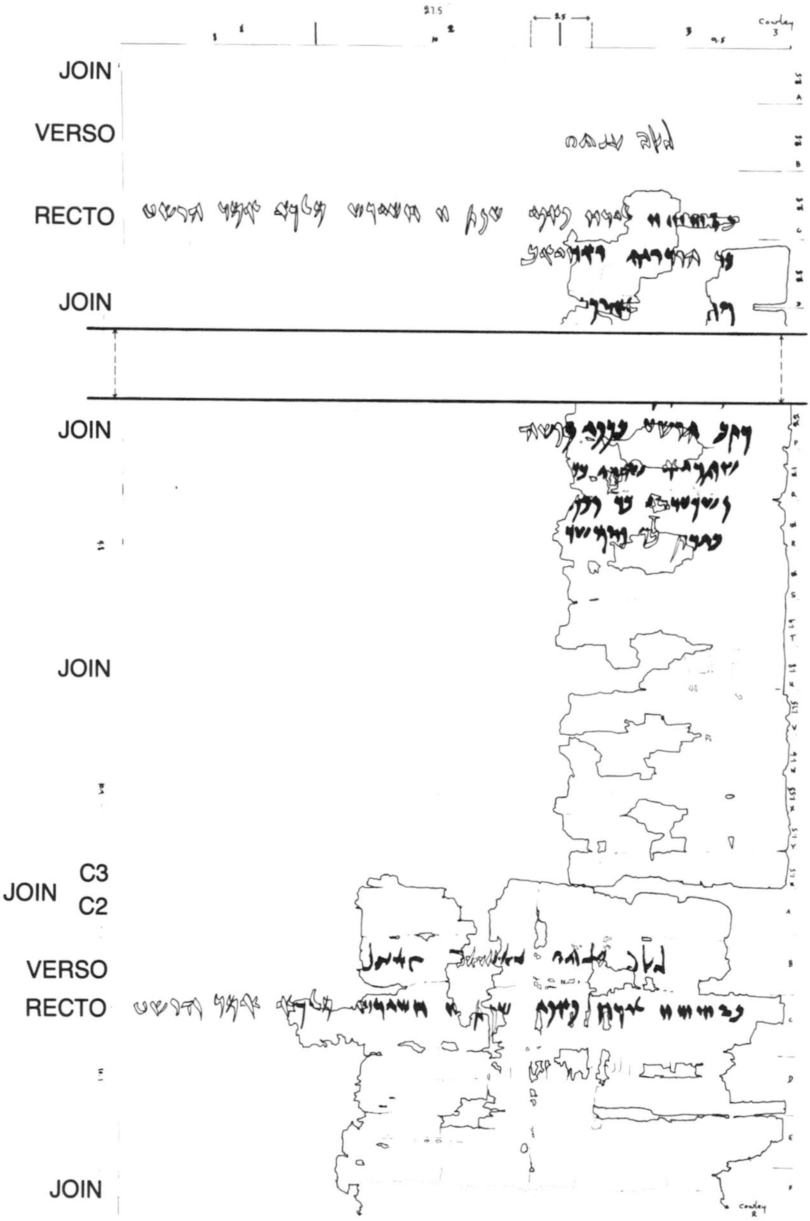

Figure 5. Two contracts written by the same scribe on the same day were cut from the same scroll, first C 3 and then C 2. Endorsment on C 2 was written on band B and restored on Band B in C 3.

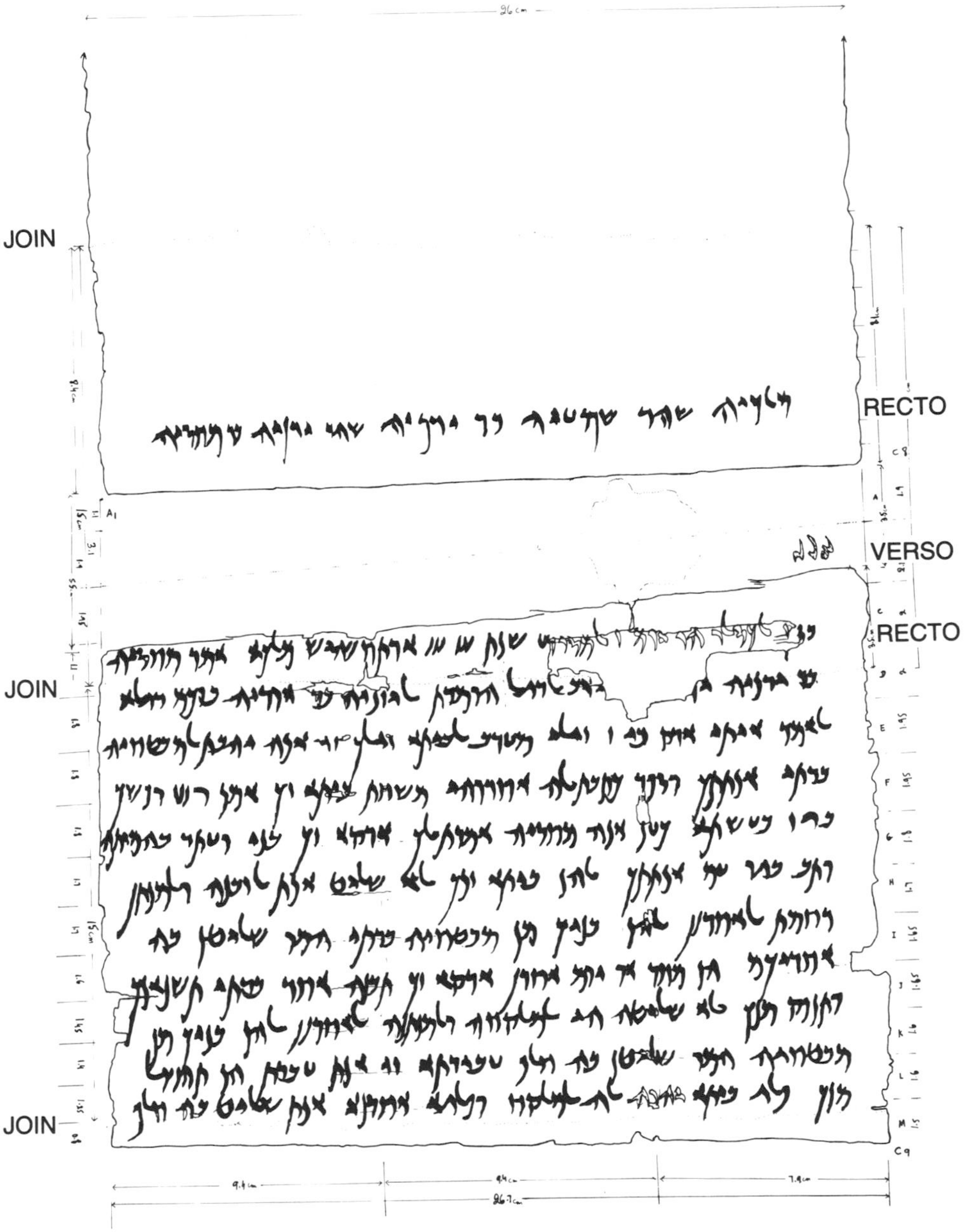

Figure 6. Two contracts written by the same scribe on the same day were cut from the same scroll, first C 8 and then C 9. Two bands, including the endorsement (on band B), of C 9 were lost.

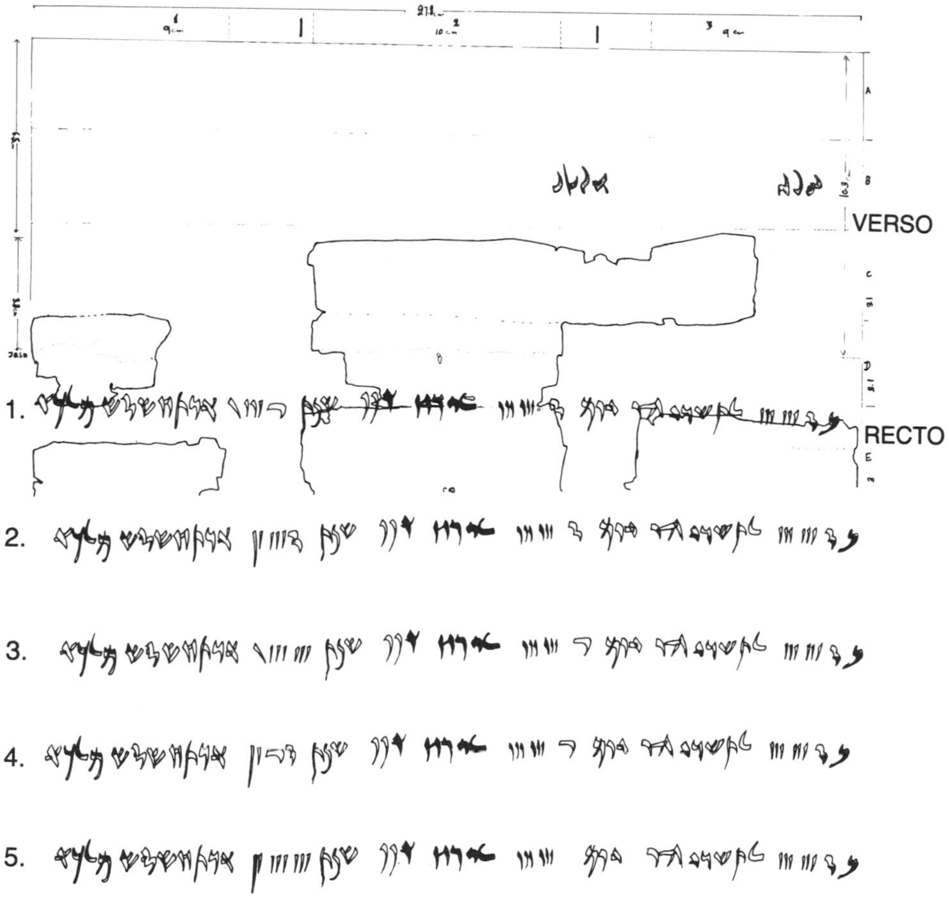

Figure 7. Five possible synchronisms for 26 Tishre and 26, 16, or 6 Epiphi between 458 and 432 B.C.E. Paleographically, 16 (Nos. 3–4) or 6 (No. 5) leave too much space. In the year date, 14 (No. 1) is more reasonable than 25 (No. 2). Date—8 November 451.

(1.) 26 Tishre = 26 Ephphi, 14 Artaxerxes = 8 November 451

(2.) 26 Tishre, 25 Artaxerxes = 6 October 440 = 26 Epiphi, 25 Artaxerxes = 5 October 440

(3.) 26 Tishre = 16 Epiphi, 7 Artaxerxes = 27 October 458

(4.) 26 Tishre = 16 Epiphi, 32 Artaxerxes = 20 October 432

(5.) 26 Tishre = 6 Epiphi, 8 Artaxerxes = 16 October 457

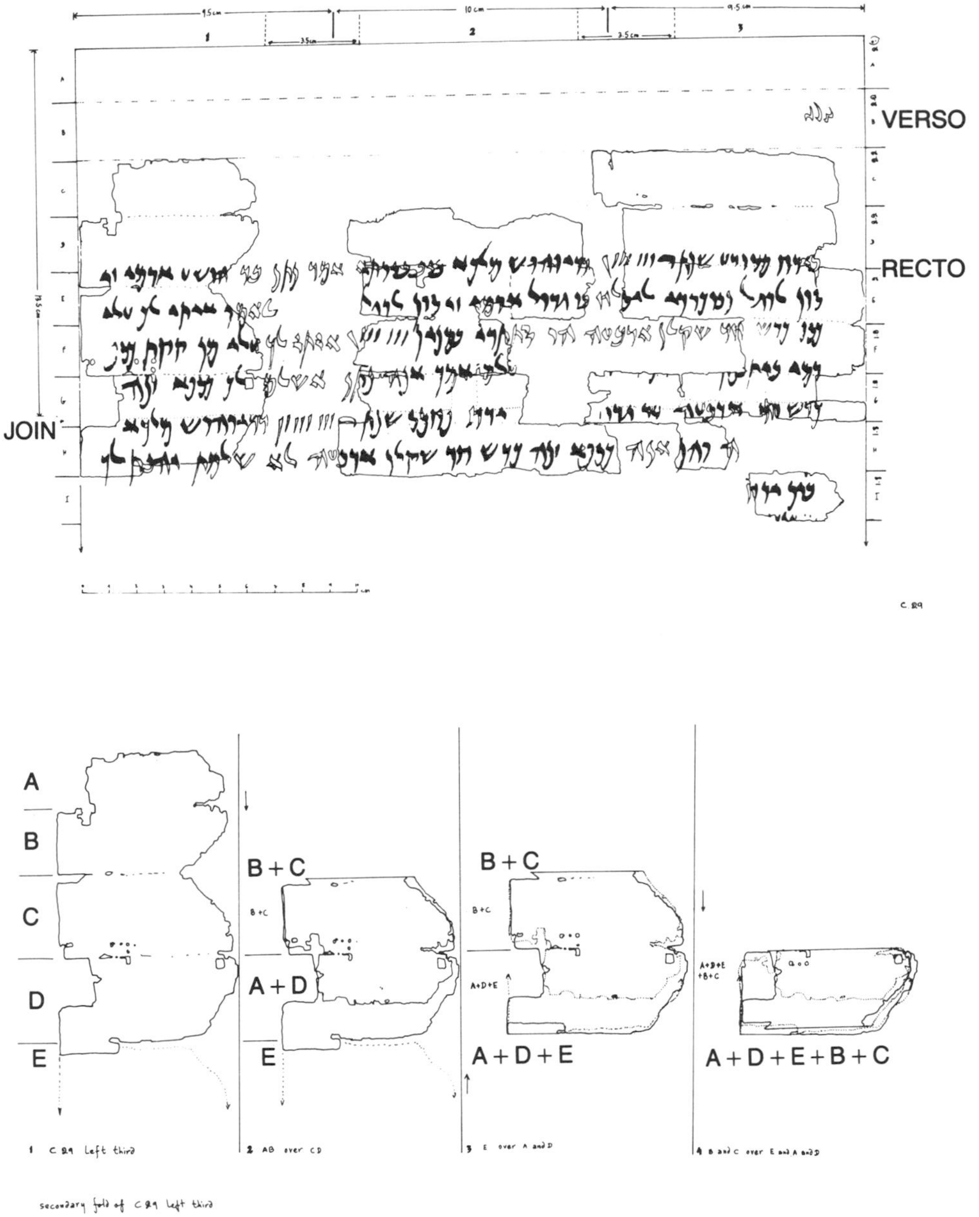

Figure 8. Top—Restoration of C 29. Bottom right fragment moved down to line 7. Endorsement restored on lost band B (verso). Bottom: mysterious, independent secondary fold of left vertical band.

References

Cowley, A. (= C)
1923 *Aramaic Papyri of the Fifth Century* B.C. Oxford: Clarendon Press.

Grelot, P.
1972 *Documents araméens d'Égypte.* Paris: Les Éditions du Cerf.

Halévy, J.
1907 *Revue sémitique* 15: 108–12.

Kraeling, E. G. (= K)
1953 *The Brooklyn Museum Aramaic Papyri.* New Haven: Yale University Press.

Porten, B.
1968 *Archives from Elephantine.* Berkeley: University of California Press.
1979 Aramaic Papyri and Parchments: A New Look. *Biblical Archeologist* 42: 74–103.

Sachau, Ed.
1911 *Aramäische Papyrus und Ostraka.* Leipzig: Hinrichs.

Sayce, A. H., and Cowley, A. E.
1906 *Aramaic Papyri Discovered at Assuan.* London: Alexander Moring.

Turner, E. G.
1978 The Terms Recto and Verso: The Anatomy of the Papyrus Roll. In *Actes du XVe congrès international de Papyrologie, I.* Papyrologica Bruxellensia, 16.

Yaron, R.
1957 The Schema of the Aramaic Legal Documents. *Journal of Semitic Studies* 2: 33–61.

The Historical, Linguistic, and Biblical Significance of the Khirbet el-Kôm Ostraca

Lawrence T. Geraty
Andrews University, Berrien Springs, Michigan

Ten years ago ostraca were discovered during John S. Holladay's salvage excavation at Khirbet el-Kôm, a site almost midway between Hebron and Lachish overlooking the Shephelah of southern Palestine (grid reference: 146.5/104.5). The earlier two inscriptions came from foundation trenches belonging to the initial Hellenistic rebuilding of the Iron II two-entry-way city gate while the later six inscriptions came from the living surface of a room belonging to the last phase of the Hellenistic rebuilding of an Iron Age house.

The most interesting ostracon (no. 3) was a bilingual which was published in 1975 (Geraty) and has received attention subsequently (Skaist 1978; Shea 1979; Naveh 1979; Hadley 1981; Geraty 1981). The first four lines are written in Aramaic script (Edomite language?) and the last five lines are written in the Greek script and language. Both halves of the inscription appear to refer to the same transaction on the same day: a payment of 32 *zuzin* (drachmas) by the Edomite shopkeeper (*kapēlos*) *Qôs-yadaʿ* to the Greek *Nikēratos* on the 12th of *Tammuz* (*Panēmos*), year 6, probably of Ptolemy II Philadelphus, i.e., 277 B.C.E. Thus the ostracon would have served as *Qôs-yadaʿ's* receipt.

The other seven ostraca, as yet unpublished, were studied in a doctoral dissertation (Geraty 1972). Six of them are in Aramaic script and the seventh is in Greek only. They add to our vocabulary and onomasticon for the period.

A number of conclusions, some of them only tentative, may be drawn from the data in this small corpus of inscriptions. The ostraca must now take their place among the few primary sources for the history of Palestine in the late fourth and early third centuries.

In 1941 Albright suggested that the Edomite occupation of the southern hill country of Judah around Hebron, Adoraim, and Marissa, which (according to 1 Esdr 4: 50) began during the exile, must have been substantially completed by the end of the sixth century since the Jewish province of the succeeding century extended southward only as far as Bethzur (Albright 1941: 14). Judging from the apparent language in ostraca nos. 1–6 (numbered sequentially as they were found), and from the name of the *kapēlos*, we have what is our first primary evidence of Edomite (or by this time, Idumean) presence in the area. The Edomites, then, were certainly in southern Judah by the early third century. Whether they were there earlier or not is difficult to decide on the basis of the earlier ostraca because the two names in ostracon no. 8 are Jewish. (The latter—along with ostracon no. 7—came from foundation trenches of the *initial* Hellenistic rebuilding of the site, whereas ostraca nos. 1–6 came from the *final* phase of Hellenistic occupation.) Theoretically ostraca nos. 7–8, being sealed in fill, could date from any time prior to their archeological context; paleographically it is possible that they are nearly contemporary with their context.

Because there is no evidence for a *bona fide* Persian period occupation of any size, Professor Holladay has suggested that the paleographical dates for the two groups of documents may help to date the two extremes of the time span of the Hellenistic occupation, which, in his opinion (based on the stratigraphy) could be as little as ten to twenty-five years but is not more than fifty to a hundred years (Holladay 1972). The initial phase of Hellenistic occupation may be due to Idumean settlement of the site but more probably to the establishment of effective Greek control in the region. We know that Alexander the Great subjugated this area before going into Egypt in 332 B.C.E. (Abel 1952: 11,12), and that after the battle of Ipsus in 301 B.C.E, Ptolemy I Soter established further control that was to last throughout the third century. If it was the Greeks who built up el-Kôm's fortifications, then (as Professor Holladay has also suggested) no special reason need be given for their abandonment of it once the surrounding country had been pacified. This would agree with the fact that there is no evidence for hostile destruction of the fortifications. If, however, the 277 B.C.E. date is accepted for ostracon no. 3 (Geraty 1972: ch. 5), it is possible that the site's demise may be connected with the fortunes of the First Syrian War when, in 276 B.C.E., Ptolemy I Soter invaded Syria but was defeated and eventually withdrew his forces all the way back to Egypt, fearing a Seleucid invasion that never materialized (Bevan 1927: 61, 62; and Tarn 1926: 155–62).

The ostraca contain further evidence for the value of *kesep*, *zuz*, *drachma*, and *ribaᶜ*, in the third century. *Qôs-yadaᶜ* was involved with average amounts of money. These may be compared with 50 drachmas for a slave girl, 100 drachmas as a reward for the recovery of three runaway slaves, and 52 drachmas for a *metrētēs* measure of oil—all from the third-century Zenon archive (Bevan 1927: 156; and Zenon papyri 59003, 59015). In the fourth century, a bushel of corn sold for between 6 and 22 drachmas; in the second century, soldiers were paid 350 drachmas a month (Bevan 1927: 17,157). Along with the inscriptional evidence for financial transactions, there is archeological evidence that *Qôs-yadaᶜ* may have been involved in weaving, though it may have been solely for his own family. His occupation as a storekeeper (*kapēlos*) appears to have brought him into contact with Nabateans, Arameans, Jews (?), Greeks, Arabs, and Egyptians (to judge from the personal names mentioned in the ostraca). Whether or not a person's ethnic or racial identity can be judged by his name, it can at least be said that Khirbet el-Kôm seems to have been a cosmopolitan military outpost in the early third century.

Though the script of the ostraca appears to be similar to, if not identical with, Aramaic, their locale, the *Qôs* name of the *kapēlos*, and the use of *bn* rather than *br* may hint at a strong Canaanite influence if not a full-blown Edomite dialect. If the language were Edomite, these ostraca doubled the number of inscriptions that at the time of the el-Kôm discovery could be considered Edomite or Idumean (Geraty 1972: 93, 94). No article appears in any of the ostraca, though that is not surprising considering the nature of the documents. The prepositions employed (*l*, *b*, *m*, and *mn*) are not distinctive. The transcription of the Greek term and name are normal except that *taw* rather than *ṭet* is the equivalent of *tau*. The orthography is defective (i.e., *tmz*, *zwzn*, and *ysp*) except for the historical spellings of *qws* and *zwzn*, which represent contractions, and the transcription of Greek *qpyls* and *nqyrts*. Besides the Edomite names *qwsydʿ* and *qwsbnh* (the former transliterated in Greek as *kos-idelē*), the following names may be added to the onomasticon: Semitic script *ḥyʾl*, *ʾṣly*, *yʿpt*, *mlḥʾ*, *ysp*, *šṭʾ*, and *ḥnʾ* (Greek *Ana*); and Greek script *Nikēratos*, *Sobbathos*, *Pestaus*, and *Domos*.

Ostraca nos. 3 and 6 may be the earliest extant indigenous Greek inscriptions to be found in Palestine. They appear to be under Semitic influence at least in the date formula, if not in the position of the verb. The transcription of the Semitic name *Qôs-yadaʿ* is normal, though both *epsilon* and *eta* are used as equivalents for the final vowel sound.

As already indicated, *Qôs-yadaʿ* is a *kapēlos*—a Greek term normally translated something like "retailer," "pedlar," or "shopkeeper" (Finkelstein 1935), in other words, someone intent on selling his wares for the sake of profit. *Kapēlos* is frequently used of a retailer of wine (Plummer 1915: 74). Well known in classical sources, the term carried a pejorative implication (Hughes 1962: 83), and that is certainly its biblical usage in Isa 1: 22 (LXX), where *kapēloi* mix their wine with water in order to cheat their buyers, and in Sir 26: 29 (LXX), where a *kapēlos* will not be judged free from sin; in 2 Cor 2: 17 Paul's opponents go about watering down (*kapēleuontes*) the word of God (cf. Barrett 1973: 103). Here at el-Kôm we have the first "real, live" evidence of a Palestinian *kapēlos*—which evidence should now be considered when defining the term during this period.

The question of paleography was thoroughly treated in the unpublished dissertation (Geraty 1972: chaps. 3 and 4). It is enough to say here that the ostraca provide the first firm third-century peg for this discipline for both the Palestinian Aramaic script and the Palestinian Greek script; even in Egypt, the formal hands of these scripts survive in few closely dated papyri, not to mention ostraca. That these results will have implications for the dating of the manuscripts at Qumran written in both Aramaic and Greek is obvious, though more detailed discussion of these implications must await further study.

As far as chronology goes—though ostracon no. 3 may be dated to 25 July 277 B.C.E. with some degree of probability—the discovery of further double dates will be necessary before the intricacies of the relationship between the Palestinian and Macedonian calendars can be satisfactorily explained. In the meantime, we must content ourselves with the contribution that these brief inscriptions have already made, meager though they are, to our knowledge of an area and era once touched on by none other than David Noel Freedman (1963: 375), to whom this essay is dedicated.

References

Abel, F. M.
1952 *Histoire de la Palestine depuis la conquête d'Alexandre jusqu'a l'invasion arabe.* Tome 1. Paris: Gabalda.

Albright, W. F.
1941 Ostracon No. 6043 from Ezion-Geber. *Bulletin of the American Schools of Oriental Research* 82: 11–15.

Barrett, C. K.
1973 *A Commentary on the Second Epistle to the Corinthians.* London: Black.

Bevan, E. R.
1927 *A History of Egypt under the Ptolemaic Dynasty.* London: Methuen.

Finkelstein, M. I.
1935 *ʾEmporos, Nauklēos* and *Kapēlos:* A Prolegomenon to the Study of Athenian Trade. *Classical Philology* 30: 320–26.

Freedman, D. N.
1963 Hebron. P. 375 in *Dictionary of the Bible*, ed. J. Hastings *et al.* New York: Scribners.

Geraty, L. T.
1972 *The Third Century B.C. Ostraca from Khirbet el-Kôm.* Harvard Dissertation.
1975 The Khirbet el-Kôm Bilingual Ostracon. *Bulletin of the Amerian Schools of Oriental Research* 220: 55–61.
1981 Recent Suggestions on the Bilingual Ostracon from Khirbet el-Kôm. *Andrews University Seminary Studies* 19: 137–40.

Hadley, T. D.
1981 The Edomite Language: What Can We Know? Cincinnati: Hebrew Union College Paper (unpublished).

Holladay, J. S.
1972 Personal communication to L. T. Geraty, dated March 6, 1972.

Hughes, P. E.
1962 *Paul's Second Epistle to the Corinthians.* Grand Rapids: Eerdmans.

Naveh, J.
1979 The Aramaic Ostraca from Tel Beer-Sheba (Seasons 1971–1976). *Tel Aviv* 6: 182–98.

Plummer, A.
1915 *A Critical and Exegetical Commentary on the Second Epistle of St. Paul to the Corinthians.* Edinburgh: Clark.

Shea, W. H.
1979 The Receipts of the Bilingual Ostracon from Khirbet el-Kôm. Berrien Springs, Michigan: Andrews University Paper (unpublished).

Skaist, A.
1978 A Note on the Bilingual Ostracon from Khirbet el-Kôm. *Israel Exploration Journal* 28: 106–8.

Tarn, W. W.
1926 The First Syrian War. *Journal of Hellenic Studies* 46: 155–62.

The Background of the Paleo-Hebrew Texts at Qumran

K. A. Mathews
Criswell Center for Biblical Studies, Dallas, Texas

Though more than thirty years of inquiry by two generations of able scholars have been given to the Essene desert commune and library, many of its most tantalizing secrets remain relatively undisturbed, having eluded modern attempts at rediscovery. For instance, while historians are agreed on the general history of Essene life at Qumran, the identities of two primary protagonists, the Teacher of Righteousness and the Wicked Priest, remain uncertain, and the background of the sect itself, whether Babylonian or Palestinian, is disputed. Again, while hundreds of variant readings from the biblical manuscripts at Qumran have been catalogued, no single reconstruction of the history of the Hebrew Bible has achieved wide acceptance. However, the successes of scholars laboring over the past quarter-century have far outnumbered failures, as evidenced not only by the amassing of details in numerous volumes but also by the evolution of methodologies developed for the particular demands of the new finds.

Paleography, particularly the troublesome paleo-Hebrew script, is a parade example of such ground-breaking efforts. F. M. Cross (1955; 1961), following the lead of W. F. Albright (1937), established an absolute chronology for the dating of Jewish square scripts during the Hellenistic and Roman periods, tracing paleographic developments from the Aramaic hand of the 4th century B.C.E. to the Nabatean and Palmyrene scripts. R. S. Hanson (1964) followed Cross by establishing a chronology for the paleo-Hebrew scripts of several Qumran texts, using the script of the Hasmonean coins as his control. While some adjustment must be made in Hanson's dates, if Meshorer's historical reconstruction of the Hasmonean coinage (1967) is followed (see Hanson 1974), the work of Hanson has served to correct the early attempts of Birnbaum (1950) and de Vaux (1949), who assigned the paleo-Hebrew materials to the 5th and 4th centuries B.C.E.

In spite of such advances, the reason why these paleo-Hebrew manuscripts existed at all, particularly at Qumran, has not been adequately addressed. The problem raised by P. W. Skehan as early as 1955 concerning paleo-Hebrew texts remains unresolved: "Leaving open the question as to by whom, and for what purpose, such texts were prepared, the materials from Qumran make it quite sure that texts in this sort of script were being currently produced in the second and first centuries B.C.E. Any theory as to who produced them, and why, will have to be broad enough to include the fact of a text of Job in such a script, of which several fragments were yielded by Cave 4 at Kh. Qumran" (1955a: 182–83). It is now possible to sketch such a theory, since more texts are now available and contemporary scholarship is closer to achieving a consensus on the general history and socio-political life of the desert sectarians.

Paleo-Hebrew at Qumran

Among the novelties in Qumran square-script texts is the appearance of the Tetragrammaton and other divine names in paleo-Hebrew characters. Examples of this phenomenon are not few in number nor limited in scope among the manuscripts. The appearance of this feature in eighteen different texts, recovered from six of the eleven caves, suggests that the practice was not uncommon (see the Appendix for the published examples). These manuscripts not only vary in kind (i.e., biblical texts, *pĕšārîm*, and sectarian texts) but also range in date from the 2nd century B.C.E. to the 1st century C.E. Some texts (e.g., 11QPs[a]) show a consistent employment of paleo-Hebrew for the divine name(s), while others show only occasional usage (e.g., 1QH).

In addition to these manuscripts there are a dozen texts completely written in paleo-Hebrew, which come from the 2nd and 1st centuries B.C.E. (see the Appendix for the published examples). All the manuscripts come from the Pentateuch with the exception of the fragments of Job; the pentateuchal texts consist of two copies each of Genesis, Exodus, and Deuteronomy, one of Numbers, and four of Leviticus (Skehan 1965: 88).

Divine Name(s)

Differentiating the holy name by a distinctive script is a feature of Jewish scribal practice found in both Greek and Hebrew texts. The remains of a Greek text of Deuteronomy (Fouad Papyrus 266), dated to the end of the 2nd century B.C.E., has the Hebrew Tetragrammaton (in "square" letters) rather than the expected Greek translation *kyrios* (Waddell 1944: 158–61). Also, fragments from Aquila's translation of Kings and Psalms (2nd century C.E.) recovered from the Cairo Genizah show the divine name in a degenerate form of paleo-Hebrew (Burkitt 1898: 15–17, pls.; Taylor 1900: 27, 72, pls. 3–8). Similarly, the Milan palimpsest of the Hexapla has, in the second column, *yhwh* written in Hebrew characters (Jellicoe 1968: 127–33; Waddell 1944: 159; see further in general C. H. Roberts 1979). From Naḥal Ḥever in Palestine comes a Greek text of the *Dodekapropheton*, written in the mid-1st century C.E. (8ḤevXII gr) which uses the same scribal convention, the use of paleo-Hebrew characters instead of *kyrios* for the Tetragrammaton (Barthélemy 1953: 24, n. 1; 1963: 168, pls. 1–2).

What could be the purpose of this practice? The use of distinguishing scripts, whether Hebrew characters in Greek texts or paleo-Hebrew insertions in "square"-letter manuscripts, may have functioned like our modern italics for the ancient Jew reading the text. At least initially, that is, the scribe may have used a different script for *yhwh* to alert the reader not to pronounce what was written. This suggestion is solely inferential, however, since we have no ancient explanation for the practice. Among the few references from antiquity that we have to this custom are those of Origen and Jerome, who allude to the writing of the Tetragrammaton with characters from "ancient times" (i.e., paleo-Hebrew).[1] They considered texts which had the divine name in "old" characters to be more accurate. Though little can be learned from their testimony, it does tell us that by the third century C.E. knowledge of the original intention of the practice seems to have been lost. Apparently, the Fathers recognized the antiquity of the practice and were so impressed with its implication for the fidelity of the scribe who produced the text that they considered manuscripts which show it to be of greater textual value.

J. P. Siegel (1971), working from tannaitic sources and the Qumran corpus, has advanced an explanation for the scribal convention. He has shown that the scribes wrote the divine name(s) in paleo-Hebrew to insure permanency in the text. From a tannaitic discussion (*y. Megillah* 1. 9) concerning the problem of erasing the divine name(s) and attendant prefixes and suffixes, Siegel discovered that the practice at Qumran paralleled the regulations set forth by the rabbis. Like the rabbis of later generations, the Essene scribe experienced the difficulties of when and how to cancel out the sacred name(s); he resolved the dilemma by writing in paleo-Hebrew characters what was too sacred to be changed.

By analogy, then, we may conclude that the Jewish scribe, in preparing Greek manuscripts, employed Hebrew letters whether "square-script" or paleo-Hebrew for a similar purpose of signaling caution for those engaged in writing and reading the text.

From the Qumran testimony and the Greek exemplars noted above, it is evident that the use of a distinctive script for *nomina sacra* was not uncommon among the Jews. The evidence shows a measure of uniformity in its regulation, much as we should expect since the practice is attested for more than two centuries among diverse scribal schools.

Manuscripts

We have stated above that the writing of the divine name(s) in paleo-Hebrew characters was prompted by two related concerns: (1) to indicate special homage for the holy name(s) and (2) to alert the scribe as to which divine name(s) and elements could not be erased. When we consider the manuscripts which are completely penned in paleo-Hebrew script, we must first ask if such concerns also were factors in creating them.

First, can we posit that the Qumran community paid special tribute to the Pentateuch (and Job) in sort of a quasi-canonical fashion? Did the Essenes deem these particular biblical books more binding than others, whether biblical or sectarian? The *pěšārîm* alone would indicate otherwise, since they show a wide interest in various books of the Hebrew Bible. Habakkuk (1QpHab), for example, is crucial to the community's understanding of its role in the "last days"; through apocalyptic interpretations of its ancient prophecies the Essenes could see themselves and their plight at the hands of the Wicked Priest. The Temple Scroll (11QTemple) could not have been regarded by its desert adherents as any less than the very words of God. Writing the whole scroll in first person, even to the point of changing biblical quotations from Moses' speeches to those of God and thereby making God the sole speaker, produced a revelatory work on the same plane as the sacred Torah itself (Yadin 1977; Milgrom 1978: 119; Levine 1978: 6, 18, 20). Such examples are too numerous and well known among the Qumran scrolls to necessitate further discussion, and these two texts alone are sufficient to dismiss any notion that the Pentateuch (and Job) alone had "proto-canonical" status among the Essenes. The evidence from the scrolls by itself is inconclusive, but the data suggest to us that a concept of canon (i.e., a closed collection of sacred books) did not exist among the Essenes; otherwise, we must conclude that their canon far exceeded in size any canon known elsewhere in Judaism, sectarian or not.[2]

Second, it would be senseless to think that the scribes who employed paleo-Hebrew script to cope with the problem of erasures would use the same device in producing whole manuscripts (Siegel 1971: 170). Evidently, as Siegel notes (1971: 170–71), a conservative circle of priestly scribes perpetuated the script.[3] A number of unanswered questions remain, however. What was the origin of this practice? Why is it found in the Pentateuch and Job alone? Why do we find it among the Essenes? Why was it rejected by the rabbis? Though the facts are scanty, a reconstruction is possible to account for the appearance of paleo-Hebrew texts at Qumran and for their perpetuation in the Essene scribal community.

Origin of Paleo-Hebrew

The paleo-Hebrew script is descended from the archaic Hebrew hand of the 7th and 6th centuries B.C.E. It survived the popularity of the Aramaic script during the Persian and Hellenistic periods probably due to its perpetuation by a small, ultra-conservative circle of Jewish scribes (Cross 1961: 189, n. 4). The late paleo-Hebrew script is not genuinely archaic but archaistic, a script which was deliberately fashioned after older models in an attempt to recapture the script of antiquity. The Hasmonean period is characterized by infatuation with the golden years of Israel's past; this is demonstrated in the official use of the old script by the Hasmonean rulers and in the deliberate archaisms of style and language found in the literature of the day.

The revival in use of the "old" script during the 2nd-1st centuries B.C.E., as evidenced by the Hebrew legends of the Hasmonean coinage, was due largely to the resurgence of Jewish nationalism at that time.[4] That paleo-Hebrew conveyed a spirit of nationalistic fervor is confirmed by its reappearance on the "Freedom of Zion" and "Redemption of Zion" coin series minted by the Jewish zealots of the First and Second Jewish Wars (Meshorer 1967: 88–91, 154–58, pls. 19–20; 92–101, 159–69, pls. 21–28; Yadin 1965: 81, pl. 19F-G; 1966a: 97–98, 108–9, 171). By the 1st and 2nd centuries C.E. paleo-Hebrew was extremely rare among the Jews, though a derivative form existed among the Samaritans; the script's use by the freedom-fighters symbolized for them a return to the days of independence experienced by the ancients and the Hasmoneans. The Zealots are known to have shared in many of the same patriotic sentiments felt by their Hasmonean predecessors (Farmer 1956: 175–86). The coins inscribed with the "ancient" script inflamed the revolutionary hearts of the people.

The use of paleo-Hebrew in the Persian and early Hellenistic periods can also be interpreted as a feature of Jewish nationalism. The Tennes rebellion against Persian domination (mid-4th century B.C.E.), in which Judah participated, created a climate which could account for the script's resurgence among the Jews during the late Persian period.[5]

The coins of the Hasmonean family reflected not only the ruler's political status with respect to the Syrians and the Sanhedrin but also the mood of his subjects. The coin sequence of Alexander Janneus is illustrative of this, since some of his coins reflect both his political ambitions and his attention to the pulse of public feeling.[6] Some coins of the flower-anchor series bearing his royal inscription were restruck while in the mint with the customary formula: "Jonathan the High Priest and the *ḥeber* of the Jews" (Meshorer 1967: nos. 17, 17a; Kindler 1974a: nos. 12–13); this change may have been a reaction to the difficulties Janneus encountered with the Pharisees, a concession by which he hoped to appease the moderate wing of the party (Kanael 1963: 44–45). The dated coins of Janneus (83 and 78 B.C.E.), which were struck in Aramaic script rather than the customary paleo-Hebrew (for which the Pharisees had little regard[7]), indicate an attempt near the end of his reign to neutralize his political opposition (Naveh 1968: 25). However, even two years before his death, as we see from the dated coins of 78 B.C.E., he still retained the title "king." From these coin changes during the reign of Janneus, we can see how the use of paleo-Hebrew reflected socio-political concerns.

The history of the Hasmonean dynasty is a story of political transition: what had begun as a religious reformation among those "zealous for the law" (1 Macc 2: 27) soon became a matter of political independence from Syria. The initial goal of the Maccabees was to rid Judea of the idolatry foisted upon the Jews during the reign of Antiochus IV. The hellenizing program promulgated by this Syrian "sinful root" (1 Macc 1: 10) culminated in the eradication of the Temple cultus and the dedication of the sacred shrine to the worship of Zeus (1 Macc 1: 54). It was this "abomination of desolation" (Dan 11: 31; 12: 11) which fueled the Maccabean uprising. Yet within the three years it took Judas Maccabeus to reverse Antiochus' desecration (167–164 B.C.E.), the interests of the Maccabean princes had become more political than religious. Their new quest was total independence from Syrian interference and sole control of Judean matters. An inner-Jewish rivalry for control of Judea developed between the hellenizing party and the "nationalists" (Schürer 1973: I, 167), but with Jonathan's acquisition of the high priesthood from Alexander Balas in 152 B.C.E. the Hasmonean family essentially won control of internal Jewish affairs. Jonathan's appetite was not so easily satisfied though, and he wished to free Judah from any external influence, an aspiration which alarmed the Syrians and ultimately led to his murder at the treacherous hands of Tryphon (1 Maccabees 12–13). Jonathan's brother and successor, Simon Maccabeus, succeeded in ousting the Syrian garrison at Jerusalem, freeing Judah from Syrian taxation, and bringing a season of peace to the Jews. During his reign, it could be said that the "yoke of the Gentiles was removed from Israel" (1 Macc 13: 41). Proof of Simon's newly won autonomy was the reckoning of chronology by his regal years and the granting of the right to mint his own coinage (which he probably did not exercise; 1 Macc 13: 41; 15: 1–9). If some of the *yhwḥnn* coins can be attributed to John Hyrcanus I, then we have evidence of Simon's immediate successor showing a growing optimism for a Judean dynasty. If not, then certainly during the time of Janneus (103–76 B.C.E.), probably about 96 B.C.E. with the defeat of Gaza and the death of Antiochus VIII, a Hasmonean could boastfully declare himself king.

This spirit of nationalism, reminiscent of the Davidic kings, under the Hasmonean regime explains why paleo-Hebrew was adopted as its official script and why the "old" characters received wider circulation in the 2nd-1st centuries B.C.E.

The literature of the Hasmoneans reflects the same nostalgia for Israel's past glory. Jewish literature of the period generally is marked by apocalyptic and wisdom compositions, but 1 Maccabees stands apart from these as a sober, simple historical account of the Maccabean wars, an account like that of the biblical books of Samuel. Though the author is not overly concerned with the miraculous or with attributing the successes of the Maccabeans to the intervention of God, he clearly is an adherent of the Maccabean pledge to the Torah (Oesterly 1953: 306–7). While some contemporary authors composed works in Greek and modeled them after Greek writers (e.g., 2 Maccabees), the author (and translator) of 1 Maccabees followed the genre and language of the biblical histories. As the biblical account traced the careers of Saul and David, and thereby dispelled any doubts about the legitimacy of the Davidic house, the author of 1 Maccabees wrote his work as an apology for Hasmonean legitimacy. Such a defense is best suited to the time of Janneus, whose authority was severely challenged by Pharisaic circles. The Pharisees questioned his fitness for the high priesthood, which would in essence threaten his civil authority over the Jews. 1 Maccabees was written as propaganda for the Hasmonean house; its method is to extol Simon by focusing on his confirmation by public proclamation as high priest "forever" (1 Macc 14: 41). The Maccabean account nicely (though modestly) parallels the second chapter of 2 Samuel, which tells of the establishment of the Davidic house at Hebron by popular demand. The author set out to prove that Hyrcanus was the rightful heir to the high priesthood, not the pretender Ptolemy. Legitimizing Hyrcanus' accession to the priesthood was tantamount to giving Janneus credibility (Goldstein 1976: 71, 77, 172).

These archaistic trappings of script and literary style associated with the Hasmoneans reflect a desire to recapture the past glory of the Jews and to kindle within the people nationalistic vision.

At Qumran, too, during this period, the archetype for the community was drawn from biblical times.[8] For instance, several sectarian compositions contain deliberate archaisms which mimic classical Hebrew style. The language, while agreeing at many points with postexilic Hebrew, has grammatical and lexical features closer to the Torah than the contemporary Hebrew style of the period. This "neo-classical" style of Hebrew, as Polzin terms it (1976: 6), illustrates the community's interest, shared with the Hasmoneans, in the distant past.[9]

Biblical Texts in Paleo-Hebrew

The tendency toward archaizing during this period was a response to the Maccabean revolution which had led to a revival of ancient Jewish traditions. Consequently, appreciation for the ancient Torah grew and with it an interest in its "ancient" script, which until then had been preserved among only a few priestly families. Paleo-Hebrew achieved wider recognition among scribal communities, and manuscripts of the Pentateuch (and Job), copied from older models, approximated an archaic appearance.

This brings us to the question, Why only the Pentateuch and Job? From the 5th century B.C.E. on, all Judahite socio-political and religious life had its roots in Ezra's "Torah-centered" community. The Law of Moses not only regulated postexilic life (as in preexilic Israel) but now actually defined what was and was not "Jewish." To be "Jewish" and to keep the covenant and law were now perceived as one tradition. The

Law became the primary distinguishing feature of Judaism rather than acknowledgment of Yahweh's acts in history; history had almost become inconsequential since the Law was now thought to have always existed (Bright 1976: 444; Mendenhall 1962: 721).

With the hellenistic reforms of Antiochus IV, as in the days of the Exile, Jewish identity was again threatened: Torah scrolls were burned and the Temple cultus was abandoned. The survival instinct of the Jews more than any other factor was responsible for the Maccabean revolt; as Farmer (1956: 48) has remarked, Jewish nationalism was not merely theocentric but "Torahcentric." The Torah, which was formative for the Jewish community, had to be defended at all costs; it became of paramount importance to the people during this time. The teaching of the Torah became the ideal, the model through which Jews must interpret their present and future experience.

Since the Torah was believed to be the oldest portion of Scripture, scribes thought it fitting to pen it in the "ancient" script. Some may have even believed Moses himself wrote the books in this way. The central place the Torah had among the Jews coupled with its known antiquity encouraged scribes to transmit it in the archaizing script.

If we are correct, why then did Job merit the distinctive script? P. W. Skehan (1955a: 183 n. 2) was near the heart of the resolution when he asked if it was "because of the association of the person of Job with patriarchal times, and the speculation which placed the composition of the Book of Job in proximity to that of the Pentateuch." W. H. Brownlee (1964: 29) correctly observed almost a decade later that use of paleo-Hebrew reflects the presumption of Mosaic authorship. If we can accept rabbinic opinion as indicative of an earlier sentiment among the Jews, we can be sure that Moses was the common denominator, since at least some Jews later believed that Moses wrote Job as well as the Torah and that the hero Job was Moses' contemporary (*b. B. Bat.* 14b-15a). The antiquity of the composition and its special association with Moses justified its writing in the "old" script.

Paleo-Hebrew Texts at Qumran

The limitations of our data prohibit us from a definitive statement as to the extent the Essene community participated in perpetuating the use of paleo-Hebrew for biblical manuscripts. There are, however, several points which are clear as a result of what has been published so far from Qumran. (1) The precautions taken to hide all the texts indicate that the Essenes considered them to be of considerable value. (2) While dates for the paleo-Hebrew manuscripts remain subject to revision since the dating of our control (i.e., the coins) is uncertain, we are generally safe in assigning most to Period I (ca. 150–31 B.C.E.).[10] (3) The practice was unevenly used among the Essenes; many more copies of pentateuchal books appear in "square" characters than in paleo-Hebrew. (4) Among the texts which have been recovered, many were skillfully worked; the script, though less familiar to the scribe than the Jewish hand, was evidently well known to his eye.[11]

Apart from these points, little is known; we are left with a number of puzzling questions. The chief is, Why would the Essenes use and preserve texts written in the script which adorned the coinage of their chief adversaries the Hasmoneans? The answer may be suggested by a reexamination of the enigmatic dominant figure of Essene history, the Teacher of Righteousness.

Following Murphy-O'Connor's reconstruction (1974; 1977) of the history of the Essenes, we can allow that the Teacher was (1) a contemporary of Jonathan, the Wicked Priest (160–143 B.C.E.), (2) a Zadokite high priest,[12] who was Jonathan's predecessor but who was never officially recognized, and (3) the primary catalyst for the sect's move to the desert community at Qumran.

After the death of the hellenizing Alkimos in 159 B.C.E., the office of high priest was left vacant for seven years, according to Josephus' account (*Ant* 20, 237).[13] The position was not immediately filled, at least officially, because Jonathan viewed the high priesthood as a potential threat to his civil authority, and also because the Syrians hoped to use the position, if necessary, for political leverage against Jonathan. However, the functions of the high priest (e.g., the Day of Atonement) could not have ceased for long and it is reasonable to suppose that the senior Zadokite priest at the time would have filled the void created by Alkimos' death (Murphy-O'Connor 1974: 230).

This Zadokite high priest is not mentioned in 1 Maccabees, not only because he was never officially installed, but also because admission of his existence would have been counter-productive to the author's aim—to legitimize Hasmonean claims. To speak of the Zadokite's position would have made Jonathan appear the usurper he actually was. By omitting reference to the Zadokite, 1 Maccabees makes Jonathan appear to be the first to break the line of hellenizing high priests (Murphy-O'Connor 1977: 114). Josephus' omission of the Zadokite was probably due to his dependence on 1 Maccabees for his account of the period.

For some time, then, the legitimate Zadokite heir officiated in the Temple, a situation warmly received by the Pious but a new problem for the civil ruler, Jonathan. Jonathan not only had an eye on the position for himself; to achieve his nationalistic ambitions he had to appeal to the wealthy hellenizing class. The Zadokite priest would have opposed concessions to the hellenizing faction and probably became obstructive to Jonathan's plans. When Jonathan received appointment as high priest, he successfully silenced the Zadokite's opposition and put him to flight (Murphy-O'Connor 1974: 231–33; 1977: 117).

The Essenes openly welcomed the deposed Zadokite priest as the rightful heir to the high priesthood and immediately acknowledged his authority over their community. Several members were persuaded by him to establish a commune in the desert in preparation for the coming dawn of the new age.

That the Teacher actually served as high priest at one time cannot be proven, but it is probable that the Teacher had been a Temple official of Zadokite lineage. The Essenes themselves were a priestly party whose members identified themselves as the "sons of Zadok." From the scrolls we see how the Teacher so completely dominates the community that we must believe this imposing figure was in line to the Zadokite high priesthood and thereby enjoyed the unquestioned loyalty of the Essene members. As a Temple official the Teacher would have had access to its archives; he probably brought a number of writings with him to the desert site. Most likely among them were manuscripts copied in paleo-Hebrew script.

While scribal activity at Qumran was greatest during Periods Ib (100–31 B.C.E.) and II (4 B.C.E.–68 C.E.), some literary activity must have occurred earlier, as sectarian works are known to have been produced then. The oldest copy of the *Rule* (1QS) comes from ca. 100–75 B.C.E. and is believed to be somewhat distant from its autograph, which would suggest a date of ca. 150–125 B.C.E. for its authorship (Cross 1980: 114, n. 7; 119, n. 18). The "Manifesto" of 1QS (8: 1–16a; 9: 13–10: 8a) is thought to reflect a period antedating the Qumran community though it was composed by the Teacher of Righteousness (Murphy-O'Connor 1969: 531). Also, we should take into account the "Hymns of the Teacher" preserved in 1QH. Among non-sectarian scrolls, the biblical manuscripts begin in quantity about 150 B.C.E.; earlier scrolls are rare and are probably master copies brought into the community at its founding, as Cross (1971: 74–75) has suggested. The writing and copying of literary documents must have been a fervent activity at Qumran from its very inception.

Paleo-Hebrew manuscripts brought to Qumran remained important to the Teacher and were perpetuated by the community because the texts in their "ancient" script evoked nostalgic memories of early Israel. While more attention would have been given to writing documents in the contemporary Jewish hand, the paleo-Hebrew manuscripts retained their popularity because they were the very works penned by Moses during his sojourn in the wilderness. The Essenes believed that their season in the desert was analogous to that of Moses and of ancient Israel when there was no king or temple but only the sacred Torah. They recognized that they were living in the last days before the coming of the messianic kingdom and were convinced that the events of Israel's formative period—the Exodus and desert sojourn—would be reenacted in preparation for the *eschaton* (Wieder 1953: 171). They thought themselves to be reconstituting the nation of Israel as it was in the days of Moses and Aaron in the desert.

The Essenes' celebration of the past was, however, not a shallow nostalgia (Freedman 1971: 141); the "sons of Zadok" will know their vindication only in the future. Thus, their focus was eschatological but modeled after the life experienced by Israel in the desert. The forty years of war projected between the Sons of Light and the Sons of Darkness correspond to the years of wilderness wanderings; each period serves as a transition period before the ultimate conquest (see 1QM 1: 16–2: 14). The elaborate description of the military camp in 1QM depicts the structure known in the wilderness as it is described in Numbers (Yadin 1962: 38–39). The laws of warfare recorded in Numbers and Deuteronomy became the prototype for the military organization and laws of war anticipated in the eschatological conflict (Yadin 1962: 4–5, 16, 38–86). So the Sinai event, which was formative in Israel's interpretation of its history, became the paradigm for the community's understanding of God's future encounter with Israel (Betz 1967: 89–99). By eschatological interpretation, the Essenes couched visions of the future coming of God in the imagery of the desert motif found in Exodus 19 and Deuteronomy 33.

The primary figure central to the story of the historical Exodus, i.e., Moses, could not be absent from the Essene reenactment in the eschatological event. Thus, the Teacher plays the same role as the historical Moses in the wilderness. As Moses gave ancient Israel its covenant, so the Teacher revealed the New Covenant to the second Israel in the wilderness. As the "new" Moses, the Teacher was God's spokesman through whom He would unveil the final, climactic events leading to the new age. The Habakkuk commentary claims that his teachings are "from the mouth of God" and his interpretations of ancient prophecy are of divine origin (1QpHab 2: 3, 8; for the New Covenant, cf. CD 6: 19; 8: 21; 19: 33; Huntjens 1974: 370–71). However, he is not the *second* Moses, as Wieder (1953) has suggested. Passages in the *Damascus Document* (CD 19: 34–20: 1) and the *Rule* (1QS 9: 9–11) prevent us from identifying the Teacher with the eschatological prophet anticipated by the community on the basis of Deut 18: 15–18. If Wieder is correct in assuming that the Teacher is the "expositor of the Law" (CD 6: 10–11), then the Teacher for the Essenes was a Moses-like figure. Wieder has shown how the epithets of Moses found in rabbinic literature are applied by the sectarians to the Teacher, which suggests that the Essenes considered the Teacher another Moses—their Moses! Essene attention to Moses is reflected also by pseudo-Mosaic writings recovered from Qumran such as the "Sayings of Moses" (1QDM), which echoes the Deuteronomic sermons of Moses in style and content.[14]

However, the new doctrine of the Teacher did not supplant the Old, for every novitiate swore to uphold the "Torah of Moses" (1QS 5: 8); rather, the New Covenant was a retelling of the Old for the present generation in the desert. Departure from the Law demanded excommunication for the violator (1QS 8: 20–23); study of the Law was given paramount importance in the life of the community (1QS 5: 11; 6: 6; 8: 15).

The Law of Moses may have been more deeply rooted in the mind of the Essene and more of a formative factor for his ideology than first discerned, if Murphy-O'Connor's theory of Essene origins is correct. While his reconstruction remains tentative, it convincingly accounts for several previously unexplained difficulties. Traditionally, the birth of the Essene movement has been explained as a local reaction to Palestinian Hellenism, but Murphy-O'Connor has suggested that its origins are in distant Babylon. At Babylon the original Essenes found themselves in a pagan environment which threatened their unique religious heritage. Like Ezra, the Essenes emphasized strict observance of the Law in the hope of maintaining fidelity to God and preserving their identity among the Gentiles. When these people returned to Palestine at the time of the Maccabean uprising, they were shocked to discover that Hellenism had made such dramatic inroads into Palestinian Judaism. The story of Essene fortunes in Palestine is the story of the Essene's encounter with Hellenistic Judaism. From the Essene viewpoint, their Palestinian brethren were repeating the mistakes which led to the Captivity (Murphy-O'Connor 1974; 1977). The Essenes believed that they alone among the Jews could rightly understand the Law, with the result that their interpretation of the Law became a rallying point for their movement.

In spite of the "Moses mentality" among the Essenes, an inventory of the Essene library indicates that the practice of writing paleo-Hebrew texts did not dominate Qumran scribal convention. By far the majority of pentateuchal texts occur in the popular "square" script, and we know that "normative" Judaism ultimately adopted the contemporary late Herodian hand for the Hebrew Bible (*m. Yad.* 4, 5). We are left with the questions, Why could the paleo-Hebrew script not supplant the Jewish hand and why did the script fall out of favor altogether among the Pharisees?

The End of Paleo-Hebrew Among the Jews

The Essenes enjoyed the "old" script but it never achieved the following the contemporary hand had known. This situation was due only in part to the traditional limitations imposed on its usage (for the Pentateuch and Job only), though this did result in the "square" characters being more familiar to the scribe. Coupled with this practical aspect was the ideological antagonism experienced between the Essenes and the Hasmonean family. The Essenes were naturally suspicious of Hasmonean policy; with Hasmonean adoption of paleo-Hebrew, the script probably lost some of its appeal and prestige for the community.

The rabbis decidedly rejected the "old" script and permitted the "square" characters only for the writing of scripture. Talmudic tradition recognizes Ezra as the first to commission the writing of the Bible in "Assyrian" (*ʾaššûrît*) characters (*b. Sanh.* 21b-22a; *t. Sanh.* 4: 7; *y. Meg.* 1: 8b). The rabbis could have no greater authority than Ezra himself to legitimize their adoption of the "square" script. The rabbinic attitude toward paleo-Hebrew was probably conditioned more by their antagonism toward those who did adopt it than anything else.

Cross (1975: 185, 291, 314) has suggested that the rejection of paleo-Hebrew script cannot be viewed as "anti-Samaritan" since the script appears among the Hasmoneans, the Essenes, and the rebels of the First and Second Jewish Wars. Within the framework of his local texts theory, Cross posits that the rabbis of the 1st-2nd centuries C.E. selected a text-type (Babylonian in origin) for the Pentateuch which was "never found in pure type in Palaeo-Hebrew" and they chose with reluctance the contemporary Herodian hand for the Hebrew Bible (1964: 289). We have already expressed some reservations about Cross's thesis. Here we wonder why the rabbis would have chosen a text only recently reintroduced to Palestine, and thus new to them, and rejected the more familiar text which was indigenous to Palestine? If the rabbis had no ill-will toward paleo-Hebrew, why would they accept a text which not only was new but also was written in the less-appealing "square" characters? Even given Cross's theory, it would not seem to have been too difficult to commission the copying of the Babylonian text-type in paleo-Hebrew if the rabbis actually approved of the script.

The rabbinic attitude toward the "old" script can be traced back to the Hasmonean-Sadducean coalition which opposed the Pharisees. Hyrcanus I and Janneus of the Hasmoneans particularly catered to the wealthy Sadducean families whose political interests paralleled their own. Heated antagonism finally erupted into outright hostilities under Janneus, when as many as 6000 Jews were massacred. D. Diringer (1950: 48–49) has suggested that the Hasmonean kings adopted the "old" script under the influence of priestly Sadducean families. This would explain why the Pharisees initially had such little regard for the script.

By the 2nd century C.E., the Sadducee controversy had long since ended with the fall of the temple aristocracy, the Essenes were dispersed, and only the Samaritan sect remained to rival rabbinism. The script used by the Samaritans, though derived from the paleo-Hebrew of the Hasmonean period, had its own independent development from the 1st century B.C.E. (Cross 1966b: 209–11; Purvis 1968). The script had been in use among the Samaritans for about two centuries by then, and if the Samaritans claimed priority for their Torah on the basis of the older script (Diringer 1950: 37), then we can see why the rabbis appealed to an authority such as Ezra to legitimize their use of the "square" script. Talmudic passages (*b. Sanh.* 21b-22a; *m. Yad.* 4: 5) indicate that the Samaritan usage of the script prevented the Jews from using it: Ezra himself had selected the "Assyrian" hand. The rabbis could not risk the potential confusion of their version of the Torah with the rival counterpart promulgated by the Samaritans—not even in script!

We cannot assume that the rabbis appreciated the archaizing script simply because some of their number supported the rebels of the Jewish wars. In fact, the attitude of the rabbis toward the Jewish revolts is not always clear. While it is true that rabbinic zeal for the Torah indirectly contributed to the two revolts, there was within the rabbinic movement a pacifist opinion. Within Pharisaism and its offspring rabbinic Judaism two opposite viewpoints emerged; they were able to coexist because each was founded on religious conviction. Even in the time of Herod, individual Pharisees showed both sympathy and intolerance for Gentile authority. During Herod's regime Pharisees on two occasions refused to take an oath of loyalty to the Empire, yet two prominent Pharisees, Pollio and Sameas, are remembered for urging the populace to accept the rule of Herod. Those who were sympathic to foreign rule were so out of the conviction that it was a punishment from God that ought to be endured and not escaped (Schürer 1973: I, 296, 314; II, 294–95).

The First Jewish War started slowly with a small group of extremists who did not have the support of the religious hierarchy (Smallwood 1976: 289–93). The tradition is unclear at points, but it appears that Yohanan ben Zakkai himself believed in Jewish submission to the Romans. At Yavneh the Jews cooperated with the Romans by opposing insurrection in exchange for the chance to preserve the remnants of their faith. For the Pharisees, acceptance of Gentile domination was tolerable as long as the Torah governed the life of the Jews (Neusner 1962: 126–28, 141; 1973: 50; 1975: 167–68). Even Simeon ben Gamaliel, who eventually joined the insurgents, initially opposed the activities of the Zealots and attempted to steer the people along a course of moderation (*JW* 2: 411–14; 4: 158–61; Rivkin 1978: 60–65).

The Bar Kokba revolt had a clearer rabbinic following. Rabbi Akiba acknowledged Kokba's messianism and authenticated the movement which ultimately called for Akiba's martyrdom. Yet other rabbis were more skeptical of Bar Kokba's revolt. As Yohanan ben Zakkai could not support the war against Rome, Gamaliel II opposed the Bar Kokba war. The retort of one rabbi to Akiba, "The grass will grow from your cheeks, Akiba, before the son of David comes" (*y. Ta'an.* 4: 5) indicates that not all condoned the Bar Kokba war.[15]

While many rabbis supported the two wars, rabbinic opinion was divided. Following the two revolts, which had brought upon the Jews only calamity and threatened the very existence of Judaism, it is not surprising that the Jews would with *little* reluctance abandon the paleo-Hebrew script which would recall only painful memories of faded dreams.

APPENDIX

Divine Names in Paleo-Hebrew at Qumran

Letters occurring in parenthesis with the divine name(s) appear in "square" characters. Both published texts and texts mentioned in preliminary reports are included.

I.	*ʾl*	
	1QpMic	Milik 1955: 77–79 (*DJD* 1)
	1QMyst	Milik 1955: 105 (*DJD* 1)
	1QH	Milik 1955: 137 (*DJD* 1)
		Sukenik 1955: pls. 35, 49
	3Q*14* (fragmentary)	Baillet 1962: 104 (*DJD* 3)
	6QHymn (2 times)	Baillet 1962: 134–35 (*DJD* 3)
	6QD (2 times)	Baillet 1962: 130 (*DJD* 3)
	4QBookPeriods	Allegro 1968: 77 (*DJD* 5) cf. Milik 1976: 249–50
	4Q*183*	Allegro 1968: 81 (*DJD* 5)
II.	*ʾly*	
	1QH	Sukenik 1955: pl. 36
III.	*(b)ʾl*	
	6QHymn	Baillet 1962: 134 (*DJD* 3)
IV.	*yhwh*	
	1QPs[b] (2 times)	Barthélemy 1955: 71 (*DJD* 1)
	1QpMic (2 times)	Milik 1955: 77 (*DJD* 1)
	1QpZeph	Milik 1955: 80 (*DJD* 1)
	2QExod[b]	Baillet 1962: 53, 55 (*DJD* 3)
	3QLam (2 times)	Baillet 1962: 95 (*DJD* 3)
	4QpPs[a] (6 times)	Allegro 1968: 43–45 (*DJD* 5)
	4Q*183* (2 times)	Allegro 1968: 82 (*DJD* 5)
	4QpIsa[a]	Allegro 1968: 14 (*DJD* 5)
	4QPBless (=4QpGen 49)	Allegro 1956: 180
	11QPs[a] (143 times)	Sanders 1965 (*DJD* 4) Yadin 1966b: 6, 8–9
	1QpHab (4 times)	Burrows et al. 1950: pls. 6, 10–11
	4QIsa[c] (occurrences unknown)	Skehan 1955b: 162
	11QLev (3 times)	van der Ploeg 1968: 154
V.	*(l)yhwh*	
	2QExod[b] (3 times)	Baillet 1962: 53–55 (*DJD* 3)
	11QPs[a] (4 times)	Sanders 1965: 36–37 (*DJD* 4) and Yadin 1966b: 6, 9
VI.	*(m)yhwh*	
	4QpPs[a]	Allegro 1968: 44 (*DJD* 5)
	11QPs[a]	Sanders 1965: 23 (*DJD* 4)

VII.	*(b)yhwh*	
	11QPs^{a} (3 times)	Sanders 1965: 25, 37 (*DJD* 4)
VIII.	*(k)yhwh*	
	11QPs^{a}	Sanders 1965: 35 (*DJD* 4)
IX.	*byhwh*	
	4QIsa^{c} (occurrences unknown)	Skehan 1955b: 162
X.	*yhwh ṣbʾwt*	
	4QIsa^{c} (occurrences unknown)	Skehan 1955b: 162
XI.	*ʾlwhynw*	
	4QIsa^{c} (occurrences unknown)	Skehan 1955b: 162
XII.	*ʾdwny ʾlwhym*	
	4QIsa^{c} (occurrences unknown)	Skehan 1955b: 162

Published or Partially Published Texts in Paleo-Hebrew at Qumran

1QLev (1Q*3*)	Barthélemy 1955: 51–52
2QpaleoLev (2Q*5*)	Baillet 1962: 56–57
6QpaleoGen (6Q*1*)	Baillet 1962: 105–6
6QpaleoLev (6Q*2*)	Baillet 1962: 106
4QpaleoExod^{l}	Skehan 1965: 88, 99
4QpaleoExod^{m}	Skehan 1955a; 1965: 98–99
11QpaleoLev	Freedman 1974 Mathews 1980

(Following Skehan 1965: 88, we count the following unpublished paleo-Hebrew manuscripts: one each of Genesis, Numbers, and Job, and two of Deuteronomy.)

Notes

1. Origen, *Comm.* on Ps 2: 2, and Jerome, *Prologus Galeatus*; for discussion of the patristic evidence, see Burkitt 1898: 15; Waddell 1944: 159; Diringer 1950: 39–40.

2. We do not mean that certain books were not more meaningful to the community than others; as we shall see below, the events recorded in the books of Moses, in particular, were essential to the way in which the community in the desert viewed itself. The Essenes were thoroughly Jewish and therefore biblical in their posture and orientation; the Hebrew Bible pervades the total life of the community (Freedman 1971). Yet it appears that they had no concept of a closed list of holy works (i.e., "books which defile the hands") such as existed in the Talmudic period; at least we can safely say that the Essenes tolerated more books than "normative" Judaism did (as suggested by the reports of Philo, Josephus, and the rabbis). S. Z. Leiman (1974: 34–37), we believe, is correct in warning against taking the Qumran evidence of canon or any other sectarian development of canon (e.g., Samaritans) as paradigmatic for normative Judaism during the period.

3. Siegel's contention that the paleo-Hebrew texts all show the Samaritan text type and thereby demonstrate their Palestinian origin should be questioned. 11QpaleoLev presents a paleo-Hebrew text which does not clearly belong to any major tradition (i.e., massoretic, Samaritan, or LXX) and cannot be safely assigned to the Samaritan type (Tov 1978–79; Mathews 1980). The local texts theory outlined by Cross (1966a; 1975; 1979) must remain tentative; there are a number of problems with its reconstruc-

tion of the history of the Hebrew Bible (Mathews 1980: 154–245; Tov 1972; 1978–79; 1980). We must await the full publication of the paleo-Hebrew texts from Cave 4 before concluding that there is clear textual affinity even among them. Furthermore, serious methodological problems exist with the procedure of assigning manuscripts to text types on the basis of comparing the number of common readings. Comparing texts primarily by quantity of readings (e.g., Cross 1955: 171–72; Freedman 1974: 33; Ulrich 1978; 1979; Barthélemy 1963) is not decisive for determining manuscript filiation (Maas 1958: 42–46).

4. The identity of the first Hasmonean to strike coins remains an unresolved problem since most are undated. Traditionally, the *yhwḥnn* coins have been ascribed to John Hyrcanus I (134–104 B.C.E.), but Meshorer (1967: 44–52; 1974) has recently called this attribution into question (also Hanson 1974). He argues that the coins are those of Hyrcanus II (76–40 B.C.E.), which make the coins of Alexander Janneus (103–76 B.C.E.) the first to have been minted. (For the traditional opinion, see Kindler 1958: 14, 16–17; 1974a: 9, 11–13 and, *contra* Meshorer, see Ben-David 1972). The resolution of the question, however, is not essential to our concerns; whether Hyrcanus or Janneus, the Hasmoneans indicate through their use of paleo-Hebrew script that they endeavored to pattern themselves after Judah's ancient kings. It would be interesting if Janneus were the first to produce Jewish coinage since he specially distinguished his autonomous claims by his "king" series, which reads "Jonathan the king" in paleo-Hebrew characters and "King Alexander" in Greek on the reverse. For the Hasmonean coinage and seals, see Meshorer 1967: 41–63, 118–26, pls. 2–5; Avigad 1975a; 1975b; Naveh 1968.

5. Coins of the 4th century B.C.E. bearing the official name of the province Judah (*yhd*) and others bearing the name of its governor (*yḥzqw hpḥh*) are inscribed in paleo-Hebrew (Meshorer 1967: 35–40, 116–17, pl. 1; Spaer 1977; Cross 1969; Rahmani 1971). Also, jar handles from the early Hellenistic period have *yhd* and *yršlm* stamped in the script (Lapp 1963; Kindler 1974b; Jeselsohn 1974; Avigad 1974). Concerning the Tennes rebellion, see Barag 1966; Cross 1969: 23; Naveh 1973: 90, n. 43.

6. The inner chronology of the Janneus coin series is uncertain; perhaps it was high priest, king, high priest (Kindler 1974a: 14–19), though Meshorer (1967) suggests that the king series was the earliest and that the high priest coins were struck during the entirety of the reign.

7. Judging from the tannaitic evidence; see our discussion below.

8. Below we will discuss how Essene life was a living replica of the Mosaic period.

9. Among many archaisms noted by Polzin (1976) in Qumran literature, we cite only two for illustration: the exensive use of the cohortative form at Qumran is probably an archaism since this form is rare in Late Biblical hebrew (1976: 54–55); the preference for placing the cardinal number before the substantive at Qumran is the older practice, uncommon in Late Biblical Hebrew (1976: 5, 60).

10. In Hanson's first study (1964), he operated under the prevalent opinion among numismatists that Hyrcanus I was first to strike Hasmonean coinage and thus assigned an early date of 225–175 B.C.E. to certain Exodus fragments (1964: 37). In light of Meshorer's revision of the coin chronology (to which he subscribes), Hanson has recently reconsidered the Exodus fragments along with the script of 11QpaleoLev, assigning a date of ca. 100 B.C.E. for 11QpaleoLev and a date slightly earlier for the Exodus texts (in his contributions to the forthcoming edition of the Cave 11 text). Perhaps the future publication of the paleo-Hebrew materials from Cave 4 will shed further light on the problem of dating the manuscripts.

11. Hanson describes the scribe of the Exodus fragments as a "careful and consistent workman" who produced a "handsome script."

12. Murphy-O'Connor (1974: 229) is dependent in this conclusion on Stegemann's study (1971) in which he notes that *hkhn*, used to refer to the Teacher (1QpHab 2: 8, and 4QpPs[a] 2: 19; esp. 3: 15), is a term always designating the high priest.

13. Josephus elsewhere gives three years (*Ant* 13, 46) for the interim period between Alkimos and the appointment of Jonathan as high priest.

14. We should ask why 1QDM does not appear in paleo-Hebrew script if it was believed to be Mosaic in authorship. Evidently, the tradition of copying the Pentateuch (and Job) in paleo-Hebrew was popular early in the community whereas pseudo-Mosaic works appeared later, were initially penned in "square" Hebrew characters, and did not carry the same force of tradition. Other, similar texts either came through an intermediary (Jubilees) or directly from God (11QTemple), and Mosiac *authorship* was not in question.

15. For a different interpretation of the Pharisaic attitude toward foreign dominance, see Allon 1961: 53–78.

References

Albright, W. F.
1937 A Biblical Fragment From the Maccabean Age: The Nash Papyrus. *Journal of Biblical Literature* 56: 145–76.

Allegro, J. M.
1956 Further Messianic References in Qumran Literature. *Journal of Biblical Literature* 75: 174–87.
1968 *Qumran Cave 4, I (4Q158–4Q186)*. With the collaboration of A. A. Anderson. Discoveries in the Judaean Desert [of Jordan] 5. Oxford: Clarendon Press.

Allon, E.
1961 The Attitude of the Pharisees to the Roman Government and the House of Herod. *Scripta Hierosolymitana* 7: 53–78.

Avigad, N.
1974 More Evidence on the Judean Post-Exilic Stamps. *Israel Exploration Journal* 24: 52–58.
1975a A Bulla of Jonathan the High Priest. *Israel Exploration Journal* 25: 8–12.
1975b A Bulla of King Jonathan. *Israel Exploration Journal* 25: 245–46.

Baillet, M.
1962 Textes des Grottes 2Q, 3Q, 6Q, 7Q à 10Q. Pp. 45–166 in *Les 'Petites Grottes' de Qumrân. Textes*. Discoveries in the Judaean Desert [of Jordan] 3, eds. M. Baillet, J. T. Milik, and R. de Vaux. Oxford: Clarendon Press.

Barag, D.
1966 The Effects of the Tennes Rebellion in Palestine. *Bulletin of the American Schools of Oriental Research* 183: 6–12.

Barthélemy, D.
1953 Redécouverte d'un chaînon manquant de l'histoire de la Septante. *Revue biblique* 60: 18–29. Rpt. as pp. 127–39 in Cross and Talmon 1975.
1955 Les Textes: Textes bibliques. Pp. 49–76 in *Qumran Cave I*. Discoveries in the Judaean Desert 1, eds. D. Barthélemy and J. T. Milik. Oxford: Clarendon Press.
1963 *Les devanciers d'Aquila*. Supplements to Vetus Testamentum 10. Leiden: E. J. Brill.

Ben-David, A.
1972 When Did the Maccabees Begin to Strike Their First Coins? *Palestine Exploration Quarterly* 124: 93–103.

Betz, O.
1967 The Eschatological Interpretation of the Sinai-Tradition in Qumran and in the New Testament. *Revue de Qumrân* 6: 89–107.

Birnbaum, S.
1950 The Leviticus Fragments from the Cave. *Bulletin of the American Schools of Oriental Research* 118: 20–27.

Bright, J.
1976 *A History of Israel*[2]. Philadelphia: Westminster Press.

Brownlee, W. H.
1964 *The Meaning of the Qumran Scrolls for the Bible*. New York: Oxford University Press.

Burkitt, F. C.
1898 *Fragments of the Books of Kings According to the Translation of Aquila*. Cambridge: University Press.

Burrows, M.; Trever, J. C.; and Brownlee, W. H.
1950 *The Dead Sea Scrolls of St. Mark's Monastery*. Vol. I. New Haven: American Schools of Oriental Research.

Cross, F. M.

1955 The Oldest Manuscripts from Qumran. *Journal of Biblical Literature* 74: 147–72. Rpt. as pp. 147–76 in Cross and Talmon 1975.

1961 The Development of the Jewish Scripts. Pp. 166–88 in *The Bible and the Ancient Near East: Essays in Honor of William Foxwell Albright*, ed. G. E. Wright. Garden City, NY: Doubleday. Rpt. 1979. Winona Lake, Indiana: Eisenbrauns.

1964 The History of the Biblical Text in the Light of Discoveries in the Judaean Desert. *Harvard Theological Review* 57: 281–99. Rpt. as pp. 177–95 in Cross and Talmon 1975.

1966a The Contribution of the Qumran Discoveries to the Study of the Biblical Text. *Israel Exploration Journal* 16: 81–95. Rpt. as pp. 278–92 in Cross and Talmon 1975.

1966b Aspects of Samaritan and Jewish History in Late Persian and Hellenistic Times. *Harvard Theological Review* 59: 201–11.

1969 Judean Stamps. *Eretz-Israel* 9: 20–27.

1971 The Early History of the Qumran Community. Pp. 70–89 in *New Directions in Biblical Archaeology*, ed. D. N. Freedman and J. Greenfield. Garden City, NY: Doubleday.

1975 The Evolution of a Theory of Local Texts. Pp. 306–20 in Cross and Talmon 1975.

1979 Problems of Method in the Textual Criticism of the Hebrew Bible. Pp. 31–54 in *The Critical Study of Sacred Texts*, ed. W. Doniger O'Flaherty. Berkeley: Graduate Theological Union.

1980 *The Ancient Library of Qumran and Modern Biblical Studies*². Grand Rapids: Baker Book House. Originally 1961. Garden City: Doubleday.

Cross, F. M., and Talmon, S.

1975 *Qumran and the History of the Biblical Text*. Cambridge: Harvard University Press.

Diringer, D.

1950 Early Hebrew Script Versus Square Hebrew Script. Pp. 35–49 in *Essays and Studies Presented to Stanley Arthur Cook*, ed. D. Winton Thomas. London: Taylor's Foreign Press.

Farmer, W.

1956 *Maccabees, Zealots, and Josephus*. New York: Columbia University Press.

Freedman, D. N.

1971 The Old Testament at Qumran. Pp. 131–41 in *New Directions in Biblical Archaeology*, ed. D. N. Freedman and J. Greenfield. Garden City, NY: Doubleday.

1974 Variant Readings in the Leviticus Scroll from Qumran Cave 11. *Catholic Biblical Quarterly* 36: 525–34.

Goldstein, J.

1976 *1 Maccabees*. Anchor Bible 41. Garden City, NY: Doubleday.

Hanson, R. S.

1964 Paleo-Hebrew Scripts in the Hasmonean Age. *Bulletin of the American Schools of Oriental Research* 175: 26–42.

1974 Toward a Chronology of the Hasmonean Coins. *Bulletin of the American Schools of Oriental Research* 216: 21–23.

Huntjens, J. A.

1974 Contrasting Notions of Covenant and Law in the Texts From Qumran. *Revue de Qumrân* 81: 261–80.

Jeselsohn, D.

1974 A New Coin Type with Hebrew Inscription. *Israel Exploration Journal* 24: 77–78.

Jellicoe, S.
1968 *The Septuagint and Modern Study*. Oxford: Clarendon Press. Rpt. 1978. Ann Arbor: Eisenbrauns.

Kadman, L.
1960 *The Coins of the Jewish War of 66–73 C.E.* Corpus Numorum Palaestinensium, 2nd series, ed. L. Kadman et al. Jerusalem: Schocken Publications.

Kanael, B.
1963 Ancient Jewish Coins and Their Historical Importance. *Biblical Archeologist* 26: 38–62.

Kindler, A.
1958 The Coinage of the Hasmonean Dynasty. Pp. 10–28 in *The Dating and Meaning of Ancient Jewish Coins and Symbols*. Numismatic Studies and Researches 2, ed. L. Kadman et al. Jerusalem: Schocken Publications.

1974a *Coins of the Land of Israel. Collection of the Bank of Israel*. Trans. R. Grafman. Jerusalem: Keter Publishing House.

1974b Silver Coins Bearing the Name of Judea from the Early Hellenistic Period. *Israel Exploration Journal* 24: 74–76.

Lapp, P. W.
1963 Ptolemaic Stamped Handles from Judah. *Bulletin of the American Schools of Oriental Research* 172: 22–35.

Leiman, S. Z.
1974 *The Canonization of Hebrew Scripture: The Talmudic and Midrashic Evidence*. Hamden, CT: The Connecticut Academy of Arts and Sciences.

Levine, B.
1978 The Temple Scroll: Aspects of its Historical Provenance and Literary Character. *Bulletin of the American Schools of Oriental Research* 232: 5–23.

Maas, P.
1958 *Textual Criticism*. Trans. B. Flowers. Oxford: Clarendon Press.

Mathews, K. A.
1980 *The Paleo-Hebrew Leviticus Scroll from Qumran*. Michigan dissertation.

Mendenhall, G.
1962 Covenant. Vol. 1, pp. 714–23 in *The Interpreter's Dictionary of the Bible*, eds. G. A. Buttrick et al. Nashville: Abingdon.

Meshorer, Y.
1967 *Jewish Coins of the Second Temple Period*. Trans. I. H. Levine. Tel-Aviv: Am-Hassefer Publications.

1974 The Beginnings of the Hasmonean Coinage. *Israel Exploration Journal* 24: 59–61.

Milgrom, J.
1978 The Temple Scroll. *Biblical Archeologist* 41: 105–20.

Milik, J. T.
1955 Les Textes: non-bibliques. Pp. 77–149 in *Qumran Cave I*. Discoveries in the Judaean Desert 1, eds. D. Barthélemy and J. T. Milik. Oxford: Clarendon Press.

1976 *The Books of Enoch. Aramaic Fragments of Qumrân Cave 4*. With the collaboration of M. Black. Oxford: Clarendon Press.

Murphy-O'Connor, J.
1969 Le genèse littéraire de la Règle de la Communauté. *Revue biblique* 76: 528–49.

1974 The Essenes and Their History. *Revue biblique* 81: 215–44.

1977 The Essenes in Palestine. *Biblical Archeologist* 40: 100–24.

Naveh, J.
1968 Dated Coins of Alexander Jannaeus. *Israel Exploration Journal* 18: 20–25.

1973 An Aramaic Tomb-Inscription Written in Paleo-Hebrew Script. *Israel Exploration Journal* 23: 82–91.

Neusner, J.

1962 *A Life of Rabban Yohanan ben Zakkai Ca. 1–80 C.E.* Studia Post-Biblica 6. Leiden: E. J. Brill.

1973 *From Politics to Piety. The Emergence of Pharisaic Judaism.* Englewood Cliffs, NJ: Prentice-Hall.

1975 *First-Century Judaism in Crisis.* Nashville: Abingdon Press.

Oesterly, W. O. E.

1953 *An Introduction to the Books of the Apocrypha.* London: SPCK.

Polzin, R.

1976 *Late Biblical Hebrew: Toward An Historical Typology of Biblical Hebrew Prose.* Harvard Semitic Monographs 12. Missoula, MT: Scholars Press.

Purvis, J. D.

1968 *The Samaritan Pentateuch and the Origin of the Samaritan Sect.* Harvard Semitic Monographs 2. Cambridge: Harvard University.

Rahmani, L. Y.

1971 Silver Coins of the Fourth Century B.C. from Tel Gamma. *Israel Exploration Journal* 21: 158–60.

Rivkin, E.

1978 *A Hidden Revolution.* Nashville: Abingdon.

Roberts, C. H.

1979 *Manuscript, Society and Belief in Early Christian Egypt.* Schweich Lectures of the British Academy for 1977. London: Oxford University Press.

Sanders, J. A.

1965 *The Psalms Scroll of Qumran Cave 11.* Discoveries in the Judaean Desert [of Jordan] 4. Oxford: Clarendon Press.

Schürer, E.

1973 *The History of the Jewish People in the Age of Jesus Christ (175 B.C.-A.D. 135).* Revised and edited by G. Vermes and F. Miller, 2 vols. Edinburgh: T. & T. Clark.

Siegel, J. P.

1971 The Employment of Paleo-Hebrew Characters for the Divine Names at Qumran in the Light of Tannaitic Sources. *Hebrew Union College Annual* 42: 159–72.

Skehan, P. W.

1955a Exodus in the Samaritan Recension from Qumran. *Journal of Biblical Literature* 74: 182–87.

1955b The Text of Isaias at Qumran. *Catholic Biblical Quarterly* 17: 158–63.

1965 The Biblical Scrolls from Qumran and the Text of the Old Testament. *Biblical Archeologist* 28: 87–100. Rpt. 1970 as pp. 240–53 in *The Biblical Archaeologist Reader III*, ed. E. F. Campbell and D. N. Freedman. Garden City: Doubleday; and as pp. 264–77 in Cross and Talmon 1975.

Smallwood, E. Mary

1976 *The Jews Under Roman Rule.* Studies in Judaism in Late Antiquity 20. Leiden: E. J. Brill.

Smith, M.

1956 Palestinian Judaism in the First Century. Pp. 67–81 in *Israel: Its Role in Civilization*, ed. M. Davis. New York: Harper and Row.

Spaer, A.

1977 Some More Yehud Coins. *Israel Exploration Journal* 27: 200–3.

Stegemann, H.

1971 *Die Entstehung der Qumrangemeinde.* Bonn: Rheinische Friedrich-Wilhelms Universität.

Sukenik, E. L.
1955 — *The Dead Sea Scrolls of the Hebrew University*. Jerusalem: The Magnes Press/The Hebrew University.

Taylor, C., ed.
1900 — *Hebrew-Greek Cairo Genizah Palimpsests from the Taylor-Schecter Collection*. Cambridge: Cambridge University Press.

Tov, E.
1972 — Lucian and Proto-Lucian. *Revue biblique* 79: 101–13. Rpt. as pp. 293–305 in Cross and Talmon 1975.
1978–79 — The Textual Character of the Leviticus Scroll from Qumran Cave 11. *Shnaton* 3: 238–44 (Hebrew).
1980 — Determining the Relationship between the Qumran Scrolls and the LXX: Some Methodological Issues. Pp. 45–67 in *The Hebrew and Greek Texts of Samuel*, ed. E. Tov. Jerusalem: Academon.

Ulrich, E. C.
1978 — *The Qumran Text of Samuel and Josephus*. Harvard Semitic Monographs 19. Missoula, MT: Scholars Press.
1979 — A Fragmentary Manuscript of 2 Samuel 14–15 from the Scribe of the *Serek Hay-yaḥad* (1QS) [4QSam[c]]. *Bulletin of the American Schools of Oriental Research* 235: 1–26.

van der Ploeg, J. M. P.
1968 — Lev. IX,23–X,2 dans un texte de Qumran [11QLev]. Pp. 153–55 in *Bibel und Qumran: Beiträge zur Erforschung der Beziehungen zwischen Bibel- und Qumranwissenschaft: Hans Bardtke zum 22. 9. 1966*, ed. S. Wagner. Berlin: Evangelische Haupt-Bibelgesellschaft.

de Vaux, R.
1949 — La Grotte des manuscrits hébreux. *Revue biblique* 56: 586–609.

Waddell, W. G.
1944 — The Tetragrammaton in the LXX. *Journal of Theological Studies* 45: 158–61.

Wieder, N.
1953 — The "Law-Interpreter" of the Sect of the Dead Sea Scrolls: The Second Moses. *Journal of Jewish Studies* 4: 158–75.

Yadin, Y.
1962 — *The Scroll of the War of the Sons of Light Against the Sons of Darkness*. Trans. C. Rabin. Oxford University Press.
1965 — The Excavation of Masada 1963/64: Preliminary Report. *Israel Exploration Journal* 15: 1–120.
1966a — *Masada: Herod's Fortress and the Zealots' Last Stand*. New York: Random House.
1966b — Another Fragment (E) of the Psalms Scroll from Qumran Cave 11 (11QPs[a]). *Textus* 5: 1–10, pls. 1–4.
1977 — *Megillat Hammiqdaš*. 3 vols. Jerusalem: Israel Exploration Society, Institute of Archeology of the Hebrew University, and the Shrine of the Book (Hebrew).

V. Other Perspectives

Material Remains and the Cult in Ancient Israel: An Essay in Archeological Systematics

William G. Dever
University of Arizona, Tucson, Arizona

Introduction

Although David Noel Freedman would insist that he is a biblical scholar rather than an archeologist, as author and editor he has consistently drawn attention to the unique value of archeology in reconstructing all aspects of the phenomenon of ancient Israel, not least its religious life and institutions.[1] It may therefore be appropriate for me as an archeologist, in this *Festschrift* honoring a friend and colleague in biblical studies, to offer a brief essay on the problems of correlating literary and non-literary remains with specific reference to the Israelite cult. For the purposes of this discussion we shall confine ourselves to the period of the Judges and the Monarchy.

We may focus on the central problem by observing that much of Syro-Palestinian archeology has been dominated until recently by biblical scholarship— particularly under the influence of the "Albright school" (of which Freedman is a prominent member). Yet, despite several generations of intensive excavation and research, and what has sometimes amounted to an obsession with "cultic" interpretation, archeology in the Holy Land appears to have produced surprisingly little direct illumination of ancient Israelite religious practice *per se.* It has recovered a great deal of the historical and cultural *milieu* from which the Hebrew Bible emerged, and in that sense archeology has helped to correct the false presuppositions on which certain schools of *Religionsgeschichte* sought to base their reconstruction of Israelite religion.[2] But as I shall attempt to show, archeology of either the "biblical" or the "secular" persuasion has scarcely augmented our understanding of the actual *cult* in ancient Israel in any specific and fundamental way.[3] Is the "silence" significant? Or is this curious failure due to the inherent limitations of archeology itself? If not, how might we proceed in the future in a manner more beneficial to both archeology and biblical criticism? In order to answer these questions let us look first at the theoretical value of archeology to the study of the cultic aspects of Israelite religion, against which we shall then measure the actual contribution.

A. The Unfulfilled Potential of Archeology for Illuminating the Cult

1. What Might Be Found to Illumine the Cult

To speculate on the potential of archeology for interpreting Israelite religious institutions and practice, we must isolate those aspects of the cult that may be expected to leave tangible traces in the archeological record, that is, the material correlates of specifically "religious" behavior. For this purpose we shall distinguish religion as "a set of beliefs concerning the supernatural nature of the universe and the moral nature of man, usually institutionalized and expressed in ritual observance"; and "cult" as "a particular system of religious worship, especially with reference to its rites and ceremonies." Extrapolating from these definitions we may then consult three basic sources: (1) what we know of Near Eastern religion in general; (2) the descriptions of religious life in ancient Israel in the Hebrew Bible (although the value of the texts is obviously limited); and (3) the artifactual discoveries made thus far in excavations in Palestine. From these sources we may thus derive a rough outline of the material remains of the Israelite cult that might be amenable to archeological investigation, somewhat as follows.

a. *Architecture.* This would include both (1) monumental structures and local shrines that served as public temples, and (2) private household shrines. Here the significant features that might reveal belief and practice are likely to be the orientation of the building, its essential plan, and in particular the arrangement and presumed function of such features as forecourt, vestibule, vestry, cella, and any attached service or residential areas. The location, size, manner of construction, and degree of sumptuousness could also yield indirect information on the relative place of the cult in society.

b. *Art.* This might include: (1) monumental art, both architectural decor (reliefs, paintings) and mobile works such as statuary; and (2) the minor arts, especially pottery and other ceramics (figurines, plaques, terra cotta stands, temple models, censers, etc.), ivory carvings, seals, and possibly textiles. In theory at least, no other category of material culture should be so readily accessible or so potentially revealing in explicating the cult as works of art.

c. *Artifacts.* The first category would include: (1) architectural furnishings, generally fixed, such as benches, altars, *favissae,* various types of stands, lavers, braziers, censers, and other obviously cultic paraphernalia; and (2) smaller, more mobile objects, whether found in temple/shrine contexts or used in everyday life, such as votives of all kinds (including foundation deposits and funeral offerings), human or animal figurines, any "magical" items (such as masks or aids in divination and incantation), and also some of the objects considered above under Art (particularly the iconographic ivories and seals). Finally, although they are more "ecofacts" than artifacts, paleo-zoological and paleo-botanical remains in possible cultic deposits do reflect human alteration and usage and constitute invaluable evidence for sacrificial customs.

d. *Texts.* The evidence provided by epigraphic remains (usually considered "literary" and thus non-artifactual) is rare in ancient Palestine, but obviously of the greatest potential importance. Types of written data applicable to the cult might include monumental or dedicatory inscriptions, incantations and other magical texts, liturgical and mythological texts, votives, funeral inscriptions, ostraca, seals, and even graffiti.

e. *Burials.* A final category of material remains, often overlooked, includes all aspects of mortuary practice which may leave unique physical evidence for interpreting such matters as popular piety, ancestral worship, and belief in life after death.

2. What is Currently Known Archeologically of the Israelite Cult

In the light of the above outline—a brief compendium of the varieties of cultic material we could reasonably expect Syro-Palestinian archeology to have produced—it is instructive to note how *scant* the actual usable data are, even after a century of exploration and discovery.

a. *Architecture.* Here the most striking fact is that no full-scale, monumental temple from ancient Israel has been found. Of the Solomonic temple of 10th-century Jerusalem no actual trace has been (or is likely to be) found. We may, of course, combine the biblical descriptions (1 Kgs 6: 2–36; 7: 13–51; 2 Chr 3: 3–5: 1; Ezekiel chaps. 40–47) and archeological finds from such sites as Ebla and Tell Tayinet in Syria and Shechem and Hazor in Palestine to elucidate the tripartite architectural plan. And the small finds from a number of sites in Syria and Palestine illustrate details described in the texts—furnishings such as altars, lavers, braziers, flesh-hooks, and shovels; as well as the Phoenician-style construction and decoration of the Jerusalem Temple.[4] The shrine of Stratum XI at Arad has been understood by the excavator as a 10th-century temple ultimately going back to the Tabernacle as a prototype and functioning as a rival of the Jerusalem Temple; but the structure is more likely to be 9th century in date and seems to be little more than a local shrine.[5]

Elsewhere, we have only the Dan sanctuary, apparently of the 10th–8th century and modelled after the Canaanite outdoor *bāmôt* or "high places"; small household shrines at 10th century Megiddo, Taʿanach, and Lachish; an 8th-century sanctuary (?), although preserved only in negative evidence, at Beersheba; and the 9th–8th century caravanserai-shrine at Kuntillet ʿAjrud in eastern Sinai.[6] None of these structures in orientation, layout, scale, or contents has shed much light on cultic practice—at least as they have been interpreted thus far (but see below). Although they may be presumed to be Yahwistic, they give no direct evidence and indicate only that they were probably designed for the presentation of food and incense offerings and simple votives of terra cotta and stone.

b. *Art and artifactual evidence.* There is so little evidence that these categories may be combined. No monumental Israelite art survives. No Israelite statuary or sculpture, large-scale iconographic representations, or paintings are known to us, save two 10th-century cultic stands from Taʿanach, with fantastic representations of what appears to be Asherah as the "Lion Lady."[7] "Furnishings" in the few attested shrines consist simply of niches and benches, presumably for placement of food or incense offerings; large platforms and several smaller "horned" altars, serving probably the same purpose; and a number of terra cotta stands that have been interpreted as censers or combination censer-libation stands.[8] (Unfortunately, no flotation analysis of paleo-zoological or -botanical remains has been done to determine the nature of possible animal sacrifices or other food-offerings.[9]) The 10th–8th/7th-century pottery occasionally found in the context of these shrines is all utilitarian rather than specifically manufactured for cultic use[10] (although that does not rule out secondary cultic use). Hundreds of female terra cottas of the so-called "Astarte" (more accurately "Asherah") type have been found, mostly Judean pillar-base figurines of the 8th-7th century B.C. Obvious fertility aspects, usually exaggerated sexual characteristics, connect these figurines with the ancient Near Eastern cult of the "Mother-goddess," but they do not specify the deity further.[11] Since these figurines are found almost without exception in domestic or tomb contexts, they are undoubtedly talismans to aid in conception and childbirth, rather than idols in the true sense, designed for sanctuary usage. It may be significant that no representations of a *male* deity in terra cotta, metal, or stone have ever been found in clear Iron Age contexts, except possibly for an El statuette in bronze from 12th-century Hazor and a depiction of an El-like stick figure on a miniature chalk altar from 10th-century Gezer, and neither is necessarily Israelite.[12]

The few specific votives we know (apart from use of the common pottery forms noted above) consist of several 9th–8th-century inscribed ceramic vessels from Hazor, el-Kôm, Arad, Beersheba, and ʿAjrud; and the inscribed stone bowls from 9th–8th century ʿAjrud.[13] Conspicuously absent are pottery workshops for the production of votives, such as those found in connection with the sacred precincts of Late Bronze Canaanite temples at Hazor and elsewhere.[14]

The well-known 9th–8th century seals and ivory plaques give us relatively abundant evidence for art and iconography in Palestine, but most of the motifs are of Phoenician derivation, and in any case they are too clearly decorative in nature to shed much light on theological conceptions, much less cultic practice.[15]

Finally, it is noteworthy that no identifiable foundation deposits or ritual-magical objects whatsoever have been found in undisputed Israelite contexts.[16]

c. *Texts.* As is well known, we have relatively little ancient Israelite epigraphic evidence in general. The ostraca witness personal names compounded with Baʿal or El. Apart from that, only a few 8th–7th-century tomb inscriptions from Jerusalem, Kh. Beit Lei, Kh. el-Kôm, and elsewhere are of obvious religious import.[17] More significant are the several recently-found graffiti and votive inscriptions on stone bowls and store-jars from the Kuntillet ʿAjrud sanctuary in the Sinai.[18] Conspicuously absent are dedicatory or incantation texts, or mythological and liturgical texts such as those from Canaanite Ugarit—except for parts of the Hebrew Bible, still almost our sole literary source for the Israelite cult (but hardly to be classed as an "archeological artifact").

d. *Burials.* Tomb offerings of the Israelite and Judean period are relatively abundant, but apart from an occasional human or zoomorphic figurine they consist overwhelmingly of quantities of common pottery, with a few items of personal adornment or utilitarian objects. Lamps, the occasional figurine, and small terra cotta "rattles" from 9th–7th-century tombs have been interpreted as cultic in nature, but there is little evidence to support this view. The basic chamber-and-bench tomb type of the 10th–7th century has not been studied in terms of the Israelite cult, but any analysis would have to begin with the observation that this tomb type seems to have been borrowed early in the Iron Age from the Aegean area via the Philistines.[19] In the disposal of the dead themselves, the normal Israelite primary extended burial—the body often deposited on a bench and subsequently removed to an adjacent repository to make room for later burials—does not seem indicative of any distinctive religious conception or practice.[20]

B. A Comparison and Critique

1. Comparison

A comparison of the theoretical agenda and actual achievement sketched above will suggest that archeology's contribution to the study of the Israelite cult has been minimal. A brief examination of recent literature (since Shiloh 1979, written in 1975) confirms the suspicion.

a. *Archeology.* On the side of archeology, we note a symposium in 1977 in Jerusalem, sponsored by the Nelson Glueck School of Biblical Archaeology, that was devoted precisely to our theme. Published now as *Temples and High Places in Biblical Times* (Biran 1981), the title is promising, but the results for our inquiry are disappointing. The majority of the essays have little to do with Palestine in the Iron Age, much less with the Israelite cult in particular. Those papers that might be relevant—on Dan, Arad, Beersheba, and ʿAjrud, for instance—offer no new data to supplement the little published evidence. Furthermore, they do not use the current archeological material to confront recent textual treatments of the central topic of the symposium, *bāmôt* or "high places," such as those of Vaughn (1974) and Barrick (1975). Finally, even a casual reading of the papers together with the published responses reveals that the biblical scholars and the archeologists participating in this potentially significant symposium were for the most part simply "talking past" each other.

b. *Biblical studies.* It is also instructive to examine the most exhaustive recent work of biblical scholarship on the subject, M. Haran's *Temples and Temple-Service in Ancient Israel* (1978). Haran's concern is almost solely with the literary tradition, for reasons he states with admirable clarity in his prologue: "The priestly source . . . rests on historical conditions that prevailed not in the post-exilic but the pre-exilic period. . . . Data available from this source . . . can properly serve as direct, substantial testimony to the cultic mannerisms, temple procedures and priestly concepts that obtained in and around the First Temple during the last third of its existence" (1978: 3). Given this presupposition, it is not surprising that Haran makes almost no use of artifactual or even textual data supplied by archeology. In discussing Israelite temples he derives a hypothetical list of 12 or 13 solely from biblical accounts. He cites the Arad sanctuary but denies that it was a temple. No Israelite "high places" have been found, since the Dan installation is neither temple nor *bāmâ* (in Haran's opinion, these are always distinct) but simply an "open-air sanctuary." Thus Iron Age cultic installations at Megiddo, Taʿanach, Tell el-Farʿah North, Lachish, and ʿAjrud are not mentioned; nor are any of the many cultic stands, censers, votives, or funeral inscriptions cited (on the above, see Haran 1978: 13–57). In the case of the one category where Haran discusses the correlation of artifacts with texts, the several 10th-century and later miniature horned incense altars, it is argued that these are irrelevant, since textual evidence shows that incense was not used before the 7th century in Israel. Haran concludes: "The truth of the matter is that archaeological evidence will remain somewhat irrelevant to the question of the place of incense in the Israelite cult until actual remains of Israelite temples eventually come to light" (1978: 237). Arad Haran has already ruled out as an Israelite temple; even so, he asserts that no incense altar was found there—ignoring the fact of the two small altars found flanking the entrance to the cella, with remains of burnt organic substance still *in situ* (cf. Haran 1978: 237; Aharoni 1968).

c. *Case-studies.* To support our indictment further, let us look at some case-studies. Arad is especially instructive. The discovery of the 9th–8th-century sanctuary by Aharoni in 1963—the first Israelite temple outside the Bible—was first hailed with excitement (and not a little envy). But faulty excavation, initial overinterpretation and pointless polemics, as well as publication that never got beyond sketchy preliminary reports, resulted in neglect by archeologists and almost all other scholars, leaving this unique find in limbo. The neglect of Arad may be rationalized by assuming that the archeological data in this case are not clear. However, more is certain than some scholars seem willing to admit: the Arad structure *is* a cultic installation, whether "temple" or *bāmâ;* its chronological range, although not precise, is 9th–8th century at *minimum* and thus contemporary with the supposedly centralized cultus in Jerusalem; its context is indisputably *Israelite;* and its plan and furnishings give *tangible evidence* of at least burnt animal and food (if not incense) offerings.

The "high place" discovered by Biran at Tell Dan has generated even more controversy. Here again, arguments over stratigraphic detail, semantic differences between "temple" and "high place" in the Bible and whether it is legitimate to connect the structure with either—important, to be sure—should not be allowed to obscure certain fundamental facts. A consensus already exists that this impressive structure and its precincts are cultic in nature, and that it was in public use at least in the 9th–8th century at a site that was one of Israel's most prominent provincial centers.

Similarly, polemics about the date, location, and even the existence of Aharoni's reconstructed "temple" at Beersheba (supposedly destroyed by Josiah's reform) should not detract from the significance of at least one discovery. The dismantled monumental "horned altar" (the first yet found) constitutes incontrovertible evidence of a local Israelite sanctuary of some sort, destroyed sometime in the 8th or the 7th century B.C. (i.e., possibly by either Hezekiah or Josiah).

Perhaps more significant than the controversy and then neglect surrounding the above is the hesitancy to deal with the sanctuary discovered most recently, one which has not yet even generated the expected dispute. The Kuntillet ʿAjrud sanctuary, excavated in 1975–76 by Zeʾev Meshel, is one of the most astonishing finds yet made in the biblical world. Here is a full-fledged cultic installation in the context of a desert fort, with inscribed votives and graffiti, the texts indicating beyond doubt that offerings were made both to Yahweh and to his "Asherah." Yet despite an Israel Museum exhibition and catalogue and several adequate preliminary reports,[21] scholars have seemed reluctant to seize upon the revolutionary implications of this material for the history of the Israelite cult. The site is certainly 9th–8th century, the language is Hebrew, and the material context of the inscriptions is Israelite-Judean. Whether one understands *yhwh wʾšrth* (the reading is indisputable) as "Yahweh and his (consort) Asherah" or "Yahweh and his Asherah-shrine," the conclusion that one is dealing with a highly syncretistic Israelite cult in the wilderness is inescapable. And the painted scenes and figures on the pithoi, however interpreted, point unmistakably in the same direction (see also below).

A word of caution is appropriate at this point. The foregoing attempt to clarify matters by emphasizing the positive aspects of the archeological record is not meant to oversimplify. However palpable and apparently self-evident archeological data may appear, one must never underestimate the necessity or the difficulty of interpreting the "facts"—whether artifacts or textual facts. This leads us to the next point.

2. A Hopeful Critique

Any critique of the failure to relate archeology creatively to the study of the Israelite cult obviously must be two-sided.

a. Archeology can certainly be faulted for its failure to produce reliable and accessible data, i.e., properly excavated, adequately interpreted, published evidence. The sad fact is that the bulk of the excavated material from ancient Palestine has been largely useless to the historian or non-specialist, and until recently even to many archeologists. The material was poorly dug, sketchily recorded, naively interpreted, rarely integrated in an overall historical-cultural explanatory framework, and frequently the basic data were not even published in catalog-fashion. The long tradition of amateurism in biblical and Syro-Palestinian archeology has resulted in a field that is characterized by arguments based on supposed "facts" that turned out to be hearsay rather than evidence. It is no wonder, then, that reconstructions based on archeology are greeted today with about as much skepticism as are the past generation's "assured results of biblical criticism." Nevertheless, as I have insisted above, even archeology of this sort has produced *some* hard data, which all too often have been ignored. And above all it must be emphasized that our branch of archeology has become much more professional in the last decade or so, and in "coming of age" is now more sophisticated in both field and analytical techniques.[22] Presently we shall see the promising implications of this development.

b. On the other hand, Biblical studies cannot escape blame entirely. The failure to engage archeology in a serious dialogue in studies of the Israelite cult may be due to several factors. First there has been the general tendency of biblical scholars since Wellhausen to be preoccupied with internal analysis of the literary sources in the Hebrew Bible. This tendency certainly marked early literary criticism; but it is scarcely less visible in later Form Criticism and Redaction-history, as well as in much of liberal and conservative biblical scholarship in Europe and America in general (the chief exception being fundamentalism, which rejected the documentary hypothesis outright—often appealing to archeology for support). Our dissatisfaction with the treatment of Haran (1978) lies precisely in his exclusive concentration on the literary sources in the Hebrew Bible; it shows how little has changed methodologically in many circles of biblical studies.[23]

Albright's well-known reaction, based on an "archeological revolution" that gave promise of external data, was correct in pointing out that the literary-critical approach, even if successful, resulted merely in a history of the *literature,* not necessarily of the religion, of ancient Israel. But that Albright's own approach was also literary may be seen from the fact that much of what he and his students called "archeology" was really the comparative study of the extra-biblical texts brought to light in excavation throughout the ancient Near East.[24] And the "Biblical archeology" movement has tended to focus even more specifically on the biblical literature. Two well-intended assumptions of this school, in my opinion, were naïve and actually diminished the value of archeology for our inquiry: (1) the notion that "religion" may be defined essentially in terms of thought, i.e., *theology* rather than cult; and (2) the assumption that theological inferences drawn from the Hebrew Bible/Christian Old

Testament are *historically* (in this case, archeologically) verifiable.[25]

A second influence in the neglect of the study of archeology and the Israelite cult stemmed from preconceived notions of Yahwism. This bias took several forms. Liberal scholars like H. G. May made pioneering use of archeology for cultic studies (1935), but the evolutionary framework into which the data were forced obscured the actual development of Israelite religion.[26] Both the *Religionsgeschichte* and "myth and ritual" schools focused specifically on the cult, but the basic conception of Israelite religion rested on philosophical presuppositions which went unchallenged by the empirical evidence of archeology. (Folklore and ethnography were adduced *a posteriori*, but in an eclectic and uncritical fashion that modern ethno-archeology would certainly reject.) Conservative biblical scholarship generally accepted the highly idealized version of Yahwism centralized in the Jerusalem cult presented in the Deuteronomic and Priestly works, and so paid little attention to the occasional disturbing discoveries of archeology. The conservative Protestant character of much American biblical scholarship (including "Biblical archeology"), despite the appeal made to archeology, tended to approach Israelite religion more in terms of theology than religious practice—almost as though the cult were something of an embarrassment.[27] Evangelical scholarship has produced a number of amateur archeologists, some of whom have been almost obsessed with cultic explanations; but this approach was always confined to the comparative study of the pre- or non-Israelite cult, so as to enhance the notion of Yahwism as pure monotheism.[28] Finally, to orthodoxy of all forms the mere suggestion of syncretism (below) was so anathema that archeology has always been regarded with great suspicion.[29]

c. A partial explanation for the minimal impact of archeology on the study of cult is, of course, simply that biblical scholarship in recent years has been unable to cope with the veritable flood of new discoveries, not to mention the necessary specialization of the field of archeology itself. That deficiency, however, is not due to methodological differences and should gradually be rectified with the progress of both disciplines. To show how archeology may contribute, we turn now to our final point.

C. A Theory and Strategy for Archeological Elucidation of the Israelite Cult

1. An Alternate Theory

In light of the impasse just described, it may be timely to advance a bold new agenda. I suggest an alternate theory to what seems to have been for too long the prevailing view: (1) the notion that Israelite "ethical monotheism" in the Monarchy was too austerely intellectual or too spiritually rarified to have developed an elaborate cultic apparatus; and (2) the contention, following the Deuteronomic and Priestly works, that Israelite worship was always centralized in Jerusalem and that the local shrines were suppressed or totally destroyed. Whatever the archeological evidence or its interpretation, neither of these views of the religion of ancient Israel can now be defended on literary or form-critical, theological, or historical grounds.

Instead, I propose, as a working hypothesis, that early Israelite religion developed gradually out of the Late Bronze and early Iron Age fertility cults of greater Canaan, and that despite the growth of a royal/priestly cultus and its theology in

Jerusalem, local cults continued to flourish and some of them reflected a highly syncretistic blend of Yahwism and pagan practice until the end of the Monarchy. "Normative Judaism," as portrayed in the Deuteronomic and Priestly literature, is a construct of the late Judean Monarchy and in particular of the exilic period. Thus our only resource for religious practice in the early formative period lies in correlating the "minority view" reflected in scattered indirect references in the Pentateuch and the Former Prophets with actual material remains of local cults unearthed by archeology. In the investigation, biblical scholars should reassess the early, relatively casual, statements mentioning "high places" in Joshua-Judges (often associated with the enigmatic "Asherah"), compared with the numerous denunciations of pagan cults in the Prophets. However, in the re-interpretation of the texts archeology may take priority, since the texts are isolated and ambiguous. These will have to be amplified and interpreted by archeology (rather than the other way around), which has only begun to sense its full explanatory potential.

The starting point for the testing of the above theory lies in the acceptance of the ever increasing body of unambiguous archeological evidence for the existence of local shrines, such as those discussed above, in particular, Dan, Arad, and ʿAjrud. The actual archeological illustration of cult paraphernalia and practice of every sort—embracing perhaps dimensions of the cult not mentioned in the Hebrew Bible—must be taken seriously.[30] The parade example thus far of archeology's revolutionary potential is the recent, dramatic confirmation of the persistence of the cult of Asherah (= Anath/Astarte), the Canaanite goddess of love and war. Here some of the long-enigmatic references in the biblical texts may finally be illuminated by the discovery of Israelite "Asherah" cult stands from 10th-century Taʿanach, and by the re-interpreted 8th-century Kh. el-Kôm funerary inscriptions, which may refer to "Asherah" in connection with Yahweh. All this is thrown into sharp relief by the 9th–8th-century sanctuary at Kuntillet ʿAjrud, with its shrine, new classes of votives, Hebrew dedicatory inscriptions, and texts mentioning both "Yahweh and his Asherah," and "Baʿal" and "El" in parallelism.[31] Now it remains to see how this alternate theory—and it is only a theory—may be tested.

2. A Deliberate Strategy

The somewhat optimistic program I shall outline assumes an awareness that archeology, particularly in the last decade, has become much more sophisticated in theory and method, and that this orientation of the "new archeology" has now begun to transform the outlook of much traditional-style "biblical" or Syro-Palestinian archeology. Elsewhere I have sketched this development and called attention to both the opportunities and the dangers it presents.[32] Here I wish only to suggest, without being exhaustive, how the fundamental insights of the newer archeology may be applied specifically to the elucidation of the Israelite cult.

Much of the new look in Syro-Palestinian archeology can be traced to a shift, for reasons beyond consideration here, away from a narrowly chronological and historical orientation, that is, from the kind of "political history" that initially seemed best suited to solving certain problems in biblical studies. The altered perspective derived first from the natural sciences and secondarily from cultural anthropology. Some of the watchwords of the "new archeology" of particular interest to the present inquiry are as follows. (1) "Systemic": the insistence that archeology is a specialized branch of anthropology that examines the material evidence for extinct societies in total cultural and environmental *context*, which entails the use of extensive multi-disciplinary and comparative (or "cross-cultural") methods. (2) "Processual": the view that archeology is concerned primarily with the variability of human behavior and thus seeks "laws" or patterns of cultural *adaptations and change*. (3) "Scientific": the assumption that archeology not only must adopt quantative-statistical and analytical techniques from the natural sciences, but must increasingly devote itself in both excavation and interpretation to the formulation and testing of hypotheses, i.e., to specific *problem-solving*.

The "systemic" concept of archeology as applied to the study of the Israelite cult would call first for the much broader examination of potential sites, areas, and installations in their *total* setting. The chronological-historical framework derived from stratigraphy and comparative typology is fundamental. But it is now clear that the comprehension of patterns of human behavior behind the archeological record requires first the use of data from all sources—artifactual, literary, paleo-environmental; and second the attempt to reconstruct the place and function of individual features in the larger cultural context. This is particularly crucial in using archeology to investigate the role of religion in primitive societies. Thus our strategy in Syro-Palestinian archeology must be deliberately to seek to locate potential cultic sites and areas in Israel, Jordan, Egypt, and Syria, and to complete large-scale exposure of appropriate Late Bronze and Iron Age levels, using the most sophisticated methods of data retrieval. From project-design to final publication, the mass of varied and complex data must be analyzed by a *truly* multi-disciplinary staff, so that the insights of archeology, history, philology, ethnography, cultural anthropology, comparative religion and literature, theology, esthetics, the history of art and technology, not to mention a number of branches of the natural sciences, can all be brought to bear on the elusive phenomenon of ancient religion and cult. Obviously this agenda is ambitious and perhaps idealistic; but the alternative is to continue to distort and even to destroy the little archeological evidence that may remain.

"Processual" for our purposes implies that archeology is capable of discerning in material remains evidence of how religion may have functioned in the adaptation of an ancient society to its natural and cultural environment, how cultic practice expressed and validated the belief-systems of that society, and how both evolved through time and circumstance. This goal of the newer archeology is even more ambitious than the above (and still hotly debated), but its application to Syro-Palestinian archeology and cultic studies should at least be tested. For instance, can we compare the archeological remains of Canaanite–Philistine and Israelite temples/shrines in number, distribution, size, artistic embellishment, or economic investment in relation to site and society, in order to determine how ancient Israel "differed"? (Here the "silence" of the archeological record may indeed be significant.) Through chemical and physical means of testing, or by high-magnification use-wear analysis, can we ascertain how implements such as "Israelite" altars, censers, and votives were actually employed, and to what degree they may reflect the fertility cult of greater Canaan rather than the Yahwistic theology of Priestly literature? On the basis of the artifactual evidence, can we trace religious syncretism in Israel through chronological and cultural *stages*, so as to offer a critique of the older evolutionary hypothesis that based itself solely on literary criticism and posited a simple evolution from polydemonism to "ethical monotheism"? These are relevant questions; since they cannot be answered satisfactorily by the literary sources alone, it is surely worthwhile to pursue archeology to its limit in our inquiry.

"Scientific" suggests methods that have already been partially introduced in the multi-disciplinary approach outlined above and promise greater precision in dating and understanding the nature and use of artifactual remains of the cult. But we can go further with the basic approach of science. We can formulate hypotheses concerning the Israelite cult on the basis of what we already know and then deliberately structure archeological research projects to test these hypotheses in order to refine them or reject them in the light of new evidence and new hypotheses. Syro-Palestinian archeology is too historically oriented ever to be truly scientific; but it could at least become more *systematic*, and thus much more productive of data that could be used by theologians and historians of religion with some confidence.

Conclusion

In this admittedly programmatic essay there are more questions than answers. But I have tried to show that the reaction against the proliferation of naïve "cultic explanations" in past has gone too far the other way,[33] that modern archeology has vast unfulfilled potential. It may be true that the relatively damp climate of central Palestine and the vicissitudes of the country's long social and political history have conspired to rob us of much of the material evidence archeology might have produced—such as the remains of the Jerusalem temple and its cultus. It is also evident that some elements of religion do not in fact lend themselves readily to archeological investigation, so that, for instance, without textual data we should be very much in the dark on most matters of religious *belief*, and even on certain aspects of practice such as priestly functions, various festal calendars, liturgy, and sacrificial systems. Above all it must be stressed that archeology is not the handmaiden of theology: by definition, it cannot validate theological propositions about the past by confirming the "historicity" of events as described in the Hebrew Bible.

Archeology does have unique potential for illuminating actual Israelite religious practice in two directions. (1) First is its ability to penetrate *behind* the later and heavily-theologized literary traditions. In doing so it may yield tangible evidence of popular religion, an independent and invaluable corrective to the "establishment" view of the texts. (2) Second, archeology can provide the essential basis for *comparative* studies, for it alone can illuminate neighboring cultures such as those of Late Bronze Age Palestine and Iron Age Philistia and Transjordan,[34] whose religious traditions will probably never be as copiously illustrated textually as those of ancient Israel are by the Bible. If "a picture is worth a thousand words," then archeology is a parallel way of viewing the ancient cult, in no way inferior to textual studies.[35]

Notes

1. One may cite Freedman's seminal essay (1965) and his more recent (if somewhat premature) focus on Ebla and Patriarchal backgrounds in recent issues of the *Biblical Archeologist*. As an editor, Freedman's contribution to archeology is seen in his 1969 work (with co-editor Jonas Greenfield) and as editor of the popular but authoritative quarterly *The Biblical Archeologist* from 1976 to 1982.

2. Albright has correctly pointed out that much of the study of the history of the religion of Israel from the time of Wellhausen on was in effect the analysis of literary tradition, and as such tended to ignore the revolutionary results of historical-archeological research. However, our point here is that while the "external evidence" of archeology may have enhanced our appreciation of the value of the biblical sources for understanding both Israelite history and theology, it has not proportionately given us an independent and direct witness to the ancient *cult*.

3. The best recent survey of the archeological material is Shiloh 1979, although this is confined to a brief description of Iron age temples/shrines and their furnishings in general. The latest analysis from a literary point of view is Haran 1978, on which see below. Our indictment, incidentally, would be even more applicable to the archeology of early Judaism and Christianity, although a discussion of that would be beyond both our scope here and our competence. The Galilee synagogue project of Eric Meyers, Carol Meyers, James F. Strange, and others is, however, most promising.

4. On the archeological evidence for the Solomonic temple and its background, see Dever 1974a and references there; and my forthcoming chapter on the art and architecture of the Solomonic era (1982c). As a prime example of the ignoring of archeology that we shall document below, note the exhaustive work of Th. A. Busink, *Der Tempel von Jerusalem, von Salamo bis Herodes I* (1970), which uses *no* archeological data.

5. See Aharoni 1968, 1969, 1973b. The confused stratigraphy and dating of Iron Age Arad are well known; for a drastic lowering of the date, for instance, of the two inscribed platters found near the cella of the sanctuary and ascribed variously by the excavator to Stratum X or VIII, see Dever 1969–70: 173 (8th century); and Cross 1979 (7th century). On the *significance* of the sanctuary, however, see below and n. 33.

6. On the "High Place" at *Dan*, see Biran 1974a, 1974b, 1980: 175–79; Stager and Wolff 1981; on Building 2081 of Stratum VA at *Megiddo*, see Loud 1948: 45, 46; on the "Cultic Structure" at *Taʿanach*, see Lapp 1964: 26–32, 1969: 42–44; Glock 1978: 1142–44; Stager and Wolff 1981; on "Cult Room 49" of Stratum V at *Lachish*, see Aharoni 1975b: 26–32, figs. 5–8, pls. 41–43; on the supposed Stratum III temple replaced by the "Basement Building" of Stratum II at *Beersheba*, see Aharoni 1973a: 16, 17; 1975a: 158–63; and cf. the critique of Yadin 1976, together with the defense of Herzog, Rainey, and Moshkovitz 1977; on *Kuntillet Ajrud*, see Meshel 1978a, 1978b, 1979; Meshel and Meyers 1976. To this list one might add a Level III "shrine" (9th century) at Tell el-Farʿah North, though this is debatable; cf. de Vaux 1951: 428; Stager and Wolff 1981. The two so-called *maṣṣēbôt* found by Kenyon in Jerusalem do not imply an 8th–7th-century cultic structure but a common house; cf. Graesser 1972: 54, 55; Shiloh 1979: 147. We do not regard the Stratum XI installation at Hazor as necessarily an Israelite shrine; see n. 12 below.

7. Lapp 1969: 42–44; Glock 1978: 1142–44. These fascinating stands, which abound in evidence for Israelite syncretistic iconography, deserve *much* more attention.

8. See the references in nn. 5, 6. Stands that may be presumed to be censers or libation holders have been studied in C. L. Meyers 1976: 73–77. Cf. nn. 7, 12.

9. Lapp (1969: 45, 46) recovered 140 astragali (not "pig," but probably sheep/goat: Stager and Wolff 1981) from the Taʿanach "Cultic Structure." Aharoni (1968: 19) noted the headless skeleton of a young lamb and pits with other bones near the large courtyard altar of the Arad sanctuary. And sheep, goat, and gazelle bones are reported to have been found in an offering bowl of the earliest phase (A) of the Dan sanctuary (Biran 1980: 175–79). But to my knowledge no flotation or wet-sieving, of the sort used to recover quantities of animal bones from the MB IIC Gezer "High Place," has yet been employed on Iron Age cultic installations.

10. See, for instance, the large collection from the Lachish sanctuary (Aharoni 1975b: pls. 41, 42), all common jugs, bowls, kraters, lamps, and chalices.

11. We desperately need a current and synthetic treatment of all the data on the Late Bronze and Iron Age figurines.

12. Yadin et al. 1961: pls. 38, 204–5; 1972: 132–34, pl. 24:c (Stratum XI); Dever *et al.* 1975:

67, 68, pls. 41:2, 75A (Stratum VI). Shiloh (1979: 150), following Yadin (1972:132–34), considers the Hazor XI statuette evidence for an Israelite cult installation; but it is clearly part of a hoard in a votive jar, and since it is classic Late Bronze in type, it is probably a holdover—even if Stratum XI is regarded as Israelite. A broken head of a male figure from near the Dan sanctuary has recently been reported (Biran 1980: 178–79), together with a painted stand of which it is probably a part (seen through the courtesy of Prof. Biran and his staff).

13. For *Hazor*, see Yadin et al. 1961: pl. 357: 4–6; 358: 4,5 (Stratum V bowl reading "Qodesh," 9th century); for *Kh. el-Kôm*, Dever 1969–70: 172–73 (8th-century bowl reading "El"); for *Arad*, Aharoni 1968: 20 (Stratum X platters inscribed with *qof, shin*, for "Qodesh"; cf. Dever 1969–70: 173, and see Cross 1979 for redating to the early 7th century); for *Beersheba*, Aharoni 1973a: pls. 42:4, 69:2 (a Stratum II krater reading "Qodesh"); for *ʿAjrud*, Meshel 1979: 30–32 (9th/8th century pithoi and two stone bowls with Yahwistic personal names and a plea for blessing (see below and n. 17).

14. See the evidence for Middle-Late Bronze Age pottery workshops cited in Dever 1974a: 43, nn. 27, 28. Aharoni (1968: 21) mentions two pottery kilns and vessels near the entrance of the Arad Strata VIII–VII sanctuary, but no details are given. The only comparable Iron Age ceramic production in a cultic context is reflected in the Asherah figurine-mould from the "Cultic Structure" at Taʿanach (Lapp 1967: 36).

15. Again, no comprehensive up-to-date study of the seals and ivories— especially with regard to iconography—can be cited. See provisionally the references in Dever 1982c, n. 61.

16. Several Iron I (12th-century) ceramic foundation deposits are known from Gezer, but these are almost certainly Philistine; cf. Dever, Lance, and Wright 1970: 23.

17. For *Jerusalem*, see Avigad 1953; for *Kh. Beit Lei*, Naveh 1963 (funereal?); for *Kh. el-Kôm*, Dever 1969–70: 169–74; and for a cave near *ʿEin-gedi*, Bar-Adon 1975. These sepulchral inscriptions have not usually been taken into account when considering the cult; but any anthropologist would quickly point out that funeral customs—particularly when combined with epigraphic evidence—may constitute prime data for the cult. Further, note that Lemaire (1977: 599–603) and Naveh (1979: 28) both now read "Asherah" in the el-Kôm Inscription 3, which, when taken with the ʿAjrud readings of "Asherah," throws dramatic light on syncretism in the Israelite cult (below).

18. Meshel 1978a; 1979: 30–32; Meshel and Meyers 1976: 6–10; cf. also below on ʿAjrud.

19. I have not yet published the evidence for this view, but it derives from comparing the Aegean-style 13th–12th-century Philistine tombs at Tell el-Farʿah South and Eitun with 10th-century and later bench-tombs from many Israelite sites; see, provisionally, Dever 1969–70: 150–51.

20. E. Meyers (1971) has studied burial customs throughout Palestine's pre-Byzantine history in order to derive a "theology of the dead," but his basic theme of secondary burial does not seem applicable to the Iron Age.

21. See references in n. 6 above.

22. See Dever 1971, 1974b, 1976, 1980, 1982a, 1982b.

23. The same criticism could be levelled at much of conservative Jewish scholarship in past, as in Y. Kaufmann's great *The Religion of Israel* (1960, 1970, 1976, cf. 1953). And the "Israeli school" today, despite its special access to archeological data, carries on biblical studies largely in isolation from archeology, both institutionally and ideologically. The best-balanced blend of archeology, history, and devout biblical criticism, in my opinion, is still seen in de Vaux's work; note his exemplary treatment of Israelite religion in 1961: 274–517 (although now dated archeologically).

24. See, for instance, the essays of Albright and Wright in Freedman and Greenfield 1969: 1–3, 170–71.

25. On the latter, see my critique of Wright and "Biblical archeology" in Dever 1980: 2–12.

26. Thus May's work on Megiddo (1935) was the first on precisely our topic and is still usable today. He later collaborated with W. C. Graham on a classic of Protestant Liberal scholarship in the evolutionary vein, now simply an historical curiosity, Graham and May 1936.

27. See, for instance, Wright 1962.

28. J. L. Kelso's publication of the excavation of Bethel is a case in point; for the refutation of his supposed MB I "shrine of the Patriarchs," see my review in Dever 1971. I have collected a vast literature on such cultic explanations among early amateur "biblical archeologists," most of them American Fundamentalists like Albright's co-director at Tell Beit Mirsim, M. G. Kyle (one of the editors of the classic series *The Fundamentals*, Dixon et al. 1910–15). See also n. 33 below.

29. The opposition of orthodoxy to archeology is nowhere more determined and outspoken than in

Israel, where excavations can and have been closed down. Elsewhere, where perhaps it is less visible, archeology is simply ignored by orthodox religionists.

30. Stager and Wolff's brilliant reconstruction (1981) of a hitherto-unrecognized oil-pressing complex associated with the Dan sanctuary (there were probably also similar complexes at Taᶜanach and Tell el-Farᶜah North) is a prime example of both the surprises archeology can produce and the new multi-disciplinary approach that we are advocating here. For the best illustration of the Dan installation (though the text still interprets it as a "libation area") see Laughlin 1981.

31. See the references in n. 6 above on ᶜAjrud; for the new reading of el-Kôm, see n. 17 above; on the Taᶜanach stand, see n. 7 above.

32. See the references in n. 22 above, especially Dever 1982b.

33. On the excesses of "cultic" interpretation in past, see n. 28 above. Yeivin (1973) has sharply criticised more recent archeologists (who, however, were presumably not religiously motivated), but he is too skeptical. Aharoni was widely accused of a cultic bias in his strategy of fieldwork, and especially in his interpretation of Beersheba, but his instincts were not altogether unsound. Wright's *Shechem: The Biography of a Biblical City* (1965) has also been criticized by both archeologists and biblical scholars; on this, see my critique in Dever 1980.

34. We now have no fewer than two dozen Late Bronze Canaanite temples from Israel (the latest from Tell Kitan, Lachish, and Mevorakh), along with the splendid Philistine temple at Tell Qasile, soon to be published by A. Mazar in two volumes in the *Qedem* series.

35. Since this chapter was written, a 12th-11th century cultic installation, with a superb bronze figure of a bull, has been found near modern Jenin, in the area of the tribal territory of Manasseh; A. Mazar will publish the find.

References

Aharoni, Y.

1968 — Arad: Its Inscriptions and Temple. *The Biblical Archaeologist* 31: 1–32.

1969 — The Israelite Sanctuary at Arad. Pp. 29–36 in Freedman and Greenfield 1969.

1973a — *Beer-sheba I. Excavations at Tell Beer-sheba, 1969–1971 Seasons*. Tel Aviv: Institute of Archaeology, Tel Aviv University.

1973b — The Solomonic Temple, the Tabernacle and the Arad Sanctuary. Pp. 1–8 in *Orient and Occident* [C. H. Gordon *Festschrift*], ed. H. A. Hoffner. Alter Orient und Altes Testament 22. Neukirchen-Vluyn and Kevelaer: Neukirchener and Butzon und Bercker.

1974 — The Horned Altar of Beer-sheba. *The Biblical Archaeologist* 37: 2–6.

1975a — Excavations at Tel Beer-sheba, Preliminary Report of the Fifth and Sixth Seasons, 1973–1974. *Tel Aviv* 2: 146–68.

1975b — *Lachish: The Sanctuary and the Residency (Lachish V)*. Tel Aviv: Institute of Archaeology, Tel Aviv University.

Avigad, N.

1953 — The Epitaph of a Royal Steward from Siloam Village. *Israel Exploration Journal* 3: 137–52.

Bar-Adon, P.

1975 — An Early Hebrew Graffito in a Judean Desert Cave. *Eretz-Israel* 12 [Glueck *Festschrift*]: 77–80 (Hebrew).

Barrick, W. B.

1975 — The Funerary Character of High Places: A Reassessment. *Vetus Testamentum* 25: 565–95.

Biran, A.

1974a — Tel Dan. *The Biblical Archaeologist* 37: 26–51.

1974b — An Israelite Horned Altar at Dan. *The Biblical Archaeologist* 37: 106–7.

1980 — Tel Dan—Five Years Later. *Biblical Archeologist* 43: 168–82.

Biran, A., ed.
1981 *Temples and High Places in Biblical Times.* Jerusalem: Nelson Glueck School of Biblical Archaeology.

Busink, Th. A.
1970 *Der Tempel von Jerusalem, von Salamo bis Herodes I.* Studia Francisci Scholten Memoriae Dicata 3. Leiden: Brill.

Cross, F. M.
1979 Two Offering Dishes with Phoenician Inscriptions from the Sanctuary of ‘Arad. *Bulletin of the American Schools of Oriental Research* 235: 75–78.

Dever, W. G.
1969–70 Iron Age Epigraphic Material from the Area of Khirbet el-Kôm. *Hebrew Union College Annual* 50–51: 139–204.

1971 Archaeological Methods and Results: A Review of Two Recent Publications. *Orientalia* 40: 461–71.

1974a The MB IIC Stratification in the Northwest Gate Area at Shechem. *Bulletin of the American Schools of Oriental Research* 216: 31–52.

1974b *Archaeology and Biblical Studies: Retrospects and Prospects.* The Winslow Lectures, Seabury-Western Theological Seminary. Evanston: Seabury-Western.

1976 Archaeology. Pp. 44–52 in *Interpreter's Dictionary of the Bible/Supplementary Volume*, ed. K. Crim et al. Nashville: Abingdon.

1980 Biblical Theology and Biblical Archaeology: An Appreciation of G. Ernest Wright. *Harvard Theological Review* 73: 1–15.

1982a Palestinian and Biblical Archaeology *ca.* 1945–1980. Forthcoming in *The Hebrew Bible and Its Modern Interpreters*, ed. G. A. Knight and G. M. Tucker.

1982b The Impact of the "New Archeology" on Syro-Palestinian Archaeology. *Bulletin of the American Schools of Oriental Research* 242: 15–28.

1982c Monumental Architecture in Ancient Israel in the Period of the United Monarchy. Forthcoming in *Proceedings of the First International Symposium of the Japan Biblical Society.*

Dever, W. G.; Lance, H. D.; and Wright, G. E.
1970 *Gezer I: Preliminary Report of the 1964–66 Seasons.* Jerusalem: Hebrew Union College Biblical and Archaeological School.

Dever, W. G., et al.
1975 *Gezer II. Report of the 1967–70 Seasons in Fields I and II.* Jerusalem: Hebrew Union College/Nelson Glueck School of Biblical Archaeology.

Dixon, A. C., et al.
1910–15 *The Fundamentals: A Testimony to the Truth.* 12 vols. Chicago: Testimony Publishing.

Freedman, D. N.
1965 Archaeology and the Future of Biblical Studies: The Biblical Languages. Pp. 294–312 in *The Bible in Modern Scholarship.* ed. J. P. Hyatt. Nashville: Abingdon.

Freedman, D. N., and Greenfield, J., eds.
1969 *New Directions in Biblical Archaeology.* Garden City, New York: Doubleday.

Glock, A. E.
1978 Ta‘anach. Vol. 4, pp. 1138–47 in *Encyclopedia of Archaeological Excavations in the Holy Land*, ed. M. Avi-Yonah and E. Stern. Jerusalem: Massada Press.

Graham, W. C., and May, H. G.
1936 *Culture and Conscience: An Archaeological Study of the New Religious Past in Palestine.* University of Chicago Publications in Religious Education: Handbooks of Ethics and Religion. Chicago: University of Chicago Press.

Graesser, C. F.
1972 Standing Stones in Ancient Palestine. *The Biblical Archaeologist* 35: 34–63.

Haran, M.
1978 *Temples and Temple-Service in Ancient Israel: An Inquiry into the Character of Cult Phenomena and the Historical Setting of the Priestly School.* Oxford: Clarendon Press.

Herzog, Z.; Rainey, A. F.; and Moshkovitz, S.
1977 The Stratigraphy at Beer-sheba and the Location of the Sanctuary. *Bulletin of the American Schools of Oriental Research* 225: 49–58.

Kaufmann, Y.
1953 *The Biblical Account of the Conquest of Palestine.* Trans. M. Dagut. Jerusalem: Magnes.
1960 *The Religion of Israel. From Its Beginnings to the Babylonian Exile.* Trans./abr. M. Greenberg. Chicago: University of Chicago Press.
1970 *The Babylonian Captivity and Deutero-Isaiah.* Trans. C. W. Efroymson. New York: Union of American Hebrew Congregations.
1976 *History of the Religion of Israel, from the Babylonian Captivity to the End of Prophecy.* Trans. C. W. Efroymson. New York: Ktav.

Lapp, P. W.
1964 The 1963 Excavations at Taʿanek. *Bulletin of the American Schools of Oriental Research* 173: 4–44.
1967 Taʿanach by the Waters of Megiddo. *The Biblical Archaeologist* 30: 2–27.
1969 The 1969 Excavations at Tell Taʿanek. *Bulletin of the American Schools of Oriental Research* 195: 2–49.

Laughlin, J. C. H.
1981 The Remarkable Discoveries at Tel Dan. *Biblical Archaeology Review* 7/5: 20–37.

Lemaire, A.
1977 Les inscriptions de Khirbet el-Qôm et l'Ashérah de Yhwh. *Revue biblique* 84: 597–608.

Loud, G.
1948 *Megiddo II. Seasons of 1935–39.* University of Chicago Oriental Institute Publication 62. Chicago: University of Chicago Press.

May, H. G.
1935 *Material Remains of the Megiddo Cult.* University of Chicago Oriental Institute Publication 26. Chicago: University of Chicago Press.

Meshel, Z.
1978a *Kuntillet ʿAjrud: A Religious Centre From the Time of the Judaean Monarchy on the Border of Sinai.* Israel Museum Catalog 175. Jerusalem: The Israel Museum.
1978b Kuntillet Ajrud. An Israelite Religious Center in Northern Sinai. *Expedition* 20: 50–54.
1979 Did Yahweh Have A Consort? *Biblical Archaeology Review* 5/2: 24–35.

Meshel, Z., and Meyers, C. L.
1976 The Name of God in the Wilderness of Zin. *Biblical Archeologist* 39: 6–10.

Meyers, C. L.
1976 *The Tabernacle Menorah: A Synthetic Study of a Symbol from the Biblical Cult.* American Schools of Oriental Research Dissertation Series 2. Missoula, MT: Scholars Press.

Meyers, E. M.
1971 *Jewish Ossuaries: Reburial and Rebirth. Secondary Burials in Their Ancient Near Eastern Setting.* Biblica et Orientalia 24. Rome: Pontifical Biblical Institute.

Naveh, J.
1961 Old Hebrew Inscriptions in a Burial Cave. *Israel Exploration Journal* 13: 74–92.
1979 Graffiti and Dedications. *Bulletin of the American Schools of Oriental Research* 235: 27–30.

Shiloh, Y.
1979 Iron Age Sanctuaries and Cult Elements in Palestine. Pp. 147–57 in *Symposia Celebrating the Seventy-fifth Anniversary of the Founding of the American Schools of Oriental Research (1970–1975),* ed. F. M. Cross. Cambridge: American Schools of Oriental Research.

Stager, L. E., and Wolff, S. R.
1981 Production and Commerce in Temple Courtyards: An Olive Press in the Sacred Precinct at Tel Dan. *Bulletin of the American Schools of Oriental Research* 243 (forthcoming).

Vaughan, P. H.
1974 *The Meaning of bāmâ in the Old Testament.* Society for Old Testament Study Monograph 3. London: Cambridge University Press.

de Vaux, R.
1951 La troisième campagne de fouilles à Tell el-Farʿah, près Naplouse. *Revue biblique* 58: 393–430; 566–90.
1961 *Ancient Israel: Its Life and Institutions.* Trans. J. McHugh. London: McGraw-Hill. Originally 1958, 1960.

Wright, G. E.
1962 Cult and History: A Study of a Current Problem in Old Testament Interpretation. *Interpretation* 16/1: 3–20.
1965 *Shechem: The Biography of a Biblical City.* New York: McGraw-Hill.

Yadin, Y.
1972 *Hazor, the Head of all Those Kingdoms.* London: Oxford University Press.
1976 Beer-Sheba: The High Place Destroyed by King Josiah. *Bulletin of the American Schools of Oriental Research* 222: 5–17.

Yadin, Y., et al.
1961 *Hazor III-IV. Plates.* Jerusalem: Magnes.

Yeivin, S.
1973 Temples That Were Not. *Eretz-Israel* 11 [Dunayevsky *Festschrift*]: 163–75 (Hebrew; English summary *28).

Two Palestinian Segments From the Eblaite Geographical Atlas

William H. Shea
Andrews University, Berrien Springs, Michigan

Since Noel Freedman first introduced me to the significance of some of the contents of the texts from Ebla, it is my pleasure to return the favor by dedicating this study of a text from that archive to him. Pettinato published this text (TM 75.G.2231) for the purpose of demonstrating that it was also known at Abū Ṣalābīkh (Pettinato 1978). The identification of this text as a geographical atlas is quite appropriate, since its 13 vertical columns (11 recto, 2 verso) record 289 place names. The geographical nature of this text is clear since the determinative for place, KI, is written after all the names. Pettinato compared the intact copy of this text that was found at Tell Mardikh in Syria with some 20 partial copies and fragments found at Abū Ṣalābīkh in Iraq (Biggs 1974: 71–76). These partial copies make up a composite text that is a duplicate of the one found at Ebla, and the Eblaite copy can be used as a framework upon which to arrange the fragments from Abū Ṣalābīkh in correct order.

The occurrence of duplicates of this and other texts at these two sites raises an interesting and debated question about the relationship between them that cannot be examined here. The most direct way in which to compare these two texts is through a transliteration of their signs; thus it was not necessary for Pettinato to translate or identify any place names in the initial publication of the Ebla text. That task remains to be addressed and the purpose of this study is to suggest some preliminary steps in that direction.

The publication of more materials from Ebla has provided a view of ancient geography from that city's vantage point that is remarkable in its extent. In addition to the 290 sites named in this atlas, Pettinato has listed some 650 place names in the toponym index to the catalogue of the tablet room archive (Pettinato 1979a: 274–79). His publication of the first 50 tablets has provided another 300 place names (Pettinato 1980a: 357–61). The full publication of the record of a military campaign against Mari has added two dozen more place names to this corpus (Pettinato 1980b: 231–45). When one discounts duplicate names in these four lists they provide an extraordinary total of over 1000 individual place names with which to deal; more are undoubtedly on the way. A whole new vista of historical geography in the third millennium B.C. has been opened up, and it will take a long time to digest and correlate all of the new material with what was previously known.

The Eblaite Geographical Atlas (EGA) is the single greatest Eblaite source of this type of information. A comparison with the other sources illustrates an important point about the EGA. Of the 307 place names listed in the publication of the first 50 texts, 131 or more than 1/3 also appear among the 650 names in the toponym index of the catalogue of texts from the tablet room. Of the two dozen place names listed as conquered in the campaign against Mari, 10 or just under half occur in either the tablet room catalogue or the first 50 texts published or both. Thus the ratio of sites recognizable in other Eblaite sources is roughly consistent between the first 50 texts and the Mari campaign text.

The situation is quite different in the case of the EGA. Of its 289 place names, only 20 or less than 10% appear in these other sources, 5 in the first 50 texts and 15 in the tablet room catalogue. More specifically, of the 80 place names examined below, none of those that appear in the second set of 30 appear in these other sources, and only two from the first set of 50 appear there (Nos. 97 and 115). Since one of these two names appears elsewhere in the EGA, it is possible that more than one site of that time was known by this name (No. 115, cf. No. 57).

This statistical difference may imply something about the location of the places named in the EGA. The cross-section of sites from the first 50 texts and the tablet room catalogue may be thought of as representing especially sites located in northern, eastern and central Syria. Greater frequency of contact with sites closer to Ebla could explain the greater number of cross-references to similar sites in these sources. The reverse may also be true: infrequent reference in the other geographical sources to sites named in the EGA could imply that they were more remote from the Eblaite heartland, farther east, north, or south. More remote locations like these would have had less frequent contacts with Ebla, and this would have led to less frequent mention of them in texts recorded there. This fits well with the fact that the places named in the two segments from the atlas studied below appear to have been located a considerable distance south of Ebla.

Before looking at these toponyms, texts from elsewhere in the ancient Near East of a similar nature might be mentioned first by way of a general introduction to this subject. Texts that convey topographical and geographical information appear to come in two main categories, those that are connected with military activities and those that are not. The Sargon Geography may be cited as an early example of the military type of statement in a rather simplified literary form (Grayson 1974: 56–64). Although this text was probably composed later than the time of Sargon of Akkad, the travels and conquests it recites go back to his time in legend at least. Sargon is now thought to have been a contemporary of the Dynasty of Ebla, and Ebla is mentioned in line 13 of his geography text. That the geographical references in this text describe conquests attributed to Sargon is evident from the way in which he is referred to at the beginning, in the middle, and at the end of the text (lines 4–5, 32, 41). The geographical references in it occur in some 30 formulaic prepositional phrases, "from X to Y" (lines 1–30). In another section of the text the travel times through these territories are listed (lines 31–40).

A text of this type has been found in the royal archive of Ebla. Pettinato refers to this text as a "military bulletin" sent back to the king of Ebla by the general of his troops in the field (Pettinato 1980b: 231–45). In 10 different sections of this text, sections that can almost be called stanzas, the general listed the towns and territories conquered stage by stage from the king of Mari. After each new list of sites he continued his report with a formulaically repeated set of verbs having to do with assaulting, besieging, and conquering them. Two dozen place names occur in this text and their relations with other geographical sources from Ebla have been mentioned above.

A geographical text which may be partly military in that it involved an expedition of troops, but which was also peaceful in nature in that no engagement was fought while they were on that expedition, is the one referred to as "The Road to Emar" (Goetze 1953: 51–72; Hallo 1964: 57–88). The scribe who recorded this itinerary listed 70 sites at which he stopped during his round trip from Larsa in Sumer to Emar on the Upper Euphrates. He also mentioned the number of days he stopped at each site, usually one day, and totaled up the time the whole trip took, 6½ months. This Old Babylonian text has provided a challenge for historical geographers who have searched for identifications and locations for its sites. Except for Emar itself, there does not appear to be any overlap in place names between this text and the one that records Ebla's campaign against Mari. If the opening phrase from each line about the number of days passed and incidental references to events were deleted from this text, the result would look much like what is proposed below for the EGA, an itinerary or list of place names visited in geographical order.

Goetze compared the Road to Emar text with the geographical data available from the Cappadocian tablets for the stops of the Old Assyrian traders who plied the caravan route from Nineveh in Assyria to Kanish in Anatolia (Goetze 1953: 64–70). The overlapping records of expenses for segments of that trip given in individual texts can be compiled into a composite picture of their journey which indicates that they utilized two dozen stopping places along the Cappadocian road. Had this compilation been made in ancient times the resulting text could well have looked something like the EGA.

Another type of non-military geographical text that may be mentioned here is that which Hallo has referred to as the list of theoretical geography. Such lists are essentially taxonomic in orientation; more specifically, they are linguistically or even orthographically oriented systems of classification. Thus the cuneiform lists of geographical names which we owe to the Babylonian academies are mainly concerned with their classification by means of 'determinatives' or 'semantic indicators' such as those for country, city, river and field; within these large groups there is a tendency to subdivide by constitutive elements into what, in transliteration, almost appears as an alphabetic order. (In HAR-ra = *hubullu* the order is cities, mountains, countries, water-ways, heavens, ziqqurrats, and fortifications.) By their very nature all these lists tell us little about the location of their topographical entries, to us the most essential element in geography (Hallo 1964: 61).

Lists of the categories of knowledge are known at Ebla for birds, fish, plants, stones, the professions of mankind, etc. (Pettinato 1979b: 256). The EGA, however, does not appear to fit into this specific category of text because none of the principles of organization for place names mentioned by Hallo above are demonstrable. Geographical features, in contrast to specific toponyms, are recognizable in this list, but they are scattered through it at irregular intervals; they are not grouped according to categories. The differences between the EGA and these lists of theoretical geography and the similarities between it and some of the other geographical texts described above suggest that the EGA should be examined for the probability that it conveys applied rather than theoretical geographical information.

Ancient Near Eastern geographical texts are, in their approach to topography and geography, either theoretical, in which case data is organized by categories, or applied, in which case the data convey practical information directly. Since the EGA does not follow the former pattern, it is reasonable to suspect that it belongs to the latter category and that its place names are listed in geographical order. If they appear only in random order it could be difficult to establish site identification even though such identifications may appear to be phonetically reasonable. If, on the other hand, these sites are listed in the order in which they were visited by, say, merchants from Ebla, then that format should provide a general region and direction in which to search for the sites. Recognition of those sites could in turn lend support to the other identifications. In practice this procedure appears to work for the two segments from this list studied below. If this principle is correct it should assist in studying the sites named in other sections of the text.

Studying the place names in the EGA is aided by the fact that its primary publication includes plates with overall photographs of both sides of the tablet and close-up views of all four quadrants of the recto. Except for a few chips and cracks, the tablet is in good condition and the photographs of it are clear enough that sign identification does not pose a great problem. In the Sumero-Eblaite writing system signs could be used either with phonetic values or as logograms. With the exception of determinatives, which designate classes of things, names consisting of a number of signs may generally be taken as having been spelled out phonetically. Signs in shorter names are more likely to consist of logograms, which can make the identification of the sites more difficult.

Even if a name is written with signs used phonetically, selecting the phonetic value intended can still pose a problem since the Sumero-Eblaite writing system was polyphonic, i.e., one and the same sign could stand for more than one sound or value. Name No. 132 below provides an illustration of this. Pettinato read its signs as *gi-bil-a-nu* (1978: 57). The *bil*-sign, however, can also be read as *bí* (Labat 1976: 111). This makes better sense of this name as Gibeon, both phonetically and according to its location in the list. Thus while sign identification does not pose a great problem with this text, sign value selection may do so on occasion.

It was noted above that there is evidence to suggest that some of the sites named in the EGA were located a considerable distance from Ebla. That being the case there obviously was a process of several steps of transmission whereby the names of those distant sites came to be recorded in the final form of the comprehensive list. It may have been merchants from Ebla who first visited these settlements and became aware of their existence. In the normal course of events the names of those settlements would have been communicated orally to such travellers by their residents. These names would then have been taken back to Ebla by those travellers either by word of mouth, which seems more likely, or possibly in some written form. Since it is unlikely that a list of place names as long as the EGA would have been compiled directly from returnees of this type, we may also expect that transmission of the names went through one or more written stages before they came to the EGA in its final form.

This hypothetical course of transmission has been reconstructed to illustrate the point that there were a number of opportunities along this course for a slip of the lip, ear, or stylus to affect the final form in which these names are preserved in the EGA. These names may have been heard differently by successive persons along the line, and the final written form may not reflect the oral form fully and accurately. Differences like these commonly reflect the phonological patterns of labials, dentals, sibilants, velars, laterals, and laryngeals, so that an interchange of consonants may be recognized when the same place name is transcribed in different writing systems. These phenomena, which have been noted in other texts from the ancient Near East, may be expected to have occurred in the texts from Ebla like the EGA. Aharoni's work may be consulted for a full discussion of these interchanges and the way in which they affect identifications in historical geography (1967: 100–112).

Excluding outright errors, written variants may also be directly related to prior forms. This can be seen readily by comparing the ways in which some of these names were written in the EGA and in copies of this text from Abū Ṣalābīkh. One difference that might be mentioned in passing here is that the scribes at Abū Ṣalābīkh appear to have been inclined to use logograms a bit more frequently than the scribes at Ebla. A handicap of the writing system in which these names are recorded is its lack of an adequate representation for the West Semitic laryngeals such as *ʿayin* (ʿ) and *ḥeth* (*ḥ*). The experience of several individuals working with Eblaite texts has indicated that these were represented especially by vowels, either written individually or with more complex syllabic signs.

The vocalization in Eblaite texts is difficult to assess at the present stage of our knowledge. Variant vocalizations of place names in different copies of the geographical atlas urge caution here. The consonants of these place names are of considerably greater importance than vowels in evaluating possible identifications. Some fluidity of sign order may also be present in texts from so early a stage in the development of writing. Name No. 140 below, *bù-gú-tá-nu*, may represent an example of this. The scribe appears to have inverted the order of the first two signs in this name, which should be read as *gú-bù-tá-nu*, for Gibbethon in the central coastal plain, according to its location in the list. The vertical lines delimiting the columns of text were incised on the tablet before the names were written down; this limitation of space may have resulted in a shortening of the form in which a few of the names were written.

With these qualifications in mind, we turn to the first segment of the EGA to be examined here. The identifications offered for some of the sites named in this segment suggest that the route followed to connect them began in Lebanon and curved south through northern Galilee to circle around Lake Huleh and then extended south down the western shore of the Sea of Galilee. From the southern end of the Sea of Galilee the route appears to have turned east and then south on the Transjordanian plateau. It appears to have returned to the Jordan Valley at its mid-point and then to the plateau to continue south until it crossed the lower Jordan Valley to its west bank. From there the route of the list appears to have crossed the central mountain ridge in an east-to-west direction by way of Michmash and Gibeon and continued down towards the coast by way of the Beth-Horon pass. The segment studied here then comes to an end with a few names that appear to correspond to those of coastal sites.

I. Eblaite Geographical Atlas, Sites Nos. 91–140 (Map 1)

Pettinato's Transliteration	Revised Reading	Proposed Identification
91. *ba-qì-a*$_5$^{ki}	*ba-qì-a*$_5$^{ki}	Beqaʿ Valley (Lebanon)
92. *a*-ḪI × ḪI^{ki}	*a*-ḪI × ḪI^{ki}	unidentified
93. *mar-da-na-ak*^{ki}	*mar-tá-na-ak*^{ki}	New Taanach
94. *áb-la*^{ki}	*áb-la*^{ki}	Abel (Beth-Maakah)
95. *úr-an*^{ki}	*úr-an*^{ki}	Yiron
96. DU^{ki}	DU^{ki}	The "Route"
97. *mu-ku*^{ki}	*mu-ku*^{ki}	Maakah
98. *ʾà-du-ru*^{ki}	*ʾà-du-ru*^{ki}	Hazor

99. *ak-šu-wa-ak*^{ki}	*ak-šu-wa-ak*^{ki}	Maakah (Huleh) Valley
100. *dag-me*^{ki}	*dag-me*^{ki}	"Fish Waters" (Lake Huleh)
101. DÚR-DÚR^{ki}	*dúr-dúr*^{ki}	Tura and Jordan Rivers
102. *a-šu*$_{12}$*-ur*^{ki}	*a-šu*$_{12}$*-ur*^{ki}	Geshur
103. *gú-a*^{ki}	GÚ-A^{ki}	"Shore of Waters" (Northeastern shore of the Sea of Galilee)
104. *a-sa-am*$_{6}^{ki}$	A-*sa-am*$_{6}^{ki}$	"Pouring of Waters" (Juncture of the Jordan River with the Sea of Galilee)
105. *ne-ra-aḫ*^{ki}	*ne-ra-aḫ*^{ki}	Marshland at the northern end of the Sea of Galilee
106. *gú-ne-er*^{ki}	GÚ-*ne-er*^{ki}	Plain of Gennesaret
107. AMBAR-*a-a*$_{5}^{ki}$	AMBAR-A-A$_{5}^{ki}$	Marshland at the southern end of the Sea of Galilee
108. *mar-a-bí-ak*^{ki}	*mar-a-bí-aq*^{ki}	New Aphek
109. *ʾà-dur-ru*^{ki}	*ʾà-dur-ru*^{ki}	Gadara
110. *šur*$_{y}$*-zu-ù*^{ki}	*šur*$_{y}$*-zu-ù*^{ki}	unidentified
111. *šur*$_{y}$*-gal*^{ki}	*šur*$_{y}$*-gal*^{ki}	unidentified
112. *ra-ga-ma-ad*^{ki}	*ra-ga-ma-at*^{ki}	Ragaba
113. *ra-ma-at*^{ki}	*ra-ma-at*^{ki}	Heights west of Ragaba
114. *a-gú-zú*^{ki}	A-GÚ-KÁ^{ki}	Entrance to the Jordan Valley
115. *zú-lum*^{ki}	ZÚ-LUM^{ki}	Date Palms (in the valley)
116. *za-me*^{ki}	*za-me*^{ki}	Damiyeh/Adam
117. *gi-a?-u*$_{9}^{ki}$	*gi*-A-BÀD^{ki}	Narrows of the Jordan River near Damiyeh
118. GÁRA-*ḫi*^{ki}	GÁRA-*du*$_{10}^{ki}$	Gilead?
119. *ʾà-zú:gú:ru*^{ki}	*ʾà-zú:gú:ru*^{ki}	unidentified
120. *pù-sa-an*^{ki}	*pù-sa-an*^{ki}	unidentified
121. *sa-ad*-NIN^{ki}	*ša*$_{10}$*-aṭ-in*$_{5}^{ki}$	(Abel-)Shittim
122. *ù-bil-la*^{ki}	*ù-bil-la*^{ki}	Abila/Abel(-Shittim)
123. GI-KU-LA-BA$_{4}^{ki}$	*gi-ḳu-la-ba*$_{4}^{ki}$	Dog Valley (Jordan valley)
124. GIŠ-GI?-TI^{ki}	GIŠ-*gi-ti*^{ki}	Forest of Gath *or* the Winepress, eastern Jordan Valley
125. GIŠ-Ù^{ki}	GIŠ-Ù^{ki}	Junction of the Jordan
126. GIŠ-Ù-GUL-LA^{ki}	GIŠ-*ù-gul-la*^{ki}	Forest of (Beth-)Hoglah
127. GIŠ-KU-LA-BA^{ki}	GIŠ-*ku-la-ba*^{ki}	Dog Forest, western Jordan Valley
128. *ra-ra*^{ki}	RA-RA^{ki}	"Springs" at Jericho
129. *ku-um*^{ki}	*qú-um*^{ki}	Khirbet el-Qubbe at the "Ascent" of the Wâdī eṣ-Ṣuweinît
130. *gi-maš-maš*^{ki}	*gi-maš-maš*^{ki}	Valley of Michmash
131. *ʾà-ru-ak-dar*^{ki}	*ʾà-ru-ak-dar*^{ki}	Mount of the Divide
132. *gi-bil-a-nu*^{ki}	*gi-bí-a-nu*^{ki}	Gibeon
133. *gir-na-ù*^{ki}	*gir-na*-Ù^{ki}	(Beth-)Ḥoron Junction
134. *tar-ma-nu*^{ki}	*tar-ma-nu*^{ki}	Yabneh?
135. *ḫar-zi-na-nu*^{ki}	*ḫar-zi-na-nu*^{ki}	Mount Zenan
136. *la-la-at*^{ki}	*(la-)la-ad*^{ki}	Lod?
137. *sa-ad*-IBILA^{ki}	*sa-ad*-IBILA^{ki}	unidentified
138. *aś-su-ud*^{ki}	*aś-su-ud*^{ki}	Ashdod
139. *su-da-an*^{ki}	*su-da-an*^{ki}	Tell Mor?
140. *pù-gú-tà-an*^{ki}	*gú-bù-tá-an*^{ki}	Gibbethon

ba-qì-a$_5$ (No. 91) can be identified directly with the name of the Beqaᶜ Valley in Lebanon. The final *a*-vowel can be interpreted as standing for *ᶜayin*. This name refers to a geographic feature, a valley, not a specific city or town. The second sign of No. 93 can also be read as *tá* (Labat 1976: 155); connecting Eblaite *mar* with Hebrew *mûr*, "to change," Dahood has suggested that No. 93 can be identified as the "Exchange" or "Market" of Taanach in central Palestine (Dahood 1981: 285, 301). The alternative, extended meaning of "changed,"

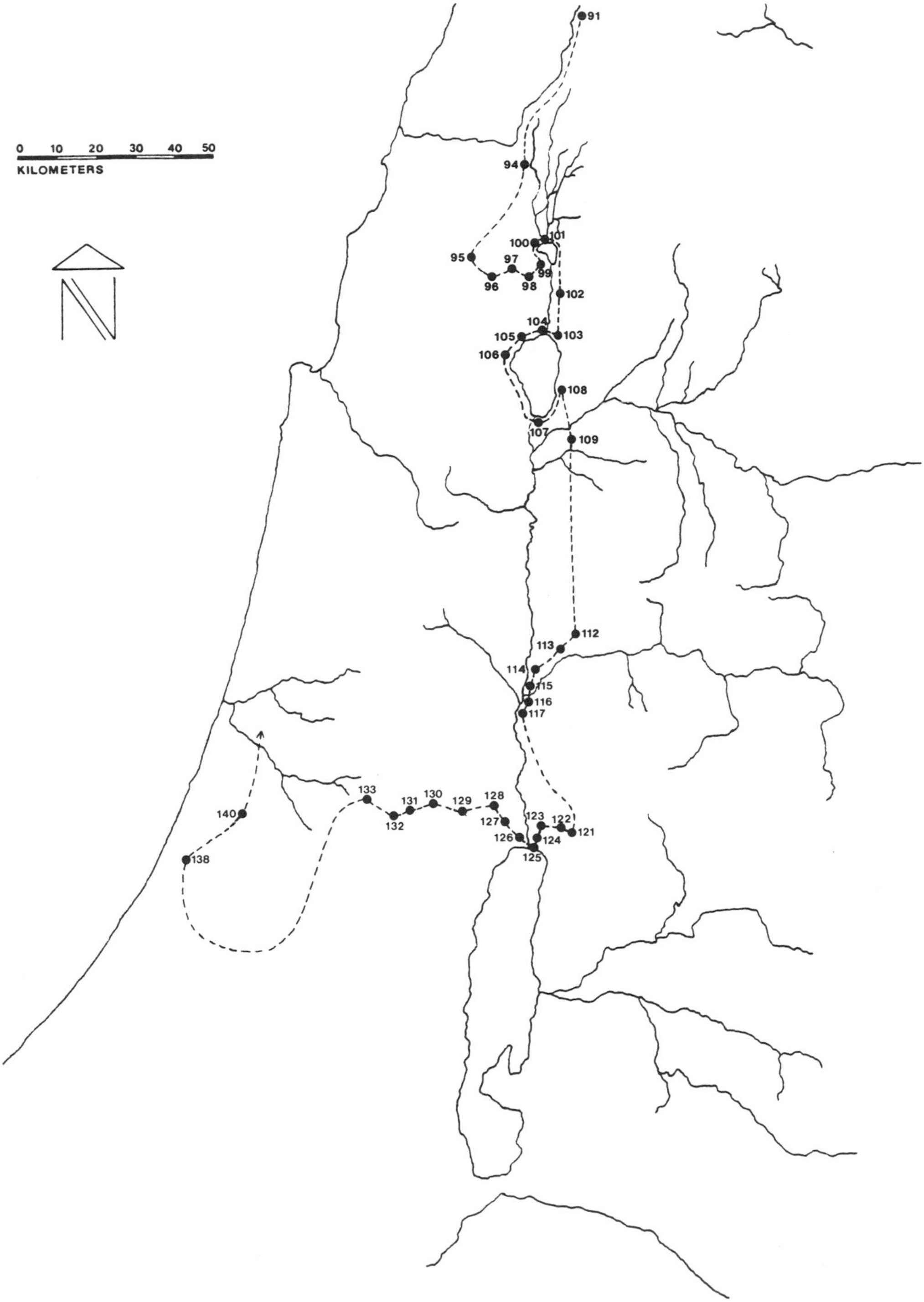
0 10 20 30 40 50
KILOMETERS
91
94
95
96
97
98
99
100
101
102
103
104
105
106
107
108
109
112
113
114
115
116
117
121
122
123
124
125
126
127
128
129
130
131
132
133
138
140

i.e., "new," may be suggested for the name's prefix, which identifies this site as New Taanach. The sense of *mar* as "new" is supported by its use with Transjordanian Aphek below (No. 108). The course of the EGA at this point locates this New Taanach north of "Old" Taanach, in the Jezreel Valley. The site of this northern Taanach has not been located. *áb-la* (No. 94) or Abel was the name of a town in the northern region of Maakah (Josh 13: 11–13), so it was later known as Abel-beth-Maakah (1 Kgs 15: 20; 2 Kgs 15: 29).

úr-an (No. 95) can be equated with biblical *yirᵓôn* (Josh 19: 38), which has been identified with modern *Yārûn*, located ten miles northwest of Hazor. For initial vowels in Eblaite standing for later *y*-, consider the probable initial *y* in place names like *a-a-za-du* (Pettinato 1980a: 357; cf. 1979a: 274) and *i-a-da-ri* (Pettinato 1979a: 277) and personal names like *i-i-bù* (Pettinato 1980a: 342; cf. 1979a: 267) and *i-a-gu-ra* (Pettinato 1979a: 270). As a precaution against placing too much stress upon vocalizations in these comparisons the differences between modern Arabic place names and their MT correspondents should be noted. Differences in vocalization also become evident from a comparison of the EGA with its Ṣalābīkh copies, where differences in vowels written with initial signs may be seen, for example, in names Nos. 14, 20, 83, 189, 196, and 205 (Pettinato 1978: 64, 66, 69).

As a logogram DU in No. 96 stands for a Semitic verb (cf. Hebrew *hālak*) which means "to go" (Labat 1976: 117). No site in Galilee has been identified with a name like this, hence it probably refers to the route travelled south here. With its middle vowel standing for *ᶜayin*, *mu-ku* (No. 97) may be taken as referring to the region of Maᶜakah mentioned above in connection with No. 94. By interpreting its initial *ᵓà*- as standing for *ḥ*- and interchanging dental *d* with *ṣ*, No. 98 can be equated with *ḥaṣôr*, i.e., Hazor. Excavations have revealed EB occupation of Hazor in Strata XXI-XIX of the Upper City (Yadin 1972: 118–20).

With an interchange in labials from *wa* to *ma*, or by reading the *wa*-sign with the ma_9 value (Labat 1976: 177), the last half of name No. 99 can be read as *ma-ak*. Final vowels vary the most when the EGA is compared with Ṣalābīkh copies; sometimes they are not represented (cf. Nos. 13, 33, 61, 66, 172, 186, 215, 238, and 270; Pettinato 1978: 64–65, 69–71). Thus *aksu-ma(ᶜ)ka* may be suggested as a fuller form of this name. Its latter half looks like a further reference to the region. The significance of what appears to be a prefix is not clear. It might tentatively be related to Hebrew *kôs*, "cup," the "cup" of Maᶜakah being interpreted as a reference to the geological depression in which Lake Huleh was located. A cognate word in Arabic is sometimes used for a cistern. This ancient name may have survived in Josephus' name, Lake Semachonitis, for this body of water, which has now been drained.

Ṣalābīkh copies supply the damaged first sign of No. 100 in the EGA, *dag*, which can be equated with the Hebrew word for "fish." *me* may be a short form of the word for "water," *ma-wu* more fully in Eblaite (Pettinato 1979b: 262), cognate with Hebrew *mayim*, *mê* in the construct form. A reversal in sign order may be suggested here to provide a construct chain relationship. "Fish Waters" may be suggested for the meaning of this name; this description fits Lake Huleh. Pettinato's reading of DÚR-DÚR for No. 101 also comes from Ṣalābīkh fragments; these signs are damaged in the EGA. These signs can be read phonetically as either *dúr* or tur_7 (Labat 1976: 221); the repetition of this sign suggests a dual or plural form. Two rivers ran into Lake Huleh from the north, and they are known today as the Tara and the Jordan (Smick 1973: 172). This name suggests a reference to the two Tura or Tara Rivers. Taking the initial *a*- of No. 102 as representing the velar *g* instead of a more commonly expected laryngeal equates this name with Geshur. A similar shift from the laryngeal *h* to the velar *k* has been suggested elsewhere in Eblaite (Pettinato 1979b: 68). Geshur was a territory in northern Transjordan west of Bashan (Deut 3: 14; Josh 12: 5).

Following a route south through Geshur along the eastern edge of the Jordan Valley would bring one first to the northeastern shore of the Sea of Galilee. Toponym No. 103 makes good sense as referring to such a location when its signs are interpreted as logograms. GÚ is the logogram for "shore" (Labat 1976: 87) and A for "water" (Labat 1976: 237), as the bilingual dictionaries of Ebla now attest (Pettinato 1979b: 262; Dahood 1981: 303, 320). The EGA then appears to turn west; travelling in that direction along the shore would bring one to the point at which the Jordan River empties into the Sea of Galilee. The first sign of No. 104 may reasonably be interpreted as the logogram A, "water." The word *sa-am*$_6$ fits well as a participle (with the vocalization as in Hebrew) from the common West Semitic root *śym*, "to put, set, place," or even "to pour" (Judg 6: 19). The pouring of these waters should therefore be the emptying of the Jordan River into the Sea of Galilee.

Several potential cognates may be cited for the final *-aḫ* of No. 105: Aramaic *'aḥw*, "(a kind of) vegetation" (Jean and Hoftijzer 1965: 9), Ugaritic *aḫ*, "meadow" (UT 355), Hebrew *'aḥû*, which refers to the reed-lined shore of the Nile in Gen 41: 2 and 18 and to a marshy plant in Job 8: 11, and Akkadian *aḫu*, "coast, shore" (Labat 1976: 87, 294). The idea of a shore being involved here is supported both by the apparent course of the EGA and by the fact that *aḫu* is the Akkadian equivalent for Sumerian GÚ that appears but two toponyms earlier. The West Semitic idea that this coastline was one of marshes is supported by the use of the logogram AMBAR, which refers to marshes, in toponym No. 107. Those marshes appear to have been located along the southern shore of the Sea of Galilee. That such marshlands were at least potentially useful in agriculture is suggested by relating *ne-er* to Hebrew *nîr* (note the similar *i*-class vowel), which refers to ground that could be broken up for cultivation (Jer 4: 3; Hos 10: 12; Prov 13: 23).

No. 106 begins with the logogram GÚ, "shore," which appeared previously in No. 103. The second element of this name is the same as that found at the beginning of the preceding name and it should mean the same thing here. The best shore of the Sea of Galilee for cultivation is that which lies along its northwestern margin, bordered by the fertile Plain of Gennesaret. No. 107 makes better sense when all of its signs are read as logograms. AMBAR is the logogram for "marshes" (Labat 1976: 219), A for "water," and A_5 for the verb "to do, make" (Labat 1976: 83). Thus this was the place where the "water makes marshes," and that designation fits the situation at the southern end of the Sea of Galilee well. Nos. 103–107 all appear to refer to geographic features along the shore of the Sea of Galilee as one traverses that shoreline from northeast to southwest. They are all apt descriptions of features found along that shoreline in that order; none of them appears to refer to sites of human settlement.

An interchange in labials from *b* to *p* (or reading *bí* as pi_5) equates No. 108 with Hebrew *'ăpēq*. Its designation as *mar-* or "New" Aphek contrasts this Transjordanian Aphek (1 Kgs 20: 26; 2 Kgs 13: 17) with the Aphek in the coastal Plain of Sharon (for *mar-* as "New," cf. No. 93 above). This inland Aphek has been identified with *Fîq*, located three miles northeast of the exit of the Jordan River from the Sea of Galilee; evidence for EB occupation has been found there. Taking the initial *'à-* of No. 109 as standing for the velar *g* (cf. No. 102) equates it with Gadara, one of the cities of the later Decapolis. It has been located at Umm Qeis, ten miles south of Aphek, and it is currently being excavated (Lux 1980: 158–62). The direction of the EGA indicates that Nos. 110 and 111 lay south of Gadara even though they have not been identified yet.

Through an interchange of the labial *m* for *b* with the third sign of No. 112 and by reading its final sign as *-at* instead of *-ad* (Labat 1976: 103), this name can be taken as *ragabat*. With loss of the final feminine *-t* this site can be identified with Ragaba. Alexander Janneus died besieging Ragaba, and its name has survived in that of the Wadi Rajib. Ramat (No. 113) is a common word for "height(s)" and, given the course of the EGA, it probably refers to heights overlooking the Jordan Valley west of Ragaba.

Pettinato read the signs of No. 114 phonetically, as *a-gú-zú*. This interpretation does not offer any readily recognizable site for identification, however; hence it appears preferable to read these signs as the logograms A-GÚ-ZÚ. As has been noted above, the logogram A stands for "water" (Nos. 103, 105, 107). GÚ appeared in two previous names as the logogram for "shore" (Nos. 103, 106). As a logogram the phonetic sign *zú* may be read as KA, "mouth" (Labat 1976: 49^2). Geographically a "mouth" refers to an entrance; the "shore" entered at this point would be the plain on the eastern side of the valley of the "waters" of the Jordan River. This toponym appears to refer to the point at which the Wadi Rajib enters the plain of the Jordan Valley after cutting down from the "heights" (No. 113) at the edge of the plateau overlooking the valley.

Phonetic *zú-lum* (No. 115) has not provided a site for identification in the east central Jordan Valley; hence it seems preferable to interpret its signs as logograms. ZÚ-LUM was read in Akkadian as *suluppu*, "date" (Labat 1976: 49^2), which may refer to the fact that the traveller who followed this route came down into the area where date palms grew when he descended into the Jordan Valley (cf. Deut 34: 3; Judg 1: 16; 3: 13; 2 Chr 28: 15). Reading the initial dental as *d* instead of *z* equates No. 116 with modern Arabic Damiyeh, biblical Adam (Josh 3: 16), which is located near the confluence of the Jabbok and Jordan Rivers. From the biblical connection of this site with events that occurred in the second millennium B.C., this place name can now be traced back into the third millennium B.C., and it still survives as the modern Arabic name for the site.

The partially damaged signs of No. 117 make better sense when they are read as logograms preceded by the West Semitic word for valley. GI/*gi* has been identified by Dahood as the phonetic equivalent of Hebrew *gê*, "valley." A is the logogram for "water," as has already been noted above, and BÀD (= u_9) is the logogram for an enclosing "wall" (Labat 1976: 105, 273). By putting these elements together this name might be translated somewhat freely as "the place (KI) where the valley (*gi*) encloses the waters (A) with a wall (BÀD)." The steep limestone cliffs or narrows through which the Jordan River flows near Damiyeh are known to have dammed the river briefly twice, in 1267 A.D. and 1927 A.D., due to earthquakes. No. 118 may be identified as *galadu*, Gilead, by interchanging the *r* in GARÁ phonetically with the lateral *l* and by reading its second sign with the alternate value of du_{10} (Labat 1976: 181). The Jabbok River divided Gilead in half (Josh 12: 2), and the EGA now appears to turn east from the Jordan Valley and head south through the southern half of that territory.

Sites Nos. 119 and 120 have not been identified yet. The first sign of No. 121 can be read as $ša_{10}$, its second sign as *aṭ*, and its third sign as in_5 (Labat 1976: 87, 103, 229). This yields *šaṭ(ṭ)in*, which is reasonably close to Hebrew *šiṭṭîm*, "acacias," the site of the last encampment of the Israelites before they crossed the Jordan (Num 25: 1; Josh 2: 1). The same results could have been reached through phonetic shifts rather than by reading these signs with different values. If this identification is correct and the interpretation of *-in* as a masculine plural ending is valid, then it offers one linguistic link between Eblaite (or the language of those who lived in this area) and Aramaic, Arabic, and Moabite, in contrast to the *-im* ending of Ugaritic, Phoenician, and Hebrew. This site is called Abel-Shittim once (Num 33: 49), but in five other biblical passages it is identified as Shittim alone. This suggests that the Abel or "meadow" associated with the grove of "acacias" should be distinguished from it in part. The EGA makes such a distinction by listing *ù-bil-a*, Abel, separately as No. 122. Khirbet el-Kefrein five miles east of the Jordan has been suggested as the location of the classical site of Abila mentioned by Josephus (*JW* 4.7.6).

The series of the next five names appears to take us across the Jordan Valley. Pettinato has read all of their signs as logograms, but only No. 125 and the prefixes written with Nos. 124–127 make good sense that way; it seems preferable to read the rest of them phonetically. The first sign of No. 123 is the Semitic word for "valley," as Dahood has pointed out, and its use has already been noted above with No. 117. The last three signs spell the name of that valley out phonetically with the common Semitic word for "dog," hence we have here the equivalent of Hebrew *gê-keleb*, "Valley of the Dog." This appears to be the name by which travellers from Ebla identified the Jordan Valley. This descriptive appellation might have derived from a comparison of the tortuosity of the river's course and the proverbial curvature of the dog's hind leg.

The logogram prefixed to the next four names stands for "wood, tree" (Labat 1976: 137). A plural or collective sense of "woods, thicket, forest" makes better sense of this word in a geographical context than the singular, "tree, wood(en object)," does. For example, the name of Dog, found in No. 127, was also seen in No. 123. The object of wood in No. 127 that corresponds with the Dog Valley of No. 123 should, therefore, be the Dog Forest, not the Dog Tree or the Wooden Dog. In Akkadian the GIŠ sign was read *iṣu* (plural *iṣṣū*), cognate with Hebrew *ʿēṣ*, and the Eblaites probably read this sign with something similar. In Hebrew this word in the singular could stand as a collective for a group of trees (Gen 1: 11; Lev 26: 20; Deut 20: 19), and I would posit the same function for this word in the Eblaite context. Toponym No. 115 appears to provide another example of a singular collective standing for a plural. The form of GIŠ that appears here was also used with the word for forest in Sumerian and Akkadian, GIŠ.TIR/^{iṣ}*qīštu* (Labat 1976: 173; Heidel 1963: 36; AHw 923). The difference here is that the name for the forest follows, rather than the word for forest.

The next name in this series can be read as the Woods of Gath (*gi-ti*) or the Winepress

(No. 124). Ugaritic demonstrates that GIŠ or *iṣu*/*ʿēṣ* could be used for vines that bore grapes by referring to wine as *dm ʿṣ* (Gordon 1965: 460); the cognate *iṣu* carries the same range of meaning in Akkadian. The second name in this Jordan Valley series was written with the logogram Ù, which served as the conjunction "and" (Labat 1976: 203). Conjunction is a grammatical term, however, and here we expect this logogram to serve a geographical function, that of designating a "junction." The eastern and western sides of the Jordan Valley meet at the river in the groove that it has cut a hundred feet below the main valley floor or *Ghor*. A thicket watered by the river has grown up there and it is known as the *Zor* (*gāʾôn* in Hebrew, Jer 12: 5).

By taking its initial vowel as standing for the laryngeal *ḥ*, No. 126 can readily be identified as the Forest of (Beth-)Hoglah. Beth-Hoglah was the first site of importance at the south end of the Jordan Valley that one came to in crossing the valley from the east side to the west side of the river (Josh 15: 5–6). It was located about five miles southeast of Jericho. The ford of the river at that point is still known as the *Hajla* ford. The next place name on the west side of the valley is named for the valley itself, the Dog Forest discussed above (No. 127). The signs of No. 128 appear to make better sense as logograms. RA is the logogram for "inundation" (Labat 1976: 151), and the repetition suggests a plural. The seasonal inundation of the Jordan River was self-evident and not localized, however; for a more localized inundation one might look to the springs at Jericho which are known as the most copious in the southern Jordan Valley.

Reading the first sign of No. 129 as *qú* (Labat 1976: 221) connects this place name with the Hebrew verb *qûm*, "to arise." That is what the landscape does going west from the Jordan Valley up into the central hill country. The verb *ʿālâ* might have been expected here instead of *qûm* since people "go up" into the western mountains from the valley, but the reference here is rather to the terrain over which people travelled; hence the "rise" of that terrain appears just as appropriate. There is a site in this area which may preserve a reference to this ancient feature. With an interchange in labials from *m* to *b* it can be related to *Khirbet el-Qubbe* which is located about 10 miles west of Jericho and a mile or two east of Michmash. Vocalizations should not be stressed, but it is interesting to note that in the Ṣalābīkh copy of this list this name was written *ku-me*.

The first sign of No. 130 identifies it as referring to a valley (cf. Nos. 117, 123). By comparison with No. 101, the reduplication of its second sign suggests some kind of special duality about this valley. The *maš* sign can also be read as *mas* (Labat 1976: 71), which suggests a relationship with the Hebrew noun *maśśāʾ*. The verb *nāśāʾ*, from which this noun is derived, is written as *nšʾ* in Ugaritic (Gordon 1965: 447), so reading this sign as either *maš* or *mas* is acceptable. This verb conveys the related ideas of (1) "to lift up," and (2) "to bear, carry." The noun derived from the first meaning refers to a "lifting up" (of hands, smoke, clouds, etc.), while the noun derived from the second refers to that which is borne or carried, a "burden." The former makes better sense in this geographical context, as a "lifting up" of two steep walls of the valley. This fits well with the configuration of the Wâdī eṣ-Ṣuweinît in the vicinity of Michmash and Geba (cf. 1 Samuel 14). This is the valley which the EGA appears to traverse according to its westerly direction and toponymic relations here. The resemblance of this Eblaite name to the later name of Michmash in the same area may be coincidental, or it may provide a partial explanation for that hitherto poorly understood place name.

The first part of toponym 131, *ʾà-ru*, can be equated readily with Hebrew *har*, "mountain," by interpreting the initial *ʾà* as standing for *he*. That yields the "mountain of *ak-dar*," with the latter element providing a description of the mountain. Given the potential interchanges involved here, Semitic words within the consonantal range of *g*/*k*/*q*—*d*/*z*/*t*/*ṭ*/*ṣ*—*r* deserve consideration. The selection is difficult and the possibilities are presented without conviction: *gdr*, "a wall of stones," *gzr*, "to cut," *ktr*, "to wear high on the head" (›"a capital, an eminence"). Between the preceding and succeeding toponyms the route of the EGA appears to cross the divide or watershed of the mountains of western Palestine, and this selection of potential modifiers fits that idea about this mountain reasonably well. Since Ramah (= "height") lies on the line of this segment of the route, the eminence upon which this town was later located might have been the one referred to here.

The second sign of No. 132 can be read as *bí* (Labat 1976: 111), which, with *-a-*

standing for *ʿayin*, equates it perfectly with Gibeon. The route of the EGA then extends down the western slope from the central ridge where portions of this EB town have been excavated at El-Jib (Pritchard 1962: 148). The *ù* of No. 133 is taken here, as with No. 125, as the logogram Ù for "Junction" (Labat 1976: 203). By reversing the laryngeal-velar interchange of Nos. 102 and 109 an original *ḫ* may be proposed for the initial consonant of this name. This suggests (Beth-)Horon Junction for the identity of this place. The natural route from Gibeon down to the coast, where the EGA now heads, runs through the junction or pass between Upper and Lower Beth-Horon, where it drops 700 feet in two miles.

The initial *tar-* of No. 134 looks like the prefix which appears to have been commonly used in the EGA for coastal sites (cf. Nos. 141–144, 160–161, 173 and later Tarshish and Tartessus). With an interchange in labials *ma-nu* might be interpreted as standing for *ba-nu* and taken as a variant form for the coastal Yabneh, later known as Yamnia. For the possible failure of the scribe to represent the initial *yōd* of *ya-ba-nu*/*ya-ma-nu*, compare the deletion of the laryngeal from the name of *ša-ḫa-ma-nu*, which was written as *śa-ma-nu* in the Ṣalābīkh copy (Pettinato 1978: 65). Written with the prefix *ḫar-* for "mountain" (cf. No. 131), No. 135 might be identified with Zenan (Hebrew *ṣĕnān*, Josh 15: 37), located in the southwestern sector of this later Judahite region. No. 136 might be Lod, but if it is I have no explanation for the reduplicated *la* other than oral or scribal error during transmission. No. 137 is not presently identifiable.

In the region through which the EGA appears to be passing at this point *ás-su-ud* (No. 138) looks most like Ashdod. The shift in sibilants from *s* to *š* presents no problems to this identification, but the absence of an expected second *dālet* does. For parallels in scribal practice to such a deletion see *a-dì-dum* (No. 25), written as *a-dì* in the Ṣalābīkh copy, and *ša-da-ba-ad* (No. 64), written as *ša-bàd* in the Ṣalābīkh copy (Pettinato 1978: 64–65; cf. also No. 66). Pettinato has held that the name of Ashdod appears in Eblaite texts which have not been published yet (Pettinato 1981: 226). No evidence for an EB occupation was found during the excavations of Ashdod, but further soundings there are said to be under consideration if references to it from Ebla can be verified. Freedman and Cross have discussed the name of Ashdod, holding that the biblical form is derived from the Canaanite form *ʾatdādu* (Cross and Freedman 1964: 48). Since the writing system in which the EGA was written does not make a distinction between the phonemes involved in this development, the evidence of EGA on this point is neutral even if it does refer to the same place.

No. 139 might be a form of the previous name that was shortened to make room in the previously incised lineations of this column of the text for the addition of a dual ending. For a similar type of development see Nos. 209–210 below. This could refer to Ashdod's port of Ashdod-Yam, located at Tell Mor. Since sign order was still somewhat fluid in this period, the first two signs of No. 140 can be reversed to make better sense of this name. *pù* can also be read as *bù* (Labat 1976: 53), and this combination yields the name of *gú-bù-ta-an*, Gibbethon, located in the central coastal region north of Ashdod (1 Kgs 15: 27; 16: 15).

Although it is difficult to identify many of the place names involved with certainty, it is plain that the EGA continues north up the coast into Phoenicia. This is evident from several aspects of the succeeding segment of the route. (1) The presence of coastal type place names, with the prefix *tar-* (Nos. 141–144, 160–161, 173). (2) Two references to the AMBAR or "marshlands" that fit well with the undrained coastal Plain of Sharon (Nos. 152, 159; cf. AMBAR in No. 107). (3) The fact that these two references to that marshland flank the name of *a-bí-ak* or the coastal Aphek (No. 154), which contrasts with the inland Aphek, *mar-a-bí-ak*, southeast of the Sea of Galilee (No. 108). (4) The presence farther along in the EGA of the name *áb-ru-ut* (No. 172), which fits reasonably well with Beirut.

From the Phoenician coast the EGA turns inland and later southwards again so that it comes down the eastern side of the Anti-Lebanon mountain range to its southern end. The segment of the EGA that starts at this point presents a new itinerary for Palestine and the names from this segment are examined below. In this segment the EGA travels first through southern Syria and northern Transjordan until it joins the previous route in Geshur and follows it around the western shore of the Sea of Galilee. From there it travels a short distance down the Jordan Valley but, instead of turning east into Transjordan, it journeys west through the Jezreel Valley. It crosses the Carmel range in the vicinity of Ibleam and then turns southeast to join the central ridge route that runs the length of the hill country of western Palestine. At the southern end of the hill country it turns east to circle around the southern end of the Dead Sea. From there it goes east into the territory of later Moab and then it continues south through Transjordan to join the Wadi Arabah, through which it finally reaches the gulf at Aqabah. The study of this segment of the EGA leaves off there.

II. Eblaite Geographical Atlas, Sites Nos. 188–219 (Map 2)

Pettinato's Transliteration	Revised Reading	Proposed Identification
188. *am-ni*^{ki}	*am-ni*^{ki}	Mount Amana
189. *bù-bù*^{ki}	*bù-bù*^{ki}	Upe (near Damascus)
190. *i-na-ḫu*^{ki}	*i-na-hu*^{ki}	Janoah
191. *i-sa-ru*^{ki}	*i-sa-rŭ*^{ki}	Geshur
192. *gú-ne-er*^{ki}	GÚ-*ne-er*^{ki}	Plain of Gennesaret Shore
193. *gú-ti-ir*^{ki}	GÚ-*ti-ir*^{ki}	Southwestern Galilee Shore
194. *sa*-NE^{ki}	*sa-ne*^{ki}	(Beth-)Shan
195. *sa-mu*^{ki}	*sa-mu*^{ki}	unidentified
196. *su-ù*^{ki}	*su-ù*^{ki}	unidentified
197. *ʾà-ra-wa-ad*^{ki}	*ʾà-ra-wa-ad*^{ki}	Harod Springs
198. *ru-bù-ù-dar*^{ki}	*ru-bù*-Ù-*dar*^{ki}	Junction with the Jezreel Valley
199. LÚ-*a-wa-ra-um*^{ki}	LÚ-*a-bì-ra-um*^{ki}	Ibleam
200. *sa-bí-ti*^{ki}	*sa-bí-ti*^{ki}	unidentified
201. *a*-BÀD^{ki}	*a-dur*$_8$^{ki}	unidentified
202. UD^{ki}	BABBAR^{ki}	Lebonah
203. BÀD^{ki}	*dur*$_8$^{ki}	(Baal-)Hazor?
204. *nìm-ma*^{ki}	*nìm-ma*^{ki}	Nob?
205. *ší-ma*^{ki}	*ší-ma*^{ki}	unidentified
206. *ì-la-lu*^{ki}	*ì-la-lu*^{ki}	Halhul
207. *a-ni*^{ki}	*a-ni*^{ki}	En-Gedi
208. ḪUL-GAL-GA-AL^{ki}	*ḫul-gal-ga-al*^{ki}	SW Dead Sea Shore Circuit
209. *da-me-gú*^{ki}	*da-me*-GÚ^{ki}	Dead Sea Shore at Admah
210. *ad-mu-ud*^{ki}	*ad-mu-ut*^{ki}	(Town of) Admah
211. *sa-dam*^{ki}	*sa-dam*^{ki}	Sodom
212. *ar-me*^{ki}	*ar-me*^{ki}	Arnon River
213. *la-ti-a*^{ki}	*la-ti-a*^{ki}	Kiriathaim
214. *ì-ti-ru*^{ki}	*ì-ṭi-ru*^{ki}	ʿAṭaroth
215. *ʾà-wu-ru*^{ki}	*ʾà-wu-ru*^{ki}	Aroer
216. *qá-rí-at*^{ki}	*qá-rí-at*^{ki}	Kiriath/Kerak
217. *sa-rí-at*^{ki}	*sa-rí-at*^{ki}	Seir
218. *ù-ba-*[*i?*]^{ki}	*ù-pá-*[*i?*]^{ki}	Punon Junction?
219. *ak-kà-bù*^{ki}	*aq-qá-bù*^{ki}	Aqabah

Amana is a name for the Anti-Lebanon range of mountains used in Assyrian inscriptions and mentioned in Song of Songs 4: 8. The reduplicated *bù* sign of No. 189 can probably be related to Hobah in this area at Abraham's time (Gen 14: 15) and, with an interchange in labials, to ʾIpwm of the Egyptian execration texts, to Apum of the Mari texts, and to Upe of the Amarna letters. The biblical and Amarna references locate the place in the vicinity of

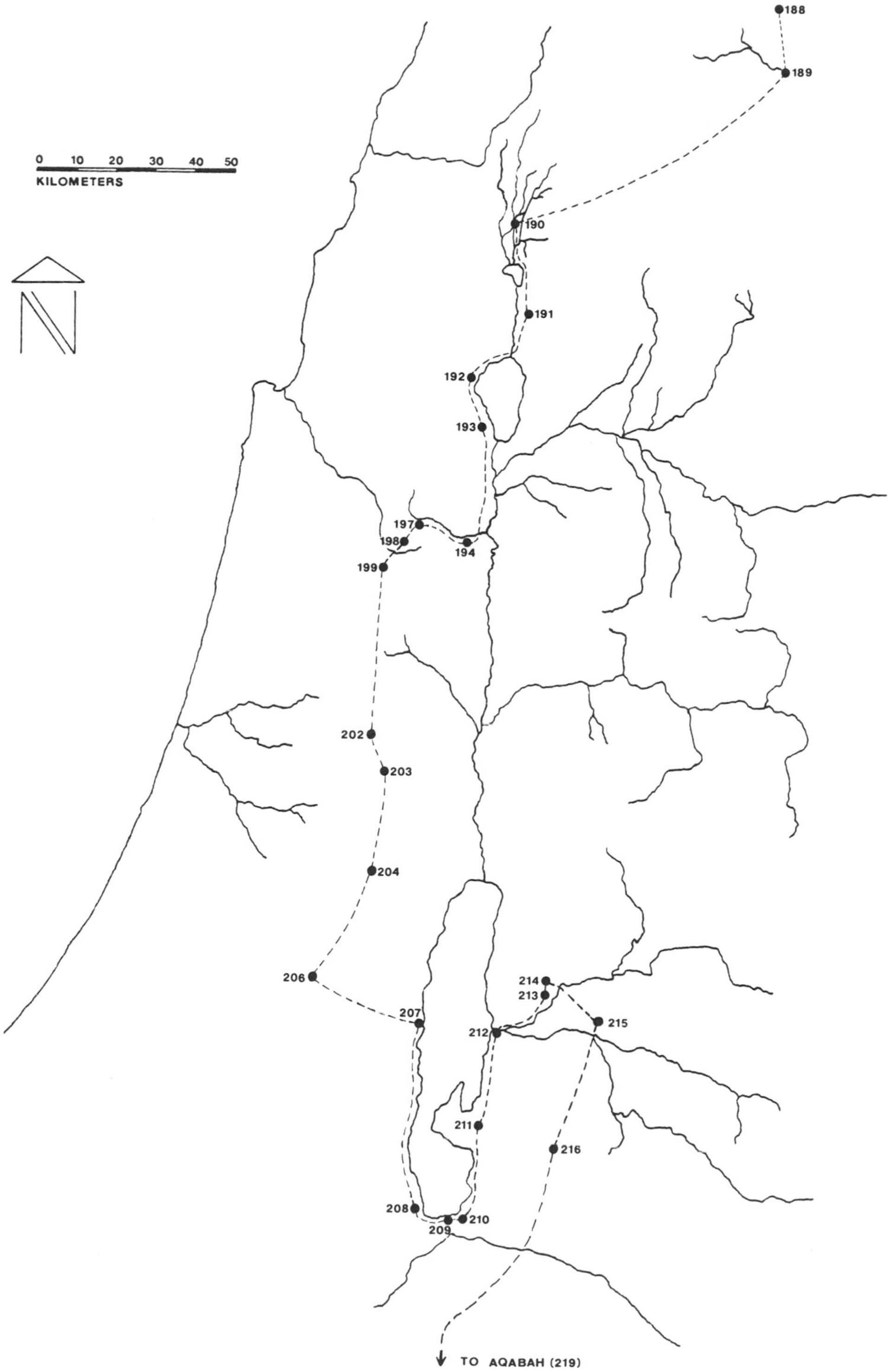

0 10 20 30 40 50
KILOMETERS
188
189
190
191
192
193
197
198
194
199
202
203
204
206
207
214
213
215
212
211
216
208
210
209
TO AQABAH (219)

Damascus. No. 190 corresponds directly to the name of the northern Israelite site of Janoah, which Tiglath-pileser III conquered along with Abel-Beth-Maakah (No. 94) according to 2 Kgs 15: 29. Its location here in this Eblaite list lends support to the identification of it with Maccabean-Herodian Ina, on the eastern slopes of Mt. Hermon.

South of Janoah (No. 190) and north of the Sea of Galilee (No. 192) one passes through the territory of Geshur, as pointed out in connection with No. 102. The similarity between the names for the territory crossed in these two instances suggests that both Nos. 191 and 102 refer to Geshur. An initial *g*- can be understood as accompanying both of their initial vowels; *sa* can be read *ša*$_{10}$ (Labat 1976: 87). No. 192 is exactly the same as No. 106, showing that the two routes converged at the northern end of the Sea of Galilee. The first sign of No. 193 is the logogram for "shore" again (Labat 1976: 87); the phonetic element *tir*/*tar* occurs commonly in connection with coastal sites in the EGA, as discussed above sub No. 134. These relations, along with the route of the EGA at this point, suggest that this toponym should be connected with the southwestern shore of the Sea of Galilee.

The Beth- or "house of" prefix known from the later place names appears to have been omitted from EGA toponyms almost routinely (cf. Nos. 94, 126, 133). That being the case, No. 194 can be equated with (Beth-)Shan quite readily. EB materials at Beth-Shan were recovered mainly from a deep sounding on the tell (Strata XI-XIII) and from the tombs (Thompson 1967: 112–14). The next two place names have not been identified. Linguistically No. 197 can be equated readily with Harod (Judg 7: 1), the name for a spring identified with ʿAin Jālûd on the northwestern slope of Mt. Gilboa.

A little more than a mile to the northwest of the Harod springs lies the site of Jezreel, for which the plain lying to the west of it was named. Through an interchange in dentals the final *-dar* of No. 198 can be interpreted as representing *zar*, the principal element in the verb "to sow," *zār(aʿ)*. This is the verb from which the place name of Jezreel ("God sows") was formed. Final vowels are the vowels most often found to be missing when the EGA is compared with its Ṣalābīkh copies, and the vocalic representation of the final *ʿayin* of this root may have been dropped due to the length of this compound geographical phrase. The *ù* may be read as the logogram Ù, which we have met before in the EGA, standing for "Junction" (cf. Nos. 125, 133). The initial *ru-bù* looks like Hebrew *rôb*, "great, abundance." These interpretations yield the combination of "Junction of abundance of the sown," a fitting description for the fertile Plain of Jezreel.

The initial *a*- of No. 199 can be taken as standing for *(y)a*, its *wa*-sign can be read as *bì* (Labat 1976: 177), through an interchange in laterals its *ra*-sign may be interpreted as representing *la*, and an *ʿayin* can be read with one of its final vowels. This yields *yabilaʿum*, which can be equated with Hebrew *yibleʿam*, i.e., Ibleam, the site which guarded the easternmost pass leading south from the Jezreel Valley. How should the logographic prefix LÚ be connected with this place name? This commonly stands for "man"; it has already been catalogued as used in the Eblaite texts with 15 place names, 35 different names for professions, and 165 personal names (Pettinato 1979a: 273–274; 1980a: 355). Its use here does not fit the first or third of these categories so it should probably be connected with the second. Establishing such a connection depends upon how one understands the meaning of the name of Ibleam. It is generally taken as referring to "the canal of the people," made up of *yābāl*, "canal" (Isa 30: 25; 44: 4), and *ʿam*, "people." If this etymology is correct, then the logogram could refer to the "man of the people's canal," possibly meaning the man or class of men who tended to the agricultural irrigation in the southeastern sector of the Plain of Jezreel. Ibleam was one of the Canaanite cities the Israelites did not conquer (Judg 1: 27), and it has been identified with Tell Belʿameh. EB II pottery was found there during a recent archeological survey (Glock 1979).

The next six toponyms are difficult to analyze and identify, but the apparent direction of the EGA through this segment suggests they were probably located somewhere along the spine of the hill country of western Palestine. No. 200, *sa-bí-ti*, could be taken as *šebet*, from *yāšab*, applied to an unspecified "dwelling" or "settlement." Derived from *šābat*, "to stop, cease," the name could be taken as referring to the end of one road and the commencement of another, possibly the central ridge route south from Shechem. The *bí*-sign could also be read as *kúm* (Labat 1976: 111) and *sa-kúm-ti* taken as referring to the geographical features of the "shoulders" of Mt. Ebal and Mt. Gerizim, though not the city of Shechem, which was not founded until MB IIA. Since No. 201, *a*-BÀD, does not make good sense when interpreted logographically ("wall of water"), its second sign can be taken as dur_8 (Labat 1976: 105); this name may be compared with No. 98 above, Hazor. No Hazor is known in the region north of the next site, however, and Addara at Khirbet ed-Deir seems too far southwest (Avi-Yonah 1966: 156). For the present, Khirbet et-Tira, a few miles south of Shechem, deserves consideration.

Since No. 202 is written with only the UD-sign, that sign should most likely be interpreted as a logogram. The four main meanings this sign conveyed as a logogram were U_4, "then," UD, "day" (*ym* in the west), UTU, "sun" (or the Eblaite sun god Sipish, Hebrew Shemesh, when used with a determinative for a god), and BABBAR, "white" (Labat 1976: 175). The first two meanings do not provide any geographically useful information and may be discarded. As a reference to the sun or sun god, Shemesh might be useful as a reference to either (Beth-)Shemesh or (En) Shemesh. The former site seems too far southwest, however, and the latter too far southeast. That leaves us with the value of BABBAR, a commonly used value at Ebla since it occurs with KÙ as part of the word for "silver" (Pettinato 1980a: 3 & passim). *lbn* is the root for "white" in the West Semitic languages (Tomback 1978: 155), and this calls to mind the name of the site of Lebonah, located on the central ridge route about 10 miles south of Shechem. The name of Lebonah means "frankincense," but that name in turn derives from the fact that the resin is white in color, so the net result of identifying this name geographically is the same. The ancient biblical name of Lebonah (Judg 21: 19) survives in the Arabic name el-Lubban.

With toponym No. 203, BÀD, we are faced with the same set of problems as in the case of No. 201, except that we are better off in terms of geographical candidates and less well off linguistically. While there is no Hazor north of Lebonah, there is Baal-Hazor (2 Sam 13: 23), located 10 miles south of it at Jebel ʿAṣur. This Eblaite toponym could correspond relatively well to that site on a geographical basis, but the linguistic case would have been stronger had an initial *a*- standing for the laryngeal *ḥ*- been written with this name, as it is in No. 201. If this toponym does not refer to that specific site, it may refer to an otherwise unspecified "walled, enclosed, or fortified" site in the area. With an interchange in labials between *m* and *b*, No. 204 might be taken as a reference to Nob (1 Sam 22: 19). No. 205 was written in the Ṣalābīkh copies as *šu-mú*, which supports the reading of *ší-ma* in the EGA (Pettinato 1978: 69), but no site or geographical feature's name resembling this has been located yet in the central hill country. Two *ḥeth*s may be taken as represented by the first two vowels of No. 206, which yields Hebrew *ḥalḥûl*, the name of a site in the hill country of Judah (Josh 15: 58). This ancient name has survived in the Arabic name for the village of *Ḥalḥul*, located three miles north of Hebron.

From this southernmost point in the central hill country, the route of the atlas now appears to turn east. Descending through the wilderness of Judah, perhaps by the Ascent of Ziz (2 Chr 20: 2–26), this route came to *a-ni*, which can be equated with the word *ʿayin*, "spring," by taking its initial vowel as standing for the laryngeal of the name. En Gedi (Josh 15: 62), "the spring of the kid," is the most impressive spring along the western shore of the Dead Sea, and in view of the subsequent course of this route it seems likely to be the spring referred to here.

Pettinato read the signs of No. 208 logographically, but they make better sense interpreted phonetically. Interpreted in this way they yield the name of *ḫul-galgal*. *ḫul* can be equated with the Hebrew verb *ḥûl*, "to turn, go around." *galgal* can be equated with the Hebrew noun *galgal*, which refers to the circular orbit of a "wheel." It is taken here in the geographical sense as referring to a circular course of travel, i.e., a circuit. Combining these two elements in order yields a compound reference to "going around the circuit." In view of the subsequent course of the route, and in contrast with the route that crossed the Jordan Valley at the northern end of the Dead Sea (Nos. 123–27), the circuit referred to here fits well with that which was travelled along the western and southern shores of the Dead Sea.

The last sign of No. 209 should be taken as the logogram for "shore," as in four previous instances (Nos. 103, 106, 192, and 193). *da-me* is the equivalent, with an interchange in dentals, of *za-me* (No. 116), identified with Arabic Damiyeh, biblical Adam, in the mid-

Jordan Valley. This name's link with that earlier one and the succeeding one here indicates that its fuller form began with an *ʾaleph* and ended with a final vowel. That equates it with biblical Admah (Gen 14: 2), just as the previous *za/da-me* was linked with biblical Adam (Josh 3: 16). The location at the south end of the Dead Sea fits the middle city of the five Cities of the Plain well geographically. Its mention here in connection with the southern shore of the Dead Sea probably means that the waters of the sea extended that far south in the Ghor in the mid-third millennium B.C.

No. 210 provides the fuller form of *ad-mu-ut* for the name of this central city of the plain. The final sign may be read as *-ut* instead of Pettinato's *-ud* (Labat 1976: 175) and the final *-t* may be interpreted as a feminine ending. Evidence for the use of *-ut* as a feminine ending has shown up in the first volume of Eblaite texts published. Tiamat is the goddess who is especially well known for having had her body divided up in the Babylonian creation story, the *Enuma eliš*. In text No. 37 of this collection her name appears written ᵈ*ti-mu-ut* (Pettinato 1980a: 255). The final *-ut* ending of her name is compatible with her gender. Final *-at* on feminine nouns in Hebrew was later reduced to *-â* (written *-ah*) in the absolute state; the final *-t* only reappeared when they were used in the construct state. Thus an earlier Eblaite *ad-mu-ut/ʾadmat* fits quite satisfactorily with later Hebrew *ʾadmâ*.

Nos. 212–214 indicate that this route turned north along the eastern shore of the Dead Sea which, as in biblical geography, took it next to Sodom, No. 211. The signs of this name are quite clear in the photograph of the text and the reading is indisputable (cf. Labat 1976: 87, 231). The vowels are of interest in this particular case since the shift from earlier Canaanite *a*-vowels to later Hebrew *o*-vowels is well known. Evidence for this shift comes from Canaanite glosses in the Amarna letters, from the vocalization of Phoenician words in other scripts, and from a comparison of Hebrew words with Akkadian (Harris 1939: 43–45; Moscati 1964: 48–49). In the Massoretic text of the Hebrew Bible this place name was vocalized *sĕdom*, but in the Dead Sea Scrolls it was written *swdm* and *swdwm* (= Sodom) and in the Septuagint *sodoma*, so the form with the two *o*-vowels probably represents a more original vocalization. This earlier Eblaite *sa-dam* can be equated quite directly with later Hebrew Sodom both linguistically and geographically.

The *me* of No. 212 may be taken as the short form of the word for "water," as it was with No. 100, and *ar* as the name for the town of Ar, located on the Arnon River (Num 21: 13–15; Deut 2: 18). Taken together these two elements appear to comprise a designation for that watercourse. Thus this route continued north from Sodom as far as the mouth of the Arnon River before it turned east into the Transjordanian plateau. Five signs would have been required to write out the full name proposed here for No. 213, but the scribe appears to have limited his writing of it to only three, possibly for reasons of space. Reconstructing the first and last signs of this name as the best candidates for such a deletion, and combining these with an interchange from *l* to *r* in the first written sign yields [*Qi-*]*-ra-ti-a*[*-im*] or Hebrew *qiryātāyim*, "two towns, twin cities." Kiriathaim is mentioned as early as the time of Abraham (Gen 14: 5); it was taken over by the Reubenites when they settled in Transjordan (Josh 13: 15, 19), and it was taken from them by the Moabites (Jer 48: 1; Ezek 25: 9; Mesha's Stela, KAI 181: 10). Glueck identified Kiriathaim with *el-Qereiyat*, north of Dibon, but he did not find any sherds there older than the Roman period (Glueck 1939: 131). I would prefer to locate Kiriathaim at either *Khirbet abu-Khirqeh* or *Khirbet Iskander* on the Wadi Wala since either of them could qualify as "twin cities" and evidence for EB occupation has been found at both.

Taking the initial vowel of No. 214 as standing for an *ʿayin*, reading its second sign as *ṭi* (Labat 1976: 69), and restoring a final *-t* which appears to have been dropped, we can identify this place name with Hebrew *ʿăṭārôt*, which was taken over by the Gadites when they settled in Transjordan (Num 32: 3, 34). Glueck identified Ataroth with *Khirbet ʿAṭṭārûs*, six miles northwest of Dibon, where he found some EB sherds there (Glueck 1939: 135). Reading *ʿayin*s with the vowels of the first two signs of No. 215 and reconstructing a sign that may have been omitted between them yields *ʿa*[*ru*]*wuʿru*, which can be identified with Hebrew *ʿărôʿēr*. This town was located on the southern border of Sihon's territory (Deut 2: 26; Josh 12: 2; Judg 11: 26, 33), hence it has been identified geographically and linguistically with *ʿarâʿir* on the northern plateau overlooking the canyon of the Arnon River. This site has been excavated, revealing an EB IV/MB I occupation (Olavarri 1969: 230–59). Locating No. 215 here indicates that the route of the atlas turned south down the King's Highway from No. 214.

No. 216 can be identified readily with the Hebrew word *qiryat*, "town." Travelling south down the King's Highway from the Arnon the Kiriath or town of importance that one most likely would have to come to would have been the site known in the Bible under three different names compounded with Kir- (Hebrew *qîr*, "wall"), which served as the capital of the Moabites and is identified today with Kerak (2 Kgs 3: 25–27; Isa 16: 7; Jer 48: 31). By reading an *ʿayin* for the first vowel and dropping the final feminine *-t*, No. 217 can be compared with the later name Seir (Hebrew *śeʿîr*). This name occurs 35 times in the Bible and refers both to Mount Seir and to the territory, occupied by the Edomites, in which Mount Seir was located. Taking this reference more generally here suggests that the route of the atlas probably crossed the northwestern corner of that territory on the way to the Wadi Arabah.

The first sign of No. 218 may be taken as the logogram for "junction," as it has been several times previously. Considering the identity and location of the succeeding place name, this junction was probably located at the point at which the route of the atlas entered the Wadi Arabah. The final sign of No. 218 is damaged, so its identity is uncertain. The second sign could be read as *pá* (Labat 1976: 43), however, which might suggest a connection with biblical Punon, identified with *Feinân* on the eastern edge of the Wadi Arabah, 25 miles south of the Dead Sea. Punon was a campsite of the Israelites as they travelled northeast (Num 33: 42–43); Glueck dated the earliest occupation at *Feinân* to the end of EB (Glueck 1935: 33).

The initial vowel of No. 219 may be taken as standing for *ʿayin*, its first sign can be read as *aq* (Labat 1976: 83), its second sign can be read as *qá* (Labat 1976: 145), or an interchange in velar from *k* to *q* can be invoked, to equate this name with modern ʿAqabah. Whether this place name refers to a town of Aqabah or to the Gulf itself is uncertain. In either case the previously unsuspected survival of this place name for more than four millennia is striking. The route of the atlas appears to turn west from this point but the names become more difficult to identify, so the study of the individual place names from this segment of the Eblaite Geographical Atlas may be concluded at this geographically logical terminus.

Conclusions

Eighty of the 290 place names in the Eblaite Geographical Atlas have been studied above, 50 from one segment of the list and 30 from another. Identifications for these place names have been suggested through a variety of different means. Some place names spelled out syllabically appear to be virtually direct equivalents of the names to which they correspond in later sources; these are the easiest to identify. In other instances different values have been suggested for the signs that make up some of the names in order to make better sense out of them. These suggestions come in a variety of forms. In some cases signs which Pettinato read as logograms have been read with syllabic values as components in Semitic names, while in other instances signs which Pettinato read with syllabic values have been read as logograms.

For the signs read as components of Semitic names, syllabic values differing from Pettinato's have been suggested in instances in which they appear to clarify the place names involved. Less major differences between the original place names and the way in which they were recorded in this text have been resolved in some instances with reference to interchanges in phonetic values that are known from other areas of comparative Semitic linguistics. Since sign order was still somewhat fluid in this early period, a few names have been explained by reversing the order of some of the signs. In a few instances it has been necessary to posit a scribal error in order to provide a more satisfactory identification. The presence of scribal variations in the writing of names in the EGA is supported by the evidence of the Ṣalābīkh copies. Finally, there are the names which consist solely of logograms; these are among the more difficult to identify.

Examining the names listed in these segments of the EGA has provided a series of identifications that can be analyzed statistically. The first major division separates them into (1) the category of toponyms which refers to human settlements—cities, towns, and villages—and (2) the category which refers to geographical features of the countryside through which the route of the EGA passed. In the first segment of the EGA analyzed above, the latter type of identification predominates, 25 to 18, with 6 names unidentified and unclassified. In the second segment, the former type of identification predominates, 18 to 8, with 6 names unidentified and unclassified. These figures indicate that about half (36) of the identifications proposed involve names for sites while the other half (33) refer to geographical features. No identifications have been proposed for a dozen out of the total of 80 names listed from these two segments of the EGA.

The relatively high proportion of names proposed for geographical features suggests an important aspect of this list. Not just a list of sites of human settlement, it also takes into account the geography in which those sites were set. The breadth of this type of reference can be seen from the variety of geographical features represented: 6 forests, 6 valleys, 5 lake shores, 3 mountains, 3 rivers, 3 springs, 2 roads, 2 marshes, 1 pass, 1 lake, and 1 plain. Some of these are better identified than others. Thirteen of these 33 identifications may be classified as good, 15 as fair, and 5 as poor. Among the good identifications of geographical features one might mention the Beqaᶜ Valley (No. 91), the marshland at the southern end of the Sea of Galilee (No. 107), *ramat*, "heights" (No. 113), the five toponyms that cross the Jordan Valley (Nos. 123–127), especially the forest of Beth-Hoglah (No. 126), and the Harod Springs (No. 197). Along with this list should be noted the geographical markers of *har*, "mountain," *gi*, "valley," GÚ, "shore," and Ù, "junction."

This high proportion of geographical features referred to among these place names indicates that the EGA is rather complete as an atlas or gazetteer. The settled sites it mentions are located within a framework of geographical surroundings. These geographical features and the sites with which they were connected both appear to have been listed in the order in which a traveller would have passed them. Thus the two segments studied from the EGA can be seen as marking out distinct and well described routes, indeed, as a kind of road map.

In view of the contents of the EGA, a suggestion may be made about its possible origin and function. It is possible to think of segments of it as having been compiled by merchants or other travellers from Ebla upon their return home; a composite—the total EGA—would have been compiled later from these individual records. In his recent summary of commerce at Ebla, Pettinato has discussed the agricultural products raised and their distribution, industries and metal technology, and Ebla's income in precious metals, semi-precious metals, and precious stones (Pettinato 1981: 156–227). Widespread trade relations were involved in this commerce. The geographical relations identified in the EGA could well have been related to Ebla's commercial relations, both as having derived from them and as providing identifiable routes for their future conduct.

The strengths and weaknesses of the identifications for specific settled sites can be evaluated in the same way in which the identifications for geographical features were treated. Nine out of 18 of the identifications proposed for site names in the first segment of the EGA studied above may be classified as good, 4 as fair, and 5 as poor. The statistics for the 18 site names from the second segment studied are about the same: 9 good, 5 fair, 4 poor. Overall this means that 18 out of 36, or one-half of the site identifications suggested, have been classified as good, 9 (one-fourth) have been classified as fair, and the other 9 (one-fourth) have been classified as poor. Among the sites whose names have been seen as good mention might be made of Maakah (No. 197), Aphek (108), Ragaba (112), Damiyeh (116), Abila (122), Gibeon (132), Gibbethon (140), Janoah (190), Halhul (206), Admah (210), Sodom (211), Seir (217), and Aqabah (219).

That even one-half of the Palestinian place names listed in the EGA can be taken as references to human settlements in this early period suggests that the Early Bronze Age was a favorable time for the peoples of this region to develop centers of occupation like those listed in this atlas. Other EB sites known in this region are not listed in the EGA and it is quite probable that the atlas does not even include the names of all the sites located along the routes it describes. Since this is only a partial list, the developments that took place under such relatively favorable conditions obviously went beyond what is indicated in this solitary literary source. A recent commentator on the settlement pattern of Palestine in the Bronze Age has noted, "The number of settlements during the EB period is particularly large" (Thompson 1979: 64). Thus a steadily accumulating body of evidence is filling out the picture of the Early Bronze Age in Palestine, and the EGA makes one of the more dramatic contributions to that picture.

Among the Palestinian sites for which identifications in the EGA have been proposed above, two may be noted for their presence in the biblical narratives of Genesis 14–19, Admah and Sodom (Nos. 210–211). The presence or absence of the names of the biblical Cities of the Plain has become a matter of considerable dispute between the two men who have served as epigraphers for the Italian Archeological Mission to Syria. The discussion of this subject began when Pettinato announced to a meeting of the Society of Biblical Literature in St. Louis on 29 October 1976 that he had identified the names of Sodom, Gomorrah, and Zoar/Bela in the Ebla tablets. The following year he published a comment to that effect in a survey article on the contents of the Eblaite archive (Pettinato 1977: 236).

A. Archi has criticized these contentions by noting that the textual evidence for these identifications has not been forthcoming and that the check of an unpublished text (TM 75.G.1992) did not provide any geographical evidence for identifying its *sa-du-ma*^{ki} with biblical Sodom (Archi 1979: 563). Pettinato responded that the tablets should be investigated further and that he preferred to identify *si-da-mu*^{ki} with Sodom (Pettinato 1980c: 213). Most recently Archi has published a review of extracts from eight unpublished texts in the interest of supporting his contention that none of the sites mentioned in them can be identified with the biblical sites of Sodom, Gomorrah, and Zoar (Archi 1981: 54–55).

Whether or not Sodom, Gomorrah, and Zoar are present in the unpublished texts that have been brought into this discussion thus far cannot be determined at present since neither Pettinato nor Archi has published them. On the other hand, neither Pettinato nor Archi has mentioned *sa-dam*^{ki} and *ad-mu-ut*^{ki} from the EGA in their dialogue over this subject, and these place names are present in a text that has been published, complete with photographs. The debate over those unpublished references loses its urgency if names that fit linguistically and geographically with two of the biblical Cities of the Plain appear in the EGA. If these names had only been found in short economic texts, like those mentioned by Archi, one might argue that they could be separated from the biblical sites in question and located in Syria. Working within the larger geographical framework of the EGA, however, one is pointed in the direction of southern Transjordan for the location and identification of these EGA toponyms.

The EGA adds some details to our knowledge about these sites and these new details aid in locating and identifying them. Four different theories about the location of the Cities of the Plain have been advocated in the past: that they lay towards the north end of the Dead Sea, either presently under the water or on land, or that they lay towards the south end of the Dead Sea, either presently under the water or on land. With the evidence now available from the EGA the locations proposed towards the north end of the Dead Sea may be discarded. The reason is that if those who travelled the route covered by the second segment of the EGA studied above had gone north from En Gedi (No. 207), they should have passed by the forests and the river junction located at the southern end of the Jordan Valley by the first segment studied above from the EGA (cf. Nos. 123–127) *before* they came to Admah and Sodom.

Given the significance of toponym No. 209, it seems likely that the southern shoreline of the Dead Sea was located in the vicinity of Admah at the time this route was recorded. It also seems likely that Sodom lay north of Admah since the route appears to continue in a northerly direction after leaving Sodom. These considerations from the EGA provide us with two geographical data about Admah and Sodom. Admah appears to have been located at the southeastern corner of the Dead Sea and Sodom lay north of it along the eastern shore. The list of the Cities of the Plain in Genesis 14 suggests that there was some order to the way in which they were listed. It is probable that they were either listed from north to south or from south to north. Correlating the biblical list with the EGA suggests the former order, since the EGA locates the first city in the biblical list north of its middle city. Thus the reason why Zeboiim and Bela/Zoar of the biblical list do not appear in the EGA is because they lay south of the Admah and travellers from Ebla turned north at that point. The absence of Gomorrah from the EGA may involve an archeological consideration which brings up the general subject of potential identifications for these cities.

Excavations (Lapp 1966a: 556–61, 1966b: 104–11, 1968a: 1–25, 1968b: 86–93; Rast and Schaub 1978a: 1–60, 1978b: 1–5; Rast 1979, Schaub 1979) and surface explorations (Albright 1924: 2–12; Rast and Schaub 1974a: 5–53, 1974b: 1–6) have identified five similar EB sites located southeast of the Dead Sea which make reasonably good candidates for the five biblical Cities of the Plain. These extend from Bab edh-Dhraᶜ in the north to Khanazir in the south. The EGA now lends some support to connecting these five archeological sites with the five biblical sites. In the first place, according to archeological correlations such as pottery dating, the EGA was found in the archive of the Ebla palace that was in use during the period of EB III during which these Transjordanian sites were occupied to their greatest extent. In the second place, the EGA locates Admah and Sodom in the same general geographical area as that in which these sites are located, around the southeastern end of the Dead Sea.

If the correlations proposed above are correct, then Bab edh-Dhraᶜ could be identified with Sodom and Admah could be identified with es-Safi. Both of these sites show signs of extensive occupation throughout the EB period, the former from the excavational evidence cited above and the latter from a surface survey examination (Rast and Schaub 1974a: 16). The site of Numeirah is located between Bab edh-Dhraᶜ and es-Safi, and thus it is a candidate for Gomorrah. Excavations at Numeirah have demonstrated a somewhat different occupational history, in that it was *only* occupied in EB III (Rast and Schaub 1978b: 6). The depth of the debris is so limited that the excavators estimate Numeirah was only occupied for about a century at the end of EB (Schaub 1979). If the EGA was compiled before the end of EB III, therefore, it might have been written down before Numeirah (= Gomorrah?) was founded.

To summarize this final point from the EGA, this concluding discussion has suggested that what can be determined about its toponyms Nos. 210 and 211 fits well with what is known about the Cities of the Plain in Genesis 14–19 and with what has recently been determined about the five significant EB sites located south-east of the Dead Sea.

References

Aharoni, Y.
1967 *The Land of the Bible*. Trans. A. F. Rainey. Philadelphia: Westminster.

Albright, W. F.
1924 The Archaeological Results of an Expedition to Moab and the Dead Sea. *Bulletin of the American Schools of Oriental Research* 14: 2–12.

Archi, A.
1979 The Epigraphic Evidence from Ebla and the Old Testament. *Biblica* 60: 556–66.
1981 Are "The Cities of the Plain" Mentioned in the Ebla Tablets? *Biblical Archaeology Review* 7: 54–55.

Avi-Yonah, M.
1966 *The Holy Land from the Persian to the Arab Conquests (536 B.C. to A.D. 640): A Historical Geography*. Grand Rapids: Baker.

Avi-Yonah, M., and Aharoni, Y.
1968 *The Macmillan Bible Atlas*. New York: Macmillan.

Baly, D., and Tushingham, A. D.
1971 *Atlas of the Biblical World*. New York: World.

Biggs, R.
1974 *Inscriptions from Tell Abū Ṣalābīkh*. Oriental Institute Publications 99. Chicago: University of Chicago.

Cross, F. M., and Freedman, D. N.
1964 The Name of Ashdod. *Bulletin of the American Schools of Oriental Research* 175: 48–51.

Dahood, M.
1981 Ebla, Ugarit, and the Bible. Afterword, pp. 271–321, to Pettinato 1981.

Glock, A. E.
1979 An Archaeological Survey of the Jenin Region. Report to the Annual Meeting of the American Schools of Oriental Research, November 16, 1979, New York.

Glueck, N.
1935 *Explorations in Eastern Palestine II.* Annual of the American Schools of Oriental Research 15. New Haven: American Schools of Oriental Research.
1939 *Explorations in Eastern Palestine III.* Annual of the American Schools of Oriental Research 18–19. New Haven: American Schools of Oriental Research.

Goetze, A.
1953 An Old Babylonian Itinerary. *Journal of Cuneiform Studies* 7: 51–72.

Gordon, C. H.
1965 *Ugaritic Textbook.* Analecta Orientalia 38. Rome: Pontifical Biblical Institute.

Grayson, A. K.
1974 The Empire of Sargon of Akkad. *Archiv für Orientforschung* 25: 56–64.

Hallo, W. W.
1964 The Road to Emar. *Journal of Cuneiform Studies* 18: 57–58.

Harris, Z. S.
1939 *Development of the Canaanite Dialects.* American Oriental Series 16. New Haven: American Oriental Society.

Heidel, A.
1963 *The Gilgamesh Epic and Old Testament Parallels.* Chicago: University of Chicago Press.

Jean, C. F., and Hoftijzer, J.
1965 *Dictionnaire des inscriptions sémitiques de l'Ouest.* Leiden: Brill.

Kraeling, E. G. H.
1956 *Rand McNally Bible Atlas.* Chicago: Rand McNally.

Labat, R.
1976 *Manuel d'épigraphie Akkadienne*[5]. Paris: Geuthner.

Lapp, P.
1966a Bâb edh-Dhrâ'. In Chronique Archéologique. *Revue biblique* 73: 556–61.
1966b The Cemetery at Bâb edh-Dhrâ', Jordan. *Archaeology* 19: 104–11.
1968a Bâb edh-Dhrâ', Perizzites and Emim. In *Jerusalem through the Ages.* The Twenty-Fifth Archaeological Convention, October 1967. Jerusalem: Israel Exploration Society.
1968b Bâb edh-Dhrâ'. In Chronique Archéologique. *Revue biblique* 75: 86–93.

Lux, U. W.
1980 Vorläufiger Bericht über die Ausgrabungen in Gadara (Umm Qēs) in Jordanien im Jahre 1979. *Zeitschrift des Deutschen Palästina-Vereins* 96: 158–62.

Moscati, S., ed.
1964 *An Introduction to the Comparative Grammar of the Semitic Languages.* Porta Linguarum Orientalium. Wiesbaden: Harrassowitz.

Olavarri, E.
1969 Fouilles à 'Arô'er sur l'Arnon. *Revue biblique* 76: 230–59.

Pettinato, G.
1977 Gli archivi reali di Tell Mardikh-Ebla. *Rivista Biblica Italiana* 25: 225–44.
1978 L'Atlante Geografico nel Vicino Oriente Antico attestato ad Ebla ed ad Abū Ṣalābīkh (I). *Orientalia* 47: 50–73.
1979a *Catalogo dei testi cuneiformi di Tell Mardikh - Ebla.* Materiali Epigrafici di Ebla 1. Naples: Istituto Universitario Orientale di Napoli.
1979b *Ebla: Un impero inciso nell'argilla.* Milan: Mondadori.
1980a *Testi amministrativi della Biblioteca L. 2769.* Materiali Epigrafici di

Ebla 2. Naples: Istituto Universitario Orientale di Napoli.

1980b Bollettino militare della campagna di Ebla contro la città di Mari. *Oriens Antiquus* 19: 231–45.

1980c Ebla and the Bible. *Biblical Archeologist* 43: 203–16.

1981 *The Archives of Ebla*. Garden City: Doubleday.

Pritchard, J. B.

1962 *Gibeon: Where The Sun Stood Still*. Princeton: Princeton University Press.

Rast, W. E.

1979 The Town Site of Bab edh-Dhra, 1979 Season. Report to the Annual Meeting of the American Schools of Oriental Research, November 16, 1979, New York.

Rast, W. E., and Schaub, R. T.

1974a Survey of the Southeastern Plain of the Dead Sea, 1973. *Annual of the Department of Antiquities in Jordan* 19: 5–53.

1974b New Discoveries in the Environs of Bab edh-Dhrâʿ. In the *Newsletter of the American Schools of Oriental Research* for April, 1974.

1978a A Preliminary Report of Excavations at Bâb edh-Dhrâʿ, 1975. *Annual of the American Schools of Oriental Research* 43: 1–32.

1978b Bab edh-Dhrâʿ and Numeira, 1977. In the *Newsletter of the American Schools of Oriental Research* for March, 1978.

Schaub, R. T.

1979 The Cemetery at Bab edh-Dhra and Numeira, 1979 Season. Report to the Annual Meeting of the American Schools of Oriental Research, November 16, 1980, New York.

Smick, E. B.

1973 *Archaeology of the Jordan Valley*. Grand Rapids: Baker.

Thompson, H. O.

1967 Tell el-Husn—Biblical Beth-shan. *Biblical Archaeologist* 30: 110–15.

Thompson, T. L.

1979 *The Settlement of Palestine in the Bronze Age*. Beihefte zum Tübinger Atlas des Vorderen Orients B 34. Wiesbaden: Reichert.

Tomback, R. S.

1978 *A Comparative Semitic Lexicon of the Phoenician and Punic Languages*. Society of Biblical Literature Dissertation Series 32. Missoula: Scholars Press.

Wright, G. E., and Filson, F. V.

1956 *The Westminster Historical Atlas to the Bible*². Philadelphia: Westminster.

Yadin, Y.

1972 *Hazor*. London: Oxford.

Baal, Lord of the Earth: The Ugaritic Baal Epic

Lawrence E. Toombs
Wilfrid Laurier University, Waterloo, Ontario

David Noel Freedman's contributions to biblical scholarship have been marked by a breadth of interest which is never submerged by his careful attention to detail. In his work the desire to see the larger significance of specific problems is everywhere apparent. Therefore, it seemed fitting in this essay to attempt an evaluation of the central theme and overall meaning of the Ugaritic Baal epic.

Almost every point made in the paper is an arena of scholarly debate. It is clearly impossible within the space available to provide detailed argumentation in support of every conclusion reached. I have been content to make the case in general terms that the unifying theme of the myth is the structure and functioning of the inhabitable earth under the lordship of Baal, and to direct the reader by means of bibliographical notes to more extensive treatments of some subjects. The references to the myth follow the system employed by G. R. Driver in *Canaanite Myths and Legends* (1956), rather than the more modern CTA and KTU systems of reference. The justification of this apparently perverse choice is that Driver's work is probably the translation of the Ugaritic texts most readily available to all potential readers of the paper. (A table supplying the UT, CTA, and KTU numbers for the cited texts follows the references.) In the main I have followed the order of the tablets as Driver presents them. In the interest of brevity I have not quoted the texts in full but have paraphrased them.

The Component Themes

In a paper originally read at the Annual Conference of the Jewish Palestine Exploration Society in 1940 and subsequently published in the *Israel Exploration Journal* (1962) and in his collected essays, *Biblical and Oriental Studies* (1976: 168–77), U. Cassuto argued that the interpretation of the Ugaritic epic of Baal as the myth of an annually recurring fertility cycle does not do justice to its complexity and comprehensiveness. Cassuto (1976: 176) saw in the character of Baal "the personification of the life-giving, life-preserving and life-renewing forces," and in that of Mot the sum total of the death-dealing and destructive powers in the universe. In his view the myth depicts a struggle on a world scale of life against death, a struggle in which the fate of plants, animals, and human beings hangs in the balance. The "message" of the myth, if one may so describe it, is optimistic. In the struggle between the mighty opposites, Baal/Life and Mot/Death, life, though brought to the point of near extinction, ultimately triumphs and rules over nature and mankind.

The starting point of this paper is Cassuto's search for the central theme which holds together the diverse elements of the Baal cycle. However, his statement of the theme is not inclusive enough to give full weight to all the component themes of the myth. In Cassuto's view the Baal cycle is a mythological statement of thoroughgoing cosmic dualism. Only two of its characters, Baal and Mot, play crucial roles. "The theme of the epic, to which, I consider, the *entire* poem is dedicated from beginning to end, throughout *all* the tablets, is the struggle between Baal and Mot" (1976: 114). The most intractable difficulty with this position is that there are two additional figures, Yam/Nahar and El, whose functions in the myth cannot readily be seen as merely subsidiary to those of Baal and Mot.

As Creator of Creatures and Father of Gods and Men, El might be expected to make a large contribution to the central theme of the myth. Cassuto (1971: 53–59), however, regards him as an otiose figure, dethroned by his sons, who have divided his kingdom and authority among them. Conrad E. L'Heureux (1979: 3–110) has argued convincingly that El is not, as many scholars contend (e.g., Roggia 1941, Kapelrud 1952, Pope 1955, Oldenburg 1969), displaced by Baal as the ultimate authority in the universe, but retains his primacy among the gods throughout the myth. The role of El in the epic is paradoxical. On the one hand, he is treated with extreme disrespect and threatened with violence by Anat (V ivb-v) and he wails and mutilates himself when he hears that Baal is dead (I* vi). On the other, he is repeatedly visited in his remote palace by gods or their messengers whenever decisions of importance must be made and is hailed as the possessor of everlasting wisdom and the bestower of good fortune (e.g., II iv 41–43).

Yam/Nahar, the lord of the chaotic waters, is an opponent of Baal whose power is such as to make the gods tremble, and to persuade the High God, El, that Baal should be made his slave (III*B 20–22, 30–36). Cassuto, however, does not recognize Yam/Nahar as an opponent of Baal in his own right, but regards him as an agent and representative of Mot. To relegate Yam/Nahar to such a dependent position appears to violate the integrity of the myth. He is one of El's sons (VI ii 18, etc.) and, because of this status, stands on a par with Baal and Mot. He is called El's beloved (VI iv 15–20), and a palace was built for him before Baal received that honor (III*C). To be sure, Mot and Yam stand in close relationship to one another, but it does not seem to be a relationship of dependence on Yam's part. When Mot attended Yam's funeral feast he felt as if he himself had died (I* i 32–33). The defeat of a lackey would not be expected to produce such an extreme feeling of despair, but the overthrow of a god of equal power might well induce Mot to see in the event an omen of things to come for himself.

Other prominent motifs which should take their place in any statement of the central theme of the myth may be mentioned briefly.

1. The fertility motif is a major concern of the texts, particularly where they deal with the protracted struggle between Baal and Mot. To an agricultural community Baal's most crucial attribute is his power to fructify the earth with his life-giving rain. When this power is interfered with, the earth produces no vegetation and "life fails among men" (III ii 17–18). The periodicity of the drought-fertility cycle is a matter of dispute. It is sometimes regarded as an annual occurrence, generated by the yearly death and resurrection of the rain god (e.g., Gaster 1961: 124–29, de Moor 1971). Others, following Cyrus Gordon (1949: 4–5), point out that only a protracted drought would put the existence of the community in jeopardy, and represent a failure of Baal. The myth itself speaks of seven-year periods of famine, and never of one-year cycles.

2. The most obvious common denominator of the various segments of the myth is the theme of contention among the gods: Baal against Yam, Anat and Baal against Mot, Anat against Yam. Athtar is a rival, verbally at least, of both Yam and Baal (III*C, III i 25–37). The contentions and violent struggles among the gods are motivated either by a desire to achieve kingship or to extend a sphere of authority already possessed. This fact draws a number of subsidiary themes into the motif of struggle: challenges issued by the rivals to one another (III*B 3–7, 31–34; II vii 45–52; I i 26–27), claims to universal kingship (II vii 49–52), demands for a palace (VI iii), and the family relationships by which their kinship is expressed and legitimated.

3. The contentions among the gods result now in victory and now in defeat, but never in the annihilation of the loser. Baal, Yam, and Mot survive the partial victories of their rivals and continue to exist and to maintain kingly rank and authority, each in his own sphere. The motif of the definition of spheres of cosmic control underlies large sections of the epic.

4. Finally, a place must be found within the central theme for the overall control of the cosmos by the High God, El. He is never physically involved in the battles among his children, but is drawn into them, often on their initiative, as arbiter and judge.

The Cosmogonic Dimensions of the Myth

It might appear that nothing short of a *Weltanschauung,* a comprehensive understanding of the nature and *modus operandi* of the cosmos, is required to unite the diversity of motifs described briefly above into a literary composition. Loren Fisher (1965: 313–24) identified the cosmic dimension of the myth with the concept of creation. He distinguished two genres of creation thought. The first, the "El type," has its analogues in physical generation (El is the father of gods and men) and in the manufacture of a new reality out of old material (El is *bny bnwt,* the creator of creatures). The second genre of creation thought, the "Baal type," is the establishment of cosmic order through a struggle among the gods out of which Baal emerges as victor and overlord.

Frank M. Cross (1973: 39–43) makes a somewhat similar distinction in a more sophisticated form. The myths in which El is active as warrior god are theogonic and have the effect of establishing him as the head of the family of gods. The narratives which depict these struggles are reflected in the theogonies of Sakkunyaton (later Sanchuniathon). In the Baal cycle El rests on his laurels and exercises the powers won in the theogonic struggles, and his children become the chief actors in a myth which is cosmogonic in its significance. El, the divine patriarch, is the transitional figure between theogonic and cosmogonic mythology. In the framework of thought developed by Cross one would naturally look for the underlying theme of the Baal epic in its understanding of the structure of reality, of the origin of that structure and of the dynamic which maintains it in operation.

Ugaritic cosmology is a variant form of the general Near Eastern perception of the nature of reality. Jacobsen (1949: 139–40) describes the Mesopotamian concept of the cosmos as an order of wills, analogous to a family or state. This order "did not appear as something given; rather it became something achieved—achieved through a continuous integration of many individual cosmic wills" (1949: 139).

Jacobsen's description may be accepted as an underlying concept of the Baal epic, if conflict and arbitration are emphasized as the means by which integration is achieved. The relatively modern notions of an evolutionary process which proceeds "with all deliberate speed" toward a solution to social problems, and of the resolution of tensions by consensus and agreement are absent from Ugaritic thought. The wills which must be integrated to produce the cosmic order are drives toward total power. Each contestant seeks to overthrow his rivals and to usurp their dominion by force. Under these conditions the establishment of order can only be the result of warfare, at times arbitrated or mitigated through arbitration by a recognized, but not all-powerful, authority. The equilibrium achieved will remain uncertain and precarious.

The functioning universe, as the Ugaritic mythographers understood it, was the result of the integration of the wills of the great powers of the cosmos through the agency of struggle. The Baal myth, however, is not a complete cosmogony. It represents only a segment of the integrative process. In the poem certain aspects of the cosmic order have been achieved and are accepted as givens. Others are worked out in the development of the myth. The central theme of the epic will be found in those elements of the cosmos the administration of which is still in a state of flux. To determine the nature and scope of these elements requires a brief description of Ugaritic cosmology as a whole.

The Structure of the Cosmos

The cultures of the ancient Near East conceived of the universe as a tripartite structure, consisting of heaven, the abode of the gods; earth, the sphere of human activity; and the underworld, the abode of the dead and of the deities who presided over their attenuated existence. The cosmology of the Baal epic diverges from this general picture in that the universe is quadripartite. Its upper level, corresponding to heaven, is the "heights of the north" (*mrym ṣpn,* I* i 11). Its basement is the underworld (*qrt mt,* II viii 11). The middle stage is divided between *ym* (sea) and *ʾarṣ* (earth).

In the "heights of the north" Baal's palace was located (I* i 9–11), as were presumably also the dwellings of the other gods. The clear exception is Mot, the god of death, whose residence was in the grime and filth of the netherworld (I* ii). The location of Yam's palace is uncertain. One would expect from the name of the deity that it would be beneath the waters of the ocean. However, the texts do not indicate that Yam's messengers had to emerge from the sea in order to reach El, and in his conflict with Baal he seems to move on the same level of reality, so to speak. In contrast, when the messengers *gpn* and *ʾugr* go from Baal to Mot they journey to the limits of the earth, raise the rocks, and descend into the depths below (II viii 1–10). For Baal and Mot to meet, Baal must descend to Mot or Mot come up to Baal. This seems to be the background of the jockeying for position between the two gods in I* iii-vi.

The location of El's palace has been the subject of considerable debate. Oldenburg (1969: 104–9), following Pope (1955: 61–81), considers that El's palace was originally in the "heights of the north." When his function as ruler was taken over by Baal, as allegedly described in the myth, El was banished to the underworld, to the confluence of the subterranean rivers. Dissatisfied with the lack of splendor of El's mansion, Baal had a new and more magnificent palace built for himself. Many scholars disagree with this position (recently Clifford 1972), and locate El's residence permanently on the summit of the cosmic mountain at the source of two rivers or oceans. It seems probable that the two streams are the waters of the upper and nether worlds. The location of El's palace on the cosmic mountain, the place where heaven, earth, and underworld are in contact with one another, and at the junction of the waters above and below the earth is a dramatic way of symbolizing El's interest in and authority over the universe in all its parts.

The mountain of the gods should not be identified exclusively with the geographical top of any particular mountain, such as Mons Cassius, Mt. Tabor, or Mt. Zion. It exists in the timeless time and spaceless space of mythology. The heights are vast beyond description. The pavilions of the gods are there, and remote from the others is the tent-palace of El, strategically located at the point of connection of the three worlds over which he rules as patriarchal head. In El's distant palace the gods meet to feast together, to present petitions to the head of the family, and to hear or dispute his decisions. What happened, or continues to happen, in this realm (the tenses have little meaning in mythological time) defines the conditions of life and determines the fate of human beings, whose existence is bound up in the cycles of chronological time.

The lowest level of the universe, deep within the mire and filth below the earth, contains the city and palace of Mot, the dreadful ruler of the underworld (II viii 10–15). Like Hades in Greek mythology, Mot does not appear at the councils of the gods on the heights. He remains in isolation in his own realm. Mot is the swallower *par excellence.* His voracious appetite threatens everyone who approaches him and in the absence of victims he devours the filth which surrounds him (I* i 19–21). His mouth reaches to earth, so that he can suck animals and mortals into his maw, and dry up the vegetation on which men and animals subsist. His insatiable hunger threatens even the sky and the stars (I* ii 1–5). Nevertheless, he remains closely related to El as his son and "beloved hero" (II vii 45–47). Lackeys of El (or of the gods) are present at his court to keep watch.

The structure and control of heaven, "the heights of the north," and "hell," the underworld realm of Mot are givens at the beginning of the Baal epic. The myth assumes that the organization of these two levels of reality is in place and functioning. It is control of the middle tier, the ocean and the dry land, which is in dispute.

Baal Becomes Lord of the Inhabited Earth

Baal possesses the power of the rain, so necessary in maintaining the life of the communities along the eastern Mediterranean coast. Yam/Nahar wields the often unruly and chaotic forces of the oceans and rivers. As the narrative begins, both deities possess their full powers and capacities but neither has a palace. The possession of a palace represents defined and acknowledged authority. The powers and attributes of Yam and Baal are inherent in their divine natures, but as yet the limits of those powers and the spheres in which they may be exercised have not been determined and will not be fixed until, with the permission of El, their palaces have been built.

To a land-based people with an agricultural economy the *ʾarṣ,* the land on which the crops grow, the animals live, and the cities of men are built, is the vital sector of the middle tier. Human beings may venture upon the sea, but it is not their home. The seafarer is an alien in a strange environment, subject to the whims and threatened by the unpredictable moods of Yam. The earth is where mankind lives, reproduces, and eventually dies. Therefore, control of the *ʾarṣ* is the prize of war in the Baal epic.

The integration of wills, to use Jacobsen's term, by which the *ʾarṣ* is administered is the reality which the human population of the *ʾarṣ* must understand and to which it must respond in the cultus. The central theme of the Baal epic may be seen as a segment of a cosmogony, dealing with the divine power structure which controls, not the universe as whole, but the inhabited earth. This may be the significance of the dictum of El repeated by Baal (V iii 29–30) after his victory over Yam, and concurred in by the warrior-goddess Anat (V iva 8, 22–23): "War on earth is opposed to my will." The sentence suggests that the establishment of peace, stability, and order in the realm of human habitation is the goal toward which the myth moves.

The first bid for power over the earth was made by Yam/Nahar. Initially, he was El's favorite among the gods and obtained his father's permission to construct a palace for himself (VI iv 11–20). This event established his right to kingship, presumably over the oceans and rivers. Yam was clearly not content to allow his authority to be limited in this manner. His messengers demanded that El surrender Baal to Yam as his slave and bondsman (III*B). What the result of Baal's servitude to Yam would have been is not specified. At the very least it would have meant that Baal's fertilizing rain would have been at the disposal of the unreliable Yam. At its most drastic earth would have been overwhelmed by the waters of the ocean. Baal's victorious battle against Yam, waged with magical weapons forged for him by the artisan god, Kothar-wa-Hasis, resulted, not in the annihilation of Prince Sea, but in his banishment to and confinement in his own proper realm (III*A 27–31, II iii 4). Prior to Baal's victory Anat made an apparently unsuccessful attempt to beat back Yam (III* A).

In this way the first stage of the integration of wills by which the *ʾarṣ* is governed was accomplished. Yam's ambition to rule the earth was thwarted and he was confined to his limited sphere of rule. Henceforth, he might threaten but could never dominate the earth. Yam's defeat insured that there would be a dry land on which human communities could subsist.

The question of who would rule the dry land was resolved by the building of Baal's palace. Permission for its construction was wrung from El with great difficulty, requiring the threats of Anat (V v 20–24) and the cajolery of Athirat/Astarte, El's consort. The palace established that Baal is *bʿl ʾarṣ,* Lord of the Earth.

The ambition of the Lord of the Earth extended, like that of Yam before him, beyond his own dominion. He aspired to universal rule, to a benevolent reign over gods and men under which his human and divine subjects would prosper (II vii 49–52). Accordingly, Baal adopted the role of challenger. The principal obstacle to his ambition was Mot, the lord of death and the underworld. Baal proposed to shut him up in one of his own graves (II vii 45–49) and to assume his kingship. What a paradise would have resulted if Baal's desire had been realized! Death's power over the earth would have been cancelled. The inhabited land would be perpetually fruitful, the flocks and herds would not sicken and die, and the curse of death would be lifted from the brow of mankind.

Mot responded to Baal's challenge by asserting his own right to rule. He would swallow Baal and entomb him in the nether world where he would remain a powerless prisoner (I* i 6–8), leaving Mot as undisputed lord of the earth.

The battles between Mot on the one side and Anat and Baal on the other need not be described in detail. The result of the contest was a draw. In spite of the sympathy of the mythographers for the cause of Baal, they acknowledged that the outcome of the struggle was a division of control of the *ʾarṣ* between Baal and Mot. The potential earthly paradise which the rule of Baal promised was not to be. Periodically, Baal must yield his lordship to Mot, and in cyclical patterns—birth–growth–death for humans and animals, seed time–maturity–harvest–death for crops, drought–fertility for the earth as a whole—Mot and Baal shared lordship over the inhabited land. The second stage of the integration of wills had been accomplished and the government of the *ʾarṣ* in the form in which the states of the eastern Mediterranean experienced it had taken shape.

Order under the Rule of Baal

The principal issues in the government of the middle tier of the cosmos were settled in the contests of Baal with Yam and Mot. The organizational structure of the earth under the kingship of Baal is described in terms of his family relationships and alliances. Broadly speaking these relationships fall into three categories: ambiguous and vacillating support, voluntary support, and dependence.

El and his consort Athirat fall into the first category. At first El favors Yam, but El acquiesces when Yam is defeated and banished by Baal (VII iv 11–20, V i 1–5). Mot is called "the hero loved of El" (I* ii 8–9), but when Mot seems to have killed Baal, El comes down from his throne and engages in a ritual of bitter mourning (I* vi 11–25). Athirat, El's consort and mother of the gods, appears at times to be hostile to Baal. Anat, in announcing Baal's death to Athirat, does so in terms which suggest that she expects her to rejoice at the news (III i 11–15). At El's request Athirat nominates her son Athtar as Baal's successor (III i 15–23). Nevertheless, she is persuaded to intercede with El on Baal's behalf in the crucial matter of the permission for a palace (II iii 31–33), and in the course of her conversation with El she acknowledges that, like Anat, she recognizes Baal as king and judge and is willing to be his cupbearer (II iv 40–46).

Since El and Athirat are the parents of the seventy gods of Ugarit, their principal interest is to maintain peace in the family, and to insure that rivalries among their children do not upset the balance of the universe over which they rule. In carrying out this delicate diplomatic task they cannot unequivocally support any of their children. However, both recognize and approve Baal's kingship in the areas under his jurisdiction.

Athtar, Athirat's nominee as successor to Baal, appears also as a rival of Yam during his period of ascendancy (III*C), but is dismissed by El as a serious contender for power. After his appointment as Baal's successor he sits on the throne of the Lord of the Earth, but his feet will not reach the footstool (III i 30–35). He voluntarily descends from the throne, disclaiming his ability to take Baal's place, but he does rule over the *ʾarṣ* during Baal's absence in the underworld (III i 37). Whether Athtar represents the morning star (Albright 1969: 187), or a fertility deity, one held in high esteem but deposed by Baal (Gese et al. 1970: 138–9), the land watered by irrigation (Gaster 1961: 126–7) or the springs and wells (Driver 1956: 28), he represents a power of fertility which could conceivably be regarded as an alternative to Baal's rain. He is a petulant, immature little god who can function only in Baal's absence but must bow to the authority of Baal when he is present. Irrigation from natural springs is the principal method of watering the land during the dry season, but it can only be auxiliary and supplementary to Baal's rain.

The deities who place their powers voluntarily at the service of Baal are Anat, *špš* and Kothar-wa-Hasis.

Anat, Baal's sister and consort, is his most ardent and valuable ally. His battles, defeats, and victories are hers as well. There is a striking parallelism between Baal's conflicts and those of Anat. Like Baal, she fights Yam (V iii 53–54) and Mot (III ii 30–37), and she is victorious in both cases. She attacks and defeats the enemies of Baal in a bloody assault, plays with their severed heads, and bathes in their blood (V ii 5–22). The warrior-goddess Anat also stands for the female powers of fertility. Her total alliance with Baal is a mythological statement of the conviction that the activities of the male and female fertility principles are synchronized with one another. They operate together in all respects, and the rule of Baal and Anat is an indissoluble unity.

The goddess *špš,* the sun deity, is somewhat ambiguous in her relationships with Baal. Her night-time journeys take her into Mot's realm and her travels during the day bring her across the sky in the dominion of Baal. However, she has a vested interest in an alliance with Baal. Without his cooling rain and his sheltering clouds her searing rays are destructive of life, and she becomes a creature of Mot (II viii 21–24). Accordingly, she volunteers to seek Baal in the underworld (III iv 20), to which she travels each night. The heat and light of the sun are necessary, along with the rains, to sustain human life. Hence, *špš* is a voluntary ally of Baal, although part of her time is spent with Mot in the underworld.

Kothar-wa-Hasis, the craftsman of the gods who builds their temples and fashions their weapons, is by his own choice on Baal's side in the battle with Yam/Nahar. He foretells Baal's victory (III*A 6–9) and designs the weapons which make that victory possible (III*A 11–24). He builds Baal's palace (II vi 16–21) and recommends that it be furnished with windows (II v 59–62), a suggestion which Baal at first rejects (II v 63–65) but later of his own accord accepts (II vii 15–19). If the artisan god may be viewed as the presiding deity of the arts and crafts, the forces governing human creativity are in the service of Baal and function as part of his world rule.

Baal's daughters (or brides), *pdry, ṭly,* and *ʾarṣy,* represent elements of the fertility of the soil other than Baal's rain (Gese et al. 1970: 164). They have no independence in the myth, but by virtue of their relationship to the rain god are completely dependent on him. Two of them, *pdry,* the dew, and *ṭly,* the mist, go with Baal into the underworld. Dew and mist are essential to agriculture in many parts of the Levant. The heavy dews and ground mists which form during the night under the clear skies of the dry season sustain the moisture level of the soil and allow vegetable crops to reach maturity. They function during the reign of Mot, apparently with his permission, but their fertilizing effect is possible only because the soil is saturated by Baal's rain during the wet portion of the annual cycle.

Baal's messenger(s), *gpn-w-ʾugr,* the deities of vineyards and irrigated fields (Gese et al. 1970: 170–1), are, as their function implies, completely dependent on

Baal and unquestioningly carry out his orders. The rain god is the undisputed lord of the fertile fields.

The ordering of the earth achieved in the Baal epic may be summarized in these terms. Rival claimants for control of the *ʾarṣ* are confined to their own spheres of power and Baal's lordship over the earth is confirmed by El and his consort when Baal is given a palace from which to exercise his kingship. However, the dubious outcome of Baal's contest with Mot means that he must share his control of the earth with his grim rival. Anat, the female power of fertility operative in the production of offspring as well as in the fertility of the soil, is the wholehearted ally of Baal and echoes his will. The minor elements in the production of fertility in the soil—dew, mist, wells and springs—are either Baal's obedient daughters or his servitors. The vineyards and irrigated fields are completely subject to his will. Except for periodic incursions into his realm of the demonic power of Death, Baal is Lord of the Earth, and all the forces and potentialities necessary for human, animal, and vegetable life are under his control. The creative powers of artisan and builder stand by his side to aid him in his rule.

The Function of the Myth

How did the Baal epic function in the life of Ugaritic society? Perhaps the variety of answers to this question offered in the literature point to the true solution. It had not a single but a multiple function. A cyclical understanding of reality lies behind the myth. However, the human being and his society are bound up in and controlled by not one cycle but many—the cycle of tides in the ocean (restless Yam attempting to push beyond his limits), the succession of day and night, the annual cycle of the seasons, the growth and death of the crops, the periodic recurrence of drought followed by seasons of plenty, the reign and death of a king and the appointment and legitimization of his successor, and the cycle of birth—maturity—reproduction—death, which provides the model for many of the other cycles.

Presumably each of the cycles had its appropriate ritual, the spoken part of which constituted its myth. The Baal epic is not any one of these myths, but a compendium of them all. It appears to be a conscious literary creation, formed out of the raw material of many myths, and designed to draw them all together within the framework of narrative poetry. The unifying concept is the achievement by Baal of lordship over the earth. It is, I believe, a gratuitous disparagement of the intellectual capacities of the ancient people to suggest that they had neither the interest nor the ability to produce such a compendium of mythic themes.

The value to the community, and especially to its priestly and political leadership, of possessing such a composite myth is apparent. It would serve as a guide to ritual activity, as a work of theological reference, and as a *credo* of Baalistic religion. Above all, it would provide divine legitimation of the customs and rituals of the Ugaritic community, a constant assurance that what was done by the temple and the royal court was in accordance with the structure of reality. Herein would lie the utility of the myth. Only if the activity of the community harmonized with divinely established reality would its continuing prosperity be assured. A document of such significance to the state would appropriately be kept in the archives of the palace.

The Baal epic does not issue from primitive, sex-ridden, and superstition-bound minds. It is a sophisticated, realistic understanding of the nature of things in pluralistic terms. Its comprehensiveness, utility, and inner consistency made it a viable alternative to the monotheistic, historically-oriented faith of Israel, similarly capable of claiming the allegiance and sustaining the intellectual, religious, and political life of human beings and their societies. It is not at all surprising that the religion which the epic represents proved so stubborn, and, one is tempted to say, so worthy an antagonist of Israel's religion.

CITED TEXTS

Driver 1956	UT	CTA	KTU
I[AB].i.1–29	62.obv.1–29	6.I.1–29	1.6.I.1–29
I[AB].vi.1–20	62.rev.38–57	6.VI.38–57	1.6.VI.38–57
I*[AB]	67	5	1.5
II[AB]	51	4	1.4
III[AB]	49	6.I.30–VI.37	1.6.I.30–VI.37
III*[AB]A	68	2.IV	1.2.IV
III*[AB]B	137	2.I-II	1.2.I-II
III*[AB]C	129	2.III(?)	1.2.III
V[AB].i-iva	^{c}nt.I-IV	3.A-D	1.3.I.1–IV.46
V[AB].ivb-vi	^{c}nt.pl.vi.IV-V	3.E-F	1.3.IV.47–VI
VI[AB].ii-iii	^{c}nt.pl.ix	1.II-III	1.1.II-III
VI[AB].iv-v	^{c}nt.pl.x	1.IV-V	1.1.IV-V

References

Albright, W. F.
1969 *Yahweh and the Gods of Canaan.* Garden City: Doubleday.

Cassuto, U.
1962 Baal and Mot. *Israel Exploration Journal* 12: 77–86.
1971 *The Goddess Anath.* Trans. I. Abrahams. Jerusalem: Magnes. Originally 1951.
1976 *Bible and Ancient Oriental Texts.* Trans. I. Abrahams. Jerusalem: Magnes.

Clifford, R.
1972 *The Cosmic Mountain in Canaan and the Old Testament.* Harvard Semitic Monographs 2. Cambridge: Harvard University Press.

Cross, F. M.
1973 *Canaanite Myth and Hebrew Epic. Essays in the History of the Religion of Israel.* Cambridge: Harvard University Press.

Driver, G. R.
1956 *Canaanite Myths and Legends.* Old Testament Studies 3. Edinburgh: T. & T. Clark.

Fisher, L. R.
1965 Creation at Ugarit and in the Old Testament. *Vetus Testamentum* 15: 313–24.

Gaster, T. H.
1961 *Thespis: Ritual, Myth and Drama in the Ancient Near East*[2]. New York: Doubleday.

Gese, H.; Höfner, M; and Rudolph, K.
1970 *Die Religion Altsyriens, Altarabiens und der Mandäer.* Stuttgart: Kohlhammer.

Gordon, C. H.
1949 *Ugaritic Literature: A Comprehensive Translation of the Poetic and Prose Texts.* Roma: Pontificum Institutum Biblicum.

Gray, J.
1965 *The Legacy of Canaan. The Ras Shamra Texts and Their Relevance to the Old Testament*[2]. Supplements to Vetus Testamentum 5. Leiden: Brill.

Jacobsen, T.
1949 Mesopotamia. Pp. 137–234 in H. Frankfurt et al., *Before Philosophy: The Intellectual Adventure of Ancient Man.* Harmondsworth: Penguin Books. Originally 1946.

Kapelrud, A. S.
1952 *Baal in the Ras Shamra Texts.* Copenhagen: G. E. C. Gad.

L'Heureux, C. E.
1979 *Rank among the Canaanite Gods. El, Baal and the Repha'im.* Harvard Semitic Monographs 21. Missoula: Scholars Press.

de Moor, J.C.
1971 *The Seasonal Pattern in the Ugaritic Myth of Baʿlu.* Alter Orient und Altes Testament 16. Neukirchen-Vluyn and Kevelær: Neukirchen Verlag and Verlag Butzon und Bercker.

Obermann, J.
1948 *Ugaritic Mythology: A Study of Its Leading Motifs.* New Haven: Yale University Press.

Oldenburg, U.
1969 *The Conflict between El and Baal in Canaanite Religion.* Supplementa ad *NUMEN*, Altera Series, Dissertationes ad Historiam Religionum 30. Leiden: Brill.

Pope, M. H.
1955 *El in the Ugaritic Texts.* Leiden: Brill.

Roggia, R. G.
1941 Alcune osservationi sul culto di El a Ras-Shamra. *Aevum* 15: 559–75.

Schmidt, W.
1961 *Königtum Gottes in Ugarit und Israel.* Beihefte zur Zeitschrift für die Alttestamentliche Wissenschaft 80. Berlin: Töpelmann.

Where Guardian Spirits Watch By Night and Evil Spirits Fail: The Zoroastrian Prototypical Heaven

Gernot L. Windfuhr
The University of Michigan, Ann Arbor, Michigan

Introduction

At the base of most grand cosmic schemes, whether the latest theories of physics aimed toward the Grand Unified Theory or the scheme posited in the Zoroastrian books, is the assumption, or hope, that nature is essentially simple and that its perplexing complexities are variations of relatively few basic phenomena.[1] Zarathushtra, who lived probably sometime between 1100 and 900 B.C.E. either in Central Asia or Sistan, profoundly changed the Iranian view of the world with his vision of time and his beliefs that this world has a beginning and an end, that the *best end* will be here, if mankind, through reason, will make the right choices based on insights into the orderly and reasoned bases of nature and the universe, and that this universe was created by Ahura Mazda so as to achieve both ultimate salvation for all and destruction of disorder and chaos, the 'evil spirit,' the LIE. This teleological world view is shared by other higher religions, such as Judaism, Christianity, and Islam, all of which originated on territory once included in the ancient Iranian empire.

In two earlier studies (Windfuhr 1976; forthcoming) I have tried to investigate what may be called the 'logical structure' implicit in Zarathushtra's thinking, especially the logic of what are generally called the 'six holy immortals,' viz., good mind, truth, rule, proper thought, completeness, and immortality. These are not only cosmological and logical principles but also creative agents as well as spiritual states, constituting, as it were, a hexagon of reasoned interrelationships and reflecting, at the same time, a set of spiritual correspondences to the six material creations of Zoroastrianism: fire, metals, water, earth, plants, and animals; the last material creation is man, who is under the guardianship of the highest creative principle, 'the holy spirit.' These material creations represent successively higher states of matter, not elements as has been assumed.

Whoever tries to penetrate the metaphoric and often enigmatic 'poetry' of the Zoroastrian world view is continuously confronted with questions related to cosmology, i.e., to the structure of the universe and its workings. The importance of cosmological assumptions in the Zoroastrian texts must be related to the function of the cosmos in the Zoroastrian *Heilsgeschichte*. If Zarathushtra's fundamental insight was that there is reason in the world of spirit, not the bickering of anthropomorphic deities, then he must also have found that there is reason in the world of matter; just as the good spiritual world was set up, so to speak, by Ahura Mazda for the struggle with the spiritual power of evil, i.e., non-reason, so the material world must have been set up by Ahura Mazda with reason. The material world is one all-encompassing skillfully designed battle-line. It is not just there, it is there for a purpose: man, who is the culminating and central creation, endowed with language to think, speak, and act with reason, and who participates in both the material and spiritual worlds, must make the cosmologically right choices, to stand 'behind' the 'fortress of reason,' which is the Zoroastrian *daēnā* 'religion, vision, conscience,' and to charge against the *aēšma*, the 'irrational fury' of the LIE, the evil spirit.

Obviously Zarathushtra inherited a long tradition of speculative thought about the spiritual and the divine, but it was he who found the reason in it. Similarly he inherited a long tradition of speculation about the cosmos, and he found the reason in it. It has long been recognized that during the long period since Zarathushtra himself the world view expressed in Zoroastrian texts has changed, that it has been adjusted to new insights and speculations within Zoroastrianism, whether or not as a result of contact with other world views, such as those of India, Mesopotamia, Egypt, and Greece. In spite of these changes, and in spite of the fact that, like other religions, Zoroastrianism was hardly ever a totally unified system, it appears that the original views continued to constitute the basic frame of reference.[2]

The following is an attempt to contribute to the understanding of a small part of that frame of reference, the sky above earth, and specifically to treat the location of a 'fortress' around the sky which is defended by the *fravašis*, who are the highest prototypical part of each man and who protect his soul and body as well as the cosmos.[3] It should be noted that the world-view investigated here is not the empirical 'realistic' one of meterology and astronomy, but the idealized 'theoretical' or 'theological' structure of heaven and the sky,[4] i.e., the view which is 'logically' abstracted from both empirical observation *and* mythology, while feeding, in its turn, both empiricist observation *and* mythology, in a continuous cycle of metaphors between the signifier and the signified.

In trying to contribute to the reconstruction of the Zoroastrian cosmos, I make three basic assumptions: (1) that the information provided by this long tradition is based on a unified view of the structure of the world, even if there sometimes seem to be contradictions; (2) that this structure is based on analogical thinking, so pervasive in Zoroastrianism, even if sometimes an analogically expected part of this system may not be explicitly described; and (3) that the basis of most, if not all, explicit and implicit (i.e., mythological) references to cosmology is the keen observation of natural phenomena, which often appear to be hidden behind a metaphoric terminology (not unlike our own technical terms); the etymologies of such terms often seem to fit the phenomena well, once the correlation between signifier and signified is recognized. While no one can hope that any such attempt can solve all or even the larger part of the problems involved even in a small sub-part of cosmology, gaining a relatively clearer picture of the underlying *Weltbild* can help resolve to some degree the many cryptic and obscure passages and references which have continued to puzzle scholarship. At the same time, it can contribute to insights into the "relative chronology" of the cosmological theory. One of the objectives along these lines is the clarification of the relationship between Zarathushtra's *Weltbild*, as expressed in his Gathas, and that of later Zoroastrian doctrine. The demonstration that a supposedly post-Zarathushtrian concept can be found behind the terminology or phraseology of a particular Gathic passage will improve the understanding of both continuity and development.[5]

Sources

Zoroastrian texts span three temporal and linguistic periods: texts in the Old Iranian language called Avestan, texts in Middle Persian, and, to a lesser extent, texts in Modern Persian.[6] For the understanding of the theological philosophy, the crucial texts are the Gathas attributed to Zarathushtra himself; these seventeen stanzaic poems, arranged into five groups according to their meter, are written in a dialect called Gathic Avestan. Next in importance are 'Younger' Avestan texts, especially the *yašts*, hymns of praise to divine beings, among whom are the god of covenant or contract Mithra, *aredvī sūrā anāhitā*, who is the female deity of water, as well as the rainbringer Sirius, and the *fravašis*, the protective spirits of the just. Specifically important for cosmology is the Middle Persian book the *Bondaheš*, the Zoroastrian "Genesis," which was completed in the main in the 9th century C.E., a final summary of received knowledge.

Many parts of the Zoroastrian cosmos remain unclear due to lack of information, seeming contradictions, elliptical and scattered statements on individual topics, and most importantly our incomplete understanding of the metaphoric language involved. Indeed, there appears to be an intentional ambivalence between the realistic and the ideal, between spiritual and material,[7] between myth and descriptive fact, especially in the ancient poetic texts. The worlds of physics, ethics, and logic were still parts of a theological universe.

A final preliminary note is necessary. Zoroastrians assume a time-space limited world. For the first 3,000 years creation was in its spiritual state; 3,000 years in its ideal material state followed.[8] After the initial 6,000 years, Ahriman and the forces of evil attacked, mixing with the good creation and attempting to destroy it. This resulted in the destruction of the original, ideal, prototypical material world and the development of the "present" shape, structure, and variety of creation. Accordingly, there is an original ideal structure and a "present" structure of the world; it is not always easy to separate these.

The Sky Above Earth

The basic structure of the sky above earth is three-fold: the atmosphere, the sky of the luminaries, and paradise.[9] The problem is the interrelationship of these and their internal structures. Among Avestan texts the most succinct description of the universe is found in Yašt 12, a hymn dedicated to Rašnu the 'judge,' who is the helper of Mithra. Both ceaselessly transverse the universe to judge, to help the truthful, and to persecute the liars. Yašt 12 appears to be an appeal to Rašnu to come down for the juridical-priestly ceremony from wherever he happens to be. In calling him the various parts of the universe are enumerated. Even though this Yašt appears to be of rather late compilation, it nevertheless antedates the Middle Persian Bondaheš by far and evidently contains much that is ancient.[10]

STRUCTURE OF UNIVERSE ACCORDING TO YAŠT 12: THE PATH OF RAŠNU

37	*garō.dmāna*	house of praise
36	*ahu vahišta*	best existence
35	*anagra raoca*	endless (lit., 'without beginning') lights
34	*hvar/xvan*	sun
33	*māh*	moon
32	*spentō. mainyara*	stars of holy spirit
31	*urvaro.ciθra*	stars with seed/nature of plants
30	*zemas.ciθra*	stars with seed/nature of earth
29	*afš.ciθra*	stars with seed/nature of water
28	*haptōiringa*	Ursa Major (north)
27	*tištrya*	Sirius (east)
26	*vanant*	Vega (west)
25	*taēra* of *haraitī*, around which stars, moon, sun revolve	
24	golden mountain *hukairya*, waters of *Aredvī* pour down onto earth	
23	mountain-high *harā*, beyond which there is no night and across which comes the sun	
22	*kuva.cit*	anywhere on earth
21	*vīmaidya*	middle of earth
20	*karana*	edges of earth
19	*sanaka*	mouth of *Rahā*
18	*aoda*	source of *Rahā*
17	tree of *saēna*–bird with seeds of plants in the middle of *vourukaša*	
16	ocean *vourukaša* filling 2/3 of earth	
15	"this" continent *xvaniraθ*	
14	continent *vouru.jarštī*	(north-east)
13	continent *vouru.barštī*	(north-west)
12	continent *vīdad.afšū*	(south-west)
11	continent *fradad.afšū*	(south-east)
10	continent *savahī*	(west)
9	continent *arzahī*	(east)

The sequence of places mentioned proceeds from lower to higher, beginning with the 7 continents on the surface of earth and ending with the ultimate, *garō.dmāna* 'the house of praise (*or* songs).' As shown, we tentatively group the places in this way: A. paradise, B. the luminaries, C. the mountains, D. the waters, E. the continents. In the following we will treat C, B, and A, in that order.

The Mountains

According to Yt. 12, Rašnu, having passed over the continents and waters, reaches three mountains.

1. *Mt. harā/haraitī berezaiti* 'high *harā*, Alborz'
2. *Mt. hukairya* 'of good deed, beneficient'
3. *Mt. taēra* of *haraitī* 'the peak of *harā*'

It has generally been assumed that *taēra*, as the summit of *harā* in the center of the earth, is identical with *hukairya*. This is unlikely; if they were identical the two mountains would not have been mentioned separately in a succinct list like that of Yt. 12. Since *harā, hukairya*, and *taēra* are each termed *gari* 'mountain,' it has generally been assumed that they were conceived of as real mountains. It is, however, more likely that *gari* is used here as a technical term, or metaphor, for 'altitude, rise above earth'; the three *gari* would refer to divisions of the atmosphere, even though their names may also be those given to concrete mountains and ranges (cf. Gnoli 1980: 147–49).

Mt. *harā*

High *harā* is said to have been the first mountain around the Eastern and Western countries (Yt. 19: 1).[11] This description of *harā*, as well as passages which state that *behind* it there is no night (Yt. 12: 23; Yt. 10: 50) and that *across* it the god Mithra comes in the morning, reaching the mountain tops before the sun (Yt. 10: 12–13, 118; Vd. 21: 5), do not suggest a mountain, but rather the circle of the horizon as well as the lowest atmospheric layer above it, i.e., the first "rise" of the atmosphere above earth (for further discussion of *harā* see below).

Mt. *hukairya* with Mt. *ushendava* and "Lake" *urvaēsa*

The golden mountain *hukairya* 'the beneficent' is directly related to the atmospheric-hydrological cycle: the waters of the water deity *anāhitā aredvī sūrā* are said to pour down from *hukairya* through a thousand golden channels at the height of a thousand men, into the ocean *vouru.kaša* (Yt. 12: 24; 5: 3) and over all the lands. The Bondaheš is more specific: by heat the waters come up from the ocean, reach Mt. *hukairya*, and go on to flow into a 'lake' called *urvaēsa* on top of *hukairya* (Bh. 12: 17); from there they flow back, purified, and pour down through another "mountain," called *ushendava*, from the height of a thousand men (Bh. 9: 8; 10: 5).[12] There is thus a 'lake' on top of Mt. *hukairya* and another 'mountain' below it which have to be identified.

Mt. *ushendava* is described in Yt. 8: 32: waters rise out of the ocean *vouru.kaša* to form clouds around this mountain, which stands in the middle of the ocean. Various etymologies previously suggested only gradually approach the proper interpretation: *ushendava* is treated as a mountain somewhere in India (based on *hindu* 'Indus'), as a mountain 'beyond natural boundaries' (*hindu* 'natural boundary'; for a survey of scholarship cf. Boyce 1975: 136), or as the mountain 'rising out of the flood' (*hindu* 'flood, water'; Humbach 1960: 42 n. 11). The proper identification, however, appears not to be a mountain but an atmospheric layer of mists and clouds below *hukairya*, which rises out of the *hindu* 'waters, rivers.'

A similarly realistic interpretation and etymology are likely for the mysterious 'Lake' *urvaēsa* on top of Mt. *hukairya*: as its etymology implies, it is the *urvaēsa* 'vortex, turning point' (from the verb *urvaēs* 'turn, revolve'), i.e., the highest point of the hydrological cycle of the hemispheric atmosphere.

"Mount" *hukairya* of the beneficent rain-clouds must therefore represent the highest layer of the atmosphere, with the vortex *urvaēsa* as its high point, and the layer of "Mount" *ushendava* below it.

There is yet another lower layer, the bluish "lake" of mist and haze, *satavaēsa*, which is above the ocean (Bh. 10: 9; Vd. 5: 77). Since *ushendava* is said to be immediately below *hukairya*, "Lake" *satavaēsa* must be the atmospheric layer directly above the ocean and the earth, equivalent to Mt. *harā*, the first rise around and above the horizon.

The structure or layering of the atmosphere is thus as follows.

"Mount"	*hukairya* 'highest layer' with "Lake" *urvaēsa*
"Mount"	*ushendava* 'middle layer'
"Lake"/"Mount"	*satavaēsa/harā* 'lowest layer'

Yt. 12 does not mention *ushendava*; either this "mountain" was considered part of *hukairya* or it is implied by the location 'middle of the earth.' Similarly, "Lake" *urvaēsa* may be "hidden" in Yt. 12 as part of Mt. *hukairya* or behind Mt. *taēra* (cf. below), while "Lake" *satavaēsa* may be implied by Mt. *harā*.

Mt. *taēra*

Taēra, 'the peak of *harā*,' is reached by Rašnu after *hukairya*. Unlike the latter, *taēra* is explicitly related not to the hydrological cycle but to the luminaries. It is located at the center of the earth; around it revolve the stars, the moon, and the sun (Yt. 12: 25; Bh. 5B: 11; 9: 6). Again, it appears not to be a 'mountain' but the rise at, and above, the center of the atmospheric hemisphere (cf. also Brunner 1975: 20 n. 13), i.e., specifically the pole. As such it is the celestial equivalent of the central point of the atmosphere, *urvaēsa* 'the vortex.'[13]

The Luminaries

After passing through the atmosphere and *taēra*, Rašnu reaches the luminaries in the sky, first the stars, then the moon, and finally the sun.

The basic structure of the sky in Yt. 12 is thus triadic. However, the stars are further divided into what appear to be a 'lower' and a 'higher' set. Of these, the lower stars are further divided, again into triadic subsets, one subset of three stars/constellations[14] and another of three star groups, identified as having the nature or seed of three of the creations.

1. *vanant* 'Vega' in the constellation Lyra; *tištrya* 'Sirius' in Canis Major; and *haptōiringa* 'Ursa Major'
2. stars with the nature/seed of water, earth, and plants.

The triadic pattern of stars is also found elsewhere in Avestan texts. Thus Yt. 8: 12 not only repeats the triad of Vega, Sirius, and Ursa Major but includes as yet another triad a subset of assistants to Sirius: *tištryaēinī*, which is the constellation Canis Minor with its main star Procyon located to the East of Orion, and near Gemini; *paoiryaēinī*, the Pleiades in Taurus; and finally *upa.paorī*, the 'pre-Pleiades' (cf. Henning 1942: 247–48). While the identity of the last set of stars is not certain, the pattern Gemini-Taurus suggests that they are to be sought in or near Aries. The sequence implied by these "assistants" of Sirius would appear to be roughly

Aries-Taurus-Gemini, covering the first quarter of the year, and followed by their "master" Sirius, who is traditionally located in Cancer (cf. Brunner 1975: 2), which is the first constellation of summer and equivalent to the fourth month of the Zoroastrian year, named after Sirius (Avestan *tištrya*, Middle Persian *tīr* or *teštar-tīr*, Modern Persian *tir*).[15] Since Sirius is considered the bringer of rain it is likely that this sub-set of three stars/constellations preceding the rising of Sirius is identical with the group of 'stars of watery nature' mentioned in Yt. 12.

The Bondaheš largely agrees with the Avestan sources. It mentions the same sub-group of 'stars of watery nature' as found in Yt. 8: 12 (Bh. 7: 1; cf. Henning 1942: 247):

Yt. 8	*upa.paoirī*	*paoiryaēinī*	*tištryaeini*	*tištrya*
Bh.	*pēš parvēz*	*parvēz*	*tlyšk*	*tištar*
	"pre-Pleiades"	Pleiades	Canis Minor with Procyon	Canis Major with Sirius

The Bondaheš is also more specific as to the stars with the nature of the creations; stars with the nature of earth are Ursa Major and Polaris; and those with the nature of plants are all other stars, which by implication would include Vega. Thus the correlation between the two sets of lower stars in Yt. 12 may be as follows:

Sirius	:: stars with aquatic nature;[16]
Ursa Major	:: stars with terrestrial nature;
Vega	:: stars with herbal nature.

There is, however, a major difference between the star pattern of the Bondaheš and that of the Avestan passages cited. The Bondaheš lists not three but four major stars/constellations. Besides Sirius, Vega, and Ursa Major, the star-generals of the East, West, and North, respectively, it adds *satavaēsa* 'Antares' (or 'Fomalhaut?', cf. Brunner 1975: 16) as the general of the warm South (cf. "Lake" *satavaēsa* discussed above), and further *mēx-i gāh* 'Polaris' as the general of all stars.[17] This would seem to imply a shift from a basic triadic system in the Avestan sources to a tetradic system by the time of the Bondaheš.

The set of "lower" stars just discussed is collectively called in the Bondaheš (Bh. 2: 2) *spihr-i stārān-i axtarī* 'the sphere of the fixed stars/constellations,' while the set of 'higher' stars, i.e., of 'the stars of the holy spirit' in Yt. 12, is identified there (Bh. 2: 9) as the *spihr stārān-i agōmēzišnīh*, 'the sphere of the unmixable stars.' These higher stars are called 'unmixable' in the Bondaheš and other sources because they are said to have been created and put in place around the sky and the first level of stars after the attack of the forces of evil in order to prevent them from carrying their pollution higher up. Like the other stars they have a major 'general,' the *xwarr-i veh-dēn-i mazdāyasnān* 'the glory of the good-religion of the Mazdayasnians,' called in Avestan, *vahvi daēnā māzdayasnī* (Yt. 10: 68; 13: 94, and elsewhere). This 'glory' of the stars was identified by Henning (1942: 240) as the Milky Way, which is also called (Bh. 5B: 27) *rāh-i kay kayus*, i.e., the path of the legendary hero-king *kava Usan* (Modern Persian *key kāvus*). Arching over and across the hemisphere of the sky and over the band of the lower constellations of the zodiac, it is like a "girdle" around the stars and the sky, tying them together and reinforcing their protective power (cf. Bailey 1943: 142–48), as it stretches across them from Gemini/Taurus in the South-East of the sky to Scorpio/Sagittarius in the North-West.

The bright line of the Milky Way is thus exactly parallel, and opposed, to the 'dark' line across the sky of *gaociθra* 'the dragon,' i.e., the fictitious line between the two lunar nodes located in Gemini (head) and Scorpio (tail).[18]

Moon, Sun, and Endless Lights

The sequence of stars-moon-sun with the sun as the highest level of luminaries is the same in all sources. There remains, however, a problem with regard to the so-called *anagra raoca* 'endless lights' or 'lights without beginning,' which are reached by Rašnu after the sun. On the one hand, they appear to be part of the spiritual heaven, i.e., paradise, together with 'best existence' and 'the house of praise,' and thus removed from material existence. On the other hand, they appear to be of material nature since they revolve like the stars, moon, and sun, as is implied in Yt. 13: 56, which states that the *fravašis* provide the proper paths for the stars, moon, sun, *and* the endless lights.

There must therefore be both material and spiritual 'endless lights.' The question then is what are the material 'endless lights' and where are they to be located. Two explanations are possible, which imply two radically different cosmological views. On the one hand, it is possible that there was a cosmological theory which assumed a boundless open universe[19] with a bounded ordered center. In this case the sun-level would be the outermost level of the central world while the 'endless lights' would be beyond it without any observable source, thus *an-agra* 'without beginning (*or* source).' On the other hand, the cosmological theory may have assumed a closed universe. In that case the 'endless lights' cannot be located beyond the level of the sun but must be located *on* the same level as the sun. This would suggest that they should be understood as lights in the night sky which illuminate the level of the sun while the sun is gone. Within this cosmological theory the epithet *an-agra* would suggest lights which have no observable stellar origin or source.

Irrespective of which alternative is the proper one (see further below), the overall structure of the luminaries in both Yt. 12 and the Bondaheš is the same.

Yt. 12	Bh. 2
sun/endless lights moon	sun/endless lights moon
'stars of holy spirit'	'unmixable stars' with Milky Way
fixed stars (calendar)	fixed stars (zodiac, calendar)

At the same time, it is worth noticing that this structure of the material sky is parallel to the structure of the atmosphere described above.

atmosphere	sky
hukairya *ushendava* *Mt. harā* 'rise' (*harā* as horizon)	sun/endless lights moon girdle of 'stars of holy spirit' fixed stars, with constellations (horizon of sky, or ecliptic)

The Seeds of Creation

The list of luminaries in Yt. 12 reflects also the interrelationship of the luminaries with the material creations, the traditional sequence of which is sky/metals-water-earth-plants-animals-man, and fire.[20]

The relationship of three of these creations with luminaries is explicitly identified in Yt. 12: there are stars with the nature or seed of water, earth, and plants, exactly following the traditional sequence of these three creations. These relationships and the sequence are also explicit in the Bondaheš (Bh. 7: 1–4), which, as mentioned, identifies as aquatic the stars around Sirius, viz., Canis Minor, the Pleiades, and the 'pre-Pleiades' (together with two lunar mansions); as terrestrial stars Ursa Major and Polaris; and all other stars, or constellations, as herbal stars.

In addition, in Bh. 7: 5, 8, the moon and the sun are said to preserve the essence or seed of the ur-animal and ur-man, while fire is said to have been created or come from the 'endless lights' (Bh. 7: 5–9). The final correlation to be made then is, by analogy, that between the original sky of the stars and constellations and the 'stars of the holy spirit' or 'unmixable stars,' which are said to have been built around the sphere of the first created sky (Bh. 2: 9). The correlations are therefore as follows:

7th creation	fire	endless lights
6th creation	man	sun
5th creation	animals	moon
		stars of the holy spirit
4th creation	plants	herbal stars
3rd creation	earth	terrestrial stars
2nd creation	water	aquatic stars
1st creation	sky	lower constellations/stars

Yt. 12 explicitly identifies only the 2nd through 4th creations as correlated to luminaries; nevertheless the fact that it lists *seven* sets of luminaries may implicitly reflect what is fully explicit in the Bondaheš, the notion of seven material/spiritual *celestial* 'guardians' of the primary essence of the material creations, intermediary to the seven *heavenly* spiritual guardians, i.e., the six holy immortals and the holy spirit.

Heaven-Paradise

The highest levels reached by Rašnu in Yt. 12 are the spiritual levels of heaven or paradise, the triad (from below) of the *anagra raoca* 'endless lights,' the central level of *vahišta ahu* 'best existence' (from which Modern Persian *behešt* 'paradise'), and finally *garō.dmāna* 'the house of praise.'

These realms are the bright shining abodes of the blessed, offering the highest state of eternal bliss, of *urvāzā* 'joy, eternal happiness' which is to be seen and recognized in the *raoca* 'the (endless) lights,' as Zarathushtra promises in the first stanza of the fundamental Yasna, Yasna 30; in Y. 30: 2 he refers to *vahištā* and its *sūcā* 'brightness,' and in Y. 30: 4 promises the *vahišta ahu* of *vohu manah*, 'good mind,' the leader of the six holy immortals.[21] Similarly, Ahura Mazda will show the soul of the just *urvāsman* in *vahišta ahu*.[22]

These abodes are ablaze like the sun. Ahura Mazda, who is allied with the holy immortals, foremost among them 'good mind,' is the good companion of *xvanvant aša* 'sun-like truth' (Y. 32: 2); he is asked to grant Zarathushtra's daughter, who is being married, the *xvanvant* 'sun-like' gain of 'good mind' (Y. 53: 4). The abodes were created by Ahura Mazda for the souls of the blessed[23] (Yt. 3: 2–3), the holy immortals and other divine entities. Therefore the souls of the blessed are said to go to the *vahištem ahum ašaonąm raocanhem vispō.xwāθrem* 'the best existence of the just, the bright providing all happiness' (Y. 16: 7; Yt. 12: 30; 9: 19; 62: 6)[24] as well as to the highest level, to the *garō.dmāna*, where praises and songs for Ahura Mazda are deposited (Y. 45: 8), a task which is performed by Mithra in later Zoroastrianism (Yt. 10: 32). Ahura Mazda is and will be the first to come here, which is the prize promised by Zarathushtra (Y. 51: 15); here is the sacrosanctum, his *asīšti* 'throne' (Insler 1975: 246), where he dwells with 'good mind' and 'truth' (Y. 44: 9) and the other holy immortals (Y. 50: 4; cf. Vd. 19: 32–36). According to the Yašt to Mithra, even Ahura Mazda venerates the latter in this *raoxšna* 'shining' house and out of here Mithra comes with his star-decked chariot (Yt. 10: 123–24).

Since light pervades all three levels, the notion of *(anagra) raoca* '(endless) lights' would thus appear to refer to, and include, the entirety of the levels, constituting both the base and the hemispheric copula, so to speak, of the spiritual sky, i.e., paradise. *Garō.dmāna*, on the other hand, appears to be the highest level within this hemisphere, so that *vahišta ahu*, while also describing the totality of bliss, would constitute the middle level, as in Yt. 12.

The Path to Paradise

For the *ašavan* 'the just, righteous' there is *hu-īti* 'a path of easy access' to the *hu-šiti* 'good dwelling places' in the 'best existence' of the 'good mind,' but *an-īti* 'no access' for the adherents of evil, for whom there will be *acišta ahu* 'the worst existence, hell' (Y. 30: 11). The same is expressed in Yt. 3: 3, which states that with the pronouncement of 'best truth,' the holy immortals will provide the path to *vahišta ahu* 'best existence,' protected by good thoughts, words, and deeds, a place only for the *ašavan* 'the just' (cf. AV Chap. 11).

The triad 'good thought, good words, good deeds,' mentioned in Yašt 3 in connection with the path to paradise, appears to refer to the steps of access to paradise to be taken by the soul after crossing the *cinvatō peretu* 'the bridge of the divider, judge' (Y. 46: 10). The three steps of *humata* 'good thoughts,' of *hūxta* 'good words,' and of *hvaršta* 'good deeds' finally lead the soul with a fourth step into the *anagra raoca* 'endless lights' (Hadoxt Nask 2: 15).

In addition, there is a preliminary step into *misvānām gātu* (Middle Persian *hamestagān*), the level of the mixed, the limbus for those whose good and evil actions are equal. It is reached by the soul immediately after crossing the Bridge (Y. 33: 1; cf. Boyce 1975: 237–44; Gignoux 1968; Klingenschmitt 1972).

The Location of Pre-Paradise

It cannot be a coincidence that the pattern of these steps through the ante-rooms to ultimate paradise (cf. Bartholomae 1904: 1819) is identical with that of both the material sky and paradise.

	Sky	Steps	Paradise
3	sun/endless lights	deeds	*garō.dmāna* 'house of praise'
2	moon	words	*vahišta ahu* 'best existence'
1	stars of holy spirit	thoughts	*anagra raoca* 'endless lights'
0	fixed stars	good/evil balanced	

Given this correspondence in pattern the question is where to locate these ante-rooms. They evidently represent the spiritual levels, since the Bridge leads from the material into the spiritual form of existence; they cannot be in ultimate paradise, nor can they be in the material sky. Yt. 12 does not give a clue. If there was the notion at that time of preliminary steps, they are not mentioned. The Vidēvdāt (19: 36) mentions only two sections, the *misvānām gātu* 'the place of the mixed' and *garō.dmāna* 'the house of praise,' apparently identifying the preliminary levels as a whole with the mixed, i.e., preliminary state, and the levels of the highest paradise summarily as 'house of praise.'

The 'house of praise' is also the highest (set of) levels in the late Pahlavi Rivayat (Chap. 23: 13); it is reached after the three steps of good thoughts, words, and deeds. There the three steps are equated with the levels of the material luminaries, viz., the stars, the moon, and the sun, respectively, and were thus considered to be correspondents to the levels of the material sky, located there spiritually. In fact, the Bondaheš not only offers the same equation between the level of the material sun/endless lights with the sun-level of the soul, and of the material moon-level with the moon-level of the soul; it also calls them 'house of praise' and 'best existence,' respectively, i.e., the terms elsewhere used for ultimate paradise. Having thus exhausted, so to speak, the traditional terminology, the levels above are termed 'throne of the holy immortals,' which is attached to 'the endless lights' where is found the 'throne of Ahura Mazda.'[25]

The material luminaries were considered not only the repositories of the seed and substance of the creations but also the 'astral' places of the souls, as shown in the following chart.

	Yt. 12	Spiritual/material*	Spiritual
III	house of praise best existence endless lights		throne of Ahura Mazda throne of holy immortals endless lights
II	sun/endless lights moon stars of holy spirit fixed stars	sun/endless lights moon unmixable stars fixed stars	house of praise = endless lights best existence (good thoughts) level of mixed stars
I	atmosphere	atmosphere	

*Bh. 3: 7; 28: 17

The overall structure is triadic; atmosphere, sky, paradise. But material and spiritual existences interlock: the material world above earth consists of two parts, the atmosphere and *material* sky, while the spiritual world consists of two parts, the pre-paradise of the *spiritual* sky and ultimate paradise.[26] Given this interlocking structure, the problem is where to locate the Bridge between the material and spiritual worlds. In order to do so, it is necessary to review the concept of *harā*.

harā

harā, the first mountain to grow around earth (Yt. 19: 1), across which Mithra comes before the sun reaches the mountain tops (Yt. 10: 12–13; 118) and beyond which there is no night, mist, or wind (Yt. 10: 50; 12: 23), was identified above as both the horizon and the first rise of the atmosphere. The term, however, is more inclusive.

The Bondaheš states that *harā*, after an initial rise of 18 years, rises further in four stages to the levels of the stars, moon, and sun, and finally to the highest height of the sky, each stage taking 200 years, for a total of 800 years (Bh. 9: 2). That *harā* reaches beyond the sun is also evidenced by Yt. 10: 50–51, which mentions that Ahura Mazda and the holy immortals built an abode for Mithra in the 'house of praise' above (*upairi*) high *harā*, in harmony with the sun (*hvare.hazaoša*), from which Mithra watches the material world. As Gershevitch (1967: 205) has suggested, *harā* as "the highest mountain on earth is also the nearest peak on which to step down [i.e., from the house of praise in paradise]. From an *anticephalic* (as against *antipodean*) point of view the *harā* may be considered the upside down *bālā-xāna* or watchtower of Mithra's heavenly *palace*."

Thus, while on the one hand the sun rises above *harā*, on the other hand, *harā* rises above the sun, i.e., to the top of the sun level. These two statements need not contradict each other,[27] once it is realized that *harā* is not a mountain but the rise and radial expansion of the sky above earth. As such it is all inclusive: it is the boundary around the entire hemisphere of the sky, that inverse celestial bowl, the lowest part and rim of which is also *harā* as horizon.

It is here that divine beings coming out of ultimate paradise cross over into or onto the highest level of 'middle' world, viz., the level of the sun/endless lights, where the divine *haoma* first placed the spiritually fashioned, star-decked *haoma*-stalk whose well-grown body was praised by Ahura Mazda and the holy immortals (Yt. 13: 90); here the holy immortals 'good mind' and *aša* 'truth' formed the *haoma*-stalk within which Zarathushtra's *fravaši* was set and then brought from the endless lights down to earth.[28] From here Haoma's priestly voice reaches *us*, i.e., up to (or out of) the lights and down around the earth and the seven continents (Yt. 10: 82). Here *haoma* is indeed *barezištē paiti barezahi haraiθyō paiti barezayå yaṭ vaocē hūkairīm nāma* 'on the highest height of *haraiti*, the high, which is (also) called *hukairya* by name (Yt. 10: 88).

As this passage indicates, this level of the sun/endless lights first reached by the divine is also called *hukairya* 'beneficent.' That, however, is also the name of the corresponding highest level of the atmosphere, a correspondence also implied when it is said that, after the freeing of the waters by *tištrya* 'Sirius,' the clouds move from the west on the path of *haoma* (Yt. 8: 33), i.e., on the atmospheric *hukairya*. Thus just as the 'highest height' of *harā* is the boundary between the outer sphere of paradise and the highest sun-level *hukairya* of the inner sphere of the sky of the luminaries, so there is a lower *harā*, the boundary between the sphere of the luminaries and the highest level *hukairya* of the atmosphere.[29]

The Bridge

The idea of the eschatological *cinvatō peretu* 'the bridge (*or* ford) of the separator' is repeatedly mentioned by Zarathushtra (e.g., Y. 46: 10–11; 51: 13). Elsewhere, the souls of the deceased as said to go up above *harā*, above the Bridge (Vd. 19: 30). Its base, according to the Bondaheš, is on the *cagād-i dāidīg* 'the lawful summit,' which is 100 men high, the place of the judgment of the souls (Bh. 9: 9; cf. Boyce 1975: 137). That place is at the base of *harā*, while the other end of the Bridge is at the highest (*bālest*) part of *harā* (Bh. 30: 22). The summit itself is said to be in the middle of the world (*miyān-i gēhān*; Bh. 9: 9). The term 'middle' suggests two locations: either the vertical middle of the earth, the zenith, or its horizontal middle, i.e., the middle between the upper hemisphere of light and the lower hemisphere of darkness. The fact that the souls of the just move *up* from that summit to the pre-paradises while the souls of the sinners fall *down* from there into the abyss of the corresponding pre-infernos (Hadoxt Nask 33–36; Gignoux 1968) indicates that the Bridge must be horizontal, i.e., from the horizon *harā* of the material world to the other side of *harā* in the spiritual world (from where the souls of the just rise, with the sun, to the spiritual abodes of their merit) (cf. Boyce 1975: 237). The direction of the Bridge is most likely due east, as the judgment and passage happen at sun-rise on the fourth day after death.

The other side of *harā* reached by the souls of the just cannot be the 'highest height' of *harā* since many souls will remain on one of the levels of the spiritual sky and will not reach ultimate paradise. Therefore, the *harā* immediately opposite the material *harā* must be the boundary of the lowest level of the bowl of the spiritual sky at horizon level.

The Fortess and the Two Watchposts

According to the Bondaheš, the spirit of the sky like a gallant warrior withstood the first onslaught of the evil spirit until Ahura Mazda made a stronger *drubuštih* 'fortress' around it. This 'fortress' is defended by the myriads of *fravašis* posed around it.[30] It is further fortified by a 'girdle,' the spiritually fashioned, star-decked 'good religion of the Mazdayasnians' (Y. 9: 26; Bh. 2: 9), i.e., the 'unmixable stars' or 'stars of the holy-spirit,' which make up the Milky Way.

This 'fortress' then must be around the lower stars and thus the lower *harā*.[31] In Middle Persian it is called *ahravān āgāhīh* which should be understood not as 'knowledge of the righteous' (Bailey 1940: 145) but as the 'watchpost' (*āgāh* 'aware, watching') 'of the just,' and thus as a rendering of Avestan *harā*, which indeed means 'watchpost.' The 'fortress' of the *fravašis* above the atmosphere then is identical with the *harā* 'watchpost' mentioned in Yt. 13: 59–60, 65, where they were positioned by the holy spirit (Yt. 13: 29) and from which they watch Ursa Major and the ocean *vourukaša*, waiting for the waters to flow again so that they can distribute them to the living members of their families. It is the *barešnu* 'height' of the sky from where they, the *upairi.kairya* 'those who act from above,' come down to their families at spring-equinox, the beginning of the new year (Yt. 13: 42), or rush down, whenever invoked, like arrows (just as did *tištrya* 'Sirius' to fight the demon of drought at the shores of ocean *vourukaša*, Yt. 8). The *fravašis* from their watchpost thus trap the forces of evil inside the boundary of the material world while at the same time being the foremost spiritual array protecting the souls of the just in pre-paradise and ultimately in paradise. And while the material stars are subject to the effects of the evil stars, i.e., the planets (cf. Bh. 5: 12), *they* are not.

Just as this lower *harā* is the watchpost of the *fravašis*, so the higher *harā* is the watchpost of Mithra, the holy immortals and the other holiest ones, from which they survey the entire spiritual and material world below. Here the souls of the most perfect just enter with their fourth step and are received by *vohu manah* 'good mind,' the doorkeeper of paradise, passing gladly on to the golden thrones of Ahura Mazda and the holy immortals in 'the house of songs' (Vd. 19: 31–32).

Gathic Evidence

It has been the standard view that the concept of the *fravaši*, as opposed to *urvan* 'soul,' developed after Zarathushtra, if shortly after him; the term is first mentioned in the "Yasna of the Seven Chapters," which is inserted in the midst of the Gathas (Y. 35–42) and is considered the earliest post-Zarathushtrian Zoroastrian(ized) text (cf. Boyce 1975: 203–5). A specific cosmological function of the *fravašis*, not mentioned yet, is their primordial choice, their electing to work for the world of *aša* 'truth' and Ahura Mazda. This choice, made at the beginning of the world, specifically prior to material creation, is concomitant with the primordial choice of the holy spirit and the evil spirit between life and non-life. The *fravašis* thus become essential agents in the preservation of the material world (cf. Yt. 13: 76; Bh. 3: 23–24; cf. also Boyce 1975: 127–28; and Windfuhr forthcoming).

The concept of *fravašis* and both their primordial choice and their 'fortress,' are, I submit, already implied in the fifth stanza of Y. 30.

ayå manivå varatā	*yę̄ drę̄gvå acišta vę̄rę̄zyō*
ašę̄m mainyuš spę̄ništō	*yę̄ xraoždištę̄ng asę̄nō vastē*
yaēcā xšnaošen ahurę̄m	*haiθyāiš šyaoθanāiš fraorę̄t mazdą̄m*

> Of these two spirits, the deceitful one chose to realize the worst. But the holiest spirit, who has clothed himself with the firmament/firmest heaven, chose the truth; so did/do those who satisfy the wise lord foremost with true/real deeds. (Y. 30: 5, cf. Insler 1975: 33)

The phrase *yaēcā xšnaošen ahurę̄m/haiθyāiš šyaoθanāiš fraorę̄t mazdą̄m* 'those who satisfy the wise lord foremost with their true/real deeds' would seem to refer to either the holy immortals or the *fravašis* of the *ašavans* 'the truth-ful' since man had not been created yet. The firmament/firmest heaven reflects one or both of the 'fortresses' around the sky. Finally, while *fraoret* here, as elsewhere, appears to be adverbial, 'foremost,' it may nevertheless be related to the etymon(s) for *fravaši* (cf. note 3) and thus anticipate the term, in spite of Insler's insistence on the translation 'continuously' (1975: 167).

Material and Spiritual Lights

The suggested correlation between the celestial boundaries and spiritual 'watchposts' is thus:

	material level	spiritual watchpost of
higher:	sun/endless lights	holy immortals, Mithra, etc.
lower:	constellations, zodiac	*fravašis*

As mentioned above, between the two, girding them and the sky, is the Milky Way, which is both material and spiritual; in it are 'stars of the holy spirit,' or 'unmixable stars,' and its spiritual epitome is the 'glory of the good religion of the Mazdayasnians.'

It was tentatively suggested above that the *anagra raoca* 'endless lights' may refer to nocturnal luminary phenomena on the level of the sun, which do not have any observable stellar source. Such lights do indeed exist: the zodiacal light and the Gegenschein or counterglow.[32] The latter is an "oval patch of faint luminosity" about 8° long and 6° wide exactly opposite the sun in the night sky; it moves along the same path as the sun, and is oriented with the sun, six months earlier and six months later. The counterglow is part of a more comprehensive phenomenon, the zodiacal light, so called because it is most visible in the region of the constellations and the zodiac. It appears after twilight in the west and before dawn in the east as a band of light above the horizon, and it extends upward to the sun's position, where it appears as the counterglow. In northern mid latitudes it is at its brightest during March and April after sunset and during September and October before dawn, i.e., around the equinoxes; it is partially (and in its higher parts totally) lost in or merged with the light of the Milky Way in summer and winter. This light is thought to result from the scattering and reflection of sunlight by interstellar dust particles.

These luminous phenomena may be the material source of the 'spiritual lights' and the *xvarena* 'light-glory' of the divine beings who occupy these regions, specifically the heroic *fravašis* and the mighty deity Mithra, who in the morning brings into existence the many shapes, who is endowed with his own light like the moon, whose face blazes like Sirius (Yt. 10: 142–43), whose one-wheeled chariot (Yt. 10: 136)[33] is on the sun's path and thus on the path of the endless lights, which do not seem to have a stellar origin. Mithra would truly be the watchful representative and nightly reflexion of the sun. This correlation would be supported by the fact that the zodiacal light is brightest around the spring and fall equinoxes, which coincide with the months called *fravartinām* 'the *fravašis*'' and *miθra(hya)* 'Mithra's' respectively; during summer and winter this light is absorbed by that of the girdle of the Milky Way, i.e., the 'stars of the holy spirit' and the 'glory of the good' Zoroastrian religion, spiritually encompassing the cosmic universe.

In this context mention should be made of another spectacular phenomenon, the noctilucent clouds. Still little understood, these are thought to be caused by the penetration of interplanetary dust particles into the atmosphere. Such clouds, forming a band some kilometers thick at an height of 82 kilometers, can be distinguished from regular clouds only when observed against the dark sky and illuminated by the sun below the horizon, after the remainder of the sky has already become dark. This phenomenon, which takes place inside the atmosphere, could also be the luminous source of the entering, by the *fravašis* and other divine beings, of the atmosphere before and after sunset.

If these interpretations prove correct, then Avestan observers must have made the distinction between light emanating from stellar sources and lights without such observable source.[34] The latter were interpreted as the visible appearance of spiritual beings, as the spiritual counterpart to the material sky, and thus of paradise.

Conclusion

Harā 'the protective shell and horizon around the sky' has to be seen in direct correlation with *hāra*, 'protecting, caring,' derived from the same root. *Hāra* is mentioned repeatedly by Zarathushtra. To be *hāra* 'caring and watching,' to defend and attack, are mutual responsibilities of human and divine beings. Zarathushtra says:

yā frasā āvišyā *yā vā mazdā pərəsaitē tayā*
yē vā kasēuš aēnaŋho *ā mazištąm (a)yamaitē būjim*
tā cašməng θwisrā hārō *aibi aša (aibi-) vaēnahī vīspā*

> What is counseled openly or what is deliberated secretly; which one is guilty of a small offense or which one will receive a major punishment: you, O Mazda, see them all through 'truth,' *hāra* 'watching/as a guardian' with the brightness of your eye. (Y. 31: 13; cf. Insler 1975: 41)

The phenomenal is not outward reality but a logically necessary correlate to inward reality. Just as both divine and human beings are in constant dialog with each other (cf. Windfuhr forthcoming), so human beings watch over each other, and divine beings watch over humans; all are part of the reasoned dialectic process of the world. The eschatologically intricate interdependence between outward cosmological and inward ethical aspects, both of which merge in the spiritual, is eloquently expressed in the very problematical second stanza of the extensive 'cosmological' Yasna 44 (cf. the widely differing translations by Humbach 1959 I: 116 and Insler 1975: 67). This stanza can only be understood properly, it seems to me, when its cosmological aspects are recognized (all the more so since this stanza is immediately followed by questions about the cause of the *ząθa* 'birth' of the world and the orderly paths of the luminaries).

kaθā aŋhēuš *vahištahyā paourvīm*
kaθē sūidyāi *yē ī paitišāt̰*
hvō zī ašā *spəntō irixtəm vispōibyō*
hārō mainyū *ahūm.biš urvaθō mazdā*

> How (is/was) the beginning of the 'best existence'? The one who in loving care (initially) sets these two (spheres/worlds) in motion for them all to be saved through his 'truth/the cosmos,' he is indeed the holy *harā* 'guardian' at *irixtem* 'the end'[35] (*or* 'of the heritage'), the friend who heals the world through his (holy) spirit, O Mazda (Y. 44: 2).

The two fortresses and guardian spheres, that of the *fravašis*, mankind's protective and prototypical highest part and that of the holy immortals, the universe's and mankind's highest powers, principles, and spiritual states,[36] would thus seem to be the luminous celestial and cosmological correlate to man's inner 'fortress of reason,' which is the Zoroastrian *daēnā* 'religion, vision and conscience,' whence he charges against the irrational fury of the phantasmagoria of the evil spirit, the LIE.

Notes

1. I would like to express my thanks here to the Near Eastern Center of the University of Arizona, Tucson for offering me the opportunity to present an earlier version of these notes, and to my students and colleagues of the Department of Near Eastern Studies at Michigan for their many comments on an earlier presentation at a departmental colloquium.

2. Cf. Boyce 1975: 131. Boyce 1975 provides the latest and most comprehensive survey and interpretation of Zoroastrian cosmology, beliefs, and customs, a major achievement in understanding Zoroastrianism, primarily from within, while adducing ample comparative data from Indian and other traditions.

3. For a detailed discussion of the concept and functions of *fravaši*, see Boyce 1975: 117–29. The etymology of this feminine noun, from **fra-var-ti*, has been much debated, since there are many roots *var*, with different meanings. It is not impossible that the term was intentionally ambi- or multivalent; so one could suggest, with reference to the Zoroastrian triad 'good thoughts, good words, good deeds,' that relevant etyma include a. *ver-* 'choose', or *vel-* 'want, choose, prefer'; b. *ver-* 'speak solemnly'; and c. *ver* 'watch' or *ver* 'protect'; thus the word means first or foremost a. choice or preference, b. promise or oath, c. protection; these together describe the highest and foremost spiritual part and quintessence of man.

4. For this distinction, see Bailey 1943: 120 and Boyce 1975: 144.

5. Some recent observations along these lines are made in Windfuhr forthcoming.

6. On the extent of Zoroastrian literature, cf. Gershevitch 1968 and Boyce 1968. The following abbreviations are used here; convenient translations or sources added in parentheses.

principal Avestan texts
Y. = Yasna (Gathas = Y. 28–34, 43–51, 53: Humbach 1959, Insler 1975; remainder: Mills 1887)
Yt. = Yašt (Lommel 1927)
Vd. = Vidēvdāt (Darmesteter 1880, 1883)
Hadoxt Nask (*idem*)

major Middle Persian texts
Bh. = (Greater) Bondaheš (B. Anklesaria 1956)
Dd. = Dādestān-i Dēnīg (T. Anklesaria, no date)
Mx. = Mēnōg-i Xrad (West 1871)
AV = Ardā Virāz Nāmag (Jamaspi-Asa and Haug 1872)
Pahlavi Rivayat (Anklesaria 1969)

7. On the intricate relationship between the spiritual and material aspects, cf. Shaked 1971.

8. On the expansion of the world-year from 6,000 to 12,000 years, cf. Boyce 1975: 286.

9. Comparisons with other cosmological systems, especially the closely related Vedic-Indic tradition (cf. Kirfel 1920 and more recently Gonda 1966) will be discussed in a subsequent study.

10. Cf. Lommel 1927: 95–101; Humbach (1960: 42 n. 12), however, argues convincingly for the relative independence of this yašt from other sources. An observation by Boyce (1970: 522) suggests that final changes in the Avestan text may have been made as late as Sasanian times.

11. It is also believed to be identical with yet another mountain, *cagād-i dāidīg* (cf. Boyce 1975: 137; Gnoli 1980: 148). Besides *harā* there appear to have been two more rings of mountains concentric with it (Yt. 19: 1).

12. In order to avoid confusion for the non-specialist terms will usually be given here in their Avestan form, even in citing Middle Persian passages.

13. *taēra* is also said to be the cause of the day-night cycle (Bh. 5B:11) and to be the mountain into which the stars, the moon and the sun go and from which they emerge again (Bh. 9: 6). These statements do not necessarily contradict the interpetation of *taēra* as the pole (as will be discussed in a forthcoming study).

14. The correlation between the modern constellations given here and ancient constellations is a little researched subject. Moreover, the names of constellations and their principal stars seem to have been used interchangeably. The identification of several of the stars is still debated, although *tištrya* 'Sirius' and *haptōiringa* 'Ursa Major' are quite certain (cf. Henning 1942).

15. It is therefore likely that the set of lower stars is based on the division of the year into 12

months and six seasonal festivals (to be discussed in a forthcoming study). The designation *tēr/tīr* for this month has been puzzling (cf. Boyce 1975: 75–76). Rather than looking for a deity *tir*, I would suggest as the original base for the month name *tištryahya taēra* 'the heliacal rise *(taēra)* of Sirius,' which fell on July 20 between 800 B.C.E. and 400 C.E. (cf. van der Waeren 1968: 244).

16. However, in Bh. 5B: 14 Sirius is said to be of 'airy' nature; air is not an 'element' traditional in Zoroastrianism and this reference reflects the later fourfold concept of elementary states.

17. Henning (1942: 242) suggested that the Avestan term *merezu* 'neck, vertebra,' occurring once evidently with cosmological connotations, in Vd. 19: 42, may be an Avestan rendering of the Greek notion of *pólos* 'pole, axis.' Bartholomae (1904: 1174) had already suggested that this passage may refer to a constellation, and he grammatically recognized *merezu* as a dual; it is indeed possible to see here a reference to the zenith and the nadir of the polar axis.

18. For this 'dragon' cf. Hartner 1938. For the 'evil' planetary oppositions to the 'good' fixed stars and constellations in Zoroastrianism, cf. Mackenzie 1968 and especially Brunner 1975, who plotted these oppositions in detail on a planispherical sky-map.

19. Cf. Needham and Wang 1959: 219–20 for similar views in some schools in China.

20. In this sequence, the position of 'fire,' which permeates all creations, is not quite clear; cf. Boyce 1975: 140–48.

21. These terms in Y. 30 have generally not been interpreted as referring to 'spatial' cosmology but rather as references to less 'concrete' spiritual aspects of Zarathushtra's message (cf., e.g., the translations by Humbach 1959 I: 116 and Insler 1975: 67).

22. According to the late Pursišnihā # 38, Darmesteter 1893 III: 53. This abode of happiness and songs, perhaps even through the etymology of the term, may, if remotely, be related to the enigmatic Greek 'plains of *ēlysion*.'

23. While there is a seeming overlap between *urvan* 'soul' and *fravaši*, Boyce 1975: 129 has shown that they were indeed conceived of as different aspects, or parts, of man.

24. Cf. the virtually literal Middle Persian rendering of this phrase in AV, Chap. 15: 10, *pahlom axvān-i ahlavān-i rōšn-i hamāg-xvārīh*.

25. The position of the 'endless lights' in the passages of the Bondaheš is not clear; it shifts from the sun-level to the level above it or is listed twice (cf. Bh. 3: 7, 28–17). For these levels in other later sources cf. Gignoux 1968.

26. Yt. 12 leaves two important questions open: first, whether at that time there existed the notion of preliminary steps; second, if it did exist, where were the steps? There are two possible locations; either they coincided with the levels of the sky, as in the other texts, or they were conceived of as the lowest part of the ultimate paradise.

On the 'level of the mixed,' see also Klingenschmitt 1972.

27. As assumed, e.g., by Mackenzie 1964: 519 n. 43.

28. For this myth, cf. Boyce 1975: 278.

29. Excluded from discussion here is the concept of *vayu* 'void, ether' (or similar interpretations), which will be discussed in another context.

30. For a detailed discussion of the fortress, see Bailey 1942: 142–48.

31. Just as this fortress in Middle Persian is named *drubuštih*, which in Avestan would be **druva paršta* 'strong backing,' so the *fravašis* themselves are called *paršta* 'backers' when protecting the heroes and believers down on earth (e.g., Yt. 13: 71).

32. I would like to thank Dr. Günther Elste, professor in the Department of Astronomy, University of Michigan, for suggesting these phenomena as lights 'which are not stars but related to the sun and zodiac.' Among many studies, see Roach and Gordon 1973 (photographs pp. X, 43). In fact, the identification of these phenomena suggested here would imply the earliest documented references to them; Zinner (1931: 500) mentions as the earliest date otherwise 1730 C.E. The relation between celestial phenomena and heroic saga in Iranian (for Indic cf. Mukherji 1905) needs a thorough review.

33. For a translation, with extensive discussion, of the *yašt* to Mithra see Gershevitch 1957; on the God specifically, pp. 35, 281, 289, 293, *et passim*; Boyce 1975: 47–52 *et passim*; Insler (1978) discusses Mithraic iconography, suggesting a correlation with the signs of the zodiac.

34. The Bondaheš remarks that the unmixable stars lack the computations of the other stars (Bh. 2: 9; cf. Henning 1942: 240). Henning also suggested that this 'higher' set of luminaries was the result of a later artificial split-up of an assumed original single set of stars, created in order to fill out a seven layer sky, under Babylonian influence (1942: 239). The evidence here, however, suggests that the two

sets must be part of the original system.

35. This passage may also refer to the final apocalyptical melting and purification of the material world (Bh. 34: 31; cf. Boyce 1975: 243–45).

36. *Harā*, the place of the watch, and *hāra*, the beneficent beings who do the watching, both derive from the Avestan verb *har(-u-)* 'watch, protect.' This, in turn, derives from the Indo-European root *ser(-u)-*. Etymologically, and remotely perhaps even conceptually, these two terms are thus related to Latin *ser-u-are* 'serve, guard' and more directly to Zeus' wife *hēra* 'the protectress' as well as to the Greek *hērōēs* 'protectors, heroes,' a term which originally may have been the designation for the protective spirits of the land (cf. Pokorny 1948 I: 910); accordingly the original Greek *hērōēs* may, however distantly, reflect a cosmological function similar to that of the Iranian *fravašis*. It should be noted that the etymologies of the Greek terms are disputed.

References

B. T. Anklesaria
1956 *Zand Ākāsīh, Iranian or Greater Bundahišn*. Bombay.
1957 *Zand-ī Vohūman Yasn*. Bombay.
1964 *Vichitakika-i Zatsparam*. Bombay.
1969 *The Pahlavi Rivayāt of Aturfarnbag and Farnbag-Sroš*. Ed. K. M. Jamaspji-Asa. Bombay.

T. D. Anklesaria
1908 *The Būndahishn*. Bombay.
no date *Dātistān-ī Dīnīk*. Part I. Bombay.

H. W. Bailey
1943 *Zoroastrian Problems in the Ninth-Century Books*. Oxford: Clarendon. Rpt. 1971.

C. Bartholomae
1904 *Altiranisches Wörterbuch*. Strassburg: Trübner. Rpt. 1961.

M. Boyce
1968 Middle Persian Literature. Pp. 32–66 in *Iranistik. Literatur*. Handbuch der Orientalistik 1.4.2.1. Leiden: Brill.
1970 On the Calendar of Zoroastrian Feasts. *Bulletin of the School of Oriental and African Studies* 33: 513–39.
1975 *A History of Zoroastrianism*. Vol. 1. Handbuch der Orientalistik 1.8.1.2.2A. Leiden: Brill.

C. Brunner
1975 The "Flights of the Sun" in Zoroastrian Eschatology. Paper delivered to the American Oriental Society, 23 April 1975.

J. Darmesteter
1880/83 *The Zend-Avesta*. Oxford: Oxford University Press. Rpt. 1965.
1892/93 *Le Zend-Avesta*. Annales du Musée Guimet. Paris.

I. Gershevitch
1967 *The Avestan Hymn to Mithra*. University of Cambridge Oriental Publications 4. Cambridge: Cambridge University Press. Originally 1959.
1968 Old Iranian Literature. Pp. 1–30 in *Iranistik. Literatur*. Handbuch der Orientalistik 1.4.2.1. Leiden: Brill.

P. Gignoux
1968 L'enfer et le paradis d'aprés les sources pehlevies. *Journal asiatique* 256: 219–45.

P. Gnoli
1980 *Zoroaster's Time and Homeland*. Seminario di studi asiatici/Series minor 7. Naples: Istituto Universitario Orientale.

J. Gonda
1966 *Loka — World and Heaven in the Veda*. Verhandelingen der Koninklijke Nederlandse Akademie van Wetenschappen, Afd. Letterkunde NR 73 # 1. Amsterdam: North-Holland Publishing.

W. B. Henning
1942 An Astronomical Chapter of the Bundahishn. *Journal of the Royal Asiatic Society* 1942/3–4: 229–48.

H. Humbach
1959 *Die Gathas des Zarathustra*. Heidelberg: Winter.
1960 Die awestische Länderliste. *Wiener Zeitschrift für die Kunde Süd- und Ostasiens* 4: 36–46.

S. Insler
1975 *The Gāthās of Zarathustra*. Acta Iranica 8. Leiden and Tehran: Brill and Bibliothèque Pahlavi.
1978 A New Interpretation of the Bull-Slaying Motif. Vol. 2, pp. 519–38 in *Hommages à Maarten J. Vermaseren*, ed. M. B. de Boer and T. A. Edridge. Leiden: Brill.

D. H. Jamaspji-Asa and M. Haug (after E. W. West)
1872 *The Book of Arda Viraf*. Rpt. 1971. Amsterdam: Oriental Press.

W. Kirfel
1920 *Die Kosmographie der Inder nach den Quellen dargestellt*. Bonn: Dümmler.

G. Klingenschmitt
1972 Avestisch *hę̄miiāsāitē* und Pahlavi *hmystk'n'*. *Münchener Studien zur Sprachwissenschaft* 30: 79–82.

H. Lommel
1927 *Die Yäšt's des Awesta*. Göttingen: Vandenhoeck und Rupprecht.
1930 *Die Religion Zarathustra nach dem Awesta dargestellt*. Tübingen: Mohr.

D. N. Mackenzie
1964 Zoroastrian Astrology in the *Bundahišn*. *Bulletin of the School of Oriental and African Studies* 27: 511–29.

K. Mukherji
1905 *Popular Hindu Astronomy*. Calcutta: Nirmal Mukherjea. Rpt. 1969.

J. Needham with L. Wang
1959 *Science and Civilization in China*. Vol. 3. Cambridge: Cambridge University Press.

J. Pokorny
1948 *Indogermanisches etymologisches Wörterbuch*. Bern: Francke.

F. Roach and J. L. Gordon
1973 *The Light of the Night Sky*. Dordrecht: Reidel.

S. Shaked
1967 Some Notes on Ahreman, the Evil Spirit, and His Creation. Pp. 227–34 in *Studies in Mysticism and Religion Presented to Gershom A. Scholem*, ed. E. E. Urbach et al. Jerusalem: Magnes.
1971 The Notions of *mēnōg* and *gētīg* in the Pahlavi Texts and their Relation to Eschatology. *Acta Orientalia* 33: 59–107.

B. L. van der Waeren
1968 *Die Anfänge der Astronomie*. Basel: Birkhäuser.

E. W. West
1871 *The Book of the Mainyo-Khard*. Stuttgart and London.

H. Willey
1938 The Pseudoplanetary Nodes of the Moon's Orbit in Hindu and Islamic Iconographies. A Contribution to the History of Ancient and Medieval Astrology. *Ars Islamica* 5: 113–54.

G. L. Windfuhr

1976 — *Vohu Manah*: A Key to the Zoroastrian World-Formula. Pp. 269–310 in *Michigan Oriental Studies in Honor of George G. Cameron*, ed. L. L. Orlin et al. Ann Arbor: Department of Near Eastern Studies, The University of Michigan.

forthcoming — The Word in Zoroastrianism. In *The Word: Religious Use of Language*, ed. R. Rappaport and L. O. Gómez.

E. Zinner

1931 — *Die Geschichte der Sternkunde*. Berlin: Springer.

The Nabateans and the Ḥismā: In the Footsteps of Glueck and Beyond

David F. Graf
The University of Michigan, Ann Arbor, Michigan

Systematic archeological surveys of Transjordan during the past half decade have now provided a basis for a critical evaluation of Nelson Glueck's important investigations of the region in the 1930's as reported in his *Explorations in Eastern Palestine* I-IV in the *Annual of the American Schools of Oriental Research* XIV (1934), XV (1935), XVIII-XIX (1939), and XXV-XXVIII (1951). At the ASOR Symposium "American Archaeological Survey in Jordan: Results and Methods," on 8 November 1980 at Dallas, Texas, these recent activities and their contribution to our understanding of historical and cultural developments in Transjordan during ancient times were briefly summarized. As was indicated by several of the participants on that occasion, it is now apparent that certain conclusions Glueck derived from his topographical work are in serious need of revision and perhaps even rejection.

Thus far, the most pointed criticisms of Glueck's pioneering effort have come from J. Maxwell Miller, co-director of the recent Central Moab survey with Jack M. Pinkerton. One of the objectives of this project was to establish precise map coordinates for the 33 sites visited by Glueck during his survey of the Moabite plateau, as well as any others discovered in the exploration of the region. The following results emerged from this effort: (1) the sites listed by Glueck represented only a good sample of the ancient settlements in central Moab; (2) Glueck's directions and estimates of distance were frequently incorrect; (3) surface pottery was often misread or even missed entirely by the earlier explorer; (4) Glueck's famous hypothesis of an occupational gap in Transjordan during the Middle and Late Bronze ages (18–13th centuries B.C.) was found to be misleading, as these periods are represented at several sites visited in the recent survey (Miller 1979a, b). In fairness to Glueck, it must be stressed that his survey of the region was limited to one week's duration and was not a multi-teamed, mobilized effort. Nevertheless, the results of the Moab survey have promoted caution and reserve concerning Glueck's generalizations about the occupational history of Transjordan.

In recent years, survey work in the Ḥismā region of southern Jordan (the area between the Gulf of ʿAqaba and the al-Sherā escarpment at Ras al-Naqb; see Map 1) has been conducted, with a primary focus on the Nabatean-Roman period (Parker 1976; Graf 1979). These reconnaissance efforts afford yet another opportunity to evaluate Glueck's findings from his exploration of Transjordan as well as to assess some of the criticisms that have been already registered about his work in this region.

I

The climatic conditions of the Ḥismā have generally been regarded as prohibitive

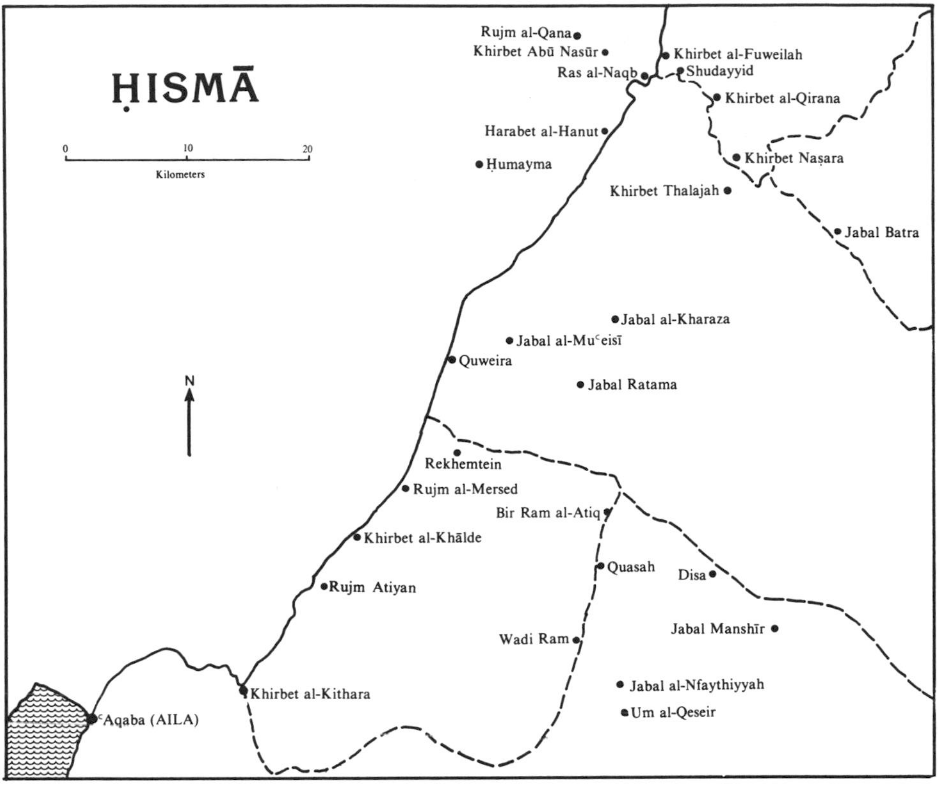

Map 1. The Ḥismā region of southern Jordan east of the *via nova*, up to the escarpment of al-Sherā.

of any extensive settlement in the region. Annual precipitation today averages less than 100 mm. in the region, as compared to more than 200 mm. at Maᶜān and other villages on the southern portion of the central Transjordanian plateau. According to modern geologists, the present phase of intense aridity began about 4000 years ago (Burdon 1959). The advanced state of arid erosion is revealed by weathered sandstone mountains protruding from the sand-drifts and mud-flats of the valley floor, which is itself broken up by gigantic wadis. Population today is scattered among only a few villages and bedouin encampments, the most notable being that at Wadi Ram, where more than a dozen springs lining the eastern side of Jabal Ram nourish a small settlement, centered around a police post.

Glueck investigated the Ḥismā desert during 6–10 April 1933, proceeding from ᶜAqaba along the ancient caravan route which cut through the Wadi Yitm and which largely corresponds to the southern end of the *via nova Traiana,* the main Roman highway that linked Aila on the Red Sea with Bostra, the capital city of *provincia Arabia.* After inspecting the Roman fort at Khirbet al-Kithara at the junction of the Wadi Imran, he diverted from this route to visit the Nabatean ruins at Wadi Ram, which were being excavated by the École Biblique Française of Jerusalem at the time. From this site, he then departed for Quweira, pausing only to investigate the Nabatean watchtower and dam at Rekhemtein, located near the old dirt track leading from Wadi Ram to the main highway (this route has now been replaced by a paved road, 4 km. further south). The ruined caravanserai, *birkeh,* and watchpost at Quweira were then explored, before Glueck proceeded northwards to the plateau along the main road leading to Ras al-Naqb and Maᶜān. The only discovery made along the way was at al-Menjir, where he found a number of Nabatean sherds by a large cistern and several Dushara niches on the face of the rocky outcrop from which the cistern had been hewn.

On the edge of the escarpment, however, Glueck found numerous Nabatean settlements, including Rujm al-Qana, Khirbet abū–Nasūr, Ras al-Naqb, Khirbet al-Fuweilah, Khirbet al-Shudayyid, Khirbet al-Qirāna, Khirbet Nasara, and Khirbet Thalajah. This evidence led Glueck to conclude that the al-Sherā plateau was intensively settled during the Nabatean period, with abundant small and large Nabatean villages scattered throughout the region. It was also observed that none of these settlements were enclosed with outer walls, implying that the edge of the plateau was not a boundary for the spread of the Nabatean kingdom, as it had been for the earlier Edomites, whose fortresses lined the undulating hills above the escarpment. Thus, Glueck concluded, "the entire Hismeh Valley . . . was in the hands of the Nabataeans, obviating the necessity of border fortresses on the edge of the Neqb" (1935: 63).

These conclusions seem somewhat premature in light of Glueck's brief exploration of the Ḥismā. The only other visit to the region he records was his later investigation of the Nabatean caravanserai and Roman castellum at Khirbet al-Khālde, as well as the small Nabatean-Roman rujm several km. further south in the Wadi Yitm (Glueck 1939: 15–19). These sites are located along the stretch of the main highway from ᶜAqaba to Maᶜān that Glueck had previously missed due to his excursion to Wadi Ram. In essence, his explorations of the extensive region (more than 4,000 sq. km.) never ventured far from the highways and main dirt tracks leading to the plateau and along the escarpment.

Therefore it is not surprising that some reservations have been expressed about Glueck's depiction of a dense Nabatean occupation in the Ḥismā. As Avraham Negev observed in his recent critique of this evidence, there seems to be in Glueck's reports a marked absence of any rural or urban settlements in the region. Aside from the large settlement at Wadi Ram, Glueck only mentions a few small sites strung along the old caravan routes. Negev further stressed other difficulties with Glueck's analysis of the evidence.

> In the survey no distinction was made between small military outposts along the road and larger agglomerations of houses. Neither could Glueck distinguish between the various phases of Nabatean occupation. The typical Nabatean pottery, which has been Glueck's faithful servant, is good for the Middle Nabatean period only, the pottery of the later phases was completely unknown to him, and research on it is still in the early stages. When all of this is taken into account, the density of Nabatean occupation in Edom may well appear somewhat different to the distribution represented on Glueck's maps (Negev 1978: 586).

Additional skepticism about Glueck's Nabatean Ḥismā hypothesis was created in 1976 by S. T. Parker's survey of the *limes Arabicus,* the Roman frontier defensive system in Jordan. For the Ḥismā, this embraced the forts and caravanserai along the main highway to ʿAqaba, namely Quweira, Khirbet al-Khālde, and Khirbet al-Kithara, all of which were visited by Glueck during his exploration of the region. However, in contrast to Glueck's apparent discovery of evidence for Nabatean occupation at all of these sites, Parker found nothing that suggested a pre-Roman Nabatean settlement at either Quweira or Khirbet al-Kithara (1980: 866). This disagreement in the interpretation of the surface finds at these sites has cast some doubt even on Glueck's ability to identify Nabatean pottery, much less distinguish the stages in its development. If these observations are correct, they also place in question Glueck's ascribing to the Nabateans over 500 sites in the Sinai, Negev, Wadi Arabah, and Transjordan.

Several comments can be offered on these criticisms. Glueck's conclusions about Nabatean settlements were primarily based on the presence at these sites of the distinctive "eggshell"-thin, plain, rouletted, or painted, reddish-buff fine ware that George and Agnes Horsfield had correctly assigned to the Nabateans in 1929. Although the precise chronological and typological development of Nabatean coarse pottery is still essentially unknown, more than half a century of excavations of Nabatean sites has provided only minimal refinement in the general outline of the classical fine ware provided by the Horsfields' work at Petra (Schmidt-Korte 1979: 14–16). This can particularly be seen by comparing Glueck's early discussion of Nabatean painted pottery (1939: 15) with the recent assessment of this peculiar ware by Peter Parr (1979: 203–9). Without this reliable guide, Glueck would possibly have designated many of the sites discovered in his survey as just Roman settlements; his acquaintance with this unique pottery makes it highly unlikely that he was wrong in his ceramic analysis when this ware was present. In Glueck's own words, "Typical Nabataean pottery, which cannot be mistaken by the veriest tyro once he has gained some acquaintance with it, was found abundantly on almost all of the approximately five hundred Nabataean sites which the expeditions of the [American] Schools [of Oriental Research] examined in southern Transjordan" (1942: 3).

Moreover, both earlier and later investigators of the disputed sites of Khirbet al-Kithara and Quweira have supported Glueck's findings. In a visit to Kithara in 1932, R. Savignac and G. Horsfield of the École Biblique had reported results similar to those of Glueck's later survey of the site. Savignac's description of their inspection of the ruins of Kithara is particularly revealing.

> Nous avons remassé dans les terres entrainées par la pluie, au nord des ruines, des fragments de poterie appartenant à deux époques nettement tranchées: une poterie rouge très fine et très bien cuite, avec un décor naturaliste de couleur violacée, dont M. Horsfield a trouvé d'innombrables spécimens parmi les plus anciennes ruines de Pétra et qu'il qualifie pour cela de poterie nabatéen; en second lieu de[s] nombreux fragments de poterie romaine et byzantine. A défaut d'autres données, ces indices archéologiques suggèrent que les Nabateens ont été les fondateurs de ce qasr, occupé plus tard par les Romains et les Byzantins (Savignac 1932: 595).

These remarks clearly indicate that the distinctive painted pottery of the Nabateans was the basis for assigning a Nabatean occupation to the site prior to the establishment of the Roman fort. Corroboration of these finds was provided in 1935, when Albrecht Alt visited Khirbet al-Kithara, as the German scholar agreed completely with Savignac's appraisal of the pottery scattered around the ruins: "Der Scherbenbelag besteht auch hier aus nabatäisch-früh-römischer und aus byzantinischer Ware" (Alt 1936a: 105). However, in contrast to Savignac and Glueck's proposal for an original Nabatean structure, Alt argued that the fort had probably been constructed and garrisoned by Nabatean subjects *after* the Roman annexation of their kingdom in A.D. 106 (1936b: 166). In defense of his thesis, Glueck contended that the strategic location of the fortress at the confluence of the Wadi Yitm and Wadi Imran demanded that a Nabatean military structure had existed prior to the Roman fortress (1939: 14). Only excavation of the site can ascertain if there is a Nabatean predecessor to the later Roman military structure. This ancillary issue should not, however, obscure the important discrepancy that exists between the findings of the explorers of the 1930's and Parker's recent survey of the site: were these early reports merely wrong or has all the evidence of a Nabatean settlement just been washed away by the seasonal rains?

In an effort to resolve this problem, a visit was made to the site in 1980 as part of our regional survey of the Ḥismā. Although intensive investigation of the fortress and its environs yielded no typical Nabatean painted pottery, other types of the unmistakable red fine ware were discovered. These included a ring base, a ribbed strap handle, and a rouletted body-sherd, all representative of traditional Nabatean ceramic form and technique. It should be noted that these finds were restricted to the northern slopes of the hill upon which the ruins of the fortress rest, just where Savignac earlier had indicated he had found examples of Nabatean ware. The confinement of the pottery to this area suggests that it was probably a dump for the debris of an earlier Nabatean settlement that was cleared off of the hill by the Romans prior to their erecting a fort or their refortification of a previous Nabatean structure.

Additional support for Glueck's interpretation of the ruins at Kithara is found at Khirbet al-Khālde, 24 km. further north in the Wadi Yitm. At this location, there is a typical Roman *castellum* just to the north of a smaller rectangular structure that has been designated a caravanserai. From Byzantine sources the fort has been identified as ancient Praesidium, where the *cohors quarta Frygum* was stationed (Bowersock 1971:

239). In Savignac's inspection of the larger structure, he observed that behind the roughly-cut granite blocks of the northern enclosure wall there was a second wall of sandstone. What particularly struck his interest was the fact that the facade of the northern gateway was also constructed with these sandstone blocks, many of which had the striated diagonal dressing which he had previously encountered at Petra and Wadi Ram and which Horsfield had styled "Nabataean" (Savignac 1932: 596 and pl. xix.2). As a consequence, he concluded that there had been at least two periods of construction for the *castellum,* with the original Nabatean fortress having undergone alteration and renovation after the Roman annexation of the Nabatean kingdom. Support for these deductions was found in the Nabatean fine ware he discovered among the abundant Roman and Byzantine sherds scattered around the ruins. According to Savignac, this Nabatean pottery was predominant at the smaller southern building and was remarkably similar to that which he had found at Kithara. In sum, he argued that both structures were originally Nabatean.

Glueck's conclusions, derived from a subsequent visit to the site, concur with those of Savignac (Glueck 1939: 15–18). Alt, however, again stubbornly maintained that the fort at Khālde originated *after* the fall of the Nabatean kingdom. The sandstone blocks with diagonal dressing, which were crucial for Savignac's ascribing the ruins of the fort to the Nabateans, were explained as simply the work of Nabatean masons employed by the Romans, though Alt did admit that the smaller structure seemed to pre-date the fort because of the preponderance of Nabatean sherds among the ruins (Alt 1936a: 103 n. 1). Glueck countered these arguments by once again pointing to the presence of "classical" Nabatean sherds at the fort, sherds which he felt had affinity with the pottery he had found in the excavations of the Nabatean temple at Khirbet Tannur, further north in Transjordan, which in his opinion dated to the early 1st century A.D. In my recent visit to Khālde, I was also struck by the amount of Nabatean painted ware in the environs of the fort, especially in a gully to the southwest of the structure, where an abundance of fine ware appears to have been washed down from the ruins. In consideration of these finds, it is somewhat difficult to sympathize with Alt's reluctance to concede that there may well have been pre-A.D. 106 Nabatean settlements at Khālde and Kithara.

Quweira is the other site in the Ḥismā where doubt has arisen about Glueck's ostensible discovery of evidence for a Nabatean settlement. These ruins, also located on the *via nova,* were described as a caravanserai, early Arab in appearance, but perhaps built over an earlier structure. Among the large quantities of Byzantine and Islamic sherds Glueck discovered, he claimed to have found also some Roman fragments and "several scraps of Nabataean ware" (Glueck 1935: 58). Alt's survey of the site produced results that were notably similar: "der überwiegend byzantinisch-arabische Scherbenbelag mit vereinzelten nabatäisch-römischen Stucken würde dazu stimmen" (Alt 1936a: 98). In contrast, Parker found only a few Roman and Byzantine sherds, and not a trace of any Nabatean or Islamic pottery (1976: 25). A visit to Quweira in 1980 confirmed the sparsity of surface pottery and also produced no distinctively Nabatean sherds.

Nonetheless, an inspection of the ruins of the watchpost on the top of the adjacent Jabal Quweira revealed a few possible Nabatean sherds and some well-cut stone blocks with Nabatean diagonal dressing. Strangely, Glueck reported only the presence of a few "indistinguishable" sherds at this small structure, and Parker does not appear to have investigated these ruins at all, though they loom just above the fort. Since it seems evident that this structure served as an observation post for the settlement in the plain below, there is some additional reason to believe that a Nabatean caravanserai or fort once existed at Quweira. Confirmation of Glueck's ceramic analysis at Kithara also militates against any distrust of his alleged finds at Quweira, at least until excavation and further research should indicate otherwise.

Still, the basic problem remains the apparent absence in the region south of the al-Sherā escarpment of any extensive Nabatean occupation. The sites so far considered in the Ḥismā, a few small military outposts and roadstations, do not constitute evidence for a dense Nabatean settlement pattern. In the desert east of the string of these forts and caravanseries, the early explorers make reference only to the Nabatean settlement at Wadi Ram and an occasional dam or rujm. Consequently, in contrast to Glueck, Manfred Weippert has characterized the region between Ras al-Naqb and ʿAqaba as basically a *Niemandsland,* devoid of any large economic or industrial complexes during the Nabatean period. In his opinion, the climatic conditions of the Ḥismā prohibited the development of urban settlements—the Nabatean sedentary occupation in southern Jordan terminated at Ras al-Naqb, at the edge of the al-Sherā escarpment, precisely where the southern frontier of the Edomite kingdom presumably existed (Weippert 1979: 88). But Weippert is careful to state that this judgment is only a general impression derived from reports of surface finds and further notes that archeological research in southern Jordan is still in its *Kinderschuhen.* The importance of recent activities in the Ḥismā is evident: what more can now be said about Nabatean occupation of this region?

II

One of the most prominent facets of Nabatean civilization was its achievement in hydraulic engineering and cultivation of semiarid regions. These technological accomplishments have frequently been praised and were specifically emphasized by Glueck: "Only an immensely able people could look at blistering wastelands, such as occur in the Wadi Arabah and the Negev of southern Israel, for instance, and envision in them productive farms and burgeoning flocks and flourishing villages connected by thronged roads, and then perform the miracle of translating such dreams into living reality, as the Nabataeans did" (1965: 5). Much of the evidence for this achievement has been revealed by recent archeological research in the Central Negev, where the Nabateans established a number of cities stretching from Petra to Gaza and al-ʾArish on the coast of the Mediterranean—Kurnub (Mampsis), Avdat (Oboda), Shivta (Subeita), Nitzana (Nessana), and Khalutza (Elusa) were the most important. The hundreds of Nabatean farms and agricultural plots also discovered in this region demonstrate the extraordinary skills of this people in channeling run-off water from the flash floods produced by seasonal rains and directing it to their terraced fields and catchment installations (Evenari, Shanan, and Tadmor 1971). This intricate system of dams, aqueducts, cisterns, and reservoirs made possible, as one writer describing this development has phrased it, "the cultivation and settlement of vast areas of the Negev, and perhaps of other desert lands hitherto written off as uncultivable and waste" (Morris 1961: 55). The reasons for not regarding the Ḥismā as *sui generis* and distinct from the pattern of Nabatean occupation of the Negev and elsewhere may now be considered.

In the first general archeological exploration of the Ḥismā, A. G. Kirkbride and G. L. Harding emphasized the surprising number of springs and sources for water supply in the region (1947: 24). These discoveries were frequently made in conjunction with their examination of the equally abundant Nabatean dams and cisterns found nestled in the weathered surfaces of many of the sandstone mountains. Similar finds were made in our 1978–80 survey of the Ḥismā and reinforce observations made by the earlier explorers. Most of these constructions were found in the large fissures that characterize the mountains of the region; the dam described by Glueck at Rekhemtein is typical: channels cut into the sides of this small hill directed the water into a cistern and trough hewn out of the sides of the cleft; access to the dam was provided by a series of steps cut into the hillside (1935: 56–57). The dams found in subsequent surveys of the Ḥismā are just as impressive as examples of Nabatean engineering skill, and have not been considered thus far in the recent discussion of the Nabatean occupation of the region.

A large conglomeration of these hydrological structures is at Jabal Kharaza, about 12 km. east of Quweira. In at least five clefts of the western face of the mountain, dams have been constructed with finely-cut stone blocks bearing the diagonal dressing of the Nabateans. If any further doubt existed of the Nabatean construction of these reservoirs, it is removed by the inscriptions in the inimitable Aramaic script of the Nabateans that are found on the sides of the fissures adjacent to the structures. In the inspection of one of these dams in 1980, faint traces of what is apparently the name of the Nabatean owner were found just several inches above the existing water level, estimated at about two meters deep, and directly facing the location, several meters above, from which the water would be drawn. The dam furthest to the south is the most elaborate: it consists of a wall about 4 m. wide and 3 m. high constructed across a large fissure, with the remains of approximately 23 arches still visible along its sides; these arches apparently served as the support for the roofing of the huge cistern, which measures 25 m. in length (Kirkbride and Harding 1947: 19–20). On the northern face of the fissure, Greek and Nabatean inscriptions have been cut into the rock, indicating the precise date of the dam and the identity of its builders: in the 41st year of the reign of the Nabatean king Aretas (IV), i.e., A.D. 32, the dam was constructed by Sab^{c} and Teudas, the sons of ʾEleh, whose name is written in Greek *(Eleos)* just above the Nabatean inscriptions of his sons (Milik 1958: 250).

The energy and time involved in building these dams suggest that Kharaza was more than just a temporary camping site or way station for Nabateans travelling to or from Petra and other major urban centers. Evidence that it was a small permanent settlement is indicated by the caves and dwelling places that have been hewn out of the sides and top of the mountain, the interiors of which have the common diagonal dressing of the Nabateans, revealing the identity of their ancient inhabitants.

Still further support for Glueck's thesis of a substantial Nabatean population in the Ḥismā is to be found in the vicinity of Kharaza. Just to the south of the mountain, a number of small catchments have been constructed in the clefts of Jabal Ratama by modern bedouin. Nabatean sherds scattered over the environs indicated that these structures probably represent renovated damming devices initially installed by Nabateans centuries ago (Graf 1979: 125). Several kilometers west of Kharaza, there is another dam constructed in a large fissure of Jabal Muʿeiṣī. Although it exhibits obvious signs of having been rebuilt in recent times, its Nabatean origin is disclosed by the diagonal dressing on the blocks still visible beneath the modern plaster and mortar carelessly smeared on the outside faces of the stone. Some 10 km. to the north of this site, there are a number of rock-cut cisterns and dams in the vicinity of Harabet al-Hanut, just before the modern highway begins its ascent of the escarpment (Kirkbride and Harding 1947: 21). The weathered South Arabian and Nabatean inscriptions adjacent to these structures, along with several Dushara niches cut into the faces of the rock, provide the only clues for identifying the ancient people who constructed and utilized these water reservoirs, but they also bear a striking resemblance to those associated with the Nabateans found elsewhere in the Ḥismā.

Another area where there is a concentration of hydrological structures is Wadi Ram, where an impressive aqueduct system conveyed water from the majestic ʿAin al-Shellaly to a large reservoir in the plain hundreds of meters below (Savignac 1932: 585–87; see Map 2). Although excavations have focused on the Nabatean temple at this site (Savignac and Horsfield 1935; D. Kirkbride 1960), a substantial part of the settlement area has also been cleared, presumably in the early 1960's by the Jordanian Department of Antiquities (cf. Starcky 1965: 979). In addition, Savignac observed several walls running east of the reservoir that he interpreted as the remains of a military enclosure (1932: 588). As a result, Wadi Ram has been described as a "large Nabatean centre, comprising a large military camp, a necropolis and a spacious temple" (Negev 1978: 586). Certainly, the numerous springs in the valley would have supported a fairly large settlement or entrepôt.

The exposing of this village complex at Wadi Ram provides support for the association of the site with the "many-columned city of Iram" mentioned in the Quran (89: 5–7), as travelers and scholars in recent times have proposed (Doughty 1888: 93–94; Starcky 1965: 978). The settlement has also been connected with the ancient Arabian tribe of the Arreni, whose major town was an important commercial center in the first century A.D. (Pliny, N.H. 6.32.157, *Arreni oppido in quod negotiatio omnis convenit),* and the settlement named Aramaua of the second century geographer Ptolemy (Sprenger 1875: 144). In fact, Aramaua heads Ptolemy's list of the inland villages of the northwestern sector of Arabia Felix, followed by Ostama and Thapaua (*Geog.* 6.7.27), which have been identified with Qurraya and Tabūk, respectively (Musil 1926: 312). The ruins at Wadi Ram may then be considered as the location of a major settlement during the Nabatean-Roman era.

Additional evidence of a large population centered around the temple at Ram can be found in the vicinity. To the east, at Um al-Qeseir in the Wadi al-Baidha, there is a Nabatean structure about 12 m. long and 5 m. wide built against a huge stone abutting Jabal Um Hariq. Adjacent Nabatean graffiti indicate it was erected by a Nabatean named Malakalatu, a priest of the goddess Alat, who is identified as "the goddess who (is to be found) at Iram" (Savignac 1932: 590–94). The function of this structure is mystifying, as there does not seem to be a spring or water source in the immediate vicinity. However, the pools in the northern cleft of Khaz Ali are just 5 km. to the southwest, and to the east, there is a Nabatean dam at Jabal al-Jadayda (Kirkbride and Harding 1947: 15–17).

Our investigation of the region also led to the discovery of other dams, one just a

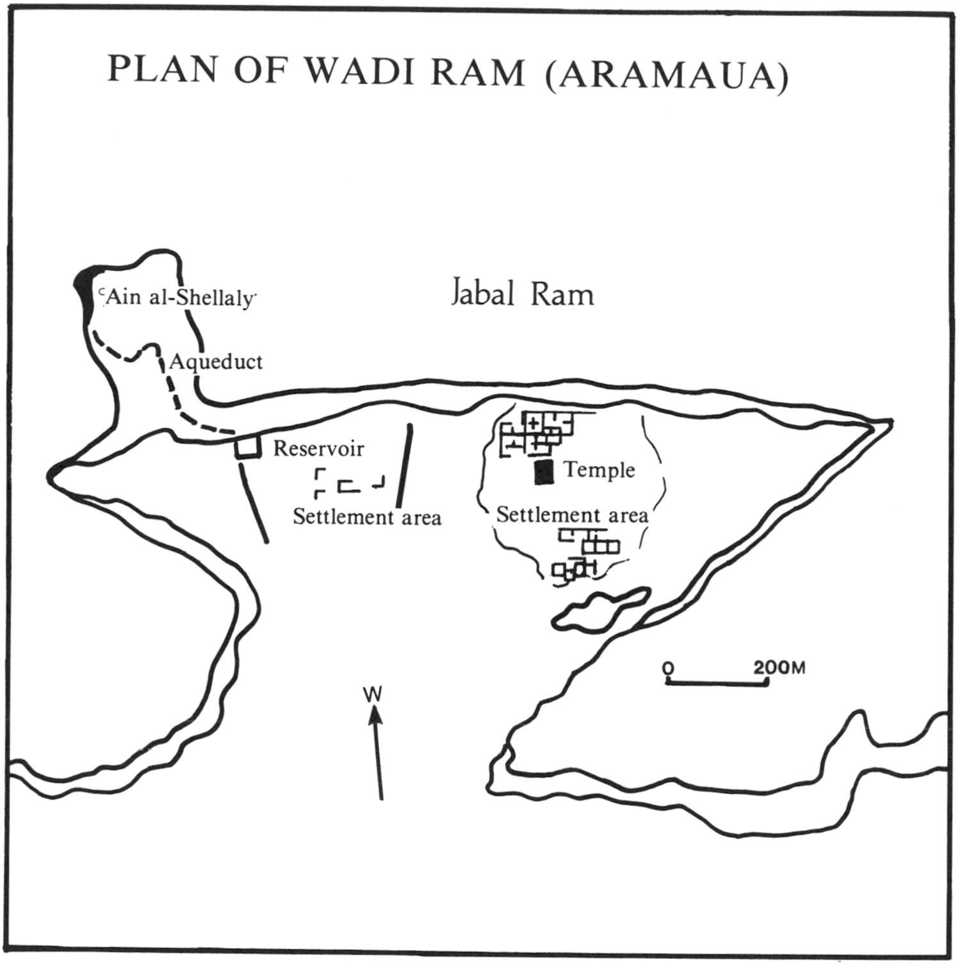

Map 2. The plan of Wadi Ram.

kilometer north of Um al-Qeseir and another 8 km. further north in the Wadi Um ʿIshrīn, though neither of these could be associated definitely with the Nabateans.

Another notable Nabatean water retention artifice in the area is that at Bir Ram al-Atiq, which stretches across the northern entrance to Wadi Ram, 10 km. from the Nabatean settlement. This dam consists of a wall about 50 m. in length with a circular well in its center and a rectangular enclosure at the eastern end; a curved wall at the western end of the structure apparently served to direct runoff water to the cistern (Kirkbride and Harding 1947: 17–18). The rectangular stone structures recently erected along the highway in Ram and the Wadi Yitm attest to the destructive forces of the winter torrent, but Nabatean sherds and diagonal dressing on the stones at Bir Ram al-Atiq reveal that it was the Nabateans whose engineering skill and creativity effectively devised the means of preserving the seasonal rains as a perennial water source. Nabatean sherds and graffiti scattered around such nearby sites as Jabal al-Nfaythiyyah, Jabal Disa, and Jabal Manshir provide further evidence of Nabatean occupation and activities in the same area.

The density and distribution of these hydrological works throughout the whole region, most of them discovered subsequent to Glueck's survey, remove any basis for assuming that the arid Ḥismā was such a hostile environment that it prevented the Nabateans from developing agricultural settlements or towns. The average rainfall in this region is only slightly less than that of the Negev and was obviously not so slight as to inhibit the use of the same ingenious water retention techniques that the Nabateans used in other desert regions: for example, the Negev cities have averaged approximately 100 mm. of rainfall per year in recent times (Shanan, Evenari, and Tadmor 1967), while the annual mean for the Ḥismā based on the past several decades of rainfall at Quweira and Wadi Ram is about 80 mm. (WPJ 1977: 16). Although the dams and cisterns discussed thus far seem basically rural in their setting, substantiating at least that there was regular pastoralist activity in the region, they also demonstrate that there may have existed other major villages in the Ḥismā besides that at Wadi Ram. Confirmation that such did exist is offered by the Nabatean ruins at Ḥumayma, where the most astounding Nabatean hydrological accomplishments in the Ḥismā are to be found, perhaps even comparable in this respect to those at the better known Nabatean cities of the Negev.

Ḥumayma, located about 13 km. west of Harabet al-Hanut, has been identified as the site of ancient Auara, an important military post during the Roman-Byzantine period (Bowersock 1971: 239; see Map 3). In Ptolemy, it is listed as one of the *poleis* of Arabia Petraea (*Geog.* 5.16.4), which, according to the Peutinger Table, was located about 30 km. south of Ṣadaqa (ancient Zadagatta) and 36 km. north of Khirbet al-Khālde (ancient Praesidium). These distances make the correlation of Auara with Ḥumayma reasonably secure. From the *Notitia Dignitatum,* an early Byzantine military document, it is further revealed that a unit of *equites sagitarii indigenae* was stationed at Auara (*Or.* 34.25; Haua[r]ae) and the contemporaneous Beersheba Edict credits the town with the second highest annual taxes of any of the military stations listed in the Transjordan sector of Palaestina Tertia (Alt 1921: 4).

Auara's connection with the Nabateans has a similar impressive documentary basis. In a fragment of Uranius' *Arabica,* the founding of the city is attributed to Aretas III, the visionary son of the Nabatean king Obodas I and later successor to his father (FGrH 675 F1b). According to this source, an oracle had instructed the young

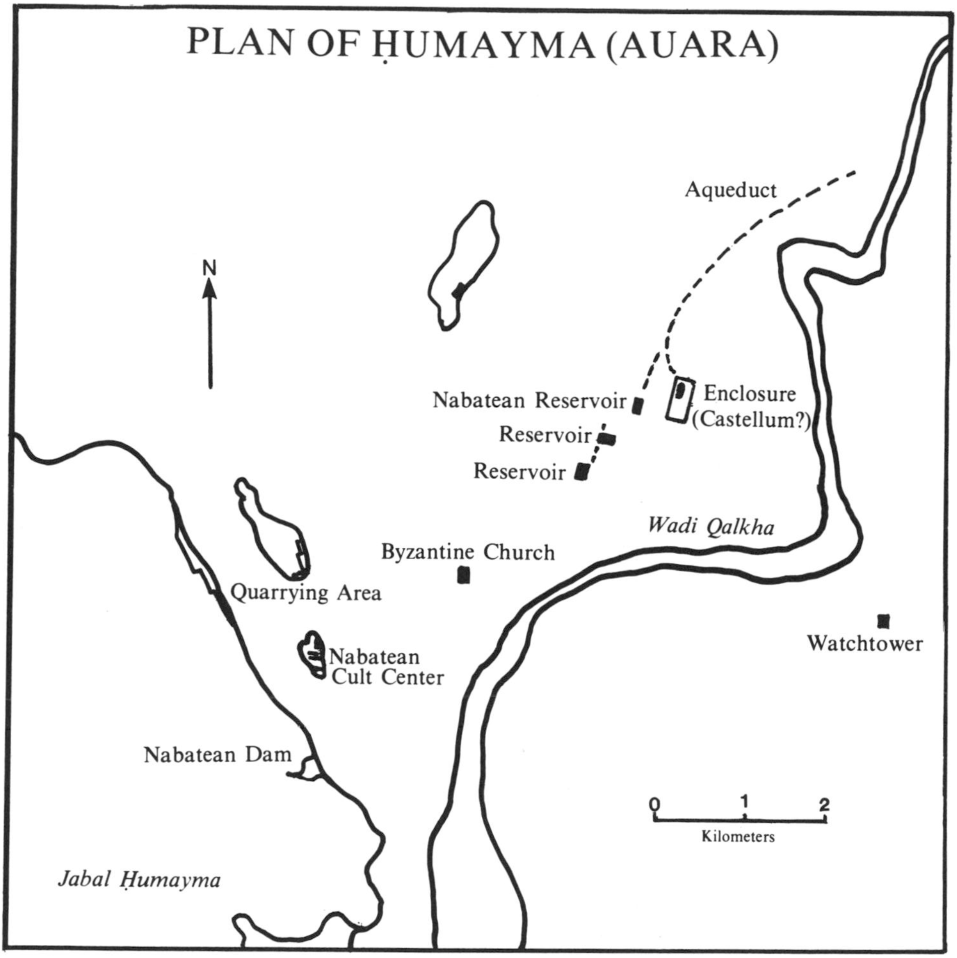

Map 3. The plan of Ḥumayma.

prince to build a city at a place called Auara, which means "white," i.e., *ḥawwara,* in Aramaic and Arabic; the town was established on the site where Aretas had a vision of a man dressed in white riding on a white camel. Since Aretas began his reign in 85 B.C., this tradition places the establishment of Auara early in the first century B.C.

In spite of these literary references attesting to Auara's importance, the site of Ḥumayma has generally been neglected by modern archeologists and explorers. Neither Savignac nor Glueck visited the site, and even Parker failed to include Ḥumayma in his survey of the *Limes Arabicus,* although the site was of known Roman military importance (cf. Weippert 1979: 88 n. 7, who summarizes this evidence, though he also omits Ḥumayma from his discussion of settlements in the Ḥismā). In contrast, R. G. Head and Agnes Horsfield collected Nabatean sherds from the site in an unrecorded visit (see Glueck 1935: 65), and Kirkbride and Harding also visited Ḥumayma, which they described as "a dreary waste of tumbled blocks" (1947: 21). Explorers of the region in the 19th century were more enthusiastic about their discovery of the site (*apud* Brünnow and Domaszewski 1904: 476–78) and those who have examined the ruins in this century have been unanimous with them in emphasizing the spectacular nature of the water system that nourished the settlement at Ḥumayma (Frank 1934: 236–37; Alt 1936a: 93–95; Stein 1940: 437). The following description of these ruins is primarily based on recent visits to the site, which were benefitted immensely by the 1979 action of the Canadian government (through UNESCO) in evacuating the modern inhabitants of Ḥumayma and resettling them in a new village adjacent to the main highway to ʿAqaba; this made it possible to investigate areas of the site previously obscured and rendered partially inaccessible.

The lack of any springs at Ḥumayma had evidently forced the settlers to construct a ground level aqueduct from ʿAin al-Qana, some 17 km. northeast of the site. This conduit ran adjacent to the Roman road, or *via nova*, whose pavement and milestones are still visible at certain stretches (Graf 1979: pl. xlv), and apparently led to several large reservoirs and cisterns within the settlement; at least its connection with an open reservoir (30 x 15 m.) to the northeast of the site is still visible. This structure is in the northwest corner of a large enclosure (208 x 150 m.), which perhaps is to be identified with the Roman *castellum* of Auara (Alt 1936a: 95). If this is the case, it is larger in total area than the sum of all the other Roman forts in the Ḥismā—Quweira, Khirbet al-Khālde, and Khirbet al-Kithara. A watchtower to the east of the settlement is the only other military installation visible in the environs. To the immediate southwest of the large enclosure is another open reservoir (28 x 17 m.), whose weathered surfaces still bear traces of Nabatean diagonal dressing. South of this structure are several other reservoirs, the largest of which was rehabilitated during the 1960's and is still used by local bedouin. It was apparently connected at one time to several small arch-covered cisterns nearby that are not now in use. Numerous small underground cisterns are also distributed throughout the extensive settlement, which comprises several square kilometers in total area. In addition, the proximity of Ḥumayma to the escarpment suggests that the drainage from the seasonal rains on the plateau, which has formed the Wadi Qalkha and its tributaries in the Ḥismā, was also an important source of water for the catchment areas in the settlement and the development of agriculture in the region.

The remains at Ḥumayma thus constitute the largest water retention system of any site known in the Ḥismā. Just how much of this extensive construction was the product of Nabatean hydrological technology cannot be determined without excavation, but the predominance of Nabatean sherds scattered over the site suggests that the pre-Roman Nabatean settlement was so sizable as to demand at least a similar system. The remains of buildings from the ancient settlement, which have largely been incorporated into the modern village, provide a similar impression, as many of the stones are dressed in Nabatean fashion. Most of these were probably quarried at Jabal Ḥumayma, to the southwest of the site, as indicated by huge vertical slices cut into its surfaces, marked by the typical striated diagonal Nabatean dressing (cf. Musil 1926: 60). Nabatean inscriptions have also been cut across these surfaces and on adjacent areas, giving further testimony to Nabatean activities in the area. In one cleft of this mountain, a dam has been constructed, with a channel cut into the surface to direct the water into an adjacent cistern. The Nabatean character of the structure is confirmed by several Nabatean inscriptions cut across one side of the fissure, bearing perhaps the names of those who utilized the device.

Further evidence of the Nabatean occupation of the site are several dwelling places and caves, cut into the surrounding mountains, reminiscent of those at Petra. Finally, there are in the far southern area of the site, carved into a protruding outcrop of Jabal Ḥumayma, the remains of what was obviously a Nabatean cultic center. Steps have been cut into the side of this mound, leading to several shafts cut into the upper surfaces which overlook a lower platform and rock-cut altar, similar in design to the famous open-air high place at Petra. There is also a Byzantine church in the same vicinity, a reminder of the importance of the site in later periods. But the overwhelming impression of the ruins is that they mark the site of one of the largest Nabatean villages in southern Jordan and certainly the largest Nabatean settlement to be found in the Ḥismā.

Ḥumayma, almost certainly ancient Auara, thus represents a major obstacle to the characterization of the Ḥismā as basically a desolate region, marked only by an isolated temple and a few caravanseries or road stations strung across its barren landscape, during the Nabatean period. This site, with its complex water system, extensive occupational remains, and Nabatean sanctuary, demonstrates that at least one other major settlement existed in the region besides that at Wadi Ram. Whether Ḥumayma functioned as an agricultural center, industrial complex, and/or entrepôt on the Nabatean route leading to Petra, cannot be determined without excavation and further exploration of the region, but that the settlement was of sizable proportions and significance is indisputable. Perhaps, with regard to the Nabatean occupational phase, Ḥumayma was even as large as most of the Negev cities of the Nabateans, if not larger than some. Unfortunately, this analogy can only be regarded as suggestive, as population estimates in modern demographic studies still are dependent on rigid formulas of a constant density for any settlement area, in spite of possible variables affecting the result (Adams 1981: 50).

However, aside from Ḥumayma and Wadi Ram, it is doubtful that there were any other major settlements in the northern Ḥismā. In Ptolemy's list of the cities in Arabia Petraea (*Geog.* 5.16.4), the only other settlements listed for southern Jordan are Characmoab (Kerak), Petra, Zadagatha (Ṣadaqa), and Adru (Udhruḥ). The fact that there were only a few large settlements in the Ḥismā is not surprising, as major sites in any area without arable land and a high annual rainfall are naturally correlated with the location of springs and other topographical features. Nonetheless, the existence of such villages as Ḥumayma and Ram in the Ḥismā must have been a stimulus to local agriculture and the establishment of small rural settlements. This is indicated as early as the second century B.C. by Diodorus Siculus, who observed that the coastal area and hinterland of the Gulf of ʿAqaba was characterized by numerous Nabatean villages and a large pastoralist population (3.43.4). The numerous dams and cisterns scattered through the region confirm the existence of just such a settlement pattern.

The distribution and abundance of Thamudic graffiti in the Ḥismā provide additional evidence of shepherds operating in the area. Consentrations of these graffiti, probably contemporaneous for the most part with the Nabatean occupation of the region, appear in valleys and bays of mountains some distance from the main tracks of the region, which supports their interpretation as the product of local villagers and pastoralists, rather than caravaneers or nomadic raiders of sedentary communities. That animal husbandry was the occupation of their authors is implied by the animal drawings that accompany these inscriptions and the peculiarity to this region of the names and genealogies mentioned in the texts (Graf 1978: 6–8). The existence of pasturage and water for flocks and herds appears to be the basis for the provenance of the graffiti. As a result of this evidence, it seems reasonable to accept Glueck's thesis that the Ḥismā desert was not an uninhabited wasteland but the location of a substantial population during the Nabatean period.

III

Several general observations can now be offered about the methodology and results of Glueck's survey of the Ḥismā. First, it is obvious that Glueck's explorations of the region never ventured far from the previously known sites adjacent to the modern highways and main desert tracks. As a result, Glueck, although familiar with the importance of Ḥumayma, excluded it from his itinerary. This has led to the site's glaring omission in some recent discussions of the region, especially those in which it is argued that Glueck exaggerated the extent of Nabatean occupation in the Ḥismā. In similar fashion, the expansive area east of the modern highway was left unexplored, leaving the impression that only a string of road stations existed in the Ḥismā. Admittedly, subsequent investigation of this region has not yielded any ruins as spectacular as Ḥumayma, but evidence has been revealed of a large Nabatean habitation active in the area. Yet, in spite of his lack of knowledge of these sites, Glueck intuitively realized the potential and possibility for the habitation of the Ḥismā by the Nabateans, based on their settlement of similar desert regions. It is then bizarre that the same scholars who commend Glueck's pioneering effort in the Negev, which transformed our image of the Nabatean settlement in that region from one of moderate to one of dense occupation, are reluctant to accept his opinion that the Nabateans had a substantial permanent population in the Ḥismā as well (e. g., see Hammond 1973: 30–31).

Furthermore, it should be emphasized that Glueck never represented his survey as completely thorough and comprehensive in this region. It is true that on occasion he could boast that he was "confident that not very many ancient sites in Edom and Moab, whose ruins have not been completely obliterated, remain undiscovered." Yet, in relating the approach and procedures of his explorations, he clearly qualified and clarified such statements: "We did not find it possible to visit all the sites we knew of, or had heard about, but had to rest content with the knowledge that . . . we had succeeded in studying a majority of the ancient sites located in this area" (Glueck 1939: xxiii and 48). Such lacunae in the archeological record of a surface reconnaissance are to be expected, as a survey is a provisional enterprise by nature (Ammerman 1981). Even intense, exhaustive coverage of a limited area is likely to miss sites, especially in a region like the Ḥismā, where sweeping sands and erosion can conceal or destroy surface remains. Thus, repeated visits to sites in our survey sometimes provided different results, a product possibly of sampling technique, but probably as much a response to the seasonal alteration of the surface area from rain and wind.

As far as Glueck's analysis of surface remains is concerned, it may be said that his observations were fundamentally accurate, as was concluded also from a recent survey in the Jordan Valley (Ibrahim, Sauer, and Yassine 1976: 45). Thus, our re-examination of the contested Nabatean sites at Kithara and Quweira provided evidence to support Glueck's diagnosis of the architectural and ceramic remains. Nevertheless, it must be confessed that several problems persist concerning the present criteria for dating surface finds. Our present knowledge of the development of Nabatean pottery only allows the assignment of sherds to periods that roughly embrace several centuries. This chronological impreciseness prohibits us from establishing that certain sites were contemporaneous, an obviously important aspect for any discussion of a settlement pattern (Parsons 1972: 142–43). The current tendency to correlate typology with political developments is also to be avoided, e.g., classifications of pre-Roman or post-Roman Nabatean pottery (Parr 1978). For all the importance that the Roman annexation in 106 A.D. must have had for the Ḥismā and other areas of the Nabatean realm, we still do not have the means to assess the waxing and waning of Nabatean culture.

None of these remarks are meant to be disparaging about the conclusions reached as a result of the Central Moab Survey, as earlier outlined by M. Miller, or those from other comparative field work in Jordan. What they rather illustrate is that Glueck's statements about the settlement patterns of any region must be analyzed independently from the results emerging from the re-evaluation of his survey elsewhere. Any categorical rejection of the findings of his Transjordanian explorations or general impugning of their accuracy is now confounded by the fact that for the Ḥismā, Glueck has proven to be a trustworthy source of information.

References

Adams, Robert McC.
1981 *Heartland of Cities.* Chicago: University of Chicago.

Alt, A.
1921 *Die griechischen Inscriften der Palaestina Tertia westlich der Araba.* Berlin/Leipzig: Deutsch-turkischen Denkmalschultz Kommandos.
1936a Der südliche Endabschnitt der römischen Strasse von Bostra nach Aila. *Zeitschrift des Deutschen Palaestina-Vereins* 59: 92–111.
1936b Rev. Glueck 1935. *Zeitschrift des Deutschen Palaestina-Vereins* 59: 163–67.

Ammerman, A. J.
1981 Surveys and Archaeological Research. *Annual Review of Anthropology* 10: 63–88.

Bowersock, G.W.
1971 A Report on Arabia Provincia. *Journal of Roman Studies* 61: 219–42.

Burdon, David J.
1959 *Handbook of the Geology of Jordan.* Amman: The Hashemite Kingdom of Jordan.

Brünnow, R., and von Domaszewski, A.
1904 *Die Provincia Arabia,* vol. I. Strassburg: Trübner.

Doughty, Charles M.
1888 *Travels in Arabia Deserta.* Vol. I. Rpt. 1979, New York: Dover.

Evenari, M.; Shanan, L. and Tadmor, N.
1971 *The Negev: The Challenge of a Desert.* Cambridge: Harvard University Press.

von Frank, F.
1934 Aus der ʿAraba I: Reiseberichte. *Zeitschrift des Deutschen Palaestina-Vereins.* 57: 191–280.

Glueck, Nelson
1934 Explorations in Eastern Palestine I. Pp. 1–113 in the *Annual of the American Schools of Oriental Research* 14. Cambridge, MA: American Schools of Oriental Research.
1935 Explorations in Eastern Palestine II. *Annual of the American Schools of Oriental Research* (1934–1935). Cambridge, MA: American Schools of Oriental Research.
1939 Explorations in Eastern Palestine III. *Annual of the American Schools of Oriental Research* 18–19 (1937–1939). Cambridge, MA: American Schools of Oriental Research.
1942 Nabatean Syria. *Bulletin of the American Schools of Oriental Research* 85: 3–8.
1951 Explorations in Eastern Palestine IV. *Annual of the American Schools of Oriental Research* 25–28. Cambridge, MA: American Schools of Oriental Research.
1965 *Deities and Dolphins: The Story of the Nabataeans.* New York: Farrar, Straus and Giroux.
1970 *The Other Side of the Jordan.* Cambridge, MA: American Schools of Oriental Research.

Graf, David F.
1978 The Saracens and the Defense of the Arabian Frontier. *Bulletin of the American Schools of Oriental Research* 229: 1–26.
1979 A Preliminary Report on a Survey of Nabatean–Roman Military Sites in Southern Jordan. *Annual of the Department of Antiquities, Jordan* 23: 121–27.

Hammond, Philip C.
1973 *The Nabataeans—Their History, Culture and Archaeology.* Studies in Mediterranean Archaeology 37. Gothenburg: Paul Atröms.

Ibrahim, M.; Sauer, J.; and Yassine, Y.
1976 The East Jordan Valley Survey, 1975. *Bulletin of the American Schools of Oriental Research* 222: 41–66.

Kirkbride, A., and Harding, G. L.
1947 Hasma. *Palestine Exploration Quarterly* 79: 7–26.

Kirkbride, D.
1960 Le Temple Nabatéen de Ramm. *Revue biblique* 67: 65–72.

Milik, J.T.
1958 Nouvelles inscriptions nabatéennes. *Syria* 35: 227–51.

Miller, J. Maxwell
1979a Archaeological Survey South of Wadi Mūjib. *Annual of the Department of Antiquities, Jordan* 23: 79–92.
1979b Archaeological Survey of Central Moab, 1979. *Bulletin of the American Schools of Oriental Research* 234: 43–52.

Morris, Y.
1961 *Masters of the Desert: 6000 Years in the Negev.* New York: G.P. Putnam's Sons.

Musil, A.
1926 *The Northern Ḥeǧaz.* New York: American Geographical Society.

Negev, Avraham
1978 The Nabataeans and the Provincia Arabia. Vol. 2.8, pp. 520–686 in *Aufstieg und Niedergang der römischen Welt,* ed. H. Temporini. Berlin: De Gruyter.

Parker, S. Thomas
1976 Archaeological Survey of the *Limes Arabicus. Annual of Department of Antiquities, Jordan* 21: 19–31.
1980 Towards a History of the Limes Arabicus. Pp. 865–78 in *Roman Frontier Studies 1979,* ed. W. W. Hanson and L. J. F. Keppie. Oxford: BAR International Series 71.

Parr, P. J.
1978 Pottery, People and Politics. Pp. 203–9 in *Archaeology in the Levant,* ed. R. Moorey and P. Parr. Warminster: Aris & Phillips, Ltd.

Parr, P. J.; Harding, G. L.; and Dayton, J.E.
1970 Preliminary Survey in N.W. Arabia, 1968. *Bulletin of the Institute of Archaeology, University of London* 8–9: 193–242.

Parsons, J. R.
1972 Archaeological Settlement Patterns. *Annual Review of Anthropology* 1: 127–50.

Savignac, R.
1932 Notes de Voyage: Le sanctuaire d'Allat à Iram. *Revue biblique* 41: 581–97.

Savignac, R., and Horsfield, G.
1935 Le Temple de Ramm. *Revue biblique* 44: 245–78.

Schmidt-Korte, K.
1979 Nabataean Pottery: A Typological and Chronological Framework. *The Second International Symposium on Studies in the History of Arabia.* Riyadh: University of Riyadh.

Shanan, L.; Evenari, M.; and Tadmor, N. H.
1967 Rainfall Patterns in the Central Negev Desert. *Israel Exploration Journal* 17: 163–84.

Sprenger, Aloys
1875 *Die alte Geographie Arabiens.* Bern: von Huber.

Starcky, J.
1965 Pétra et la Nabatène. Vol. 7, cols. 886–1017 in *Supplément au dictionnaire de la Bible,* ed. L. Pirot et al. Paris: Letouzey et Ané.

Stein, Sir Aurel
1940 Surveys on the Roman Frontier in Iraq and Transjordan. *Geographical Journal* 95: 428–39.

Weippert, M.
1979 Nabatäisch-römische Keramik aus *Hirbet Dōr* im südlichen Jordanien. *Zeitschrift des Deutschen Palaestina-Vereins* 95: 87–110.

WPJ
1977 *National Water Master Plan of Jordan.* Amman: Department of Natural Resources.

Matthew 12:40 as an Interpretation of 'The Sign of Jonah' Against its Biblical Background

George M. Landes
Union Theological Seminary, New York

I must confess at the outset that I have undertaken this study with some trepidation, since its subject matter falls a bit 'outside the camp' of one for whom the OT has been his principal claim to scholarly expertise. However, my own extensive research in the book of Jonah, and especially recently in the history of its interpretation, has inevitably drawn my attention to the intriguing NT appropriation of Jonah tradition. Because I have not been altogether satisfied with the way NT scholars have interpreted Matt 12: 40 in the Matthean rendition of that tradition, despite the riskiness of the venture, I have decided to try my own hand at explaining what I think might be involved here. I happily dedicate this study to my esteemed friend, respected colleague in OT scholarship, and fellow student of the late W.F. Albright, David Noel Freedman, whose own scholarly endeavors on more than one occasion have dared to suggest some bold new interpretations of previously well-worked-over biblical material. Though I do not anticipate my efforts here will be either as exciting or provocative as his have been, perhaps they will at least have some heuristic value in stimulating a reassessment of the meaning of Matt 12: 40 and its background that might prove to be more convincing than the one herein offered.

I. The Problems With the Traditional Interpretations of Matt 12: 40

Within the Matthean pericope (Matt 12: 38–42) which introduces and also seems to present at least two different interpretations of what the unusual genitival expression 'the sign of Jonah' might signify, it is perhaps v 40 which has confronted exegetes with the most perplexing problems of understanding. For not only is this verse unique to Matthew, its Lukan counterpart (Luke 11: 30) being contentually at variance, it also seems to convey an interpretation of the sign of Jonah quite unlike that given in Matt 12: 41 and its precise parallel in Luke 11: 32. Of course it may be argued, as it sometimes has been, that neither Matt 12: 40 nor 12: 41 (= Luke 11: 32) reflect Jesus' own understanding of the sign of Jonah (assuming its origin actually goes back to him, which is not universally accepted), and in the absence of any genuinely original Dominical sayings having been preserved within the Gospel traditions that interpreted what this unique phrase meant, the early Church (or more precisely, what has been called the 'Q community'), most likely some time prior to the composition of Matthew and Luke, generated what it conceived to be the meaning of Jesus' usage, reflected now preeminently in Matt 12: 40 and Luke 11: 30, subsequently embellished in the final redaction of these Gospels by Matt 12: 41 and Luke 11: 32. In this essay, I shall focus primarily on the Matthean material, which in my view, because of the obvious differences between Matt 12: 40 and Luke 11: 30, can be legitimately treated on its own.[1] Moreover, without completely ignoring the pertinent results of redaction- and history-of-traditions-criticism, my approach will be to ask what Matt 12: 40 within 12: 38–41,[2] in its present final arrangement and contiguity, might have meant to Matthew and his community. I shall proceed on the assumption that the extant form and ordering of these verses can be properly assigned to Matthew himself, and even though this has been questioned, the arguments against it are not for me compelling.[3] Thus my working hypothesis is that Matt 12: 40 and 12: 41 were placed together, not principally because they both made use of traditions stemming from the OT book of Jonah, but because they both were understood to have an underlying coherence in their indication of what the sign of Jonah meant.

In his 1971 monograph, *The Sign of Jonah in the Theology of the Evangelists and Q,* Richard A. Edwards has formally typed Matt 12: 40 as one example among ten (including parallels) in Matthew and Luke of what he calls an 'eschatological correlative' (47–58). From the standpoint of form, the latter consists of an opening protasis clause introduced variously by the Greek adverbs *kathōs, hōsper,* or *hōs,* with its verb occurring in either the past or present tense, followed by an apodosis usually introduced by the Greek adverb *houtōs,* with its verb always being the future tense form of the verb 'to be' (*estai*), to which is linked the phrase 'the Son of Man,' either as subject of this verb, or in a genitival phrase frequently after *hē parousia* as subject (Edwards 1971: 49–51). In Matt 12: 40, the protasis is introduced by *hōsper,* followed by the verb 'to be' in the past tense, while the apodosis begins with *houtōs*, followed by *estai* with 'the Son of Man' as its subject. Translated, it reads, "For just as Jonah was in the belly of the sea monster three days and three nights, so the Son of Man will be in the heart of the earth three days and three nights."

Most important for our purposes here is assessing the implications of the synonymous parallelism between the phrase in the protasis, 'in the belly of the sea monster,' and its analogue in the apodosis, 'in the heart of the earth.' There would seem to be fairly common consensus today among NT interpreters that this parallelism, particularly because of its association with the 'three days, three nights' motif, was intended to indicate a death-resurrection theme, so that the meaning would be: for just as the prophet Jonah had been brought to the verge of death in the sea and had been delivered, so will the Son of Man experience actual death and burial in the heart of the earth before being raised to life. Under this interpretation, the only sign to be given to 'this evil and adulterous generation' (Matt 12: 39) is the sign of Jesus'[4] death and resurrection, and the phrase 'the sign of Jonah' has to be construed as an objective genitive, i.e., indicating the sign which Jonah experienced in his being swallowed by the sea monster and then regurgitated. However, a careful scrutiny of what is being correlated in Matt 12: 40 raises a serious question about this interpretation.

First of all, it is of some interest to note that the phrase 'in the heart of the earth' is unique: it occurs only here in the NT, nowhere in the OT or, as far as I have been able to ascertain, in pre-Christian Jewish literature. The normal expression in the OT is 'in the heart of the sea(s)' (*bilbab yamîm* or *bĕlēb yām*, cf. Exod 15: 8; Ezek 27: 4,

25–27; 28: 2, 8; Ps 46: 3; Prov 23: 34; 30: 19; Jonah 2: 4). I am convinced that Seidelin (1952: 130) is correct when he concludes that the words 'in the heart of the earth' have been created by the author of Matt 12: 40 under the influence of the psalm in Jonah 2, where in the LXX of v 4 we have the phrase *eis bathē kardias thalassēs* ("into the depths of the heart of the sea"), while v 7 opens with the words, *katebēn eis gēn* ("I descended into the earth"). Thus in Matt 12: 40, *en tē kardia tēs gēs* represents a combination and rephrasing of words drawn from the LXX of Jonah 2, vv 4 and 7. For the author, Jonah's being *en tē koilia tou kētous* ("in the belly of the sea monster") was the same thing as being *en tē kardia tēs gēs* ("in the heart of the earth"), i.e., in the underworld, the realm of death, which he applies to Jesus' death. Though both 'sea' and 'earth' are often used to refer to the netherworld in the OT, and theoretically at least, the writer could have employed the phrase *en tē kardia tēs thalassēs* in his composition of Matt 12: 40b, doubtless he was moved to create a new phrase employing 'earth' instead of 'sea' because Jesus' death was in no way related to a sea experience, unlike the situation with Jonah.[5] In any event, Matt 12: 40 in its present context functions as the First Evangelist's initial explanation of the meaning of the sign of Jonah, pointing to a future three-day, three-night sojourn of the Son of Man/Jesus in the realm of the dead, on the analogy of the prophet Jonah's identical short-term residence in the belly of the sea monster, which, to Matthew and his community, would stand for the netherworld, because Jonah 2: 1 was interpreted in light of the following psalm (Jonah 2: 3–10) with its netherworld imagery.

But if this is correct, what then would be the meaning of the sign given? In what sense would Jesus' future brief stay in Hades be a sign? If anything, it would appear to be basically a negative sign, an indication of defeat and humiliation. But could this be the very point that Matthew wanted to represent Jesus as making in his response to the scribes and Pharisees' demand for a sign? Given the fact that within the Jewish conception of the Messiah as well as the 'son of man' figure in Dan 7: 13-14 and in Jewish apocalyptic sources,[6] there was no thought that both of these figures suffered and died as a substitute for humanity and as a way of initiating the divine salvation (cf. Jenni 1962: 365a), could the implication of Matt 12: 40 be that Jesus as the Son of Man must suffer and die before triumphing over death, that indeed the way to salvation leads only through his real and necessary death, for only in this fashion could death be truly conquered? Thus in responding to the scribes and Pharisees' request for a sign, is Jesus saying that his message and mission are not genuinely authenticated except through the offense of his death (cf. Seidelin 1952: 130–31)? Such an interpretation is conceivable, but hardly likely in the total context of Matthew's Gospel, in which not simply Jesus' death but also, and most crucially, his resurrection are together seen as validating his messiahship.[7] Why then is the focus in Matt 12: 40 more upon death than upon death *and deliverance*? It is clear that if Matthew understood the latter as Jesus' interpretation of the sign of Jonah, he had the scriptural basis for formulating the correlative from the book of Jonah much more explicitly in that direction than the present form in v 40. Thus, combining elements from Jonah 2: 1 and 11, a correlative stressing both death and deliverance might have read something like the following: "For just as Jonah was in the belly of the sea monster three days and three nights and then was cast out on the dry land, so will the Son of Man be in the heart of the earth three days and three nights and then be raised from the dead." It has been argued, of course, that the twice repeated words "three days and three nights" clearly indicate a limited sojourn of Jonah and the Son of Man in the netherworld, and hence point to a deliverance, at least by implication.[8] But aside from the fact that it seems rather strange that well before he first introduces the passion theme (by Jesus to his disciples, Matt 16: 21) Matthew should make initial reference in such an indirect and elliptical way to Jesus' resurrection as a sign to his opponents, the whole context against which the Demand-for-a-Sign motif is set does not make a sign of the future death and resurrection of Jesus an appropriate response to the scribes and Pharisees' request.

Though it is quite conceivable that Matthew and his community viewed Jesus' resurrection as a sign verifying his messianic claim (Gschwind 1911: 159), even though in his Gospel Matthew never explicitly calls it a sign (leaving aside for the moment the possibility that Matt 12: 39–40 might be interpreted in this way), it is more questionable whether the Pharisees, despite their well-known belief in resurrection as a divinely instigated event, would have accepted Jesus' allusion to his future resurrection as potentially fulfilling what they wanted in a sign, assuring them beyond doubt (i.e., without any requirement of faith) that his authority and mission were truly from God. Indeed from within Matthew's own special tradition (Matt 27: 62–66; 28: 11–15), it seems clear that the Pharisees were not impressed with the reality of Jesus' resurrection, for when the guard whom they had helped post at Jesus' tomb to prevent his disciples from coming and stealing the body and then proclaiming his resurrection reported to the Jewish leadership what had happened at the tomb, instead of giving credence to the fact that Jesus had risen, they bribed the soldiers to spread the rumor that Jesus' disciples had in fact stolen his body.[9] But even granting theoretically, within the context of Matthew 12, that the Pharisees might have accepted the sign of Jonah, as defined by Matt 12: 40, as a sign suitably pointing to the confirmation of Jesus' messianic claims, it seems doubtful, on the one hand, that Jesus would seriously undercut the meaning of his categorical refusal to give a sign like the Pharisees demanded ("but no sign shall be given . . .") by conceding to do precisely that, and on the other, by seemingly accepting the legitimacy of their demand (which he does nowhere else, cf. Matt 16: 1, 4), that he would tacitly allow them to delay the obligation to repentance and faith until the event of his resurrection, something that conforms neither with the absolute character of Jesus' unconditional and unpostponable demand for a present decision nor with his understanding that the demand for a sign beyond that which they are able to see already in his ministry of teaching and healing is an expression of a reprehensible desire (Vögtle 1953: 243, 254).

Of course it may be replied that none of this is relevant because Matt 12: 40 is a secondary interpolation, representing words never spoken by Jesus, or if so, not for their present setting in Matthew (Cope 1976: 41; Vögtle 1953: 240, 248–63; Seidelin 1952: 120, 128). Created within the Q community sometime after Pentecost, the verse was not originally intended as an explanation of the sign of Jonah, but was composed to provide an OT prophetic witness to the Passion theme of the suffering and death of the Son of Man as a necessary preliminary to his marvelous deliverance. Later, because of the comparison with Jonah, and also because what Jesus may have meant by the sign of Jonah was either no longer fully understood or had become lost, or perhaps even more because by this time within the early church Jesus' resurrection had come to be viewed as a sign of his messiahship, the verse was placed in its present context in Matthew as an additional interpretation of the sign of Jonah. I would have no quarrel with this sketch of the origin and history of development of Matt 12: 40 if I was as convinced as many NT scholars seem to be of its secondary character in Matt 12: 38–42, or of its incompatibility with other features in Matthew (e.g., the three-day motif already mentioned, or the way Matthew typically introduces an OT citation, cf. Stendahl 1968: 132–33). It is because I think Matt 12: 40 has an understanding that conjoins well not only with its immediate context but also with its larger setting in the Gospel as a whole, that a fresh examination of its meaning and function is warranted, and to that I now turn.

II. Matt 12: 40 in the Context of Matthew

In a correlative form like Matt 12: 40, what is crucial for its understanding is determining the nature of its *tertium comparationis*. Basically three elements are comparatively aligned between the protasis and apodosis of this verse: the figures of Jonah and the Son of Man; the places where they sojourn; and the time-span of their sojourning. As we have seen above, if the thrust is primarily on the place of residence, thus emphasizing the death experience of Jonah and Jesus, respectively, this hardly provides an adequate definition for a sign intended to authenticate Jesus' messianic mission, which for Matthew, as well as all the other NT writers, could not be limited to Jesus' death alone but must also include his resurrection. On the other hand, if the stress is on the short duration of Jonah's and the Son of Man's stay in the netherworld, thus pointing to the imminence of their deliverance, this also creates a problem by appearing to make Jesus approve a demand that he does not accept as legitimate, and then grant a sign like he said he would not give, while at the same time apparently relieving the scribes and Pharisees of any immediate obligation to repent and believe in what Jesus was saying and doing. Is there an understanding of Matt 12: 40 that avoids these problems, yet also makes tolerably good sense in the context?

Is it possible that the *tertium comparationis* in Matt 12: 40 is somewhat more subtle and less explicit than hitherto supposed, emphasizing neither the place where Jonah and the Son of Man dwelt, nor the time they spent there, but rather *what they did* while residing for three days and three nights 'in the belly of the sea monster' and 'in the heart of the earth,' respectively? At first glance, this suggestion seems rather far-fetched, since it has no formal expression in the wording of the verse. Yet neither does the idea of deliverance, except by inference from the words 'three days and three nights.' Could then Matthew have understood another inference as more important in this context, an inference based not upon the three-days, three-nights motif, but upon the locative expressions, the interest being *in what happened* 'in the belly of the sea monster' and 'in the heart of the earth' while Jonah and the Son of Man were in these places? Let us pursue this idea further and see where it might lead.

If we turn to the book of Jonah, and especially to the psalm in chap. 2,[10] we can observe right away that from Jonah's perspective several things happen between his being cast overboard by the sailors (1: 15) and his being deposited back safely on the dry land by the fish (2: 11). First of all, he cries to Yahweh for help while still in the sea, shown through the imagery of the psalm to be the netherworld, the region of death.[11] Secondly, Yahweh responds to his cry by appointing a great fish to swallow Jonah (2: 1), an action which the prophet clearly interprets as a divine rescue from almost certain death (2: 3, 7). Thirdly, Jonah prays while in the belly of the fish (2: 2), praising Yahweh for heeding his plea for help and delivering him from death (2: 3–10). Perhaps it was this last event which most caught the attention of Matthew, for what he perceives Jonah to be saying is not simply a prayer of thanksgiving, but a bearing witness to the death-conquering power of Yahweh, culminating in the proclamation: "Salvation belongs to Yahweh!" (2: 10). As one who has experienced not only what it is like to be in the clutches of death, but also to be removed from those clutches, Jonah can give expression to the divine power that liberates from death, and do so, moreover, even before the full effects of that power have become manifest, i.e., prior to his own 'resurrection,' so to speak, when the fish, at Yahweh's command, returns him to the dry land.

Is there something in this line of interpretation that provided for Matthew the *tertium comparationis* between Jonah 'in the belly of the sea monster' and the Son of Man 'in the heart of the earth'? On the basis of NT tradition, which tends to be rather reticent when it comes to saying anything about the activity of Jesus between his burial and resurrection (Jeremias 1949: 199), the question is not easily answered in the affirmative. For the most part, the Gospel writers were content merely to say that after his death Jesus was buried and then raised on the third day (cf. also 1 Cor 15: 3–4), and although it seems to be a clear inference in Acts 2: 31 and Rom 10: 7 that before his resurrection Jesus was in Hades or the Abyss, there is not the slightest hint in either of these texts of anything Jesus might have done while there. Moreover, in most of the other NT passages which have traditionally been thought to reflect Jesus' descent to Hades after his death on the cross (e.g., Luke 23: 43; Eph 4: 7–10[12]; Rev 1: 18, in addition to Matt 12: 40; for the problematics surrounding 1 Pet 3: 18–22, 4: 5–6, see further below), there is no allusion to any action of Jesus in the netherworld. However, there are three NT texts which, while not addressing the issue directly, do seem to provide some rather tantalizing hints which possibly suggest what the signification of the correlation in Matt 12: 40 may have been.

The first of these, interestingly enough, is within Matthew's own special tradition in 27: 51–54, where, after recording the death of Jesus (v 50), he describes the cataclysmic reaction to it both on earth and in the realm of the dead:

> [51]At that, the veil of the Temple was torn in two from top to bottom; the earth quaked; the rocks were split; [52]the tombs were opened and the bodies of many holy men rose from the dead, [53]and these, after his resurrection, came out of the tombs, entered the Holy City and appeared to a number of people. [54]Meanwhile the centurion, together with the others guarding Jesus, had seen the earthquake and all that was taking place, and they were terrified and said, "In truth this was a son of God." (Jerusalem Bible)

Might Matthew have though there was a relationship between the Son of Man being 'in the heart of the earth' (12: 40) and the events narrated in 27: 52–53? Admittedly, the wording of the latter does not make this immediately obvious. However, since vv 51–53 are set against the background of Jesus' death, and v 53 makes clear that the event described in v 52 must have taken place *before* Jesus' resurrection, it is not inconceivable that Matthew may have visualized some connection between Jesus' brief presence in Hades after his death and the 'awakening' (*ēgerthēsan*) of "the bodies of many holy men." Two distinguishable moments seem to be constitutive of the resurrection being portrayed: first, the awakening of the righteous dead in their tombs, which might also be described as their vivification in the netherworld, and second, their coming out of the tombs after Jesus' resurrection to appear to many in Jerusalem. The agentless passive verb for 'awaken' (*ēgerthēsan*) suggests, as this situation often does in the NT, that the 'awakener' is God, but might not Jesus have been thought to have played some role in conjunction with awakening? Presumably not as God's agent of it himself, since nowhere in Matthew's Gospel is Jesus ever described as raising anyone from the dead through God's Spirit (as he does, e.g., exorcise demons through the Spirit, cf. Matt 12: 28), but recalling the analogy with Jonah discussed above, perhaps the idea was that God awakened Jesus and then 'the holy ones' in the netherworld as he once rescued Jonah from death in the sea. Then Jesus would have proclaimed the divine salvation prior to his own and the righteous dead's coming out of their tombs to appear once again on earth, just as Jonah sang a psalm praising God's liberation from death before he was released from the fish back on to the dry land. The sequence of events evoked by Jonah 2 would thus suggest the explicit and implied sequence underlying Matt 27: 50–53: the experience of death, the saving from death, announcement of the divine deliverance, the return to life on earth.[13] Moreover, it can be observed that just as the focus in Matt 12: 40 is more upon death than upon death and deliverance, the same is true for Matt 27: 50–53, though obviously v 53 is more explicit about a resurrection taking place than 12: 40. It also seems significant for this interpretation that Matt 27: 51–53 has been inspired by the stirring prophetic vision of Ezekiel (37: 1–14; note esp. the LXX translation of vv 7, 12–14), as pointed out by Meier (1979: 34) and others. Ezekiel's prophecy of the revival of the dead house of Israel is in the form of a proclamation or announcement of Israel's rising to new life prior to its fulfillment.[14] This fits well our view that Matthew may have envisioned Jesus after his death in Hades, first announcing the divine salvation before it begins to be carried out in his own resurrection and that of the righteous. The great eschatological event, therefore, is not initiated by resurrection, but rather by the death of Jesus, i.e., by his proclamation of God's liberation of the dead 'in the heart of the earth.'[15]

III. Matt 12: 40 in Relation to John 5: 25–29 and 1 Peter 3: 18–22 and 4: 5–6

A second NT passage which might possibly bear some relation to the interpretation of Matt 12: 40 being proposed here is John 5: 25-29, which reads:

> [25]Truly, truly, I say to you, the hour is coming, and now is, when the dead will hear the voice of the Son of God, and those who hear will live.
>
> [26]For as the Father has life in himself, so he has granted the Son also to have life in himself, [27]and has given him authority to execute judgment, because he is the Son of man. [28]Do not marvel at this; for the hour is coming when all who are in the tombs will hear his voice and come forth, [29]those who have done good, to the resurrection of life, and those who have done evil, to the resurrection of judgment. (RSV)

Most NT critics, and especially Johannine scholars, whom I have consulted, either do not mention the tradition of Jesus' descent into Hades as having some underlying relationship with the conceptuality in these verses (an exception would be Selwyn 1946: 346–51), or they reject it outright (Jeremias 1949: 201). However, the temporal perspective in vv 28–29 is solely future,[16] and the moment referred to "when all who are in the tombs will hear his [the Son of Man's] voice and come forth" cannot be within Jesus' earthly ministry, but only after his death. However, whether John would have conceived this moment as in any sense having first occurred immediately after Jesus' death and before his resurrection is quite problematic, even doubtful, since nowhere else in John's Gospel do we find a hint that he knew of any tradition about the activity of Jesus between his death and resurrection. Nonetheless, since the eschatological outlook of vv 26–30 is not unlike that in many Synoptic passages (Brown 1966: 220), perhaps it should not be completely ruled out that John has taken over and reshaped in terms of his own perspective some of the ideas that I have intimated might lie behind Matt 12: 40 and 27: 51–53. These ideas would involve the role of Jesus as the Son of Man,[17] who after his death announces life to the entombed pious dead. To these ideas John has added the notions of Jesus as life-giver (5: 21), not simply life-announcer, and also dispenser of judgment "to those who have done evil" (5: 27, 29–30), notions which do not appear to be implicit in either Matt 12: 40[18] or 27: 51–53, though in the later development of the descent tradition among the Church Fathers in the 2nd and 3rd centuries, they came to play a role.

A third NT passage that has sometimes been associated with Matt 12: 40 because both were thought to reflect the tradition of Jesus' descent to Hades after his death, is 1 Pet 3: 18–22, 4: 5–6. However, since Dalton's thorough reexamination of the interpretation of these verses in 1 Peter (Dalton 1965), it is clear that this text has nothing to do with the descent tradition.[19] Thus, when 1 Pet 3: 18 speaks of Christ "being put to death in the flesh but made alive in the spirit," this refers to his resurrection effected by the Holy Spirit, not to his vivification in Hades following his crucifixion (Dalton 1965: 103–34). The "spirits in prison" to which Christ is said to have gone (*poreutheis,* not *katabainō*, 'descend') and preached (1 Pet 3: 19) are not all the dead in Hades (whether righteous or wicked or both), but the evil angels who led humanity into the wickedness that provoked the Flood, to whom Christ proclaims judgment and condemnation on his *ascent* through the lower heavens to his exaltation at the right hand of God (1 Pet 3: 22; Dalton 1965: 135–62). Finally, 1 Pet 4: 6 says nothing about the gospel being preached; it is rather Christ as judge of the living and the dead *who has been preached* (cf. v 5) by Christian preachers to those who have since died (and hence were *alive* when they heard the preaching) so that they might live the new life of the Spirit, even though in the eyes of some they seemed condemned as mortal beings to death (Dalton 1965: 257–72). Dalton's interpretation makes much more plausible sense over against the traditional one, if Peter's words are to serve their intended purpose as helpful consolation to the early Christians in their beleaguered situation.[20] But this means that Dalton has effectively removed any close relationship between 1 Pet 3: 18–22, 4: 5–6 and Matt 12: 40 and 27: 51–53. Only one set of general similarities remains: Jesus makes a proclamation to certain ones among the dead following his own death and does so in their place of incarceration. But for 1 Peter, what Jesus proclaimed, and precisely where and under what circumstances he proclaimed it, are all quite different from the conceptions that possibly provide the background to the Matthean texts.

IV. Matt 12: 40 and the Apocryphal Jeremiah Logion in Justin and Irenaeus

The theme of a divine figure entering the netherworld to proclaim salvation to the righteous dead is encountered in its most clear-cut form for the first time in Christian circles in an apocryphal saying attributed to the prophet Jeremiah by the 2nd century Church Fathers Justin (*Dialogue with Trypho*, 72) and Irenaeus (*Epideixis* 78; *Adversus Haereses* III.20.4; IV.22.1, 33.1, 12; V.31.1).[21] Although not attested earlier, the citation could well have been a part of a now lost apocryphal book of Jeremiah or corpus of Jeremiah quotations used by the early Christians (including possibly even Matthew himself, but see further on this below) as messianic prooftexts in the latter part of the 1st century, and so it deserves some attention here. Indeed, in one of his references to the saying, Irenaeus directly associates it with Matt 12: 40 in support of the affirmation that immediately after dying on the cross, Jesus did not depart on high, leaving his body to the earth, but dwelt for three days in the place where the dead were (*Adv. Haer.* V.31.1). To my knowledge this is the earliest connection of Matt 12: 40 with the so-called descent tradition.

Justin is the first to quote the Jeremiah saying (ca. 160 A.D.), which may be translated from his Greek as follows: "The Lord God from Israel remembered the dead who slept in the dust of the earth, and he descended to them to proclaim to them his salvation."[22]

The background and origin of this saying are unfortunately shrouded in obscurity. The fact that it occurs neither in the MT nor versional witnesses to the early Hebrew text of Jeremiah, that its thought and language do not conform to that know from the canonical Jeremiah,[23] and that its principal themes do not find any striking parallels in either the OT[24] or in other pre-Christian Jewish literature,[25] lends credence to the supposition that the saying is apocryphal, and that it has a non-Jewish, most likely Christian provenance.[26] Though it seems unwise to reject Justin's claim that the saying was present in the book of Jeremiah known to him, it is highly doubtful that this was a proto-MT form of the book,[27] rather than a Christian version that had been midrashically edited and expanded.[28] Traces of the one-time existence of such a work seem to be reflected in various Christian writings (beyond those of Justin and Irenaeus) when they refer to other non-canonical sayings attributed to the prophet Jeremiah.[29] Interestingly, one of these references occurs in the NT in our Gospel of Matthew (27: 9–10), suggesting the intriguing possibility that already by the last quarter of the 1st century A.D. an apocryphally embellished Christian edition of Jeremiah existed, from which a Gospel writer like Matthew could draw messianic prooftexts.[30] If so, could the Jeremiah citation of Justin and Irenaeus have been already present in some form in that book and through that have become known to Matthew?

It would seem quite unlikely, yet the following observations should be made. According to *Adv. Haer.* IV.27.1–2, Irenaeus would appear to have derived at least some of his information about the descent tradition (cf. IV.27.2) from what he had heard from "a certain presbyter," who he says had obtained his knowledge "from those who had seen the apostles, and from those who had been their disciples" (IV.27.1), thereby tracing it back to the 1st century A.D. Scholars who have given close attention to the origin and background of the Jeremiah Logion are generally agreed that it goes back at least as far as the first part of the 2nd century (MacCulloch 1930: 89; Bieder 1949: 140), even though its first recorded appearance is not until past the middle of that century at Ephesus, where presumably Justin wrote his *Dialogue with Trypho*. Its Asia Minor connection is strengthened by the fact that Irenaeus also came from that area, and doubtless learned of it there before he moved to Gaul as Bishop of Lyons. But none of this really lends much support to a pre-2nd century origin for the Logion, nor to its spread as far south as Syrian Antioch, where the Gospel of Matthew is now generally thought to have been written. It is perhaps worth noting, however, that Ignatius of Antioch, at the beginning of the 2nd century, provides the earliest patristic references to the descent tradition (note esp. *Epistle to the Magnesians* 9: 2; cf. MacCulloch 1930: 83), though not in a form that indicates any possibly direct connection with the Jeremiah Logion. Thus, it is not at all clear that Gschwind (1911: 220) was right in concluding that Matthew was familiar with the Jeremiah saying in one of the forms in which Irenaeus presents it because of the connection with Matt 27: 52–53. The present tendency is to argue that the influence went in the opposite direction, that it is the Jeremiah citation which was shaped in light of scripture passages—most notably Dan 12: 2, Matt 27: 52, and 1 Pet 4: 6 (Bieder 1949: 152)—rather than the reverse. The influence of Dan 12: 2 on *both* Matt 27: 52 and the Jeremiah saying seems clear enough, but whether either of these in turn was shaped by the other is far less certain. Moreover, despite an apparent terminological coincidence between 1 Pet 4: 6 and the Jeremiah Logion, Dalton's decisive removal of the 1 Peter passage from having any connection with the descent tradition makes it very risky to posit its influence on the author of the Jeremiah text, particularly in light of the fact that no patristic writer before Clement of Alexandria at the end of the 2nd century ever makes mention of 1 Pet 4: 6 as one of the scriptural supports for the descent tradition.

What may we conclude, then? Matt 12: 40 and 27: 52–53 do seem to bear an intriguing implicit relationship to the conceptuality manifest much more explicitly in the apocryphal Jeremiah citation of Justin and Irenaeus, but the possibility that Matthew may have become acquainted with these ideas through an apocryphally expanded edition of Jeremiah which he may have had at his disposal appears to be rather remote, and certainly not demonstrable on the basis of our present evidence. The most that can be said is that Matthew may have already been developing a belief about Jesus' activity 'in the heart of the earth' which was later to receive its clearest articulation in the Jermiah Logion.[31]

V. The Interpretation of Matt 12: 40 in its Context

Returning now to Matt 12: 40: if behind this verse there does lie some such idea as Jesus proclaiming God's liberation to the righteous dead as Matthew's premier interpretation of what Jesus meant by the sign of Jonah, how does this fit into the context of 12: 38–41? It has often been argued that the motif of 'preaching' (whether of liberation or judgment) could never constitute the meaning of a 'sign' (Howton 1962: 389; Jeremias 1965: 409), first, because the definition of 'sign' implied in the scribes and Pharisees' request (12: 38) must be consistent with the conclusion of Jesus' answer, ". . . except the sign of the prophet Jonah" (12: 39), i.e., a divine wonder immediately authenticating Jesus' messiahship (Vögtle 1953: 244; Seidelin 1952: 119), and second, because the association of Jonah with the word 'sign' must refer to the miraculous deliverance of the prophet from the fish, since this is deemed the only event in the book of Jonah that aptly qualifies as a 'sign' (Jeremias 1965: 409). The operative definition of 'sign' throughout most of Matt 12: 38–39 is indeed that of a verification wonder, but, as we contended earlier, such a definition fits poorly in the expression 'the sign of Jonah,' since it would imply Jesus' acceptance of his opponents' request as ultimately legitimate, thereby canceling any significance to his initial words of refusal, but also, and more seriously, releasing the scribes and Pharisees from Jesus' customary appeal for repentance and faith until after his resurrection, something granted no one else. Thus, when Jesus uses the words 'the sign of Jonah,' he probably does *not* have in mind the same meaning for 'sign' as in his adversaries' request. But what other type(s) of meaning might he have had in mind?

To answer this question we need to remind ourselves briefly of those places, first in the OT, where a 'sign' is brought into connection with a prophetic figure. Though the OT never uses the expression 'the sign of (name of prophet),'[32] it can speak of a prophet giving, announcing, or telling about a sign, usually originating from Yahweh (Isa 7: 11,14; 19: 20; 37: 30; 38: 7; 55: 13; 66: 19; Jer 32: 20–21; 44: 29; Ezek 14: 8; 20: 12,20; cf. also Deut 13: 2–3; 1 Sam 2: 34; Ps 74: 9), or of a prophet acting out a sign (Ezek 4: 3), or even becoming a sign himself (Isa 8: 18; 20: 3). Few of these signs are miraculous or supernatural, though this is not automatically precluded (cf. Isa 37: 30; Jer 32: 20–21). Often they are not something that will happen immediately, but in the more or less distant future. Though they may serve to confirm an action or word from Yahweh (e.g., 2 Kgs 20: 8), they may also function to impart knowledge (Ezek 14: 8), assure defense and deliverance (Isa 19: 20), evoke faith (Isa 7: 9,11), and produce remembrance (Isa 55: 13) (Helfmeyer 1974: 170–88). In Jer 44: 29–30 the sign is a future event whose announcement in the present serves as a sign to the remnant of Judah that Yahweh will surely judge them, while in Isa 66: 19, where admittedly the context is somewhat obscure, the sign seems to be in the very words of 'the survivors to the nations,' proclaiming to the nations Yahweh's fame and glory (cf. Westermann 1969: 425). These last two examples seem to me to be instructive when considering the function of Matt 12: 40, as we shall see below.

When we turn to the NT we likewise find that the word 'sign' is not always used in the same way but can denote any kind of outward indication of an inner or hidden purpose, not necessarily supernatural in character, though certainly more often than in the OT the word does seem to indicate a prodigious act or event (Richardson 1962: 346a). But important for our purposes here is how Matthew himself employed the word 'sign.' Outside of the two Demand-for-a-Sign pericopes (12: 38–41;16: 1,4[33]), he uses it only four times. In 24: 24, where Jesus speaks of false messiahs and prophets arising and showing "great signs and wonders, so as to lead astray, if possible, even the elect," the word 'sign' obviously refers to some kind of wondrous prodigy. Perhaps also in 24: 3, when the disciples ask Jesus, "What will be the sign of your coming and of the close of the age," they may anticipate something supernatural, though possibly nothing more than a visibly striking or unusual portent that would unmistakably point to Jesus' parousia and the manifestation of the end-time. Jesus' response in 24: 29–30 need not indicate anything more than this, though the meaning of the phrase 'the sign of the Son of Man in heaven' (v 30) is much disputed, and the precise content of the sign is not stated. However, I am inclined to agree with those who do not see the sign as the Son of Man himself (e.g., Rengstorf 1971: 236–38), but, as the context suggests, as something that clearly precedes the Son of Man's coming, announcing his advent in some awesome fashion, possibly with a blaze of heavenly light effectively counterposed against all the darkness described in v 29, and to which the words 'great glory' might point. Of interest is the fact that the sign is a future phenomenon announced in the present, and that it functions as a warning of the onset of judgment (recall Jer 44: 29–30 above), as the mourning response of 'the tribes of the earth' suggests when the latter behold the sign (Tödt 1965: 80). Finally, the kiss Judas gives Jesus in the Garden of Gethsemane is called a 'sign' (26: 48), indicating in this context a customary physical gesture functioning for the somewhat unusual purpose of confirming Jesus' identity to the chief priests and elders. From this survey, we see that Matthew's understanding of a sign was not univocal, nor was it narrowly limited to some type of divine authentication wonder.

But, it might be countered, does not Matthew's particular usage in the expression 'the sign of Jonah' signal a definition of 'sign' that must refer it to a miraculous event, since for Matthew's audience, what else in the book of Jonah other than the prophet's marvelous deliverance from the fish would warrant the designation 'sign'? It is true, of course, that 1st century B.C.-A.D. Jewish writings alluding to the Jonah story never fail to mention this event (cf. 3 Macc 6: 8; Josephus *Antiq*. 9. 213; also Jeremias 1965: 409, n.24), but in light of Matthew's flexible understanding of the word 'sign,' the fact that in 12: 40 he does not stress Jonah's deliverance but rather his sojourn in the belly of the sea monster, and that he appends 12: 41 as a further explication of the meaning of the sign of Jonah, is it not reasonable to infer that for Matthew and his readers another feature from the Jonah story might be understood as explaining the sign of Jonah, viz., the prophet's proclaiming God's salvation prior to his ultimate deliverance?

Though it is likely that in pre-Matthean tradition the saying in 12: 41 did not originally function as an indication of the meaning of the sign of Jonah (though it may have already in Q, cf. Edwards 1971: 83), it definitely seems to serve this purpose in the final form of Matthew's Gospel. Moreover, if our interpretation of how Matthew may have understood 12: 40 is in the right direction, it can be seen not only how this prepares the way for 12: 41, but also how both verses cohered in explaining what Matthew thought the sign of Jonah meant, and in what sense they provided an appropriate answer of Jesus in the context of the Jewish leaders' demand for a sign.

In my view, Matt 12: 40 and 12: 41 were thought to share a common theme —the proclamation of Jonah—albeit derived from different parts of the Jonah story, and thus employed with different meanings. However, the predominant stress in 12: 40 lies not on the Jonah side of the correlation, but with the Son of Man. As Jonah was, so the Son of Man will be in the netherworld acclaiming the divine liberation from death, but unlike Jonah, he will have an audience:[34] the righteous dead, to whom his words are addressed as a preface to resurrection, first his own, then theirs (applying the background of Matt 27: 52–53 discussed above). For Matthew, this was the first meaning of the sign of Jonah (thus construing it as a subjective genitive: the sign that Jonah and the Son of Man give), a sign of the gracious divine word of salvation announced to "the holy ones" in the tombs by the Son of Man "in the heart of the earth." It is therefore a sign not at all like the one the scribes and Pharisees were demanding (and hence we have no contradictory concession to Jesus' categorical denial of a sign), because its enactment is future, not immediate, and because it does not function to verify unequivocally Jesus' present messianic role. Ironically, to his opponents' request for "a sign from heaven" (Matt 16: 1, and undoubtedly this is the type of sign meant in 12: 38), Jesus counters with what we might call "a sign from Hades," since that is where the sign will be manifest through the Son of Man. But how does this sign function meaningfully as an apt response to the scribes and Pharisees' demand?

In Matt 12: 38 Jesus castigates the *present* generation, epitomized by the scribes and Pharisees, as 'evil and adulterous,' because they seek the wrong kind of sign. For them he has only what is ultimately a sign of the Son of Man (12: 40b), which refers to a future act for the benefit of *past* generations, the past generations of the *righteous* (whether the patriarchs and prophets would be in mind, as later traditions indicated, or all the righteous, is of no importance at this point), but which is given to the present evil generation as a warning sign, a warning that they will not hear the Son of Man's joyous word of salvation *in the future* (not even if they should die before Jesus). However, they *can* hear it *now* through Jesus, and proleptically receive the salvation he has come to bring by responding to his words and deeds. In effect these are the only immediate 'signs' he has to give. And what if they do not respond?

In Matt 12: 41 they are presented with another interpretation of the sign of Jonah that answers this question. This interpretation also refers to a *past* generation, this time that of the wicked Ninevites, who upon hearing Jonah's proclamation of *judgment*, repented and were delivered. Again we are confronted with a warning sign, a warning that unless the scribes and Pharisees repent *now* in the face of Jesus' admonitions, the proclamation they will hear at the final judgment will not be one of salvation, but of condemnation, preeminently from the repentant Ninevites! Thus the sign of Jonah is a proclamation of salvation and judgment—salvation to the righteous dead of the past, judgment to the unrighteous living of the present—both as a warning to the contemporary evil generation that without an immediate positive response to Jesus, the final reckoning will only spell disaster. The experience of salvation will not come for them, as it will for the past generation of the pious, unless like them, they too respond in faith and repentance. Moreover, there is nothing greater than the proclamation of Jesus and the Son of Man. No other divine acts will surpass or replace what he has said and done. Therefore it is absolutely crucial that Jesus' hearers respond in the present, for in the eschatological future there will only be condemnation and death.

My study of the scholarly literature on Matt 12: 40 has impressed me with the fact that those who have endeavored to make sense of this verse within its biblical setting have been unable to do so without resorting to extrapolation, i.e., inferring from what is plainly stated meanings that are assumed to be implicit in the background. Obviously, my own effort has been no exception. W. F. Albright used to warn his students of the dangers of extrapolation in historical reconstruction, and I am fully conscious of similar risks in exegetical interpretation. I am therefore under no illusion that what I have suggested as possibly Matthew's understanding of 12: 40 in its context solves all the problems raised by this puzzling verse. Indeed, it probably poses others. Nonetheless, I dare to think that what has been proposed here does offer a plausible explanation for what Matt 12: 40 seems to presuppose, and also one which links well with the way Matt 12: 41 is made to explicate the sign of Jonah. Moreover, it reflects an interpretation of Jonah 2: 1 in relation to the psalm in Jonah 2 that does not have to resort either to Jonah's or Jesus' 'resurrection' to be comprehensible, but which appropriates themes characteristic both of the Gospel tradition about Jesus and the message of the book of Jonah: the themes of the proclamation of God's liberating salvation and the assurance of the divine judgment when there is no repentance.

Notes

1. Both Matt 12: 40 and Luke 11: 30 are clearly similar in form, but not in content. Because it is not essential to my presentation here, I shall not go into the question of whether Luke 11: 30 represents the oldest form of the explanation of the sign of Jonah, as many have thought, nor shall I examine the nature of the relationship between Luke 11: 30 and Matt 12: 40. For discussion of these matters, see Vögtle 1953: 248–49, 252, and Edwards 1971: 37, 85, 96–97.

2. Matt 12: 42 will be left aside, since it has only a somewhat tangential bearing on the meaning of the sign of Jonah.

3. The fact that Justin in his *Dialogue with Trypho* (107.2) refers quite directly to the Matthean pericope on the request for a sign but does not clearly indicate that the quote from Jonah 2: 1 was in his text of Matt 12: 39–41, is no solid evidence that Matt 12: 40 is a post-Matthean interpolation in the first Gospel (against Stendahl 1968: 132–33). See Edwards 1971: 97. Actually, after literally quoting Matt 12: 39, Justin in his very next words could well suggest he was aware of the presence of v 40: "And since [Jesus] spoke this obscurely, it was to be understood by the audience that after His crucifixion He should rise again on the third day." (Translation from Roberts and Donaldson 1950: 252.)

4. Certainly the tradition in its final form clearly understood the identification of Jesus with the Son of Man.

5. Reicke (1946: 246) calls attention to certain instances in the Gospel accounts of Jesus' passion where language is borrowed from various OT psalms of lament in which the psalmist's distress is sometimes portrayed as a struggle in the waters of death, thus providing a basis for the early Christians to use similar language in describing Jesus' suffering and death. However, in Matt 12: 40, the author has studiously avoided this usage.

6. Esp. the sixth vision in 4 Ezra 13 and in the Similitudes of the Ethiopic 1 Enoch. Cf. Tödt 1965: 22–31.

7. Particularly instructive here is Matt 27: 51–54, where immediately after the indication of Jesus' death (v 50), the Evangelist inserts from his own special material a description of certain apocalyptic phenomena that directly follow—indeed are precipitated by—Jesus' "yielding up his spirit," including the opening of the tombs, the resurrection of "the bodies of many holy men," and by implication, Jesus' own resurrection (v 53), culminating in the confession of the centurion and his companions testifying to the validity of Jesus' messianic title as Son of God (v 54). For further comments on this text, see below.

8. Even though the temporal phrase is somewhat at odds with the usual NT indication of Jesus' resurrection "on the third day" (which obviously conforms best with the chronology of the Passion story in all the Gospels), the fact that in 27: 63 Matthew has the chief priests and Pharisees quote Jesus as having said he would rise "after three days" (which does not seem to be a direct allusion to 12: 40) suggests that for Matthew there was no serious discrepancy between "on the third day" (16: 21; 17: 23; 19: 19), on the one hand, and "after three days" or "three days and three nights," on the other. Mark regularly has "after three days" (8: 31; 9: 31; 10: 34), even though his Passion story represents Jesus' death and burial as taking place on the day before the sabbath (15: 39, 42–46), his resurrection on the

day after the sabbath (16: 1–6). In light of this, the temporal datum alone in Matt 12: 40 should not be cited as evidence that this verse cannot have had a reference to the resurrection (see, e.g., Vögtle 1953: 258).

9. Though it is true that in Matt 28: 11–12 the Pharisees are not singled out as among those bribing the soldiers, there seems no good reason to doubt their knowledge of and approving complicity in this act.

10. Though many OT scholars have deemed this psalm to be a secondary interpolation within the book of Jonah, this would hardly have been the view of Matthew's time, when the psalm would have been read as integral to the book as a whole. As already indicated above, the wording of Matt 12: 40b shows that its author was familiar with the psalm. For scholarly efforts to give a plausible contextual interpretation of the psalm, see my own study (Landes 1967), and most recently that of Ackerman (1981), whose analysis differs somewhat from mine.

11. Note such expressions as "the belly of Sheol" (2: 3), "the deep" (Heb *mĕṣûlâ*), "the heart of the seas," "the flood" (Heb *nāhār*) (2: 4), "the deep" (Heb *tĕhôm*) (2: 6), "the earth" and "the Pit" (2: 7), all typical OT underworld terminology.

12. Eph 4: 9–10 is the only place in the NT where the key verb "to descend" (*katabainō*) is employed with Christ as subject, but the meaning of the closely associated words in v 9, "into the lower parts of the earth" (*eis ta katōtera merē tēs gēs*), is much controverted. Though the words *ta katōtera merē*, when conjoined with *tēs gēs*, seem at first glance to be an obvious reference to the netherworld, Barth (1974: 433–34) has argued most persuasively that in the context of Ephesians they are more probably equivalent to "the low region of the earth" or "the earth down here," denoting Christ's incarnation and especially his crucifixion, rather than his descent into Hades (434). Of course Matthew need have looked no further than the book of Jonah itself for the clear portrayal of a descent into Sheol, since this is the way Jonah's journey from Joppa (1: 3) to the "heart of the seas" (2: 3) is depicted in chaps. 1–2 (note the key verb *YRD*, 'to descend,' in 1: 3, 5 and 2: 7). It is quite conceivable, therefore, that Matthew understood a descent underlying 12: 40, simply on the basis of the analogy with the book of Jonah. For comparatively recent good summary discussions of "the descent into Hades" tradition in the NT and early Christian literature, see Robinson (1962) and Perrot (1968).

13. In the Jonah story, of course, the prophet does not actually experience death, but the fact that his being cast into the sea is depicted as a descent into Sheol was enough to suggest a valid analogy between Jonah in the belly of the sea monster and the Son of Man in the heart of the earth. Moreover, that Jonah does something while inside the sea monster may not be irrelevant to assigning a corresponding activity to the Son of Man in Hades (against Bieder 1949: 43). Matt 27: 54 might seem to pose a problem for our interpretation of the preceding verses, since it seems to suggest that the resurrection of "the holy ones" actually took priority over that of Jesus. However, though a number of scholars have adjudged the words "after his resurrection" (v 53) to be either a late apologetic gloss to support the affirmation that Christ is "the first fruits of those who have fallen asleep" (1 Cor 15: 20; cf. also Rom 8: 29; Col 1: 18) or a corruption of an original *meta tēn egersin autōn*, "after *their* resurrection," referring to "the holy ones" (Allen 1912: 296; Schweizer 1975: 516), these critical strictures receive no significant support from the history of the textual witness to v 53, and it is likely the verse is original as it stands. If so, then, for Matthew, the emergence of "the holy ones" from their tombs and subsequent appearance in Jerusalem were not among "the things happening" (*ta ginomena*) which the centurion and his guards saw at the cross, but which they became aware of only later. Thus these events are recounted here proleptically to show their intimate connection with the *death* of Jesus, i.e., with his presence "in the heart of the earth" and the activity associated with that.

14. Interestingly, with the OT, it is almost paradigmatic that Yahweh's great salvatory deeds are first announced before they are carried out. For the Exodus, cf. Gen 15: 13–16; Exod 3: 10,12; 14: 13–18. Second Isaiah is in essence a dramatic prophetic proclamation of the new exodus, Yahweh's work in bringing Israel back to Palestine from Babylonian captivity, before it is actually accomplished. Similarly with the two 'resurrection' passages in the OT (Isa 26: 19 and Dan 12: 1–2): neither recounts the event as having taken place; they announce its advent in the future.

15. For the presentation of the resurrection as a 'liberation-wonder' (*Befreiungswunder*), esp. in Matt 27: 51–54, see the study of Kratz 1973: 38–47.

16. Unlike v 25, where the addition of the words "and now is" indicates that the dead who will hear the voice of the Son of God are not just the already physically dead, but also the spiritually dead who presently can hear and respond to Jesus' call to life during his early ministry. I am inclined to agree with

Brown (1966: 218–21) that v 25 does not belong with the unit vv 26–30, but with vv 19–25, which, because of their parallelism in thought with vv 26–30, probably "represent a rethinking of the same sayings of Jesus at a later date, when realized eschatology had come to the fore as an answer to the delay in the second coming" (Brown 1966: 220).

17. I am aware that the expression "son of man" in v 27 is anarthrous, but the context militates against construing the words to mean simply a human being. Perhaps, unaccountably, John is rendering the words in their original Semitic form, as, e.g., in Dan 7: 13, where they are likewise anarthrous (also in the LXX). See Brown 1966: 215.

18. However, we shall see below that the idea of judgment is very much involved in Matt 12: 41, and what significance this has for 12: 38–41.

19. In his comparatively recent commentary on 1 Peter, Kelly (1969) appears to be in thorough agreement with Dalton's interpretation of 1 Pet 3: 18–22, 4: 5–6.

20. Perrot (1968: 27, n. 26) does not acknowledge this point in his criticism of Dalton's interpretation of 1 Pet 4: 5–6.

21. For the most thorough scholarly discussions of this saying, see Gschwind 1911: 199–227, and Bieder 1949: 135–53. In the matter of the attribution of the saying to Jeremiah, Irenaeus is inconsistent, once assigning it to Isaiah (*Adv. Haer.* III.20.4), once to "the prophet" (unidentified, V.31.1), once quite imprecisely to "others" (IV.33.12), or without any reference to authorship at all (IV.33.1), in addition to the two times (IV.22.1, *Epid.* 78) he agrees with Justin in crediting it to Jeremiah. Selwyn (1946: 346) considers the reference to Isaiah as due to a *lapsus calami*, while Bieder (1949: 136) concludes from all the citations that it was a matter of indifference to Irenaeus who spoke the words.

22. A comparison of Justin's Greek with the five Latin renderings of the citation by Irenaeus (the sixth, in *Epid.* 78, is extant only in an Armenian translation) does tend to justify the conclusion that Irenaeus was not dependent upon Justin for his versions of the text (Gschwind 1911: 200), but it does not necessarily mean that he had before him several different manuscript witnesses to the quotation (against Gschwind 1911: 211), since his variant readings could well be due to quoting from memory (MacCulloch 1930: 89), or even intentionally paraphrasing. However, at the beginning of the quotation in Irenaeus' renditions, the persistence of the divine title, *Dominus sanctus Israel* ("the Lord, the Holy One of Israel," cf. *Adv. Haer.* III.20.4; IV.22.1; *Epid.* 78; and note also the shortened form, *Dominus sanctus*, in IV.33.12), over against Justin's somewhat awkward Greek, *kyrios ho theos apo Israēl*, does suggest that the original Greek reading may have been *kyrios ho hagios tou Israēl*, which Justin or his source had either miscopied or corrupted (Gschwind 1911: 212). The only other major difference between the texts of Irenaeus and Justin is in the concluding words, where on three occasions Irenaeus replaces the word 'to announce' with other terms meaning variously 'to deliver' (IV.33.1), 'to raise up' (IV.33.12), or 'to rescue' (V.31.1). But whether this indicates two variant traditions of the saying, one stressing originally only the proclamation of salvation to the dead, the other only their deliverance from death, the latter antedating the former (so Gschwind 1911: 216–17; contrast Bieder 1949: 139–40, 149–50), is difficult to determine on the basis of our present limited evidence. Since for Irenaeus (on the basis of *Epid.* 78, *Adv. Haer.* III.20.4 and IV.22.1) the proclaiming was clearly for the purpose of salvation, it is likely he saw no major difference between the two readings, and his choice of words was probably determined by his own predilections in each context.

23. This is perhaps best illustrated by Gschwind's unsatisfying effort to reconstruct the original Hebrew form of the saying (Gschwind 1911: 214–15), but it is also indicated when one sees how unconvincing are the places that have been proposed for the setting of the saying within Jeremiah's prophecies, e.g., after 22: 12 (Bieder 1949: 140, referring to Hennecke), or between vv 19 and 20 in Jeremiah 11 (Selwyn 1946: 346, n.22). It is possible, however, as Bieder has suggested (152), that the descent tradition was linked to Jeremiah because of the prophet's suffering which brought him to the pit (cf. Jer 45: 6 LXX).

24. The motif of Yahweh proclaiming salvation to his people, usually through a prophet or prophet-like figure, is common in the OT, though not in the context of Sheol addressed to Israelites who have already died. Only Ezekiel 37 begins to move in this direction. It is true, of course, that the divine title, "Holy One of Israel," originates in the OT, and even occurs twice in Jeremiah (50: 29; 51: 5), but this is the only phrase in the saying that seems in any way reminiscent of Jeremiah's language, and even then it is not one of the prophet's typical appellations for Yahweh (as it is, e.g., in Isaiah). The words "who slept in the dust of the earth" seem to be dependent upon Dan 12: 2 (certainly not

Jeremiah), interestingly in its Greek rendering as represented in Theodotion's recension (though the verb has been changed, probably in light of Matt 27: 52; cf. Hart 1907: 70).

25. It is therefore difficult to agree with Hart (1907: 69) that the saying may have once been a part of a traditional Jewish exposition of the prophets.

26. With the presence of the key verb form *katebē*, "he descended," the Logion would appear to be the earliest unambiguous witness to the descent tradition within Christian circles. However, that it originated as part of an early Christian homily from which it was excerpted and inserted into the text of Jeremiah seems highly unlikely (Bieder 1949: 151, against Swete 1894: 59 and MacCulloch 1930: 89).

27. Against Bieder 1949: 140, who thinks Justin must have been correct in his reproach of the Jews for expunging the Jeremiah saying from their canonical text, which would presumably have been the same as the one Justin used, but without the deletion. Justin may indeed have thought this is what the Jews had done (because of the way Christians were using the saying in their interpretation of Jesus), but Trypho's response to him seems more in keeping with the reality of the situation when he says the substance of Justin's accusation is incredible.

28. Cf. Atzberger 1896: 139, n.3. Gschwind (1911: 200–1) thinks the Jeremiah citation had been added to a *Jewish* midrashically redacted edition of Jeremiah, but this seems unlikely, for reasons already outlined above (the Jewish Aramaic insertion of Jer 10: 11 would not be a real prototypical parallel). It is also possible that the saying was a part of a completely apocryphal book of Jeremiah, perhaps even an apocalypse like the Assumption of Moses or the Apocalypses of Baruch, but it is very doubtful that either Justin or Irenaeus, in pursuit of their apologetic intentions, would quote a text as scriptural from a work generally known, especially by Jews, as non-canonical.

29. For discussion of these writings, see Gschwind 1911: 203–6. Bieder (1949: 151) adds two Syriac sources. 1 Macc 2: 1–2 refers to several otherwise unattested Jeremiah sayings which are said to be in the *apographai* (RSV, "records"). Were these "records" already the beginning of a corpus of non-canonical words of Jeremiah?

30. In his commentary on Matthew, Jerome says the quote in 27: 9–10 is to be found in a Hebrew scroll which he calls *Apocryphum Jeremiae*. There is no good reason to question the existence of this work (Gschwind 1911: 204), but whether the Jeremiah citation of Justin and Irenaeus was ever composed in Hebrew seems doubtful. Recent NT scholars have tended to reject Matthew's assigning the quote in 27: 9–10 to Jeremiah, seeing it rather as based upon Zech 11: 13. However, as Lohmeyer (1958: 378–79) has pointed out, the Matthean citation departs radically from both the MT and LXX of Zech 11: 13, and appears to be a new literary creation, picking up on the "thirty pieces of silver" and "potter" in Zech 11: 13, and the purchase of the Potter's Field in Jer 32: 1–33: 13. Since Matthew clearly thought this saying belonged to Jeremiah (the textual evidence against this is not weighty), it seems plausible to conclude that he found it in a version of Jeremiah containing apocryphal sayings. That he would not have been troubled by a saying based upon a combination of prophetic texts is obvious from Matt 11: 5–6, and that an apocryphon would be formed from the words of both Zechariah and Jeremiah evokes no surprise in view of Zechariah's own appropriation of Jeremiah on more than one occasion (cf. Zech 1: 4 with Jer 18: 11 and 35: 15; Zech 3: 8 and Jer 23: 5).

31. Where of course the reference is to God, not to Jesus. But also contemporary with the Jeremiah Logion is the earliest non-canonical account of Jesus' passion in the so-called Gospel of Peter, where in lines 39–42 there is not only an allusion to the descent tradition, but also to the motif of Jesus' "preaching" to the dead while in Hades. Precisely what Jesus preached is not specified in this text. For a translation, see James 1924: 90–94, and the discussion in MacCulloch (1930: 297) and Dalton (1965: 25).

32. Despite the fact that four OT prophets make use of the word 'sign,' we never hear of a 'sign of Isaiah,' or 'sign of Jeremiah,' or 'sign of Ezekiel.' This type of expression also never occurs in pre-Christian Jewish literature, as far as I am aware, so its presence on the lips of Jesus in the form "the sign of Jonah" appears to be unique and unparalleled.

33. I intentionally omit 16: 2–3, with its reference to "the signs of the times," since textually these verses do not appear to be genuine to Matthew, but constitute an editorial gloss shaped in light of Luke 12: 54–56 (Schweizer 1975: 333).

34. Of course, by the 1st century A.D., interpreters of the Jonah Psalm could well have thought *Jonah's* words were heard by the inhabitants of Hades, since they identified "the belly of the sea-monster" with the netherworld.

References

Ackerman, J. S.
1981 Satire and Symbolism in the Song of Jonah. Pp. 213–46 in *Traditions in Transformation: Turning Points in Biblical Faith* [Frank Moore Cross 60th Birthday Festschrift], ed. B. Halpern and J. Levenson. Winona Lake, Indiana: Eisenbrauns.

Allen, W. C.
1912 *A Critical and Exegetical Commentary on the Gospel According to S. Matthew*. The International Critical Commentary. Edinburgh: T. and T. Clark.

Atzberger, L.
1896 *Geschichte der christlichen Eschatologie innerhalb der vornicänischen Zeit*. Freiburg: Herder'she Verlagshandlung.

Barth, M.
1974 *Ephesians 4–6*. Anchor Bible 34A. Garden City: Doubleday.

Bieder, W.
1949 *Die Vorstellung von der Höllenfahrt Jesu Christi. Beitrag zur Entstehungsgeschichte der Vorstellung vom sog. Descensus ad inferos*. Abhandlungen zur Theologie des Alten und Neuen Testaments 19. Zürich: Zwingli-Verlag.

Brown, R. E.
1966 *The Gospel According to John (i-xii)*. Anchor Bible 29. Garden City: Doubleday.

Cope, O. L.
1976 *Matthew: A Scribe Trained for the Kingdom of Heaven*. The Catholic Biblical Quarterly Monograph Series 5. Washington, D.C.: The Catholic Biblical Association of America.

Dalton, W. J.
1965 *Christ's Proclamation to the Spirits: A Study of 1 Peter 3: 18–4: 6*. Analecta Biblica 23. Rome: Pontifical Biblical Institute.

Edwards, R. A.
1971 *The Sign of Jonah in the Theology of Evangelists and Q*. Studies in Biblical Theology, Second Series, 18. London: SCM.

Gschwind, K.
1911 *Die Niederfahrt Christi in die Unterwelt. Ein Beitrag zur Exegese des Neuen Testamentes und zur Geschichte des Taufsymbols*. Neutestamentliche Abhandlungen. II Band 3./5. Heft. Münster: Aschendorffsche Verlagsbuchhandlung.

Hart, J. H. A.
1907 Scribes of the Nazarenes. The Gospel According to St. Luke and the Descent into Hades. *The Expositor* 7: 53–71.

Helfmeyer, F. J.
1974 *ʾôth*. Vol. I, pp. 167–88 in *Theological Dictionary of the Old Testament*, ed. G. Botterweck and H. Ringgren, trans. J. Willis et al. Grand Rapids: Eerdmans.

Howton, J.
1962 The Sign of Jonah. *Scottish Journal of Theology* 15: 288–304.

James, M. R.
1924 *The Apocryphal New Testament*. Oxford: The Clarendon Press.

Jeremias, J.
1949 Zwischen Karfreitag und Ostern: Descensus und Ascensus in der Karfreitagstheologie des Neues Testamentes. *Zeitschrift für die neutestamentliche Wissenschaft* 42: 194–201.

1965 *Iōnas*. Vol. III, pp. 406–10 in *Theological Dictionary of the New Testament*, ed. G. Kittel, trans. G. Bromiley. Grand Rapids: Eerdmans.

Jenni, E.
1962 Messiah, Jewish. Vol. K-Q, pp. 360–65 in *The Interpreter's Dictionary of the Bible*, ed. G. Buttrick et al. Nashville: Abingdon.

Kelly, J. N. D.
1969 *A Commentary on the Epistles of Peter and Jude*. Black's NT Commentaries. London: Adam and Charles Black.

Kratz, R.
1973 *Auferweckung als Befreiung. Eine Studie zur Passions- und Auferstehungstheologie des Matthäus (besonders Mt 27, 62–28, 15)*. Stuttgart: Katholisches Bibelwerk.

Landes, G. M.
1967 The Kerygma of the Book of Jonah: The Contextual Interpretation of the Jonah Psalm. *Interpretation* 31: 3–31.
1976 Jonah, Book of. Pp. 488–91 in *The Interpreter's Dictionary of the Bible: Supplementary Volume*, ed. Keith Crim et al. Nashville: Abingdon.

Lohmeyer, E.
1958 *Das Evangelium des Matthäus*. 2 Aufl. ed. W. Schmauch. Göttingen: Vandenhoeck und Ruprecht.

MacCulloch, J. A.
1930 *The Harrowing of Hell: A Comparative Study of an Early Christian Doctrine*. Edinburgh: T. and T. Clark.

Meier, J. P.
1979 *The Vision of Matthew: Christ, Church, and Morality in the First Gospel*. New York: Paulist.

Perrot, C.
1968 La descente du Christ aux enfers dans la Nouveau Testament. *Lumière et Vie* XVII, No. 17: 5–29.

Reicke, B.
1946 *The Disobedient Spirits and Christian Baptism*. København: Ejnar Munksgaard.

Rengstorf, K.
1971 *Sēmeion*. Vol. VII, pp. 200–61 in *Theological Dictionary of the New Testament*, ed. G. Kittel, trans. G. Bromiley. Grand Rapids: Eerdmans.

Richardson, A.
1962 Sign in the NT. Vol. R-Z, pp. 346–47 in *The Interpreter's Dictionary of the Bible*, ed. G. Buttrick et al. Nashville: Abingdon.

Roberts, A., and Donaldson, J.
1950 *The Ante-Nicene Fathers: Translations of the Writings of the Fathers Down to A.D. 325*. Vol. I. Grand Rapids: Eerdmans.

Robinson, J. M.
1962 Descent into Hades. Vol. A-D, pp. 826–28 in *The Interpreter's Dictionary of the Bible*, ed. G. Buttrick et al. Nashville: Abingdon.

Schweizer, E.
1975 *The Good News According to Matthew*, trans. D. Green. Atlanta: John Knox.

Seidelin, P.
1952 Das Jonaszeichen. *Studia Theologica* 5: 119–31.

Selwyn, E. G.
1946 *The First Epistle of St. Peter*. London: Macmillan.

Swete, H. B.
1894 *The Apostle's Creed: Its Relation to Christianity*. London: C. J. Clay.

Stendahl, K.
1968 *The School of St. Matthew and Its Use of the Old Testament*. Philadelphia: Fortress.

Tödt, H. E.
1965 *The Son of Man in the Synoptic Tradition*. Philadelphia: Westminster.

Vögtle, A.
1953 Der Spruch vom Jonaszeichen. Pp. 230–77 in *Synoptischen Studien. Festschrift für Alfred Wikenhauser*. München: Karl Zink.

Westermann, C.
1969 *Isaiah 40–66. A Commentary*, trans. D. Stalker. The Old Testament Library. Philadelphia: Westminster.

Jewish Reaction to Christian Borrowings

Cyrus H. Gordon
New York University, New York City

Taken on its own terms, Christianity is The True Israel. The Old Testament basis for a radical reform of Judaism is the call for a *brit ḥadaša*[1], "a new covenant" or "a new testament." Jeremiah[2] insists on the need for a *brit ḥadaša* so there is no doubt that the concept and terminology are pre-Christian. Indeed, the Qumran Scrolls, which show no trace of Christianity, stress initiation into the *brit,* by which is meant the Qumran community and the ideals for which it stood. For Christianity, from the start, emphasis on the *brit ḥadaša* has been paramount. The success of Christianity has caused Judaism to softpeddle Jeremiah's *brit ḥadaša,* with the result that for the Jews the Covenant remains the "Old" one that God made with ancient Israel, with no reference to any new covenant, even though the latter is called for by a major Old Testament prophet.

The thesis of this article is that Jewish elements stressed by Christianity have tended to be played down by Judaism, by way of reaction. Accordingly, Christianity has determined to a great extent what Judaism has become. Obviously there are areas of universal accord where this could not be the case. Just because Christianity continued the Old Testament injunctions outlawing murder and theft, Judaism could not and did not take an opposing view. However, Christianity has accorded to the Ten Commandments a highly honored place, so much so that although Judaism could not remove the list from its place in The Law of Moses,[3] it did eliminate it from the prayer book. Reform Judaism has in modern times reintroduced an emphasis on The Ten Commandments, an emphasis still absent from traditional liturgies.[4]

One of the archeological surprises of this century is the early synagogue at Dura-Europos (third century A.D.). In it the walls were covered with frescoes of Old Testament scenes.[5] Churches, at Dura-Europos and elsewhere, all later than the early Dura synagogue, continued the tradition of illustrating biblical scenes, adding New Testament episodes. But the Dura-Europos evidence points to the priority of synagogue art. Pictorial art characterizes other old excavated synagogues. Beth Alfa in Israel is perhaps the best preserved example; there the mosaic floor, while including purely Hebraic themes (such as the sacrifice of Isaac), highlights the signs of the zodiac, with the central divine figure depicted like Helios in his chariot drawn by four horses. We need not delve into the phenomenon of syncretism. For present purposes suffice it to note that synagogue art, including the representation of animals and people, was common during the early Christian centuries. There were different schools of thought in interpreting the Commandment against images. The rabbis disagreed amongst themselves as to whether the Commandment banned only three-dimensional graven images or whether two-dimensional paintings, drawings, and mosaics were also forbidden. As a matter of fact, the Commandment is directed against artistic representations when such figures are worshipped.[6] Indeed the Mishnaic treatise *ʿAvoda Zara* ("Idolatry") permits Jews to make and sell idols for a living, because images do not become idols until they are worshipped.[7] Thus a Jewish sculptor is allowed to sell statuary that his customers will subsequently transform into idols by worshipping them.

Christianity, too, has harbored divergent attitudes regarding the intent of the Commandment against images. The Iconoclastic Movement in the Byzantine Church may have been of relatively short duration,[8] but it did take place in a major branch of Christianity that both before and after was and remains devoted to the adoration of images. Roman Catholicism has developed religious art to points of excellence and heights of glory culminating in the Renaissance art of the Church, developments which have rubbed off, in varying degree, on the Protestant churches. But what interests us here is the undeniable fact that while the Church emphasized religious art, the Synagogue abandoned it with the result that there has been almost no synagogue painting since the passing of Greco-Roman antiquity.[9]

Baptism is another "old Hebrew custom." Baptism in the Jordan had an honored place in Israel long before St. John baptized Christ. Naaman turned to the Prophet Elisha for healing and was instructed to immerse himself seven times in the Jordan.[10] Naaman was at first skeptical, but when he at last followed the instructions of the Prophet, he was cured of his dire ailment. Judaism still retains vestiges of ritual baptism. For Orthodox Jewish women, it is *de rigeur* to wash away their menstrual impurity in a *miqve* ("ritual pool"). In strict Orthodox communities like Williamsburg, N.Y., even pious men purify themselves in a *miqve* prior to every Sabbath. Moreover, Orthodox conversion to Judaism is completed only through total immersion in the *miqve.* Christianity has stressed baptism, so much so that some churches call themselves "Baptist." As a result, no Jew (or for that matter Gentile) ever refers to Judaism as "baptistic".

In Old Testament times, the Hebrews kneeled in prayer. Deutero-Isaiah predicts the day when everyone will kneel to the God of Israel.[11] Even a late book of the Old Testament describes the pious Jew Daniel as kneeling when praying to God.[12] Christianity in its churches has continued the old Hebrew tradition of kneeling. Judaism has just about eliminated it.[13] Kneeling benches are found in many churches, but never in synagogues.

The Qumran discoveries after World War II were disturbing not only to many Christians, but also and for other reasons to many Jews.[14] Qumran was a monastic community and what could be more "un-Jewish" than monasticism? Jews were tacitly assumed to be "in this world" and not out of it. It was "natural" for Christians to have religious communities in monasteries or nunneries because the latter were "Christian" institutions. Then came Qumran: a Jewish religious community quite "out of this world." Christ was baptized by John only a few miles north of Qumran while that Jewish monastic community was still functioning. There could be no doubt about it; the Christians of the "New Testament" continued monastic institutions of their Jewish predecessors. We are confronted with the same old story: once the Christians made much of religious communities separated from the mainstream of secular life, the Jews gave them up and eventually forgot that they ever had them.

The most instructive document on the Qumranic way of life is the Manual of Discipline (1QS).[15] It spells out the ideals and the rules of initiation into the community, of how members must conduct themselves and relate to each other, and of how offenders are to be chastised and, if necessary, excommunicated. The tradition of this Jewish Manual of Discipline was continued by Christian monastic orders after Jews had given up monasticism and all its trappings, including all manuals of discipline. The earliest Christian manual of discipline (*regula* is the Latin term) on record is the one formulated by the Coptic Church Father Pachomius (died 346), who founded monasteries in Egypt and formulated the *Regula* for them. Jerome (died 421) made the *Regula* of Pachomius available in Latin translation so that it reached Western Europe. This in turn inspired St. Benedict (6th century) to formulate the *Regula* for his Benedictine monasteries. Since then every monastic order has had its own *regula.* A detailed comparison of the Rule of St. Benedict with the Qumran Manual of Discipline shows that the tradition is in a straight line. Judaism has lost all awareness of its monasteries and their *regulae.* Christianity, in building up the institution of religious communities and providing each order with its *regula,* inclined the Jews to give up their monasteries and relegate their manuals of discipline to oblivion. But the first *regula* on record is no longer St. Benedict's, nor even Pachomius', but the Hebrew Manual of Discipline from Qumran.[15a]

One of the most prominent scrolls from Qumran is the War Scroll (1QM). The Qumran community saw itself as the army of God destined to wage the final war to victory over the forces of evil. Indeed the War Scroll includes the battle-plans leading to that Cosmic Victory, which was viewed as imminent, much as it is in the Gospels.[16] The Church has retained the concept of "The Church Militant" with the result that Judaism has lost all semblance of any "Synagogue Militant." We are of course speaking of the mainstream of "normative"[17] Judaism. There were always militaristic pockets of Judaism, ranging from the Elephantine Colony of the fifth century B.C., to the bloody Messianic uprising against Rome under Bar Kokhba in A.D. 132–135. In the Middle Ages there was an interest in far-off segments of the Jewish People capable of waging war against their foes and repossessing the Holy Land.[18] But prior to developments in modern Zionism between the two World Wars,[19] it is fair to say that normative Judaism had no notion of any Synagogue Militant, while Christianity, if not waging Crusades by force of arms, at least always continued some concept of a Church Militant.

Old Testament prophets looked forward to a Kingdom of God in which nature would be changed where necessary to make a better world. Thus even vicious beasts would have to alter their *modus vivendi.* Lions are to give up eating flesh and instead feed on grass like cattle. Vipers will become harmless.[20] Moreover, Judaism in communities like Qumran expected the Kingdom of God under Messianic[21] supervision to come soon (as also in the Gospels). Sex, which causes so much trouble in this world, will not be operative in the next, according to Christ. In the Kingdom of Heaven, men and women will not be joined in sex and matrimony.[22] Christianity has fostered a keen interest in life after death, the return of the Messiah, and the Kingdom of Heaven. While Judaism could not and did not divest itself of messianism and the notion of the world to come,[23] the mainstream deemphasized unworldly concerns. Human relations were stressed: if we please our fellow man, God is satisfied with us; if we fail to please our fellow man, God is not satisfied with us.[24] If you are planting a sapling and someone tells you the Messiah is arriving, finish planting the sapling before you go to greet the Messiah.[25] The business of this world takes priority and must not be neglected through preoccupation with the next world. There are extremes of worldliness and of unworldliness in both Judaism and Christianity, but it is an "educated guess" to say that in the social psychology of the people who call themselves "Jews" and "Christians" it is the latter who have been more concerned with Heaven, Hell and the Messianic Age.

It stands to reason that since Judaism has softpeddled what Christianity has borrowed and emphasized, Judaism could stress what Christianity rejected or failed to emphasize. Since Jesus took a relaxed approach to the Sabbath,[26] Judaism could and did remain as sabbatarian as ever. Jesus did not value ritual purity highly, proclaiming that what matters is not what goes into a person's mouth but what comes out of it.[27] Orthodox Judaism has therefore been left free to make of *kašrut* a strict and elaborate system going far beyond biblical regulations. By relieving Christians of the burden of the Law,[28] the New Testament had the effect of bolstering the onerous definition of traditional Judaism as the following of the 613 commandments (the *miṣvot)* embodied in the Torah. Salvation through faith in Christ eliminated the need for Christians to abide by hundreds of Mosaic precepts.

The most positive effect that Christianity has exerted on traditional Judaism is in the realm of learning. To be sure, learning and teaching are among the *miṣvot.*[29] Though Christianity has always had its revered scholars,[30] the fact is that in Christianity the gate to salvation is faith. Every religious system worthy of the name puts a premium on good deeds. Christianity and Judaism are no exceptions. Faith is *one* of the gates to salvation in Judaism, but in Christianity it is *the* gate. Religionists are familiar with another gateway to salvation: knowledge. We need not digress on Gnosticism, which requires *esoteric* knowledge for the initiated. We may instead call attention to the Old Testament[31] and Qumranic[32] emphasis on knowledge through study in the service of "The God of Knowledge."[33] Classical rabbinic Judaism, as spelled out in the *Pirqe Avot,* requires study as a way of life. To be a first-class person, scholarship is indispensable. The greatest of avoidable blights is ignorance. The *ʿam ha-areṣ* ("ignoramus"), even though he may commit no evil deeds, has no status in this world or in the next.[34] It takes scholarship to enter the "academy on earth"; and in heaven, the "academy on high" admits only those who have earned admission to the "academy below." Works and faith are crowns of glory, but without scholarship they cannot save us from being ignoramuses. The inordinate stress that normative Judaism has placed on learning is such that it is hard to point out many distinguished Jews in any generation who were not people of the book: whether in scholarship, literature, or science.[35]

I have tried to qualify my generalizations sufficiently for setting forth what I consider to be a useful principle of wide application, actually far wider than I have spelled out or can anticipate.[36] I have been pondering this principle for several years, while testing it through observation and primary texts. If I have not qualified every jot and tittle, and then requalified every qualification, that is because such precision can kill any broad principle worth teaching, worth learning, worth writing or worth reading. I once had an erudite, well-meaning colleague of blessed memory, whom I forbear to name (*de mortuis nihil nisi bonum).* He came to class one day and announced: "Today we shall learn one of the most important laws of Hebrew grammar. But before I teach you that law, I must discuss the seventeen exceptions to it." The law is in fact important, and the seventeen exceptions are real. But by the time he got through with the exceptions, no one had any strength or attention left for the law.

Notes

1. For present purposes, a simplified transliteration (without finesse in vowel quantities, etc.) is preferable to a precise but cumbersome system, e.g., *bĕrîṯ ḥăḏāšā(h)*.

2. Jer 31: 31–34.

3. Exod 20: 2–17; Deut 5: 6–21.

4. E.g., Birnbaum 1949.

5. *Encyclopaedia Britannica, Micropaedia* III: 603, notes merely that at Dura were found a synagogue and a church, both of the third century, with wall paintings of importance for the study of Jewish and early Christian art.

6. Exod 20: 5; Deut 5: 9.

7. This permissiveness was prompted by the need to allow Jews to earn a living through their skills. Uncompromising strictness in such matters could lead only to economic ruin.

8. Little more than half a century (from 730 to 787).

9. There are, of course, exceptions. For example, in the so-called Tomb of Esther and Mordechai in Hamadan, there are two prominent icons, one of Moses, the other of Aaron. This atypical Jewish veneration of tombs of "saints" and images of holy personages reflects the Shiite environment of Iran.

10. 2 Kings 5, note particularly verses 10 and 14.

11. Isa 45: 23.

12. Dan 6: 11.

13. The *ʿAlenu* prayer states that "we kneel and bow" before God (Birnbaum 1949: 413), but actual kneeling is limited to the Day of Atonement; even then it is often the cantor alone who kneels and prostrates himself.

14. A convenient Hebrew edition of the Qumran scrolls (with vocalization and German translation) has been published by Lohse (1964). For an English translation, see Gaster (1976). For a popular account of the needless anxieties and foibles, see Edmund Wilson (1969).

15. *Serek ha-Yaḥad,* which the Jesuit fathers P. Boccaccio and G. Berardi render in Latin *Regula unionis*.

15a. For the essential facts about Saint Pachomius, his monasteries and his Rule, see *Encyclopaedia Britannica, Micropaedia* VII: 663–64. For the Rule of Saint Benedict, see Verheyn (1935).

16. E.g., Matt 24: 44; 25: 13.

17. This adjective is applicable to Jews with a western, secular education. It would not apply to large groups of Hasidim who anticipate the early return of the Messiah and enroll school children as soldiers in the Armies of God. I have seen the children's military ID cards with rank and serial number. However, these Hasidim have no weaponry or military hardware of any kind; their "Synagogue Militant" is purely verbal, with no military capability.

18. The exotic narrative of Eldad the Danite (9th century) is one of many such tales that surfaced over a long span of time, through the Middle Ages and afterwards.

19. Prior to the outbreaks in 1936, the large majority of the Jews in Palestine did not want independent nationhood but preferred to leave civil and military affairs in the hands of the British Mandate. It was the curtailing of Jewish immigration to the "homeland" during the Hitler period, when immigration was needed most, that impelled the Jews of Palestine to fight for statehood.

20. Isa 11: 6–9.

21. The Manual of Discipline has the Kingdom inaugurated by (1) The Prophet, (2) The Messiah of Aaron, and (3) The Messiah of Israel. The Messiah of Aaron is the anointed High Priest or religious chief, while the Messiah of Israel is the anointed King or secular ruler. In Christianity all three offices (Prophet, Priest and King) are combined in Christ. The War Scroll provides the forty-year time-table of the battles between the forces of Goodness/Light (= God) and Evil/Darkness (= Belial).

22. Mark 12: 25.

23. *Ha-ʿolam ha-ze,* "This World," is frequently contrasted with *ha-ʿolam ha-ba,* "The World to Come," in rabbinic literature. The point we are making has to do with actual social psychology, not with official inherited doctrine.

24. *Pirqe Avot* 3: 10 (*Prayer Book* 13). Accordingly, this humanistic standard is built into the classical formulation of rabbinic Judaism.

25. This has been highlighted by the late Abba Hillel Silver in *Where Judaism Differed* (1956).

26. E.g., Mark 2: 23–28.

27. Mark 7: 15–23.

28. See 1 Cor 10: 25–27; Gal 2:21; 3: 5–6, 23–25; etc.

29. E.g., Deut 6: 6–7.

30. Origen, Jerome, Augustine, Thomas Aquinas, Luther, Calvin and many others, ancient and modern, come to mind.

31. The Torah is not simply a spiritual way of life, it is also a *sefer,* a "written document," which must be studied constantly (Josh 1: 8). Wisdom literature embodied this component of Hebraism, note especially Ecclesiastes (12: 12), who got an overdose of book-learning. Throughout historic Judaism, study is not merely meritorious; it is a sacrament, a *miṣva* rooted in the Torah.

32. The Manual of Discipline calls for the entire membership of the community to engage in an obligatory, intensive program of study. That this ideal was implemented is clear from the excavated scriptorium and from the great number of scrolls found in the Qumran caves.

33. See, e.g., 1 Sam 2: 3.

34. The *Pirqe Avot* spells this out. Hillel (*Avot* 2: 5, Prayer Book 6) goes so far as to declare that no ignoramus can rightly be called a *ḥasid,* a "pious man". Piety is more than absence of sin, for, if that were the case, dumb animals might qualify for sainthood. The true *ḥasid* had to be endowed with human excellence, including the grace that only knowledge can bestow.

35. Times are changing so fast that we will be on safer ground if we qualify our statements "as of 1945" (when the Second World War ended). Up to that time the high proportion of Jews among university students, scholars, and scientists (including Nobel laureates) made of them an intellectual elite. With the breakdown of their traditional values and discipline, their record is deteriorating.

36. Additional applications of the theme (e.g., circumcision) will be obvious to the reader.

References

Birnbaum, P.
1949 *Daily Prayer Book.* New York: Hebrew Publishing Company.

Gaster, T. H.
1976 *The Dead Sea Scriptures*[3]. Garden City: Doubleday/Anchor Press.

Lohse, E.
1964 *Die Texte aus Qumran.* Munich: Kösel–Verlag.

Silver, A. H.
1956 *Where Judaism Differed.* New York: Macmillan.

Verheyn, B., trans.
1935 *The Holy Rule of Our Most Holy Father Benedict*[8]. Atchison, Kansas: The Abbey Student Press.

Wilson, E.
1969 *The Dead Sea Scrolls 1947–1969.* New York: Oxford University Press.

Humanism and the Rise of Hebraic Studies: From Christian to Jewish Renaissance

M. H. Goshen-Gottstein
The Hebrew University of Jerusalem

This paper will explore some aspects of interconnected and parallel features in the development of 16th-century Humanism as a cultural-educational-academic ideal, on the one hand, and of the science of Judaism in its 19th-century expression, on the other.[1] To be sure, the very term 'Humanism' has attracted a fair number of senses. First and foremost is the sense of concentrating on human achievements, away from medieval transcendentalism, coupled with appreciation of the 'pure sources' of knowledge and aesthetic form. In spite of the 18th- and 19th-century senses of Humanism, Humanities as pursued in our institutions of higher learning are an ultimate institutionalized concretization of those ideals which symbolized the 15th-century break with the Middle Ages.[2] The anti-transcendental enlightenment of the 18th century gave a new twist to the sense of 'Humanism,' just as a century later new overtones clung to this term in the terminology of the philosophy of historical materialism. Yet, by and large, it is the offshoots of 15th-century philological Humanism that are decisive for our understanding of certain parallels between the rise of post-medieval Christian Hebraic studies and the emergence of the 19th-century academic revival of Jewish studies.

2. The major thrust of Humanist endeavor was the attempt to renew direct inspiration from ancient sources, the cultural ideal of pushing beyond the darkness of the Middle Ages and reaching back to the beauty, purity, and uncorruptedness of the ancient originals. The medieval concentration on trans-human values was to yield to the rediscovery of human creativity. On the operational level this meant fashioning anew through inspiration from ancient human creativity, whether in art, literature, or thought. It was not the one ever-flowing divine source that was to provide the waters of life, but the once-flowing human *fons*. That *fons,* for each creation, had to be uncovered afresh.

3. In a specific sense, the age of Humanism was the heyday of philology. Throughout the Middle Ages texts had been available in the one and only language of learning. Latin style had become corrupted by semi-vulgar intrusions and the sources had become contaminated from generation to generation. Humanistic cleansing of sources, then, meant for the student of culture the conscious search for classical language models and the working out of first principles for textual preferences. Those philologians began their task by working on Latin texts. But soon they were to set out for unknown territory.

4. The 15th century has become for us the great watershed between Latin-centered inquiry and the beginning of openness towards non-Latin cultures. In a way,

each century since then has broadened our knowledge by offering keys to previously unknown languages and texts—whether from Near Eastern or Far Eastern countries, the older or the newer world, contemporary or buried for thousands of years. But the decisive beginning can be traced to the influx of Greek refugees from the Byzantine territories that were finally taken by Turkish armies. The gradual Greek infiltration into Italy which preceded the final large-scale influx is not part of our theme. For our purpose one point should be emphasized: by the second half of the 15th century the Humanist ideal had begun to embrace Greek as well as Latin sources. Greek refugees had brought with them 'pure sources' from which insight could be gained and misconceptions corrected. Without the preceding incorporation of Greek sources into the Humanist *Weltbild,* Hebraic studies would hardly have found their place in the world of the Christian Renaissance around 1500.[3]

5. There was, of course, a major difference. The Greek refugees to Italy's shores were brothers in Christ. To be sure, they were regarded as dangerous heretics, and the history of the great schism had poisoned the relationship between the churches of West and East for centuries. But they were Christians—and for some time various efforts had been going on to heal the old rifts between various churches, including some Eastern and African monophysite rites. Accepting sources in Greek was not the same as opening the gates to Hebraic learning. But it proved a decisive precedent for broadening the Humanist ideal. The thirst for drinking from new sources was there, even though the purity of those sources was, theologically speaking, rather dubious.

6. This must suffice, for the moment, as backdrop for one of the most amazing features of the transition from the Middle Ages to Modernity: the Hebraic component of the Humanist revival. In the present framework we can but hint at the developments that made this phenomenon possible. Perhaps, first and foremost, the general feeling of malaise within the Church of the 15th century: there was a widespread readiness to believe that the Church could be healed of its many ills through the discovery of hidden knowledge that would bring about rejuvenation, revival, and new certainty. Such knowledge was to be gained from hidden sources, such as those available in the secret doctrines of the Jews. Once those secrets were uncovered, not only would the Church regain its power but the truth of its teachings vis-à-vis Judaism would emerge triumphant. Put differently, the official interest of prominent Church circles in Kabbalistic writings was probably the most powerful motive for the study of Hebraic sources.

7. This motive joined the primary ideal of Humanist ideology. The slogan *ad fontes* applied to classical literature as it applied to the Bible. The Latin Bible, however highly praised, was known to be a translation, even though pious statements attributed to it the authority of the original. Yet in the very same year, 1516/17, Christian printers in Venice and Basel made available to the learned public the Bible in its original languages, Hebrew and Greek.[4] This was, of course, immediately followed by the Alcalá Polyglot and other products of the printing presses in many major centers.

8. It is of no use to speculate how the Hebraic studies of 1510-1520 would have progressed without the rapid new developments in printing. The growth of Humanist ideology, Hebraic learning, and the printing trade went hand in hand. Many printers were the patrons of scholars, and in some places—like Basel—the activity of printers was perhaps more of a driving power than that of the established university authorities.

Some Churchmen—like Cardinal Egidio de Viterbo, one of the leading patrons of Hebraic studies in the early 16th century—were ardent Humanists; the commitment of others, like Luther, has remained a matter of dispute. Yet a decade later the former lines of distinction had become blurred. Humanist ideology or not, Hebraic knowledge had become a must, not only for the student of Bible and related fields, but for everyone who wanted to be part of learned society. *Homo trilinguis*—the man knowledgeable in the three languages (Latin, Hebrew, Greek)—was the educational ideal, perhaps the one clearly defined ideal of language education that lasted until its final collapse in our own time.

9. Hebraic knowledge was the final step in the development of the trilingual ideal. But, theologically speaking, Hebrew was regarded as the source of all language. The fast-growing knowledge of Comparative Semitics, between ca. 1525 and 1550, not only established Hebrew as the 'mother' of its daughters—i.e., the other Semitic languages then known; in the very process the biblical statements about the language of creation enhanced the standing of Hebraic knowledge for centuries to come. In fact, only in the framework of the 18th-century Enlightenment was Hebrew finally dethroned, even though its position as a major component of Humanist knowledge remained untouched.

10. The above is not intended to detail all the components of the Hebraic revival as part of Renaissance Humanism, but rather to paint in some bold strokes the picture of the rise of Humanist ideals in which Hebraic learning, in its broadest sense, became so prominent. The story would not be complete without our looking at major political-cultural events that occurred in the 15th century and changed the attitude of the Christian world vis-à-vis the Muslim powers. Moreover, without the claims of the Reformation, which pushed the *ad fontes* ideal towards the *sola scriptura* demand, the feud between the old and the new churches might not have caused competition for Hebraic excellence. These and other forces combined in such a way that around 1600 practically all of Hebraic literature—biblical, rabbinic, medieval—was available to Christian Hebraists, and many scholars who specialized in other areas of Humanist interest had at least a fair working knowledge of what were by then regarded as standard Jewish writings.

11. To be sure, it is always the initial stage that is most revolutionary. Let us envisage a person born about five centuries ago and passing away as an old man in the mid-16th century. As a little child he would have been a contemporary of Pico della Mirandola, the first prominent Renaissance genius to take up Hebraic studies seriously, as part of his Kabbalistic researches.[5] As a youth he would have witnessed the publication, in 1506, of the first Hebrew grammar, by one of the foremost Humanists of the Germanic area, Johannes Reuchlin. As an adult he would have learned of the immense progress made by the first representatives of Semitic philology and biblical exegesis who used Jewish sources, such as Conrad Pellican in Zurich or Sebastian Münster in Basel; he might have seen the polyglot volumes of the Bible printed for Cardinal Ximenes de Cisneros in Alcalá and the Hebrew text produced by Bomberg in Venice. Finally—as an old man—his Hebraic knowledge might have undergone systematization as part of a new derivational linguistic model as evolved in the 1550's by Canini. At that point new Bible translations from the Hebrew would have come to his notice, editions of medieval exegetes, philosophers, and scientists. The next generation was to take less impressive strides; but much knowledge needed

to be consolidated before the Hebraic heritage, as transmitted by Jews for centuries, became fully incorporated into Humanist consciousness.

12. If there is substance to the claim that the Humanist component of the Renaissance around 1500 is a major signpost along the path from Middle Ages to Enlightenment, then the rise of Hebraic knowledge—both as regards language and Jewish studies in general—was one of its outstanding features. Whatever changes the concept of Humanism underwent in the centuries to follow, Hebraic studies occupied a place of honor as long as European academic education drew its strength at least from an image of the ideal of *humaniora*. But one must always be fully aware that this was the ideal of an exclusively Christian elite. The services of Jewish teachers had been necessary at the very beginning, when the great competed for men such as Elija Levita or Obadiah Sforno to introduce them into the intricacies of that strange language and its treasures. By the middle of the 16th century those services were needed no more. Jewish authorities led a shadow existence in the ever-growing literature, to be quoted as proof and counterproof in learned dispute. There was no place for living Jews to partake in the intellectual development of post-Humanist days unless they were ready to turn their back on their own heritage. There was hardly a place in Europe where Jews could live unmolested in those centuries and often enough they were happy to escape with their lives. Not for them the progress from Renaissance Humanism to Enlightenment.

13. Three centuries thus passed from the time that Jewish teachers had put the keys to the treasures of Jewish knowledge into the hands of Christian Humanists, roughly speaking from 1500 till about 1800. Some members of a tiny new Jewish elite—heirs to the small circle of the Berlin Enlightenment of the 1760's and 1770's, hopefully breathing the air full of promises of equality—were allowed, for the first time, to present themselves for academic study.[6] Even though the old Humanist ideal had long been dulled by generations of academic establishment, the halls of Academe still echoed that learning as the basis of comprehensive education. To the extent that Jewish students about 1800 wished to partake of that education, they met with the standardized Hebraic knowledge that had become part of Humanities since the days when Reuchlin had broken new ground.

14. In our present context it is permissible to stress the one aspect of the Jewish Renaissance, in the early days of the emancipation of Jews, that involves the rise of Hebraic studies, the aspect in which we see an expression of a new type of Jewish Humanism.[7] On the one hand, emancipation and equality—on the level of academic studies—meant that the Jewish student was allowed to avail himself of what the University had to offer, provided he was ready and willing to play according to the rules set by the host-culture. European culture in 1800 had become a value to be coveted by Jews, a goal to be reached, a fund of knowledge and attitudes to be assimilated. The fossilized heritage of Humanism, as transmitted in the academies of the German and French empires, thus became part and parcel of what the aspiring Jewish student of the early 19th century had to acquire as his entrance-ticket. On the other hand, however, that very same fossilized Humanist ideal got a new lease on life as a model for imitation. It was, perhaps, rather natural that among that first generation of Jewish students exposed to University life, the Humanist model should spark off the idea that they should approach the sources of Judaism in the same way and spirit they had been taught to approach the sources of Greek and Latin antiquity.

The uncovering of those sources would shed light on their own past, would show Judaism in its true and original light, would force the educated world around them to acknowledge the manifold cultural values of Jewish heritage, would result in rebirth and honor to Judaism, which was about to recover its rightful place in a world of enlightenment, emancipation, and equality.

15. Hebraic studies, quite unwittingly, did thus become again a centerpiece of an attempt at cultural renaissance—this time as part of a world trying to rebuild itself in the wake of the Enlightenment and the Napoleonic wars. In hindsight, the formulations by the founding fathers of *Wissenschaft des Judentums*—from the first attempts by Leopold Zunz in 1818 and the first formalized program in 1822—seem like a blueprint for Jewish cultural renaissance conceived as a copy of the Humanist Renaissance three centuries previously, though without any expressed consciousness of similarities. It is only in hindsight that the component of philological study of Hebraic sources emerges strikingly.

16. From the vantage point of the late 20th century the preeminence of philology ought to be stressed. In the model of 1500 and of 1800 it is philology that is the driving force toward uncovering the Hebraic sources. To be sure, the 19th century is usually conceived of as putting historical-evolutionary thought at the center. Yet there is no historical or literary or philosophical approach but through the texts. Texts must be discovered, studied, edited—only thus will the true picture of Israel's spiritual world emerge, only thus can its hidden value be presented to the world. The manuscripts saved from the ravages of centuries of persecutions are but the remaining stones; the newly emerging practitioner of the science of Judaism is the one who will re-erect the palace of Jewish culture and learning in its original splendor. We find no indication that Zunz and his small band of fellow-workers consciously tried to imitate the feats of great Renaissance philologists like Lorenzo Valla, Erasmus, Scaliger. But I do not think that we exaggerate if we claim that the renaissance of Hebraic studies in the 19th century became a version of the 16th-century model. The philologist became the spearhead of antiquarian drive proclaiming afresh the slogan *ad fontes*.

17. The very facts of the history of 19th-century science of Judaism seem to indicate that the expectations of a Jewish renaissance as a result of a large-scale academic interest in Hebraic studies were not as unreasonable as we might think today. In a world of Idealistic philosophy such high hopes could possibly be entertained, even though some of the founding-members of Zunz's little group soon chose other personal paths. It would, therefore, be less than fair if, in hindsight, we belittle the harbingers of the Jewish Hebraic renaissance of the 19th century because they could not visualize the limitations. A model of Jewish Humanist revival in the post-Napoleonic world could hardly have achieved what its youthful protagonists had hoped for, and the kind of learning pursued never had the ideology of the 16th-century network of *collegium trilingue* to back it up. The Hebraic learning of the 16th century was part of an encompassing ideology, and even though the numbers of scholars involved was limited, the overall impact was considerable. The 19th-century Jewish attempt could really never aspire to exercise any influence beyond a rather limited circle. A Humanist Hebraic revival, by its very nature, could never bring about the kind of rejuvenation of Judaism that would have made the historic treasures of Judaism part of an all-embracing common Judeo-Christian milieu. Other forces were to emerge that created new constellations. But old-new problems and hopes remain.

Notes

1. This is a version of one paper in a series dealing with aspects of the rise of Hebraic studies in post-medieval Europe and the place of Jewish Studies as a developing field of academic inquiry. David Noel Freedman and I have often discussed questions of Biblical Studies and positions of Judaism and I know how deeply interested he is in these issues. I should, therefore, like to accompany my good wishes upon his having traversed the first half of his life span with this tentative version of some of my reflections rather than with some pages of philological erudition. This is the first English formulation of these problems; for a tentative Hebrew formulation of some ideas see *World Union of Jewish Studies Newsletter* 19 (1981) 3-8.

2. Differences of periodization between the beginnings of Humanism in Italy and elsewhere in Europe are of little consequence for our discussion. They may, however, explain the earlier Italian Quattrocento stirrings and Cinquecento interest in ancient manuscripts as well as the first applications of philological method by a scholar like Lorenzo Valla in the mid-fifteenth century.

3. Half a century later guardians of Christian orthodoxy who fought what they regarded as Judaizing influences in exegesis blamed the previous influence of Greek "heretical" literature as having paved the way. Details of sources will, in general, be quoted only in my forthcoming book on the rise of Hebrew Studies in Europe.

4. The basic difference in textual character between the edition of the New Testament by Erasmus and the first Rabbinic Bible by Felix Pratensis is a matter of considerable interest for the *textus receptus* question that was to occupy students of biblical philology till our days. But when those first products of Hebrew and Greek Bible printing came on the market, nobody could evaluate those problems. For our presentation here, I mention the major enterprises of 1518 rather than the odd attempt of the learned Giustiniani in 1516, whose polyglot edition of the Psalms remained virtually unknown.

5. In another context I hope to deal with the question of how at the very same time—i.e., in the seventies of the 15th century—Hebrew knowledge could be pursued both by a leading Humanist in Ficino's circle in Florence and by a representative of violent Dominican missionary efforts like Petrus Nigri.

6. The history of the partial admittance of Jews to study medicine is another matter. Generally speaking, Jews could previously hardly fulfill the conditions for being accepted for study. The personal history of a man like Moses Mendelssohn is more telling than anything.

7. In the framework of a holistic interpretation of nineteenth century Jewish intellectual history additional points would have to be discussed. The counterpoint structure of the present paper should thus not be taken as an analysis of all the component features.

Prague Structuralism in American Biblical Scholarship: Performance and Potential

Stanislav Segert
University of California, Los Angeles, California

The term "structuralism" entered English only recently. The *Encyclopaedia Britannica* (1974, IX: 620) relates it to American structural linguistics, inaugurated in the 1930's by Leonard Bloomfield, and to the Prague school.* Neither of these trends has excited much interest on the part of American biblical scholarship. If the use of American linguistic structuralism in biblical scholarship has been limited to technical studies dealing with linguistic features of biblical texts and with biblical languages in general, however, the impact of American structuralist literary criticism on the study of biblical literature is somewhat more visible. References to Prague structural studies were quite rare before 1970 (cf., e.g., Buss 1969: 47 n. 91; 48–49 n. 97). Even when structuralism began to attract the attention of American biblical scholars, in about 1970, the response was limited. The real development of structuralist biblical studies dates in fact from 1974, when a special issue of *Interpretation* (28 #2) was published, and the journal *Semeia: An Experimental Journal for Biblical Criticism* and its supplements began to appear.

The overwhelming majority of publications using a structuralist approach are based on the structuralism of the French type. Its influence may be attributed to two factors: the interest of leading French structuralists in the Bible and the considerable impact of French structuralism on literary criticism in general. Introductory surveys and anthologies of structuralism in the 'seventies broadened the interest of American biblical scholars. Like their colleagues in other fields, they studied the sources of French structuralism as they became available in translation: the linguistic theories of Ferdinand de Saussure, the works of the Russian formalists from the 1920's and—to a lesser extent—the basic literature of Prague structuralism from the 1920's and 1930's.

Some ideas of the Prague structuralists came to the attention of American scholars through the work of French—and to a lesser extent— German structuralists (cf. Broekman 1973: 98), but direct access to the basic studies of Prague structuralism still remains somewhat difficult, especially in comparison with French structuralism. Even though many important Prague school papers from the 1920's and 1930's were originally published in French, German, and English, they are not easily available, and very few of the Czech and Russian publications have been translated. These rather superficial reasons may account for the relatively slight interest of American scholars in Prague structuralism. (Short surveys of Prague structuralism are given by Trnka et al. 1958/1964/1970; Kučera 1964; Garvin 1969; Matejka 1976; detailed reports may be found in Vachek 1964 and Holenstein 1976.)

Nonetheless, the fact that several leading representatives of the Prague structuralist school specialized in the study of English language and literature may yet help to gain them an audience in English-speaking countries. The founder and first president of the Prague Linguistic Circle, Vilém Mathesius (1882–1945), was professor of English language and literature at Charles University in Prague (Wellek 1976). Several of his students and assistants—Bohumil Trnka, René Wellek, Josef Vachek — became prominent scholars in the field. Interest in English studies has continued among the younger generation of the Prague structuralist school. Jan Firbas has applied the "functional sentence perspective" approach to English syntax, and Jiří Levý (1926–1967) studied the structure of English verse.

An even more important factor in disseminating the ideas of Prague structuralism has been the pedagogical and scholarly activity of its representatives at American universities. René Wellek, who has taught in the United States since 1939, has greatly influenced American literary scholarship as professor of comparative literature at Yale University and author of many books and articles. The late Roman Jakobson came to New York during World War II; his work there with Claude Lévi-Strauss was instrumental in the formation of French structuralism. Jakobson's students at Columbia and later at Harvard and the Massachusetts Institute of Technology have done much to develop and proselytize structuralist methods in linguistics and literary criticism. Rare is the structuralist study in America that does not cite the work of Roman Jakobson.

Not surprisingly, American scholars of Czech origin—Paul L. Garvin at SUNY/Buffalo, Thomas Winner and Henry Kučera at Brown University, Ladislav Matejka at the University of Michigan, Lubomír Doležel at the University of Toronto, František Svejkovský at the University of Chicago—have made particularly important contributions to structuralism here. They might even be considered a new American generation of Prague structuralists. Moreover, during and after his term as Visiting Professor at Indiana University, Josef Vachek wrote a substantial introduction to the theory and practice of the Prague Linguistic School and edited a collection of representative studies (Vachek 1964; 1966). After presentation in anthologies (Garvin 1964) and surveys (Wellek 1969; T. C. Winner 1973; 1976), recently the works of Jan Mukařovský (1891–1975), the foremost representative of Prague structuralism in aesthetic and literary studies, have been made available in translation (1977; 1978; cf. Wellek 1977).

Neither in Prague nor in America have Czech structuralists been active enough in biblical and related studies to influence their development. Among the regular members of the Prague Linguistic Circle there were no Semitists, Classicists, or Bible scholars. A modern translator of the New Testament into Czech, Professor František Žilka (1871–1944) of John Huss Evangelical Theological Faculty lectured on Bible translation to the Circle in 1941 (cf. also Žilka 1936), and his successor, Josef Bohumil Souček (1902–1972) took pains to acquaint his students in the New Testament with the principles of structuralism. Yet in the area of biblical studies the impact of Prague structuralism in its home country was slight. (For use of structuralist methods in the study of Hebrew biblical poetry, cf. Segert 1953: 496–97; 1969: 312, 321.)

Interestingly enough, a young Dutch scholar, Christian Donner (1980), who studied in Prague, has interpreted the indications of content and intent in the margins of the Czech Kralice Bible translation of 1593 (reedited in 1601 and 1875) as structuralism *avant la lettre*. In fact, however, Czech Brethren adopted the common traditional medieval interpretive tradition.

In America, too, biblical topics are rare among structuralists of the Prague variety. Roman Jakobson devoted an important study to glossolalia (1966) because of its linguistic rather than biblical interest. But interdisciplinary seminars in which semiotic and structural approaches to literature and the Bible are prominent have been started recently at the University of Toronto by Lubomír Doležel, former student of Mukařovský, and by Daniel Patte, who applies French structuralist methodology to the study of the New Testament.

What follows is an attempt to show how certain features of Prague structuralism have been applied in American biblical scholarship. It makes no claim to comprehensiveness nor does it aim to compare Prague structuralism to other varieties of structuralist thought.

The common foundation of all structuralist trends is the attention they pay to parts as they relate to each other and to the whole (cf. Jakobson 1974: 11; quoted in Matejka 1976b: 508). In Prague structuralism the emphasis on these relations has never led to a disregard for reality. Phonological oppositions and systems, for example, are always related to phonetic entities. Reference to the real world is never excluded from semantic considerations. In the study of both grammatical systems and literary structures, meaning occupies a prominent place. The origin and development of the products of language and art are explained by the study of their functions with respect to real individuals and real societies.

The phenomenological and functionalist character of Prague structuralism provides its basic coherence. The combination of linguistic and literary study resulted not only from the interests of individual scholars, such as Vilém Mathesius, Nikolaj Trubetzkoy, and Roman Jakobson, but also from the logic of structuralism itself, which clearly distinguishes levels of analysis without isolating them. This broad base enables Prague structuralism to study many kinds of phenomena from many angles. By combining syntagmatic and paradigmatic approaches and taking into account both spatial and temporal sequences and their interrelation, it can pinpoint phenomena on various levels. By showing how the levels interconnect, it can help to reach a synthesis. All phases of development can be appropriately studied: transversal cuts serve as a basis for synchronic analysis of the entire system as projected at a given point in time; diachronic studies connect isolated phenomena in different phases, but duly respect their position and function within the system as determined by synchronic analysis.

The inner coherence of Prague structuralism has allowed it to adopt other elements without becoming eclectic or syncretistic and prevented it from turning into an exclusive system. Both the principles themselves and empirical observation of its development prove how open a system it actually is.

Openness and cooperation beyond the boundaries of nations, schools, and established disciplines have characterized Prague structuralism since its inception. Its founders gladly acknowledged their indebtedness to their teachers at Prague University: philosopher Tomáš Garrigue Masaryk (1850–1937) (cf. Mathesius 1911/1964: 32 n. 7), linguist Josef Zubatý (1855–1932), and professor of aesthetics Otakar Zich (1879–1934). When, during the 'twenties, Prague became a major center for

Russian emigrés, Roman Jakobson, Sergej Karcevskij (1887–1955), and Nikolaj Trubetzkoy (1890–1938) brought with them the ideas of Moscow formalism and the linguistic schools of Kazan (Vachek 1966: 7–8, 18) and Geneva. Visiting lecturers from many European countries and the active participation by Prague structuralists in international scholarly congresses furthered connections between scholars and disciplines. *Gestalt*-psychology, relational logic, and phenomenology all enhanced structuralist methods.

The achievements of American acoustic phonetics and communication theory contributed directly to Jakobson's attempt to describe phonological systems in terms of binary distinctive features. And again Jakobson enriched the semiotic theories of Edmund Husserl and Ferdinand de Saussure (cf. Holenstein 1976; 1975; 1977) by using the semiotic concepts of Charles Sanders Peirce (cf. Bruss 1978). More recently the methods of Prague structuralism have been organically and fruitfully combined with generative and transformational approaches to language. And in general, the extensive and intensive participation of representatives of the Prague school in both Czechoslovakia and America in a number of collective publications demonstrates the continuing cooperative openness of their *hairesis*.

Publications meant to inform American students of the Bible about modern linguistic and literary methods are now beginning to give Prague structuralism its due. In his useful survey (1978) Robert Detweiler conveniently summarizes Jakobson's six functions of language. Robert M. Polzin's study of Biblical structuralism (1977) also provides useful information about Jakobson's work. Moreover, Polzin effectively uses some of the concepts and approaches developed by Jakobson in conjunction with the methods of the French structuralists. Polzin's evaluation of the *Form-Critical Problem of Hexateuch* by Gerhard von Rad (1938/1960) from the viewpoint of Jakobson's structural approach is especially interesting: he finds considerable convergence in their methods. Edgar V. McKnight (1978: 104–26) discusses Jakobson's theories in detail and quotes some of his critics—Michael Riffaterre and Jonathan Culler—as well. He also comments on studies by Donald Davie and Stanley E. Fish and gives a brief treatment of the ideas of Jan Mukařovský (106–7, 149–50).

In his stimulating survey of literary criticism, Norman H. Petersen (1978) evaluates some commonly used forms of literary criticism as presented by René Wellek and Austin Warren (1956) and the communications model of Roman Jakobson. He then applies some of the principles in an analysis of time in Mark's narrative and in a study of narrative and the real world in Luke's Gospel and in Acts.

In discussing the theory and practice of translation, Eugene A. Nida (1964; 1969) quotes Jakobson's concepts of function in language and effectively uses them to explain the process and function of translation (1964: 3–4, 37–38, 45–46, 173). He also mentions Vladimír Procházka's attempt to apply structuralist principles to the practice of translation (1964: 161, 164).

Though M. O'Connor quotes Jakobson often in his recent book on Hebrew verse structure (1980: cf. 617, 588), he limits himself to three of his articles, two of which concentrate on verse.

Jakobson's six functions of language have been used effectively by Dan O. Via (1975: 24, 101–3, cf. 37), without reference to the primary source.

Generally speaking, quotations from Prague structuralist studies have increased in number rather than effectiveness. Often they seem little more than ornamental.

Only Nida, Polzin, and Petersen have actually incorporated the concepts and methods of Prague structuralism into their own work, and to this writer's knowledge, no complete analysis of a biblical text based solely on Prague structuralism has yet been published. Not even the straightforward analytical techniques used so effectively by Jakobson and Lévi-Strauss (1962) in their famous study of Baudelaire's "Les Chats" have found a following among Bible students, whereas they have based many analyses on methods of French structuralism, which ultimately go back to the structural analysis of Russian fairy-tales by Vladimir Propp, modified by A.-J. Greimas to conform to Jakobson's six functions of language.

The founder of the Prague linguistic circle, Vilém Mathesius, published a study dealing with the potentiality of linguistic phenomena at the beginning of his scholarly career, in 1911. In 1944, at the end of his life, he summarized his experiences and his suggestions for new programs for scholarly research and for cultural life in general in a book under the title of *Možnosti, které čekají* (*Waiting opportunities*). His ideas and those of his followers still have considerable potential in both theoretical and applied linguistics and literary criticism and may also be of interest for the study of the Bible.

This also holds true for Jiří Levý's pioneering research in the application of statistical methods to the study of prosodical systems and verse structures (1969b; 1970). Bible scholars may also benefit from Levý's innovative approach to the art of translation. Both Levý's book (1963, German translation 1969a) and a more theoretically oriented study by the Slovak literary scholar Anton Popovič (1975) deserve to be made available in English. Josef Vachek's research into the characteristics of the written language as such, based on English and Czech material and already available in English (1976), should also attract the attention of students of the Scriptures.

Research in the more specialized area of "functional sentence perspective"—the relation of previously known information (theme) to the new information (rheme)—or "communicative dynamism" was initiated by Vilém Mathesius in 1939. The articles in English by František Daneš (1964) and Jan Firbas (1964) further develop the theme/rheme distinction, which parallels the topic/comment distinction in American linguistics. The former distinction is especially useful in the study of narratives, where it can help to overcome limitations resulting from the traditional notion of the sentence as the highest unit of linguistic analysis. It can also help to develop a viable method for the study of higher units in "discourse analysis" or "text linguistics" and be effectively applied to determining the relation of B-units to A-units in parallelistic poetry.

The functional approach of Prague structuralism is not limited to language and literature. The concept of structure developed by Jan Mukařovský may be used as a model for studying complexes of traditions—historical, religious and the like—and their mutual interrelations. Religious syncretism in the Old Testament and the diverse traditions behind the New Testament may also be studied along these lines.

Approaches developed or suggested by members of the Prague structuralist school might help to clear up some persistent problems in the theory and practice of interpretation and establish new and viable methodology. Such a methodology should (1) be based on language as both foundation and model; (2) apply to all kinds of biblical texts; (3) have the ability to handle texts in all phases of development and interpretation: pre-canonical, canonical, and post-canonical; (4) be both integral and integrated; and (5) be exact, yet simple. It should proceed from language, from insights into structure, to literary analysis. The linguistic and the literary model together then serve as a basis for revealing the function of the text.

All levels of analysis are interrelated in that they all deal with sign systems: words, sentences, paragraphs, discourses or strophes, and higher, functional or literary units. The appropriate forms of linguistic and literary analysis are applied accordingly: phonology, semantics, syntax, "supra-syntax," and various kinds of literary analysis. The various methods of biblical scholarship—textual and literary criticism, criticism of form, genre, audience, redaction, tradition—may be applied as well. Most of them operate on more than one level. The interdependence of levels is a corollary to the interdependence of various stages in the development of a text. Its growth from small units to larger ones and eventually to entire "books" can be traced with the help of transversal cuts, which allow comprehensive study of each stage in the structures at any given time. The opposition of segments, their mutual place in the larger structure as well as their various functions—often varying in time—can be identified and described according to these patterns. The functional aspect as directed to a goal is aptly characterized by the concept of "teleonomy," which is related to "teleology" as scientific astronomy is to astrology (cf. Holenstein 1976: 118–19). This directional orientation may be considered germane to the aim of the biblical message itself.

A unified approach to the structures of language, literature, and function, which in the study of the Bible is religious and historical, follows appropriate codes. Syntagmatic (sequence in text or in time) and paradigmatic (the related building blocks of the structures or systems) analysis provides a firm basis for studies concentrating on immanent features as well as for comparative studies.

By distinguishing various analytical levels (linguistic, literary, and functional), we point to their mutual interdependence. Their hierarchical relationship allows us to use a lower level pattern as a model for analyzing higher levels. Roman Jakobson cited the observation that lyrical poetry tends to use the first person, and historical narrative the third (1935/1974: 419; quoted in Wellek and Warren 1956: 228, 307). Applying this observation, we may define at least some literary genres according to syntactic and some additional semantic criteria. For example, a speech of God in the first person is revelation, in second person a command or prohibition. The sentences of apodictic law (expressed in prohibitions and commands in the second person singular or plural) are distinct from those of casuistic law (expressed by conditional sentences, with the verb mostly in the third person).

The sequence in which we decode levels of linguistic analysis is dictated by practical considerations. When dealing with inflected languages such as Biblical Greek and Biblical Hebrew and Aramaic, in which full vocalization gives sufficient morphological information, we begin with syntactic analysis, preferably according to dependency syntax. Combining this with semantic analysis will provide enough information to establish the meaning of the sentence. It will also provide sufficient basis for the analysis of suprasyntactic relations, both within the immediate context and beyond it.

The second stage of interpretation will treat those phenomena used for literary effect. Many features already determined during the linguistic analysis will be evaluated according to their function at this stage, which can also be characterized as stylistic analysis (cf. Kučera 1968). Parallel syntactic and semantic features will show the parallelistic structure of ancient Hebrew poetry. Phonetic features such as repetition of certain second patterns and regular distribution of stress may point to poetic assonance and rhythmical arrangement. The study of poetic "figures" depends on a semantic analysis of words within their context. Suprasyntactical observations provide the basis for determining the compositional or redactional structure of literary units. Syntagmatic relations may be traced in a broader context, while paradigmatic relations make themselves felt in identical or similar words or structures both within and outside a given unit.

The third and final step in this unified system of interpretation may be characterized as functional. The device of synchronic transversal cuts makes it possible to trace the changing functions of a given unit through different periods. This approach also enables us to include later traditions of interpretation while preserving contact with the "canonical" meaning and function of the text. The device of "transversal cuts" may be also applied in the analysis of narratives. The mutual relationships of actants (which does not remain always unchanged throughout the story, cf., e.g., 1 Sam 28: 15–19) can be more adequately traced in its dynamism than in the application of more rigid patterns derived from different literary traditions.

Biblical scholars have certain methodological advantages due to the limits of their field; in some way these may be compared to "laboratory conditions" in the "hard" sciences. The material which they analyze is by definition limited by the boundaries of the canon; differences in languages, traditions, and historical background notwithstanding, the texts are relatively homogeneous. Even if the original functions of some of them were different, the fact that they have been received into the canon determines their message and consequently their interpretation on the basic level. The application of a structuralist approach to so clearly defined a corpus should contribute to the refining of analytical and synthetical methods of interpretation.

In the preceding we have tried to show how Prague structuralism may serve as a tool for the better understanding of biblical texts. The relative simplicity of its approach does not conceal the fact that language itself is a system of systems. This is to be reflected in the study of texts and their functions, which is modeled after the study of language.

Note

*The author would like to express his thanks for providing useful suggestions and data, for sending of offprints and preprints, and for other help to professors Vít Bubeník (St. John's, Newfoundland), Lubomír Doležel (Toronto), Thomas Eekman (Los Angeles), Paul L. Garvin (Buffalo), George Gibian (Ithaca), Elmar Holenstein (Bochum), Ladislav Matejka (Ann Arbor), and René Wellek (New Haven) as well as Alfred M. Johnson (Cary, North Carolina), for his suggestions to be used in a further publication. The author is especially indebted to Professor Michael Henry Heim (Los Angeles) for his valuable help in improving both the presentation and the English style.

References

Bailey, R[ichard], W.; Matejka, L[adislav]; and Steiner, P[eter], eds.

1978 *The Sign: Semiotics Around the World*. Michigan Slavic Contributions 9. Ann Arbor: Michigan Slavic Publications.

Broekman, Jan M.

1973 *Structuralisme: Moskou-Praag-Parijs*. Amsterdam: Athenaeum.

1974 *Structuralism: Moscow, Prague, Paris*. Dordrecht/Boston: Reidel.

Bruss, Elizabeth N.

1978 Peirce and Jakobson on the Nature of the Sign. Pp. 81–98 in Bailey et al. 1978.

Buss, Martin J.

1969 *The Prophetic Word of Hosea: A Morphological Study*. Beihefte zur Zeitschrift für die Alttestamentliche Wissenschaft 111. Berlin: Töpelmann.

Crenshaw, James

1975 Journey into Oblivion: A Structural Analysis of Gen. 24: 1–19. Pp. 99–112 in Wittig 1975.

Daneš, František

1964 A Three-Level Approach to Syntax. *Travaux Linguistiques de Prague* 1: 225–40.

De George, Richard T., and De George, Fernande M., eds.

1972 *The Structuralists: From Marx to Levi-Strauss*. Garden City, New York: Doubleday.

Detweiler, Robert

1978 *Story, Sign and Self: Phenomenology and Structuralism as Literary Critical Methods*. Semeia Supplements. Philadelphia: Fortress.

Doležel, Lubomír

1964 Vers la stylistique structurale. *Travaux Linguistiques de Prague* 1: 257–66.

1967 The Typology of the Narrator: Point of View in Fiction. Vol. 1, pp. 541–52 in *To Honor Roman Jakobson*. The Hague/Paris: Mouton.

1969 A Framework for the Statistical Analysis of Style. Pp. 10–25 in Doležel and Bailey 1969.

1975 Cf. *Semeia* 1: 268, 2: 651–56.

1980 Truth and Authenticity in Narrative. *Poetics Today* 1: 7–25.

Doležel, Lubomír, and Bailey, Richard W., eds.

1969 *Statistics and Style*. New York: American Elsevier.

Donner, Christian

1980 Some Elements of Structural Analysis in the Notes of the Bible of Kralice. *Communio viatorum* (Praha) 23: 57–64.

Firbas, Jan

1964 On Defining the Theme in Functional Sentence Analysis. *Travaux Linguistiques de Prague* 1: 267–80.

Garvin, Paul L.

1964 *A Prague School Reader on Esthetics, Literary Structure and Style*^{2}. Washington: Georgetown University Press.

1969 The Prague School of Linguistics. Pp. 229–38 in *Linguistics Today*, ed. Archibald A. Hill. New York: Basic Books.

1976 Linguistic and Literary Study—A Sociocultural Perspective. Presented at the International Symposium on Semiotics and Theories of Symbolic Behavior in Eastern Europe and the West. Brown University, Providence, Rhode Island. 14–17 April 1976.

1977 Linguistics and Semiotics. *Semiotica* 20: 101–10.

1978 Structuralism, Esthetics and Semiotics. Presented at the International Conference on the Semiotics of Art. Ann Arbor, Michigan. May 1978.

Holenstein, Elmar
1974 *Jakobson, ou le structuralisme phénomenologique*. Paris: Seghers.
1975 Jakobson and Husserl: A Contribution to the Genealogy of Structuralism. *The Human Context* 7: 61–85.
1976 *Roman Jakobson's Approach to Language: Phenomenological Structuralism*. Bloomington: Indiana University Press.
1977 Jakobson's Contribution to Phenomenology. Pp. 145–162 in *Roman Jakobson: Echoes of His Scholarship*. Lisse: de Ridder.
1979 Prague Structuralism—A Branch of the Phenomenological Movement. Vol. 1, pp. 71–97 in *Linguistic and Literary Studies in Eastern Europe*, ed. John Odmark. Amsterdam: Benjamins.

Jakobson, Roman
Selected Writings. The Hague/Paris: Mouton.
1971 I. *Phonological Studies*². Originally 1962.
1971 II. *Word and Language*.
1977 III. *Poetry of Grammar and Grammar of Poetry*.
1966 IV. *Slavic Epic Studies*.
1974 V. *On Verse, Its Masters and Explorers*.
1935 Randbemerkungen zur Prosa des Dichters Pasternak. *Slavische Rundschau* 7: 357–73. Reprinted in *Selected Writings* V: 416–32.
1960 Closing Statement: Linguistics and Poetics. Pp. 350–77 in *Style in Language*, ed. Thomas E. Sebeok. Cambridge, Massachusetts: The M.I.T. Press. (1966). Rpt. as pp. 85–122 in De George and De George 1972.
1963 Efforts toward a Mean-Ends Model of Language in Interwar Continental Linguistics. In *Trends in European and American Linguistics 1930–1950* I. Utrecht. Rpt. as pp. 481–85 in Vachek 1964.
1966 Glossolalie. *Tel Quel* 26: 3–9.
1971 *Studies in Verbal Art: Texts in Czech and Slovak*. Michigan Slavic Contributions 4. Ann Arbor: Czechoslovak Society of Arts and Sciences in America, and the Department of Slavic Languages and Literatures of the University of Michigan.
1974 *Main Trends in the Science of Language*. New York: Harper & Row.

Jakobson, Roman, and Halle, Morris
1971 *Fundamentals of Language*². The Hague: Mouton. Originally 1956.

Jakobson, Roman, and Lévi-Strauss, Claude
1962 "Les Chats" de Charles Baudelaire. *L'Homme* 2: 5–21. English translations in Lane 1970: 202–21, and in De George and De George 1972: 124–46.

Johnson, Alfred M., Jr.
1979 *A Bibliography of Semiological and Structural Studies of Religion*. Pittsburgh: Pittsburgh Theological Seminary.

Kučera, Henry
1964 The Czech Contribution to Modern Linguistics. Pp. 93–104 in *The Czechoslovak Contribution to World Culture*, ed. Miroslav Rechcigl, Jr. The Hague: Mouton.
1968 An Outline of a Model of Stylistic Analysis. Vol. 2, pp. 1060–74 in *Czechoslovakia Past and Present*, ed. Miroslav Rechcigl, Jr. The Hague: Mouton.

Lane, Michael, ed.
1970 *Introduction to Structuralism*. New York: Basic Books.

Levý, Jiří
1957 *České theorie překladu*. Praha: Státní nakladatelství krásné literatury, hudby a umění.
1963 *Umění překladu*. Praha: Československý spisovatel.
1969a *Die literarische Übersetzung: Theorie einer Kunstgattung*. Trans. Walter

Schamschula. Frankfurt.

1969b Mathematical Aspects of the Theory of Verse. Trans. as pp. 95–112 in Doležel and Bailey 1969.

1970 Generative poetics. Pp. 518–57 in *Sign, Language, Culture,* ed. A. J. Greimas and Roman Jakobson. Janua Linguarum, Series Maior 1. The Hague/Paris: Mouton.

McKnight, Edgar V.

1978 *Meaning in Texts: The Historical Shaping of a Narrative Hermeneutics.* Philadelphia: Fortress.

Matejka, Ladislav

1976a Preface. Pp. xi-xxxiv in Matejka 1976b.

Matejka, Ladislav, ed.

1976b *Sound, Sign and Meaning: Quinquagenary of the Prague Linguistic Circle.* Michigan Slavic Contributions 6. Ann Arbor: Department of Slavic Languages and Literatures of the University of Michigan.

Matejka, Ladislav, and Titunik, Irwin R.

1976 *Semiotics of Arts: Prague School Contributions.* Cambridge, Massachusetts: MIT Press.

Mathesius, Vilém

1911/1964 *O potenciálnosti jevů jazykových* (1911). Trans. as On the Potentiality of the Phenomena of Language, p. 1–32 in Vachek 1964.

1939 O tak zvaném aktuálním členění věty. *Slovo a slovenost* 5: 171–74. Rpt. as pp. 234–42 in Mathesius 1947.

1944 *Možnosti, které čekají.* Praha: Laichter.

1947 *Čeština a obecný jazykozpyt.* Praha: Melantrich.

1975 *A Functional Analysis of Present Day English on a General Linguistic Basis,* trans. Libuše Dušková, ed. Josef Vachek. The Hague: Mouton/Prague: Academia.

Mukařovský, Jan

1977 *The World and Verbal Art. Selected Essays.* Trans. and ed. John Burbank and Peter Steiner. Foreword by René Wellek. New Haven: Yale University Press.

1978 *Structure, Sign and Function. Selected Essays.* Trans. and ed. John Burbank and Peter Steiner. New Haven: Yale University Press.

1979 *Aesthetic Function, Norm and Value as Social Facts.* Trans. Mark E. Suino. Michigan Slavic Contributions 3. Ann Arbor: Department of Slavic Languages and Literatures of the University of Michigan. Originally 1970.

Nida, Eugene A.

1964 *Toward a Science of Translating: With Special Reference to Principles and Procedures Involved in Bible Translating.* Leiden: Brill.

O'Connor, M.

1980 *Hebrew Verse Structure.* Winona Lake, Indiana: Eisenbrauns.

Patte, Daniel

1975 Structural Network in Narrative: The Good Samaritan. Pp. 77–98 in Wittig 1975.

1976 *What is Structural Exegesis?* Guides to Biblical Scholarship. Philadelphia: Fortress.

Patte, Daniel, and Patte, Aline

1978 *Structural Exegesis: From Theory to Practice.* Philadelphia: Fortress.

Petersen, Norman R.

1978 *Literary Criticism for New Testament Critics.* Guides to Biblical Scholarship. Philadelphia: Fortress.

1980 The Composition of Mark 4: 1–8: 26. *Harvard Theological Review* 73: 185–217.

Polzin, Robert M.
1977 — *Biblical Structuralism: Method and Subjectivity in the Study of Ancient Texts*. Semeia Supplements. Philadelphia: Fortress.

Popovič, Anton
1975 — *Teória umeleckého překladu: Aspekty textu a literárnej metakomunikácie*. Bratislava: Tatran.

Procházka, Vladimír
1942 — Poznámky k překladatelské technice. *Slovo a slovesnost* 8: 1–20. Trans. by Paul L. Garvin as Notes on Translating Technique, pp. 93–112 in Garvin 1964.

Richter, Wolfgang
1971 — *Exegese und Literaturwissenschaft: Entwurf einer alttestamentlichen Literaturtheorie und Methodologie*. Göttingen: Vandenhoeck und Ruprecht.

Robertson, David
1976 — Bible as Literature. Pp. 547–51 in *The Interpreter's Dictionary of the Bible: Supplementary Volume*, ed. Keith Crim et al. Nashville: Abingdon.

Rudy, Stephen
1976 — Jakobson's Inquiry into Verse and the Emergence of Structural Poetics. Pp. 477–520 in Matejka 1976b.

Segert, Stanislav
1953 — Vorarbeiten zur hebräischen Metrik I-II. *Archiv Orientální* 21: 481–542.
1969 — Versbau und Sprachbau in der althebräischen Poesie. *Mitteilungen des Instituts für Orientforschung* 15: 312–21.

Stankiewicz, Edward
1974 — Poetics and Linguistics. Vol. 12, pp. 629–59 in *Current Trends in Linguistics*, ed. T. Sebeok. The Hague: Mouton.

Svejkovský, František
1974 — Theoretical Poetics in the Twentieth Century. Vol. 12, pp. 863–941 in *Current Trends in Linguistics*, ed. T. Sebeok. The Hague: Mouton.

Travaux Linguistiques de Prague.
1964 — *L'école de Prague d'aujourd'hui*. Praha: Academia. Reprint: University, Alabama: University of Alabama Press, 1966.

Trnka, Bohumil
1981 — *Selected Papers in Structural Linguistics*. The Hague: Mouton.

Trnka, B[ohumil] and others
1958/1964 — Prague Structural Linguistics. *Philologia Pragensia* 1 (1958): 33–40. Trans. as pp. 468–80 in Vachek 1964; and rpt. as pp. 73–84 in Lane 1970.

Vachek, Josef
1976 — *Selected Writings in English and General Linguistics*. Prague: Academia; The Hague: Mouton.

Vachek, Josef, ed.
1964 — *A Prague School Reader in Linguistics*. Bloomington: University of Indiana Press.
1966 — *The Linguistic School of Prague: An Introduction to its Theory and Practice*. Bloomington: University of Indiana Press.

Via, Dan O.
1975 — *Kerygma and Comedy in the New Testament: A Structuralist Approach to Hermeneutics*. Philadelphia: Fortress.

Wellek, René
1936 — The Theory of Literary History. *Travaux du Cercle Linguistique de Prague* 6: 173–91.
1963 — The Revolt against Positivism in Recent European Literary Scholarship. Pp. 256–81 in *Concepts of Criticism*. New Haven: Yale Univer-

sity Press. Essay originally 1946.

1969 *The Literary Theory and Aesthetics of the Prague School*. Michigan Slavic Contributions 2. Ann Arbor: Department of Slavic Languages and Literatures of the University of Michigan. Also pp. 275–305 in Wellek 1970.

1970 *Discriminations: Further Concepts of Criticism*. New Haven: Yale University Press.

1976 Vilém Mathesius (1882–1945), Founder of the Prague Linguistic Circle. Pp. 6–14 in Matejka 1976b.

1977 Foreword. Pp. vii-xiii in Mukařovský 1977.

Wellek, René, and Warren, Austin

1956 *Theory of Literature*[3]. New York: Harcourt, Brace and World. Originally 1949.

Winner, Irene Portis

1978a Cultural Semiotics and Anthropology. Pp. 335–63 in Bailey et al. 1978.

1978b The Semiotic Character of the Aesthetic Function as Defined by the Prague Linguistic Circle. Pp. 407–40 in McCormack, W. C., and Wurm, S. A., eds., *Language and Thought*. The Hague: Mouton.

Winner, Thomas C.

1973 The Aesthetics and Poetics of the Prague Linguistic Circle. *Poetics* 8: 77–96.

1976 Jan Mukařovský: The Beginnings of Structural and Semiotic Aesthetics. Pp. 433–55 in Matejka 1976.

1978 On the Relation of Verbal and Non-Verbal Art in Early Prague Semiotics: Jan Mukařovský. Pp. 227–37 in Bailey et al. 1978.

Wittig, Susan, ed.

1975 *Structuralism: An Interdisciplinary Study*. Pittsburgh: Pickwick.

Žilka, František

1936 Starý a nový překlad Nového zákona. *Slovo a slovesnost* 2: 106–12.

Prophet, Poet, Shaman: The Bible and the Literature of Western America

David Robertson
University of California, Davis, California

One of the strategies I have used now for several years in teaching the Bible as Literature is based ultimately on the assumption that meaning, like energy, exists in discrete quanta. These quanta are not strung out on a discursive line, so that you can move up the line by a series of more or less even, logical steps. Rather they exist in orbits that can be reached only by a leap that is comparable to seeing all-at-once a gestalt pattern.

In my class I read several passages of history, until the students have thoroughly adopted the mind set we use in processing historical writing. Then I read them certain portions of the Bible and ask if a leap is required to understand them. The students usually respond, "No leap is required." I follow the same procedure with excerpts from theological texts. Again the typical answer is, "No." Then I read them several literary texts, Shakespeare, Faulkner, Bellow, for example, until they are in the literary frame of mind. Then, once more, I read various passages from the Bible. This time, except maybe for passages from the Book of Job, the answer is almost always, "Yes, a leap is required. A rearrangement of our mental antennae, receivers, and amplifiers is needed before we can understand the words of the Bible in a literary way."

The experience of my students testifies to the fact that, in our culture at least, between the way Gibbon writes about Julius Caesar and the way Shakespeare writes about him is a sizable chasm, bridgeable only by a fundamental change of mind set. One question I find interesting is this: do comparable differences, though of smaller magnitude, exist within each of these larger frames of reference? That is, within the discipline of history, say, do various historians speak history in an importantly different way, in a way different enough to require little leaps to make it from one to the other? Surely the answer is "Yes," though I know too little about the discipline of history to name some instances.

A possible instance in literature is the subject of this paper. I have felt for some time that a fundamental difference exists between the way modernist poets, like Pound, Eliot, and Stevens, use poetic language, and the way certain western American poets, like Robinson Jeffers, Kenneth Rexroth, and Gary Snyder, use it. Assuming that this difference is quantum mechanical, I will use the same strategy here that I use in my class on the Bible as Literature. I will juxtapose passages from Wallace Stevens, whose language is, I think, most purely modernist, and poems of Gary Snyder, who speaks most purely this other poetic dialect.

First, here are the two poets confronting animals.

Wallace Stevens, from "Thirteen Ways of Looking at a Blackbird"

II

I was of three minds,
Like a tree
In which there are three blackbirds.

V

I do not know which to prefer,
The beauty of inflections
Or the beauty of innuendoes,
The blackbird whistling
Or just after.

IX

When the blackbird flew out of sight,
It marked the edge
Of one of many circles.[1]

Gary Snyder, "Water"

Pressure of sun on the rockslide
Whirled me in a dizzy hop-and-step descent,
Pool of pebbles buzzed in a Juniper shadow,
Tiny tongue of a this-year rattlesnake flicked,
I leaped, laughing for little boulder-color coil—
Pounded by heat raced down the slabs to the creek
Deep tumbling under arching walls and stuck
Whole head and shoulders in the water:
Stretched full on cobble—ears roaring
Eyes open aching from the cold and faced a trout.[2]

Next, compare their advice to beginners.

Wallace Stevens, from "Notes Toward a Supreme Fiction"

Begin, ephebe, by perceiving the idea
Of this invention, this invented world,
The inconceivable idea of the sun.

You must become an ignorant man again
And see the sun again with an ignorant eye
And see it clearly in the idea of it.[3]

Gary Snyder, from "What You Should Know to be a Poet"

all you can about animals as persons.
the names of trees and flowers and weeds.
names of stars, and the movement of the planets and the moon.

your own six senses, with a watchful and elegant mind.

at least one kind of traditional magic:
divination, astrology, the *book of changes*, the tarot;

. . . .

childrens' games, comic books, bubble-gum,
the weirdness of television and advertising.[4]

Or, again, here are the two poets talking about poetry, Stevens explicitly and Snyder implicitly.

Wallace Stevens, from "Of Modern Poetry"

The poem of the mind is the act of finding
What will suffice. It has not always had
To find: the scene was set; it repeated what
Was in the script.
                    Then the theatre was changed
To something else. Its past was a souvenir.
. . . .
. . . . It has
To construct a new stage. It has to be on that stage
And, like an insatiable actor, slowly and
With meditation, speak words that in the ear,
In the delicatest ear of the mind, repeat,
Exactly, that which it wants to hear, at the sound
Of which, an invisible audience listens,
Not to the play, but to itself, expressed
In an emotion as of two people, as of two
Emotions becoming one. The actor is
A metaphysician in the dark, twanging
An instrument, twanging a wiry string that gives
Sounds passing through sudden rightnesses, wholly
Containing the mind, below which it cannot descend,
Beyond which it has no will to rise.[5]

Gary Snyder, "Everybody Lying on Their Stomachs, Head Toward the Candle, Reading, Sleeping, Drawing"

The corrugated roof
Booms and fades night-long to

        million-darted rain
    squalls   and

        outside

        lightning

Photographs in the brain
Wind-bent bamboo.
                    through

the plank shutter
set

Half-open   on eternity.[6]

And, finally, here are Stevens and Snyder practicing what they preach.

Wallace Stevens, "Of Mere Being"

The palm at the end of the mind,
Beyond the last thought, rises
In the bronze decor,

A gold-feathered bird
Sings in the palm, without human meaning,
Without human feeling, a foreign song.

You know then that it is not the reason
That makes us happy or unhappy.
The bird sings. Its feathers shine.

The palm stands on the edge of space.
The wind moves slowly in the branches.
The bird's fire-fangled feathers dangle down.[7]

Gary Snyder, "Regarding Wave"

The voice of the Dharma
the voice
now

A shimmering bell
through all

Every hill   still.
Every tree alive. Every leaf.
All the slopes   flow.
old woods, new seedlings,
tall grasses, plumes.

Dark hollows; peaks of light.
wind stirs the cool side
Each leaf living.
All the hills.

The Voice
is a wife
to

him still

ōṃ   ah   hūṃ[8]

I assume that the tone and syntax of Stevens's language is familiar to us, the kind of poetic talk we are accustomed to hearing. The question is: as you go from Stevens to Snyder, is a leap of considerable magnitude required before the latter can be understood? I think the answer is "Yes." But, assuming once more that meaning exists in quanta, I do not wish to demonstrate this difference by discussing the two poets and their poems discursively, but to set up a series of parallels, or appositions, to their poems, and hope that one or more of these appositions will cause the mind to make the mental leap from Stevens's orbit to Snyder's.

Here, then, is the first apposition: Escher's lithographs over against Nikolaïdes' *The Natural Way to Draw.*[9] In Escher's prints people go up stairs only to go down them, water falls down only to double back upon itself and fall once more. An artist makes a drawing showing a hand holding a globe; reflected in the globe is the artist with his hand holding the globe. "Print Gallery" is a particularly interesting variation on this theme. It depicts a man looking at prints, one of which is not only a print but the city surrounding the print gallery, and in the city is a woman looking out a window at none other than the man in the gallery. Most of Escher's lithographs trace the geometrical figure of a loop, which seems an appropriate image of modernity, as I am using that word. We moderns are fascinated by that which loops back upon itself, Strange Loops, Douglas Hofstadter calls them in his book, *Gödel, Escher, Bach.*[10]

As possibly the modernist poet par excellence, Stevens writes poems in which strange loops are made, and many of which are themselves strange loops: the flight of the blackbird draws a circle around the observer; to wash the sun clean of our ideas of it leaves us with the idea of the sun; an audience watches itself act; beyond the last thought is a thought, or more precisely put, beyond the last thought is not a real bird but a highly contrived, imaginary one whose feathers would fit perfectly the bronze decor in Yeats's Byzantium. For Stevens, it seems, the mind has difficulty getting beyond the poem and the poem has difficulty getting beyond the mind.

Contrast Escher with Nikolaïdes. He says that one aspect of the natural way to draw is not to look at the object, then down at the paper to draw the figure you remember the object makes (the innuendo of the object, Stevens might say), but rather to move the pencil on the paper along the edge of the object while you look at the object. In this way a contact is made and kept with the object, not only by the eye but also by the pencil. The line from object to eye to pencil and back to the object again describes a geometrical figure, not of a loop, but of a triangle, because at each of the three points real contact is made. And this triangle is parallel, in Snyder's poems, to the triangle of bamboo, plank shutter, and observer, or to the triangle of Voice, words that resonate with it, and hearer. Every time Stevens tries to get out of himself he doubles back upon himself. Snyder, on the other hand, makes contact. Not only does he see the trout eye to eye and hear the Voice, but in writing his poems he keeps his ear cupped to the sound of that Voice and his eye on the trout, analogous to the way the student of Nikolaïdes keeps his eye on the contour of the flower or on the gesture of the person.

The second apposition is a contrast between self-referential and referential language. Terence Hawkes has a particularly clear and succinct summary of the view that poetic speech is self-referential. He is speaking of the Russian formalists and especially of the late Roman Jakobson.

> For it is of the distinctive essence of the aesthetic use of language . . . that it is self-conscious; concerned *above all* to draw attention to its *own nature*, its own sound-patterns, diction, syntax, etc. and *not* to refer primarily to some "reality" beyond itself. . . . As a result it systematically undermines the sense of any "natural" or "transparent" connection between signifier and signified, sign and object. . . . Verbal art, seen thus, is not referential in mode, and does not function as a transparent "window" through which the reader encounters the poem's or the novel's subject." Its mode is auto-referential; it is its own subject.[11]

Over against this quote place the following one by Charles Peirce.

> A *sign* . . . is a First which stands in such a genuine triadic relation to a Second, called its *object*, as to be capable of determining a Third, called its *interpretant*, to assume the same triadic relation to its Object in which it stands itself to the same Object.[12]

Closely related to this pair of quotes is another pair that contrasts absence over against presence. Here is Hawkes summarizing what he feels is one of Jacques Derrida's most important points.

> Our traditional commitment to the voice as the primary communicative instrument also commits us, in Derrida's view, to a falsifying "metaphysics of presence," based on an illusion that we are able, ultimately, to "come face to face once and for all with objects." That is, that some final, objective, unmediated "real world" exists, about which we can have concrete knowledge. Derrida sees this belief in "presence" as the major factor limiting our apprehension of the world: a distorting insistence that, in spite of our always fragmentary experience, somewhere there must exist a redeeming and justifying *wholeness*.[13]

Over against Derrida as interpreted by Hawkes, consider David Wilson.

> Nature is present to naturalists the way God is to saints or the past is to humanists—not simply as a matter of fact but as an insistent and live reality.[14]

What is crucial on one side of the above pairs is that words in poetry loop back upon themselves, becoming their own signified, leaving a void in the direction in which they might, if they were ordinary words, be taken to point. What is crucial on the other side is that words, even poetic words, not be removed from the triangle of communication, in which someone by means of words communicates something to someone else. Words must, therefore, remain open directional channels, or communication will fail. It follows from this way of looking at poetic words that the two someones and the something are of greater importance than the words themselves. And, when that something is nature, then the most important thing words communicate is not an object, but a presence, a presence that Wilson's quote calls attention to. Similarly, if through Snyder's words we hear that greater Voice, then his words have served him and the reader well. Furthermore, any attempt to make the words of his poems into a voice by making them auto-referential will violate them. Such a violation will be more or less obvious, because his words will resist such an attempt.

Briefly my last two oppositions are:

"as if" *over against* "is"

and

piano and guitar *over against* the camera

Stevens is pre-eminently a poet of supposition. Words like "as if," "might be," and "like" are sprinkled evenly over his garden of verses. To suppose is to haul anchor up from reality in order to float more freely over the waters of fancy. And since music of all the arts is most free of an objective world, it is not surprising that Stevens' favorite images of the poet are the pianist at the keyboard extemporizing and the guitarist making up the words to his songs as he goes along. "The Man with the Blue Guitar"[15] may be the prototypical Stevens poem in that it consists of 33 different ways to sing the same song.

In short, Stevens believes that, because the non-human world is inherently meaningless, the poet must compose fictions, and these fictions, if they suffice, allow us to compose ourselves in the face of this meaninglessness. Snyder, on the other hand, believes that the world as a whole makes human sense and is full of power that, if tapped, gives direction, brings order, heals, in short, suffices. The task is not to compose our own music, but to listen to the music nature is always composing, not only for us but for all living things. A Snyder poem is, then, not a piano, an instrument so good at composing its own world that most people, even listening to program music after having read the program notes, have great difficulty envisioning the scene described. Rather, one of his poems is a camera, or better, a lens, where we are the film and the world is the light. The function of this lens is to transmit and focus the light of the world onto the film of our minds.

I believe that literary criticism is always after the fact. That is, literary critical theories arise to help people understand literature that already has been written. So criticism is partly a descriptive science, any one of whose theories applies only to the literature that that particular theory comes into existence to explain. Any one literary theory is partly also a sort of lab manual: follow these directions and literature you thought opaque will become clear. Perhaps the easiest way to determine the limits of any theory is to follow its directions until you no longer get satisfactory results, that is, until even after following a theory's hermeneutical instructions, you still cannot make sense of a body of literature. Of course, you have to be careful here. New Critics applied their theory to Milton, and instead of recognizing that their results were negative, they concluded that Milton was not as good a poet as everyone had thought.

With the above understanding of literary criticism in mind, here is the main point of this paper: in testing the poetry of Robinson Jeffers, Kenneth Rexroth, and Gary Snyder, as well as others like them, you will get the most satisfactory results if you use these assumptions.

1) The world is not made up of words (that is, is neither created by nor consists of words), nor is the world of meaning primarily made up of words. Knowledge of both of these worlds can, however, be mediated by words. The task at hand is not to invent but to discover the world. Assume discovery, not invention.

2) Neither the world nor the things in it are primarily a language, and so are not signs of anything. Rather, they are presences. The function of poetic language is not to treat objects as counters in a game of "as if," but be a medium through which objects can make themselves known to us. Assume revelation, not signification.

3) Language refers, though, of course, not in any simple-minded or one-dimensional way. Assume referential, not self-referential.

4) The relation between signifier and signified is not arbitrary. It may be aggravatingly difficult to say what the relation is. The relation may in fact border on the magical. However that may be, access to the root of the word gives access to the root of (the) matter. A Snyder poem that in an especially clear way brings this assumption into play is "Wave," which begins

Grooving clam shell,
streakt through marble,
sweeping down ponderosa pine bark-scale
rip-cut tree grain
sand dunes, lava
flow

Wave wife
woman—wyfman—
"veiled; vibrating; vague"
sawtooth ranges pulsing;
veins on the back of the hand.[16]

So, assume correspondence, not coincidence.

5) Content is of very great importance, and though it can be known only through a particular form, it transcends that form, as the person the body. Assume you must go beyond formality and formalism.

6) There is a power without and a power within, and when the two dance in step, healing and health come naturally. Assume ecology.

Let me return now to the strategy of presenting patterns of literary gestalt, this time with some biblical passages.[17]

The lion roars: who can help feeling afraid?
The Lord Yahweh speaks: who can refuse to prophecy?
(Amos 3:8)

Yahweh Sabaoth, the God of Israel, says this: Amend your behavior and your actions and I will stay with you here in this place. Put no trust in delusive words like these: This is the sanctuary of Yahweh, the sanctuary of Yahweh, the sanctuary of Yahweh!
(Jer 7: 3–4)

For thus says the Lord Yahweh, the Holy One of Israel:
Your salvation lay in conversion and tranquillity;
your strength, in complete trust;
and you would have none of it.

"No," you said, "we will flee on horses."
So be it, flee then!
And you add, "In swift chariots."
So be it, your pursuers will be swift too.
(Isa 30: 15–16)

This language is closer to Snyder's than to Stevens's, or so it seems to me. If it is, then the instructions I have just enumerated will yield significantly greater results when experimenting on biblical texts than a lab manual written from the point of view, or at least, too exclusively from the point of view, of New Criticism, Form Criticism, Structuralism, semiology, or the like.

Yet quite obviously, there are differences between Amos, Jeremiah, and Isaiah on the one side and Snyder on the other. Maybe three terms—prophet, poet, and shaman—can be used adequately to summarize the similarities and differences between the biblical writers and Snyder and, at the same time, to explain why all of them stand over against Stevens. Both prophet and shaman assume discovery, revelation, referential language, primacy of content, and ecology. Both work within the triangle of communication, speak of presences, and search for what "is." The main difference between them is this: the prophet's triangle stands upright, the shaman's lies flat. That is, the shaman assumes that the natural world is full of presences, the prophet that the Presence resides in a world above nature. Consequently, for the prophet salvation is possible, for the shaman only healing.

The poet (and quite obviously the term is used here to refer to "modernist" practitioners of that profession), on the other hand, assumes invention, signification, self-referential language, primacy of form, and a world irretrievably fractured into atoms and wholes irreparably divided into parts. In such a situation about the only thing words can possibly do is loop back upon themselves in strange ways, and in so doing create fictions. All the world's a theater, constructed out of words, without actors, in which the audience projects itself onto the stage and delivers soliloquies. Absent are both object and listener.

Here is the poet Stevens.

> How simply the fictive hero becomes the real;
> How gladly with proper words the soldier dies,
> If he must, or lives on the bread of faithful speech.[18]

Here is the prophet Moses.

> Man does not live on bread alone but . . . on everything
> that comes from the mouth of Yahweh.
> (Deut 8: 3)

Here is the shaman Snyder, his poem "Source."

> Cloud finger dragons dance and
> tremble down the ridge
> and spit and spiral snow then pull in
> quivering, on the sawtooth
> spine
>
> Clears up, and all the stars.
> the tree leaves catch
> some extra tiny source
> all the wide night
>
> Up here
> Out back
> drink deep
> that black light.[19]

Notes

1. Stevens 1954: 92–94.
2. Snyder 1969: 10.
3. Stevens 1954: 380.
4. Snyder 1967: 40.
5. Stevens 1954: 239–40.
6. Snyder 1967: 28.
7. Stevens 1966: 117–18.
8. Snyder 1967: 35.
9. Nikolaïdes 1975.
10. Hofstadter 1979.
11. Hawkes 1977: 86.
12. Sebeok 1978: 217.
13. Hawkes 1977: 145–46.
14. Wilson 1978: 1.
15. Stevens 1954: 165–84.
16. Snyder 1967: 3.
17. All biblical quotations are from the Jerusalem Bible.
18. Stevens 1954: 408.
19. Snyder 1974: 26.

References

Hawkes, T.
1977 *Structuralism and Semiotics.* Berkeley: University of California Press.

Hofstadter, D.
1979 *Gödel, Escher, Bach.* New York: Basic Books.

Nikolaïdes, K.
1975 *The Natural Way to Draw.* Boston: Houghton Mifflin.

Sebeok, T. A., ed.
1978 *Sight Sound and Sense.* Bloomington: Indiana University Press.

Snyder, G.
1967 *Regarding Wave.* New York: New Directions.
1969 *Riprap.* San Francisco: Four Seasons Foundation. Originally 1959.
1974 *Turtle Island.* New York: New Directions.

Stevens, W.
1954 *Collected Poems.* New York: Knopf.
1966 *Opus Posthumous.* New York: Knopf.

Wilson, D.
1978 *In The Presence of Nature.* Amherst: University of Massachusetts Press.

Bibliography of the Works of David Noel Freedman

M. O'Connor
Ann Arbor, Michigan

I. The Bible and the Ancient Near East

A. Books, papers, and notes
B. Contributions to reference works
C. Book reviews

II. Modern Intellectual History

D. Books, papers, and articles

III. Popular, Devotional, and Ephemeral Works

E. Books and articles
F. Book reviews

IV. Editorial Work

G. Books outside series
H. The Anchor Bible
I. American Schools of Oriental Research Publications
J. The Computer Bible Series
K. The International Concordance Library
L. Consulting Editorial Work
M. Special Editorial Work
N. Journals

A Note on the New American Bible

This is a reader's bibliography, not a bibliographer's, and therefore a few words of explanation may be wanted; it is one reader's bibliography, and therefore a few words of justification may be needed. The listing is complete to the end of 1981, though some pieces of devotional ephemera from the 'fifties may have been lost track of and some further items dated 1981 may yet appear; all items dated 1982 or marked forthcoming (f/c) refer to work completed and in press. A few works in preparation are referred to in this note. Non-print media are not represented here.

The first three sections list Freedman's own work over the past two dozen years, and the fourth section records his editorial labors; incidental contributions to journals he has edited are listed in IV.N. The division of materials over the first three sections is not meant to be prejudicial, as I shall try to explain.

Section I. The works here constitute Freedman's scholarly contribution to Near Eastern and biblical studies. The range is evident, so it may be useful to mark out principal areas of study, proceeding from least to most important.

(1) *Qumranic studies*. The major papers are 1962a, 1968d, 1974b; relevant reviews and notes are 1949, 1957, 1959.

(2) *Orthographic studies*. The major work is the earliest, Cross and Freedman 1952; subsequent studies include Freedman 1962a, 1969b, 1969c, and Freedman and Ritterspach 1967.

(3) *Studies in the Tetragrammaton*. Two papers only, both major, Freedman 1960b and Freedman and O'Connor 1980.

(4) *Poetic studies*. (a) *Early work*. Cross and Freedman 1947, 1948, 1953a, 1955, 1972, and 1975. (b) *Studies since 1960 in non-prophetic poetry*. Work on poetic structure is chiefly represented in the fifteen papers and four notes collected in 1980a, which must be supplemented by the inaugural paper of this phase of work, 1960c, as well as by the major paper of Freedman and Franke-Hyland 1973, and the smaller pieces 1963b and 1964c; since the gathering of 1980a, other work has been done, 1980b, 1981a, 1981b, 1982a, 1982b, and the forthcoming paper. (c) *Studies in the eighth-century prophets*. The work underway since the early 'seventies with F. I. Andersen finds its first monument in Andersen and Freedman 1980; the Anchor Bible volume on Amos and Micah is in preparation. Though Freedman 1955 is superseded by *Hosea*, Freedman 1979a retains some interest.

(5) *The History of Israelite Literature*. Whether Freedman will bring to completion the work he has long projected under this title, I cannot say; some of the materials are to hand: 1963c is programmatic; 1961, 1962k, 1969d, 1973c, 1975c, 1976d, 1976e, and 1979c are basic; 1960a, 1963a, 1964b, and 1967b are tangential.

The listing of these five areas is problematic: fundamental concerns with historical study and with Israelite theology are obscured here; the constant attention to grammatical phenomena on all levels cannot be highlighted directly.

Section II. Grouped together here are materials tangential to the major enterprise of Near Eastern studies as Freedman has undertaken it. Along with Freedman's most controversial work, this section includes his least appreciated labors, those involving scholarly biography. The major realms can be listed. (1) Scholarly biography, whether obituary, appreciation, or biography and bibliography in the amplest sense. (2) Archeological reporting, chiefly on Ashdod (add to the materials here Cross and Freedman 1964, Dothan and Freedman 1967, and Freedman 1967c and 1979d, from Section I) and Tell Mardikh (add from Section I Freedman 1979e). (3) Reflection on the scholarly study of the Bible (add from Section I Freedman 1965) and of religion in general.

Section III. The sermons written by Freedman alone and in collaboration with his Princeton Theological Seminary classmate T. A. Gill are among the most moving pieces in the entire body of work. The work written for children and young people seems to be of little interest. The few pieces of religious-political speculation from the 'fifties are dated.

Section IV. The material is for the most part self-explanatory. All the categories remain open except for I and M; Freedman has handed on the editorship of the publications of the American Schools, and complexities in the estate of William Foxwell Albright make it unlikely that Freedman will continue to serve as Albright's literary executor.

Sigla and structure. In Part I.B., * indicates contributions of under one hundred words. In Part II.D., * indicates contributions written for children, young people, and their teachers. Only materials in Section I are lettered to coordinate various publications within a single year; the letter sigla span the three parts of Section I.

The material in Section I is ordered by category (books, papers, and notes; contributions to reference works; book reviews), by authorship (DNF alone; with others), by type of contribution (books; contributions to books; contributions to periodicals), then alphabetically (in case of contributions, by book or periodical rather than article title). Sections II and III follow the same pattern, *mutatis mutandis*. In Sections IV, all parts are arranged by year, except for IV.H. and IV.J., which are arranged alphabetically.

There are 152 entries in Section I (A: 78 entries; B: 52 entries; C: 22 entries); 27 entries in Section II; 62 entries in Section III (E: 37 entries; F: 25 entries); and 112 entries in Section IV (G: 6 entries; H: 36 entries; I: 24 entries; J: 24 entries; L: 14 entries; N: 6 entries; and K and M, 1 entry each), a total of 353 entries, slightly fewer than the number of years Enoch lived on earth before he was assumed into heaven.

I. The Bible and the Ancient Near East

I. A. Books, papers, and notes

A1. F. M. Cross and DNF
1947 — A Note on Deuteronomy 33: 26. *Bulletin of the American Schools of Oriental Research* 108: 6–7.

A2. [F. M. Cross and DNF]
1948 — *The Evolution of Early Hebrew Orthography: The Epigraphic Evidence.* Johns Hopkins Dissertation [nominally submitted by DNF]. 260 pp. Revised as Cross and Freedman 1952.

A3. F. M. Cross and DNF
1948 — The Blessing of Moses [Deuteronomy 33]. *Journal of Biblical Literature* 67: 191–210. See [Cross and Freedman 1950].

A4. DNF
1949 — The "House of Absalom" in the Habakkuk Scroll [4QpHab 5: 9, a literal, not symbolic term; note, e.g., 1 Macc 11: 70]. *Bulletin of the American Schools of Oriental Research* 114: 11–12.

A5. [F. M. Cross and DNF]
1950 — *Studies in Ancient Yahwistic Poetry*. Johns Hopkins Dissertation [nominally submitted by F. M. Cross]. 358 pp. Various chapters published, usually in revised form, as Cross and Freedman 1948, 1953a, 1955; the whole published without revision but with a postscriptum as Cross and Freedman 1975. A small offset edition of the unrevised dissertation appeared in 1964.

A6. DNF
1951a — The Orthography of the Masoretic Text of the Pentateuch (abstract). *Journal of Biblical Literature* 70: iv.

A7. F. M. Cross and DNF
1951 — The Pronominal Suffixes of the Third Person Singular in Phoenician [notably KAI 10, 24, 26, cf. KAI 189]. *Journal of Near Eastern Studies* 10: 228–30.

A8. 1952 — *Early Hebrew Orthography: A Study of the Epigraphic Evidence.* American Oriental Series 36. New Haven: American Oriental Society. viii + 77. See [Cross and Freedman 1948].

A9. DNF
1953a — Notes on Genesis [grammar in 1: 9, 11; 2: 20; 3: 17; the text of 4: 22; verse in 5: 29; 12: 1–2; 14: 4, 6, 19–20]. *Zeitschrift für die Alttestamentliche Wissenschaft* 64: 190–94.

A10. F. M. Cross and DNF
1953a — A Royal Song of Thanksgiving: II Samuel 22 = Psalm 18. *Journal of Biblical Literature* 72: 15–34. See [Cross and Freedman 1950].

A11. 1953b — Josiah's Revolt Against Assyria [esp. in 2 Chronicles 34]. *Journal of Near Eastern Studies* 12: 56–58.

A12. DNF
1954 — The Book of Ezekiel. Studia Biblica 27. *Interpretation* 8: 446–71.

A13. 1955 — PŠTY [*pištay*] in Hosea 2: 7. *Journal of Biblical Literature* 74: 275.

A14. F. M. Cross and DNF
1955 — The Song of Miriam [Exodus 15]. *Journal of Near Eastern Studies* 14: 237–50. See [Cross and Freedman 1950].

A15. DNF
1956 — The Babylonian Chronicle. *The Biblical Archaeologist* 19: 50–60. Rpt. 1961 as pp. 113–27 in *The Biblical Archaeologist Reader, 1,* ed. G. E. Wright and D. N. Freedman. Garden City: Doubleday. (See G1 below further).

A16. 1957 The Prayer of Nabonidus [4QPrNab]. *Bulletin of the American Schools of Oriental Research* 145: 31–32.

A17. 1958 Jonah 1: 46 [read a form of *ḥwb*, not of *ḥšb*]. *Journal of Biblical Literature* 77: 161–62.

A18. 1960a History and Eschatology: The Nature of Biblical Religion and Prophetic Faith. *Interpretation* 14: 143–54.

A19. 1960b The Name of the God of Moses. *Journal of Biblical Literature* 79: 151–56.

A20. 1960c Archaic Forms in Early Hebrew Poetry [Judg 5: 26; 2 Sam 22: 16; Deut 33: 11b; Num 23: 10b; 21: 17–18; 21: 27b; Ps 29: 1–2; Exod 15: 6, 9, 16]. *Zeitschrift für die Alttestamentliche Wissenschaft* 72: 101–7.

A21. R. M. Grant in collaboration with DNF
1960 *The Secret Sayings of Jesus: The Gnostic Gospel of Thomas*. With a translation by W. R. Schoedel. Garden City: Doubleday [hardcover, 206 pp.; Dolphin paperback, 198 pp.] and London: Collins [paperback, 192 pp.]. Trans. 1960 into German as *Geheime Wörter Jesu* by S. George with a translation by H. Quecke and with a contribution by J. B. Bauer. Frankfurt-am-Main: Heinrich Scheffler. 228 pp. Also trans. 1962 into Dutch as *Het Thomas Evangelie* by J. Mooy. Utrecht: Aula Boeken. 188 pp. [Jacket design for original hardcover edition by Edward Gorey.]

A22. DNF
1961 The Chronicler's Purpose. *Catholic Biblical Quarterly* 23: 436–42.

A23. DNF and E. F. Campbell
1961 The Chronology of Israel and the Ancient Near East. A. Old Testament Chronology [Freedman]. B. The Ancient Near East: Chronological Bibliography and Charts [Campbell]. Pp. 203–28 in *The Bible and the Ancient Near East: Essays in Honor of William Foxwell Albright*, ed. G. E. Wright. Garden City: Doubleday. Rpt. 1965 as pp. 265–87 of paperback reissue. Volume rpt. with original pagination, 1979, Winona Lake, Indiana: Eisenbrauns.

A24. DNF
1962a The Massoretic Text and the Qumran Scrolls: A Study in Orthography. *Textus* 2: 87–102. Rpt. 1975 as pp. 196–211 in *Qumran and the History of the Biblical Text*, ed. F. M. Cross and S. Talmon. Cambridge: Harvard University Press.

A25. 1963a On Method in Biblical Studies: The Old Testament. *Interpretation* 17: 308–18.

A26. 1963b The Original Name of Jacob [in Deut 33: 28]. *Israel Exploration Journal* 13: 125–26.

A27. 1963c The Law and the Prophets. *Supplements to Vetus Testamentum* 9: 250–65. Rpt. 1974 as pp. 5–20 in *The Canon and Masorah of the Hebrew Bible: An Introductory Reader*, ed. S. Z. Leiman. The Library of Biblical Studies. New York: Ktav.

A28. 1964a A Second Mesha Inscription [cf. KAI 181: 1–2]. *Bulletin of the American Schools of Oriental Research* 175: 50–51.

A29. 1964b Divine Commitment and Human Obligation: The Covenant Theme. *Interpretation* 18: 419–31.

A30. F. M. Cross and DNF
1964 The Name of Ashdod. *Bulletin of the American Schools of Oriental Research* 175: 48–50.

A31. DNF
1965 Archaeology and the Future of Biblical Studies: The Biblical Languages. Pp. 294–312 in *The Bible in Modern Scholarship: Papers Read at the One Hundredth Meeting of the Society of Biblical Literature*, ed. J. P. Hyatt.

Nashville: Abingdon.

A32. 1967a — The Song of the Sea. Pp. 1–10 in *A Feeling of Celebration: A Tribute to James Muilenburg*, ed. R. Shukraft. San Anselmo, California: San Francisco Theological Seminary. Rpt. as pp. 179–86 in Freedman 1980a.

A33. 1967b — The Biblical Idea of History. *Interpretation* 21: 32–49.

A34. M. Dothan and DNF 1967 — *Ashdod I. The First Season of Excavations 1962*. ʿAtiqot English Series VII. Jerusalem: The Department of Antiquities and Museums, [The State of] Israel. 171 pp. + 28 plates.

A35. DNF and A. Ritterspach 1967 — The Use of *Aleph* as a Vowel Letter in the Genesis Apocryphon. *Revue de Qumran* 6: 293–300.

A36. DNF 1968a — The Structure of Job 3. *Biblica* 49: 503–8. Rpt. as pp. 323–28 in Freedman 1980a.

A37. 1968b — Isaiah 42: 13. *Catholic Biblical Quarterly* 30: 225–26. Rpt. as pp. 345–46 in Freedman 1980a.

A38. 1968c — The Elihu Speeches in the Book of Job. *Harvard Theological Review* 61: 51–59. Rpt. as pp. 329–37 in Freedman 1980a. Trans. 1968 into Japanese in *Kirisutokyo Ronshū* [*The Journal of Christian Studies*] #14 [In Honor of Prof. Junichi Asano]: 25–37.

A39. 1968d — The Old Testament at Qumran. *McCormick Quarterly* 21 #3 (March 1968): 299–306. Rpt. 1969 as pp. 131–41 in *New Directions in Biblical Archaeology*, ed. DNF and J. C. Greenfield. Garden City: Doubleday. (See G3 below further.)

A40. 1969a — The Burning Bush [Exod 3: 2–3]. *Biblica* 50: 245–46.

A41. 1969b — Orthographic Peculiarities in the Book of Job. *Eretz-Israel* 9 [W. F. Albright Volume]: 35–44.

A42. 1969c — The Orthography of the Arad Ostraca. *Israel Exploration Journal* 19: 52–56.

A43. 1969d — The Flowering of Apocalyptic [Daniel, Qumran]. *Journal for Theology and the Church* 6 [Apocalypticism]: 166–74.

A44. 1970 — "Mistress Forever." A Note on Isaiah 47, 7. *Biblica* 51: 538.

A45. DNF and F. I. Andersen 1970 — Harmon in Amos 4: 3. *Bulletin of the American Schools of Oriental Research* 198: 41.

A46. DNF 1971a — The Structure of Psalm 137. Pp. 187–205 in *Near Eastern Studies in Honor of William Foxwell Albright*, ed. H. Goedicke. Baltimore: Johns Hopkins Press. Rpt. as pp. 303–21 in Freedman 1980a.

A47. 1971b — Is Justice Blind? (Is 11, 3f). *Biblica* 52: 536.

A48. 1971c — A Note on Judges 15: 5. *Biblica* 52: 535.

A49. 1971d — II Samuel 23: 4. *Journal of Biblical Literature* 90: 329–30. Rpt. as pp. 343–44 in Freedman 1980a.

A50. F. M. Cross and DNF 1971 — An Inscribed Jar Handle from Raddana. *Bulletin of the American Schools of Oriental Research* 201: 19–22.

A51. DNF 1972a — The Refrain in David's Lament over Saul and Jonathan. Pp. 115–26 in *Ex Orbe Religionum: Studia Geo Widengren Oblata. 1*, ed. C. J. Bleeker et al. Studies in the History of Religions (Supplements to *NUMEN*) 21. Leiden: Brill. Rpt. as pp. 263–74 in Freedman 1980a.

A52. 1972b — Prolegomenon. Pp. vii-lvi in George Buchanan Gray, *The Forms of Hebrew Poetry Considered with Special Reference to the Criticism and Interpretation of the Old Testament*. The Library of Biblical Studies

[Reprint of the Original 1915 Edition]. New York: Ktav. The Annotated Bibliography on Hebrew Poetry from 1915 to the Present was compiled with the help of Bonnie Kittel. Rpt. without the bibliography as pp. 23–50 in Freedman 1980a.

A53. 1972c — The Broken Construct Chain. *Biblica* 53: 534–36. Rpt. as pp. 339–41 in Freedman 1980a.

A54. 1972d — Acrostics and Metrics in Hebrew Poetry. *Harvard Theological Review* 65: 367–92. Rpt. as pp. 51–76 in Freedman 1980a.

A55. 1973a — God Almighty in Psalm 78, 59. *Biblica* 54: 268. Rpt. as p. 347 in Freedman 1980a.

A56. DNF and C. Franke-Hyland 1973 — Psalm 29: A Structural Analysis. *Harvard Theological Review* 66: 237–56.

A57. DNF 1974a — Strophe and Meter in Exodus 15. Pp. 163–203 in *A Light Unto My Path: Old Testament Studies in Honor of Jacob M. Myers*, ed. H. N. Bream, R. D. Heim, and C. A. Moore. Gettysburg Theological Studies IV. Pittsburgh: Temple University Press. Rpt. as pp. 187–227 in Freedman 1980a.

A58. 1974b — Variant Readings in the Leviticus Scroll from Qumran Cave 11 [11QpaleoLev]. *Catholic Biblical Quarterly* 36/4 [P. W. Skehan Number]: 525–34. For the proper siglum assignment see J. A. Fitzmyer, S. J. 1975. Correction. *Catholic Biblical Quarterly* 37: 238. For the complete text see K. Mathews. 1980. *The Paleo-Hebrew Leviticus Scroll from Qumran*. Michigan Dissertation. The final publication will be D. N. Freedman and K. A. Matthews. *The Paleo-Hebrew Leviticus Scroll from Qumran Cave 11*. With a contribution by R. S. Hanson

A59. 1975a — The Aaronic Benediction (Numbers 6: 24–26). Pp. 35–47 in *No Famine in the Land: Studies in Honor of John L. McKenzie*, ed. J. L. Flanagan and A. W. Robinson. Missoula/Claremont: Scholars Press/The Institute for Antiquity and Christianity. Rpt. as pp. 229–42 in Freedman 1980a.

A60. 1975b — Early Israelite History in the Light of Early Israelite Poetry. Pp. 3–35 in *Unity and Diversity: Essays in the History, Literature, and Religion of the Ancient Near East*, ed. H. Goedicke and J. J. M. Roberts. Baltimore: The Johns Hopkins University Press. Rpt. as pp. 131–66 in Freedman 1980a.

A61. 1975c — "Son of Man, Can These Bones Live?"—The Exile. *Interpretation* 29/2 [John Bright Number]: 171–86. With the help of M. O'Connor.

A62. F. M. Cross and DNF 1975 — *Studies in Ancient Yahwistic Poetry*. Society of Biblical Literature 21. Missoula: Scholars Press. viii + 191 pp. See [Cross and Freedman 1950].

A63. DNF 1976a — Divine Names and Titles in Early Hebrew Poetry. Pp. 55–107 in *Magnalia Dei, The Mighty Acts of God: Essays on the Bible and Archaeology in Memory of G. Ernest Wright*, ed. F. M. Cross, W. E. Lemke, and P. D. Miller. Garden City: Doubleday. Rpt. as pp. 77–129 in Freedman 1980a.

A64. 1976b — The Twenty-Third Psalm. Pp. 139–66 in *Michigan Oriental Studies in Honor of George G. Cameron*, ed. L. L. Orlin et al. Ann Arbor: Department of Near Eastern Studies, The University of Michigan [distributed by Eisenbrauns]. Rpt. as pp. 275–302 in Freedman 1980a.

A65. 1977 — Pottery, Poetry, and Prophecy: An Essay on Biblical Poetry [The Society of Biblical Literature Presidential Address for 1976]. *Journal of Biblical Literature* 96: 5–26. Rpt. 1979 as pp. 77–100 in *The Bible in its Literary Milieu: Contemporary Essays*, ed. V. L. Tollers and J. R. Maier. Grand Rapids: Eerdmans. Also rpt. as pp. 1–22 in Freedman 1980a.

A66. 1978 — Psalm 113 and the Song of Hannah. *Eretz-Israel* 14 [H. L. Ginsberg Volume]: 56–69. With the assistance of Clayton Libolt. Rpt. as pp. 243–61 in Freedman 1980a.

A67. 1979a — Problems of Textual Criticism in the Book of Hosea. Pp. 55–76 in *The Critical Study of Sacred Texts*, ed. W. D. O'Flaherty. Berkeley Religious Studies Series. Berkeley: Graduate Theological Union [Lancaster-Miller].

A68. 1979b — Early Israelite Poetry and Historical Reconstructions. Pp. 85–96 in *Symposia Celebrating the Seventy-Fifth Anniversary of the Founding of the American Schools of Oriental Research (1900–1975)*, ed. F. M. Cross. Zion Research Foundation Occasional Publications 1–2. Cambridge: The American Schools of Oriental Research. Rpt. as pp. 167–78 in Freedman 1980a.

A69. 1979c — The Age of David and Solomon. Pp. 101–25, 327–29 in *The World History of the Jewish People. First Series: Ancient Times. Volume 4. The Age of the Monarchies. Part I. Political History*, ed. A. Malamat. Jerusalem: Massada. With the help of M. O'Connor.

A70. 1980a — *Pottery, Poetry, and Prophecy: Studies in Early Hebrew Poetry*. Winona Lake, Indiana: Eisenbrauns. A reprinting, with a foreword by F. M. Cross, a preface by the author, and indexes, of DNF 1967a, 1968a, b, c, 1971a, d, 1972a, b, c, d, 1973a, 1974a, 1975a, b, 1976a, b, 1977, 1978, 1979b (15 papers and 4 notes), xiv + 376 pp.

A71. 1980b — The Poetic Structure of the Framework of Deuteronomy 33. Pp. 25–46 in *The Bible World: Essays in Honor of Cyrus H. Gordon*, ed. Gary Rendsburg et al. New York: Ktav and the Institute of Hebrew Culture Education of New York University.

A72. 1980c — Foreword. Pp. 13–15 in Millard C. Lind, *Yahweh is a Warrior: The Theology of Warfare in Ancient Israel*. Scottsdale, Pennsylvania: Herald Press.

A73. F. I. Andersen and DNF
1980 — *Hosea*. Anchor Bible 24. Garden City: Doubleday. xviii + 701 pp.

A74. DNF
1981a — Preface. Pp. 7–8 in *Chiasmus in Antiquity*, ed. J. W. Welch. Hildesheim: Gerstenberg.

A75. 1981b — Temple [Made] Without Hands. Pp. 21–30 in *Temples and High Places in Biblical Times*, ed. A. Biran et al. Jerusalem: The Nelson Glueck School of Biblical Archaeology of the Hebrew Union College.

A76. 1982a — On the Death of Abiner [2 Sam 3: 33–34]. In *Love and Death in the Ancient Near East: Essays in Honor of Marvin H. Pope on the Occasion of His Sixty-fifth Birthday*, ed. J. H. Marks and R. M. Good. Guilford, Connecticut: Four Quarters Publishing.

A77. 1982b — Discourse on Prophetic Discourse [Micah 1, 3]. In *The Quest for the Kingdom of God: Studies in Honor of G. E. Mendenhall*, ed. H. B. Huffmon, F. A. Spina, and A. R. W. Green. Winona Lake, Indiana: Eisenbrauns.

A78. f/c — On Prose Particles in the Poetry of the Primary History. In *A Festschrift for Samuel Iwry*, ed. A. Kort and S. Morschauser. Baltimore: Johns Hopkins Press.

I. B. Contributions to Reference Works

* under 100 words

Biblisch-Historisches Handwörterbuch, ed. B. Reicke and L. Rost. 3 vols. Göttingen: Vandenhoeck und Ruprecht, 1962 [-1966].

B1. DNF 1962b	Ältester. Band I, Sp. 76–77.

The Interpreter's Dictionary of the Bible, ed. G. A. Buttrick et al. Nashville and New York: Abingdon Press, 1962.

B2. DNF *1962c	D (Deuteronomist). Vol. A-D, p. 756.
B3. 1962d	Documents. Vol. A-D, pp. 860–61.
B4. *1962e	E (Elohist). Vol. E-J, p. 1.
B5. *1962f	Elohist. Vol. E-J, p. 94.
B6. *1962g	H [Holiness Code]. Vol. E-J, p. 503.
B7. 1962h	Hexateuch. Vol. E-J, p. 597–98.
B8. *1962i	J [Jahwist]. Vol. E-J, p. 777.
B9. *1962j	P. Vol. K-Q, p. 617.
B10. 1962k	Pentateuch. Vol. K-Q, p. 711–27.

*Dictionary of the Bible*², ed. J. Hastings, rev. F. C. Grant and H. H. Rowley. New York: Charles Scribner's Sons, 1963. All the entries except the one on Mari are revisions of entries in the first edition of the *Dictionary*.

B11. DNF 1963d	Armour, Arms. Pp. 54–55.
B12. 1963e	Army. Pp. 55–56.
B13. 1963f	Calneh, Calno. P. 119.
B14. 1963g	Camel. Pp. 119–20.
B15. 1963h	Chariot. P. 131.
B16. *1963i	Ezion-Geber. P. 285.
B17. 1963j	Hazor. P. 368.
B18. 1963k	Hebron. P. 375.
B19. 1963l	High Place, Sanctuary. Pp. 382–84.
B20. 1963m	Horse. P. 397.
B21. 1963n	Jachin and Boaz. P. 452.
B22. 1963o	Mari. P. 618
B23. 1963p	Millo. P. 660.
B24. 1963q	Mining and Metals. Pp. 660–61.
B25. 1963r	Nob. Pp. 700–1.
B26. 1963s	Plain, Cities of the. P. 776.
B27. 1963t	Sisera. P. 923.
B28. 1963u	Taanach. P. 948.

New Catholic Encyclopedia, ed. W. J. McDonald et al. New York: McGraw-Hill, 1967.

B29. DNF 1967c	Azotus (Ashdod). Vol. I, pp. 1144–45.

Theologisches Wörterbuch zum Alten Testament, ed. G. J. Botterweck and Helmer Ringgren. Stuttgart: Kohlhammer, 1973–.

B30. DNF and J. Lundbom
1973 — *beṭen*. Band I, Sp. 616–20.
B31. 1977a — *dôr*. With a contribution by G. J. Botterweck. Band II, Sp. 181–94.
B32. 1977b — *ḥādal*. Band II, Sp. 748–55.
B33. 1977c — *ḥānan*. With a contribution by H.-J. Fabry. Band III, Lieferung 1, Sp. 23–40.
B34. 1978a — *ḥārâ*. With a contribution by G. J. Botterweck. Band III, Lieferung 2/3, Sp. 182–88.
B35. 1978b — *ḥāraṣ*. With a contribution by G. J. Botterweck. Band III, Lieferung 2/3, Sp. 230–34.
B36. 1981a — *jṣt*. Band III, Lieferung 6/7, Sp. 840–43.
B37. 1981b — *jāqad*. Band III, Lieferung 6/7, Sp. 845–49.
B38. DNF and M. O'Connor
1980 — *JHWH*. Band III, Lieferung 4/5, Sp. 533–54.
B39. f/c — *kĕrubîm*.
B40. f/c — *kuttōnet*.
B41. f/c — *māgēn*.
B42. DNF and B. E. Willoughby
f/c — *mal'ak*.

Theological Dictionary of the Old Testament, ed. G. J. Botterweck and Helmer Ringgren; trans. D. E. Green, J. T. Willis, G. Bromiley. Grand Rapids: Eerdmans, 1975–.

B43. DNF and J. Lundbom
1975 — *beṭen*. Vol. II, pp. 94–99.
B44. 1978c — *dôr*. With a contribution by G. J. Botterweck. Vol. III, pp. 169–81.
B45. 1980 — *ḥādal*. Vol. IV, pp. 216–21.
(further contributions to appear, as sub the German original above)

Diccionario Teologico del Antiguo Testamento, ed. G. J. Botterweck and H. Ringgren; trans. A. de la Fuente and J. L. Zubizaretta. Madrid: Ediciones Christiandad, 1978–.

B46. DNF and J. Lundbom
1978d — *beṭen*. Tomo I, pp. 622–27.
(further contributions to appear, as sub the German original above)

Interpreter's Dictionary of the Bible. Supplementary Volume, ed. K. A. Crim et al. Nashville: Abingdon, 1976.

B47. DNF
1976c — Ashdod. Pp. 71–72. With the help of M. O'Connor.
B48. 1976d — Canon of the Old Testament. Pp. 130–36. With the help of M. O'Connor.
B49. 1976e — The Deuteronomic History. Pp. 226–28. With the help of M. O'Connor.
B50. DNF and M. O'Connor
1976 — Bastard. Pp. 92–93.

The International Standard Bible Encyclopedia, ed. G. W. Bromiley et al. Grand Rapids: Eerdmans, 1979.

B51. DNF
1979d — Ashdod. Vol. 1, pp. 314–16.

New Catholic Encyclopedia. Volume XVII. Supplement: Change in the Church, ed. T. C. O'Brien et al. New York: McGraw Hill, 1979.

B52. DNF

1979e — Ebla. P. 198.

I. C. Book Reviews

C1. DNF

1950 — Old Testament Literature, 1949 [brief notes on 84 books]. *Interpretation* 4: 78–88.

C2. 1951b — J. Touzard. 1949. *Grámmaïre hebraïque, abrégée*. Paris: Gabalda. *Journal of Biblical Literature* 70: 174–75.

C3. 1952 — H. J. Schoeps. 1950. *Aus frühchristlicher Zeit. Religionsgeschichtliche Untersuchungen*. Tübingen: Mohr. *Journal of Biblical Literature* 71: 58–60.

C4. 1953b — E. R. Thiele. 1951. *The Mysterious Numbers of the Hebrew Kings*. Chicago: University of Chicago Press. *Journal of Bible and Religion* 21: 122, 124.

C5. 1953c — T. W. Auer. 1951. *Die Pharaonen des Buches Exodus*. Regensburg: F. Pustet. *Journal of Biblical Literature* 72: 271.

C6. 1959 — K. Stendahl, ed. 1957. *The Scrolls and the New Testament*. New York: Harper. *Journal of Biblical Literature* 78: 326–34.

C7. 1960d — Z. Vilnay. 1960. *The Guide to Israel*. Cleveland: World. *Journal of Biblical Literature* 79: 293.

C8. 1962l — Y. Kaufmann. 1960. *The Religion of Israel . . . to the Babylonian Exile*. Chicago: University of Chicago Press. *Journal of Biblical Literature* 81: 185–90.

C9. 1964c — S. Gevirtz. 1963. *Patterns in the Early Poetry of Israel*. Chicago: University of Chicago Press. *Journal of Biblical Literature* 83: 201–3.

C10. 1964d — J. Gray. 1963. *I & II Kings*. Philadelphia: Westminster. *Journal of Biblical Literature* 83: 310–13.

C11. 1966 — J. Bonsirven. 1964. *Palestinian Judaism in the Time of Jesus Christ*. New York: Holt, Rinehart, and Winston. *Journal of Ecumenical Studies* 3: 554–55.

C12. 1969e — R. E. Brown, J. A. Fitzmyer, and R. E. Murphy, eds. 1968. *The Jerome Biblical Commentary*. Englewood Cliffs: Prentice-Hall [reviewer for the Old Testament]. *Catholic Biblical Quarterly* 31: 405–8.

C13. 1971e — G. W. Buchanan. 1970. *The Consequence of the Covenant*. Leiden: Brill. *Catholic Biblical Quarterly* 33: 554–57.

C14. 1972e — T. H. Gaster. 1969. *Myth, Legend and Custom in the Old Testament*. New York: Harper and Row. *Journal of American Oriental Society* 92: 185–86.

C15. F. M. Cross and DNF

1972 — Some Observations on Early Hebrew [Review of D. W. Goodwin. 1969. *Text Restoration Methods in Contemporary U.S.A. Biblical Scholarship*. Naples: Istituto Orientale]. *Biblica* 53: 413–20.

C16. DNF

1973b — W. L. Holladay. 1972. *A Concise . . . Lexicon of the Old Testament . . . Koehler . . . and Baumgartner*. Grand Rapids, Michigan: Eerdmans. *Interpretation* 27: 102–4.

C17. 1973c J. Sanders. 1972. *Torah and Canon*. Philadelphia: Fortress.
Journal of Biblical Literature 92: 118–19.

C18. 1973d A. A. van Ruler. 1973. *The Christian Church and the Old Testament*. Grand Rapids, Michigan: Eerdmans.
Journal of Biblical Literature 92: 119–22.

C19. 1975d J. Gutmann, ed. 1972. *No Graven Images: Studies in Art and the Hebrew Bible*. New York: Ktav.
Journal of Ecumenical Studies 12: 590–92.

C20. 1976c W. D. Davies. 1974. *The Gospel and the Land*. Berkeley: University of California Press.
Journal of Biblical Literature 105: 503–6.

C21. 1982c John Bright. 1981. *A History of Israel*[3]. Philadelphia: Westminster.
Biblical Archeologist 45: 61.

C22. 1982d A. R. Ceresko. 1980. *Job 29–31 in the Light of Northwest Semitic*. Biblica et Orientalia 36. Rome: [Pontifical] Biblical Institute Press.
Journal of Biblical Literature 101.

II. Modern Intellectual History

II. D. Books, papers, and articles

D1. DNF
1951 — James Anderson Kelso In Memoriam. *Bulletin of the American Schools of Oriental Research* 124: 11–12.

D2. 1961 — Portrait of an Archaeologist [W. F. Albright at 70]. *Presbyterian Life* 14 #4 (December 1961): 7–11.

D3. 1962 — Letter from Ashdod: A Report of Excavations 1962. *Pittsburgh Perspective* 3 #4 (December 1962): 17–19, 39.

D4. 1963 — The Second Season of Ancient Ashdod. *Biblical Archaeologist* 26: 134–39.

D5. 1963 — Modern Scripture Research and Ecumenism [chiefly Protestant-Catholic contact]. *Pittsburgh Perspective* 4 #3 (September 1963): 15–22.

D6. W. F. Albright and DNF
1963 — The Continuing Revolution in Biblical Research: [A] Setting for the Anchor Bible. *Journal of Bible and Religion* 31: 110–13.

D7. DNF
1964 — Excavating in an Old Testament Town [Ashdod]. *Presbyterian Life* 17 #6 (March 1964): 5, 10–15, 30–32.

D8. 1965 — Toward a Common Bible? Pp. 133–49 in *Scripture and Ecumenism: Protestant, Catholic, Orthodox and Jewish*, ed. L. J. Swidler. Pittsburgh: Duquesne University Press.

D9. 1966 — William F. Albright. Pp. 380–86 in *Tendenzen der Theologie im 20. Jahrhundert*, ed. H. J. Schultz. Stuttgart: Kreuz-Verlag. Volume rpt., 1967.

D10. 1968 — *The New World of the Old Testament* [Inaugural Lecture as Professor of Hebrew and Old Testament Literature, Delivered 7 May 1968]. San Anselmo, California: San Francisco Theological Seminary. 15 pp.

D11. 1969 — Archaeology in the Promised Land—1968. *Action/Reaction* 2 #2 (Winter 1969): 8–10.

D12. 1970 — The American Schools of Oriental Research. *Qadmoniot* 3 #2: 75–76 (in Hebrew).

D13. 1972 — William Foxwell Albright In Memoriam. *Bulletin of the American Schools of Oriental Research* 205: 3–13. Rpt. as pp. 24–34 in Freedman, MacDonald, and Mattson 1975.

D14. 1974 — James Alan Montgomery. Pp. 594–96 in *Dictionary of American Biography, Supplement 4*, ed. J. A. Garraty, and E. T. James. New York: Charles Scribner's Sons.

D15. 1975 — In Memoriam G. E. Wright. *Bulletin of the American Schools of Oriental Research* 220: 3.

D16. DNF and A. T. Kachel, eds.
1975 — *Religion and the Academic Scene* [Essays by Krister Stendahl, Theodore A. Gill, and Robert Bellah]. Waterloo, Ontario: Council on the Study of Religion in cooperation with the Program on Studies in Religion and the Office of Religion and Ethics of the University of Michigan. Introduction by Freedman, pp. vi-viii.

D17. DNF with the assistance of R. B. MacDonald and D. L. Mattson
1975 — *The Published Works of William Foxwell Albright: A Comprehensive Bibliography* [preceded by seven memorial tributes]. Cambridge: The American Schools of Oriental Research.

D18. L. G. Running and DNF
1975 — *William Foxwell Albright: A Twentieth Century Genius*. New York: Two Continents Publishing Group/Morgan Press.

D19. DNF
1977 Ebla is a Four-Letter Word. *LSA Magazine* (Ann Arbor) for Spring 1977: 8–9, 17–18. Rpt. 1980, in *The Imprint of the Stanford Library Associates* (Palo Alto: Associates of the Stanford University Libraries) 6 #2 (October 1980): 20–24.

D20. 1978 The Ebla Tablets and the Abraham Tradition. Pp. 67–77 in *Reflections on Mormonism: Judaeo-Christian Parallels*, ed. T. G. Madsen. Religious Studies Monograph Series 4. Provo, Utah: Religious Studies Center, Brigham Young University.

D21. 1978 A City Beneath the Sands [Tell Mardikh]. Pp. 182–95 in *Science Year: The World Book Science Annual 1978*. Chicago: Field Enterprises Educational Corporation.

D22. 1978 The Real Story of the Ebla Tablets, Ebla and the Cities of the Plain. *Biblical Archeologist* 41: 143–64.

D23. 1979 The Tell Mardikh Excavations, the Ebla Tablets, and their Significance for Biblical Studies. *Near East Archaeological Society Bulletin* NS #13: 5–35.

D24. 1980 On Studying the Bible. P. 5 in *Recommending and Selling Biblical Reference Works* [ed. S. J. Anderson]. Grand Rapids, Michigan: Eerdmans.

D25. 1981 Frank Moore Cross, Jr.: An Appreciation. Pp. 3–7 in *Traditions in Transformations: Turning Points in Biblical Faith*, ed. B. Halpern and J. Levenson. Winona Lake, Indiana: Eisenbrauns.

D26. 1981 "Epigraphic Evidence from Ebla . . .": A Correction [*in re* A. Archi; cf. Freedman 1978/D22]. *Biblica* 62: 103.

D27. DNF and B. E. Willoughby
1981 Archeology and the Bible: Volunteer and Student Programs; Archeology and the Bible: Recent Discoveries. *Your Church* (King of Prussia, Pennsylvania) 27 #1: 24, 26, 30–34.

III. Popular, Devotional, and Ephemeral Works

III. E. Books and articles

*written for children, young people or their teachers

E1. *DNF and J. D. Smart
1949 — *God Has Spoken*. Philadelphia: Westminster.

E2. DNF
1950 — When Saints Were Sinners. *The Dawn* 21 #2 (March-April 1950): 2–3.

E3. *1950 — Family Life in the Old Testament. *Growing* 2 #3 (April-June 1950): 4–6.

E4. *1950 — The Birth of a Nation. *Junior-Hi Kit* #7 (September 1950): 111–14.

E5. *1950 — The Bible Tells the Truth. *Opening Doors* 2 #2 (January-March 1950): 10–11.

E6. 1951 — The Key to Old Testament History. *The Dawn* 22 #3 (May-June 1951): 2–3.

E7. 1951 — Israel in God's Redemption Plan. *The Dawn* 22 #4 (September-October 1951): 213.

E8. 1951 — Abraham, God's Pioneer. *Westminster Teacher* 2 #1 (October-December 1951): 23–24.

E9. DNF and D. M. Thompson (*manu secunda*)
1951 — Pioneers for God: The Beginnings of the Hebrew Nation. *Crossroads* 2 #1 (October-December 1951): 43–59, 61.

E10. DNF and D. M. Thompson
1951 — The American Heritage. *Western Watch* 2 #4 (15 September 1951): 3–10.

E11. 1953 — The Key to Old Testament History. *Western Watch* 4 #4 (15 October 1953): 15–19. Rpt. 1954, as The Key to the Old Testament, in *The Dawn* 25 #2 (March-April 1954): 2–3.

E12. DNF
1955 — A Passover Question [the hardening of Pharaoh's heart]. *The Dawn* 26 #2 (March-April 1955): 1.

E13. 1955 — God Compassionate and Gracious [Inaugural Lecture as Professor of Hebrew and Old Testament Literature in Western Theological Seminary] [Exod 34: 6–7]. *Western Watch* 6 #1 (1 March 1955): 6–24.

E14. 1955 — Bridging the Gulf. *Western Watch* 6 #4 (15 December 1955): 9–17. Rpt. 1980 as pp. 98–105 in *The Messiahship of Jesus: What Jews and Jewish Christians Say*, ed. A. W. Kac. Chicago: Moody Press. Abridged as E17.

E15. 1956 — Question and Answer [Exod 20: 5–6]. *The Dawn* 27 #1 (January-February 1956): 6.

E16. *1956 — Why Should the Innocent Suffer? [Job]. *Discovery* 8 #4 (July-September 1956): 3–4.

E17. 1956 — Jew and Christian: Is Reconciliation Possible? *Presbyterian Life* 9 #5 (3 March 1956): 10–11, 26–27. Rpt. 1956 in *Israel's Anchorage* [Australian organ of the Jewish Evangelical Witness] 10 #3 (September-November 1956): 8–11.

E18. 1956 — The Unity of the Bible. *Western Watch* 7 #4 (15 December 1956): 7–14. Rpt. 1980 as pp. 173–84 in *The Messiahship of Jesus: What Jews and Jewish Christians Say*, ed. A. W. Kac. Chicago: Moody Press.

E19. DNF and T. A. Gill
1956 — [Three Sermons on Jeremiah:] The Next Step. Who Would Valiant Be. Changed Gods. *The Pulpit* 27 #9 (September 1956): 10–12; 27 #10 (October 1956): 11–13 = 27: 291–93; 27 #11 (November 1956): 16–19 = 27: 328–31.

E20. 1957 What Next? [Jeremiah 4]. *The Pulpit* 28 #2 (February 1957): 22–24 = 28: 70–72.

E21. DNF
1958 The Sabbath and the Lord's Day. *Presbyterian Life* 11 #2 (January 1958): 30–31.

E22. 1959 The Dead Sea Scrolls: The Library of the Essenes. *Carnegie Magazine* 33 #2 (February 1959): 60–63, 65.

E23. 1959 The Slave of Yahweh [The Suffering Servant]. *Western Watch* 10 #1 (March 1959): 1–19.

E24. DNF and T. A. Gill
1959 Great Expectations [on Jeremiah and Baruch]. *The Pulpit* 30 #4 (April 1959): 14–15 = 30: 110–11.

E25. DNF
1960 Question and Answer [on Esau's birthright]. *The Dawn* 31 #5 (November-December 1960): 4.

E26. 1961 *Let My People Go* [Jeremiah 34]. A Sermon Preached 12 November 1961. University Park, Pennsylvania: The Office of the University Chaplain, The Pennsylvania State University. 6 pp.

E27. 1962 When Did Christ Die? [on Qumran and the Johannine chronology of Holy Week]. *Pittsburgh Perspective* 3 #1 (March 1962): 52–57.

E28. 1964 *Naboth's Vineyard*. A Sermon Preached 26 January 1964. University Park, Pennsylvania: The Office of the University Chaplain, The Pennsylvania State University. 6 pp.

E29. 1964 The Hebrew Old Testament and the Ministry Today: An Exegetical Study of Leviticus 19: 18b. *Pittsburgh Perspective* 5 #1 (March 1964): 9–14, 30.

E30. 1965 The Biblical Idea of History. A One Hundredth Anniversary Sermon Preached, at the Grosse Pointe Memorial Church, 10 October 1965. Pp. 11–16 in *The Shape of the Church and the Future*. Grosse Pointe Farms: United Presbyterian Church in the U.S.A.

E31. *1965 Amos and the Judgment of God. *Opening Doors* 17 #3 (April-June 1965): 4–6.

E32. 1966 Religious Freedom and the Old Testament. Pp. 83–94 in *Religious Liberty: An End and a Beginning. The [Vatican II] Declaration on Religious Freedom: An Ecumenical Discussion*, ed. J. C. Murray. New York: Macmillan.

E33. 1967 Another View of the Middle East Crisis. *Presbyterian Life* 20 #18 (15 September 1967): 28–29. With letters to the editor, all negative, in *Presbyterian Life* 20 #20 (15 October 1967): 6, 43.

E34. 1969 An Essay on Jewish Christianity. *Journal of Ecumenical Studies* 6 #1 (Winter 1969): 81–86.

E35. 1972 State of Religion. *The Ann Arbor News* for 21 May 1972 at section 4, p. 41, cols. 4–6.

E36. C. B. Templeton, with DNF, T. A. Gill, W. Summerscales, and T. Harpur, eds.
1973 *Jesus: The Four Gospels . . . Combined in One Narrative and Rendered in Modern English*. New York: Simon and Schuster/ Toronto: McClelland and Stewart.

E37. DNF
1977 Afterword. Pp. 338–44 in Rudolf Augstein, *Jesus Son of Man*, trans. H. Young. Preface by Gore Vidal. New York: Urizen.

III. F. Book reviews

F1. DNF 1949
R. M. Grant. 1948. *The Bible in the Church: A Short History of Interpretation*. New York: Macmillan.
Monday Morning 14 #7 (14 February 1949): 15–16.

F2. 1950
J. A. Brewer. 1949. *The Book of the Twelve Prophets*. New York: Harper.
Theology Today 7: 128–30.

F3. 1950
Recent Literature on the Old Testament [notably Dorothy C. Wilson. 1949. *Prince of Egypt*. Philadelphia: Westminster].
Western Watch 1 #1 (January 1950): 8–10.

F4. 1951
J. Paterson. 1950. *The Praises of Israel: Studies Literary and Religious in the Psalms*. New York: Charles Scribner's Sons.
Theology Today 8: 271–73.

F5. 1951
H. H. Rowley. 1950. *From Joseph to Joshua: Biblical Traditions in the Light of Archaeology*. London: The British Academy.
Westminster Bookman 10 #4 (June 1951): 12–13.

F6. 1952
G. Walter. 1952. *Caesar: A Biography*. Trans. E. Craufurd. New York: Charles Scribner's Sons.
Western Watch 3 #2 (15 March 1952): 19–20.

F7. 1953
G. A. Buttrick et al., eds. 1952. *The Interpreter's Bible I* [General Articles, Genesis, Exodus]. Nashville: Abingdon-Cokesbury.
Western Watch 4 #2 (15 March 1953): 20–21.

F8. 1953
J. B. Pritchard, ed. 1950. *Ancient Near Eastern Texts Relating to the Old Testament*. Princeton: Princeton University Press.
Western Watch 4 #2 (15 March 1953): 21.

F9. 1955
For Antiquarians Only [Review of C. A. Muses, ed. 1954. *The Septuagint Bible* (The Charles Thomson Translation). Indian Hills, Colorado: Falcon's Wing Press]. *The Christian Century* 72 #9 (2 March 1955): 272.

F10. 1955
A New Light on the Past [Review of E. Wilson. 1955. *The Scrolls from the Dead Sea*. New York: Oxford University Press]. *Pittsburgh Press* for 23 October 1955.

F11. 1956
G. A. Buttrick et al., ed. 1956. *The Interpreter's Bible V* [Ecclesiastes, Song of Songs, Isaiah, Jeremiah]. Nashville: Abingdon.
Westminster Bookman 15 #3 (September 1956): 7–9.

F12. 1958
More About Scrolls [Review of F. M. Cross. 1958. *The Ancient Library of Qumran and Modern Biblical Studies*. Garden City: Doubleday; and M. Burrows. 1958. *More Light on the Dead Sea Scrolls*. New York: Viking].*Pittsburgh Press* for 11 May 1958 at section 5, p. 8, col. 6.

F13. 1958
M. Burrows. 1955. *The Dead Sea Scrolls*. New York: Viking; and C. T. Fritsch. 1956. *The Qumran Community: Its History and Scrolls*. New York: Macmillan.
Theology Today 15: 422–25.

F14. 1958
D. Baly. 1957. *The Geography of the Bible*. New York: Harper.
Westminster Bookman 17 #1 (March 1958): 1–2.

F15. 1959
A. R. Johnson. 1955. *Sacral Kingship in Ancient Israel*. Cardiff: University of Wales Press.
Theology Today 15: 571–73.

F16. 1959
U. Simon. 1958. *Heaven in the Christian Tradition*. New York: Harper.
Westminster Bookman 18 #3 (September 1959): 5–7.

F17. 1960
H. H. Rowley. 1957. *The Faith of Israel: Aspects of Old Testament Thought*. Philadelphia: Westminster.
Pittsburgh Perspective 1 #1 (March 1960): 21–22.

F18. 1960
A. J. Heschel. 1955. *God in Search of Man: A Philosophy of Judaism*.

New York: Farrar, Straus, and Cudahy.
Pittsburgh Perspective 1 #2 (June 1960): 22–23.

F19. 1961 R. H. Pfeiffer. 1961. *Religion in the Old Testament*. New York: Harper.
Westminster Bookman 20: 4–6.

F20. 1962 I Recommend [notices on books by Bright, Eichrodt, Kaufmann, Noth, and von Rad]. *Monday Morning* 27 #11 (21 May 1962): 22.

F21. 1963 G. von Rad. 1961. *Genesis: A Commentary*, trans. J. Marks. Philadelphia: Westminster.
Theology Today 20: 114–18.

F22. 1964 W. H. Brownlee. 1964. *The Meaning of the Qumran Scrolls for the Bible*. New York: Oxford University Press.
Pittsburgh Perspective 5 #2 (June 1964): 33–34.

F23. 1964 H. H. Rowley. 1963. *From Moses to Qumran*. New York: Association Press.
Presbyterian Outlook 146 #23 (June 1964): 15.

F24. 1964 B. W. Anderson, ed. 1963. *The Old Testament and Christian Faith: A Theological Discussion*. New York: Harper and Row.
Theology Today 21: 225–28.

F25. 1968 C. Westermann. 1967. *Handbook to the Old Testament*. Trans. R. H. Boyd. Minneapolis: Augsburg.
Action/Reaction 1 #3 (Spring 1968): 11.

IV. Editorial Work

IV. G. Books Outside Series

G1. G. Ernest Wright and DNF, eds.
1961 *The Biblical Archaeologist Reader {1}*. Garden City: Doubleday (original paper edition). Volume rpt. 1961, Chicago: Quadrangle Books. Doubleday reissues after 1964 bear the title *The Biblical Archaeologist Reader, 1*. Volume also rpt. 1975, Missoula: Scholars Press. Volume also rpt. 1978, Cambridge: American Schools of Oriental Research. Preface by DNF, pp. ix-xii.

G2. E. F. Campbell, Jr., and DNF, eds.
1964 *The Biblical Archaeologist Reader, 2*. Garden City: Doubleday. Volume rpt. 1975, Missoula: Scholars Press. Volume also rpt. 1978, Cambridge: American Schools of Oriental Research. Preface by DNF, pp. vii-xi.

G3. DNF and J. C. Greenfield, eds.
1969 *New Directions in Biblical Archaeology*. Garden City: Doubleday. Volume rpt. 1971 in paper. Preface by Freedman and Greenfield, pp. ix-xi.

G4. E. F. Campbell, Jr., and DNF, eds.
1970 *The Biblical Archaeologist Reader, Volume III*. Garden City: Doubleday. Preface by Campbell and Freedman, pp. vii-viii.

G5. {E. F. Campbell, Jr., and DNF, eds.}.
1979 *Seisho kōkogaku nyūmon* {*Introduction to the Archeology of the Bible*} by G. E. Wright, B. M. Metzger and others. Trans. Yasuo Shiono. Seisho no kenkyū {Studies on the Bible} Series 1. Tokyo: Kyobunkan. {A selection of six essays from Campbell and Freedman 1964 = *BAR* 2 and Campbell and Freedman 1970 = *BAR* 3, with a conspectus of those two volumes and Wright and Freedman 1961. The essays are: I. R. H. Smith, The Tomb of Jesus (*BAR* 3); II. G. E. Wright, Samaria (*BAR* 2); III. B. M. Metzger, Antioch-on-the-Orontes (*BAR* 2); IV. B. Kanael, Ancient Jewish Coins and their Historical Importance (*BAR* 3); V. R. B. Y. Scott, Weights and Measures of the Bible (*BAR* 3); and VI. H. O. Thompson, Science and Archaeology (*BAR* 3).}

G6. E. F. Campbell and DNF
f/c *The Biblical Archaeologist Reader 4*. Philadelphia: The American Schools of Oriental Research. Preface by Freedman.

IV. H. The Anchor Bible

Edited by William Foxwell Albright and DNF from 1956 until Albright's death in 1971 (during which period the first eighteen volumes were published), and since by DNF alone, and published by Doubleday and Company in Garden City, New York.

H1. W. F. Albright and C. S. Mann
1971 *Matthew*. AB 26.

H2. F. I. Andersen and DNF
1980 *Hosea*. AB 24.

H3. M. Barth
1974a *Ephesians 1–3*. AB 34.

H4. 1974b *Ephesians 4–6*. AB 34A.

H5. R. G. Boling
1975 *Judges*. AB 6A.

H6. 1982 *Joshua*. With an introduction by G. E. Wright. AB 6.

H7. J. Bright
1965 *Jeremiah*. AB 21.

H8. R. E. Brown, S. S.
1966 *The Gospel According to John (i-xii)*. AB 29.
H9. 1970 *The Gospel According to John (xiii-xxi)*. AB 29A.
H10. 1982 *The Epistles of John*. AB 30.
H11. G. W. Buchanan
1972 *To the Hebrews*. AB 36.
H12. E. F. Campbell, Jr.
1975 *Ruth*. AB 7.
H13. M. Dahood, S. J.
1966 *Psalms I (1–50)*. AB 16.
H14. 1968 *Psalms II (51–100)*. AB 17.
H15. 1970 *Psalms III (101–150)*. With a contribution by T. Penar. AB 17A.
H16. J. A. Fitzmyer, S. J.
1981 *The Gospel According to Luke (I-IX)*. AB 28.
H17. J. M. Ford
1975 *Revelation*. AB 38.
H18. J. A. Goldstein
1976 *I Maccabees*. AB 41.
H19. L. F. Hartman, C. SS. R, and A. A. Di Lella, O. F. M.
1978 *The Book of Daniel*. AB 23.
H20. D. R. Hillers
1972 *Lamentations*. AB 7A.
H21. P. K. McCarter, Jr.
1980 *I Samuel*. AB 8.
H22. J. L. McKenzie
1968 *Second Isaiah*. AB 20.
H23. C. A. Moore
1971 *Esther*. AB 7B.
H24. 1977 *Daniel, Esther, and Jeremiah: The Additions*. AB 44.
H25. J. Munck
1967 *The Acts of the Apostles*. With contributions by W. F. Albright and C. S. Mann. AB 31.
H26. J. M. Myers
1965a *I Chronicles*. AB 12.
H27. 1965b *II Chronicles*. AB 13.
H28. 1965c *Ezra. Nehemiah*. AB 14.
H29. 1974 *I and II Esdras*. AB 42.
H30. W. F. Orr and J. A. Walther
1976 *I Corinthians . . . With a Study of the Life of Paul*. AB 32.
H31. M. Pope
1965 *Job*[1]. AB 15. *Job*[3], 1973.
H32. 1977 *Song of Songs*. AB 7C.
H33. B. Reicke
1964 *The Epistles of James, Peter, and Jude*. AB 37.
H34. R. B. Y. Scott
1965 *Proverbs. Ecclesiastes*. AB 18.
H35. E. A. Speiser
1964 *Genesis*. AB 1.
H36. D. Winston
1979 *The Wisdom of Solomon*. AB 43.

IV. I. American Schools of Oriental Research Publications

Published by the Schools in Cambridge, Massachusetts.

Annuals of ASOR (AASOR)

I1. E. M. Meyers; A. T. Kraabel; and J. F. Strange
1976 *Ancient Synagogue Excavations at Khirbet Shemaʿ, Upper Galilee, Israel 1970–1972*. AASOR 42. Published for the Schools, Durham: Duke University.

I2. DNF, ed.
1978 *Preliminary Excavation Reports: Bâb edh-Dhraʿ, Sardis, Meiron, Tell el-Hesi, Carthage (Punic)*. AASOR 43.

I3. DNF, with the help of J. M. Lundquist, ed.
1979 *Archeological Reports from the Tabqa Dam Project—Euphrates Valley, Syria*. AASOR 44.

I4. N. L. Lapp, ed.
1981 *The Third Campaign at Tell el-Fûl: The Excavations of 1964*. AASOR 45.

Bulletin of the American Schools of Oriental Research/Supplement[al] Studies (BASOR/SS).

I5. C. T. Fritsch, ed.
1975 *Studies in the History of Caesarea Maritima*. The Joint Expedition to Caesarea Maritima I. BASOR/SS 19. Published for the Schools, Missoula: Scholars Press.

I6. C. B. Moore, ed.
1974 *Reconstructing Complex Societies: An Archaeological Colloquium . . . 1972*. BASOR/SS 20.

I7. G. M. Landes, ed.
1975 *Report on Archaeological Work at Ṣuwwānet eth-Thanīya, Tananir, and Khirbet Minḥa (Munḥata)*. BASOR/SS 21. Published for the Schools, Missoula: Scholars Press.

I8. A. Ben-Tor
1978 *Cylinder Seals of Third-Millennium Palestine*. BASOR/SS 22.

Dead Sea Scrolls Committee Publications. Edited by F. M. Cross, DNF, and J. M. Sanders.

I9. J. C. Trever [et al.]
1972 *Scrolls from Qumrân Cave I: The Great Isaiah Scroll, the Order of the Community, the Pesher to Habakkuk*. Published for the Schools through the Albright Institute for Archaeological Research and by the Shrine of the Book, both in Jerusalem, and produced by William Clowes and Sons of London. (Edition with both color and b&w plates.)

I10. 1974 *Scrolls from Qumran Cave I: The Great Isaiah Scroll, the Order of the Community, the Pesher to Habakkuk*. (Edition with b&w plates only.)

Dissertation Series/ASOR (DASOR)

I11. A. R. W. Green
1975 *The Role of Human Sacrifice in the Ancient Near East*. DASOR 1. Published for the Schools, Missoula: Scholars Press.

I12. C. L. Meyers
1976 *The Tabernacle Menorah*. DASOR 2. Published for the Schools, Missoula: Scholars Press.

I13. V. H. Matthews
1978 *Pastoral Nomadism in the Mari Kingdom (ca. 1830–1760 B.C.)*. DASOR 3.

I14. B. Lewis
1980 *The Sargon Legend: A Study of the Akkadian Text and the Tale of the Hero Who Was Exposed at Birth*. DASOR 4.

Excavation Reports/ASOR (ERASOR)

I15. W. E. Rast, ed. A. E. Glock
1978 *Taanach I. Studies in Iron Age Pottery*.

I16. J. A. Blakely and L. E. Toombs, ed. K. G. O'Connell, S. J.
1980 *The Tell el-Hesi Field Manual*. The Joint Archaeological Expedition to Tell el-Hesi 1.

I17. J. A. Callaway et al.
1980 *The Early Bronze Age Citadel and Lower City at Ai (et-Tell)*. Reports of the Joint Archaeological Expedition to Ai (et-Tell) 2.

Monograph Series/ASOR (MASOR)

I18. R. T. Anderson
1978 *Studies in Samaritan Manuscripts and Artifacts: The Chamberlain-Warren Collection*. MASOR 1.

I19. Z. Zevit
1980 *Matres Lectiones in Ancient Hebrew Epigraphs*. MASOR 2.

I20. J. H. Charlesworth with G. T. Zervos
1981 *The New Discoveries in St. Catherine's Monastery: A Preliminary Report on the Manuscripts*. MASOR 3. Foreword by DNF, pp. xi-xii.

Zion Research Foundation Occasional Publications

I21. F. M. Cross, ed.
1979 *Symposia Celebrating the Seventy-Fifth Anniversary of the Founding of the American Schools of Oriental Research (1900–1975)*. ZRFOP 1–2 [!].

Volumes *hors serie*

I22. E. F. Campbell and R. G. Boling, eds.
1976 *Essays in Honor of George Ernest Wright* [Reprint of *Bulletin of the American Schools of Oriental Research* 220/221].

I23. M. K. Lyons, M. D.
1978 *The Care and Feeding of Dirt Archeologists*.

I24. R. S. Hanson
1980 *Tyrian Influence in the Upper Galilee*. Meiron Excavation Project #2.

IV. J. The Computer Bible Series.

Edited by J. Arthur Baird and DNF, and published by Biblical Research Associates in Wooster, Ohio.

J1. F. I. Andersen and A. D. Forbes
1972 *A Synoptic Concordance to Hosea, Amos, Micah*. CBS 6.

J2. 1976a *A Linguistic Concordance of Ruth and Jonah: Hebrew Vocabulary and Idiom*. CBS 9.

J3. 1976b *Eight Minor Prophets {Hosea, Joel, Amos, Obadiah, Micah, Nahum, Habakkuk, and Zephaniah}: A Linguistic Concordance*. CBS 10.

J4. 1978a *A Linguistic Concordance of Jeremiah: Hebrew Vocabulary and Idiom*. CBS 14.

J5. 1978b *A Linguistic Concordance of Jeremiah: Common Names*. CBS 14A.

J6. J. A. Baird
1971 *A Critical Concordance to the Synoptic Gospels*. CBS 1. (Revised edition of a 1969 private publication.)

J7. R. A. Martin
1977 *Syntactical and Critical Concordance to the Greek Text of Baruch and the Epistle of Jeremiah*. CBS 12.

J8. P. M. K. Morris and E. James
1975 *A Critical Word Book of Leviticus, Numbers, Deuteronomy*. CBS 8. Published for BRA, Missoula: Scholars Press.

J9. n.d. *A Critical Word Book of the Pentateuch*. CBS 17.

J10. A. Q. Morton and S. Michaelson
1971 *I, II, III John: Forward and Reverse Concordance and Index*. CBS 3.

J11. 1974 — *A Critical Concordance to the Gospel of John*. CBS 5.
J12. 1976 — *A Critical Concordance to the Acts of the Apostles*. CBS 7.
J13. A. Q. Morton; S. Michaelson; and J. D. Thompson
1977 — *A Critical Concordance to the Letter of Paul to the Romans*. CBS 13.
J14. 1979 — *A Critical Concordance to I and II Corinthians*. CBS 19.
J15. 1980 — *A Critical Concordance to the Letter of Paul to the Galatians*. CBS 21.
J16. n.d. — *A Critical Concordance to the Letter of Paul to the Ephesians*. CBS 22.
J17. n.d. — *A Critical Concordance to the Letter of Paul to the Philippians*. CBS 23.
J18. n.d. — *A Critical Concordance to the Letter of Paul to the Colossians*. CBS 24.
J19. H. V. D. Parunak
1979 — *Linguistic Density Plots in Zechariah*. CBS 20.
J20. Y. T. Radday
1971 — *An Analytical, Linguistic Concordance to the Book of Isaiah*. CBS 2.
J21. 1973 — *An Analytical, Linguistic, Key-Word-In-Context Concordance to the Books of Haggai, Zechariah, and Malachi*. CBS 4.
J22. Y. T. Radday and G. M. Leb
1978 — *An Analytical, Linguistic, Key-Word-In-Context Concordance to Esther, Ruth, Canticles, Ecclesiastes, and Lamentations*. CBS 16.
J23. 1979 — *An Analytical, Linguistic, Key-Word-In-Context Concordance to the Book of Genesis*. CBS 18.
J24. Y. T. Radday; G. M. Leb; and L. Natziz
1977 — *An Analytical, Linguistic, Key-Word-In-Context Concordance to the Book of Judges*. CBS 11.
J25. J. B. Tyson and T. R. W. Longstaff
1978 — *Synoptic Abstract*. CBS 15.

IV. K. The International Concordance Library

Edited by J. Arthur Baird and DNF, and published by Biblical Research Associates in Wooster, Ohio.

K1. W. E. Aufrecht and (for EDP) J. C. Hurd
1975 — *A Synoptic Concordance of Aramaic Inscriptions (According to H. Donner & W. Roellig)*. ICL 1. Published for BRA, Missoula: Scholars Press.

IV. L. Consulting Editorial Work

L1. J. M. Allegro
1958 — *The People of the Dead Sea Scrolls*. Garden City: Doubleday.
L2. 1960 — *The Treasure of the Copper Scroll*. Garden City: Doubleday.
L3. G. A. Buttrick et al., eds.
1962 — *The Interpreter's Dictionary of the Bible*. 4 vols. Nashville: Abingdon.
L4. G. Cornfeld
1962 — *From Daniel to Paul: Jews in Conflict with Graeco-Roman Civilization*. New York: Macmillan.
L5. 1964 — *Pictorial Biblical Encyclopedia*. New York: Macmillan.
L6. Catholic Biblical Association
1970 — *The New American Bible Translated From the Original Languages With Critical Use of All the Ancient Sources by Members of the Catholic Biblical Association of America. Sponsored by the Bishops' Committee of the Confraternity of Christian Doctrine*. New York and elsewhere: P. J. Kenedy and Sons and others. [See special note *ad finem*.]
L7. G. J. Botterweck and H. Ringgren, eds.
1973— — *Theologisches Wörterbuch zum Alten Testament* (Band I, 1973; Band II, 1977; Band III, in publication). Stuttgart: Kohlhammer.
L8. 1974— — *Theological Dictionary of the Old Testament* (Vol. I, 1974, revised 1977; Vol. II, 1975; Vol. III, 1978; Vol. IV, 1980). Trans. J. T. Willis,

G. Bromiley, D. Green. Grand Rapids, Michigan: Eerdmans.

L9. 1978— *Diccionario Teologico del Antiguo Testamento* (Tomo 1, 1978). Trans. A. de la Fuente and J. L. Zubizaretta. Madrid: Ediciones Christiandad.

L10. Avram Kampf
1975 *Jewish Experience in the Art of the Twentieth Century*. New York: The Jewish Museum.

L11. Benjamin Mazar, assisted by G. Cornfeld
1975 *The Mountain of the Lord*. Garden City: Doubleday.

L12. Wendell Phillips
1975 *An Explorer's Life of Jesus*. New York: Two Continents Publishing Group/Morgan Press.

L13. G. Cornfeld
1976 *Archaeology of the Bible: Book by Book*. New York: Harper and Row.

L14. J. L. Gardner et al., eds.
1981 *Reader's Digest Atlas of the Bible*. Pleasantville, New York: The Reader's Digest Association.

IV. M. Special Editorial Work

As literary executor for W. F. Albright.

M1. W. F. Albright
1972 Neglected Factors in the Greek Intellectual Revolution. *Proceedings of the American Philosophical Society* 116: 225–42.

IV. N. Journals

N1. *Western Watch*
Member, Editorial Committee, vols. 1–3 (1950–1952).
Managing Editor, vols. 4–8 (1953–1957).

N2. *Journal of Biblical Literature*
Associate Editor, vols. 72–73, 1953–1954.
Editor, vols. 74–78, 1955–1959. Reports of the editor appear in the first part of each volume edited: 75 (1956) xiii; 76 (1957) xiv; 77 (1958) xvi; 78 (1959) xvii-xix; 79 (1960) xii.

N3. *Presbyterian Life*
Columnist, "We've Been Asked," 1953–1955. 6 #21 (31 October 1953) 28 [Genesis 28; Joshua 7–8]. 6 #25 (26 December 1953) 37 [the hardening of Pharaoh's heart; Isaiah's messianism]. 7 #4 (20 February 1954) 33–34 [Genesis 1; Joshua 10]. 7 #11 (29 May 1954) 30 [Conquest; cherubs]. 7 #15 (24 July 1954) 28 [Hebrew words in English; Esau's birthright]. 7 #17 (4 September 1954) 26 [manuscripts; prophets]. 7 #23 (27 November 1954) 28 [commandments; prophets; feasts]. 8 #1 (8 January 1955) 36 [resurrection; Genesis 15]. 8 #5 (5 March 1955) 35 [angels; Nazirites]. 8 #8 (16 April 1955) 37 [tithing; Baalzebub]. 8 #12 (11 June 1955) 34 [jealous God; sour grapes]. 8 #16 (6 August 1955) 37 [Gen 9: 25; Daniel in Ezek 14: 13].

N4. *Bulletin of the American Schools of Oriental Research*
Editor, #215 (October 1974)–#231 (October 1978).

N5. *Newsletter* [of the American Schools of Oriental Research]
Editor, 1976–1979 (runs from July-August 1976 to May 1977, numbered #1/2–10; from July 1977 to June 1978, numbered #1–8; and from August 1978 to June 1979, numbered #1–8; and from August 1979 until November 1979, #1–4 of that run) with incidental contributions: "ASOR Publication Policy," 1975 #2 (September 1975): 1–4 (before Freedman's editorship); "The Jerusalem [ASOR Anniversary] Conference," 1976 #7 (February 1976): 1–4 (before Freedman's editorship); "A Tour of the Tells," 1976 #5 (November 1976): 1–10; "Tourists on Parade," 1976 #6 (November 1976, sic): 1–9; "An

Abandoned Site Near Ramallah," 1976 #7 (December 1976): 15; "A Note on ASOR Publications," 1977 #3 (November 1977): 11; and, with other members of the Publications Committee, "ASOR Publication Policy," 1979 #7 (May 1979): 1–5 (after Freedman's editorship).

N6. *Biblical Archeologist*
Editor, Volume 39–45, 1976–1982. The Column "A Letter to the Readers" was occasionally written by DNF. 40 #1 (March 1977) 2–4 [Ebla]. 40 #2 (May 1977) 46–48 [sanctuaries and temples; Exodus 15; Psalm 78]. 40 #3 (September 1977) 94–97 [Qumran; dereliction of duty, his own; quoted by H. Shanks. 1978. Leading Scholar Calls for Prompt Publication *BAR* 4 #1 (March 1978): 2–3]. 40 #4 (December 1977) 134: The Flood and Other Matters. 41 #1 (March 1978) 2 [magic; seals; jewelry]. 41 #2 (June 1978) 42: "The [Biblical] City and the County [Jordan Valley]." 41 #3 (September 1978) 82–83: Ancient Woman, Future [Qumran] Temple, and Current Study. 42 #1 (Winter 1979) 4 [genealogies, etc.]. 42 #2 (Spring 1979) 68 [documents, etc.]. 42 #3 (Summer 1979) 132 [the Aleppo Codex, etc.]. 43 #1 (Winter 1980) 4 [archeology, etc.]. 43 #2 (Spring 1980) 68 [Ebla; Turin Shroud, etc.]. 43 #3 (Summer 1980) 132 [Persepolis; G. G. Cameron, etc.] 43 #4 (Fall 1980) 196 [Ebla; etc.]. 44 #1 (Winter 1981) 4 [the Adon letter; *i.m.* H. T. Frank, etc.]. 44 #2 (Spring 1981) 68 [Sodom; Ebla; Aphek, etc.]. 44 #3 (Summer 1981) 132 [Ebla; Funeral rites; etc.].

A Note on the New American Bible

Since there has been some misunderstanding concerning Freedman's role in the New American Bible, a word of explanation is in order. In the war years, the American Roman Catholic community set out to provide a new English-language Bible, translated from the original sources rather than from the Latin version associated with St. Jerome. Working with the Bishops' Committee of the Confraternity of Christian Doctrine, the members of the Catholic Biblical Association of America produced, in several volumes published through the 'fifties and 'sixties, the CCD Bible. When it came time to reissue these materials in a single volume, changes in textual study and scholarly understanding necessitated revision of the parts finished earliest. By this time, further, the American Roman Catholic church had been mandated, along with all Roman Catholics, to embrace the work of other Christians in scriptural study; the Second Vatican Council had urged that "with the approval of Church authority, . . . translations be produced in cooperation with separated brothers." In undertaking the final version of the CCD Bible, now named the New American Bible, the Catholic Biblical Association rose to the conciliar occasion, and the final body of the editors and translators included, beyond fifty Roman Catholic priests and one sister, several ordained ministers of the United Presbyterian Church U.S.A. It is as a member of a committee of fifty-four people that Freedman is to be associated with the NAB.

Since it is sometimes stated in print that Freedman translated and annotated the NAB Book of Genesis, we need to be more specific. At the request of the editorial chair for the Old Testament, the late Louis F. Hartman, and of the editorial vicechair, the late P. W. Skehan, Freedman wrote an introduction to Genesis, a set of explanatory notes, and a group of textual notes, and prepared a new translation of the book—all with a distant eye on the already published CCD versions. All of Freedman's materials were submitted to the committee and revised by it; the committee of the CBA is responsible for the final NAB version.

Thanks for aid in the labor of compilation to J. Kselman and J. Jensen in Washington, D.C.; R. G. Boling and E. F. Campbell in Chicago; J. A. Baird in Wooster; and L. E. Fyfe, L. O. Gómez, D. F. Graf, Li Chi, and B. E. Willoughby in Ann Arbor.